aback' *adv:*—**taken aback** surprised.

aban'don *vb* **1** to give up (*abandon the attempt*). **2** to depart from for ever, desert (*abandon his wife and children*):—*n* freedom from care (*dance with gay abandon*).

aban'doned *adj* **1** deserted (*an abandoned house*). **2** immoral, shameless (*abandoned young women*).

abase' *vb* to humble (*abase oneself*):—*n* **abase'ment**.

abashed' *adj* embarrassed, ashamed.

abate' *vb* to lessen (*storms abating*):—*n* **abate'ment**.

abattoir [a-bat-wär'] *n* a place where animals are killed before being sold as meat.

abb'ess *n* the chief nun in a convent.

abb'ey *n* **1** a monastery or convent. **2** a church, once part of a monastery or convent.

abb'ot *n* the chief monk in a monastery.

abbre'viate *vb* to shorten (*abbreviate a word*):—*n* **abbrevia'tion**.

ab'dicate *vb* to give up high office, esp a throne:—*n* **abdica'tion**.

ab'domen *n* the part of the body between the breast and the thighs:—*adj* **abdom'inal**.

abduct' *vb* to kidnap:—*n* **abduc'tion**:—*n* **abduc'tor**.

aberra'tion *n* **1** a wandering from the right or usual way (*to steal in a moment of aberration*). **2** a wandering of the mind.

abet' *vb* to help or encourage esp in evil (*aid and abet a criminal*):—*n* **abet'tor**.

abey'ance *n:*—**in abeyance** out of use for the time being.

abhor' *vb* to loathe:—*n* **abhor'rence**.

abhor'rent *adj* loathsome.

abide' *vb* **1** to put up with (*she cannot abide untidiness*):—**abide by** to obey, to remain true to (*abide by the rules*).

abid'ing *adj* lasting (*an abiding love*).

abil'ity *n* **1** skill or power to do a thing (*the ability to do the job*). **2** cleverness (*pupils of ability*).

ab'ject *adj* miserable, wretched (*abject poverty*).

abjure' *vb* to swear to give up.

ablaze' *adj and adv* on fire, in flames.

ab'le *adj* **1** having skill or power to do a thing. **2** clever:—*adv* **ab'ly**.

abnor'mal *adj* different from the usual (*abnormal levels of lead*):—*adv* **abnor'mally**.

abnormal'ity *n* unusual quality.

aboard' *adv and prep* on board, on a ship, train, aeroplane, etc.

abode' *n* (*fml or hum*) house, home (*our humble abode*).

abol'ish *vb* to put an end to, to do away with (*abolish slavery*).

aboli'tion *n* putting an end to something:—*n* **aboli'tionist**.

abom'inable *adj* hateful.

abom'inate *vb* to hate very much:—**abomi-na'tion**.

Aborig'inal *n* any of the original inhabitants of Australia.

aborigines [ab-ō-rij'-in-eez] *npl* the original inhabitants of a country.

abor'tive *adj* unsuccessful because done too soon (*an abortive attempt*).

abound' *vb* to be plentiful (*large houses abound there*).

about' *adv and prep* **1** concerning (*a letter about money*). **2** around (*dash about the house*). **3** near to (*somewhere about here*). **4** nearly (*costing about £5*). **5** on the point of (*just about to go*).

above' *adv and prep* **1** over (*pictures above the fireplace/a flat above the shop*). **2** higher (than) (*above average*).

above'board' *adj* honest, fair.

abra'sion *n* an injury caused by rubbing or scraping.

abreast' *adv* side by side (*competitors running abreast*):—**abreast of the times** up-to-date.

abridge' *vb* to make shorter (*abridge the story*):—*n* **abridg'(e)ment**.

abroad' *adv* **1** out of one's country (*holidays abroad*). **2** far and wide (*spread the news abroad*).

abrupt' *adj* **1** sudden, hasty (*an abrupt departure*). **2** discourteous (*an abrupt reply*):—*adv* **abrupt'ly**:—*n* **abrupt'ness**.

ab'scess *n* a boil, a gathering of pus in some part of the body.

abscond' *vb* to run away secretly and suddenly, esp after doing wrong (*abscond with the firm's money*).

ab'seil *vb* to go down a very steep slope, such as a cliff face or a very tall building, using a rope secured at the top and passed round the body in a kind of harness.

absence *see* **absent**[2].

ab'sent[1] *adj* not present (*absent from school/absent friends*).

absent[2] *vb* to keep away:—*n* **ab'sence**.

absentee' *n* one who is not present.

ab'sent-mind'ed *adj* not thinking of what one is doing.

ab'solute *adj* 1 complete (*absolute perfection*). 2 free from controls or conditions (*absolute power*):—*adv* **ab'solutely**.

absolution *see* **absolve**.

absolve' *vb* to set free, as from guilt or punishment (*absolve from blame*):—*n* **abso-lu'tion**.

absorb' *vb* 1 to soak up (*a material that absorbs liquid*). 2 to take up all the attention of.

absorbed *adj* giving the whole mind to (*people absorbed in their work*).

absorb'ent *adj* drinking in:—*also n*.

absorp'tion *n* 1 act of absorbing. 2 full attention.

abstain' *vb* 1 to keep oneself from, to hold back from (*abstain from smoking*). 2 not to vote (*three voted against and two abstained*):—*n* **abstain'er**:—*n* **absten'tion**.

abstem'ious *adj* sparing in food and drink, or pleasures (*an abstemious life*).

abstention *see* **abstain**.

ab'stinence *n* the act of holding back from (*abstinence from alcohol*):—*adj* **ab'stinent**.

ab'stract *n* a summary (*an abstract of the lecture*):—*adj* existing in the mind only.

abstruse' *adj* difficult to understand, obscure.

absurd' *adj* foolish:—*n* **absurd'ity**.

abund'ance *n* more than enough, plenty (*an abundance of apples this year*):—*adj* **abund'ant**:—*adv* **abund'antly**.

abuse [a-bûz'] *vb* 1 to make wrong use of (*abuse power*). 2 to ill-treat, to maltreat, esp physically or sexually (*abuse their children*). 3 to use insulting language (*a drunk abusing the barman*):—*n* **abuse** [a-bus].

abus'ive *adj* 1 ill-treating, cruel (*abusive treatment*). 2 insulting (*abusive language*):—*adv* **abus'ively**.

abut' *vb* to touch or lean upon.

abys'mal *adj* very great.

abyss *n* a very deep pit or ravine.

acacia [a-kā'-shi-a] *n* a type of flowering shrub.

academ'ic *adj* 1 of or concerning education, esp in a college or university (*an academic career*). 2 not practical or useful, theoretical (*of academic interest*):—*n* **academi'cian**.

acad'emy *n* 1 a school for special studies (*a military academy*). 2 a society for advancing arts and sciences (*the Royal Academy*).

accede' *vb* 1 to agree to (*accede to a request*). 2 to come to office (*accede to the throne*).

accel'erate *vb* to increase speed:—*n* **accel-era'tion**.

accel'erator *n* a device that controls the speed of a motorcar.

ac'cent *n* 1 a special emphasis given to part of a word (*the accent is on the first syllable*). 2 the mark that indicates such emphasis. 3 a way of speaking peculiar to certain persons or groups (*a Scottish accent*):—*vb* **accent'** to emphasize a certain part of a word.

accent'uate *vb* to emphasize (*a dress accentuating the blue of her eyes*).

accept' *vb* 1 to receive something offered (*accept the gift with thanks/accept his apology*). 2 to regard as true, reasonable, satisfactory, etc (*accept his excuse/accept their criticism*):—*n* **accept'ance**.

accept'able *adj* 1 pleasant to receive (*a very acceptable gift*). 2 satisfactory, good enough (*acceptable work*). 3 allowable, tolerable (*acceptable levels of radiation*).

ac'cess *n* a way or means of approach.

access *add*:—*vb* to find (information) on a computer file (*access secret data illegally*).

access'ible *adj* 1 easily approached (*an accessible manager*). 2 easily reached (*villages that are scarcely accessible*). 3 easily obtained or understood (*accessible information*):—*n* **accessibil'ity**.

access'ion *n* 1 a coming to high office (*accession to the throne*). 2 addition (*new accessions to the books in the library*).

access'ory *n* 1 an assistant, esp in crime. 2 an additional part or tool (*car accessories*). 3 an additional item worn with a woman's clothes (*accessories such as handbags*).

ac'cident *n* 1 an unexpected happening (*we met by accident*). 2 an unexpected event that causes

STUDENTS'
ENGLISH
DICTIONARY

GEDDES &
GROSSET

Key to pronunciation

The following list has been followed
for vowel sounds:

ā	as in fate
ä	as in far
å	as in fall
a	as in fat
ee	as in me
è	as in her
e	as in met
ë	as in air
ê	as in the
î	as in pine
i	as in pin
ō	as in note
ö	as in move
o	as in not
oi	as in boy
ou	as in pound
û	as in tube
ü	as in bull
u	as in tub

The French nasal sounds are given as (ng)
Where c is hard it is given as k, as in cat
j = dg, g or j as in bridge, gentle, jack
ks = x as in explain
kw = qu as in queen
s = s as in mass
z = s as in was
zh = s as in measure

Abbreviations used in this book

abbr	abbreviation
adj	adjective
adj	adjectives
adv	adverb
advs	adverbs
Amer	American
aux	auxiliary
cap	capital
conj	conjunction
demons	demonstrative
esp	especially
f	feminine
fml	formal
gram	grammar
hum	humorous
inf	informal
interj	interjection
lit	literary
mus	music
n	noun
npl	noun plural
ns	nouns
pers	personal
pl	plural
pp	past participle
prep	preposition
pt	past tense
RC	Roman Catholic
relig	religion
sing	singular
usu	usually
vb	verb

This edition published 2003 by Geddes & Grosset,
David Dale House, New Lanark, ML11 9DJ, Scotland.

© 2003 Geddes & Grosset

ISBN 1 84205 215 2

Printed and bound in Poland

damage or injury (*a road accident*):—*adj* **acciden'tal.**

acclaim' *vb* to greet with applause.

acclama'tion *n* a shout of joy or approval.

acclim'atize *vb* to accustom to a new climate or situation:—*n* **acclimatiza'tion.**

accolade [ak-kô-lãd'] *n* **1** the touching on the shoulder with a sword in the ceremony of making someone a knight. **2** praise or approval (*receive accolades for his bravery*).

accom'modate *vb* **1** to provide lodgings for (*accommodate the travellers in the hotel*). **2** to have space for (*a garage accommodating three cars*). **3** to supply with (*accommodate them with a loan*). **4** to make suitable, to adapt (*accommodate his way of life to his salary*).

accom'modating *adj* obliging (*an accommodating friend*).

accommoda'tion *n* lodgings (*provide accommodation for tourists*).

accom'paniment *n* the music played with a singer or player.

accom'panist *n* one who plays the accompaniment for a singer or player.

accompany [ak-kum'-pê-ni] *vb* **1** to go with (*accompany her to the concert*). **2** to join a singer or player by playing a musical instrument.

accom'plice *n* a helper, esp in crime (*the burglar's accomplice*).

accom'plish *vb* to perform successfully, to finish (*accomplish the task*).

accom'plished *adj* **1** finished (*the accomplished task*). **2** skilled (*an accomplished pianist*).

accom'plishment *n* **1** something done successfully. **2** completion.

accord' *vb* **1** to agree (*his account of the accident accords with hers*). **2** to give (*accord them a warm welcome*):—*n* agreement:—**of one's own accord** by one's own wish.

accord'ance *n* agreement.

accord'ingly *adv* therefore.

according to *prep* **1** in keeping with (*act according to the rules*). **2** as stated by (*according to the teacher*).

accor'dion *n* a portable musical instrument played by keys and worked by bellows:—*n* **accor'dionist.**

accost' *vb* to speak to first, to address.

account' *vb* (*fml*) to consider, to reckon (*account him an honest man*):—*n* **1** a statement of money

received and paid, a bill. **2** a report, description (*an account of the accident*):— **account for** give an explanation of (*account for his absence*):—**of no account** of no importance:—**on account of** because of.

account'able *adj* responsible (*not accountable for his brother's crime*).

account'ancy *n* the work of an accountant.

account'ant *n* one who keeps or examines money accounts.

accoutrements [ak-kü'trê-mênts] *npl* equipment, esp originally that of a soldier (*the accoutrements necessary for playing golf*).

accred'ited *adj* recognized, official (*accredited representatives*).

accre'tion *n* increase in size by growth or addition.

accrue' *vb* to come to as an addition (*savings accruing interest*).

accum'ulate *vb* **1** to increase, to heap up (*rubbish accumulated*). **2** to collect (*accumulate wealth*).

accumula'tion *n* growth, a large collection.

ac'curacy *n* exactness, precision.

ac'curate *adj* **1** correct, exact (*an accurate answer*). **2** correct, careful (*an accurate worker*):—*adv* **ac'curately.**

accur'sed *adj* lying under a curse, doomed.

accusa'tion *n* a charge brought against anyone.

accuse' *vb* to charge with wrongdoing (*accuse them of stealing cars*):—*n* **accus'er.**

accused' *n* one charged with wrongdoing (*the accused was found guilty*).

accus'tom *vb* to make well known by use (*accustom oneself to a different climate*).

accus'tomed *adj* **1** usual (*his accustomed evening walk*). **2** used (to), familiar with (*not accustomed to being treated rudely*).

ace [ãs] *n* **1** one at cards, dice or dominoes. **2** someone good at sports:—**within an ace of** on the very point of.

acer'bic *adj* sharp, bitter (*an acerbic wit*):—*n* **acer'bity.**

acet'ic *adj* sour, of vinegar.

acetylene [a-se'-ti-leen] *n* a gas used for giving light and heat, and commonly used with oxygen for welding or cutting metal.

ache [ãk] *vb* to be in or to give prolonged pain:— *n* a prolonged or throbbing pain.

achieve' *vb* **1** to succeed in doing (*achieve what we set out to do*). **2** to gain (*achieve success*).

achieve'ment n **1** something done successfully (*the achievement of his aims*). **2** a feat (*a remarkable achievement*).

a'cid adj sour, sharp to the taste:—n a sour substance.

acid rain n rain which has been polluted by acid from factory waste, car exhausts, etc and which is harmful to the environment

acid test n a test that indicates the worth or value of something (*the acid test of his invention will be if it works*).

acid'ity n sourness.

acknowledge [ak-nä'-lêj] vb **1** to admit as true (*acknowledge that he was wrong/acknowledge defeat*). **2** to admit the receipt of (*acknowledge the letter*):—n **acknow'-ledg(e)ment**.

acme [ak'-mee] n the highest point (*the acme of perfection*).

acne [ak'-nee] n a skin disease.

acolyte [a'-ko-lît] n an assistant or follower.

a'corn n the fruit or seed of the oak tree.

acous'tic adj **1** having to do with hearing and sound (*the acoustic problems of the old hall*). **2** (*of a musical instrument*) making its natural sound, not electric (*an acoustic guitar*).

acous'tics npl the science of sound.

acquaint' vb **1** to make familiar with (*acquaint oneself with the new system*). **2** to inform (*acquaint them with the facts*).

acquaint'ance n **1** a person one knows (*friends and acquaintances*). **2** knowledge (*a slight acquaintance with the plays of Shakespeare*).

acquiesce [ak-kwi-es] vb to agree to; to allow to happen without protesting (*acquiesce in their proposals*):—n **acquies'cence**.

acquire' vb to gain, to obtain.

acquire'ment n knowledge or skill gained by personal effort.

acquisi'tion n **1** the act of acquiring (*the acquisition of wealth*). **2** something acquired (*a valuable acquisition*).

acquis'itive adj eager to obtain and possess:—n **acquis'itiveness**.

acquit' vb **1** to declare innocent. **2** to conduct oneself (*acquit oneself well*).

acquit'tal n a setting free.

acre [ä-kêr] n a measure of land (= 4046.9 square metres or 4840 square yards).

a'creage n the number of acres in a piece of land.

ac'rid adj sharp and bitter in taste or smell (*the acrid atmosphere in the smoky room*).

acrimony [ak'-ri-mê-ni] n bitterness of words or temper:—adj **acrimo'nious**.

ac'robat n a tight-rope or trapeze artiste:—adj **acrobat'ic**:—npl **acrobat'ics**.

act vb **1** to do (*act quickly*). **2** to conduct oneself (*act wisely*). **3** to perform on the stage. **4** to produce an effect (*drugs acting quickly*):—n **1** a deed (*a kind act*). **2** a law. **3** a part of a play.

ac'tion n **1** something done (*take swift action*). **2** a movement (*good wrist action*). **3** the producing of an effect. **4** the events in a narrative or drama. **5** a battle. **6** a lawsuit.

ac'tionable adj giving cause for a lawsuit.

ac'tive adj **1** energetic (*active children*). **2** taking part, involved (*an active member of the club*). **3** being in action, working, operative (*an active volcano*).

activ'ity n **1** energy. **2** occupation or pastime (*spare-time activities*).

ac'tor n a man who performs in a play.

ac'tress n a woman who performs in a play.

ac'tual adj **1** real, not imaginary (*actual children, not characters in a television play*). **2** true (*the actual cost of the repairs*).

actual'ity n reality.

ac'tually adv really, as a matter of fact.

acu'men [acû'mên or ac'ûmên] n keenness of mind (*business acumen*).

ac'upuncture n a treatment used in complementary medicine in which fine needles are inserted into the skin at certain points along energy paths known as meridians.

acute' adj **1** coming to a sharp point. **2** sharp-witted. **3** (*of emotions or diseases*) intense but short-lasting:—adv **acute'ly**.

acute angle n an angle less than 90°.

ad'age n a proverb, an old, wise saying.

ad'amant adj determined, firm (*adamant that they were right*).

adapt' vb **1** to make suitable, to fit to a different use (*adapt the evening dress for day wear*). **2** to change, adjust (*adapt to new surroundings*).

adapt'able adj easily fitted to new uses or conditions:—n **adaptabil'ity**.

adapta'tion n the action or result of adapting.

add *vb* **1** to join one thing to another. **2** to increase (*add to their misery*). **3** to say further (*add a word of thanks*).

adden'dum *n* (*pl* **adden'da**) something added, esp to a book or document.

ad'der *n* a small poisonous snake, a viper.

ad'dict *n* a person who is dependent on and so unable to give up a habit, esp a harmful one such as drug-taking (*a drug addict*).

addict'ed *adj* dependent on, unable to give up (*addicted to alcohol/an addicted drug-user*):—*n* **addic'tion**.

addi'tion *n* **1** act of adding. **2** something added (*an addition to the family*):—*adj* **addi'tional**.

address' *vb* **1** to speak to (*address the crowds*). **2** to direct a letter. **3** to direct one's attention or energy to (*address the task*):—*n* **address'**, **ad'dress** **1** the place where a person lives or works. **2** the directions on a letter or envelope. **3** a formal talk (*the head teacher's address on speech day*). **4** skill (*with great address*).

adduce' *vb* (*fml*) to put forward (*adduce a reason for their behaviour*).

ad'enoids *npl* soft, natural growth at the back of the nose that hinders breathing.

adept [a'-dept *or* ê-dept'] *adj* very skilful (*adept at tennis*):—*n* one who is skilled.

adequate [a'-dee-kwât] *adj* **1** enough (*adequate supplies*). **2** satisfactory (*adequate for the job*):—*adv* **ad'equately**:—*n* **ad'equacy**.

adhere [ad-heer'] *vb* **1** to stick (to). **2** to remain loyal to (*adhere to one's principles*):—*n* **adher'ence**.

adher'ent *adj* sticking (to):—*n* a follower, a supporter (*an adherent of Karl Marx*).

adhesion [ad-hee'-zhên] *n* the act of sticking (to).

adhe'sive *adj* sticky:—*n* a sticky substance, glue.

adieu [a-dû'] *interj* farewell, goodbye:—*n* (*pl* **adieus** *or* **adieux** [a-dûz']) a farewell.

adjacent [ad-jâ'-sênt] *adj* lying near (to) (*the fire spread to adjacent buildings*).

ad'jective *n* a word that describes a noun:—*adj* **adjecti'val** [ad-jek-tî'-vêl]:—*adv* **adjecti'vally**.

adjoin'ing *adj* lying next to (*adjoining houses*).

adjourn [ad-jèrn'] *vb* **1** to put off to another time (*adjourn the meeting*). **2** to go to another place (*adjourn to the next room*):—*n* **adjourn'ment**.

adjudicate [ad-jü'-di-kât] *vb* to act as a judge in a competition, etc.

adjudica'tion *n* a sentence or award.

adju'dicator *n* one who acts as judge or referee in a matter.

ad'junct *n* something added or joined (*an adjunct to the business*).

adjust' *vb* **1** to set right. **2** to put in order:—*adj* **adjust'able**:—*n* **adjust'ment**.

admin'ister *vb* **1** to manage, to govern (*administer the firm's finances*). **2** to carry out (*administer the law*). **3** (*fml*) to give (*administer medicine*).

administra'tion *n* **1** the management of a business or a government. **2** people involved in this:—*adj* **admin'istrative**.

admin'istrator *n* a person who works in administration (*hospital administrators*).

ad'mirable *adj* deserving admiration or praise (*admirable work*):—*adv* **ad'mirably**.

ad'miral *n* the highest rank of naval officer.

ad'miralty *n* the government department that controls naval affairs.

admira'tion *n* a feeling of pleasure and respect (*look at the painting with admiration*).

admire' *vb* to think very highly of (*admire her work*):—*n* **admir'er**.

admiss'ible *adj* allowable.

admis'sion *n* **1** permission to enter (*women being refused admission*). **2** the amount payable for entry (*admission £4*). **3** a confession (*an admission of guilt*).

admit' *vb* **1** to allow to enter (*the ticket admits two people*). **2** to accept as true or just (*admit that they are right*). **3** to confess (*admit his crime*).

admit'tance *n* (*fml*) right or permission to enter (*fail to gain admittance*).

admit'tedly *adv* it cannot be denied.

admix'ture *n* **1** the act of mixing. **2** that which is mixed with something else.

admon'ish *vb* to give a warning or scolding to:—*n* **admoni'tion**:—*adj* **admon'itory**.

ado [a-dö'] *n* fuss, trouble (*let us get on our way without further ado*).

adoles'cence *n* the period when one is adolescent.

adolescent [a-do-les'-ênt] *adj* growing up from youth to manhood or womanhood:—*n* a person of either sex when adolescent.

adopt' *vb* **1** to take as one's own (*adopt a child*). **2** to take over and use (*adopt foreign customs*).

3 to choose formally (*adopt a candidate*):—*n* **adop'tion**.

ador'able *adj* lovable.

adore' *vb* **1** to worship (*adore God*). **2** to love or like very much (*adore their mother/adore spicy food*):—*n* **adora'tion**.

adorn' *vb* to decorate, to make beautiful (*adorn the tree with fairy lights*).

adorn'ment *n* an ornament.

adrift' *adj* and *adv* floating without control.

adroit [a-droit'] *adj* skilful, clever (*adroit at handling difficult situations*):—*adv* **adroit'ly**:—*n* **adroit'ness**.

adulation [a-dû-lā'-shên] *n* insincere or extreme praise, flattery.

ad'ult, adult' *adj* **1** grown-up (*an adult animal*). **2** suitable or designed for adults (*adult entertainment*):—*n* **ad'ult** a grown-up person.

adul'terate *vb* to lower in value by mixing with something of less worth (e.g. to mix wine with water, gold with tin, etc):—*n* **adultera'tion**.

adul'tery *n* unfaithfulness to the promises made to one's partner at marriage:—*n* **adul'terer**:—*f* **adul'teress**.

advance' *vb* **1** to put forward (*advance a theory*). **2** to go forward (*armies advancing*). **3** to help promote (*advance the cause of freedom*). **4** to lend (*the bank advanced him £500*):—*n* **1** a forward movement (*the advance of the army*). **2** progress (*little advance in the discussions*). **3** a loan (of money), esp a payment made before the normal time (*an advance on his pay*). **4** increase (*any advance on £500 for this picture?*):—**in advance** in front; before.

advanced' *adj* **1** far on (in life, time, etc) (*of advanced years/an illness at an advanced stage*). **2** at a high level, not elementary (*advanced studies*). **3** modern and new and sometimes not yet generally accepted (*advanced ideas*).

advance'ment *n* improvement.

advantage [ad-vän'-têj] *n* **1** a better position or something that puts one in a better position (*he has the advantage of being older*). **2** gain, profit, benefit (*little advantage in having a car if you can't afford to run it*).

advanta'geous *adj* profitable; helpful:—*adv* **advanta'geously**.

ad'vent *n* a coming, an arrival (*the advent of train travel*).

Ad'vent *n* the period from the fourth Sunday before Christmas to Christmas Day.

adventitious [ad-ven-tish'-ês] *adj* accidental, happening by chance.

adven'ture *n* an exciting or dangerous deed or undertaking.

adven'turer, adven'turess (*f*) *n* **1** one who seeks adventures. **2** one who lives by his or her wits.

adven'turous *adj* **1** daring, eager for adventure (*adventurous children*). **2** dangerous, involving risk (*an adventurous journey*).

ad'verb *n* a word that modifies the meaning of a verb, an adjective or another adverb:—*adj* **adver'bial**.

ad'versary *n* an enemy.

ad'verse *adj* acting against, unfavourable (*adverse weather conditions/adverse criticism*):—*adv* **ad'versely**.

adver'sity *n* misfortune.

ad'vert short for **advertisement**.

advertise' *vb* to make known to the public:—*n* **ad'vertiser** *or* **advertis'er**.

advert'isement *n* an announcement to the public.

advice' *n* **1** a helpful opinion offered to another (*seek expert financial advice*). **2** a formal letter, etc, giving information (*a sales advice*).

advis'able *adj* wise; correct in the circumstances:—*n* **advisabil'ity**.

advise' *vb* **1** to give advice (*advise them to leave*). **2** to inform (*advise us of the cost*).

advis'er *n* one who gives advice.

advis'ory *adj* for the purpose of giving advice.

ad'vocate *n* **1** one who speaks for another. **2** a lawyer who pleads a cause in court, esp in Scotland:—*vb* to recommend, to speak in favour of (*advocate a change of climate for his health*).

adze [adz] *n* a tool for shaping wood.

aegis [ee'-jis *or* ä'-jis] *n* protection and support (*under the aegis of the government*).

aeon, eon [ee'-on] *n* an age, a period of time too long to be measured.

aerate [ã'-er-ãt] *vb* to put air or other gas into (*aerate soft drinks*).

aerial [ã'-ri-al] *adj* of or from the air (*aerial photography*):—*n* a wire or rod, etc, for receiving radio waves or television signals.

aerobat'ics *npl* difficult exercises performed by an aircraft.

aer'odrome *n* a starting and landing place for aircraft, now usu used for military or private

pural to *n* **1** the highest male voice. **2** a low female voice, properly called **contralto**:—*also adj*.

aeronautics [ā-rō-nã'-tiks] *n* the science of the operation and flight of aircraft.

aer'oplane *n* a heavier-than-air flying machine with wings.

aer'osol *n* **1** a liquid under pressure in a container which is released in a fine spray (*deodorants in the form of aerosols*). **2** the container for this (*aerosols of perfume*).

aesthetic [is-the'-tik] *adj* having to do with beauty (*practical buildings but ugly from an aesthetic point of view*):—*n* **aesthe'tics** the study of beauty.

affable [af'-êbl] *adj* pleasant, polite, easy to talk with:—*n* **affability**:—*adv* **affably**.

affair' *n* **1** business (*affairs of state*). **2** a matter, a concern (*no affair of yours*). **3** happenings or events connected with a particular person or thing (*the Watergate affair*). **4** a love affair.

affect' *vb* **1** to act upon (*a disease affecting his eyes*). **2** to move the feelings (*deeply affected by his death*). **3** to pretend (*affect grief*).

affect'ed *adj* full of affectation (*an affected young woman*).

affecta'tion *n* manner or behaviour that is not natural, pretence (*her helplessness is just an affectation*).

affec'tion *n* fondness, love.

affec'tionate *adj* loving:—*adv* **affec'tion-ately**.

affidavit [af-fi-dā'-vit] *n* a written statement made on oath.

affil'iated *adj* joined or connected (*affiliated organizations*):—*n* **affilia'tion**.

affin'ity *n* **1** relationship (*languages having an affinity with each other*). **2** attraction (*an affinity between them*).

affirm' *vb* to state with certainty.

affirma'tion *n* **1** a statement. **2** a solemn statement of the truth.

affir'mative *adj* answering 'yes':—*n* an answer meaning 'yes':—**answer in the affirmative** to say 'yes'.

affix' *vb* to fasten to, to add (*affix a stamp to the envelope*):—*n* **affix** a prefix or suffix, an addition to a word to alter its meaning.

afflict' *vb* to cause pain, distress, etc, to (*she is afflicted with poor health/the economic problems afflicting the country*).—*n* **af-flic'tion**.

affluence *n* wealth.

affluent [af'-flö-ênt] *adj* wealthy.

afford' *vb* **1** to be able to pay for (*unable to afford a holiday*). **2** to be able to do, spend, etc, something without trouble, loss, etc (*unable to afford the time*). **3** (*fml*) to give (*the occasion afforded him much pleasure*).

affray' *n* an outbreak of fighting in public, a disturbance.

affront [af-frunt'] *vb* to insult (*he was affronted at being offered money*):—*n* an insult (*an affront to his pride*).

afloat *adj and adv* floating.

afoot' *adv* about to happen (*trouble afoot*).

afore'said *adj* already mentioned.

afraid *adj* frightened.

afresh' *adv* again (*begin afresh*).

aft *adj and adv* at or near the stern of a ship.

after *adv and prep* **1** later in time (than) (*after the meal*). **2** behind (*come after them*).

af'termath *n* the period of time, or consequences, following an unpleasant or unfortunate event (*the aftermath of the war*).

afternoon' *n* the time from noon to evening.

afterthought *n* **1** a fresh thought after an act or speech. **2** something added or done later, not part of an original plan (*a garage added as an afterthought*).

af'terwards *adv* later.

again [ê-gen'] *adv* once more.

against [ê-genst'] *prep* **1** in opposition to (*people against the new law*). **2** supported by (*lean against the wall*).

agate [a'-gãt] *n* a very hard precious stone.

age *n* **1** the length of time a person or thing has lived or existed. **2** (*inf*) a long time (*wait ages for a bus*). **3** the state of being old (*improve with age*). **4** a particular period in history (*the Stone Age*):—*vb* **1** to become old. **2** to make old (*worry has aged her*).

aged *adj* **1** [ā'-jêd] old. **2** [ājd] at the age of (*boys aged ten*).

age'less *adj* never becoming old.

a'gency *n* the office or business of an agent.

agen'da *n* a list of matters to be discussed at a meeting.

a'gent *n* **1** someone or something that acts (*cleaning agents that harm the skin*). **2** a person who acts on behalf of someone else.

agglomera'tion *n* a heap (*an agglomeration of litter*).

ag'gravate *vb* **1** to make worse (*aggravate the situation by losing his temper*). **2** (*inf*) to make angry (*children aggravating their mother*):—*adj* **ag'gravating**:—*n* **aggrava'tion**.

ag'gregate *n* a total (*an aggregate of goals*).

aggres'sion *n* **1** an attack. **2** hostile feelings.

aggres'sive *adj* **1** always ready to attack, quarrelsome. **2** forceful, determined (*an aggressive sales campaign*):—*adv* **ag-gres'sively**.

aggres'sor *n* the first to attack.

aghast [a-gast'] *adj* amazed, horrified (*be aghast at their behaviour*).

agile [a'-djîl] *adj* quick of movement, nimble:—*n* **agil'ity**.

ag'itate *vb* **1** to excite, to make anxious (*delay agitates her*). **2** to try to stir up public feeling (*agitate for prison reform*). **3** (*fml*) to shake (*agitate the bottle*):—*n* **agita'tion**.

ag'itator *n* one who tries to cause public discontent or revolt.

agnos'tic *n* one who believes that the existence of God cannot be proved.

ago' *adv* in the past (*a long time ago*).

agog' *adj* eager, excited (*children waiting all agog for the pantomime to begin*).

a'gonizing *adj* **1** causing great pain. **2** causing great distress.

a'gony *n* **1** great pain (*in agony from a gunshot wound*). **2** great distress (*the agony of divorce*).

agrarian [ag-rä'-ri-ên] *adj* having to do with the land (*the agrarian revolution*).

agree' *vb* **1** to be of the same opinion (*agree that everyone should go*). **2** to be alike (*statements that agree*). **3** to suit (*a climate that agrees with her*).

agree'able *adj* **1** pleasant (*an agreeable climate*). **2** ready to agree (*we were not all agreeable to vote that way*):—*adv* **agree'-ably**.

agree'ment *n* **1** sameness of opinion (*in agreement about the new plans*). **2** likeness (*little agreement in their statements*). **3** a contract (*sign an agreement*).

agricul'ture *n* the science of cultivating the land, farming:—*adj* **agricul'tural**.

aground' *adv* on or on to the sea bed.

ahead' *adv* **1** in front (*go on ahead to clear the way*). **2** forward, for the future (*plan ahead*).

ahoy' *interj* a call used by sailors.

aid *vb* to help:—*n* help.

aide-de-camp [åd'-dê-ko(ng)] *n* (*pl* **aides-de-camp**) an officer in attendance on a king, general or other high official.

Aids, AIDS *n* a serious disease which affects the body's immune system, greatly reducing resistance to infection. (*A*cquired *I*mmune *D*eficiency *S*yndrome).

ail'ing *adj* **1** unwell (*his ailing wife*). **2** weak (*the country's ailing economy*).

aileron [ål'-ê-ron] *n* a flap on the wing tip of an aeroplane.

ail'ment *n* a minor illness.

aim *vb* **1** to point a weapon (at). **2** to intend, to try (*aim to win*):—*n* **1** the act of aiming a weapon. **2** intention, goal, purpose (*our aim is to win*).

aim'less *adj* without purpose (*aimless discussions*).

air *n* **1** the mixture of gases composing the earth's atmosphere. **2** a light breeze. **3** a tune (*play a familiar air*). **4** manner (*an air of confidence*). **5** *pl* a manner that is not genuine (*put on airs*):—*vb* **1** to expose to fresh air (*air the room by opening the windows*). **2** to expose to warm air, to dry (*air clothes*). **3** to speak openly about (*air one's views*).

air'borne *adj* **1** carried about by air (*seeds that are airborne*). **2** in the air, in flight (*we will be airborne shortly*).

air'craft *n* (*pl* **air'craft**) a flying machine.

air'field *n* a starting and landing place for aircraft.

air'gun *n* a gun worked by releasing compressed air.

air'ily *adv* in an airy manner.

air'ing *n* **1** act of exposing to fresh or warm air. **2** an outing in the open air.

air'less *adj* stuffy.

air'line *n* a company providing regular aircraft services.

air'liner *n* a large passenger aircraft.

air pocket *n* a stream of air that carries an aircraft suddenly up or down.

air'port *n* a station for passenger aircraft.

air raid *n* an attack by aircraft.

air shaft *n* a passage for air into a mine.

air'ship *n* an aircraft kept aloft by a gas-filled balloon and driven by a motor.

air'tight *adj* so sealed that air can pass neither in nor out (*preserve fruit in an airtight bottle*).

air'y *adj* **1** with plenty of fresh air (*an airy room*). **2** lacking seriousness (*an airy disregard for authority*).

aisle [îl] *n* **1** the side part of a church, often separated from the central part by a row of pillars. **2** a passage in a church.

ajar' *adv* partly open (*doors left ajar*).

akim'bo *adv* with the hand on the hip and the elbow outwards (*arms akimbo*).

akin' *adj* similar (*problems akin to ours*).

alabas'ter *n* a soft marble-like stone.

alac'rity *n* quickness and eagerness (*accept the offer with alacrity*).

alarm' *n* **1** a warning of danger (*hear the fire alarm*). **2** sudden fear (*news causing alarm*):— *vb* to frighten.

alarm'ing *adj* frightening:—*adv* **alarm'ingly**.

alarm'ist *n* one who needlessly spreads frightening news or rumours:—*adj* causing needless fear.

alas' *interj* a cry of grief or pity.

al'batross *n* a large white seabird.

albeit [ål-bee'-it] *conj* (*fml*) although.

albi'no *n* a person or animal with white skin and hair and pink eyes.

al'bum *n* **1** a blank book into which may be put autographs, photographs, stamps, etc. **2** a long-playing record (*the group's latest album*).

albumen [al-bû'-mên] *n* the white of an egg.

alchemy [al'-kê-mi] *n* the chemistry of the Middle Ages, esp the study of matter in order to find a means of changing other metal into gold:—*n* **al'chemist**.

al'cohol *n* **1** pure spirit. **2** strong drink containing such spirit (*addicted to alcohol*).

alcohol'ic *n* someone who is addicted to alcohol:—*adj* having to do with alcohol (*alcoholic drinks*).

al'cove *n* a recess, a section of a room, etc, that is set back from the main part.

alder [ål'-dêr] *n* a tree common in wet ground.

ale *n* a light-coloured beer.

alert' *adj* **1** attentive (*sentries must be alert on duty*). **2** quick (*mentally alert*):—*n* warning of danger:—*n* **alert'ness**.

alfal'fa *n* a green plant used as cattle food.

al'gebra *n* a method of calculation in which letters and symbols are used to represent numbers:—*adj* **algebraic** [-ā'-ik].

alias [ā'-li-as] *adv* otherwise (*Fred Jones, alias Martin Smith*):—*n* a false name (*the alias adopted by the spy*).

alibi [a'-li-bî] *n* the plea that one was elsewhere when a crime was committed (*establish an alibi*).

alien [ā'-li-yên] *adj* **1** foreign (*find ourselves in an alien land*). **2** different, strange (*attitudes that are alien to ours*):—*n* **1** a foreigner, a person who is not a naturalized citizen of the country where he or she is living. **2** a being from another world.

a'lienate *vb* to make unfriendly (*alienate his family with his violence*).

alight'[1] *vb* **1** to get down (from) (*alight from the bus*). **2** to settle upon (*butterflies alighting on the leaves*).

alight'[2] *adv* on fire.

align [a-lîn'] *vb* **1** to put in line, to straighten. **2** to join, ally oneself with (*align himself with the enemy*):—*n* **align'ment**.

alike' *adj* like, similar:—*adv* in the same way.

alimen'tary canal *n* the passage through the body by which food is received and digested.

al'imony *n* the money payable regularly by a man or woman to his or her former wife or husband after legal separation or divorce.

alive' *adj* **1** living (*wounded soldiers still alive*). **2** lively (*eyes alive with excitement*). **3** aware of (*alive to danger*).

alkali [al'-ka-lî] *n* a substance such as potash or soda that neutralizes acids and unites with oil or fat to form soap.

all *adj* **1** every one of (*all the girls*). **2** the whole of (*all the cake*):—*n* **1** everyone (*all left*). **2** everything (*eat it all*):—*adv* wholly, entirely.

allay' *vb* to calm (*allay their fears*).

allege [al-ledj'] *vb* to state without proof (*allege that he had been attacked*):—*n* **alle-ga'tion**.

alleg'iance *n* loyalty.

allegory [al'-lê-gê-ri] *n* a story with a hidden meaning different from the obvious one:—*adj* **allegor'ical**.

alle'gro *adv* (*mus*) briskly.

al'lergy *n* a reaction of the body to some substance (*come out in a rash because of an allergy to cats*):—*adj* **aller'gic**.

alleviate [al-lee'-vee-āt] *vb* to lessen (*alleviating pain*):—*n* **allevia'tion**.

alley [al'-lā] *n* a narrow walk or passage.

alliance [a-lī'-êns] *n* a union between families, governments, etc.

allied *see* **ally**.

al'ligator *n* a type of crocodile.

allitera'tion *n* the repetition of a letter or sound at the beginning of two or more words close to one another.

al'locate *vb* to share out, to distribute (*allocating tasks to each of the children*):—*n* **alloca'tion**.

allot' (**allot'ted, allot'ting**) to give a share, to distribute (*allot the money collected to various charities*).

allot'ment *n* 1 act of allotting. 2 a small piece of land for growing vegetables, etc.

allow' *vb* 1 to permit (*allow them to go*). 2 to provide, to set aside (*allow three hours for the journey*).

allow'able *adj* permissible.

allow'ance *n* a sum of money granted for a special purpose (*a dress allowance*):—**make allowance for** take into consideration.

al'loy *n* a mixture of metals.

allude' *vb* to refer to, to mention (*allude to several new developments in his speech*):—*n* **allu'sion**:—*adj* **allu'sive**.

allure' *vb* to attract (*allure them to new jobs with promises of high salaries*):—*n* attraction, charm (*the allure of the stage*):—*n* **allure'ment**:—*adj* **allur'ing**.

allusion *see* **allude**.

alluvium [al-lû'-vi-êm] *n* soil left by a flood:—*adj* **allu'vial**.

ally [al-lī'] *vb* to join with another for a special purpose (e.g. by marriage or by treaty) (*ally ourselves with the French against the Germans*):—*adj* **allied** [al-līd']:—*n* **al'ly** 1 a helper (*one of the*

Prime Minister's closest allies). 2 a nation bound to another by treaty of friendship (*a victory for the allies against the enemy*).

almanac [al'-mê-nak] *n* a book containing a calendar and information about anniversaries, tides, stars and planets, etc.

almighty *adj* 1 (*often cap*) all-powerful (*Almighty God*). 2 (*inf*) very great, strong, loud, etc (*an almighty crash*):—*n* **The Almighty** God.

almond [a'-mând] *n* the nut of the almond tree.

almoner [al'-mo-nêr *or* ä'-monêr] *n* formerly, a medically trained social worker attached to a hospital.

al'most *adv* nearly (*almost midnight/almost at my mother's house/she almost fell*).

alms [ämz] *npl* money given to the poor.

aloe [al'-ō] *n* a plant with a bitter juice used in medicines.

aloft' *adv* high up in the air (*hold the banner aloft*).

alone' *adj and adv* 1 without company (*live alone/go on holiday alone*). 2 taken by itself (*money alone is not enough*).

along'side *adv and prep* by the side of (*draw up alongside their car*).

aloof' *adv* apart, distant (*stand aloof from his friends' quarrelling*):—*adj* distant, cool (*aloof people who do not make friends*):—*n* **aloof'ness**.

aloud' *adv* so as can be heard (*read aloud*).

alp *n* a high mountain.

alpa'ca *n* 1 a llama with long fine wool. 2 the cloth made from this wool.

al'pha *n* the first letter in the Greek alphabet.

al'phabet *n* the set of letters used in writing a language:—*adj* **alphabet'ical** (*in alphabetical order*).

al'pine *adj* having to do with high mountains, esp the Swiss Alps (*alpine plants*).

already *adv* 1 before this time, previously (*I have already seen the film*). 2 now or before the expected time (*are you leaving already?*).

Alsa'tian *n* a large dog somewhat like a wolf.

altar [âl'-têr] *n* 1 a raised place or table on which sacrifices are offered. 2 a communion table.

alter [âl'-têr] *vb* to change (*alter one's lifestyle/alter a dress/town centres that have altered*):—*n* **altera'tion**.

alterca'tion *n* a noisy quarrel.

alternate [ål-tèr'-nêt] *adj* **1** first one coming, then the other (*a pattern with alternate squares and circles*). **2** every second (*visit on alternate Tuesdays*):—*adv* **alter'-nately**:—*vb* **alternate** [ål'-têr-nåt] **1** to do, use, cause, arrange, etc, by turns (*alternating reading with watching television*). **2** to happen by turns (*rainy days alternated with dry ones*):—*n* **alterna'tion**.

alter'native *n* **1** a choice between two things (*the alternatives are to go or stay*). **2** (*inf*) a choice of two or more possibilities:—*adj* offering such a choice:—*adv* **alter'natively**.

although' *conj* though.

al'titude *n* height.

al'to *n* **1** the highest male voice. **2** a low female voice, properly called **contralto**:—*also adj*.

altogeth'er *adv* **1** wholly (*not altogether satisfied*). **2** including everything (*£20 altogether*). **3** on the whole (*altogether the holiday was a success*).

al'truism *n* acting to please others rather than oneself:—*n* **al'truist**:—*adj* **altruis'tic**.

alumin'ium *n* a soft, white, light metal.

al'ways *adv* at all times.

amal'gam *n* a mixture, esp of mercury with another metal.

amal'gamate *vb* to unite, to join together (*amalgamate the clubs/the clubs amalgamated*):—*n* **amalgama'tion**.

amanuensis [a-man-û-en'-sis] *n* one who writes what another dictates.

amass' *vb* to collect a large amount of.

amateur [am'-at-ûr *or* am'-atèr] *n* **1** one who takes part in any activity for the love of it, not for money (*a tennis tournament open only to amateurs*). **2** a person without skill or expertise in something (*repairs carried out by an amateur*):—*n* **am'ateurism**.

amateur'ish *adj* inexpert, unskilful (*his amateurish repair of the fence*).

amaze' *vb* to astonish (*her rudeness amazed me/amazed by his skill*):—*n* **amaze'ment**.

am'azon *n* a tall strong woman.

ambass'ador *n* a high-ranking official appointed to represent his or her government in a foreign country:—*adj* **ambassado'rial**.

am'ber *n* a clear yellowish substance used for ornaments:—*adj* **1** made of amber (*amber beads*). **2** brownish-yellow (*amber eyes*).

ambergris [am'-bêr-grees] *n* a white, waxy, sweet-smelling substance obtained from the whale and used in making perfume.

ambidex'trous *adj* able to do things equally well with either hand.

ambig'uous *adj* having more than one meaning (*the ambiguous statement left him in doubt*):—*n* **ambigu'ity**.

am'bit *n* **1** the space round about (*the ambit of the grounds*). **2** limits (*the ambit of his power*).

ambition [am-bish'-ên] *n* **1** desire for power, determination to succeed (*people of ambition struggling for promotion*). **2** a goal, aim (*his ambition is to play football for his country*):—*adj* **ambi'tious**.

am'ble *vb* **1** to walk at an easy pace (*ambling along although late for school*). **2** (*of a four-legged animal*) to move the two right legs together then the two left:—*n* **1** an easy pace. **2** a slow walk:—*n* **am'bler**.

ambro'sia *n* in classical mythology, the food of the gods.

am'bulance *n* a vehicle for carrying the sick or injured.

am'bush *n* **1** a body of people so hidden as to be able to make a surprise attack on an approaching enemy. **2** the place where such people hide. **3** a surprise attack made by people in hiding (*killed in a terrorist ambush*):—*vb* to lie in wait, to attack from an ambush.

ameliorate [a-mee'-li-ê-råt] *vb* **1** to make better (*medicines ameliorating her condition*). **2** to grow better (*conditions have ameliorated slightly*):—*n* **ameliora'tion**.

amen [ä'-men *or* a-men'] *interj* may it be so!; so be it.

amenable [a-mee'-nê-bêl] *adj* ready to be guided or influenced (*amenable to your suggestions/amenable people*).

amend' *vb* **1** (*fml*) to change for the better (*amend your ways*). **2** to correct (*amend the author's manuscript*). **3** to alter slightly (*amend the law*):—**to make amends** to make up for a wrong done.

amend'ment *n* **1** improvement. **2** an alteration (e.g. in a law).

amenities [a-mee'-nê-tees] *npl* things that make life easier or more pleasant (*the amenities of* *the town, such as the library, cinema, theatre, etc*).

amethyst [am'-ee-thist] *n* a precious stone of a bluish-violet or purple colour.

amiable [ăm'-i-êbêl] *adj* friendly, pleasant (*an amiable young man/in an amiable mood*):—*n* **amiability**.

amicable [a'-mik-êbêl] *adj* friendly (*settle the dispute in an amicable way*).

amid', amidst' *preps* in the middle of, amongst.

amid'ships *adv* in or towards the middle of a ship.

amiss' *adv* wrong (*something amiss*):—**take amiss** to take offence at.

ammo'nia *n* 1 a strong-smelling, colourless gas. 2 a solution of ammonia gas and water (*ammonia may be used for cleaning*).

ammuni'tion *n* 1 powder, bullets, shells, etc. 2 facts, etc, used against someone in an argument, etc.

amnesia [am-nee'-zi-a] *n* loss of memory (*a blow to the head caused his amnesia*).

am'nesty *n* a general pardon (*an amnesty for all political prisoners*).

amoeba [a-mee'-ba] *n* (*pl* **amoe'bae**) a tiny living creature found in water:—*adj* **amoe'bic**.

amok' *adv*:—**to run amok** to go mad with the desire to kill.

among', amongst' *preps* 1 in the middle of (*a house among the trees/roses amongst the weeds*). 2 in shares or parts to each person (*share the chocolate among you*). 3 in the group of (*the best among his novels*).

am'orous *adj* feeling or expressing love or sexual desire (*amorous glances*).

amount' *vb* 1 to add up to (*bills amounting to £ 3000*). 2 to be equal to (*a reply amounting to a refusal*):—*n* the sum total.

ampere [am'-per] *n* the unit used in measuring electric current.

am'persand *n* a character (&) that stands for 'and' (*Jones & Son*).

amphibian [am-fib'-i-an] *n* 1 a creature that can live both on land and in water (*frogs are amphibians*). 2 a vehicle designed to move over land or water. 3 an aircraft that can take off from or land on either land or water:—*adj* **amphib'ious**.

am'phitheatre *n* an oval or circular theatre or building in which the seats rise in tiers around and above a central stage or arena.

am'ple *adj* 1 large (*a lady with an ample bosom*). 2 enough, sufficient, more than enough (*ample time to get there/ample opportunity*).

amplification *see* amplify.

am'plifier *n* an instrument for making sounds louder.

am'plify *vb* 1 to enlarge (*amplify his statement with further details*). 2 to make louder (*amplify the music from the guitar*):—*n* **amplifica'tion**.

am'plitude *n* size, extent, abundance.

am'ply *adv* fully, sufficiently (*amply paid*).

am'putate *vb* to cut off (a limb):—*n* **ampu-ta'tion**.

amuck' *same as* amok.

am'ulet *n* an ornament worn as a charm against evils.

amuse' *vb* 1 to entertain, to give pleasure (*amuse the children by reading to them*). 2 to make laugh or smile (*amused by the comedian's jokes*):—*adj* **amus'ing**.

amuse'ment *n* 1 pleasure, entertainment (*play the piano purely for her own amusement*). 2 entertainment, pastime (*a wide variety of amusements, such as darts, dominoes, table tennis*).

ana'chronism [an-ak'-ro-nizm] *n* 1 the mistake of placing a person or thing in the wrong period of time. 2 a thing or custom that is far behind the fashion.

anacon'da *n* a large snake of South America.

anaemia [an-eem'-ia] *n* a condition caused by lack of red corpuscles in the blood.

anaem'ic *adj* 1 suffering from anaemia. 2 pale, colourless (*wearing an anaemic shade of pink*). 3 lifeless, lacking spirit (*an anaemic performance*).

anaesthes'ia *n* loss of feeling.

anaesthetic [an-ês-thet'-ik] *n* a substance that causes loss of feeling for a time, either in the whole body (**general anaesthetic**) or in a limited area of the body, such as a leg (**local anaesthetic**) (*given an anaesthetic before the operation*):—*also adj*:—*vb* **anaesthetize** [an-ees'-thêt-îz].

anaesthetist [an-ees'-thêt-ist] *n* one who gives anaesthetics.

an'agram *n* a word or words formed by arranging the letters of a word or phrase in a new order (*e.g. mite from time*).

anal'ogous *adj* similar (*in a situation analogous to our own*).

anal'ogy *n* **1** likeness (*the analogy between the human heart and a pump*). **2** the process of reasoning based on such similarity (*explain the movement of light as an analogy with that of water*).

an'alyse *vb* to break a thing up into its parts or elements (*analyse the food for signs of poison/ analyse the facts and figures*).

analysis [a-na-li-sis] *n* (*pl* **ana'lyses**) **1** the process of analysing (*subject the food to analysis*). **2** a statement of the results of this. **3** *short for* **psychoanalysis**:—*adj* **an-alyt'ical**.

an'alyst *n* one who analyses, esp in chemistry.

analytical *see* **analysis**.

an'archist *n* one who wishes to do away with all government.

an'archy *n* **1** lawlessness. **2** absence of government.

anathema [a-na'-thê-ma] *n* **1** a solemn curse. **2** a thing accursed or hateful. **3** something or someone that one detests or strongly disapproves of (*bullying is an anathema to him*).

anat'omy *n* **1** the study of the way the body is put together (*study anatomy*). **2** the cutting up of a body to study its parts and their relation to each other. **3** (*often hum*) the body (*leaving some parts of his anatomy uncovered*):—*adj* **anatom'ical**:—*n* **anat'omist**.

ancestor [an'-ses-têr] *n* forefather, a person from whom one is descended:—*adj* **an-ces'tral**.

an'cestry *n* line of forefathers.

anchor [an'-kêr] *n* **1** a heavy iron hook that grips the sea bed and holds a ship at rest in the water. **2** a person or thing that provides support, stability or security (*his wife was an anchor to him*):—*vb* **1** to hold fast by an anchor. **2** to drop an anchor:—**to weigh anchor** to take up an anchor before sailing.

an'chorage *n* a place where a ship can anchor.

an'chorite *n* a hermit.

an'chovy *n* a small strong-tasting fish of the herring family.

ancient [ân'-shênt] *adj* **1** old, existing since early times (*ancient customs*). **2** belonging to old times (*ancient civilizations*). **3** (*inf*) very old (*still wearing that ancient coat*):—**the ancients** those who lived long ago, esp the Greeks and Romans.

ancillary [an-sil'-ê-ri] *adj* supporting, helping, subsidiary (*doctors and ancillary medical staff*).

andante [an-dan'-te] *adj* (*mus*) with slow and graceful movement.

an'ecdote *n* a short, interesting or amusing story about a person or event.

anemometer [a-ne-mo'-mêtêr] *n* an instrument for measuring the force of the wind.

anemone [a-ne'-mo-ni] *n* the wind-flower, a kind of garden plant with red, purple or white flowers.

an'eroid *adj*:—**aneroid barometer** an instrument for measuring air pressure without the aid of a fluid.

anew' *adv* (*fml or old*) again, in a new or different way (*begin the attempt anew*).

angel [ân'-jêl] *n* **1** in Christianity, a spirit created to serve God (*angels are usually shown in pictures with wings and wearing white*). **2** a very good and helpful person (*she was an angel to lend me the money*):—*adj* **angel'ic**.

an'ger *n* a feeling of rage or fury:—*vb* to enrage (*angered by his rudeness*).

angina [an-jî'-na] *n* a disease of the heart, causing sudden, sharp pains.

angle¹ *n* **1** the space between two meeting lines (*an angle of 90°*). **2** a corner (*a room full of angles*). **3** point of view (*looking at things from the parents' angle*).

angle² *vb* **1** to fish with hook and bait. **2** to try to get by indirect means (*angle for an invitation*).

Ang'lican *adj* of the Church of England:—*also n*.

ang'ling *n* the art of fishing with a rod:—*n* **ang'ler**.

Ang'lo- *prefix* English; of England.

ango'ra *n* a long-haired wool from a goat.

an'gry *adj* feeling or showing anger (*an angry man/angry words*):—*adv* **ang'rily**.

anguish [ang'-gwish] *n* very great pain, of body or mind (*suffer anguish until the lost child was found*).

ang'ular *adj* **1** sharp-cornered (*an angular building*). **2** thin and bony (*clothes hanging loosely on her angular body*).

an'imal n **1** a living being with the power to feel and to move at will. **2** such a living being other than human beings (*care about animals as well as people*). **3** a four-footed creature, as distinct from a bird, fish or insect. **4** a wild or uncivilized person.

an'imate vb **1** to give life to. **2** to enliven, to make lively and interesting (*need to animate our weekly discussions*):—adj **living**.

anima'tion n liveliness, excitement.

animos'ity n strong dislike, hatred, enmity (*cause animosity between neighbours*).

ank'le n the joint that connects the foot with the leg.

an'nals npl a record of events written year by year (*the annals of the parish from early times*):—n **an'nalist**.

anneal' vb to harden (glass or metals) by exposing to great heat.

annex' vb **1** to add to the end (*annex a personal note to her report*). **2** to take possession of (*small countries annexed by the emperor*):—n **annexation**.

an'nexe n a part added to or situated near a building (*the school annexe*).

annihilate [an-nī'-il-āt] vb to destroy completely (*annihilate the entire army/annihilate their argument*):—n **annihila'tion**.

anniver'sary n the yearly return of the date on which some event occurred and is remembered (*their wedding anniversary/the anniversary of the end of the war*).

an'notate vb to write notes upon:—n **anno-ta'tion**.

announce' vb to make known (*announce their engagement*):—n **announce'ment**.

announ'cer n in broadcasting, one who makes known the programmes or reads news items.

annoy' vb to vex; to tease; to be troubled by something one dislikes:—n **annoy'ance**.

an'nual adj **1** yearly (*her annual salary*). **2** happening every year or only once a year (*an annual festival*):—n **1** a plant lasting only for one year. **2** a book of which a new edition is published yearly (*children's annuals published for Christmas*):—adv **an'nually**.

annu'ity n a sum of money payable yearly.

annul' vb (**annul'led, annul'ling**) to declare that something is not valid, to cancel (*annul a marriage/annul a contract*):—n **an-nul'ment**.

anoint' vb to put oil on, esp with the intention of making holy.

anom'aly n something unusual, irregular or not normal (*a bird with no wings is an anomaly/anomalies in the tax system*):—adj **anom'alous**.

anon[1] adv (*old or hum*) soon (*see you anon!*).

anon[2] abbr of **anonymous** (*the author of the poem is anon*).

anonymous [an-on'-im-ês] adj nameless, of unknown name (*an anonymous donor*):—n **anonym'ity**.

anorex'ia n an eating disorder in which someone refuses to eat in order to lose weight, although already very thin:—adj **anorex'ic**.

answer [än'-sêr] vb **1** to reply to (*answer a letter/answer her questions*). **2** to be suitable, to fit (*answer the firm's needs/answer the description*). **3** to accept blame for or punishment (*have to answer for one's crimes*). **4** to be responsible to (*answer to a new boss*):—n **1** a reply. **2** a solution (to a problem).

an'swerable adj open to blame for (*answerable for the damage*).

ant n a small, busy insect.

antag'onism n opposition, enmity (*cause antagonism between the partners*).

antag'onist n an opponent.

antagonis'tic adj opposed to, hostile.

antag'onize vb to make an enemy of (*antagonize neighbours with noisy behaviour*).

Antarc'tic adj of South Polar regions.

anteced'ent adj (*fml*) going before (*antecedent events*):—npl **anteced'ents** the previous family, history, etc, of a person.

an'tedate vb **1** to belong to an earlier time or period than (*events that antedate their quarrel*). **2** to write a date on earlier than the date of writing (*antedate a cheque*).

an'tediluvian adj **1** (*Bible*) before the Flood. **2** old-fashioned (*antediluvian ideas*).

an'telope n a graceful, delicate animal like the deer.

antenatal [an-ti-nā'-têl] adj before birth (*antenatal exercises*).

anten'na n **1** (*pl* **anten'nae**) the feeler of an insect. **2** (*pl* **anten'nas**) (*esp Amer*) an aerial.

anter'ior adj **1** (*fml*) earlier (*anterior events*). **2** situated near or nearer the front (*the anterior bones of the skull*).

an'teroom n a room leading to another room (*the anteroom to the doctor's surgery*).

an'them n a hymn or song of praise to God.

anthol'ogy n a collection of pieces of poetry or prose by different authors.

anthracite [an'-thra-sît] n a type of coal that burns almost without flame or smoke.

an'thrax n a disease attacking sheep or cattle and sometimes infecting men.

anthropoid [an'-thro-poid] adj like a human being (*anthropoid apes*).

anthropol'ogy n the study of man in relation to his surroundings.

an'ti- prefix against.

antibiot'ic n a substance produced by living things, used in medicine to destroy bacteria that cause disease (*given an antibiotic, such as penicillin, to cure a sore throat*):—also adj.

antic'ipate vb **1** to expect (*anticipate trouble at the football match*). **2** to take action in advance of (*we anticipated their arrival at the camp by getting there first*). **3** to foresee (*anticipate how they would act*):—n **anticipa'tion**.

anticli'max n an unexpectedly dull ending to a striking series of events (*after the weeks of preparation, the actual festival seemed an anticlimax*).

an'tics npl absurd or exaggerated behaviour (*the antics of the clowns*).

anticy'clone n a widespread area of cool, dry air, accompanied by fair weather.

an'tidote n a medicine that counteracts the effects of poison or disease (*given an antidote when bitten by a snake*).

an'timony n a bluish-white metal.

antip'athy n dislike, opposition to (*feel antipathy towards the man who caused the accident*).

antipodes [an-ti'-po-dez] npl places on the surface of the earth exactly opposite to each other.

antiqua'rian n one who studies or collects things of an earlier period in history:—also adj.

antiquary [an'-tik-wa-ri] n same as **antiquarian**.

an'tiquated adj old-fashioned, out of date (*antiquated ideas*).

antique [an-teek'] adj **1** made in an earlier period and usu valuable (*antique furniture*). **2** (*fml*) connected with ancient times:—n a piece of furniture, jewellery, etc, made in an earlier period and considered valuable.

antiquity [an-tik'-wê-ti] n **1** ancient times, esp those of the Greeks and Romans. **2** great age.

antisep'tic adj having the power to kill germs:—n an antiseptic substance (*clean the wound with an antiseptic*).

antithesis [an-tith'-ê-sis] n (*pl* **antith'eses**) **1** contrast of ideas, emphasized by similarity in expressing them. **2** the exact opposite:—adj **antithet'ical**.

ant'ler n a branch of a stag's horn:—adj **ant'lered**.

an'tonym n a word meaning the opposite of (*ugly is the antonym of beautiful*).

an'vil n an iron block on which a smith hammers or shapes metal.

anxious [ang'-shus] adj worried about what will happen or has happened (*anxious parents waiting for their lost children/anxious about flying*):—n **anxiety** [ang-zî'-ê-ti].

aorta [ā-or'-ta] n the great artery leading from the heart, carrying blood to all parts of the body.

apace' adv (*fml or old*) quickly (*work went on apace*).

apart' adv separately (*married but now living apart*).

apartheid' n a policy of racial segregation implemented in South Africa.

apart'ment n **1** a room (*the private apartments that cannot be visited in the palace*). **2** a set of rooms rented as lodgings (*a holiday apartment in a boarding house*). **3** (*Amer*) a flat (*share an apartment*).

a'pathy n lack of feeling or interest (*people failing to vote in the election because of apathy*):—adj **apathet'ic**.

ape n a tailless monkey (e.g. gorilla, chimpanzee, orangutan, gibbon):—vb to imitate exactly.

aperitif n a drink taken before meals to stimulate the appetite (*a glass of sherry or other aperitif*).

ap'erture n an opening, a hole (*peek through an aperture in the fence*).

apex [ā'-peks] n (*pl* **a'pexes** or **a'pices**) the top or highest point (*the apex of the triangle/the apex of his career*).

aphorism [a'-for-izm] n a short wise saying, a maxim

apiary [ā'-pi-êr-i] n a place where bees are kept, a beehouse, a number of hives

apiece' adv to or for each one (*cakes costing 40p apiece*).

aplomb' *n* confidence in oneself (*handle the awkward question with aplomb*).

apocalyp'tic *adj* **1** telling of great misfortune in the future (*apocalyptic warning about what will happen to the environment*). **2** relating to an event of great importance, particularly an event of disastrous or catastrophic importance.

apoc'ryphal *adj* not likely to be genuine, doubtful or untrue (*the stories about his adventures are thought to be apocryphal*).

apologet'ic *adj* making excuses, expressing regret (*an apologetic refusal to the invitation*).

apol'ogize *vb* to express regret for a fault or error, to say one is sorry (*apologize for being late*).

apol'ogy *n* an admission that wrong has been done, an expression of regret.

apoplexy [a'-po-plek-si] *n* sudden paralysis caused by the bursting of a blood vessel in the brain:— *adj* **apoplec'tic.**

apos'tasy *n* the giving up of one's faith or accepted principles:—*n* **apos'tate:**—*vb* **apos'tasize.**

apostle [a-pos'-êl] *n* **1** one sent to preach the gospel. **2** one of the twelve disciples of Christ. **3** a supporter of a new system or theory (*an apostle of low-fat diets*).

apostrophe [a-pos'-tro-fi] *n* **1** the breaking off during a speech to address directly some person or object absent or present. **2** a mark (') indicating the possessive case or omission of certain letters.

apoth'ecary *n* (*old*) one who prepares and sells drugs for medical purposes.

appal [ap-pâl'] *vb* (**appalled', appal'ling**) to shock, to horrify (*appalled at the state of the starving children*).

appal'ling *adj* shocking, terrible, horrific.

apparatus [ap-pa-rã'-tês] *n* **1** tools or equipment for doing work (*gymnastic apparatus/laboratory apparatus*). **2** organization, system (*the apparatus of government*).

appar'el *n* clothing:—*vb* (*old*) to dress.

apparent [ap-pã'-rênt *or* ap-pâ'-rênt] *adj* **1** easily seen, evident (*it was apparent that he was very ill/worries that were apparent to everyone*). **2** seeming but not necessarily real (*her apparent concern for her friend*).

appar'ently *adv* evidently, seemingly.

appari'tion *n* **1** someone or something that appears suddenly (*an apparition stumbling out of the fog*). **2** a ghost.

appeal' *vb* **1** to make an earnest and strong request for (*appeal for money to feed her children*). **2** to carry (a law case) to a higher court. **3** to interest, to please (*films that appeal to me*):—*also n.*

appear' *vb* **1** to come into sight (*figures appearing out of the mist*). **2** to seem (*she appears sad*):—*n* **appear'ance.**

appease' *vb* **1** to calm, to make peaceful (*appease the angry father by apologizing*). **2** to satisfy by giving what is wanted (*appease their curiosity*):—*n* **appease'ment.**

appella'tion *n* (*fml*) name, title (*his official appellation*).

append' *vb* to add, to attach (*append their signatures to the document*).

appen'dage *n* **1** something added or attached (*signatures as appendages to the document*). **2** something forming a part or attached to something larger or more important (*appendages, as elephants' trunks*).

appendici'tis *n* a painful disease of the appendix, usu requiring surgical removal.

appen'dix *n* (*pl* **appen'dixes** *or* **appen'dices**) **1** information added at the end of a book. **2** a short, closed tube leading off the bowels.

appertain' *vb* (*fml*) to belong, to relate to (*matters appertaining to the situation*).

ap'petite *n* desire to have something, esp food or pleasure (*invalids with little appetite for hospital food/no appetite for love*).

ap'petizer *n* something eaten or drunk to stimulate the appetite (*savouries served as an appetizer*).

appetiz'ing *adj* increasing the desire for food (*appetizing smells from the kitchen*).

applaud' *vb* to praise by clapping or shouting (*applauded warmly by the audience*):—*n* **applause'.**

ap'ple, *n* a fruit:—**apple of the eye** a person or object held very dear.

appli'ance *n* an instrument intended for some particular use (*modern kitchen appliances*).

ap'plicable *adj* that may be applied, suitable under the circumstances (*rules not applicable to the situation*):—*n* **applicabil'ity.**

ap'plicant *n* one who asks for, a person who applies for or makes a formal request for (*several applicants for the post*).

applica'tion *n* **1** the act of applying. **2** a formal request (*make an application for a council grant*). **3** perseverance, hard work (*application is required to pass the exams*).

apply' *vb* **1** to put or spread on (*apply the ointment to the wound*). **2** to use (*apply force*). **3** to pay attention (to), to concentrate (*apply oneself to one's work*). **4** to ask for, to put in a formal request for (*apply for the post of manager*). **5** to concern or be relevant to (*the usual rules apply*).

appoint' *vb* **1** to choose for a job or position (*appoint her to the post of manager*). **2** (*fml*) to fix or decide on (*appoint a date for the meeting*).

appoint'ment *n* **1** a post or position (*a teaching appointment*). **2** a meeting arranged for a certain time (*have several appointments today/a doctor's appointment*).

appor'tion *vb* to divide out into fair shares (*apportion blame*).

ap'posite *adj* apt, suitable to the circumstances (*apposite remarks*).

apprais'al *n* the assessment of the value or quality of (*give an appraisal of his assistant's work*).

appraise' *vb* to judge the value, quality, ability, etc, of (*appraise her suitability for the job*).

appre'ciable *adj* enough to be noticed (*no appreciable difference*):—*adv* **appre'ciably**.

appre'ciate *vb* **1** to recognize the value or good qualities of, to enjoy (*appreciate good food*). **2** to understand fully, to recognize (*I appreciate your concern*). **3** to be grateful for (*appreciate your kindness*). **4** to rise in value (*houses appreciating in value*).

apprecia'tion *n* **1** a good or just opinion of (*audiences showing their appreciation by applauding*). **2** gratitude (*in appreciation of his good work*). **3** understanding (*some appreciation of your problem*). **4** incr ease in value (*appreciation of property values*).

appre'ciative *adj* **1** willing to understand and praise justly (*appreciative of good music/an appreciative audience*). **2** grateful (*appreciative of his kindness*):—*adv* **appre'ciatively**.

apprehend' *vb* **1** (*fml*) to arrest, to seize (*apprehended by the police*). **2** (*fml or old*) to understand (*apprehend his actions*).

apprehen'sion *n* **1** (*fml*) fear, dread (*view the arrival of the new manager with some apprehension*). **2** (*fml*) arrest, seizure (*the apprehension of the bank robbers*). **3** (*fml*) understanding (*no apprehension of the difficulties involved*).

apprehen'sive *adj* afraid of what may happen, anxious (*apprehensive about the exams*).

apprent'ice *n* one who is learning a trade or skill while working at it:—*vb* to bind by agreement to serve as an apprentice.

apprent'iceship *n* the time served as an apprentice.

apprise' *vb* to inform (*apprise them of the facts*).

approach' *vb* **1** to move nearer (to) (*approaching the village/Christmas is approaching*). **2** to seek an opportunity to speak to someone (*approach him for a donation to the charity*):—*n* **1** act of approaching. **2** the way leading to a place.

approach'able *adj* **1** able to be approached (*villages not approachable by the road in winter*). **2** easy to speak to (*he's unfriendly and not at all approachable*).

approba'tion *n* praise, approval.

appro'priate *vb* **1** to take and use as one's own (*appropriate the firm's money*). **2** to set apart for a particular purpose or use (*money appropriated by the government for training*):—*adj* suitable: *ns* **appro-pria'tion**, **appro'priateness**.

approve' *vb* **1** to think well of, to accept (*approve of your choice*). **2** to agree to, to accept (*approve the application*):—*n* **approv'al**:— **on approval** for a period of trial before purchase.

approx'imate *vb* to come near to (*a story approximating to the truth*):—*adj* nearly correct (*an approximate price*).

approx'imately *adv* nearly (*approximately 9 o'clock/approximately four miles*).

approxima'tion *n* a nearly correct result (*the figure is an approximation*).

apricot [ăp'-ri-kot] *n* an orange-yellow fruit of the peach family.

A'pril *n* the fourth month of the year.

a'pron *n* a garment or cloth worn in front to protect the clothes.

apropos of [a-pro-pō'] *prep* relating to, concerning (*apropos of your suggestion*).

apt *adj* **1** suitable, appropriate (*an apt reply*). **2** ready to learn (*an apt pupil*). **3** having a tendency to (*a car that is apt to break down*).

apt'ly *adv* fitly.

apt'itude *n* skill, cleverness (*an aptitude for foreign languages*).

apt'ness *n* suitability (*the aptness of the remark*).

aquarium [a-kwë'-ri-um] *n* (*pl* **aquariums** or **aquaria**) a tank for (live) fish and water animals and water plants.

aqua'tic *adj* **1** living or growing in water (*aquatic plants*). **2** taking place in water (*aquatic sports*).

aqueduct [a'-kwee-dukt] *n* **1** a man-made channel for carrying water. **2** a bridge built to carry water.

aqueous [a'-kwi-us] *adj* of or like water, watery (*an aqueous solution*).

aq'uiline *adj* hooked like the beak of an eagle (*an aquiline nose*).

ar'able *adj* fit for ploughing.

arbiter [är'-bi-têr] *n* one chosen by the parties concerned to settle a dispute, an umpire (*appoint an arbiter in the dispute between unions and management*).

ar'bitrary *adj* **1** not decided by rules, laws, etc, but by a person's own opinion (*a decision that was completely arbitrary/an arbitrary choice*). **2** uncontrolled, unrestrained (*arbitrary power/an arbitrary ruler*):—*adv* **ar'bitrarily**.

ar'bitrate *vb* to act as an umpire or referee, esp in a dispute (*asked to arbitrate in the dispute between neighbours*):—*n* **ar'bitrator**.

arbitra'tion *n* the settling of a dispute by an arbitrator (*disputes going to arbitration*).

ar'bour *n* a shady recess in a garden.

arc *n* **1** a curve. **2** a part of the circumference of a circle.

arcade' *n* **1** a covered walk. **2** a covered street containing shops.

arch[1] *n* a curved structure, usu supporting a bridge or roof.

arch[2] *adj* cunning, roguish (*an arch smile*):—*adv* **arch'ly**:—*n* **arch'ness**.

arch- *prefix* chief.

archaeology [ar-kā-ol'-odj-i] *n* the study of the remains and monuments of ancient times:— *adj* **archaeolog'ical**:—*n* **archaeol'ogist**.

archaic [ar-kā'-ik] *adj* **1** old-fashioned (*archaic medical methods*). **2** (*of words*) no longer in current use (*'methinks' is an archaic expression for 'I think'*).

ar'chaism *n* a word or expression not in present-day use.

archan'gel *n* an angel of the highest rank.

archbish'op *n* a chief bishop, with other bishops under his rule.

archdea'con *n* a church rank next in importance to that of bishop.

archduke' *n* a prince, esp of the royal family of Austria.

arch'er *n* one able to use a bow and arrow.

arch'ery *n* the art of shooting with bow and arrow.

archipelago [ar-ki-pel'-a-gō] *n* (*pl* **archipelagos** or **archipelagoes**) **1** a sea dotted with many islands. **2** a group of islands.

architect [ar'-ki-tekt] *n* **1** one who plans buildings. **2** a person who plans, designs or creates something (*the architect of our modern political system*).

architec'ture *n* **1** the art or science of planning or designing buildings (*study architecture*). **2** a special fashion in building (*Gothic architecture*):—*adj* **architec'tural**.

archives [ar'-kīvz] *npl* **1** historical records (*the firm's archives go back to the early 19th century*). **2** the place where they are kept:—*n* **ar'chivist**.

arc'tic *adj* very cold (*arctic conditions*).

ar'dent *adj* eager, enthusiastic, passionate (*ardent fans/ardent lover*):—*adv* **ar'dently**.

ar'dour *n* enthusiasm, passion (*with patriotic fervour/the ardour of her lover*).

ar'duous *adj* difficult, requiring much effort (*an arduous task/an arduous climb*).

ar'ea *n* **1** any open space, place, region (*a residential area/dry areas of the world*). **2** a subject, topic or activity (*in the area of politics*). **3** the extent of a surface (*a room 16 square metres in area*). **4** an enclosed court, esp a sunken one between a house and the street.

are'na *n* **1** an open space of ground for contests or games. **2** area of activity or conflict (*the arena of party politics*).

ar'gent *n* the silver of a coat of arms.

ar'gosy *n* a large ship, esp a merchant ship, of olden times.

ar'gue *vb* **1** to give reasons for believing something to be true (*argue against uniting the two firms*). **2** to discuss in an unfriendly or quarrelsome way (*argue about whose toy it is*). **3** to quarrel (*brother and sister are always arguing*):—*adj* **ar'guable**.

ar'gument *n* **1** reasons for holding a belief (*the argument for going to college*). **2** a dispute, an unfriendly discussion (*an argument about money*). **3** a quarrel. **4** a summary of a book.

argumen'tative *adj* given to discussing or disputing (*argumentative people unable to discuss calmly/in an argumentative mood*).

a'rid *adj* **1** very dry (*arid soil/arid areas of the world*). **1** unproductive, uninteresting (*arid discussions*):—*n* **arid'ity**.

aright' *adv* (*old*) correctly (*did I hear you aright?*).

arise' *vb* (*pt* **arose**, *pp* **aris'en**) **1** to come into being, to appear (*difficulties that may arise/when the need arises*). **2** to result from (*matters arising from our discussion*). **3** (*old*) to get up (*arise and go*).

aristoc'racy *n* **1** government by the nobility of birth. **2** the nobility.

aris'tocrat *n* a person of noble birth:—*adj* **aristocrat'ic**.

arith'metic *n* the science of numbers; the art of working with numbers:—*adj* **arith-met'ical**.

ark *n* a wooden chest (e.g. *Ark of the Covenant*):— **the Ark** the vessel in which Noah was saved from the Flood.

arm *n* **1** one of the upper limbs, the part of the body from the shoulder to the hand. **2** anything resembling this (*the arm of the chair*). **3** the part of a garment that covers the arm. **4.** power (*the arm of the law*). **5** *pl* **arms** weapons or armour used in fighting. **6** *pl* the badge of a noble family, town, etc (*coat of arms*):— *vb* **arm 1** to take up weapons. **2** to provide with weapons.

arma'da *n* a fleet of armed ships (*the Spanish Armada*).

armadil'lo *n* a South American animal with a bony protective shell.

ar'mament *n* **1** the guns on a ship, tank, etc. **2** all the weapons used in war.

armistice [är'-mês-tis] *n* in war, an agreement to stop fighting for a time.

arm'let *n* a band worn round the arm (*mourners with black armlets*).

armor'ial *adj* relating to arms in heraldry.

ar'mour *n* **1** protective covering. **2** (*old*) a metal covering worn by soldiers to protect their bodies. **3** the tank force of an army.

ar'moury *n* a place for keeping arms.

arm'pit *n* the hollow under the shoulder, between the arm and the body.

arm'y *n* **1** a large number of soldiers organized for war. **2** a large number of persons engaged on a common task (*an army of voluntary workers*).

aro'ma *n* a pleasant smell (*the aroma of newly baked bread*).

aroma'tic *adj* sweet-smelling (*aromatic cooking herbs*).

around' *prep* **1** on all sides of or in a circle, about (*flowers grew around the tree/children dancing around the maypole*). **2** here and there, at several places in (*books lying around the room*). **3** approximately (*around 4 o'clock/around four miles away*). **4** near to (*restaurants around here*):—*adv* **1** on every side, here and there (*pick up the books lying around*). **2** in the surrounding area (*he's somewhere around*). **3** available (*no money around*). **4** in the opposite direction (*turn around*).

arouse' *vb* **1** to stir up (*arouse their anger*). **2** to make awake or active (*arouse them from sleep*).

arraign [ar-rān'] *vb* **1** to accuse publicly (*arraign on a charge of murder*). **2** to find fault with, criticize strongly (*arraign the press for not respecting their privacy*):—*n* **arraign'ment**.

arrange' *vb* **1** to put into order (*arrange the books on the shelves*). **2** to make plans, to make preparations for (*arrange a meeting*):—*n* **arrange'ment**.

ar'rant *adj* thoroughly (bad), out-and-out (*an arrant coward*).

ar'ras *n* a hanging of ornamental cloth on a wall.

array' *vb* **1** to set in order (*soldiers arrayed for battle*). **2** to dress up (*dancers arrayed in beautiful ballgowns*):—*n* **1** order. **2** dress.

arrears *npl* that which remains unpaid or undone (*her rent is in arrears/pay the arrears on their TV rental*).

arrest' *vb* **1** to take as prisoner, esp in the name of the law. **2** (*fml*) to catch or attract (*arrest the* *attention of the crowd*). **3** to stop (*arrest the economic growth of the country*):—*n* **1** the act of stopping. **2** the act of arresting in the name of the law.

arriv'al *n* **1** the act of arriving (*the late arrival of the visitors*). **2** one who arrives (*recent arrivals in the village*).

arrive' *vb* **1** to come (*the day of the wedding arrived*). **2** to reach (*arrive home*).

ar'rogant *adj* proud, haughty (*too arrogant to listen to others' advice*):—*n* **ar'rogance**.

ar'row *n* a pointed stick or similar missile for shooting from a bow.

ar'rowroot *n* a West Indian plant from which an edible starch is obtained.

ar'senal *n* a place where weapons of war are made or stored, usu on behalf of a government.

ar'senic *n* a toxic chemical poison.

ar'son *n* the crime of setting fire to property on purpose.

art *n* **1** a particular ability or skill (*the art of conversation/the art of cooking*). **2** (*fml*) cunning, trickery (*get her own way by art*). **3** the practice of painting, sculpture, and architecture, etc (*studying art at college*). **4** examples of painting, sculpture, etc (*a gallery showing modern art*):—**the Arts** subjects of study that are intended to broaden the mind rather than (or as well as) to teach practical skill.

ar'tery *n* a tube carrying blood from the heart.

artesian [ar-tee'-zhên] *adj:*—**artesian well** a well made by digging so deep that pressure forces the water up.

art'ful *adj* deceitful, cunning (*an artful child/an artful dodge*):—*adv* **art'fully**.

ar'tichoke *n* **1** (**globe artichoke**) a tall plant, somewhat like a thistle, part of the leaves of which can be eaten. **2** (**Jerusalem artichoke**) a type of sunflower with edible underground stems.

ar'ticle *n* **1** a thing (*articles of clothing*). **2** an essay on a single topic in a newspaper, periodical or encyclopedia. **3** a single item in a list or statement (e.g. a treaty). **4** *pl* a written agreement (*articles of apprenticeship*).

articulate [ar-tik'-û-lêt] *adj* **1** distinct, clear (*articulate speech*). **2** able to express oneself

clearly:—*vb* [ar-tik'-û-lãt] **1** to join together (*bones articulated with others*). **2** to speak distinctly (*articulate your words so that you can be heard at the back*).

articula'tion *n* **1** a joint. **2** the act of joining. **3** forming of sounds in speech.

artifice [ar'-ti-fis] *n* **1** a trick (*use artifice to gain entrance*). **2** trickery (*gain entrance by artifice*).

artific'ial *adj* **1** man-made and so not natural (*artificial flowers/artificial light*). **2** not genuine, unnatural (*an artificial smile*):—*n* **artificiality**.

artil'lery *n* **1** big guns. **2** the part of an army that cares for and fires such guns.

ar'tisan *n* a skilled manual workman.

ar'tist *n* **1** a professional painter (*Constable and other British artists*). **2** one skilled in some art (*a culinary artist*). **3** an artiste.

artiste [ar-teest'] *n* a public entertainer, such as a professional singer or dancer.

artis'tic *adj* **1** having to do with art or artists (*artistic works*). **2** having or showing love for what is beautiful (*an artistic child/an artistic flower arrangement*).

ar'tistry *n* artistic skill.

art'less *adj* simple, sincere:—*adv* **art'lessly**.

asbes'tos *n* a soft white mineral that cannot burn.

ascend' *vb* (*fml*) **1** to go upwards (*the lift ascended*). **2** to climb (*ascend the mountain*).

ascen'dancy, ascen'dency *ns* controlling power.

ascen'sion *n* act of rising.

ascent' *n* (*fml*) **1** act of going up (*the ascent of the hill*). **2** an upward slope (*a rocky ascent*).

ascertain' *vb* to find out (*ascertain facts*).

ascet'ic *n* one who gives up bodily pleasure to improve spiritually, a hermit:—*also adj:*—*n* **ascet'icism**.

ascribe' *vb* to explain as the result of something else (*ascribe his behaviour to his violent upbringing*).

aseptic [ã-sep'-tik] *adj* not causing disease or decay (*aseptic conditions necessary in a hospital*).

ash[1] *n* a tree.

ash[2] *n or* **ash'es** *npl* the dust left after anything has been burned.

ashamed' *adj* feeling shame (*ashamed of his actions*).

ash'en adj greyish-white like ashes, very pale (*ashen with grief*).

ashore' adv on or to land (*go ashore*).

aside' adv 1 on one side (*put some money aside every week for a holiday*). 2 to one side, apart (*take her aside to tell her the secret*).

as'inine adj very foolish (*asinine ideas*).

ask vb 1 to request (*ask for directions*). 2 to inquire (*ask how old they are*).

askance' adv sideways; out of the corners of the eyes:—**to look askance at** to consider with disapproval or suspicion.

askew [as-kû'] adv to one side, crookedly (*wear his cap askew*).

asleep' adj and adv sleeping (*remain asleep despite the noise*).

asp n a small poisonous snake.

aspar'agus n a plant, the tops of which can be eaten as a vegetable.

as'pect n 1 (*fml*) appearance (*of frightening aspect*). 2 the direction in which a building, etc, faces (*a house with a southern aspect*). 3 a particular part or feature of something (*consider the financial aspects of the situation*).

as'pen n a type of poplar tree.

asper'ity n roughness, harshness (*reply with asperity*).

asper'sion n damaging or unkind critical remarks (*make aspersions about his ability*).

asphalt [as'-falt] n a type of pitch used in road-making.

asphyx'iate vb to choke, to suffocate:—n **asphyxia'tion**.

aspira'tion n eager desire, ambition (*aspirations to greatness*).

aspire' vb to try very hard to reach (something ambitious, difficult, etc) (*aspire to high office in the government*).

as'pirin n a drug that relieves pain.

ass [as] n 1 a donkey. 2 a foolish person.

assagai same as **assegai**.

assail' vb (*fml*) to attack (*assail him with violent blows/assail them with questions*).

assail'ant n an attacker.

assas'sin n one who kills by surprise or secretly.

assas'sinate vb to murder by surprise or treachery, often for political reasons (*try to assassinate the president*):—n **assassi-na'tion**.

assault' n a sudden violent attack:—vb to attack.

assay' n a test of the quality of a metal, to find out how far it is pure or an alloy:—vb to test the quality, esp of metals.

assegai [as'-sê-gî] n a South African spear.

assem'ble vb 1 to bring or put together (*assemble the family together/assemble all the parts*). 2 to come together (*people assembling in the town centre*):—n **assem'blage**.

assem'bly n a gathering of people to discuss and take decisions (*school assembly*).

assent' vb to agree (*assent to the proposal*):—n consent; permission.

assert' vb to state firmly (*assert that he is innocent*):—**to assert oneself** to stand up for one's rights.

asser'tion n a firm statement.

asser'tive adj confident, tending to assert oneself.

assess' vb 1 to fix an amount payable (*assess your tax contribution*). 2 to estimate the value, worth, quality, etc, of (*assess his worth to the firm*):—n **assess'or**.

assess'ment n the amount or value fixed.

as'sets npl the entire property of a person or company:—**an asset** a help, an advantage (*he is an asset to the team*).

assidu'ity n close attention to a task.

assid'uous adj 1 steadily attentive, careful (*assiduous in his duties*). 2 hard-working, diligent (*assiduous pupils*).

assign' vb 1 to give as a share, duty, task, etc (*assign household tasks to each of the children*). 2 to appoint (*assign three men to the job*). 3 to fix, to name (*assign Wednesdays for our meetings*).

assigna'tion n an appointment to meet, esp secretly (*an assignation with her lover without her husband's knowledge*).

assign'ment n the share or amount (of work, etc) given to a person or group.

assim'ilate vb to take in and absorb (*plants assimilating food from the soil/assimilate people from different countries into America/try to assimilate the facts*):—n **assi-mila'tion**.

assist' vb to help (*assist with teaching duties/assist her in cooking the meal*).

assis'tance n help, aid.

assis'tant n 1 a helper (a teacher and two nursery assistants). 2 a person who serves in a shop, etc.

assiz'es npl law courts held at intervals in each English county for dealing with serious criminal cases.

associate [as-sō'-shee-āt] vb 1 to keep company with, to join with (associate with criminals). 2 to join or connect in the mind (associate childhood with happiness):—n a companion, a partner, a colleague.

associa'tion n 1 act of associating. 2 a group of persons meeting for a common purpose (an athletics association). 3 the bringing together of connected ideas (the association of home with security).

association football n eleven-a-side football played under the rules of the Football Association.

as'sonance n the rhyming of vowels but not consonants.

assort'ed adj mixed (a bag of assorted sweets):—**ill-assort'ed** badly matched (an ill-assorted pair).

assort'ment n a mixed collection (an assortment of books sold as one lot).

assuage [as-swāj'] vb to make less, to ease (assuage his thirst/try to assuage their grief).

assume' vb 1 to take for granted (assume that he is honest). 2 to take over (assume responsibility for the running of the school). 3 (fml) to put on, to pretend (assume an air of innocence although guilty). 4 (fml) to take on, to begin to have (the situation gradually assumed the quality of a nightmare).

assump'tion n 1 act of assuming (his assumption of the leadership). 2 something supposed, but not proved, to be true (making an assumption that he is guilty before his trial/proceed on the assumption that he is innocent).

assur'ance n 1 confidence (a post requiring a great deal of assurance). 2 a promise (you have my assurance that I shall be there). 3 a form of life insurance.

assure' vb 1 to make certain (his success in his career is now assured). 2 to tell as a sure fact, to state positively (I assure you that everything possible has been done).

assur'edly adv certainly.

as'ter n a star-like flower.

as'terisk n a star-shaped mark (*) used in printing.

astern' adv at or towards the back of a ship.

asthma [as'-ma or as'-thma] n a disease marked by difficulty in breathing:—adj **asthmat'ic**.

aston'ish vb to surprise greatly, to amaze (we were astonished at the news):—n **as-ton'ishment**.

astound' vb to shock with surprise, to surprise greatly.

astrakhan [as-trê-kan'] n a rough, black, curling wool.

as'tral adj belonging to the stars.

astray' adv out of the right way (parcels that have gone astray).

astride' adv with the legs apart or on each side of a thing.

astrin'gent adj 1 helping to close open wounds, cuts or pores (astringent lotions). 2 stern, severe (astringent comments):—n **astrin'gency**.

astrol'ogy n the study of the stars in order to learn about future events:—n **astrol'oger**.

as'tronaut n a member of the crew of a spaceship.

astronom'ical adj 1 connected with astronomy. 2 extraordinarily great (an astronomical sum of money).

astron'omy n the scientific study of the stars:—n **astron'omer**.

astute' adj clever, shrewd (an astute businessman):—n **astute'ness**.

asun'der adv apart, into parts (a house ripped asunder by the explosion/a family torn asunder by a feud).

asyl'um n 1 a place of refuge or safety (seek political asylum in another country). 2 (old) a home for the care of helpless or weak-minded people.

ate pt of **eat**.

atheism [ā'-thee-izm] n the belief that there is no God.

a'theist n one who believes that there is no God:—adj **atheis'tic**.

ath'lete n one good at sports, esp outdoor sports.

athlet'ic adj 1 having to do with sport or athletics (athletic events). 2 physically strong and active (athletic young people).

athlet'ics npl field sports (e.g. running, jumping, etc) (an athletics club).

at'las n a book of maps.

at'mosphere n 1 the air surrounding the earth. 2 the gas surrounding any star. 3 the air in a particular place (a stuffy atmosphere in the hall). 4 the feelings given rise to by an incident, place, story, etc, mood (*a friendly atmosphere*).

atmospher'ic *adj* **1** connected with the air (*atmospheric conditions*). **2** creating a certain atmosphere or mood (*atmospheric music*).

at'oll *n* a ring-shaped coral island.

at'om *n* **1** the smallest possible particle of an element that can be shown to have the properties of that element. **2** anything very small (*not an atom of truth*).

atom'ic *adj* connected with atoms.

atomic energy *n* the power obtained by separating the electrical units in an atom.

atone' *vb* to make up for, to pay for a wrong (*atone for his crime by paying compensation to his victim*):—*n* **atone'ment**.

atro'cious *adj* **1** very cruel or wicked (*atrocious crimes*). **2** very bad (*atrocious weather*).

atroc'ity *n* a very cruel act.

at'rophy *n* a wasting away (*suffering from atrophy of the muscles*).—*also vb.*

attach' *vb* to join (by tying, sticking, etc) (*attach the rope to the boat*).

attaché [at-ta'-shā] *n* an official on the staff of an embassy.

attaché case *n* a small case for papers, etc.

attached' *adj* **1** joined on to (*read the attached document*). **2** fond of (*she is very attached to her sister*).

attach'ment *n* **1** something joined on (*a food mixer with various attachments*). **2** fondness (*feels a strong attachment to his old school*).

attack' *vb* **1** to use force against, to begin to fight against (*armies attacking each other*). **2** to speak or act strongly against (*attack the politician in a newspaper article*). **3** to begin to deal with vigorously, to tackle (*attack the pile of correspondence*):—*also n*:—*n* **attack'er.**

attain' *vb* to reach (*attain a position of power/attain one's goal*).

attain'able *adj* able to be reached.

attain'ment *n* **1** act of attaining (*the attainment of early ambitions*). **2** something, such as a skill or ability, learned successfully (*attainments in the field of music*).

attempt' *vb* to try to do (*attempt to cheat*):—*n* an effort (*an attempt at cheating*).

attend' *vb* **1** to be present at (*attend the meeting of the committee*). **2** to take care of (*doctors attending to their patients/attend to the needs of the patient*). **3** (*fml*) to fix the mind on (*attend to what the teacher is saying*). **4** to wait on (*the queen -attended by her ladies-in-waiting*).

attend'ance *n* **1** presence. **2** the persons present.

attend'ant *n* **1** one who waits on. **2** a servant.

atten'tion *n* **1** care (*a wound in need of urgent attention*). **2** heed, notice (*pay attention to what is said/attract her attention*). **3** concentration (*her attention tends to wander*).

atten'tive *adj* giving attention, paying heed (*attentive pupils*).

atten'uate *vb* **1** to make thin (*illness had attenuated her limbs*). **2** to become thinner, to grow less (*the force of the storm attenuated*).

attest' *vb* to bear witness to, to vouch for (*attest to the truth of her statement*):—*n* **attesta'tion.**

at'tic *n* a room just under the roof of a house.

attire' *vb* to dress (*attired in silk*):—*n* dress.

at'titude *n* **1** position of the body (*artists painting models in various attitudes*). **2** way of thinking or behaving (*a hostile attitude*).

attorney [at-tur'-ni] *n* **1** a lawyer. **2** one appointed to act for another:—**power of attorney** the right to act on another's behalf.

attract' *vb* **1** to cause to come nearer (*magnets attracting steel*). **2** to cause to like or desire (*always attracted to amusing people*). **3** to arouse (*attract their attention*).

attrac'tion *n* **1** act of attracting (*the attraction of moths to the light/the attraction of television for children*). **2** the power to attract (*her attraction lies in her personality*). **3** something that attracts (*the attractions of the holiday resort*).

attrac'tive *adj* **1** having the power to attract, interesting, pleasing, etc (*an attractive offer*). **2** good-looking, pretty, handsome (*an attractive young woman*).

attrib'utable *adj* able to be attributed (*crimes easily attributable to him*).

attrib'ute *vb* **1** to think of as being caused by (*attribute his silence to guilt*). **2** to regard as being made, written, etc, by (*attribute a play to Shakespeare*):—*n* **at'-tribute** a quality, a characteristic (*the right attributes for the job*).

attri'tion *n* **1** act of wearing down strength, confidence, etc (*a war of attrition*). **2** a wearing away by rubbing, friction.

attune vb to make to agree, bring into harmony (*unable to attune our ideas to theirs*).

aubergine [ō'-ber-jeen] n a vegetable with a shiny, dark purple skin, often egg-shaped or long and pear-shaped, used in cooking, Also called **eggplant**.

auburn adj reddish-brown.

auction n a public sale at which an object is sold to the person offering the highest price or bid.

auctioneer n the person who conducts the sale at an auction.

audacious adj 1 bold, daring (*an audacious scheme*). 2 bold, shameless (*an audacious young woman*):—n **audacity**.

audible adj able to be heard (*a voice scarcely audible*):—n **audibility**.

audience n 1 the people who listen (e.g. to a speech, concert, etc). 2 an interview granted by a ruler or person of high authority (*an audience with the pope*).

audit vb to examine accounts to see if they are correct:—also n:—n **auditor**.

audition n a test given to an actor or singer to see how good he or she is (*hold auditions for the part of Hamlet*).

auditorium n the part of a hall open to the audience.

auditory adj having to do with the sense of hearing (*auditory organs*).

auger n a tool for boring holes.

augment vb to increase (*augment income*):—n **augmentation**.

augur n an ancient Roman priest who foretold the future:—also vb:—**to augur well** to be a good sign for the future.

augury n a sign of the future.

august adj (*fml*) noble, worthy of reverence (*an august personage*).

August n the eighth month of the year.

auk n a northern sea bird expert at swimming and diving.

aunt [änt] n the sister of one's mother or father.

au pair [ō-pär'] n a young person from abroad who helps with childcare and domestic work in exchange for board and a small salary.

aural adj having to do with the ear or hearing (*aural comprehension tests*).

aureole n in paintings, the gold circle around the head of saints or holy persons, a halo.

aurora n 1 the dawn. 2 the brightness seen in the sky in the extreme north or south (e.g. *the Aurora Borealis* or Northern Lights).

auspice n:—**under the auspices of** with the approval and help of (*a conference organized under the auspices of the university*).

auspicious adj promising future good (*an auspicious beginning*).

austere adj 1 simple and severe (*an austere way of life*). 2 stern (*her austere manner*). 3 plain, without decoration (*an austere room*):—n **austerity**.

authentic adj true, genuine (*an authentic signature/authentic documents*):—n **au-thenticity**.

authenticate vb to show the authenticity of, to prove genuine.

author n 1 a writer of books, etc. 2 (*fml*) a person who creates or begins something (*the author of this particular scheme*):—n **authorship**.

authoress n a female writer.

authoritative adj 1 having or showing power (*an authoritative tone of voice*). 2 reliable, providing trustworthy information (*an authoritative book on a subject*).

authority n 1 the power or right to rule or give orders (*the authority to sack people*). 2 a person or group of persons having this power or right.

authorize vb to give to another the right or power to do something (*authorizing him to sign the firm's cheques*).

autism [o'-tism] n a condition in which someone has unusual difficulty in communicating or in relating to other people or the world around them:—adj **autistic**.

auto- prefix self.

autobiography n the story of a person's life written by himself or herself.

autocrat n an all-powerful ruler:—n **autocracy**.

autocratic adj 1 like or belonging to an autocrat. 2 commanding in manner, expecting obedience (*an autocratic father*).

autograph n a person's own handwriting or signature.

automatic adj 1 working by itself (*an automatic washing machine*). 2 done without thought (*automatic process of breathing/an automatic response*):—adv **automatically**.

automation n the act of replacing human labour by machines.

autom'aton *n* (*pl* **autom'atons** *or* **autom'ata**) **1** a self-moving machine, a robot. **2** a person who acts in a mechanical manner, without thought or feeling.

aut'omobile *n* (*fml*) a motorcar.

auton'omy *n* the right of people, an organization, etc, to self-government (*regions demanding a degree of autonomy from central government*):— *adj* **auton'omous**.

autop'sy *n* an examination of a dead body to discover the cause of death.

au'tumn *n* one of the four seasons of the year, between summer and winter.

autum'nal *adj* having to do with autumn (*autumnal colours*).

auxil'iary *n* a person or thing that helps (*nursing auxiliaries*):— *also adj.*

avail' *vb* to make use of (*avail oneself of any help offered*):— *n* use, help.

avail'able *adj* at hand if wanted (*all the available money/not so far available*).

avalanche [av'-al-änsh] *n* **1** a great mass of snow, earth and ice sliding down a mountain. **2** a great amount (*an avalanche of offers*).

av'arice *n* greed for gain and riches:— *adj* **avaric'ious.**

avenge' *vb* to take revenge for a wrong (*to avenge her brother's death by killing his murderer. to avenge herself on her attacker by damaging his car*):— *n* **aven'ger.**

av'enue *n* **1** a way of approach. **2** a broad street. **3** a double row of trees, with or without a road between them.

aver' *vb* (**averred'**, **aver'ring**) (*fml*) to state as a fact (*aver that he is innocent*).

av'erage *n* the figure found by dividing the total of a set of numbers by the number of numbers in the set:— *adj* **1** calculated by finding the average of various amounts, etc (*average expenditure per person*). **2** ordinary (*the average person/his work is average*):— *vb* to find the average.

averse' *adj* not in favour of.

aver'sion *n* **1** dislike (*have an aversion to people smoking*). **2** something disliked (*housework is one of her pet aversions*).

avert' *vb* to turn away (*avert one's eyes*).

aviary [ā'-vi-êri] *n* a place for keeping birds.

avia'tion *n* the science of flying aircraft.

a'viator *n* an airman.

av'id *adj* eager, keen (*an avid reader/avid for news*):— *n* **avid'ity.**

avoca'do *n* a pear-shaped fruit with a hard, dark green skin, soft, pale green flesh and a large stone, used in salads, etc.

avoid' *vb* to keep away from (*avoid trouble/avoid walking in the streets at night/avoid inquisitive neighbours*):— *adj* **avoid'able:**— *n* **avoid'ance.**

avoirdupois [av-er-dê-poiz'] *n* a system of weights in ounces, pounds, etc (as distinct from metric).

await' *vb* (*fml*) to wait for (*await further instructions*).

awake' *vb* (*pt* **awoke'**, *pp* **awok'en**) **1** (*fml*) to rouse from sleep (*the noise awoke me*). **2** (*fml*) to stop sleeping (*we awoke early*). **3** to stir up, to rouse (*awake old memories*):— *adj* **1** not sleeping (*people not yet fully awake*). **2** aware of, conscious of (*awake to the dangers*).

awak'en *vb* **1** to awake. **2** to rouse (*awaken old fears*).

award' *vb* to give after judgment or examination (*award compensation for his injuries/award him first prize*):— *n* what is awarded, a prize.

aware' *adj* **1** having knowledge of, interested, concerned (*young people who are politically aware*). **2** conscious of (*aware of the difficulties*).

awe *n* fear mixed with respect or wonder (*look at the huge cathedral with awe/hold his grandfather in awe*).

awe'some *adj* **1** causing awe (*the awesome sight of the huge waterfall*). **2** (*inf*) excellent, marvellous (*an awesome achievement/an awesome performance*).

aw'ful *adj* **1** very bad or unpleasant, terrible (*an awful accident*). **2** (*inf*) very great (*I am in an awful hurry*). **3** (*old or lit*) causing awe (*the awful sight of the towering mountain*).

aw'fully *adv* (*inf*) very (*awfully kind*).

awk'ward *adj* **1** clumsy, unskilled (*awkward with his hands*). **2** difficult to use or deal with (*furniture of an awkward shape/awkward customers*). **3** inconvenient (*an awkward time*):— *adv* **awk'wardly.**

awl *n* a tool for making holes in leather.

awn'ing *n* a covering, usu of canvas, to provide shelter from sun or rain.

awry [a-rī'] *adj* twisted not straight (*with hats awry*):—*adv* **1** crookedly. **2** wrongly, amiss (*plans that went awry*).

axe *n* **1** a tool for hewing or chopping. **2** to dismiss someone suddenly (*axe workers*). **3** to end or cancel something suddenly (*axe TV programmes*)

ax'iom *n* a statement accepted as true without need for proof.

ax'is *n* (*pl* **ax'es**) the straight line, real or imaginary, on which a body turns (*the axis of the earth*).

axle [aks-1] *or* **axle-tree** *n* the pole on which a wheel turns.

ay, aye [ī] *adv* yes, yes, indeed.

azure [ā'-zhêr] *adj* sky-blue:—*n* **1** a bright blue colour. **2** the sky.

B

bab'ble *vb* **1** to make indistinct sounds (*babies babbling in their prams*). **2** to chatter continuously and without making much sense (*what's he babbling about?*). **3** to make a sound, as of running water (*brooks babbling*):—*n* **1** indistinct sounds, **2** foolish chatter. **3** murmur, as of a stream.

ba'bel *n* a confused noise (*unable to hear above the babel of the party*).

baboon' *n* a type of large monkey.

ba'chelor *n* **1** an unmarried man. **2** one who has passed certain university examinations (*a bachelor of science*).

bacillus [ba-sil'-ês] *n* (*pl* **bacilli** [ba-sil'-î]) a type of bacterium often causing disease.

back *n* part of the body, that which is behind:— also adj and adv:—*vb* **1** to go or move backwards (*back out of the garage*). **2** to support (*back plans for expansion*).

back'bite *vb* to speak ill of an absent person:— **back'biting** (*tired of all the backbiting in the office*).

back'bone *n* **1** the spine. **2** firmness, determination. **3** the chief support (*workers who are the backbone of the industry*).

back'er *n* a supporter or helper (*financial backers of the scheme*).

back'fire *n* an explosive noise made by a motor vehicle:—*vb* **backfire'1** to explode. **2** (*of a plan*) to go wrong in such a way that it harms its maker.

back'gammon *n* an indoor game played with draughtsmen and dice.

back'ground *n* **1** the area behind the principal persons in a picture, scene or conversation. **2** a series of events connected with or leading up to something (*the background to the quarrel between the families*). **3** a person's origins, upbringing, education, etc (*come from a wealthy background*).

back'hand *n* **1** writing in which the letters slope backwards. **2** in tennis, a stroke played with the hand turned outwards.

back'hand'ed *adj* **1** made with the back of the hand. **2** indirect and sometimes with a double meaning (*backhanded compliments*).

back num'ber *n* **1** an earlier copy of a newspaper or magazine. **2** a person (or thing) past his or her best or most useful (*actors who are back numbers now*).

back'pack *n* a large bag with straps carried on the back by hikers, etc to hold their luggage:—*vb* to travel from place to place with your belongings in a backpack:—**back'packer** *n*.

back'slide' *vb* to turn away from what one has accepted as good or true:—*n* **back'slid'er**.

back'ward *adj* **1** towards the back (*a backward glance*). **2** less advanced in mind or body than is normal for one's age. **3** behind others in progress (*backward countries*). **4** shy, reserved (*too backward to be noticed in a crowd*):—*n*. **back'wardness**.

back'water *n* **1** a piece of water supplied by a river, but not out of its current. **2** a remote or backward place, unaffected by modern progress.

back'woods *npl* land not cleared of forest.

back'woodsman *n* one out of touch with modern ideas.

bac'on *n* pig's flesh, salted and dried.

bacteria [bak-tee'-ri-a] *npl* (*sing* **bacte'rium**) very tiny living things that are often the cause of disease.

bacteriol'ogy *n* the study of bacteria:—*n* **bacteriol'ogist**.

badge *n* something worn as a sign of membership, office, rank, etc (*a school badge on a blazer*).

bad'ger *n* a night animal that lives in a burrow:— *vb* to worry, to pester (*badger their mother for more pocket money*).

bad'inage *n* playful talk in which insults are exchanged light-heartedly.

bad'minton *n* a game like tennis played with shuttlecocks as balls.

baf'fle *vb* **1** to puzzle, to bewilder (*baffled by the exam question/police baffled by the crime*). **2** to make someone's efforts useless (*baffle the enemy's attempt to gain entrance*):—*n* **baf'flement**.

bag *n* **1** a container. **2** the number of birds or animals shot on one outing:—*vb* (**bagged'**, **bag'ging**) **1** to put into a bag (*bag all this stuff for taking to the rubbish dump*). **2** (*inf*) to take possession of (*bag that empty table*). **3** to catch or kill (*bag a few rabbits*). **4** to hang loosely, to bulge (*trousers bagging at the knee*).

bagatelle [ba-ga-tel'] *n* **1** a game played on a board in which the players try to strike balls into holes with a cue. **2** a thing of no importance (*the cost was a mere bagatelle to someone as rich as she is*).

bag'gage *n* **1** luggage. **2** stores of a moving army. **3** (*old*) a saucy young woman.

bag'gy *adj* **1** loose (*wear fashionable baggy trousers*). **2** out of shape (*trousers baggy at the knees*).

bag'pipes *npl* a musical wind instrument in which a bag serves as bellows.

bail[1] *n* **1** one ready to pay a sum of money to obtain freedom for a person charged with a crime until the day of his or her trial. **2** the sum so charged, which is lost if the person does not appear for trial:—*also vb*.

baguette [bag'et] *n* a long crusty loaf of bread.

bail[2] *n* a small bar placed on the top of the stumps in cricket.

bail[3] *see* **bale**[2].

bail'iff *n* **1** a law officer (*bailiffs sent to evict tenants for non-payment of rent*). **2** the manager of a farm or estate.

bait *n* **1** food to trap or attract animals or fish. **2** a temptation (*shops offering free goods as a bait to customers*):—*vb* **1** to put bait on a hook or in a trap. **2** to torment (*pupils baiting the new boy because he was so small*).

baize *n* a coarse woollen cloth used mainly for coverings or linings.

bake *vb* **1** to dry and harden by fire. **2** to cook in an oven.

bak'er *n* one who makes or sells bread.

bak'ery *n* a place where bread is made.

bak'ing pow'der *n* a powder containing baking soda, used instead of yeast in baking.

balalaika [ba-la-lī'-ka] *n* a type of guitar used in Russia.

bal'ance *n* **1** a pair of weighing scales. **2** equality of weight, power, etc (*the major countries of the world trying to achieve a balance of power*). **3** a state of physical steadiness (*lose one's balance*). **4** a state of mental or emotional steadiness (*while the balance of her mind was disturbed*). **5** the difference between the amount of money possessed and

the amount owed:—*vb* **1** to make equal. **2** to keep steady or upright (*acrobats balancing themselves on a tightrope*). **3** to add up two sides of an account to show the difference between them:—**in the balance** doubtful; about to be decided.

balance sheet *n* a statement of two sides of an account.

bal'cony *n* **1** a railed platform outside a window or along the wall of a building. **2** an upper floor in a hall or theatre.

bald *adj* **1** without hair (*a bald old man*). **2** bare, without the usual or required covering (*bald tyres*). **3** plain (*the bald truth*):—*n* **bald'ness**.

bal'derdash *n* senseless talk, nonsense.

baldric [bål'd-rik] *n* (*hist*) a crossbelt from shoulder to waist.

bale[1] *n* a large bundle or package (*a bale of hay*).

bale[2], **bail** *vb* to throw water out of a boat, a little at a time.

bale'ful *adj* threatening (*children running away under the baleful eye of the policeman*).

balk, baulk [båk] *ns* a large beam of timber:—*vb* **1** to stop short of, to be reluctant or unwilling to be involved in (*balk at actually committing a crime*). **2** to prevent (*balk the opposition's attempt at winning*).

ball[1] *n* **1** anything round in shape (*a ball of wool*). **2** a round or roundish object used in games (*a tennis ball/a golf ball/a rugby ball*). **3** a rounded part of something (*the ball of the foot*).

ball[2] *n* a party held for the purpose of dancing:— *n* **ball'room**.

ball'ad *n* **1** a simple poem relating a popular incident. **2** a short, romantic song.

ball'ast *n* heavy material carried in a ship or other vehicle to keep it steady.

ball'-bearings *npl* small metal balls that help a machine to work more smoothly.

ballerin'a *n* a female ballet dancer.

ballet [bal'-ā] *n* a performance in which dancing, actions and music are combined to tell a story.

ball game *n* **1** any game played with a ball. **2** (*Amer*) baseball. **3** (*inf*) situation (*a different ball game*).

ballis'tics *npl* the science of the flight of missiles through space:—*adj* **ballis'tic**.

balloon' n 1 a small brightly coloured rubber bag that can be blown up and used as a toy or as a decoration at parties, etc. 2 originally, a large bag of light material that floats in the air when filled with air or light gas, often equipped with a basket for carrying passengers.

balloon'ist n one who goes up into the air in the basket attached to a balloon.

ball'ot n a way of voting secretly by putting marked cards into a box:—also vb:—n **ball'ot box.**

ball'point n a pen that writes by means of a small rotating ball fed by a tube of ink.

balm [bäm] n 1 a sweet-smelling oil. 2 a pain-relieving ointment. 3 something that heals or soothes (a balm to his wounded pride).

balm'y adj gentle, soft (balmy breezes).

bal'sa n an American tree with light, corky wood.

bal'sam n 1 a flowering plant. 2 a sweet-smelling, healing oil.

bal'uster n a post or small pillar supporting a rail.

bal'ustrade n a row of balusters joined by a rail.

bamboo' n a giant tropical reed from which canes, etc, are made.

bamboo'zle vb 1 to puzzle, mystify (motorists bamboozled by the road directions). 2 to deceive, trick (bamboozle the old lady into believing that he was a doctor).

ban n an order forbidding something (impose a ban on smoking in public places):—vb (**banned'**, **ban'ning**) to forbid (banned from driving).

banal [bên-al'] adj unoriginal, commonplace; uninteresting (a few banal remarks):—n **banal'ity.**

band¹ n 1 anything used to bind or tie together (a band to tie her hair back). 2 a strip of cloth round anything (skirt waistbands).

band² n a group of persons united for a purpose, esp to play music together:—vb to join (together) (local people banding together to fight crime).

ban'dage n a strip of cloth used in dressing a wound or injury:—also vb.

bandan'a, bandan'na n a brightly coloured handkerchief often worn round the neck.

ban'dit n an outlaw, a robber.

ban'dy¹ vb:—**to bandy words** to quarrel.

ban'dy², ban'dy-legged adjs having legs curving outwards.

bane n 1 (old) a poison (rat bane). 2 ruin. 3 a cause of ruin or annoyance (that child is the bane of our existence).

bane'ful adj causing harm, hurtful.

bang n 1 a sudden loud noise (the door shut with a bang). 2 a blow or knock (get a bang on the head):—vb 1 to close with a bang (the door banged shut). 2 to hit or strike violently, often making a loud noise (children banging drums/ banged on the leg by a supermarket trolley). 3 to make a sudden loud noise (guns banging away).

ban'gle n a ring worn on the wrist or ankle.

ban'ish vb 1 to order to leave the country (banished from his native land). 2 to drive away (banish all their doubts):—n **ban'-ishment.**

ban'ister n a post or row of posts supporting a rail at the side of a staircase.

ban'jo n a stringed musical instrument played with the fingers.

bank n 1 a ridge or mound of earth, etc (banks of snow at the edge of the road/stand on a grassy bank full of wild flowers). 2 the ground at the side of a river, lake, etc. 3 a place where money is put for safekeeping:—vb 1 to heap up (snow banked up at the sides of the road). 2 to cover a fire with small coal to make it burn slowly. 3 to put money in a bank. 4 to make an aeroplane slope one wing tip down when turning.

bank'er n 1 one who runs or manages a bank. 2 one who holds the money staked in gambling games.

bank'ing n the business of a banker.

bank'rupt n one who is unable to pay his or her debts (declared bankrupt):—also adj:—n **bank'ruptcy.**

ban'ner n a flag.

banns npl the announcement in church or in a public place of an intended marriage.

ban'quet n a feast.

banshee' n in Ireland, a fairy once supposed to wail near a house when someone in it was about to die.

ban'tam n a small fowl.

ban'ter vb to poke fun at; to tease:—also n.

ban'yan n the Indian fig tree.

bapt'ism n 1 the ceremony by which one is received into the Christian Church. 2 a first experience of something, an initiation:—*adj* **baptis′mal**.

baptize′ *vb* **1** to dip in or sprinkle with water as a sign of receiving as a Christian (*baptize the baby*). **2** to christen or give a name to (*she was baptized Mary Jones*).

bar *n* **1** a solid piece of wood, metal, etc, that is longer than it is wide (*a gold bar/a bar of chocolate*). **2** a length of wood or metal across a door or window to keep it shut or prevent entrance through it (*iron bars on the prison windows*). **3** an obstacle (*a bar to progress*). **4** the bank of sand, etc, at the mouth of a river which hinders entrance. **5** a counter at which food or drink may be bought and consumed (*a sandwich bar*). **6** a counter at which alcoholic drinks are served (*place two beers on the bar*). **7** a place where alcoholic drinks are sold, a public house (*the Station Bar*). **8** the rail behind which a prisoner stands in a court of law. **9** all the barristers and advocates in a court. **10** a division in music:—*vb* (**barred′, bar′ring**) **1** to fasten with a bar or belt (*bar the door*). **2** to hinder or prevent (*bar their advance*). **3** to forbid, to ban (*bar women from joining the club*):—*prep* except.

barb *n* a backward-curving spike on a fish-hook or arrow.

barbar′ian *n* **1** an uncivilized person. **2** one who does not respect the arts or learning.

barbar′ic *adj* connected with barbarism.

bar′barism *n* the state of being uncivilized.

barbar′ity *n* savage cruelty.

bar′barous *adj* **1** savage, uncivilized (*a barbarous tribe*). **2** cruel (*his barbarous treatment of prisoners of war*).

bar′becue *n* **1** a framework on which meat, etc, may be cooked over a charcoal fire, usu outside. **2** a large outdoor party where food is cooked on a barbecue:—*vb* to cook on a barbecue (*barbecuing steaks*).

barbed *adj* having a barb or barbs, having sharp points facing in more than one direction.

bar′ber *n* a man's hairdresser.

bar′bican *n* a tower over the gateway of a castle to defend the drawbridge.

bar code *n* a pattern of vertical lines of differing widths that represent numbers. It is printed on

something, such as an item for sale, and contains information, such as the price, which can be scanned by a computer.

bard *n* **1** a Celtic minstrel. **2** a poet.

bare *adj* **1** uncovered (*bare hillsides/bare floors*). **2** empty (*bare cupboards*). **3** naked (*children stripped bare*):—*vb* to uncover, to expose (*bare his chest/dogs baring their teeth*).

bare′back *adj, adv* without a saddle.

bare′faced *adj* shameless.

bare′ly *adv* **1** only just. **2** scarcely.

bar′gain *n* **1** an agreement about buying and selling. **2** an agreement. **3** something bought cheaply:—*vb* **1** to argue about the price before paying. **2** to make an agreement:—**to bargain for** to expect:—**into the bargain** in addition.

barge *n* a flat-bottomed boat for carrying cargoes on inland waters:—*vb* to move clumsily and often rudely (*barge on to the bus in front of us*).

bar′itone *n* a male singing voice that can go neither very high nor very low.

bark¹ *n* the outer covering of a tree:—*vb* to scrape the skin off (*bark one's shin*).

bark² *n* the noise made by a dog, wolf, etc:—*also vb*.

bark³, barque *n* (*old or lit*) **1** a three-masted sailing ship. **2** a boat.

bar′ley *n* a grain used for making malt.

bar′maid, bar′man *ns* one who serves drinks at a bar.

bar mitz′vah *n* a ceremony held on the thirteenth birthday of a Jewish boy by which he becomes an adult.

barn *n* a farm building for the storage of grain, hay, etc.

bar′nacle *n* a type of shellfish.

barn dance *n* a country dance.

baro′meter *n* **1** an instrument for measuring air pressure, thus showing what the weather may be. **2** something that indicates change (*opinion polls are a barometer of the popularity of the government*).

bar′on *n* a nobleman of the lowest rank:—*f* **bar′oness**.

bar′onet *n* a titled rank just below that of a nobleman:—*n* **bar′onetcy**.

bar′ony *n* the rank or lands of a baron:—*adj* **baron′ial**.

baroque [ba-rok′] *adj* (*esp of a style of art and architecture*) decorated in an exaggerated, ornate way:—*n* a style of architecture in which fantastic decoration is used.

barque *see* **bark.**

bar'rack *n* (*usu pl*) a building for housing soldiers:—*vb* to jeer at, to shout insults to (*crowds barracking the politicians*).

bar'rage *n* **1** a bar across a river to make the water deeper. **2** a concentration of heavy gunfire on a certain area. **3** a large number (of questions, etc) made rapidly one after the other (*a barrage of comments from the audience*).

bar'rel *n* **1** a round wooden cask or container with flat ends and curved sides (*a barrel of beer*). **2** the tube of a gun.

bar'ren *adj* **1** producing no fruit or seed (*barren apple trees*). **2** (*old*) unable to produce young, infertile (*barren women*). **3** unable to produce crops (*barren soil*). **4** useless, not productive (*barren discussions*):—*n* **bar'renness.**

bar'ricade *n* a barrier, often temporary and quickly constructed, to prevent people passing or entering:—*also vb.*

bar'rier *n* **1** a kind of fence put up to control or restrain (*barriers along the sides of the street to keep the crowds back*). **2** an obstacle (*a barrier to progress*). **3** something that separates or keeps people apart (*a language barrier*).

bar'rister *n* a lawyer with the right to plead a case in court.

bar'row *n* **1** a small hand-cart (*wheel grass cuttings away in a barrow*). **2** (*old*) a mound over a grave.

bar'ter *n* trade by exchange of goods instead of money payments:—*vb* to trade by barter, to exchange.

bas'alt *n* a dark volcanic rock.

base[1] *n* **1** that on which a thing stands or is built up (*the base of the column*). **2** the place in which a fleet or army keeps its main stores and offices. **3** a fixed point in certain games:—*vb* **1** to use as a foundation or grounds (*base one's decision on the evidence*). **2** to establish, to place (*a company based in Wales*).

base[2] *adj* low, worthless, vile (*a base villain/a base act*):—*adv* **base'ly.**

base'ball *n* an American game played with bat and ball.

base'less *adj* without foundation, groundless (*baseless suspicions*).

base'ment *n* the ground floor, below ground level.

bash *vb* to beat, to hit with great force.

bash'ful *adj* modest, shy (*too bashful to speak in public*).

bas'ic *adj* **1** providing a foundation or beginning (*the basic rules of science/basic steps in mathematics*). **2** without more than is necessary, simple, plain (*a room with basic furniture*).

basil'ica *n* a church.

bas'ilisk *n* in fable, a serpent whose look was said to kill.

bas'in *n* **1** a deep broad dish (*a pudding basin*). **2** a hollow place containing water. **3** a dock. **4** the land drained by a river.

bas'is *n* (*pl* **bas'es**) that on which a thing is built up, the foundation or beginning (*arguments that have a firm basis*).

bask *vb* **1** to lie in the sun. **2** (*fml*) to enjoy (*bask in his employer's approval*).

bas'ket *n* a container made of thin sticks or coarse grass plaited together (*a basket of groceries*).

bas mitz'vah *n* a ceremony for a Jewish girl similar to a **bar mitz'vah.**

bas-relief [bäs'-rê-leef'] *n* a sculpture in which the figures or objects stand out a little way above the background of the material on which they are carved.

bass[1] [bâs] *n* **1** the lowest part in music. **2** the lowest male voice.

bass[2], **basse** *n* a type of fish.

bassoon' *n* a musical wind instrument, with low notes only.

baste *vb* **1** to beat, to thrash. **2** to drip or pour fat on meat while roasting. **3** to sew with long loose stitches.

bas'tion *n* **1** a tower jutting out from the wall of a fort to allow the defenders to aim arrows, bullets, etc, at the flanks of the attackers. **2** a person or thing that provides strong support or defence (*the last bastions of the traditional village way of life*).

bat[1] *n* a piece of wood prepared for striking a ball in certain games:—*vb* to use the bat for striking the ball:—*n* **bat'sman** (*in cricket*) the player at the wicket.

bat[2] *n* a flying creature with a body like a mouse and large wings.

batch n 1 a quantity of bread, etc, baked at one time. 2 a set or group (*a new batch of army recruits*).

bat'ed adj:—**with bated breath** hardly breathing at all because of nervousness, fear, etc.

bath n 1 act of washing the body. 2 a large vessel in which the body is washed. 3 a large tank in which one can swim:—vb to wash the body in a bath.

bath chair n a wheeled chair for invalids or people who cannot walk.

bathe vb 1 to apply water to in order to clean (*bathe the wound*). 2 to go for a swim (*bathe in the sea*):—n act of swimming or playing in water:—n **bath'er**.

bath'os n an unintended contrast between the important and the trifling.

bat'man n an officer's servant in the army.

bat'on n 1 a short stick used by the conductor of a band or choir. 2 a short club carried by policemen as a weapon. 3 a stick passed by one member of a team of runners to the next runner in a relay race.

batsman see **bat**.

battal'ion n a body of infantry, about 1000 strong.

bat'ten[1] n 1 a long board or strip of wood. 2 a strip of wood used to fasten down the hatches of ships:—vb to close firmly with battens.

bat'ten[2] vb:—**to batten on** to live well or thrive by taking advantage of someone else (*landlords battening on their poor tenants*).

bat'ter vb to beat with violence:—n a paste of flour and liquid mixed together for cooking.

bat'tering ram n a heavy piece of wood with an iron head formerly used for battering down castle walls or doors.

bat'tery n 1 a group of guns and the people who serve them. 2 a number of connected cells for providing or storing electric current. 3 a violent attack (*arrested for assault and assault*).

bat'tle n 1 a fight between armies, fleets, etc. 2 a struggle (*a battle for promotion*):—vb to fight or struggle (*battling for top place in the league*).

bat'tledore n a small bat used in playing with a shuttlecock.

bat'tlement n the top wall of a castle, with openings through which weapons can be aimed.

baub'le n a small, worthless ornament or piece of jewellery (*baubles on the Christmas tree*).

baulk see **balk**.

bawl vb to shout or cry loudly:—also n.

bay[1] adj reddish-brown:—n a bay horse.

bay[2] n 1 an inlet of the sea. 2 a recess in a wall.

bay[3] n the laurel tree.

bay[4] n the bark of a dog, the low cry of a hunting dog:—**to stand at bay** to stop running away and turn to defend oneself:—**to keep at bay** to keep at a safe distance:—vb to give the bark or cry of a dog (*hounds baying*).

bay'onet n a dagger-like weapon for fixing on to a rifle:—vb to stab with a bayonet.

bay win'dow n a window built into a section of the wall that juts out.

bazaar' n 1 in the East, a marketplace or group of shops. 2 a sale of articles held to raise money for a special purpose (*a church bazaar in aid of roof repairs*).

beach' n the shore of a sea or lake:—vb to run or pull (a vessel) on to a beach (*beach the canoe*).

beach'comber n 1 in the Pacific, one who lives by what he or she finds on the beach (e.g. pearls, wreckage). 2 an idler about harbours or beaches.

bea'con n 1 a signal fire. 2 a high hill on which a beacon could be lighted. 3 a signal of danger.

bead n 1 a small object, usu round, of glass or other material, with a hole through it for a string (*a necklace of coloured beads*). 2 a drop or bubble (*beads of sweat*). 3 pl a rosary.

bead'le n a minor official in a church or college.

bead'y adj small and bright (*with beady eyes*).

beag'le n a small hunting dog.

beak n the bill of a bird.

beak'er n 1 a large drinking cup (*a beaker of cocoa*). 2 a glass vessel used in scientific experiments.

beam n 1 a thick piece of wood. 2 a main timber in a building. 3 the greatest breadth of a ship. 4 a ray of light. 5 radio waves sent out in one particular direction, as a ray:—vb to smile brightly (*beam with pleasure*).

bean n a plant whose seed or seed pod is eaten as a vegetable (*green beans/runner beans*).

bear[1] vb (pt **bore**, pp **borne**) 1 (fml) to carry (*bearing gifts*). 2 to put up with (*bear the pain*). 3 to support (*bear his weight*). 4 to have or show (*still* *bearing a scar*). **5** to move (*bear left*). **6** (*pp* **born**) to bring into existence. **7** (*pp* **borne**) to produce (*bear fruit*).

bear[2] *n* a wild animal with long hair and claws.

bear'able *adj* able to be put up with (*pain scarcely bearable*).

beard [beerd] *n* the hair on the chin and lower jaw:—*vb* to defy openly (*beard the lion in its den*).

bear'er *n* a carrier (*the bearer of bad news*).

bear gar'den *n* a noisy and disorderly place.

bear'ing *n* **1** the way a person holds himself or herself or behaves (*of noble bearing*). **2** direction (*lose one's bearings*). **3** connection, influence (*their statement had no bearing on our decision*).

bear'skin *n* a tall furry cap worn by the Guards in the British Army.

beast *n* **1** a four-footed animal. **2** a person who behaves in an animal-like way, a hateful person:—*adj* **beastly**:—*n* **beast'liness**.

beat *vb* (*pt* **beat**, *pp* **beat'en**) **1** to strike several times. **2** to defeat or win against (*beat the home team*). **3** to throb (*with heart beating*):—*n* **1** a repeated stroke. **2** a policeman's round. **3** a regular rhythm (e.g. the pulse, a drum).

beat'er *n* one who, by beating grass or bushes, drives animals or birds into the open to be hunted (*grouse beater*).

beatific *adj* blissful (*a beatific smile*).

beau [bō] *n* (*pl* **beaux**) **1** (*old*) a man who is taken up with matters of dress and manners, a dandy. **2** (*old or fml*) a male sweetheart (*her latest beau*).

beau'tify *vb* to make beautiful (*girls beautifying themselves at the mirror*).

beauty [bū'-ti] *n* **1** that which is pleasing to the senses. **2** a beautiful woman (*she was a beauty in her youth*). **3** (*inf*) a very fine specimen (*his new car is a real beauty*). **4** (*inf*) advantage (*the beauty of the job is the short hours*):—*adj* **beau'tiful**.

beav'er *n* **1** an animal that can live both on land and in water. **2** the fur of the beaver. **3** (*old*) the part of a helmet that covered the face.

beck *n*:—**at the beck and call of** ready to do whatever is wanted by someone (*she is at the beck and call of the whole office*).

beck'on *vb* to make a sign inviting a person to approach (*beckon to them to move forward*).

become *vb* (*pt* **became**[1], *pp* **become**[1]) **1** to come to be (*become a fine young woman/become a doctor*). **2** to suit (*green becomes her*).

becom'ing *adj* **1** (*fml*) fitting, suitable, appropriate (*behaviour that was far from becoming in the circumstances*). **2** suiting the wearer (*a becoming dress*).

bed *n* **1** a thing to sleep or rest on. **2** the channel of a river. **3** a piece of ground prepared for growing flowers, plants, etc.

bed'clothes *npl* the coverings on a bed.

bed'ding *n* bedclothes.

bedeck' *vb* (*old or fml*) to ornament (*bedeck herself in diamonds*).

bed'lam *n* a scene of noisy uproar and confusion (*it was bedlam at the children's party*).

bedrag'gled *adj* wet and dirty, muddy (*bedraggled from her walk through the storm*).

bed'ridden *adj* having to stay permanently in bed (*bedridden invalids*).

bed'rock *n* **1** the solid rock underlying the broken rock formations near the earth's surface. **2** basic facts or principles (*the bedrock of his beliefs*).

bed'room *n* a room for sleeping in.

bed'stead *n* a frame for supporting a bed.

bee *n* a flying, honey-making insect.

beech *n* a type of tree:—*n* **beechnut**.

beef *n* the flesh of an ox or cow.

beefburger *see* **hamburger.**

beef'eater *n* a member of the royal guard at the Tower of London, who wears Elizabethan dress.

beef'tea[1] *n* a thin beef soup for invalids.

beefy *adj* (*inf*) very strong, muscular (*beefy rugby players*).

bee'hive *n* a place where bees are kept, often dome-shaped.

bee'line *n* the shortest way:—**make a beeline for** to go directly and quickly towards (*make a beeline for the prettiest girl at the party*).

beer *n* a drink made from barley and hops.

bees'wax *n* the wax made by bees for their honeycombs:—*vb* to polish with beeswax.

beet *n* a plant with a root eaten as a vegetable (*also* **sugar beet**).

beet'le[1] *n* a common insect:—*vb* (*inf*) to hurry, to scurry (*beetle off home*).

beet'le[2] *n* a heavy wooden tool that, when thrust down on e.g. paving stones, beats them into place.

beet'le[3] *vb* to jut, to hang over (*cliffs beetling over the sea*).

beet'le-browed' *adj* having prominent eyebrows.

beet'root *n* the root of the beet.

befall' *vb* (*pt* befell', *pp* befall'en) (*fml*) to happen (*troubles that befell her*).

befit' *vb* (befit'ted, befit'ting) (*fml*) to suit, to be proper for (*his behaviour does not befit a man of his position*).

befit'ting *adj* suitable (*behave with a befitting degree of modesty*):—*adv* befit'tingly.

before'hand *adv* earlier (*pay for the tickets beforehand*).

befriend' *vb* to act as a friend to, to be kind to (*befriend the orphan girl*).

beg *vb* (begged', beg'ging) 1 to ask for money (*beg on the streets*). 2 to ask earnestly (*beg for forgiveness/beg a favour*):—**to beg the question** to take a fact for granted without proving its truth.

beget' *vb* (*pt* begot', *pp* begot'ten, *prp* be-get'ting) 1 (*old*) to give life to (*beget four sons*). 2 (*fml*) to be the cause of (*war begets misery*).

beg'gar *n* one who asks for money or food.

beg'gary *n* extreme poverty.

begin' *vb* (*pt* began', *pp* begun', *prp* begin'-ning) 1 to start (*begin to play/the trouble began in June*). 2 to be the first to do or take the first step in doing (*begin the discussion*).

begin'ner *n* one starting to learn (*a beginners' class*).

begone' *interj* go away!

bego'nia *n* a plant with brightly coloured flowers.

begrudge' *vb* 1 to give unwillingly (*begrudge spending money on bus fares*). 2 to envy someone the possession of (*begrudge the girl her success as a dancer*).

beguile [bê-gïl'] *vb* (*fml*) 1 to deceive, to trick (*beguile the old lady into giving them money*). 2 to make pass pleasantly (*beguile away the evening hours*).

behalf' *n*:—**on behalf of** in the name of (*speak on behalf of his mother*).

behave' *vb* 1 to conduct oneself. 2 to conduct oneself well. 3 to act.

behav'iour *n* conduct.

behead' *vb* to cut off the head.

behest' *n* (*fml*) command (*we went at his behest*).

behind'hand *adv* late.

behold' *vb* (*pt*, *pp* beheld') to see; to watch:—*n* behold'er.

behold'en *adj* obliged (to someone), owing gratitude to (*beholden to the people who had brought her up*).

behove', behoove' *vb*:—**it behoves** (*fml*) it is necessary or proper for (*it behoves you to be polite to your parents*).

belab'our *vb* (*fml*) to beat soundly (*belabour him with a large stick*).

belat'ed *adj* too late (*a belated apology*).

belay' *vb* on ships, to secure a rope by winding it around something.

belch *vb* to send out forcefully, esp wind through the mouth.

beleaguer [bê-lee'-gêr] *vb* 1 to surround with troops, to besiege (*beleaguer the city*). 2 to worry or pester continuously (*the press beleaguering the police for a statement*).

bel'fry *n* a bell tower.

belie' *vb* to give a wrong idea of (*her smile belied her feelings of sadness*).

belief' *n* 1 faith (*belief in God*). 2 trust (*shake her belief in his ability*). 3 opinion (*it is my belief that she is guilty*).

believe' *vb* 1 to accept as true or real (*believe in ghosts*). 2 to trust (*believe in her husband*). 3 to have faith, esp in God. 4 to think:—*adj* believ'able:—*n* make-believe pretence.

believ'er *n* one who has faith, esp in God.

belit'tle *vb* to make to seem small or unimportant (*belittle his achievements*).

bell *n* a hollow metal vessel that gives a ringing sound when struck.

belle *n* a lady of great beauty.

belles-lettres [bel'-letr] *npl* (*fml*) literature, such as poetry, essays, novels, criticisms.

bel'licose *adj* (*fml*) eager to fight, warlike:—*n* bellicos'ity.

belligerent [bel-lì'-jê-rênt] *adj* 1 angry and ready to fight or quarrel (*in belligerent mood*). 2 (*fml*) taking part in war (*belligerent nations*):—*n* a nation or person taking part in war.

bel'low *vb* 1 to shout loudly (*bellow to his children to make less noise*). 2 to roar (*bulls bellowing*):—also *n*.

bel'lows npl an instrument that makes a draught of air by forcing wind out of an airtight compartment.

bell tent n a cone-shaped tent.

bel'ly n 1 the part of the human body between the breast and thighs. 2 the under part of an animal's body:—vb to bulge out (sails bellying in the wind).

belong' vb 1 to be the property (of). 2 to be a member. 3 to be connected with.

belong'ings npl the things that are one's own property.

beloved [bê-luv'-êd or bê-luvd'] adj greatly loved:—n one who is greatly loved (having lost his beloved).

belt n 1 a strap or band for putting round the waist. 2 a leather band used to carry the motion of one wheel on to another in a piece of machinery. 3 a space that is much longer than it is broad (a belt of trees dividing two fields). 4 an area that has a particular quality or characteristic (the industrial belt of the country). 5 (inf) an act of hitting, a blow:—vb 1 to put on a belt. 2 to hit with a strap. 3 to hit, to attack with blows (belt his brother):—**below the belt** 1 below the waistline. 2 unfair.

bemoan' vb to lament (bemoan her fate).

bemused' adj confused, bewildered (motorists bemused by the traffic system/wearing a bemused expression).

bench n 1 a long seat (children sitting on benches in the school hall). 2 a worktable (benches in the science lab). 3 the seat of a judge in court. 4 all the judges, as a body.

bench'mark n 1 a mark on a fixed object indicating height. 2 a standard for judging or measuring (his work was regarded as a benchmark for that of his classmates).

bend vb (pt, pp **bent**) 1 to curve (a road bending sharply). 2 to make to curve (bend the branch). 3 to incline the body, to stoop (bend to pick up a coin):—n 1 a curving turn on a road. 2 an angle.

benedic'tion n blessing:—adj benedic'tory.

benefac'tor n one who gives help to another:—f **benefac'tress**.

beneficial [be-nê-fish'-êl] adj helpful, having a good effect (a diet beneficial to health).

beneficiary [be-nê-fi'-shi-êri] n 1 one who receives money or property by will. 2 one who benefits from another's kindness.

ben'efit n 1 advantage, gain (the benefits of a healthy lifestyle/advice that is of benefit to us). 2 the money to which an insured person has the right when unemployed, ill, etc:—vb 1 to do good to (the holiday clearly benefited her). 2 to be of advantage to (he benefited from having educated parents).

bene'volence n kindness, generosity.

bene'volent adj kindly, generous.

benign [bê-nîn'] adj 1 kindly, gentle (a benign smile). 2 not malignant, not cancerous (a benign tumour):—adv benign'ly.

bent[1] pt, pp of **bend**.

bent[2] adj (inf) dishonest (a bent lawyer).

bent[3] n a natural skill in or liking for (a musical bent).

benzene [ben'-zeen] n a colourless liquid obtained from coal tar.

benzine [ben'-zeen] n a type of petrol.

bequeath' vb to leave by will (bequeath her jewellery to her granddaughter).

bequest' n the money or property left by will; a legacy.

berate' vb to scold.

bereave' vb (pt, pp **bereaved** or **bereft**) to take away (war bereft her of her sons):—n **bereave'ment**.

bereaved' adj having lost, by death, a near relative (the bereaved mother):—n one who has lost a relative by death (comfort the bereaved).

bereft' adj having been deprived of something (so amazed that she was bereft of words).

beret [be'-rā] n a round flat cap with no peak or brim.

beri-beri n a disease caused by lack of certain vitamins.

ber'ry n a small fruit containing seeds.

ber'serk adj uncontrollably angry (he went berserk when he saw the damage).

berth n 1 the place where a ship lies when at anchor or in dock. 2 a place for sleeping in a ship or train:—vb to moor a ship:—**to give a wide berth to** to keep well clear of (give a wide berth to troublemakers).

beseech' vb (pt, pp **besought'** or **beseeched'**) (fml) to ask earnestly, to beg for (beseech her employer not to dismiss her):—adv **beseech'ingly**.

beset' *vb* (**beset'**, **beset'ting**) to attack from all sides, to surround (*trouble beset them from all sides*):—**besetting sin** the sin to which a person is most easily tempted (*extravagance is her besetting sin*).

besiege' *vb* **1** to surround a fortress with soldiers in order to bring about its capture. **2** to surround, to crowd round (*reporters besieging the princess on her tour*). **3** to overwhelm (*reporters besieging the police with questions*):—*n* **besieg'er**.

besom [beez-'êm *or* bez-'êm] *n* a broom.

besot'ted *adj* silly, muddled (*besotted with love*).

bespat'ter *vb* to sprinkle (with dirt, etc) (*traffic bespattering pedestrians with mud*).

best *adj* (*superl of* **good**) good in the utmost degree (*his best attempt*):—*vb* to do better than, to win against (*best them in their attempt at victory*).

best'ial *adj* like an animal, beastly, disgusting (*a bestial crime*).

bestial'ity *n* animal-like behaviour.

bestow' *vb* (*fml*) to give (to) (*bestow a gift of money*).

bestride' *vb* to sit or stand across something, with a leg on either side of it.

bet *n* money put down in support of an opinion, to be either lost or returned with interest, a wager:—*vb* (**betting, bet**) to stake money in a bet.

betake' *vb*:—**betake oneself to** (*old or fml*) to go (*betake oneself to the hospital*).

betide' *vb* (*fml or lit*) to happen (*whatever may betide*).

betok'en *vb* to be a sign of, to indicate (*houses betokening great wealth*).

betray' *vb* **1** to give up to an enemy. **2** to be false to, to be a traitor to (*betray one's country*). **3** to reveal, to show (*nervousness betraying guilt*):—*n* **betray'er**.

betray'al *n* act of betraying.

betroth' *vb* to promise in marriage:—*n* **betroth'al**.

between *prep* **1** the space, time, etc, separating (two things) (*between meetings*). **2** connecting one from or to the other (*the bond between them*).

betwixt' *prep* between.

bev'el *vb* (**bev'elled, bev'elling**) to cut to a slope:—*n* a sloping edge.

bev'erage *n* a drink.

bev'y *n* **1** a group (*a bevy of beautiful girls*). **2** a flock of birds.

bewail' *vb* (*fml*) to lament aloud, to regret (*bewail the loss of his fortune*).

beware' *vb* to be cautious or careful of (*warned to beware of thieves*).

bewil'der *vb* to puzzle, to confuse:—*adj* **bewil'dering**:—*n* **bewil'derment**.

bewitch' *vb* **1** to put under a spell. **2** to charm, to fascinate (*he was bewitched by her beauty*):—*n* **bewitch'ment**.

bewitch'ing *adj* charming, fascinating (*a bewitching smile*).

beyond' *prep* on the farther side of:—*adv* at a distance.

bezique' *n* a game of cards.

bias [bî'-ês] *n* **1** the greater weight on one side of a bowl that causes it to roll off the straight. **2** an unreasonable dislike (*a bias against foreigners*). **3** a preference (*a bias towards blonde women*). **4** in dress-making, a line across the weave of a fabric:—*vb* to incline to one side, to prejudice (*his early childhood had biased him against foreigners*).

bi'as(s)ed *adj* prejudiced.

bib *n* a cloth tied under a child's chin to keep him clean while eating.

Bib'le *n* the Holy Scriptures of the Christian religion:—*adj* **bib'lical**.

bibliography [bib-lee-o'-gra-fi] *n* a list of books dealing with a particular subject:—*n* **biblio'grapher**:—*adj* **bibliograph'ical**.

bib'liophile *n* (*fml*) a lover of books.

bicentenary [bî-sen-tee'-nê-ri] *n* the two hundredth year (after a certain event).

biceps [bî'-seps] *n* a muscle in the upper part of the arm.

bick'er *vb* to quarrel frequently over unimportant things.

bi'cycle *n* a machine with two wheels which can be ridden on:—*also vb*.

bid *vb* (*pt* **bid** *or* **bade**, *pp* **bid'den** *or* **bid**, *prp* **bid'ding**) **1** to offer (*bid £400 for the vase at the auction*). **2** to ask, to order (*bid them come in*):—*n* **1** an offer of money, esp at a sale. **2** a strong effort (*make a bid to take over the company*).

bid'der *n* one offering a price.

bide *vb* (*pt, pp* **bi'ded** *or* **bode**):—**bide one's time** to wait for a good opportunity (*biding his time until he tries to get her job*).

biennial [bî-en'-ni-êl] *adj* **1** lasting for two years (*biennial plants*). **2** happening every second year (*a biennial event*):—*n* a plant that flowers only in its second year, then dies:—*adv* **bien'nially**.

bier [beer] *n* a stretcher for carrying a dead body or coffin to the grave.

big'amy *n* the state of having two wives or two husbands at the same time:—*n* **big'a-mist**:—*adj* **big'amous**.

bight *n* a bay.

big'ot *n* one who accepts without question certain beliefs and condemns the different beliefs held by others (*a religious bigot*):—*adj* **big'oted**:—*n* **big'otry**.

bi'jou *adj* small and neat (*a bijou residence*).

bikini *n* a two-piece swimsuit for women.

bilateral [bî'-la-tê-rêl] *adj* **1** two-sided. **2** concerning two parties (*a bilateral agreement*).

bil'berry *n* a small blue berry, the whortleberry.

bile *n* **1** a fluid, coming from the liver, that aids digestion. **2** (*fml*) anger (*arouse his bile*).

bilge *n* **1** the bulging part of a cask. **2** the broadest part of a ship's bottom. **3** the rubbish that collects there. **4** (*inf*) nonsense (*talking bilge*).

bilingual [bî-ling'-gwêl] *adj* able to speak two languages.

bil'ious *adj* **1** relating to bile. **2** sick (*feeling bilious*):—*n* **bil'iousness**.

bilk *vb* to cheat, to defraud.

bill[1] *n* **1** (*old*) a battle-axe with a long handle. **2** a tool for pruning. **3** the beak of a bird.

bill[2] *n* **1** the form of a proposed law, as put before parliament for discussion. **2** a statement of money owed for things bought (*ask the waiter for the bill*). **3** a printed notice (*a bill on the noticeboard announcing the meeting*):—*vb* to advertise by bills.

bil'let *n* a lodging, esp for soldiers:—*vb* to lodge (e.g. soldiers) in people's houses.

billet-doux [bi'-lā-dö] *n* (*fml*) a love letter.

bill'hook *n* a tool for pruning.

billiards [bil'-yardz] *n* a game, played on a cloth-covered table, with cues and balls.

bil'lion *n* **1** in Britain, one million millions. **2** in America and often now in Britain, one thousand millions.

bil'low *n* a great wave of the sea:—*vb* to swell out:—*adj* **bil'lowy**.

bil'ly-goat' *n* a male goat.

bin *n* **1** a large box for corn, meal, etc (*a bread bin*). **2** a container for rubbish.

bind *vb* (*pt, pp* **bound**) **1** to tie (*bind the wound with bandages*). **2** to fasten together (*bind his hands together*). **3** to cover (a book) (*a book bound in leather*). **4** to put an edging on (*bind the seams of the dress*). **5** (*fml*) to put under an obligation (*the contract binds you to pay me £1000 per month*):—**bind oneself** to promise.

bind'ing *n* the cover and sewing of a book.

bin'nacle *n* a box in which the compass of a ship is kept.

binoc'ulars *npl* a pair of fieldglasses.

biochem'istry *n* the chemistry of living things:—*adj* **biochem'ical**:—*n* **biochem'ist**.

biodegrad'able *adj* decaying naturally as the result of the action of bacteria and so not causing pollution to the environment (*plastic is not biodegradable*).

biog'rapher *n* a writer of biography (*the biographer of Margaret Thatcher*).

biog'raphy *n* the written life story of a person:—*adj* **biograph'ical**.

biol'ogy *n* the study of life and living creatures:—*adj* **biolog'ical**:—*n* **bio'logist**.

bipar'tite *adj* having two parts.

bi'ped *n* an animal with two feet.

bi'plane *n* an aeroplane with two wings, one above the other.

birch *n* **1** a tree. **2** a bundle of sticks tied together at one end and used for flogging:—*vb* to flog with a birch (*wrongdoers used to be birched*).

bird *n* a creature with feathers and wings that usu flies.

birth *n* **1** the act of being born (*happy at the birth of her son*). **2** the beginning (*the birth of civilization*).

birth'day *n* the day on which one is born, or its anniversary.

birth'mark *n* a mark on the body from birth (*a purple birthmark on her face*).

birth'right *n* any right one possesses by birth.

bis'cuit *n* a dry bread made into flat, crisp cakes.

bisect' *vb* (*fml*) to cut into two equal parts (*bisect the circle*).

bish'op *n* in the RC Church or Church of England, the chief clergyman of a district.

bish'opric *n* 1 the office of a bishop. 2 the district in which a bishop has powers.

bis'muth *n* a reddish-white metal.

bison [bī'-sên] *n* a type of wild ox.

bit *n* 1 a small piece (*tear the paper to bits*). 2 a piece of (*a bit of cake/a bit of advice*). 3 part (*the bit in the film where the hero dies*). 4 a tool for boring holes. 5 the metal bar attached to the bridle, and put in the mouth of a horse.

bite *vb* (*pt* **bit**, *pp* **bit'ten**) 1 to cut, pierce, etc, with the teeth (*the dog that bit the postman/bite the apple*). 2 to take the bait (*fish biting today*):—*n* 1 the amount bitten off. 2 the wound made by biting. 3 a taking of the bait by fish.

bit'ing *adj* 1 sharp (*biting wind*). 2 hurtful (*a biting remark*):—*adv* **bit'ingly**.

bit'ter *adj* 1 sharp to the taste (*bitter oranges*). 2 severe, piercing (*the bitter cold*). 3 painful (*from bitter experience*). 4 feeling or showing hatred, hostility, envy, disappointment, etc (*feeling bitter about her divorce/a bitter quarrel*):—*adv* **bit'terly**:—*n* **bit'terness**.

bit'tern *n* a bird like a heron.

bitumen [bi'-tû-mên *or* bi-tû'-mên] *n* a substance like pitch, used to make roads, etc.

bi'valve *n* an animal or fish whose shell is in two parts joined by a hinge-like cartilage:—*adj* **bival'vular**.

bivouac [bi'-vö-ak] *n* an open-air camp, made from such materials as lie to hand:—*vb* to spend the night in a bivouac.

biweek'ly *adj* 1 happening once every two weeks (*a biweekly magazine*). 2 twice in one week (*biweekly meetings*).

bizarre [bi-zär'] *adj* strange, peculiar, weird (*his bizarre appearance/a bizarre crime*).

blab *vb* (**blabbed'**, **blab'bing**) (*inf*) to tell a secret, sometimes intentionally (*blab to the teacher about his friends playing truant/blab the secret to her mother*).

black *n* 1 a dark colour like coal. 2 a member of one of the dark-skinned races of people:—*also*

adj:—*n* 1 to make black (*black his eye in a fight*). 2 to clean with black polish (*black his shoes*). 3 to impose a ban on, to refuse to handle (*strikers blacking goods from factories not on strike*):—*n* **black'ness**.

black art *n* magic.

black'bird *n* a type of thrush.

black'board *n* a dark-coloured board used for writing on with a light-coloured chalk.

black'en *vb* 1 to make black (*smoke blackening the walls*). 2 to become black or dark (*skies blackening*).

blackguard [bla'-gärd] *n* a rascal, a very bad person.

black'ing *n* a black polish (e.g. for shoes).

black'leg *n* one who goes on working when his or her fellow workers are on strike.

black'list *n* a list of persons suspected of doing wrong.

black'mail *vb* to obtain money by threatening to reveal a secret:—*also n*:—*n* **black'-mailer**.

black'out *n* 1 a sudden putting out of all lights (*a blackout caused by an electrical power failure*). 2 a period when all lights must be put out or covered (*blackouts ordered by the government to guard against enemy air attacks*). 3 a sudden, short loss of consciousness (*have a blackout after hitting her head on a beam*).

black'smith *n* a metal-worker who works with iron.

blad'der *n* 1 a bag-like part of the body in which urine collects. 2 a bag of thin leather, rubber, etc, containing air (*the bladder of a football*).

blade *n* 1 a leaf (of grass, corn, etc). 2 the cutting part of a sword or knife. 3 the flat part of an oar.

blame *vb* 1 to find fault with (*I don't blame you for being angry*). 2 to regard as guilty or responsible (*blame him for his brother's death/blame the rise in prices on the government*):—*n* 1 fault. 2 guilt:—*adj* **blame'less**:—*adj* **blame'worthy**.

blanch *vb* 1 to become white (*blanch with terror at the sight of the gunman*). 2 to put into boiling water for a few minutes (*blanch almonds to remove their skins*).

blancmange [blâ-mo(ng)j'] *n* a jelly-like milk pudding.

bland *adj* 1 so mild as to be almost tasteless (*bland food*). 2 so mild or gentle as to be without personality or emotion (*bland smiles/ bland articles about the government's problems*).

blan'dishment *n* (*fml*) flattery, coaxing.

blank *adj* **1** not written on or marked (*blank sheets of paper*). **2** empty, without expression (*blank faces*):—*n* an empty space (*leave blanks for unanswered questions in the exam paper*).

blank cartridge *n* a cartridge without a bullet.

blank verse *n* poetry with no rhymes.

blan'ket *n* **1** a woollen, etc, bedcovering. **2** a covering (*a blanket of snow*).

blare *vb* to make a loud sound (*trumpets blaring*):—*also n.*

blar'ney *n* flattering talk.

blasé [blä'-zā] *adj* tired of pleasure through having too much of it (*blasé about travelling after so many holidays abroad*).

blaspheme [blas-feem'] *vb* **1** to speak mockingly or disrespectfully of God. **2** to swear or curse (*drunks blaspheming when thrown out of the pub*):—*n* **blasphem'er**:—*adj* **blas'phemous**:—*n* **blas'phemy**.

blast *n* **1** a sudden, strong gust of wind. **2** a loud sound (*the blast of a trumpet*). **3** an explosion (*killed in the bomb blast*):—*vb* **1** to blow up or break up by explosion (*blast rock*). **2** to make a loud noise (*music blasting from the radio*). **3** (*old or lit*) to cause to wither (*frost blasted the oak trees*). **4** to ruin (*blast their hopes*). **5** (*inf*) to criticize severely (*the critics blasted their performance*).

blatant [blā'-tênt] *adj* very obvious, shameless (*a blatant disregard for the law*).

blaze[1] *n* **1** a bright fire or flame (*dry wood makes a good blaze*). **2** a bright glow of light or colour (*the garden was a blaze of colour in the summer*). **3** a large, often dangerous, fire (*several people killed in the blaze*). **4** an outburst (*leave in a blaze of anger*):—*vb* **1** to burn brightly. **2** to shine like a flame.

blaze[2] *n* a mark, esp as made on a tree by cutting off a piece of bark:—*vb* to show a trail by such marks.

blaz'er *n* a kind of jacket (*school blazers*).

blaz'on *vb* to make known in a very obvious way (*newspapers blazoning the scandal*).

bleach *vb* **1** to make white or whiter (*hair bleached by the sun*). **2** to become white:—*n* a

substance that bleaches (*soak sheets in diluted bleach*).

bleak *adj* **1** dreary, cold (*a bleak winter's day*). **2** not hopeful or encouraging (*a bleak future*):—*n* **bleak'ness**.

blear'y-eyed *adj* with eyes unable to see properly (*bleary-eyed from lack of sleep*).

bleat *vb* to cry, as a sheep:—*also n.*

bleed *vb* (*pt, pp* **bled**) **1** to lose blood. **2** to take blood from (*doctors used to bleed people to treat disease*). **3** (*inf*) to take money from illegally or dishonestly (*moneylenders bleeding their clients*).

blem'ish *n* a stain, a fault:—*vb* to stain; to spoil.

blench *vb* to go back or aside in fear.

blend *vb* to mix together (*blend the cake ingredients/blend colours*):—*n* a mixture.

bless *vb* **1** to pronounce holy (*bless the new church*). **2** to ask God's favour for (*priests blessing newborn children*).

blessed [-ed *or* -t] *adj* **1** holy (*blessed saints*). **2** happy, fortunate.

bless'ing *n* **1** a thing that brings happiness (*the blessing of children*). **2** a prayer (*say a blessing at the christening*).

blight *n* **1** a disease in plants that causes them to wither. **2** a cause of ruin (*the blight of all their hopes*):—*vb* **1** to cause to wither. **2** to ruin.

blind *adj* **1** having no sight. **2** unable or unwilling to understand (*blind to the truth*). **3** closed at one end (*a blind alley*):—*n* **1** a window screen. **2** (*inf*) a pretence (*his business was a blind for drug-smuggling*):—*vb* **1** to make blind. **2** to dazzle (*blinded by the light*):— *adv* **blind'ly**:—*n* **blind'ness.**

blind'fold *vb* to cover the eyes with a bandage:— also *adj.*

blink *vb* **1** to wink. **2** to twinkle (*lights blinking*):—*n* **1** a glimpse. **2** a quick gleam of light.

blink'er *n* a piece of leather put over a horse's eyes to prevent it seeing sideways.

bliss *n* **1** great happiness. **2** the happiness of heaven.

bliss'ful *adj* very happy.

blis'ter *n* a bag of skin containing watery matter (*blisters on their feet after the long walk*):—*vb* to raise a blister.

blithe, blithe'some *adj* joyful, merry.

bliz'zard *n* a violent storm of wind and snow.

bloat'ed adj blown out, swollen (*I feel bloated after the large meal*).

blob n a drop, a small round mass (*a blob of paint*).

block n 1 a solid piece of wood, stone, etc (*a block of stone/a block of ice*). 2 the piece of wood on which people were beheaded. 3 a group of connected buildings (*a block of flats*). 4 a piece of wood in which a pulley is placed. 5 an obstacle (*a block to further progress*):—vb to stop the way.

blockade' n the surrounding of a place with soldiers and/or ships to prevent people and food from going in or leaving:—*also vb*.

block'head n a stupid fellow.

blond adj having fair hair and skin:—f **blonde**:— *also ns*.

blood n 1 the red liquid in the bodies of people and animals. 2 family or race (*of noble blood*).

blood'hound n a large dog much used in tracking.

blood'less adj 1 without blood or killing (*a bloodless victory*). 2 pale, anaemic. 3 without spirit or energy.

blood'shed n the spilling of blood, slaughter.

blood'shot adj (*of the eye*) red and inflamed with blood.

blood'thirsty adj eager to shed blood, taking pleasure in killing.

blood vessel n a vein or artery.

blood'y adj 1 bleeding, covered with blood (*a bloody nose*). 2 stained with blood (*a bloody handkerchief*). 3 with much death or killing (*a bloody battle*).

bloom n 1 a blossom, a flower (*the first blooms of spring*). 2 the state of flowering (*flowers in bloom*). 3 freshness, perfection (*in the bloom of youth*):—vb to blossom.

blot n 1 a spot or stain, often of ink. 2 disgrace (*a blot on the family's honour*). 3 something that spoils something beautiful or good (*high-rise flats are a blot on the beautiful landscape*):—vb (**blot'ted, blot'ting**) 1 to spot, to stain, esp with ink. 2 to dry ink with blotting paper.

blotch n a large spot or mark (*a blotch of ink/red blotches on her skin*).

blot'ter n a sheet or pad of blotting paper.

blot'ting pap'er n soft paper for drying ink.

blouse n a loose upper garment.

blow[1] vb (pt **blew**, pp **blown**) 1 to cause air to move. 2 to breathe hard (at or into) (*blow into one's*

hands to warm them). 3 to pant (*blowing hard after a climb*):—vb **blow up** to destroy by explosives.

blow[2] n 1 a stroke. 2 a misfortune.

blow[3] vb (pt **blew**, pp **blown**) to bloom.

blow'lamp n a lamp producing heat by a rush of air.

blow'y adj (*inf*) windy (*a blowy day*).

blub'ber n the fat of whales, etc:—vb (**blub'bered, blub'bering**) to weep noisily.

blud'geon n a short club:—vb to strike repeatedly with something heavy (*bludgeoned to death*).

blue n 1 a primary colour, as that of the sky on a clear day. 2 a university award for excellence in sport:—*also adj*.

blue'bell n 1 in Scotland, the wild hyacinth. 2 the harebell.

blue'bottle n a large bluish fly.

blue'jacket n a sailor.

blue pet'er n a signal flag flown by a ship about to sail.

blue'print n 1 a photographic print of a plan for a structure (*the blueprints for the new office block*). 2 a detailed plan or scheme (*a blueprint for success*).

blue riband n the highest honour.

blue'stocking n a learned woman, esp one who shows off her learning.

bluff n 1 a cliff, a steep headland. 2 a pretence (*their threat to kill the hostage was just a bluff*):—adj frank and abrupt but good-natured:—vb to try to deceive by a show of boldness (*they said they had guns but we knew they were bluffing*).

blun'der vb 1 to make a foolish mistake (*you blundered when you mistook her for her mother*). 2 to stumble about or into something (*blundering about in the dark looking for candles*):—*also n*.

blun'derbuss n an old type of gun, short with a wide mouth.

blunt adj 1 not sharp (*blunt knives*). 2 short and plain in speech (*a blunt young man*). 3 outspoken (*a few blunt remarks*):—vb 1 to make less sharp. 2 to weaken.

blur n 1 an indistinct mass (*people only a blur in the distance*). 2 a stain, a blot, a smear:—vb (**blurred'**, **blur'ring**) to make unclear (*blur his vision*/*blur memories*).

blurb *n* a short description of something written to make people interested in it (*the blurb on a paperback*).

blurt *vb* to speak suddenly or thoughtlessly (*blurt out the truth to the teacher*).

blush *vb* to become red in the face from shame, modesty, etc:—*n* the reddening of the face so caused:—*adv* **blush'ingly**.

blus'ter *vb* **1** (*of wind*) to blow violently. **2** to talk boastfully, noisily or threateningly:—*n* boastful, noisy or threatening talk.

bo'a *n* **1** a snake that kills by crushing its victim. **2** a scarf of fur or feathers.

bo'a constric'tor *n* a type of boa.

boar *n* **1** a male pig. **2** a wild pig.

board *n* **1** a long, broad strip of timber (*nail boards together to make a raft*). **2** food (*ask for board as well as lodging*). **3** persons who meet at a council table (*board of directors*). **4** the deck of a ship. **5** *pl* the stage. **6** a flat surface, often marked with a pattern on which certain games are played (*a Scrabble board*):—*vb* **1** to cover with boards (*board the broken windows up*). **2** to supply with food and accommodation (*board the pupils during term time*). **3** to take meals, and usu have accommodation, in (*workers boarding at my mother's house*). **4** to enter a ship. **5** to get on to (*board a bus*).

board'er *n* one who receives food and lodging at an agreed price.

board'ing house' *n* a house where food and lodging may be obtained.

board'ing school' *n* a school in which pupils live as boarders.

boast *vb* **1** to speak with too much pride about oneself or one's belongings, etc (*boast about his victory*/*boast about her big house*). **2** to possess (something to be proud of) (*a town boasting three theatres*):—*n* proud speech; a proud claim.

boast'ful *adj* fond of or given to boasting.

boat *n* **1** a ship, esp a small one. **2** a dish shaped like a boat (*a gravy boat*):—*vb* to go in a boat:—*n* **boat'man**.

boatswain [bōs'-ên] *n* a petty officer on board ship.

bob *vb* (**bobbed'**, **bob'bing**) **1** to move quickly up and down (*boats bobbing up and down on the water*). **2** to cut short (*bob her hair*):—*also n*.

bob'bin *n* a pin or cylinder round which thread is wound, a reel.

bode *vb*:—**bode ill** *or* **well** to be a bad *or* good sign of future events (*the team's victory bodes well for the championship*).

bod'ice *n* **1** a woman's tight-fitting, sleeveless garment worn on the upper body. **2** the upper part of a woman's dress (*a dress with a low-cut bodice*).

bod'ily *adj* having to do with the body (*convicted of doing bodily harm to her*):—*adv* by taking hold of the body (*remove him bodily from the building*).

bod'kin *n* **1** a needle-like instrument for piercing holes. **2** a blunt needle with a large eye for threading tape through a hem.

body *n* **1** the physical structure of a human being or animal. **2** the main part of anything (*the body of the text of the book*/*the body of the hall*). **3** a group of persons (*a body of spectators*). **4** a dead body, a corpse (*police looking for a body*).

bod'yguard *n* a guard to protect a person from attack.

bog *n* soft, wet ground, a marsh.

bog'ey, bog'y *n* **1** (*also* **bogeyman**) a goblin, an imaginary evil spirit. **2** an object of fear (*the bogey of unemployment*). **3** in golf, the score in which a good player should complete a round.

bog'gle *vb* **1** to be unwilling (to do something), to hesitate (*boggle at the thought of swimming in the cold sea*). **2** (*inf*) to be amazed or confused (*my mind boggled at his impertinence*).

bog'ie *n* **1** a low truck. **2** a four-wheeled truck supporting the front of a railway engine.

bog'us *adj* not genuine, sham (*a bogus workman*/*a bogus passport*).

bogy *see* **bogey**.

bohem'ian *n* anyone who pays little heed to the customs or conventions of the time.

boil[1] *vb* **1** to bubble from the action of heat (*water boiling*). **2** to cook in boiling water (*boil the potatoes*):—*n* **boil'er**.

boil[2] *n* a painful swelling containing poisonous matter.

bois'terous *adj* **1** stormy. **2** noisy and cheerful (*a boisterous party*).

bold *adj* 1 daring, brave. 2 large and clear (*bold type*).

bold'ness *n* courage.

bole *n* the trunk of a tree.

bole'ro *n* a Spanish dance:—*n* **bol'ero** a short jacket.

boll *n* a seed-container, as of the cotton or flax plant.

bol'lard *n* a short thick post used to prevent motor vehicles from going on part of a road.

boll weev'il *n* an insect that destroys cotton bolls.

bol'ster *n* a long pillow:—*vb* to hold up, to support (*get a loan to bolster up the firm's financial state*).

bolt *n* 1 an arrow. 2 a thunderbolt. 3 a bar of a door:—*vb* 1 to fasten with a bolt. 2 to run away (*horses bolting in fright*). 3 to eat too quickly (*bolt one's food*).

bomb *n* a hollow metal missile containing high explosive, gas, etc (*buildings blown up by a bomb*):—*vb* to attack with bombs (*the enemy airforce bombing the city*).

bombard' *vb* 1 to fire many guns at. 2 to direct many questions, statements of criticism, etc, at (*reporters bombarding the police with questions about the murder*):—*n* **bombard'ment**.

bombardier [bom-bê-deer'] *n* a non-commissioned officer in the artillery.

bom'bast *n* words that sound important but mean little:—*adj* **bombas'tic**.

bomb'shell *n* a very surprising piece of news, often bad news (*the closing of the factory was a real bombshell to the town*).

bon'bon *n* (*fml*) a sweet.

bond *n* 1 that which binds (*the bond of friendship/the bond between twins*). 2 a written agreement, esp to pay money. 3 a government store in which goods are kept until the taxes on them are paid. 4 (*fml*) *pl* chains, fetters (*prisoners in bonds*).

bon'dage *n* slavery.

bone *n* 1 the hard substance forming the skeleton of human beings and animals (*flesh and bone*). 2 any one of the pieces of this (*break a bone in the leg*):—*vb* to take out the bones from (*bone fish*).

bon'fire *n* a large, open-air fire.

bon'net *n* 1 a headdress. 2 the metal cover of a motor engine.

bon'ny *adj* 1 pretty. 2 healthy-looking.

bonus [bō-nês] *n* an extra payment, made for a special effort or services (*a productivity bonus/a Christmas bonus*).

bon'y *adj* 1 having many bones (*bony fish*). 2 having protruding bones (*a bony man*).

boob'y *n* a stupid person.

booby prize *n* a prize given to the worst performer.

booby trap *n* a trap hidden in a place so obvious that no one suspects it.

book[1] *n* printed matter, bound between covers.

book[2] *vb* to reserve in advance (*booked a hotel room/book theatre tickets*)

book'ing of'fice *n* an office at which tickets are sold (*the booking office at the station*).

book'ish *adj* fond of reading or study.

book'keeper *n* one who keeps accounts:—*n* **book'keeping**.

book'maker *n* (*also* (*inf*) **bookie**) one who makes his or her living by betting.

book'worm *n* one who reads a great deal.

boom[1] *n* 1 a long pole to stretch the bottom of a sail. 2 a barrier set across a harbour entrance or river.

boom[2] *n* a long deep sound:—*also vb*.

boom[3] *n* a time of rapid increase or growth (*a tourist boom/a baby boom*):—*vb* to increase or grow quickly (*business is booming*).

boom'erang *n* a curved throwing stick that returns to the thrower, used by Australian Aboriginals:—*vb* (*of an action, plan, etc*) to go wrong in such a way that harm or damage is caused to the person responsible.

boon *n* 1 (*old*) a favour, a special request. 2 an advantage, a blessing.

boor *n* a rough, ill-mannered person:—*adj* **boor'ish**.

boot[1] *n* 1 a covering for the foot and lower leg. 2 the storage place for luggage at the back of a motor car. 3 *pl* a hotel servant who cleans the boots and shoes:—*vb* to kick (*boot the ball into play*).

boot[2] *vb* (*old*) to be of advantage.

boot'leg *vb* to smuggle (alcoholic liquor):—*n* **boot'legger**.

booth *n* 1 a tent at a fair. 2 a covered stall at a market. 3 a small, enclosed structure (*a phone booth*).

boot'y *n* 1 goods seized and divided by the victors after a battle. 2 goods taken by thieves.

boracic [bor-as'-ik] *adj* connected with borax.

bor'ax *n* a salt used for cleaning and healing.

bor'der *n* 1 the outer edge of anything (*a hand-kerchief with a lace border/a white border round the picture*). 2 the boundary between two countries (*show one's passport at the border*). 3 a flowerbed round a lawn, etc (*borders of pansies*):—*vb* to be next to (*the farm bordering ours*):—**border (up)on** to come close to, to be almost (*a crime bordering on treason*).

bore[1] *vb* to make a hole in:—*n* 1 the hole made by boring. 2 the greatest breadth of a tube, esp of a gun.

bore[2] *vb* to weary by uninteresting talk, etc (*an audience bored by a long speech*):—*n* a person whose talk is wearisome:—*adj* **bor'ing**.

bore[3] *n* a large tidal wave.

boreas [bor'-ee-ês] *n* the north wind:—*adj* **bor'eal**.

bored *adj* weary and dissatisfied with one's circumstances (*bored children with nothing to do*).

bore'dom *n* the state of being bored.

born *pp* of **bear**, sense 6.

borne *pp* of **bear**, senses 1–5, 7.

bor'ough *n* a town with powers of self-government and certain other privileges granted by royal charter.

bor'row *vb* to ask or receive as a loan (*borrow money from the bank/borrow a library book*):—*n* **bor'rower**.

bor'stal *n* formerly, a special kind of prison for young lawbreakers.

borzoi [bor'-zoi] *n* a Russian wolfhound.

bosh *n* (*inf*) foolish talk.

bosom [bö-sêm] *n* 1 the breast (*an ample bosom*). 2 (*lit or fml*) the heart, considered as the seat of desires and feelings (*hope stirred in his bosom*):—*adj* close, well-loved (*bosom friends*).

boss[1] *n* a knob.

boss[2] *n* (*inf*) a master, a manager(ess):—*vb* 1 to be in charge. 2 to order about (*older boys bossing younger ones*).

boss'y *adj* (*inf*) fond of ordering others about (*bossy people/in a bossy manner*).

bot'any *n* the science or study of plants:—*adjs* **botan'ic**, **botan'ical**:—*n* **bot'anist**.

botch *n* (*inf*) a badly done piece of work:—*vb* to do (a job) badly or roughly.

both'er *vb* 1 to annoy (*stop bothering your mother for sweets*). 2 to trouble oneself (*don't bother to get up*):—*n* a trouble.

bot'tle *n* 1 a container, usu of glass, with a narrow neck. 2 (*inf*) courage, boldness (*lose one's bottle*):—*vb* to put into bottles (*bottle wine*).

bottle'neck *n* 1 a narrow or busy part of a road where traffic has to slow down or stop 2 something that slows down progress (*production held up by a bottleneck in the system*).

bot'tom *n* 1 the lowest part (*at the bottom of the well/the bottom of the cupboard*). 2 the buttocks:—*adj* lowest (*the bottom drawer/the bottom flat*):—*adj* **bot'tomless**.

boudoir [bö-dwär'] *n* (*fml*) a lady's private room.

bough [bou] *n* (*fml*) the branch of a tree.

bought *pt* of **buy**.

bouillon [bö-yo(ng)'] *n* a strong broth.

boul'der *n* a large smooth stone.

boulevard [böl'-vär] *n* a wide street, with trees planted along either side.

bounce *vb* to jump or rebound suddenly (*balls that bounce easily/children bouncing with joy*):—also *n*.

bounc'ing *adj* big, strong (*a bouncing baby*).

bound[1] *n* a limit or boundary beyond which one must not go:—*vb* to form a limit or boundary.

bound[2] *vb* to jump, to leap:—also *n*.

bound[3] *adj* 1 on the way to (*homeward bound*). 2 (*pt of* **bind**). 3 obliged (*feel bound to report him*). 4 sure (to do something) (*bound to fail*). 5 tied (*with bound hands*). 6 covered (*bound books*).

boun'dary *n* 1 an outer limit. 2 a border.

bound'less *adj* without limit, endless (*with boundless energy*).

boun'tiful *adj* (*fml*) giving generously.

boun'ty *n* (*fml*) 1 generosity, kindness. 2 a gift of money above what is earned.

bouquet [bö'-kä] *n* 1 a bunch of flowers. 2 perfume of wine.

bourgeois [bör'-jwä] *n* a middle-class citizen:—*adj* 1 middle-class. 2 dull and unwilling to change (*young people accusing their parents of being bourgeois*).

bourgeoisie [bör-jwä-zee'] *n* the middle class.

bout *n* 1 a period or action (*bouts of activity*). 2 an attack (of illness) (*a bout of flu*). 3 a contest (*a boxing bout*).

boutique n [bŏ-teek'] a small shop selling fashionable clothes (*a boutique selling only designer clothes*).

bov'ine adj 1 like an ox. 2 slow and stupid.

bow[1] [bou] vb 1 to bend, esp in respect or greeting (*bow to the queen*). 2 to lower (*bow his head*):—n a bending of the head or body in respect or greeting.

bow[2] [bō] n 1 a weapon for shooting arrows. 2 a looped knot. 3 a stick for playing a stringed instrument (e.g. the violin).

bow[3] [bou] n the curved front part of a ship.

bowed adj bent, stooping (*with head bowed in prayer*).

bow'els npl 1 the inside of the body, the intestines. 2 the organ by means of which waste matter is expelled from the body.

bow'er n (*fml*) a shady recess in a garden.

bowie-knife [bou'-wee-] n a long curved hunting knife.

bowl[1] [bōl] n a roundish dish or basin (*a pudding bowl*).

bowl[2] [bōl] n 1 a heavy wooden ball. 2 pl the game played with such balls:—vb 1 to play bowls. 2 to deliver the ball at cricket.

bowleg'ged [bō'-] adj having legs wide apart at the knees, bandy-legged.

bowl'er[1] n one who bowls.

bowl'er[2], **bowl'er hat'** n a round stiff hat.

bowl'ine n 1 a rope on a sailing ship. 2 a knot that does not slip.

bowl'ing green n a lawn prepared for the game of bowls.

bowsprit [bō'-] n a pole sticking out from the front of a ship.

bow'string n the string of a bow.

bow win'dow [bō'-] n a window built into a section of wall that curves out and back.

box[1] n a type of hardwood tree.

box[2] n 1 a case or container (*a box of chocolates/boxes of books*). 2 in a theatre, a separate compartment with seats, overlooking the stage:—vb to put in a box (*a job boxing apples*).

box[3] vb 1 to strike (*box the boy's ears*). 2 to fight in sport, wearing padded gloves:—n **box'er**.

box'ing n the sport of fighting with padded gloves on.

Boxing Day n the day after Christmas Day.

box'-room n a storage room in a house.

boy n 1 a male child (*have two boys and a girl*). 2 a young male person:—n **boy'hood**.

boy'cott vb to refuse to have any dealings with (*workers boycotting firms whose employees are not union members*):—also n.

Boy Scout n formerly the name given to a member of an international youth organization for boys, now **Scout**.

bra n (*abbr of* **brassiere**) a supporting undergarment worn by women over the breasts.

brace n 1 a support. 2 a pair or a couple (*a brace of pheasants*). 3 a boring tool. 4 pl crossed straps for holding up trousers:—vb to steady or prepare oneself (*brace yourself for some bad news*).

brace'let n an ornament for the wrist.

brac'ing adj giving strength (*a bracing climate*).

brack'en n a type of fern.

brack'et n 1 a support for something fixed to a wall (*lights supported by brackets*). 2 pl marks in printing to enclose a word, as {}, [] or ():—vb 1 to enclose in brackets (*bracket the information*). 2 to link or connect (*bracket the two cases together*).

brack'ish adj having a salty taste (*brackish water*).

brad, n a headless nail.

brad'awl n a boring tool.

brag n a boast:—vb (**bragged'**, **brag'ging**) to boast (*brag about the cost of her jewels*).

brag'gart n a boaster:—adj boastful.

braid vb to twist together into one (*braid her hair*):—n 1 a plait of cords or of hair so twisted together. 2 a narrow edging of decorated tape.

braid'ed adj edged with braid.

Braille n a system of printing for blind people in which the letters of the alphabet and numbers are printed as raised dots that can be read by touching them.

brain n 1 the soft matter within the skull, the centre of the nervous system (*an operation on the brain*). 2 cleverness, intelligence (*the job requires someone with brains*). 3 (*inf*) someone very clever or intelligent:—vb to dash the brains out.

brain'less adj stupid.

brain'y adj (*inf*) clever.

braise vb to stew in a closed pan (*braise beef*).

brake[1] n 1 a fern. 2 a clump of bushes or undergrowth.

brake[2] n 1 a large wagon. 2 an apparatus for slowing or stopping a vehicle:—vb to apply the brake (brake sharply).

bram'ble n a prickly bush, esp the blackberry bush.

bran n the husks of corn when separated from the grain.

branch n 1 a shoot growing out of the trunk or one of the boughs of a tree. 2 any connected part of a larger body (e.g. office, store, bank, etc) (branches responsible to head office):—vb to divide into branches (the road branches here):—**branch out 1** to begin something new (after working for the family firm, he's branching out on his own). 2 to expand (the firm is branching out into computers).

brand n 1 a burning piece of wood. 2 a mark made with a hot iron to identify cattle, etc. 3 a trademark, a special make of article (several brands of tinned soup). 4 variety (his own brand of humour):—vb 1 to mark with a hot iron (brand cattle). 2 to mark down (as being bad).

bran'dish vb to wave, to shake (brandish a sword in the air).

bran'dy n a strong drink made from wine.

brasier see brazier.

brass n 1 an alloy of copper and zinc. 2 (inf) impudence (have the brass to call me a liar). 3 (inf) money (made his brass in industry):—adj brass'y.

brass'iere see bra.

brat n an ill-mannered child.

brava'do n pretended courage, boastful talk.

brave adj courageous, daring (a brave man/a brave action):—vb 1 to defy (brave the opposition). 2 to face with courage (brave the dangerous journey):—n a North American Indian warrior.

brav'ery n courage, daring.

bravo [brä'-vō] interj well done!

brawl vb to quarrel noisily (drunks brawling in the pub):—n a noisy row:—n brawl'er.

brawn n 1 muscle, strength. 2 a type of pressed meat.

brawn'y adj muscular, strong.

bray vb to make a loud, harsh sound, as an ass:—also n.

braz'en adj 1 made of brass. 2 impudent, bold (a brazen young woman):—vb to face boldly and impudently.

braz'en-faced adj impudent.

braz'ier, bras'ier n 1 a worker in brass. 2 an iron frame for holding fire.

breach n 1 act of breaking (a breach of the law). 2 (fml) a gap (breach in the wall). 3 a fault (breach in security). 4 a quarrel, separation (breach between two sections of the club):—vb to make a gap or opening in.

bread n a food made from flour or meal and baked.

breadth n the distance from side to side, width.

bread'winner n the person whose earnings supply the needs of the family.

break vb (pt broke, pp bro'ken) 1 to separate into two or more parts, usu by force (break his leg). 2 to become unusable or in need of repair (the machine is broken). 3 to tame (break in the new horses). 4 to fail to keep (break a promise/break the law). 5 to tell gently (break the news). 6 to go with force (break out from the prison). 7 to do better than (break a record):—n 1 an opening. 2 a separation. 3 a pause:—adj break'able.

break'age n 1 a breaking. 2 the thing broken.

break'er n a wave broken by rocks.

breakfast [brek'-fêst] n the first meal in the day:—vb to eat breakfast.

break'neck adj dangerously fast (at breakneck speed).

break'through n an important new development (a breakthrough in the treatment of cancer).

break'water n a wall to break the force of the waves.

bream n a freshwater fish.

breast n 1 (fml) the front part of the body from the neck to the stomach, the chest (a soldier stabbed in the breast). 2 each of the milk-producing glands in a female:—vb 1 to face (breast the waves). 2 to touch (breast the tape). 3 to come to the top of (breast the hill).

breast'plate n armour for the breast.

breath n 1 the air taken into and put out from the lungs. 2 a gentle breeze.

breathe vb 1 to take air into one's lungs and put it out again. 2 (fml) to live (while he breathes he will be loyal). 3 (fml) to whisper (breathe a reply in her ear).

breath'less adj 1 out of breath, panting (breathless after climbing the hill). 2 excited, eager (in breathless expectation):—adv breath'lessly.

breech n 1 the back part of a gun barrel. 2 pl **breech'es** trousers, esp those fastening just below the knee.

breed vb (pt, pp **bred**) 1 to produce young (rabbits breeding rapidly). 2 to keep (animals) for the purpose of breeding young (he breeds Alsatians). 3 to be the cause of (breed disaster):—n a type, variety, species (a breed of cattle/a new breed of men).

breed'ing n 1 the bearing of offspring. 2 good manners.

breeze n a light wind.

breez'y adj 1 windy. 2 lively (in a breezy manner):—adv **breez'ily**.

breth'ren npl (old or relig) brothers.

brev'ity n (fml) shortness (the brevity of the statement).

brew vb 1 to make (beer). 2 to make (tea). 3 to be about to start (a storm brewing/trouble brewing):—n the mixture made by brewing:—n **brew'er**.

brew'ery n a factory where beer is made.

briar see **brier**.

bribe n a reward offered to win unfairly favour or preference (get into the country by bribing the border guard):—vb to win over by bribes:—n **brib'ery**.

bric-à-brac [brik'-a-brak] n small ornaments (a shelf covered by bric-à-brac).

brick n 1 a block of baked clay. 2 (inf) a good or helpful person.

brick'bat n a piece of criticism (a play receiving only brickbats).

brick'layer n one who builds with bricks.

brid'al adj concerning a bride or a wedding (the bridal party).

bride n a woman about to be married, or newly married.

bride'groom n a man about to be married, or newly married.

brides'maid n a girl who attends the bride at a wedding.

bridge[1] n 1 a roadway built across a river, etc. 2 the small deck for a ship's captain. 3 the piece of wood that supports the strings of a violin, etc:—vb 1 to build a bridge over. 2 to close a gap or pause to make a connection (bridging the awkward silence with a few remarks).

bridge[2] n a card game.

brid'le n 1 the head straps and metal bit by which a horse is guided. 2 a check (act as a bridle on her extravagance):—vb 1 to put a bridle on (bridle a horse). 2 to check (bridle his anger). 3 to toss the head in anger, etc (bridle at his criticism). 4 to show anger or indignation.

brief n a summary of a law case for use in court:—adj short (a brief statement):—vb to provide with a summary of the facts.

brief'case n a case for carrying papers.

bri'er, bri'ar n a thorn bush, the wild rose.

brigade[1] n an army unit consisting usu of three battalions.

brigadier[1] n an officer commanding a brigade.

brig'and n (old) a member of a band of robbers.

bright adj 1 shining (a bright light). 2 strong, vivid (a bright red colour). 3 lively, cheerful (the invalid is a bit brighter). 4 clever (a bright pupil):—n **bright'ness**.

bright'en vb to make or become bright (candles brightening the room/something to brighten her mood).

brill n a type of flatfish.

brill'iant adj 1 sparkling. 2 very bright. 3 very clever:—n a diamond:—ns **bril-l'iance, brill'iancy**.

brim n 1 the rim (the brim of the cup). 2 the edge (the brim of the hat).

brim'ful, brim'ming adj full to the brim (glasses brimful with wine).

brim'stone n sulphur.

brin'dled adj marked with streaks (a brindled terrier).

brine n salt water:—**the bri'ny** the sea.

bring vb (pt, pp **brought**) 1 to fetch, to carry (bring food with you/bring a friend to the party). 2 to cause (death bringing sadness and grief):—**bring about** to cause to happen:—**bring off** to succeed (bring off a victory):—**bring up** 1 to rear, to educate (bring up three children). 2 to raise (a subject for discussion).

brink n 1 the edge of a steep place (at the brink of the waterfall). 2 the edge, the point (on the brink of disaster).

brisk adj keen; lively:—adv **brisk'ly**:—n **brisk'ness**.

bris'ket n a cut of meat from the breast of an animal.

bris'tle n a short, stiff hair:—vb to stand on end.

brist'ly adj having bristles, rough (a bristly chin).

brit'tle adj hard but easily broken (brittle wood/brittle bones).

broach vb 1 (fml) to open up (broach a new bottle of wine). 2 to begin to speak of (broach the question of money).

broad [bråd] adj 1 wide (a broad piece of ribbon). 2 not detailed, general (a broad description). 3 (of speech) with a strong local accent:—n **broad'ness.**

broad'cast vb (pt, pp broadcast) 1 to make widely known (broadcast his views to the whole office). 2 to send out by radio or television (broadcast the match). 3 to scatter widely (broadcast seed):—also n.

broad'en vb to make or become broad or broader (broaden the road/the road broadens here).

broad'-mind'ed adj ready to listen to and consider opinions different from one's own, liberal.

broad'sheet n 1 a piece of paper printed on one side. 2 a newspaper of large format, a quality newspaper (he buys a broadsheet, not a tabloid).

broad'side n 1 the firing of all the guns on one side of a ship at the same time. 2 a sheet of paper printed on one side. 3 a verbal or written attack.

broad'sword n a sword with a broad blade.

brocade' n a silk cloth with a raised pattern.

broccoli [bro'-co-li] n a green vegetable.

brochure [bro'-shör] n a small book, a pamphlet (a brochure advertising the hotel).

brock n a badger.

brogue [brög] n 1 a strong shoe. 2 a strong accent, esp an Irish one.

broil vb to cook over a fire, to grill.

brok'er n 1 one who buys and sells for others for a commission. 2 a stockbroker.

bron'chial adj having to do with the **bronchi,** the branches of the windpipe to the lungs.

bronchi'tis n an illness affecting the windpipe to the lungs.

bron'co, bron'cho n (Amer) a half-tamed horse.

bron'tosaurus n a very large plant-eating dinosaur.

bronze n 1 an alloy of copper and tin. 2 a reddish-brown colour:—vb to give or become a reddish-brown colour.

brooch n an ornamental pin.

brood vb 1 to sit on eggs. 2 to think deeply or anxiously about (brood about her money problems):—n 1 children. 2 a family of young birds.

brood'y adj 1 hatching eggs. 2 badly wanting to have children (feels broody when she looks at a newborn baby).

brook¹ n a small stream.

brook² vb (fml) to bear, to tolerate (brook no interference).

broom n 1 a plant with yellow flowers. 2 a brush, esp one of twigs.

broom'stick n the handle of a broom.

broth n a meat soup with vegetables.

broth'er n (pl broth'ers or (old or relig) breth'ren) 1 a son of the same parents. 2 a member of the same group.

broth'erhood n 1 the relation of a brother. 2 a group with one common purpose.

broth'erly adj of or like a brother.

brougham [brö'-êm or brö'-êm] n a light carriage.

brought pt of **bring.**

brow n 1 the forehead. 2 the jutting-out edge of a cliff or hill (the brow of the hill).

brow'beat vb to bully (browbeat the younger boy into doing his work).

brown adj of a dark colour:—also n:—vb to make or become brown.

brown'ie n 1 a kindly fairy. 2 formerly, a junior member of the Girl Guides, now **Brownie Guide.**

brown study n deep thought.

browse vb 1 to feed upon (cows browsing in the fields). 2 to glance through a book (browse through the catalogue).

bruise n a dark spot on the skin, caused by a knock:—vb to cause a bruise on (bruise her face in the accident/apples bruised by falling from the tree).

brunette [brû-net'] n a woman with dark brown hair.

brunt n the main force or shock of something, the worst effects (the mother bore the brunt of the father's violence).

brush n 1 an instrument for cleaning, sweeping or smoothing. 2 an instrument for putting paint on to something. 3 the tail of a fox. 4 small trees and bushes. 5 a short battle. 5 (inf) a slight disagreement or hostile encounter (a brush with the police):—vb 1 to clean with a brush. **2** to touch lightly (*brush her cheek with his lips*).

brush'wood *n* **1** small trees and bushes. **2** a thicket.

brusque [brûsk *or* brusk] *adj* blunt, rude and abrupt in speech or manner:—*adv* **brusque'ly:**—*n* **brusque'ness**.

Brussel sprout *n* a small, round, green vegetable like a very small cabbage.

brut'al *adj* cruel, savage (*a brutal murder*).

brutal'ity *n* cruelty, savagery.

brute *n* **1** an animal. **2** (*inf*) a cruel person (*he was a brute to leave her like that*).

brut'ish *adj* savage, animal-like.

bub'ble *n* a film of water or other liquid, containing air (*bubbles in the glasses of champagne*):—*vb* to form bubbles:—*adj* **bubbly**.

buc'caneer *n* a pirate.

buck *n* **1** a male deer, goat, rabbit, etc. **2** (*old*) a dandy, a lively young man:—*vb* to jump straight up with the back arched.

buck'et *n* a vessel for carrying water, a pail.

buck'le *n* a fastener for joining the ends of a belt or band:—*vb* **1** to fasten (*buckle on his belt*). **2** to bend out of shape (*metal buckling in the intense heat*).

buck'ler *n* (*old*) a small shield.

buck'shot *n* a type of shot for killing big game.

buck'skin *n* a soft leather.

bucol'ic *adj* connected with country life, rustic (*a bucolic poem*).

bud *n* a leaf or flower before it opens:—*vb* (**bud'ded, bud'ding**) to put out buds.

Buddhist *n* a person who believes in the religious teaching of Buddha:—**Buddhism** *n*.

bud'ding *adj* promising (*a budding young artist*).

budge *vb* (*inf*) to move, to stir (*I can't budge this heavy wardrobe/she won't budge from that seat*).

budgerigar [bu-jê-ri-gär'] *n* a type of small parrot that can be trained to talk.

bud'get *n* **1** a statement of government taxation and intended spending for the coming year. **2** a plan to ensure that household expenses or those of a firm or organization will not be greater than income (*keep within our monthly budget*):—*vb* **1** to make such a plan (*I try to budget but I always seem to spend too much*). **2** to allow for something in a budget (*they hadn't budgeted for such a large phone bill*).

buff *n* **1** a type of leather. **2** a pale dull yellow colour:—*adj* light yellow.

buffalo *n* (*pl* **buffalos** *or* **buffaloes**) a type of ox.

buffer *n* an apparatus to lessen the force of a collision or shock.

buffet[1] [bö'-fâ] *n* **1** a sideboard. **2** a counter or bar at which refreshments may be obtained (*the station buffet*). **3** a meal, often cold, set out on tables so that people can help themselves (*have a buffet supper*).

buffet[2] [buf'-fet] *n* (*fml*) a blow, a slap (*give his son a buffet on the side of the head*):—*vb* **1** to strike. **2** to knock about (*boats buffeted by strong winds*).

buffoon' *n* **1** a clown. **2** a person who plays the fool.

bug *n* **1** a blood-sucking insect (*bedbugs*). **2** any insect (*bugs crawling over our picnic*). **3** (*inf*) an infection (*a stomach bug*). **4** (*inf*) a hidden microphone used to record other people's conversations secretly (*a bug in his hotel room*). **5** a defect or error in a computer program or system.:—*vb* (**bugged'**, **bug'ging**) (*inf*) **1** to install or use a hidden microphone (*bug his room*). **2** (*inf*) to annoy (*what's bugging you?*).

bug'bear *n* a cause of fear or anxiety (*sudden redundancy is one of the bugbears of modern times*).

bug'le *n* **1** a hunting horn. **2** a trumpet:—*n* **bug'ler**.

build [bild] *vb* (*pt, pp* **built**) to put together materials in order to make something, to construct:—*n* **build'er**.

build'ing *n* the thing built.

bulb *n* **1** the round root of certain flowers. **2** a pear-shaped glass globe surrounding the element of an electric light.

bulb'ous *adj* bulb-shaped, swollen.

bulge *n* a swelling:—*vb* to swell out (*his muscles are bulging after weight-training*):—*adj* **bulg'y**.

bulim'ia *n* an eating disorder in which bouts of over-eating are followed by bouts of vomiting in order to lose weight:—**bulim'ic** *adj*.

bulk *n* **1** the size, esp of large things (*the package is not heavy but its sheer bulk makes it difficult to move*). **2** the main part (*the bulk of their money goes on housing*):—**in bulk** in a large quantity:—*vb* to make fuller, to increase in size (*use gel to bulk out her hair*):—**bulk large** (*fml*) to be important or prominent (*education does not bulk large in his plans*).

bulk'head *n* an inside wall between one part of a ship and another.

bulk'y *adj* very large and awkward to move or carry.

bull[1] *n* the male ox, elephant, whale, etc.

bull[2] *n* a ruling by the pope.

bull'dog *n* **1** a type of dog. **2** a person who will not give in easily.

bull'dozer *n* a heavy tractor for clearing away obstacles and making land level.

bul'let *n* a lead ball shot from a rifle or pistol.

bul'letin *n* **1** a short, official report of news. **2** a printed information sheet or newspaper (*the company bulletin*).

bul'letproof *adj* not able to be pierced by bullets (*a bulletproof vest*).

bull'finch *n* a songbird.

bull'frog *n* a large frog.

bull'ion *n* uncoined gold and silver in lumps.

bull'ock *n*. a young bull.

bull's-eye[1] *n* **1** the centre of a target. **2** a shot that hits it. **3** a type of sweet.

bul'ly *n* a person who uses his or her strength to hurt or to terrify those who are weaker:—*vb* to intimidate, oppress or hurt (*bullying younger boys/bullied people into doing what he wants*).

bul'rush *n* a tall weed.

bulwark [búl'-wêrk] *n* **1** a defensive mound. **2** a protection. **3** the part of a ship's side that comes above deck level.

bum'blebee *n* a large type of bee.

bump *n* **1** a heavy blow, or the dull noise made by it (*receive a bump on the head in the accident*). **2** a lump caused by a blow:—*vb* to knock against.

bum'per *n* **1** (*old*) a full glass or cup. **2** a protective bar at the front and the back of a motor car:—*adj* unusually large or full (*a bumper harvest*).

bump'kin *n* an awkward country fellow.

bump'tious *adj* conceited, too full of oneself.

bun *n* **1** a small cake. **2** a rounded mass of hair.

bunch *n* **1** a group or collection of things of the same kind (*a bunch of flowers/a bunch of bananas/a bunch of keys*). **2** (*inf*) a group of people (*her friends are a nice bunch*):—*vb* to come or put together in groups or bunches (*traffic bunching on motorways/players bunched up on the field*).

bun'dle *n* a collection of things tied together:—*vb* **1** to tie in a bundle (*bundle up the old clothes for the jumble sale*). **2** to force to go in a hurry (*bundle the children off to school*).

bung *n* a large stopper for a barrel:—*vb* to stop up (*bung up the hole*).

bun'galow *n* a low house usu of one storey.

bun'gee jumping *n* the act of jumping from a high place while the ankles are secured by an elastic cord.

bung'hole *n* the hole in a barrel.

bun'gle *vb* to do badly or clumsily (*bungle a deal and lose the firm money*):—*also n*.

bun'ion *n* a swelling on the foot, esp on the big toe.

bunk *n* **1** a narrow bed, esp in a ship. **2** one of a pair of beds placed one above the other (*bunk beds*).

bun'ker *n* **1** a ship's coal store. **2** a large chest for storing coal. **3** a sand-filled hollow on a golf course.

bun'kum *n* foolish talk.

bun'ting *n* **1** a material used for making flags. **2** flags.

buoy [boi] *n* an object floating in a fixed position to show ships the safe course:—*vb* **1** to keep afloat. **2** to support, to keep high (*profits buoyed up by the export market/buoy up his hopes*). **3** to raise the spirits of (*thoughts of going home buoyed him up*).

buoy'ant *adj* **1** floating, able to float easily (*cork is a buoyant material*). **2** cheerful, optimistic (*in buoyant mood*):—*n* **buoy'-ancy.**

bur, burr *n* the prickly seed container of certain plants.

bur'ble *vb* **1** to murmur. **2** to talk in a confused way.

bur'den *n* **1** a load. **2** the chorus of a song. **3** the leading idea (of):—*vb* to load heavily.

bur'densome *adj* (*fml*) heavy and difficult (*a burdensome task*).

bur'dock *n* a weed with burs.

bureau [bû'-rō] *n* (*pl* **bu'reaux** *or* **bu'reaus**) **1** a writing desk with drawers (*an antique bureau*). **2** an office (*an accommodation bureau/an exchange bureau*).

bureaucracy [bû-rok'-rê-si] *n* **1** a system of government by paid officials working for a government (*the Civil Service bureaucracy*). **2** these officials taken as a group. **3** a system of doing things officially, often unnecessarily complicated and time-consuming (*complain about the bureaucracy involved in getting a licence*).

burette' *n* a glass tube for measuring liquids.

bur'geon *vb* **1** to bud (*plants burgeoning*). **2** to grow or develop quickly, to flourish (*the economy is burgeoning*).

bur'ger *n see* **hamburger**.

burgh [bu-rê] *n* the Scottish form of **borough**.

bur'glar *n* a thief who breaks into a house.

bur'glary *n* the crime of housebreaking.

bur'gle *vb* to commit burglary.

bur'ial *n* the act of putting into a grave.

burlesque [bur-lesk'] *n* a comic or mocking imitation, a parody, a caricature:—*also adj and vb*.

bur'ly *adj* stout, big and strong (*troublemakers thrown out by burly doormen*).

burn *vb* (*pt, pp* **burnt** *or* **burned**) **1** to be alight, to give out heat (*wood that burns easily*). **2** to be on fire (*the house is burning*). **3** to destroy or damage by fire (*all their possessions were burnt in the blaze*). **4** to hurt or injure by fire (*he was badly burnt in the fire*). **5** to be very hot (*burn with fever*). **6** to feel great anger, passion, etc:— *n* a hurt caused by fire (*receive severe burns in the fire*).

burn'er *n* the part of a stove, etc, from which the flame comes.

burn'ish *vb* to polish:—*also n*.

burr *n* **1** a throaty sounding of the letter *r*. **2** a bur.

bur'row *n* a hole in the earth made by certain animals, e.g. rabbits, foxes, etc:—*vb* **1** to make by digging (*burrow a hole*). **2** to search for something (*burrow in her pocket for keys*).

bur'sar *n* the treasurer of a school or college.

burst *vb* (*pt, pp* **burst**) **1** to break in pieces (*the balloon burst*). **2** to rush, to go suddenly or violently (*burst into the room*):—*n* a sudden outbreak (*a burst of applause*).

bur'y *vb* **1** to put into a grave. **2** to put under ground.

bus *n* a large road vehicle for carrying passengers (short for **omnibus**):—*vb* (**bussed', bus'sing** *or* **bused', bus'ing**) to transport by bus (*bus the children to school*).

bus'by *n* a tall fur cap, worn by certain soldiers.

bush *n* **1** a small low tree. **2** wild, uncleared country; forest country.

bush'el *n* a measure (8 gallons) for grain, etc.

bush'y *adj* **1** full of bushes. **2** thick-growing (*bushy hair*).

bus'iness *n* **1** one's work or job (*selling furniture is his business*). **2** trade and commerce (*a career in business*). **3** a matter that concerns a particular person (*none of your business*):—**bus'inesslike** *adj*.

bus'ker *n* a street musician.

bust *n* **1** the shoulders and breast. **2** a statue showing only the head, shoulders and breast of a person (*a bust of Shakespeare*).

bus'tard *n* a large bird.

bus'tle[1] *vb* to move about busily and often fussily (*bustling about preparing a meal*):—*n* noisy movement, hurry.

bus'tle[2] *n* a frame or pad once worn to hold out the back of a woman's skirt.

bus'y *adj* **1** always doing something (*too busy to visit her family*). **2** at work, engaged in a job, etc (*he's busy and will ring you back*). **3** full of people, traffic, etc (*busy shops/busy streets*):— *vb* to occupy (*busy oneself with Christmas preparations*):—*adv* **bus'ily**.

bus'ybody *n* one who shows too much interest in the affairs of others, a meddler.

but'cher *n* **1** one who kills and sells animals for food. **2** a cruel killer (*the leader of the enemy army was a butcher*):—*vb* **1** to kill for food. **2** to kill cruelly.

but'chery *n* cruel slaughter.

but'ler *n* the chief manservant in a household, formerly in charge of the wine cellar.

butt[1] *n* **1** a large barrel. **2** the thicker end of a thing (*the butt of a rifle*):—*vb* to strike with the head or horns (*butted by a ram*).

butt[2] *n* **1** a mark to be shot at. **2** the mound behind the targets for rifle practice. **3** a person who is always being made fun of (*the butt of his jokes*).

but'ter *n* an oily food made from milk.

but'tercup *n* a common yellow wild flower.

but'terfly *n* **1** an insect with large colourful wings. **2** a frivolous unreliable person.

but'termilk *n* the milk that remains after the butter has been made.

but'terscotch *n* a hard toffee.

but'ton *n* **1** a knob or disc to fasten one part of a garment to another. **2** something shaped like a button, esp a knob or switch on an electrical appliance (*press the red button to switch on*). **3** *pl* a boy servant in uniform:—*vb* to fasten with buttons (*button up your coat*).

but'tonhole *n* **1** a hole for a button. **2** a flower worn in a buttonhole:—*vb* to stop and hold in conversation (*he buttonholed me and bored me with his holiday plans*).

but'tress *n* **1** a support for a wall. **2** a support, a reinforcement (*his wife's money was a buttress to the firm in the early days*):—*vb* **1** to build a support for. **2** to support or strengthen (*a firm buttressed by sales of older products*).

bux'om *adj* jolly, plump.

buy *vb* (*pt, pp* **bought**) to obtain by paying for.

buy'er *n* **1** one who buys. **2** one whose job is to buy goods (*the buyer in the dress department*).

buzz *n* a humming noise:—*also vb*.

buz'zard *n* a type of hawk.

by and by *adv* soon (*I'll see you by and by*).

bye *n* **1** in cricket, a run made from a ball that is not hit. **2** in a competition, a pass without contest into the next round.

bye-law *see* **bylaw**.

by'-election *n* an election held when the person elected at a general election has resigned or has died.

by'gone *adj* (*fml*) past (*in bygone days*):—*npl* **by'gones** past events.

by'law, bye'-law *n* a law made by a local council or other body and applying to the area in which the body has authority.

by'pass *n* a road round a town to avoid busy areas:—*vb* to go around, to avoid.

by'play *n* action carried on aside.

by'-product *n* something made in the course of making a more important article.

by'road *n* a side road.

by'stander *n* an onlooker, a spectator (*bystanders at the accident scene giving statements to the police*).

byte [bît] *n* the unit of storage in a computer memory.

by'word *n* **1** a common saying. **2** something or someone that represents or is typical of a quality, type, etc (*the firm is a byword for reliability/ our employer is a byword for injustice*).

C

cab *n* **1** (*old*) a horse carriage for public hire. **2** the driver's part of a railway engine or lorry. **3** a taxi.

cabal [ka-bal'] *n* **1** a group of people who make secret plans, often for political reasons (*a cabal formed to bring down the government*). **2** a secret plot.

cabaret [ka'-ba-rã] *n* a form of light entertainment consisting of songs and dancing, usu performed in a nightclub or restaurant (*diners watching the cabaret*).

cab'bage *n* a kind of common vegetable with eatable green leaves.

cab'in *n* **1** a small simple house, a hut (*a holiday cabin*). **2** a room on a ship for accommodation of passengers. **3** the space available for passengers or crew on an aircraft. **4** the covered part of a yacht.

cab'inet *n* **1** a display case. **2** a piece of furniture with drawers (*a filing cabinet*). **3** a case or container for a radio, television, etc. **4** the chief ministers in a government.

cab'inetmaker *n* one who makes furniture, a skilled joiner.

cab'le *n* **1** a strong rope, often of wire. **2** a chain. **3** an undersea telegraph line. **4** a bundle of electric wires enclosed in a pipe. **5** a message sent by cable:—*vb* to send a message by cable.

cab'legram *n* a more formal name for cable, sense 5.

cable television *n* a television service which is supplied by using underground wires.

cacao [ka-kä'-ō *or* ka-kã'-ō] *n* the tree from whose seeds chocolate and cocoa are made.

cache [cash] *n* **1** a hiding place (*the miser's cache for his money*). **2** something hidden away (*police discovered a cache of weapons in the cellar*).

cack'le *n* **1** the sound of the hen or goose. **2** noisy chatter (*the cackle of women gossiping*). **3** loud unpleasant laughter (*try to ignore the cackle of her friends*):—*also vb*.

cacophony [ka-ko'-fo-ni] *n* (*fml*) loud and unpleasant mixture of different sounds:—*adj* **caco'phonous**.

cac'tus *n* (*pl* **cac'ti**) a thick prickly plant.

cad *n* a dishonourable fellow (*a cad to steal his girlfriend's money*).

cadav'erous *adj* pale and sickly looking (*cadaverous cheeks*).

cad'die *n* one who carries a golfer's clubs.

cad'dy *n* a small box for holding tea.

cad'ence *n* **1** a fall of the voice at the end of a sentence. **2** the rise and fall of sound, esp at the end of a piece of music.

cadet' *n* **1** one training to be an officer in the armed forces. **2** a schoolboy receiving military training. **3** (*fml*) a younger son.

cadge *vb* (*inf*) to beg or borrow (*he's always cadging cigarettes*):—*n* **cad'ger**.

caesura [siz-û'-rê] *n* a pause about the middle of a line of poetry.

ca'fé *n* [ka-fã] tea or coffee house, an inexpensive restaurant serving light meals.

cafeteria [ka-fe-tee'-ri-a] *n* a restaurant with a self-service bar.

caffeine [ka'-feen] *n* a drug, present in tea and coffee.

cage *n* **1** a box, with one or more walls consisting of bars or wire-netting, in which animals or birds may be kept. **2** a lift for taking men down a mine:—*vb*. to shut up in a cage or prison (*cage the rabbits/cage the prisoners*).

cairn *n* a pointed heap of stones, set up as a monument or landmark.

cairn terrier *n* a breed of small dog.

caisson [käs'-on] *n* a watertight chest to enable men to work on foundations, etc, under deep water.

cajole' *vb* to persuade by flattery, to coax (*we cajoled her into lending us her car*):—*n* **cajol'ery**.

cake *n* **1** a sweetened bread. **2** a type of biscuit (*oatcake*). **3** a small flat lump (*a cake of soap*).

cal'abash *n* **1** a tree bearing large melon-like fruits, or gourds. **2** a hollowed-out gourd used as a water bottle, etc.

calam'ity *n* **1** a disaster (*the earthquake was a calamity for the whole area*). **2** a serious misfortune (*losing his job was a calamity for the family*):—*adj* **calam'itous**.

cal'careous [kal-kā'-ri-ês] *adj* containing chalk or lime.

cal'cium *n* the metal found in chalk or lime.

cal'culate *vb* **1** to work with numbers. **2** to estimate (*calculate the cost of the repair work*). **3** to count on, to rely on (*we didn't calculate on having bad weather*):—*adj* **cal'culable**.

cal'culating *adj* **1** far-seeing. **2** self-centred.

calcula'tion *n* **1** the art of counting (*the calculation of the cost*). **2** a sum (*make a mistake in the calculation*).

cal'culus *n* a method of calculation, involving very small quantities.

cal'endar *n* a table showing the relation of the days of the week to the dates of a particular year.

cal'ender *n* a machine for rolling paper in its manufacture.

calf[1] *n* (*pl* **calves**) the young of the cow elephant, whale, etc.

calf[2] *n* (*pl* **calves**) the fleshy part at the back of the leg below the knee.

calf'skin *n* a type of leather made from a calf's skin.

cal'ibre *n* **1** the breadth of the inside of a gun barrel. **2** quality, ability (*workers of the highest calibre*).

cal'ico *n* cotton cloth.

calif *see* **caliph**.

caligraphy *see* **calligraphy**.

calipers *see* **callipers**.

caliph, calif, khalif [kā'-lif *or* kal'-if] *n* in the Islamic religion, a title given to a successor of Mohammed.

calk *see* **caulk**.

call *vb* **1** to name (*call her daughter Amy*). **2** to cry out (*call out in pain/call a warning to her friend*). **3** to ask to come (*call the next witness*). **4** to make a short visit (*call on her mother on her way home*):—*n* **1** a cry (*a call for help*). **2** a short visit. **3** a telephone call. **4** need, demand (*there is no call for that vegetable here*):—**a close call** a narrow escape.

callig'raphy, calig'raphy *n* **1** handwriting. **2** the art of writing well.

call'ing *n* (*fml*) profession or employment.

cal'lipers, cal'ipers *npl* **1** an instrument for measuring round objects. **2** Also called **cal'liper splint** *n* a splint made of two metal rods with straps attached fitted to the leg to enable the wearer to walk.

cal'lous *adj* hardened, unfeeling, insensitive (*his callous treatment of animals/a callous disregard for her grief*):—*n* **cal'lousness**.

cal'low *adj* immature, lacking experience (*require an experienced worker, not a callow youth*).

calm *adj* **1** quiet, still (*a calm day*). **2** unexcited, not agitated (*remained calm when the building went on fire*):—*n* **1** stillness. **2** freedom from excitement (*admire her calm during the bomb scare*):—*vb* to make calm:—*n* **calm'ness**.

Cal'or gas[1] *n* a tradename of a fuel gas stored in bottles, etc.

cal'orie *n* **1** a measure of heat. **2** a unit for measuring the energy value of food (*diet by reducing the number of calories eaten*).

cal'umet *n* the North American Indian pipe of peace.

cal'umny *n* (*fml*) an untrue story intended to blacken the character of another person:—*vb* **calum'niate**.

calve *vb* to give birth to a calf.

calyp'so *n* a West Indian folk song.

cal'yx *n* the cup of a flower.

cam *n* part of a machine that changes a turning movement into a straight one.

cam'ber *n* a slightly curving surface, as on a road.

cam'bric *n* a fine white linen.

cam'corder *n* a portable video camera that records pictures and sound.

cam'el *n* an animal of the desert, with one hump (*called* **dromedary**) or two humps (*called* **bactrian**) that can store water.

cam'eo *n* a precious stone with a raised design with figures carved on it, often of a different colour.

cam'era *n* an apparatus for taking photographs:—**in camera** in secret (*the trial was heard in camera*).

cam'isole *n* a woman's light undergarment worn on the upper part of the body (*wear a camisole under her blouse*).

camp *n* **1** a place where people live in tents, caravans, huts, etc (*a holiday camp/a military camp*). **2** a group of tents, caravans, huts or other kinds of temporary shelter:—*vb* to stay in or set up a camp.

campaign' *n* **1** a battle or series of battles in a war. **2** any series of actions, meetings, etc. directed to one purpose (*a campaign to save the village* *school*):—*vb* to take part in or conduct a campaign (*campaigning against the motorway*).

cam'phor *n* a whitish, strong-smelling solid gum.

cam'pus *n* (*Amer*) the grounds of a college.

can[1] *vb* am (*also* is, are) able.

can[2] *n* a small metal container:—*vb* (**canned'**, **can'ning**) to put into tins to preserve (*employed to can vegetables*).

canal' *n* a man-made waterway.

cana'ry *n* a songbird often kept as a cage bird:—*adj* bright yellow.

can'cel *vb* (**can'celled, can'celling**) 1 to cross out. 2 to put off:—*n* **cancella'tion**.

can'cer *n* 1 a harmful, sometimes fatal growth in the body (*receive surgery for cancer of the lung*). 2 a growing evil (*meaningless violence is a cancer in modern society*).

Cancer *n* 1 a group of stars. 2 a sign of the zodiac.

candelab'rum *n* (*pl* **candelab'ra**) an ornamental candlestick holding several candles.

can'did *adj* saying what one thinks, frank (*my candid opinion/a candid person*):—*adv* **can'didly**.

can'didate *n* 1 one who offers himself or herself for a post or for election (*interview candidates for the job of manager*). 2 one who sits an examination:—*n* **can'didature**.

can'dle *n* a bar of wax or tallow containing a wick for lighting.

Can'dlemas *n* 2nd February, the day on which the Presentation of Christ in the Temple is commemorated in RC churches.

can'dlepower *n* the light given by one candle as a unit in the measurement of light.

can'dlestick *n* a holder for a candle.

can'dour *n* frankness.

can'dy *n* 1 sugar hardened by boiling. 2 in the US, any sweet or sweets (*a box of candy*):—*vb* to preserve by boiling with sugar.

cane *n* 1 a hard hollow reed, as bamboo, sugar cane, etc. 2 an easily bent stick. 3 a walking stick (*an old man leaning on his cane*):—*vb* to beat with a cane.

cane sug'ar *n* sugar from the sugar cane.

can'ine *adj* having to do with dogs:—*n* one of the pointed teeth in the front of the mouth (*also* **canine tooth**).

can'ister *n* a small box or tin (*a canister of tea*).

can'ker *n* 1 a quickly spreading sore (*canker in the dog's ear*). 2 a disease of plants (*tree canker*). 3 any growing evil (*drug addiction is a canker in modern society*).

can'nery *n* a factory where food is canned.

can'nibal *n* 1 a person who eats human flesh. 2 an animal that eats flesh of its own species:—*n* **can'nibalism**.

can'non *n* 1 a large gun. 2 a stroke at billiards:—*vb* 1 to make a cannon at billiards. 2 to knock against (*rush on to the bus and cannon into the people coming off*).

cannonade' *n* a continued firing of many guns.

can'nonball *n* an iron ball fired from a cannon.

can'ny *adj* careful and shrewd (*canny when it comes to money matters*).

canoe [ka-nö'] *n* a light boat moved by paddles.

can'on *n* 1 a law, esp of the Church. 2 a clergyman with duties in a cathedral.

canon'ical *adj* according to the law of the Church.

can'onize *vb* in the RC Church, to recognize as a saint:—*n* **canoniza'tion**.

canon law *n* the laws of the Church.

can'opy *n* a hanging cover forming a shelter above a throne, bed, etc (*a canopy over the porch to keep out the sunlight*).

cant[1] *n* 1 a special way of speaking used by a particular group of people (*thieves' cant*). 2 hypocritical or insincere talk (*just political cant*).

cant[2] *vb* to tilt up (*the ship began to cant*):—*n* a tilt (*a table with a definite cant*).

cantank'erous *adj* cross and unreasonable (*a cantankerous old man always complaining about the children playing*).

canta'ta *n* a piece of choral music.

canteen' *n* 1 a refreshment shop in a camp, factory, office, etc. 2 a box containing a set of knives, forks and spoons (*a canteen of cutlery*).

can'ter *vb* to gallop, but not very quickly (*horses cantering over the meadow*):—*also n*.

can'tilever *n* a large supporting bracket for a balcony, bridge, etc.

can'to *n* a division of a long poem.

can'ton *n* a district with certain rights of local government, as in France and Switzerland.

can'vas *n* 1 a coarse cloth. 2 the sails of a ship. 3 an oil painting (*sell a canvas by Picasso*).

can'vass *vb* to go around asking for votes or orders (*politicians knocking on people's doors to canvass for votes*):—*n* **can'vasser**.

can'yon *n* a pass between cliffs, a ravine.

cap *n* 1 a covering for the head with no brim or only part of one (*boys wearing school caps*). 2 a cover or top piece (*the cap of a bottle*):—*vb* (**capped'**, **cap'ping**) 1 to put a cap on (*cap the bottle*). 2 to improve on (*cap his opponent's performance*). 3 to choose for a team (*capped for his country at rugby*). 4 to impose an upper limit on (*cap local authority spending*).

cap'able *adj* 1 able to (*capable of doing better*). 2 likely to (*capable of committing violent acts*). 3 able to do things well, competent, efficient (*a capable manager*):—*n* **capabil'ity**.

capa'cious *adj* wide, roomy (*a capacious handbag*).

capac'ity *n* 1 ability to hold or contain (*a capacity of 10 gallons/a seating capacity of 2000*). 2 ability to produce perform, experience, etc (*a great capacity for hard work*). 3 (*fml*) position (*in his capacity as chairman*).

cape[1] *n* a short cloak for covering the shoulders, a sleeveless cloak.

cape[2] *n* a headland.

cap'er[1] *vb* to jump about playfully (*children capering about in excitement*):—*n* 1 a jump or leap. 2 a prank, a mischievous act.

cap'er[2] *n* a bush whose seeds are used for flavouring (*fish with a caper sauce*).

capil'lary *adj* very small and thin, hair-like:—*npl* **capil'laries** the small blood vessels.

cap'ital *adj* 1 chief (*the capital city*). 2 punishable by death (*a capital offence*). 3 (*inf*) excellent (*capital entertainment*):—*n* 1 the top of a column or pillar. 2 the chief city. 3 money, esp when used for business (*borrow capital from the bank*). 4 a large letter, as used first in proper names.

capital punishment *n* punishment by death (*murderers used to be subjected to capital punishment*).

cap'italist *n* a wealthy businessman.

capit'ulate *vb* to surrender on conditions (*the enemy capitulated when they were surrounded*):—*n* **capitula'tion**.

cap'on *n* a domestic cock castrated and fattened for eating.

caprice' *n* a sudden desire or fancy, a whim (*a caprice made her change her plans*).

capri'cious *adj* changeable, unreasonable (*too capricious to be relied on*).

capsize' *vb* to upset (*boats capsizing*).

cap'stan *n* an iron post that, when turned, winds or unwinds a cable.

cap'sule *n* 1 a hollow pill containing medicine. 2 the part of a spacecraft containing the instruments and crew.

cap'tain *n* 1 a commander. 2 an officer. 3 a leader (*the captain of the football team*):—*also vb*.

caption [kap'-shên] *n* the heading over (or under) a newspaper report or picture.

cap'tivate *vb* to charm, to fascinate (*captivated by her beauty*).

cap'tive *n* a prisoner.

captiv'ity *n* the state of being a prisoner.

cap'tor *n* one who takes prisoner.

cap'ture *vb* 1 to take prisoner, to catch (*capture convicts trying to escape*). 2 to take control of (*capture the castle/capture the imagination*):—*n* 1 act of taking prisoner. 2 the thing so taken.

car *n* 1 a wheeled vehicle (*a tramcar*). 2 a motorcar. 3 a carriage (*the dining car in the train*).

carafe [ka-räf'] *n* a glass bottle (*a carafe of wine*).

car'amel *n* 1 burnt sugar used as colouring in cooking (*ice cream flavoured with caramel*). 2 a type of sweet (*chew a caramel*).

car'at *n* 1 a measure ($^1/_{24}$) of the purity of gold. 2 a jeweller's weight.

car'avan *n* 1 a vehicle containing living quarters, formerly drawn by a horse but now usu by a car (*tow a caravan/holiday in a caravan*). 2 in the East, a company of people travelling together for safety.

caravan'serai *n* an Eastern inn or rest-house.

car'away *n* a plant whose seeds are used to flavour cakes.

car'bine *n* a short rifle, used by soldiers on horseback.

carbohy'drate [karbōhīdrāt'] *n* a substance, such as sugar, found in foods that gives you energy. 2 lines

carbol'ic a'cid *n* a disinfectant made from coal tar.

car'bon *n* 1 one of the nonmetallic elements. 2 pure charcoal:—*adjs* **carbona'ceous**, **car-bon'ic**.

carbon dio'xide *n* a gas without colour or smell which is breathed out by people and animals.

carbon monox'ide *n* a poisonous gas, without colour or smell, emitted by the exhaust systems of cars, etc.

carbon paper *n* prepared paper used in making copies of letters as they are written.

carbonif'erous *adj* producing coal.

car'buncle *n* 1 a red precious stone. 2 a large boil.

car'burettor (-er) *n* the part of a motor engine in which air is mixed with petrol, etc, to make a vapour that will burn.

car'cass, car'case *n* the dead body of an animal (*carcasses in a butcher's shop*).

card[1] *n* a small piece of thick paper for various purposes (*playing cards/business cards/membership card/credit card*).

card[2] *vb* to comb wool or flax before making it into thread:—*n* an instrument for combing wool or flax:—*n* **card'er**.

card'board *n* stiff thick paper.

car'diac *adj* having to do with the heart (*cardiac disease*).

car'digan *n* a knitted woollen jacket with buttons.

car'dinal *adj* very important, principal (*a cardinal virtue*):—*n* in the RC Church, a high-ranking official with the right to take part in the election of the pope.

car'diograph *n* an instrument for recording the movements of the heart.

care *n* 1 worry (*a life full of care*). 2 attention (*read the article with care*). 3 supervision (*in the care of a social worker*):—*vb* to be concerned or interested (*I don't care what you say*). 2 to look after (*cares for her neighbour's children*). 3 to have a liking or love (for) (*still cares for his wife*).

career' *n* one's work or profession in life (*a career in law*):—*vb* to move at full speed (*the car careered downhill out of control*).

care'ful *adj* 1 taking trouble. 2 cautious:—*adv* **care'fully**.

care'less *adj* taking little or no trouble:—*adv* **care'lessly**:—*n* **care'lessness**.

caress' *vb* to touch or stroke lovingly (*caressed her cheek*):—*also n*.

car'et *n* a sign (/) to show that something has been missed out in writing.

care'taker *n* one who looks after a building or place.

car'go *n* the goods carried by a ship, plane, etc (*a cargo of tropical fruit*).

caribou [ka-ri-bü'] *n* the North American reindeer.

car'icature *n* a picture that shows people or things as worse or uglier than they really are, to make others laugh at them:—*vb* to draw a caricature:—*n* **caricatur'ist**.

caries [kā'-ri-eez] *n* (*fml*) decay of bone, esp of the teeth.

carillon [ka-ril'-yon] *n* 1 a set of bells with which a tune can be played. 2 the tune so played.

car'mine *n* a bright red colour.

car'nage *n* widespread killing, slaughter (*the carnage of World War I*).

car'nal *adj* 1 having to do with the body rather than the spirit. 2 sexual or sensual (*carnal desire*).

carna'tion *n* a sweet-smelling flower, usu coloured white, pink or red.

car'nival *n* 1 a time of feasting and merriment (*an annual street carnival*). 2 a funfair (*the carnival is in town*).

car'nivore *n* a flesh-eating animal (*lions are carnivores*):—*adj* **carniv'orous**.

car'ol *n* a song of joy, esp one sung at Christmas:—*vb* (**car'olled, car'olling**) to sing joyfully.

carot'id *n* having to do with the two large arteries in the neck.

carous'al *n* (*fml*) a noisy drinking party.

carouse [kê-rouz'] *vb* (*fml*) to drink freely.

carp[1] *vb* to find fault or complain, often unreasonably (*carping about petty details*).

carp[2] *n* a freshwater fish.

car'penter *n* one who makes the wooden framework for houses, ships, etc:—*n* **car'pentry**.

car'pet *n* 1 a thick covering of wool or other material for a floor. 2 a covering (*a carpet of leaves*):—*vb* 1 to cover with a carpet (*carpeted the stairs*). 2 to cover (*snow carpeting the fields*). 3 (*inf*) to scold, to reprimand (*carpet him for being late*).

car'pet-bag *n* a travelling bag made of carpeting.

car'riage *n* 1 act of carrying. 2 the price of carrying (*carriage extra*). 3 the way one stands or moves (*she has a noble carriage*). 4 a vehicle with wheels (*a royal carriage/a railway carriage*).

car'rier *n* 1 one who carries or transports goods. 2 anyone or anything that carries (*a carrier of disease*).

car'rier pigeon n a pigeon used for carrying letters.

car'rion n rotten flesh (*vultures feeding on carrion*).

car'rot n a reddish root vegetable.

car'ry vb **1** to take from one place to another (*carry chairs from the van to the hall*). **2** to go from one place to another (*the sound of his voice carried all over the room*). **3** to have or hold (*carry great responsibility/carry a whole range of goods*):—**carry on 1** to continue to do (*carry on speaking*). **2** to behave badly or in an uncontrolled manner:—**carry out** to perform (*carry out the operation*).

cart n a two-wheeled vehicle or wagon for carrying goods:—vb to carry by cart (*cart the rubbish to the dump*):—n **cart'er**.

car'tilage n an elastic substance surrounding the joints of bones.

cartog'raphy n the art of map-making:—n **cartog'rapher**.

car'ton n a cardboard box (*a carton of milk*).

cartoon' n a comic drawing:—n **cartoon'ist**.

car'tridge n the container for the explosive that fires the bullet or shell from a gun.

carve vb **1** to cut into a special shape (*carve a piece of wood into the shape of an animal*). **2** to make by cutting wood or stone (*carve animals out of stone*). **3** to cut into slices (*carve the meat*).

car'ver n **1** one who carves. **2** a carving knife.

cascade' n **1** a waterfall. **2** something like a waterfall (*a cascade of hair down her back*).

case[1] n **1** a box or container (*a watch in a case/a case of wine*). **2** a covering (*seed cases of plants*). **3** a suitcase. **4** a piece of furniture for displaying or containing things (*a glass case in the jewellery shop/a bookcase*).

case[2] n **1** an event, instance or example (*in that case you must go now/it's a case of having to spend less/a case of measles/a case of blackmail*). **2** a person having medical, etc, treatment (*a psychiatric case*). **3** a statement of facts and arguments or reasons (*there's a good case for believing him*). **4** a question to be decided in a court of law, a lawsuit.

case'ment n **1** a window that opens on hinges. **2** a window frame.

cash n **1** coins or paper money, not cheques or credit cards, etc. **2** immediate payment rather than by credit or hire purchase (*a discount for paying cash*). **3** (*inf*) money generally (*make a lot of cash*):—vb to turn into money (*cash traveller's cheques*).

cash dispenser *see* **cash machine**.

cashier [kash-eer'] n one who has charge of money:—vb to dismiss (an officer from the army, navy, etc) in disgrace.

cash machine n a machine from which you can obtain money from your bank account using a special plastic card supplied by the bank or a credit card and your PIN (personal identification number), also called **cash dispenser**.

cash'mere n a fine woollen material.

cas'ing n the outside covering.

casino [ka-see'-no] n a hall for dancing or gambling.

cask n a barrel.

cas'ket n a jewel case.

casque [käsk] n a helmet.

cass'erole n **1** a heat-resisting dish in which food can be cooked in an oven and then served at table. **2** the food so prepared (*a beef casserole*).

cassette' n a flat plastic case containing tape for recording or playing back sounds or pictures.

cass'ock n a long robe worn by clergymen and those taking part in services.

cass'owary n a running bird like the ostrich.

cast vb (*pt, pp* **cast**) **1** to throw (*cast a pebble in the pool*). **2** to throw off (*snakes casting their skins*). **3** to shape (melted metal) in a mould. **4** to give parts to actors in (*cast his new play*):—n **1** a throw. **2** a squint (in the eye). **3** a model made in a mould. **4** the actors in a play.

castanets [kas-tan-etz'] npl pair(s) of wooden shells held by Spanish dancers and struck against each other to make a rattling noise.

cast'away n a shipwrecked person.

caste n in India, the social class or rank into which one is born.

cas'tellated adj having battlements.

caster *see* **castor**.

cas'tigate vb (*fml*) to scold or criticize severely (*employees castigated for arriving late*):—n **castiga'tion**.

cast'ing n anything shaped in a mould.

casting vote n an extra vote allowed to the chairman of a meeting when the votes of the others are equally divided.

cast ir'on *n* iron that has been melted and shaped in a mould:—*adj* very strong.

cas'tle *n* **1** a large building, usu one strengthened against attack (*Windsor Castle*). **2** a piece in chess:—**castles in the air** a daydream.

cas'tor, cas'ter *n* **1** a small jar or bottle with holes in the top for sprinkling salt, sugar, etc. **2** a small wheel on a piece of furniture, making it easy to move (*a wardrobe on castors*).

cas'tor oil *n* an oil used as medicine.

cas'tor sug'ar *n* very fine sugar.

casual [ka'-zhū-êl] *adj* **1** happening by accident (*find out from a casual remark*). **2** not regular (*casual work in the summer*). **3** uninterested (*casual attitude to his work*). **4** not careful, not thorough (*take a casual glance at the page*). **5** informal (*casual clothes*):—*adv* **cas'ually.**

cas'ualty *n* **1** an accident (*there's been a casualty at the mine*). **2** an injured or wounded person (*no casualties in the train accident*). **3** something that is damaged or destroyed as a result of an event (*the library has closed—a casualty of spending cuts*).

cat *n* **1** a common domestic animal with soft fur and sharp claws. **2** a genus of wild animals (*lions are members of the cat family*).

cat'aclysm *n* **1** a great flood. **2** a sudden complete change, upheaval or disaster (*the cataclysm of revolution*).

catacomb [ka'-ta-küm] *n* an underground tomb.

catafalque [ka'-ta-falk] *n* a covered platform on which a coffin may be placed.

cat'alogue *n* a complete list arranged in a special order so that the items can be found easily (*a catalogue of the books in the library*):—*vb* to make a list (*cataloguing the books according to the alphabetical order of the authors' surnames*).

cat'alyst *n* **1** a substance that aids a chemical reaction but is not itself changed. **2** something or someone that causes a change in a situation or has a marked effect on the course of events (*World War I was a catalyst for social change*).

cat'amaran' *n* a boat made in two parts joined by a bridge.

cat'apult *n* **1** (*old*) a machine used for hurling heavy stones in war. **2** a Y-shaped stick with elastic for shooting stones, etc.

cat'aract *n* **1** a waterfall. **2** a disease of the eye, causing gradual loss of sight.

catarrh' *n* **1** the fluid coming from the nose and eyes of a person with a cold. **2** a cold in the head causing inflammation of the lining of the nose.

catas'trophe [-fâ] *n* a sudden great disaster (*the flood was a catastrophe for the whole area*):—*adj* **catastroph'ic.**

catch *vb* (*pt, pp* caught) **1** to take and hold (*catch the ball*). **2** to capture (*catch the remaining prisoners*). **3** to become accidentally attached or held (*her skirt caught on the door handle*). **4** to surprise in the act of (*catch him stealing*). **5** to succeed in hearing (*catch what he said*). **6** to get by infection (*catch measles from his sister*). **7** to be in time for, to get on (*catch the first bus in the morning*):—*n* **1** the act of catching. **2** the number of fish caught at one time. **3** a fastener (*a gate catch*). **4** a snag (*a catch in the plan*). **5** a song in which the same words and tune are repeated by several singers starting at different times.

catch'y *adj* memorable and attractive (*a catchy tune*).

cat'echism *n* a book in which information is given by means of question and answer.

cat'echize *vb* **1** to ask questions and teach the answers by heart. **2** to examine by asking difficult questions.

categor'ical *adj* definite (*give a categorical denial*):—*adv* **categor'ically.**

cat'egory *n* a class or group of things in a system of grouping (*various categories in the dog-judging competition/books in categories of fiction, non-fiction and reference*).

cat'er *vb* **1** to supply with food and drinks, esp at social occasions (*the firm catering for the wedding reception*). **2** to provide what is needed or desired by (*cater for a wide range of tastes*):—*n* **cat'erer.**

cat'erpillar *n* **1** the worm-like grub of the butterfly and other insects. **2** an engine that moves on metal belts instead of wheels.

cat'erwaul *vb* to cry like a cat.

cat'gut *n* a cord made from the inside parts of certain animals and used as strings for violins, harps, guitars, etc.

cathe'dral *n* the chief church in a district in which a bishop has his throne.

cath'ode *n* the negative pole of an electric current.

cathode ray tube *n* in television, the device that throws the picture on the screen.

cath'olic *adj* wide-ranging, broad, including many different things (*a catholic taste in reading*):—*n* **catholic'ity**.

Cath'olic *n* a member of the Roman Catholic Church:—*also adj*

cat'kin *n* the furry blossom of the willow, hazel, etc.

cat's-paw' *n* a person who is used by another to do unpleasant or risky tasks.

cat'tle *npl* cows, bulls and oxen.

caucus [kå'-kês] *n* a small group within a body who decide what it should do (*a member of the caucus of the political party*).

cau'dal *adj* having to do with the tail.

caught *pt of* **catch**.

caul'dron *n* a large boiling-pot (*the witch's cauldron*).

caul'iflower *n* a type of cabbage, of which the white flower is eaten as a vegetable.

cause *n* **1** something or someone that produces an effect or result (*an electrical fault was the cause of the fire/he was the cause of his father's unhappiness*). **2** the reason for an action, a motive (*no cause to treat her so badly/little cause for complaint*). **3** a purpose, aim (*in the cause of peace*):—*vb* to make happen.

cause'way *n* **1** a road raised on a mound above the level of the surrounding country. **2** a paved road.

caus'tic *adj* **1** burning (*a caustic chemical substance*). **2** bitter, severe, sarcastic (*caustic remarks*):—*adv* **caus'tically**.

cau'terize *vb* to burn with caustic or a hot iron (*cauterize the wound*).

cau'tion *n* **1** carefulness, esp in order to avoid risk or danger (*cross the busy road with caution*). **2** warning (*receive a caution from the police to stop speeding*):—*vb* **1** to warn against possible danger (*caution children against talking to strangers*). **2** to give a warning, often with the threat of future punishment (*this time the police just cautioned him for careless driving*).

cau'tious *adj* careful, showing caution (*a cautious driver/cautious about spending a lot of money*).

cavalcade' *n* a procession (*a cavalcade of decorated lorries*) (originally, of people on horseback).

cavalier' *n* **1** a horseman. **2** a follower of King Charles I in the Civil War in the 17th century:—*adj* offhand, casual and disrespectful (*a cavalier disregard for other people's feelings*):—*adv* **cavalier'ly**.

cav'alry *n* horse-soldiers.

cave *n* a hollow place under the ground or in a rock:—**cave in** to fall in over a hollow.

caveat [ka'-vä-at] *n* (*fml*) a warning (*you should buy the used car with the caveat that a mechanic check it*).

cave'man *n* **1** (*old*) one who, in the earliest times, lived in a cave. **2** a man with very rough manners, esp towards women.

cav'ern *n* a large cave.

cav'ernous *adj* large and hollow, like a cavern (*the lion opened its cavernous mouth*).

caviar(e)' *n* a dish made from the roe (eggs) of the sturgeon and similar fish.

cav'il *vb* (**cav'illed, cav'illing**) to find fault without reason.

cav'ity *n* **1** a hollow place. **2** a hole (*a cavity in his tooth*).

cayenne [cä-yen'] *n* a very hot red pepper.

CCTV (*abbr of* **closed circuit television**) a type of surveillance camera system (*The thieves were seen on CCTV robbing the jeweller's shop*).

CD *n* (*abbr of* **compact disc**) a small mirrored plastic disc storing music or images that are read optically by a laser beam.

cease *vb* **1** to stop (*soldiers ordered to cease firing/the factory has ceased making weapons*). **2** to come to an end (*the noise finally ceased*).

cease'less *adj* endless, continuous (*ceaseless chatter*).

ce'dar *n* **1** a large cone-bearing tree. **2** its wood.

cede *vb* (*fml*) to give up (*ceding their land to the enemy*).

ceil'ing *n* **1** the inside roof of a room. **2** the greatest height to which a particular aircraft can climb. **3** an upper limit (*a wages ceiling of 3%*).

cel'andine *n* a flower of the poppy family.

cel'ebrant *n* the priest performing a ceremony, one who celebrates, one who takes part in a ceremony.

cel'ebrate *vb* **1** to perform (a religious ceremony). **2** to honour an event by feasting and rejoicing (*celebrate her birthday*):—*n* **celebra'tion**.

cel'ebrated *adj* famous (*the celebrated artist*).

celeb'rity *n* a famous person (*the new hall was opened by a local celebrity*).

cel'ery *n* a kind of vegetable, of which the green stem is eaten either cooked or raw.

celes'tial *adj* **1** heavenly (*celestial beings such as angels*). **2** having to do with the sky (*celestial bodies such as planets*).

cel'ibacy *n* the state of being unmarried.

cel'ibate *adj* unmarried, not having sexual relationships (*priests who must remain celibate*).

cell *n* **1** a small, bare room, esp in a prison or monastery. **2** a compartment in a honeycomb. **3** a single unit of the living matter of the body (*red blood cells*). **4** a unit of an electric battery. **5** a small group of people working for the same end (*a terrorist cell*).

cello *short for* **violoncello**.

Cel'lophane *n* a trademark for a transparent wrapping material (*wrap the flowers in cellophane*).

cel'lular *adj* **1** having cells, made up of cells (*cellular tissue*). **2** containing tiny hollow spaces allowing air to pass through (*a cellular blanket*).

cel'luloid *n* a transparent plastic material that looks like ivory.

cel'lulose *n* a substance obtained from wood or plants and used in making paper, artificial silk, film, etc.

Cel'sius *adj* the same as **centigrade**.

cement' *n* any powder that, mixed with liquid, forms a solid material used to make things stick together (*bricks stuck together with cement*):— *vb* **1** to join with cement. **2** to unite closely (*cement their relationship by marrying*).

cem'etery *n* a burial ground.

cen'otaph *n* a monument to a person or persons who are buried elsewhere, esp soldiers killed in war.

cen'ser *n* a vessel in which incense is burnt.

cen'sor *n* one who examines letters, books, films, etc, to see if they contain anything harmful to society (*censors removing anything obscene in the film*):—*also vb*:—*n* **cen'sorship**.

censor'ious *adj* (*fml*) fault-finding, severely critical (*difficult to satisfy such a censorious person*).

cen'sure *vb* to criticize harshly, to rebuke strongly, to blame (*censuring him for his disgraceful behaviour*):—*also n*.

cen'sus *n* **1** an official regular counting of a country's population. **2** an official counting of other things (*take a traffic census on the new motorway*).

cent *n* **1** a hundred (e.g. ten per cent). **2** (*Amer*) a coin that is one hundredth part of a dollar.

cen'taur *n* in Greek stories, an imaginary creature, half man and half horse.

centena'rian *n* a person a hundred years old.

centenary [sen-teen'-êr-i] *n* the hundredth year after a certain event (*the centenary of the opening of the school*).

centen'nial *adj* happening once every hundred years.

cent'igrade *adj* divided into one hundred degrees (*centigrade thermometer*).

cent'imetre *n* one hundredth part of a metre.

cent'ipede *n* an insect with many feet.

cen'tral *adj* **1** in the middle (*the central barrier in a motorway*). **2** chief (*the central character in the novel*).

cen'tralize *vb* to bring together to one place (*regions objecting to government being centralized*):—*n* **centraliza'tion**.

cen'tre *n* **1** the middle point or part of anything (*the centre of the circle/the centre of the town*). **2** a place where certain activities or facilities are concentrated (*a shopping centre*). **3** a political position that is not extreme (*people in the centre of the party*):—*vb* **1** to put into the middle (*centred the picture on the wall*). **2** to collect or concentrate at or around (*interests centring on sport*).

centrif'ugal *adj* moving away from the centre.

centu'rion *n* (*old*) the captain of a hundred men, esp in the Roman army.

cen'tury *n* **1** a hundred years. **2** in cricket, a hundred runs.

ceram'ic *adj* having to do with pottery.

ceram'ics *n* the study of pottery.

ce'real *adj* having to do with corn:—*n* **1** any grain that can be eaten (*wheat and barley are cereals*). **2** food made from such grain, often eaten at breakfast.

cer'ebral *adj* **1** having to do with the brain (*a cerebral tumour*). **2** intellectual rather than emotional (*cerebral poetry*).

ceremo'nial *n* the actions connected with a ceremony (*the ceremonial of a coronation*):—*adj* having to do with a ceremony.

ceremo'nious adj (fml) full of ceremony, very formal (ceremonious events).

cer'emony n 1 the performing of certain actions in a fixed order for a religious or other serious purpose (a wedding ceremony/a coronation ceremony). 2 formal behaviour, formality (an occasion of great ceremony).

cerise [ser-eez'] n a light-red colour:—adj cherry-coloured.

cer'tain adj 1 sure (a certain victory). 2 particular (certain people).

cer'tainly adv 1 undoubtedly. 2 willingly.

cer'tainty n 1 the state of being certain or sure (I can say with certainty that he will fail). 2 that which is certain (it's a certainty that they will succeed).

certificate n a written statement of fact (birth certificate/a certificate of insurance).

cer'tify vb 1 to confirm formally the truth of a statement (certify that he is the owner of the car). 2 officially to declare insane (the patient was certified and sent to a mental hospital).

cessa'tion n (fml) a stoppage (a truce following the cessation of hostilities).

ces'sion n (fml) the act of giving something to another (the cession of land to the enemy).

cess'pool n a pool or hole in which filthy water collects.

chafe vb 1 to warm by rubbing. 2 to make sore or wear away by rubbing. 3 to be angry.

chaff n 1 the husks of corn. 2 anything worthless. 3 joking talk, good-humoured teasing:—vb 1 to talk jokingly. 2 to tease (chaff her about her new boyfriend).

chaf'finch n a songbird.

chagrin [shag-reen' or shag'rên] n a feeling of anger and disappointment (their chagrin when someone put in a higher bid).

chain n 1 a number of metal rings joined together to form a rope (the dog was fastened to the fence by a chain/prisoners in chains/a silver chain round her neck). 2 a number of connected facts or events, a series (a chain of events). 3 a measure of length (22 yards). 4 a range (of mountains):—vb to bind or fasten with a chain (chain the dog to the fence).

chair n 1 a movable seat with a back. 2 chair person. 3 the seat or place of an official (e.g. of

a professor in a university or a person controlling a meeting). 4 a professorship:—vb 1 to be in charge of (a meeting (chairing the annual general meeting). 2 to carry shoulder-high as a sign of honour (chaired the captain of the winning team off the field).

chair'man, chair'person, chair'woman n one who presides at or controls a meeting.

chaise [shãz] n (old) a light carriage for one or two people.

chalet [sha'-lã] n 1 a wooden house or hut with a steeply sloping roof, common in Switzerland. 2 a wooden house or hut used by holidaymakers, etc.

chal'ice n (old) 1 a drinking cup. 2 a cup with a stem, used in church services.

chalk n 1 a soft white limestone. 2 a pencil of chalk used for writing on a blackboard:—vb to mark with chalk:—adj **chalk'y**.

chal'lenge vb 1 to call on another to fight or play a match to see who is the better (challenge him to a duel/challenge him to a game of darts). 2 to doubt the truth of (challenge his statement that the substance was safe/challenge his right to be present):—n 1 the daring of another to a contest. 2 an order given by a sentry to stop and say who one is. 3 a statement or action that questions or disputes something (a challenge to the leader's authority). 4 a difficult or stimulating task (regard his new job as a challenge):—n **chal'lenger**.

cham'ber n 1 (old) a room. 2 a room in which an assembly, such as Parliament, meets (the chamber of the House of Commons). 3 an administrative group (the Chamber of Commerce). 4 the part of a gun in which the cartridge is held.

chamber music n music written to be played in a room rather than a hall.

cham'berlain n 1 an official in a king's household. 2 a city treasurer.

chameleon [kêm-eel'-yên] n a type of lizard that can change the colour of its skin.

chamois [sham'-wä] n 1 an Alpine antelope. 2 [sham'-i] a soft leather.

champ vb to chew noisily with the teeth (horses champing hay).

champagne [sham-pãn'] n a type of sparkling French wine.

cham'pion n 1 one who has beaten all his or her rivals or opponents (*the club tennis champion*). 2 one who fights for a certain cause, or for another person (*a champion of animal rights*):— vb to defend or support (*champion the cause of freedom*).

cham'pionship n 1 a series of contests or matches to discover the champion. 2 the state of being a champion.

chance n 1 accident (*we met by chance*). 2 opportunity (*the chance to get a better job*). 3 risk (*take a chance and try to escape*):— vb 1 (*fml*) to happen (*I chanced to see him yesterday*). 2 to risk (*it may rain on our picnic but we'll just have to chance it*):—adj accidental (*a chance meeting*).

chan'cel n the altar end of a church.

chan'cellor n 1 a high government official. 2 the chief judge of England. 3 the head of a university:—**Chancellor of the Exchequer** in Britain, the chief minister of finance in the government.

chan'cery n a high court of law.

chandelier [shan-de-leer'] n a hanging frame with branches to hold lamps (formerly candles).

chand'ler n 1 (*old*) a seller of candles. 2 a dealer in general stores (*a ship's chandler*).

change vb 1 to become different (*her lifestyle has changed/the wind changed*). 2 to make different (*change one's attitude/change one's clothes*). 3 to put or take one thing in place of another, to exchange (*change one's library books*):—n 1 a difference or alteration (*see a change in her/a change in the direction of the wind*). 2 money given in return for money received (*given the wrong change by the shop assistant*). 3 small coin (*I have only a £10 note—I have no change*):—adj **change'-able**:— adj **change'less**.

change'ling n a child supposed to be put by fairies in the place of another.

chan'nel n 1 the course of a river. 2 the deep part of a river where ships can sail safely. 3 a narrow sea.

chant vb 1 to sing. 2 to recite slowly in a singing voice:—n 1 a song. 2 a way of singing sacred music.

chan'ter n the finger-pipe of a bagpipe.

chanty see **shanty**.

chaos [kā'-os] n a state of utter confusion, disorder (*the chaos in the room after the children's party*).

chaot'ic adj completely without order or arrangement (*chaotic traffic conditions in the snow*).

chap¹ vb (**chapped', chap'ping**) to crack (*hands chapped by the cold*):—n a crack in the skin, caused by cold and wet.

chap² n (*inf*) a man, a fellow (*a friendly chap*).

chap'el n 1 a small church. 2 a private church.

chaperon [sha'-pê-rōn] n 1 esp formerly, an older woman who accompanies a younger one when she goes out. 2 a person who supervises young people on an outing (*the chaperon of the Sunday-school group*):—vb to act as chaperon to.

chap'lain n 1 the clergyman serving a private chapel. 2 a clergyman with the army, navy or air force.

chap'let n a wreath for the head (*a chaplet of flowers*).

chap'man n (*old*) one who buys or sells articles from door to door.

chap'ter n 1 a division of a book. 2 a meeting of the canons of a cathedral.

chap'ter-house n the building in which a chapter is held.

char¹ vb (**charred', char'ring**) 1 to burn in part (*furniture charred in the fire*). 2 to burn the outside (*char the steak*).

char² vb (**charred', char'ring**) (*inf*) to do odd cleaning jobs in another's house (*she chars for the minister*).

charabanc [shar'-a-bang] n (*old*) a motor coach.

char'acter n 1 a letter or figure or, as in Chinese, a sign standing for a whole word. 2 a person's nature as known by words, deeds, etc. 3 a reputation (*not of very good character*). 4 a person in a story or play (*the chief characters in the novel*). 5 (*inf*) an odd, humorous or interesting person (*he's quite a character*). 6 (*inf*) a person (*a nasty character*).

characteris'tic n a single point in a person's character, a special and recognizable quality in someone or something (*generosity is not one of his characteristics/a characteristic of the disease*):—adj typical (*symptoms characteristic of the disease*).

char'acterize vb 1 to be characteristic or typical of (*conduct characteristic of an unhappy child*). 2 (*fml*) to describe as (*characterize the terrorist attack as a bid for freedom*).

charade [shê-räd'] n 1 a word game. 2 something that is easily seen to be false or a pretence (*the trial was just a charade as they had decided he was guilty*).

char'coal n partly burnt wood used as fuel (*steak grilled over charcoal*).

charge vb 1 to ask a price (*charge £6 a ticket*). 2 to accuse (*charge him with murdering his brother*). 3 to rush (*children charging into the room*). 4 to attack at speed (*charge the enemy*). 5 to fill with electricity (*charge the battery*). 6 (*fml*) to load, fill (*charge one's glass*). 7 to tell a person to do something as a duty (*charge them with getting the groom to the church*):—n 1 a load of electricity. 2 a price (*the hotel's exorbitant charge*). 3 a duty, esp that of a clergyman. 4 a violent attack. 5 an accusation (*bring a charge of murder*):— adj **charge'able**:—**take charge** to take command, take control.

chariot n 1 (*old*) a horse-drawn cart used in war. 2 a state carriage.

charioteer n (*old*) the driver of a war chariot.

charity n 1 love as a Christian duty. 2 kindness to others. 3 generosity in giving to the poor:—adj **char'itable**. 4 an organization that raises money to help people in need or other good causes (*collecting money in aid of a children's charity*).

charlatan [shar'-lê-tan] n one who deceives by pretending to have special knowledge or skill (*the supposed doctor was a charlatan*).

charm n 1 a magic spell (*the witch reciting a charm*). 2 an object or words possessing magical power (*wear a charm*). 3 attractiveness of character, a pleasant quality (*succeed in deceiving people because of her great charm*). 4 pl (*fml*) beauty (*use her charms to get her way*):—vb 1 to put under a spell (*charmed by the wizard*). 2 to delight (*charmed by her personality*).

char'nel house n a house where dead bodies or the bones of the dead are put.

chart n 1 a map, esp one for sailors. 2 a paper showing a graph or diagram (*a chart showing production progress*).

char'ter n a written paper granting certain rights:—vb to hire (*charter a boat*).

char'woman n a woman hired for odd work about the house.

char'y adj (**char'ier, char'iest**) careful, cautious (*chary of talking to strangers*).

chase[1] vb 1 to run after (*chase the man who had stolen the old lady's bag*). 2 to drive away (*chase the boys who were stealing the apples*):—n a pursuit, a hunt.

chase[2] vb to engrave or cut figures on metal.

chasm n 1 a wide deep crack in the surface of the earth, a gorge. 2 a wide gap or difference of opinion, attitudes, feelings, etc (*the chasm between the two families*).

chassis [sha'-see] n the base frame of a vehicle.

chaste adj pure, esp sexually (*young women expected to remain chaste before marriage*).

chasten [châs'-ên] vb to teach by suffering or punishment (*chastened by the thought that he had caused his brother's death*).

chastise' vb to punish by beating:—n **chastise'ment**.

chas'tity n purity.

chat vb (**chat'ted, chat'ting**) to talk about unimportant matters (*chat on the phone to her friend*):—n a friendly talk.

chateau [sha-tō'] n (pl **chateaux**) a French castle or country house.

chat'tels npl movable belongings, esp in the phrase **goods and chattels** all one's possessions.

chat'ter vb 1 to talk quickly and continuously, usu about something unimportant (*children chattering when the teacher was out of the room*). 2 to make meaningless sounds (*monkeys chattering*):—also n:—n **chat'terer**.

chat'terbox n one who chatters a great deal.

chauffeur [shō-fêr' or shô-fêr'] n a person employed to drive someone's car (*the prime minister's chauffeur*):—also vb.

chauvinism [shō'-vin-izm] n too great pride in one's own country, leading to a dislike of foreigners:—n **chau'vinist**.

cheap adj 1 of a low price. 2 of little value.

cheap'en vb to lessen the price or value of.

cheat vb to deceive, to use unfair means:—n 1 a trick. 2 a swindler.

check vb 1 to stop. 2 to slow down. 3 to scold. 4 to look at something to see if it is correct or in order:—n 1 a sudden halt or obstacle. 2 a control. 3 a ticket to prove ownership:—adj divided into or marked by squares.

check'ers, chequ'ers *npl* the game of draughts.

check'mate *n* the winning move in chess:—*vb* to defeat another's plans.

ched'dar *n* a variety of cheese.

cheek *n* **1** the side of the face (*kiss her on the cheek*). **2** (*inf*) impudence (*have the cheek to call me a liar*).

cheek'y *adj* impudent (*cheeky children/a cheeky remark*).

cheep *n* **1** a faint squeak, a chirp (*the cheep of a young bird*). **2** a sound (*not a cheep out of the children*):—*also vb*.

cheer *n* **1** (*old*) mood, disposition (*be of good cheer*). **2** food. **3** a shout of joy or encouragement (*the cheers of the football supporters*):—*vb* **1** to brighten up (*cheered him up by taking him to the cinema/cheer the room up with some new curtains*). **2** to encourage, esp by shouts (*cheering on their football team*).

cheer'ful *adj* **1** happy and lively (*a cheerful person/a cheerful mood*). **2** bright and attractive (*cheerful colours*).

cheer'less *adj* sad, gloomy (*a cheerless room*).

cheer'y *adj* bright, cheerful (*a cheery greeting*):—*n* **cheer'iness**.

cheese *n* a solid savoury food made from milk.

cheese'-paring *adj* mean, unwilling to spend money (*too cheese-paring to go on holiday*).

chee'tah *n* a wild animal like the leopard.

chef *n* a head cook.

chem'ical *adj* having to do with chemistry:—*n* a substance studied in chemistry.

chemise *n* (*old*) a woman's undergarment.

chem'ist *n* **1** one who studies or works in chemistry. **2** one who sells medicines (*buy painkillers from the chemist*).

chem'istry *n* the science that separates and studies the substance of which all things are made up.

cheque *n* a written order to a banker to pay out a sum of money from one's account.

cheque book *n* a book of blank cheque forms.

chequ'ered *adj* **1** marked in squares of different colours (*a chequered pattern*). **2** containing good and bad (*a chequered career*).

chequers *see* **checkers**.

cher'ish *vb* **1** to treat lovingly, to hold dear (*cherish his only daughter*). **2** to keep in the

mind or heart (*cherish hopes of becoming wealthy/cherish her memory*).

cheroot [shê-röt'] *n* a type of cigar.

cher'ry *n* **1** a small stone-fruit. **2** a tree bearing cherries.

cher'ub *n* (*pl* **cher'ubs** *or* **cher'ubim**) **1** an angel. **2** in art, an angel pictured as a winged child. **3** a beautiful and innocent-looking child.

cherub'ic *adj* angelic.

chess *n* a game of skill, played on a chequered board.

chess'man *n* a piece used in chess.

chest *n* **1** a large strong box. **2** the bony upper part of the body, from the shoulders to the lowest ribs.

chest'nut *n* **1** a nut. **2** a tree bearing chestnuts. **3** a reddish-brown horse. **4** a joke long known to everyone (*a comedian telling that old chestnut*):—*adj* reddish-brown.

chev'ron *n* a V-shaped strip of cloth worn on the sleeve as a sign of rank.

chew *vb* to crush with the teeth.

chic [sheek] *adj* smart, fashionable (*chic dress shop*).

chican'ery *n* trickery (*persuaded the old lady to leave him her money by chicanery*).

chick, chick'en *n* a young fowl.

chick'en-heart'ed *adj* not brave, timid.

chick'enpox *n* an infectious disease involving fever and red itchy spots, usu affecting children.

chick'weed *n* a weed liked by birds.

chic'ory *n* a plant used in salads or in cooking, also sometimes mixed with coffee.

chide *vb* to scold (*chiding the children for talking in class*).

chief *adj* **1** highest in rank (*the chief clerk*). **2** most important, main (*the chief crops of the country*):—*n* a head, a leader:—*adv* **chiefly**.

chief'tain *n* a chief, the head of a clan or tribe.

chiffon [shi'-fon(g)] *n* a thin silky cloth.

chil'blain *n* a sore on the hands or feet caused by cold.

child *n* (*pl* **chil'dren**) **1** a boy or girl (*I have lived here since I was a child*). **2** a son or daughter (*they have two children*):—*n* **child'hood**.

child'care *n* the care of children, especially by people other than the parents, when they are at work (*Most of her salary goes to pay for childcare*).

child'ish *adj* **1** like a child (*childish voices*). **2** silly, immature (*their childish behaviour in not speaking to their neighbours*).

child'like adj having the good qualities of a child (a childlike belief that everything will be all right).

child'minder n a person who is paid to look after other people's children, usually in her own home.

children see **child**.

chill n 1 coldness (a chill in the air). 2 an illness caused by cold (catch a chill). 3 coldness of manner, unfriendliness:—vb 1 to make cold (children chilled after their walk in the snow). 2 to make cold without freezing (chill the wine). 3 to discourage (chill their hopes):—adj cold (a chill wind).

chil'li n (pl chillies) the small red or green seed pod of a type of hot pepper, used in cooking spicy food.

chill'y adj 1 cold (a chilly day). 2 unfriendly (a chilly welcome).

chime n 1 the sound of a bell. 2 the music of bells. 3 pl a set of bells:—vb to ring musically:—**chime in** to agree.

chim'ney n 1 a passage by which smoke may escape. 2 a narrow crack in the side of a mountain.

chim'ney pot n a pipe at the top of a chimney.

chim'ney stack n a group of chimney pots.

chim'ney sweep n one who cleans chimneys.

chimpanzee' n a type of ape of Africa.

chi'na n 1 a fine thin earthenware. 2 cups, plates, etc, made of this (put out the best china for her guests).

chinchil'la n 1 a small animal valued for its fur. 2 its fur.

chink[1] n a very narrow opening (peer through a chink in the door).

chink[2] n a ringing or jingling sound (the chink of money in his pockets):—vb to jingle.

chintz n a gaily patterned cotton material.

chip n 1 a small piece (wood chips). 2 a small piece of deep-fried potato (fish and chips). 3 a counter or token used in games:—vb (**chipped'**, **chip'ping**) 1 to cut into small pieces (chip potatoes). 2 to break off a small piece, often accidentally (wood chipped off the wardrobe).

chip'munk n a type of squirrel found in North America.

chiropodist [ki-rop'-o-dist] n one who treats corns and other foot troubles.

chirp vb to make a short sharp whistling sound (birds chirping):—also n.

chirp'y adj cheerful, bright (a chirpy shop assistant/in a chirpy mood).

chis'el n a tool used for cutting or chipping wood, stone, etc:—also vb (**chis'elled**, **chis'elling**).

chit n 1 a written note (sign a chit to get notebooks for the classroom). 2 a bold or forward girl (object to being spoke to like that by a chit of a girl).

chiv'alry n 1 (old) the rules of good behaviour laid down for knights in the Middle Ages, gentlemanly behaviour. 2 good manners, esp towards women:—adjs **chival'-ric**, **chiv'alrous**.

chlo'ride n a mixture of chlorine with another substance.

chlorine [klô'-reen] n a poisonous gas.

chlor'oform n a liquid whose vapour causes loss of consciousness, an anaesthetic.

chlor'ophyll n the green colouring matter of plants.

chock'-full adj (inf) completely filled (trains that were chock-full/a garden chock-full of weeds).

choc'olate n a drink or sweetmeat made from cacao seeds:—adj chocolate-coloured, i.e. dark brown.

choice n 1 act of choosing (he left his job by choice). 2 that which is chosen (like their choice of song/Italy was her first choice):—adj very good, excellent (choice fruit).

choir [kwîr] n 1 a group of singers. 2 the part of the church where the choir sits.

choke vb 1 to be unable to breathe (people choking in the fumes from the fire). 2 to prevent breathing by pressing the windpipe (choke his victim to death). 3 to block up (drains that had become blocked):—n 1 a fit of choking or its sound. 2 a valve that controls the flow of air in a carburettor.

chol'era n a serious stomach illness, common in hot countries.

chol'eric adj (fml) easily made angry (choleric old men/of a choleric disposition).

choose vb (pt chose, pp cho'sen) to take what one prefers (choose a dish from the menu/choosing the members of his team/he has chosen between the two jobs).

chop vb (**chopped'**, **chop'ping**) 1 to cut with a quick strong blow (chop his head off). 2 to cut into pieces (*chop the meat up*):—*n* a piece of pork or mutton on a rib bone (*a lamb chop*).

chop'per *n* (*inf*) a helicopter.

chop'py *adj* rough (*a choppy sea*).

chops *npl* the jaws (*dogs licking their chops*).

chop'sticks *npl* two small sticks used by the Chinese instead of a knife and fork.

chor'al *adj* having to do with a chorus or choir (*choral music*).

chord [kord] *n* 1 the playing of several musical notes at once in harmony. 2 the straight line joining two points on a curve.

chore *n* an odd job about the house (*chores such as washing up*).

chor'ister *n* a singer in a choir.

chor'us *n* 1 a group of singers and dancers. 2 a song or part of a song in which all may join (*ask the audience to sing the chorus*):—*vb* to sing or speak together ('*Goodbye,*' *chorused the children to their teacher*).

chough [chuf] *n* a red-legged bird of the crow family.

christen [kris'-ên] *vb* 1 to baptize (*have their son christened in church*). 2 to name (*she calls herself Kate although she was christened Catherine*):—*n* **chris'tening**.

Chris'tendom *n* 1 all Christians. 2 the parts of the world where people believe in Christ.

Chris'tian *adj* having to do with Christ and his teaching:—*n* a believer in Christ.

Christian name *n* the name given at christening.

Christmas [kris'-mês] *n* 25 December, the day each year on which the birth of Christ is celebrated.

chroma'tic *adj* 1 having to do with colours. 2 coloured.

chromatic scale *n* (*mus*) a scale made up of semitones.

chrom'ium *n* a bright metal.

chron'ic *adj* lasting for a long time (*a chronic illness*).

chron'icle *n* 1 a record of events, set down in the order in which they happened (*a chronicle of the events leading up to the war*):—*also vb*:—*n* **chron'icler**.

chronolog'ical *adj* arranged in order of time (*announce the dates of the meetings in chronological order*).

chronom'eter *n* an instrument for measuring time extremely accurately.

chrysalis [kris'-êl-is] *n* an early stage in the life of a flying insect, when it is shut up in a shell-like cover until its wings grow.

chrysan'themum *n* a garden plant with a large, bushy flower.

chub'by *adj* plump (*chubby babies*).

chuck *vb* 1 to tap gently (under the chin). 2 (*inf*) to throw (*chuck the apple core into the rubbish bin*).

chuck'le *vb* to laugh quietly (*chuckling over his comic*):—*also n*.

chum *n* (*inf*) a close friend (*old school chums*):—*adj* **chum'my**.

chunk *n* a thick piece (*a chunk of cheese*).

church *n* 1 a building set aside by Christians for the worship of God. 2 a group of Christians having the same beliefs and organization. 3 the body of Christians. 4 the body of clergy.

churchwar'den *n* one who helps to look after a church.

church'yard *n* a burial ground round a church.

churl *n* (*old*) a rough ill-mannered fellow.

chur'lish *adj* ill-mannered and bad-tempered (*a churlish fellow who liked nobody/his churlish behaviour*):—*n* **chur'lishness**.

churn *n* a vessel or machine for making butter:—*vb* to shake (cream) so as to make butter.

chute [shöt] *n* 1 a waterfall. 2 a sloping passage or slide (*children sliding down the chute in the playground*).

ci'der *n* a strong drink made from apple juice.

cigar' *n* a roll of tobacco leaves for smoking.

cigarette' *n* tobacco finely cut and rolled in thin paper for smoking.

cin'der *n* burned coal.

cin'ema *n* 1 a building in which films ar e shown. 2 the making of films.

cin'namon *n* 1 an East Indian tree. 2 a spice made from its bark, used in cooking.

ciph'er *n* 1 a nought (0). 2 any figure from 1 to 9. 3 a person or thing of no importance (*just a cipher in the organization*). 4 a method of secret writing, a code (*a message written in cipher*). 5 letters, esp initials, written one on top of another, to form a single design.

cir'cle *n* 1 a perfectly round figure. 2 a group of people (*a small circle of close friends*):—*vb* 1 to move round (*dancers circling the room*). **2** to draw a circle around (*circled the correct word*).

cir'clet *n* an ornamental ring for the head.

circuit [sèr'-kêt] *n* **1** a path round (*the earth's circuit round the sun*). **2** the act of moving round (*do a circuit of the city walls*). **3** the journey of a judge round a district to hold courts of law in several places. **4** the path of an electric current.

circuitous [ser-kû-it-ês] *adj* roundabout, indirect (*a circuitous route to avoid the city centre*).

cir'cular *adj* (*of a circular shape*):—*n* a letter, copies of which are sent to many people (*sent a circular to the parents about school sports day*).

cir'cularize *vb* to send circulars to (*circularize the members to get their views*).

cir'culate *vb* **1** to move in a circle or a fixed path (*water circulating in the pipes of the heating system*). **2** to pass round, to spread (*circulate information*). **3** to move from one person to another (*a hostess circulating among the guests*).

circula'tion *n* **1** the act of circulating. **2** the movement of the blood through the body. **3** the number of readers (of a newspaper, etc).

circum- *prefix* round, round about.

circumci'sion *n* a ceremony by which baby boys are received into the Jewish religion:—*vb* **circumcise'**.

circum'ference *n* the line marking the limits of a circle.

cir'cumflex *n* an accent mark (^) on vowels in certain languages.

circumlocu'tion *n* a roundabout way of saying something (*uses circumlocution instead of saying straight out what he means*):—*adj* **circumlocu'tory**.

circumnav'igate *vb* (*fml*) to sail round (*circumnavigate the world*).

cir'cumspect *adj* careful, cautious (*be more circumspect and do not rush to change jobs*):—*n* **circumspec'tion**.

cir'cumstance *n* **1** (*usu pl*) a condition relating to or connected with an act or event (*the circumstances surrounding her death/in the circumstances the police let him go*). **2** *pl* state of affairs, position (often financial) (*in very bad circumstances*).

circumstan'tial *adj* (*of information or evidence concerning a crime*) consisting of details that strongly suggest something but do not prove it.

circumvent' *vb* to get the better of (*try to circumvent the tax laws/circumvent the problem*).

cir'cus *n* **1** an entertainment given largely by skilled acrobats and trained animals. **2** a building or group of houses arranged in a circle, usu found in place names.

cirrus [sir'-ês] *n* (*pl* **cir'ri**) a high, fleecy type of cloud.

cis'tern *n* a tank for storing water.

cit'adel *n* a fortress in a city.

cita'tion *n* **1** a summons to a law court. **2** a short passage taken from something written or spoken, a quotation.

cite *vb* **1** to call to appear in court. **2** to quote. **3** to give as an example.

cit'izen *n* **1** an inhabitant of a city. **2** a member of a state.

cit'izenship *n* being, or having the rights of, a citizen.

cit'rus *adj* of a group of related fruits, including the lemon, orange, lime and grapefruit.

cit'y *n* a large town, usu with a cathedral.

civ'et, **civ'et cat** *n* **1** a small African or Asian animal. **2** the perfume obtained from it.

civ'ic *adj* **1** having to do with a city (*a civic function*). **2** having to do with citizens or citizenship (*one's civic duty*):—*npl* **civ'ics** the study of the rights and duties of citizens.

civ'il *adj* **1** having to do with citizens (*civil disorder*). **2** having to do with those citizens who are members of neither the armed forces nor the clergy (*civil, not military, government*). **3** polite (*shop assistants who are scarcely civil*):—*adv* **civ'illy**.

civil'ian *n* one not in the armed forces.

civil'ity *n* politeness.

civiliza'tion *n* **1** a well-organized and refined society (*the ancient civilizations of Greece and Egypt*). **2** the state of being civilized (*living with a savage tribe far from civilization*).

civ'ilize *vb* **1** to teach how to live in a properly organized society (*local tribes civilized by the invaders of the island*). **2** to make more polite and well-mannered:—*adj* **civ'ilized**.

civil servant *n* a government servant not in the armed forces.

civil war *n* a war between citizens of the same state.

clad *pp* of **clothe**.

claim *vb* to demand as a right (*claimed the throne/ claiming his share of his late father's money*):— also *n*.

claim'ant *n* one who claims.

clairvoy'ant *n* one claiming the power of clairvoyance (*a clairvoyant telling people's futures*):—also *adj*.

clam *n* a type of shellfish.

clam'ber *vb* to climb with difficulty, to scramble (*children clambering over the rocks*):—also *n*.

clam'my *adj* damp and sticky (*clammy hands/the weather was clammy before the storm*).

clam'orous *adj* noisy (*clamorous protesters*).

clam'our *n* loud shouting, a general outcry, esp demanding something (*a clamour from the audience to get their money back*):—*vb* to shout (for something).

clamp *n* a band or instrument used for holding things firmly together:—*vb* to fasten with a clamp.

clan *n* a group of families related by blood and ruled by a chief:—*n* **clans'man**.

clandes'tine *adj* secret, underhand (*a clandestine meeting*).

clang *n* a loud ringing sound, as of metal against metal:—*vb* to make this noise (*the iron gates clanged shut*).

clank *n* a short sharp sound (*the clank of chains*):—also *vb*.

clan'nish *adj* keeping to one's own group and not mixing with others.

clap *vb* (**clapped'**, **clap'ping**) **1** to smack the hands together noisily (*the audience clapped when the singer appeared*). **2** to slap or tap, usu in a friendly way (*clap him on the back in congratulation*). **3** to put suddenly and quickly (*clap the wrongdoers in jail*):—*n* **1** the noise made by clapping the hands. **2** a sudden sound (e.g. of thunder).

clap'per *n* **1** an instrument for making a clapping noise. **2** the tongue of a bell.

clap'trap *n* insincere or pretentious talk, nonsense.

claret *n* **1** a kind of red wine. **2** a dark red colour (*a velvet dress of claret*).

clarify *vb* to make clear or clearer (*clarifed the instructions/clarifying the situation*):—*n* **clarifica'tion**.

clarinet [kla'-ri-net *or* kla-ri-net'], **clar'ionet** *n* a musical wind instrument, usu of wood.

clar'ion *n* a shrill trumpet:—*adj* clear and loud (*a clarion call to action*).

clar'ity *n* clearness (*the clarity of his speech/the clarity of the instructions*).

clash *n* **1** to strike together noisily (*clash the cymbals*). **2** to disagree strongly about (*the two sides clashed over money*). **3** (*of events*) to happen at the same time (*the concert clashed with my birthday party*):—*n* **1** the loud noise of two objects coming violently together. **2** a quarrel.

clasp *n* **1** a metal fastener (*the clasp of a brooch*). **2** a firm hold (*hold her hand in a firm clasp*):— *vb* **1** to fasten. **2** to hold firmly (*clasp her mother's hand/clasp her to his bosom*).

class *n* **1** a group of persons or things of the same kind (*plants divided into classes*). **2** a group of pupils or students. **3** a rank, a standard of excellence (*of the first class*). **4** the system according to which people are divided into social groups. **5** one of these social groups (*the upper class*):—*vb* to put in a class, to regard as being of a certain type (*he classes all women as inferior/class him as being unfit for work*).

clas'sic *adj* of the best kind or standard:—*n* **1** a great writer or book. **2** *pl* **clas'sics** Greek and Latin literature.

clas'sical *adj* **1** classic. **2** having to do with Greek and Latin literature.

clas'sify *vb* to arrange in classes (*classified the books as fiction or non-fiction*):—*n* **classifica'tion**.

clat'ter *vb* to make rattling noises (*clattered up the wooden stairs*):—*n* a rattling noise.

clause *n* **1** a part of a sentence. **2** a section of an agreement (*a clause in the contract allowing either side to withdraw*).

clav'icle *n* the collarbone.

claw *n* **1** the hooked nail of a bird or animal. **2** a foot with such nails:—*vb* to scratch or tear with claws or nails (*clawed at his face with her nails*).

clay *n* a moist sticky earth that hardens when dried:—*adj* **clay'ey**.

clay'more *n* a large two-edged sword once used by Scottish Highlanders.

clean *adj* **1** free from dirt (*clean hands/a clean shirt*). **2** pure, free from guilt, evil, crime, etc (*a* *clean life/a clean record*). **3** complete (*a clean break*):—*adv* completely (*the handle came away clean in my hand*):—*vb* to remove dirt, dust, etc, from (*cleaned the dress/cleaning the kitchen*):—*n* **clean'er**.—*n* **clean'ness**.

cleanly [klen'-li] *adj* having clean habits (*a cleanly animal*):—*adv* in a clean manner, neatly:—*n* **cleanliness** [klen'-li-nês].

cleanse [klenz] *vb* to make clean or pure (*the lotion cleansed her skin/cleansing his soul*).

clear *adj* **1** easy to hear, see or understand (*a clear description*). **2** bright (*clear skies*). **3** free from difficulties or obstacles (*the way is now clear to go on with our plans*). **4** obvious (*a clear case of guilt*):—*vb* **1** to make or become clear (*the skies cleared*). **2** to prove innocent (*clearing his name*). **3** to remove difficulties or obstacles from (*clear the way*). **4** to pass through or over (*clear the fence*):—*adv* **clear'ly**.

clear'ance *n* **1** act of clearing (*the clearance of trees/the clearance of goods from the shelves*). **2** permission for something to be done (*receive clearance from the Foreign Office*).

clear'ing *n* part of a forest cleared of trees.

cleav'age *n* **1** a splitting. **2** a separation.

cleave[1] *vb* (*fml*) to stick to (*cleave to an old way of life/cleave to their principles*).

cleave[2] *vb* to split, to cut apart (*cleave a tree*).

cleav'er *n* a butcher's chopper.

clef *n* a mark to show the pitch in music.

cleft *n* a crack, a split.

cleg *n* a gadfly, a horsefly.

clematis [klem'-a-tis] *n* a climbing plant.

clem'ent *adj* **1** mild (*clement weather*). **2** merciful, kindly (*a clement judge*):—*n* **clem'ency**.

clench *vb* to press tightly together (*clench one's fist/clench one's teeth*).

cler'gy *n* the ministers and priests of the Christian religion.

cler'gyman *n* a minister.

cler'ic *n* a clergyman.

cler'ical *adj* **1** having to do with the clergy. **2** having to do with a clerk (*clerical work*).

clerk [klark] *n* an office employee doing written work.

clev'er *adj* **1** able to learn quickly. **2** able to do things well with the hands, skilful:—*adv* **clev'erly**:—*n* **clev'erness**.

clew *n* **1** a ball of thread. **2** the corner of a sail.

cliché [klee'-shā] *n* a stock phrase in common use.

click *n* a light sharp sound (*the click of her heels*):—*also vb*.

cli'ent *n* **1** a customer (*a hairdresser's clients*). **2** one who employs a member of some profession (*a lawyer's clients*).

clientele [klî-ên-teel'], **clientèle** [klee-ên-tel'] *n* all the clients of a lawyer or customers of a shopkeeper.

cliff *n* a high steep rock face.

cli'mate *n* the usual weather conditions of a place:—*adj* **clima'tic**.

cli'max *n* the highest or most exciting point, the most dramatic moment (*the climax of his career/the climax of the play*).

climb *vb* to go up, using the hands and feet:—*n* **climb'er**.

clinch *vb* **1** to settle (*clinched the deal*). **2** in boxing, to stand so close that no strong punches may be given.—*also n*.

cling *vb* (*pt, pp* clung) **1** to stick to (*mud clinging to her shoes*). **2** to hold firmly to (*clung to her mother's skirt*).

clin'ic *n* a building or a part of a hospital for people needing special treatment or advice (*a skin clinic*):—*adj* **clin'ical**.

clink *n* a sharp thin ringing sound:—*also vb*.

clip[1] *vb* (clipped', clip'ping) to cut (*clip the hedge*):—*n* **1** the thing clipped. **2** a sharp blow.

clip[2] *n* a fastener:—*vb* (clipped', clip'ping) to fasten together.

clip'per *n* **1** an instrument for clipping (*nail clippers*). **2** a fast sailing ship.

clique [kleek] *n* a small group of people who keep together, not mixing with others.

cloak *n* **1** a loose outer garment. **2** a means of hiding (some activity) (*a cloak for his drug smuggling*):—*vb* **1** to cover as with a cloak. **2** to conceal.

cloak'room *n* **1** a room where one can leave outer garments, packages, etc, in a public place. **2** a lavatory (*a downstairs cloakroom*).

clock *n* **1** an instrument for telling the time. **2** an ornamental pattern on the side of a sock or stocking.

clock'wise *adj* going round in the direction of the hands of a clock.

clock'work n machinery like that of a clock:—**like clockwork** regularly and smoothly.

clod n **1** a lump of earth. **2** a stupid fellow.

clod'hopper n a rough stupid person.

clog n a shoe with a wooden sole:—vb (**clogged'**, **clog'ging**) to block, to choke (clog the drains).

clone n **1** an animal or plant that has been produced artificially from the cells of another one and is, therefore, absolutely identical to it. **2** a person or thing that is very like someone or something else (The teenagers all wear the same clothes and look like clones of each other):—vb to produce an exact copy of an animal or plant from its cells.

clois'ter n **1** a monastery or convent. **2** a covered walk in a monastery or convent.

close[1] [klōz] vb **1** to shut (close the gates). **2** to finish" (close the meeting). **3** to bring or come near together (his arms closed around her):—n the end.

close[2] [klōs] adj **1** shut in. **2** stuffy (the air was close in the crowded hall). **3** near (a close result). **4** near, not far (the station is quite close). **5** mean (close with money).

closed circuit television n a television system, in which the cameras and monitors operate within a limited area, such as a public building, used for surveillance and crime detection, often called **CCTV**.

close-fist'ed adj mean.

clos'et n a large cupboard:—vb to shut up (closeted themselves in a private room).

clo'sure n (fml) closing, end (the closure of the factory).

clot n a soft lump formed from liquid (a clot of blood):—vb (**clot'ted**, **clot'ting**) **1** to form into clots. **2** to thicken (clot the cream).

cloth n a material made by weaving threads of wool, cotton, etc.

clothe vb (pt, pp **clothed** or **clad**) to put clothes on (clothe herself in silk).

clothes [klō(th)z] npl garments.

clothes horse n a frame on which clothes are hung to dry.

cloth'ier n a seller of cloth or clothes.

cloth'ing n garments (warm clothing).

cloud n **1** a mass of water vapour floating high up in the air. **2** a great many (a cloud of insects). **3** a cause of gloom or trouble (a cloud on their

happiness):—vb to darken:—adjs **cloud'y**, **cloud'less**.

cloud'burst n a sudden violent rainstorm.

clove n **1** a plant bud used as a spice. **2** a part of a garlic bulb.

clo'ven adj split.

clo'ven-foot'ed, **clo'ven-hoofed** adjs having the foot or hoof cloven, as the ox.

clo'ver n a three-leaved plant grown as food for cattle.

clown n **1** a fool. **2** one who plays the fool to amuse others:—vb to play the fool (boys clowning around).

cloy vb **1** to cause dislike by giving too much (cloying the appetite). **2** to become unpleasant by being tasted or experienced too often (sweet things tend to cloy).

club n **1** a heavy stick. **2** a golf stick. **3** a group of people who meet for a common purpose. **4** their meeting place (construct a golf club). **5** a place, usually one selling drinks, where people go to listen to music and dance. **6** pl a suit of playing cards:—vb (**clubbed'**, **club'bing**) **1** to beat with a club (club him to death). **2** to join together (club together to buy a present).

cluck n the sound made by a hen.

clue n a fact that, when understood, helps one to find the answer to a problem, a hint (police looking for clues/find a clue to her whereabouts).

clump n a closely packed group, a cluster (a clump of trees):—vb to walk heavily (clump angrily upstairs).

clum'sy adj **1** awkward in movement, shape, etc (awkward with his hands/an awkward size). **2** badly done (a clumsy apology):—n **clum'siness**.

clus'ter n a number of things growing very close together, a closely packed group (a cluster of grapes):—vb to grow or stand close together.

clutch vb **1** to seize (clutched the rope that was thrown). **2** to hold tightly (clutches her bag):—n **1** a firm hold. **2** pl power, control (in the clutches of criminals). **3** eggs being hatched at one sitting. **4** in a motor car, a lever that puts an engine in or out of action.

clut'ter vb to fill or cover untidily (papers cluttering the desk):—n an untidy mass.

co- prefix together.

coach n **1** (old) a closed four-wheeled horse carriage. **2** a railway carriage. **3** a bus (holiday by coach). **4** a private teacher (employ a coach to improve their son's French). **5** one who trains sportsmen or athletes (an athletics coach):—vb **1** to give private lessons (coach him in French). **2** to prepare (someone) for a contest (coach the football players).

coag'ulate vb to make into or become a soft solid or thickened mass (blood coagulating):—n **coagula'tion**.

coal n a black substance dug from a coal mine, used as fuel for fires.

coalesce [kō-al-es'] vb (fml) to join together, to unite, to merge (different attitudes begin to coalesce).

coali'tion n **1** a joining together. **2** the joining together of different political parties for a special purpose (a country ruled by a coalition).

coal scuttle n a fireside container for coal.

coal tar n a black liquid made from coal.

coarse adj **1** rough (coarse material). **2** rude, vulgar, unrefined (a coarse sense of humour):—adv **coarse'ly**:—n **coarse'ness**.

coars'en vb to make coarse (hands coarsened by washing floors).

coast n the side of the land next the sea:—vb **1** to sail alongside the coast. **2** to move without the use of power (cars coasting downhill). **3** to go on without much effort (coast along without doing much studying):—adj **coast'al**.

coast'guard n the coast police (an empty boat spotted by coastguards).

coast'line n the line of the coast or shore.

coat n **1** an outer garment with sleeves. **2** the natural cover of an animal (e.g. hair, wool, fur). **3** anything that covers (a coat of paint):—vb to cover (biscuits that were coated with chocolate).

coat'ing n a covering.

coat of arms n the design on the shield or badge of a nobleman.

coax vb to get someone to do something by speaking kindly or petting.

cob n **1** a head of wheat. **2** a strong pony.

cobalt [kō'-bält] n **1** a metal. **2** a blue colouring matter made from it.

cob'ble vb **1** (old) to mend (shoes) (he cobbled boots). **2** to mend or put together roughly (cobble together a makeshift table):—n a cobblestone.

cob'bler n a mender of shoes.

cob'blestone n a rounded stone used in paving roads.

cob'ra n a poisonous snake found in India.

cob'web n the spider's web.

cocaine' n a drug that deadens pain.

cochineal [ko-chi-neel'] n **1** an insect. **2** the scarlet dye got from the dried bodies.

cock n **1** a male bird. **2** a tap. **3** the hammer of a gun:—vb **1** to turn upwards, to tilt (cock his hat). **2** to raise, to cause to stand up (the dog cocked its ears). **3** (of a gun) to draw back the hammer before firing.

cock'-and-bull' adj quite unbelievable (a cock-and-bull story).

cockatoo' n a type of parrot.

cock'erel n a young cock.

cock-eyed' adj **1** squint-eyed. **2** foolish, absurd (cock-eyed schemes).

cock'le n a type of shellfish.

cock'leshell n **1** the shell of the cockle. **2** a small light boat.

Cock'ney n one born in East End London:—also adj.

cock'pit n **1** (old) a pit in which cocks were made to fight each other. **2** the pilot's place in an aircraft.

cock'roach n the black beetle.

cocks'comb n the red crest on a cock's head.

cock'sure adj too sure, overconfident.

cock'tail n a strong drink made by mixing several drinks, usu alcoholic, together.

co'co, co'coa n a tropical palm tree, on which the coconut grows.

co'coa n **1** a powder made from cacao seeds. **2** a drink made from this powder.

co'conut n the fruit of the coco palm.

cocoon' n a silky case spun by many insects in the chrysalis state.

cod n a large sea fish.

cod'dle vb **1** to pet, to treat with too much care (coddles her youngest child). **2** to cook gently (coddle eggs).

code n **1** a collection of laws, rules or signals (the Highway Code). **2** a method of sending secret messages by using signs or words (try *to decipher the message in code/the Morse Code*).

codicil [kod'-i-sil] *n* a note added at the end of a will.

coerce' *vb* to make to do, to force (*enemy soldiers coercing the villagers into providing accommodation*):—*n* **coer'cion**:—*adj* **coer'cive**.

coe'val *adj* of the same age or time:—*also n*.

coexist' *vb* to live at the same time or place with another, esp peacefully (*the warring neighbours finally succeeded in coexisting happily*):—*n* **coexist'ence**.

coffee *n* a drink made from the seeds of the coffee tree.

coffer *n* a strong box for holding money or valuable things.

coffin *n* a box in which a dead body is put for burial.

cog' *n* the tooth of a wheel.

cogent [kō'-jênt] *adj* persuasive, convincing (*cogent arguments*):—*n* **co'gency**.

cognac [kon'-yak] *n* a kind of French brandy.

cog'nate *adj* having the same origin or source (*cognate words*).

cog'nizance *n*:—**take cognizance of** (*fml*) to take into consideration (*take cognizance of everyone's opinion*).

cog'nizant *adj* having knowledge or information, aware (*fully cognizant of the problems*).

cog'wheel *n* a wheel with teeth by means of which it turns another wheel.

cohab'it *vb* to live together, esp as husand and wife without being married:—*n* **co-habita'tion**.

cohere' *vb* 1 (*fml*) to stick together (*a substance to make the surfaces cohere*). 2 to be clear and logical (*an argument that does not cohere*).

coher'ent *adj* clear and logical (*a coherent argument*):—*n* **coher'ence**.

cohe'sion *n* 1 the force that makes the parts of a body stick together. 2 coherence:—*adj* **cohe'sive**.

co'hort *n* 1 a company of Roman soldiers. 2 a group or band of people (*cohorts of his followers*).

coif [koif] *n* (*old*) a close-fitting cap.

coiffure [kwä-fêr'] *n* a style of hairdressing.

coil *vb* to wind in a series of rings (*a snake coiling itself round a tree*):—*n* a ring or rings into which a rope, etc, is wound.

coin *n* a metal piece of money:—*vb* 1 to make money out of metal. 2 to invent (*coin a word*).

coin'age *n* 1 the act of coining. 2 all coined money. 3 the coined money in use in a particular country. 4 a newly invented word.

coincide' *vb* (*fml*) 1 to happen at the same time (*their arrival coincided with our departure*). 2 to be in agreement (*their opinions coincide*).

coin'cidence *n* the accidental happening of one event at the same time as another (*it was a coincidence that we both arrived together*):—*adjs* **coin'cident, coinciden'tal**.

coke *n* coal from which gas has been extracted, used as fuel.

col'ander *n* a strainer.

cold *adj* 1 not hot or warm (*a cold day/cold food*). 2 without emotion or passion, unenthusiastic (*his performance left me cold*). 3 unfriendly (*a cold welcome*):—*n* 1 absence of heat (*cannot stand the cold*). 2 an illness caused by cold (*catch a cold*).

cold-blood'ed *adj* 1 having blood colder than the air or water, as fish, snakes, etc. 2 completely unfeeling, cruel (*cold-blooded murder*).

cold'ness *n* 1 absence of heat. 2 lack of feeling. 3 unfriendliness.

cold-shoul'der *vb* to treat in an unfriendly way (*former friends cold-shouldering him after he cheated*).

col'ic *n* a sharp pain in the stomach.

collab'orate *vb* 1 to work with another, esp in writing or study (*collaborating on a book*). 2 to work with another to betray secrets, etc (*collaborating with the enemy*):—*ns* **collabora'tion, collab'orator**.

collapse' *n* 1 a fall (*the collapse of the bridge*). 2 a sudden loss of consciousness. 3 a failure (*the collapse of the firm/the collapse of the talks*):—*vb* 1 to fall down (*the bridge collapsed*). 2 to fall down unconscious (*collapsing in the extreme heat*). 3 to fail completely (*the company collapsed*).

col'lar *n* 1 the part of the clothing that covers or surrounds the neck. 2 a strap or band put round the neck of an animal:—*vb* (*inf*) to take hold of, to seize (*police collaring criminals*).

collate' *vb* 1 to put together and compare, as books, manuscripts, etc. 2 to arrange sheets of paper in the right order before binding them into a book.

collat'eral *adj* **1** connected but less important, additional (*collateral aims*). **2** distantly related (*a collateral branch of the family*):—*n* security pledged for the repayment of a loan.

col'league *n* a fellow worker.

collect' *vb* **1** to bring together (*collect the glasses*). **2** to come together (*a crowd collected*). **3** to gather and keep things of the same kind (*collect stamps*). **4** to obtain money by contributions (*collecting for charity*).

collect'ed *adj* calm, cool.

collec'tion *n* **1** act of collecting. **2** the things collected. **3** the gathering of money for a special purpose:—*n* **collec'tor**.

collec'tive *adj* taken as a whole, joint (*our collective strength*):—*n* a collective enterprise, as a farm:—*adv* **collec'tively**.

col'leen *n* an Irish girl.

col'lege *n* **1** a society of learned or professional people (*the Royal College of Surgeons*). **2** a part of a university where students live and are taught (*an Oxford college*). **3** a place of further education.

collide' *vb* to run into, to strike against (*collide with another car/two cars colliding*):—*n* **colli'sion**.

col'lie *n* a sheepdog.

col'liery *n* a coal mine.

collision *see* **collide**.

collo'quial *adj* conversational, having to do with the spoken language of ordinary people (*colloquial language*).

collo'quialism *n* a popular but not literary expression.

collu'sion *n* a secret agreement to do something wrong (*witnesses acting in collusion to deceive the courts*).

col'on *n* **1** a mark of punctuation (:). **2** a part of the bowel.

colonel [kèr'-nêl] *n* the officer commanding a regiment of soldiers.

colon'ial *adj* having to do with a colony.

col'onist *n* a settler in a colony.

col'onize *vb* to form or set up a colony in (*the British colonized parts of Canada*).

colonnade' *n* a row of columns or pillars.

col'ony *n* **1** a community of settlers in a new land. **2** the place in which they settle.

colos'sal *adj* very big, gigantic.

col'our *n* **1** a quality that objects have and that can be seen only when light falls on them (*what colour is her new dress?/bright colours such as red and yellow*). **2** paint (*watercolours*). **3** redness (of the face) (*brings colour to her cheeks*). **4** a skin colour varying with race (*discrimination on the grounds of colour*). **5** vividness (*a description full of colour*). **6** *pl* a flag:—*vb* **1** to paint, to put colour on or into (*colour the walls yellow*). **2** to give interesting qualities to, to exaggerate (*an account coloured by her imagination*). **3** to affect (*a view of life coloured by childhood experiences*). **4** to blush (*colouring with embarrassment*).

col'our-blind *adj* unable to see the difference between colours or certain colours.

col'ourful *adj* **1** full of colour, bright. **2** vivid and interesting (*a colourful account*).

col'ourless *adj* **1** without colour. **2** uninteresting (*a colourless description/a colourless young woman*).

colt *n* a young horse.

col'umbine *n* **1** a kind of wild flower. **2** a female character in pantomime.

col'umn *n* **1** a pillar used to support or ornament a building. **2** something similar in shape (*a column of smoke*). **3** a body of troops standing one behind the other in one or more lines. **4** a row of numbers, one below the other. **5** a narrow division of a page:—*adj* **col'umnar**.

col'umnist *n* the writer of a regular series of articles for a newspaper.

co'ma *n* a long-continuing unconscious state (*in a coma after the head injury*).

comatose [kō'-ma-tōz] *adj* **1** in a coma. **2** (*inf*) very sleepy, drowsy (*comatose after a large lunch*).

comb *n* **1** a toothed instrument for disentangling and arranging hair, wool, etc. **2** the crest of a cock:—*vb* to disentangle or arrange with a comb.

com'bat *vb* (**com'batted, com'batting**) to fight against, to try to defeat, destroy, etc (*combat disease*):—*n* a fight.

com'batant *n* one taking part in a fight:—*also adj*.

com'bative *adj* liking to fight (*in a combative mood*).

combina'tion *n* **1** a joining together, a union (*a combination of the new and the old/work in com-*

bination with overseas firms). **2** *pl* a one-piece undergarment covering the body and the legs.

combine' *vb* to join together (*he combines wit and skill/the two firms have combined*).

com'bine har'vester *n* a machine that cuts corn, separates grain from chaff, and binds the remainder.

combust *vb* to burn.

combus'tible *adj* able to take light and burn.

combus'tion *n* the process of burning.

come [kum] *vb* (*pt* came, *pp* come) to move towards (*opposite of* go):—*n* com'ing:—**come across** to discover (something) by accident (*come across some valuable books in an old shop*):—**come to pass** (*old or fml*) to happen (*it came to pass that they married*).

come'dian *n* **1** a performer who tells jokes, a comic. **2** one who is always trying to make others laugh:—*f* comedienne'.

com'edy *n* **1** a light or amusing play with a happy ending. **2** an amusing happening, the amusing side of something (*the comedy of the situation*).

comely [kum'-li] *adj* (*old or fml*) pleasant-looking, graceful (*a comely young woman*):—*n* come'liness.

comes'tibles *npl* (*fml*) food.

com'et *n* a bright heavenly body, seen only rarely, with a tail of light.

comfit [kum'-fit] *n* a type of sweetmeat.

com'fort *vb* to give comfort to, to cheer (someone) up (*comfort the widow at the funeral*):—*n* **1** the state of being free from anxiety, worry, pain, etc, and having all one's physical needs satisfied, ease (*a life of comfort*). **2** something that satisfies one's physical needs (*all modern comforts*). **3** strength, hope, sympathy, etc (*offer comfort to the widow*). **4** the cause of comfort to others (*a comfort to her mother*).

com'fortable *adj* **1** at ease, free from anxiety, worry, etc (*not feel comfortable in her presence*). **2** providing comfort, soft and restful, relaxing (*a comfortable bed*).

com'forter *n* (*old*) a woollen scarf.

com'ic *adj* **1** having to do with comedy (*a comic act/comic opera*). **2** amusing, laugh-able (*a comic situation*):—*also n*.

com'ical *adj* funny, amusing (*look comical in that funny hat*).

com'ma *n* a mark of punctuation (,).

command' *vb* **1** to order (*command them to come at once*). **2** to be in charge (of). **3** to control. **4** to overlook (a place) (*command a view of the sea*):—*n* **1** an order. **2** mastery.

commandant' *n* an officer in charge of a place or of troops.

commandeer' *vb* to take over private property for military use (*commandeered the houses for soldiers' lodgings*).

command'er *n* **1** an officer in charge of troops. **2** an officer in the navy.

command'ing *adj* arousing respect.

command'ment *n* an order, a law.

command'o *n* **1** a group of soldiers trained for tasks of special difficulty. **2** a soldier so trained.

commem'orate *vb* to make people remember something by holding a service or doing something special (*commemorating those who died in the war*):—*n* com-memora'tion.

commence' *vb* (*fml*) to begin:—*n* com-mence'ment.

commend' *vb* **1** to praise (*her teaching was highly commended*). **2** (*fml*) to recommend (*I commend you to try the new restaurant*).

commend'able *adj* deserving praise.

commenda'tion *n* praise.

commen'surate *adj* equal or like in value or amount (*a salary commensurate with your abilities*).

com'ment *vb* **1** to say something about, to remark on (*friends commenting on her unhappiness*). **2** to write notes in explanation of:—*n* **1** a remark. **2** an explanation.

com'mentary *n* **1** a series of remarks or notes. **2** a book explaining another book. **3** a spoken description of an event as it happens:—**running commentary** a description of an event as it happens, given by an onlooker.

com'mentator *n* **1** one who comments. **2** the writer or speaker of a commentary.

com'merce *n* the buying and selling of goods, trade.

commer'cial *adj* **1** having to do with trade or commerce (*commercial law*). **2** profit-making (*not a commercial proposition*).

commercial traveller *n* (*esp old*) a firm's representative, a rep.

commin'gle *vb* (*fml*) to mix together (*pity commingling with anger*).

commis'erate *vb* to pity, to sympathize with (*commiserate with her on her misfortune*).

commisera'tion *n* pity, sympathy.

commissariat [ko-mi-së'-ri-êt] *n* the army department in charge of food and other stores.

commis'sion *n* **1** act of committing. **2** an order for a work of art (*receive a commission to paint the president's portrait*). **3** a group of people appointed to study and report on a particular matter (*a member of a Royal Commission*). **4** money paid to someone who has helped to arrange a business deal (*his commission for selling the painting/the commission paid by the writer to his agent*):—*vb* to give an order or request to, to appoint (*commission him to paint a portrait*).

commissionaire' *n* a uniformed attendant at the entrance to certain public buildings (*a hotel commissionaire*).

commis'sioner *n* **1** one given a special duty to perform. **2** a member of a commission appointed to report on a particular matter.

commit' *vb* (**commit'ted, commit'ting**) **1** to perform or do, esp something illegal (*commit a crime*). **2** to make a definite agreement (that one will do something) (*commit oneself to raising £1000 for the charity*). **3** to give (someone) into care (*he committed his brother to a mental hospital*). **4** (*fml*) to put in or on (*commit the facts to paper/commit the body to the fire*).

commit'ment *n* **1** the act of committing (*the commitment of facts to paper*). **2** a promise, a duty, an obligation (*family commitments*). **3** state of being dedicated or devoted (*looking for someone with commitment to his work*).

commit'tal *n* the act of committing, esp of sending someone to prison, etc (*his committal to an open prison*).

commit'tee *n* a group of people appointed from a larger body to manage its affairs or perform a particular duty (*the committee of the local tennis club*).

commo'dious *adj* (*fml*) having plenty of room, roomy (*a commodious flat*).

commod'ity *n* (*often pl*) a thing produced to be sold, an article of commerce (*household commodities*).

com'modore *n* a high-ranking officer in a navy or air fleet.

com'mon *adj* **1** belonging to everyone, of no special rank or quality (*their common desire to be free*). **2** found everywhere (*a common wild flower*). **3** ordinary (*a common member of the public*). **4** frequent (*a common occurrence*). **5** rough, vulgar, regarded as being low-class (*regarded as common because of her dress and speech*):—*n* **1** land belonging to or open to the community (*the village common*). **2** *pl* the common people (not the nobles). **3** *pl* **Com'mons** the members of the House of Commons as a body.

com'monly *adv* usually (*Francis, commonly known as Frank*).

com'moner *n* **1** one of the common people, one who is not a noble (*princes marrying commoners*).

com'monplace *n* a well-known remark, an ordinary or unoriginal remark:—*adj* ordinary, not regarded as special (*a commonplace speech/foreign holidays are regarded as commonplace nowadays*).

com'mon sense' *n* practical good sense, knowledge of how to act in everyday matters (*brilliant but with little common sense*).

com'monwealth *n* **1** a state in which everyone has a say in the type of government. **2** a group of states united by certain common interests.

commo'tion *n* confused movement, disorder (*awakened by a commotion in the street*).

commu'nal *adj* shared by all (*a communal changing room*).

commune' *vb* (*fml*) to talk together (with), to exchange thoughts or feelings with (*claims he can commune with plants*).

commu'nicable *adj* **1** able to be passed to others (*a communicable disease*). **2** able to be communicated or explained to others (*ideas only communicable to experts*).

commu'nicant *n* one who receives Holy Communion.

commu'nicate *vb* **1** to make known to, to tell (*communicate the facts to her*). **2** to get in touch with (*communicate with each other by phone*). **3** to make known information, ideas, feelings, etc, clearly to others (*necessary to be able to communicate in this job*). **4** to pass (something) to another (*communicate a disease*).

communica'tion n **1** a message (receive a secret communication). **2** a means of communicating (telephone communications).

commun'icative adj talkative, ready to give information (find the witnesses not very communicative).

commun'ion n fellowship:—**Holy Communion** the sacrament of the Lord's Supper.

com'munism n the belief that all property should belong to the whole community and none to the individual.

com'munist n a believer in communism:—adj **communis'tic**.

commun'ity n the whole body of the people living in a town, district, country, etc (the mining disaster affected the whole community).

commute' vb **1** to travel daily from the place where one lives to another place where one works (commute by rail). **2** to change into something less unpleasant (commute the death sentence to one of life imprisonment):—adj **commut'able**:—n **commu-ta'tion**.

commu'ter n one who commutes (commuters affected by the rail strike).

compact' adj **1** tightly packed, firm (a compact mass of sand). **2** fitted neatly together in a small space (a compact kitchen). **3** short, concise (a compact account of the events/a compact style):—n **com'pact** a flat case for face powder:—n **compact'ness**.

com'pact² n (fml) an agreement, a treaty, a contract (sign a compact).

com'pact disc n a small hard plastic disc on which sound or information is recorded in a form readable by laser beam, often called **CD**.

compan'ion n **1** a friend, a person, etc, who regularly accompanies another (his dog was his constant companion/miss his companions at the club). **2** one who goes with or accompanies (her companion on her walk). **3** a person employed to live with someone and keep him or her company (the old lady's companion). **4** one of a matching pair or set of things (the companion to this volume):—n **compan'ionship**.

compan'ionable adj liking company (companionable people missing a social life).

compan'ionway n stairs on a ship from deck to cabin:—also **compan'ion-lad'der**.

com'pany n **1** a number of people gathered together by chance or invitation (tell the assembled company the facts). **2** being together with another or others (enjoy his company). **3** a group of persons who have put together money to run a business. **4** a group of people working together (a theatrical company). **5** a body of soldiers commanded by a captain. **6** the crew of a ship.

com'parable adj **1** able to be compared (a comparable job). **2** nearly or just as good as (a book that is comparable with the greatest novels).

compar'ative adj judged alongside something else, relative (comparative luxury).

compare' vb **1** to consider things together to see how they are like and how different (compare the two accounts of the accident). **2** to point out the likeness between (compare his novels to those of Dickens).

compar'ison n **1** act of comparing (a small city in comparison with London). **2** likeness, similarity (no comparison between fresh food and frozen).

compart'ment n **1** a part (e.g. of a drawer) divided off from the rest. **2** one of the small rooms in a railway carriage.

compass [kum'-pês] n **1** a direction-finding instrument containing a magnetic needle. **2** the range of musical notes. **3** (fml) scope (not within the compass of his power). **4** pl **com'passes** an instrument for drawing circles.

compas'sion n pity, sympathy (show compassion for the refugees).

compas'sionate adj feeling or showing pity.

compat'ible adj **1** able to exist together peacefully (husband and wife who are not compatible). **2** in agreement with (their accounts of the accident are not compatible).

compat'riot n one of the same country, a fellow countryman.

com'peer n a person of equal rank or status (his compeers in the House of Commons).

compel' vb (**compelled'**, **compel'ling**) to make to do, to force (compel him to pay his share):—adj **compel'ling**.

compen'dious adj containing a great deal of information in a small space.

compen'dium n a book dealing briefly with many different aspects of a subject (a compendium of sport).

com'pensate vb 1 to give something to make up for harm or injury done (*compensate him for his injury at work*). 2 to undo or counteract the effect of a disadvantage, loss, etc (*her aunt's love compensated for her parents' neglect*).

compensa'tion n something given to make up for harm or injury.

compere n a person who talks between and introduces items of entertainment (*the compere at the variety show*):—vb to act as a compere (*he compered the show*).

compete' vb 1 to try to do better than one's fellows in work, games, etc (*two teams competing for a place in the final/two firms competing for a government grant*). 2 to take part in the hope of winning a prize (*a record number of teams competing*).

com'petence, com'petency ns 1 ability, skill (*no one doubts his competence as a statesman*). 2 (*old*) a sufficient amount of money to live on.

com'petent adj 1 good at one's job (*a competent teacher*). 2 well done (*a competent job*). 3 (*fml*) having the necessary powers (*a court not competent to deal with the matter*):—adv **com'petently**.

competi'tion n 1 the act of competing, rivalry (*much competition for the post of manager*). 2 a contest for which a prize is offered (*enter the golf competition*). 3 people competing for a prize, etc (*the competition is very strong*).

competi'tive adj encouraging competition or rivalry (*a competitive industry*).

competi'tor n 1 one who competes (*line up the competitors in the race*). 2 a rival (*a shop charging less than its competitors*).

compile' vb to collect (facts and figures, etc) and put together in a book:—n **com·pil'er**:—n **compila'tion**.

complac'ence, complac'ency ns satisfaction, esp self-satisfaction.

complac'ent adj too satisfied with oneself and one's actions etc (*he's complacent about his position as champion but there are many new young players in the competition*).

complain' vb 1 to grumble (*complaining about the cold weather*). 2 to say that one is not satisfied (*complain to the manager about the faulty goods*).

complain'ant n one who accuses another of an offence against the law.

complaint' n 1 a grumble (*complaints about the weather*). 2 an expression of dissatisfaction (*write a letter of complaint to the manager*). 3 an illness (*childhood complaints*). 4 an accusation (*lodge a complaint against his noisy neighbour*).

complaisant [kom-plez'-ênt] adj obliging, ready to please (*a complaisant husband*):—n **complais'ance**.

com'plement n 1 that which completes (*a good wine is a complement to a good meal*). 2 the number or quantity needed to make something complete (*have their full complement of office staff*).

complemen'tary adj adding what is necessary to make complete (*a wine that is complementary to the meal/a complementary amount*).

complementary medicine n a range of therapies other than the usual scientific medical treatments, including herbal medicine, homoeopathy and acupuncture.

complete' adj 1 finished (*a task that will soon be complete*). 2 whole (*a complete set of Shakespeare's plays*). 3 perfect (*a complete gentleman*):—vb 1 to finish (*complete the task*). 2 to make whole (*complete their happiness*):—n **comple'tion**.

com'plex adj 1 having many parts (*complex machinery*). 2 not simple (*a complex plan*):—n 1 a group of connected or similar things (*a shopping complex/a leisure complex*). 2 an abnormal mental state, often caused by past experiences or suppressed desires or fears, that influences a person's behaviour (*a persecution complex/have a complex about being small*).

comple'xion n the colour of the face:—**put a different complexion on** to make seem quite different.

complex'ity n 1 the state of being complex. 2 difficulty (*deal with the complexities of the situation*).

compli'ant adj giving in easily to others (*so compliant that everyone takes advantage of him*):—n **compli'ance**.

com'plicate vb to make difficult (*it will complicate matters if we travel separately*).

com'plicated adj 1 difficult to understand (*a complicated problem*). 2 confusing because of having many parts (*a complicated machine*).

complica'tion n **1** a confused state of affairs. **2** an event or fact that makes things more difficult.

complic'ity n helping to do something wrong (*accused of complicity in the robbery*).

com'pliment n **1** praise, a flattering remark (*pay her a compliment on her appearance*). **2** pl (*fml*) good wishes (*compliments of the season/free wine with the compliments of the owner*):—vb to praise, to express admiration.

complimen'tary adj **1** flattering, showing admiration (*complimentary remarks*). **2** free (*complimentary tickets*).

comply' vb **1** to agree to (*complying with their request*). **2** to obey (*complied with the rules*).

compo'nent n a part necessary to the whole object (*car components*).

comport' vb (*fml*) to behave (*comport oneself with dignity*).

compose' vb **1** to make up by putting together. **2** to write (*compose a poem/compose a piece of music*). **3** to calm (*take time to compose oneself*).

composed' adj calm.

compos'er n one who writes music.

com'posite adj made up of several parts (*a composite picture painted by all the children in the class*).

composi'tion n **1** act of putting together. **2** the arrangement of parts to form a pleasing whole (*studying the composition of the chemical*). **3** the thing composed or written (*children writing a composition/a composition for violins*). **4** a mixture (*a chemical composition*).

com'post n rotting vegetable matter, etc, used as a fertilizer (*a compost heap*).

compo'sure n calmness.

com'pote n preserved or stewed fruit (*compote and cream for dessert*).

compound¹ vb **1** to put together, to mix (*a pain-killer compounded of two chemicals*). **2** to increase greatly (*the usual difficulties compounded by bad weather conditions*):—adj **com'pound**, made up of two or more parts (*a compound substance*):—n a mixture of two or more substances.

com'pound² n the yard or garden round a building.

comprehend' vb **1** to understand (*unable to comprehend his attitude*). **2** (*fml*) to include (*his estate comprehends all the land from the sea to the castle*).

comprehen'sible adj able to be understood (*his speech was scarcely comprehensible*).

comprehen'sion n the power of understanding (*beyond our comprehension*).

comprehen'sive adj taking in as much as possible (*a comprehensive survey*).

compress' vb to press together, to press together into a smaller space (*compress all his belongings into a small case/compress all his material into a ten-minute speech*):—n **com'press** a soft pad (*a cold compress to reduce the swelling*):—n **compres'sion**.

comprise' vb to be made up of (*a committee comprising only women/a house comprising three bedrooms and three public rooms*).

com'promise vb **1** to reach agreement by giving way on certain points (*we couldn't agree on a holiday destination so we both had to compromise and choose somewhere acceptable to both of us*). **2** to leave open to suspicion or criticism (*politicians compromising themselves by accepting hospitality from business firms*):—n an agreement reached when each party gives way on certain points.

compul'sion n **1** force (*they left only under compulsion*). **2** an irresistible urge (*a sudden compulsion to run away*).

compul'sory adj forced, compelled (*the wearing of school uniform is compulsory/compulsory safety helmets*).

compunc'tion n regret, feeling of guilt (*feel no compunction about leaving work early*).

compute' vb (*fml*) to calculate or estimate (*compute the likely cost*):—n **computa'tion**.

comput'er n an electronic machine capable of storing and processing large amounts of information and of doing calculations:—**comput'erize** vb **1** to store (information) on a computer (*begin to computerize hospital records*) **2** to use computers to do the work connected with something (*Production at the factory has now been fully computerized*):—**computeriza'tion**.

com'rade n a friend, a companion.

com'radeship n good fellowship.

con vb (**conned'**, **con'ning**) **1** (*old*) to study closely, to learn by heart. **2** (*inf*) to deceive, to trick (*con him into lending her money*).

con'cave *adj* hollow, curved inwards (like a saucer).

conceal' *vb* to hide, to keep from others (*conceal the money/conceal his feelings*).

conceal'ment *n* 1 act of concealing. 2 hiding place.

concede' *vb* 1 to admit as true (*conceding that we may be wrong*). 2 to give up (*conceded his right to a part of his father's estate*).

conceit' *n* 1 too high an opinion of oneself. 2 (*fml*) a fanciful or imaginative idea (*a poem full of conceits*).

conceit'ed *adj* too proud of oneself, vain (*so conceited that she couldn't imagine losing the contest*).

conceiv'able *adj* able to be thought of or imagined (*it was hardly conceivable that they were still alive*).

conceive' *vb* 1 to grasp clearly with the mind. 2 to imagine. 3 to become pregnant.

con'centrate *vb* 1 to bring together to one point. 2 to bring all the powers of the mind to bear on. 3 to make a substance stronger by reducing its volume. 4 to pack tightly:—*n* a concentrated substance:—*n* **concen-tra'tion**.

concen'tric *adj* having the same centre (*concentric circles*).

con'cept *n* a general idea (*scientific concepts*):—*adj* **conceptual**.

concep'tion *n* 1 act of conceiving. 2 an idea.

concern' *vb* 1 to have to do with (*the problem concerns all of us*). 2 to take interest (*concern themselves in other people's business*). 3 (*fml*) to be anxious about (*his absence concerned us*):—*n* 1 an affair (*his financial concerns*). 2 interest (*of little concern to other people*). 3 anxiety (*the invalid's condition giving cause for concern*). 4 a business (*a profitable concern*).

concern'ing *prep* having to do with, about (*problems concerning work*).

con'cert *n* a musical entertainment.

concert'ed *adj* planned together, worked out together (*a concerted effort*).

concerti'na *n* a musical wind instrument containing bellows, played by hand.

concerto [kon-tsher'-to] *n* a musical composition for a solo player accompanied by an orchestra.

conces'sion *n* 1 the action of giving up (*the concession of his claim to his father's estate*). 2 a thing conceded, a favour (*he always wore jeans, but as a concession to his mother he agreed to wear a suit to the dinner party*).

conch [kon(g)k] *n* a type of seashell.

concil'iate *vb* 1 (*fml*) to make less angry or more friendly (*try to conciliate her by bringing her some flowers*). 2 to create peace between (*conciliate the two parties in the dispute*).

concilia'tion *n* the bringing together in peace or friendship of those who have quarrelled (*attempts at conciliation between the two sides*).

concil'iatory *adj* calming, peace-making (*some conciliatory words*).

concise' *adj* short and to the point, brief (*a concise account of the events*):—*n* **con-cise'ness**.

con'clave *n* 1 the meeting of cardinals to choose a new pope. 2 a meeting held in private (*a meeting in conclave*).

conclude' *n* 1 (*fml*) to end, to bring to an end (*conclude the meeting*). 2 to arrange, to settle on (*concluding an agreement*). 3 to come to believe after consideration of the facts (*from the evidence we concluded that he was guilty*).

conclu'sion *n* 1 (*fml*) end (*at the conclusion of the meeting*). 2 the idea finally reached after thinking something out (*come to the conclusion that he was innocent*).

conclu'sive *adj* convincing, putting an end to doubt (*conclusive evidence*).

concoct' *vb* 1 to make by mixing (*concocting something for dinner*). 2 to make up, invent (*concocted an excuse for being late*).

concoc'tion *n* food or drink made by mixing several things.

concom'itant *adj* (*fml*) accompanying, going together (*an important job and its concomitant responsibilities*):—*also n*.

con'cord *n* (*fml*) 1 agreement (*little concord among the committee members*). 2 peace and friendship (*neighbouring countries living in concord*).

concord'ance *n* a book listing in alphabetical order all the words occurring in another book and exactly where they occur.

concor'dat *n* a treaty.

con'course *n* 1 a large open space for people (*the railway station concourse*). 2 (*fml*) a gathering, a crowd.

con'crete *adj* 1 solid, having a real bodily existence (unlike an idea) (*concrete evidence*).

2 definite (*no concrete plans*):—*n* a mixture of cement, sand and gravel with water.

concur' *vb* (**concur'red, concur'ring**) to agree (*we concurred with their plans*).

concur'rence *n* (*fml*) agreement (*the concurrence of their opinions*).

concur'rent *adj* happening at the same time (*current events/concurrent prison sentences*):—*adv* **concur'rently**.

concus'sion *n* a temporary injury caused to the brain by a violent blow on the head (*suffer concussion when he fell on the concrete floor*).

condemn' *vb* **1** to blame. **2** to find guilty. **3** to name a punishment for a guilty person:—*n* **condemna'tion**.

condem'natory *adj* laying the blame on.

condense' *vb* **1** to make shorter or smaller (*condense his original speech into a few sentences*). **2** to make a substance more solid (e.g. to change vapour into liquids):—*n* **condensa'tion**.

condescend' *vb* to agree to do something supposedly beneath one's dignity, usu in an ungracious, patronizing manner (*she condescended to speak to the workers*):—*adj* **condescend'ing**:—*n* **condescen'sion**.

con'diment *n* anything sharp-tasting eaten with food to bring out its flavour or taste (*salt and pepper and other condiments*).

condi'tion *n* **1** state (*furniture in poor condition/patients in no condition to be sent home*). **2** something that must be or happen before something else can take place (*a condition of the agreement/he can go on condition that he reports to the police*).

condi'tional *adj* depending on something else happening (*a conditional acceptance to university/an acceptance to university conditional on his passing his exams*).

condol'ence *n* (*often pl*) expression of sympathy (*express our condolences to the widow*).

condone' *vb* to forgive, to allow wrong to be done without making it known or punishing it (*condone his bad behaviour because of his unhappy home life*).

con'dor *n* a large vulture

conduc'ive *adj* helping to produce (*circumstances not conducive to good health*).

conduct' *vb* **1** to lead, to guide (*conduct us to our seats*). **2** to carry (*pipes conducting water*). **3** to direct (*conducted the orchestra*). **4** (*fml*) to behave (*conduct oneself well*):—*n* **con'duct** behaviour.

conduct'or *n* **1** the director of an orchestra. **2** the person who takes the fares on a bus. **3** a substance that passes on heat or electricity to something else:—*f* **conduct'ress**.

conduit [kon'-dit] *n* a pipe or channel made to carry water.

cone *n* **1** a figure with a circular base and a pointed top. **2** the fruit of pines and firs. **3** any object shaped like a cone (*an ice-cream cone*).

coney *see* **cony**.

confec'tionery *n* **1** cakes and sweets. **2** a shop selling confectionery.

confed'erate *adj* joined together by agreement (*confederate states*):—*n* a supporter, a helper, often in wrongdoing (*the bully and his confederates*).

confedera'tion *n* a group of states that have agreed to act together.

confer' *vb* (**conferred', confer'ring**) **1** to talk together (*conferring over the plans*). **2** to give (*confer an honour on him*).

con'ference *n* a meeting held to discuss matters (*an international conference on the environment*).

confess' *vb* **1** to own up, to admit (*confess to the crime/confess one's sins*). **2** to tell one's sins to a priest.

confes'sion *n* an account of the wrong one has done (*make a confession to the police*).

confes'sional *n* the box or small room in which a priest hears confessions.

confes'sor *n* a priest who hears confessions.

confet'ti *n* small pieces of coloured paper thrown at newly married people.

confidant' *n* a person trusted with a secret:—*f* **confidante'**.

confide' *vb* to give or tell something to a person one trusts (*confide her personal problems to a friend/confide in a friend*).

confid'ing *adj* trusting (*a confiding nature*).

con'fidence *n* **1** trust (*gain his confidence*). **2** belief in one's own abilities (*lose one's confidence*).

con'fident *adj* having no fear of failure (*confident competitors/confident of success*):—*adv* **con'fidently**.

confiden'tial *adj* **1** trusted (*a confidential secretary*). **2** secret (*confidential information*):—*adv* **confiden'tially**.

configura'tion n (fml) shape.

confine' vb 1 to shut up (confine prisoners in a cell). 2 to keep within limits (confine yourself to subjects that you know about):—n a limit, a boundary.

confine'ment n 1 imprisonment (sentenced to a confinement of 5 years). 2 childbirth.

confirm' vb 1 to say that something is undoubtedly certain or true (confirm her alibi). 2 to give final approval to (confirmed his appointment as governor).

confirma'tion n 1 proof (receive confirmation of his innocence). 2 the ceremony or sacrament by which one becomes a full member of certain churches.

confirmed' adj settled, habitual (a confirmed bachelor).

con'fiscate vb to seize a person's private property, esp as a punishment (customs officials confiscating illegal drugs/the teacher confiscated the sweets):—n **confisca'tion**.

conflagration n (fml) a great fire.

con'flict n 1 a state of disagreement (unions in conflict with management). 2 a fight (armed conflict):—vb **conflict'** to disagree, to clash (modern ideas that conflict with traditional ones).

conflict'ing adj 1 going against each other, fighting or quarrelling (on conflicting sides). 2 clashing, disagreeing (conflicting opinions).

con'fluence n 1 a flowing together. 2 the meeting of streams:—adj **con'fluent**.

conform' vb 1 to act or think like most other people, to accept the laws and customs of the time or place (people who want to rebel and don't want to conform). 2 to obey, to be in accordance with (conform to school rules/conform to safety standards).

conforma'tion n the way in which a thing is put together, shape (the conformation of the crystal).

conform'ity n 1 behaviour, attitudes, etc, that are the same as most people's. 2 agreement, obedience (in conformity with the law/not in conformity with safety standards).

confound' vb 1 to defeat completely. 2 to confuse. 3 to surprise.

confront' vb to meet face to face (confront the enemy/confront the problems):—n **con-fronta'tion**.

confuse' vb 1 to put into disorder, to muddle (confuse the arrangements/confuse the argument). 2 to puzzle, to bewilder (confused by the questions in the official form). 3 to mistake one person or thing for another (confuse the two sisters).

confu'sion n 1 disorder (a room in total confusion). 2 puzzlement, bewilderment (confusion over the meaning of the word).

confute' vb to prove (someone) wrong, to prove untrue (confute their argument/confute their accusation):—n **confuta'tion**.

congeal' vb 1 to freeze. 2 to become solid and stiff (blood congeals).

congen'ial adj 1 having the same likes and dislikes (a congenial companion). 2 pleasing (a congenial climate).

congen'ital adj dating from birth (a congenital brain defect).

conger [kon(g)'-gêr] n a sea eel.

congest'ed adj 1 overcrowded (congested roads). 2 too full of blood (congested arteries):—n **congest'ion**.

conglom'erate adj stuck together in a lump:—n 1 a rock of different kinds of pebbles sticking together. 2 a large corporation formed by merging several different firms (an international conglomerate).

conglomera'tion n a mixed collection (a conglomeration of old toys).

congrat'ulate vb to express pleasure at another's success, a happy event, etc (congratulate him on getting into the football team/congratulate him on his engagement:—n **congratula'tion**:—adj **congra'tulatory**.

con'gregate vb to meet together, to form a crowd (the villagers congregated in the church hall).

congrega'tion n a gathering of people, esp at a church service.

con'gress n 1 a formal meeting of statesmen, etc, to settle certain questions. 2 **Con'gress** the parliament of the USA:—adj **congres'sional**.

con'gruent adj suitable, agreeing, congruous (behaviour congruent with his position):—n **congru'ity**.

con'gruous adj suitable, congruent (punishment congruous with the crime).

con'ic, con'ical adjs cone-shaped.

con'ifer *n* a cone-bearing tree:—*adj* **conif'erous**.

conjec'tural *adj* due to guesswork, not certain (*opinions that are purely conjectural*).

conjec'ture *vb* to guess, to suppose:—*n* guess.

conjoin' *vb* (*fml*) to join together (*conjoin in marriage*).

conjoint' *adj* (*fml*) joined together, united:—*adv* **conjoint'ly**.

con'jugal *adj* having to do with marriage (*conjugal bonds*).

con'jugate *vb* to give the forms (i.e. mood, tense, person, etc) of a verb:—*n* **conju-ga'tion**.

conjunc'tion *n* **1** connection. **2** in grammar, a joining word:—*adj* **conjunc'tive**.

conjunc'ture *n* (*fml*) a combination of events or situations, esp one causing difficulties (*a depressing conjuncture in their lives*).

conjure [kun'-jêr] *vb* to do magic, to do tricks so quickly and skilfully that the onlooker cannot see how they are done.

con'jurer *n* one who entertains by doing tricks.

connect' *vb* **1** to join together (*connect the two pipes*). **2** to see that a thing or idea is related to another, to associate in the mind (*he didn't connect the middle-aged woman with the girl he used to know/the police are connecting the two murders*).—**well-connect'ed** related to important or powerful people.

connec'tion *n* **1** something that joins (*a loose connection between the two pipes*). **2** a relation by blood or marriage. **3** something that makes one think of a certain person, place, event, etc, when one sees another (*police making a connection between the crimes*).

connexion *same as* **connection**.

connive' *vb* to pretend not to see wrongdoing (*her parents connived at the girl's truancy*):—*n* **conni'vance**.

connoisseur [kon-ês-sèr'] *n* one with good knowledge of something and the ability to tell what is bad from what is good (*a connoisseur of wine/a connoisseur of opera*).

connota'tion *n* what is suggested by a word in addition to its actual meaning ('*armchair' has connotations of comfort*).

connote' *vb* to suggest in addition to the actual meaning (*the word 'plump' usually connotes cheerfulness*).

connu'bial *adj* (*fml*) having to do with marriage or married life (*connubial bliss*).

con'quer *vb* **1** to win by war (*conquer the neighbouring state*). **2** to defeat (*conquer the enemy/conquer his opponent*). **3** to overcome (*conquer her fears*):—*n* **con'queror**.

con'quest *n* **1** act of conquering. **2** the thing gained by force.

consanguin'ity *n* blood relationship.

con'science *n* one's sense of right and wrong (*have a bad conscience about her treatment of her friend*).

conscien'tious *adj* careful to do one's duty at work (*conscientious pupils*):—*n* **con-scien'tiousness**.

conscientious objector *n* one who, in war, refuses to fight because he or she believes it is wrong to do so.

con'scious *adj* **1** knowing what is going on around one (*badly hurt but still conscious*). **2** aware (*conscious that he was being watched*):—*n* **con'sciousness**.

con'script *n* one made by law to serve in the armed services.

conscrip'tion *n* act of making people serve in the armed services by law.

con'secrate *vb* **1** to make holy, to offer to God (*consecrate a new church*). **2** to devote, to set apart (*consecrate his life to helping others*):—*n* **consecra'tion**.

consec'utive *adj* following one after the other, in the correct order (*consecutive numbers/on consecutive days*).

consen'sus *n* general agreement (*fail to reach a consensus on the issue*).

consent' *vb* to agree, to give one's permission (*to consent to the operation*):—*n* agreement, permission.

con'sequence *n* **1** a result, an effect (*have to face the consequences of their actions*). **2** importance (*matters of no consequence*).

con'sequent *adj* (*fml*) following, resulting (*his illness and consequent death*).

consequen'tial *adj* **1** following upon. **2** self-important.

conser'vatism *n* dislike of changes, esp in the way of governing.

conser'vative *adj* disliking change:—*n* a member of a British political party.

conservatoire [kon-ser-vê-twär'] *n* a school of music.

conser'vatory *n* a glasshouse for plants, a greenhouse.

conserve' *vb* 1 to keep (something) as it is (*conserving the environment*). 2 to keep from being wasted (*conserved our supplies*):—*n* a fruit preserved in sugar, jam:—*n* **conserva'tion**.

consid'er *vb* 1 to think about (*consider what's best to do*). 2 to think seriously (*take time to consider before acting*). 3 to take into account (*consider the effect on others*). 4 to regard as (*considered him a hero*).

consid'erable *adj* fairly large, great (*a considerable amount of money/considerable influence*).

consid'erate *adj* thoughtful for others.

considera'tion *n* 1 serious thought (*give consideration to her future*). 2 thought for others and their feelings (*show consideration to elderly people*). 3 a payment or reward (*do the work for a consideration*).

consid'ering *prep* allowing for.

consign' *vb* (*fml*) 1 to deliver to, to put in (*consign the body to the grave*). 2 to send (*goods consigned to you by rail*).

consign'ment *n* the goods sent (*a consignment of drugs found by police*).

consist' *vb* to be made up of (*a stew that consists of lamb and vegetables*).

consist'ency *n* 1 degree of thickness (*the consistency of the jam*). 2 the quality of being consistent.

consist'ent *adj* 1 fixed, having a regular pattern (*show consistent improvement*). 2 agreeing with (*action consistent with the company's policy/a statement not consistent with the previous one*). 3 always thinking or acting on the same principles (*the judge's punishments are harsh but he is always consistent*).

consola'tion *n* 1 comfort (*bring consolation to the bereaved*). 2 a person or thing that brings comfort in sorrow or sadness (*the new baby was a consolation to the unhappy family*).

console' *vb* to comfort in sorrow (*consoling the unhappy little girl with some sweets*):—*adj* **consol'atory**.

consol'idate *vb* 1 to make solid or firm, to strengthen (*consolidating your present position*). 2 to unite or combine (*consolidated four small firms into one large one*):—*n* **consolida'tion**.

con'sonance *n* (*fml*) agreement.

con'sonant *n* a speech sound or letter other than a vowel:—*adj* in agreement with.

con'sort *n* a partner, a husband or wife (*the queen's consort*):—*vb* **consort'** (*fml*) to go about together, to associate with (*object to his daughter consorting with criminals*).

conspic'uous *adj* easily seen, very noticeable (*a conspicuous sight in her red coat*).

conspir'acy *n* 1 a coming together to plan wrongdoing (*arrested on charges of conspiracy*). 2 a plot (*discover the conspiracy to kill the king*).

conspire' *vb* 1 to plan secretly together to do something unlawful (*terrorists conspiring to bring down the government*). 2 to unite (*events that conspired to bring about his ruin*):—*n* **conspir'ator**.

con'stable *n* a policeman.

constab'ulary *n* the police force.

con'stant *adj* 1 never stopping (*constant noise/constant rain*). 2 unchanging (*temperatures at a constant level*). 3 (*fml*) faithful, loyal (*friends for ever constant*):—*n* **con'stancy**.

con'stantly *adv* 1 again and again, nearly always, regularly (*children constantly nagging*). 2 without stopping (*lights burning constantly*).

constella'tion *n* a group of stars.

consterna'tion *n* great surprise, dismay (*to our great consternation our team lost*).

con'stipated *adj* having difficulty in clearing the bowels:—*n* **constipa'tion**.

constit'uency *n* the people of a district who elect a member of parliament.

constit'uent *adj* being part of, forming (*the constituent parts of the machine*):—*n* 1 a necessary part (*a constituent of the chemical compound*). 2 a member of a constituency (*a meeting of the MP's constituents*).

con'stitute *vb* 1 (*fml*) to be (*his dismissal constitutes a breach of the rules*). 2 to make up, to form (*twelve months constitute a year/five people constitute the committee*).

constitu'tion *n* 1 the way something is made up (*the constitution of the committee*). 2 the general health of the body (*have a strong constitution*). 3 the body of law in keeping with which a country is governed.

constitu'tional *adj* having to do with the laws of a country:—*n* (*old or hum*) a short walk taken to improve the health.

constrain' *vb* to force, to compel (*you must not feel constrained to go/I feel constrained to write and complain*).

constraint' *n* 1 force, compulsion (*leave only under constraint*). 2 a limit or restriction (*no constraints on your freedom*). 3 strained manner, lack of friendliness (*aware of a certain constraint between husband and wife*).

constrict' *vb* 1 to make smaller or narrower, to make tight (*a drug constricting blood vessels*). 2 to prevent free movement (*constricted by lack of money*):—*n* **con-stric'tion**.

constric'tor *n* a large snake that crushes its prey.

construct' *vb* 1 to build (*construct a new block of flats*). 2 to make by putting the parts together (*construct a theory*).

construc'tion *n* 1 act of constructing. 2 the thing constructed (*a large construction*). 3 the way of arranging words to give a certain meaning. 4 (*fml*) meaning (*what construction do you put on his statement?*).

construc'tive *adj* useful and helpful (*constructive criticism*).

construe' *vb* 1 to translate into another language. 2 to explain, to interpret (*construing his remark as an insult*).

con'sul *n* 1 a person appointed to look after the interests of his own country in a foreign country. 2 one of the two chief magistrates of ancient Rome.

con'sular *adj* having to do with a consul.

con'sulate *n* the office of a consul.

consult' *vb* 1 to ask advice, information or help from (*consult a doctor*). 2 to discuss matters with (*consult his partners*). 3 to look up (*consult a dictionary*):—*n* **consul-ta'tion**.

consul'tant *n* one able to advise, esp a doctor who is an expert in one branch of medicine (*a chest consultant*).

consume' *vb* 1 to eat (*consume quantities of chocolate*). 2 to use up (*consume our supply of firewood*). 3 to destroy, to waste (*a building consumed by fire*).

consum'er *n* one who buys or uses (*consumers' rights*).

con'summate *vb* to finish, to make complete or perfect (*the award consummated his life's work*):—*adj* complete, perfect (*a consummate performance*):—*n* **consumma'tion**.

consump'tion *n* 1 the act of using. 2 the amount used (*a low electricity consumption*). 3 (*old*) a disease of the lungs (tuberculosis).

consump'tive *adj* suffering from the disease of consumption:—*also n.*

con'tact *n* 1 touch (*eyes that had come into contact with dangerous chemicals/in contact with someone with measles*). 2 communication (*keep in contact with old friends*):—*vb* to get in touch with, to communicate with (*contact her by phone*).

contact lens *n* a small round piece of thin plastic or glass placed on the front of the eye to make the wearer see better.

contag'ious *adj* (*of disease*) able to be passed on by touch, quickly spreading to others:—*n* **contag'ion.**

contain' *vb* 1 to have in it (*a bucket containing a gallon of water*). 2 to keep control of (*contain the fire*).

contain'er *n* anything made in order to hold something else in it (*a plant container*).

contam'inate *vb* to make dirty, infected or impure, to pollute (*chemical waste contaminating the water*):—*n* **contamina'tion.**

contemn' *vb* (*old or lit*) to look down on, to despise.

con'template *vb* 1 to look at thoughtfully (*contemplating the bottom of his glass*). 2 to think deeply about (*contemplated her future with gloom*). 3 to think of doing (*contemplate emigrating*):—*n* **contempla'tion.**

contemplative [kon'- *or* kon-tem'-] *adj* 1 thoughtful (*in contemplative mood*). 2 spending much time in prayer.

contempora'neous *adj* (*fml*) existing or happening at the same time (*contemporaneous events*).

contem'porary *adj* 1 belonging to the same time (*contemporary musicians/a contemporary record of the war*). 2 modern (*contemporary styles*):—*n* one who lives at the same time as another (*a contemporary of Bach*).

contempt' *n* the feeling that another person or thing is worthless and to be looked down on, scorn (*the wealthy businessman's contempt for unsuccessful people*).

contemp'tible *adj* deserving to be looked down on (*contemptible behaviour*).

contemp'tuous *adj* showing contempt or scorn (*a contemptuous smile*).

contend' *vb* **1** to struggle against (*contend against financial difficulties*). **2** to compete (*contending for the trophy*). **3** to maintain, to state (*contended that he was innocent*):—*n* **contend'er**.

con'tent' *n* that which is in something else (*the content of his speech*).

content² *adj* satisfied, pleased, not wanting more than one has (*content with their humble way of life/content with his exam results*):—*also vb and n*:—*n* **content'ment**.

conten'tion *n* **1** disagreement, dispute (*much contention in the town about the new road*). **2** competition (*in contention for the trophy*). **3** an opinion (*his contention is that he is innocent*).

conten'tious *adj* quarrelsome (*contentious neighbours*).

contest' *vb* **1** to try to prove wrong (*contest their accusation of theft*). **2** to try hard to gain (*contest the boxing title*):—*n* **con'test 1** a struggle (*a contest for promotion*). **2** a competition (*an athletics contest*).

contes'tant *n* one who contests (*the contestants in the TV quiz show*).

con'text *n* **1** the part of a book from which a shorter passage has been taken. **2** circumstances, surrounding conditions (*in the context of his unhappy childhood*).

contig'uous *adj* (*fml*) touching, next to, neighbouring (*his farm and contiguous farms*):—*n* **contigu'ity**.

con'tinence *n* self-control.

con'tinent¹ *adj* able to control oneself, esp one's bladder and bowels.

con'tinent² *n* one of the large land masses in the world (e.g. Africa):—**the Continent** Europe.

continent'al *adj* having to do with a continent, esp Europe (*continental travel*).

contin'gency *n* something that may happen but is not certain to do so (*prepared for all possible contingencies*).

contin'gent *adj* **1** happening only if something else happens first (*success contingent upon hard work*). **2** accidental (*contingent advantages*):—*n* a body of soldiers, scouts, etc.

contin'ual *adj* **1** going on all the time (*live in continual fear*). **2** happening again and again, repeated (*continual interruptions*).

contin'uance *n* the going on or lasting of.

continua'tion *n* **1** act of going on or carrying on. **2** something that continues from something else (*this is a continuation of the street where they live*).

contin'ue *vb* **1** to go on doing (*continue working although in pain*). **2** to carry on with later (*continue with his work after dinner*). **3** to go or move further (*the forest continuing as far as one can see*). **4** to remain (*continued in the same job*).

continu'ity *n* uninterrupted connection, the fact or quality of being continuous (*ensure continuity of supplies*).

contin'uous *adj* **1** never stopping (*continuous noise*). **2** unbroken (*a continuous line*).

contort' *vb* to twist out of shape (*his face contorted in rage*).

contor'tion *n* **1** act of twisting. **2** a twisting of the body.

contor'tionist *n* one who entertains people by twisting his or her body into strange shapes, an acrobat.

con'tour *n* **1** an outline, a shape (*the smooth contours of the piece of sculpture*). **2** a line drawn on a map through all places of the same height.

con'traband *n* **1** goods that it is forbidden by law to bring into the country. **2** goods brought into the country against the law:—*adj* (*of goods*) forbidden by law.

contract' *vb* **1** to arrange by agreement (*contract an alliance/contract to build the house*). **2** to make or become smaller or shorter (*metals contract as they cool*). **3** to begin to have (*contract a fatal illness*):—*n* **con'tract** a legal written agreement (*sign a contract*).

contrac'tion *n* **1** something becoming smaller or shorter. **2** a shortened form ('*I'm*' *is a contraction of* '*I am*').

contrac'tor *n* one who undertakes to do certain jobs (*a building contractor*).

contradict' vb **1** to say the opposite (*his story contradicts hers*). **2** to say that something is not true (*she contradicted what he said about the accident*):—n **contradic'tion**.

contradic'tory adj saying the opposite (*contradictory statements*).

contral'to n the deepest singing voice of a woman.

contrap'tion n an unusual machine or instrument (*an inventor always building strange contraptions*).

contrari'ety, contra'riness ns opposition.

contrary [kon'-tra-ri or kon-trä'-ri] adj **1** opposite (*hold contrary opinions/opinions contrary to ours*). **2** always choosing to act differently from others, difficult to deal with:—n **con'trary** the opposite (*on the contrary*).

contrast' vb **1** to put things together to show clearly the differences between them (*contrast their neat garden with our untidy one*). **2** to appear very different from (*a black dress contrasting with her blonde hair*):—n **con'trast** a clear difference.

contravene' vb to break (a law):—n **contra-ven'tion**.

contrib'ute vb **1** to give part of what is needed (*contributing to her leaving present/contributed £20 to the charity*). **2** to write something for (*contribute several articles to the magazine*):—n **contri-bu'tion**:—n **contrib'utor**.

contrib'utory adj giving a share, helping.

con'trite adj showing or feeling guilt or sorrow (*a contrite apology*):—n **contri'tion**.

contri'vance n **1** act of contriving. **2** an invention, an apparatus (*a contrivance for opening gates automatically*).

contrive' vb **1** to succeed in, usu with difficulty (*contriving to hold a surprise party for her*). **2** to succeed in bringing about, usu with difficulty (*contrived a meeting between the two rivals*).

control' n **1** power over the movements and actions of another person or thing (*a country under the control of a tyrant*). **2** power over one's own thoughts and feelings (*esp self-control*) (*keep her temper under control*). **3** pl those parts of a machine that start, stop or change the movement of all other parts (*the controls of the plane*):—vb (**controlled'**, **control'ling**) **1** to have power or authority over (*controlled the whole department*). **2** to direct the movements of (*con-*

trol the car). **3** to hold back, to restrain (*control yourself*). **4** to regulate, to cause to keep to a fixed standard (*control prices*):—n **control'ler**.

control tower n an airport building from which messages are sent by radio to aircraft, telling them when and how it is safe to land or take off.

controver'sial adj causing controversy (*a controversial decision*).

con'troversy n disagreement, dispute (*much controversy over the council's decision to close the local school*).

con'trovert vb to deny the truth of (*a statement that cannot be controverted*).

contuma'cious adj (*fml*) openly unwilling to obey, stubborn:—ns **con'tumacy, con-tuma'ciousness**.

contume'lious adj (*fml*) proud and scornful.

con'tumely n (*fml*) insulting language or treatment (*treat people of other races with contumely*).

contuse' vb (*fml*) to bruise (*the boxer's face contused by punches*).

contu'sion n (*fml*) a bad bruise.

conun'drum n a riddle.

convalesce' vb to recover gradually after an illness (*home from hospital to convalesce*):—n **convales'cence**:—adj and n **convales'cent**.

convec'tion n warming by the spreading of heat from a portion of water or air to that surrounding it until a current of warmth is set up.

convec'tor n a heater that works by convection.

convene' vb **1** to call together (*convened a meeting*). **2** to meet (*the committee convening for an emergency meeting*).

conven'er n **1** one who calls members to a meeting. **2** the chairman of a committee.

conven'ience n **1** quality of being convenient (*come at your convenience/the convenience of the house to the station/the convenience of her kitchen*). **2** comfort (*a house full of modern conveniences*).

conven'ient adj **1** suitable, not causing trouble or difficulty (*find a convenient date/when it is convenient to you*). **2** easy to reach, accessible (*a house convenient for the railway station*). **3** easy to use or manage (*a convenient size of house*).

con'vent n a house of nuns:—adj **con-ven'tual**.

conven'ticle n a secret religious meeting.

conven'tion n **1** a large meeting called for a special purpose (*a convention on mental health*). **2** an agreement (*a convention to ban nuclear* *weapons*). **3** a way of behaving that has been in use for so long that it is regarded as necessary, a custom (*a common convention when meeting someone new is to shake hands/a matter of convention*).

conven'tional *adj* **1** following convention (*a conventional way of behaving*). **2** accepting the manners and ideas of others, not original (*a very conventional person*).

converge' *vb* to move from different directions towards one point (*converging on the town from all directions*):—*n* conver'gence:—*adj* conver'gent.

convers'ant *adj* having knowledge of (*not conversant with modern methods*).

conversa'tion *n* talk, speech with others.

conversa'tional *adj* having to do with conversation (*in conversational tones*).

conversa'tionalist *n* one who is good at talking easily with others.

converse'¹ *vb* (*fml*) to talk.

con'verse² *n* the exact opposite (*the converse of what he says is true*):—*also adj*.

con'verse'ly *adv* looked at in the opposite way.

conver'sion *n* a change, esp in belief or way of life (*his conversion to Christianity*).

convert' *vb* **1** to change from one state or form to another (*coal converted to gas/a sofa that converts to a bed/convert dollars to sterling*). **2** to get another to change his or her ideas, esp on religion:—*n* **con'vert** one who has changed his or her beliefs or way of life.

convert'ible *adj* able to be changed into something else (*a sofa convertible to a bed/a convertible sofa*).

con'vex *adj* curved outwards (like a saucer when upside down):—*n* convex'ity.

convey' *vb* **1** to carry, to take from one place to another (*pipes conveying oil/buses conveying children/lorries conveying food*). **2** to pass (e.g. property) from one person to another. **3** to make known (*convey our apologies to our hostess*).

convey'ance *n* **1** any kind of vehicle that carries people or things (*go by public conveyance rather than private car*). **2** the document by which property is passed from one person to another.

convey'ancing *n* the preparing of the papers to make a change in ownership lawful.

convict' *vb* to prove guilty, esp in a court of law (*convict him of robbery with violence*):—*n* **con'vict** a person imprisoned for a crime.

convic'tion *n* **1** a proving guilty (*the conviction of the accused*). **2** a strong belief (*a woman of strong convictions/deep, religious conviction*).

convince' *vb* to persuade a person that something is true (*convincing the teacher of his innocence/I am convinced he is lying*).

convinc'ing *adj* **1** able to convince (*a convincing argument*). **2** clear (*a convincing victory*).

conviv'ial *adj* fond of good company, cheerful:—*n* conviviality.

convoca'tion *n* a meeting, esp of clergy.

convoke' *vb* to call together.

convolu'tion *n* **1** a twist (*a carving with curves and convolutions*). **2** complication (*the convolutions of the plot*).

convol'vulus *n* a kind of climbing plant.

convoy' *vb* to go with to protect (*a warship convoying ships across the Atlantic/parents convoying children to and from school*):—*n* **con'voy** **1** warships accompanying other ships to protect them. **2** the ships so protected. **3** a number of army wagons travelling together for protection.

convulse' *vb* **1** to shake violently (*convulsing with laughter*). **1** to agitate, to disturb (*a country convulsed with revolution*).

convul'sion *n* a fit, shaking (*go into convulsions/suffer from convulsions*).

convul'sive *adj* sudden and jerky (*convulsive movements*).

con'y, con'ey *n* (*pl* con'ies) **1** a rabbit. **2** a rabbit-skin.

coo *vb* to make a sound, as a dove:—*also n*.

cook *vb* to prepare food by heating it:—*n* one who prepares food for eating.

cook'ery *n* the art of preparing food.

cook'ie *n* **1** a small bun. **2** (*Amer*) a biscuit.

cool *adj* **1** slightly cold, pleasantly cool (*a long cool drink*). **2** calm, not easily excited (*keep cool in difficult situations*):—*vb* **1** to make or become colder (*drinks cooling in the fridge*). **2** to become calmer or less keen (*she was very angry but she's cooled down/he was in love with her but he's cooled off*):—*n* **cool'ness**.

cool'ly *adv* calmly, without excitement

coop n a cage for hens or small animals (a chicken coop):—vb to shut up in a small space (cooped up in a small airless office).

coop'er n one who makes barrels.

coop'erate, co-op'erate vb to work or act together (pupils cooperating on a project/the public co-operating with the police):—n coopera'tion, co-opera'tion.

coop'erative, co-op'erative adj 1 willing to work with others, helpful (the cooperative attitude of the staff). 2 made, done, etc, by people working together (a cooperative effort/a cooperative farm).

co-operative society n a society, open to everyone, that opens shops and divides the profits among its members.

co-opt' vb to elect into a society or committee by the votes of the members.

coor'dinate, co-or'dinate vb to make things work or happen together for the same purpose (co-ordinate her movements/coordinate the various parts of the campaign/coordinate our efforts):—npl coor'dinates figures that indicate a position on a map or squared paper:—n coordina'tion, co-ordina'tion.

coot n a water bird.

co'pal n a gum out of which varnish is made.

cope[1] n a cloak-like garment worn by a clergyman on certain occasions.

cope[2] vb to deal with, esp successfully (coping with tired children/single mothers finding it difficult to cope/unable to cope with his work).

cop'ing n the top row of stones on a wall.

cop'ing stone n a top stone, sloping down to let the rain run off.

co'pious adj plentiful (copious supplies of food).

cop'per n 1 a reddish metal. 2 (old) a penny or halfpenny. 3 a large boiler of copper.

cop'perplate n 1 large, clear handwriting. 2 a plate of copper on which something has been engraved. 3 a print made from it.

cop'pice, copse ns a small wood, a group of bushes growing close together.

cop'ra n the dried inside of the coconut.

copse see coppice.

cop'y n 1 a thing done or made in exactly the same way as another (keep a copy of the letter/this picture's not by Picasso—it's a copy). 2 a single example of a newspaper, magazine, book, etc

(order several copies of the book). 3 written material given to the printer for printing:—vb to imitate, to make a copy of.

cop'yright n the right, given to one person or publisher only, to print and sell books, music or pictures for a certain number of years.

coquette' n a woman who flirts.

coquet'tish adj intended to attract attention from men (a coquettish glance).

cor'acle n a boat made of basketwork covered with skins.

cor'al n a rock-like material built up under the sea from the skeletons of tiny creatures (polyps).

cord n 1 a thin rope, a thick string (tie the box up with cord). 2 a length of electrical cable or flex attached to an electrical apparatus. 3 a part of the body resembling this (the spinal cord/vocal cords).

cord'age n a number of ropes, esp those in the rigging of a ship.

cor'dial adj 1 very friendly (a cordial welcome). 2 heartfelt (cordial thanks):—n a refreshing drink.

cordial'ity n friendliness (greet his guests with great cordiality).

cor'dite n a smokeless explosive used instead of gunpowder.

cor'don n a line of soldiers, police, etc, to prevent people from entering an area (crowds kept back from the accident by a police cordon):—vb to surround with a cordon (police cordoned off the area and the house held by the gunman).

cor'duroy n a strong cotton cloth with raised cord-like lines running from one end to the other (trousers made of brown corduroy).

core n 1 the central part of a fruit in which the seeds are stored (apple core). 2 the innermost part, the most important part (the core of the problem).

cork n 1 the cork tree or its bark. 2 a stopper made from cork (the cork from a wine bottle):—vb to stop a bottle with a cork.

cork'screw n an instrument for taking the cork out of a bottle.

cor'morant n 1 a large greedy sea bird. 2 (inf) a greedy person.

corn[1] n 1 a grain-bearing plant, as wheat, oats, etc. 2 the seeds of cereal plants, (esp in Britain) wheat, (*Amer*) maize:—*vb* to put salt on to pre-serve (*corned beef*).

corn² *n* a hard painful growth on the toe or foot.

corn'cob *n* a head of maize.

corn'crake *n* a bird that nests in cornfields.

cor'nea *n* the transparent covering of the eyeball.

cor'ner *n* 1 the meeting place of two walls (*a table standing in the corner*). 2 a bend in a road (*the car took the corner too quickly*). 3 a difficult position (*he is in a tight corner financially*):—*vb* 1 to drive into a position from which there is no escape (*cornered the wild animal and shot it/police succeeded in cornering the escaped prisoner*). 2 to put into a difficult situation (*corner the politician by asking awkward questions*). 3 to gain sole control of (*corner the market in pine furniture*).

cor'nerstone *n* 1 a stone put at the corner of the foundations of a new building. 2 something very important, something on which everything is based (*the cornerstone of the firm's success*).

cor'net *n* a type of trumpet.

corn'flour *n* flour made from maize (*thicken the sauce with cornflour*).

corn'flower *n* a blue flower.

cornice [kor'-nis] *n* 1 a plaster decoration running round the top of the wall of a room (*a cornice of flowers*). 2 an ornamental line of stone sticking out at the top of the wall of a building.

corol'la *n* the petals of a flower.

corol'lary *n* something that must be true if another thing is proved true.

corona'tion *n* the crowning of a king or queen.

cor'oner *n* an officer of the law who holds an inquiry in the case of sudden or violent death (*a case sent to the coroner*).

cor'onet *n* a small crown (*brides wearing coronets of flowers*).

cor'poral¹ *adj* (*fml*) having to do with the body (*corporal punishment*).

cor'poral² *n* the lowest noncommissioned officer in the army.

corporal punishment *n* punishing by beating the body.

cor'porate *adj* 1 forming one group (*several individual colleagues forming a corporate body*). 2 of or shared by all the members of a group (*corporate responsibility*):—*adv* cor'porately.

corpora'tion *n* 1 a group of people allowed by the law to act as one person in certain cases (e.g. in business matters) (*the British Broadcasting Corporation*). 2 (*inf*) fatness in the middle of the body (*get a corporation in middle age*).

corporeal [kor-pō'-ri-êl] *adj* (*fml*) 1 having to do with the body but not the spirit (*corporeal needs such as food*). 2 material, not spiritual (*the corporeal world*).

corps [kôr or kâr] *n* 1 a large body of soldiers, a division of an army. 2 a group of people working together for one purpose (*the Diplomatic Corps*).

corpse *n* the dead body of a human being.

cor'pulent *adj* (*fml*) fat, stout (*Father Christmas, corpulent and jolly*):—*n* cor'pulence.

corpus'cle *n* a tiny body, esp one of those making up a large part of the blood of human beings and animals (*red and white corpuscles*):—*adj* corpus'cular.

corral' *n* an enclosure for horses or cattle.

correct¹ *adj* right, having no mistakes (*the correct spelling*):—*vb* 1 to set right, to remove mistakes from (*correct her spelling*). 2 to point out or mark mistakes (*corrected the pupil's homework*):—*n* correct'ness.

correc'tion *n* 1 act of correcting. 2 the right thing put in place of a mistake (*write corrections in red*). 3 (*old or fml*) punishment (*a house of correction*).

correc'tive *adj* putting right or improving what is wrong (*corrective treatment/corrective punishment*):—*also n*.

cor'relate *vb* to show the connection between two or more things (*medical researchers correlating old age with certain illnesses*).

correla'tion *n* connection (*a correlation between ill health and poverty*).

correspond' *vb* 1 to write letters to (*correspond with a friend overseas*). 2 to fit in with, to agree with (*your written statement does not correspond with your spoken one*). 3 to be like, to be the equivalent of (*the elephant's trunk corresponding to the human nose*).

correspond'ence *n* 1 all the letters a person or office sends or receives. 2 likeness.

correspond'ent *n* 1 one who writes letters to another (*the two old friends have been correspond-*

ents for many years). **2** one who sends special reports to a newspaper (*a foreign correspondent*).

correspond'ing *adj* like or similar.

cor'ridor *n* an indoor passage (*several doors leading off the hotel corridor*).

corrob'orate *vb* to support or confirm the story or idea of another (*a statement corroborating other evidence*):—*n* **corrobora'tion**:—*adj* **corrob'orative**.

corrode' *vb* to eat or wear away slowly (*rust corroding the metal*):—*n* **corro'sion**.

corro'sive *adj* able to eat away (*acids are corrosive substances*):—also *n*.

corrugated iron *n* sheets of iron with an uneven wavy surface.

corrupt' *vb* to make or become evil or morally bad (*young people corrupted by drug-dealers*):—*adj* **1** evil (*corrupt drug-dealers*). **2** ready to act dishonestly for money (*corrupt officials accepting bribes*):—*n* **corrup'tion**:—*adv* **corrupt'ly**.

cor'sair *n* **1** a pirate. **2** a pirate ship.

cor'set *n* a stiff tight-fitting undergarment (*corsets worn by women to make them look slimmer/corsets worn by people with back problems*).

cortege [kor-tezh'] *n* a procession, as at a funeral.

corvette' *n* a small fast warship.

cosmet'ic *n* something used to make the face and hair more beautiful (*cosmetics such as lipstick and blusher*):—*adj* **1** intended to improve the appearance (*cosmetic preparations/cosmetic surgery following a car accident*). **2** dealing only with outside appearances (*cosmetic changes to the law*).

cos'mic *adj* **1** having to do with the universe. **2** (*inf*) very great (*changes of cosmic proportions*).

cosmol'ogy *n* the study of the universe as a whole.

cosmopol'itan *adj* **1** consisting of people from many different parts of the world (*a cosmopolitan city*). **2** having or showing wide experience of different people and places (*a cosmopolitan attitude*).

cos'mos *n* the whole universe (*all the planets in the cosmos*).

cos'set *vb* to treat with great or too much kindness, to pamper (*cosseting her by giving her breakfast in bed*).

cost *vb* (*pt*, *pp* **cost**) **1** to be on sale at a certain price (*apples costing 20 pence each*). **2** to cause loss or suffering (*the battle cost many lives*):—*n* **1** the price (*the cost of the house*). **2** loss (*at the cost of many lives*). **3** *pl* the money needed to pay for a lawsuit (*lose the case and have to pay costs*).

cos'ter, cos'termonger *n* a street seller of fruit and vegetables.

cost'ly *adj* having a high price, dear (*costly silk clothes*).

cos'tume *n* **1** the clothes worn in a special place or at a special time (*bathing costume/in Victorian costume*). **2** a woman's jacket and skirt, a suit.

costum'ier *n* a maker or seller of costumes.

co'sy *adj* pleasantly comfortable or warm (*a cosy room/cosy pyjamas*):—*n* a teapot or egg cover:—*adv* **co'sily**.

cot *n* **1** a small bed with movable sides for a child. **2** (*old*) a small house.

cot'erie *n* a small group of people with shared interests who wish to exclude other people (*a coterie of people art lovers*).

cotillion [ko-til'-yon], **cotillon** [co-tee'-yo(ng)] *n* a lively dance.

cot'tage *n* a small house:—*n* **cot'tager**.

cot'ton *n* **1** a soft white substance got from the cotton plant. **2** thread or cloth made of cotton:—also *adj*.

cot'tonwool *n* cotton before it is made into thread or cloth (*wipe the wound with cottonwool*).

cotyledon [ko-ti-lee'-dèn] *n* the seed leaf of a plant.

couch *vb* (*fml*) to put into words (*couch his statement in simple words*):—*n* a sofa, something on which one lies.

couchant [kö-shênt] *adj* (*of an animal*) lying on all four paws (*a statue of a lion couchant*).

cou'gar *n* the puma, a wild animal of the cat family.

cough [kof] *vb* to force air noisily from the throat, often to clear it of some matter or phlegm:—*n* **1** a noisy forcing of the air from the throat. **2** an illness marked by frequent coughing (*have a bad cough*).

coun'cil *n* a number of people chosen to make decisions for a larger number (*town council*).

coun'cillor *n* a member of a council.

coun'sel n 1 (fml) advice (refuse to listen to his father's counsel). 2 professional advice given by a counsellor (debt counsel). 3 the lawyer who presents a case in a law court:—vb (**coun'selled**) to advise.

counselling n the act of listening to people's difficulties or problems and giving professional advice as to how to cope with them or solve them (They were given counselling after being held hostage).

coun'sellor n an adviser, one who gives (professional) advice on a variety of personal problems (a marriage guidance counsellor).

count¹ vb 1 to number (count the people as they enter). 2 to consider (count him among her friends). 3 to matter (money doesn't count with her):—n a numbering (a count of the votes).

count² n a foreign nobleman.

coun'tenance n (fml) 1 the face (a beautiful countenance). 2 the expression of the face (a fierce countenance):—vb (fml) to tolerate, to allow (refuse to countenance such behaviour).

coun'ter n 1 a person or thing that counts (the counters of votes at elections). 2 a small flat object used in some games instead of money. 3 the table in a shop across which goods are sold:—vb to act in order to oppose or defend onself against (counter the enemy attack by bringing in more soldiers).

coun'ter- prefix against, opposite to.

counteract' vb to undo or prevent the effect of by opposite action (a drug that counteracts the effect of the poison).

count'erattack n an attack made in reply to an enemy attack:—also vb.

coun'ter-attraction n something that attracts away from something else (the live theatre faces the counter-attractions of television and the cinema).

counterbal'ance vb to put something of equal weight or importance on the other side (the expense of the project is counterbalanced by its usefulness).

coun'terblast n a strong statement of the case against (write a counterblast to her critics).

coun'terclaim n a request made in reply to a request for something else by another (she claimed against his insurance for car damage and he issued a counterclaim).

counterfeit [koun'-têr-feet] vb 1 to copy or imitate in order to deceive (accused of counterfeiting twenty-pound notes). 2 (fml) to pretend (counterfeit cheerfulness):—adj 1 not real. 2 made like in order to deceive. 3 pretended:—n something copied, not real or true:—n **coun'terfeiter**.

coun'terfoil n the part of a (postal order, cheque, receipt, ticket, etc) kept by the giver or sender.

countermand' vb to withdraw an order or give an opposite order to replace it.

coun'terpane n a cover for a bed.

coun'terpart n a person or thing almost exactly the same as another (his counterpart in the opposing team).

coun'terpoint n (mus) the art of arranging two tunes so that they can be played together.

coun'ter-revolu'tion n an attempt to undo the work of an earlier revolution:—adj and n **coun'ter-revolu'tionary**.

coun'tersign vb to sign in addition to another to show that his or her name is properly signed (a cheque countersigned on the back).

coun'tess n the wife of a count or of an earl.

count'less adj too many to be counted (countless visitors).

coun'try n 1 the land of one nation or people. 2 the land outside and away from towns (a quiet holiday in a cottage in the country). 3 an area or stretch of land (hilly country):—adj having to do with the country rather than the town (country districts).

coun'tryman n 1 one living away from towns (countrymen who go to the market in town). 2 one belonging to the same nation (meet a fellow countryman in a foreign country).

coun'tryside n country areas (paint pictures of the English countryside/admire the beauty of the countryside).

coun'ty n a part of a country, operated for administrative purposes.

coup [kö] n a sudden successful action (pull off a coup by taking business away from their competitors).

coupé [kö-pâ'] n a covered two-seater motor car or carriage.

couple [kup'-êl] n 1 (inf) two. 2 a man and his wife:—vb 1 to join (coupling the carriage to the *train/bad weather coupled with illness kept many people away*). **2** to link or associate with (*their names have been coupled*).

coup'let *n* two lines of poetry, one after the other, that rhyme.

coup'ling *n* a joining link, as that between two railway carriages.

cou'pon *n* **1** a ticket that can be exchanged for money or goods. **2** an entry form (*fill in a coupon to try to win a holiday*).

cour'age *n* bravery.

coura'geous *adj* brave, fearless.

courgette' [kürjet'] *n* a type of long vegetable of the marrow family with dark green skin and white flesh, also called **zucchini**.

cour'ier *n* **1** a messenger (*packages delivered by courier*). **2** a guide in charge of a party of travellers.

course *n* **1** the way along which a thing moves or runs (*the course of the river/the usual course of events*). **2** the ground on which a race is run or golf is played. **3** a number of lectures or lessons given for the same purpose (*take a course in English literature*). **4** a row of stones, all at the same height, in a wall. **5** part of a meal served at the one time (*a meal consisting of three courses*):— *vb* **1** to hunt, esp hares, with dogs. **2** (*fml*) to move quickly (*tears coursing down her cheeks*).

cours'er *n* a fast horse.

cours'ing *n* hunting with greyhounds.

court *n* **1** a place marked out for tennis, squash rackets, etc. **2** a king and queen and all their advisers and attendants. **3** the building in which judges hear cases and give decisions. **4** all the judges and officials in a court of law. **5** attentions paid to someone to gain favour (*pay court to her in the hope that she would marry him/pay court to wealthy people*):— *vb* **1** to pay attention to a woman with a view to marrying her. **2** (*fml*) to try to gain (*court the audience's approval*). **3** to act in a way that is likely to bring about (something unpleasant) (*court disaster*).

courteous [kèrt'-yês] *adj* polite, considerate and respectful (*a courteous young man/a courteous reply*).

courtesy [kèr'-tê-si] *n* politeness, good manners (*treat people with courtesy/have the courtesy to apologize*).

cour'tier *n* one who attends the court of a king or queen.

court'ly *adj* polite and dignified (*courtly manners*).

court martial *n* (*pl* **courts mar'tial**) a military or naval court, with officers acting as judges.—*vb* **court-martial** (**court-mar'tialled, court-mar'tialling**) to try by court martial (*court-martialled for taking leave without permission*).

court'ship *n* the courting or wooing of a lady.

court'yard *n* an open space shut in by walls or houses on every side.

cous'in *n* the child of an uncle or aunt.

cove *n* a small bay (*build sandcastles in a sandy cove*).

cov'enant *n* a written agreement (*sign a covenant to give money regularly to a charity*):—*vb* to enter into written agreement, to promise

cov'er *vb* **1** to spread over (*cover the table with a cloth/the ground covered in snow*). **2** to protect (*cover her eyes in the sunlight*). **3** to wrap (up) (*covering her head from the cold*). **4** to include (*the cost covers accommodation and meals*):—*also n.*

cov'ering *n* anything that covers (*a covering of snow*).

covering letter *n* a letter that explains why papers included with it are being sent.

cov'erlet *n* the cover of a bed.

covert [kuv'-êrt] *adj* secret, hidden (*exchange covert glances/the covert activities of the spy*):— *n* a group of bushes or trees in which hunted birds or animals can hide.

covet [kuv'-êt] *vb* to want to have something belonging to another (*she coveted her friend's diamond ring*):—*adj* **cov'etous**:—*n* **cov'etousness**.

covey [ku'-vi] *n* **1** a family of partridges. **2** a flock of game birds.

cow *n* the female of certain animals (e.g. of the ox, elephant, whale).

cow'ard *n* one easily frightened in face of danger.

cow'ardice *n* fear of danger (*his cowardice in running away*).

cow'ardly *adj* having no bravery, showing fear (*too cowardly to admit his mistakes*).

cow'boy *n* (*Amer*) a man who looks after cattle on a ranch.

cow'er *vb* to crouch or shrink back out of fear (*covered in a corner as the bully threatened him with his fists*).

cow'herd *n* one who looks after cows.

cowl *n* **1** a hood, as on a monk's robe. **2** a metal cover for a chimney.

cow'rie, cow'ry *n* a small shell used as money in parts of Africa and Asia.

cow'slip *n* a kind of yellow wild flower like the primrose.

cox *vb* to act as coxswain, to steer a boat.

cox'comb *n* (*old*) *same as* **cock'scomb**, one foolishly proud of dress and appearance:—*n* **cox'combry**.

coxswain [kok'-sên *or* kok'-swên] *n* **1** the steersman of a boat. **2** an officer in charge of a ship's boat and its crew.

coy *adj* **1** shy, bashful, esp excessively so. **2** reluctant to give information (*coy about her age*):—*adv* **coy'ly**.

coyote [ko-yō'-ti *or* ki'-yot] *n* a type of wolf, found in North America.

crab *n* **1** a ten-legged sea creature with a shell. **2** a wild apple, a sour-tasting apple.

crab'bed *adj* bad-tempered, cross (*crabbed old men/in a crabbed mood*).

crack *n* **1** a sudden sharp noise (*the crack of a gun being fired*). **2** a break in which the parts remain together (*a crack in the china vase*). **3** a sharp blow (*a crack on the head*):—*also vb*:—*adj* very good.

cracked *adj* **1** broken, but not into pieces. **2** (*inf*) crazy, mad (*don't listen to him—he's completely cracked*).

crack'-brained *adj* (*inf*) mad, crazy (*a crack-brained scheme*).

crack'er *n* **1** a small firework. **2** a crisp biscuit (*crackers with cheese*).

crack'le *vb* to go on making short sharp noises, to rustle (*dry leaves crackling as they walked*):—*n* the act or sound of crackling.

crack'ling *n* the hard outer skin of roast pork.

cra'dle *n* **1** a baby's bed that can be rocked or swung. **2** the wooden frame under a ship when being built, **3** a frame to protect a broken limb:—*vb* to lay or rock as in a cradle (*cradling the head of the dying man in her arms*).

craft *n* **1** cleverness, esp in deceiving (*gain entry to the house by craft*). **2** a trade needing special skill, esp with the hands (*a craft such as woodworking*). **3** a ship (*a seaworthy craft*).

crafts'man *n* a skilled workman, esp with the hands:—*ns* **craft(s)'manship**.

craft'y *adj* good at deceiving, cunning (*criminals too crafty to get caught by the police*):—*adv* **craft'ily**.

crag *n* a steep, rough rock:—*adj* **crag'gy**.

cram *vb* (**crammed', cram'ming**) **1** to fill very full (*cram the suitcase full of clothes*). **2** to learn many facts in a short time.

cram'mer *n* a teacher who prepares someone for an examination by making him or her learn many facts in a short time.

cramp *n* a sudden sharp pain in a muscle (*suffer from stomach cramps*):—*vb* to prevent free movement, to hinder (*lack of money cramps his style*).

cran'berry *n* a sour red berry.

crane *n* **1** a long-legged, long-necked water bird. **2** a machine for raising heavy weights:—*vb* to stretch out one's neck (*craning his neck to see over the crowd*).

cranium [krā'-ni-êm] *n* (*fml*) the skull (*suffer injury to the cranium*):—*adj* **cra'nial**.

crank *n* **1** in machines, a part that changes an up-and-down or side-to-side movement into a round-and-round movement (or the other way round). **2** a person with fixed obsessive ideas, a person with strange ideas (*a health-food crank*):—*vb* to turn or wind.

cran'ny *n* a small narrow opening, a crack (*insects in the crannies of the walls*).

crape *n* a thin cloth, usu black

crash *vb* **1** to fall with a loud noise (*the vase crashed to the floor*). **2** to dash violently against something (*crashing his fist into her face*):—*n* **1** the loud noise of a breakage or collision. **2** the sudden failure of a business (*the crash of his firm in the recession*).

crass *adj* very stupid, insensitive.

crate *n* a large box or packing case, with spaces between the boards.

cra'ter *n* **1** the bowl-shaped mouth of a volcano. **2** a deep wide hole in the earth.

cravat' *n* a piece of cloth worn round the neck (*a silk cravat tucked into the neck of his shirt*).

crave *vb* **1** (*fml*) to beg for (*crave forgiveness*). **2** to desire very much (*craving a long cool drink/ craved admiration*).

crav'en *n* (*fml*) a coward:—*adj* cowardly (*craven behaviour*).

crav'ing n a strong desire.

crawfish see **crayfish**.

crawl vb 1 to move with the body on or near the ground, to move on the hands and knees (crawl along the tunnel/children learning to crawl). 2 to move slowly (time crawled past):—n 1 act of crawling. 2 a stroke in swimming.

cray'fish, craw'fish n a type of lobster.

cray'on n a stick of coloured chalk, a coloured pencil:—vb to draw with crayons.

craze vb to drive mad:—n a popular fashion, a temporary enthusiasm for (a 1970s' craze for flared trousers).

crazy adj 1 (inf) mad (he must be crazy to think that). 2 very enthusiastic, liking very much (crazy about horror films/crazy about the girl next door).

crazy pavement n a pavement made of stones of odd shapes and sizes.

creak vb to make a harsh squeaking sound (stairs creaking as he crept upstairs):—also n:—adj **creaky**.

cream n 1 the oily part of the milk that rises to the top, and from which butter is made. 2 the best of anything (the cream of the local footballers). 3 a cream-like substance for rubbing into the skin (hand cream). 4 the colour of cream.

cream'ery n a place where milk is made into butter and cheese.

cream'y adj like cream (a creamy dessert).

crease n 1 a mark made by folding, crushing or pressing. 2 one of the lines marking out a cricket pitch:—vb to make creases in (her skirt creased by sitting too long).

create [kree-āt'] vb 1 to bring into existence (God created the world). 2 to make (create a bad impression/create a fuss/fashion designers creating a new line).

crea'tion n 1 act of creating. 2 anything made or invented (designers showing the latest creations).

crea'tive adj 1 involving creation (the creative process). 2 able to create or invent, producing original ideas and works (a creative writer).

crea'tor n one who creates or invents:—**the Creator** God.

creature [kree'-tyêr] n 1 anything created, esp human beings, animals, and other living things. 2 one who depends on another's favour and does what he or she says (the king's creatures).

crèche [kresh] n a day nursery for small children.

cred'ence n belief, trust (give no credence to what he says).

creden'tials npl papers saying that the owner of them may be trusted (ask candidates for the job for their credentials).

cred'ible adj able to be believed (a scarcely credible story):—n **credibility**.

cred'it n 1 belief, trust in (place no credit in their policies). 2 approval or praise (give credit for his capture of the thief). 3 a cause of honour (a credit to his school). 4 a system of buying goods or services and paying for them later (buy the video on credit). 5 the quality of being able to pay debts (her credit is good). 6 the money a person has in a bank (an account in credit):— vb 1 to believe. 2 to sell or lend in trust. 3 to write in on the credit side of an account. 4 to consider as having (a good quality).

cred'itable adj deserving praise (a creditable achievement).

credit card n a plastic card with which goods can be purchased and paid for later.

cred'itor n one to whom money is owed.

cred'ulous adj too ready to believe, too trusting (credulous creatures who would believe anything):—n **credulity**.

creed n 1 that which one believes, esp in religion (people of every creed). 2 a statement of one's faith or beliefs.

creek n 1 a small bay. 2 a narrow inlet. 3 a small river.

creel n a fisherman's basket.

creep vb (pt, pp **crept**) 1 to move with the body on or near the ground (insects creeping over the grass). 2 to move slowly and silently (creep upstairs). 3 to shiver with horror (her flesh crept at the ghostly sight).

creep'er adj a plant that grows along the ground or up walls, trees, etc.

creep'y adj (inf) eerie (a creepy story/a creepy old house).

cremate' vb to burn a dead body to ashes.

crema'tion n act of cremating.

cremato'rium n a place where dead bodies are cremated (attend a funeral ceremony in the crematorium).

cren'ellated adj having battlements.

creole [kree-yōl'] *n* a person born in the West Indies or South America but of European race.

creosote [kree'-o-sōt] *n* an oily liquid taken from tar and used to disinfect or preserve from decay.

crepe [krāp] *n* 1 a soft light cloth with a finely lined and folded surface (*a dress of blue crepe*). 2 crinkly rubber (*shoes with crepe soles*). 3 any crinkly material (*crepe paper*).

crepus'cular *adj* having to do with twilight (*crepuscular light*).

crescendo [krê-shen'-dō] *n* 1 a sign used in writing music. 2 a gradual increase in volume of sound.

cres'cent *n* 1 the shape of the moon in its first and last quarter. 2 a narrow tapering curve. 3 a curving street:—*adj* shaped like a crescent.

cress *n* an eatable water plant.

crest *n* 1 a tuft or comb on the head of certain birds (*a cock's crest*). 2 a bunch of feathers on the top of a helmet. 3 a sign or badge of family, seen on coats-of-arms, writing paper, etc. 4 the top of a slope, wave, etc (*surfing on the crest of a wave*):—*vb* to get to the top of.

crest'fallen *adj* sad, disappointed (*feel crestfallen at missing the party*).

cret'in *n* 1 a person who is mentally subnormal. 2 (*inf*) a fool:—*n* **cret'inism**.

crevasse' *n* a deep crack in a glacier.

crev'ice *n* a crack or opening (*crevices in the stone wall*).

crew *n* 1 the sailors of a ship. 2 a gang.

crib *n* 1 a baby's bed. 2 something copied dishonestly from someone else. 3 a translation of a text:—*vb* (**cribbed'**, **crib'bing**) to copy unfairly the work of another.

crib'bage *n* a card game.

crick *n* a painful stiffness, esp of the neck:—*vb* to cause this (*cricked her neck looking over her shoulder*).

crick'et[1] *n* a small jumping insect.

crick'et[2] *n* an outdoor game played with a bat and ball:—*n* **crick'eter**.

cri'er *n* (*old*) one whose job it is to read notices to the public (*the town-crier*).

crime *n* a breaking of the law (*the crime of murder*).

crim'inal *adj* 1 against the law (*convicted of a criminal act*). 2 wrong, wicked (*it was criminal to cut down such a beautiful tree*):—*n* one who breaks the law.

criminol'ogist *n* one who studies the causes and prevention of crime:—*n* **criminol'ogy**.

crimp *vb* 1 to compress into small folds or ridges (*crimp the cloth*). 2 to make to curl (*crimp her hair*).

crim'son *n* a deep red colour:—*also adj*:—*vb* to make or become red.

cringe *vb* 1 to shrink back in fear (*cringe from the bully/dogs cringing at the sight of the whip*). 2 to behave too humbly towards (*cringe in the presence of the boss*).

crink'le *vb* to twist or bend into many folds, to wrinkle:—*n* a fold or wrinkle.

crinoline [krin'-o-leen] *n* a stiff petticoat, made to stick out by hoops.

crip'ple *n* (*offensive*) one who is unable to use some or all of his limbs:—*vb* 1 to make unable to move freely, to make lame (*crippled his legs in the accident*). 2 to make less strong, less efficient, etc (*crippling the country's economy*).

cris'is *n* (*pl* **crises** [krī'-seez]) 1 a turning point at which things must become either better or worse (*the crisis of the illness*). 2 a very serious state of affairs (*the firm recovered from a financial crisis*).

crisp *adj* 1 hard but easily broken (*crisp biscuits*). 2 tight (*crisp curls*). 3 fresh and firm (*crisp apples*). 4 firm and clear (*give crisp orders*). 5 dry and clear (*a crisp day*):—*vb* to curl or twist:—*adv* **crisp'ly**.

criterion [krī-tee'-ree-on] *n* (*pl* **crite'ria**) a rule or standard with which things may be compared in order to judge their value, a test (*criteria used in judging a novel*).

crit'ic *n* 1 one who judges something by pointing out its good and bad points (*a theatre critic*). 2 one who finds fault, a person who expresses dislike and disapproval of (*one of the government's critics*).

crit'ical *adj* 1 pointing out both good and bad (*a critical analysis of the play*). 2 hard to please, ready to find fault (*a very critical person/in a critical mood*). 3 having to do with a crisis (*a critical point in his career*). 4 most important (*at the critical moment*).

crit'icism *n* 1 judgment (*literary criticism*). 2 fault-finding (*a plan open to criticism/tired of her constant criticism*).

crit'icize vb 1 to point out the good and bad in (*the journalist appointed to criticize the play*). 2 to find fault with (*always criticizing his clothes*).

critique [krit-eek'] n an essay in which a criticism is made.

croak vb to make a low hoarse noise in the throat (*frogs croaking/croaking because of a sore throat*):—adj **croak'y**.

crochet [krō'-shā] n a type of knitting done with one hooked needle:—vb to make crochet (*crocheting a tablecloth*).

crock[1] n a pot or jar (*a crock of salt*).

crock[2] n an old broken-down animal or person:—vb to injure.

crock'ery n earthenware or china cups, plates and other dishes.

croc'odile n a large reptile that can live both in water and on land.

crocodile tears npl pretended sorrow or grief (*she seemed upset when we left but I think it was a case of crocodile tears*).

cro'cus n a spring plant grown from a bulb with yellow, purple or white flowers.

croft n a very small farm:—n **croft'ing**.

croft'er n a small-farmer, esp in the Scottish Highlands.

croissant n [kwa'song] a light crescent-shaped roll made of flaky pastry eaten at breakfast.

crom'lech n a group of standing stones set up in ancient times.

crone n (*old*) an old woman.

cron'y n (*inf*) a close friend (*have a glass of beer with his cronies*).

crook n 1 a bend, curve (*in the crook of one's arm*). 2 a stick, hook-shaped at one end, as carried by a shepherd or bishop. 3 (*inf*) a dishonest person, a criminal (*a crook who eventually went to jail*):—vb to bend, to shape like a hook.

crook'ed adj 1 not straight, twisted (*a crooked stick/a crooked smile*). 2 dishonest, illegal (*a crooked business deal*). 3 dishonest, not to be trusted (*a crooked businessman*):—n **crook'edness**.

croon vb to sing softly (*crooning a lullaby to the child*).

crop n 1 a pocket in the throat of birds in which the food is partly digested before passing to the stomach. 2 a riding whip. 3 the whole amount of grain, fruit, etc, growing or gathered at one place or time (*the wheat crop/a fine crop of green beans/a disappointing crop of apples*). 4 a short haircut:—vb (**cropped', crop'ping**) 1 to cut short (*crop his hair*). 2 to bite off (*sheep cropping the grass*). 3 to sow or gather (a crop):—**crop up** to turn up unexpectedly (*difficulties that cropped up/one of the subjects that crop up*):—**come a cropper** 1 to fall heavily (*coming a cropper on the icy surface*). 2 to fail completely (*he came a cropper when he tried to expand his business*).

croquet [krō'-kā] n a game in which wooden balls are hit through hoops with long hammer-shaped wooden clubs.

cro'sier, cro'zier n the staff of office, or crook of a bishop or abbot.

cross n 1 a mark made by drawing one straight line across another, e.g. +, x. 2 one piece of wood fastened across another in the shape of a cross. 3 anything made in the shape of a cross (*wear a cross round her neck*). 4 the sign of the Christian religion. 5 (*old*) a cross-shaped wooden frame to which criminals were fixed as a punishment. 6 a place where roads meet. 7 a monument in the shape of a cross (*a cross in the middle of the village*). 8 a source of suffering or sorrow (*a cross to bear*). 9 an animal or plant that is the offspring of different breeds or varieties (*a mule is a cross between a horse and an ass*):—vb 1 to draw a line through or across (*cross out the mistakes*). 2 to go from one side to the other side (*cross the road*). 3 to pass across each other (*the roads cross before the village*). 4 to put or place something across or over something of the same type (*crossing her fingers*). 5 to hinder, to obstruct (*he doesn't like to be crossed*):—adj angry, bad-tempered (*feeling cross about ripping her tights*):—**cross'er** n **cross'ly** adv **cross'ness** n.

cross'bow n a bow fixed across a support or stand on to which the string was looped when drawn back, then fired by a trigger.

cross'breed n a mixture of two breeds:—also vb.

cross-coun'try adj going across fields, etc, instead of along roads (*people taking part in a cross-country race*).

cross-exam'ine vb to ask a person questions about a statement he or she has made to test its truth, esp in a court of law (*cross-examine the witness for the defence*):—*n* **cross-examina'tion.**

cross'-eyed *adj* squinting.

cros'sing *n* a place at which one may cross a street, river, etc (*cross the road at the pedestrian crossing by the school*).

cross'-pur'pose *n*:—**to be at cross-purposes** to disagree with another through a misunderstanding (*they were at cross-purposes—they were talking about different people without realizing it*).

cross-question *vb* to cross-examine.

cross-re'ference *n* the mention in a book of another passage or book in which the same subject is discussed.

cross'roads *n* the place where two roads cross.

cross'word *n* a word puzzle with squares and clues.

crot'chet *n* **1** a note in music. **2** a strange desire or idea, a whim. **3** a hook.

crot'chety *adj* **1** (*old*) having strange desires or ideas. **2** cross, bad-tempered (*a crotchety old man*).

crouch *vb* to bend low (*crouch down to look at the plant*).

croup[1] *n* the hind-quarters of a horse.

croup[2] *n* a disease of the throat in children.

croup'ier *n* the person who takes in and gives out the money at a gambling table.

crow *n* **1** a large black bird. **2** the cry of a cock (*sleepers disturbed by the crow of the cock*). **3** a baby's cry of pleasure (*crows of delight*):—*vb* **1** to cry like a cock. **2** (*of a baby*) to make sounds expressing pleasure. **3** (*inf*) to boast (*crowing about his new car*):—**as the crow flies** following the straightest and shortest way from one place to another.

crow'bar *n* a bar of iron used to raise heavy objects (*prise the load up with a crowbar*).

crowd *n* a large number of people gathered together, esp into a small space (*a crowd packed the hall*):—*vb* **1** to come together in large numbers (*the villagers crowded together in the square*). **2** to fill too full by coming together in (*crowd the streets*).

crowd'ed *adj* full of people or objects.

crown *n* **1** an ornamental headcovering worn by a king or queen as a sign of office. **2** a wreath worn on the head (*a crown of flowers*). **3** the top of certain things (*the crown of the hill/the crown of the head/the crown of the hat*). **4** (*old*)

a five-shilling piece:—*vb* **1** to put a crown on (*crown the king*). **2** to finish with a success (*the award crowned a fine career*). **3** (*inf*) to hit on the head (*crowned him with an iron bar*).

crown prince *n* the prince who will be the next king.

crow's-feet *npl* the little lines on the face at the outside eye-corners.

crozier *see* **crosier.**

crucial [krö′-sh-êl] *adj* of the greatest importance, needing a clear decision (*take the crucial step of resigning/the next game is a crucial one for the championship*).

cru'cible *n* a melting pot.

cru'cifix *n* a figure of Christ on a cross.

crucifix'ion *n* act of crucifying:—**the Crucifixion** the crucifixion and death of Jesus Christ.

cru'cify *vb* **1** to put to death by fastening on a cross. **2** to treat cruelly, to deal with severely (*a politician crucified by the press about his private life*).

crude *adj* **1** rough (*crude garden furniture*). **2** in the natural state (*crude oil/crude sugar*). **3** coarse, vulgar, not refined (*crude manners/crude voices*):—*n* **crud'ity.**

cru'el *adj* **1** taking pleasure in making others suffer, hard-hearted (*a cruel tyrant*). **2** causing pain (*a cruel blow/cruel punishment*):—*n* **cru'elty.**

cru'et *n* a small bottle for vinegar, salt, etc.

cruise [kröz] *vb* **1** to sail here and there, often now for pleasure. **2** to travel at the speed that uses up least fuel:—*also n.*

cruis'er *n* a fast warship.

crumb *n* **1** a very small bit, esp of bread (*biscuit crumbs*). **2** a small piece (*a crumb of comfort*).

crum'ble *vb* **1** to break into small bits or dust (*crumble the bread*). **2** to fall to pieces or into dust (*ancient walls gradually crumbling*). **3** gradually to get into a poor state and come to an end (*empires crumbling/hope crumbling*).

crum'pet *n* a thin flat cake with holes in it (*a toasted crumpet*).

crum'ple *vb* **1** to press into many folds, to crush out of shape (*crumpling her dress*). **2** to fall down suddenly (*she crumpled down in a faint*). **3** to collapse, to fail (*all resistance to the enemy suddenly crumpled*):—*also n.*

crunch *vb* to crush noisily with the teeth (*the dog crunching a bone*):—*also n.*

crusade *n* **1** an attempt by Christian armies to win back control of the Holy Land from non-Christians. **2** any attempt by a number of people to do what is considered to be good or work against what is considered to be evil (*a crusade against corruption among officials*):—*n* **crusad'er.**

crush *vb* **1** to squeeze or press together with force. **2** to press out of shape. **3** to defeat completely:—*n* the crowding together of things or persons.

crush'ing *adj* overwhelming.

crust *n* the hard outside of anything (e.g. bread):—*vb* to cover with a crust.

crust'y *adj* **1** having a crust (*a crusty pizza base*). **2** short-tempered (*a crusty old man*):—*adv* **crust'ily.**

crutch *n* **1** a stick, with a top made to fit under the armpits, to support lame people. **2** a person or thing that provides help and support (*regard her religion as a crutch*).

crux *n* the most important or difficult part of a matter, issue, etc (*lack of money is the crux of the problem*).

cry *vb* **1** to make shrill loud sounds of weeping, joy, etc (*cried for help*). **2** to weep. **3** to shout:—*also n.*

cry'ing *adj* needing to be put right (*a crying need for more books*).

crypt *n* a cellar under the floor of a church, often used as a burial place.

cryp'tic *adj* difficult to understand, sometimes intentionally so (*a cryptic remark/a cryptic crossword*).

cryp'togram *n* anything written in code.

crys'tal *n* **1** a clear, bright glass. **2** a hard glassy-looking stone. **3** one of the regular shapes in which the atoms of certain bodies are arranged:—*also adj.*

crys'talline *adj* **1** clear (*crystalline water*). **2** made of or like crystal.

crys'tallize *vb* **1** to form into crystals. **2** to make or become clear or definite (*plans beginning to crystallize*):—*n* **crystalliza'tion.**

cub *n* **1** the young of certain animals (e.g. the bear, fox, etc). **2** formerly, a Cub Scout, a member of the junior section of the Scout Association.

cube *n* **1** a solid body with six equal square sides. **2** the answer got by multiplying a number twice by itself (e.g. $2 \times 2 \times 2 = 8$, therefore 8 is the **cube** of 2, 2 is the **cube root** of 8).

cu'bic *adj* **1** cube-shaped. **2** having to do with cubes.

cu'bicle *n* **1** a small bedroom in a dormitory or large sleeping room. **2** a compartment in a larger room (*changing cubicles at the swimming pool*).

cu'bit *n* an ancient measure of length (about 45–56 centimetres).

cuckoo [kö'-kö] *n* a bird that lays its eggs in the nests of other birds.

cu'cumber *n* a creeping plant with a long green fruit much used in salads.

cud *n* the food that certain animals bring up from their stomachs to chew again.

cud'dle *vb* **1** to hug lovingly (*cuddled the baby*). **2** to lie close and comfortably (*children cuddling up to keep warm*).

cud'gel *n* (*fml*) a short thick stick, a club:—*vb* (**cud'gelled, cud'gelling**) (*fml*) to beat with a cudgel.

cue *n* **1** a word or sign that reminds a person of what to say or do next (*the last words of an actor's speech act as a cue to the next speaker*). **2** the long stick used for striking the balls in billiards.

cuff[1] *n* the part of a sleeve near the wrist.

cuff[2] *n* a blow (*a cuff on the ear*):—*also vb.*

cuirass [kwi-ras'] *n* (*old*) a piece of armour to protect the breast and back.

cuisine [kwee-zeen'] *n* a style of cooking (*French cuisine/Italian cuisine*).

cul-de-sac [köl'-dê-sak] *n* a street closed at one end.

cul'inary *adj* having to do with cooking (*culinary skills*).

cull *vb* **1** to gather, choose or select (*information culled from many sources*). **2** to select and kill (unwanted animals in a group) (*cull seals to reduce their numbers*).

cul'minate *vb* to reach the highest point (*small battles culminating in a full-scale war/a fine career culminating in a knighthood*):—*n* **culmina'tion.**

cul'pable *adj* deserving to be blamed, guilty (*she was caught but they were equally culpable*):—*n* **culpabil'ity.**

cul'prit *n* a wrongdoer, one accused of a crime (*catch the culprit committing the crime*).

cult *n* a particular, often temporarily, fashionable system of beliefs, esp religious.

cul'tivate *vb* 1 to prepare (land) for the growing of crops. 2 to make to grow (*cultivating several types of vegetable*). 3 to improve (the mind) (*reading books and listening to music to cultivate her mind*):— *n* **cultiva'tion**:— *n* **cul'tivator**.

cul'ture *n* 1 the character of an age and people as seen in customs, arts, etc (*learn about Roman culture*). 2 learning and good taste (*people of culture*). 3 the rearing of creatures or growing of plants in conditions not natural to them:— *adj* **cul'tural**.

cul'tured *adj* having learning and good taste (*cultured people interested in the arts*).

cul'vert *n* a tunnel for carrying water under a road, railway, etc.

cum'bersome *adj* 1 heavy and difficult to move (*cumbersome parcels/cumbersome furniture*). 2 slow and inefficient (*a cumbersome method of government*).

cum'merbund *n* a sash or waistband.

cu'mulative (*fml*) growing gradually larger by being added to (*cumulative damage to the environment/frequent small doses of a drug with a cumulative effect*).

cu'mulus *n* a mass of white rounded cloud.

cuneiform [kū'-ni-form] *n* the writing of the peoples of ancient Persia, Babylon, etc:— *adj* wedge-shaped.

cun'ning *adj* 1 clever, skilful, craft (*a cunning trick*). 2 good at deceiving (*a cunning cheat*). 3 clever (*a cunning device*):— *n* skill, deceit.

cup *n* a small drinking vessel:— *vb* (**cupped'**, **cup'ping**) to put into the shape of a cup (*cup her hands round the flower/cup his hands to catch the ball*).

cupboard [kub'-êrd] *n* a shelved place for storing food, dishes etc.

cup'ful *n* the amount a cup holds.

Cu'pid *n* the ancient Roman god of love.

cu'pola *n* a rounded dome.

cur *n* 1 a dog of no fixed breed, a mongrel. 2 a low mean person.

cu'rate *n* a member of clergy who assists a vicar or parish priest:— **cu'racy**.

cu'rative *adj* helping to cure or heal (*water said to have curative powers*):— also *n*.

cura'tor *n* one in charge of a museum, art gallery, etc.

curb *vb* to control, to keep in check (*curb his anger/curb their expenditure*):— *n* 1 anything that controls or holds in check (*a curb on their expenditure*). 2 a chain or strap fastened to the bit in a horse's mouth.

curd *n* 1 a solid substance that forms in sour milk, and from which cheese is made. 2 a type of jam (*lemon curd*).

cur'dle *vb* to thicken, to become solid (*a creamy sauce curdling when boiled*).

cure *n* 1 act of healing. 2 that which heals or gives back health (*a cure for cancer*). 3 (*fml*) the care of souls:— *vb* 1 to heal. 2 to preserve meat, fish, etc.

cur'few *n* 1 (*old*) a bell rung in the evening as a signal to put out all lights. 2 a military order for people to be indoors and keep the streets empty after a certain hour (*impose a curfew after the riots*). 3 the time at which people have to be indoors.

cu'rio *n* a rare object of interest to collectors.

curios'ity *n* 1 the desire to learn, or to find out about (*a child showing curiosity about how the car works/full of curiosity about her neighbours' lives*). 2 a rare or strange object (*an antique shop full of curiosities*).

cu'rious *adj* 1 wanting to learn (*curious about the origin of mankind*). 2 wanting to know the private affairs of others (*neighbours curious about where she goes in the evenings*). 3 strange (*rather a curious figure/it's curious that he has disappeared*).

curl *vb* 1 to form into ringlets. 2 to twist round and round (*smoke curling from the chimney*). 3 to play at the game of curling:— *n* a ringlet.

cur'lew *n* a long-legged, long-billed bird.

curl'ing *n* a winter game played on ice, involving sliding heavy smooth stones.

cur'ly *adj* having curls (*curly hair*).

curmud'geon *n* a bad-tempered person (*a curmudgeon complaining about the child*).

cur'rant *n* 1 a small dried grape (*buns made with currants*). 2 a type of berry growing on certain shrubs (*redcurrants*).

cur'rency *n* 1 the money in present use in a country. 2 the state of being widely known (*the currency of the rumours*).

cur'rent *adj* **1** in general use (*words no longer current*). **2** belonging to the present time (*current fashions*):—*n* **1** a stream of water or air moving in a certain direction. **2** a flow of electricity.

cur·ric'ulum *n* a course of study at a school, university, etc (*several foreign languages on the curriculum*).

cur'ry[1] *n* a dish of meat, vegetables, etc, cooked with a hot-tasting sauce.

cur'ry[2] *vb* to rub down a horse with a comb:—
curry favour to try to win the favour of another by pleasing (*curries favour with the teacher by giving her presents*).

cur'ry-comb *n* a comb for rubbing down a horse.

curse *vb* **1** to use bad language (*drunks cursing in the streets*). **2** to call down harm and evil upon (*cursed the man who killed her son*):—*n* **1** the wish that another may suffer harm and evil (*put a curse on his enemy*). **2** a great evil or cause of suffering (*the curse of drug-dealing*). **3** a swear word.

cur'sive *adj* (*of handwriting*) so written that the pen, pencil, etc, need not be lifted until a word is complete, flowing.

cur'sor *n* a movable pointer on a computer screen which shows, for example, where the next piece of text should be typed.

cur'sory *adj* quick, careless (*give the instructions a cursory glance*).

curt *adj* **1** abrupt, rude (*a curt answer/he was very curt with us*). **2** brief, abrupt (*a curt reply*):—*n* **curt'ness**.

curtail' *vb* (*fml*) to cut short (*have to curtail our holiday/curtailing our spending*):—*n* **curtail'ment**.

cur'tain *n* a cloth hung up to darken, or to hide things behind it:—*also vb*.

curt'sy, curt'sey *n* a low bow made by women (*a curtsy to the queen*):—*also vb*.

cur'vature *n* a bending or curving (*suffer from curvature of the spine*).

curve *n* **1** a line that is not straight and that changes direction without angles (*a curve on the graph*). **2** something shaped like this (*curves in the road/her attractive curves*):—*vb* to bend into a curve.

cur'vet *n* a little jump into the air by a horse:—*vb* to give a jump, to jump about.

cush'ion *n* **1** a cloth bag, filled with soft material, for sitting, leaning or kneeling on. **2** anything

that takes the force of a blow or shock (*his savings acted as a cushion when he lost his job*):—
vb to lessen a blow or shock (*his savings cushioned him from the blow of redundancy*).

cus'tard *n* a dish of milk, eggs and sugar, baked or boiled.

cus·to'dian *n* a keeper, one who takes care, esp of a museum or other public building.

cus'tody *n* **1** care (*a mother given custody of her children*). **2** safekeeping (*leave her jewellery in the custody of the bank*). **3** imprisonment (*taken into custody while awaiting trial*).

cus'tom *n* **1** the usual way of doing something (*traditional country customs*). **2** something done often as a habit (*it was her custom to have an afternoon nap*). **3** the buying of certain things at one particular shop, etc (*threaten to take her custom elsewhere when the assisant was rude*). **4** *pl* the taxes payable on goods brought into a country. **5** *pl* the office where such taxes are paid, or the officials collecting them.

cus'tomary *adj* usual (*the customary route for his walk*).

cus'tomer *n* one who usu buys things (in a particular shop) (*the local shop with a few regular customers*).

cut *vb* (**cut**, **cut'ting**) **1** to make an opening with a sharp instrument (*cut her hand*). **2** to divide into pieces with a sharp instrument (*cut up the meat*). **3** to shorten or shape by cutting (*cut his hair*). **4** to divide a pack of cards. **5** to lessen (*cut costs*). **6** to refuse to look at or speak to (*cut his old friend dead*):—*n* **1** an opening made by cutting (*a cut in the cloth*). **2** a wound (*a deep cut in her leg*). **3** the way a thing is shaped (*the cut of her coat/a haircut*). **4** a lessening (*a cut in their budgets*). **5** a piece of meat (*an expensive cut of meat*).

cut'back *n* a reduction in the amount of something (*cutbacks in public spending*).

cute *adj* (*inf*) cunningly clever (*he was too cute to be caught/a cute trick*).

cu'ticle *n* the outer skin of a plant or of the body.

cut'lass *n* a short curving sword.

cut'lery *n* knives, forks, spoons, etc.

cut'let *n* a rib and the meat attached to it, a chop (*lamb cutlets*).

cut'ter *n* **1** a light sailing boat. **2** the tailor who cuts out the cloth.

cut'ting *adj* hurting the feelings (*a cutting remark*):—*n* **1** a piece of a plant cut off for replanting (*take cuttings from the geranium*). **2** a piece cut out of a newspaper (*save cuttings about the pop star*). **3** a passage cut through rock for a road or railway.

cut'tlefish *n* a sea creature that gives out a black liquid when attacked.

CV (*abbr for* **curriculum vitae**) a list of a person's educational and professional qualifications and details of previous jobs (*enclose a CV with the completed application form*).

cy'ber ca'fé [sī'-ber ka-fā] *n* a ca'fé which provides computer terminals so that customers can browse the Internet.

cyclamen [sik'-lê-mên] *n* a kind of bulb plant with coloured flowers.

cy'cle *n* **1** a series of events that are regularly repeated in the same order (*the cycle of the seasons*). **2** a number of stories, songs, etc, about the same person or event (*a Schubert song cycle*). **3** (*inf*) a bicycle:—*vb* to ride a bicycle (*cycling to school*).

cy'clic *adj* happening in cycles.

cy'clist *n* one who rides a bicycle.

cy'clone *n* a violent storm of wind.

cy'clostyle *n* a machine for printing copies of a written stencil.

cy'clotron *n* a machine used in splitting atoms.

cyg'net *n* a young swan.

cyl'inder *n* **1** a solid or hollow shape with circular ends and straight sides. **2** an object or container shaped like this (*a cylinder of oxygen*):—*adj* **cylin'drical**.

cym'bal *n* one of two brass plates used as a musical instrument and struck together to make a clanging noise.

Cymric [kim'-rik] *adj* Welsh.

cynic [sin'-ik] *adj* one who believes that people do not do things for good or kindly reasons but for their own advantage (*cynics who believe that politicians are interested only in keeping their seats*):—*also adj:—adj* **cyn'ical**:—*n* **cyn'icism**.

cynosure [sin'-ō-shêr] *n* anything that attracts attention (*in her beautiful dress she was the cyonosure of all eyes at the ball*).

cypher *same as* **cipher**.

cy'press *n* an evergreen tree with dark leaves.

cyst *n* a small bag full of liquid that forms on or in the body (*have a cyst removed from his scalp*).

czar *n* same as **tsar**:—*f* **czari'na**.

D

dab vb (**dabbed, dab'bing**) to touch or hit gently with something soft or damp (*dab the wound with cotton wool*):—n **1** a gentle touch (*give the wet ink a dab with some blotting paper*). **2** a small lump of anything soft or damp (*a dab of butter*). **3** a flatfish:—**a dab hand** (*inf*) an expert (*a dab hand at carpentry*).

dab'ble vb **1** to splash, to wet (*dabble her fingers in the water*). **2** to take up in a small way (*dabble in witchcraft*):—n **dab'bler**.

dab'chick n a small water bird.

dace n a small river fish.

dachshund [däks'-hünt] n a small dog with a long body and short legs.

dado [dā'-dō] n a border of wood or paint round the lower part of the walls of a room.

daf'fodil n a yellow bell-shaped spring flower.

daft adj (*inf*) foolish, silly (*a daft idea/daft behaviour*).

dag'ger n a short sharp-pointed sword.

dahlia [dā'-li-a] n a garden flower.

dai'ly adj happening every day (*a daily walk to the park*):—also adv:—n a daily newspaper.

daily help n one who is employed from day to day to help with housework.

daintily adv **1** in a dainty way (*dress daintily*). **2** with very great care (*eat daintily*):—n **dain'tiness**.

dain'ty adj small, delicate and pretty (*a dainty little girl/dainty porcelain*).

dai'ry n a place where milk is sold, or made into butter or cheese:—ns **dai'rymaid, dai'ryman**.

dais [dā'-is] n a low platform (*a speaker addressing the school from a dais*).

dai'sy n a kind of common wild flower.

dale n a valley, esp in northern England (*the Yorkshire Dales*).

Dalma'tian n a large spotted dog.

dal'ly vb **1** to move slowly or waste time (*dallying to school*). **2** to play with, toy with (*dallied with the idea of emigrating*):—n **dal'liance**.

dam[1] n a wall to stop or control the flow of water (*the dam in the river*):—vb (**dammed', dam'ming**) to keep back by a dam.

dam[2] n (*of animals*) a mother.

dam'age n **1** injury, harm (*storms causing a lot of damage/rumours doing damage to his*

reputation). **2** pl money paid to make up for loss or harm (*sue the driver of the car that hit her for damages*):—vb to harm.

dam'ask n **1** cloth with designs woven into it. **2** the red colour of the damask rose.

dame n **1** the status of a lady of the same rank as a knight. **2** a comic woman in a pantomime, usu played by a man.

damn vb **1** to send to everlasting punishment (*damn his soul*). **2** to condemn, to declare to be bad (*a play damned by the critics*). **3** to curse (*damn you!*):—n a curse.

dam'nable adj hateful, terrible, deserving to be condemned or disapproved of (*what damnable weather!/a damnable cheek!*).

damna'tion n everlasting punishment.

damp adj slightly wet (*damp hair/damp clothes*):—n slight wetness:—vb to make slightly wet (*damp her hair*):—n **damp'-ness**.

damp'en vb **1** to make or become damp (*dampen the shirt before ironing*). **2** to make less strong, etc (*dampen his enthusiasm*).

damp'er n a device in a chimney to control the flow of air.

dam'sel n (*old*) a girl.

dam'son n a small dark plum.

dance vb **1** to move in time to music. **2** to move in a lively way (*children dancing about in excitement*):—n **1** act of dancing. **2** a social gathering for the purpose of dancing (*invite her to a formal dance*):—n **danc'er**.

dan'delion n a wild plant with a yellow flower.

dan'dle vb to move (a baby) up and down on the knee (*dandling a baby on her knee*).

dan'druff, dan'driff n small pieces of dead skin on the scalp.

dan'dy n a man who pays much attention to his appearance and clothes:—adj **dan'di-fied**.

Dane n a native of Denmark:—**Great Dane** a very large breed of dog.

dan'ger n **1** the risk of hurt or harm (*with her life in danger*). **2** something that may cause harm, injury, death, etc (*wild animals that are a danger to the villagers/the dangers of modern living*).

dan'gerous adj full of risks (*a dangerous journey*).

106

dang'le vb to hang loosely (*with her bag dangling from her wrist*).

dank adj cold and damp (*a dank cellar*).

dap'per adj small and neat (*a dapper little man*).

dap'ple, dap'pled adjs marked with spots of a different shade (*dappled ponies*).

dare vb 1 to be brave enough (to), to undertake to do (*he dared to ask the boss for more money/who would dare to climb Everest?*). 2 to challenge (*dare the boy to climb to the roof*):—n a challenge.

dare'devil n one ready to face any danger.

dar'ing adj brave, fearless (*a daring young man/a daring attempt*):—n courage.

dark adj 1 without light (*dark nights/dark rooms*). 2 having black or brown hair (*a dark girl*). 3 evil (*dark deeds*):—n **dark'ness**.

dark'en vb to make or become darker (*a complexion darkened by the sun*).

dar'ling n one dearly loved:—also adj.

darn vb to mend holes in clothes:—also n.

dart n 1 a pointed weapon thrown by hand. 2 a sudden quick movement (*in one dart the child escaped*). 3 in needlework, a small pleat. 4 pl a game in which darts are thrown at a target:—vb to move quickly (*the child darted out of the door*).

dash vb 1 to run quickly. 2 to smash against (*waves dashing against the rocks*). 3 to discourage (*dash all their hopes*):—n 1 a quick movement. 2 a small amount (*a dash of milk*). 3 a mark of punctuation (—).

dash'board n the instrument board in a car.

dash'ing adj 1 active, showy. 2 smart.

das'tard n (*old*) a coward:—adj **das'tardly**.

data npl (*now often regarded as a singular noun*) a known fact or piece of information (*consider all the data relating to population/process computer data*).

data'base n a collection of data that is stored in a computer.

date[1] n 1 the day and month and/or year in which something happened or is going to happen (*the date of the next meeting*). 2 (*inf*) an arrangement to meet at a certain time, esp a social meeting with a member of the opposite sex:—vb 1 to write the date on (*dated the letter*). 2 (*inf*) to make a date, to see often a member of the opposite sex (*dating the boy next door*):—**date from**

to have a beginning at a certain time (*houses dating from the 18th century*):—**out of date** no longer in use (*machinery that is out of date*).

date[2] n the eatable fruit of the date palm.

date'line n the line in the Pacific where one day is regarded as beginning and another as ending.

datum [dā'-têm] sing of **data**.

daub vb 1 to put on in lumps or smears (*clothes daubed with mud/daub paint on*). 2 to paint roughly (*daub the walls red with paint*):—n 1 a smear (*a daub of mud*). 2 a bad painting (*I will not hang his daubs on my wall*).

daughter [dā'-têr] n a female child.

daugh'ter-in-law n (*pl* **daugh'ters-in-law**) the wife of a son.

daunt vb to make less brave, to discourage (*she refused to be daunted by the remarks of her critics/not be daunted by the difficulty of the journey*).

dauphin [dō'-fin] n (*old*) the eldest son of the king of France.

daw'dle vb to move slowly, often stopping, to waste time (*dawdling along, late for school*).

dawn vb to grow light:—n 1 the beginning of day. 2 a beginning (*at the dawn of civilization*):—**dawn upon** to become clear eventually (*it suddenly dawned on me that I was on the wrong train*).

day n 1 daylight. 2 twenty-four hours.

day'break n the beginning of day, dawn (*set out on our journey at daybreak*).

day'dream vb to dream while awake (*daydream of being rich one day*):—also n.

day'light n the light of day.

daze vb to confuse, to bewilder (*dazed by the bang on the head/dazed by the bad news*):—n confusion.

daz'zle vb 1 to prevent from seeing clearly with strong light (*car headlights dazzling rabbits*). 2 to confuse or impress (*dazzled by her beauty*).

dea'con n 1 a clergyman inferior in office to a priest. 2 a church official:—f **dea'coness**.

dead adj 1 without life (*dead bodies*). 2 dull, lifeless (*a dead expression*). 3 absolute, complete (*come to a dead stop*). 4 not working (*the phone is dead*):—adv 1 completely (*dead tired*). 2 straight (*dead ahead*):—n 1 a dead person (*prayers for the dead*). 2 the quietest time (*dead of night*).

dead'beat *adj* tired out, exhausted (*deadbeat after the long walk*).

dead'en *vb* to dull, to lessen (*deaden the pain/ deaden the sounds*).

dead heat' *n* a race in which two or more competitors finish at the same time.

dead'line *n* a time by which something must be done (*Tomorrow is the deadline for applications for the job*).

dead'lock *n* a complete disagreement (*talks between the two sides have reached deadlock*).

dead'ly *adj* 1 causing death (*a deadly disease/a deadly blow*).2 (*inf*) very boring (*what a deadly talk!*):—*n* **dead'liness**.

deadly night'shade *n* a plant with poisonous berries (*kill his victim with deadly nightshade*).

dead wood *n* useless, unneeded material or people (*clear out the dead wood from the staff*).

deaf *adj* 1 unable to hear. 2 unwilling to listen (*deaf to our request for mercy*):—*n* **deaf'ness**.

deaf'en *vb* to make deaf (*noise that would deafen one*).

deaf-mute' *n* a person who is both deaf and dumb.

deal[1] *n* 1 an amount (*a great deal of money/a good deal of rain*). 2 the giving out of playing cards. 3 a business agreement (*sign an important export deal*):—*vb* (*pt, pp* **dealt**) 1 to give out (cards). 2 to cope with, to handle (*deal with the problem*). 3 to do business with (*will deal only with the owner of the firm*).

deal[2] *n* a board of fir or pine wood:—*also adj.*

deal'er *n* 1 one who buys and sells (*a dealer in antiques*). 2 one who gives out playing cards in a game.

deal'ings *npl* acts of business, relations (*wish to have no further dealings with them*).

dean *n* 1 the chief of the clergy who staff a cathedral. 2 the head of a university faculty.

dear *adj* 1 well loved (*my dear mother*). 2 high in price (*dear food/leeks are dear today*):—*n* a loved person:—*adv* dearly:—*n* **dear'ness**.

dear'ly *adv* 1 with great affection. 2 at a high price.

dearth *n* want, scarcity (*there is a dearth of talent in the show/a dearth of fresh food*).

death *n* state of being dead.

death duties *npl* the part of a dead person's property that must be paid as tax.

death'ly *adj and adv* like death (*deathly pale*).

death'trap *n* (*inf*) a place that is very dangerous (*the floor of that old cottage is a real deathtrap*).

death war'rant *n* an order for a person's execution.

debac'le, de'bacle *n* 1 a complete failure (*the concert was a debacle*). 2 defeat (*the battle turned into a debacle for our army*).

debar' *vb* (**debarred', debar'ring**) to shut out from (*people debarred from entering the club/former members debarred from the club*).

debase' *vb* to lower in value, importance or character (*a coinage now debased/debasing oneself by lying*):—*n* **debase'ment**.

debat'able *adj* doubtful, open to question (*a debatable point*).

debate' *n* 1 an argument (*much debate over where to go on holiday*). 2 the formal discussion of a question in public (*a debate in parliament*):—*vb* 1 to argue. 2 to discuss.

debauched' *adj* leading a life of self-indulgence, usu including drinking too much and immorality (*debauched people becoming alcoholics*).

debauch'ery *n* a state of self-indulgence and immorality.

debil'itate *vb* to weaken (*debilitated by a long illness*).

debil'ity *n* weakness (*the debility of the invalid*).

deb'it *n* the written note in an account book of a sum owed:—*vb* to note the sum owed.

debonair [deb-ê-när'] *adj* cheerful, pleasant and elegant (*a debonair young man*).

débris, debris [dã'-bree or deb'-ree] *n* 1 the remains of something broken, destroyed, etc, wreckage (*the debris of the crashed plane*). 2 rubbish, litter, etc (*clear up the debris after the party*).

debt *n* anything owed.

debt'or *n* one who owes.

debut [dã'-bö] *n* a first appearance in public (*a young actress making her debut*).

debutante [dã'-bö-to(ng)t] *n* a young lady making her first appearance in society or at court.

dec'ade *n* 1 a period of ten years. 2 (*inf*) a long time (*I haven't seen her in decades*).

dec'adence *n* a time or state of becoming worse in an artistic or moral sense, decay (*the decadence of the Roman empire/lead a life of decadence*):—*adj* **dec'adent**.

decaf'feinated [dee-kaf'-in-āted] *adj* of coffee, having had most of the caffeine removed, often abbreviated to **decaf**.

dec'agon *n* a figure with ten sides:—*adj* **decag'onal**.

Dec'alogue *n* the ten commandments in the Bible.

decamp' *vb* to go away secretly (*decamp without paying their bills*).

decant' *vb* to pour carefully from one vessel to another (*decant wine from a bottle into a carafe*).

decant'er *n* a stoppered bottle in which wine or spirits is served.

decap'itate *vb* to cut off the head of:—*n* **de-capita'tion**.

decath'lon *n* an athletics event in which people compete in ten different sports.

decay' *vb* **1** to go rotten (*teeth decaying*). **2** to fall into ruin (*buildings decaying from lack of maintenance*):—*also n*.

decease' *n* (*fml*) death:—*vb* to die:—*also n*.

deceased' *adj* dead:—*n* a dead person (*bury the deceased*).

deceit' *n* anything said or done to deceive, trickery (*capable of great deceit/use deceit to get the old lady's money*):—*adj* **deceit'ful**.

deceive' *vb* to make someone believe what is not true, to trick (*deceive them into believing he was a real doctor*):—*n* **deceiv'er**.

Decem'ber *n* the twelfth month of the year.

decency *see* **decent**.

decen'nial *adj* happening every ten years.

de'cent *adj* **1** pr oper, not shocking (*a low neckline that was scarcely decent/think it scarcely decent for her to marry so soon after her husband's death*). **2** reasonable, satisfactory (*get a decent meal*):—*n* **de'cency**.

decen'tralize *vb* to divide power among several authorities instead of giving it all to one (*decentralizing power from central government to the individual regions*).

decep'tion *n* **1** act of deceiving. **2** a trick, pretence (*gain entrance by a deception*):—*adj* **deceptive**.

dec'ibel [des'] *n* a unit for measuring how loud something is.

decide' *vb* **1** to make up one's mind (*decided to go on holiday*). **2** to settle a question, etc (*a goal deciding the match*).

decid'ed *adj* **1** firm. **2** definite.

decid'edly *adv* undoubtedly (*feel decidedly unwell*).

decid'uous *adj* having leaves that fall off in autumn.

dec'imal *adj* counted by tens, hundreds, etc:—*n* a fraction worked out to the nearest tenth, hundredth, etc.

decimal system *n* a system of weights, measures and money based on multiplying and dividing by ten.

dec'imate *vb* **1** to kill every tenth man. **2** to destroy a large number (*a people decimated by famine*).

deciph'er *vb* to work out the meaning of (*decipher her bad handwriting/decipher the enemy's code*).

deci'sion *n* **1** act of deciding. **2** a judgment (*the judge's decision is final/come to a decision*). **3** (*fml*) firmness (*act with decision*).

decisive [dee-sîz'-iv] *adj* **1** firm (*stop changing your mind and be decisive*). **2** settling a matter finally (*a decisive battle*).

decis'ively *adv* firmly, clearly.

deck *vb* (*fml*) to cover, to decorate (*deck the room with holly/deck oneself out in one's best*):—*n* the covering or floor on a ship.

declaim' *vb* to speak with feeling (*declaim a sermon against immorality*):—*n* **decla-ma'tion**:—*adj* **declam'atory**.

declare' *vb* **1** to make known, to announce (*declared war/declaring their intention to marry*). **2** to state firmly ('*I am going home early,*' *she declared*):—*n* **declara'tion**.

declen'sion *n* **1** the grammatical case-endings of nouns or adjectives. **2** a falling away from a higher standard.

decline' *vb* **1** to refuse (*decline the invitation*). **2** to slope downwards. **3** to become worse or weaker (*her state of health is declining*). **4** to give the cases of a noun or adjective:—*n* a gradual worsening or weakening (*a noticeable decline in standards*).

decliv'ity *n* a downward slope.

decode' *vb* to work out the meaning of a message in code.

decompose' *vb* to decay, to rot (*vegetables decomposing on the compost heap/bodies decomposing in the heat*):—*n* **decomposi'tion**.

decontam'inate vb to free from what is infectious or harmful (*decontaminating the radioactive area*):—n **decontamina'tion**.

dec'orate vb **1** to make beautiful or ornamental (*decorating the Christmas tree*). **2** to put wallpaper, paint, etc, on the walls of (*decorate the kitchen*). **3** to give a badge or medal of honour to (*decorate the soldiers for bravery*):—n **decora'tion**.

dec'orative adj ornamental (*a fireplace that was purely decorative*).

dec'orator n one who paints and papers houses.

decorous [dek-ôr'-ês or dek'-or-ês] adj proper, correct, acceptable (*decorous behaviour*).

deco'rum n correct and proper behaviour (*behave with decorum at the formal dinner*).

de'coy n anything intended to lead people, animals, etc, into a trap (*use her child as a decoy to get her into the car*):—vb to lead into a trap, to trick into a place of danger by using a decoy (*decoy him into the cellar by saying his son was there*).

decrease' vb to become or make less (*the number of pupils is decreasing/decrease the amount of money allowed*):—n **de'crease** a lessening (*a decrease in the number of patients*).

decree' n **1** an order or law (*a decree forbidding hunting*). **2** a judgment at law:—vb to make a decree.

decrep'it adj broken down with age (*decrepit old man/decrepit old furniture*):—n **decrep'itude**.

decry' vb (**decried'**, **decry'ing**) to speak against (*decry the government's policy*).

ded'icate vb **1** to set apart for a special purpose (*dedicating his life to medicine*). **2** to offer to God. **3** to write another's name at the beginning of a book to show that one thinks highly of him or her:—n **dedi-ca'tion**:—adj **ded'icatory**.

deduce' vb to work out a truth from things already known (*from the evidence the police deduced that he was guilty*):—adj **de-duc'tive**.

deduct' vb to subtract, to take away (*deduct the price of the broken vase from her wages*).

deduc'tion n **1** an amount taken away (*tax deductions from her salary*). **2** a conclusion worked out from things already known (*the deduction made by the police*).

deed n **1** that which is done, an act (*a brave deed/a foolish deed*). **3** a written agreement (*sign a deed transferring her house to her son*).

deem vb (fml) to judge, to consider (*deem him unworthy to marry her son*).

deep adj **1** going far down (*a deep hole/a deep lake*). **2** difficult to understand (*thoughts too deep for me/a very deep person*). **3** strongly felt (*deep feelings*). **4** cunning (*a deep plot*). **5** (of sounds) low in pitch. **6** (of colour) strong, dark, intense (*a deep purple*):—n the sea.

deep'en vb to become or make deep (*his voice deepened/deepen the hole*).

deer n a swift-moving animal with hooves and horns (e.g. the stag, reindeer, etc).

deer'stalk'er n **1** one who hunts deer. **2** a cap worn by such a sportsman.

deface' vb to damage, to spoil the appearance of (*deface the walls with graffiti*):—n **deface'ment**.

defam'atory adj doing harm to a person's good name (*defamatory remarks*).

defame' vb to speak ill of unfairly (*defaming her by calling her a liar when everyone knows she is truthful*):—n **defama'tion**.

default' n **1** failure to do what is necessary. **2** failure to pay a debt:—also vb:—n **de-fault'er**.

defeat' vb **1** to beat in a fight or contest. **2** to make to fail:—n a lost fight or contest.

defeat'ist adj expecting or being ready to accept defeat or failure (*don't be so defeatist—if you start work now you could still pass your exams*):—n a defeatist person:—n **defeat'ism**.

de'fect[1] n a fault or flaw (*a defect in the dress material/a defect in his character*).

defect[2] vb to desert a country, army, group or political party to join an opposing one (*soldiers defecting to the enemy/voters defecting to another party*):—n **defec'tion**.

defec'tive adj **1** below average or normal (*mentally defective*). **2** faulty, flawed (*defective goods*).

defence' n **1** act of holding off an attack (*join in the defence of the city against the invaders*). **2** that which protects (*thick castle walls acting as a defence*). **3** the arguments in favour of an accused person, esp in a court of law.

defence'less adj without protection (*defenceless children*).

defend' vb **1** to protect or guard against attack (*defend the city against the invaders*). **2** to give reasons in support of one's ideas (*defend their economic policy*). **3** to present the case for an accused person (*the barrister defending the accused*).

defend'ant *n* in law, the person accused.

defens'ible *adj* able to be defended (*behaviour that is scarcely defensible*).

defens'ive *adj* **1** suitable for defence, protecting (*defensive weapons*). **2** ready to defend from attack (*she always adopts a defensive attitude against criticism*):—*n* state of defending.

defer[1] *vb* (**deferred'**, **defer'ring**) to put off until later (*defer the meeting planned for today*):—*n* **defer'ment**.

defer[2] *vb* (**deferred'**, **defer'ring**) to give in to another's wishes from respect (*defer to more experienced people*).

defer'ence *n* respect (*treat elderly people with deference*).

deferen'tial *adj* respectful.

defi'ance *n* defiant behaviour (*in defiance of her teachers/in defiance of the law*).

defi'ant *adj* fearlessly and boldly refusing to obey (*a defiant child/a defiant attitude*).

defic'iency *n* lack, want (*a deficiency of vitamin C*).

deficient [de-fish'-ênt] *adj* lacking something, not having something one should have (*a diet deficient in fresh fruit/deficient in common sense*).

deficit [def-is-it] *n* the amount by which a sum of money falls short of what is needed, a shortage (*annual accounts showing a deficit of thousands of pounds*).

defile[1] *vb* to make dirty or corrupt (*defiling the minds of children*):—*n* **defile'ment**.

defile[2] *vb* to march in line:—*n* a narrow valley.

define' *vb* **1** to mark out the limits of (*define the boundary of his estate*). **2** to explain exactly (*defining a difficult word/define your terms*).

definite *adj* fixed, certain (*definite plans*).

defini'tion *n* an exact meaning or explanation.

defin'itive *adj* **1** clear and certain. **2** final.

deflate' *vb* **1** to let the air out of (*deflating tyres*). **2** to reduce, esp someone's pride, importance, etc:—*n* **defla'tion**.

deflect' *vb* to make to change direction, to turn aside (*deflect the blow with his arm/deflect her from her chosen career*):—*n* **deflec'tion**.

defor'est *vb* to clear of forest.

deforesta'tion *n* the act of cutting down or burning a lot of trees in an area.

deform' *vb* to spoil the shape or appearance of (*her beauty was deformed by a birthmark/deform the landscape with buildings*).

deformed' *adj* badly or unnaturally shaped:—*n* **deform'ity**.

defraud' *vb* to cheat (*defraud the old man of his savings*).

defray' *vb* (*fml*) to pay the cost of (*defrayed the travel costs*).

deft *adj* skilful (*deft fingers/deft at pottery/a deft handling of the situation*):—*n* **deft'-ness**.

defunct' *adj* dead, out of existence (*customs now defunct*).

defy' *vb* **1** to challenge. **2** to refuse to obey or to respect. **3** to care nothing for.

degen'erate *vb* to become worse, to lose good qualities (*the meeting started off well but degenerated into a loud argument*):—*also adj*:—*n* a person whose character has become worse (*a moral degenerate*):—*ns* **degen'eracy**, **degenera'tion**.

degrade' *vb* **1** to lower in rank or importance. **2** to disgrace (*the family were degraded by their son's brutal behaviour*):—*n* **degrada'tion**.

degree' *n* **1** a step or stage (*be promoted by degrees/make progress by degrees*). **2** (*old*) a rank (*ladies of high degree*). **3** a unit of measurement for heat, angles, etc. **4** the title given by a university to those who reach a certain standard of learning.

de'hydrate *vb* **1** to take the water out of (*dehydrated vegetables*). **2** to lose water from the body (*dehydrated from walking in the severe heat*).

deign [dān] *vb* to do something as if it were a favour (*deign to accept his gift*).

deity [dee'-i-ti] *n* a god or goddess:—**the Deity** God.

deject'ed *adj* sad, discouraged (*feel dejected when he failed to win*):—*n* **dejec'tion**.

delay' *vb* **1** to put off till later (*delaying the start of the meeting*). **2** to make late (*a plane delayed by fog*). **3** to wait before going on (*we delayed a bit before starting out*):—*also n*.

delec'table *adj* (*fml*) delightful, very pleasing (*the creamy dessert was a delectable sight*).

delecta'tion *n* (*fml*) delight, enjoyment (*for your delectation*).

del'egate *vb* **1** to send a person to act or speak for others. **2** to give certain powers to another:—*n* one acting or speaking for others (*our union delegate at the conference*).

delega'tion *n* a body of delegates.

delete' *vb* to rub out, to cross out (*deleting the second paragraph of the report*):—*n* **dele'tion**.

deleterious [del-i-teer'-i-us] *adj* hurtful (*a way of life deleterious to his health*).

Delft *n* a type of pottery.

delib'erate [-āt] *vb* **1** (*fml*) to think over carefully, to consider (*take time to deliberate whether to go or not/deliberating on his financial problems*). **2** to talk over (*deliberated with his colleagues about the correct course of action*):—*adj* [-ēt] **1** done on purpose (*a deliberate attempt to hurt her*). **2** slow (*with a deliberate tread*).

delibera'tion *n* **1** (*fml*) careful thought. **2** discussion.

del'icate *adj* **1** fine, easily hurt or damaged (*delicate skin/delicate china*). **2** fine, dainty (*delicate features*). **3** not very healthy, easily made ill (*his wife is delicate/of a delicate constitution*). **4** light, subtle (*delicate shades of pink/delicate flavours*):—*n* **del'icacy**.

delicates'sen *n* a shop, or part of one, that sells cold meats and cheese and speciality foods from other countries.

delic'ious *adj* very pleasing, esp to the taste (*delicious food/delicious smells*).

delight' *n* great joy or pleasure (*take delight in reading/one of the delights of living in the country*):—*vb* to gladden, to give great joy (*delighted by the news*).

delight'ful *adj* causing delight, pleasant (*a delightful day/a delightful personality*).

delim'it *vb* to mark the boundaries of, to fix the extent of.

delin'eate *vb* **1** to draw the outline of. **2** to describe:—*ns* **delinea'tion, delin'eator**.

delin'quency *n* **1** (*fml*) failure to do duty (*the soldier's delinquency in being asleep on duty*). **2** wrongdoing, minor crime (*juvenile delinquency*).

delin'quent *adj* **1** (*fml*) not doing one's duty. **2** doing wrong, committing minor crimes (*delinquent young people*):—*n* **1** one not doing one's duty. **2** a wrongdoer, especially a young one.

deli'rious *adj* **1** wandering in the mind (*delirious after the blow to his head*). **2** highly excited (*children delirious with excitement at the idea of going to the pantomime*):—*n* **delir'ium**.

deliv'er *vb* **1** (*fml*) to set free, to rescue (*deliver them from slavery*). **2** to hand over (*deliver the parcel*). **3** to make (a speech). **4** to aim (*deliver a blow*).

deliv'ery *n* **1** childbirth (*present at the delivery of his son*). **2** a giving out of letters (*postal delivery*). **3** manner of speaking in public (*a clear delivery*).

dell *n* a small valley.

del'ta *n* the land between the branches of a river with two or more mouths.

delude' *vb* to deceive, to trick (*deluding his parents into thinking she was staying at a friend's house*).

del'uge *n* a great flood.

delu'sion *n* a mistaken belief (*parents under the delusion that their children were studying*).

delu'sory *adj* s (*fml*) deceiving, misleading.

delve *vb* (*old*) to dig, to search deeply (*delving in her bag for change/delved into old records for details of her family history*).

demagogue [dem'-ê-gog] *n* **1** a leader of the people. **2** one who, in speeches, tries to play upon the feelings of his audience.

demand' *vb* **1** to ask for firmly or sharply (*demand to see the manager/demand his rights*). **2** require or need (a situation demanding tact):—*n* **1** a claim. **2** a pressing request.

de'marcate *vb* to mark out the boundaries or limits of (*demarcating the various jobs in the factory*):—*n* **demarca'tion**.

demean' *vb* to lower (oneself) (*refuse to demean oneself to associate with a thief*).

demean'our *n* (*fml*) behaviour, manner (*a cheerful demeanour*).

dement'ed *adj* mad, out of one's mind (*demented with grief*).

demer'it *n* (*fml*) a fault, a bad quality (*the demerits of the system*).

demi- *prefix* half.

dem'igod *n* in fable, one half-human, half-divine.

demise' *n* **1** (*fml*) death (*after the demise of his father*). **2** end, often due to failure (*the demise of his business*).

demob'ilize *vb* **1** to release from the army. **2** to break up an army and let the soldiers return to their homes.

democ'racy *n* **1** government by the people. **2** a state that is governed by the people or by persons elected by the people.

dem'ocrat *n* one who believes in democracy:—*adj* **democrat'ic**.

demol'ish *vb* **1** to pull down (*demolish the dangerous old buildings*). **2** to destroy (*demolish their argument*):—*n* **demoli'tion**.

de'mon *n* an evil spirit, a devil.

demoniacal [dee-mên-î'-êk-êl] *adj* **1** devilish. **2** cruel.

demonol'ogy *n* **1** the study of evil spirits. **2** a book about evil spirits.

dem'onstrate *vb* **1** to show (*demonstrating his skill in carpentry/demonstrated his affection by bringing her flowers*). **2** to show how something works (*demonstrate the new washing machine*). **3** to take part in a public show of strong feeling or opinion, often with marching, large signs, etc (*students demonstrating against cuts in grants*).

demonstra'tion *n* **1** a proof (*flowers in demonstration of his affection*). **2** actions taken by a crowd to show their feelings (*a demonstration against racism*). **3** a display to show how something works (*a demonstration of the new vacuum cleaner*).

demon'strative *adj* **1** indicating the person or thing referred to (*a demonstrative pronoun*). **2** quick to show feelings, showing feelings openly (*a demonstrative person/so demonstrative that she gave him a hug*).

dem'onstrator *n* one who shows how something works.

demor'alize *vb* to weaken the courage or self-confidence of (*a defeat that demoralized the troops*):—*n* **demoraliza'tion**.

demur' *vb* (**demurred'**, **demur'ring**) to express doubt or objection (*demur at lending her car to the group*):—*also n*.

demure' *adj* serious and modest in manner (*a demure young girl*):—*n* **demure'ness**.

den *n* **1** the home (cave, hole, etc) of a wild beast (*the lion's den*). **2** a secret meeting place (*a den of thieves*). **3** (*inf*) a small room for studying in.

denial *see* **deny**.

denigrate [den'-i-grāt] *vb* to speak ill of, to belittle (*denigrating his achievements*):—*n* **denigra'tion**.

den'im *n* a cotton material used for overalls, etc (*jeans made of blue denim*).

den'izen *n* (*fml or lit*) an inhabitant (*the denizens of the deep*).

denom'inate *vb* to give a name to.

denomina'tion *n* **1** (*fml*) a name (*a firm trading under another denomination*). **2** a class or unit of measurement or money (*coins of low denomination*). **3** all those sharing the same religious beliefs.

denomina'tional *adj* having to do with a religious group or sect.

denom'inator *n* the number below the line in a vulgar fraction (*in $^3/_4$ the denominator is 4*).

denote' *vb* **1** to be a sign of, to mean (*a silence that probably denoted guilt/a sign denoting a missing word*).

dénouement [dā-nö'-mo(ng)] *n* the point in the telling of a story at which all difficulties or doubts are settled.

denounce' *vb* to speak openly against, to accuse publicly (*the headmaster denounced the culprits at assembly*):—*n* **denuncia'tion**.

dense *adj* **1** thick (*dense fog*). **2** closely packed (*a dense crowd*). **3** stupid (*dense pupils*).

dens'ity *n* the thickness of anything.

dent *n* a hollow made by a blow or by pressure on the surface (*a dent in his car after the collision/the dent in the pillow made by her head*):—*also vb*.

dent'al *adj* having to do with the teeth (*dental treatment*).

dent'ist *n* one who takes out or repairs bad teeth, makes false teeth, and in general cares for the teeth of others:—*n* **dent'istry**.

dent'ure *n* a set of artificial teeth.

denuda'tion *n* the wearing away by the weather of the surface of the earth, and the laying bare of rocks underneath it.

denude' *vb* to make bare or naked, to strip (*trees denuded of leaves*).

denunciation *see* **denounce**.

deny' *vb* **1** to say that something is not true (*deny that he is guilty/deny the accusations*). **2** to refuse (*deny them the opportunity to go to the concert*):—*n* **deni'al**.

deod'orant *n* a liquid or powder that takes away or hides bad smells (*an underarm deodorant*).

deod'orize vb (fml) to take away the smell from.

depart' vb **1** (fml) to go away, to set out (the train departs from platform 6/we depart at dawn). **2** to cease to follow (depart from our usual routines). **3** (fml) to die (depart this life):—n **depart'ure.**

depart'ment n a separate part (the sales department/the history department).

depart'ment store n a large store that has many different sections, each selling a different type of goods.

departure see **depart.**

depend' vb **1** to be likely to happen only under certain conditions (our holiday depends on our having enough money). **2** to trust, to rely on (depend on his assistant). **3** to need for one's support (charities depend on the public for donations).

depend'able adj trustworthy (dependable employees).

depend'ant n one who looks to another for support or livelihood (have a wife and three children as dependants).

depend'ence n the state of depending.

depend'ency n a country governed by another country.

depend'ent adj **1** relying on another for support (countries dependent on foreign aid). **2** to be decided by (whether we have a picnic is dependent on the weather).

depict' vb **1** to describe (the book depicts Victorian London). **2** to draw, paint, etc (a painting depicting a cornfield).

depil'atory adj used to remove hair (a depilatory cream):—also n.

deplete' vb to lessen in amount, size or numbers (the number of spectators was depleted by the weather):—n **deple'tion.**

deplor'able adj very bad, regrettable (deplorable behaviour).

deplore' vb to regret, to express disapproval of (deploring their behaviour).

deploy' vb to spread out over a wide front (deployed troops):—n **deploy'ment.**

depop'ulate vb to take away the people living in a certain area (the area is now depopulated because of lack of jobs):—n **depop'ulation.**

deport' vb **1** to send a person out of the country in punishment (formerly criminals were deported to Australia). **2** (fml) to behave (oneself) (deport oneself well).

deporta'tion n act of sending out of the country.

deport'ment n (fml) the manner in which one stands, moves, etc (improve one's deportment).

depose' vb to remove from high office or the throne (deposing the king).

depos'it vb **1** (fml) to lay down (deposit the books on the table). **2** to put in a safe place (depositing her jewellery in the bank):—n **1** an amount paid into a bank (make several large deposits). **2** a first payment towards a larger amount (put down a deposit on a TV set). **3** solid matter in liquid, collecting at the bottom (the deposit at the bottom of a bottle of wine).

deposi'tion n **1** the act of deposing. **2** the act of depositing. **3** a statement made on oath.

depos'itory n a storehouse.

depot [dep'-ō] n **1** a storehouse. **2** a military station or headquarters. **3** a garage for buses.

deprave' vb to make wicked.

depraved' adj wicked (worried about such depraved people associating with children):—n **depravity** [dee-prav'-i-ti].

dep'recate vb to express disapproval of (deprecating any form of violence):—n **deprecation.**

dep'recatory adj **1** full of regret, apologetic (confess his wrongdoing with a deprecatory smile). **2** expressing disapproval (a deprecatory statement on the use of violence).

depreciate [de-pree'-shi-āt] vb **1** to lower the value of (houses depreciating in value/cars depreciating rapidly). **2** (fml) to represent as being of little value (try to depreciate his contribution):—n **depreciation.**

depreda'tion n (fml) plundering, stealing (the depredations of war).

depress' vb **1** to press down, to lower (depress the lever to start the machine). **2** to make sad (winter depresses him).

depress'ion n **1** gloom, sadness (suffer from depression). **2** a hollow (a depression in the soil where the box had stood). **3** low atmospheric pressure, causing unsettled or stormy weather.

depriva'tion n **1** loss (the deprivation of their rights). **2** want, hardship (live in deprivation).

deprive' vb to take away from (war depriving them of their father/people deprived of their rights).

depth n **1** deepness (*the depth of the water*). **2** strength (of feeling) (*the depth of her love/the depth of public feeling*).

depths npl the deepest or most central part (*in the depths of the ocean/the depths of winter*).

deputa'tion n a group of persons speaking or acting for others (*a deputation sent to ask the boss for a wage increase*).

depute [de-pût'] vb **1** to send someone to act or speak for others. **2** to hand over to someone else to do (*deputing the task of collecting the money to him*):—adj acting for another.

dep'utize vb to take the place of, to act for (*deputizing for the head teacher at the parents' meeting*).

dep'uty n one acting for another (*the head teacher's deputy*).

derail' vb to cause to leave the rails (*trains derailed in a collision*):—n **derail'ment**.

deranged' adj mad, insane (*so deranged that he is a danger to himself and others*).

der'elict adj left as useless (*derelict old houses*):—also n.

derelic'tion n (*fml*) neglect (*dereliction of duty*).

deride' vb to laugh at, to make fun of (*deriding his efforts to jump the high wall*).

deri'sion n mockery.

derisive [de-rî'-siv] adj mocking (*derisive laughter/derisive remarks*).

deriva'tion n the history of a word back to its earliest known form.

deriv'ative n a word made from another word:—adj not original, copying others (*a derivative style of painting*).

derive' vb **1** to obtain from (*deriving comfort from their presence/derive cheese from milk*). **2** to come from (*a word derived from Latin/her popularity derives from her pleasantness*).

dermatol'ogy n the study of the skin and its diseases:—n **dermatol'ogist**.

derog'atory adj insulting, indicating disapproval and scorn (*make derogatory remarks about management*).

der'rick n a type of crane (used in drilling oil wells).

des'cant n a second tune played at the same time as and generally higher than the main tune for contrast:—vb **descant'** to talk at length.

descend' vb **1** (*fml*) to climb down (*descending the mountain*). **2** to attack (*thieves descended*

on the travellers*). **3** to have as an ancestor (*descended from Queen Anne*).

descend'ant n one having a certain person as an ancestor (*a descendant of Queen Anne*).

descent' n **1** (*fml*) act of climbing down (*the descent of the mountain*). **2** a slope (*a slippery descent*). **3** a sudden attack (*the terrorists' descent on the tourists*). **4** a line of ancestors (*proud of his royal descent*).

describe' vb **1** to tell what happened (*describing the visit of the president/described how the accident happened*). **2** to tell what a thing or person is like (*asked to describe her attacker*):—n **descrip'tion**:—adj **descrip'tive**.

descry' vb (*old*) to catch sight of, esp something a long way off (*descried a ship on the horizon*).

des'ecrate vb to treat something holy insultingly, to put something holy to a bad use (*desecrating the altar of the church*):—n **desecra'tion**.

des'ert[1] adj without inhabitants (*a desert island*):—n a large area of barren, often sandy, land (*camels in the desert*).

desert'[2] vb **1** to leave, to run away from (*desert his wife and children*). **2** to go away from (one's duty) (*soldiers deserting their posts*): —n **deser'tion**.

desert'er n one who leaves the army, navy, etc, without permission.

deserts' n that which is deserved (good or bad) (*receive a reward or a punishment according to one's deserts/get one's just deserts*).

deserve' vb to be worthy of (*deserve a medal for bravery*):—adj **deserv'ing**.

deser'vedly adv justly (*punished deservedly*).

des'iccate vb to dry (*desiccated coconut*):—n **desicca'tion**.

design' vb **1** to make a plan of (*design a swimming pool/design clothes*). **2** to plan, to intend (*a scheme designed to save money*):—n **1** a plan or drawing of something to be made (*the design for the new building*). **2** a plan, a purpose (*they met by design*). **3** a pattern (*a checked design*).

des'ignate vb **1** to name (*an area designated a bird sanctuary*). **2** to point out (*crosses on the map designating churches*). **3** to appoint to a particular post or position (*designated sportswoman of the year*):—adj appointed to a post, but not yet in it (*managing director designate*).

designa'tion n (fml) name, title (a firm trading under a new designation).

design'er adj made by a famous designer and bearing a label with that name on it (unable to afford designer clothes).

design'ing adj always planning cunningly or to gain advantage (a designing woman looking for a rich husband).

desir'able adj 1 much wanted (a desirable job). 2 arousing longing for (a desirable woman):— n desirabil'ity.

desire' vb 1 (fml) to wish for, to long for (desiring happiness). 2 to be sexually attracted to:— n 1 a longing, a wish (their desire for peace/express a desire to emigrate). 2 a strong wish for sexual relations. 3 something or someone that is desired (his heart's desire).

desir'ous adj (fml) wanting, eager for (desirous of peace).

desist' vb (fml) to stop, to leave off (ordered to desist from threatening people).

desk n a table for reading or writing at.

des'olate adj 1 deserted and miserable (a desolate part of the world). 2 miserable, lonely (desolate at the death of her husband):—vb to lay waste.

desola'tion n 1 loneliness, grief (the desolation of the widow). 2 a wilderness (areas of desolation).

despair' vb to be without hope, to give up hope (despair of ever getting a job):—n hopelessness.

despatch see dispatch.

des'perate adj 1 hopeless, and therefore ready to take risks (a desperate criminal/prisoners desperate to escape). 2 without hope (a desperate cause). 3 urgent and despairing (a desperate appeal for help):—n despera'tion.

despic'able adj mean, deserving to be despised (a despicable trick).

despise' vb to look down upon, to consider worthless (despised him for hitting a child).

despite' prep in spite of.

despond'ent adj without hope, downcast (despondent after her failure in the exam):—n despond'ency.

des'pot n a ruler with power to do as he pleases without opposition, a tyrant:—adj despot'ic:—n des'potism.

dessert' n the sweet course at the end of a meal (have fresh fruit for dessert).

destina'tion n the place to which a person or thing is going (arrive at our destination).

des'tine vb to mark out for a special purpose (a young man destined for greatness).

des'tiny n a power that seems to arrange people's lives in advance, fate.

des'titute adj in great want, very poor (homeless and destitute):—n destitu'tion.

destroy' vb 1 to break to pieces (a house destroyed by fire). 2 to ruin (destroying all our hopes). 3 to kill (a poison that destroys rats).

destroy'er n 1 one who destroys. 2 a fast-moving warship.

destruc'tible adj able to be destroyed.

destruc'tion n 1 act of destroying (the destruction of the house by fire). 2 ruin (the destruction of our hopes/the destruction of the Roman empire). 3 death (the destruction of the rats by poison).

destruc'tive adj 1 causing ruin (destructive fire). 2 unhelpful (destructive criticism).

des'ultory adj without plan or method, rambling (a desultory discussion).

detach' vb 1 to unfasten (detach the lead from the dog's collar). 2 to take away from the rest (a group of soldiers detached to guard the castle).

detach'able adj able to be detached (a coat with a detachable hood).

detached' adj 1 separate, not joined to others (a detached house). 2 not influenced by others, impartial (take a detached view/a detached judgment).

detach'ment n 1 a group of soldiers taken away from a larger group. 2 freedom from prejudice, impartiality (judges require detachment).

detail' vb 1 (fml) to give a very full account or description (detailing the tasks to be carried out). 2 to set apart for a particular job (detailed soldiers to guard the castle):—n de'tail, detail' a small part or item (the plan has been drawn up but not the details).

detailed' adj very full and exact (a detailed report).

detain' vb 1 to prevent from leaving or doing something, to delay (detained by several telephone calls/the doctor has been detained). 2 to arrest, to keep in custody (detained by the police):—n deten'tion.

detect' vb 1 to find out, to notice, to discover (detect smoke/detect a note of sadness). 2 to investigate and solve (*police detecting a murder*):—*n* detec'tion.

detec'tive *n* one whose job it is to find those guilty of crimes (*detectives seeking clues*).

detention *see* detain.

deter' *vb* (deterred', deter'ring) to keep from, to discourage (*deterred from leaving by fear*).

deter'gent *adj* cleansing:—*n* a chemical material used instead of soap for washing and cleansing (*wash clothes in detergent*).

deter'iorate *vb* to become worse (*the invalid's condition is deteriorating*).

determina'tion *n* strength of will, firmness (*have the determination to succeed*).

deter'mine *vb* **1** to fix, to decide on (*determine the date for the meeting*). **2** to find how exactly (*determining the cause of the accident*).

deter'mined *adj* strong-willed (*a determined young woman/a determined attitude*).

deter'rent *n* something that keeps people from acting in a certain way (*prison acting as a deterrent to those who might break the law*):—*also adj*.

detest' *vb* to hate, to loathe (*detest violence*):—*adj* detest'able:—*n* detesta'tion.

dethrone' *vb* to put off a throne:—*n* de-throne'ment.

det'onate *vb* to explode (*a bomb detonated by remote control*):—*n* deto-na'tion.

det'onator *n* a mechanism that sets off an explosion.

de'tour *n* a roundabout way (*forced to make a detour to avoid the city centre*).

detract' *vb* to take away from (*a crack detracting from the value of the antique vase/detract from our enjoyment*):—*n* de-trac'tion.

det'riment *n* (*fml*) harm, damage, disadvantage (*to the detriment of his health/with inevitable detriment to his reputation*).

detrimen'tal *adj* harmful, disadvantageous (*conditions detrimental to health/detrimental effects*).

deuce [dûs'] *n* **1** in cards, the two of any suit. **2** in tennis, forty to each side. **3** the devil.

dev'astate *vb* **1** to lay waste (*war devastating the country*). **2** to overwhelm with grief or disappointment (*devastated at the news of her death/devastated by his defeat in the championship*):—*n* devasta'tion.

devel'op *vb* **1** to grow bigger or better (*he is developing into a fine young man/the plan is slowly developing*). **2** to make to grow bigger or better (*exercises to develop muscles/develop the scheme further*). **3** in photography, to treat a film with chemicals to make the picture appear.

devel'opment *n* **1** growth (*watch the child's development/the development of the business*). **2** a stage of growth (*the latest development*). **3** a new product or invention (*exciting developments in the car industry*).

de'viate *vb* to turn aside (*deviating from the usual procedure*).

devia'tion *n* a turning aside from the normal or expected course (*little deviation from her routine*).

device' *n* **1** a plan, scheme, trick (*a supposed illness that was just a device to get off work*). **2** an invention, a tool or mechanism (*a labour-saving device for the kitchen/an explosive device*). **3** an emblem or sign (*the heraldic device on the family crest*).

dev'il *n* **1** an evil spirit. **2** Satan. **3** a very wicked person. **4** one who does detailed or routine work for a professional man (e.g. a lawyer, printer, etc).

dev'ilish *adj* very evil (*a devilish plan*).

dev'il-may-care' *adj* carefree, ready to risk everything (*a devil-may-care attitude*).

dev'ilment, dev'ilry *ns* mischief, naughtiness (*children full of devilment*).

de'vious *adj* **1** roundabout, indirect (*a devious route*). **2** not direct, not straightforward and honest (*use devious means to get his own way/a very devious person*).

devise' *vb* to plan, to invent, to work out, esp cleverly (*devising a scheme*).

devoid' *adj* lacking in, free from (*devoid of humour/devoid of trouble*).

devolu'tion *n* **1** the handing on of tasks or duties to another in a less important position. **2** the act of handing on certain powers to a regional government by a central government.

devolve' *vb* **1** to hand on (*property devolving to his daughter on his death*). **2** to fall upon as a task or duty (*work that devolved on his assistants*).

devote' *vb* to give up wholly to (*devoting his life to helping the poor*).

devot'ed *adj* loving (*her devoted parents*).

devotee [dev-o-tee'] *n* a very keen follower.

devo'tion *n* **1** great love, dedication (*her devotion to her children*). **2** (*fml*) prayer (*at her devotions*).

devour' vb **1** to eat greedily (*devour the chocolate*). **2** to destroy (*a forest devoured by fire*). **3** to possess completely (*devoured by hate/devoured by jealousy*). **4** to read eagerly (*devour the story hungrily*).

devout' adj **1** given to prayer and worship, religious (*a devout Christian*). **2** sincere, deeply felt (*it is our devout hope that we will be able to help*).

dew n tiny drops of water that fall on the ground when air cools during the night:—adj **dew'y**.

dexter'ity n cleverness with the hands, skill (*admire the dexterity of the juggler*):—adj **dext'(e)rous**.

dhow [dou'] n an Arab trading vessel.

diabetes [dî-ê-bee'-tês] n a disease causing too much sugar in the body (*suffer from diabetes and have to take insulin*):—adj and n **diabet'ic**.

diabolic [dî-a-bol'-ik], **diabol'ical** adjs **1** devilish. **2** very wicked, very cruel (*a diabolical plan to murder his wife*). **3** (inf) very bad (*her cooking is diabolical*).

diadem [dî'-a-dem] n a type of crown.

diaeresis [dî-er'-ê-sis] n a mark (¨) over a vowel to show that it is to be pronounced separately (e.g. naïve [na-eev])

diagnose' vb to decide by examining a sick person the kind of illness that he or she has (*diagnosing chickenpox/diagnose the patient as having chickenpox*):—n **diagno'sis**.

diag'onal adj going from corner to corner:—n a line joining opposite corners.

diag'onally adv at a slant (*a path going diagonally across a field*).

di'agram n a plan or sketch, a drawing made to help to explain something (*a diagram of the parts of the body*).

di'al n **1** the face of a watch or clock (*a watch with a digital dial*). **2** the numbered disc or pad by means of which one rings a telephone number:—vb (**di'alled, di'alling**) to ring a telephone number (*dial 999*).

di'alect n the way of speaking in a particular part of a country (*the Cornish dialect*).

di'alogue n a conversation between two or more people (*the play is a dialogue between two old men about the past*).

diam'eter n a straight line passing from one side of a circle to the other through its centre:—dia-

metrically opposed exactly opposite (*hold diametrically opposed views*).

di'amond n **1** a hard, very valuable precious stone. **2** pl a suit of playing cards.

diamond wedding n the sixtieth anniversary of marriage.

diaphragm [dî'-a-fram] n **1** a muscle separating the chest from the abdomen. **2** a plate or skin separating one part of an instrument from another.

di'arist n one who keeps a diary (*Samuel Pepys was a famous diarist*).

diarrhoea [dî-a-ree'-a] n looseness of the bowels (*suffering from diarrhoea*).

di'ary n a book in which one writes something every day (*write her appointments in her diary/write an account of her day in her diary*).

di'atribe n a bitter attack in words, violent criticism (*listen to her diatribe against the government's economic policy*).

dib'ble, dib'ber ns a pointed tool to make holes for planting seeds.

dice pl of **die²**:—vb to cut into pieces shaped like cubes (*dicing vegetables for soup*).

Dic'taphone n the trademark for a machine for recording and playing back what is spoken into it.

dictate' vb **1** to speak aloud something to be written down by another (*dictating letters for his secretary to type*). **2** to give orders, to order about (*workers trying to dictate how the factory should be run*). **3** to fix, to determine (*the amount of work done by the charity is dictated by money*):—n **dicta'tion**.

dicta'tor n one person with complete power of government (*a people terrified of the dictator*):—n **dicta'torship**.

dictato'rial adj **1** like a dictator (*a dictatorial manner*). **2** liking to order others about (*so dictatorial that people will not work for her*).

diction n **1** choice of words (*poetic diction*). **2** way of speaking (*clear diction/try to improve her diction*).

dic'tionary n a book in which words are arranged in alphabetical order and their meanings and other information about them given.

dic'tum n (pl **dic'ta** or **dictums**) **1** a saying, a maxim ('*Do as you would be done by' is a well-known dictum*). **2** an opinion formally given (*the judge's dictum*).

didac'tic adj **1** meant to teach a lesson (didactic poetry). **2** too eager to teach or give instructions (a very didactic person/a didactic way of talking).

did'dle vb (inf) to trick, to cheat (diddling his boss by taking money from the till).

die[1] vb **1** to stop living. **2** to fade away (hope died).

die[2] n **1** (pl **dice**) a small cube, its sides marked with numbers from 1 to 6, used in games of chance. **2** (pl **dies**) a stamp for marking designs on paper, coins, etc.

dies'el engine n an engine that works by burning heavy oil.

di'et n **1** food, the type of food on which one lives (a healthy diet/a vegetarian diet). **2** a course of limited foods designed to lose weight, treat a medical condition, etc (go on a strict diet/a calorie-controlled diet):—vb to eat certain foods only, esp in order to lose weight.

di'etary adj concerning diet (religious dietary restrictions).

dietet'ic adj having to do with diet (a dietetic expert):—n **dieti'cian.**

dif'fer vb **1** to be unlike (people differing from each other in their attitude to money/differ in size). **2** to disagree (two sides differing over the site of the new building/agree to differ).

dif'ference n **1** unlikeness (a marked difference in the state of her health/the difference between the two cars). **2** a disagreement, a quarrel (settle their difference).

different adj **1** unlike, not the same (sisters quite different from each other/a different hairstyle). **2** (inf) unusual, special (well, her new hairstyle is certainly different).

differen'tial adj changing to suit different conditions:—also n.

differential gear n a mechanism on an axle between two wheels, enabling each wheel to turn at a different speed.

differen'tiate vb **1** to see or point out the difference between (able to differentiate a robin from a sparrow). **2** to make different (what differentiates the two models of car?). **3** to treat differently (differentiating between men and women in terms of salary).

difficult adj **1** hard to do (a difficult task). **2** hard to please (a difficult old woman). **3** troublesome (a difficult period):—n **dif-ficulty.**

dif'fident adj shy, not sure of oneself (a diffident young woman/diffident of expressing opinions in public):—n **dif'fidence.**

diffuse [dif-fûz'] vb (fml) to spread widely (diffusing light/diffused happiness):—adj diffuse [dif-fûs'] **1** widely spread (diffuse light). **2** long-winded, wordy (a diffuse style of writing):—n **diffu'sion.**

dig vb (**digged', dig'ging**) **1** to turn up earth or soil. **2** to prod, to poke (dig her in the ribs). **3** (inf) to search (dig in her handbag for her keys):—n a prod, a sharp push:—n **dig'ger.**

digest' vb **1** to dissolve in the stomach (digest a heavy lunch). **2** to think over and understand fully (take time to digest what he said):—n **di'gest** (fml) a summary, a short account (prepare a digest of the evidence given at the trial).

digest'ible adj able to be digested (able to eat foods that are easily digestible).

diges'tion n the process of digesting food.

diges'tive adj concerning digestion (the human digestive system).

dig'it n **1** any figure from 0 to 9. **2** (fml) a finger or toe:—adj **dig'ital.**

dig'ital adj **1** showing information in the form of numbers (a digital watch). **2** recording or transmitting information as numbers in the form of very small signals. **3** to do with the fingers or toes.

digitalis [di-dji-tä'-lis] n a drug made from the foxglove.

dig'ital tele'vision n a system of television in which the picture is transmitted as a digital signal and decoded by a device attached to the viewer's television set.

digital video disk see **DVD.**

dig'nified adj noble in manner, stately (dignified behaviour/a dignified exit/a dignified old lady).

dig'nify vb **1** to give grace or nobility to (a procession dignified by the presence of the mayor). **2** to give an important-sounding name to something (dignifying his patch of grass with the title of lawn).

dig'nitary n a person of high rank (a formal dinner attended by local dignitaries).

dig'nity n **1** goodness and nobleness of character, worthiness (human dignity). **2** seriousness, calmness, formality (the dignity of the situation/

keep her dignity while being booed by the crowd). **3** high rank (*confer the dignity of knighthood on him*).

digress' *vb* to speak or write on a subject other than the one being considered (*keep digressing from the main issue/unable to follow the speaker as he often digresses*):—*n* **digres'sion.**

dike, dyke *n* **1** a ditch or wall. **2** a bank built up to hold back the sea or floods.

dilap'idated *adj* completely worn out, falling to bits (*dilapidated property/in a dilapidated condition*):—*n* **dilapida'tion.**

dilate' *vb* **1** to become larger or wider (*eyes dilating in fear*). **2** to cause to become larger or wider (*a substance that had dilated her pupils*).—*ns* **dilata'tion, dila'tion.**

dil'atory *adj* slow, given to wasting time (*dilatory in answering correspondence*).

dilem'ma *n* a choice between two things or actions, usu equally unpleasant.

dilettante [di-le-tan'-ti] *n* one who studies a subject slightly or carelessly (*a musical dilettante*):—*adj* having no deep interest.

dil'igent *adj* very careful, painstaking, hard-working (*diligent pupils/diligent workers*):—*n* **dil'igence.**

dil'ly-dal'ly *vb* (*inf*) to waste time, to wait about (*dilly-dallying instead of getting down to work*).

dilute' *vb* **1** to water down, to reduce in strength by adding water or another liquid (*diluting lime juice with water*). **2** to weaken in force, effect, etc (*the president's power has been diluted/try to dilute the force of her critical speech with a smile*):—*n* **dilu'tion.**

dim *adj* **1** faint, not bright (*a dim light*). **2** indistinct (*a dim figure in the distance*). **3** (*inf*) not bright, not understanding clearly (*she's a bit dim*):—*vb* (**dimmed', dim'ming**) to make or become dim (*dim the lights/the lights dimmed in the theatre*).

dime *n* in US, a silver coin that is a tenth part of a dollar, ten cents.

dimen'sion *n* **1** the measure of length, breadth and depth (*a beast of huge dimension*). **2** (*often pl*) size, extent (*take the dimensions of the room*).

dimin'ish *vb* to make or become less (*enthusiasm has gradually diminished/strength diminished by a poor diet*).

diminu'tion *n* a lessening.

dimin'utive *adj* very small, tiny (*diminutive little girls/look diminutive beside the tall man*):—*n* a word or part of a word suggesting smallness (e.g. *-kin* in lamb*kin*).

dim'ple *n* a small hollow, esp on the cheek or chin:—*vb* to show dimples (*dimpling prettily as she smiled*).

din *n* a continued loud noise (*complain about the din from the neighbour's television*):—*vb* (**dinned', din'ning**) **1** to go on saying the same thing again and again (*try to din the information into her*). **2** to make a continued loud noise (*music from her car radio dinning in our ears*).

dine *vb* to eat dinner (*dining at 8 o'clock/dined on pheasant*):—*n* **din'er.**

dinghy [ding'-gi] *n* a small boat, a ship's boat.

din'gle *n* a small shady valley.

din'gy *adj* dull, dirty-looking, faded (*dingy wallpaper/a dingy room/dingy colours*):—*n* **din'giness.**

din'ner *n* the principal meal of the day (*eat dinner in the evening*).

dinosaur [dī'-no-sår] *n* a very large lizard-like animal of prehistoric times.

dint *n*:—**by dint of** by means of (*succeed by dint of sheer hard work*).

diocese [dī'-o-sis] *n* the district under the care of a bishop:—*adj* **diocesan** [dī-o-si-san].

dip *vb* (**dipped', dip'ping**) **1** to put into liquid for a moment (*dip the biscuit in chocolate sauce/dip his bread in the soup*). **2** to lower sheep into a liquid that disinfects them or kills insects. **3** to lower for a short time (*dip his headlights*). **4** to take a sudden downward slope (*the road suddenly dipped*):—*n* **1** (*inf*) a quick wetting, a bathe (*go for a dip in the river*). **2** a liquid or semi-liquid substance into which something is dipped (*a cheese dip*). **3** a cleansing liquid for dipping sheep. **4** a downward slope (*a dip in the road*).

diphthe'ria *n* an infectious throat disease.

diph'thong *n* two vowels joining to make one sound (e.g. encyclopædia).

diplo'ma *n* a printed paper showing that a person has passed certain examinations.

diplo'macy *n* **1** the discussing of affairs and making of agreements with foreign countries (*solving the differences between the two countries by* *diplomacy rather than war*). **2** the ability to get people to do things without annoying them (*use diplomacy to get his friends to stop quarrelling*).

dip'lomat *n* **1** one who represents his or her country in discussions with foreign governments. **2** one good at managing people (*you have to be a bit of a diplomat to be a good personnel officer*).

diplomat'ic *adj* **1** having to do with or good at diplomacy. **2** tactful (*a diplomatic reply*).

dipsoma'nia *n* an uncontrollable longing for alcohol:—*n* **dipsoma'niac.**

dire *adj* very great, extreme, terrible (*in dire poverty/in dire need of food/in dire trouble*).

direct' *adj* **1** straight (*the most direct route*). **2** without any other reason or circumstances coming between (*his illness is a direct result of damp housing*). **3** saying openly what one thinks (*a very direct person/a direct way of speaking*):—*vb* **1** to point or aim at (*direct a gun at him*). **2** to show or tell the way to (*direct her to the station*). **3** to control (*direct the whole operation*). **4** (*fml*) to order (*direct her to go immediately*). **5** to address (*direct his remarks to us*).

direc'tion *n* **1** the way in which one is looking, pointing, going, etc (*in a northerly direction/have no sense of direction*). **2** control (*the direction of the military operation*). **3** an order (*obey directions*). **4** an address. **5** *pl* information as to how to do something (*get directions to the station/read the directions for putting the machine together*).

direct'ly *adv* **1** in a direct manner (*tell her directly what he thinks of her behaviour*). **2** at once, very soon (*I'll be with you directly*).

direct'or *n* **1** one of a group of people who manage a business, etc (*on the board of directors*). **2** a person in charge of putting on a play or making a film.

direc'tory *n* a book containing people's names, addresses, telephone numbers, etc (*a telephone directory*).

dirge *n* a song of mourning, a lament (*play a dirge at the funeral*).

dirk *n* a kind of short dagger.

dirt *n* **1** anything not clean (*remove the dirt from the wound/brush the dirt from the clothes*). **2** (*inf*) gossip, scandal (*spread dirt about her*). **3** (*inf*) something obscene.

dirt'y *adj* **1** unclean (*dirty hands/dirty clothes*). **2** mean or unfair (*a dirty trick*). **3** (*inf*) obscene (*dirty books*). **4** (*of weather*) rough:—*also vb.*

disa'ble *vb* **1** (*fml*) to take away the power from (*disabled from voting*). **2** to cripple (*disabled by the accident*):—*ns* **disabil'ity, disa'blement.**

disabuse' *vb* to free from wrong ideas (*disabusing him of the idea that he is in charge*).

disadvan'tage *n* something unfavourable or harmful to one's interests, a drawback (*a disadvantage to be small in a basketball team*):—*adj* **disadvantage'ous.**

disadvan'taged *adj* suffering from a disadvantage, esp with regard to one's economic situation, family background, etc.

disaffec'ted *adj* discontented, disloyal (*a leader deserted by disaffected followers*):—*n* **disaffec'tion.**

disagree' *vb* **1** to differ (*the two accounts of the event disagree*). **2** to have different opinions, etc (*two sides disagreeing*). **3** to quarrel (*children disagreeing*). **4** to have a bad effect on (*food that disagrees with her*):—*n* **disagree'ment.**

disagree'able *adj* unpleasant (*a disagree-able old woman/a disagreeable situation*).

disallow' *vb* (*fml*) to refuse to allow (*disallowed by a local law to play football there*).

disappear' *vb* **1** to go out of sight (*the sun disappearing behind a cloud*). **2** to leave or become lost, esp suddenly or without explanation (*two children have disappeared*). **3** to cease to exist (*a species of bird that has disappeared*):—*n* **disap-pear'ance.**

disappoint' *vb* **1** to fail to do what is hoped or expected. **2** (*fml*) to fail to fulfil (*disappoint their hopes*). **3** to cause sorrow by failure (*she was disappointed at losing the race/disappoint the children by not coming*):—*n* **disappoint'ment.**

disapproba'tion *n* (*fml*) an opinion that something is wrong or bad (*express his disapprobation of the proposals*).

disapprove' *vb* to believe that something is wrong or bad (*disapproving of the new changes in education*):—*n* **disapprov'al.**

disarm' *vb* **1** to take away weapons from (*police disarming the gunman*). **2** to do away with weapons (*countries beginning to disarm*). **3** to make less angry, to charm (*disarmed by her frankness/a disarming smile*).

disarm'ament *n* doing away with weapons of war (*a supporter of nuclear disarmament*).

disarrange' *vb* (*fml*) to set in the wrong order, to untidy (*the wind had disarranged her hair*):—*n* **disarrange'ment**.

disas'ter *n* **1** a great misfortune (*a firm affected by financial disaster*). **2** an accident affecting many people or causing much damage (*natural disasters such as floods and earthquakes*). **3** a complete failure (*an attempt at dressmaking that was a complete disaster*):—*adj* **disas'trous**.

disband' *vb* to break up and separate (*disband his private army/the club has disbanded*):—*n* **disband'ment**.

disbelieve' *vb* to refuse to believe (*see no reason to disbelieve his statement*):—*n* **disbelief'**.

disburse' *vb* (*fml*) to pay out money (*disbursing money for travelling expenses*):—*n* **disburse'ment**.

disc, disk *n* **1** a round flat object (*wear an identity disc*):—*see also* **disk**. **2** a gramophone record (*recorded on disc*). **3** a layer of cartilage between the bones of the spine.

discard' *vb* to throw away (*discard old furniture*).

discern' *vb* (*fml*) to make out (*just able to discern a figure in the distance/discern a hint of cinnamon in the pudding/finally discern his true character*).

discern'ible *adj* able to be seen (*no discernible improvement*).

discern'ing *adj* having good judgment (*a discerning judge of character/a discerning reader*).

discern'ment *n* judgment, wisdom.

discharge' *vb* **1** to unload (*a plane discharging its passengers*). **2** to set free (*discharge the prisoner*). **3** to fire (*discharged the gun*). **4** to send away (*discharge the members of the jury*). **5** to give or send out (*a wound discharging pus*). **6** to do, to carry out (*discharge one's duty*). **7** to pay (*discharge one's account*):—*n* **dis'charge 1** act of discharging. **2** the matter coming from a sore or wound (*a bloody discharge*).

disci'ple *n* a person who believes in the teaching, etc, of another, a follower (*Christ's disciples/disciples of Picasso*).

disciplina'rian *n* one who controls others firmly or severely:—*adj* **dis'ciplinary**.

dis'cipline *n* **1** training of mind or character (*the discipline of the monks' way of life*). **2** ordered behaviour (*the discipline shown by the soldiers*). **3** punishment (*pupils claiming unfair discipline*). **4** a branch of knowledge (*study other disciplines as well as science*):—*vb* **1** to train to be obedient (*a well-disciplined team*). **2** to punish (*disciplining his son by not allowing him to go to the cinema*).

disc' jockey *n* someone who introduces and plays recorded pop music on a radio or television programme or at a club.

disclaim' *vb* to refuse to accept, to say that one has nothing to do with (*disclaim all knowledge of the incident/disclaim any responsibility*).

disclaim'er *n* a denial (*issue a disclaimer that the politician was involved in the affair*).

disclose' *vb* **1** to make known (*disclosing family secrets/disclosed his whereabouts*). **2** to uncover (*disclose the contents of the box*).

disclo'sure *n* the telling or showing of something previously hidden (*disclosures made in the newspapers about a member of the royal family*).

dis'co *n* a club to which people go to dance to recorded pop music.

discol'our *vb* to spoil the colour of, to stain (*teeth discoloured by smoking*):—*n* **dis-colora'tion**.

discom'fit *vb* **1** (*fml*) to defeat (*discomfiting the enemy army*). **2** to make uneasy, to embarrass (*discomfited by her staring at him*).

discom'fiture *n* **1** defeat. **2** unease, embarrassment.

discom'fort *n* the fact or state of being uncomfortable:—*vb* to make uncomfortable.

discompose' *vb* (*fml*) to trouble, to make to feel uneasy (*not at all discomposed by the news*):—*n* **discompo'sure**.

disconcert' *vb* to make uneasy (*disconcerted by the fact that he ignored her*).

disconnect' *vb* **1** to unfasten (*disconnect the carriages from the train*). **2** to break the connection (*disconnect a gas supply*).

disconnect'ed *adj* showing little connection between (*a disconnected stream of words*).

discon'solate *adj* sad, disappointed (*disconsolate because of her cancelled holiday*).

discontent' *n* the state of not being satisfied, displeasure (*a sign of discontent in the workforce*):—*adj* **discontent'ed**:—*n* **dis-content'ment**.

discontin'ue *vb* to stop or put an end to (*discontinue the bus service/discontinuing that range of goods*).

dis'cord *n* **1** two or more notes of music that sound unpleasing when played together. **2** (*fml*) disagreement, quarrelling (*marital discord/some discord between the families*):—*adj* **discord'ant**.

dis'count *n* a reduction in the cost or price of (*receive a discount on the car for paying cash/a discount on goods sold to staff*):—*vb* **discount' 1** to give a discount. **2** to regard as unimportant or untrue (*discount anything they say since they have no knowledge of the situation*).

discoun'tenance *vb* (*fml*) to show disapproval of (*discountenancing the behaviour of the young*).

discour'age *vb* **1** to dishearten (*his early failure discouraged him*). **2** to persuade not to do (*smoking is discouraged here*):—*n* **discour'agement**.

dis'course *n* a speech, a lecture (*a long discourse on manners delivered by the head teacher*):—*vb* **discourse'** to talk.

discourt'eous *adj* rude, impolite:—*n* **dis-court'esy**.

discov'er *vb* **1** to find (*discover America/discover a great new restaurant*). **2** to find out (*discover the truth about him/discover how to work the machine*).

discov'erer *n* an explorer.

discov'ery *n* **1** act of finding (*a voyage of discoveries*). **2** the thing found (out) (*a number of important discoveries*).

discred'it *vb* **1** to refuse to believe (*discrediting all he says*). **2** to cause to be disbelieved (*theories discredited by experts*). **3** to damage the good reputation of (*try to discredit the government*):—*n* shame, dishonour (*bring discredit on his family*).

discred'itable *adj* shameful (*discreditable behaviour*).

discreet' *adj* thinking carefully before acting or speaking, cautious, not saying anything that is likely to cause trouble (*discreet behaviour/be discreet about her boss's affairs*).

discrep'ancy *n* the difference between what a thing is and what it ought to be or is said to be (*a discrepancy between the two accounts of the accident/a discrepancy between the amount of money taken in and the amount in the till*).

discre'tion *n* **1** discreetness (*you can rely on her discretion—she won't tell anyone*). **2** judgment,

caution (*use your discretion on how much to charge*).

discrim'inate *vb* **1** to see differences, however small. **2** to show judgment:—*n* **dis-crimina'tion**.

discrim'inating *adj* having good judgment.

discur'sive *adj* **1** rambling. **2** dealing with many subjects (*a discursive report*).

discuss' *vb* to talk about, to consider:—*n* **discus'sion**.

disdain' *vb* to look down upon, to be too proud to, to refuse because of pride (*disdain our company/ disdain our offers of help*):—*n* scorn:—*adj* **disdain'ful**.

disease' *n* an illness or unhealthy condition (*kidney disease/disease of oak trees/violence is a disease of today*).

diseased' *adj* suffering from a disease (*diseased fruit trees*).

disembark' *vb* to put or go on land from a ship (*disembark at dawn*):—*n* **disembarka'tion**.

disembod'y *vb* to free from the body (*disembodied spirits*):—*n* **disembod'iment**.

disenchant' *vb* to free from mistaken beliefs (*many former admirers have been disenchanted by her behaviour*).

disenfranchise *see* **disfranchise**.

disengage' *vb* **1** to free or disconnect (*disengage the clutch*). **2** to stop fighting (*troops disengaging*).

disentan'gle *vb* **1** to take the knots out of (*disentangling the string*). **2** to free from a position that is difficult to escape from (*disentangled herself from an unhappy marriage*). **3** to separate from a confused condition (*disentangle the truth from a mass of lies*).

disfa'vour *n* dislike, lack of approval (*look upon the new building with disfavour*).

disfig'ure *vb* to spoil the appearance of (*a face disfigured by a huge scar*):—*n* **disfig'urement**.

disfran'chise, dis'enfran'chise *vbs* to take away the right to vote:—*ns* **disfran'chise-ment, disenfran'chisement**.

disgorge' *vb* **1** to bring up what has been eaten (*disgorge a small bone*). **2** to pour out or allow to pour out (*crowds disgorging from the cinema/ smoke disgorging from factory chimneys*).

disgrace' *n* **1** shame, loss of favour or respect (*bring disgrace on his family*). **2** a person or thing that should cause shame (*work that is a disgrace*):—*vb* to bring shame or dishonour upon (*disgracing his family by going to prison*).

disgrace'ful *adj* shameful.

disguise' *vb* to change the appearance of, to change so as not to be recognized:—*n* changed dress or appearance so as not to be recognized.

disgust' *n* strong dislike, loathing (*look with disgust at the rotting meat/feel disgust for his evil behaviour*):—*vb* to cause to loathe or hate (*disgusted by the smell of rotting meat/disgusted by his cruel treatment of his wife*).

disgust'ing *adj* sickening (*a disgusting mess*).

dish *n* 1 a broad open vessel for serving food (*a casserole dish*). 2 a particular kind of food (*a French dish*). 3 food mixed and prepared for the table (*a dish of meat and potatoes*):—*vb* to put into a dish (*dish the potatoes*):—**dish out 1** to distribute and give out (*dish out leaflets to people*). 2 (*inf*) to give out generously (*dish out compliments*).

disheart'en *vb* to discourage (*disheartened by his failure*).

dishevel [dis-shev'-êl] *vb* (**dishev'elled, dishev'elling**) to untidy (*hair dishevelled by the wind*).

dishon'est *adj* not honest (*dishonest salesman/dishonest means*):—*n* **dishon'esty**.

dishon'our *n* shame, disgrace (*bring dishonour on his family by stealing*):—*vb* 1 to bring shame on (*dishonour his regiment*). 2 (*fml*) to treat in a shameful way (*dishonour his wife*).

dishon'ourable *adj* not honourable, shameful (*dishonourable conduct*).

disillu'sion *vb* to free from a wrong idea or belief (*disillusion her that he was not interested only in her money/disillusioned with the legal system*):—*n* **disillu'sionment**.

disinclina'tion *n* unwillingness (*a disinclination to cooperate with others*).

disinclined' *adj* unwilling (*disinclined to believe her*).

disinfect' *vb* to free from infection (*disinfect the wound/disinfect the toilet*):—*n* **disin-fec'tion**.

disinfec'tant *adj* destroying germs, killing infection:—*n* a disinfectant substance (*clean the bathroom with a disinfectant*).

disingen'uous *adj* not saying what one thinks, insincere, cunning (*it was disingenuous of her to claim to be innocent*).

disinher'it *vb* to take from a son or daughter the right to receive anything by the will of a dead parent.

disin'tegrate *vb* 1 to break up into parts (*a damp cardboard box that just disintegrated*). 2 to fall to pieces (*plans disintegrating/families disintegrating*):—*n* **disintegra'tion**.

disinter' *vb* (**disinter'red, disinter'ring**) to take out of a grave (*permission to disinter the corpse*):—*n* **disinter'ment**.

disin'terested *adj* favouring no side (*referees must be disinterested*).

disjoin' *vb* (*fml*) to separate.

disjoint'ed *adj* having no clear connection between ideas, rambling (*a disjointed piece of prose/a few disjointed ideas*).

disk *n* a circular plate, coated with magnetic material, on which data can be recorded in a form that can be used by a computer:—*see also* **disc**.

dislike' *vb* not to like (*dislikes her very much/disliking her habit of asking questions/dislike tasteless food*):—*also n*.

dis'locate *vb* 1 to put out of joint (*dislocated a bone in his foot*). 2 (*fml*) to throw into disorder (*dislocating the computer system*):—*n* **disloca'tion**.

dislodge' *vb* to move from its place (*dislodging the fish bone from his throat/dislodge the stone from the horse's hoof*).

disloy'al *adj* 1 unfaithful (*disloyal to her husband*). 2 not true to (*disloyal to their leader*):—*n* **disloy'alty**.

dis'mal *adj* dark, gloomy (*a dismal place/a dismal mood*).

disman'tle *vb* to take to pieces (*dismantling the machine*).

dismay' *vb* to make afraid, anxious, discouraged, etc (*they were dismayed to find the door locked/dismayed at the news of his disappearance*):—*also n*.

dismem'ber *vb* to cut or tear to pieces (*dismember the murdered man*).

dismiss' *vb* 1 to send away (*dismiss the visitor with a wave of her hand/dismiss ideas of promotion*). 2 to send away from one's job (*dismiss him for dishonesty*):—*n* **dis-mis'sal**.

dismount' *vb* to get down from a horse, etc (*dismounting from his bicycle*).

disobey' vb to refuse to do what one is told (*disobeying orders/disobey his boss*):—n **disobed'ience:**—adj **dis-obed'ient.**

disoblig'ing adj not helpful, not cooperative (*in a disobliging mood*).

disor'der vb to put things out of their places, to untidy:—n 1 untidiness (*criticize the disorder of the room*). 2 disturbance, riot (*the meeting broke up in disorder*). 3 illness, disease (*a disorder of the stomach*).

disor'derly adj 1 untidy (*a disorderly office*). 2 out of control (*a disorderly crowd*).

disor'ganize vb to put out of order, to throw into confusion (*wedding plans totally disorganized when the bride changed her mind*):—n **disorganiza'tion.**

disown' vb to refuse to have anything to do with, to refuse to acknowledge as belonging to oneself (*disowned his son because of his dishonest behaviour*).

dispar'age vb to suggest, esp unfairly, that something or someone is of little value or importance (*disparaging his achievements*):—n **dispar'agement.**

dis'parate adj unlike, completely different (*totally disparate personalities*).

dispar'ity n difference, inequality (*the disparity in age between husband and wife*).

dispas'sionate adj not influenced by emotion, taking no side, impartial (*a dispassionate account of the accident*).

dispatch', despatch' vb 1 to send off (*dispatch a letter/dispatch a messenger*). 2 (*old*) to kill. 3 (*fml*) to do quickly (*dispatch several pieces of work*):—n 1 act of sending off (*the dispatch of a letter*). 2 a written official report (*a dispatch from the military line/mentioned in dispatches*). 3 (*fml*) quickness in doing (*act with dispatch*).

dispel' vb (**dispelled', dispel'ling**) to drive away, to make disappear (*dispel all doubts*).

dispense' vb 1 (*fml*) to give out (*dispensing money to the poor/dispense justice*). 2 to prepare and give out (medicines):—**dispense with** to do without (*dispense with the need for regular checking*).

dispens'able adj able to be done without (*workers regarded as being dispensable*).

dispens'ary n a place where medicines are prepared and given out.

dispensa'tion n a permission, often from the church, not to do something (*by dispensation of the bishop*).

dispens'er n 1 one who prepares medicines. 2 a machine from which something can be obtained by the insertion of money (*a soap dispenser/a drinks dispenser*).

disperse' vb to scatter (*crowds dispersing/clouds dispersed by the wind*):—ns **dis-per'sal, disper'sion.**

dispir'ited adj discouraged, in low spirits (*feel dispirited after his defeat*).

displace' vb 1 (*fml*) to put out of place (*papers displaced by the burglar*). 2 to take the place of (*displacing his wife in his affections*).

displace'ment n 1 act of displacing. 2 the amount of liquid put out of place when an object is placed in it.

display' vb 1 to show, to make obvious (*displaying one's lack of knowledge*). 2 to put where it can be easily seen (*display ornaments in a glass-fronted cabinet/display the paintings in a gallery*):—n 1 show (*goods on display*). 2 a parade. 3 an exhibition (*a display of the work of local artists*).

displease' vb to anger, to annoy (*displeased by their failure*).

displeas'ure n annoyance (*show his displeasure by frowning*).

disport' vb (*fml*) to play about, to amuse oneself actively (*children disporting themselves on the beach*).

dispos'al n 1 act of getting rid of (*the disposal of rubbish*). 2 the way that people or things are arranged (*the disposal of the troops*). 3 use (*a firm's car at his disposal*).

dispose' vb 1 (*fml*) to arrange (*troops disposed in battle formation*). 2 (*fml*) to make willing (*I am not disposed to be of assistance to them*). 3 to get rid (of) (*disposing of the evidence*).

disposi'tion n 1 arrangement (*the general's disposition of the troops*). 2 a person's character as revealed by his or her normal behaviour (*of a bad-tempered disposition*).

dispossess' vb to take away from (*dispossess them of their houses*).

dispropor'tion n lack of proper or usual relation between things (*a disproportion between his height and weight*).

dispropor'tionate adj too great (or too small) in the circumstances (a head disproportionate to her body).

disprove' vb to prove to be false (difficult to disprove his allegations).

disput'able adj doubtful, open to question (it is disputable if the land belongs to him/a disputable point).

disputa'tion n an argument, a debate.

disputa'tious adj (fml) fond of argument.

dispute' vb 1 to argue, to quarrel (farmers disputing whose land it is). 2 to refuse to agree with, to question the truth or rightness of (dispute the truth of what he said/dispute his right to the throne):—also n.

disqual'ify vb 1 to make unable (his ill-health disqualified him from joining the army). 2 to put out of a competition, etc, usu for breaking a rule (a relay team disqualified for dropping the baton):—n disqualifica'tion.

disqui'et n anxiety (feel disquiet when the children were late):—vb to make anxious:—n disqui'etude.

disquisi'tion n (fml) a long written report or a long speech on a subject.

disregard' vb to take no notice of (disregard the rules/disregard safety instructions):—n neglect.

disrepair' n a bad state due to lack of repairs (property in disrepair).

disrep'utable adj 1 having a bad character. 2 in a bad condition, shabby.

disrepute' n disgrace, bad reputation (bring his team into disrepute by using drugs).

disrespect' n rudeness, failure to behave in a proper way (show disrespect to his elders by being very late):—adj disrespect'ful.

disrobe' vb (fml) to take off clothing, esp ceremonious or official clothing (judges disrobing).

disrupt' vb to put into a state of disorder (disrupt the traffic/a strike disrupting holiday flights):—n disrup'tion.

disrup'tive adj causing disorder (disruptive pupils/disruptive behaviour).

dissat'isfied adj not satisfied, discontented (a dissatisfied customer/dissatisfied with the result).

dissat'isfy vb to fail to satisfy, to displease (a standard of work that dissatisfied the teacher):—n dissatisfac'tion.

dissect' vb 1 to cut into separate parts in order to examine (dissecting a rat in the biology class). 2 to study carefully (dissect the election result):—n dissec'tion.

dissem'ble vb to pretend not to be what one is, to hide (one's feelings, intent, etc) (he said he loved her but he was dissembling):—n dissem'bler.

dissem'inate vb (fml) to spread far and wide (disseminating information):—n dissemi-na'tion.

dissen'sion n disagreement, quarrelling (the proposal caused some dissension among committee members).

dissent' vb to disagree, to think differently from (the vote was almost unanimous but one committee member dissented):—also n.

Dissent'er n an English Protestant who does not agree with the teachings of the Church of England.

dissen'tient adj (fml) disagreeing (a few dissentient voices):—also n.

disserta'tion n a lecture or essay (students required to write a dissertation).

disser'vice n a bad turn (do him a disservice by letting him copy your homework).

dissev'er vb to cut in two (dissever the connection).

dis'sident adj disagreeing:—n a person who disagrees with a government's policies, esp one who is punished (political dissidents).

dissim'ilar adj unlike (have totally dissimilar tastes).

dissim'ulate vb (fml) to pretend not to be what one is, to hide (one's feelings) (he acted as though he was interested but he was dissimulating):—n dissimula'tion.

dis'sipate vb 1 to scatter (a crowd that dissipated when the police arrived). 2 to spend or use wastefully (dissipating a fortune on gambling). 3 to waste (dissipate the natural resources of the country):—n dissipa-tion.

dis'sipated adj given to living wildly, indulging in drinking and foolish or dangerous pleasures (dissipated young men/lead a dissipated life).

disso'ciate vb 1 to separate from (try to dissociate his private life from his public one). 2 to refuse to be connected with (dissociating oneself from the behaviour of one's workmates):—n dissocia'tion.

dis'solute *adj* living wickedly, immoral (*dissolute drunks/a dissolute life*).

dissolu'tion *n* **1** act of dissolving (*the dissolution of Parliament/the dissolution of the Roman empire*). **2** death, decay.

dissolve' *vb* **1** to make or become liquid by placing in liquid (*dissolving pills in water*). **2** to break up, to put an end to (*dissolve Parliament/dissolve a marriage*).

dis'sonant *adj* harsh-sounding (*dissonant sounds*):—*n* **dis'sonance**.

dissuade' *vb* to advise not to do (*try to dissuade them from resigning*):—*n* **dissua'-sion**:—*adj* **dissua'sive**.

dis'taff *n* a stick to which wool is attached in spinning.

dis'tance *n* **1** being far off (*live at a distance from her mother*). **2** the space between two points or places (*a distance of three miles between the villages*). **3** (*fml*) unfriendliness (*notice a certain distance in his manner*).

dis'tant *adj* **1** far off (*travel to distant lands*). **2** not close (*a distant relative*). **3** cold or unfriendly in manner (*he seemed rather distant to his old friends*).

distaste' *n* dislike (*look at her dirty fingernails with distaste*).

distaste'ful *adj* unpleasant (*a distasteful duty to have to declare people redundant/a subject that is distasteful to her*).

distem'per *n* **1** a disease of dogs. **2** (*old*) an oilless paint for walls.

distend' *vb* to stretch, to swell (*children's stomachs distended from lack of food in the famine area*):—*n* **disten'sion**.

distil' *vb* (**distilled'**, **distil'ling**) **1** to fall in drops. **2** to purify a substance by heating it until it turns into vapour, and then cooling the vapour until it becomes liquid.

distilla'tion *n* act of distilling.

distil'ler *n* a maker of whisky or other spirit.

distil'lery *n* a factory where whisky, etc, is made.

distinct' *adj* **1** separate (*two distinct types of bird*). **2** easily heard, seen, etc (*a distinct improvement*).

distinc'tion *n* **1** difference (*make a distinction between primary and secondary pupils*). **2** excellence (*a writer of distinction*). **3** a special mark of honour (*win a distinction for bravery*).

distinct'ive *adj* different in a special way (*a distinctive style of dressing/wear a distinctive perfume*).

distinct'ness *n* clearness.

disting'uish *vb* **1** to see or point out the differences (between) (*unable to distinguish one twin from the other/distinguish right from wrong*). **2** to make different (*the ability to speak distinguishes humans from animals*). **3** to make (oneself) outstanding (*distinguish himself in battle*). **4** to see, to make out (*be just able to distinguish a figure in the distance*).

disting'uished *adj* famous (*a distinguished writer*).

distort' *vb* **1** to twist out of shape (*a face distorted in agony*). **2** to give a false meaning to (*the facts distorted by some newspapers*):—*n* **distor'tion**.

distract' *vb* to draw the attention away (*distract him from his work*).

distract'ed *adj* almost mad with grief or anxiety (*parents distracted by the loss of their children*).

distrac'tion *n* **1** anything that draws the attention away (*too many distractions for her to be able to study properly*). **2** confusion of mind (*driven to distraction by the constant noise*).

distrain' *vb* (*fml*) to seize goods as payment of debt:—*n* **distraint'**.

distraught' *adj* almost mad with grief or anxiety (*a distraught mother looking for her missing child*).

distress' *n* **1** great pain or anxiety (*an accident victim in great distress*). **2** suffering caused by lack of money (*in financial distress*). **3** danger (*a ship in distress*):—*vb* to cause anxiety, sorrow or pain.

distrib'ute *vb* **1** to give out, to give each his or her share (*distributing food to the poor*). **2** to spread out widely (*hamburger restaurants distributed throughout the country*):—*n* **distribu'tion**.

distrib'utor *n* **1** one who gives away or shares out. **2** part of a motor engine.

dis'trict *n* **1** part of a country. **2** an area marked off for some special purpose.

distrust' *vb* to have no confidence or belief in (*distrust that old car/have a distrust of strangers*):—*n* doubt, suspicion:—*adj* **dis-trust'ful**.

disturb' *vb* **1** to throw into disorder (*disturb the papers on the desk*). **2** to trouble (*disturbed by the lack of news*). **3** to interrupt (*disturb his sleep*).

disturb'ance n **1** disorder, riot (*police called to a disturbance in the local pub*). **2** disarrangement (*notice the disturbance of the papers on his desk*). **3** an interruption (*unable to work with all the disturbance*). **4** mental illness (*suffer an emotional disturbance*).

disun'ion n (*fml*) separation, disagreement.

disuse' n a state of not being used, neglect (*old laws fallen into disuse*):—*adj* **disused'**.

ditch n a long narrow trench for carrying away water:—*vb* to make a ditch.

dit'to n the same as before, indicated by the sign " (used to show that the same word phrase, figure, etc, is to be repeated, in writing, often shortened to **do**.).

dit'ty n a short simple song.

diurnal [dī-èr'-nêl] *adj* **1** daily (*a diurnal occurrence*). **2** taking one day (*the diurnal rotation of the earth*). **3** active or happening during the day (*diurnal animals*).

divan' n **1** a long low sofa without back or arms. **2** a kind of bed like this.

dive *vb* **1** to plunge into water head first. **2** to move quickly downwards (*rabbits diving into holes*):—*n* **1** a plunge. **2** a sudden downward move.

div'er n **1** one who, with special equipment, is able to work under water (*deep-sea divers*). **2** a diving bird.

diverge' *vb* to go off in a different direction, to branch in different directions (*the road and railway line diverging near the village/that is where our opinions diverge*):—*n* **diver'gence**:—*adj* **diver'gent**.

divers [dī'-verz] *adj* (*old*) several, various (*divers people were present/for divers reasons*).

diverse' *adj* different, unlike (*have many diverse reasons to go/people of diverse backgrounds*).

divers'ify *vb* to make or become different (*diversifying their range of goods/engineering firms diversifying into computers*).

diver'sion n **1** (*fml*) amusement (*swimming and other diversions for the children*). **2** something that distracts the attention (*his friend created a diversion while he stole sweets from the shop*). **3** a turning aside from the main route (e.g. to avoid an obstacle) (*a diversion ahead because of roadworks*).

divers'ity n difference, variety.

divert' *vb* **1** to turn in another direction (*divert the traffic on to a side road*). **2** to draw away (*diverting their attention from their personal problems*). **3** to amuse (*diverted by the clown's antics*).

divert'ing *adj* amusing.

divest' *vb* **1** to take away, to strip (*divest the tyrant of his power*). **2** to take off, esp ceremonial clothes (*bishop divesting himself of his robes*).

divide' *vb* **1** to break up into parts (*dividing the class into three groups*). **2** to share out (*divide the chocolate among them*). **3** to separate (*a wall divided the gardens*). **4** in arithmetic, to see how many times one number is contained in another.

div'idend n **1** a number to be divided. **2** a share of profit. **3** the rate at which the profits of a company are divided among shareholders.

divid'ers npl an instrument for measuring distances on paper, etc.

divine' *adj* **1** of or belonging to God. **2** (*inf*) extremely good (*a divine dancer*):—*n* a clergyman:—*vb* **1** to foretell, to guess (*divining the future*). **2** to learn or discover by intuition, insight (*divine a sudden change in her manner*):—*n* **divina'tion**.

divin'ing rod n a Y-shaped rod, usu of hazel, used to find underground water.

divin'ity n **1** a god. **2** the study of religion.

divis'ible *adj* able to be divided.

divi'sion n **1** act of dividing (*the division of responsibility*). **2** one of the parts into which something is divided (*the sales division of the firm*). **3** disagreement (*some division in the family*). **4** a large army group.

divi'sional *adj* having to do with a division (*the divisional head*).

divi'sor n the number by which another number (the **dividend**) is divided in a sum.

divorce' n **1** legal permission to separate from one's married partner and to marry someone else if so desired. **2** separation:—*vb* **1** officially to end a marriage (*parents who are divorcing*). **2** to separate (*try to divorce his private life from his public life/he seems divorced from reality*).

divulge' *vb* to make known, to reveal (*divulging secrets to the press/divulge information about the robbery to the police*).

Diwali *n* a Hindu festival held in the autumn, particularly associated with Lakshmi, the goddess of prosperity.

DIY *n* the act of making, repairing or decorating things yourself, as opposed to employing a tradesman, an abbreviation of do-it-yourself.

diz'zy *adj* giddy, having the feeling that everything is spinning around (*children whirling around until they are dizzy/feel dizzy at the top of a ladder*):—*n* **diz'ziness.**

do[1] *vb* (*pt* **did**, *pp* **done**) **1** to perform, to carry out (*do his duty*). **2** to attend to (*do the dishes*). **3** to act or behave (*do as you are told*). **4** to be enough or suitable (*will this hat do for the wedding?*).

do[2] *see* **ditto.**

do'cile *adj* easily managed, controlled or influenced, quiet (*a docile pony/docile children*).—*n* **docil'ity.**

dock[1] *n* a common weed.

dock[2] *vb* to cut short, to remove part of (*dock the dog's tail*).

dock[3] *n* **1** an enclosure in a harbour where enough water can be kept to float a ship when it is being loaded or unloaded repaired, etc. **2** the box in which prisoners stand in a court of law:—*vb* to sail into dock (*when the ship was docking/dock the ship*).

dock'et *n* a label tied to goods (*a docket listing the contents*).

dock'yard *n* a place where ships are built and repaired.

doc'tor *n* **1** one who is qualified by medical training to attend the sick and injured. **2** one who receives a degree granted by universities to those learned in a certain field (*a doctor of philosophy*):—*vb* **1** to give medical treatment to (*doctoring her cold with aspirin and hot drinks*). **2** to make different in order to deceive, to tamper with (*doctor the evidence*).

doc'torate *n* the degree of doctor.

doc'trinal *adj* having to do with a doctrine or set of beliefs held by a religious society (*doctrinal differences between the two faiths*).

doctrinaire' *adj* believing in or trying to put into action a system of ideas without considering the practical difficulties of doing so.

doc'trine *n* a set of beliefs held by a person or group (*the Protestant doctrine/socialist doctrine*).

doc'ument *n* a written or printed paper that can be used as proof (*secret government documents/documents of sale*):—*vb* to bring forward written evidence (*local history that is well documented*).

documen'tary *adj* **1** having to do with documents (*documentary evidence*). **2** giving facts and explanations (*a documentary film*):—*also n.*

dod'der *vb* to move unsteadily or shakily (*an elderly man doddering along*).

dodge *vb* **1** to make a quick movement to avoid someone or something (*succeed in dodging the blow/dodge the police*). **2** to avoid by cleverness or trickery (*politicians dodging reporters' questions*):—*n* **1** a quick movement aside (*a footballer making a sudden dodge to the right*). **2** a trick (*up to his old dodges*).

dod'ger *n* a trickster, one not to be trusted.

do'do *n* (*pl* **do'does** *or* **do'dos**) a type of flightless bird no longer in existence (*dead as the dodo*).

doe *n* the female of many animals (e.g. deer, rabbit, etc).

doff *vb* (*fml*) to take off (*doff his cap*).

dog *n* **1** a common domestic animal. **2** (*hum or contemp*) a fellow:—*vb* (**dogged'**, **dog'-ging**) to follow closely, to pursue (*dog his footsteps/a family dogged by bad luck*).

dog'cart *n* a two-wheeled cart or carriage.

dog col'lar *n* **1** a collar for a dog. **2** a clergyman's collar.

dog days *npl* the Northern hot season in July and August.

doge [dōzh *or* dō'-jā] *n* formerly the chief magistrate in Venice or Genoa.

dog'eared *adj* with the corners of the pages turned down (*a dogeared paperback*).

dog'fish *n* a type of small shark.

dog'ged *adj* determined, unwilling to give in (*a dogged attempt to get to the top*):—*n* **dog'gedness.**

dog'gerel *n* bad poetry.

dog'ma *n* a belief or set of beliefs put forward by an authority to be accepted as a matter of faith (*Christian dogma/tired of his political dogma*).

dogmat'ic *adj* **1** relating to dogma (*dogmatic theology*). **2** holding one's beliefs very strongly and expecting other people to accept them without question (*so dogmatic about the best way to educate children*):—*n* **dog'matism.**

dog rose n the wild rose.

Dog Star n Sirius, the brightest of the fixed stars.

dog'watch n on a ship, a short watch of two hours.

doil'y, doy'ley n a small fancy napkin or mat (*the doily under the cake*).

dol'drums npl seas near the equator where there is little or no wind:—**in the doldrums** in a sad mood.

dole vb to give out shares of, often in small amounts (*dole out daily rations to the refugees/dole out pocket money*).

dole'ful adj gloomy, sad (*looking doleful/doleful news*).

doll n a toy in the shape of a person (*a baby doll*).

dol'lar n an American, Australian or Canadian coin (= 100 cents).

dol'lop n (*inf*) a lump, esp of something soft (*a dollop of mashed potato*).

dol'men n a group of upright stones supporting a large flat piece of stone, dating from ancient times.

dol'orous adj (*fml*) sad, sorrowful:—n **dol'our**.

dol'phin n a sea animal like the porpoise, belonging to the whale family.

dolt n a stupid person.

domain' n **1** the land one owns. **2** the country one rules. **3** an area of interest, knowledge, influence, etc (*lie within the domain of science fiction*).

dome n **1** a rounded top on a building. **2** something of this shape (*the dome of his bald head*):—adj **domed**.

domes'tic adj **1** belonging to or having to do with the house (*appliances for domestic use*). **2** concerning one's personal or home life (*domestic happiness*). **3** tame and living with or used to people (*domestic animals*). **4** having to do with one's own country (*goods sold on the domestic market*). **5** (*inf*) interested in and good at cooking, housework, etc (*she's very domestic*):—n a house servant.

domes'ticated adj **1** accustomed to living near and being used by people (*domesticated animals*). **2** fond of and/or good at doing jobs associated with running a house (*a domesticated person*).

domestic'ity n **1** home life. **2** the state of being fond of and good at running a home.

dom'icile n (*fml*) a house, a home, the place where a person is living.

dom'inant adj **1** controlling others (*a dominant personality*). **2** most important (*the dominant issue at the meeting*):—n **dom'i-nance**.

dom'inate vb **1** to have complete control over (*dominate the meeting/dominate the rest of the class*). **2** to be the most important (*financial problems that dominated his thoughts*). **3** to rise high above (*mountains dominating the village*):—n **domina'tion**.

domineer' vb to bully (*tired of being domineered by his elder brother*).

domin'ion n **1** rule, government (*an emperor holding dominion over millions of people*). **2** the territory governed (*the vast dominions of the empire*).

dom'ino n **1** a loose cloak with a hood and a mask that covers half the face. **2** pl **dom'-inoes** a game played with small flat pieces of wood, ivory, etc, marked with dots.

don' n a teacher in a university or college.

don² vb (**donned'**, **don'ning**) (*fml*) to put on (*don his coat*).

donate' vb to give, esp to a charity, etc, to contribute (*donating hundreds of pounds to a children's charity*):—n **dona'tion**.

done pp of **do**:—adj (*inf*) utterly exhausted (*completely done after the long walk*).

do'nor n **1** one who gives or contributes (*money given to the charity by anonymous donors*). **2** a person who provides blood for transfusion, organs for transplantation, etc (*a blood donor/a kidney donor*).

doom n death, ruin, destruction, terrible and inevitable fate (*meet one's doom*):—vb to cause to suffer something unavoidable and terrible, such as death, ruin or destruction (*doomed to a life of unemployment*).

dooms'day n the day of judgment at the end of the world.

dope n **1** (*inf*) an illegal drug (*smuggling dope*). **2** (*inf*) a fool, a stupid person:—vb to give a drug to.

dor'mant adj not at present active (*a dormant volcano*).

dor'mer n a small window in a sloping roof.

dor'mitory n a sleeping room with many beds (*the dormitories in the boarding school*).

dor'mouse n (*pl* **dor'mice**) a small mouse-like animal that sleeps in winter.

dor'sal *adj* having to do with the back (*the dorsal fin of the shark*).

dor'y *n* a sea fish (often **John Dory**).

do'sage *n* the amount to be given in a dose (*exceed the recommended dosage*).

dose *n* the amount of medicine given at one time (*a dose of cough mixture*):—*vb* to give medicine to (*dosing herself with cough mixture*).

doss'ier *n* a collection of papers dealing with one particular subject or person (*firms keeping dossiers on members of staff*).

dot *n* a small point or mark (*a pattern of black and white dots*):—*vb* (**dot'ted, dot'ting**) to mark with dots:—**dotted with** having (things) placed here and there (*a sky dotted with stars*).

do'tage *n* the weak-mindedness of old age (*an old man in his dotage*).

do'tard *n* one whose mind is weakened by age.

dote *vb* 1 to show great fondness of, esp in a foolish way (*doting on his daughter and thinking she can do no wrong*). 2 (*old*) to become weaker in mind when old.

dou'ble *adj* 1 twice as much as usual or normal (*a double helping of pudding/his income is double that of his brother*). 2 for two people (*a double bed/a double ticket*). 3 forming a pair (*a double window/double yellow lines*). 4 combining two things or qualities (*a double meaning/a double life*):—*n* 1 twice the amount (*double the price*). 2 a person or thing looking the same as another (*the double of her mother at that age*). 3 a glass of spirits holding twice the standard amount. 4 a running pace (*leave at the double*):—*vb* 1 to multiply by two, to cause to become twice as large or numerous. 2 to fold in two (*doubling the blanket for extra warmth*). 3 to have two uses, jobs, etc (*the sofa doubles as a bed*):—*adv* **doub'ly**:—**dou'ble back** to turn back in the opposite direction, esp unexpectedly.

doub'le-bass' *n* a large, low-toned stringed instrument.

double-deal'ing *n* deceit, dishonesty:—*adj* devious, not to be trusted (*a double-dealing business partner*).

doub'let *n* 1 a close-fitting body garment worn by men in the 14th to 17th centuries. 2 one of a pair of words having the same meaning.

doubloon' *n* an old Spanish gold coin.

doubt *vb* to be uncertain about, to be unwilling to believe or trust (*doubt his word/I doubt whether they'll come*):—*n* 1 a feeling of uncertainty. 2 distrust:—*adj* **doubt'-ful:**—*adv* **doubt'less**.

douche [dōsh] *n* a stream of water directed on to the body to clean it:—*also vb*.

dough [dō] *n* 1 flour moistened with water and pressed into a paste ready for baking (dough for making bread). 2 (*inf*) money.

dough'nut *n* a type of sweet cake in the shape of a ring.

doughty [dou'-ti] *adj* (*old*) brave (*a doughty warrior*).

dour [dör] *adj* silent and unsmiling, gloomy (*in a dour mood/a dour person*).

douse, dowse *vb* 1 to drench in water (*dousing the fire/douse him with a bucket of water*). 2 to put out (*douse the candles*).

dove *n* a bird of the pigeon family.

dove'-cot(e) *n* a pigeonhouse.

dove'tail *n* a sticking-out end of wood shaped like a dove's tail to fit into a hole in another piece of wood to lock the two together:—*vb* to fit neatly or exactly together (*plans neatly dovetailing with theirs*).

dow'ager *n* the title given to the widow of a nobleman.

dow'dy *adj* badly or shabbily dressed, unfashionable, drab (*a dowdy woman/dowdy clothes*):—*n* **dow'diness**.

down[1] *prep* in a descending direction in, on, along or through (*water flows down/go down the hill*):—*adv* 1 from a higher to a lower position, to a lying or sitting position (*she fell down*). 2 towards or to the ground, floor or bottom (*climb down*). 3 to or in a lower status or in a worse condition (*prices are going down*). 4 from an earlier time (*down the ages*). 5 in cash. 6 to or in a state of less activity (*the children quietened down*):—*adj* 1 occupying a low position, esp lying on the ground. 2 depressed (*she is feeling down*):—*n* 1 a low period. 2 (*inf*) a dislike:—*vb* 1 to go or cause to go or come down. 2 to defeat. 3 to swallow.

down[2] *n* the fine soft feathers of a bird (*the down of a swan/pillows filled with down*):—*adj* **down'y**.

down^3 *n* an area of low grassy hills.

down'-and-out' *adj* having no job and no money, and often no money (*down-and-out people sleeping rough under the bridge*):—*n* a down-and-out person.

down'cast *adj* 1 directed downwards (*with eyes downcast*). 2 sad, in low spirits (*feel downcast at the news of his failure*).

down'fall *n* 1 ruin, fall from power, prosperity, etc (*over-confidence led to his downfall*). 2 a heavy fall of rain.

down'-heart'ed *adj* discouraged, in low spirits (*down-hearted after the failure of his business*).

download *vb* to copy or transfer data or a program from one computer to another.

down'pour *n* a heavy fall of rain (*get soaked in the downpour*).

down'right *adj* 1 thorough, complete (*a downright lie*). 2 frank, straightforward, saying exactly what one thinks (*a downright kind of man*).

downsize *vb* to reduce the number of people who work in a company, usually in order to reduce costs (*reduce the workforce*).

dow'ry *n* the property a woman brings to her husband at marriage.

dowse *see* **douse**.

doxol'ogy *n* a short hymn of praise to God.

doy'ley *see* **doily**.

doze *vb* to be half asleep (*dozing in his chair after lunch*):—*n* light sleep.

doz'en *n* twelve.

drab *adj* 1 of a dull greyish-brown colour (*wearing drab clothes*). 2 dull, uninteresting (*lead a drab existence*).

drachma *n* formerly the currency unit of Greece, until the introduction of the euro in 2002.

draft *n* 1 a number of soldiers picked to go somewhere on duty. 2 a written order to pay money. 3 a rough copy or plan of work to be done (*a draft of his essay*):—*vb* 1 to prepare a plan or rough copy (*draft the contract*). 2 to pick and send off (*draft police to control the football crowds*).

drafts'man *same as* **draughtsman**.

drag *vb* (**dragged**, **drag'ging**) 1 to pull along with force (*drag the fallen tree*). 2 to trail on the ground (*with her long skirt dragging in the mud*). 3 (*inf*) to go very slowly (*the evening seemed to drag*). 4 to search underwater with hooks or a

net (*drag the canal for the dead body*):—*n* anything that causes to go slowly.

drag'net *n* a net to be drawn along underwater.

drag'on *n* 1 in fables, a winged monster. 2 a fierce, stern person.

drag'onfly *n* a winged insect.

dragoon' *n* a horse soldier:—*vb* to force to obey, to bully into (*dragoon them into helping him paint the house*).

drain *vb* 1 to draw off liquid by pipes, ditches, etc (*drain the water tank*). 2 to empty completely (*drain his glass*). 3 to cause to become dry as liquid flows away (*drain the plates*):—*n* a pipe or channel to carry away liquid (*a blocked drain*).

drain'age *n* all the means used to draw water away from a certain area.

drake *n* a male duck.

dram *n* 1 a small measure of weight ($^1/_{16}$ ounce). 2 a small drink of whisky, etc.

dram'a *n* 1 a play (*a television drama*). 2 plays as a branch of literature and as a performing art (*study drama*). 3 an exciting event, a series of exciting events (*a real-life hospital drama*). 4 excitement (*a life that seems full of drama*).

dramat'ic *adj* 1 having to do with drama (*a dramatic society/a dramatic representation of the novelist's life*). 2 sudden or exciting (*a dramatic improvement*). 3 showing too much feeling or emotion (*she's so dramatic about the least thing*).

dramat'is perso'nae *n* a list of the characters in a play.

dram'atist *n* a writer of plays.

dram'atize *vb* 1 to turn into a stage play (*dramatizing a novel*). 2 to exaggerate the importance or significance of (*she dramatized what was a minor injury/a situation that was dramatized by the press*):—*n* **dramatiza'tion**.

drape *vb* 1 to cover or decorate with cloth, etc, in folds (*drape the sofa with a large length of brown velvet*). 2 to cause to hang or rest loosely (*draping his legs over the end of the sofa*).

drap'er *n* one who sells clothes.

drap'ery *n* 1 cloth, linen. 2 a draper's shop.

dras'tic *adj* acting with strength or violence, thorough (*take drastic measures*).

draught [dräft] *n* 1 the amount taken in one drink (*a long draught of cold beer*). 2 a stream of air through a room (*draughts coming in the window*). 3 the depth a ship sinks in water. 4 *pl* a game in which round pieces are moved about on a squared board.

draughts'man n 1 a piece in a game of draughts. 2 a man whose job it is to draw plans for buildings, etc.

draught'y adj cold because of a stream of air (large draughty rooms).

draw vb (pt **drew**, pp **drawn**) 1 to pull along or towards (a tractor drawing a trailer/draw a gun out/drew a file from the cabinet). 2 to move towards or away from (the crowd drew nearer/the car drew away from the kerb). 3 to attract (try to draw his attention to the lack of money). 4 to receive money (as wages, for a cheque, etc) (draw £1500 per month). 5 to make a picture or pictures of, usu with a pencil, crayons, etc (ask the child to draw a picture of the house/draw his mother). 6 (of a game or contest) to end with nobody winning (the two football teams drew). 7 (of a ship) to sink to a certain depth in the water:—n 1 an attraction (the new singer is a real draw at the club). 2 a game or contest won by nobody (the football match ended in a draw). 3 the selecting of winning tickets in a raffle, lottery, etc:—**draw the line at** to refuse to have anything to do with (draw the line at lying):— **draw up 1** to stop (cars drawing up at the kerb). 2 to prepare, esp in writing (draw up a contract).

draw'back n a disadvantage (he found his poor eyesight a drawback).

draw'bridge n a bridge that can be lifted at one end to prevent crossing.

draw'er n 1 a sliding box or container in a table, cupboard, etc. 2 pl (old) an undergarment with legs for the bottom part of the body.

draw'ing n 1 a picture made with a pencil, crayons, etc (a pen-and-ink drawing of the house). 2 the art of making such pictures (study drawing).

drawing room n a sitting room, esp a large one in which guests are received.

drawl vb to speak slowly or lazily (drawl his words in an irritating way):—also n.

dray n a long low cart for heavy loads.

dread n fear, terror (live in dread of being attacked):—adj causing great fear, terrible:—vb to fear greatly (dread losing his job).

dread'ful adj 1 terrible (a dreadful accident/a dreadful storm/in dreadful pain). 2 very unpleasant, bad (a dreadful noise/a dreadful dress).

dread'locks npl hair that is twisted into long thick braids hanging down from the scalp.

dread'nought n a type of heavy battleship.

dream n 1 the ideas or fancies passing through the mind of a person sleeping. 2 memories of the past or thoughts of what may happen (dreams of becoming a millionaire). 3 state of being occupied by one's thoughts, daydream. 4 (inf) a beautiful or wonderful person or thing (a dream of a dress):—vb (pt, pp **dreamt** or **dreamed**) 1 to have dreams. 2 to imagine.

dream'er n one more interested in thoughts or fancies than facts.

dream'y adj given to or relating to daydreaming (a dreamy kind of person/in a dreamy mood).

drear'y adj cheerless, gloomy (a dreary November day/a dreary style of decoration).

dredge[1] n a machine for bringing up mud, fish, etc, from the bottom of a river or the sea:—vb 1 to bring up with a dredge (dredge up the body from the river bed). 2 to clear with a dredge (dredging the canal). 3 to mention something from the past (dredge up the old scandal about her).

dredge[2] vb to sprinkle with (dredging biscuits with sugar).

dredg'er n a ship fitted to clear mud from the channel in a river or harbour.

dregs npl tiny pieces of matter that sink to the foot of a standing liquid (wine dregs/coffee dregs).

drench vb 1 to make very wet (get drenched in the storm). 2 to force (an animal) to drink.

dress vb 1 to put on clothes (dress oneself/dress the child warmly). 2 to wear evening or formal dress (do we have to dress for dinner?). 3 to straighten, to set in order (dress the shop window). 4 to bandage (dress a wound). 5 to prepare for use (dress a turkey for the oven):— n 1 clothing (casual dress). 2 a woman's outer garment (a summer dress):—**dress up 1** to put on the clothes of another person, nation, etc (dress up for the fancy-dress party). 2 to put on one's best clothes (dress up for the formal ball).

dress circle n the first-floor gallery in a theatre.

dress'er n 1 a kitchen sideboard (*plates displayed on the dresser*). 2 one who helps an actor or actress to dress.

dress'ing n 1 the ointments, bandages, etc, put on a wound. 2 something put on as a covering (*give the plants a dressing of fertilizer*). 3 sauce for food, esp a mixture of oil and vinegar, etc, for putting on salads.

dress'ing gown n a loose garment worn over night clothes or underclothes.

dress rehear'sal n a practice before a performance, in the appropriate costume.

dress'y adj 1 (*inf*) fond of nice clothes (*a dressy young man*). 2 elegant or elaborate, suitable for special occasions (*dressy clothes*).

drib'ble vb 1 to fall or let fall in small drops (*water dribbling from the tap*). 2 to allow saliva to run from the mouth (*babies dribbling*). 3 to keep a moving ball under control by little kicks or taps (*a footballer dribbling towards the goal*).

drib'let n a small amount (*water coming out in driblets*).

drift n 1 that which is driven by wind (e.g. snow, sand) or water (e.g. seaweed). 2 meaning (*I didn't get the drift of his speech*):—vb 1 to be driven by wind or water current (*boats drifting*). 2 to do something aimlessly (*just drifting without any ambition*).

drift'er n a fishing boat using **drift nets** (i.e. nets kept near the surface of the water by cork).

drill[1] n 1 a tool for boring holes (*an electric drill*). 2 training practice (*military drill*). 3 procedures to be followed in a certain situation, such as an emergency (*fire drill*):—vb 1 to make holes with a drill (*drill holes for screws/drill for oil*). 2 to teach something by making learners do it again and again (*drill the class in spelling rules*). 3 to practise military exercises (*soldiers drilling*).

drill[2] n 1 a machine for sowing seeds. 2 a row of seeds:—vb to sow in rows.

drily see **dry**.

drink vb (pt **drank**, pp **drunk**) 1 to swallow (a liquid) (*drink milk*). 2 to take alcoholic liquids, esp in too great amounts (*her husband drinks*):—n 1 an act of drinking (*have a drink of water*). 2 a liquid suitable for drinking (*soft drinks*). 3 alcoholic liquids (*take to drink*). 4 a glass of alcoholic liquid (*buy the drinks*).

drip vb (**dripped**[1], **drip'ping**) to fall or let fall in drops (*water dripping from the ceiling/his umbrella dripping water*):—n a drop (*drips from the ceiling*).

drip'ping n the fat that drips from roasting meat.

drive vb (pt **drove**, pp **driv'en**) 1 to control or guide (a car, etc) (*drive a sports car*). 2 to ride in a motor car or other vehicle (*driving with his friends to the seaside*). 3 to force or urge along (*drive cows to market*). 4 to hit hard (*drive the nail through the wood*):—n 1 a ride in a carriage or motor car. 2 a private road up to a house. 3 a hard hit (at a ball). 4 energy.

driv'el n (*inf*) foolish talk, nonsense (*talk a lot of drivel*):—vb (**driv'elled**, **driv'elling**) to talk nonsense (*drivel on about unimportant problems*).

driv'er n 1 one who drives (*lorry drivers*). 2 a golf club with a wooden head.

driz'zle vb to rain in small drops:—n a fine rain (*get caught in the drizzle*).

droll adj amusing, odd (*a droll child/a droll story*).

drom'edary n a camel with one hump on its back.

drone n 1 the male or non-working bee. 2 a lazy person (*the drones in the office*). 3 a humming sound (*the drone of traffic*). 4 the bass pipe of a bagpipe:—vb 1 to make a humming sound (*an aeroplane droning overhead*). 2 to speak boringly (*the speaker droned on as most of the audience left*).

droop vb 1 to hang down (*with the hem of her dress drooping*). 2 to become weak (*drooping visibly after a hard day at the office*):—also n.

drop n 1 a very small amount of liquid (*not a drop spilled*). 2 the act of falling (*a drop in temperature*). 3 the distance that one may fall (*a drop of 300 feet from the castle wall*). 4 a small hard sweet:—vb (**dropped**[1], **drop'ping**) 1 to fall or let fall in drops. 2 to fall or let fall (*drop a plate on the floor/the dish dropped to the floor*). 3 to fall or cause to fall to a lower level or amount (*the price dropped sharply/forced to drop his speed*). 4 to stop seeing, talking about, doing, etc (*we've discussed this too long—let's drop the subject*).

drought [drout] n a long spell of dry weather, lack of rain, dryness (*crops dying in the drought*).

drove n a herd or flock on the move (*a drove of cattle*).

drov'er n one who drives cattle.

drown vb 1 to die under water by water filling the lungs (*drown while trying to rescue his friend from the river*). 2 to kill by keeping under water (*drown the kittens in the canal*). 3 to flood, to submerge (*farmland drowned by the floods*). 4 to put too much liquid in or on (*meat drowned in a sickly sauce*). 5 to prevent from being heard by making a noise (*her speech was drowned by the noise of the traffic*).

drow'sy adj sleepy (*feeling drowsy after a large lunch*):—n **drow'siness**.

drub vb (**drubbed'**, **drub'bing**) to beat, to thrash (*drub the other team*):—n **drub'bing**.

drudge vb to work hard, to slave (*drudging away in the factory*):—n one who does hard or boring work (*drudges washing dishes in the hotel kitchen*).

drud'gery n dull or hard work.

drug n 1 any substance used as or in a medicine (*pain-killing drugs*). 2 a substance that causes sleep or loss of feeling, esp a habit-forming one (*drugs such as cocaine and heroin*):—vb (**drugged'**, **drug'ging**) to give drugs to in order to make insensible (*drug him before kidnapping him*).

dru'id n a priest of the Celts in ancient Britain before the Christian era.

drum n 1 a musical instrument in which skin is stretched tightly over the ends of a box and then beaten to produce a booming sound. 2 the tight skin across the inside of the ear. 3 something shaped like a drum (*an oil drum*):—vb (**drummed'**, **drum'ming**) 1 to beat a drum. 2 to make a noise by beating or tapping (*drumming impatiently on the table/drumming her fingers impatiently on the table*):—n **drum'mer**.

drum'stick n a stick for beating a drum.

drunk adj overcome or overexcited by too much strong drink (*too drunk to drive*):—n **drunk'enness**.

drunk'ard n one who is often drunk.

dry adj 1 not wet or damp (*paint not yet dry/is the washing dry?*). 2 with little rainfall (*a dry spell/dry parts of the world*). 3 not legally allowed to sell alcohol (*dry areas of America*). 4 not sweet (*a dry wine*). 5 (inf) thirsty (*dry after their long walk*). 6 uninteresting (*a very dry book*). 7 (of humour) quiet, not easily noticed:—

vb to make or become dry (*dried the washing on the radiators/paint taking a long time to dry*):—adv **dri'ly**, **dry'ly**:—n **dry'ness**.

dry'ad n a mythical spirit of the woods.

dry'-clean' vb to clean with chemicals instead of water:—n **dry'-clean'er**.

dry dock n a dock out of which water can be drained so that a ship may be repaired.

dry rot n a disease of wood that makes it crumble away (*houses affected by dry rot*).

dry'salter n (old) one who sells dyes, chemicals, etc:—n **dry'saltery**.

du'al adj consisting of two, double (*dual controls in the car used by the driving instructor/have dual nationality/play a dual role in the film*):—n **dual'ity**.

dual carriageway n a wide road which has a strip of grass or barrier in the middle to separate two lines of traffic moving in opposite directions.

dub vb (**dubbed'**, **dub'bing**) 1 to make someone a knight by touching him with a sword. 2 to give a nickname or title to (*dubbed 'Ginger' by his friends*).

dub'bin, **dub'bing** ns a grease for softening leather.

du'bious adj 1 feeling doubt (*I am rather dubious about his suitability for the job*). 2 causing doubt, of uncertain worth, etc, possibly dishonest (*of dubious character*):—n **dubiety** [dû-bī'-ê-ti].

du'cal adj having to do with a duke.

ducat [duk'-êt] n (old) a gold or silver coin once used in Europe.

duch'ess n the wife or widow of a duke.

duch'y n 1 the lands of a duke. 2 a country ruled by a duke.

duck[1] n 1 a type of common waterfowl, both domestic and wild, whose flesh is used as a food (*ducks swimming on the pond/duck served in orange sauce*). 2 in cricket, a score of 0 by a batsman:—**break one's duck** to score one's first run.

duck[2] vb 1 to plunge or dip under water (*duck her in the river*). 2 to bend to avoid something or to avoid being seen (*duck to avoid hitting his head on the branch/duck down behind the window to avoid being seen by the police*). 3 to avoid or dodge (*duck his responsibilities*).

duck[3] n 1 a strong cotton material. 2 pl clothes made of duck.

duck'ling n a young duck.

duck'weed n a water plant.

duct n 1 a pipe or tube for carrying liquid, gas, electric wires, etc (*air-conditioning ducts*). 2 a tube in the body or in plants through which fluid, etc, passes (*tear ducts*).

dud adj (*inf*) of no use (*dud fireworks/a dud manager*):—*also* n.

dud'geon n annoyance, anger (*leave the meeting in high dudgeon*).

due adj 1 owed. 2 proper. 3 expected:—*adv* directly:—n 1 an amount owed. 2 a right. 3 pl a sum payable:—**due to** caused by.

du'el n 1 an arranged fight between two armed people (*challenge him to a duel when he insulted his honour*). 2 a contest or struggle between two people (*a duel of wits*):—*also* vb (**duelled'**, **duel'ling**).

duet' n a piece of music for two singers or players (*pianists playing a duet*).

duff'el, duff'le n a rough woollen cloth (*a duffel coat*).

duff'er n (*inf*) a stupid or slow-thinking person (*too much of a duffer to pass the exam*).

duff'le see **duffel**.

dug n an animal's teat or nipple from which its young suck milk.

dug'out n 1 an underground shelter (*a military dugout*). 2 a boat made from a hollowed-out tree.

duke n 1 the highest rank of nobleman. 2 in some parts of Europe, esp formerly, a ruling prince.

duke'dom n the lands or title of a duke.

dul'cet adj (*often hum*) sweet, tuneful (*good to hear your dulcet tones*).

dul'cimer n a musical instrument played by small hammers striking strings, the forerunner of the piano.

dull adj 1 slow, stupid (*a dull pupil*). 2 uninteresting (*a dull TV show/rather a dull young woman*). 3 cloudy, sunless, gloomy (*a dull, wet day*). 4 not bright (*dull colours*). 5 not sharp (*a dull pain/a dull noise*):—vb to make dull, to blunt:—n **dull'ness**.

dulse n an eatable seaweed.

du'ly adv 1 properly, fitly (*duly elected MP for the area*). 2 at the due and proper time (*the taxi they ordered duly arrived*).

dumb adj 1 unable to speak (*people who have been dumb since birth*). 2 silent (*remain dumb throughout the policeman's questioning/struck dumb with amazement*). 3 (*inf*) stupid, unintelligent (*she's obviously a bit dumb*):—n **dumb'ness**.

dumb'bells npl weights used when exercising the arm muscles (*dumbbells used in weight training*).

dumbfound' vb to astonish greatly (*she was dumbfounded by his rude behaviour*).

dum'my n 1 a model of the human figure, used for displaying or fitting clothes (*a tailor's dummy*). 2 an imitation article (*dummies in the window, not real boxes of chocolate*):—adj pretended, not real.

dump vb 1 to throw away, to get rid of (*dump rubbish*). 2 (*inf*) to let fall or set down heavily (*dump his suitcase on the doorstep*). 3 to sell goods in another country at a low price:—n 1 a rubbish heap (*take the rubbish to the council dump*). 2 a military store (*an ammunition dump*). 3 (*inf*) a dirty, untidy or uninteresting place (*the flat's a real dump*). 4 pl low spirits.

dumper truck, dump truck n a heavy lorry the back of which can be tilted back and up to unload cargo such as earth, gravel, rocks, etc.

dump'ling n a food consisting of a thick paste, sometimes rolled into balls, or sometimes filled with fruit or meat.

dun[1] adj of a pale yellowish or greyish-brown colour (*a horse of a dun colour*).

dun[2] vb (**dunned'**, **dun'ning**) to press for payment (*creditors dunning him for money*).

dunce n a slow learner, a stupid pupil (*the class dunce*).

dune [dûn] n a low sandhill, esp on the seashore (*children playing on the dunes*).

dung n the waste matter passed from the bodies of animals (*dung used as a fertilizer by farmers*):—vb to mix dung with earth to fertilize it.

dung'arees, dungarees' npl outer garments worn to protect the clothing (*workmen in dungarees*).

dun'geon n a dark prison, an underground prison cell (*the dungeons beneath the castle*).

duodenum [du-o-dee'-nêm] n part of the bowel:—adj **duode'nal.**

dupe vb to cheat (*duping the old lady by pretending to be a telephone engineer*):—n one who is cheated or deceived.

dup'licate *adj* exactly the same, exactly like another (*duplicate keys*):—*n* an exact copy (*keep a duplicate of the letter in the office files*):—*vb* to make a copy or copies of (*duplicating the documents for the meeting*):—*n* duplica'tion.

dup'licator *n* a machine for making many copies.

duplicity [dö-plis'-i-ti] *n* deceit, trickery.

dur'able *adj* **1** lasting, hard-wearing (*trousers of a durable material*). **2** lasting or able to last (*hopes of a durable peace are fading*):—*n* durabil'ity.

dura'tion *n* the time for which a thing lasts (*for the duration of the storm/a disease of short duration*).

duress' *n* use of force, threats, etc (*agree to go only under duress*).

du'ring *prep* **1** in the course of (*he died during the night*). **2** throughout the time of (*a shortage of food during the war*).

dusk *n* partial darkness, twilight (*dusk sets in early in the winter*).

dust *n* tiny dry particles of earth or matter (*dust settling on the furniture*):—*vb* **1** to remove dust (*dust the piano*). **2** to sprinkle with powder (*dust the cake with icing sugar*):—*adj* dust'y.

dust'bin *n* a container for household rubbish.

dust'er *n* a cloth for removing dust, etc (*polishing the silver with a duster*).

dust'man *n* a man who removes household rubbish.

du'tiable *adj* able to be taxed (*dutiable goods such as wine and spirits*).

du'tiful *adj* obedient, careful to do one's duty (*a dutiful son*).

du'ty *n* **1** that which one ought to do (*do one's duty as a responsible citizen*). **2** an action or task requiring to be done, esp one attached to a job (*perform his duties as a junior doctor/on night duty*). **3** a tax on goods (*duty paid on cigarettes*).

duvet [dü'vā] *n* a large quilt for a bed filled with down, feathers or other light material and used instead of blankets.

DVD [*abbr for* **digital video disk**] a kind of compact disk on which particularly large amounts of information, especially photographs and video material, can be stored.

dwarf *n* (*pl* **dwarfs** *or* **dwarves**) **1** a person, animal or plant much smaller than is the average. **2** in fairy tales, a creature like a very small man who has magical powers (*dwarfs and fairies*):—*adj* undersized, very small (*dwarf fruit trees*):—*vb* to make seem small (*he was so tall that he dwarfed the rest of the team*):—*adj* dwarf'ish.

dwell *vb* (*pt, pp* **dwelt** *or* **dwelled'**) **1** (*old or lit*) to live in (*dwell in a house by the sea*). **2** to talk or think much about (*try not to dwell on your health problems*).

dwell'ing *n* (*fml or old*) a house.

dwin'dle *vb* to grow gradually less or smaller (*his hopes of success dwindled/the population of the village is dwindling*).

dye *vb* to give a new colour to, to stain (*dye a white skirt red*):—*n* a colouring substance:—*n* dy'er.

dyke *see* **dike.**

dynam'ic *adj* active, energetic (*a dynamic new salesman*).

dynam'ics *n* the science of matter and movement.

dyn'amite *n* a powerful explosive (*bridges blown up with dynamite*).

dyn'amo *n* a machine for making electric current.

dynasty [din'-ês-ti] *n* a line of rulers of the same family (*the Tudor dynasty in England*):—*adj* dynas'tic.

dys'entry *n* a disease of the bowels.

dyslex'ia *n* difficulty with reading and spelling caused by a slight disorder in the brain.

dyspep'sia *n* (*fml*) indigestion (*suffering from dyspepsia after a heavy meal*).

dyspep'tic *n* one suffering from dyspepsia:—*adj* **1** suffering from dyspepsia. **2** relating to dyspepsia (*a dyspeptic condition*). **3** (*inf*) bad-tempered (*a dyspeptic old man*).

E

each *pron, adj* every one taken singly or separately (*each pupil is to bring money for the school trip/give a cake to each of the children*).

eager *adj* full of desire, keen (*eager to learn/eager pupils/eager for news*):—*n* **eagerness**.

eagle *n* a large bird of prey.

eagle-eyed *adj* having very keen sight (*the eagle-eyed teacher saw the children exchange notes*).

eaglet *n* a young eagle.

ear[1] *n* 1 the organ of hearing. 2 the ability to hear the difference between sounds (*a musical ear*). 3 attention (*have the king's ear*).

ear[2] *n* a head or spike of corn.

earache *n* a pain in the ear.

eardrum *n* the tight skin across the inside of the ear that enables one to hear sounds.

earl *n* a British nobleman, in rank above a viscount but below a marquis.

earldom *n* the lands or title of an earl.

early *adj* 1 before the time arranged (*the baby's early arrival*). 2 near the beginning (*in the early part of the century*). 3 belonging to the first stages of development, etc (*early musical instruments*). 4 (*fml*) soon (*we look forward to an early reply*):—*adv* 1 near the beginning (of a period of time, etc) (*early in the afternoon*). 2 sooner than usual, sooner than expected, sooner than often, etc (*arrive early for work*).

earmark *vb* to set aside for a special purpose (*earmark some money for their children's education*).

earn *vb* 1 to get in return for work (*earn £15,000 per year*). 2 to deserve (*earn their respect*).

earnest[1] *adj* 1 serious. 2 determined:—*n* **earnestness**:—**in earnest** meaning what one says (*they thought he was joking about leaving but he was in earnest*).

earnings *npl* wages, money paid for work done (*pay tax on earnings*).

earring *n* an ornament worn on the ear.

earshot *n* the distance within which one can hear something (*be quiet—he's within earshot*).

earth *n* 1 the planet on which we live (*people used to think that the earth was flat*). 2 the world as opposed to heaven (*heaven and earth*). 3 dry land, the ground or soil (*the earth, sea and sky/*

fill a plant pot with earth*). 4 the hole of a fox, badger, etc. 5 the wire connecting an electrical apparatus to the ground:—*vb* to connect an electrical apparatus to the ground:—**earthen** *adj*

earthenware *n* dishes or other vessels made of baked clay, pottery.

earthly *adj* having to do with the world, of wordly rather than heavenly things (*earthly pleasures*).

earthquake *n* a shaking movement of the surface of the earth.

earthwork *n* a defensive wall of earth.

earthy *adj* 1 like or of earth (*an earthy smell*). 2 coarse, not refined (*earthy humour*).

earwig *n* a small insect formerly thought to enter the head by the ear.

ease *n* 1 freedom from anxiety or pain (*a mind at ease*). 2 lack of difficulty (*do the job with ease*). 3 freedom from work, rest, comfort (*a life of ease*). 4 naturalness (*ease of manner*):—*vb* 1 to lessen (*easing the pain/the pain has eased*). 2 to move gently or gradually (*ease the piano through the door*).

easel *n* a stand to hold a picture, blackboard, etc, upright (*an artist's easel*).

east *n adj and adv* one of the four chief points of the compass, the direction in which the sun rises:—*adjs* **eastern**, **eastwards**:—**the East** the countries of Asia.

Easter *n* a religious feast during which Christians commemorate the rising of Christ from the dead.

easterly *adj* from or towards the east (*easterly winds*).

easy *adj* 1 not difficult (*easy tasks/easy exams*). 2 free from anxiety or pain (*an easy mind*). 3 comfortable (*an easy life*). 4 relaxed, leisurely (*walk with an easy stride*).

easy-chair *n* a comfortable armchair (*a three-piece suite of a sofa and two easy-chairs*).

easy-going *adj* not easily worried or angered (*an easy-going mother who is not upset by her children's noise*).

eat *vb* (*pt* **ate**, *pp* **eaten**) 1 to chew and swallow, as food (*eat a lot of chocolate/eat only vegetarian food*). 2 to wear away (*acids eating metal*).

eating disorder *n* an emotional disorder which is characterised by an irrational attitude towards food, either an abnormal avoidance of it or a craving for it.

eaves *npl* that part of the roof that comes out beyond the walls.

eaves'drop *vb* (**eaves'dropped, eaves'drop-ping**) to try to hear what others are saying to each other privately (*find out their secrets by eavesdropping on their conversation/open the door suddenly and find her eavesdropping*):—*n* **eaves'dropper.**

ebb *n* **1** the flowing back of the tide. **2** a falling away or weakening (*the ebb of the emperor's power*):—*vb* **1** to flow back (*the tide ebbing*). **2** to grow less, weak, faint, etc (*enthusiasm began to ebb*).

eb'ony *n* a hard black wood:—*adj* **1** made of ebony (*the ebony keys on the piano*). **2** black (*an ebony skin*).

ebul'lient *adj* full of energy and excitement (*so ebullient that he makes everyone feel enthusiastic/in ebullient mood after his success*).

eccentric [ek-sen'-trik] *adj* **1** odd, strange (*an eccentric old woman/eccentric behaviour*). **2** (*of circles*) not drawn round the same centre:—*n* a person who behaves in an odd or unusual manner (*one of the village's eccentrics*).

eccentric'ity *n* **1** strangeness of behaviour (*the eccentricity of his style of dressing*). **2** a strange or unusual habit (*one of his eccentricities*).

ecclesias'tic, ecclesias'tical *adjs* having to do with the church or clergy:—*n* **ecclesi-as'tic** a clergyman.

echo [e'-kō] *n* (*pl* **e'choes**) **1** the repeating of a sound by the reflection of sound waves from a surface (*hear the echo in the cave*). **2** an imitation (*work that is a mere echo of Shakespeare*):—*vb* **1** to repeat, to throw back a sound (*the cave echoed back his shout*). **2** to imitate (*echoing their leader's behaviour*).

eclec'tic *adj* (*of people, beliefs, ideas, tastes, etc*) not restricted to any one system, etc, choosing from or using a whole range of (*an eclectic taste in books/an eclectic range of music*).

eclipse' *n* **1** the cutting off of the light from the sun by the moon coming between it and the earth. **2** the darkening of the face of the moon by the earth coming between it and the sun. **3** a failure caused by the unexpected success of another (*a writer who suffered an eclipse when younger writers gained popularity*):—*vb* **1** to cut off the light from, to darken. **2** to make another seem inferior by outdoing (*eclipsing her husband as a painter/eclipsed by her beautiful talented sister*).

ecol'ogy *n* **1** the science of the life of things in their physical surroundings (*study ecology*). **2** the relation of plants and living creatures to each other and to their surroundings (*pollution affecting the ecology of the area*):—**ecolog'ical** *adj.*

e-commerce *n* electronic commerce, business conducted on-line.

econo'mic *adj* **1** having to do with economics (*the government's economic policy*). **2** designed to give a profit (*charge an economic rent/not economic for the shop to open in the evening*).

econo'mical *adj* careful of money, not wasteful (*an economical meal/be economical with cream in cooking*).

econo'mics *n* the study of the means of increasing the wealth of a community or nation.

econ'omist *n* one who studies economics.

econ'omize *vb* to spend or use carefully, to save, to be economical (*economizing on petrol by walking to work*).

econ'omy *n* **1** careful management of the wealth, money, goods, etc, of a home, business or country. **2** sparing use of money (*have to practise economy*).

e'cosystem *n* all the plants and living creatures that live in an area and depend on each other together with their habitat (*The ecosystem of the lakeshore is being threatened by factory waste*).

ec'stasy *n* great delight or joy (*religious ecstasy/be in ecstasies after her victory*).

ecstat'ic *adj* delighted, carried away by joy (*ecstatic at the birth of their child/ecstatic people celebrated their win on the pools*).

ecumen'ical *adj* having to do with the whole Christian church (*the ecumenical movement*).

eczema [ek-zee'-ma] *n* a skin disease.

ed'dy *n* a whirling current of water or air, a whirlpool or whirlwind (*eddies of mist on the mountain tops*):—*vb* to move in eddies (*mist eddied round the mountain tops*).

edelweiss [ādl'-vîs] *n* a small white flower found in the Alps.

E'den *n* (in the Old Testament) the garden of Adam and Eve, paradise.

edge *n* **1** the sharp side of a blade (*put an edge on the knife*). **2** a border or boundary (*the edge of the lake*). **3** keenness, sharpness (*a wit with an edge/add an edge to her appetite*):—*vb* **1** to move gradually, esp with small sideways movements (*edged his way towards the front of the queue/edging away from their angry mother*). **2** to put a border on (*edge a lawn with flowers/ edge a handkerchief with lace*).

edge'ways, edge'wise *adjs* sideways (*get the wardrobe through the door edgeways*).

edg'ing *n* a border or fringe (*the edging on the woollen shawl*).

ed'ible *adj* able or fit to be eaten (*food that is scarcely edible/edible berries*).

edict [ee'-dikt] *n* an order by a ruler or government.

edification *see* **edify**.

ed'ifice *n* (*fml*) a large building (*large edifices built by rich Victorian merchants*).

ed'ify *vb* to improve the mind or character (*a lecture designed to edify the children*):—*n* **edifica'tion**.

ed'it *vb* to prepare for printing or publication (*edited a manuscript*).

edi'tion *n* the number of copies of a book or newspaper published at one time (*the late edition of the newspaper*).

ed'itor *n* **1** one who edits (*the editor of a manuscript*). **2** one who collects the material for a newspaper or magazine and selects what is to be published or who is in charge of a newspaper or part of a newspaper (*a fashion editor*):— *f* **ed'itress**.

edito'rial *adj* of an editor:—*n* an article by the editor or someone chosen by him or her on a matter of immediate interest (*an editorial on the country's economic situation*).

ed'ucate *vb* to teach or train (*educating children to the age of sixteen*):—*n* **educa'tion**.

educa'tional *adj* having to do with education (*educational opportunities*).

educa'tionist *n* one who studies methods of education.

ed'ucative *adj* (*fml*) helping to educate (*educative techniques*).

eel *n* a snake-like fish.

e'en [een] (*old or lit*) *short for* **even**.

e'er [ër] (*old or lit*) *short for* **ever**.

ee'rie, ee'ry *adj* strange and frightening (*eerie sounds in the night/the eerie feeling of a graveyard at night*).

efface' *vb* to rub out:—*n* **efface'ment**:—**efface oneself** to try to avoid being noticed.

effect' *n* **1** result, power to bring about a change (*a medicine that had little effect/angry words that had no effect on the child's behaviour*). **2** impression (*flower arrangements creating a colourful effect*). **3** *pl* goods, property (*personal effects*). **4** *pl* the imitation of natural lighting and sounds in a play, film, etc (*special effects in the horror film*):—*vb* to bring about, to succeed in doing, to produce (*effecting a market change*).

effec'tive *adj* **1** doing what is intended or desired, successful (*an effective cure*). **2** striking (*an effective use of colour*). **3** actual, real (*in effective control of the film*). **4** in operation, working (*a new system of taxation effective from next week*).

effec'tual *adj* (*fml*) able to produce the result desired (*seeking effectual measures against crime*).

effem'inate *adj* womanish, unmanly (*a man walking in an effeminate way*):—*n* **effem'inacy**.

effervesce' *vb* to bubble or sparkle (*champagne effervescing in the glasses*):—*n* **ef-ferves'cence**.

efferves'cent *adj* **1** bubbling, sparkling (*effervescent wine*). **2** lively and enthusiastic (*young people in an effervescent mood*).

effete' *adj* **1** worn out, feeble (*an effete political system*). **2** lacking vitality, feeble (*rather an effete young man*).

effica'cious *adj* able to produce the result desired (*efficacious remedies*):—*n* **efficacy**.

effi'cient *adj* **1** able to do what is necessary or intended without wasting time, energy, etc (*an efficient filing system*). **2** good at one's job, capable (*an efficient administrator*):—*n* **effi'ciency**.

effigy *n* **1** a likeness in the form of a picture, statue or carving (*stone effigies of Buddha*). **2** the head on a coin. **3** an imitation figure of a person (*burn an effigy of Guy Fawkes*).

effluent *adj* flowing out from:—*n* **1** the discharge of liquid waste matter, sewage, etc (*the effluent from the factory*). **2** a stream flowing from a larger stream:—*n* **efflu'ence**.

effort n **1** an energetic attempt (*make a real effort to arrive on time*). **2** the making use of strength or ability (*take a lot of effort to move the rock*).

effort'less adj with ease, without trying hard (*playing with effortless skill/what seemed an effortless victory*).

effront'ery n open impudence, shameless rudeness (*have the effrontery to call me a liar*).

efful'gence n (*fml*) a flood of light, brightness.

efful'gent adj (*fml*) very bright, shining brightly.

effu'sive adj expressing one's feelings too freely, pretending to feel more than one really feels (*an effusive welcome by the hostess*):—n effu'siveness.

egg n **1** an oval object, usu covered with a hard brittle shell, laid by a bird, reptile, etc, from which a young one is hatched. **2** such an object laid by the domestic hen used as food (*have a boiled egg for breakfast*). **3** in the female mammal, the cell from which the young is formed, the ovum.

egg on vb to try to get somebody (to do something), to urge, to encourage (*egg his friend on to steal the apples*).

eggplant see aubergine.

eg'lantine n the sweet-brier, the wild-rose bush.

ego n the image a person has of his or herself; self confidence; egotism.

ego'ism n selfishness, the belief that the best guide to action is what is good for oneself.

eg'oist n a selfish person, one who believes in and practises egoism (*such an egoist that she sees things only from her point of view*):—adj egois'tic.

eg'otist n one always talking of himself or herself (*he's such an egotist that he bores everyone with tales of his personal life*):—n eg'otism:—adjs egotis'tic, egotis'tical.

egregious [e-gree'-ji-ês] adj (*fml*) outstanding, extraordinarily bad (*unable to overlook such egregious errors*).

e'gress n **1** (*fml*) a way out (*two means of egress from the building*). **2** the right or power of going out (*no egress through his property*).

e'gret, n a small white heron.

eider [ī'-dêr] n the Arctic duck.

ei'derdown n a warm bedcovering stuffed with the soft feathers of the eider.

eisteddfod [i-steth'-vod] n a Welsh national festival of song, music, dancing and poetry.

ei'ther pron and adj one or other of two (*either book will do/either of the restaurants is suitable*).

ejac'ulate vb **1** to say something suddenly, to exclaim ('*I don't believe it,' he ejaculated*). **2** to eject discharge fluid, esp semen, from the body:—n ejacula'tion.

eject' vb to throw out (*people employed to eject troublemakers from the club*).

ejec'tion n **1** act of throwing out. **2** putting somebody out of a house rented by him or her (*the ejection of tenants for non-payment of rent*).

eke vb:—**eke out 1** to cause to last longer (*eke out the coal by burning wood with it/eking out the meat in the stew with lots of vegetables*). **2** to manage with difficulty to make (a living, etc) (*eke out a livelihood by doing people's washing*).

elab'orate adj **1** worked out with great care (*elaborate preparations*). **2** having many parts (*elaborate machines*). **3** very decorative (*an elaborate carving*):—vb **1** to work out very carefully, to add to and improve upon (*elaborating their plans*). **2** to explain fully (*elaborate on what you said*):—n elabora'tion.

e'land n a type of South African deer.

elapse' vb (*fml*) to pass (*a few years had elapsed*).

elas'tic adj able to stretch or be stretched easily, but returning immediately to its former shape (*a skirt with an elastic waistband*):—n a strip of material lined with rubber to make it elastic.

elastic'ity n springiness.

elate' vb to make very glad or proud (*elated by the news of his victory*):—n ela'tion.

el'bow n **1** the joint between the forearm and upper arm. **2** a sharp bend or corner (*an elbow in the pipe*):—vb to push with the elbow.

eld'er[1] adj older (*a younger sister and an elder brother*):—n **1** an older member of a community (*the elders of the tribe*). **2** an official in certain churches (e.g. the Presbyterian).

eld'er[2] n a small tree with purple berries.

eld'erly adj old, getting old (*seats reserved for elderly people*).

eld'est adj oldest (*her eldest daughter*).

elect' *vb* **1** (*fml*) to choose (*elect to go by train*). **2** to choose by voting (*elect a new president*):—*adj* chosen:—*n* **1** those chosen. **2** those chosen by God.

elec'tion *n* act of choosing, esp by vote (*a general election*).

electioneer' *vb* to try to get people to use their votes in a certain way (*politicians going round the country electioneering*).

elec'tor *n* one with the right to vote (*politicians trying to convince the electors*).

elec'toral *adj* having to do with electors (*the electoral roll*).

elec'torate *n* all those having the right to vote on a certain occasion (*a proportion of the electorate do not bother to vote*).

elec'tric *adj* **1** having to do with electricity. **2** exciting, thrilling (*an electric performance*):—*npl* electric fittings.

elec'trical *adj* having to do with electricity, worked by electricity.

electri'cian *n* one who works with electricity or electrical apparatus.

electri'city *n* an energy produced by chemical or other action, a natural force that can be harnessed to give heat, light and power.

elec'trify *vb* **1** to put electricity into (*electrify the railway line*). **2** to thrill (*electrified by the orchestra's performance*).

elec'trocute *vb* to kill by electricity (*in some states of the USA convicted murderers are electrocuted*):—*n* **electrocu'tion.**

elec'trode *n* either of the two conductors through which electricity enters or leaves something, such as a battery.

electrodynam'ics *n* the science of electric currents.

electrol'ysis *n* **1** the treatment of a substance by passing an electrical current through a liquid. **2** the destruction of hair roots by means of an electric current (*facial hair removed by electrolysis*).

elec'tron *n* the negative electrical unit in an atom.

electron'ic *adj* of a device, having many small parts, such as microchips and transistors, which control and direct an electric current (*an electronic calculator*).

electron'ics *n* the branch of technology that is concerned with electronic devices such as computers and televisions.

elec'troplate *vb* to cover with a thin coat of metal by means of electricity (*electroplated cutlery*).

el'egant *adj* **1** graceful, smart, stylish (*an elegant woman/an elegant suit*). **2** stylish, polished (*an elegant style of writing*):—*n* **el'egance.**

elegi'ac *adj* having to do with an elegy, expressing sadness (*elegiac verses*).

el'egy *n* a mourning or sorrowful poem.

el'ement *n* **1** a necessary part (*have all the elements of a good crime novel/a sensible economic policy is a vital element of government*). **2** a substance that cannot be broken down into any other substances and from which all other things are made up (*elements such as hydrogen*). **3** *pl* knowledge without which a subject cannot be properly understood (*fail to grasp the elements of mathematics*). **4** *pl* nature, the weather (*exposed to the elements without shelter*).

elemen'tal *adj* **1** having to do with elements, like the powers of nature (*the elemental forces of nature*). **2** basic (*elemental truths*).

elemen'tary *adj* **1** having to do with the beginning (*elementary steps in mathematics*). **2** simple, easy (*elementary questions*).

el'ephant *n* a large very thick-skinned animal with a trunk and ivory tusks:—**white elephant** a gift or purchase that turns out to be of no use, a useless possession that is troublesome to keep up or retain (*those large china dogs that they gave us are a real white elephant—they need so much dusting*).

elephan'tine *adj* huge, clumsy (*pieces of furniture of elephantine proportions*).

el'evate *vb* **1** (*fml*) to make finer, better, more educated, etc (*elevating the minds of his pupils*). **2** to raise to a higher place or rank (*elevated him to the peerage*).

eleva'tion *n* **1** the act of raising. **2** (*fml*) a hill (*from an elevation above the city*). **3** height (*at an elevation of 1500 metres*). **4** a plan showing a building as seen from one side. **5** the angle measuring height.

el'evator *n* (*esp Amer*) a lift (*take the elevator to the top floor*).

elf *n* (*pl* **elves**) in fairy tales, a mischievous fairy:—*adjs* **elf'in, elf'ish, elv'ish.**

elicit [e-lis'-it] *vb* to draw out by asking questions (*eliciting information from the prisoners*).

elide' vb to run two sounds together so that only one of them is heard (e.g. *he's* for *he is*):—n **eli'sion.**

eli'gible adj able to be chosen, suitable (*eligible for the post/interview the eligible candidates*):—n **eligibil'ity.**

elim'inate vb to get rid of (*eliminating him from our list of suspects/eliminate errors from the manuscript*):—n **elimina'tion.**

elision see **elide.**

élite [ā-leet'] n a group that is at a higher level or rank, professionally, socially or in ability, etc (*the élite of the tennis club/the élite of Victorian society*).

elix'ir n (old) a magic liquid that, alchemists believed, could change any metal into gold, or enable people to live for ever.

elk n a type of large deer.

ellipse' n an oval figure. ·

ellip'sis n the leaving out of certain words needed for complete understanding of a sentence.

ellip'tic, ellip'tical adjs 1 of or lik e an ellipse. 2 having to do with an ellipsis, having a word or words missed out.

elm n a type of tree.

elocu'tion n the art or way of speaking well (*taking elocution lessons*).

e'longate vb 1 to make longer (*figures in the painting that are too elongated*). 2 to stretch out (*feel that the speaker had unnecessarily elongated his speech*):—n **elonga'tion.**

elope' vb to leave home secretly with one's lover (*decided to elope when their parents forbade them to marry*):—n **elope'ment.**

el'oquent adj 1 able to speak well, esp in public and express one's ideas and opinions effectively (*an eloquent speaker*). 2 showing or using such an ability (*an eloquent appeal to possible blood donors*):—n **el'oquence.**

else adj 1 besides, also (*what else did he say?/who else spoke?*). 2 other than that already mentioned (*someone else/decide to live somewhere else*).

elsewhere' adv in another place (*unhappy in his job and applying for jobs elsewhere*).

elu'cidate vb (fml) to explain, to make clear (*try to elucidate the scope of the problem/I do not understand; can you elucidate?*):—n **elucida'tion.**

elude' vb 1 to escape or avoid by quickness, cleverness or trickery (*eluding the policy by going down a side road*). 2 to be difficult, etc, to understand or remember (*a name that eludes me/a cure for cancer that has eluded the researchers*).

elu'sive adj 1 hard to remember, express, identify, etc (*an elusive perfume*). 2 hard to catch or track down (*elusive criminals*).

elves, elvish see **elf.**

Elys'ium n the heaven of Greek mythology:—adj **Elys'ian.**

ema'ciate vb to become or make very thin, to waste away (*emaciated by her long illness*):—n **emacia'tion.**

email n 1 electronic mail, a system for sending communications from one computer to another, using a telephone connection and a modem. 2 a message sent by email:—vb to send a (message) by email (*email the list of club members*).

e'manate vb (fml) to come from (*interesting smells emanating from the kitchen/information emanating from an unknown source*):—n **emana'tion.**

eman'cipate vb to free from control (*emancipate from slavery*):—n **emancipa'tion.**

emas'culate vb 1 to remove the sexual organs of (a male animal), to castrate. 2 to take away force and strength of (*a new law that has been emasculated by amendments in parliament*).

embalm' vb to preserve a dead body with spices.

embank'ment n a mound of stones and earth built to shut in a river or to carry a road, railway, etc, over low ground.

embar'go n (pl **embar'goes**) an official order forbidding something, esp trade with another country (*put an embargo on trade with countries practising racism*).

embark vb 1 to put or go on board ship. 2 to start (upon) (*embarking on a new career*):—n **embarka'tion.**

embar'ass vb 1 to cause to feel shy or uncomfortable (*embarrass her by paying her compliments*). 2 to involve in difficulties (*find himself financially embarrassed*):—n **embarr'assment.**

em'bassy n 1 the duties of an ambassador. 2 the house of an ambassador. 3 a group of people sent by a country to act for it in another country.

embel'lish vb **1** to make beautiful (a plain black hat embellished with pink ribbons). **2** to make more interesting, etc, by adding exaggerated or untrue details (embellish the tales of his travels):—n embell'ishment.

em'bers npl **1** live cinders of a dying fire (stare into the embers of the fire). **2** the fading remains (try to rekindle the embers of their love affair).

embezz'le vb to steal money that one has been trusted with by other people:—n em-bezz'lement.

embit'ter vb to make feel bitter, to increase anger or hatred (embittered by the disloyalty of his followers).

embla'zon vb **1** to show in a very noticeable or bold way (adverts for the product emblazoned on the billboards). **2** to adorn (shields, etc) with a heraldic design.

em'blem n an object that is regarded as a sign of something (the dove is the emblem of peace):—adjs emblema'tic, emblema'tical.

embod'iment n a living example (he is the embodiment of the old-fashioned gentleman/the embodiment of politeness).

embod'y vb **1** to give a solid form to, to express in a real or physical form (a country's constitution that embodies the principles of freedom). **2** to include (a computer system embodying many new features).

embold'en vb to give courage, to make bold (emboldened by the silence they moved forward).

emboss' vb to make a raised pattern on (embossing leather with a pattern/with the firm's name and address embossed on the writing paper).

embrace' vb **1** to hold in the arms, to hug (embracing his wife fondly). **2** to include (a speech that embraced many topics):—n a holding in the arms, a hug (a farewell embrace).

embra'sure n a loophole, a door or window set in side walls that slope outward to make a broad approach to it.

embroca'tion n an ointment for rubbing on sprains, etc (athletes applying embrocation to stiff limbs).

embroi'der vb **1** to decorate with needlework (embroidering a handkerchief with a border of roses). **2** to add interesting or exaggerated details to a story (embroidered the account of his unhappy childhood).

embroi'dery n **1** the art of decorating with needlework. **2** the act of adding interesting or exaggerated detail to. **3** decorative needlework.

embroil' vb to lead into trouble or a quarrel (become embroiled in his brother's quarrel with the neighbours).

embryo [em'-bri-ō] n **1** the form of any creature before it is born or grows (an egg containing the embryo of a chicken). **2** the beginning stage of anything (plans that are yet in embryo).

embryon'ic adj **1** in an early stage (the embryonic foetus). **2** not yet fully grown or developed (the embryonic stages of our plans).

emend' vb to correct (emend the manuscript).

emenda'tion n a correction.

em'erald n a bright green precious stone:—adj bright green (an emerald dress).

emerge' vb **1** to come out (swimmers emerging from the water). **2** to become known (facts beginning to emerge/it emerged that she had been in prison):—n emer'gence:—adj emer'gent.

emer'gency n a state of affairs requiring immediate action (call 999 in an emergency/use one's savings only in an emergency).

em'ery n a very hard mineral, made into powder and used for polishing or sharpening metals.

emet'ic adj causing one to throw up all that is in the stomach (give an emetic substance to one who has taken poison):—n an emetic medicine.

em'igrant n one who emigrates:—also adj.

em'igrate vb to leave one's country and go to live in another (emigrating to find work overseas):—n emigra'tion.

em'inence n **1** (fml) a high place, a hill (the view from the eminence above the town). **2** fame (achieve eminence as an artist). **3** the title given to a cardinal in the RC Church.

em'inent adj distinguished, very well-known (one of our most eminent writers).

emir [em-eer'] n an Arab chief.

em'issary n (fml) one sent as a representative or negotiator, often to perform a secret or unpleasant task.

emit' vb (emit'ted, emit'ting) to send or give out (chimneys emitting smoke/emit a cry of pain):—n emis'sion.

emol'lient adj (fml) softening:—n a cream or lotion that softens the skin.

emol'ument n, **emol'uments** npl (fml) wages, salary (an emolument of £20,000 per annum).

emo'tion n 1 strong or deep feeling (emotions such as love and hate). 2 the moving or upsetting of the mind or feelings (overcome by emotion).

emo'tional adj 1 of the emotions (emotional problems). 2 causing or showing deep feelings (an emotional farewell). 3 easily moved by emotion (a very emotional young woman).

em'peror n the ruler of an empire:—f **em'press.**

em'phasis n (pl emphases) 1 the added force with which certain words or parts of words are spoken (place the emphasis on the first syllable). 2 special meaning, value, importance, etc (the emphasis in the firm is on efficiency).

em'phasize vb 1 to say with emphasis (emphasizing the first syllable of the word). 2 to call attention to specially, to stress (emphasized the trustworthiness of his friends).

empha'tic adj forceful, firm and definite (an emphatic denial).

em'pire n 1 a group of countries under the rule of one of their number. 2 a large industrial organization controlling many firms (a carpet empire).

empir'ical adj guided by one's own experience, observation or experiment and not on theory (require empirical evidence).

employ' vb 1 to give work to (a firm employing hundreds of factory workers). 2 (inf) to use (employed tact).

employ'ee, employee' n one paid to work for another person or for a firm (sack several employees).

employ'er n one who gives work to another.

employ'ment n job, occupation (seek employment in industry).

empor'ium n (pl empor'ia or empor'iums) 1 a market. 2 a large store in which many different kinds of things are sold.

empow'er vb to give the right or power to (police empowered to stop and search cars).

empress see **emperor.**

emp'ty adj having nothing inside (empty barrels/empty shops):—vb 1 to take everything out of (empty the bottle/empty the barrel of beer). 2 to become empty (shops emptying at closing time):—n **emp'tiness.**

empyre'an n (fml) the sky:—also adj.

emu [ee-mû] n a large Australian flightless bird.

em'ulate vb (fml) to try to be as good as or better than (try to emulate his elder brother on the football field).

emula'tion n act of emulating, rivalry.

emul'sion n a mixture of two liquids that remain separate until shaken up (e.g. oil and vinegar).

enab'le vb to give the power or means to do something (more money enabling the firm to expand).

enact' vb 1 to lay down by law, to pass a law (laws enacted in the last session of parliament). 2 to act, perform (enact scenes from Shakespeare).

enact'ment n a law.

enam'el n 1 a smooth, glossy coating put on metals or wood to preserve or decorate them. 2 the outer covering of the teeth:—vb (**enam'elled, enam'elling**) to cover with enamel.

ena'mour vb 1 (fml) to fill with love (he is enamoured of a very young girl). 1 to like very much, to be very fond of (she is not enamoured of her new job).

encamp' vb to pitch a camp (soldiers encamped at the gates of the city):—n **en-camp'ment.**

encase' vb to put in a case or covering (encasing the broken leg in plaster).

enchant' vb 1 (old) to put a magic spell on (the enchanted wood). 2 to delight (children enchanted by the ballet):—n **enchant'er:**—f **enchant'ress:**—n **enchant'ment.**

encir'cle vb to surround (a field encircled by trees/troops encircling the enemy):—n **en-cir'clement.**

enclose' vb 1 to shut in, to fence in (enclosing the garden within a wall). 2 to send with a letter (enclose an application form).

enclo'sure n 1 a space shut or fenced in (an enclosure for ponies). 2 something sent with a letter (a cheque sent as an enclosure).

encom'ium n (fml) great praise.

encom'pass vb 1 to surround. 2 to include or comprise (a course encompassing a wide range of subjects).

encore [on(g)-kōr] adv again, once more:—n 1 a call to a performer to repeat something or perform something else. 2 the repetition of part of a performance or a further performance by the same person or people given after the main performance:—also vb.

encoun'ter n 1 a meeting, esp an unexpected one (a brief encounter with an old friend). 2 a fight or quarrel (an encounter between the opposing armies):—vb to meet (encountered her ex-husband in the street/encountering several problems).

encour'age vb 1 to make bold (their victory encouraged the troops). 2 to urge on (encouraging the pupils to stay on at school):—n **encour'agement**.

encroach' vb to go upon another's land, etc, to intrude on (accusing his neighbour of encroaching on his property):—n **en-croach'ment**.

encrust' vb to cover with a crust or hard outer layer (a crown encrusted with diamonds/shoes encrusted with mud).

encum'ber vb 1 to overload (donkeys encumbered with heavy loads). 2 to make it difficult for a person to move or act freely or easily (travel is difficult if you are encumbered with young children).

encum'brance n 1 a load. 2 something that makes it difficult to move or act freely (travellers with the encumbrance of heavy luggage).

encyclical [en-sîk'-li-kêl] n a letter addressed by the pope to all Roman Catholics.

encycloped'ia, encyclopaed'ia n a book or set of books containing information about every subject or about every branch of one subject.

encycloped'ic adj very detailed or complete (encyclopedic information).

end n 1 the last part of anything (the end of the book/the end of the journey). 2 death (meet a violent end). 3 purpose or aim (with this end in view/strive towards such an end):—vb to bring or come to an end (ending his life/the book ends happily).

endan'ger vb to put someone or something in a dangerous or harmful situation (endanger their health by smoking):—**endan'gered** adj in danger or at risk, especially of ceasing to exist (trying to conserve an endangered species).

endear' n to make dear (she endeared herself to him by being kind to his mother).

endear'ment n an act or word showing love (whisper endearments to his sweetheart).

endeavour [en-dev'-êr] vb to try, to try hard (endeavouring to win):—n attempt, effort (make every endeavour to succeed).

endem'ic adj found specially among one people or in one place (endemic diseases).

end'less adj 1 having no end (an endless conveyor belt). 2 seemingly having no end (the endless noise).

endorse' vb 1 to sign one's name on the back of a cheque or document. 2 to express approval or support (his proposals endorsed by the committee/endorsing the new product):—n **endorse'ment**.

endow' vb 1 to give so much money for a certain purpose that each year there is enough interest to carry it on. 2 to give, to grant (endowed with great charm):—n **endow'ment**.

endur'ance n the ability to endure or bear patiently (the marathon race is a test of endurance/bear pain with endurance).

endure' vb 1 (fml) to last (houses built to endure). 2 to bear patiently (enduring much pain). 3 to put up with (hard to endure noisy neighbours).

en'ema n an injection of liquid to cleanse the bowels.

en'emy n 1 one who is unfriendly, one who acts against another (make a lot of enemies in business). 2 those with whom one is at war (form an alliance against the enemy):—also adj.

energet'ic adj active, powerful, vigorous.

en'ergize vb to give energy to (healthy food energizing him).

en'ergy n active power, force, vigour (set about the work with energy/lack energy since her illness).

e'nervate vb to make weak (extreme heat enervating him).

enfee'ble vb (fml) to weaken (a country enfeebled by war and famine).

enfilade' vb to fire at a line from one end towards the other end:—also n.

enforce' n to cause to be obeyed or carried out (police enforcing traffic laws):—n **en-force'ment**.

enfranchise [en-fran'-shîz] vb 1 (fml) to set free (enfranchise slaves). 2 to give the right of voting to (fight for enfranchising women):—n **enfran'chisement**.

engage' vb 1 (fml) to bind oneself by a promise, to promise (engage to pay the money back in instalments). 2 to begin to employ (engaging a gardener). 3 to begin fighting (the armies engaged at dawn). 4 to busy (oneself) with (engage onself in household activities). 5 to attract and keep (engaging the child's attention).

engag'ing *adj* pleasing, attractive (*an engaging smile*).

engage'ment *n* 1 (*fml*) a written agreement (*unable to meet all his financial engagements*). 2 a promise to marry (*announce their engagement*). 3 an arrangement to meet someone, an appointment (*a previous engagement*). 4 a battle (*an engagement that ended the war*).

engen'der *vb* (*fml*) to give rise to, to be the cause of (*poverty that engendered crime and violence*).

en'gine *n* 1 a machine that produces power (*a car engine*). 2 a railway locomotive.

engineer' *n* 1 one who looks after engines. 2 one who makes or designs machinery, roads, bridges, etc:—*vb* to arrange for or cause something to happen, usu by clever, cunning or secret means (*engineered a suprise party for her birthday/engineering his son's promotion*).

engineer'ing *n* the science of making and using machines.

engraft' *vb* to fit on to so that it becomes one with (*engraft a shoot onto the plant*).

engrain' *n* to make sink deeply in (*a sense of what is right engrained in her/dirt engrained in his skin*).

engrave' *vb* 1 to cut or carve on metal, stone, wood, etc (*engraving his name on the trophy that he won/engrave flowers on the table top*). 2 to cut a picture on a metal plate in order to print copies of it.

engrav'ing *n* a print from an engraved plate.

engross' *vb* to take up one's whole time or attention (*children engrossed by the film*):—*n* **engross'ment**.

engulf' *vb* to swallow up (*a flood that threatened to engulf the town/people engulfed with grief*).

enhance' *vb* to increase in amount, value, importance, etc, to increase, to improve (*qualifications enhancing her job prospects/a colour that enhanced her beauty*):—*n* **enhance'ment**.

enig'ma *n* a person or thing that is difficult to understand, a mystery (*we've known her for years but she is still a bit of an enigma to us/her background is an enigma to us*).

enigma'tic, enigma'tical *adjs* having to do with an enigma, mysterious (*an enigmatic smile*).

enjoin' *vb* (*fml*) to order (*enjoin the troops to march*).

enjoy' *vb* 1 to take pleasure in (*enjoy reading/enjoying a walk in the hills*). 2 to possess (*enjoy good health/enjoy a comfortable income*):—*adj* **enjoy'able**:—*n* **enjoy'ment**.

enlarge' *vb* 1 (*fml*) to make larger (*enlarging the lawn*). 2 to reproduce (a photograph) on a larger scale. 3 to talk at length about (*enlarge on his previous comments*).

enlarge'ment *n* 1 act of making larger. 2 a larger copy of a photograph.

enlight'en *vb* (*fml*) to give more and correct information or knowledge about (*enlighten me as to the cause of the fire*):—*n* **en-light'enment**.

enlist' *vb* 1 to join the armed forces. 2 to obtain support (*enlist friends to help paint the house*). 3 to obtain from (*enlist help from the neighbours*):—*n* **enlist'ment**.

enliven *vb* to brighten, to cheer (*enliven a dull party*).

en'mity *n* ill-will, hatred, unfriendliness, hostility (*the enmity between the two families/feelings of enmity towards his brother*).

enno'ble *n* 1 (*fml*) to make noble (*the king ennobling him*). 2 to make better, more honourable, etc (*suffering is said to ennoble some people*):—*n* **enno'blement**.

ennui [on'wee] *n* (*fml*) boredom, weariness, lack of interest in everything.

enor'mity *n* 1 immensity (*the enormity of the task*). 2 a great wickedness (*the enormity of the crime*). 3 a crime, an act of great wickedness (*enormities committed during the war*).

enor'mous *adj* huge, very large (*an enormous creature/enormous sums of money*).

enquire *see* **inquire**.

enrage' *vb* to make very angry (*enraged by the child's impertinence*).

enrap'ture *n* (*fml*) to fill with delight (*enraptured by the dancer's performance*).

enrich' *vb* 1 to make rich (*a country enriched by its oil resources*). 2 to improve greatly in quality (*enriching the soil/enrich the mind*):—*n* **enrich'ment**.

enrol(l)' *vb* (**enrol'led, enrol'ling**) 1 to write (a name) in a list (*enrol her daughter in the ballet class*). 2 to join or become a member (*decide to enrol in the aerobics class*):—*n* **enrol'ment**.

ensconce' *n* (*fml or hum*) to establish or settle in a safe, secret, comfortable, etc, place (*ensconcing himself in the most comfortable chair*).

ensemble [å(ng)-sâm'-bêl] *n* **1** a group of musicians regularly performing together (*a woodwind ensemble*). **2** clothing made up of several items, an outfit (*wear a green ensemble to the wedding*). **3** all the parts of a thing taken as a whole (*the furniture of the room forms a pleasing ensemble*).

enshrine' *n* **1** (*fml*) to put in a holy place (*holy relics enshrined in a casket*). **2** to hold dear (*memories enshrined in her heart*).

en'sign *n* a flag.

enslave' *vb* (*fml*) to make a slave of (*enslaved by her beauty*).

ensnare' *vb* (*fml*) to catch in or as if in a trap or snare (*ensnaring a rich husband*).

ensue' *vb* to follow upon, to result from (*the fire and the panic that ensued*).

ensure' *vb* to make sure (*he ensured that his family was well provided for/ensuring their success*).

entail' *vb* **1** to leave land or property to an heir with the condition that he must not sell any of it. **2** to make necessary, to involve (*a post that entails much hard work*):—*n* land or property so left.

entangle *vb* **1** to cause to become twisted, tangled or caught (*a bird entangled in wire netting/a long scarf entangled in the rose bushes*). **2** to get into difficulties or complications (*become entangled in an unhappy love affair*).

entang'lement *n* a difficult situation, involvement (*his entanglement with the police*).

en'ter *vb* **1** to go or come into (*entered the building by the back door*). **2** to become a member of (*enter politics*). **3** to put down in writing (*entering the money spent*).

enteric *adj* (*fml*) having to do with the bowels.

en'terprise *n* **1** an undertaking or project, esp one that is difficult or daring (*a new business enterprise*). **2** willingness to take risks or to try out new ideas (*show enterprise by starting their own business*).

en'terprising *adj* having or showing enterprise (*an enterprising young man/an enterprising scheme*).

entertain' *vb* **1** to receive as a guest (*entertain him to dinner*). **2** to please, to amuse (*a magician to entertain the children at the birthday party*). **3** (*fml*) to consider (*refuse to entertain the idea*).

entertain'ment *n* **1** the act of entertaining (*the entertainment of dinner guests/the entertainment of children at the party*). **2** amusement (*chil-*

dren seeking entertainment). **3** something that entertains, such as a public performance (*a musical entertainment*).

enthral' *vb* (**enthralled', enthral'ling**) to delight, to enchant (*enthralled by her performance*).

enthrone' *vb* (*fml*) to place on a throne (*enthroning the new king*):—*n* **enthrone'ment**.

enthuse' *vb* to be, become or cause to be enthusiastic, to show enthusiasm (*enthusing over the new fashions*).

enthus'iasm *n* great eagerness, keenness (*show no enthusiasm for the new game/play the game with great enthusiasm*).

enthus'iast *n* one who is very keen (*a football enthusiast*).

enthusias'tic *adj* full of enthusiasm (*enthusiastic about the new house/enthusiastic filmgoers*).

entice' *vb* to tempt, to attract by offering something (*enticing the child into his car by giving her sweets*):—*n* **entice'ment**:—*adj* **entic'ing**.

entire' *adj* whole, complete (*paint the entire house/spend her entire fortune*):—*adv* **en-tire'ly**.

entir'ety *n* completeness.

enti'tle *vb* **1** to give a right to (*a ticket entitling us to attend the exhibition*). **2** to give a name to (*a book entitled 'Green Dragons'*).

en'tity *n* **1** existence. **2** anything that exists (*separate political entities*).

entomol'ogy *n* the study of insect life:—*n* **entomol'ogist**.

en'trails *npl* the bowels, the internal organs of the body (*a sheep's entrails*).

entrance¹ *vb* to delight, to fill with wonder (*children entranced by the lights on the Christmas tree*).

entrance² *n* **1** coming or going in (*applaud the entrance of the actor*). **2** a place by which one enters (e.g. a door or gate) (*the side entrance of the building*).

en'trant *n* one who puts his or her name in for or joins (*entrants in the race/the youngest entrant won the competition*).

entrap' *vb* (**entrapped', entrap'ping**) to catch in a trap or by a trick.

entreat' *vb* (*fml*) to ask earnestly (*entreat her to help him*).

entreat'y *n* an earnest request (*the tyrant refused to listen to her entreaties for mercy*).

entrée [on(g)'-trä] *n* a main course at dinner.

entrench' vb **1** to dig ditches around, thus putting oneself in a strong position (with the enemy army entrenched across the river). **2** to establish firmly or in a strong position (entrenched in that job for years/entrenched in old-fashioned ideas and attitudes).

entrust' vb to give into the care of (entrust her children to him).

en'try n **1** act of entering (try to gain entry to the locked building/their country's entry into the war). **2** a way in (the entry to the block of flats). **3** something written in a diary, cash book, etc (read out the entry for yesterday).

entwine' vb to twist round (lovers walking with fingers entwined/trees entwined with ivy).

enu'merate vb to name one by one (enumerating the articles of clothing needed):—n **enumera'tion**.

enun'ciate vb to speak or state, to pronounce (enunciating his words clearly):—n **enuncia'tion**.

envel'op vb to cover or surround completely (mountains enveloped in mist/a long coat enveloping a small figure).

en'velope n **1** a wrapper or cover, esp one made of paper for a letter (address the envelope).

enven'om vb (fml) **1** to poison (an envenomed dagger). **2** to fill with hatred (insults envenomed with hatred).

en'viable adj causing envy, very desirable (an enviable lifestyle).

en'vious adj full of envy, jealous (friends envious of her achievement/envious neighbours looking at her new car).

envi'ronment n **1** surroundings. **2** all the conditions and surroundings that influence human character. **3** the natural world in which people, animals and plants live (pollution affecting the environment:—adj **environmen'tal** adj.

envi'rons npl (fml) the suburbs and outskirts of a town (a map of the city and environs).

envis'age vb (fml) to picture to oneself (I could not envisage myself agreeing to such a plan/impossible to envisage him as a young man).

en'voy n a messenger, esp one sent to speak for his or her government in another country (envoys sent to discuss a peace treaty with the king of France).

en'vy n **1** a feeling of discontent caused by someone else's good fortune or success, esp when one would like these for oneself (try to hide their envy at his winning the lottery/his success arousing envy/look with envy at her new car). **2** something that causes envy (a dress that was the envy of her friends):—vb to feel envy towards or at (envy him his good luck/envy her beauty).

eon see **aeon**.

epaulette [ep'-o-let] n a flap of material, sometimes of another colour, worn on the shoulder of a uniform jacket (a soldier's epaulettes).

ephemeral [e-fem'-er-êl or e-feem'-êr-êl] adj lasting for only a short time (ephemeral pleasures/ephemeral fashions in dress).

ep'ic n **1** a long poem telling of heroic deeds (Homer's 'Iliad' is a famous epic). **2** a story, film, etc, dealing with heroic deeds and exciting adventures (watch an epic about the Roman empire):—adj of or like an epic, heroic, in the grand style (an epic journey).

ep'icure n one fond of eating and drinking, one who likes to choose food and drink with great care.

epicure'an n one fond of pleasure, esp eating and drinking:—also adj.

epidem'ic n a disease or condition that attacks many people at the same time (an epidemic of influenza/a measles epidemic).

epider'mis n (fml) the outer skin.

epidi'ascope n (fml) a lantern for projecting films, slides or shapes on to a screen.

ep'igram n a short, clever, neatly worded saying:—adj **epigramma'tic**.

ep'igraph n an inscription, esp one carved in stone.

epilep'sy n a disease causing fits of unconsciousness and sudden attacks of uncontrolled movements of the body:—adj and n **epilep'tic**.

ep'ilogue n **1** a speech addressed to the audience at the end of a play (the epilogue in 'Hamlet'). **2** a part or section added at the end of a book, programme, etc.

Epiph'any n the revealing of Jesus Christ to the Magi, or three wise men from the east.

epis'copacy n government of the church by bishops.

epis'copal adj having to do with bishops.

episcopa'lian adj believing in episcopacy (an episcopalian church).

ep'isode n **1** a particular event or a series of events that is separate from but forms part of a larger whole (*enjoy the episode in the novel where the hero meets an elephant/episodes in her youth that she wants to forget*). **2** a part of a radio or television serial that is broadcast at one time (*miss last week's episode*).

episod'ic *adj* consisting of events not clearly connected with each other.

epis'tle *n* (*fml or hum*) a letter, esp a long one.

ep'itaph *n* words referring to a dead person, inscribed on his or her tombstone.

ep'ithet *n* an adjective that describes a quality of a person or thing.

epitome [e-pi'-to-mee] *n* **1** a person or thing that is a perfect example of a quality, type, etc (*she is the epitome of kindness/he is the epitome of the English country gentleman*). **2** something that in a small way perfectly represents a larger or wider idea, issue, etc (*the family's hardship was the epitome of the poverty affecting the whole country*). **3** (*fml*) a summary, an abstract (*an epitome of the talks given at the conference*).

epit'omize *vb* **1** to be an epitome of (*she epitomizes the dumb blonde/the strike epitomizes the country's industrial problems*). **2** (*fml*) to summarize, to describe briefly (*epitomizing the lecture in a few paragraphs*).

e'poch *n* **1** a period of time in history, life, etc, esp one in which important events occurred (*an epoch characterized by wars*). **2** the start of such a period.

e'poch-mak'ing *adj* of great importance (*epoch-making medical discoveries*).

equable [ek-wa-bêl] *adj* **1** calm, even-tempered (*remain equable when everyone else was becoming annoyed*). **2** not changing suddenly, neither very hot nor very cold (*equable temperatures/an equable climate*).

e'qual *adj* **1** the same in size, number, value, etc (*earn an equal amount of money*). **2** able (to do something) (*not equal to the task*):—*n* a person the same as another in rank or ability (*her intellectual equal*):—*vb* (**e'qualled**, **e'qualling**) to be equal to (*sales figures that equal last year's*).

equal'ity *n* the state of being equal (*fighting for equality of women in salary scales/seeking racial equality*).

e'qualize *vb* to make or become equal (*the home team equalized*).

equanimity [ek-wa-ni'-mi-ti] *n* (*fml*) calmness of temper (*he never loses his equanimity*).

equate' *vb* **1** to state that certain things are equal. **2** to think of as equal or the same (*equating financial success with happiness*).

equa'tion *n* a statement that two things are equal (*a mathematical equation*).

equa'tor *n* an imaginary line round the earth, halfway between the poles.

equato'rial *adj* **1** having to do with the equator (*an equatorial climate*). **2** on or near the equator (*the equatorial rain forest*).

equerry [e'-kwe-ri] *n* one who attends on a king or prince.

eques'trian *adj* **1** on horseback (*an equestrian statue*). **2** having to do with horse riding (*equestrian skills*):—*n* a horseman or horsewoman.

equi- *prefix* equal.

equidis'tant *adj* equally distant (*a village equidistant from the two cities*).

equilat'eral *adj* having all sides equal (*equilateral triangles*).

equilib'rium *n* **1** a balance between equal weights (*scale in equilibrium*). **2** steadiness (*a disease of the ear affecting his equilibrium*). **3** balanced state of the mind, emotions, etc (*try to maintain his equilibrium in a difficult situation*).

equine [e'-kwîn] *adj* (*fml*) of or like a horse.

equinox [e'-kwi-nox] *n* either of the two times in the year at which the sun crosses the equator and day and night are equal:—*adj* **equinoc'tial**.

equip' *vb* (**equipped'**, **equip'ping**) to give the things necessary for doing a job, to fit out (*equip a new operating theatre/equip themselves with climbing gear*).

equip'ment *n* outfit, the set of things needed for a particular activity (*mountaineering equipment/video equipment*).

e'quitable *adj* fair, just (*an equitable share of his father's money*).

e'quity *n* fairness, justice (*try to establish equity in sentencing criminals*).

equiv'alent *adj* **1** equal in value, amount, meaning, etc (*a sum of money equivalent to £5000*):—*n* an equivalent thing (*the equivalent of 500 grams*).

equiv'ocal *adj* of doubtful meaning, capable of meaning two or more things (*politicians giving equivocal answers*).

equiv'ocate *vb* to say things that may be understood in more than one way, often in order to avoid telling the truth without telling a lie (*politicians equivocating rather than giving straight answers*):—*n* **equi-v'ocation.**—*n* **equiv'ocator.**

era [ee'-ra] *n* **1** a long period of time, starting from some important or particular event (*the Elizabethan era*). **2** a period of time marked by an important event or events (*the era of the steam engine*).

erad'icate *vb* to root out, to destroy completely (*eradicating weeds from the garden/eradicate corruption/try to eradicate violence*):—*n* **eradica'tion.**

erase' *vb* to rub out, to remove (*erasing pencil marks from the manuscript/erased all memories of him from her mind/erase a recording from a videotape*).

era'sure *n* a rubbing out.

ere [ér] *adv, conj and prep* (*old or lit*) before (*ere break of day*).

erect' *adj* standing up straight (*soldiers standing erect*):—*vb* **1** to build (*erect blocks of flats*). **2** to set upright (*erect a tent*):—*n* **erec'tion.**

erg *n* the unit of energy of work in calculations in physics.

er'mine *n* **1** a type of weasel. **2** its white winter fur (*robes trimmed with ermine*).

erode' *vb* to destroy or wear away gradually (*rocks eroded by the sea/a need for low prices eroding standards of quality*):—*n* **ero'sion.**

erot'ic *adj* having to do with love or sexual desire (*erotic literature*).

err *vb* (*fml*) to make a mistake, to do wrong (*admit that he erred in leaving his wife*).

err'and *n* **1** a short journey made to give a message, deliver goods, etc, to someone (*send the child on an errand*). **2** the purpose of such a journey (*accomplish her errand*).

err'ant *adj* **1** (*old*) wandering (*knight errant*). **2** (*fml*) wrongdoing (*errant husbands*).

errat'ic *adj* not steady, irregular, uneven, unpredictable (*people of erratic behaviour/an erratic sales pattern*).

erra'tum *n* (*pl* **erra'ta**) (*fml*) an error in a book.

erro'neous *adj* wrong, mistaken (*create an erroneous impression*).

er'ror *n* **1** a mistake (*a spelling error*). **2** the state of being mistaken (*a letter sent to your address in error*).

erst'while *adj* (*fml*) former (*his erstwhile friend*).

er'udite *adj* having or showing much knowledge, learned, well-read (*an erudite man/an erudite lecture*).

erudi'tion *n* learning.

erupt' *vb* to break or burst out (*volcanoes erupting/father erupting in anger*).

erup'tion *n* act of breaking or bursting out (e.g. of a volcano).

es'calate *vb* **1** to rise (as if on a moving staircase) (*house prices escalating*). **2** to increase in intensity (*a war escalating rapidly*).

es'calator *n* a moving staircase (*go to the second floor on the escalator*).

es'capade *n* a foolish or risky adventure (*childhood escapades such as stealing apples from orchards/the romantic escapades of the actress*).

escape' *vb* **1** to get out of the way of, to avoid (*escape punishment*). **2** to free oneself from (*escape from prison*). **3** to leak (*gas escaping*). **4** to avoid being noticed, remembered, etc (*a name that escapes me*):—*n* **1** act of escaping. **2** a leakage.

escarp'ment *n* the steep side of a hill or rock.

eschew' *vb* (*fml*) to keep away from, to avoid (*try to eschew crowded places/aim to eschew trouble*).

escort' *vb* to go with as a guard, as a partner, to show the way or as an honour (*supply ships escorted by a warship/escort the members of the audience to their seats/escort his cousin to the ball*):—*n* **es'cort 1** a guard, a bodyguard (*ships acting as an escort to the royal yacht*). **2** a partner, a companion (*he was her escort to the ball*).

escudo *n* formerly the currency unit of Portugal, until the introduction of the euro in 2002.

Es'kimo *n* a member of a group of people who live in Northern Canada, parts of Alaska, Greenland and parts of Siberia, many of whom, especially in North America and Greenland, prefer to be called **Inuit** and regard Eskimo as offensive.

esoter'ic *adj* (*fml*) understood by certain people only, esp those with a special knowledge or interest, obscure, mysterious (*poetry of a rather esoteric nature*).

espar'to *n* a type of grass used for making paper.

espe'cial adj (fml) more than ordinary, particular (an especial favourite of hers/with especial care).

espe'cially adv specially, particularly, markedly (especially pleased to see her today).

espionage [es'-pi-on-azh] n spying (involved in espionage during the war).

esplanade' n 1 a public walk along the sea front. 2 a level space for walking.

espouse' vb (fml) to support (espousing the cause of nationalism):—n **espous'al**.

espy' vb (fml or hum) to catch sight of (espied a figure in the distance).

es'quire n a title added to a man's name in politeness, esp when addressing envelopes (abbr **esq.**) (e.g. James Smith, Esq.).

essay' vb (fml or old) to try (foolish to essay that task):—n **es'say 1** (fml or old) an attempt (an unsuccessful essay at climbing the mountain). **2** a written composition (pupils asked to write an essay on holidays).

es'sence n 1 the nature or necessary part of anything (confidence could be said to be the essence of success). 2 a substance obtained from a plant, etc, in concentrated form (vanilla essence).

essen'tial adj 1 necessary, very important, that cannot be done without (essential equipment for diving/it is essential to take warm clothing). 2 of the basic or inner nature of something, fundamental (the essential difference between the two methods).

estab'lish vb 1 to set up (establish a local branch of the society/take time to establish a new business). 2 to place or fix in a position, etc, usu permanently (establish herself as the local bridge expert). 3 to prove, to show to be true (establish an alibi).

estab'lishment n 1 act of setting up (the establishment of a new business). 2 a group of people employed in an organization, the staff of a household (in charge of a large establishment). 3 a place of business, the premises of a business organization or large institution (an educational establishment):—**the Establishment** the people holding important positions in a country, community, etc, and usu supporting traditional ways, etc.

estate' n 1 all one's property and money (on her death her estate is to be divided between her children). 2 area of land, esp in the country, with one owner (owns a large estate in the north of Scotland). 3 (old) political or social group or class (the Church was one of the Three Estates). 4 (fml or old) condition (the holy estate of matrimony).

estate a'gent n one who buys and sells property on behalf of others.

esteem' vb to think highly of (the artist's work is highly esteemed):—n respect, regard (hold him in high esteem as a teacher).

es'timable adj 1 worthy of respect (people of estimable worth). 2 able to be estimated (a contribution that is scarcely estimable).

es'timate vb 1 to judge size, amount, etc, roughly, to guess (estimating the distance at six miles). 2 to calculate the probable cost of (estimate the repairs to the house at £1000):—n 1 an opinion. 2 a judgment as to the value or cost of a thing.

estima'tion n 1 judgment (give his estimation as to the value of the vase). 2 opinion (of someone) (she was not a good artist in his estimation/ go down in their estimation).

estrange' vb to make unfriendly (her parents are estranged from each other/her estranged partner):—n **estrange'ment**.

es'tuary n the mouth of a river as far as the tide flows up it.

etch vb to cut a picture on a metal plate by use of acids in order to print copies of it.

etch'ing n a picture printed by etching (etchings of the harbour hanging on the wall).

eter'nal adj 1 everlasting, without beginning or end (believe in eternal life). 2 seeming never to stop (tired of their eternal arguments).

eter'nity n 1 everlasting existence, with no beginning and no end, unending life after death. 2 (inf) a very long time (wait an eternity for a bus).

ether [ee'-thêr] n 1 the clear upper air. 2 formerly, an invisible substance supposed to fill all space and to pass on electric waves. 3 a colourless liquid, often formerly used as an anaesthetic.

ethe're'al adj 1 of the ether. 2 delicate and light, fairy-like (an ethereal beauty).

eth'ical adj 1 having to do with right and wrong (the doctor's behaviour was not considered ethical). 2 relating to ethics (ethical problems).

eth'ics n 1 the study of right and wrong. 2 rules

or principles of behaviour (*the ethics of protecting a member of the family from the police*).

eth'nic *adj* having to do with human races or their customs, food, dress, etc (*ethnic restaurants*).

ethnol'ogy *n* the study of human races:—*n* **ethnol'ogist**.

etiquette [e'-ti-ket] *n* the rules of polite behaviour, good manners (*a book on wedding etiquette*).

etymol'ogy *n* **1** the study of the history of words. **2** derivation, an explanation of the history of a particular word (*dictionaries giving etymologies*):—*adj* **etymolog'ical**:—*n* **etymol'ogist**.

EU [*abbr for* European Union] a group of European countries which have joined together for economic and political purposes (*Britain is a member of the EU*).

eucalyptus [û-kal-ip'-tês] *n* **1** an Australian gum tree. **2** the oil from its leaves, used in the treatment of colds.

eucharist [û'-kar-ist] *n* the sacrament of the Lord's Supper.

eu'logize *vb* (*fml*) to praise, to speak highly of (*eulogizing over the meal she served*):—*n* **eu'logist**:—*adj* **eulogis'tic**.

eu'logy *n* (*fml*) praise.

eunuch [û'-nuk] *n* a man made incapable of fathering children.

euphemism [û'-fem-izm] *n* the use of mild words or phrases to say something unpleasant (e.g. *fairy tale* for *lie*):—*adj* **eu-phemis'tic**.

euphon'ious *adj* pleasing to the ear (*euphonious sounds from the orchestra*).

euphony [û'-fo-ni] *n* (*fml*) pleasantness of sound.

eurhyth'mics *n* the art of moving gracefully in time to music.

eur'o *n* the common unit of currency in the following European countries: Austria, Belgium, Finland, France, Germany, Greece, Ireland, Italy, Luxembourg, the Netherlands, and Portugal.

European Union *see* **EU**.

euthanasia [û-thana-ā'-zi-a] *n* painless killing, esp of a person suffering from a painful incurable disease (*she believes in euthanasia but it is illegal*).

evac'uate *vb* **1** to go away from (a place) (*evacuating the area as the enemy army approached*). **2** (*fml*) to make empty (*evacuate the bowels*).

2 to send to a place of safety in wartime (*children evacuated from areas likely to be bombed in World War II*):—*n* **evacua'tion**.

evade' *vb* **1** to keep oneself away from (*evading the police/evade an attack*). **2** to dodge, to find a way of not doing something, esp by using trickery, deception, etc (*evaded military service by pretending to suffer from asthma*). **3** to refuse to answer directly (*evade the question*):—*n* **eva'sion**.

eval'uate *vb* to work out the value of (*difficult to evaluate his success as a writer on such little evidence*):—*n* **evalua'tion**.

evanes'cent *adj* passing or disappearing quickly (*evanescent snowflakes/evanescent fame*).

evangel'ic, evangel'ical *adjs* **1** having to do with the Gospels. **2** accepting the Bible as the only guide to faith.

evan'gelist *n* **1** one of the four Gospel writers. **2** a preacher of the Gospel.

evap'orate *vb* **1** to turn into vapour and disappear (*the water in the puddles soon evaporated*). **2** to disappear (*all hope gradually evaporating*):—*n* **evapora'tion**.

evasion *see* **evade**.

eva'sive *adj* **1** having the purpose of evading (*take evasive action*). **2** not straightforward, not frank (*give evasive answers*).

eve *n* **1** (*old*) evening. **2** the day before (*Christmas Eve*). **3** the time before an important event (*on the eve of the battle*).

e'ven *adj* **1** level (*an even temperature*). **2** smooth (*even ground*). **3** equal (*scores now even*). **4** divisible by 2 (*even numbers*). **5** calm (*of even temper*):—*adv* just (*even as we speak*):—*vb* **1** to make smooth or level (*even the ground*). **2** to make equal (*even the score*):—*n* **e'venness**.

e'vening *n* the close of day.

event' *n* **1** anything that happens, an incident (*the events leading up to the war*). **2** a single race or contest at sports or races (*athletic events*).

event'ful *adj* full of interesting or exciting happenings (*an eventful life/an eventful day*).

even'tual *adj* happening as a result, final (*his criminal behaviour and eventual imprisonment*).

eventual'ity *n* a possible happening (*try to allow for any eventuality in planning the celebration*).

even'tually *adv* finally, at length (*after many attempts, he eventually passed the exam*).

ev'er adv always, at all times.

ev'ergreen n a tree or plant that has green leaves all the year round:—adj always green (evergreen trees).

everlast'ing adj 1 never ending (everlasting life). 1 seemingly without end, frequent (their everlasting complaints).

evermore' adv for ever (promise to love her for evermore).

ev'ery adj each one (every child was present).

ev'eryday adj 1 happening every day (everyday duties). 2 usual, ordinary (everyday clothes).

evict' vb to put out of a house or off land by order of a court (evict tenants for not paying rent):—n evic'tion.

ev'idence n 1 information given to show a fact is true (produce evidence of his innocence). 2 the statement made by a witness in a court of law (give evidence at the murder trial).

ev'ident adj clear, easily understood, obvious (it was evident that she was ill/her evident unhappiness).

e'vil adj 1 wicked, bad, sinful (an evil man/evil deeds). 2 unpleasant, nasty (an evil smell):—n 1 wickedness (feel surrounded by evil in that house). 2 anything bad or harmful (the evils of the world).

evince' vb (fml) to show (evincing no feelings of shame).

evoke' vb 1 to call up (evoking memories of childhood). 2 to give rise to, to cause (her tears evoked sympathy from the crowd):—n evoca'tion.

evolu'tion n 1 the belief that life began in lower forms of creature and that these gradually changed over millions of years into the highest forms, such as humans (Darwin's theory of evolution). 2 development (the evolution of a modern political system).

evolve' vb 1 to work out (evolving an efficient filing system in the office). 2 to develop gradually (a system of efficient government evolved).

ewe [û] n a female sheep (ewes and rams).

ewer [û'-êr] n a large water jug.

exacerbate [eks-as'-êr-bãt] vb to make worse (lack of money exacerbating their feeling of misery/she had applied a cream that exacerbated her rash):—n exacerba'tion.

exact' adj absolutely correct, accurate in every detail (the exact measurements/an exact copy of the antique vase). 2 showing or taking great care (require to be very exact in that kind of work):—vb 1 to force to make payment. 2 to demand and obtain.

exact'ing adj needing much work or attention (an exacting job).

exact'itude n (fml) great care or accuracy (count the votes with great exactitude).

exag'gerate vb 1 to speak or think of something as being better or more (or worse or less) than it really is (exaggerating her unhappiness to gain people's sympathy). 2 to go beyond the truth in describing something (you can't believe what she says—she always exaggerates):—n exaggera'tion.

exalt' vb 1 (fml) to raise in power or rank (he has been exalted to general). 2 to praise highly (exalt God):—n exalta'tion.

exam'ine vb 1 to look at closely and carefully in order to find out something (the doctor examined the child/customs officials examining luggage). 2 to question (witnesses examined by the prosecuting barrister). 3 to test a learner's knowledge by questions (examine the pupils in French):—n exa-mina'tion:—n exam'iner.

examinee' n one who is being examined.

exam'ple n 1 one thing chosen to show what others of the same kind are like, a model (an example of the artist's work/an example of his bad behaviour). 2 a person or thing deserving to be imitated (the saint's patience was an example to us all).

exas'perate vb to make angry (exasperating their mother with their endless questions):—n exaspera'tion.

ex'cavate vb 1 to uncover by digging (excavating Roman remains). 2 to dig up, to hollow out (excavate a building site):—n ex'cavator.

excava'tion n 1 act of excavating. 2 a hole or trench made by digging.

exceed' vb 1 to go beyond (exceed the speed limit). 2 to be greater or more numerous than (a price not exceeding £5000).

exceed'ingly adv very, extremely (exceedingly difficult tasks).

excel' vb (excelled', excel'ling) to do very well at, to get exceptionally good at (excel at tennis/excel at playing the piano).

ex'cellence *n* perfection, great merit (*recognize her excellence as a musician/the excellence of his work*).

Ex'cellency *n* a title given to ambassadors, governors, etc.

ex'cellent *adj* very good, of a very high standard (*excellent work/an excellent performance*).

except[1] *vb* (*fml*) to leave out (*only children are excepted from the admission charge*).

except[2], **except'ing** *preps* leaving out (*everyone except my brother*).

excep'tion *n* a person or thing that does not follow the rule (*everyone will pay an admission fee with the exception of old-age pensioners*):—**take exception** to object (*took exception to his remarks*).

excep'tional *adj* different from others, unusual, remarkable (*show exceptional understanding/have an exceptional musical talent*):—*adv* **excep'tionally**.

excerpt [ek'-serpt] *n* a short passage taken out of a longer piece of writing or music.

excess' *n* 1 too much (*an excess of alcohol*). 2 the amount by which a thing is too much (*the bill was wrong and we paid an excess of £5*). 3 bad and uncontrolled behaviour (*his drunken excesses*).

exces'sive *adj* more than is right or correct (*an excessive amount of salt in the soup/excessive alcohol in his blood/find the price excessive*).

exces'sively *adv* very.

exchange' *vb* to give one thing and receive another in its place (*exchanging his pounds for dollars*):—*n* 1 the act of exchanging (*an exchange of views/give food in exchange for gardening work*). 2 a place where merchants meet to do business. 3 the changing of the money of one country into that of another. 4 a telephone headquarters.

exchequ'er *n* that part of the government that looks after the nation's money (*Chancellor of the Exchequer*).

excise[1] *n* a tax on certain goods made within the country.

excise[2] *vb* to cut out, to cut away (*surgeons excising the diseased tissue*):—*n* **exci'sion**.

excit'able *adj* easily excited.

excite' *vb* 1 to stir up feelings of happiness, expectation, etc (*children excited by thoughts of Christmas*). 2 to rouse (*exciting feelings of envy in her friends*):—*n* **excite'ment**.

exclaim' *vb* to cry out suddenly ('*What's this?*' *she exclaimed in surprise*):—*adj* **ex-clam'atory**.

exclama'tion *n* a word or words said suddenly or with feeling (*utter an exclamation of amazement*).

exclamation mark *n* a mark of punctuation (!).

exclude' *vb* 1 to shut out (*exclude air from the bottle*). 2 to leave out (*excluding her from membership of the club*). 3 to leave out, not to include (*the price excludes drinks*):—*n* **exclu'sion**.

exclu'sive *adj* 1 open to certain people only (*an exclusive club*). 2 sole (*your exclusive role*). 3 not shared (*exclusive rights*):—*adv* **exclu'sively**.

excommun'icate *vb* to expel from the Church:—*n* **excommunica'tion**.

ex'crement *n* waste matter put out from the body (*stepped in dog's excrement*).

excrescence [eks-kres'-êns] *n* something that grows out from the surface, spoiling its appearance (*ugly blocks of flats like an excrescence on the landscape*).

excrete' *vb* to put out what is useless from the body (*excreting abnormal quantities of urine*):—*adj* **excre'tory**.

excru'ciating *adj* 1 very great, intense (*an excruciating pain in his back*). 2 terrible, very bad (*an excruciating performance on the violin*).

ex'culpate *vb* (*fml*) to free from blame (*try to exculpate oneself from the charges of theft*).

excur'sion *n* a trip made for pleasure, an outing (*children on a bus excursion to the seaside*).

excuse [eks-kûz'] *vb* 1 to let off (*excused from playing games because of illness*). 2 to forgive, to overlook (*excuse her late arrival/excusing her for being late*). 3 to give reasons showing or intended to show that someone or something cannot be blamed (*nothing could excuse such behaviour*):—*n* [eks-kûs'] a reason given for failure or wrongdoing:—*adj* **excus'able**.

ex'ecrable *adj* (*fml*) horrible (*an execrable crime/execrable weather*).

ex'ecrate *vb* to curse, to express or feel hatred for (*execrating his action in killing his brother*):—*n* **execra'tion**.

ex'ecute *vb* **1** to perform (*executing a dance step*). **2** to carry out (*execute orders*). **3** to put to death by law (*execute murderers*).

execu'tion *n* **1** the carrying out, performance, etc, of something (*execution of orders/execution of difficult dance steps*). **2** skill in performing music. **3** the act of putting to death by order of the law.

execu'tioner *n* an officer who puts to death condemned criminals.

exec'utive *adj* **1** concerned with making and carrying out decisions, esp in business (*an executive director/executive powers*). **2** having the power to carry out government's decisions and laws:—*n* **1** one involved in the management of a firm. **2** the part of government that puts laws, etc, into effect.

exec'utor *n* one who sees that a dead person's written will is carried out (*appoint two executors*):—*f* **exec'utrix**.

exem'plary *adj* **1** admirable, worth copying, giving a good example (*an exemplary piece of work/exemplary conduct*). **2** (*fml*) serving as a warning (*the judge gave him an exemplary sentence*).

exem'plify *vb* **1** to be an example (*this machine exemplifies the firm's high standard of work*). **2** to illustrate by example (*exemplify the problems*).

exempt' *vb* to free from, to let off (*exempt certain goods from tax/exempt him from military service*):—*adj* free:—*n* **exemp'tion**.

ex'ercise *n* **1** an action performed to strengthen the body or part of the body. **2** a piece of work done for practice. **3** training (*military exercises*). **4** use (*the exercise of patience*):—*vb* **1** to use, to employ (*exercising patience*). **2** to perform some kind of physical exercises. **3** to give exercise to, to train (*exercise the horses*).

exert' *vb* to apply (*exert influence to get his son a job/have to exert force*):—**exert oneself** to try hard.

exer'tion *n* effort (*tired after the exertion of climbing the hill*).

exhale' *vb* to breathe out:—*n* **exhala'tion**.

exhaust' *vb* **1** to use up completely (*exhaust our food supplies*). **2** to tire out (*the journey exhausted her*). **3** to say everything possible about (*exhaust the subject*):—*n* **1** a passage by which used steam or gases are carried away from an engine (*a car's exhaust*). **2** these gases.

exhaust'ing *adj* very tiring (*an exhausting journey/an exhausting day*).

exhaus'tion *n* **1** the state of being tired out. **2** lack of any strength.

exhaus'tive *adj* **1** very thorough, complete (*an exhaustive search*). **2** dealing with every possible aspect of a subject.

exhib'it *vb* **1** to show in public (*exhibit Picasso's early works/exhibit roses at the flower show*). **2** (*fml*) to display, to show (*exhibiting no sign of emotion*):—*n* a thing shown in public.

exhibi'tion *n* **1** act of exhibiting. **2** a collection of many things brought together to be shown to the public (*an art exhibition*).

exhibi'tionist *n* one who behaves in such a way as to draw attention to himself or herself.

exhib'itor *n* one who exhibits at a show (*exhibitors in the art gallery*).

exhil'arate *vb* to make lively or happy (*a swim in cold water exhilarating him*):—*n* **exhilara'tion**.

exhort' *vb* (*fml*) to encourage, to urge strongly (*exhorting them to try harder*):—*n* **exhorta'tion**.

exhume' *vb* to dig up a body from a grave (*police getting permission to exhume the body for examination*):—*n* **exhuma'tion**.

exi'gency *n* (*fml*) a state of affairs requiring immediate action, a pressing demand (*the harsh exigencies of war*).

ex'igent *adj* (*fml*) **1** requiring immediate action (*exigent circumstances*). **2** severe, exacting (*an exigent employer*).

exig'uous *adj* (*fml*) small, not enough (*exiguous amounts of money*).

ex'ile *n* **1** long or unwilling absence from one's home or country (*an ex-general forced to live in exile*). **2** a person living in a country other than his or her own (*exiles talking about the old country*):—*vb* to send someone out of his or her own country as a punishment (*they were exiled for taking part in a conspiracy against the government*).

exist' *vb* **1** to be. **2** to live:—*n* **exis'tence**:—*adj* **exis'tent**.

ex'it *n* **1** a way out (*several exits in the large hall*). **2** a going out (*an orderly exit by the crowd*):—*also vb*.

ex'odus *n* a going out or away by many people (e.g. the departure of the Jews from Egypt) (*an exodus of people to the seaside in the summer*).

exon'erate vb to free from blame (the judge exonerated the accused):—n **exonera'tion**.

ex'orb'itant adj far too much, far too great (exorbitant prices/exorbitant demands):—n **exorb'itance**.

ex'orcise vb to drive out evil spirits (exorcising the haunted house).

ex'orcism n act of exorcising:—n **ex'orcist**.

exot'ic adj 1 foreign, introduced from another country (exotic fruits). 2 striking and unusual (exotic clothes).

expand' vb 1 to make or become larger (metals expand when heated). 2 to spread out (his face expanded in a smile/the form has expanded). 3 to become more friendly or talkative (guests beginning to expand after a few drinks).

expanse' n a wide area (an expanse of green).

expan'sion n act of expanding.

expan'sive adj 1 wide (an expansive gesture with his arms). 2 ready to talk freely (become expansive when drunk).

expatiate [eks-pā'-shi-āt] vb (fml) to speak or write at length about (expatiating on his political views).

expatriate [eks-pā'-tri-āt] vb to send someone out of his own country:—n one living or working in a country other than his or her own (expatriates living abroad for tax reasons).

expect' vb 1 to wait for (expect a letter from her daughter). 2 to think it likely that something will happen (she expects to arrive today). 3 to require as a right or duty (teachers expecting obedience from the pupils).

expec'tancy n state of being expectant.

expec'tant adj hopeful, waiting for something to happen (children with expectant faces on Christmas morning):—**expectant mother** a woman who is pregnant.

expecta'tion n 1 hope that something will happen (enter the competition full of expectation). 2 that which is expected (have high expectations on entering the competition).

expec'torate vb (fml) to spit or cough out from the lungs or throat.

expe'dience, expe'diency ns doing things not because they are right or moral but because they are likely to be successful or to one's advantage

(the government were not interested in people's feelings—it was a question of expedience).

expe'dient adj 1 wise or desirable in a particular case (politically expedient). 2 bringing immediate advantage, although not necessarily right or moral:—n a plan or action that solves an immediate difficulty.

expedite [eks'-ped-īt] vb to make happen more quickly (use her father's influence to expedite her promotion).

expedi'tion n 1 a journey made for a particular purpose (on a shopping expedition). 2 (fml) speed (carry out the tasks with expedition).

expedi'tious adj (fml) speedy (expeditious methods):—adv **expedi'tiously**.

expel' vb (expelled', expel'ling) 1 to drive out (air expelled from the lungs). 2 to force to go away (foreign journalists expelled from the war zone). 3 to dismiss officially from a school, club, etc (expel pupils for drug-taking):—n **expul'sion**.

expend' vb to spend, to use up (expend all his energy).

expen'diture n 1 the amount spent (try to reduce your annual expenditure). 2 the act of spending (the expenditure of money).

expense' n 1 cost (purchase the car at his own expense). 2 spending of money, etc.

expen'sive adj dear, costing much (expensive clothes/an expensive house).

expe'rience n 1 a happening in one's own life. 2 knowledge gained from one's own life or work:—vb 1 to meet with. 2 to feel. 3 to undergo.

exper'iment n something done so that the results may be studied, a test (scientific experiments):—vb to do an experiment (object to scientists experimenting on animals):—adj **experimen'tal**.

expert' adj very skilful (an expert tennis player):—n **ex'pert** one having special skill or knowledge (an expert in antiques).

ex'piate vb (fml) to pay for wrongdoing by undergoing punishment or suffering (do penance to expiate his sins):—n **expia'tion**.

expiration n (fml) 1 act of breathing out. 2 end (the expiration of the contract).

expire' vb 1 (fml) to die (soldiers expiring on the battlefield). 2 (fml) to breathe out. 3 to come to an end (a bus pass that has expired).

expi'ry *n* end (*expiry of the lease on the flat*).

explain' *vb* 1 to make clear (*explain the instructions*). 2 to give reasons for (*explain his absence*).

explana'tion *n* a statement of the meaning of or the reasons for.

explan'atory *adj* helping to make clear (*explanatory notes*).

expletive [eks-plee'-tiv] *n* 1 a swear word (*drunks issuing a stream of expletives*):—*adj* serving to fill out.

explic'able *adj* able to be explained (*behaviour that seems scarcely explicable*).

explicit [eks-plis'-it] *adj* 1 stating exactly what is meant (*explicit instructions*). 2 with full details, with nothing hidden (*explicit sex scenes*).

explode' *vb* 1 to burst or blow up with a loud noise (*a bomb exploding/a gas boiler exploding*). 2 to show to be untrue, to destroy (*explode a myth*).

ex'ploit *n* 1 a brave or outstanding deed (*a film about the exploits of pilots during World War II*):—*vb* to make use of, esp for selfish reasons (*rich employers exploiting illegal immigrants by paying low wages*):—*n* **exploita'tion**.

explore' *vb* 1 to examine closely (*explore all possibilities*). 2 to travel through a country to find out all about it:—*n* **explora'tion**:—*n* **explor'er**.

explo'sion *n* 1 going off or bursting with a loud noise. 2 an outburst (*an explosion of anger*).

explo'sive *adj* able to cause an explosion:—*n* any substance that will explode (*the police found explosives in a barn*).

expo'nent *n* 1 one who explains and supports a theory, belief, etc (*an exponent of Marxism*). 2 one who is good at (*an exponent of mime*).

export' *vb* to send goods to another country:—*n* **ex'port** an article that is exported:—*n* **exporta'tion**.

expose' *vb* 1 to uncover (*dig and expose the roots of the tree/exposing white teeth/expose her legs to the sun*). 2 to make known the truth about (*newspapers exposing scandals about politicians*). 3 to allow light to fall on (a photographic film).

exposi'tion *n* 1 (*fml*) a collection of things brought together to be shown to the public (*an exposition of modern art*). 2 a full explanation (*an exposition of the company's sales policy*).

expos'tulate *vb* to try to get someone to think differently, to argue (*expostulating with his colleague for dismissing his secretary*):—*n* **expostula'tion**.

expo'sure *n* 1 act of exposing (*exposure to the sun/the newspaper's exposure of fraud*). 2 the effect on the body of being out in cold weather for a long time (*climbers dying of exposure*).

expound' *vb* (*fml*) to explain fully (*expound his theory*).

express' *vb* 1 to put into words, to state (*expresses his ideas*). 2 to make known by words or actions (*express her anger by stamping her feet*):—*adj* 1 swift (*by express post*). 2 clearly stated (*express instructions*):—*n* a fast train.

express'ly *adv* 1 clearly (*I expressly forbade you to do that*). 2 specially, with a certain definite purpose.

expres'sion *n* 1 a word or phrase (*foreign expressions*). 2 the look on one's face (*a surprised expression*). 3 ability to read, play music, etc, with meaning or feeling.

express'ive *adj* with feeling or meaning (*expressive eyes*).

expulsion *see* expel.

expunge' *vb* to rub out, to wipe out (*expunging some passages from the book/expunge the tragedy from your memory*).

ex'purgate *vb* to cut out of a book unsuitable or objectionable passages:—*n* **expur-ga'tion**.

ex'quisite, exquis'ite *adj* 1 beautiful and delicate, very fine (*exquisite china/exquisite workmanship/exquisite beauty*). 2 (*fml*) strongly felt, acute (*exquisite pain*).

extant' *adj* still existing (*customs still extant*).

extempora'neous *adj* (*fml*) unprepared (*an extemporaneous speech*).

extem'pore *adv and adj* without preparation (*speak extempore at the meeting*).

extem'porize *vb* 1 to speak without preparation. 2 to make up music as one is playing.

extend' *vb* 1 to stretch out (*extend his arms*). 2 to reach or stretch (*a forest extending for miles*). 3 to offer (*extend an invitation*). 4 to make longer or bigger (*extend the garden*).

exten'sion *n* 1 an addition (*build an extension to the house*). 2 an additional period of time (*get an extension to write his essay*).

exten'sive *adj* 1 large (*extensive grounds*). 2 wide, wide-ranging (*extensive interests*).

extent' *n* 1 the area or length to which something extends (*the extent of his estate*). 2 amount, degree (*the extent of the damage*).

exten'uate vb (fml) to make excuses for in order to make seem less bad (nothing could extenuate such behaviour):—n **ex-tenua'tion**.

exten'uating adj making a crime, etc, seem less serious by showing there is some excuse for it (extenuating circumstances).

exte'rior adj outer (exterior walls):—n the outside.

exter'minate vb to kill to the last one, to destroy completely (exterminating rats on the farm):— n **extermina'tion**.

exter'nal adj on the outside (external walls).

extinct' adj 1 no longer found in existence (an extinct species). 2 no longer burning (extinct volcanoes).

extinc'tion n 1 act of destroying. 2 the state of being no longer living (species threatened with extinction). 3 the putting out of (the extinction of lights/the extinction of fires).

exting'uish vb 1 to put out (extinguish the fire). 2 to put an end to (extinguish all hope).

ex'tirpate vb (fml) to destroy completely, to root out (a tyrant extirpating all opposition to him/ attempt to extirpate poverty from our society):— n **extirpa'tion**.

extol' vb (extolled', extol'ling) (fml) to praise highly (extol the merits of the new product/extol her daughter's virtues).

extort' vb to take from by force or threats (bullies extorting money from younger boys):—n **extor'tion**.

extor'tionate adj 1 far too expensive (extortionate prices). 2 asking too much (extortionate demands).

ex'tra adj additional, more than is usual, expected or necessary (workers asking for extra money/ require extra workers):—adv more than usually:—n something additional (school fees and extras such as dancing).

extract' vb 1 to draw, take or pull out (extract teeth/try to extract information). 2 to select a passage from a book:—n **ex'tract** 1 a passage taken from a book (a book of extracts from Shakespeare's plays). 2 a substance drawn from a material and containing all its qualities (yeast extract).

extrac'tion n 1 act of drawing out (the extraction of teeth). 2 connection with a certain family or race (Spanish by extraction).

ex'tradite vb to hand over a foreign criminal to the police of his own country:—n **ex-tradi'tion**.

ex'tramur'al adj 1 organized for those who are not members (e.g. of a university) (extramural studies). 2 separate from or outside the area of one's studies (extramural activities).

extraneous [eks-trā'-ni-ês] adj having nothing to do with the subject.

extraor'dinary adj 1 very unusual, remarkable (what extraordinary behaviour). 2 (fml) additional to what is usual or ordinary (an extraordinary meeting of the committee).

extraterres'trial adj existing or happening beyond the earth's atmosphere (the possibility of extraterrestrial life).

extrav'agance n 1 wasteful spending. 2 wastefulness.

extrav'agant adj 1 spending or using a great deal, wasteful (extravagant use of materials/live in an extravagant way). 2 spending foolishly (an extravagant young woman). 3 foolish and improbable (extravagant schemes).

extreme' adj 1 farthest away (the extreme ends of the continent/at the extreme edge of the forest). 2 greatest possible (in extreme pain). 3 far from moderate, going beyond the limits, not sharing the views of the majority (extreme views/extreme members of the party). 4 intense, strong, not ordinary or usual (calling for extreme measures of punishment):—n 1 the end, the farthest point (the extremes of the earth). 2 something as far or as different as possible from something else (the extremes of wealth and poverty). 3 the greatest or highest degree (the extremes of heat in the desert).

extrem'ist n one who holds extreme ideas (a political extremist):—also adj.

extrem'ity n 1 the farthest point (the extremities of the earth). 2 (fml) a situation of great misfortune, distress or danger (in an extremity of poverty). 3 (fml) the farther parts of the body, i.e. the hands and feet (poor circulation in her extremities).

ex'tricate vb to set free from a difficult position (extricating the dog from the hole in which he was stuck/extricate the firm from its financial difficulties).

exu'berant adj 1 vigorous, strong (exuberant growth of plants). 2 in high spirits (in exuberant mood):—n **exu'berance**.

exude' *vb* to ooze out, to give off (*exuding perspiration/exude confidence*).

exult' *vb* to rejoice very much, to express joy (*exulting over their victory*):—*adj* **exul'tant**:—*n* **exulta'tion**.

eye *n* **1** the organ by means of which we see. **2** a small hole in a needle. **3** the seed bud of a potato:—*vb* **1** to look at, to watch closely (*eying his friend's cake with envy/eyed the policeman warily*).

eye'-opener *n* something very surprising.

eye'sore *n* something very ugly (*high-rise flats that are an eyesore on the landscape*).

eye'witness *n* one who sees an event happen (*eye-witnesses of the accident*).

eyrie, eyry [ee'-ri] *n* **1** the nest of a bird of prey, esp an eagle. **2** a building in a very high place. **3** a very high place.

F

fa'ble *n* a short story, usu about animals, etc, who talk and behave like human beings, intended to teach people to do what is right and good (*Aesop's fable about the fox and the grapes*).

fab'ric *n* 1 the framework of a building (*the fabric of the building is crumbling*). 2 manufactured cloth (*a woollen fabric*).

fab'ricate *vb* to make up or invent (*fabricating an excuse*):—*n* **fabrica'tion**.

fab'ulous *adj* 1 (*fml*) existing only in fable or legend (*the dragon is a fabulous animal*). 2 (*inf*) wonderful, marvellous, very good (*a fabulous dress/a fabulous performance*).

facade [fa-säd'] *n* 1 the front of a building. 2 outer appearance (*frightened in spite of his brave facade*).

face *n* 1 the front part of the head, from forehead to chin (*a beautiful face*). 2 the front part of anything (*break the face of his watch*):—*vb* 1 to stand looking towards, to turn towards (*a house facing south*). 2 to meet or encounter boldly (*face the enemy army/face his problems*). 3 to cover with a surface of different material (*face the wall with plaster*).

facet [fas'-êt] *n* 1 one of many small sides, as of a diamond. 2 an aspect (*a humorous facet to the situation*).

facetious [fa-see'-shês] *adj* 1 fond of joking, intended to make people laugh (*a facetious person*). 2 intended to be amusing, often in an inappropriate situation (*object to his facetious remarks in sad circumstances*):—*n* **face'tiousness**.

facial [fā'-shêl] *adj* having to do with the face (*facial hair*).

facile [fas'îl] *adj* 1 done with ease, often done too easily (*a facile victory*). 2 without depth, superficial (*a facile remark*).

facil'itate *vb* to make easy (*facilitating the bill's progress through parliament*).

facil'ity *n* 1 (*fml*) ease, skill (*perform the tasks with facility*). 2 *pl* the means or conditions for doing something easily.

facsimile [fak-sim'-i-li] *n* 1 an exact copy (*a facsimile of the legal document*). 2 an image produced by facsimile transmission (*also* **fax**):—

facsimile transmission a system of transmitting written, printed or pictorial documents over the telephone system by scanning it and reproducing the image after transmission.

fact *n* 1 something known to be true or to have happened (*geographical facts about the country*). 2 truth (*it is a fact that the earth is round*). 3 in law, a deed, an event (*after the fact*).

fac'tion *n* 1 a group of people acting for their own interests against those of a party or society (*rival factions*). 2 (*fml*) disagreement, dispute (*obvious faction within the political party*).

fac'tious *adj* (*fml*) relating to faction, quarrelsome.

fac'tor *n* 1 one who does business for another, one who manages another's land '*the estate's factor*'. 2 a cause, element (*one of the factors in his lack of success*). 3 a number that goes exactly into another number.

fac'tory *n* a building where large quantities of goods are made (*a car factory*).

fac'tual *adj* having to do with facts (*a factual, rather than fictional, account of the war*).

fac'ulty *n* 1 a special ability (*a faculty for putting people at their ease*). 2 the power to do something (*the faculty of speech*). 3 a department of a university in which related subjects are taught (*the science faculty*).

fad *n* 1 (*inf*) an unreasonable like or dislike for something (*a child with lots of fads about food*). 2 a craze, a short-lived fashion (*one of the fads of the 1960s*).

fade *vb* 1 to wither. 2 to lose colour. 3 to disappear gradually (*hopes fading*).

fag *vb* (**fagged'**, **fag'ging**) (*inf*) to cause to become tired (*the long journey fagged her out*):—*n* (*inf*) 1 tiring or unpleasant work (*find gardening a fag*). 2 a schoolboy forced to do odd jobs for a senior.

Fahrenheit [fah'rinhît] *adj* of a scale of temperature in which the freezing point of water is 32° and the boiling point is 212°.

fail *vb* 1 not to succeed (*fail his driving test/fail in his attempt at the record*). 2 to break down (*a car engine that failed*). 3 to disappoint (*feel that she failed her mother*). 4 to owe so much money that one cannot pay one's debts (*a firm that is bound to fail*).

fail'ing *n* a fault, a weakness (*laziness is his major failing*).

fail'ure *n* **1** lack of success (*disappointed at their failure in the tournament*). **2** one who has not succeeded (*regard himself as a failure*). **3** a breakdown (*engine failure*).

fain *adj* (*old or lit*) glad:—*adv* gladly.

faint *vb* to become weak, to fall down unconscious (*faint from lack of food*):—*n* act of falling down unconscious:—*adj* **1** weak, dizzy. **2** lacking clearness or brightness (*writing grown faint over the years*). **3** slight (*chances of winning are now faint*).

fair[1] *adj* **1** light in colour, having light-coloured hair (*one daughter is fair and the other dark*). **3** quite good (*a fair piece of work*). **3** just (*a fair sentence given by the judge*). **4** (*of weather*) not rainy (*hope the weather will be fair for the picnic*). **5** (*old or lit*) attractive (*a fair young maiden*).

fair[2] *n* **1** a market or sale, often with shows and amusements. **2** a trade exhibition (*a book fair*).

fair'ly *adv* quite (*fairly sure that he is guilty*/*do fairly well*).

fair-mind'ed *adj* just.

fair'ness *n* justice (*dispute the fairness of the referee's decision*).

fair'way *n* **1** the deep part of a river where ships usually sail. **2** the part of a golf course where the grass is cut short.

fair'y *n* an imaginary small being, supposed to have magic powers.

fair'ylike *adj* light, dainty.

faith *n* **1** belief, esp in God (*lose one's faith*). **2** trust, confidence (*have faith in her ability*). **3** religion (*Christianity and other faiths*). **4** one's word of honour (*keep faith with his friends*).

faith'ful *adj* **1** true to one's friends or one's promises (*the king's faithful followers*). **2** loyal to one's marriage vows (*a faithful wife*). **3** true to the facts or an original (*a faithful account of the situation*/*a faithful copy*).

faith'less *adj* (*fml*) disloyal (*faithless friends*).

fake *n* someone or something that deceives by looking other than he, she or it is (*that painting is not an original Picasso—it's a fake*):—

vb **1** to change something so that it falsely appears better, more valuable, etc (*faking the experiment's results*). **2** to copy something so as to deceive (*faked his father's signature on a cheque*). **3** (*inf*) to pretend (*fake illness to get off school*).

fakir [fa-keer'] *n* in the East, a holy man.

fal'con *n* a bird of prey trained to hunt smaller birds.

fal'conry *n* hunting with falcons.

fall *vb* (*pt* **fell**, *pp* **fallen**) **1** to drop down (*trip over a stone and fall*). **2** to become less or lower (*prices falling*). **3** to hang down (*hair falling to her waist*). **4** to happen or occur (*Christmas falls on a Sunday*). **5** to enter into a certain state or condition (*fall asleep*/*fall silent*). **6** to be taken by an enemy (*Rome fell to the enemy*). **7** to be killed in battle (*soldiers who fell in World War I*):—*n* **1** a drop or descent (*injured in a fall from the cliff*). **2** a lessening or lowering (*a fall in the birth rate*). **3** loss of power (*predict the government's fall*). **4** a waterfall. **5** (*Amer*) autumn:—**fall back** to go back:—**fall on** or **upon** to attack:—**fall out** (*inf*) to quarrel:—**fall through** to fail (*plans falling through*).

fallacy [fal'-ê-si] *n* a wrong idea or belief, usu one that is generally believed to be true, false reasoning (*it is a fallacy that more expensive things are always of better quality*):—*adj* **falla'cious**.

fallible [fal'-ibl] *adj* (*fml*) able to make mistakes (*all human beings are fallible*):—*n* **fallibil'ity**.

fall'out *n* particles of radioactive dust that is in the air after a nuclear explosion.

fal'low *adj* ploughed but left unsown for a year (*fields lying fallow*):—*also n*.

fallow deer' *n* a small yellowish-brown deer.

false *adj* **1** not true (*a false account of what happened*). **2** disloyal (*false friends*). **3** not real, artificial (*a false beard*):—*ns* **false'ness**, **fals'ity**.

false'hood *n* (*fml*) a lie (*tell falsehoods*).

falset'to *n* an unnatural high-pitched singing voice.

fals'ify *vb* to alter in order to deceive (*an accountant falsifying the firm's books*):—*n* **falsifica'tion**.

falsity *see* **false**.

falter [fäl'-ter] *vb* **1** to speak or say in an uncertain or hesitant way (*'I didn't know what to say,' she faltered*/*falter out a few words of apology*).

2 to stumble (*he faltered as he went down the slippery steps*).

fame *n* the state of being well known for what one has done (*prefers personal happiness to fame*).

famed *adj* (*fml*) well-known (*famed for her cooking*).

familiar *adj* **1** well-known because often seen (*a familiar figure in the village*). **2** having good knowledge of (*familiar with the layout of the town*). **3** too friendly, disrespectful (*object to his talking to her in such a familiar way*):—*n* **1** a close friend. **2** the animal companion of a witch:—*n* **familiar'ity**.

familiarize *vb* to make used to (*familiarizing himself with the rules of the game*).

family *n* **1** a household, parents and children. **2** one's children (*a couple with no family*). **3** people descended from the same ancestors. **4** a group of things in some way related to each other (e.g. races, animals, etc).

family tree *n* a chart which shows the members of a family and their ancestors and their relationship to each other.

famine *n* a great shortage of food (*people dying of starvation in the famine*).

famish *vb*:—**to be famished** (*inf*) to be very hungry.

famous *adj* well-known to all (*famous artists/a famous building/a famous painting*).

fan[1] *n* an instrument or machine causing a current of air (*use an electric fan in hot weather*):—*vb* (**fanned', fan'ning**) to move the air with a fan:—**fan out** to spread out over a wider front (*police fanning out over the fields to look for evidence in the murder case*).

fan[2] *n* a keen follower or supporter (*football fans*).

fanatic *n* one who holds a belief, esp a religious or political belief, so strongly that he or she can neither discuss it reasonably nor think well of those who disagree with it (*a health food fanatic*):—*n* **fanat'icism**.

fanat'ical *adj* having the views of a fanatic (*fanatical about cleanliness*).

fan'ciful *adj* **1** imaginative, inclined to have strange, unreal ideas (*a fanciful child*). **2** imaginary, unreal (*fanciful ideas*).

fan'cy *n* **1** (*fml*) the imagination (*poets relying on fancy*). **2** a false idea or belief, something

imagined (*just an old woman's fancy*). **3** a sudden desire (*a pregnant woman with a fancy for oranges*). **4** a liking for, often a romantic one (*a fancy for the girl next door*):—*adj* not plain, ornamented:—*vb* **1** to imagine (*he fancied that he saw a ghost*). **2** (*inf*) to like (*fancying a drink*). **3** to be romantically or sexually attracted to (*the boss fancies his secretary*).

fan'fare *n* the sounding of many trumpets or bugles in greeting (*a fanfare introducing the queen's entry*).

fang *n* **1** a long, pointed tooth (*the fangs of the wolf*). **2** the poison tooth of a snake.

fan'light *n* a window over a door.

fantasia [fan-tā'-zi-a] *n* a light or fanciful piece of music.

fantas'tic *adj* **1** strange or weird (*amazed by her fantastic appearance*). **2** created in the mind, fanciful, unrealistic (*fantastic hopes of wealth*). **3** (*inf*) very large (*a fantastic sum of money*). **4** (*inf*) very good, excellent (*a fantastic performance*).

fan'tasy *n* **1** a highly imaginative composition (*a musical fantasy*). **2** an unusual or far-fetched idea, a dream (*have fantasies about lying on a sun-drenched beach*).

far *adj* distant (*far places*):—*adv* at a distance in time, space or degree (*travel far*).

farce *n* **1** a stage play intended only to arouse laughter. **2** a laughable or ridiculous situation (*the trial was a farce—they had already decided he was guilty*).

far'cical *adj* laughable. ridiculous.

fare *vb* (*fml or old*) to be or do (ill or well):—*n* **1** food. **2** the cost of a travel ticket (*unable to afford the rail fare*). **3** a passenger on a bus or taxi (*taxi drivers picking up fares*).

farewell' *interj* goodbye.

far'-fetched *adj* so unlikely as to be almost impossible (*far-fetched stories of his adventures*).

farm *n* an area of land prepared for crops and herds by one owner:—*vb* to use land as a farm (*farm the land next to ours*):—*n* **farm'er**:—**farm out** to give out to be done by others (*farm out work*).

farm'stead *n* a farm and the buildings on it.

farrier *n* one who shoes horses.

far'row *n* a family of baby pigs born at the same time.

far'-see'ing adj wise.

far'thing n a British coin (= ¼ old penny) no longer in use.

fas'cinate vb to attract or interest very strongly, to charm (she was fascinated by his travel stories/her beauty fascinating him):—n **fascina'tion**.

fascism [fash'-izm] n a right-wing, nationalist political movement originating in Italy:—n and adj **fasc'ist**.

fash'ion n 1 the way in which a thing is done or made (paint after the fashion of Van Gogh). 2 the kinds of clothes popular at a certain time (1920s fashion):—vb to shape, to make (fashion a figure out of clay).

fash'ionable adj 1 following a style that is currently popular (fashionable clothes/fashionable women/fashionable furniture). 2 used or visited by people following a current fashion (a fashionable hotel).

fast[1] vb to do without food, esp for religious reasons (Muslims fasting during Ramadan/patients fasting before being operated on):—n act or time of fasting.

fast[2] adj 1 firm, fixed (make fast the rope). 2 quick, swift (at a fast pace):—adv 1 firmly (made fast). 2 quickly (run fast). 3 (old) near.

fasten [fas'-ên] vb 1 to fix firmly (fasten the gate). 2 to fix to (fasten a brooch to her dress).

fast'ener, **fast'ening** ns a device that joins together or fixes one thing to another (a zip fastener).

fast food n hot food that is prepared and served very quickly, often taken away to be eaten (fast food like fish and chips).

fastid'ious adj hard to please (fastidious about what she eats):—n **fastid'iousness**.

fast'ness n a fort.

fat adj well-fed, fleshy:—n 1 an oily substance in animal bodies (cut the fat off the meat). 2 this substance or the oily substance found in some plants when in solid or almost solid form, used as a food or in cooking (fry in vegetable fat).

fatal [fã'-têl] adj 1 causing death (a fatal accident). 2 bringing danger or ruin, or having unpleasant results (it's fatal to mix wine and spirits at parties).

fat'alism n the belief that one's future is decided and cannot be changed (unable to try to overcome his disability because of his fatalism):—n **fat'alist**:—adj **fatalis'tic**.

fatal'ity n 1 death caused by accident, war, etc (a bomb attack resulting in several fatalities). 2 (fml) deadliness (the fatality of certain diseases).

fate n 1 an imaginary power that is supposed to decide future events before they happen (decide to take no action and leave it up to fate). 2 what will happen to one in the future (a judge deciding the accused's fate).

fat'ed adj decided by fate, unavoidable.

fate'ful adj important for one's future (a fateful decision).

fa'ther n 1 a male parent. 2 a person who begins, invents or first makes something (the father of the English navy). 3 a priest:—vb 1 to be the father of (father several children). 2 to start an idea or movement (fathered the Scout movement).

fa'therland n one's native country.

fath'om n a measure of 6 feet or 1.8 metres, esp of depth of water:—vb to understand fully.

fatigue [fa-teeg'] n 1 weariness, great tiredness (suffering from fatigue after climbing the mountain). 2 an unpleasant or tiring job:—vb to tire out.

fat'ten vb to make fat (fattening turkeys for Christmas).

fat'ty adj containing fat.

fat'uous adj foolish, stupid (a fatuous thing to say):—ns **fatu'ity**, **fat'uousness**.

fault n 1 a mistake (the accident was his fault). 2 a weakness in character (his main fault is laziness). 3 an imperfection, something wrong with something (a fault in the machine). 4 a break in rock that then drops below the rest:—adj **fault'less**.

fault'y adj having a fault, imperfect (a faulty electric appliance).

faun n in Roman legend, a god, half-man and half-beast.

fauna [fã'-na] n all the animals found in a country or region.

fa'vour n 1 a feeling of kindness or approval towards (look with favour on the suggestion). 2 an act done out of kindness (do him a favour and give him a lift to work). 3 something (e.g. a flower, rosette, etc) worn as a sign of good will or support (*favours worn by the politician's supporters*):—*vb* **1** (*fml*) to show more kindness to one than to another (*favour his son over his daughter*). **2** to prefer (*she favours the yellow dress*). **3** to give an advantage (*the weather favoured the other team*).

fa'vourable *adj* kindly, helpful (*favourable weather conditions*).

fa'vourite *n* a person or thing preferred to others (*accused of being the teacher's favourite*):—*also adj*.

fa'vouritism *n* showing more liking for one person than for others (*show favouritism to the youngest of her children*).

fawn¹ *n* **1** a young fallow deer. **2** a yellowish-brown colour:—*adj* yellowish-brown.

fawn² *vb* to flatter or behave like a slave to gain another's favour (*fawning on his rich uncle so that he would leave something in his will*):—*adj* **fawn'ing.**

fax *n* **1** a machine that sends and receives documents electronically along a telephone line and then prints them out, also called **fax machine**, **2** a document sent in this way:—*vb* to send by fax machine (*fax the exam results*).

fear *n* dread, terror, anxiety (*have a fear of spiders/the noises in the night filled her with fear*):—*also vb.*

fear'ful *adj* **1** apprehensive and afraid (*fearful of being attacked*). **2** terrible (*a fearful storm/a fearful sight*). **3** (*inf*) very bad, very great (*what fearful cheek!*)

fear'less *adj* unafraid (*fearless explorers*).

fear'some *adj* (*fml*) causing fear (*a fearsome sight*).

feas'ible *adj* possible, able to be done (*a feasible plan/it is not feasible to use that method*):—*n* **feasibil'ity.**

feast *n* **1** a meal with plenty of good things to eat and drink. **2** something extremely pleasing (*the view was a feast for the eyes*). **3** a day or period of time kept in memory of a religious event, such as Christmas:—*vb* **1** to eat well. **2** to provide a good meal for others.

feat *n* a deed notable for courage, skill, etc.

feath'er *n* one of the growths that cover a bird's body:—*vb* to line or cover with feathers:—

feather one's nest to make a profit for oneself out of work done for others.

fea'ture *n* **1** an outstanding part of anything (*his eyes are his most striking feature*). **2** a special long article in a newspaper (*a feature on children's rights*). **3** *pl* the face (*have small neat features*):—*vb* to give or have a position, esp an important one (*money features largely in his life*).

Feb'ruary *n* the second month of the year.

feck'less *adj* helpless, ineffectual (*so feckless she can't boil an egg*).

fec'und *adj* (*fml*) fertile, fruitful (*fecund soil/a fecund imagination*):—*n* **fecun'dity.**

fed'eral *adj* united under one central government, but keeping local control of certain matters.

fed'erate *vb* to join together in a federal union.

federa'tion *n* **1** a group of states that give up certain of their powers to a common central government. **2** a joining together of certain groups of people.

fee *n* **1** a payment made for special professional services, a charge or payment (*a lawyer's fee*). **2** money paid for entering or being taught in a school, college, etc.

fee'ble *adj* very weak (*the old lady has grown very feeble/hear a feeble cry*):—*n* **fee'bleness.**

feed *vb* (*pt, pp* **fed**) **1** to give food to (*feed the children early*). **2** to eat (*cats feeding on mice*). **3** to provide what is necessary for (*feed the furnace/feed the imagination*). **4** to put into (*feed data into the computer*):—*n* food.

feed'back *n* information about how good or bad something or someone has been (*feedback about the athlete's performance*).

feel *vb* (*pt, pp* **felt**) **1** to touch (*feel the bump on his head*). **2** to find out by touching (*feel the quality of the cloth*). **3** to experience or be aware of (*feel a sudden anger/feel the cold*). **4** to believe or consider (*feel that she is too old*). **5** to be moved by, to have pity (*feel for the orphaned children*):—*n* the sense of touch, a quality as revealed by touch (*the smooth feel of silk*).

feel'er *n* **1** the thread-like organ of touch of an insect. **2** something said to try to get others to give their opinions (*put out feelers to test the market*).

feel'ing *n* **1** the sense of touch (*lose the feeling in the fingers of her right hand*). **2** emotion (*a* *feeling of sadness*). **3** kindness for others (*have no feeling for the orphaned children*). **4** an impression or belief (*I have a feeling that he is lying*):—*adj* able to understand the emotions of others.

feet *see* **foot**.

feign [fān] *vb* to pretend (*feign sleep*).

feint [fānt] *n* a pretended movement:—*also vb*.

feld'spar, fel'spar *n* a rock-forming mineral.

felicita'tions *npl* (*fml*) good wishes (*offer him their felicitations on his engagement*).

felic'itous *adj* (*fml*) well chosen (*a few felicitous phrases*).

felic'ity *n* (*fml*) **1** great happiness (*find felicity in marriage*). **2** suitability (*the felicity of his remarks*).

feline [fee'-līn] *adj* **1** cat-like. **2** of the cat family.

fell¹ *n* a bare hill, esp in northern England.

**fell² ** *adj* (*old*) cruel, savage (*a fell blow*).

fell³ *vb* to cut down, to knock down (*felled trees for firewood*).

fell'ow *n* **1** one of a pair (*the fellow to the glove*). **2** a companion and an equal (*school fellows*). **3** a member of a learned society or a college. **4** (*inf*) a man (*quite a nice fellow*).

fell'owship *n* **1** company (*seek the fellowship of his colleagues*). **2** friendship (*feelings of fellowship among the staff*). **3** an association (*a church youth fellowship*). **4** a grant of money given to someone to enable him or her to do advanced studies.

fel'on *n* (*fml*) a criminal (*convicted of being a felon*).

fel'ony *n* (*fml*) a serious crime (*commit a felony*):—*adj* **felo'nious**.

felspar *see e* **feldspar**.

felt¹ *pt* and *pp* of **feel**.

felt² *n* a coarse cloth made of wool and hair (*a felt hat*).

fe'male *n* **1** a girl or woman (*the changing area for females*). **2** an animal or bird that can bear offspring (*our dog is a female*):—*also adj*.

fem'inine *adj* **1** having the qualities considered suitable or essential for a woman (*wear feminine clothes*). **2** of a woman (*a feminine voice*).

fem'inism *n* the belief that men and women should have equal rights:—*n* **fem'inist**.

feminin'ity *n* the state of being female or womanly (*the feminity of her style of decoration*).

femur [fee'-mur] *n* (*fml*) the thighbone (*break his femur*):—*adj* **fem'oral**.

fen *n* a marsh, an area of flat, wet, low-lying land.

fence *n* **1** a wall made of wood or of wooden posts and wire to enclose a field (*a fence made of wire netting*). **2** (*inf*) a receiver of stolen goods (*the burglars handed on the stolen jewellery to a fence*):—*vb* **1** to put a fence round (*fence in the garden*). **2** to take part in sword-play. **3** to avoid giving direct answers to questions, esp by quibbling over minor points:—**sit on the fence** to give no decision either way, to be neutral (*sit on the fence and not give one's support to either side*).

fenc'ing *n* **1** the materials for making a fence. **2** sword-play as a sport.

fend *vb* **1** to keep off, to turn aside (*fend off blows/fend off attackers*). **2** to look after (*fend for oneself*).

fen'der *n* **1** a guard around the fireplace. **2** a rope pad to protect the side of a ship when at a pier.

fen'nel *n* a sweet-smelling plant used as a herb and vegetable.

fer'ment *n* **1** that which causes fermentation. **2** excitement (*children in a state of ferment before Christmas*):—*vb* **ferment'** **1** to cause or undergo fermentation (*ferment beer*). **2** to excite (*ferment trouble among the workers*).

fermenta'tion *n* a chemical change that causes solids to break up and mix and liquids to froth and bubble (e.g. the action of yeast in beer, etc).

fern *n* a plant with no flowers and feathery leaves.

fero'cious *adj* fierce, cruel, savage (*a ferocious dog/a ferocious attack*):—*n* **fero'city**.

fer'ret *n* a small weasel-like animal used in hunting rabbits:—*vb* **1** to search busily and persistently (*ferreting about in the cupboard*). **2** to find something carefully hidden (*ferret out her secret diary/ferret out details of her past*).

ferrule [fer'-êl] *n* the metal cap on the end of a cane or umbrella.

fer'ry *vb* **1** to carry over water in a boat or aeroplane (*ferrying passengers to the island*). **2** to transport (*ferried the children to and from school*):—*n* **1** a boat that ferries (*the ferry that sank*). **2** the place where a ferry crosses.

fer'tile *adj* **1** able to produce much, fruitful (*fertile land*). **2** inventive (*a fertile imagination*):—*n* **fertil'ity**.

fer'tilize vb to make fertile or fruitful, to enrich (*fertilizing the soil with manure*).

fer'tilizer n a material mixed into soil to make it more fertile.

fer'vent adj eager, very keen, sincere (*a fervent supporter of the local team*).

fer'vid adj (*fml*) very keen, intense (*a fervid desire*).

fer'vour n keenness, strength of feeling (*speak with great fervour*).

fes'ter vb **1** (*of a wound*) to become full of poisonous matter, to become infected. **2** to give rise to bitter feelings, to become bitter (*memories of the insult festering in his mind/resentment festered over the years*).

fes'tival n **1** a day or number of days spent in joy, merrymaking, etc (*a religious festival*). **2** a season of plays, films, concerts, etc (*a musical festival*).

fes'tive adj gay, joyous (*a festive occasion*).

festiv'ity n gaiety, merrymaking (*join in the festivities*).

festoon' n a drooping chain of flowers, ribbons, etc, put up as a decoration, a hanging garland:— n to decorate with festoons, etc (*a room festooned with balloons*).

fetch vb **1** to go and bring (*fetch water from the well*). **2** to be sold for (*an antique vase fetching £2000*).

fetch'ing adj attractive (*a fetching red hat*).

fête [fet] n a day of public enjoyment and entertainment held usu out of doors and often to collect money for a special purpose (*a church fête*):— vb to show honour to, to make much of (*villagers fêting the famous writer when he came home*).

fet'id adj evil-smelling, stinking (*fetid air*).

fet'ish n **1** an object that is worshipped and believed to possess magic power. **2** something regarded with too much attention or respect (*make a fetish of cleanliness*).

fet'lock n **1** the tuft of hair on the back part of a horse's foot. **2** that part of a horse's hoof.

fet'ter n a chain for the feet (*prisoners in fetters to stop them running away*):— vb **1** to fasten with fetters. **2** to hinder, to restrain (*fettered by a very tight budget*).

fet'tle n condition, fitness (*a team in fine fettle for the game*).

feu [fû] n the right to possess land and buildings in return for a fixed yearly payment.

feud [fûd] n lasting quarrelling or strife between persons or families or clans, etc (*a feud between the families for 200 years*).

feudal [fû'-dal] adj having to do with feudalism.

feu'dalism n a system under which land was held in return for military or other service.

feu du'ty n the payment made for a feu.

fe'ver n **1** a disease causing great heat in the body (*scarlet fever*). **2** an abnormally high body temperature (*symptoms of flu such as fever and aching limbs*). **3** excitement (*in a fever of impatience*).

fe'vered, **fe'verish** adjs **1** hot with fever (*the child is feverish/a fevered brow*). **2** excited (*with feverish haste*).

fez n a brimless red cap with a black tassle.

fiancé [fee-ân(g)'-sâ] n a man engaged to be married:—f **fiancée**.

fias'co n (*pl* **fias'coes** or **fias'cos**) a complete failure, a laughable failure (*the amateur show was a complete fiasco*).

fib n a not very serious lie or untruth (*children scolded for telling fibs*):—vb (**fibbed'**, **fib'bing**) to tell untruths:—n **fib'ber**.

fi'bre n **1** a thread-like part of an animal or plant (*cotton fibres/nerve fibres*). **2** a material made of fibres (*woollen fibre for spinning*).

fi'brous adj made of fibres (*a fibrous substance*).

fib'ula n (*fml*) the outer of the two bones between the knee and the ankle (*fracture her fibula*).

fick'le adj quickly changing, not faithful (*a fickle lover*):—n **fick'leness**.

fic'tion n **1** a made-up story (*the account of the event was a complete fiction*). **2** the art of writing stories (*works of fiction*). **3** novels (*publish fiction*).

ficti'tious adj imaginary, invented (*fictitious characters/a fictitious village*).

fid'dle n a violin:—vb **1** to play the violin. **2** to play about with (*a girl fiddling with her hair*). **3** to prepare or alter dishonestly to one's own advantage (*an accountant fiddling the books*):—n **fidd'ler**.

fidd'lesticks interj (*old*) nonsense.

fidel'ity n **1** faithfulness, loyalty (*rely on his followers' fidelity*). **2** exactness (*the fidelity of the translation*).

fid'get vb to move about restlessly (children fidgeting with impatience):—also n.

field n 1 open country. 2 an enclosed area of ground. 3 a battlefield. 4 a sports ground:—vb to catch and return a ball.

field day n 1 a day spent in military exercises. 2 a day of great activity.

field'fare n a type of thrush.

field'glass'es npl a pair of telescopes fitted together for outdoor use, binoculars.

field'mar'shal n an army officer of the highest rank.

fiend n 1 a devil. 2 a very cruel person (the guard in the prisoner of war camp was a real fiend):—adj fiend'ish.

fierce adj wild, angry (a fierce tiger/a fierce wind/a fierce look):—n fierce'ness.

fiery [fi-ri] adj 1 having to do with fire. 2 easily angered or excited.

fig n the fig tree or its fruit.

fight vb (pt, pp **fought**) 1 to use force against another (boys fighting). 2 to take part in war or battle (armies fighting). 3 to quarrel, to argue (brother and sister always fighting). 4 to try hard to succeed (fighting for his life):—n 1 a struggle in which force is used, a battle. 2 a hard effort (a fight for poor people to survive).

fig'ment n:—a figment of one's imagination something that one has imagined and that has no reality (the ghostly figure was a figment of her imagination).

fig'urative adj not having the usual or literal meaning (a figurative use of the word).

fig'ure n 1 the shape of the body (have a slim figure). 2 a person (see three figures in the distance). 3 lines drawn to show a shape, a geometrical shape (a hexagonal figure). 4 a number from 0 to 9. 5 a price (the house will fetch a high figure). 6 a diagram or illustration (number the figures in the book):—vb 1 to work out the answer to a sum or problem. 2 to appear (she figures in his account of the event). 3 (inf) (esp Amer) to think or consider (I figure he will arrive soon).

fig'urehead n 1 a carved figure fixed on the front of a ship (a figurehead in the shape of a woman's head). 2 a person who has a high position but no real power (the owner is now just a figurehead in the company).

figure of speech n the use of words in an unusual meaning or order to express ideas with greater clarity or feeling.

fil'ament n 1 a very thin thread. 2 the thin wire in an electric-light bulb.

fil'bert n a hazelnut.

filch vb (inf) to steal (filch bars of chocolate from the shop).

file[1] n 1 a number of papers arranged in order (a file relating to the house sale). 2 any device that keeps them in order (a cardboard file). 3 in a computer, a collection of related information stored under a particular name. 4 a row of persons one behind the other (a file of school-girls):—vb 1 to put in place in a file (file the correspondence). 2 to walk in file (people filing out of church).

file[2] n a tool with a rough face for smoothing or cutting:—vb to smooth or cut away with a file (filing her nails/filed through the metal bars).

fil'ial adj having to do with a son or daughter (filial duty).

fil'ibuster n a pirate:—vb to try to stop a debate ending by making unnecessarily long speeches.

fil'igree n very delicate ornamental work done with fine gold or silver thread.

fil'ings npl the metal fragments rubbed off by a file (iron filings).

fill vb 1 to make full (fill the bathtub with hot water/the news filled him with sadness). 2 to become full (the hall filled quickly). 3 to stop up (fill the holes in the wall). 4 to occupy (fill a teaching post):—n as much as fills or satisfies, often to a great extent (have one's fill of the excellent food/have one's fill of his advice).

fill'et n 1 a ribbon worn around the head. 2 boneless meat or fish (fillet of plaice):—vb to take the bones out of.

fil(l)'ibeg n a kilt.

fill'ip n encouragement, incentive, stimulus (give a fillip to their sales).

fill'y n a young female horse.

film n 1 a thin skin or covering (a film of dust over the furniture). 2 the thin roll of celluloid on which the pictures are taken by a camera. 3 a cinema picture (a horror film):—vb to take a moving picture.

film star n a popular film actor or actress.

fil'ter n a strainer, a device through which liquid is passed to cleanse it:—vb to cleanse or separate by passing through a filter (*filter the coffee*).

filth n 1 dirt, foulness (*clean the filth from his clothes*). 2 evil talk, obscene literature (*the filth in pornographic literature*).

filth'y adj 1 very dirty (*filthy clothes after walking through the mud*). 2 disgusting, obscene (*filthy phone calls*).

fin n a small wing-like organ by means of which a fish swims.

fi'nal adj 1 last (*the final chapter of the book*). 2 putting an end to (*my final offer/the judge's decision is final*):—n **final'ity**:—adv **fi'nally**.

finale [fi-na'-lä] n the last part of a piece of music, play, etc (*the whole cast took part in the finale*).

fi'nance n 1 money matters (*seek a career in finance*). 2 pl money resources (*keep his finances in order*):—vb **finance'** to find or provide the money for (*financing his son's business venture*):—adj **finan'cial**.

finan'cier n 1 one skilled in finance. 2 one who is able to provide large sums of money for business undertakings (*the financier of the new business*).

finch n one of many kinds of small singing birds.

find vb (pt, pp **found**) 1 to come upon what one is looking for (*find the lost ring*). 2 to discover (*he was too late to find oil*). 3 to decide after inquiry (*found the accused guilty*):—n a valuable discovery.

find'ing n a decision or opinion reached after an inquiry (*the jury's findings*).

fine¹ adj 1 very thin or small (*fine bones*). 2 excellent (*a fine performance*). 3 delicate, beautiful (*fine china*). 4 bright, sunny (*a fine day/fine weather*). 5 healthy (*ill yesterday but feeling fine today*). 6 slight (*a fine distinction*).

fine² n money paid as a punishment:—vb to punish by fine (*fined for a driving offence*).

fine arts npl painting, sculpture and music.

fin'ery n rich and colourful clothing or decoration (*wedding guests in their finery*).

finesse [fi-nes'] n great skill and cleverness (*handle the situation with great finesse*).

fing'er n one of the five points that extend from the hand or glove:—vb to touch with the fingers (*finger the piano keys/fingered the material*):—**have at one's fingertips** to have ready knowledge of (*have the facts of the situation at their fingertips*).

fing'ering n the use of the fingers in playing a musical instrument.

fing'ermark n a dirty mark made by the fingers (*fingermarks on the furniture*).

fing'erprint n 1 the mark made by the tips of the fingers (*burglars who left no fingerprints anywhere*). 2 an ink print of the lines on the fingertips for identification purposes (*a police file of fingerprints*).

fin'icky adj 1 fussy, too particular (*finicky tastes in food/a finicky eater*). 2 needing much attention to detail (*a finicky job*).

fin'ish vb 1 to bring to an end (*unable to finish the job*). 2 to come to an end (*the show finished early*):—n 1 the end (*the finish of the race/the finish of the job*). 2 extra touches to make perfect (*furniture with a fine finish/manners lacking finish*).

finite [fī'-nît] adj having an end, limited (*human knowledge is finite*).

fiord, fjord [fee'-ord] n a long narrow bay running inland between steep rocky hills.

fir n a cone-bearing (coniferous) tree.

fire n 1 something burning giving out heat and light (*a coal fire*). 2 an apparatus for heating (*a gas fire*). 3 (*fml*) keenness (*patriotic fire*):—vb 1 to set on fire (*fire the house*). 2 to bake (*fire pottery*). 3 to cause to explode (*firing a gun*). 4 to arouse keenness (*fired them with enthusiasm*). 5 (*inf*) to dismiss (from a job) (*fired his assistant for unpunctuality*).

fire'arm n a gun, rifle or pistol (*the police issued with firearms*).

fire'brand n 1 (*old*) a piece of burning wood. 2 one who stirs up trouble (*a political firebrand*).

fire brigade', fire ser'vice n a body of people trained to put out fires.

fire en'gine n an engine or pump for putting out fires.

fire escape n a long ladder or steps by which people may escape from a burning building.

fire'fighter n a person who is trained to put out fires.

fire'fly *n* an insect that glows in the dark.

fire'guard *n* a wire screen to prevent live coals from leaving the fireplace (*prevent the children touching the fire by putting up a fireguard*).

fire'man *n* 1 a man trained to put out fires (*saved from the burning house by firemen*). 2 one who puts fuel on a fire or furnace.

fire'place *n* a framed opening in the wall of a house to hold a fire (*a marble fireplace*).

fire'proof *adj* which cannot be set on fire (*fireproof material for children's clothes*).

fire'works *npl* toy explosives (e.g. rockets, squibs, etc) set off in the dark for show (*let off fireworks on 5th November*).

firm[1] *adj* 1 steady, not easily moved (*a table that is not quite firm*). 2 determined (*a firm refusal/she was quite firm about not going*):—*n* **firm'ness**.

firm[2] *n* a business company organized to manufacture or trade in goods (*a publishing firm*).

fir'mament *n* the sky or heavens.

first *adj* before all others (*the first person to arrive/his first visit*):—*adv* 1 before all others (*speak first*). 2 before doing anything else (*speak first and then act*).

first aid *n* treatment given to an injured person before the doctor arrives, simple medical attention (*receive first aid when she fainted at the football match*).

first'-born *n* (*fml*) eldest child.

first name *n* a person's personal name which comes before the family name or surname and is given at birth, also called **forename** and sometimes **Christian name** (*His first name is Joe.*)

fis'cal *adj* having to do with the management of public money (*the fiscal year*).

fish *n* an animal with gills and fins, living in water:—*vb* 1 to try to catch fish (*fishing in her bag for her keys*). 2 (*inf*) to search for (*fishing in her bag for her keys*). 3 (*inf*) to try to get by indirect means (*fish for compliments*).

fish'ery *n* 1 the industry of catching fish. 2 a place where fish can use be caught.

fish'monger *n* one who buys and sells fish.

fish'y *adj* 1 of or like fish (*a fishy smell*). 2 doubtful, arousing suspicion (*rather a fishy story/fishy circumstances*).

fis'sile *adj* 1 easily split (*fissile wood*). 2 capable of undergoing nuclear fission.

fission [fish'-ên] *n* the splitting into parts.

fiss'ure *n* a deep crack (*a fissure in the rock*).

fist *n* the hand tightly shut (*fight with their fists*).

fist'icuffs *npl* (*inf*) fighting with the fists (*solve the problem with fisticuffs*).

fit[1] *adj* 1 suitable, proper, right (*a fit person for the job/not fit behaviour/food not fit to be eaten*). 2 in good health:—*n* the particular way in which something fits (*a good fit/a tight fit*):—*vb* (**fit'ted, fit'ting**) 1 to be of the right size (*a coat that fits beautifully*). 2 to suit (*a punishment that fits the crime*). 3 to make suitable (*fit the punishment to the crime*).

fit[2] *n* 1 a sudden attack of illness, fainting, etc (*epileptic fits*). 2 a sudden feeling (*a fit of anger*).

fit'ful *adj* occurring in short periods, not regularly and steadily (*in fitful bursts of energy/fitful sleep*).

fit'ness *n* suitability (*question his fitness for the job*).

fit'ter *n* one who puts the parts of machinery together.

fit'ting *adj* suitable, proper (*fitting behaviour/a fitting end to his career*):—*n* 1 a thing fixed in position (*kitchen fittings*). 2 the trying on of clothes to see if they fit (*a fitting for a wedding dress*).

fives *n* a game in which a ball is hit by hand or bat against a wall.

fix *vb* 1 to make firm (*fix the loose tiles*). 2 to arrange (*fixing a meeting*). 3 to fasten (*fixed a brooch to her dress*). 4 to repair (*fix the broken radio*). 5 (*inf*) to arrange the result of dishonestly (*fix the result of the election*):—*n* (*inf*) a difficulty.

fix'ative *n* a substance used to fix colours in paintings, photographs, etc, glue.

fixed *adj* firm, not moving or changing (*a fixed stare/a fixed price*):—*adv* **fix'edly**.

fix'ture *n* 1 anything fastened in place (*bathroom fixtures*). 2 an arrangement to play a game, etc, on a certain date (*a cancelled fixture*).

fizz *vb* to release or give off many bubbles (*champagne fizzing in the glass*):—*n* 1 bubbles of gas in a liquid (*champagne that has lost its fizz*). 2 the sound of fizzing. 1 (*inf*) enthusiasm, liveliness, excitement (*the fizz went out of the party*).

fizz'le *vb* to fail, to come to nothing (*after an enthusiastic start out plans fizzled out*).

fjord *see* **fiord**.

flab'bergast *vb* to astonish (*flabbergasted by the expense of the holiday*).

flab'by *adj* **1** soft, hanging loosely (*flabby muscles*). **2** having soft loose flesh (*get flabby after giving up sport*):—*n* **flab'biness**.

flaccid [flak'-sêd] *adj* soft and weak, flabby (*flaccid muscles*).

flag[1] *n* **1** a square or oblong piece of material with a pattern on it representing a country, party, association, etc (*the French flag*). **2** a coloured cloth or paper used as a sign or signal (*red flags at dangerous beaches*):—*vb* (**flagged'**, **flag'ging**) **1** to signal with flags (*flag dangerous beaches*). **2** to cause a vehicle to stop by signalling to the driver (*police flagging down speeding motorists*).

flag[2] *n* a flowering plant that grows in wet ground.

flag[3] *n* a flat paving stone.

flag[4] *vb* (**flagged'**, **flag'ging**) (*fml*) to become tired (*flagging after a hard day's work*).

flagellate [fla'-jel-āt] *vb* (*fml*) to whip the body:—*n* **flagella'tion**.

flageolet [fla-jol-et'] *n* a type of flute.

flag'on *n* a large or wide bottle (*a flagon of wine*).

flagrant [flā'-grênt] *adj* done without concealment, shameless (*a flagrant disobeying of the rules*).

flag'ship *n* **1** the ship carrying an admiral. **2** the finest or most important of a group or list of products, projects, etc (*the book that was the flagship of the publisher's list*).

flail *n* a hand instrument for threshing corn:—*vb* **1** to beat with, or as if with, a flail. **2** to wave or swing about wildly (*with arms flailing*).

flair *n* **1** a natural ability (*a flair for languages/a flair for organizing*). **2** style, stylishness, an original and attractive quality (*dress with flair*).

flake *n* **1** a small thin piece of anything, esp a small loose piece that has broken off something (*flakes of paint/flakes of chocolate*). **2** a very light piece (e.g. of snow):—*vb* to come off in flakes (*paint flaking off*):—*adj* **flak'y**.

flamboy'ant *adj* **1** very brightly coloured or decorated (*flamboyant clothes*). **2** showy and confident (*a flamboyant person/with flamboyant gestures*).

flame *n* a tongue of fire, a blaze (*a candle flame*):—*vb* **1** to burn brightly (*the fire flamed

suddenly*). **2** (*inf*) to become suddenly angry (*she was flaming*).

flam'ing *adj* **1** burning with flames. **2** passionate, violent (*in a flaming temper*). **3** very bright (*flaming red hair*).

flamin'go *n* (*pl* **flamin'goes**) a brightly coloured water bird with long legs and neck.

flam'mable *adj* likely to catch fire and burn easily (*clothes made of a flammable material*).

flange *n* a sticking-out rim, as on a wheel that runs on rails.

flank *n* **1** the fleshy part of an animal's side (*stroke the horse's flank*). **2** the side of anything (e.g. an army, a mountain etc):—*vb* to be at the side of, to move to the side of (*the prisoner flanked by the policemen*).

flan'nel *n* **1** a soft woollen cloth (*blankets made of flannel*). **2** a small piece of material used for washing the face, etc.

flannelette' *n* an imitation flannel made from cotton.

flap *n* **1** anything fixed at one end and hanging loose, esp part of a garment (*the flap of the tent*). **2** the sound made by such a thing when it moves (*the flap of the washing on the line*). **3** (*inf*) panic, agitation (*don't get in a flap*):—*vb* (**flapped'**, **flap'ping**) **1** to flutter, to move up and down, to make a sound as of fluttering (*clothes flapping on the line*). **2** (*inf*) to get into a panic, to become confused or excited (*people flapping in an emergency*).

flare *vb* **1** to blaze up, to burn brightly but unsteadily (*a match flared in the darkness*). **2** to spread outwards (*trousers flaring out at the bottoms*):—*n* **1** a bright unsteady light. **2** a light used as a signal (*ships firing off emergency flares*). **3** a gradual widening out, esp of a skirt.

flash *n* **1** a quick or sudden gleam (*a flash of light*). **2** (*inf*) a moment (*all over in a flash*). **3** anything lasting for a very short time (*a flash of humour*). **4** a device for producing a short burst of electric light used to take photographs in the dark:—*vb* **1** to shine out suddenly (*lights flashing*). **2** to move very quickly (*days seeming to flash past*).

flash'light *n* **1** an electric torch (*find his way in the dark by flashlight*). **2** a short burst of electric light used to take photographs in the dark.

flash'y adj gaudy, showy (flashy clothes/a flashy car).

flask n 1 a kind of bottle. 2 a pocket bottle (a hip flask of brandy). 3 a vacuum flask.

flat adj 1 level (flat land). 2 uninteresting, dull and lifeless (things a bit flat after Christmas). 3 (of music) below the right note. 4 lying full length (people flat on the ground after the explosion). 5 deflated, without enough air in it (a flat tyre). 6 emphatic, firm (a flat denial). 7 no longer fizzy (champagne gone flat):—n 1 a level area (cycle on the flat). 2 the flat part or side (with the flat of my hand). 3 a home occupying one storey or part of a storey of a building (a second-floor flat). 4 a musical sign (b) showing that a note is to be played a semitone lower. 5 a flat tyre:—n flat'ness.

flat rate n a fixed price for each of a number of things that is the same in all cases (charge a flat rate for car hire).

flat'ten vb to make flat (flatten out the un-even ground).

flat'ter vb 1 to praise over much or insincerely (flatter his mother by complimenting her on her dress because he wanted to borrow the car). 2 to make appear better than is true (candlelight flatters her):—n flat'terer.

flat'tery n insincere praise.

flat'ulence n wind in the stomach or bowels:—adj flat'ulent.

flaunt vb to show off, to try to draw attention to (flaunt his wealth by buying expensive clothes/flaunt her figure by wearing tight clothes).

flaut'ist [flâ'-tist], **flutist** ns a flute-player.

fla'vour n 1 a taste (have the flavour of strawberries). 2 the taste special to a thing:—vb to add something to a dish in order to improve its taste (flavour the sauce with herbs/flavour the ice cream with vanilla).

fla'vouring n something added to improve the taste (artificial flavouring).

flaw n 1 a crack, a defect, imperfection (the flaw reduces the price of the antique vase). 2 any weakness that makes a person or thing less than perfect, less effective, etc (flaws in her character/spot the flaws in his argument):—adj flaw'less.

flax n a plant whose fibres are made into linen.

flax'en adj 1 like or of flax. 2 light yellow in colour (flaxen hair).

flay vb 1 to strip the skin off (flaying the dead horse). 2 to whip violently and cruelly (Roman soldiers flayed prisoners). 3 to criticize severely (a play flayed by critics).

flea n a small, jumping, bloodsucking insect (dogs with fleas).

fleck n a spot (flecks of soot on the white washing/flecks of white on the cat's black fur):—vb to mark with spots (black fur flecked with white).

fledg'ling n a young bird learning to fly.

flee vb (pt, pp fled) to run away, to run away from (villagers fleeing from the invading army).

fleece n the woolly coat of a sheep or similar animal:—vb 1 to cut the wool off (shepherds fleecing sheep). 2 (inf) to overcharge (fleece the customers).

fleet[1] n 1 a large number of ships, motorcars, aeroplanes, etc, together. 2 a large group of warships commanded by an admiral.

fleet[2] adj (fml) quick-moving (fleet of foot):—vb (fml) to pass quickly (time fleeting past).

fleet'ing adj (fml) passing quickly (fleeting moments).

fleet'ness n quickness.

flesh n 1 the soft substance that covers the bones of an animal to form its body (the trap cut into the rabbit's flesh). 2 this as food (animals that eat flesh rather than grass). 3 the eatable part of fruit (the flesh of a melon). 4 the body. 5 the desires of the body.

flesh'ly adj having to do with the body and its desires.

flesh'y adj fat (fleshy arms).

flew pt of **fly**.

flex vb to bend (flexing his muscles/flex one's toes):—n a cord of rubber-covered wires used to carry electric currents.

flex'ible adj 1 easily bent (flexible tubing). 2 easily changed, adaptable (flexible plans). 3 willing and able to change according to circumstances, adaptable (flexible people):—n flexibil'ity.

flick vb to strike lightly and quickly (flick a piece of dirt from his sweater/flick the light switch on):—also n.

flick'er vb **1** to shine or burn unsteadily (a candle flickering). **2** to flutter, to move quickly and lightly (with eyes flickering):—also n.

flier see **fly**.

flight n **1** the act of flying (birds shot down in flight). **2** the act of running away (the flight of the refugees). **3** the movement or path of a thing through the air (the flight of an arrow). **4** a journey made by air (a long-distance flight). **5** a number of birds flying together (a flight of geese). **5** a set of stairs or steps (a flight of wooden stairs).

flight attendant n a person whose job it is to look after passengers in an aircraft.

flight'y adj **1** changeable, unreliable (flighty young girls).

flim'sy adj **1** thin (a dress of flimsy material). **2** not strong, easily broken or destroyed (a flimsy box). **3** weak (a flimsy excuse).

flinch vb to draw back in fear or pain (flinched as the bully raised his hand).

fling vb (pt, pp **flung**) **1** to throw (fling papers on the floor). **2** to move suddenly and forcefully (fling from the room in a temper):—n **1** a throw (with one fling of the hammer). **2** a Scottish Highland dance.

flint n **1** a hard stone (rock containing a lot of flint). **2** a piece of hard mineral from which sparks can be struck (a flint for his lighter):—also adj.

flip vb (**flipped'**, **flip'ping**) **1** to turn over lightly but sharply (flip over the pages of the book). **2** to toss (flip a coin in the air):—also n.

flip'pant adj not serious, disrespectful (a flippant remark):—n **flip'pancy**.

flip'per, n a limb used by certain sea creatures (e.g. seal, turtle, penguin) when swimming.

flirt vb **1** to show interest in for a time only (flirt with the idea of emigrating). **2** to behave towards another as if attracted by or in order to attract (she was flirting with all the men at the party):—n one who plays at making love:—n **flirta'tion**.

flirta'tious adj fond of flirting.

flit vb (**flit'ted**, **flit'ting**) **1** to move quickly and lightly (bees flitting from flower to flower/flit from one idea to another). **2** (Scot) to move from one house to another.

float vb **1** to remain on the surface of a liquid (rafts floated on the water/swimmers floating on

their backs). **2** to start (a new business or company) by selling shares to the public. **3** to suggest, to put forward (float a few ideas at the meeting):—n **1** anything that floats (e.g. a raft, a buoy, etc) or helps to make something else float (e.g. the floats of a seaplane). **2** a low cart for carrying cattle, etc.

floata'tion, flota'tion n the starting of a company (the floatation of the company on the stock market).

flock[1] n **1** a company of birds or animals (a flock of sheep). **2** a number of people together (people arriving in flocks). **3** a congregation (a priest and his flock):—vb to come together in a crowd (people flocking to the sales).

flock[2] n **1** a tuft or flake of wool. **2** waste wool used for stuffing cushions, etc (a mattress made of flock).

floe n a large sheet of floating ice.

flog vb (**flogged'**, **flog'ging**) to beat, to thrash (flog wrongdoers):—n **flog'ging**.

flood n **1** an overflowing of water on to dry land. **2** a rush (of water, people, etc) (a flood of correspondence). **3** the flowing in of the tide:—vb **1** to overflow, to cover with water (water flooding the town). **2** to arrive in great quantities (letters flooded in).

flood'gate n a gate that when shut prevents the flow of water.

flood'light n a very bright lamp directed on to the outside of a building at night to light it up:—also vb:—n **flood'lighting**.

flood tide n the rising or inflowing tide.

floor n **1** the bottom surface of a room on which one walks (an uncarpeted floor). **2** any bottom surface (the floor of the ocean). **3** all the rooms, etc, on the same level in a building (rent the first and second floors):—vb **1** to make a floor (floor the room with pine). **2** to knock down (the boxer floored his opponent with one blow). **3** (inf) to ask someone a question that he or she cannot answer (completely floored by one of the exam questions).

flop vb (**flopped'**, **flop'ping**) **1** to sit or fall down heavily or loosely (flop down exhausted in a chair). **2** to hang or swing heavily or loosely (long hair flopping). **3** to fail completely, to be unsuccessful (the play flopped):—n a complete failure.

flop'py adj hanging loosely, not stiff (a floppy hat).

floppy disk n a small disk made of magnetic material on which computer data is stored and which can be removed from the computer. See **hard disk**.

flo'ra n all the plants in a country or region.

flor'al adj having to do with flowers (a floral arrangement/a floral pattern).

flor'id adj 1 red in colour (a florid complexion). 2 showy, over-elaborate, ornate (a florid style of decoration).

flor'in n a British coin worth two shillings, replaced by the 10 penny piece.

flor'ist n one who grows or sells flowers (ask the florist to make up a bouquet).

floss n 1 rough silk. 2 any fluffy substance. 3 waxed thread for cleaning between the teeth.

flotation see **floatation**.

flotil'la n 1 a small fleet. 2 a fleet of small ships.

flot'sam n floating wreckage (the flotsam from the wrecked ship).

flounce[1] vb to move sharply or quickly (flounced out in a temper):—also n.

flounce[2] n a gathered strip of cloth sewn by its upper edge round a skirt or dress and left hanging (a skirt with lace flounces).

floun'der[1] n a type of flatfish, the fluke.

floun'der[2] vb 1 to struggle helplessly or awkwardly (walkers floundering in the mud). 2 to be in doubt as to what to say next, to hesitate, to struggle when speaking (he lost his notes and floundered helplessly when giving the lecture).

flour n the meal of wheat, etc, ground into powder (wholemeal flour).

flourish [flur'-ish] vb 1 to get on well, to be very successful, to prosper (a company that is flourishing). 2 to grow well, to bloom (flowers flourished). 3 to wave about in a showy manner (flourish his letter of acceptance):—n 1 spoken words or handwriting that attract attention by being unusual. 2 a sudden short burst of music (a flourish of trumpets). 3 a bold sweeping movement or gesture (open the door to his guests with a flourish).

floury adj 1 covered with flour (floury hands). 2 like flour (floury potatoes).

flout vb to pay no attention to, to disobey openly and scornfully (flouting the school rules).

flow [flō] vb 1 to move steadily and easily, as water (tears flowing/keep the traffic flowing). 2 to proceed evenly and continuously (conversation flowing). 3 to fall or hang down loosely and freely (hair that flowed to her waist). 4 to be plentiful (the wine was flowing at the party):—n 1 a flowing movement, a stream. 2 the rise of the tide. 3 a continuous stream or supply (the flow of conversation/a flow of information).

flow chart n a diagram showing the sequence of stages in a process or system (a flow chart of the production process).

flow'er n 1 a blossom. 2 the best part of (the flower of the nation's young men):—vb to blossom or bloom.

flow'ery adj 1 full of flowers (flowery meadows). 2 patterned with flowers (a flowery wallpaper). 3 ornate, over-elaborate (flowery language).

fluc'tuate vb 1 to rise and fall, as a wave (prices fluctuating). 2 to vary, to change continually and irregularly (opinions that fluctuate):—n **fluctua'tion**.

flue n a passage in a chimney for carrying away air or smoke.

flu'ent adj able to speak or write quickly and easily (fluent in French/a fluent French speaker):—n **flu'ency**.

fluff n any soft or feathery material (fluff from blankets on his dark suit/the fluff on new-born chickens).

fluffy adj like fluff, soft and downy (fluffy little ducklings).

flu'id adj 1 able to flow, flowing. 2 able to change quickly (fluid arrangements). 3 smooth and graceful (dance with fluid movements):—n any substance that flows, as liquid or gas.

fluke[1] n 1 a type of flatfish, the flounder. 2 a tiny worm that causes disease in sheep.

fluke[2] n 1 the part of an anchor that hooks into the seabed. 2 one of the pointed parts on a whale's tail.

fluke[3] n (inf) a lucky chance (win by a fluke).

flum'mox vb to confuse, to disconcert (completely flummoxed by his frank questions).

flunk'ey n 1 a uniformed servant, a footman. 2 (inf) a person who treats someone else with too much respect and humility (a wealthy filmstar surrounded by flunkeys).

fluorescence [flŏ-êr-es'-êns] *n* a quality in certain substances that enables them to give very bright light for quite low expenditure of electricity.

fluoresc'ent *adj* having or showing fluorescence (*fluorescent paint*).

flu'oride *n* a chemical compound containing fluorine which is sometimes added to toothpaste and water supplies to prevent tooth decay.

flur'ry *n* **1** confused movement (*in a flurry of excitement when the visitors were due*). **2** a sudden rush of air, rain, etc (*a flurry of snow*):—*vb* to make anxious or confused (*unexpected visitors always flurried her*).

flush *vb* **1** to become suddenly red in the face (*flush with embarrassment/flushed with the heat*). **2** to cleanse by a flow of water (*flush the toilet*).—*n* **1** a sudden redness in the face (*heat bringing a flush to her face*). **2** a rush of water. **3** freshness, vigour (*in the first flush of youth*):—*adj* **1** (*inf*) having plenty of money (*he's flush since he's just been paid*). **2** level (*flush with the wall*).

flus'ter *vb* to make confused, to over-excite (*get flustered in an emergency*):—*also n.*

flute *n* **1** a wooden musical wind instrument. **2** a shallow hollow carved in a pillar:—*vb* **1** to play the flute. **2** to carve hollows or grooves.

flutist *same as* **flautist.**

flutt'er *vb* **1** to move the wings up and down without flying (*moths fluttering*). **2** to move about quickly (*flags fluttering in the breeze/fluttered her eyelashes*):—*n* **1** quick movement (*with a flutter of her eyelashes*). **2** (*inf*) excitement (*the handsome new arrival caused a flutter among the girls in the office*). **3** (*inf*) a bet, a gamble (*have a flutter on the horses*).

flux *n* **1** a flowing. **2** a state of continued change (*plans in a state of flux*). **3** a substance that helps metals to melt and join.

fly *vb* (*pt* flew, *pp* flown) **1** to move through the air on wings (*birds flying*). **2** to travel by aeroplane (*prefer to fly than go by train*). **3** to move quickly (*I must fly—I'll be late*). **4** to run away (*fly from the invading army*):—*n* **1** a common flying insect (*the house fly*). **2** a fishing hook covered with feathers to make it look like a fly. **3** (*old*) a one-horse carriage. **4** a flap, esp that closing the entrance to a tent:—*n* **fli'er, fly'er.**

fly'leaf *n* a blank page at the beginning or end of a book (*write a message on the flyleaf of the book that he gave her as a birthday present*).

fly'over *n* a bridge which carries a main road over another main road.

fly'paper *n* a sticky paper for catching and killing flies.

fly'wheel *n* a heavy wheel that helps to control the speed at which a machine works.

foal *n* a young horse or ass:—*vb* to give birth to a foal.·

foam *n* bubbles on the top of liquid, froth (*the foam on a glass of beer*):—*vb* to gather or produce foam (*a mad dog foaming at the mouth*).

fob *n* **1** a small pocket for a watch. **2** an ornamental watch chain:—*vb* (**fobbed'**, **fob'-bing**) to get rid of another by giving him or her something of little value (*fob the buyer off with a fake instead of a genuine Renoir/we wanted a final decision but he fobbed us off with some vague promises*).

fo'cal *adj* **1** of a focus. **2** central, main (*the room's focal point is a marble fireplace*).

fo'c'sle *see* **forecastle.**

fo'cus *n* (*pl* **fo'ci** [fō-ki] *or* **fo'cuses**) **1** a point at which rays of light meet. **2** a centre of interest or attention (*the beautiful woman was the focus of everyone's attention*):—*vb* **1** to bring to bear on one point (*focus his attention on the firm's financial problems*). **2** to get a clear image in the lens of a camera before taking a photograph.

fod'der *n* dried food for cattle.

foe *n* (*fml*) an enemy (*the foreign foe/regard his rival as a foe*).

foetus [fee'-tês] *n* the young animal or human in the egg or womb.

fog *n* a thick mist.

fogey, fogy [fō'-gi] *n* a person whose ideas are out of date (*teenagers think he was an old fogey for not liking loud pop music*).

fog'gy *adj* **1** misty (*a foggy day*). **2** confused, vague (*have just a foggy impression of what she looked like*).

foi'ble *n* (*fml*) a weakness in character (*his inability to be on time was one of his foibles*).

foil[1] *vb* to cause to fail, to defeat (*foil their attempt to burgle his house*).

foil² *n* **1** a very thin sheet of metal (*aluminium foil*). **2** the metal in which a precious stone is set. **3** anything placed alongside something else to make it show to advantage (*black was the perfect foil for her pale complexion*).

foil¹ *n* a blunt sword used in fencing.

foist *vb* by a trick, to get rid of something worthless or unwanted to another (*try to foist his old furniture on us/unwanted visitors foisting themselves on us*).

fold¹ *vb* **1** to bend one part of a thing over to cover another part (*fold the blanket in two*). **2** to enclose (*fold her in his arms*):—*n* **1** a line or crease made by folding (*iron out the folds in the sheets*). **2** the part doubled over.

fold² *n* a place where sheep are kept.

fold'er *n* a stiff cover for holding papers, letters, etc (*keep his insurance documents in a folder*).

fo'liage *n* (*fml*) the leaves of trees (*a plant with silvery green foliage*).

fo'lio *n* **1** a sheet of paper once folded. **2** the largest size of printed volume.

folk *n* **1** (*inf*) people (*the friendly folk next door*). **2** the people of a country or a particular part of a country (*townsfolk*). **1** (*inf*) *pl* relatives, parents (*take him home to meet her folks*).

folk'lore *n* all the stories, songs, beliefs, etc, that have been passed on from one generation of people to another (e.g. *folk dance, folk song, folk tale*).

fol'low *vb* **1** to go or come after (*follow her mother down the path*). **2** to be next in order to (*autumn follows summer*). **3** to go along (*follow the mountain path*). **4** to accept as a leader or a teacher (*follow Jesus*). **5** to result from (*disease that followed the famine*). **6** to understand (*I don't follow what you mean*).

fol'lower *n* a supporter (*followers of the football team*).

fol'lowing *n* all one's supporters (*a football team with a huge following*):—*adj* next in order (*the following day*).

fol'ly *n* **1** foolishness (*their folly is lending him money*). **2** a foolish act (*regret their follies*).

foment' *vb* **1** to bathe with hot water. **2** to apply hot bandages to. **3** to stir up (*fomenting civil unrest*).

fond *adj* **1** having a love or liking for (*fond of music/fond of her parents*). **2** loving (*fond glances*).

3 foolishly loving, indulged, doting (*spoilt by fond parents*). **4** hoped for but not likely to be realized (*fond hopes*):—*n* **fond'ness**.

fond'le *vb* to stroke, to touch lovingly (*fondling the dog's ear*).

font *n* **1** the basin holding the water for baptism. **2** a set of type of the same size and face (*also* **fount**).

food *n* that which can be eaten (*a shortage of food*).

food chain *n* a series of living things, each of which feeds on one below it in the series.

fool¹ *n* **1** a silly or stupid person (*he was a fool to leave his job*). **2** (*old*) a jester (*the fool in Shakespeare's plays*):—*vb* **1** to deceive (*succeed in fooling the police*). **2** to behave as if one were a fool (*fool around with the children*).

fool² *n* crushed fruit mixed with milk or cream.

fool'ery *n* foolish behaviour.

foolhar'dy *adj* foolishly bold, taking unnecessary risks, reckless (*it was foolhardy of her to climb the hill on her own/foolhardy swimmers going out of their depth*).

fool'ish *adj* silly, stupid (*a foolish thing to do/a foolish young man*):—*n* **fool'ishness**.

fool'proof *adj* unable to go wrong even when foolishly used (*the filing system is meant to be foolproof*).

fools'cap *n* large (folio) size writing or printing paper.

foot *n* (*pl* **feet**) **1** the part of the leg below the ankle. **2** the lowest part of anything (*the foot of the stairs/the foot of the page*). **3** a measure of length equal to 12 inches. **4** foot-soldiers:—*vb* (*inf*) to pay (*foot the bill*).

foot'ball *n* **1** a large ball for kicking. **2** a ball game for a team of eleven players, soccer.

foot'hills *npl* low hills at the bottom of mountains (*the foothills of the Himalayas*).

foot'hold *n* **1** a safe place for the feet (*footholds in the rock*). **2** a secure position from which to make progress (*try to get a foothold in industry*).

foot'ing *n* **1** a safe place for the feet (*a climber seeking a footing*). **2** balance (*miss his footing and fall*). **3** foundation, basis (*a business on a firm footing*). **4** relationship (*on a friendly footing with the boss*).

foot'lights *npl* lights on the floor at the front of the stage in a theatre.

foot'man *n* a uniformed manservant.

foot'note *n* a note at the foot of a page (*footnotes explaining part of the text*).

foot'pad[1] *n* (*old*) a robber.

foot'print *n* the mark left by a foot (*police examining footprints at the murder scene*).

foot'sore *adj* tired by much walking.

foot'step *n* the sound or mark made by the foot of someone walking (*hear footsteps behind me*).

fop *n* (*old*) a man who takes too much interest in his clothes (*a fop who is not interested in anything but his appearance*):—*n* **fop'pery**:—*adj* **fop'pish**.

for'age *n* food for cattle or horses:—*vb* **1** to gather forage. **2** to go out and look for food. **3** to search, to hunt, to rummage (*foraging around in the cupboard*).

for'ay *n* **1** a raid (*a foray into enemy territory to look for food*). **2** a vigorous but brief attempt to be involved in a different activity, profession, etc (*he made an unsuccessful foray into politics and decided to stick to the legal profession*):—*also vb.*

forbear'[1] *vb* (*pt* **forbore'**, *pp* **forborne'**) **1** to hold oneself back from doing (*forbear from critizing his son*). **2** (*old*) to be patient.

for'bear[2], **fore'bear** *n* an ancestor.

forbear'ance *n* **1** patience. **2** self-control.

forbid' *vb* (*pt* **forbade'**, *pp* **forbid'den**) to order not to do (*forbid his son to drive his car*).

forbid'ding *adj* rather frightening (*rather a forbidding expression*).

force *n* **1** strength, power (*the force of the wind*). **2** violence (*have to use force to get him into the car*). **3** an organized body of people (*the police force*). **4** *pl* the army, navy and airforce. **5** a person or thing that has great power (*a force in the local council*):—*vb* **1** to make (somebody do something) (*force him to lend them money*). **2** to get something by strength, violence or effort (*forcing his way through the crowd*). **3** to grow plants out of season under artificial conditions.

forced *adj* unnatural, strained (*a forced smile*).

force'ful *adj* strong, energetic (*a forceful speech/a forceful personality*):—*adv* **force'fully**.

for'ceps *n* a pincer-like instrument used by doctors and dentists to hold, lift or grip things.

for'cible *adj* done by force (*forcible entry to the house*).

ford *n* a place where a river is shallow enough to be crossed:—*vb* to wade across.

fore *adj* and *adv* in front:—*interj* (*in golf*) look out!

fore'arm[1] *n* the arm from the elbow to the wrist (*tennis players have strong forearms*).

forearm'[2] *vb* to arm or prepare in advance (*forearmed by a list of the questions the audience were likely to ask*).

forebear *see* **forbear**.

forebod'ing *n* a feeling that evil is going to happen (*a foreboding that he was going to die in the battle/look upon the future with foreboding*).

fore'cast *vb* (*pt, pp* **fore'cast**) to say what will happen in the future (*impossible to forecast the result of the match/try to forecast the result of the general election*):—*also n.*

forecastle [fōr'-käsl], **fo'c'sle** [fōk'-sêl] *ns* **1** the raised deck at the front of a ship. **2** the crew's quarters beneath that deck.

fore'father *n* an ancestor (*his forefathers went from Ireland to America*).

fore'finger *n* the finger next to the thumb (*point with his forefinger*).

fore'front *n* the front part (*in the forefront of the campaign against nuclear weapons*).

forego'[1] *vb* (*pt* **fore'went**, *pp* **fore'gone**) to go before, to precede.

forego'[2] *see* **forgo**.

forego'ing *adj* earlier, previous (*the foregoing passage in the book*).

foregone conclusion *n* an ending that can be foreseen with certainty (*it was a foregone conclusion that he would win*).

fore'ground *n* **1** the nearest objects shown in a picture (*a house in the background and two figures in the foreground*). **2** the nearest part of a view.

forehead [for'-id] *n* the part of the face above the eyebrows (*frown lines in her forehead*).

for'eign *adj* **1** belonging to or concerning another country (*foreign customers/a foreign holiday*). **2** strange (*meanness was foreign to her nature*). **3** out of place (*a foreign body in her eye*).

for'eigner *n* a person from a country other than one's own.

fore'land *n* a headland, a cape.

fore'leg *n* one of the front legs of an animal (*the racehorse broke its foreleg*).

fore'lock n a lock of hair on the forehead.

fore'man n **1** the man in charge of a group of workers (*the foreman on the building site*). **2** the chief person in a jury (*the foreman of the jury delivered the verdict*).

fore'most adj **1** most famous, best (*the foremost writer of his generation*). **2** most important (*the foremost issue before the committee*).

forename see **first name**.

foren'sic n having to do with the law or courts of law (*forensic medicine*).

fore'runner n **1** (*old*) one who goes before with a message or announcement. **2** an ancestor (*one of her forerunners was an explorer*). **3** a person or thing that comes before another (*a forerunner of the jet plane*).

foresee' vb (pt **foresaw'**, pp **foreseen'**) to see what is going to happen (*no one could have foreseen the accident*).

foreshad'ow vb to be a sign of future events (*his personal defeat in his own event foreshadowed the defeat of the whole team*).

fore'shore n the part of the shore between high and low water marks.

foreshort'en vb to draw objects in such a way that the parts farthest from the eye are shorter and so seem farther away in the picture.

fore'sight n the ability to guess and prepare for future events (*have the foresight to save for his old age*).

for'est n a large area covered by trees and undergrowth.

forestall' vb to anticipate what another is going to do and act before him or her (*her brother was going to tell her mother what she had done but she forestalled him by telling her mother herself*).

for'ester n an officer in charge of a forest.

for'estry n the study of planting and looking after forests.

fore'taste n an advance idea of what something is like (*a foretaste of what will happen to the firm when he is in charge*).

foretell' vb (pt, pp **foretold'**) to say what will happen in future, to prophesy (*claim to be able to foretell the future from the stars/she foretold that he would go to prison*).

fore'thought n care that the results of actions will be good (*have the forethought to book tickets in advance*).

forewarn' vb to warn in advance (*try to forewarn his brother that their father was angry*).

fore'word n a piece of writing at the beginning of a book to explain its purpose.

for'feit vb to lose or give up a right as a punishment (*forfeit his right to the throne/forfeited our respect by his behaviour*):—n that which is so lost or given up, a fine.

forgath'er vb to meet together (*forgather in the bar for a drink before dinner*).

forge n **1** a blacksmith's workshop. **2** a furnace for heating metal:—vb **1** to beat hot metal into shape. **2** to make by hard effort (*forging a new career*). **3** to imitate something in order to deceive (*forged the old man's signature on the will*).

forg'ery n **1** act of imitating something dishonestly, esp another's writing. **2** the imitation so made (*this is not his handwriting on the will—it's a forgery*).

forget' vb (pt **forgot'**, pp **forgot'ten**) to fail to remember (*she forgot his name/forget to bring her notes*).

forget'ful adj bad at remembering (*get forgetful as she grows older*):—n **forget'fulness**.

forget'-me-not n a small blue flower.

forgive' vb **1** to pardon (*forgive her disloyalty*). **2** to stop being angry or bitter towards, to stop blaming or wanting to punish (*forgive his son for crashing the car*):—n **forgive'ness**:—adj **forgiv'able**.

forgiv'ing adj quick to forgive (*a forgiving nature*).

forgo', **forego'** vb to give up, to do without (*make up her mind to forgo meat for life*).

fork n **1** an instrument with two or more pointed prongs used for digging, eating, etc. **2** a place where two roads meet. **3** a place where a tree or branch divides:—vb **1** to raise or dig with a fork (*fork the hay/fork the soil*). **2** to divide into branches (*the road forks outside the village*).

forlorn' adj left alone, miserable (*stand forlorn on the platform after he had gone*).

forlorn' hope n a plan that no one expects to succeed (*it was a forlorn hope that they would be in time to catch the train*).

form n **1** shape (*geometric forms such as triangles/a cake in the form of a train*). **2** a paper so printed that a message or information can be written in prepared spaces (*fill in an application form for the job*). **3** kind (*training in* several different forms). **4** a long bench (*sitting on forms in the school hall*). **5** a class in school. **6** arrangement (*poetic form*). **7** a fixed way of doing things (*the correct form of the wedding ceremony*):—*vb* **1** to make, to cause to take shape (*how do you form the past tense of the verb?/form the matches into a triangle/children forming an orderly queue*). **2** to come into existence, to take shape (*icicles forming on the edge of the garage roof/ideas slowing forming in her mind*).

form'al *adj* **1** following the accepted rules or customs (*a formal invitation*). **2** stiff in manner (*rather a formal old woman*).

formal'ity *n* **1** stiffness of manner. **2** something done only to carry out a rule (*sending you a letter of acceptance was a pure formality*). **3** care to follow rules and customs (*observe the formalities of the wedding ceremony*).

for'mat *n* the general shape and size of anything (*the format of the book*):—*vb* to prepare a computer disk so that data can be recorded and stored on it.

forma'tion *n* **1** act of forming. **2** an orderly arrangement (*planes flying in formation*).

form'ative *adj* helping to shape or develop (*in her formative childhood years*).

form'er *adj* earlier, past (*in former times*):—*pron* the person or thing previously mentioned.

form'erly *adv* in earlier times (*he formerly worked in a bank*).

for'midable *adj* **1** to be feared (*her mother seems rather formidable*). **2** difficult (*a formidable task*).

form'ula *n* (*pl* **form'ulae** *or* **form'ulas**) **1** a fixed arrangement of words. **2** a rule in arithmetic set down with signs or letters so that it can be used for any sum. **3** in chemistry, the use of signs or letters to show how substances, etc, are made up. **4** a statement of a principle accepted to cover differences of opinion.

form'ulate *vb* (*fml*) to express or set down clearly (*find it difficult to formulate her objections*).

forsake' *vb* (*pt* **forsook'**, *pp* **forsak'en**) to give up, to abandon (*forsake his family/forsake her religion*).

forswear' *vb* (*pt* **forswore'**, *pp* **forsworn'**) **1** (*old*) to give up altogether (*forswear smoking*). **2** (*fml*) to say what is not true when on oath.

fort *n* a place prepared for defence against an enemy.

forte[1] [for'-tā] *n* one's strong point, the thing at which one is best (*tact is not her forte*).

forte[2] [for'-tā] *adv* (*mus*) loud.

forth *adv* **1** onward in time place or order (*from that time forth*). **2** out (*go forth*).

forthcom'ing *adj* **1** about to happen, coming soon (*the forthcoming election*). **2** open, responsive (*a forthcoming personality*).

forth'right *adj* saying what one thinks (*a forthright person/a forthright reply*).

forthwith' *adv* (*fml* or *old*) at once (*she was told to leave forthwith*).

fortifica'tion *n* anything built or dug to protect defenders.

for'tify *vb* **1** to strengthen or enrich (*a fortified wine/cereal fortified with vitamins*). **2** to build defences around (*fortify the city against attack*).

fortiss'imo *adv* (*mus*) very loud.

for'titude *n* ability to suffer without complaint, courage, patience (*the dying woman bore her pain with fortitude*).

fort'night *n* two weeks.

fort'nightly *adj and adv* once in two weeks (*a fortnightly publication*).

fort'ress *n* a place prepared with strong defences against attackers (*a fortress built on the hill to repel invaders*).

fortu'itous *adj* (*fml*) happening by chance, accidental (*a fortuitous meeting*).

for'tunate *adj* lucky (*a fortunate young lady/come at a fortunate time*).

for'tune *n* **1** luck, chance (*she had the good fortune to win the lottery*). **2** wealth, a large amount of money (*make a fortune on the stock exchange*). **3** the supposed power that affects one's life (*fortune is on his side*).

for'um *n* (*pl* **for'ums** *or* **for'a**) **1** (*old*) the market place in a Roman town. **2** any place of public discussion (*the local pub is a forum for all local issues*). **3** a meeting involving a public discussion (*a forum on the subject of the local traffic policy*).

for'ward *adv* towards the front (*step forward*) (*also* **for'wards**):—*adj* **1** advancing (*a forward movement*). **2** near the front (*the forward part of the bus*). **3** in advance (*forward planning*). **4** developing more quickly than usual (*forward* *plans*). **5** bold, not shy (*a forward young woman*):—*vb* **1** to help forward (*forwarding our plans*). **2** to send on (*forward mail*).

fos'sil *n* **1** the remains of a plant or animal that have hardened into stone and so been preserved in shape in rock or earth. **2** a person whose ideas are out of date (*children regarding their parents as old fossils*).

fos'ter *vb* **1** to look after for a time, to bring up a child that is not one's own (*fostering the boy while his mother was unable to look after him*). **2** to encourage (*foster hopes/foster her daughter's talent*).

fos'ter-child *n* a child nursed and brought up by one not its parent:—*also ns* **fos'ter-brother, fos'ter-sister.**

fos'ter-father, fos'ter-mother *ns* those who bring up the child(ren) of other parents.

foul *adj* **1** dirty, disgusting (*a foul smell/a foul mess*). **2** stormy (*foul weather*). **3** against the rules (*foul play*). **4** nasty (*he was foul to his wife*). **5** obscene, bad (*use foul language*):—*vb* **1** to make or become dirty (*fouling the streets*). **2** to become entangled (*ropes getting fouled*). **3** to break the rules of a game (*foul his opponent*):—*n* an act against the rules of a game (*the referee said she committed a foul*).

foul play *n* **1** unfair play. **2** violence or murder (*police suspected foul play when they saw the body*).

found¹ *pt of* **find.**

found² *vb* **1** to start from the beginning, to set up (*found a new club*). **2** to give money to start a school, hospital, etc:—*n* **found'er.**

founda'tion *n* **1** the lowest part of a building upon which the walls stand (*lay the foundations of the new theatre*). **2** the amount of money given to start a school, hospital, etc. **3** the place started with such money.

foun'der *vb* **1** to fill with water and sink (*ships foundering*). **2** to come to nothing, to fail (*our plans foundered*).

found'ling *n* a child left by its parents and found by others .

foun'dry *n* a workshop where metals are melted and shaped.

fount *n* **1** (*old*) a spring of water. **2** (*fml*) a cause or beginning (*the fount of knowledge*). **3** a set of type of the same size and face (*also* **font**).

foun'tain *n* **1** a spring of water. **2** a jet of water thrown into the air from a pipe (*take a drink from the drinking fountain in the park*). **3** (*fml*) a beginning or source (*the fountain of knowledge*).

foun'tain pen *n* a pen containing a supply of liquid ink.

fowl *n* a bird, esp the farmyard cock or hen (*a boiling fowl*).

fowl'er *n* one who hunts or traps wild birds.

fox *n* **1** a dog-like animal with red fur and a bushy tail (*a fox killed by the hunt*). **2** a cunning or deceitful person:—*f* **vix'en.**

fox'glove *n* a plant with pink, white or purple bell-like flowers.

fox'trot *n* a ballroom dance.

fox'y *adj* **1** cunning (*with foxy cleverness*). **2** like a fox (*a foxy smell*). **3** reddish-brown (*hair of a foxy colour*). **4** sexually attractive (*a foxy lady*).

foy'er [foi'yā] *n* an entrance hall (*hotel foyer*).

fracas [fra'-kä] *n* an uproar, a noisy quarrel (*a bit of a fracas in the pub last night*).

frac'tion *n* **1** a part of a whole. **2** a small part (*a fraction of the cost*). **3** in arithmetic, part of a whole number, e.g. $\frac{1}{2}$, $\frac{1}{4}$, etc.

frac'tional *adj* very small (*a fractional improvement*).

frac'tious *adj* quarrelsome, easily angered, cross (*fractious children*).

frac'ture *n* **1** a break (*a fracture in the pipe*). **2** the breaking of a bone:—*vb* to break, to suffer a fracture (*fracturing a bone in his leg*).

fra'gile *adj* **1** easily broken (*fragile goods*). **2** not strong (*fragile after her illness*).

frag'ment *n* **1** a part broken off (*fragments of china*). **2** a small part (*not a fragment of common sense*):—*vb* **fragment'** to break into fragments.

frag'mentary *adj* made up of a number of pieces, with no clear connection between parts (*fragmentary evidence*).

fra'grance *n* **1** scent, sweet smell (*the fragrance of flowers*). **2** scent, perfume (*market a new fragrance*).

fra'grant *adj* sweet-smelling (*fragrant flowers*).

trail *adj* **1** weak, feeble, delicate (*frail old ladies*). **2** (*old*) easily tempted to do wrong.

frail'ty *n* weakness (*the frailty of the invalid*).

frame vb **1** to make, to construct (*framing a sentence/framed a reply/frame a plan*). **2** to put in a frame (*frame the painting*). **3** (*inf*) to cause someone to seem guilty of a crime (*they framed him by putting the stolen goods in his garden shed*):— n **1** the supports around which the rest of a thing is built (*the frame of the ship*). **2** the border of metal, wood, etc, placed around a picture (*a photograph frame*). **3** the body (*of slender frame*).

frame'work n the supports around which the rest of a thing is built (*the framework of the ship/the framework of their plans*).

franc n a currency unit, formerly of France, Belgium and Luxembourg (now the euro).

franchise [fran'-shīz] n **1** the right to vote, esp in elections to parliaments (*when women got the franchise*). **2** a special right given or sold by a company to one person or group of people to sell the company's goods or services in a particular place (*a hamburger franchise*).

Francis'can n a friar of the order of St Francis.

frank[1] adj **1** saying what one really thinks, forthright (*a frank person/a frank reply*). **2** open, honest-looking (*a frank face*):— n **frank'ness**.

frank[2] vb to put an official mark on a letter.

frank'fur'ter n a long thin smoked sausage.

frank'incense n a gum giving a sweet-smelling smoke when burned.

fran'tic adj **1** very anxious or worried (*frantic about her missing children/frantic mothers*). **2** wildly excited, hurried (*frantic pace of modern life*).

frater'nal adj brotherly (*fraternal love*).

frater'nity n **1** a group of people meeting for a common purpose. **2** (*fml*) the state of being brothers or like brothers.

frat'ernize vb to mix with in a friendly or brotherly way (*accused of fraternizing with the enemy*).

frat'ricide n **1** the murder of a brother (*accused of fratricide*). **2** one who murders his or her brother (*a convicted fratricide*).

fraud n **1** dishonesty (*found guilty of fraud for embezzling money*). **2** a deceiving trick (*carry out a number of frauds on trusting old women*). **3** a person who deceives (*the doctor turned out to be a fraud*).

fraud'ulent adj dishonest (*fraudulent behaviour*).

fraught adj **1** full of, loaded (*a situation fraught with danger*). **2** tense and anxious (*feeling fraught before the exam*). **3** tense (*have a fraught day*).

fray[1] n **1** a fight. **2** a noisy quarrel.

fray[2] vb **1** to wear away by rubbing (*rubbing against the wall had frayed the rope*). **2** to become worn at the edges (*material fraying easily*). **3** to upset, to exasperate (*with nerves frayed*).

freak n **1** a living creature of unnatural form. **2** a strange, unexpected happening (*by some freak snow fell in July*):— adj strange, unusual (*a freak accident*).

freak'ish adj **1** very unusual, strange (*a freakish result*). **2** changing the mind suddenly (*freakish and unreliable*).

freck'le, n a brownish-yellow spot on the skin:— adj **freck'led**.

free adj **1** at liberty, able to do what one wants (*former prisoners now free/animals free to wander*). **2** not forced or persuaded to act, think, speak, etc, in a particular way (*the right to free speech*). **3** not occupied (*no rooms free in the hotel*). **4** generous (*free with his money*). **5** costing nothing (*free goods/goods given free*). **6** open, frank (*a free manner*):— n **1** to set at liberty (*freeing the prisoner*). **2** to set free from (*freed him from his responsibility*).

free'dom n **1** the state of being at liberty (*prisoners enjoying their freedom*). **2** the right to act, think, speak, etc, as one pleases without interference (*freedom of speech*). **3** the state of being without pain (*freedom from pain*). **4** the unrestricted use of something (*have the freedom of the house*).

free'hand n drawn by hand (*draw a map of the British Isles freehand*).

free'hold n land possessed completely, and so free from all payments except taxes.

free'lance n one, esp a journalist or artist, who works for himself and not any group or organization:— vb to work in such a way (*freelancing for various newspapers*).

free'man n one who is given the freedom of a town, i.e. is allowed certain rights in the town as an honour.

free'ma'son n one belonging to a certain secret society whose members try to help each other:— n **freema'sonry**.

free-range adj of eggs, laid by hens which are allowed to move around freely.

free'thinker n one who tries to work out his or her own ideas about God and religion.

free trade n the exchanging of goods without making a customs charge on imports.

freeze vb (pt **froze**, pp **fro'zen**) 1 to harden because of cold (a dessert left to freeze). 2 to become or make into ice (the pond sometimes freezes). 3 to be very cold (it's freezing today). 4 to make (food) very cold so as to preserve it (freeze raspberries).5 to become suddenly still (he froze when he saw the gunman).

freez'er n a piece of electrical equipment or a compartment of a refrigerator which freezes and preserves food at very low temperatures.

freight [frāt] n 1 the cargo of a ship. 2 the load on a goods train. 3 the cost of transporting goods (freight included in the price of the goods).

freight'er n a cargo ship.

French fries another name for chips. See **chip**.

fren'zied adj wild, uncontrolled (a frenzied attack on the victim).

fren'zy n 1 a sudden attack of madness (kill his friend in a frenzy).2 uncontrollable excitement or feeling (the fans at the pop concert worked themselves into a frenzy).

fre'quency n 1 the number of times something happens (increase the frequency of his visits to his father). 2 the number of waves, vibrations, etc, per second.

fre'quent adj happening often, common (a frequent occurrence):—vb [free-kwent'] to visit often (frequent the local wine bar).

fres'co n (pl **fres'coes** or **fres'cos**) a picture painted on plaster.

fresh adj 1 new (no fresh news). 2 not tired (feeling fresh after a night's sleep). 3 cool (fresh air). 4 not stale (fresh bread). 5 not frozen or canned (fresh vegetables). 6 not salted (fresh butter).

fresh'en vb 1 to make or become fresh (the air has freshened). 2 to cause to become less untidy, etc (freshen oneself up for dinner).

fresh'et n 1 a river in flood. 2 a stream of fresh water.

fret vb (**fret'ted**, **fret'ting**) 1 to wear away by rubbing (rope becoming fretted). 2 to worry, to be anxious, to be discontented (children fretting while their mother is away).

fret'ful adj troubled, peevish, irritable (overtired children getting fretful).

fret'saw n a very narrow saw used in fretwork.

fret'work n a way of cutting pieces out of thin wood so as to make ornamental designs.

friable [frī'-êbl] adj (fml) easily crumbled or made into powder.

fri'ar n a member of one of several Roman Catholic religious orders.

fri'ary n a convent of friars.

fric'tion n 1 rubbing, a rubbing together (a rope worn by friction). 2 the resistance felt when one object is moved against another (friction between the wheels of a car and the road). 3 disagreement (some friction between the two departments).

Friday n one of the seven days of the week, between Thursday and Saturday.

fridge n a refrigerator.

friend n a close companion:—**Society of Friends** the religious group also known as the Quakers.

friend'ly adj 1 kind (friendly people). 2 fond of or liking one another (they have been friendly since their schooldays):—n **friend'liness**.

friend'ship n the state of being friends (form a friendship/value her friendship).

frieze n a decorative border round the top of the wall of a room.

frig'ate n a small fast warship.

fright n a sudden feeling of fear, a shock (take fright and run away/get a fright when she saw the strange man).

fright'en vb to make afraid (the strange noise frightened the children).

fright'ful adj 1 dreadful, causing fear (a frightful experience when the car crashed/the corpse was a frightful sight). 2 (inf) very bad, dreadful (wearing a frightful dress/the film was frightful).

frig'id adj 1 (fml) cold, frozen (the frigid areas of the world). 2 cold and unemotional, unfriendly (give a frigid stare/a frigid welcome). 3 having no sexual desire:—n **fri-gid'ity**.

frill n 1 a loose ornamental edging of cloth gathered or pleated at one end and sewn on to a garment. 2 an unnecessary ornament (a plain room with no frills):—adj **frill'y**.

fringe n 1 an ornamental edging of hanging threads (*a skirt with a fringe round the hem*). 2 hair arranged to fall over the forehead (*a fringe nearly covering her eyes*). 3 the edge (*the fringe of the lake*):—vb to border.

fripp'ery n cheap or showy ornaments.

frisk vb to jump and dance about, to play about joyfully (*lambs frisking about*).

frisk'y adj playful, active (*old people frisky for their age*).

fritt'er n any sweet or tasty food cut small, fried in batter and served hot (*banana fritters*):—vb to waste (*frittering away money on sweets/fritter away her time*).

frivol'ity n fun, lack of seriousness.

friv'olous adj 1 interested only in amusement (*frivolous nature/a frivolous man*). 2 not taking important matters seriously, flippant (*make frivolous comments*). 3 not serious, playful, light-hearted (*frivolous pleasures*).

frizz vb to curl (*frizz her hair by perming*).

frizz'le vb 1 to curl. 2 to fry with a hissing noise (*bacon frizzling in the pan*).

fro adv:—to and fro forward and back again (*wander to and fro along the sea front*).

frock n 1 a woman's outer garment (*a summer frock*). 2 the long loose-sleeved gown worn by a monk, etc.

frock'coat n a double-breasted knee-length jacket formerly worn by men.

frog n a four-footed land and water creature (*tadpoles growing into frogs*).

frolic vb (**frol'icked, frol'icking**) to play about, to dance or jump about happily (*children frolicking around the garden/lambs frolicking*):—n a trick played for fun, lively amusement.

frol'icsome adj playful, ready for fun (*frolicsome puppies*).

frond n a leaf, esp of a palm or fern.

front n 1 the forward part of anything. 2 in war, the place where the fighting is going on (*news from the front*):—also adj:—vb to face, to stand before.

front'age n the front of a building (*a marble frontage*).

front'al adj having to do with the front (*a frontal attack*).

fron'tier n the boundary between one country and another (*show passports at the frontier*).

fron'tispiece n the picture at the beginning of a book, opposite the title page.

frost n frozen dew or moisture freezing (*young plants killed by a late frost*):—vb 1 to cover with frost (*fields frosted over in winter*). 2 to cover with icing (*frost the birthday cake*). 3 to treat glass so that it cannot be seen through (*frosted glass on the bathroom window*).

frost'bite n injury caused to the body by very severe cold:—adj **frost'bitten**.

frost'ing n icing for cakes (*pink frosting on the birthday cake*).

frost'y adj 1 covered with frost (*frosty roofs*). 2 cold because of frost (*a frosty day*). 3 unfriendly (*a frosty manner*).

froth n a mass of tiny bubbles on the surface of liquid, foam (*the froth on a glass of beer*):—vb to throw up froth (*beer frothing in the glass*):—adj **froth'y**.

frown vb to wrinkle the forehead, to scowl, to look angry (*frown at the children's bad behaviour/frown in disapproval*):—also n:—**frown on** to discourage, to disapprove of (*frown on staff leaving early*).

frow'zy adj 1 (*fml*) stuffy (*frowzy old women*). 2 untidy, shabby (*a frowzy room*).

fruc'tify vb (*fml*) 1 to cause to bear fruit. 2 to bear fruit.

fru'gal adj 1 careful, not wasteful (*he's frugal with money*). 2 very small, meagre (*a frugal meal*):—n **frugal'ity**.

fruit n 1 the part of a plant that produces the seed, esp when eaten as a food (*apples, pears and other fruits*). 3 result (*the fruits of his research*).

fruit'erer n one who sells fruit and vegetables.

fruit'ful adj 1 (*old*) fertile. 2 having good results (*fruitful discussions*).

frui'tion n fulfilment, a successful ending (*plans finally coming to fruition*).

fruit'less adj unsuccessful (*a fruitless search*).

frump n a badly or unfashionably dressed woman (*she's such a frump although she is very wealthy*).

frustrate' vb 1 to make to fail (*frustrating their attempt*). 2 to cause to have feelings of disappointment or dissatisfaction (*frustrated by the dullness of her job/delays that frustrated her*):—n **frustra'tion**.

fry[1] vb to cook in fat (*fry bacon*):—n anything fried.

fry[2] n (*pl* **fry**) young fishes.

fuchsia [fū'-sha] *n* a shrub with long hanging bell-shaped flowers.

fud'dle *vb* to make stupid or confused (*fuddled with drink*).

fudge *n* a soft sweet:—*interj* (*old*) nonsense!

fuel [fū'-êl] *n* 1 material to keep a fire going (*coal and logs as fuel*). 2 material used for producing heat or power by burning (*high fuel bills because of the central heating system*).

fu'gitive *n* one who is running away:—*adj* 1 (*fml*) passing quickly (*fugitive hours*). 2 escaping (*fugitive prisoners*):—*n* a person who flees from danger, pursuit or duty.

fugue [fūg] *n* a musical composition.

ful'crum *n* (*pl* **ful'crums** *or* **ful'cra**) the support on which a lever rests as it moves.

fulfil' *vb* (**fulfilled'**, **fulfil'ling**) 1 to carry out successfully, to complete (*fulfil tasks/fulfil promises*). 2 to satisfy, to meet (*fulfil the entrance requirements*):—*n* **fulfil'ment**.

full *adj* 1 holding as much as possible (*a full bucket of water*). 2 complete (*a full report*):—*n* **full'ness**.

full *vb* to clean and thicken cloth:—*n* **full'er**.

full'-blown *adj* fully opened (*full-blown roses*).

ful'mar *n* a type of sea bird.

ful'minate *vb* 1 (*fml*) to thunder. 2 to speak loudly and threateningly (*father fulminating about her coming in late*):—*n* **fulmi-na'tion**.

ful'some *adj* overmuch (*fulsome praise/fulsome apologies*).

fum'ble *vb* 1 to feel for something one cannot see (*fumbling in the dark for the light switch*). 2 to handle clumsily (*fumble the catch and drop the ball*).

fume *n* smoke, vapour (*paint fumes/petrol fumes*):—*vb* 1 to give off fumes. 2 (*inf*) to show anger (*fuming about his insulting remarks*).

fu'migate *vb* to disinfect by means of fumes (*fumigating the room after the patient died of an infectious fever*):—*n* **fumiga'tion**.

fun *n* merriment, amusement, enjoyment (*children having fun in the park*):—*adj* amusing, enjoyable (*have a fun time*).

function *n* 1 the work that a thing is made or planned to perform, use (*the function of the clutch in a car/the function of the liver*). 2 duties (*his function is to supervise the workers*). 3 (*fml*) a public ceremony or party (*the firm's Christmas function*):—*vb* 1 to work as intended. 2 to act.

func'tional *adj* designed with a view to its use (*functional rather than decorative furniture*).

func'tionary *n* (*fml*) an official (*council functionaries*).

fund *n* 1 an amount laid aside till needed (*a Christmas fund*). 2 money collected or kept for a purpose (*the church repair fund*).

fundamen'tal *adj* having to do with the beginning or most necessary parts of something, of great importance (*the fundamental principles of mathematics/a fundamental difference*):—*also n*.

fundamen'talism *n* the belief that the whole of the Bible is to be taken literally.

fu'neral *n* 1 burial of the dead. 2 the ceremonies performed at burial.

fune'real *adj* gloomy, sad, dark (*funereal music/a funereal atmosphere*).

fun'gal *adj* having to do with or caused by a fungus (*a fungal infection*).

fun'gus *n* (*pl* **fun'gi** *or* **fun'guses**) 1 a mushroom, toadstool or similar plant. 2 an unhealthy growth on an animal or plant (*roses affected by a fungus*).

funk *vb* (*inf*) to fear to do, to be frightened (*funk telling his mother about the broken window*):—*n* a state of fear (*in a funk about telling his parents about failing his exams*).

fun'nel *n* 1 a hollow cone used for pouring liquids into bottles etc (*use a plastic funnel to pour cooking oil into a bottle*). 2 a passage by which smoke etc, escapes (*the funnel of a steamship*).

fun'ny *adj* 1 amusing, humorous (*a funny joke*). 2 strange, odd (*he's a funny man—he doesn't like chocolate*).

fur *n* 1 the short soft hair of certain animals (*a cat's fur*). 2 the skin of an animal with the hair still attached, used as a garment (*wear a stole made of silver fox fur*). 3 a coating (e.g. on the tongue).

fur'bish *vb* to polish, to make bright by rubbing (*furbish the family silver*).

furious *see* **fury**.

furl *vb* to roll up (a sail, flag, etc).

fur'long *n* the eighth part of a mile (220 yards).

furlough [fur'-lō] *n* (*fml*) permission to be absent from work for a certain time (*obtain furlough from the army*).

fur'nace n an enclosed place in which great heat can be produced by fire (*a furnace for melting iron ore/a furnace that provides the office's central heating*).

fur'nish vb **1** to provide what is necessary (*furnish them with all the necessary information*). **2** to put tables, chairs, beds and other necessary articles in a house (*furnish the house gradually*).

fur'nishings npl the fittings in a house.

fur'niture n the articles (tables, chairs, etc) needed in a house or office.

furore [fû-rō'-rä] n great excitement or eagerness (*the furore of the wedding preparations*).

fur'rier n one who deals in furs.

fur'row n **1** the trench cut in the earth by a plough. **2** a wrinkle (*furrows in her brow*):—vb **1** to plough. **2** to wrinkle (*furrowed her brow*).

fur'ry adj covered with fur (*furry toy animals*).

further adv **1** besides (*he is hardworking—further, he is honest*). **2** farther (*unable to go any further without a rest*):—adj **1** more distant. **2** more (*no further use*):—vb to help forward (*furthering the cause of freedom*).

furthermore adv besides, in addition (*he is poor—furthermore he is homeless*).

furthermost adj most distant (*the furthermost point in the British Isles*).

fur'tive adj stealthy, done secretly (*cast a furtive look around before letting herself into the house*).

fu'ry n rage, great anger (*fly into a fury on discovering the damage to his property*):—adj **fu'rious.**

fuse[1] vb **1** to melt by heat (*lead fuses at a low temperature*). **2** to melt together as a result of

great heat (*copper and tin fuse to form bronze*). **3** (*of an electrical appliance or circuit*) to stop working or cause to stop working because of the melting of a fuse (*fusing all the lights*). **4** to join together (*ideas that fused*):—n easily melted wire used to complete an electric current.

fuse[2] n a tube of slow-burning substance used to explode shells, bombs, dynamite, etc (*light the fuse*).

fuselage [fû'-zê-läj] n the body of an aeroplane.

fusillade[1] n **1** the firing of many guns together. **2** (*fml*) a rapid, continuous stream (*a fusillade of criticism*).

fu'sion n **1** act of melting (*a metal formed by the fusion of two other metals*). **2** a joining together to make one (*a literary work that is a fusion of several different styles*).

fuss n anxiety or excitement over unimportant things.

fuss'y adj worrying over details, hard to please.

fus'ty adj stuffy, having a stale smell (*fusty unused rooms*).

futile adj having no useful result (*a futile search/futile attempts*):—n **futil'ity.**

fu'ture adj about to happen, coming (*present and future projects*):—n the time to come (*in the future we will take more care/the future of the factory is uncertain*).

fuzz n **1** a mass of fine light hair or similar substance (*apricots covered in fuzz*). **2** (*inf*) the police.

fuzz'y adj **1** covered in fuzz (*toy fuzzy animals*). **2** not clear, blurred (*a fuzzy television picture*).

G

gab vi to chatter or talk idly:—n idle chat:—**gift of the gab** the ability to speak well or at length (*it is important for salespeople to have the gift of the gab*).

gab'ble vb to talk too quickly and not very clearly (*she was so upset after the accident that she was just gabbling/police unable to understand her gabbled account of the event*):—n quick unclear talk (*the gabble of excited children*).

gab'erdine n a strong cloth usu of wool.

ga'ble n the pointed top to the end wall of a building with a sloping roof.

gad vb (**gad'ded, gad'ding**) (*inf*) to go around from place to place, usu in order to amuse oneself (*she was gadding about the town while everyone else was working*).

gad'fly n a cattle-biting fly.

gad'get n a small useful tool or machine (*labour-saving kitchen gadgets*).

gaff n 1 a stick with an iron hook used for landing fish. 2 a pole to which the top end of certain types of sails is fixed.

gaffe n a mistake, a blunder, an unintentional social mistake (*I committed a gaffe when I asked how his wife was—they are divorced*).

gaff'er n 1 (*old*) an old man (*gaffers of the village sitting on a bench in the sun*). 2 the man in charge of a group of workmen.

gag vb (**gagged', gag'ging**) to stop somebody speaking by forcibly stopping the mouth (*burglars gagging the bank staff*):—n 1 something put in the mouth to prevent speech (*use a scarf as a gag*). 2 a joke (*comedians telling the same old gags*).

gage n 1 something given as a sign that a promise will be kept, a pledge. 2 (*old*) something (e.g. a glove) thrown down as a challenge.

gag'gle n 1 a flock of geese. 2 a disorderly group of people (*a gaggle of neighbours gossiping about the accident*).

gai'ety n fun, enjoyment (*the gaiety of the wedding reception/the gaiety of the children playing*).

gai'ly see **gay**.

gain vb 1 to obtain (*gain an advantage/gain support for the scheme*). 2 to have an increase in (*gain weight/gain speech*). 3 to reduce between oneself and someone or something (*gain on the car in front*). 4 (*fml*) to reach (*gain the safety of her home*):—n profit, advantage.

gain'ful adj (*fml*) paid, profitable (*gainful employment*).

gait n manner of walking (*walk with a rolling gait*).

gait'er n a covering of cloth leather, etc, for the lower leg and ankle.

ga'la n 1 a day or time of feasting and rejoicing (*a miners' gala*). 2 a meeting for certain sports (*a swimming gala*).

gal'antine n cooked chopped veal or chicken served cold in its own jelly.

gal'axy n 1 a belt of stars stretching across the sky (e.g. the Milky Way). 2 a company of well-known, impressive, etc, people (*a galaxy of stars at the film premiere*).

gale n a strong wind (*ships wrecked in the gale*).

gall[1] [gål] n 1 a fluid that comes from the liver and helps the body to digest food. 2 (*fml*) bitterness of feeling, hatred (*full of gall at being beaten*). 3 (*inf*) impudence (*have the gall to come uninvited*).

gall[2] n a painful sore, esp on a horse, caused by rubbing:—vb 1 to make sore by rubbing. 2 to annoy or irritate (*it galls her to think that he earns more than she does*).

gall[3] n a nut-like growth on oaks and other trees.

gal'lant adj (*fml*) brave, noble (*a gallant soldier*):—adj **gallant'** (*esp old*) polite and attentive to women (*be gallant and open the door for the lady*).

gal'lantry n 1 (*fml*) bravery (*receive a medal for gallantry in battle*). 2 (*esp old*) politeness to women (*show his gallantry by placing his cloak on the ground for the queen to walk on*).

gal'leon n (*old*) a large sailing ship with several decks, as used by the Spaniards in the 15th and 16th centuries.

gal'lery n 1 a raised floor over part of a church, theatre, etc (*a good view of the stage from the front row of the gallery*). 2 a narrow passage in a mine. 3 a room in which pictures, etc are displayed (*an exhibition of modern art at the local gallery*).

gal'ley *n* **1** (*old*) a long low ship with sails and oars. **2** a ship's kitchen.

gal'ley slave' *n* (*old*) a slave made to work at the oars of a galley.

gallivant' *vb* to go about amusing or enjoying oneself (*spend her time gallivanting instead of looking for a job*).

gal'lon *n* a measure for liquids or grain (= 8 pints or 4.546 litres).

gal'lop *n* a horse's fastest speed:—*vb* **1** to go at a gallop (*racehorses galloping to the finish*). **2** (*inf*) to move or do very quickly (*children galloping through their homework so that they can watch TV*).

gal'lows *n or npl* a wooden frame for hanging criminals.

galore' *adj* in plenty (*bargains galore at the sales*).

galosh' *n* an overshoe, usu of rubber, to protect the shoes in wet weather.

gal'vanism *n* the use of electric currents in medical treatment.

gal'vanize *vb* **1** to give an electric shock. **2** to put on a coat of metal by electricity, to electroplate. **3** to rouse to activity (*galvanized into action under threat of losing his job*).

galvano'meter *n* an instrument for measuring electric currents.

gam'bit *n* **1** in chess, opening moves in which one piece is given up to gain a strong position for others. **2** (*often* **opening gambit**) a starting move, action, remark, etc (*the new manager's opening gambit was to say that there would be redundancies*).

gam'ble *vb* **1** to play for money, to bet. **2** to take risks (*the burglars gambled on there being no one in the house*):—*n* a risk:—*n* **gam'bler**:—*n* **gam'bling**.

gamboge [gam-bōzh'] *n* **1** a gum used for colouring. **2** a deep yellow colour.

gam'bol *vb* (**gam'bolled**, **gam'bolling**) to jump about playfully:—*also n*.

game[1] *n* **1** a sporting contest (*interested in games such as football and hockey*). **2** a single part of a set into which a game is divided (*lose a game at tennis*). **3** an amusement or diversion, a pastime (*it was just a game—not to be taken seriously*). **4** (*inf*) a scheme, a trick (*wonder what his little game is*). **5** birds or animals hunted for sport (*shoot game such as pheasants*):—*adj* **1** brave, plucky (*game enough to go on playing after being injured*). **2** willing, ready (*if you want to go to the cinema, I'm game*):—*vb* to gamble (*to make money gaming*):—**make game of** (*fml*) make fun of, mock (*make game of him for being small*).

game[2] *adj* lame, injured (*his game leg*).

game'keeper *n* one who looks after birds or animals that are to be hunted (*a gamekeeper on the grouse moors*).

gam'in *n* a cheeky quick-witted street child, a street urchin.

gam'ing *n* gambling (*lose a fortune on gaming*).

gam'mon *n* the end piece of a side of bacon, salted and smoked (*a slice of grilled gammon*):—*vb* to talk nonsense, to deceive.

gam'ut *n* **1** the musical scale. **2** all the known musical notes. **3** the whole range of anything (*the gamut of emotions*).

gan'der *n* a male goose.

gang *n* **1** a group of people working on the same job (*the gang working on the new road*). **2** a group of criminals working together (*the gang that raided the bank*).

gang'er *n* (*inf*) the foreman of a gang of workers.

gang'lion *n* (*pl* **gang'lions** *or* **gang'lia**) **1** a collection of nerve cells. **2** a swelling.

gan'grene *n* the rotting away of a part of the body (*have his foot amputated because of gangrene*):—*adj* **gan'grenous**.

gang'ster *n* a member of an organized gang of criminals (*local shopkeepers terrorized by gangsters threatening to rob them*).

gang'way *n* **1** a movable footbridge from a ship to the shore. **2** a passage between rows of seats (*the gangway in a theatre*).

gan'net *n* a sea bird.

gaol [jāl], **gaolbird**, **gaoler** *same as* **jail**, **jailbird**, **jailer**.

gap *n* **1** an opening (*a gap in the fence*). **2** a space between (*bridge the gap between the banks*). **3** space (*the gap in his knowledge*).

gape *vb* **1** to stare open-mouthed (*stand gaping at the piles of gold*). **2** to be wide open (*the entrance to the cellar gaped open*).

gap year *n* a year's break taken by students, especially between school and university, usually spent travelling, doing voluntary work overseas etc.

gar'age n **1** a building in which a motor car can be kept (*a garage attached to the house*). **2** a shop where motorcars are repaired.

garb n (*old*) dress, clothes:—vb (*old*) to clothe (*garbed in silk*).

gar'bage n **1** (*esp Amer*) waste food, rubbish (*household garbage*). **1** (*inf*) nonsense, anything of little value (*newspaper reporting that was nothing but garbage*).

gar'bled adj mixed up and muddled (*a garbled account of the accident*).

gar'den n a piece of land on which flowers or vegetables are grown:—vb to look after a garden, often as a hobby (*try to find time to garden*):—n **gar'dener**.

gargan'tuan adj huge, gigantic (*a gargantuan appetite*).

gar'gle vb to wash the throat with a mouthful of liquid by blowing it up and down in the back of the mouth (*gargling to cure a sore throat*):—n a liquid prepared for gargling.

gar'goyle n a grotesquely or fancifully carved spout to carry away water from a roof gutter (*a cathedral with gargoyles*).

gar'ish adj flashy, unpleasantly bright (*garish colours*).

gar'land n a wreath of flowers (*wear a garland round her neck*):—vb to decorate with a garland.

gar'lic n a plant with a strong-smelling bulb used in cookery (*chop up cloves of garlic*).

gar'ment n (*fml*) any article of clothing (*a shop selling only ladies' garments*).

gar'net n a red mineral, sometimes a precious stone.

gar'nish vb to decorate (*garnish the dish with parsley*).

gar'nishing n that which decorates, decoration (*use watercress as garnishing*).

garr'et n a small room just under the roof of a house, an attic (*servants sleeping in the garret*).

garr'ison n the soldiers sent to a place to defend it:—vb to send soldiers to defend (*troops garrisoning the coastal towns*).

garrotte [gar-rot'] vb (*old*) to kill or make senseless by stopping the windpipe, esp with wire (*robbers garrotting their victims*).

garr'ulous adj given to talking too much (*garrulous neighbours standing gossiping*):—ns **garrul'ity**, **garr'ulousness**.

gar'ter n **1** a band of elastic to hold up a stocking. **2** the badge of the Order of the Garter, the highest rank of knighthood in Britain.

gas n **1** matter in the form of an air-like vapour. **2** any of various gases or mixtures of gases used as fuel (*natural gas/coal gas*). **3** the vapour given off by a substance at a certain heat. **4** (*Amer*) petrol.

gas'eous adj of gas (*gaseous fumes*).

gash n a wide deep wound or cut:—vb to cut deep (*gash his thumb with a carving knife*).

gas'ket n a thin pad for tightening the cylinder head of an engine.

gas mask n a mask that enables one to breathe when surrounded by poisonous gas (*gas masks issued to everyone in World War II*).

gas meter n an instrument that measures the amount of gas used to heat or light a house (*read the gas meter*).

gas'oline n (*esp Amer*) petrol.

gasom'eter n a large tank for storing gas.

gasp vb **1** to breathe with difficulty, to pant (*gasping for breath*). **2** to draw in the breath suddenly through the mouth (*gasp in horror at the sight*):—n the act or sound of gasping (*his dying gasp/a gasp of horror*).

gas'sy adj full of gas, fizzy (*gassy drinks*).

gas'tric adj having to do with the stomach (*a gastric complaint*).

gastri'tis n a disease of the stomach.

gastronom'ic, gastronom'ical adjs having to do with gastronomy (*the gastronomic delights of France*).

gastron'omy n the art of good eating.

gate n **1** a movable frame of wood, iron, etc, to close an opening in a wall or fence (*the garden gate*). **2** an entrance or way out, esp in an airport (*the boarding gate*). **3** the number of people who pay to see a game (*expecting a large gate for the football match*). **4** the total sum of money paid for entrance to a sports ground.

gâteau [ga'-tō] n (*pl gâteaux or gâteaus*) a large cake, often filled and decorated with cream (*a chocolate gateau for desert*).

gate'crash vb to attend a party, etc, without an invitation.

gate'crasher n a person who gatecrashes (*police sent to get rid of the gatecrashers*).

gate'legged ta'ble n a table with a folding leg that is opened outwards to support a leaf.

gate'way n 1 the opening closed by a gate (*the gateway to the orchard*). 2 the way or path to (*the gateway to a successful career*).

gath'er vb 1 to bring or come together (*a crowd gathered*). 2 to collect, to pick (*gather wild flowers*). 3 to draw cloth together in small folds (*a skirt gathered at the waist*). 4 to guess, to come to the conclusion (*we gather that he is ill*):—n a fold in cloth held in position by thread.

gath'ering n 1 a meeting (*a gathering of protesters against the motorway*). 2 (*old*) a sore containing infected matter.

gauche [gōsh] adj awkward and clumsy, apt to say or do the wrong thing in company (*a gauche young girl/it was gauche of her to mention his personal problems in public*).

gaucho [gou'-tsho] n a South American cowboy.

gaudy [gă'-di] adj showy, flashy, too bright (*gaudy colours*):—n gau'diness.

gauge [găj] vb 1 to measure (*instruments that gauge the diameter of the wire*). 2 to make an estimate of (*gauging the strength of the wind from the movement of trees*). 3 to make a judgment about, to judge (*try to gauge his likely reaction*):—n 1 a measuring-rod. 2 a measuring instrument. 3 the distance between the two rails of a railway. 4 a help to guessing accurately (*a reliable gauge of his character*).

gaunt adj very thin, haggard (*the gaunt faces of starving people*).

gaunt'let n 1 (*old*) an iron glove worn as part of a suit of armour. 2 a type of glove covering the wrist (*driving gauntlets*):—**run the gauntlet** to be criticized or attacked from all sides (*have to run the gauntlet of a lot of newspaper articles on his private life*):—**throw down the gauntlet** to challenge (*throw down the gauntlet and challenge him to a tennis match*).

gauze n a light cloth that one can see through (*bandages of gauze*).

gav'el n a small wooden hammer used to call a meeting to order (*the auctioneer's gavel*).

gawk'y, gawk'ish adjs clumsy, awkward (*gawky teenagers*).

gay adj 1 homosexual (*gay men/a gay bar*). 2 lively, fond of enjoyment, cheerful (*in a gay mood/gay music/streets gay with Christmas lights*):—adv gai'ly.

gaze vb to look hard at without looking away (*gaze at him in disbelief/gazing into space*):—n a fixed look.

gazelle' n a small antelope.

gazette' n a government news sheet containing official notices, appointments, etc.

gazetteer' n a book listing places in alphabetical order and telling where they can be found on a map (*a world gazetteer*).

gear n 1 the set of tools, equipment, etc, used for a particular job, sport, expedition, etc (*camping gear*). 2 any arrangement of levers, toothed wheels, etc, that passes motion from one part of a machine to another (*put the car into reverse gear*).

gear'ing n any arrangement of toothed wheels working into each other to pass motion.

geese see **goose**.

geisha [gā'-sha] n a Japanese dancing girl.

gel n a smooth, soft substance resembling jelly, often used in products for the skin or hair (*shower gel*).

gel'atine n a jelly-like substance made from boiled-down bones, etc, used as a thickening agent in jellies, etc.

geld vb to take away from a male the power of having offspring (*gelded horses*).

geld'ing n a gelded horse.

gel'ignite n a powerful explosive (*blow up the bridge with gelignite*).

gem n 1 a precious stone. 2 anything or anyone that is thought to be especially good (*the gem of his stamp collection/her mother is a gem*).

gen'der n (*gram*) 1 a grouping of nouns roughly according to the sex (masculine, feminine or neuter) of the things they name. 2 the sex of a person or animal (*discriminated against on the grounds of gender*).

gene n any of the basic elements of heredity passed from parents to their offspring, that cause the offspring to have certain features that the parents have.

geneal'ogist n one who studies genealogy.

genealogy [jee-nee-al'-o-ji] n 1 the tracing of the history of a family to discover all its ancestors and branches. 2 a diagram showing this:— **genealog'ical.**

gen'era see **genus.**

gen'eral adj 1 including every one of a class or group (a general lowering of prices throughout the industry/wet weather that is general throughout the country). 2 not specialized (general knowledge). 3 common, usual, normal (the general procedure). 4 taken as a whole, overall (the invalid still has a weak arm but her general condition is good). 5 widespread, public (information that has become general). 6 without details (a general report):—n 1 a high-ranking army officer. 2 the commander of an army.

general'ity n (fml) the majority (the generality of people).

gen'eralize vb 1 to work out from a few facts an idea that covers a great number of cases (you must not generalize from just two examples). 2 to talk in general terms without details (generalizing about educational problems):—n **generaliza'tion**.

gen'erally adv in most cases (generally it is warm in summer).

gen'erate vb to bring into life, to produce, to be the cause of (a meeting generating ideas/a misunderstanding that generated ill-feeling in the office).

genera'tion n 1 the act of bringing into existence or producing (the generation of new ideas). 2 a single step in family descent (three generations at the old man's birthday party). 3 people living at the same time (most of the people of her generation are dead).

gen'erator n a machine for producing electricity, steam, etc.

generic adj applies to a member of a group or class, see **genus**:—(of a drug, etc) a product not patented or sold with a brand name.

gen'erous adj 1 giving or given freely and gladly (generous hosts/generous donors). 2 ready to see the good in others:—n **gen-eros'ity**.

gen'esis n (fml) beginning, origin:—n **Gen'esis** the first book of the Bible.

genet'ic adj of genes, of genetics (a genetic defect).

genetic fingerprinting n the process of analysing DNA patterns using body tissues, such as blood and saliva, in order to establish someone's identity, used particularly in crime detection.

genet'ics n the science of breeding and family characteristics.

ge'nial adj friendly in manner, cheerful (genial hosts/new neighbours who seem genial).

genie [jee'-nee] n (pl **genii** [jee'-nee-î]) a good or evil spirit in Eastern tales (the genie of the lamp in the tale of Aladdin).

gen'ital adj having to do with sexual reproduction (genital organs).

ge'nius[1] n 1 extraordinary skill or ability (amazed at the genius of Shakespeare). 2 a person of extraordinary intelligence (Einstein was a genius). 3 (inf) a natural ability (a genius for offending people).

ge'nius[2] n (pl **genii** [jee'-nee-î]) (fml) the spirit of a place (a castle thought to have an evil genius).

genteel' adj over-refined in manners, affected (use a genteel voice on the telephone).

gentian [jen-shên] n a plant with blue flowers grown in some mountainous areas.

gen'tile adj non-Jewish:—also n.

gentil'ity n the state of having good manners or being of good birth.

gen'tle adj 1 (old) well-born (people of gentle birth). 2 not rough or violent in manner, unwilling to hurt anyone (her gentle handling of the situation/gentle with the injured animal):—n **gen'tleness**:—adv **gen'tly**.

gen'tleman n 1 (old) a man of good birth. 2 a well-mannered and kindly man (he was a gentleman and rose to give the old lady his seat in the bus):—adj **gen'tlemanly** well-mannered.

gen'try n the people of good but not noble birth (landed gentry).

gen'uflect vb (fml) to bend the knee in respect (courtiers genuflecting before the king):—n **genuflec'tion**.

gen'uine adj 1 true, real (a genuine Van Gogh painting). 2 sincere, without pretence or dishonesty (feel genuine concern for her situation):—n **gen'uineness**.

ge'nus n (pl **gen'era**) a kind or class of animals, plants, etc, with certain characteristics in common:—adj **gener'ic**.

geog'raphy n the study of the surface of the earth and its climate, peoples, cities, etc:—n **geog'rapher**:—adjs **geograph'ic, geo-graph'ical**.

geol'ogy n the study of the rocks, etc, forming the earth's crust:—n **geol'ogist**:—adj **geolog'ical**.

geom'etry n a branch of mathematics dealing with the measurement of lines, figures and solids:— adjs **geomet'ric, geomet'rical.**

gera'nium n a strongly scented plant, with red, pink or white flowers.

germ n 1 a tiny living cell that has the power to grow into a plant or animal. 2 the beginning of anything (*the germ of an idea*). 3 a disease-carrying microbe (*a disinfectant claiming to kill all germs*).

germane' adj (*fml*) having to do with the subject, connected (*remarks that were not germane to the discussion*).

ger'micide adj killing germs:—also n.

ger'minal adj just beginning to grow (*in a germinal form*).

ger'minate vb to begin to grow (*seeds germinating*).

gerryman'der vb to make use of unfair methods in an election, to arrange the boundaries of or divide an area for voting in order to give unfair advantages to one party in an election.

ger'und n part of a verb that acts as a noun.

gesta'tion n 1 the carrying of a child in the womb (*the gestation period of nine months*). 2 the coming to birth from the stage of a seed. 3 gradual development (*the gestation of a work of art*).

gestic'ulate vb to make meaningful signs with the hands while speaking, usu for emphasis (*gesticulating wildly/gesticulate to her to go away*):—n **gesticula'tion.**

ges'ture n 1 a movement of the hands, head, etc, to express feeling (*with a gesture of despair*). 2 an action showing one's attitude or intentions (*a gesture of friendship*):—vb to make a gesture.

get vb (*pres p* **getting,** *pp* **got** *or* **gotten**) 1 to obtain (*get money*). 2 to reach (*get there*). 3 to become (*get older*).

gewgaw [gū'-gä] n (*fml*) a showy but worthless ornament (*buy gewgaws as souvenirs of their foreign holiday*).

geyser [gī'-zêr *or* gee'-sêr] n 1 a hot water spring that shoots up into the air (*geysers in Iceland*). 2 a kind of gas or electric water heater (*the geyser in the bathroom*).

ghast'ly adj 1 (*fml or lit*) deathly pale (*his face ghastly with fear*). 2 horrible, terrible (*a ghastly murder/a ghastly experience*). 3 (*inf*) very bad, ugly, etc (*a ghastly mistake/a ghastly dress*). 4 (*inf*) unwell, upset (*feel ghastly after a drinking bout*):—n **ghast'liness.**

gherkin [ger'-kin] n a small cucumber used for pickling.

ghetto [ge'-tō] n (*pl* **ghet'tos** *or* **ghet'toes**) 1 the Jewish quarter of a town. 2 a part of a city, often poor, in which a certain group of people, often immigrants, lives.

ghost n the spirit of a dead person appearing to one living:—adjs **ghost'like, ghost'ly:—n ghost'liness.**

ghoul [göl] n 1 a spirit said to prey on corpses. 2 a person who takes an unusually great interest in death, disaster and other horrible things (*ghouls at the scene of the fatal accident*):— adj **ghoulish.**

gi'ant n 1 in fairy stories, a huge man (*the giant in 'Jack and the Beanstalk'*). 2 a person of unusually great height and size (*the giants in the basketball team*). 3 a person of very great ability or importance (*one of the political giants of the 19th century*):—f **gi'antess.**

gibber [jib'-êr] vb 1 to talk at length but unintelligibly, to talk nonsense (*what's he gibbering about?*). 2 to make meaningless sounds (*monkeys gibbering/gibbering with fear*).

gib'berish n nonsense, meaningless words (*talk gibberish*).

gib'bet n a wooden frame for hanging criminals, or for displaying the bodies of executed criminals.

gibbon [gĭ-bên] n a type of ape.

gibe vb to mock, to jeer at (*gibe at their ragged clothes/gibing at his attempts to climb the tree*):— also n.

gib'lets npl the eatable inside parts of a fowl (*choice giblets*).

gid'dy adj 1 dizzy (*feel giddy at the top of the ladder*). 2 changeable, not serious in character, fond of amusement (*giddy young girls*):—n **gid'diness.**

gift n 1 a present (*Christmas gifts*). 2 a natural ability to do something (*a gift for public speaking*):—vb to give as a present (*money gifted by former pupils*).

gift'ed adj having exceptional natural ability (*gifted children*).

gig n 1 (old) a light two-wheeled carriage. 2 (inf) a single booking for a jazz or pop band, etc, a single night's performance.

gigan'tic adj huge, giant-like (a gigantic machine).

gig'gle vb to laugh quietly, but in a silly way (children giggling at the practical joke).

gigot [ji'-gêt] n a leg of mutton.

gild vb to cover with gold (a gilded statue).

gill[1] [jil] n a quarter of a pint.

gill[2] [gil] n the organ through which a fish breathes.

gil'lie n (Scot) a gamekeeper.

gil'lyflower n the wallflower or pink.

gilt adj covered with gold or gold paint (a gilt brooch):—n the gold or imitation of gold used in gilding.

gilt-edged' adj very safe (a gilt-edged investment).

gim'crack adj worthless, badly made, flimsy (gimcrack furniture).

gim'let n a small tool with a screw point for boring holes in wood.

gim'mick n an ingenious gadget or device to attract attention (a sales gimmick).

gin[1] n a strong drink flavoured with juniper berries (gin and tonic).

gin[2] n 1 a trap or snare (a rabbit caught in a gin). 2 a machine for separating cotton from its seeds.

gin'ger n 1 a hot-tasting root used as a spice (crystallized ginger/chop ginger for an Indian dish). 2 a reddish-yellow colour (ginger hair):—vb to stir up, to enliven.

gin'gerbread n treacle cake flavoured with ginger.

gin'gerly adv carefully, cautiously (walk gingerly on the icy road).

gingham [ging'-êm] n a striped or checked cotton cloth (gingham tablecloths).

gip'sy, gyp'sy n a member of a wandering people who travel about in caravans (a gipsy woman telling fortunes).

giraffe' n an African animal with a very long neck and long legs.

gird vb (pp **girt**) 1 (fml or old) to tie round (gird her waist with a silken sash). 2 to fasten on with a belt (girded on his sword). 3 to prepare for action.

gir'der n a heavy beam of iron or steel used to bridge an open space when building.

gir'dle n 1 a kind of belt. 2 (fml or lit) anything that surrounds (a girdle of green around the village):—vb to surround as with a belt.

girl n 1 a female child (a baby girl). 2 a young woman. 3 a daughter (they have two boys and a girl):—n **girl'hood**.

Girl Guide n a member of an international youth organization for girls.

girl'ish adj like or of a girl (a girlish figure/girlish laughter).

girt pp of **gird**.

girth n 1 the measurement around the waist (a man of enormous girth). 2 the distance around something cylindrical in shape (the girth of the tree). 3 a strap that holds the saddle in place on a horse's back.

gist [jist] n the meaning, the most important part (follow the gist of what he was saying).

give vb (pt **gave**, pp **given**) 1 to make a present of (give him a book for Christmas). 2 to hand over to (give the money to the bank). 3 to allow (given a chance). 4 to utter (give a shout). 5 to produce (cows giving milk). 6 to organize, to hold (give a party). 7 to yield, bend, break, etc (the heavy door gave under pressure):—n **giv'er**:—**give away** 1 to give as a gift. 2 to tell something secret (give away their hiding place):—**give ground** to go backwards (the army had to give ground):—**give in** to admit defeat (after a long argument he gave in and admitted he was wrong):—**give out** to report (give out the news of her death):—**give up** 1 to leave to be taken by others (give up a seat to an old lady). 2 to stop (give up smoking). 3 to lose hope (so long unemployed that he has given up):—**give way** 1 to stop in order to allow somone or something to pass (give way to traffic coming from the right). 2 to be replaced by (anger that gave way to fear). 3 to break and fall (a bridge that gave way):—**give and take** allowing some of another's views to be correct.

giz'zard n the second stomach of a bird.

gla'cial adj 1 of ice. 2 icy, very cold (glacial winds). 3 (fml) very cold in manner (a glacial stare).

glacier [glas'-i-êr] n a large slow-moving river of ice.

glad adj pleased, cheerful (glad for her success):—n **glad'ness**.

glad'den vb to make glad (news that gladdened his heart).

glade n (fml) a clear space in a wood.

glad'iator n in Ancient Rome, a man trained to fight with other men or wild animals for public entertainment:—adj **gladiator'ial**.

gladio'lus n (pl **gladio'li**) a plant of the iris family.

glam'our n apparent charm and attractiveness that depends entirely on the outer appearance, dress, etc (the glamour of the filmstar/the glamour of the stage):—adj **glam'orous**.

glance n a quick look (give a glance over her shoulder):—vb 1 to look at for a moment (glance at the newspaper). 2 to hit the side of something and fly off in another direction (the bullet glanced off the wall). 3 to gleam (lights glancing on the sea).

gland n an organ in the body that produces certain fluids necessary to the health of the body (the thyroid gland):—adj **glan'dular**.

glare n 1 a dazzling light (the glare of the car's headlights). 2 an angry or fierce look (give her a glare for going before him in the queue):—also vb.

glar'ing adj 1 having a fierce look. 2 very obvious (a glaring error).

glass n 1 hard, easily broken transparent material (a door made of glass). 2 a mirror (look in the glass/a looking glass). 3 a glass drinking vessel (a glass of milk). 4 pl a pair of spectacles (wear dark glasses):—adj **glass'y** adj 1 like glass (a glassy pond). 2 lifeless, having a fixed expression (glassy eyes/a glassy stare).

glaze vb 1 to fit with glass (glaze the new windows). 2 to cover with a smooth shiny surface (glaze a cake with icing/glazed fruit). 3 to become fixed or glassy-looking (eyes glazing over):—n a smooth shiny surface (a glaze on the tiles).

gla'zier n one who fixes glass in windows.

gleam n 1 a small ray of light, esp one that disappears quickly (the gleam of a match in the darkness). 2 a temporary appearance of some quality (a faint gleam of humour/a gleam of hope):—vb 1 to shine softly (lights gleaming/polished tables gleaming). 2 to be expressed with a sudden light, to be bright (eyes gleaming with excitement/excitement gleamed in her eyes).

glean vb 1 (old) to gather the corn left by the reaper. 2 to pick up by the way (glean information).

glee n 1 pleasure, joy (full of glee at their victory). 2 a song with several different parts to be sung together.

glee'ful adj joyful (gleeful at his enemy's defeat).

glen n (Scot) a narrow valley.

glib adj 1 quick to answer, able to find words easily, fluent (a glib salesman). 2 spoken fluently and without hesitation (a glib reply):—n **glib'ness**.

glide vb to move smoothly or without effort (skiers gliding down the mountain).

glid'er n an aircraft with no engine.

glim'mer vb to burn low and unsteadily, to shine faintly (a candle glimmering at the end of the dark passage):—n 1 a low and unsteady light (the glimmer from the candle) 2 a slight sign or amount (a glimmer of hope).

glimpse n a quick or passing view of (catch a glimpse of her in the crowd):—vb to see for a moment only (glimpsing her red hat in the crowd).

glint vb to flash, to sparkle (eyes glinting with anger):—n 1 a brief flash of light. 2 a brief indication (glint of anger in her eyes).

glist'en vb (esp of wet or polished surfaces) to shine, to give a bright, steady light, to sparkle (dew drops glistening on the grass/bodies glistening with sweat):—also n.

glis'ter vb (old) to sparkle, to give a bright flickering light:—also n.

glit'ter vb to sparkle, to give a bright flickering light (stars glittering in the clear sky/diamonds glittering at her throat):—also n.

gloam'ing n twilight.

gloat vb to look at with greedy or evil enjoyment (gloat over her neighbour's misfortune/a miser gloating over his gold).

glob'al adj 1 affecting the whole world (a global issue like poverty). 2 relating to or including the whole of something (The industry is seeking a global pay settlement).

globaliza'tion n the process by which a business firm or organization begins to operate on an international basis (the globalization of the insurance industry).

global warming n a gradual increase in the world's temperatures believed to be caused, in part at least, by the **greenhouse effect** (see below).

globe n 1 a ball, a sphere. 2 anything ball-shaped (a new globe for the light). 3 the earth (from all *parts of the globe).* **4** a map of the earth printed on to a ball.

glob'ular *adj* ball-shaped.

glob'ule *n* a drop, a very small ball (*globules of wax from a candle*).

gloom *n* **1** darkness. **2** sadness.

gloom'y *adj* **1** dark, dim (*gloomy corridors*). **2** sad-looking, depressed (*gloomy about the future/in a gloomy mood*).

glorify *vb* **1** to praise or worship (*glorifying God*). **2** to make seem better, more beautiful, more important, etc, (*a book that glorified war*):—*n* **glori'fication**.

glor'ious *adj* **1** splendid, magnificent (*a glorious summer's day/a glorious sunset*). **2** famous (*a glorious victory/glorious deeds*).

glo'ry *n* **1** honour, fame (*win glory on the battle-field*). **2** brightness, beauty, splendour (*the glory of the sunset*). **3** worship, adoration (*glory to God in the highest*). **4** a special cause for pride, respect, honour, etc (*one of the glories of British justice*):—*vb* to take pride in, to rejoice (*glorying in one's freedom/gloried in her success*).

gloss[1] *n* a bright or shiny surface:—*vb* to give a shine to:—**gloss over** to try to make appear pleasing or satisfactory.

gloss[2] *n* **1** a note written in the margin or between lines (*a gloss explaining the word*). **1** an explanation, interpretation (*politicians putting different glosses on the situation*):—*vb* to provide with glosses, to annotate (*expressions that need to be glossed*).

glos'sary *n* a list of words with their meanings (*a glossary of cooking terms in the recipe book*).

gloss'y *adj* smooth and shining (*glossy hair*).

glot'tis *n* the opening at the upper end of the windpipe.

glove *n* a covering of cloth or leather for the hand, each finger being separately covered (*gloves wet from throwing snowballs*).

glov'er *n* one who makes or sells gloves.

glow *vb* **1** to give out light and heat but no flame (*coal glowing in the grate/a cigarette glowing in the dark*). **2** to look or feel warm or red (*cheeks glowing after exercise*):—*n* **1** a bright steady light (*the glow of the furnace*). **2** a warm look or feeling (*a healthy glow after their walk*). **3** a good feeling (*feel a glow of satisfaction*).

glow'ing *adj* **1** full of praise (*a glowing account of her work*). **2** giving out heat (*glowing coal*).

glow'er *vb* to give an angry look (*glower at the person who bumped his car*).

glow'-worm *n* an insect that sends out a light in the dark.

glu'cose *n* grape sugar, a natural sugar found in fruits and plants.

glue *n* a sticky substance used for sticking things together:—*vb* to stick with glue (*gluing the pieces of the vase together/glued the newspaper cuttings in a scrapbook*).

glue'y *adj* sticky.

glum *adj* **1** sad, gloomy (*glum expressions*). **2** downcast (*feel glum about the future*).

glut *vb* (**glut'ted, glut'ting**) **1** to fill too full, to supply with more than is needed (*glut the market with cheap foreign goods*). **2** to stuff, to gorge oneself (*glutted with food*):—*n* too great an amount (*a glut of soft fruit on the market*).

glu'tinous *adj* (*fml*) sticky (*a glutinous substance*).

glutt'on *n* **1** one who eats too much. **2** (*inf*) a person who is always ready for more (*a glutton for work*).

glutt'onous *adj* greedy, too fond of food.

glutt'ony *n* a fondness for eating a good deal, love of food (*disgusted by his gluttony*).

glycerine [glis'-êr-ēn] *n* a colourless sweet liquid obtained from fats.

GM [*abbr for* **genetically modified**] *n* food, such as a plant, whose genetic material or structure has been altered by technological means to improve growth or treat disease.

gnarled [narled'] *adj* twisted and having a rough surface (*gnarled tree trunks/hands gnarled with age*).

gnash [nash] *vb* to strike the teeth together, to grind the teeth, often as a sign of emotion (*gnash his teeth in rage*).

gnat [nat] *n* a small biting insect.

gnaw [nå] *vb* **1** to keep on biting at in order to wear away gradually (*dogs gnawing bones*). **2** to continued distress to (*guilt gnawing away at her*).

gnome [nōm] *n* in fairytales, a mischievous fairy supposed to live underground.

gnu [nö] *n* a large African antelope.

go *vb* (*pt* **went**, *pp* **gone**) **1** to move (*go backwards*). **2** to become (*go mad/go white-haired with* *age*):—*n* **go'ing:**—**go for** to attack (*the dog went for the postman*):—**go hard with** (*fml*) to turn out badly for (*it went hard with our army in the battle*):—**go in for** to take interest in (*she works hard and doesn't go in for hobbies*):—**go under** to fail (*hope that the firm does not go under*).

goad *n* a sharply pointed stick to urge forward cattle;—*vb* **1** to urge on, to prod (*goad them into action*). **2** to annoy (*goaded the man into striking him*).

go-ahead *adj* ready to try out new ideas (*a go-ahead firm*):—*n* permission to proceed (*get the go-ahead for the new road*).

goal *n* **1** an aim, target, object of one's efforts (*his main goal in life*). **2** in some games, the wooden frame through which players try to pass the ball (*the goalkeeper guarding the goal in the hockey match*). **4** a score at football, hockey, etc (*the team that scored a goal*).

goal'keeper *n* the player who defends a goal.

goat *n* an animal with horns, related to the sheep.

goatee' *n* a neat pointed beard on a man's chin.

gob'ble *vb* **1** to eat quickly (*children gobbling down their food before going out to play*). **2** to make a noise like a turkey.

gob'bledygook *n* language which seems meaningless because of the use of difficult words and complicated sentence structures (*This official document is full of gobbledygook*).

go'-between *n* one who arranges an agreement between two other parties (*act as a go-between in the talks between the firms*).

gob'let *n* a drinking cup without a handle (*silver wine goblets*).

gob'lin *n* in fairytales, a mischievous fairy.

God *n* the Creator of the world, the Supreme Being:—*n* **god** any being worshipped for having more than natural powers (*the Roman god of war*).

godd'ess *n* **1** a female god (*the Greek goddess of beauty*). **2** a woman of superior charms or excellence.

god'father *n* one who makes the promises for a child at baptism:—*f* **god'mother:**—*also* **god'child, god'daughter, god'son.**

god'-fearing *adj* deeply religious (*a god-fearing old man/a god-fearing people*).

god'less *adj* (*fml*) living as if there were no God, wicked (*a godless people*).

god'like *adj* **1** like God. **2** like a god (*a godlike beauty*).

god'ly *adj* religious, following God's laws (*a godly man/a godly life*):—*n* **god'liness.**

god'send *n* an unexpected piece of good luck (*her father's cheque was a godsend*).

gog'gle *vb* to look with wide-open or rolling eyes (*goggling at the piles of gold*).

gog'gles *npl* a type of spectacles, esp those worn to protect the eyes (*machine operators wearing protective goggles*).

goitre [goi'-têr'] *n* a diseased swelling on the neck.

go'-kart *n* a small racing vehicle made of an open frame on four wheels with an engine (*go-kart racing*).

gold *n* **1** a precious metal (*rings made of gold*). **2** wealth, money (*a miser counting his gold*). **3** the colour of gold (*hair of gold*).

gold'en *adj* **1** made of gold. **2** of the colour of gold (*golden sands/golden hair*). **3** valuable (*a golden opportunity*).

golden mean *n* the middle way, neither too much nor too little (*he wants to go out all the time and his parents want him to study—they must find the golden mean*).

golden wedding *n* the fiftieth anniversary of marriage (*an old couple celebrating their golden wedding*).

gold'field *n* an area in which gold is to be found.

gold'finch *n* a beautiful singing bird.

gold'fish *n* a small red Chinese carp.

gold leaf *n* gold beaten out into a thin sheet.

gold'smith *n* a worker in gold.

golf *n* an outdoor game played with clubs and a hard ball (*play a few rounds of golf*):—*also vb.*

gon'dola *n* **1** a long narrow boat used on the canals of Venice. **2** the car of an airship. **3** a set of shelves in a shop for displaying goods.

gondolier [gon-dol-eer'] *n* a man who rows a gondola.

gone *pp* of **go.**

gong *n* a flat metal plate that makes a ringing sound when struck (*sound the gong for dinner*).

good *adj* **1** right, morally acceptable, virtuous (*a good deed/a good life*). **2** of a high quality (*a good performance/good eyesight*). **3** pleasant, agreeable, welcome (*good news/good to see some sun-*

shine). **4** fit, competent (*a good teacher*). **5** well-behaved (*tell the children to be good*). **6** kindly (*the good fairy in the story*). **7** clever (*good at maths*). **8** fit to be eaten (*good fruit affected by the bad*).**9** beneficial (*food that is good for one*):—*npl* **goods 1** movable property (*stolen goods*). **2** things for buying or selling (*a range of electrical goods*).

goodbye' *n and interj* a farewell greeting.

good-for-noth'ing *adj* useless, worthless (*her good-for-nothing husband*):—*also n.*

Good Friday *n* the Friday before Easter on which the crucifixion and death of Christ are commemorated.

good-look'ing *adj* handsome.

good'ly *adj* considerable (*a goodly sum of money*).

good-na'tured *adj* kindly (*good-natured neighbours*).

good'ness *n* the quality of being good.

goodwill' *n* **1** kindly feeling (*full of goodwill even towards people who treat her badly*). **2** the good name and popularity of a shop or business (*the price she was charging for her shop took into consideration the goodwill of the business*).

goog'ly *n* in cricket, a ball that swerves one way and breaks the other.

goose *n* (*pl* **geese**) **1** a web-footed farmyard fowl. **2** (*fml or old*) a foolish person (*she was a goose to believe him*).

goose'berry *n* **1** a thorny shrub. **2** its eatable berry. **3** an unwanted third person when two people, esp lovers, want to be alone.

goose flesh *n* a roughness or bumpiness of the skin due to cold or fear.

gore[1] *vb* to wound with a tusk or horn (*a farmworker gored by a bull*).

gore[2] *n* (*fml or lit*) blood from a dead or wounded person, esp when formed into solid lumps (*a battlefield covered in gore/a film with too much gore*):—*adj* **gor'y.**

gorge *n* **1** (*old*) the throat (*a bone stuck in his gorge*). **2** (*found in place names*) a deep narrow pass between hills (*the Cheddar Gorge*):— **make one's gorge rise** to sicken, to fill with disgust:—*vb* to overeat, to eat greedily.

gor'geous *adj* **1** splendid, magnificent, richly decorated or coloured (*walls covered with gorgeous tapestries/gorgeous silks and satins*).

2 (*inf*) very beautiful and glamorous (*gorgeous models*).**3** (*inf*) giving much pleasure, marvellous (*a gorgeous meal/a gorgeous day*).

gor'gon *n* **1** in Greek fable, a female monster whose look turned people to stone. **2** an ugly or frightening person (*no one visits her as her mother is a real gorgon*).

Gorgonzo'la *n* a blue-veined, strong-tasting Italian cheese.

gorill'a *n* a large ape.

gorse *n* a prickly evergreen bush with yellow flowers, furze, whin (*a hillside covered in gorse*).

gory *see* **gore.**

gos'hawk *n* a large short-winged hawk.

gos'ling *n* a young goose.

gos'pel *n* **1** the teaching of Jesus Christ. **2** the story of the life of Christ as written by Matthew, Mark, Luke or John. **3** any complete system of beliefs (*spread the gospel of a healthy diet*). **4** (*inf*) the truth (*I thought his story was untrue but he swore that it was gospel*). **5** religious music in a popular or folk style and black American in origin.

goss'amer *n* **1** cobweb-like threads floating in the air or resting on bushes. **2** any very light material (*a wedding veil of gossamer*):—*adj* very light.

gos'sip *n* **1** one who likes to hear and spread news about the private affairs of others (*the village gossips starting whispering in the post office*). **2** idle talk (*spread gossip about her*):—*vb* **1** to spread stories about others. **2** to talk idly or chatter, often about other people (*neighbours gossiping over the fence*).

Goth'ic *adj* in the pointed-arch style of architecture common in the Middle Ages.

Gou'da *n* a mild, round Dutch cheese.

gouge [gouj] *n* a chisel with a curving blade for cutting grooves:—*vb* **1** to make a groove or hole in (*gouging holes in the paintwork*). **2** to scoop out, to force out (*gouge her eyes out as a torture*).

gourd *n* **1** a large fleshy fruit (e.g. cucumber, melon). **2** the hollow skin of a gourd used as a bottle or a cup.

gour'mand *n* **1** (*fml*) a greedy eater, a glutton. **2** one who likes good food, often to excess.

gourmet [gŏr'-mā] *n* one who is a good judge of wines and food (*a restaurant guide written by a gourmet*).

gout *n* a disease causing painful swelling of the joints.

gov'ern *vb* **1** to control and direct the affairs of (*the prime minister and cabinet govern the country*). **2** to control, to guide, to influence (*price of goods governed to some extent by demand/a business policy governed by several factors*). **3** to exercise restraint over, to control, to regulate (*try to govern her temper*).

gov'erness *n* a woman who looks after and teaches children in their home.

gov'ernment *n* **1** the act or way of ruling (*a democratic system of government*). **2** the group of people who direct the affairs of a country (*ministers resigning from the government*):—*adj* **government'al.**

gov'ernor *n* **1** in America, a person who is elected as head of a state (*the Governor of Texas*). **2** a member of the committee of people who govern a school, hospital, etc (*on the school's board of governors*). **3** (*old*) a person governing a province or colony (*the former governor of Australia*). **4** a device that controls the speed at which an engine works.

gown *n* **1** a woman's dress, usu formal (*an evening gown*). **2** a long robe worn by members of clergy, teachers, lawyers, etc (*students required to wear academic gowns to graduate*).

grab *vb* (**grabbed', grab'bing**) **1** to take hold of with a sudden quick movement (*grab the child to prevent her being run over/a robber grabbing the money from the bank clerk*). **2** to get or take something quickly and sometimes unfairly (*grab a sandwich/grab her seat*). **3** (*inf*) to affect, to influence, to find favour with (*how does a trip to the cinema grab you?*):—*also n*.

grace *n* **1** the mercy or kindness of God. **2** a sense of what is right or decent (*he finally had the grace to apologize*). **3** a delay allowed as a favour (*a few days' grace to repay the loan*). **4** beauty and effortlessness of movement (*dance with grace*). **5** a short prayer said at meal times. **6** a title of respect used to dukes, archbishops, etc:—*n* **1** to honour (*grace the dinner with her presence*). **2** to adorn (*flowers gracing the table*).

grace'ful *adj* beautiful in appearance or movement (*graceful dancers*).

gra'cious *adj* kind, pleasant, polite (*our gracious hostess*).

grada'tion *n* **1** arrangement in order (*a gradation from light to dark*). **2** progress step by step (*gradations in promotion to the top*).

grade *n* **1** a placing in an order according to one's merit, rank, performance, etc (*grades achieved in exams*). **2** rank (*various grades in the army*):—*vb* **1** to arrange in grades (*grade the wool according to quality/grading eggs according to size*). **2** to pass or change from one thing to another gradually (*blues and reds grading into purple*).

gra'dient *n* **1** a slope (*the child tumbled down the steep gradient*). **2** the steepness of a slope (*the gradient of the hill/a gradient of 1 in 7*).

grad'ual *adj* slow and steady, little by little (*a gradual improvement/a gradual rise in temperature*).

grad'uate *vb* **1** (*fml*) to divide into stages or equal spaces (*a thermometer graduated in degrees/a graduated tax system*). **2** to receive a university degree:—*n* one who holds a university degree (*a graduate of Edinburgh University*).

gradua'tion *n* the receiving of a university degree.

graf'fiti *npl* (*sing* **graffito** rare) writing or drawings, often humorous or rude, scribbled or sprayed unofficially or illegally on walls or other surfaces in public places (*The new bus shelter is covered in graffiti already*).

graft[1] *vb* **1** to fix a piece cut from one plant on to another so that it grows into it. **2** to put skin cut from one part of the body on to another part (*graft skin from his thigh to his arm after he was scalded*). **3** to replace an organ of the body by one belonging to someone else, to transplant (*graft a kidney from his brother in the patient*):—*n* the cutting or skin so grafted.

graft[2] *n* (*inf*) **1** bribery and corruption (*accused of graft by his political opponents*). **2** wealth made by illegal use of office. **3** hard work (*make money by sheer hard graft*).

Grail *see* **Holy Grail.**

grain *n* **1** a seed of wheat, corn, etc. **2** corn in general (*grain ground into flour*). **3** a very small hard particle (*a grain of salt*). **4** a very small amount (*not a grain of truth in it*). **5** the smallest measure of weight (1 pound = 7000 grains).

6 the pattern of markings in wood, leather, etc:—*vb* to imitate the grain of wood when painting doors, etc.

gram, gramme *n* the basic unit of weight in the metric system.

gram'mar *n* the science of the correct use of language:—**gramma'rian**.

grammat'ical *adj* correct in grammar (*a grammatical sentence*).

gramme *see* gram.

gram'ophone *n* (*old*) an instrument on which sound recorded on a specially prepared disc can be played back, a record-player.

gram'pus *n* **1** a whale. **2** a dolphin.

gran'ary *n* a storehouse for grain.

grand *adj* **1** noble, magnificent, splendid (*a very grand procession/generals looking very grand in their uniforms*). **2** important, proud, too proud (*grand ladies looking down on poor people/too grand to go out for a drink with his old colleagues*). **3** (*inf or dial*) pleasant (*a grand day*). **4** wonderful, highly respected (*a grand old man*). **5** dignified (*write in a grand style*):—*n* **grand'eur**.

grandee' *n* a Spanish nobleman of high rank.

grandeur *see* grand.

grand'father *n* the father of one's father or mother:—*f* **grand'mother:**—*also* **grand'-parent, grand'child, grand'son, grand'-daughter.**

grandil'oquent *adj* (*fml*) using important-sounding words (*a grandiloquent style of prose*):—*n* **grandil'oquence.**

gran'diose *adj* meant to be splendid, intended to be impressive (*he has grandiose ideas but no money to carry them out*).

grand pia'no *n* a large piano in which the strings are horizontal.

grand'stand *n* rows of seats built on a rising slope to allow people a good view of a sports contest.

gran'ite *n* a hard rock (*houses built of granite*).

gran'ny *n* **1** (*inf*) an old woman (*the kind of clothes worn by grannies*). **2** (*inf*) a grandmother (*a little girl asking for her granny*).

grant *vb* **1** to give, to agree to, to allow (*grant him permission to go/grant him a favour*). **2** (*fml*) to admit as true (*I grant that he is hardworking*):—*n* something allowed or given, esp money given for a certain purpose (*a grant to insulate their house/student grants*).

gran'ular *adj* **1** of or like grains (*granular substances like salt*). **2** rough to the touch, rough in appearance (*rather granular skin*).

gran'ulate *vb* to break into grains or small pieces (*granulated sugar*).

gran'ule *n* a small grain (*granules of sugar*).

grape *n* the fruit of the vine (*wine made from grapes*).

grape'fruit *n* a large yellowish sharp-tasting fruit (*have half a grapefruit for breakfast*).

graph *n* a diagram in which different numbers, quantities, etc, are shown by dots on a piece of squared paper, and then joined up by lines so that they can be easily compared (*a graph showing the annual variations in sales*).

graph'ic *adj* **1** so well told that the events, etc, can be seen in the mind's eye (*a graphic description of what was going on in the war zone*). **2** drawn, concerned with drawing, painting, etc (*the graphic arts*):—**graph'ics** *npl* information in the form of illustrations or diagrams (*The graphics in the book make the text easier to understand*).

graph'ite *n* blacklead as used in pencils.

grap'nel *n* **1** an anchor with several arms. **2** a grappling iron.

grap'ple *vb* **1** to fight hand to hand, to take hold of and struggle with (*grapple with the burglar who had entered his house*). **2** to struggle with (*grappling with maths for the exam*).

grasp *vb* **1** to take firm hold of (*grasp his hand in farewell*). **2** to understand (*unable to grasp the urgency of the situation*):—*n* **1** firm hold (*shake his hand in a grasp*). **2** reach (*the job was within his grasp*). **3** understanding (*a good grasp of the subject*).

grasp'ing *adj* mean, always wanting more money (*grasping moneylenders/grasping merchants overcharging customers*).

grass *n* the common plant covering of the ground, usu green.

grass'hopper *n* a small jumping insect.

grass widow *n* a woman whose husband is away from home a great deal (*she's a grass widow while her husband is away at international conferences*).

grate[1] *n* a metal frame in a fireplace for holding the fire (*a fire burning steadily in the grate*).

grate² vb **1** to break down by rubbing on something rough (*grate cheese*). **2** to make a harsh sound, as of metal rubbing on metal (*chalk grating on a blackboard*). **3** to annoy, to irritate (*a voice that really grates on people*).

grate'ful adj thankful (*grateful for your help/with grateful thanks*).

grat'er n an instrument with a rough surface for breaking down to crumbs or powder (*a cheese grater*).

gratifica'tion n pleasure, satisfaction (*a sense of gratification at finishing the job on time*).

grat'ify vb **1** to please, to delight (*we were gratified to hear that they liked our present*). **2** to satisfy (*able to gratify her desire to go to the opera*).

grat'ing n a framework of metal bars.

gratis [grä-tis] adv for nothing, free of charge.

gratitude n thankfulness (*express his gratitude for their help/be filled with gratitude for her kindness*).

gratu'itous adj **1** unasked for, unwanted (*gratuitous advice*). **2** unnecessary, unjustified (*scenes of gratuitous violence in the film*).

gratu'ity n (*fml*) a tip, a money gift to a servant or employee (*the waiter's gratuities*).

grave¹ n the hole dug in the earth for a dead body.

grave² adj serious, important (*a matter of grave importance/wear a grave expression*).

grave³ vb (pp **grav'en**) (*old*) to engrave.

grav'el n **1** small stones or pebbles (*throw gravel at the bedroom window to wake her*). **2** a mixture of small stones and sand used to make the surface of roads and paths (*the child fell on the gravel*).

grave'stone n a memorial stone placed over a grave.

grave'yard n a piece of land set aside for graves.

gravitate vb **1** to move towards the centre. **2** to move in a certain direction as if drawn there by some force (*children gravitating towards the toy shop*):—n **gravita'tion**.

grav'ity n **1** seriousness, importance (*understand the gravity of the situation*). **2** (*fml*) weight. **3** the force drawing bodies towards the centre of the earth (*the force of gravity*).

grav'y n the juice got from meat when it is being cooked, often thickened and served as a sauce with the meat.

gray adj (*esp Amer*) grey.

gray'ling n a freshwater fish of the salmon family.

graze¹ vb **1** to touch or rub against lightly in passing (*the car grazed the garage door*). **2** to scrape along the surface:—n **1** a passing touch. **2** a scraping of the skin (*bandage the graze on the child's knee*).

graze² vb to eat growing grass, to feed on grass (*cows grazing in the field*).

gra'zier n (*old*) one who feeds cattle on grass and prepares them for market.

grazing n land with grass suitable for feeding cattle (*hire out the grazing to a neighbouring farmer*).

grease n **1** fat in a soft state (*the grease from cooking bacon*). **2** fatty or oily matter (*use grease on his hair/lubricate the hinges with grease*):—vb to smear with grease:—adj **greas'y**.

great adj **1** large in amount, number or size (*a great crowd*). **2** important (*a great painting/a great discovery*). **3** famous (*a great leader*). **4** long in time (*a great age*). **5** more than is usual (*great kindness*). **6** noble. **7** having possessed and made full use of extraordinary ability. **8** (*old*) pregnant (*great with child*):—n **great'ness**.

great-grand'father n the father of one of one's grandparents:—f **great-grand'-mother**:—also **great-grand'parent, great-grand'child**, etc.

greed n **1** the desire to have more and more for oneself (*the greed of the miser as he got more and more money*). **2** love of eating (*eat not from hunger but from greed*).

greed'y adj always wanting more than one has (*greedy miser/greedy eaters*):—n **greed'iness**.

green adj **1** the colour of grass (*a green dress*). **2** fresh, not ripe (*green bananas*). **3** inexperienced (*young workers so green that they believed his jokes*):—n **1** green colour (*she always wears green*). **2** a piece of ground covered with grass (*the village green*). **3** pl green vegetables (e.g. cabbage) (*children told to eat their greens*). **4** concerned with the protection and conservation of the environment (*discussing green issues in parliament*).:—n **green'ness**.

green'ery n green plants, foliage (*arrange the flowers with some greenery*).

green'gage n a type of plum.

green'grocer n one who sells fruit and vegetables.

green'horn n (*inf*) a young and inexperienced person (*employ a greenhorn and pay him hardly anything*).

green'house n a glasshouse for growing plants (*grow tomatoes in a greenhouse*).

green'house effect n an increase in the earth's atmosphere of the amount of carbon dioxide and other gases that trap the heat of the sun and prevent it from escaping into space, thought to be a major cause of **global warming** (*see above*).

green'room n a rest-room for actors in a theatre.

greet vb **1** to welcome (*greet the guests at the front door*). **2** to speak or send good wishes to someone (*greeted his neighbours in the street*). **3** to receive (*greet the news with relief/the statement was greeted with disbelief*).

greet'ing n **1** welcome (*a few words of greeting to the guests*). **2** (*often pl*) good wishes (*send greetings to her parents*).

grega'rious adj **1** (*fml*) living in flocks or herds (*gregarious animals*). **2** fond of company (*too gregarious to live alone*).

grenade' n a small bomb thrown by hand.

grey adj **1** black mixed with white in colour (*a grey dress*). **2** of the colour of hair whitened by age (*grey hair*):—*also n*.

grey'hound n a lean fast-running dog, used in dog-racing.

grid n **1** a framework of metal bars (*a grid to keep cattle from leaving the field*). **2** a gridiron. **3** a large number of electric wires, railways, etc, crossing and going in different directions. **4** the division of a map into squares to make map-reading easier.

grid'dle n a flat iron plate for baking cakes, etc, on a fire or the top of a stove.

grid'iron n **1** a framework of iron bars used for cooking meat over a fire (*grill steaks over a gridiron*). **2** a field for American football.

grief n great sorrow (*their grief at their friend's death*):—**come to grief** to fail, to suffer a misfortune (*they'll come to grief if they oppose his scheme*).

griev'ance n a cause of complaint (*workers giving management a list of grievances*).

grieve vb **1** to sorrow, to mourn (*widows grieving for their dead husbands*). **2** (*fml*) to cause sorrow (*it grieved him to leave her*).

griev'ous adj (*fml*) **1** causing pain or sorrow (*grievous loss*). **2** severe, serious (*grievous bodily harm*).

griff'in, griff'on n an imaginary monster with an eagle's head and wings and a lion's body.

grill n **1** a framework of metal bars used in cooking, a device on a cooker that directs heat downards for cooking meat, toasting bread, etc (*brown the dish under the grill*). **2** food cooked on a grill (*a mixed grill*). **3** a grille:—*vb* **1** to cook on a grill (*grill the steak*). **2** (*inf*) to question intensively (*grilled by the police*).

grille n a framework of metal bars fitted into a counter, a door or outside a window (*bank staff protected by a grille*).

grilse n a young salmon.

grim adj **1** angry-looking, unsmiling (*look grim when he heard the news*). **2** unpleasant, depressing (*the grim prospect of unemployment*). **3** severe, harsh (*a grim struggle for survival*). **4** stubborn, determined (*with grim determination*):—*n* **grim'ness**.

grimace [gri-mâs'] vb to twist the face to show one's feelings (*grimacing with disgust at the sight*):—*also n*.

grime n dirt, filth (*the grime on the city buildings*):—*adj* **grim'y**.

grin vb (**grinned', grin'ning**) to smile widely in pleasure:—*also n*.

grind vb (*pt, pp* **ground**) **1** to rub or crush to powder (*grind the coffee*). **2** to sharpen by rubbing (*grind the knives*). **3** to press together noisily (*grind his teeth*). **4** (*inf*) to work hard (*grind away at her studies*):—*n* hard and uninteresting work.

grind'er n a person or thing that grinds (*a coffee grinder*).

grind'stone n a wheel of hard stone for sharpening or polishing.

grip vb (**gripped', grip'ping**) **1** to take a firm hold of, to hold very tightly (*a child gripping his mother's hand*). **2** to seize the attention of (*an audience gripped by the play*):—*n* a firm or tight hold (*keep a tight grip on his wallet*).

gripe vb **1** (*fml*) to cause a sharp pain in the stomach. **2** (*inf*) to complain (*always griping about something*):—*n* **1** a pain in the stomach. **2** (*inf*) a complaint.

gris'ly adj dreadful, frightening (*the grisly sight of the headless corpse*).

grist n:—**grist to the mill** something that brings profit or advantage (*we'll accept anything for the jumble sale—all is grist to the mill*).

gris'tle n a tough elastic substance surrounding the joints of the bones (*unable to eat the meat that was full of gristle*):—adj **grist'ly**.

grit n 1 grains of sand or dust (*spread grit on icy roads*). 2 courage, determination (*it took grit to face up to the bullies*):—vb (**grit'ted, grit'ting**) 1 to press (the teeth) tightly together. 2 to spr ead grit on roads.

grizz'led adj (*fml*) having grey or greyish hair (*grizzled old men*).

grizz'ly n a large fierce North American bear.

groan vb to utter a low, deep sound expressing pain or anxiety (*victims groaning with pain after the accident/groaned in despair*):—also n.

groat n (*old*) a silver coin worth fourpence.

groats npl the grain of oats with the husks removed.

gro'cer n one who sells dry and tinned foods, tea, sugar and household supplies (*prefer the grocer's shop to the supermarket*).

gro'ceries npl goods sold by a grocer.

grog n (*old*) a mixture of strong drink and cold water.

grog'gy adj not steady on the feet, weak (*feeling groggy after the operation*).

groin n the hollow part of the body where the legs join the trunk (*strain a muscle in the groin*).

groom n 1 a person who cares for horses (*the grooms at the racing stables*). 2 a man who is being married (*the bride and groom*).

groom'sman n the 'best man' (i.e. a friend who accompanies a man at his wedding).

groove n a long narrow hollow, as that made by a tool in wood (*the groove in a record/the groove for a sliding door*):—vb to make a groove in.

grope vb to feel for something unseen by feeling with one's hands (*groping for the light switch*).

gross adj 1 fat and overfed (*feel gross beside the slender models*). 2 coarse, vulgar, impolite (*gross behaviour/gross language*). 3 very noticeable, glaringly obvious (*gross negligence*). 4 whole, complete, total (*gross weight/gross profit*):—n 1 twelve dozen. 2 the whole.

gross'ness n rudeness, vulgarity (*the grossness of his behaviour*).

grotesque¹ adj 1 strangely shaped, distorted, fantastic (*grotesque masks*). 2 ridiculously

exaggerated, unreasonable, absurd, foolish (*a grotesque distortion of the truth/look grotesque in clothes too young for her*).

grott'o n (*pl* **grott'oes**) a cave, often an articial one in a park, etc (*Santa's grotto*).

ground¹ n 1 the surface of the earth, land (*dead birds falling to the ground/plant seeds in the ground*). 2 a piece of land used for a particular purpose (*sports ground*). 3 (*often pl*) a reason (*grounds for complaint*). 4 pl the tiny pieces of matter that sink to the bottom of a liquid (*coffee grounds*). 5 pl the land surrounding a large house, castle, etc (*extensive grounds*):—vb 1 (*of a ship*) to run ashore (*ships grounded in the storm*). 2 (*of an aeroplane*) to come to or keep on the ground (*ground aeroplanes in bad weather conditions*). 3 to base (*an argument that is grounded on lies*). 4 to teach the basic facts to (*ground the pupils in mathematics*).

ground² pp of **grind**.

ground floor n the storey of a building on the same level as the ground.

ground'ing n knowledge of the elementary part of a subject (*receive a good grounding in English grammar*).

ground'less adj without a reason (*fears that proved groundless*).

ground'sel n types of weed.

grounds'man n the man in charge of a sports field.

ground staff n those who service an aeroplane and do other duties connected with it while it is on the ground.

ground'swell n 1 long rolling waves. 1 a sudden and quickly developing growth of feeling among a lot of people (*a groundswell of public opinion in favour of conserving the environment*).

ground'work n work that must be done well in the beginning if later work on the subject or task is to succeed (*a book that required a great deal of groundwork in the form of research/lay the groundwork for talks between the heads of state*).

group n 1 a number of persons or things taken together (*a group of horses/a group of languages/a drama group*). 2 a set of people who play or sing together (*a pop group*):—vb to put or go into a group (*group the books according to subject*).

grouse¹ n a small fowl hunted on the moors as game.

grouse² *vb* (*inf*) to grumble, to complain (*grousing about the high prices*):—also *n*.

grove *n* (*fml*) a small wood.

grov'el *vb* (**grov'elled, grov'elling**) **1** to lie face downwards in humility or fear (*grovel before the emperor*). **2** to humble oneself, to behave with humility (*grovel to her father for a loan*).

grow *vb* (*pt* **grew**, *pp* **grown**) **1** to become bigger (*children growing*). **2** (*of plants*) to have life (*plants that can grow in any soil*). **3** to become (*grow old*). **4** to plant and rear (*grow potatoes in the back garden*):—*n* **growth**.

growl *vb* to utter a low harsh sound, as a dog when angry (*growling at the children who were disturbing him*):—also *n*.

grown-up' *n* a fully grown person (*children wishing to have dinner with the grown-ups*).

growth *see* **grow**.

groyne *n* a breakwater.

grub *vb* (**grubbed'**, **grub'bing**) **1** to dig, to root out (*grub out all the weeds*). **2** to search for by digging (*pigs grubbing around for food*). **3** (*inf*) to search around for (*reporters grubbing around for information*):—*n* the form of an insect when it comes out of the egg.

grub'by *adj* dirty (*children grubby after a day's play/wash his grubby clothes*).

grudge *vb* **1** to be unwilling to give (*grudging the money spent on travelling to work*). **2** to be displeased by another's success, to envy (*grudge the actor his part in the play*):—*n* a deep feeling of ill-will, dislike, resentment, etc (*bear a grudge against his brother for marrying his girlfriend*).

gru'el *n* (*old*) a light food made by boiling meal in water.

gruel'ling *adj* very difficult and tiring (*a gruelling climb up the mountain*).

grue'some *adj* horrible, very unpleasant (*a gruesome murder/the gruesome sight of rotting meat*).

gruff *adj* **1** deep and rough (*a gruff voice*). **2** rough, angry-sounding (*a gruff reply*).

grum'ble *vb* to complain, to express discontent (*grumbling about being overworked*):—also *n*:—*n* **grum'bler**.

grum'py *adj* (*inf*) cross, ill-tempered (*feeling grumpy first thing in the morning*).

grunt *vb* to make a noise like a pig (*he grunted that he was too busy to talk*):—also *n*.

guano [gwä'-nō] *n* a rich manure made from the dung of sea birds.

guarantee [ga-rên-tee'] *n* **1** a promise to pay money on behalf of another person if that person fails to pay money he or she has promised to pay. **2** one who undertakes to see that another keeps his promise, esp to repay money, a guarantor. **3** a promise, usu in the form of a written statement, that if an article bought is unsatisfactory, it will be repaired or replaced (*a manufacturer's guarantee*). **4** a thing that makes something likely or certain (*there's no guarantee that we will have enough money*):—*vb* **1** to promise (*guaranteed that he'd be there*). **2** to undertake to see that a promise is kept (*guaranteeing that the money will be repaid*).

gua'rantor *n* one who hands over something as a guarantee and loses it if the promise is not kept.

guard *vb* **1** to watch over, to protect (*guard the children*). **2** to defend against attack (*guard the city from enemy attack*):—*n* **1** something that protects (*a fire guard/guards to protect players' shins*). **2** a person, such as a soldier or prison officer, who watches over a person or place to prevent escape, attack, etc. **3** a group of persons whose duty it is to watch over and defend something or someone (*the changing of the guard at Buckingham Palace*). **4** the official in charge of a train. **5** a position in which one can defend or protect oneself, a state of watchfulness (*be on his guard walking through the unlit streets*).

guard'ed *adj* careful, cautious (*give a guarded reply*).

guar'dian *n* **1** (*fml*) a keeper (*the guardian of the castle*). **2** a person who has the legal duty to take care of a child (*when her parents were killed her uncle was appointed her guardian*).

guava [gwä'-vä] *n* a tropical tree or its fruit.

gud'geon *n* **1** a small freshwater fish. **2** a metal pin used to join up parts of a machine, etc.

guerril'la, guerril'la *n* a member of an unofficial small military group that makes sudden, unexpected attacks (*the president and his staff were ambushed by guerrillas in the mountains/guerrilla warfare*).

guess *vb* **1** to put forward an opinion or solution without knowing the facts (*I would guess that it* *is a distance of twenty miles/try to guess the weight of the cake*). **2** (*inf*) (*esp Amer*) to suppose, to consider likely (*I guess you might know him*):—*n* an opinion or judgment that may be wrong as it is formed on insufficient knowledge (*I think he's about 60 but it's just a guess*).

guess'work *n* a number of connected guesses (*reach the right answer by guesswork*).

guest *n* **1** a visitor to a house (*be rude to her mother's guests/have guests for Christmas dinner*). **2** one staying in a hotel (*have room for twenty guests*).

guffaw *vb* to laugh loudly or rudely (*guffawed at his vulgar jokes*):—*also n*.

guide *vb* **1** to lead to the place desired (*guiding guests to their seats*). **2** to show the way (*guide them up the mountain*). **3** to direct, to influence (*be guided by one's common sense*).—*n* **1** one who shows the way (*a mountain guide*). **2** an adviser, a person who directs or influences one's behaviour (*his father was also his guide and friend*). **3** a guidebook (*a guide to Amsterdam*). **4** one who leads people around a place, pointing out things of interest (*a guide taking tourists round the castle*). **5** a thing that helps one to form an opinion or make a calculation (*sales as a guide to the firm's financial situation*).

guide'book *n* a book describing a place and giving information about it.

guild *n* a group of people who meet for a particular purpose (formerly, the members of one trade) (*the Young Mothers' Guild of the local church*).

guid'ance *n* help and advice (*career guidance*).

guilder *n* formerly the currency unit of the Netherlands, until the introduction of the euro in 2002.

guile *n* (*fml*) deceit, trickery, cunning skill (*use guile to gain access to the old lady's house*):— *adjs* **guile'ful, guile'less**.

guillemot [gil'-ê-mot] *n* a swimming and diving bird.

guillotine [gil'-o-teen] *n* **1** a machine formerly used in France for beheading persons. **2** a machine for cutting paper.

guilt *n* **1** the fact of having done wrong, the fact of having committed a crime (*the police established his guilt*). **2** blame or responsibility for wrongdoing (*where the guilt lies*). **3** a sense of shame, uneasiness, etc, caused by the knowl-

edge of having done wrong (*unable to sleep because of feelings of guilt/racked with guilt*):—*adj* **guilt'less**.

guilt'y *adj* **1** having done wrong, having broken a law (*found guilty of the crime*). **2** responsible for behaviour that is morally wrong or socially unacceptable (*a local authority guilty of spending too much money on hospitality*). **3** feeling or showing a sense of guilt or shame (*feel guilty about keeping them waiting*).

guinea [gin'-i] *n* (*old*) a British gold coin worth 21 shillings.

guin'ea fowl *n* a large spotted eatable bird.

guin'ea pig *n* **1** a small animal like a rabbit. **2** a person made use of for the purpose of an experiment (*guinea pigs for their mother's cookery experiments*).

guise *n* **1** dress. **2** appearance.

guitar' *n* a six-stringed musical instrument.

gulch *n* a rocky valley.

gules *n* red (in heraldry).

gulf *n* **1** an inlet of the sea, a long bay. **2** a deep hollow. **3** an area of serious difference or separation (*a gulf between brother and sister*).

gull[1] *n* a long-winged sea bird.

gull[2] *vb* (*old*) to cheat, to deceive (*gulled into lending her money*):—*n* one who has been cheated, one easily deceived.

gull'et *n* the food passage from the mouth to the stomach, the throat (*get a piece of food stuck in her gullet*).

gull'ible *adj* easily deceived (*so gullible that she believed him when he said he wasn't married*).

gull'y *n* a deep channel worn by running water.

gulp *vb* **1** to eat quickly, to swallow in large mouthfuls (*gulped his food down and rushed out*). **2** to make a swallowing movement (*gulp with fear as he saw the policeman*):—*also n*.

gum[1] *n* the flesh in which the teeth are set.

gum[2] *n* **1** the sticky juice of trees. **2** a liquid used for sticking things together (*children using gum to stick pieces of coloured paper on cardboard*):—*vb* (**gummed', gum'ming**) to stick with gum (*gum the cuttings into a scrapbook*).

gum'boil *n* a painful swelling on the gum.

gum'boot *n* a rubber boot (*children wearing gumboots to walk in the muddy fields*).

gum'my *adj* sticky.

gump'tion *n* common sense, good sense (*not have the gumption to think for herself*).

gun *n* any weapon that fires bullets or shells by means of explosive:—*vb* (**gunned'**, **gun'ning**) to shoot or hunt with a gun.

gun'boat *n* a small warship.

gun'cotton *n* an explosive.

gun'dog *n* a dog trained to accompany hunters and to fetch game shot down.

gun'metal *n* **1** a mixture of copper and tin. **2** a dull-grey colour (*shoes of gunmetal*).

gunnel *see* **gunwale**.

gun'ner *n* a man trained to fire large guns.

gun'nery *n* the science of large guns and their management.

gun'powder *n* a type of explosive.

gun'running *n* taking guns into a country against its laws (*terrorists involved in gunrunning*).

gun'shot *n* **1** the firing of a gun (*hear gunshot the night his neighbour was murdered*). **2** the distance a gun can fire (*within gunshot*).

gun'smith *n* one who makes or repairs guns.

gunwale [gun'-el], **gun'nel** *n* the upper edge of a ship's side.

gur'gle *vb* **1** to flow with a bubbling sound (*water gurgling from the taps*). **2** to make a noise resembling this (*babies gurgling in their prams*):—*also n*.

gush *n* a sudden or strong flow (*a gush of water from the tap/a gush of blood from the wound/a gush of enthusiasm*):—*vb* **1** to flow out strongly (*water gushing from the taps/blood gushing from the wound*). **2** to talk as if one felt something very deeply, to speak insincerely (*gushing about how grateful she was*).

guss'et *n* a triangular piece of cloth put into a garment to strengthen part of it.

gust *n* a sudden violent rush of wind (*papers blown away by a gust of wind*).

gus'to *n* keen enjoyment, eagerness (*eat the meal with gusto/play the piano with gusto*).

gus'ty *adj* **1** windy (*a gusty day*). **2** in short violent bursts (*a gusty wind*).

gut *n* **1** a tube in the body that takes the waste matter from the stomach. **2** a strong cord used for violin strings, fishing lines, etc. **3** *pl* (*inf*) the bowels, intestines (*a bad pain in the guts*). **4** *pl* (*inf*) bravery, courage (*not have the guts to admit the truth*):—*vb* (**gut'ted**, **gut'ting**) **1** to take out the inner parts (*gut the fish*). **2** to remove or destroy all except the walls of a building (*fire gutted the house*).

gutta-percha *n* a substance like rubber, made from the juice of certain trees.

gut'ter *n* **1** a passage at the edge of a roof or at the side of the road to carry away water (*blocked gutters*). **2** the lowest poorest level of society (*she was born in the gutter but became famous*):—*vb* to run down in drops, as wax on a candle.

gut'tural *adj* **1** having to do with the throat. **2** made or seeming to be made in the throat, harsh (*a guttural accent*).

guy[1] *n* a rope to steady anything (e.g. a tent).

guy[2] *n* **1** a figure of Guy Fawkes burned on 5th November in Britain in memory of the time when he tried to blow up the Houses of Parliament in London in 1605 (*children making a guy for their bonfire*). **2** (*inf*) a strange-looking or strangely dressed person (*look a real guy in that outfit*). **3** (*inf*) (*esp Amer*) a person (*quite a nice guy*).

guz'zle *vb* (*inf*) to eat or drink greedily (*guzzling all the ice cream*).

gymkha'na *n* a sports meeting for races, horse racing, horse jumping, etc (*children riding ponies at the local gymkhana*).

gymna'sium *n* (*pl* **gymna'sia** *or* **gymna'si-ums**) a room or hall fitted out for bodily exercise (*the school gymnasium*).

gym'nast *n* one skilled in gymnastics:—*adj* **gymnas'tic**.

gymnas'tics *npl* exercises to develop the muscles of the body.

gyp'sum *n* a chalk-like mineral used in making plaster of Paris.

gypsy *see* **gipsy**.

gyrate [jî-rāt'] *vb* **1** to spin round (*a spinning top gyrating*). **2** to move in circles (*dancers gyrating to the music*):—*n* **gyra'tion**.

gy'roscope *n* an instrument that is sometimes used to keep steady ships, aircraft, etc.

H

habeas corpus [hā'-bee-ês kor'-pês] *n* a rule by which a person detained in prison must be brought before the courts.

hab'erdasher *n* one who sells needles, thread and small articles of dress.

haberdash'ery *n* a haberdasher's shop or goods.

hab'it *n* **1** a fixed way of doing something without having to think about it, one's ordinary way of doing things, something that a person does regularly (*he goes home by the path through the woods out of habit/it is her habit to go for a walk before going to bed*). **2** dress, esp of a monk or rider.

hab'itable *adj* that may be lived in (*houses that are scarcely habitable*).

hab'itat *n* the place or surroundings in which a plant or animal is usu found (*the usual habitat of the badger*).

habita'tion *n* **1** the act of living in a place (*houses unfit for human habitation*). **2** the place where one lives (*squalid habitation*).

habit'ual *adj* **1** usual. **2** having formed a certain habit (*habitual drunkard*).

habit'uate *vb* (*fml*) to make used to (*become habituated to a hot climate*).

hack¹ *vb* **1** to cut roughly or unevenly (*hack meat into chunks/hack a way through the jungle*). **2** to kick (*hack an opponent's leg in the football game*):—*n* a cut, a kick.

hack² *n* **1** a hired horse. **2** a person hired to do uninteresting written work for low payment (*employed as a hack in the advertising firm*). **3** (*inf*) a journalist (*all the hacks were at the scene of the accident*).

hack'le *n* **1** a feather in the neck of a farmyard cock. **2** a steel comb for flax:—**make the hackles rise** to make someone angry (*his critical remarks made her hackles rise*).

hack'ney carriage *n* (*old*) a carriage that may be hired, a taxi.

hack'neyed *adj* overused and therefore uninteresting (*listen to the politician's hackneyed ideas*).

had'dock *n* a sea fish of the cod family, used as food.

Hades [ha'-dez] *n* **1** in ancient legend, the home of the dead. **2** hell.

haemorrhage [hem'-or-êj] *n* a sudden bleeding:—*vb* to bleed in this way (*he haemorrhaged after his operation*).

haft *n* (*fml or lit*) a handle (*the haft of a sword*).

hag *n* an ugly old woman.

hag'gard *adj* pale, thin-faced and tired-looking (*looking haggard after being up all night*).

hag'gis *n* (*Scot*) a dish in which the heart, liver, etc, of a sheep are minced and boiled in a sheep's stomach bag with oatmeal and seasoning.

hag'gle *vb* to try to get a seller to lower his or her price (*in some countries customers are expected to haggle with merchants*).

hail¹ *n* **1** frozen rain. **2** a shower of anything (*a hail of arrows*):—*vb* **1** to rain hail (*it was hailing when we left*). **2** to pour down.

hail² *vb* **1** to call to, to greet (*she hailed her neighbour cheerfully*). **2** to shout to a person to try to catch his or her attention (*hail a taxi*):—*interj* a call of greeting:—**hail from** to come from (*he hails from the Highlands*).

hair *n* any or all of the thread-like growths covering the skin of men and animals (*losing his hair as he gets older*):—*adjs* **hair'less**, **hair'y**:—**to split hairs** to point out differences so slight that they could be overlooked.

hair'breadth, **hair's-breadth** *ns* a very small distance (*the bullet missed him by a hair's-breadth*).

hair'dresser *n* one who cuts, arranges, etc, hair (*a hairdresser perming hair*).

hair'-raising *adj* terrifying (*travelling with him is hair-raising as he drives so fast*).

hake *n* a fish like the cod, used as food.

halal *n* meat from an animal that has been killed according to Muslim law.

hal'berd *n* (*old*) a battle-axe fixed on to the shaft of a spear.

hal'cyon *n* the kingfisher:—*adj* calm, peaceful:—**halcyon days** a time of happiness and peace (*recall the halcyon days of her youth*).

hale *adj* healthy, full of vigour (*old men who are still hale and hearty*).

half *n* (*pl* **halves**) one of two equal parts (*she cut the apple and gave her sister half*):—*also adj*.

half'-brother *n* a brother by one parent only.

half-crown' n (old) a British coin worth two shillings and sixpence, in use until 1970.

half-heart'ed adj lacking enthusiasm, not eager (make a half-hearted attempt).

half-sister n a sister by one parent only.

half-sov'ereign n (old) a British gold coin formerly worth ten shillings.

half-wit'ted adj 1 weak in mind (not really responsible for his actions as he is half-witted). 2 foolish, idiotic (a half-witted scheme).

hal'ibut n a large flatfish, used as food.

hall n 1 a large public room (a concert hall). 2 the room or passage at the entrance to a house (stand in the hall waiting for her hostess). 3 (usu found in place names) a large country house.

hallelujah [hal-ê-lŏ'-ya] n a song of praise to God:—interj Praise to God!.

hall'mark n 1 a mark stamped on things made of gold or silver to show the quality of the gold or silver used. 2 anything that shows the quality of a person, thing, etc (politeness is the hallmark of a gentleman).

hallo', hello', hullo' interjs a greeting.

halloo' n and interj a hunting cry:—also vb.

hall'ow vb 1 to make holy (the hallowed ground of the churchyard). 2 to treat as being holy.

Hallowe'en' n the eve of All Saints' Day (i.e. 31st October) (in legend witches are supposed to be seen on Hallowe'en).

hallucina'tion n 1 the experiencing of seeing something that is not there (hallucination can be the result of drug-taking). 2 something imagined as though it is really there (he thought he saw a ghost but it was a hallucination).

ha'lo n 1 a circle of light around the sun or moon. 2 a coloured ring round the head of a holy person in a painting (the Virgin Mary with a halo).

halt[1] vb to stop (the guard halted the train/halt progress/the car halted):—n 1 a stopping place (several halts on the bus journey). 2 a stop (trains coming to a halt).

halt[2] vb 1 (old) to limp (halting badly after the accident to his leg). 2 to hesitate (a reader halting over some difficult words):—adj lame, limping.

halt'er n 1 a rope or strap fitted on to the head of a horse for leading it. 2 a rope for hanging a person:—**halt'erneck** the neck of a dress or top

formed by a strap that goes round the wearer's neck leaving the shoulders bare.

halve vb to cut or break into halves (halve the apple/halving the cost).

halves see half.

hal'yard n a rope for raising or lowering a sail or flag.

ham n 1 the back of the thigh (strain a ham muscle). 2 the thigh of a pig salted and dried and used as food (slices of baked ham). 3 (inf) a bad actor who exaggerates his or her actions and speech (Hamlet performed by a real ham).

ham'burger n a flat round cake made of minced beef, fried or grilled and usually eaten in a bread roll, also known as **burger** or **beefburger.**

ham'let n a small village (a hamlet of just a few cottages).

ham'mer n 1 a tool for driving nails, beating metal, etc. 2 part of a machine or apparatus that strikes (the hammers in a piano):—vb 1 to drive or beat with a hammer (hammer the nail into the wall). 2 to strike hard (police hammering at the door):—**hammer and tongs** with all one's strength (they were arguing away—going at it hammer and tongs).

ham'mock n a bed of a strip of canvas or network hung up at the ends (lying on a hammock in the garden).

ham'per[1] n a large basket (a picnic hamper).

ham'per[2] vb to prevent from moving freely (a tight skirt that hampered her movements/hamper progress).

ham'ster n a rodent like a small rat, often kept as a pet.

ham'string n the tendon behind the knee (strain a hamstring playing football):—vb (pt, pp **ham'strung**) 1 to make lame by cutting the hamstring. 2 to prevent from acting freely (they were hamstrung by lack of money).

hand n 1 the end of the arm below the wrist. 2 a worker (a factory hand). 3 a sailor on a ship (all hands on deck!). 4 the cards given to one player in a card game (deal someone a good hand). 5 one's style of writing (write in a neat hand). 6 the pointer of a clock or watch (the minute hand). 7 a measure of 0.1 metres used in measuring a horse's height at the shoulder:—vb to give with the hand (hand him the book).

8 a share, a part, an influence (*suspect he had a hand in the robbery*):—**hand in glove with** in league with (*suspect that the house owner was hand in glove with the burglar to get insurance money*):—**hand-to-hand** at close quarters (*hand-to-hand combat*):—**hand-to-mouth** with only just enough money to live on with nothing for the future (*earns so little that the family lives a hand-to-mouth existence*):—**out of hand** out of control (*the party got out of hand and the police came*):—**upper hand** control (*he had the upper hand in the tennis match*):—**to wash one's hands of** to refuse to have anything more to do with (*if you won't take any notice of my advice I am washing my hands of you*).

hand'bag *n* a small bag carried by people to contain their personal possessions.

hand'bill *n* a small printed notice (*handbills advertising the jumble sale*).

hand'book *n* a small useful book giving information or instructions (*a handbook explaining the parts of the car*).

hand'cuff *vb* to put handcuffs on (*the police handcuffed the criminal*):—*npl* **hand'cuffs** metal rings joined by a chain, locked on the wrists of prisoners.

hand'ful *n* **1** as much as can be held in one hand (*children giving a handful of nuts each*). **2** a small number or amount (*only a handful of people turned up*).

hand'icap *vb* (**hand'icapped, hand'icap-ping**) **1** in sports or races to give a certain advantage to weaker competitors so that they have an equal chance of winning. **2** to hinder, to put at a disadvantage (*in the race she was handicapped by a knee injury/a firm handicapped by having too little capital*):—*n* **1** in sports or games, an arrangement that allows all competitors to start with an equal chance of winning. **2** a hindrance, a disadvantage (*her lack of height is a handicap in netball*). **3** a physical or mental disability.

hand'icraft *n* skilled work done by hand:—*n* **hand'icraftsman**.

hand'iwork *n* **1** work done with one's own hands (*examples of the pupils' handiwork on show in the classroom*). **2** something bad done or caused by someone (*they think the fire in the school was the handiwork of a former pupil*).

hand'kerchief *n* a cloth for wiping the nose.

handle *vb* **1** to feel, use or hold with the hand (*wash your hands before handling food*). **2** to deal with (*handle the situation well*):—*n* that part of a thing made to be held in the hand (*the handle of the cup*).

hand'lebar *n* the bent rod with which one steers a bicycle.

hand'some *adj* **1** good-looking (*a handsome young man*). **2** generous (*a handsome gift*).

hand'writing *n* the way one writes.

hand'y *adj* **1** clever in using one's hands, skilful (*handy around the house*). **2** useful and simple (*a handy little gadget*). **3** ready, available (*keep a torch handy*). **4** near (*a house handy for the station*):—*n* **hand'iness**.

hang *vb* **1** (*pt, pp* **hung**) to fix one part to something above and allow the rest to drop (*hang the picture from a hook/hang the curtains from a rail*). **2** to remain steady in the air, as certain birds (*hawks hanging*). **3** to let fall (*hang her head in shame/with hair hanging down her back*). **4** (*pt, pp* **hanged'**) to kill a criminal by putting a rope round the neck and then letting him or her drop suddenly so that the neck is broken (*we no longer hang criminals in Britain*).

hang'ar *n* a shed in which aeroplanes are kept.

hang'er *n* that by or from which a garment is hung (*clothes on metal hangers/coat-hangers*).

hang'er-on *n* (*pl* **hang'ers-on**) one who supports another in the hope of gaining some advantage (*since she won the lottery she has been surrounded by hangers-on*).

hang'ings *npl* curtains or material hung on the walls as decoration (*admire the splendid hangings in the palace*).

hang'man *n* one whose job it was to hang criminals.

hank *n* a coil of thread or wool.

hank'er *vb* to desire greatly, to long for (*hankering after a holiday in the sun*).

hank'y-pank'y *n* (*inf*) deceit, trickery, sexually improper behaviour of a minor kind (*some hanky-panky at the office party*).

han'som *n* (*old*) a two-wheeled cab.

Han'ukah *n* an eight-day Jewish festival taking place in November or December.

haphaz'ard adj chance, unplanned (the town had developed in a haphazard way/holiday plans that are rather haphazard):—adv **haphaz'ardly**.

hap'less adj (fml) unfortunate, unlucky (the hapless victim).

hap'ly adv (old) 1 by chance. 2 perhaps.

hap'pen vb 1 to take place (a terrible thing happened). 2 to come about by chance (it happened that they arrived at the same time).

hap'pening n an event (an unfortunate happening).

hap'py adj 1 lucky (by a happy chance). 2 pleased, joyous (she was happy to see him). 3 pleasant, joyful (a happy occasion). 4 suitable (a happy turn of phrase):—n **hap'piness**.

hap'py-go-luck'y adj not easily worried, carefree (too happy-go-lucky to worry about the future).

harangue [ha-rang'] n a loud speech:—vb to speak loudly and forcefully (the manager haranguing the work force about the importance of being on time).

har'ass vb 1 to attack again and again (troops harassing the enemy army). 2 to worry or disturb constantly or frequently (children harassing their mother for more pocket money).

har'binger n a sign of what is to come or happen (swallows are harbingers of summer).

har'bour n 1 a place of safety for ships. 2 a place of shelter (they regarded his house as a harbour for criminals):—vb 1 to give shelter (it is an offence to harbour criminals who are wanted by the police). 2 to keep in the mind (harbour resentment).

hard adj 1 firm, solid (a hard substance). 2 unfeeling, unkind, cruel (a hard master/a hard look). 3 difficult (a hard task). 4 harsh, severe (a hard punishment/a hard life):—adv 1 with force (hit him hard/raining hard). 2 with great effort (work very hard). 3 close (follow hard on his heels). 4 with great attention (stare hard):—**hard of hearing** fairly deaf:—**hard up** (inf) having little money.

hard cash n ready money (she had no hard cash but she could pay by credit card).

hard disk n a magnetic disk inside a computer on which data and programs are stored. See **floppy disk**.

hard'en vb to make hard or harder (leave the toffee to harden/harden one's heart).

hard-head'ed adj clever, practical, not influenced by emotion (hard-headed businessmen).

hard-heart'ed adj unfeeling, having no pity (hard-hearted people who gave no money to the beggars).

hard'iness n toughness, strength.

hard'ly adv 1 almost not (we hardly ever see her). 2 only just, not really (I hardly know him). 3 with difficulty (she could hardly hear him).

hard'ness n the state of being hard (the hardness of the plastic).

hard'ship n poor or difficult conditions (poor people enduring hardship).

hard'ware n 1 household articles made of metal (a shop selling hardware). 2 the mechanical and electronic components of a computer system.

hard words npl angry words (she and her father had hard words before she left home).

hard'y adj 1 strong, tough (have to be hardy to work such long hours out in the winter cold). 2 (old) bold (hardy warriors).

hare n a fast-running animal with rabbit-like ears and long hind legs:—**hare and hounds** a game in which some people (the hounds) chase others (the hares) across country by following a trail of paper scattered by them.

hare'bell n a bluebell-shaped wild flower.

hare'brained adj thoughtless, rash (a harebrained scheme/it was harebrained of her to leave her job).

hare'lip n an upper lip divided in the centre, like that of the hare.

harem [hä'-rêm or ha-reem'] n 1 in Muslim countries, the part of the house where the women live. 2 the women themselves.

har'icot bean n a type of vegetable.

hark vb to listen:—**hark back 1** to begin speaking again about something already discussed (he keeps harking back to his original point). 2 to mention events or subjects of an earlier time (she keeps harking back to how things were in their youth).

har'lequin n a kind of clown, dressed in a suit of colours and often wearing a mask.

har'lot n (fml or old) a woman who earns her living immorally, a prostitute.

harm n hurt, damage, wrong (do his reputation harm/try to cause harm to his rival):—also vb:—adjs **harm'ful**, **harm'less**.

harmon'ic adj having to do with harmony.

harmon'ica n a mouth organ.

harmon'ics n the study of harmony in music.

harmo'nious adj 1 pleasant-sounding (*harmonious sounds*). 2 friendly (*a harmonious atmosphere/relations between them are not harmonious*). 3 pleasant to the eye (*a harmonious combination of colours*).

harmo'nium n a musical wind instrument, like a small organ.

har'monize vb 1 to cause to be in harmony or agreement, to be in harmony or agreement (*colours that do not really harmonize*). 2 to play or sing notes that sound pleasantly with others.

har'mony n 1 agreement, friendship (*they used to be enemies but they now live in harmony*). 2 the pleasant effect made by parts combining into a whole (*the harmony of colours in the flower garden*). 3 the playing at one time of musical notes that are pleasant when sounded together. 3 pleasant sound.

har'ness n the straps, etc, by which a horse is fastened to its load:—vb to put a harness on:—**to die in harness** to die while still doing one's job (*he did not retire—he died in harness*).

harp n a stringed musical instrument played by the fingers:—also vb:—n **harp'ist:—harp on** to keep on talking about one subject (*I wish he would stop harping on about his unhappy childhood*).

harpoon' n a long spear used in hunting whales:—vb to strike with a harpoon.

harp'sichord n an old-time string instrument played by striking keys (as a piano).

har'py n 1 in ancient fables, a monster, half-woman, half-bird. 2 a cruel or nasty woman.

har'ridan n a bad-tempered old woman (*the pupils regard their new leader as an old harridan*).

har'rier n 1 a small dog used in hunting hares. 2 pl a club of cross-country runners.

har'row n a frame with iron spikes or teeth for breaking up lumps of earth in ploughed land.

har'rowing adj very distressing (*seeing her father die in the accident was a harrowing experience for her*).

har'ry vb 1 to keep attacking, to lay waste, to plunder, to raid (*harry the enemy's borders*). 2 (*fml*) to keep on annoying (*harried by people to whom she owes money*).

harsh adj 1 rough and unpleasant to hear, see, etc (*a harsh voice/harsh colours*). 2 unkind, severe, cruel (*a harsh sentence/a harsh attitude*).

hart n a stag or male deer.

hartebeest [har'-tê-beest] n the South African antelope.

ha'rum-sca'rum adj thoughtless, wild (*too harum-scarum to worry about studying*).

har'vest n 1 the time when the ripe crops are cut and gathered in (*take on extra staff for the harvest*). 2 the crops so gathered:—vb to cut and gather in (*harvesting grapes*):—n **har'vester**.

hash n 1 a dish of minced meat. 2 (*inf*) something done badly, a mess (*make a hash of the job*).

hasp n a clasp, a catch for a door, fastened by a padlock.

has'sle (*inf*) vb to annoy someone, especially by repeatedly asking them to do something:—n a difficult or troublesome situation (*finding enough volunteers is a real hassle*).

hass'ock n a footstool, a cushion for kneeling on.

haste n speed, hurry (*change the subject with haste/make haste*).

hasten [hās'-ên] vb (*fml*) to hurry (*worry hastened his death/hasten home*).

hast'y adj 1 done in a hurry (*eat a hasty meal*). 2 done too quickly, rash (*a hasty decision*). 3 quick to lose one's temper.

hat n a head-covering.

hatch' vb 1 to produce (young) from eggs (*hens hatching chicks*). 2 to break out of the egg (*chickens hatching*). 3 to work out in secret (*hatch a cunning scheme*):—n the young hatched from eggs.

hatch' n 1 an open space in a wall or roof or the deck of a ship. 2 a half door (*a serving hatch between the kitchen and dining room*).

hatch' vb to decorate (in drawing, stone-carving) with thin lines.

hat'chet n a small axe:—**bury the hatchet** to end a quarrel (*they did not speak for years but they've now buried the hatchet*).

hatch'way n an opening in the ship's deck through which cargo is loaded.

hate vb to dislike greatly (*hating his job/hate her sister*):—n great dislike (*full of hate for his rival*).

hate'ful adj deserving or causing hate (a hateful job/a hateful person).

ha'tred n great dislike (look at his rival with hatred).

hat'ter n one who makes or sells hats.

hat'-trick n **1** the scoring of three goals in a match (the football player scored a hat-trick). **2** the taking of three wickets with successive balls at cricket. **3** the act of achieving something three times.

haugh'ty adj proud, behaving as if one were better than others (a haughty young woman/a haughty expression):—n **haught'iness**.

haul vb to pull by force, to drag (haul the fishing nets up/hauling the felled trees from the forest):—n **1** a pull (give the rope a haul). **2** an amount taken or caught (e.g. of fish).

haul'age n **1** the carrying of goods by cart or lorry. **2** the amount charged for so carrying goods (add the haulage to the price of the goods).

haul'ier n a carter.

haunch n the thick part of the body around the hips (squat on his haunches).

haunt vb **1** to visit again and again, to go often to (haunt the local cinema). **2** to visit as a ghost (supposedly haunted by a grey lady). **3** to be always in the thoughts of someone (she was haunted by thoughts of his wretched appearance):—n a place often visited.

haunt'ed adj visited by ghosts (a haunted castle).

hautboy [hō'-boi] n (old) an oboe, a shrill wind instrument.

have vb (pt, pp had; indicative I have, he has; we, they have) **1** to possess, to own, to hold (he has a fast car/I have a book). **2** to be forced to do (he has to leave tomorrow):—**to have to do with** to be concerned in (he has nothing to do with the affair).

ha'ven n **1** (old) a harbour. **2** (fml) a place of safety, a shelter (the hostel is a haven for the homeless).

hav'ersack n a bag carried on the back, used for carrying food, etc, on a journey.

hav'oc n destruction, ruin (the storm created havoc in town/create havoc with our plans).

haw n the berry of the hawthorn.

hawk[1] n a bird of prey:—vb to hunt with a hawk.

hawk[2] vb **1** to sell from door to door (tinkers hawking things to housewives). **2** to try to get

people interested in (hawk around his ideas for a film):—n **hawk'er**.

haw'ser n a thick strong rope, often of steel, a cable.

haw'thorn n a thorny tree with white or red flowers and small berries.

hay n grass cut and dried (give hay to the horses).

hay'cock n hay piled neatly in a field.

hay fever n an illness caused by dust or pollen (sufferers from hay fever sneezing uncontrollably).

hay'rick, hay'stack ns a large pile of hay.

hay'wire adj (inf) tangled up, mixed up, in a state of disorder (the computer system went haywire).

haz'ard n **1** risk (allow for driving hazards such as icy roads). **2** (fml) chance (a game of hazard). **3** a piece of rough ground or a sand trap on a golf course:—vb **1** to risk (hazard his earnings on a bet on a horse). **2** to put in danger (hazarding their lives to save others). **3** to put forward (hazard a guess).

haz'ardous adj risky (a hazardous journey).

haze n **1** a thin mist (an early morning haze over the fields). **2** vagueness of mind (in a haze about the future).

ha'zel n **1** a tree with eatable nuts. **2** a reddish-brown colour (eyes of hazel).

ha'zy adj **1** misty (hazy weather). **2** not clear (only a hazy idea of what is involved). **3** doubtful (she's a bit hazy about what happened):—n **haz'iness**.

head n **1** the top part of the body. **2** a person's mind (have a good head). **3** a chief person, a head teacher (the head of the department). **4** the top or front part (the head of the procession). **5** a division in an essay or speech (a chapter divided into various heads). **6** the beginning of a stream. **7** a piece of high land jutting out into the sea:—vb **1** to be first (heading the list). **2** to direct (headed the firm). **3** to strike (a ball) with the head:—adj **1** belonging to the head. **2** chief, principal (the head teacher). **3** coming from the front (head winds).

head'ache n pain in the head (suffer from headaches).

head'dress n a covering for the head (the bride's headdress).

head'er n (inf) **1** a fall or dive forwards (slip and take a header into the water). **2** the act of hitting a ball with the head.

head'gear n a covering for the head.

head'ing n the words written at the top of a page or above a piece of writing (a chapter divided into various headings).

head'land n a piece of high land jutting out into the sea.

head'light n a light at the front, esp a motor vehicle (see the headlights of an approaching car).

head'line n **1** the line in large print above a piece of news in a newspaper (have a quick look at the headlines). **2** the line of print at the top of a page of a book.

head'long adv **1** hastily and rashly (rush headlong into one impossible job after another). **2** with the head first (fall headlong into the mud):—adj **1** rash. **2** head-first (a headlong fall).

head'man n the chief man in a village, etc.

headmas'ter n the male head of a school:—f **headmis'tress**.

head'quarters n the office of those who are in control or command (the firm's headquarters are in London).

head'ship n the position of a head teacher.

heads'man n (old) one who cut off the head of a guilty criminal.

head'stone n the stone placed over a dead person's grave in his or her memory.

head'strong adj determined to have one's own way (so headstrong that he refused to listen to anyone's advice).

head'way n advance, improvement (boats making little headway against the storm/he is not making much headway with his plans to emigrate).

head'y adj **1** excited (the heady feeling of success/heady with triumph). **2** strong, having a quick effect on the senses (a heady wine).

heal vb to make or become well or healthy, to cure (a wound that would not heal/given ointment to heal the wound).

heal'er n one who heals or cures (a faith healer).

health n **1** the state of being well. **2** the state of being free from illness (in sickness and in health).

health'ful adj (fml) causing good health.

health'y adj **1** having good health (a healthy young woman/in a healthy state). **2** causing good health (a healthy climate/a healthy diet).

heap n a number of things lying one on top of another (a heap of leaves/a heap of old newspapers):—vb to put one on top of another, to pile (leaves heaped up against the door/heap the old newspapers together).

hear vb (pt, pp **heard**) **1** to perceive sounds by the ear. **2** to listen (wait and hear what they say).

hear'er n one who listens.

hear'ing n **1** the power to hear sounds (have sharp hearing). **2** the distance at which one can be heard (they made remarks about him within his daughter's hearing). **3** the examining of evidence by a judge.

heark'en vb (old) to listen carefully.

hear'say n what people say though not perhaps the truth, gossip (no one knows why she left—it's all hearsay).

hearse n a car or carriage for a coffin at a funeral.

heart n **1** the organ that keeps the blood flowing through the body (suffer from heart disease). **2** the central or most important part of anything (the heart of the forest/the heart of village life). **3** the centre of a person's thoughts and emotions (know in his heart that he was dying). **4** the cause of life in anything. **5** enthusiasm, determination (the heart went out of them when their leader died). **6** kindly feelings, esp love (he had given her his heart). **7** pl a suit of playing cards. **8** a thing shaped like a heart (a valentine with hearts in it):—**learn by heart** to memorize:—**take to heart** to feel deeply about (take her criticism to heart).

heart'ache n sorrow (the heartache of losing a child).

heart attack n a sudden, painful, sometimes fatal, medical condition in which the heart stops working normally (He died of a heart attack).

heart'broken adj overcome by sorrow or grief (heartbroken by his wife's death).

heart'burn n a burning feeling in the throat or stomach, caused by indigestion.

heart'en vb to encourage, to cheer up (heartened by winning the first game).

heart'felt adj sincere (their heartfelt thanks).

hearth n **1** the floor of a fireplace. **2** the fireside (sit by the hearth).

heart'ily adv sincerely (thank him heartily for his help).

heart'less adj having no kind feelings (heartless people/heartless remarks).

heart-rending adj causing great sorrow or grief (the heart-rending sobs of the child).

heart's-ease n the pansy.

heart'sick adj (old) very sad or sorrowful.

heart'y adj 1 cheerful, sometimes too cheerful (he annoys people by being so hearty first thing in the morning). 2 sincere (hearty thanks). 3 healthy (hale and hearty). 4 large (a hearty breakfast).

heat n 1 hotness, warmth (the heat of the sun/the effect of heat on metal). 2 anger, excitement (in the heat of the moment). 3 a division of a race from which the winners go on to the final:—vb to make or become warm or hot (a small fire to heat a large room/heat the soup).

heat'ed adj angry (a heated argument).

heath n 1 a stretch of wasteland, a moor (Hampstead Heath). 2 a low-growing ever-green shrub.

heath'en n one who knows nothing of God (missionaries sent to convert the heathens):—also adj.

heath'er n a low-growing shrub with purple or white flowers, found on moors or mountains.

heat'wave n a long spell of hot weather (forbidden to use garden hoses during the heatwave).

heave vb 1 to lift, to raise with effort (heave the luggage into the car boot). 2 to move up and down regularly (shoulders heaving with laughter). 3 to pull hard (sailors heaving ropes). 4 to utter with effort (heave a sigh of relief):—n 1 an upward throw. 2 a pull:—**heave to** (of a ship) to stop moving.

hea'ven n 1 the sky. 2 the everlasting presence of God. 3 the dwelling place of the gods. 4 the happiness enjoyed by good people after death (Christians believe that people go to heaven after death).

hea'venly adj 1 having to do with heaven or the sky. 2 (inf) delightful (a heavenly dress/a heavenly performance).

hea'vy adj 1 having weight, of great weight (lead is a heavy metal/how heavy is the parcel?). 2 of more than the usual size, amount, force, etc (heavy traffic/heavy losses in the battle). 3 dull, dark and cloudy (a heavy sky). 4 sleepy (children with heavy eyes/heavy with tiredness). 5 sad (with heavy heart). 6 difficult to digest (a heavy meal/a heavy book). 7 busy, full of activity (a heavy day/a heavy programme):—n hea'viness.

heavy-duty adj strong and not easily damaged or worn out (heavy-duty boots).

He'brew n 1 the language of the Jewish people. 2 a Jew:—also adj:—adj Hebra'ic.

heck'le vb to put difficult questions to a public speaker (a politician heckled by his opponent's supporters):—n heck'ler.

hec'tic adj 1 feverish. 2 flushed with fever.

hec'to- prefix one hundred.

hec'togram n one hundred grams.

hec'tor vb to try to frighten by bullying, to shout at (their father tried to hector them into studying).

hedge n 1 a fence of bushes, shrubs, etc (plant a hedge along the front of the garden). 2 means of defence or protection (as a hedge against inflation):—vb 1 to surround with a hedge (hedge the garden). 2 to avoid giving a clear, direct answer (politicians hedging when asked questions).

hedge'hog n a small animal covered with prickles, that can roll itself into a ball.

hedge'row n a line of bushes, shrubs, etc, forming a hedge.

heed vb to pay attention to, to notice (you should heed your parents' advice):—n care, attention (pay little heed to his work):—adjs heed'ful, heed'less.

heel[1] n 1 the back part of the foot (have blisters on her heel). 2 the part of a shoe, etc, under the heel of the foot (shoes with high heels):—vb 1 to strike with the heel (heeling the ball away). 2 to put a heel on (have the boots heeled):—**bring to heel** to get control over (bring the rebels to heel):—**down at heel** poorly or untidily dressed:—**take to one's heels** to run away (he took to his heels when he saw the public).

heel[2] vb to lean over to one side (boats heeling over in the storm).

hef'ty adj 1 rather heavy, big and strong (a hefty young woman). 2 large and heavy (a hefty load).

3 powerful (*a hefty blow*). **4** (*inf*) large, substantial (*a hefty salary*).

hei'fer *n* a young cow.

height [hīt] *n* **1** the distance from top to bottom (*the height of the fence*). **2** the state of being high (*his height is an advantage in some games*). **3** a high place (*be afraid of heights*). **4** a hill (*scale the heights above the town*). **5** the highest degree of something (*the height of summer/the height of her acting career*).

height'en *vb* **1** to make higher (*heighten the fence*). **2** to increase (*heighten the tension/heighten the dramatic effect*).

heinous [hee'-nês] *adj* very bad, wicked (*a heinous crime*).

heir [ēr] *n* one who receives property or a title after the death of the previous owner (*as his uncle's heir he inherited the estate*):—*f* **heir'ess**.

heir appar'ent *n* one who has the right to a title or property on the death of the owner.

heir'loom *n* a valuable object that has been the property of a family for many generations (*her diamond brooch is a family heirloom*).

hel'icopter *n* a type of aeroplane with propellors that enable it to go straight up or down (*survivors rescued from the sea by helicopter*).

he'liograph *n* an instrument for sending signals by reflecting sunlight.

he'liotrope *n* **1** a garden plant with purple flowers. **2** a purple colour (*a dress of heliotrope*):— also *adj*.

he'lium *n* a very light gas.

hell *n* **1** in some religions, the place where the wicked suffer after death. **2** everlasting banishment from God. **3** a place of great evil or suffering.

Hellen'ic *adj* Greek (*Hellenic culture*).

Hell'enism *n* Greek art and learning.

hell'ish *adj* **1** having to do with or like hell. **2** (*inf*) very bad, extremely unpleasant (*a hellish crime*).

hello *see* **hallo.**

helm *n* a steering wheel or handle on a ship:—**at the helm** in control or command (*the firm's owner has retired and there is a new man at the helm*).

hel'met *ns* **1** (*old*) head armour. **2** a protective covering for the head (*motorcyclists wearing helmets*).

helms'man *n* the steersman.

help *vb* **1** to aid, to assist (*help the old lady across the road/help them to find the book*). **2** to give what is needed (*help him to vegetables*). **3** to serve someone in a shop (*can I help you?*). **4** to make it easier for something to happen (*it would help if he left*). **5** to avoid (doing) (*she could not help laughing*):—*n* aid, assistance:—*n* **help'er.**

help'ful *adj* **1** willing to help (*helpful neighbours*). **2** useful (*a helpful suggestion*).

help'ing *n* one's share of a dish of food (*a second helping of pudding*).

help'less *adj* unable to help oneself (*helpless children*).

help'mate, help'meet *ns* (*old*) a helper, one's husband or wife.

hel'ter-skel'ter *adv* **1** in a hurry and confusion, (*the children ran helter-skelter from the bus to the beach*):—*n* a twisting downward slide at a fair.

hem *n* the border of a garment folded back and sewn (*put a hem on the skirt to shorten it*):—*vb* (**hemmed, hem'ming**) to sew a hem:—**hem in** to surround closely (*a house hemmed in by blocks of flats*).

hem'isphere *n* **1** half of the world. **2** a map showing half of the world.

hem'lock *n* a poisonous plant.

hemp *n* **1** a grass-like plant from whose fibres ropes are made. **2** a narcotic drug from the plant.

hen *n* a female bird, esp a farmyard fowl (*keep hens for their eggs*).

hen'bane *n* a poisonous plant.

hence *adv* **1** (*old*) from this place (*get thee hence!*). **2** (*fml*) from this time on (*a week hence*). **3** for this reason (*I injured my arm—hence the bandage*).

henceforth', hencefor'ward *advs* (*fml*) from this time on (*henceforth they will work at another branch of the firm*).

hench'man *n* a follower, a trusty supporter (*a people oppressed by the dictator and his henchmen*).

hen'coop *n* a cage for a hen.

hen'pecked *adj* ordered about by one's wife (*so henpecked that he is not allowed out with his friends*).

hep'tagon *n* a seven-sided figure.

her'ald *n* **1** (*old*) one who makes important announcements to the public. **2** an official who keeps records of coats of arms. **3** a sign of something to come (*flowers that are a herald of spring*):—*vb* **1** to announce the approach of someone or something (*heavy footsteps heralded his approach*). **2** to be a sign of (*flowers heralding the arrival of spring*).

her'aldry *n* the study of coats of arms and the history of noble families:—*adj* **heral'dic**.

herb *n* **1** any plant whose stem dies away during the winter. **2** a plant used for medicine or flavouring food (*add herbs to the spaghetti sauce*).

herba'ceous *adj* having to do with or full of herbs:—**herba'ceous border** a flowerbed with plants that flower year after year.

herb'al *adj* of herbs (*herbal remedies*).

herb'alist *n* one who studies or sells herbs (*go to a herbalist for a cure for his allergy*).

her'bivore *n* a grass-eating animal (*sheep are herbivores*):—**herbiv'orous** *adj* eating grass or herbs (*herbivorous animals such as cows*).

herculean [her-kû-lee'-ên] *adj* requiring great effort, very difficult (*a herculean task*).

herd *n* **1** a flock of animals (*a herd of cows/a herd of deer*). **2** a large crowd of people (*herds of people doing Christmas shopping*). **3** a herdsman:—*vb* **1** (*inf*) to crowd or collect together (*people herded into the hall to hear the speaker*). **2** to look after a herd (*herd the cows in the field*). **3** to drive (*herd the cows to market*).

herds'man *n* one who looks after a herd.

here'about(s) *advs* about here.

hereaf'ter *adv* after this time:—*n* the life after death.

hered'itary *adj* passed on from parents to children (*a hereditary disease*).

hered'ity *n* the passing on of qualities of character, etc, from parents to children (*health factors associated with heredity*).

her'esy *n* an opinion that contradicts accepted ideas, esp in religion.

her'etic *n* one who teaches a heresy:—*adj* **heret'ical**.

her'itable *adj* able to be passed on from parents to children (*heritable property*).

her'itage *n* **1** that which is passed on to one by one's parents (*the farm was part of his heritage*). **2** things that have been passed on from earlier generations (*the art collection is part of our national heritage*).

hermaphrodite [her-maf'-ro-dît] *n* an animal or plant with the characteristics of both sexes.

hermet'ically *adv* so tightly (sealed) as to keep out all air (*keep the food in a hermetically sealed tin to prevent it going rotten*).

her'mit *n* one who lives alone or away from other people, often originally for religious reasons.

her'mitage *n* the dwelling of a hermit.

her'nia *n* a break in the wall of muscle in the front of the stomach (*have an operation to repair a hernia*).

he'ro *n* (*pl* **he'roes**) **1** a brave person, someone admired for his brave deeds (*treated as a hero for saving the cat from the fire*). **2** the chief character in a play or novel (*the hero of the novel is a young boy*):—*f* **her'oine**.

hero'ic *adj* **1** brave (*heroic deeds*). **2** having to do with heroes (*heroic legends*).

her'oin *n* a habit-forming drug obtained from opium.

heroine *see* **hero**.

her'oism *n* bravery (*receive a medal for his heroism in battle*).

her'on *n* a water bird with long legs and neck (*a heron catching fish*).

her'ring *n* a small sea fish used as food.

herring-bone' *adj* with a pattern like the backbone of a herring (*a herring-bone tweed*).

hes'itance, hes'itancy, hesita'tion *ns* doubt, act of hesitating, indecision (*her hesitance about accepting the invitation*).

hes'itant *adj* doubtful, undecided (*a hesitant person/a hesitant step/a hesitant remark*).

hes'itate *vb* **1** to stop for a moment before doing something or speaking (*she hesitated before answering the question*). **2** to be undecided (*they are hesitating about whether to go or not*).

het'erodox *adj* having opinions different from those of the majority:—*n* **het'ero-doxy**.

heterogeneous [het-er-ô-jee'-nee-ês] *adj* (*fml*) of different kinds (*a heterogeneous mix of nationalities*).

hew *n* (*fml*) to cut by a number of strong blows, to chop (*hew down a tree*).

hex'agon *n* a six-sided figure:—*adj* **hexag'-onal**.

hexam'eter *n* a line of verse containing six metrical feet.

hey'day n full strength, the time of life when one's abilities, etc, reach their full power (*when silent films were in their heyday*).

hiatus [hī-ā'-tês] n 1 a break in a piece of writing or a speech (*notice a hiatus in the play*). 2 a gap (*the talks resumed after a week's hiatus*).

hi'bernate vb to pass the winter in sleep, as certain animals do (*squirrels and hedgehogs hibernating*):—n **hiberna'tion**.

hic'cup n 1 a sudden short stoppage of the breath. 2 the sound caused by this. 3 a small delay or interruption (*a hiccup in our timetable because of the absence of one of the speakers*):—vb (**hic'cupped, hic'cupping**) to have hiccups.

hick'ory n an American tree with very hard wood.

hide[1] vb (hid, pp **hid'den**) 1 to put or keep out of sight (*hide the presents from the children until Christmas/hide the evidence from the police*). 2 to keep secret (*hide her disappointment*):—n a camouflaged place used by bird-watchers, hunters, etc.

hide[2] n the skin of an animal (*an elephant's hide*).

hide'bound adj narrow-minded, unwilling to change one's ideas (*hidebound people who automatically dislike new fashions and attitudes*).

hide'ous adj 1 frightful (*a hideous scream*). 2 very ugly (*a hideous dress*).

hide'out n a place to hide (*a hideout in the forest where they were safe from enemies*).

hid'ing n a thrashing, a beating (*their father threatened them with a hiding if they got into trouble again*).

hie vb (old or hum) to go quickly (*hie thee to the town*).

hi'erarchy n 1 an arrangement in order, putting the most important first (*his place in the firm's hierarchy*). 2 the group of people in an organization who have power or control.

hi'eroglyph, hieroglyph'ic [hî-êr-ō-glif(-ik)] n s a picture or sign standing for a letter, as in ancient Egyptian writing.

hieroglyph'ics [hî-êr-ō-glif-iks] n 1 a system of writing that uses hieroglyphs. 2 (*inf*) writing that is difficult to read.

hig'gledy-pig'gledy adj and adv (*inf*) very untidy, in disorder (*clothes lying higgledy-piggledy around her bedroom*).

high adj 1 being a certain distance up (*a wall six feet high*). 2 being above normal level (*high blood pressure/a high temperature*). 3 raised above (*a high window*). 4 of important rank (*high officials*). 5 morally good (*of high ideals*). 6 dear (in price) (*high costs*). 7 (*of meat*) not fresh (*game that is high*):—also adv:—**on one's high horse** wanting to be treated with great respect, haughty (*when anyone criticizes her she gets on her high horse and won't speak to anyone*).

high'-born adj (*fml*) belonging to a noble family (*high-born young men*).

high'brow adj 1 interested only in things requiring great learning (*highbrow people*). 2 relating to things requiring great learning (*highbrow literature*):—also n.

high-flown adj full of long and unusual words (*a high-flown style of writing*).

high-hand'ed adj using power without thought for the rights or feelings of others (*the new boss has a very high-handed approach to the work force*).

high'lander n one who lives in the mountains.

high'lands npl the mountainous part of a country, esp in Scotland (**the Highlands**).

high'ly adv greatly, very (*highly amused/highly spiced/highly unlikely*).

high'ly strung', high'-strung adjs very nervous, easily excited (*she's very highly strung and easily gets upset*).

high-mind'ed adj noble and virtuous in character (*too high-minded even to tell a white lie*).

high'ness n a title of honour given to sons or daughters of kings or queens.

high'road n 1 a main road. 2 the easiest or most direct way (*the highroad to happiness*).

high school n a school educating up to an advanced standard.

high seas npl the open seas (*pirates sailing the high seas*).

high'-spirited adj 1 lively and energetic, cheerful (*high-spirited children*). 2 nervously active, frisky (*high-spirited horses*).

high-strung see highly strung.

high tea n afternoon tea with a cooked dish (*have fish and chips for high tea*).

high-tech adj using very advanced modern machinery and methods, especially electronic ones, also **hi'-tech**.

high water *n* high tide.

high'way *n* a public road.

high'wayman *n* (*old*) one who attacks and robs travellers.

hi'jack *vb* to take control of a vehicle illegally during a journey (*terrorists hijacking a plane*):— **hi'jacker** *n*.

hike *vb* to go on a long walk in the country, esp over rough ground (*hiking over the moor on Saturday mornings*):— *n* **hik'er.**

hila'rious *adj* **1** extremely amusing (*a hilarious account of the party/hilarious jokes*). **2** noisily merry (*a hilarious party*):— *n* **hi-lar'ity.**

hill *n* a low mountain.

hill'ock *n* (*fml*) a small hill.

hill'y *adj* abounding with hills (*hilly ground*).

hilt *n* the handle of a sword or dagger.

hind[1] *n* a female deer.

hind[2] *adj* at the back (*the dog's hind legs*).

hind'er[1] *adj* at the back.

hin'der[2] *vb* to stop or delay the advance or development of, to put difficulties in the way of (*hinder progress/hinder them in their escape plan*).

hind'most *adj* (*old*) last of all, farthest back.

hin'drance *n* something or someone that makes action or progress difficult (*the new assistant was more of a hindrance than a help/her injured arm was a hindrance in her work*).

Hindu' *n* a believer in Hinduism.

Hin'duism *n* a religion held by many in India and believing in many gods.

Hindusta'ni *n* the chief language of northern India.

hinge *n* a folding joint to which a door or lid is fixed so that it can turn on it (*gate hinges in need of being oiled*):— *vb* **1** to fix hinges to (*the cupboard door is hinged on the right*). **2** to depend (*his promotion hinges on passing the exam*).

hint *vb* to suggest indirectly (*she hinted that he was not completely honest*):— *n* **1** an indirect suggestion (*he received a hint that the firm would be sold*). **2** a helpful suggestion (*mother's cookery hints*). **3** a small amount (*a hint of parsley*).

hin'terland *n* the country inland from a port or stretch of coast.

hip[1] *n* the upper part of the thigh (*stand with her hands on her hips*).

hip[2] *n* the fruit of the wild rose.

hip pock'et *n* a pocket at the back of the trousers (*have his wallet sticking out of his hip pocket*).

hippopot'amus *n* (*pl* **hippopot'amuses** *or* **hippopot'ami**) a large wild river animal found in Africa.

hire *n* **1** the hiring of something (*a boat for hire*). **2** the money paid for the use of a thing or for the work of another (*pay the hire of the hall in advance*):— *vb* **1** to get the use of a thing by paying for it (*hire a yacht for a week*). **2** to lend to another for payment (*hiring out his boat to tourists*).

hire'ling *n* (*fml*) one who works for someone else.

hire-pur'chase *n* the getting of a thing on hire until one has paid its whole cost, when it becomes one's own property (*buy their furniture on hire-purchase*).

hirsute [hir'-sût *or* hir-sût'] *adj* hairy (*a very hirsute young man*).

hiss *vb* to make a sound like that of the letter *s*, often as a sign of disapproval (*the audience hissed at the comedian's bad jokes*):— *n* the act or sound of hissing (*the hiss of a snake*).

histor'ian *n* a writer of history (*a historian specializing in the Tudor period*).

histor'ic *adj* of outstanding importance (*a historic battle*).

histor'ical *adj* having to do with history (*historical studies*).

his'tory *n* **1** the study of past events (*study British history at college*). **2** an accurate account of past events, conditions, ideas, etc (*the history of the English language/told him her life history*).

histrion'ic *adj* (*fml*) **1** having to do with actors or acting. **2** behaving or done in too theatrical a way, esp in showing insincere feelings (*her histrionic behaviour in public embarrassed him*).

histrion'ics *npl* **1** (*fml*) play-acting. **2** exaggerated theatrical behaviour showing insincere feelings.

hit *vb* (**hit**, **hit'ting**) **1** to strike (*hit the ball with the racket/hit his attacker in the face*). **2** to reach, to arrive at (*hit a bad patch*):— *n* **1** a blow. **2** a success (*the show was a hit*).

hitch *vb* **1** to hook or fasten (on to) (*hitch the carriage on to the train*). **2** to try to get a life in someone else's car (*try to hitch to Birmingham*):— *n* **1** a jerk, a pull (*give his trousers a* *hitch*). **2** a type of knot. **3** a difficulty, a snag (*a slight hitch in the proceedings*).

hi-tech *adj* using very advanced modern machinery and methods, especially electronic ones, also **high-tech.**

hith'er *adv* (*fml or old*) to this place (*come hither*):—**hither and thither** back and forward, here and there.

hith'erto *adv* (*fml*) until now (*hitherto he has been punctual but he was late today*).

HIV (*abbr for* Human Immunodeficiency Virus) a virus that affects the body's immune system and causes infections or illnesses which can lead to **Aids.**

hive *n* **1** a home made for bees. **2** a place of great activity (*the small office was a real hive of industry*).

hoar *n* white frost:—*adj* **hoary.**

hoard *n* a hidden store (*the miser's hoard of gold*):—*vb* **1** to store secretly (*a miser hoarding gold coins*). **2** to collect, to lay in a store of (*hoard food in case there is a shortage*).

hoard'ing *n* a high wooden fence on which posters are often stuck.

hoar'frost *n* frozen dew.

hoarse *adj* having a rough or husky voice (*children hoarse from shouting*).

hoar'y *adj* **1** white or grey from age or frost (*his hoary head*). **2** (*fml*) very old (*hoary traditions*).

hoax *n* a trick or joke intended to deceive (*the phone call about the fire was a hoax*):—*vb* to deceive, to trick.

hob *n* an iron shelf at the side of the fireplace for pots, etc.

hob'ble *vb* **1** to limp (*hobbling in shoes that were too tight*). **2** to tie the legs of a horse to one another to stop it running away.

hob'by *n* a favourite subject or interest for one's spare time, an interesting pastime (*work so hard that they had no time for hobbies/play golf as a hobby*).

hob'byhorse *n* **1** a rocking horse. **2** a horse on a merry-go-round. **3** a favourite subject that a person is constantly referring to (*the behaviour of young people today is one of his hobbyhorses*).

hob'goblin *n* in fairy stories, a mischievous fairy.

hob'nail *n* a nail with a thick head used in horseshoes, boots, etc:—*adj* **hob'nailed.**

hob'nob *vb* (**hob'nobbing, hob'nobbed**) **1** (*old*) to drink together. **2** to be friends with, to associate socially with, usu with someone in a higher social position.

hock *see* **hough.**

hock'ey *n* a team game played with a ball and sticks curved at the end (*there are eleven players in a hockey team*).

ho'cus-po'cus *n* trickery, deception, talk or behaviour designed to draw attention away from what is actually happening (*the conjurer's hocuspocus*).

hod *n* a V-shaped wooden container on a pole used for carrying bricks, etc.

hoe *n* a garden tool for loosening the earth around plants:—*vb* to dig with a hoe (*hoeing the weeds*).

hog *n* **1** a pig. **2** a greedy or filthy person (*he's such a hog that he ate all the food before the others arrived*).

Hogmanay' *n* (*Scot*) the last day of the year (*have a party on Hogmanay*).

hoist *vb* to lift, to raise, esp by some apparatus (*hoist the load with a crane*):—*n* a lift for goods.

hoi'ty-toi'ty *adj* (*inf*) thinking oneself very important (*she's too hoity-toity to talk to her old neighbours*).

hold *vb* (*pt, pp* **held**) **1** to have or take in the hand(s) or arms (*hold a newborn baby/holding a knife in one hand*). **2** to bear the weight of, to support (*the bridge wouldn't hold them*). **3** to be able to contain (*a jug holding two litres*). **4** to have (an opinion) (*he holds the view that all men are equal*). **5** to cause to take place (*hold a meeting*):—*n* **1** grasp (*have a firm hold of the wheel*). **2** the lowest part of a ship, where the cargo is stored:—**hold forth** (*fml*) to speak in public or at length (*held forth about his political opinions*):—**hold one's own** to keep one's advantages without gaining any more (*held his own in a fight*):—**hold up 1** to attack and rob. **2** to delay, to hinder. **3** to last. **4** to raise. **5** to support:—**hold with** to agree with (*he does not hold with new educational ideas*).

hold'er *n* one who holds or possesses (*the holder of the lease*).

hold'ing *n* **1** a small rented farm. **2** the amount possessed (*his financial holding in the firm*).

hole *n* **1** a hollow or empty space in something solid (*a hole in the road*). **2** an opening (*a hole in the fence*). **3** an animal's den (*the fox's hole*). **4** (*inf*) a difficulty (*in a bit of a hole financially*):—*vb* to make a hole in (*a ship holed by a rock*).

hole'-and-cor'ner *adj* secret and dishonest (*have a hole-and-corner affair with his secretary*).

hol'iday *n* a day or period of rest or amusement (*their annual holiday*):—*n* **hol'iday-maker**.

ho'liness *n* the state of being holy:—**Holiness** a title given to the pope.

holl'and *n* a coarse linen.

holl'ow *adj* **1** not solid (*hollow balls/hollow metal cylinders*). **2** empty inside (*hollow trees*). **3** worthless (*a hollow victory*). **4** not sincere (*hollow promises*). **5** sounding as if coming from a hollow place, echoing (*hollow sounds*):—*n* **1** a sunken place, something hollow (*hollows in the cheeks*). **2** a low place between folds, ridges, etc. **3** a valley:—*vb* **1** to make hollow. **2** to take out the inside. leaving the surrounds untouched (*hollow out the melon*).

holl'y *n* a prickly evergreen tree with red berries (*decorations of holly at Christmas*).

holl'yhock *n* a kind of tall garden flowering plant.

holm oak [hōm'-] *n* the evergreen oak.

hol'ocaust *n* **1** (*old*) the burning of an animal as a sacrifice. **2** killing or destruction on a huge scale, often by fire (*fear a nuclear holocaust*).

hol'ogram *n* a three-dimensional photographic image created by using a laser beam.

hol'ograph *n* a document wholly in one's own handwriting (*a will in the form of a holograph*).

hol'ster *n* a pistol case that can be fixed to a belt (*remove his gun from his holster*).

holt *n* **1** a wood. **2** a woody hill.

ho'ly *adj* **1** good and trying to be perfect in the service of God (*holy men*). **2** set aside for the service of God (*holy places*).

Holy Grail *n* in Christian belief, the bowl used by Christ at the Last Supper, in which later were received the last drops of his blood.

Holy Week *n* the week before Easter.

Holy Writ *n* the Bible.

hom'age *n* **1** (*old*) the promise to do certain duties for an overlord. **2** respect, things said or done to show great respect (*come to do homage at the great man's funeral/pay homage to the famous writer*).

home *n* **1** one's house, the place where one lives (*the doctor visited her in her home*). **2** where one was born, the place where a person or thing originally comes from (*the home of jazz*). **3** a place where children without parents, old people, people who are ill, etc, are looked after (*an old people's home*):—*adj* **1** having to do with one's home (*home comforts*). **2** made or done at home (*home cooking*):—*adv* to or at home (*go home*).

home'ly *adj* **1** plain, simple (*homely tastes*). **2** like home, comfortable (*a homely place*).

Home Office *n* the British government department that sees that peace is kept within the country (represented in Parliament by the **Home Secretary**).

home'sick *adj* having a longing for home (*homesick at boarding school*):—*n* **home'-sickness**.

home'spun *n* cloth made in the home:—*adj* **1** made of cloth spun at home. **2** plain and simple (*homespun remedies*).

home'stead *n* a house with grounds and outhouses around it, esp a farm.

home'wards *adv* (*fml*) towards home (*travel homewards*).

hom'icide *n* **1** the act of killing another human being (*guilty of homicide*). **2** one who kills another human being (*homicides in jail*):—*adj* **homici'dal**.

hom'ily *n* **1** a sermon. **2** a long, boring talk containing advice about good or correct behaviour (*grandfather is always giving the children a homily on the importance of doing homework*).

hom'ing *adj* able to find the way home (*a homing pigeon*).

hom'iny *n* maize crushed to powder and boiled in water or milk.

homoeopath'ic *adj* having to do with homoeopathy (*homoeopathic remedies*).

homoeopathy [hō-mi-op'-êthi] *n* the curing of diseases by giving medicine that would cause a mild form of the disease in a healthy person (*homoeopathy is a branch of alternative medicine*).

homogeneous [ho-mō-jee'-ni-ês] *adj* of the same kind, having all the parts of the same kind (*a homogeneous group of people*):—*n* **homogene'ity**.

hom'onym *n* a word sounding the same as another but having a different meaning (e.g. here, hear).

hone n a smooth stone for sharpening knives, etc:—vb **1** to sharpen on a hone (*honing the kitchen knives*). **2** to sharpen or make effective (*hone his wit*).

honest [on'-ĕst] adj **1** free from deceit, upright, truthful, not cheating, stealing, etc (*honest workers*). **2** open and frank (*to be honest with you*). **3** typical of an honest person, open (*an honest face*). **4** true (*an honest report*):—n **hon'esty**.

honey [hun'-i] n a sweet fluid collected by bees, etc, from flowers.

hon'eycomb n the waxy cells in which bees store their honey.

hon'eyed adj sweet but often insincere (*honeyed words*).

hon'eymoon n the holiday taken by a newly married couple immediately after marriage.

hon'eysuckle n a sweet-smelling climbing plant (*honeysuckle surrounding the door*).

honora'rium n (**honora'riums** or **hono-ra'ria**) (*fml*) a sum of money given to someone who does unpaid work, a voluntary payment made for professional services (*receive a small honorarium for looking after the club's accounts*).

hon'orary adj **1** unpaid (*honorary secretary of the organization*). **2** given to a person as a mark of respect for his or her ability (*an honorary degree*).

honour [on'-or] n **1** good name, reputation (*fight for his country's honour*). **2** high principles and standards of behaviour (*a man of honour*). **3** glory (*bring honour to the school*). **4** a person or thing that brings pride or glory (*he is an honour to the school*). **5** a title of respect used when talking to or about certain important people such as judges, mayors, etc. **6** respect (*in honour of the dead*):—vb **1** to respect. **2** to raise in rank or dignity. **3** to pay (a bill) when due.

hon'ourable adj **1** worthy of respect or honour (*honourable deeds*). **2** honest, of high principles (*an honourable man*). **3** just. **4** a title of respect used to the children of certain nobles and to certain members of parliament.

hood n **1** a covering for the head and neck (*the monk's hood*). **2** anything hood-shaped (*the hood of a pram*). **3** a V-shaped cloth lined with coloured silk worn over the shoulders by holders of a university degree.

hood'wink vb to deceive (*hoodwink her into lending him money*).

hoof n (pl **hooves** or **hoofs**) the horny part of the foot in certain animals (*a horse's hoof*).

hook n **1** a piece of metal or plastic bent for catching hold of or for hanging things on (*a hook on the bathroom door for dressing gowns*). **2** a short curved cutting instrument:—vb **1** to catch, hold or fasten with a hook (*hook a large salmon*):—adjs **hooked**, **hook-shaped**:—**by hook or by crook** by any means, fair or unfair (*he will get the money by hook or by crook*).

hook'ah n an Eastern tobacco pipe with a long tube by which the smoke is sucked down into a bowl of water.

hool'igan n a street rough, a ruffian (*young hooligans fighting in the street and damaging property*):—n **hool'iganism**.

hoop n **1** a band of metal around a cask. **2** a large ring of wood, metal, etc (*dogs jumping through hoops*).

hooping cough see **whooping cough**.

hoop'oe n a beautiful crested bird.

hoot vb **1** to cry as an owl. **2** to make a loud noise of laughter or disapproval (*hooting with laughter*). **3** to sound a horn (*the car driver hooted his horn at the pedestrian*):—n **1** the cry of an owl. **2** the sound of a hooter. **3** a shout of laughter or disapproval.

hoot'er n **1** a steam whistle. **2** an instrument that makes a hooting sound (*the factory hooter*). **1** (*inf*) a nose (*a big red hooter*).

hooves see **hoof**.

hop[1] vb (**hopped**, **hop'ping**) **1** to jump on one leg (*hurt his foot and have to hop to the car*). **2** to jump (*he hopped over the wall*):—n a jump, esp on one leg.

hop[2] n a plant with bitter-tasting cones used in making beer.

hope vb to wish and expect what is good in future (*he hopes for better things/she hopes to get a job soon*):—n a wish or expectation for the future (*her hopes of getting to university/live in hope*).

hope'ful adj **1** full of hope (*in a hopeful mood*). **2** giving cause for hope (*hopeful signs*).

hope'less adj **1** without hope. **2** giving no cause for hope (*a hopeless cause*). **3** (*inf*) poor, not good (*a hopeless cook*).

hop'per *n* a large narrow-necked funnel for feeding grain into a mill.

horde *n* 1 a wandering tribe. 2 a huge crowd (*hordes of people at the January sales*).

hori'zon *n* 1 the line along which earth and sky seem to meet. 2 the breadth of one's understanding and experience (*extend his horizons by studying*).

horizon'tal *adj* parallel to the horizon, flat, level (*in a horizontal line*).

horn *n* 1 a hard pointed growth on the heads of some animals (*a bull's horns*). 2 anything shaped like a horn (e.g. snail's feelers). 3 a musical wind instrument (*play the French horn*). 4 on a motor car, an instrument that makes warning noises (*sound his horn for the sheep to get out of the way*):—*adj* made of horn.

horned *adj* having horns (*horned cattle*).

horn'et *n* a large stinging insect of the wasp family.

horn'pipe *n* 1 a lively dance, a sailor's dance. 2 music for such a dance.

hor'oscope *n* 1 a plan showing the positions of the stars in the sky at a particular time, esp the hour of one's birth, made in the belief that from it future events can be foretold (*cast a horoscope*). 2 a forecast of a person's future based on such a plan (*horoscopes printed in the newspapers*).

hor'rible *adj* 1 causing horror, dreadful, terrible (*a horrible accident*). 2 (*inf*) unpleasant, nasty (*a horrible person/horrible weather*).

hor'rid *adj* 1 (*fml*) horrible, dreadful (*horrid crimes*). 2 (*inf*) horrible, unpleasant, nasty (*a horrid girl*).

hor'rify *vb* to shock (*we were horrified to hear the news of his accident*).

hor'ror *n* 1 terror, great fear or dislike (*have a horror of snakes*). 2 (*inf*) a horrible or disagreeable person or thing (*the child is a real horror*).

horse *n* 1 an animal that can be used for riding on or pulling loads. 2 cavalry. 3 a padded block on four legs used by gymnasts in vaulting.

horse chest'nut *n* 1 a type of tree. 2 its nut.

horse'man *n* a rider on horseback.

horse'manship *n* skill in riding horses.

horse'play *n* rough play (*children breaking things while indulging in horseplay*).

horse'power *n* the pulling power of a horse taken as a measure of power, equal to the power needed to raise 33,000 pounds one foot in one minute (*the horsepower of a vehicle*).

horse'rad'ish *n* a plant with a sharp-tasting eatable root used for a sauce or relish (*roast beef with horseradish*).

horse sense *n* common sense (*he is brilliant academically but has no horse sense*).

horse'shoe *n* 1 a curved iron shoe for horses. 2 anything of this shape (*a lucky cardboard horseshoe given to the bride*).

hors'y *adj* 1 having to do with horses. 2 resembling a horse (*horsy features*).

horticul'tural *adj* having to do with gardening or growing plants, vegetables, etc.

hor'ticulture *n* the art or science of gardening or growing flowers, vegetables, etc.

horticul'turist *n* one skilled in gardening.

hosan'na *n* a cry of praise to God.

hose *n* 1 (*fml*) stockings, socks, etc (*a shop selling hose*). 2 a movable pipe of rubber plastic, etc, used for carrying water (*a garden hose*):—*vb* to spray with a hose.

ho'sier *n* one who sells hose, shirts and men's undergarments.

ho'siery *n* the articles sold by a hosier.

hos'pice *n* 1 (*old*) a place of rest or shelter for travellers. 2 a hospital for sufferers of incurable diseases (*cancer patients in hospices*).

hos'pitable *adj* kind to guests and visitors (*she was very hospitable to the visitors and gave them tea and cakes*).

hos'pital *n* a building for the care of the sick.

hospital'ity *n* kindness to guests and visitors, often including offering them food and drink.

host¹ *n* 1 one who receives guests (*their host at the dinner party*). 2 (*old*) an innkeeper or hotelkeeper:—*vb* to act as a host (to a party, television show, etc).

host² *n* 1 (*old*) an army. 2 a very large number (*a whole host of people came to the meeting*).

host³ *n* in the Roman Catholic church, the bread consecrated during the Mass.

hos'tage *n* one held prisoner until certain conditions have been carried out (*the hijackers of the plane took passengers with them as hostages*).

hostel

hos'tel n a building in which persons away from home (students, travellers, etc) may pay to stay if they agree to keep its rules.

hos'telry n (old) an inn.

hostess see **host**.

hos'tile adj 1 unfriendly (hostile towards anyone who disagrees with her). 2 having to do with an enemy (hostile troops).

hostil'ity n 1 unfriendliness. 2 enmity. 3 pl warfare.

hot adj 1 very warm (a hot day). 2 easily excited (a hot temper). 3 having a sharp, burning taste (hot food).

hot'bed n 1 in a garden, a piece of earth kept warm so that plants will grow in it more quickly. 2 a place where things develop quickly (a hotbed of rebellion).

hot'-blood'ed adj easily angered.

hotch'-potch n a disorderly mixture (the room is a hotch-potch of different kinds of furniture).

hot dog n a hot sausage, usually a frankfurter, served on a long bread roll.

hotel' n a building where people may live and eat when away from home, an inn (stay at a hotel when away on business).

hot-head'ed adj easily excited, rash (he's so hot-headed that he rushes into things without thinking).

hot'house n a glasshouse kept warm so that plants may be grown out of season.

hot'pot n a stew (a Lancashire hotpot).

hot-tem'pered adj easily angered (so hot-tempered that children are afraid of him).

hough [hok], **hock** ns the joint in the middle of an animal's back leg.

hound n 1 a hunting dog (foxhounds). 2 (inf) a worthless rascal (that thieving hound):—vb to hunt:—**hound out** to drive out (hounded out of the village by racists).

hour [our] n 1 sixty minutes. 2 the twenty-fourth part of a day. 3 the time fixed for doing something, the time at which something is usu done (business hours).

hour'glass n a sand-filled glass for measuring time.

hour'ly adj happening every hour (hourly reports).

house n 1 a building in which people, often a family, live. 2 a place or building used for a particu-

lar purpose (a public house). 3 a theatre audience (a large house at the evening performance). 4 a business firm (a famous fashion house). 5 a school boarding house:—vb [houz] 1 to provide a house for. 2 to shelter.

house'boat n a boat used as a home (a houseboat on the Thames).

house'breaker n one who forces his way into a house to steal.

house'hold n all who live in a house (the whole household helped with the cooking):—adj having to do with those who live in it (household pets/household insurance).

house'holder n one who owns or rents a house (he just rents a room in their house—he is not the householder).

household name n a person or thing spoken of in every home (the TV personality is a household name).

house'keeper n a person in charge of a house (the widower employed a housekeeper).

house'maid n a woman servant who helps to clean a house.

house'warming n the first party given after going to live in a new house (give a housewarming in their new flat).

house'wife n 1 a woman who works at home looking after her house and family and cooking, cleaning, etc. 2 [huz'-if] (old) a pocket case for needles and thread.

hov'el n a poor, dirty house (disease spreads rapidly in those hovels).

hov'er vb 1 to stay in the air without moving (hawks hovering). 2 to stay near, to loiter (hover around to try and talk to the TV celebrity).

hov'ercraft n a type of vehicle or boat that can skim over the surface of smooth land or water on a cushion of air.

howev'er adv 1 in whatever way (get there however we can). 2 no matter how (however bad the conditions). 3 yet (he is very old—however he is healthy).

howl vb to give a long, loud cry, as a dog or wolf (the wind howling/people howling with mirth). 2 to wail, to cry (children howling with pain):—also n.

howl'er n (inf) a silly laughable mistake (spelling howler).

hoy'den n a rude, bold girl.

hub n **1** the central part of a wheel. **2** a centre of interest or activity (*the area is the hub of the business community*).

hub'bub n confused noise (*unable to hear what she was saying in the hubbub at the airport*).

huck'ster n one who sells things from door to door or in the street (*hucksters trying to sell cheap souvenirs to tourists*).

hud'dle vb to crowd together (*people huddling together for warmth*):—n a close crowd (*in a huddle to discuss the plan*).

hue[1] n (*fml or lit*) **1** colour (*materials of every hue*). **2** shade of a colour.

hue[2] n:—**hue and cry 1** pursuit after a criminal. **2** a noisy expression of anger, a noisy protest (*a hue and cry after the new road was cancelled*).

huff n a fit of temper (*he goes into a huff when he does not get his own way*).

huffy adj easily angered.

hug vb (**hugged'**, **hug'ging**) **1** to hold tightly in the arms, to take lovingly in the arms. **2** to keep close to (*cars hugging the side of the road in the fog*):—n a close grip, an embrace (*an affectionate hug*).

huge adj very big, enormous (*a huge monster/a huge sum of money*):—n **huge'ness**.

hulk n **1** the body of an old disused ship. **2** anything difficult to move (*a hulk of an old wardrobe*).

hulk'ing adj big and awkward (*a hulking old chest of drawers*).

hull n **1** the outer covering of a grain or seed. **2** the frame or body of a ship.—vb to strip off the husk (*hull raspberries*).

hullo *see* **hallo.**

hum vb (**hummed'**, **hum'ming**) **1** to make a buzzing sound (*bees humming/machines humming*). **2** to sing without words or with the mouth closed (*hum a tune as she works*):—n **1** a buzzing noise (*the hum of machinery*). **2** the noise made by a bee when flying.

hu'man adj having to do with mankind (*human diseases/human remains*).

humane' adj kindly, merciful (*it is humane to put to sleep very ill animals*).

hu'manism n **1** love of literature and learning. **2** the belief that Man is the most important subject of study (*she believes in humanism, not Christianity*):—n **hu'manist.**

humanita'rian n one who works to lessen human suffering (*humanitarians who go to famine areas to help the local people*):—*also adj.*

human'ity n **1** all mankind. **2** kindness, feeling for others (*he is cruel and totally lacking in humanity*).

hu'manize vb **1** to civilize. **2** to make gentler (*marriage seemed to humanize him*).

hum'ble adj thinking oneself unimportant, not proud, seeking no praise (*too humble to see that she was being taken advantage of/show a humble attitude to his senior colleagues*):—vb **1** to make humble (*humbling herself by begging for her job back*). **2** to lessen the importance or power of (*humble the proud king*):—*adv* **hum'bly.**

hum'ble bee n the bumblebee, a large wild bee.

hum'ble pie':—**to eat humble pie** to have to admit that one is in the wrong after being sure that one was right.

hum'bug n **1** pretence, dishonest talk or behaviour that is intended to deceive people and win their support or sympathy (*he pretended to be interested in charity but it was just humbug*). **2** a cheat, a person who pretends to be something he or she is not:—vb (**hum'bugged, hum'bugging**) to cheat, to deceive.

hum'drum adj dull, ordinary (*lead a humdrum existence*).

hu'merus n the bone that extends from the shoulder to the elbow.

hu'mid adj moist, damp (*a humid heat/humid weather*).

humid'ity n dampness, the amount of moisture in the air.

humil'iate vb to lessen the importance or power of, to lower the dignity or pride of (*humiliating her in front of the rest of the class by making her stand in the corner*):—n **humilia'tion.**

humil'ity n the state of being humble (*people in lower positions in the firm were expected to behave with humility*).

hum'ming-bird n a brightly coloured tropical bird whose wings make a humming sound when it is flying.

hum'mock n a small hill.

hu'morist n one who writes or talks amusingly (*a humorist who has had several books published*).

hu'morous adj **1** funny, amusing (tell a humorous story). **2** having or displaying a sense of humour (a humorous person).

hu'mour n **1** a comical or amusing quality (a sense of humour/see the humour in the situation). **2** a state of mind, mood (in a good humour).

hump n a rounded lump, esp on the back (camels have humps).

hump'back n a person with a lump on his or her back.

hump'backed adj having or resembling a humpback (a humpbacked bridge).

hu'mus n rotted leaves, etc, mixed into the earth (humus fertilizing the soil).

hunch n **1** a rounded hump, esp on the back. **2** (inf) an intuitive feeling, a hint (I have a hunch that she is hiding something).

hunch'back n a person with a hunch on his or her back:—adj **hunch'backed**.

hun'dred n ten times ten:—adj **hun'dredth**.

hun'dredfold n a hundred times as much (he promised to repay the favour a hundredfold).

hun'dredweight n a weight = 112 pounds (abbr **cwt**) (a hundredweight of coal).

hun'ger n **1** a strong desire for food (try to suppress his hunger until lunchtime). **2** lack of food (die of hunger). **3** any strong desire (a hunger for fame):—vb **1** (old) to feel hunger. **2** to desire greatly (hunger for love).

hunger strike n public refusal to eat any food (prisoners going on hunger strike).

hun'gry adj **1** needing food, feeling or showing hunger (hungry children asking for food). **2** having a strong need or desire for (hungry for love).

hunk n (inf) a large piece (a hunk of cheese).

hunt vb **1** to chase wild animals in order to kill or capture them (hunting stags). **2** to look for (hunting for his other sock). **3** to follow in order to catch (police hunting the escaped prisoner):—n **1** the act of hunting. **2** a group of people who meet to hunt wild animals.

hunt'er n **1** one who hunts (fhunt'ress). **2** a horse trained for hunting foxes.

hunts'man n one who hunts.

hur'dle n **1** a gate-like movable frame of wood or metal. **2** a wooden frame over which people or horses must jump in certain races (the horse refused to jump the last hurdle). **3** hindrance, obstacle (their major hurdle is lack of money).

hurd'y-gurd'y n a musical instrument played by turning a handle, a barrel organ.

hurl vb **1** to throw with force (hurling a brick through the window/hurl abuse). **2** to play hurley.

hurl'ey, hurl'ing ns an Irish game like hockey played with a ball and sticks.

hur'ly-bur'ly n confusion, great noise (in the hurly-burly of the guests arriving).

hurrah' interj a cry of joy.

hur'ricane n a violent storm, a very strong wind (parts of America flattened by a hurricane).

hur'ried adj **1** done quickly, often too quickly, hasty (a hurried exit/a hurried reply).

hur'ry vb **1** to do or go quickly (hurrying to catch a train). **2** to make to go quickly (hurried the children along):—n haste, speed (in a hurry).

hurt vb (pt,pp **hurt**) **1** to cause pain to, to wound, to injure (hurt his hand on broken glass). **2** to upset (hurt by his remarks):—n (fml) **1** a wound, an injury. **2** harm.

hurt'ful adj harmful (hurtful remarks).

hurt'le vb to move with force and speed through the air (sledges hurtling down the snowy slopes).

hus'band n a married man (husband and wife):—vb to use or spend carefully (husband their resources).

hus'bandry n **1** (old) farming. **2** (fml) careful spending.

hush n silence, stillness (in the hush of the evening/a hush descended on the room):—vb **1** to make silent, to quieten (try to hush the children). **2** to become silent (ask the children to hush):—**hush up** to prevent something becoming generally known (try to hush up the family scandal):—interj quiet! silence!

husk n the dry outer covering of a grain or seed, or of certain fruits.

husk'y[1] adj **1** hoarse, dry and rough (a husky voice). **2** hefty, strong.

husk'y[2] n an Arctic sledge dog.

hus'sy n a bold, cheeky girl (a brazen hussy).

hus'tings npl **1** formerly, the platform from which candidates for the British Parliament used to address electors before an election, or the place where votes were cast. **2** the proceedings such as the making of speeches at a parliamentary election. **3** political campaigning.

hust'le vb **1** to hurry (*hustling the new laws through*). **2** to push roughly (*hustle them into a taxi*):—*also n.*

hut n a small, roughly built house, a wooden shed (*a garden hut*).

hutch n a box-like cage for rabbits.

hy'acinth n a bulbous plant with bell-like flowers (*plant hyacinths to bloom indoors at Christmas*).

hy'brid n a plant or animal resulting from the mixing of two different kinds or species, a mongrel (*a mule is a hybrid of a horse and a donkey*):—*adj* bred from two different kinds.

hy'dra n in Greek myths, a many-headed monster whose heads grew again when cut off.

hydrangea [hî-drān'-jä] n a garden shrub with large heads of brightly coloured flowers.

hy'drant n a pipe from the main water pipe of a street from which water (e.g. for a hose) may be drawn direct (*firemen attaching their hose to a hydrant*).

hydraul'ic adj worked by the pressure of water or other liquid (*hydraulic brakes*).

hy'dro- prefix having to do with water.

hydroelec'tric adj having to do with electricity obtained by water power.

hy'drogen n an invisible gas with no colour or smell that with oxygen forms water.

hydropho'bia n **1** rabies. **2** fear of water. **3** the inability to swallow water.

hy'droplane n a speedboat that skims the surface of the water:—*also vb.*

hyena [hî-ee'-nä] n a dog-like animal that eats dead flesh (*hyenas make a sound like a human laughing*).

hy'giene n **1** the study of clean and healthy living. **2** clean and healthy living (*careful about personal hygiene*).

hygien'ic adj having to do with hygiene, clean (*a kitchen that was not hygienic*).

hymn [him] n a song of praise, esp to God.

hym'nal, hym'nary ns a book of hymns.

hy'perac'tive adj too active and unable to sit still for very long (*a hyperactive child*).

hyper'bole n a figure of speech by which a statement is exaggerated in a striking way:— *adj* **hyperbol'ic**.

hypercrit'ical adj too critical (*people who are hypercritical of the young*).

hy'permarket n a very large supermarket.

hy'phen n a short dash (-) between syllables or between words joined to express a single idea.

hypno'sis n a sleep-like state in obedience to the will of another who can then make the sleeper do as he or she says (*she wondered if hypnosis could cure her addiction to smoking*).

hypnot'ic adj producing sleep (*a hypnotic state*).

hyp'notism n the art of producing hypnosis.

hyp'notist n one who has the power to hypnotize others.

hyp'notize vb to will a person into a sleep-like state and to perform certain actions while in it.

hypochondria [hî'-pō-kon'-dri-a] n a condition in which someone is overanxious about their health, constantly believing that they are ill when they are not (*she is physically healthy but she's a hypochondriac*):—**hypochondriac** n a person who suffers from hypochondria.

hypoc'risy n the pretence of being good or of having beliefs or feelings that one does not have (*it was hypocrisy for him to read a passage in church about loving his neighbour and then go home and beat his wife*).

hyp'ocrite n one who pretends to be good but is not so, a person who says one thing and does another (*hypocrites who pretend to be good Christians but treat the poor badly*).

hypocrit'ical adj not sincere, false.

hypoder'mic adj **1** under the skin. **2** used for injecting a drug under the skin (*a hypodermic syringe*):—n a medical instrument for injecting a drug under the skin.

hypot'enuse n the side opposite the right angle of a triangle.

hypother'mia n a serious medical condition in which the body temperature is much lower than normal because of prolonged exposure to cold.

hypoth'esis n an idea accepted as true for the basis of an argument, something supposed true but not proved so:—*adj* **hypo-thet'ical**.

hys'sop n a sweet-smelling plant.

hyste'ria n **1** a disorder of the nerves, causing a person to laugh or cry violently without reason, have imaginary illnesses, etc (*she suffers from* *bouts of hysteria*). **2** lack of control, uncontrolled excitement (*the mass hysteria of the crowd when the president was killed*).

hyster'ics *n* **1** a fit of hysteria (*she went into hysterics when she heard of his death*). **2** (*inf*) an uncontrollable fit of laughter (*the audience were in hysterics at the comic's jokes*).

hyster'ical *adj* **1** suffering from hysteria. **2** caused by hysteria (*a hysterical illness*). **3** (*inf*) very funny (*a hysterical sight*).

I

i'amb, iam'bus *ns* a metrical foot of one short followed by one long syllable:—*adj* **iam'bic**.

i'bex *n* a wild mountain goat with large horns.

i'bis *n* a long-legged water bird.

ice *n* **1** frozen water (*take some ice from the fridge for the drinks*). **2** an ice cream (*buy ices for the children*):—*vb* **1** to cool in ice. **2** to cover with icing.

ice'berg *n* a great mass of ice floating in the sea (*the ship hit an iceberg*).

ice'breaker *n* a ship designed for cutting its way through ice floes.

ice cream *n* **1** cream or a mixture of creamy substances flavoured and frozen (*a shop selling ice cream*). **2** a portion of ice cream (*buy two ice creams*).

ice floe *n* a large sheet of floating ice.

ice pack *n* masses of floating ice packed closely together.

ichthyosaurus [ik-thi-o-sår'-ês] *n* a huge fish-like lizard of very ancient times.

i'cicle *n* a long, hanging pointed piece of ice formed by the freezing of falling water (*icicles hanging from the roof*).

i'cing *n* a mixture of fine powdery sugar with liquid used to cover cakes (*cover the cake with chocolate icing*).

i'con *n* **1** a religious picture or statue, an image. **2** a famous person or thing that many people admire and regard as a symbol of a way of life, set of beliefs etc (*Princess Diana was regarded as an icon by many*). **3** a small symbol on a computer screen which represents a program or file (*click on that icon using the mouse*).

icon'oclasm *n* **1** the breaking of religious images. **2** the attacking or destruction of long-established ideas or customs.

icon'oclast *n* **1** one who breaks or destroys religious images. **2** one who attacks or destroys widely accepted and long-established ideas or customs (*the new manager was regarded as an iconoclast because he wanted to change the firm's system of accounts*):—*adj* **iconoclas'tic**.

i'cy *adj* **1** very cold (*icy weather*). **2** covered with ice (*icy roads*). **3** unfriendly (*an icy stare*).

ide'a *n* **1** a plan, thought or suggestion (*I have an idea for a book*). **2** a picture in the mind (*an idea of the house that they are looking for*). **3** an opinion or belief (*political ideas*).

ide'al *n* **1** a perfect example (*her ideal of what a husband should be*). **2** (too) high principles or perfect standards, a person's standard of behaviour, etc (*a person of high ideals*):—*adj* **1** perfect (*an ideal wife/an ideal job*). **2** extremely suitable (*a tool that is ideal for the job*). **3** expressing possible perfection that is unlikely to exist (*ideal happiness*).

ide'alism *n* the desire to achieve perfection, the state of having (too) high principles or perfect standards (*he is full of idealism about marriage*):—*n* **ide'alist**:—*adj* **idealis'tic**.

ide'alize *vb* to think of as perfect or better than reality (*he gives an idealized account of life at the beginning of the century*).

iden'tical *adj* **1** the very same (*this is the identical car that was here yesterday*). **2** the same, exactly alike (*they were wearing identical dresses*).

identification *n* **1** act of recognizing (*identification of the badly injured body was difficult*). **2** something that is proof of or a sign of identity (*in case you are under age you require identification to get into the club*). **3** the feeling that one shares ideas, feelings, etc, with another person (*her identification with the unhappy woman whom she was reading about*).

iden'tify *vb* **1** to think of as being the same (*she identifies wealth with happiness*). **2** to recognize as being a certain person or thing (*she had to identify her dead husband in the police mortuary*). **3** to discover or r ecognize (*identified the cause of the problem*).

iden'tity *n* **1** (*fml*) the state of being the same. **2** who a person is (*have to prove her identity*).

ideol'ogy *n* a system of ideas (*political ideologies*).

id'iocy *n* **1** the state of being an idiot. **2** a foolish action (*the idiocies committed by fast drivers in the fog*).

id'iom *n* **1** a way of saying things that is found only in a certain language or dialect (*the*

English idiom). **2** a group of words that together have an unexpected meaning (*the expression 'white elephant' is an idiom*).

idiomat'ic *adj* **1** having an unusual or unexpected meaning (*the expression 'passed away' is idiomatic*). **2** having to do with everyday speech (*idiomatic English as spoken by native speakers*).

idiosyncrasy [id-i-o-sin(g)'krě-si] *n* an odd way of behaving (*it is one of her idiosyncrasies to talk to herself*).

idiosyncrat'ic *adj* peculiar to oneself (*an idiosyncratic habit of putting salt on pudding*).

id'iot *n* **1** (*old or fml*) a person with very low intelligence. **2** a foolish or stupid person (*he was an idiot to drive without a licence*).

idiot-proof *adj* very easy to use or understand (*an idiot-proof mobile phone*).

i'dle *adj* **1** doing nothing, not working, not in use (*workers forced to be idle for lack of work/machines lying idle*). **2** lazy (*idle people who don't want to work*). **3** having no effect or results (*idle threats*):—*vb* **1** (*fml*) to be idle, to do nothing (*enjoy idling on holiday*). **2** (*of a machine*) to run without doing work (*the car engine was idling*):—*n* **i'dleness**:—*n* **i'dler**:—*adv* **i'dly**.

i'dol *n* **1** a statue or other object that is worshipped (*heathens worshipping idols*). **2** a person regarded with too great love and respect (*he made an idol out of his father*).

idol'ater *n* one who worships idols:—*f* **idol'atress**.

idol'atrous *adj* having to do with the worship of idols.

idol'atry *n* **1** the worship of idols. **2** too great love and respect (*his idolatry of his father*).

i'dolize *vb* to love or admire very greatly (*idolizing his wife although she is not very pleasant*).

idyll [i'-dil *or* i'-dil] *n* a story of simple country life (*an idyll about a shepherd and his sweetheart*).

idyll'ic *adj* **1** perfectly happy , pleasant (*an idyllic marriage*). **2** charming, pictur esque (*a cottage in an idyllic setting*).

ig'loo *n* an Eskimo house made of blocks of frozen snow.

ig'neous *adj* (*of rocks*) formed from lava.

ignite' *vb* **1** to set fire to (*drop a match and ignite the petrol*). **2** to catch fire (*the petrol leaking from the car ignited*).

igni'tion *n* **1** act of setting fire to. **2** the part of a motor engine that sets fire to the fuel that drives the engine (*turn the key in the ignition*).

igno'ble *adj* **1** (*fml*) mean, dishonourable (*an ignoble action*). **2** (*old*) of low birth.

ignomin'ious *adj* shameful, disgraceful, damaging to one's pride or good name (*an ignominous defeat for her team by a much weaker team*).

ig'nominy *n* public disgrace, shame, the loss of one's pride or good name (*soldiers enduring the ignominy of being dismissed from the army*).

igno'ramus *n* a person with little or no knowledge (*she's an ignoramus about cooking*).

ig'norance *n* **1** want of knowledge (*his ignorance of mathematics*). **2** lack of awar eness or knowledge (*his ignorance of what they were really doing*).

ig'norant *adj* **1** having little or no knowledge (*ignorant about financial matters*). **2** unawar e of (*he was ignorant of the true facts*).

ignore' *vb* to take no notice of, to refuse to pay attention to (*she completely ignored her old friend/try to ignore her problems/ignoring his advice*).

iguana [ig-wä'-na] *n* a large lizard.

ill *adj* **1** sick (*ill patients*). **2** bad (*ill health*). **3** evil, harmful (*ill luck*):—*n* **1** evil, harm (*wish him ill*). **2** tr ouble (*all the ills of the world*):—*adv* badly (*treat him ill*).

ill-advised' *adj* unwise (*an ill-advised action*)

ill'-bred' *adj* badly brought up, rude (*ill-bred children with bad manners*).

ille'gal *adj* against the law:—*n* **illegal'ity**.

ileg'ible *adj* that cannot be read, badly written (*illegible handwriting*).

illegit'imate *adj* born of unmarried parents (*his illegitimate daughter*):—*n* **illegit'i-macy**.

ill-fa'voured *adj* (*fml*) ugly-looking, unattractive (*an ill-favoured woman*).

ill-gott'en *adj* gained unfairly or unjustly.

illib'eral *adj* (*fml*) **1** narrow-minded (*illiberal attitudes*). **2** not generous (*illiberal hosts/illiberal helpings*).

illic'it *adj* unlawful, against the law (*the illicit trade in drugs*).

illit'erate *adj* **1** unable to read or write (*illiterate people seeking help with reading lessons*). **2** uneducated (*an illiterate note*):—*n* **illit'eracy**.

ill'judged' adj unwise (an ill-judged remark).

ill'-mann'ered adj rude, impolite (ill-mannered people pushing to the front of the queue).

ill nat'ure n bad temper.

ill-na'tured adj bad-tempered, spiteful (an ill-natured old man/an ill-natured reply).

ill'ness n sickness, the state of being unwell (off work because of illness/childhood illnesses).

illog'ical adj 1 not using reasoning, not reasonable (illogical people). 2 against the rules of reasoning (his action was completely illogical).

ill-starred' adj unlucky (the ill-starred production of the play which closed after two weeks).

ill-tem'pered adj having a bad temper, angry (she's always ill-tempered first thing in the morning).

ill-treat' vb 1 to handle roughly (ill-treat the delicate material). 2 to behave roughly to, to be cruel to (she ill-treats her children).

illum'inate vb 1 (old) to light up (strings of little lights illuminating the garden). 2 (of books, etc) to decorate with bright colours (early illuminated manuscripts prepared by monks). 3 to explain, to make clear (could you illuminate a few points in the legal agreement).

illumina'tion n (fml) 1 a light. 2 decorative lights (the town's Christmas illuminations). 3 a picture or decoration painted on a page of a book (illuminations on early manuscripts). 4 explanation, clarification (a few points in need of illumination).

illu'mine vb 1 to light up. 2 to make clear.

illu'sion n 1 deception (an optical illusion). 2 a wrong belief, a false idea (she had illusions that she was very beautiful).

illu'sionist n one who performs tricks that deceive the eye, a conjuror.

illu'sory adj deceiving, imaginary, unreal (an illusory victory).

ill'ustrate vb 1 to make clear by examples (illustrating the movement of traffic by a diagram). 2 to provide pictures for a book or magazine (she illustrates children's books).

illustra'tion n 1 an example that makes something easier to understand or demonstrates something (an illustration of his meanness). 2 a picture in a book or magazine (colour illustrations).

ill'ustrative adj helping to explain (illustrative examples).

illus'trious adj (fml) famous (illustrious former pupils).

im'age n 1 a likeness, form (made in the image of Christ). 2 a likeness or copy of a person, etc, made of stone, wood, etc (images of the saints). 3 a statue or picture that is worshipped (heathens worshipping golden images). 4 a picture formed of an object in front of a mirror or lens. 5 a picture in the mind (have an image of what life would be like in ten years). 6 the impression which a person, organization gives to the public (We must improve the firm's image). 7 a figure of speech (a piece of prose full of images).

im'agery n figures of speech, words chosen because they call up striking pictures in the mind (the poet's use of imagery).

imag'inary adj existing in the mind only, not real (a child with an imaginary friend).

imagina'tion n 1 the power of inventing stories, persons, etc, creative ability (require a lot of imagination to write for children/a play showing a great deal of imagination). 2 the power of forming pictures in the mind (able to see it all in her imagination). 3 the seeing or hearing of things that do not exist (she said that she heard noises in the night but it was just her imagination).

imag'inative adj 1 having a good imagination (an imaginative person). 2 demonstrating imagination (an imaginative production of the play/imaginative designs).

imag'ine vb 1 to form a picture in the mind (I can imagine her reaction). 2 to form ideas of things that do not exist or of events that have not happened (she imagined that she met an alien). 3 to suppose (I imagine that he will arrive on time).

imbecile [im'-be-seel] adj 1 weak-minded. 2 foolish, stupid (an imbecile thing to do):—n 1 (fml) a weak-minded person. 2 a fool, an idiot:—n **imbecil'ity**.

imbibe' vb (fml or hum) to drink (imbibing several pints of beer).

imbue' vb to fill with (imbued with a desire to win).

im'itate vb to copy, to try to be, behave or look the same as (imitating his voice/imitate her style of writing):—n **im'itator**.

imita'tion n 1 act of imitating. 2 a copy (not the original painting but an imitation).

im'itative adj **1** done as a copy (an imitative piece of work). **2** fond of copying (an imitative poet).

immac'ulate adj **1** (old) pure. **2** spotless (immaculate white shorts). **3** perfect (an immaculate performance).

immate'rial adj unimportant (it is immaterial how you get here as long as you do).

immature' adj **1** unripe. **2** not full-grown. **3** lacking experience and wisdom:—n **im-maturity**.

immeas'urable adj huge (immeasurable damage).

imme'diate adj **1** happening at once (an immediate improvement). **2** direct, without anyone or anything coming between (her immediate successor). **3** near, close (her immediate surroundings).

imme'diately adv **1** at once (you must reply immediately). **2** closely (houses immediately next to the station).

immemo'rial adj too long ago to be remembered, ancient (there has been a church in the village from time immemorial).

immense' adj huge (an immense improvement/an immense stretch of grassland):—n **immens'ity**.

immerse' vb **1** to put into water (immersing the vegetables in boiling water). **2** to give one's whole attention to (immerse oneself in one's work).—n **immer'sion**.

immersion heater n an electric heater fitted inside a tank to heat the water in it.

im'migrant n one who immigrates (America is a country with immigrants from many parts of the world).

im'migrate vb (fml) to enter a country not one's own and settle there:—n **immi-gra'tion**.

im'minent adj just about to happen, near in time (in imminent danger):—n **im'minence**.

immo'bile adj not moving, unable to move (lying there immobile as if dead/he is immobile since breaking both legs):—n **im-mobil'ity**.

immod'erate adj more than is proper, uncontrolled (immoderate expenditure).

immod'est adj (fml) **1** shameless, indecent (the immodest behaviour of the women/an immodest dress). **2** not modest (an immodest pride in his own achievements):—n **immod'esty**.

im'molate vb (fml) to offer in sacrifice (immolating herself as a sacrifice to the god).

immor'al adj wrong, evil, wicked (immoral actions/an immoral person):—n **immo-ral'ity**.

immor'tal adj **1** living for ever. **2** famous for all time (Shakespeare is immortal).

immortal'ity n **1** everlasting life. **2** undying fame (the undoubted immortality of Shakespeare).

immor'talize vb **1** to make immortal. **2** to make famous for all time (she was immortalized in a poem by her lover).

immov'able adj **1** not able to be moved (immovable objects). **2** not changing easily (immovable opinions).

immune' adj **1** free from, specially protected from (immune from taxation). **2** not to be infected by (immune from chickenpox as she has had it already):—n **immun'ity**.

im'munize vb to inject disease germs into the blood stream to cause a mild attack of an illness and so make the person immune from it (immunizing the children against measles).

immure' vb (fml) to imprison (immured behind stone walls).

immut'able adj (fml) unchangeable (immutable laws).

imp n **1** in fairy tales, an evil spirit. **2** a mischievous child (the little imp stole an apple).

im'pact n **1** the force with which one thing strikes another (thrown out of the car by the impact of it hitting the wall). **2** a collision (the car was wrecked on impact with the wall). **3** a strong effect or impression (the impact on the audience of the politician's speech).

impair' vb to make worse, to weaken (his vision is impaired).

impale' vb to fix upon something sharp, to pierce (he fell out of the window and was impaled on the railings below).

impal'pable adj (fml) **1** not able to be felt by touch (an impalpable lump that showed up on X-ray). **2** not easily understood (impalpable philosophic theories).

impart' vb (fml) **1** to tell (impart new information). **2** to give (impart courage to his troops).

impar'tial adj fair, just, not taking sides (an impartial judgment).

impartial'ity n fairness, treating all parties or persons in the same way.

impass'able adj unable to be passed or crossed (roads impassable because of snowdrifts).

impasse [im'-pas] n a point in an argument on which those taking part are unable to agree (man-

agement and workers have reached an impasse over pay).

impass'ioned *adj* full of strong feeling, very earnest (*an impassioned plea for mercy*).

impass'ive *adj* **1** not showing strong feeling (*a totally impassive expression*). **2** calm, unexcited (*he remained impassive as the judge passed sentence*).

impa'tient *adj* not willing to wait, easily angered by delay (*a very impatient person/in an impatient mood*):—*n* **impa'tience**.

impeach' *vb* **1** to charge with a crime, esp treason. **2** to charge an important officer of state with crime before the House of Lords (*politicians impeached for accepting bribes*). **3** (*fml*) to raise doubts about (*impeach the character of the manager*):—*n* **impeach'ment**.

impecc'able *adj* faultless (*his behaviour was impeccable*).

impecu'nious *adj* (*fml or hum*) having no money, poor (*impecunious students unable to afford books*).

impede' *vb* **1** to prevent from moving freely (*impeded by her tight skirt*). **2** to delay (*impeding progress*).

imped'iment *n* **1** something that prevents or delays movement (*lack of money was an impediment to the expansion of the firm*). **2** a physical or nervous condition that makes it difficult to speak clearly (*a slight speech impediment*).

impel' *vb* (**impelled'**, **impel'ling**) to urge on (*the assistant was so rude that the customer felt impelled to write to the manager*).

impend'ing *adj* about to happen (*the impending general election*).

impen'etrable *adj* **1** unable to be passed through (*impenetrable enemy lines*). **2** (*fml*) not able to be understood (*an impenetrable piece of prose*).

impen'itent *adj* (*fml*) not sorry for having done wrong.

imper'ative *adj* **1** commanding. **2** necessary, urgent (*it is imperative that we get more supplies*).

impercep'tible *adj* that can scarcely be seen or noticed, very small, slight (*an imperceptible difference*).

imper'fect *adj* having faults, not perfect (*goods that are slightly imperfect*).

imperfec'tion *n* a fault, a flaw (*slight imperfections in the china/imperfections in her character*).

impe'rial *adj* **1** having to do with an empire or emperor, royal (*Britain's former imperial power*). **2** (*of weights and measures*) according to the standard legal in the UK:—*n* **1** a size of paper. **2** a small beard on the lower lip.

impe'rialist *n* one who believes that a strong and advanced nation should rule less advanced nations:—*n* **impe'rialism**.

impe'ril *vb* (**imper'illed**, **imper'illing**) (*fml*) to put in danger (*careless driving imperils lives*).

impe'rious *adj* commanding, liking to give orders, haughty (*an imperious manner*).

imper'ishable *adj* (*fml*) that cannot be destroyed, everlasting (*imperishable memories*).

imper'meable *adj* waterproof.

imper'sonal *adj* **1** not influenced by personal feelings (*an impersonal account of the situation/impersonal places like hospitals*). **2** (*of verbs*) occurring only in the third person singular, usu with 'it' as the subject.

imper'sonate *vb* to pretend to be someone else (*she impersonated her older sister to get into the club*).

imper'tinent *adj* cheeky, purposely disrespectful (*punish the impertinent children*):—*n* **imper'tinence**.

imperturb'able *adj* calm, not easily excited or worried (*she remained imperturbable amid the confusion*).

imper'vious *adj* **1** that cannot be passed through (*a substance impervious to liquids*). **2** taking no notice (of) (*impervious to criticism*).

impetigo [im-pe-tī'-gō] *n* a skin disease.

impet'uous *adj* acting without thinking first, rash, hasty (*an impetuous young woman/regret his impetuous decision*):—*n* **impetuos'ity**.

im'petus *n* **1** the force with which something moves. **2** energy.

impinge' *vb* **1** to come into contact with, to make an impression on (*scarcely impinged on his consciousness*). **2** to interfere with, to trespass on (*impinging on his rights as an individual*).

im'pious *adj* (*fml*) having no respect for God or religion:—*n* **impi'ety**.

imp'ish *adj* mischievous (*an impish sense of humour*).

implac'able *adj* **1** not easily calmed. **2** unforgiving.

implant' *vb* **1** to plant firmly. **2** to place in. **3** to teach.

im'plement *n* a tool, an instrument (*garden*

implements):—*vb* **implement'** to put into practice (*implement an agreement*).

im'plicate *vb* to show that a person is involved or connected with (an affair), to mix up in (*when he was arrested his statement implicated two of his friends*).

implica'tion *n* something hinted at but not said openly (*by implication he was accusing her of lying*).

impli'cit *adj* 1 understood but not said (*his implicit criticism*). 2 unquestioning, without doubts (*implicit faith*).

implore' *vb* to ask earnestly, to beg (*imploring him to forgive her*).

imply' *vb* to suggest something without saying it openly, to hint (*he implied that she was lying*).

impolite' *adj* (*fml*) rude, ill-mannered (*impolite table manners*).

impol'itic *adj* unwise in the circumstances (*it was impolitic of him to sack the worker*).

impon'derable *adj* of which the results cannot be foreseen (*the effects of the new tax are imponderable*).

import' *vb* to bring in goods from abroad (*import wine from Australia*):—*n* **im'port**er.

im'port² *n* 1 meaning (*not fully understand the import of his remarks*). 2 importance (*matters of great import*).

import'ant *adj* 1 deserving great attention (*an important book*). 2 having results that affect many people (*important decisions*). 3 having a high position (*important people in the land*):—*n* **impor'tance**.

impor'tunate *adj* keeping on asking for what one wants (*importunate in their demands*).

importune [im-por'-tûn *or* im-por-tûn'] *vb* (*fml*) to keep on asking for (*they importuned the king to save their friend from hanging*):—*n* **importu'nity**.

impose' *vb* 1 to lay on (as a duty, tax, etc). 2 to make to accept (*imposing his authority on others*):—**impose upon** to take advantage of, to exploit, to make unfair demands on (*they imposed upon her by getting her to babysit free of charge*).

impos'ing *adj* important-looking, stately (*an imposing building*).

imposi'tion *n* 1 the act of laying upon (*the imposition of taxes*). 2 a tax. 3 an unfair demand (*it was an imposition to get him to give her a lift to*

work every day). 4 a punishment exercise (*pupils given an imposition for being late*).

impos'sible *adj* not able to be done or achieved (*an impossible dream*):—*n* **im-possibil'ity**.

impos'tor *n* one who deceives by pretending to be someone else, a deceiver (*they realized he was an impostor when the real policeman turned up*).

im'potent *adj* 1 lacking power, helpless, weak (*impotent against the force of the storm/full of impotent rage*). 2 (*of men*) lacking in sexual power:—*n* **im'potence**.

impound' *vb* 1 to shut in, as cattle in a pen (*impound the dog in the Dog and Cat Home*). 2 to take or seize by power of the law (*impound his car which was illegally parked*).

impov'erish *vb* to make poor (*impoverished because of his wife's extravagance*):—*n* **impov'erishment**.

imprac'ticable *adj* impossible to carry out, not able to be done (*plans that are totally impracticable*):—*n* **impracticabil'ity**.

impreca'tion *n* (*fml*) a curse (*the old woman was muttering imprecations under her breath*).

impreg'nable *adj* (*fml*) not able to be taken by attack (*an impregnable fortress*).

impreg'nate *vb* 1 to fill with (*water impregnated with salt*). 2 to fertilize or make pregnant.

impress' *vb* 1 to mark by pressing into, to stamp (*impress a pattern on the clay pots before baking them*). 2 to fix in the mind (*try to impress the details in her memory*). 3 to stress, to emphasize the importance of (*impress the need for haste upon them*).

impress'ion *n* 1 the mark left by pressing or stamping (*the impression of his heel in the mud*). 2 the number of copies of a book printed at one time. 3 an effect on the mind or feelings (*his appearance creates a bad impression*). 4 a not very clear idea or memory (*I had a vague impression that she left early*). 5 an attempt to copy in a humorous way someone else's voice, behaviour, appearance, etc (*he does impressions*).

impress'ionable *adj* easily influenced (*impressionable people were deceived by him*).

Impress'ionism *n* an attempt by a group of artists to represent through imaginative use of colour, etc, scenes just as they appeared to them at a certain moment.

impress'ionist *n* **1** an artist believing in Impr essionism. **2** a person who does impr essions of people, esp as a form of theatrical entertainment:—*also adj*.

impress'ive *adj* **1** important-looking (*an impressive building*). **2** causing deep feeling, such as admiration (*an impressive performance*).

imprima'tur *n* permission to print a book.

imprint' *vb* **1** to make a mark by pressing or printing. **2** to fix in the memory (*her sad expression is imprinted on my memory*):—*n* **im'print 1** that which is imprinted. **2** a publisher's name, address, etc, on a book.

impris'on *vb* to put into prison, to shut in.

impris'onment *n* the act of imprisoning or the state of being imprisoned (*the accused is facing imprisonment*).

improb'able *adj* not likely (*an improbable ending to the story*):—*n* **improbabil'ity**.

impromp'tu *adj* not prepared (*an impromptu speech*):—*adv* without preparation.

improp'er *adj* **1** wrong (*accused of improper use of the company's funds*). **2** not suitable, not polite (*improper behaviour on such a formal occasion*). **3** indecent (*make improper suggestions to a female colleague*).

improper fraction *n* a fraction greater than 1 (e.g. $\frac{5}{2}$).

impropri'ety *n* (*fml*) incorrect or impolite behaviour (*accused of impropriety in conducting the legal case*).

improve' *vb* to make or become better (*do something to improve the situation/a patient beginning to improve*):—*n* **improve'ment**.

improv'ident *adj* (*fml*) having no thought for the future, wasteful of money and goods (*improvident people who do not save for their old age*):—*n* **improv'idence**.

im'provise *vb* **1** to make something from material that is available (*improvising a shelter*). **2** to make something up at the moment required without preparation (*the pianist had no music so had to improvise*):—*n* **improvisa'tion**.

impru'dent *adj* rash, acting without forethought, unwise (*it was imprudent of her to give up her job before she found another one*):—*n* **impru'dence**.

im'pudent *adj* disrespectful, cheeky (*the impudent child put her tongue out at the teacher*):—*n* **im'pudence**.

impugn [im-pûn'] *vb* (*fml*) to question the truth of (*she impugned his sincerity*).

im'pulse *n* **1** a force causing movement (*an electrical impulse*). **2** a sudden desire or decision to act at once (*she bought the new dress on impulse*).

impuls'ive *adj* **1** done without forethought (*an impulsive decision to buy an expensive dress*). **2** acting without thinking first (*an impulsive young man*):—*n* **impuls'iveness**.

impun'ity *n* freedom from punishment or loss (*he cannot go around upsetting everyone with impunity*).

impure' *adj* **1** dirty, polluted (*impure water*). **2** mixed with something else (*impure drugs*). **3** sinful (*impure thoughts*):—*n* **im-purity**.

impute' *vb* **1** to consider guilty of. **2** to consider to be the cause of.

inabil'ity *n* lack of power, state of being unable (*his inability to control his dog*).

inaccess'ible *adj* not to be reached or approached (*villages made inaccessible by the storm*).

inacc'urate *adj* **1** not correct (*an inaccurate answer to the mathematical problem*). **2** not exact (*an inaccurate description*):—*n* **inacc'uracy**.

inac'tion *n* idleness, lack of action (*local councillors accused of inaction following the floods*).

inac'tive *adj* **1** not taking much exercise (*inactive office workers*). **2** no longer working or operating (*an inactive volcano*). **3** not taking an active part (*inactive members of the political party*).

inadequate [in-ad'-i-kwät] *adj* **1** not good enough (*inadequate attempts*). **2** not sufficient (*inadequate supplies*):—*n* **inad'equacy**.

inadmiss'ible *adj* not able to be allowed (*evidence that is inadmissible in court*).

inadvert'ent *adj* **1** without care or attention (*inadvertent damage*). **2** unintentional (*an inadvertent insult*):—*n* **inadver'tence**.

inadvert'ently *adv* unintentionally (*he inadvertently damaged his neighbour's gate with his car*).

ina'lienable *adj* that cannot be given or taken away (*his inalienable right to a fair hearing*).

inane' *adj* foolish, silly (*make inane remarks*):—*n* **inan'ity**.

inan'imate *adj* without life (*inanimate objects*).

inapp'licable *adj* not suitable, not appropriate (*inapplicable remarks*).

inappreci'able *adj* very small, slight (*an inappreciable difference*).

inappro'priate *adj* not suitable (*an inappropriate remark/wear inappropriate clothes*).

inapt' *adj* not suitable, not appropriate (*inapt humorous remarks at a serious meeting*).

inartic'ulate *adj* 1 not clear (*an inarticulate account*). 2 unable to express oneself clearly (*too inarticulate to give a clear account of the accident*).

inartis'tic *adj* 1 not interested in art. 2 without taste (*an inartistic flower display/an inartistic person*).

inatten'tion *n* lack of attention (*accused of inattention to his work*).

inatten'tive *adj* not attending, neglectful (*inattentive pupils*).

inaud'ible *adj* that cannot be heard (*inaudible remarks/the speaker was inaudible at the back of the hall*).

inaug'urate *vb* 1 to start off with a ceremony. 2 to do something special to mark the beginning:—*n* **inaugura'tion**:—*adj* **inaug'ural**.

inauspic'ious *adj* unlucky, being a sign of ill luck to come (*an inauspicious beginning*).

in'born *adj* apparently existing in one since birth, natural (*an inborn ability to play musical instruments*).

in'bred *adj* having become part of one's nature as a result of early training (*her inbred politeness*).

incal'culable *adj* very great, too many or too much to be counted (*incalculable damage*).

incandes'cent *adj* white or glowing when hot:—*n* **incandes'cence**.

incanta'tion *n* words sung or spoken as a spell or charm (*witches reciting an incantation*).

incap'able *adj* 1 not good at one's job. 2 not able, helpless:—*n* **incapabil'ity**.

incapac'itate *vb* to make unfit or unable (*incapacitated by his injured leg*).

incapac'ity *n* 1 unfitness. 2 lack of ability.

incar'cerate *vb* (*fml or hum*) to imprison (*incarcerated in a dungeon*):—*n* **incar-cera'tion**.

incar'nate *adj* enclosed in a body, given human form (*he seemed to be the devil incarnate*).

incarna'tion *n* the act of taking form as a human body.

incau'tious *adj* (*fml*) not careful, rash (*incautious remarks*).

incen'diary *n* 1 one who deliberately sets fire to a building, etc (*the judge sentenced the incendiary to prison*). 2 an incendiary bomb (*the terrorists placed incendiaries in the basement of the building*):—*adj* 1 meant to cause fire (*incendiary bomb/incendiary device*). 2 meant to stir up trouble (*incendiary remarks*):—*n* **incen'diarism**.

in'cense[1] *n* a mixture of spices burned to give a sweet-smelling smoke.

incense'[2] *vb* to make angry (*he was incensed when the boy broke his window*).

incen'tive *n* something for which one is prepared to work hard, a reason for action (*award a prize as an incentive to the pupils*).

incep'tion *n* (*fml*) a beginning (*the firm was successful from its inception*).

incer'titude *n* the state of being not certain.

incess'ant *adj* not stopping, going on all the time (*incessant rain/her incessant complaining*).

inch *n* the twelfth part of a foot in length:—*vb* to move a little at a time (*try to inch nearer the front of the crowd*).

inchoate [in'-ko-āt] *adj* (*fml*) just begun, not fully formed (*inchoate plans*).

in'cidence *n* 1 the extent or rate of frequency of something (*the incidence of burglaries in the area*). 2 the direction in which a ray of light or heat falls upon a surface.

in'cident *n* 1 a happening, an event (*it was rather a sad incident in his life*). 2 an event involving violence or law-breaking (*police called to an incident in the pub*).

inciden'tal *adj* 1 happening as a result, though not the most important one (*an incidental effect of the meeting*). 2 accompanying (*incidental music to the play*).

inciden'tally *adv* by the way (*incidentally, it has started to rain*).

incin'erate *vb* to burn to ashes (*incinerating the rubbish*).

incin'erator *n* a furnace for burning anything to ashes.

incip'ient *adj* beginning (*an incipient infection*).

inci'sion *n* 1 act of cutting. 2 a cut, a deep cut (*the incision made by the surgeon*).

inci'sive *adj* clear and sharp, to the point (*incisive criticism/incisive comments*).

inci'sor n a cutting tooth in the front of the mouth.

incite' vb 1 to stir up, to urge on (a speech that incited the crowd to burn the prison down):—n **incite'ment**.

incivil'ity n rudeness (his incivility in shutting the door in her face).

inclem'ent adj (fml) 1 stormy, unpleasant (inclement weather). 2 merciless (an inclement judge):—n **inclem'ency**.

inclina'tion n 1 a slope (a slight inclination in the road). 2 a bow (with an inclination of his head). 3 a liking, preference (have an inclination to travel). 4 a tendency (an inclination to pessimism).

incline' vb 1 to slope. 2 to bend (incline the head). 3 to move gradually off the straight way:—**be inclined to 1** to feel a desire or preference (I am inclined to accept their story). 2 to have a tendency to (he is inclined to be lazy):—n **in'cline** a slope.

include' vb to count as a part or member (including them on the invitation list):—n **inclu'sion**.

inclu'sive adj including everything mentioned or understood (Monday to Friday inclusive/a price inclusive of postage).

incog'nito adv in disguise, under a false name (the princess was travelling incognito so as not to be recognized).

incoher'ent adj 1 having no clear connection between the parts, muddled (an incoherent account of what had happened). 2 not speaking or writing clearly, difficult to follow or understand (she was so upset that she was incoherent):—n **incoher'ence**.

incombust'ible adj not able to be burnt, fireproof (incombustible waste products).

in'come n the money earned or gained (his annual income).

income tax n the tax charged on income.

incommen'surate adj (fml) out of proportion, not enough (salaries incommensurate with their qualifications).

incommode' vb (fml) to cause trouble to, to disturb (unwilling to incommode him by staying longer).

incom'parable adj 1 that cannot be equalled (an incomparable performance). 2 having no equal (an incomparable pianist).

incompat'ible adj 1 unable to get on together (they loved each other but they were totally incompatible). 2 not in agreement (the statements from the witnesses were incompatible):—n **incompatibil'ity**.

incom'petent adj 1 unable to do one's job well, unskilful (an incompetent manager). 2 not good enough (an incompetent piece of work):—ns **incom'petence, incom'petency**.

incomplete' adj unfinished (the poet's final work is incomplete).

incomprehen'sible adj that cannot be understood (incomprehensible behaviour).

inconceiv'able adj unable to be imagined (it seemed inconceivable that she could treat her own child so cruelly).

incon'gruous adj 1 (fml) not agreeing with (incongruous accounts of the event). 2 not suitable to (the house looks incongruous in that area). 3 laughably out of place (wear a totally incongruous outfit to the ceremony):—n **incongru'ity**.

inconsequen'tial adj 1 not consistent or logical. 2 of little or no importance, of no value (inconsequential comments).

inconsid'erable adj very small, of no importance (a not inconsiderable sum of money).

inconsid'erate adj having no thought for the feeling of others, thoughtless (it is inconsiderate to play loud music late at night).

inconsis'tent adj 1 not agreeing with what was said or done before or elsewhere (the judge's decision is inconsistent with the one he made last week). 2 changeable, erratic (her work is extremely inconsistent). 3 contradictory (sending his children to private school is inconsistent with his political views):—n **inconsis'tency**.

inconsol'able adj not to be comforted (the inconsolable widow).

inconspic'uous adj not easily seen (try to make herself inconspicuous in the crowd by wearing dark clothes).

incon'stant adj 1 often changing. 2 not always behaving in the same way:—n **in-con'stancy**.

incontest'able adj that cannot be doubted, undeniable (incontestable proof).

incon'tinent adj unable to control one's bladder and/or bowels (incontinent elderly people):—n **incon'tinence**.

incontrovert'ible *adj* that cannot be denied (*incontrovertible evidence*).

inconven'ience *n* trouble, annoyance (*apologize for any inconvenience caused by his absence*):—*vb* (*fml*) to cause trouble or difficulty (*visitors who inconvenienced them by staying too late*).

inconven'ient *adj* causing trouble, unsuitable (*come at an inconvenient time*).

incor'porate *vb* 1 to bring together in one (*incorporating the smaller firm in the international company*). 2 to make to form a part of, to include (*incorporate their suggestions in his report*):—*n* incorpora'tion.

incorpor'eal *adj* (*fml*) having no body.

incorrect' *adj* 1 wrong (*incorrect answers*). 2 not according to accepted standards (*incorrect behaviour*).

incorr'igible *adj* too bad to be corrected, very bad (*an incorrigible liar*).

incorrupt'ible *adj* 1 (*fml*) that cannot rot or decay. 2 not to be bribed (*incorruptible officials*).

increase' *vb* to make or become greater in size or number (*the number of club members has increased/the temperature has increased*):—*n* in'crease a rise in amount, numbers or degree (*an increase in membership/an increase in temperature*).

incred'ible *adj* 1 unbelievable, hard to believe (*I find his story completely incredible*). 2 amazing, wonderful (*it was an incredible performance*):—*n* incredibil'ity.

incred'ulous *adj* not willing to believe, unbelieving (*she gave him an incredulous look*):—*n* incredu'lity.

in'crement *n* an increase in money or value, often in salary (*receive an annual increment*).

incrim'inate *vb* to show that a person has taken part in a crime (*the accused tried to incriminate several other people in the bank robbery*).

in'cubate *vb* 1 to sit on eggs, to keep eggs warm till the young come out of them. 2 (*of eggs*) to be kept warm until the young birds come out. 3 (*of a disease or infection*) to develop until signs of disease appear. 4 to be holding in one's body an infection that is going to develop into a disease (*she must have been incubating chickenpox*).

incuba'tion *n* 1 act of incubating. 2 the time between the catching of a disease and the showing of symptoms (*the incubation period of measles*).

in'cubator *n* 1 an apparatus for hatching eggs. 2 an apparatus for keeping alive premature babies.

in'cubus *n* (*pl* in'cubuses *or* in'cubi) a cause of great anxiety or worry.

in'culcate *vb* to teach by frequent repetition (*inculcating in children the importance of getting qualifications*).

in'culpate *vb* (*fml*) to show that a person shares guilt or blame (*try to inculpate his friend in the crime*).

incum'bent *adj* resting on as a duty (*it is incumbent upon him to support his leader*):—*n* the member of clergy in charge of a certain church.

incur' *vb* (incurred', incur'ring) 1 to bring upon oneself (*incur the wrath of his father*). 2 to fall into (*incur huge debts*).

incur'able *adj* that cannot be cured (*incurable diseases*).

incu'rious *adj* not curious, not wanting to find out (*incurious about what goes on in the rest of the world*).

incur'sion *n* a raid, a sudden quick attack (*enemy forces making incursions into our territory*).

indebt'ed *adj* owing thanks (*indebted to them for their help*):—*n* indebt'edness.

inde'cent *adj* 1 not decent, morally offensive, improper (*indecent remarks*). 2 not suitable, not in good taste (*marry in indecent haste after her husband's death*):—*n* inde'cency.

indeci'pherable *adj* that cannot be read or made out (*indecipherable handwriting/an indecipherable code*).

indeci'sion *n* doubt, hesitation, inability to make up one's mind (*full of indecision about whether to change jobs or not*).

indeci'sive *adj* 1 uncertain, having difficulty in making decisions (*too indecisive to make up her mind and stick to the decision*). 2 settling nothing (*an indecisive verdict*).

indec'orous *adj* not proper, not acceptable (*criticized for her indecorous behaviour*).

indeco'rum *n* improper, unacceptable behaviour.

indeed' *adv* truly (*yes indeed he will be there*).

indefat'igable *adj* never becoming tired (*indefatigable in their attempts to help her*).

indefens'ible *adj* that cannot or should not be defended (*his attitude towards her is indefensible*).

indefin'able *adj* that cannot be clearly described or explained (*an indefinable difference*).

indef'inite *adj* 1 not fixed or exact, without clearly marked outlines or limits (*guests staying for an indefinite time*). 2 not clear, not precise, vague (*give indefinite replies*).

indel'ible *adj* that cannot be rubbed out or removed (*an indelible stain*).

indel'icate *adj* 1 slightly indecent, improper (*indelicate language for a lady*). 2 lacking in tact (*an indelicate question*):—*n* **in-del'icacy**.

indemnifica'tion, indem'nity *ns* a sum of money paid to make up for something (*receive indemnification for the damage*).

indem'nify *vb* to pay something to someone to make up for what he or she has lost (*indemnified her for the damage to her car*).

indent' *vb* 1 to make a notch or zig-zag in (*a coastline indented by the sea*). 2 to begin a line in from the margin. 3 to order goods in writing (*the soldier indented for a new uniform*):—*n* **in'dent** an order for goods.

indenta'tion *n* 1 a notch or piece cut out of a straight edge (*the indentations in the coastline*). 2 the starting of a line in from the margin.

inden'ture *n* a written agreement between two parties, esp a master of a trade and an apprentice.

indepen'dence *n* freedom to act or think as one likes, freedom (*a colony that gained independence several decades ago*).

indepen'dent *adj* 1 thinking and acting for oneself (*too independent to let others tell her what to do*). 2 free from control by others (*independent countries*). 3 having enough money to live without working or being helped by others (*financially independent/a woman of independent means*).

indescrib'able *adj* that cannot be described (*indescribable cruelty*).

indestruc'tible *adj* that cannot be destroyed (*indestructible courage*).

indeter'minate *adj* not fixed, uncertain (*indeterminate plans*).

in'dex *n* (*pl* **in'dices**) 1 the pointer on the dial or scale of an instrument. 2 something that indicates or points to (*the results of the opinion poll are an index to public opinion*). 3 (*pl* **in'dexes**) an alphabetical list of names, subjects, etc, at the end of a book (*consult the index to see on what page the battle is mentioned*).

In'dian *adj* 1 of India. 2 having to do with North American Indians.

Indian corn *n* maize.

Indian file *n* a line of persons, one following the other (*mourners walking past the grave in Indian file*).

Indian ink *n* a black ink that makes a lasting mark.

Indian summer *n* a spell of fine warm weather in late autumn.

in'dia-rub'ber *n* a piece of rubber used for rubbing out pencil marks.

in'dicate *vb* 1 to point out, to show (*arrows indicating the way to the X-ray department*). 2 to be a sign of (*her attitude indicates an unwillingness to go*). 3 to show to be necessar y or desirable (*drastic action is indicated*).

indica'tion *n* a sign (*she gave no indication that she intended leaving*).

indic'ative *adj* showing, being a sign of (*a rash indicative of measles*).

in'dicator *n* 1 a needle or pointer on a machine that indicates something or gives information about something (*the indicator on the petrol gauge*). 2 one of the lights on a car that flashes to show which way the car is turning.

indict [in-dît'] *vb* to accuse of a crime (*he was indicted on a charge of murder*).

indictment [in-dît'-ment] *n* an accusation made before a court or magistrate.

indiff'erence *n* lack of interest.

indiff'erent *adj* 1 taking no interest, not caring (*indifferent to the suffering of others/indifferent to whether he goes or stays*). 2 neither good nor bad (*rather an indifferent musical performance*).

in'digence *n* (*fml*) want, poverty.

indig'enous *adj* born or growing naturally in a country (*plants indigenous to Britain/the indigenous people of the country*).

in'digent *adj* (*fml*) needy, poor (*indigent people with not enough money to live on*).

indigest'ible adj not easily digested (food that he finds indigestible).

indiges'tion n illness or pain caused by failure to dissolve food properly in the stomach (certain foods give her indigestion).

indig'nant adj angry, annoyed by what is unjust (she was indignant at the way she had been treated by the sales assistant/an indignant customer):—n **indigna'tion**.

indig'nity n treatment that makes one feel shame or loss of respect (suffer the indignity of being taken to the police station for questioning).

in'digo n a blue dye:—adj deep blue.

indirect' adj 1 not leading straight to the destination, roundabout (take an indirect route home). 2 not direct, not straightforward, not frank (give indirect answers to the questions). 3 not intended, not directly aimed at (an indirect result of the meeting).

indiscreet' adj 1 unwise, thoughtless. 2 done or said without thought of results.

indiscre'tion n 1 thoughtless behaviour. 2 an act done without thought of its results.

indiscrim'inate adj taking no notice of differences, choosing without care (indiscriminate in their choice of books/indiscriminate killing of hostages).

indispens'able adj that cannot be done without (no one is really indispensable).

indisposed' adj (fml) 1 unwilling (indisposed to do as he asks). 2 unwell (the speaker is indisposed).

indisposi'tion n (fml) a slight illness (unable to attend because of a slight indisposition).

indispu'table adj that cannot be denied or contradicted (his indisputable right to vote as he pleases).

indissol'uble adj 1 that cannot be melted or dissolved. 2 lasting (an indissoluble bond between them).

indistinct' adj not clear (her voice on the telephone was indistinct).

indisting'uishable adj that cannot be made out (the twins were indistinguishable from each other).

indite' vb (old) to write, to make up (inditing a report on the conference).

individ'ual adj 1 single (label each individual item). 2 intended for, used by, etc, one person only (individual attention). 3 special to one person (a very individual style of painting):—n 1 a single person (the rights of the individual). 2 (inf) a person (a strange individual).

individ'ualism n the belief that the rights of the single person are more important than those of society.

individ'ualist n one who believes in doing things in his or her own way (an individualist who disregards fashion).

individual'ity n one's own character (express her individuality in her style of dress).

individ'ually adv separately, one by one (they went individually to see the head teacher).

indivis'ible adj that cannot be divided (an indivisible number).

indoc'trinate vb 1 to instruct in a belief (indoctrinating children with the idea that qualifications are important). 2 to bring to accept a system of belief unquestioningly (indoctrinating children with his own political ideas).

in'dolent adj lazy (he's too indolent to get out of bed and look for a job):—n **in'do·lence**.

indom'itable adj not to be overcome, unwilling to admit defeat (her indomitable spirit).

indoor' adj done in a house or building (an indoor sport).

indoors' adv within doors, inside a house (hold the party indoors).

indu'bitable adj that cannot be doubted (his indubitable skill at the job).

induce' vb 1 to lead on to do, to persuade (inducing her to go back to school). 2 to bring about (induce feelings of excitement in the audience).

induce'ment n something that leads one to try to do something, an attractive reason for doing something (offer her the inducement of a company car to get her to stay).

induct' vb to put into a new office or position (induct a new priest).

induc'tion n 1 the ceremony at which someone is introduced to a new office or position. 2 an introduction into a new job, company, organization, etc (an induction course for new employees). 3 a way of r easoning by which a law or principle is worked out from the study of numerous examples. 4 the passing of electricity or magnetism from one body to another without their being in direct contact.

induc'tive *adj* starting from examples and working out a law to cover them (*inductive reasoning*).

indulge' *vb* **1** to take pleasure in something, without trying to control oneself (*indulging in too much rich food*). **2** to give in to the wishes of (*indulge her child too much/indulge oneself by going on a shopping trip*).

indul'gence *n* **1** act of indulging. **2** in the RC church, a setting free from the punishment due to sinners.

indul'gent *adj* kindly, easygoing, ready to give in to the wishes of others (*parents who are too indulgent*).

indus'trial *adj* having to do with the manufacturing of goods (*an industrial, rather than an agricultural, country*).

industrial action *n* protest action, often strike action, taken by workers over pay, working conditions, redundancies, etc.

indus'trialist *n* one who owns or runs an industrial organization.

indus'trious *adj* hard-working, busy (*industrious children studying for their exams*).

in'dustry *n* **1** (*fml*) the ability to work hard (*he owes his success to industry as well as ability*). **2** in trade or commer ce, the work that is done to make goods ready for selling, the manufacturing and selling of goods (*workers involved in industry rather than agriculture*).

ine'briate *vb* to make drunk (*to become inebriated after a few beers*):—*n* a drunkard:—*also adj.*

ined'ible *adj* that should not or cannot be eaten (*salty food that was totally inedible*).

ineffable *adj* (*fml*) too wonderful to be described (*her ineffable beauty*).

ineffec'tive *adj* useless, having no effect (*ineffective methods/ineffective people*):—*n* **ineffec'tiveness.**

ineffec'tual *adj* **1** not having the desired effect (*ineffectual remedies*). **2** powerless, not able to get things done (*ineffectual people*).

inefficacy *n* (*fml*) failure to have effect (*the inefficacy of the medical treatment*).

inefficient [in-ê-fish'-ênt] *adj* **1** not good at one's job, unable to do the job required (*sack the inefficient workers*). **2** not pr oducing results in the

best, quickest and cheapest way (*inefficient methods of production*):—*n* **ineffic'iency.**

inel'egant *adj* not elegant, lacking in grace or style (*an inelegant dresser*).

inel'igible *adj* not suitable to be chosen or to include (*ineligible to stand for election*).

inept' *adj* **1** clumsy, awkward (*an inept attempt at making a dress*). **2** foolishly unsuitable (*embarrass them by her inept remarks*).

inept'itude *n* **1** clumsiness, awkwardness. **2** foolish unsuitability.

inequal'ity *n* lack of equality, unevenness (*inequalities in the law*).

ine'quitable *adj* unfair, unjust (*an inequitable distribution of money*).

inerad'icable *adj* (*fml*) that cannot be done away with or changed (*ineradicable flaws in the system*).

inert' *adj* **1** without the power to move (*lying inert on the bed as if dead*). **2** not wanting to tak e action, not taking action (*she remained inert as though she could not think of what to do*). **3** not acting chemically when combined with other substances (*inert gases*).

iner'tia *n* **1** unwillingness or inability to move (*feelings of inertia caused by the heat*). **2** the inability of matter to set itself in motion or to stop moving.

inessen'tial *adj* not necessary (*no money for inessential foods*).

ines'timable *adj* (*fml*) **1** of very great value, that cannot be valued (*advice of inestimable worth*).

inev'itable *adj* certain to happen (*defeat seemed inevitable*):—*n* **inevitabil'ity.**

inexact' *adj* not quite correct (*an inexact science/inexact figures*):—*n* **inexact'itude.**

inexcus'able *adj* that cannot be forgiven or pardoned (*inexcusable behaviour*).

inexhaust'ible *adj* that cannot be used up or worn out (*seemingly inexhaustible supplies of food*).

inex'orable *adj* **1** not able to be stopped or changed by one's efforts (*the inexorable process of ageing*). **2** not able to be persuaded to act differently (*an inexorable opponent*).

inexpen'sive *adj* cheap, not dear (*inexpensive presents for Christmas stockings*).

inexpe'rience *n* lack of skill or practice (*the accident was caused by the driver's inexperience*):—*adj* **inexpe'rienced.**

inex'pert adj not skilled.

inex'plicable adj that cannot be explained (inexplicable delays).

inexpress'ible adj that cannot be put into words (inexpressible grief).

inex'tricable adj that cannot be disentangled (an inextricable involvement in an unhappy relationship).

infall'ible adj 1 unable to mak e a mistake (supposedly infallible judges). 2 that cannot fail (supposedly infallible methods):—n **infallibil'ity**.

in'famous adj having a bad reputation, famous for something bad or wicked (infamous criminals):—n **in'famy**.

in'fancy n 1 babyhood (she died in infancy). 2 the early stages of anything (the computer industry was in its infancy then).

in'fant n a very young child.

infant'icide n the murder of a newborn child (she was found guilty of infanticide).

in'fantile adj 1 childish (the infantile behaviour of the two women). 2 having to do with infants (infantile diseases).

in'fantry n foot-soldiers.

infat'uated adj loving foolishly or unreasonably (the young girl is infatuated with a much older man):—n **infatua'tion**.

infect' vb 1 to pass on a disease to another (the hotel worker infected others with the illness). 2 to make impure by spreading disease into it (food that is infected). 3 to pass on or spr ead (infect others with his love of life).

infec'tion n the passing on or spreading of disease, or anything harmful.

infec'tious adj that can be passed on to others (infectious diseases/infectious laughter).

infer' vb (**inferred'**, **infer'ring**) 1 to work out an idea from the facts known (what can we infer from the evidence given). 2 (inf) to suggest by hints.

in'ference n 1 an idea worked out from the known facts. 2 a hint.

infe'rior adj 1 of lesser value or importance (people of inferior qualifications were promoted before her). 2 of bad quality (inferior goods):—n a person lower in rank (he is her inferior in the company's staff structure).

infer'nal adj 1 (fml) having to do with hell (the infernal regions). 2 (inf) extremely unpleasant,

very annoying (that infernal noise/that infernal cat next door).

infer'no n a very hot place (the burning factory was an inferno where several people died).

infest' vb to be present in very large numbers in (a building infested with mice).

in'fidel n 1 one who does not believe in Christianity. 2 an unbeliever.

infide'lity n disloyalty, unfaithfulness (his wife's infidelity/his infidelity to his leader).

in'filtrate vb 1 to pass through, a few at a time (soldiers infiltrating enemy lines). 2 to enter and secretly and gradually become part of, usu with an unfriendly purpose (enemy spies infiltrated the government department):—n **infiltra'tion**.

in'finite adj 1 having neither beginning nor end, limitless (infinite space). 2 (inf) very great (infinite patience).

infin'ity n 1 space, time or quantity that is without limit or is immeasurably great or small (the grassy plains seemed to stretch into infinity). 2 an indefinitely large number, quantity or distance.

infinites'imal adj tiny, too small to be seen or noticed easily (infinitesimal differences).

infirm' adj weak, sickly (infirm old people unable to live alone).

infirm'ary n a hospital.

infirm'ity n illness, weakness (old people suffering from a range of infirmities).

inflame' vb 1 to set on fire. 2 to excite. 3 to anger.

inflamm'able adj 1 easily set on fire (children's nightware should not be made of inflammable material). 2 excitable.

inflamma'tion n a swelling on part of the body, accompanied by heat and pain (inflammation of the tonsils).

inflamm'atory adj causing excitement or anger (an inflammatory speech).

inflate' vb 1 to puff up (her success inflated her sense of her own importance). 2 to make to swell by filling with air or gas (inflate the tyre/inflating the balloon). 3 to incr ease in price or value (inflate house prices).

infla'tion n 1 act of inflation. 2 a situation in a country's economy where prices and wages keep forcing each other to increase:—adj **infla'tionary**.

inflec'tion same as **inflexion**.

inflex'ible adj **1** that cannot be bent, stiff and firm (inflexible materials). **2** not easily changed (inflexible attitudes). **3** not giving in (we tried to persuade her to change her mind but she was inflexible):—n **in-flexibil'ity**.

inflex'ion, inflec'tion n **1** a change in the form of a word to show its relation to other words in the sentence. **2** a change in the tone of the voice (her anger was obvious from the inflexion in her voice).

inflict' vb to force something unpleasant or unwanted on someone (inflict pain on his parents/inflict a heavy burden on them).

inflic'tion n **1** suffering. **2** punishment.

in'fluence n **1** the ability to affect other people or the course of events (his childhood unhappiness had an influence on his way of thinking). **2** the power to make requests to those in authority (he has some influence with the local authorities):—vb to have an effect on (she tried not to influence the decision).

influen'tial adj having power, important (influential people in the community).

influen'za n a type of infectious illness, usu causing headache, fever, a cold, etc.

in'flux n (fml) a flowing in (an influx of cheap foreign toys on the market).

inform' vb **1** to tell, to give information (inform her of the changes/inform him that she was leaving). **2** to teach, to give knowledge to. **3** to tell facts to the police or authorities about a criminal, etc (he informed against his fellow thieves).

inform'al adj **1** without ceremony (an informal dance). **2** not bound by rules or accepted ways of behaving (an informal agreement). **3** suitable for ordinary everyday situations (informal clothes/informal speech):—n **informal'ity**.

inform'ant n one who informs (when she heard the news she did not believe her informant).

informa'tion n facts told, knowledge in the form of facts, news, etc (receive information about new products/gather information about foreign customs).

information technology n the use of computers and other electronic equipment to produce, store and communicate information.

inform'ative adj giving news or facts (an informative TV documentary).

inform'er n one who gives away the plans of others (a police informer).

infre'quent adj not happening often:—n **infre'quency**.

infringe' vb **1** to br eak (infringing a local parking regulation). **2** to interfer e with (infringe his rights as an individual):—n **infringe'ment**.

infu'riate vb to madden, to make very angry (she was infuriated by his superior attitude to women).

infuse' vb **1** to put into (infuse some enthusiasm into the class). **2** to steep in hot liquid (as in making tea) (infusing camomile to make a herbal tea).

infu'sion n **1** act of infusing. **2** a liquid given taste or colour by something steeped in it (an infusion of camomile).

inge'nious adj **1** having good or new ideas, inventive (ingenious at thinking of ways to keep the children entertained). **2** cleverly thought out (an ingenious plan).

ingenu'ity n **1** cleverness, inventiveness (the ingenuity of the plan). **2** the ability to invent, cleverness (use her ingenuity to make a meal from very few ingredients).

ingen'uous adj lacking cunning or deceit, simple, having little experience of life (an ingenuous young country girl):—n **in-gen'uousness**.

ing'le-nook n a corner near the fire.

inglo'rious adj (fml) shameful (an inglorious defeat).

in'got n a bar or block of metal, esp gold or silver, got from a mould.

ingrained' adj fixed firmly in (an ingrained sense of duty/ingrained dirt).

ingratiate [in-grä'-shi-ãt] vb to try to obtain another's favour (she tried to ingratiate herself with the manager to get promotion).

ingrat'itude n lack of thankfulness (showing nothing but ingratitude to her parents).

ingre'dient n one of the things in a mixture (the ingredients for a cake/the ingredients for a happy life).

inhab'it vb to live in (an area mainly inhabited by retired people).

inhab'itable adj that can be lived in (houses that are inhabitable).

inhab'itant n one who lives in a certain place (the older inhabitants of the village).

inha'lation n **1** act of breathing in (*the inhalation of car exhaust fumes*). **2** something that is breathed in (*prepare an inhalation to try to cure her cold*).

inhale' vb to breathe in (*inhaling the smoke from other people's cigarettes*).

inharmo'nious adj **1** (*fml*) not friendly (*an inharmonious relationship*). **2** unmusical (*an inharmonious composition*).

inhere' vb (*fml*) to exist in as a quality or necessary part of.

inher'ent adj natural, existing in one since birth (*his inherent kindness*).

inher'it vb **1** to receive something from another at his or her death (*inherited his father's estate*). **2** to receive certain qualities through one's parents (*inherit his mother's good looks*):—n **inher'itor**.

inher'itance n that which is inherited (*he has spent most of his inheritance already*).

inhib'it vb **1** to pr event or hinder, to hold back from doing (*a tight skirt that inhibited walking/ a financial situation that inhibited expansion of the company*). **2** to mak e someone inhibited (*his presence seems to inhibit her*).

inhib'ited adj unable to relax and express one's feelings in an open and natural way (*too inhibited to speak in public*).

inhibi'tion n a belief or fear of which one is not aware but which may prevent one from performing certain actions (*have inhibitions about being seen in a swimsuit*).

inhos'pitable adj not welcoming visitors, not kind to strangers (*it was inhospitable not to offer the visitors anything to eat or drink*).

inhu'man adj cruel, merciless (*an inhuman tyrant/ inhuman actions*):—n **inhuman'ity**.

inim'ical adj hostile, not favourable, harmful, acting against (*an inimical environment/conditions inimical to growth*).

inim'itable adj that cannot be copied, excellent (*an inimitable performance*).

iniq'uitous adj very unfair, unjust, wicked (*an iniquitous system of taxation*).

iniq'uity n wickedness, evil (*an act of great iniquity*).

ini'tial adj first, happening at the beginning (*the initial reaction was favourable*):—vb (**ini'tialled**,

ini'tialling) to mark or write one's initials (*initial the order form to authorize it*):—npl **ini'tials** the first letters of each of a person's names.

ini'tiate vb **1** to begin (*initiating a new system of accounting*). **2** to teach the ways of a society to a new member (*the boys initiated their friend into their gang*):—n **ini-tia'tion**.

ini'tiative n **1** the ability to mak e decisions and take action without asking for help and advice (*he had to use his initiative when he was stranded on the island*). **2** the first movement or action that starts something happening (*take the initiative in organizing the jumble sale*).

inject' vb **1** to put into the bloodstream through a hollow needle (*injected with a drug to fight the infection*). **2** to put in (*her arrival injected some life into the party*):—n **injec'tion**.

injudi'cious adj (*fml*) unwise, thoughtless (*an injudicious remark*).

injunc'tion n **1** (*fml*) a command (*obey his mother's injunction to be home before midnight*). **2** an order from a court of law forbidding or ordering certain action (*he took an injunction out against the newspaper to prevent it printing a story about him*).

in'jure vb **1** to hurt (*she was badly injured in the car accident*). **2** to harm, to damage (*the incident injuring his reputation*).

inju'rious adj (*fml*) harmful, wrongful (*smoking is injurious to health*).

in'jury n **1** damage, harm, hurt (*an accident that caused injury to his spine/injury to his reputation*). **2** a physical hurt or wound (*he died later from his injuries*).

injus'tice n **1** unfairness (*feel there was injustice in the way he was treated*). **2** an unfair act (*complain about the injustices of the system*).

ink n a coloured liquid used for writing or printing:—vb to mark with ink.

ink'ling n a hint, a slight idea (*she doesn't have an inkling about what's going on*).

ink'stand n a vessel for holding ink.

ink'y adj **1** stained with ink (*inky hands*). **2** dark (*an inky sky*).

inlaid see **inlay**.

in'land n the part of a country away from the sea coast or border:—adj **1** having to do with a country's own affairs (*inland trade*). **2** away from the coast or border (*inland waterways*):— *also adv.*

inlay' *vb* (*pt,pp* **inlaid'**) to decorate by filling carved designs with gold, silver, ivory, etc (*the box is inlaid with precious stones*):—*adj* **inlaid':**—*n* **in'lay.**

in'let *n* **1** a way in (*a fuel inlet*). **2** a small bay (*boats sheltering in an inlet*).

in'mate *n* one living in a house, hospital, etc.

in'most *adj* farthest in (*the inmost depths of the cave*).

inn *n* a house where travellers may pay to eat, drink or stay for the night.

in'ner *adj* farther in (*the inner room*).

in'nermost *adj* farthest in (*her innermost thoughts*).

inn'ings *n* in cricket, the time spent batting or the score made by a player or a team.

inn'keeper *n* one who is in charge of an inn.

inn'ocence *n* freedom from blame or wickedness (*the innocence of the young children/try to prove his innocence*).

inn'ocent *adj* **1** not guilty (*innocent of the crime/ innocent people accused*). **2** having no knowledge or experience of evil (*innocent young children*).

innoc'uous *adj* harmless (*drugs thought to be innocuous/a perfectly innocuous remark*).

innova'tion *n* **1** a new way of doing something, a new thing or idea (*innovations in marketing methods*). **2** the introduction of new things or ideas (*he is set in his ways and dislikes innovation*).

innuen'do *n* (*pl* **innuen'does** *or* **innuen'dos**) **1** a way of speaking that makes one understand what is meant without actually saying it (*a newspaper that goes in for innuendo*). **2** an indirect hint (*he made innuendoes about where she got all the money*).

innu'merable *adj* too many to be counted (*innumerable objections to the scheme*).

inoc'ulate *vb* to infect slightly with the germs of a disease to prevent more serious infection (*inoculating the children against measles*):—*n* **inocula'tion.**

inoffen'sive *adj* not causing harm or trouble (*a quiet inoffensive man/be insulted at a perfectly inoffensive remark*).

inop'erative *adj* not working (*machines in the factory inoperative because of lack of orders*).

inop'portune *adj* happening at the wrong time, inconvenient (*arrive at an inopportune moment*).

inor'dinate *adj* too great (*spend an inordinate amount of time shopping*).

inorgan'ic *adj* having nothing to do with living creatures.

inorganic chemistry *n* the chemistry of substances without life (e.g. rocks, metals, etc).

in'quest *n* a legal inquiry to decide the cause of a person's sudden death (*at the inquest a verdict of accidental death was given*).

inquire', enquire' *vb* **1** to ask (*inquire the way to the station*). **2** to ask for information about (*inquire about times of trains to London*). **3** to try to discover the facts of (*the police are inquiring into the accident*).

inquir'ing *adj* seeking information, curious (*an inquiring mind*).

inquir'y, enquir'y *n* **1** a question (*reply to his inquiry about times of trains*). **2** a careful search for information, an investigation (*an official inquiry into the train accident*).

inquisi'tion *n* **1** (*fml*) an official inquiry (*subjected to an inquisition about his movements on the previous evening*). **2** (*old*) an examination consisting of a series of questions (*the Spanish Inquisition*):—*n* **inquis'itor.**

inquis'itive *adj* seeking information, esp about other people (*inquisitive neighbours*).

inquisito'rial *adj* trying to get information by every method possible.

in'road *n* a raid, a sudden attack:—**make inroads into** to use up a large amount of (*the visitors made inroads into her food supplies*).

insane' *adj* **1** mad (*a murderer declared insane*). **2** (*inf*) very unwise (*it was insane to give up his job*).

insan'itary *adj* dirty, causing disease (*living in insanitary conditions*).

insan'ity *n* madness.

insatiable [in-sā′-shi-a-bêl] *adj* that cannot be satisfied, greedy (*an insatiable appetite/his insatiable curiosity*).

inscribe' *vb* to write in a book or on stone, etc (*the words inscribed on the tombstone*).

inscrip'tion *n* words written on something, often as a tribute (*the inscription on the tombstone*).

inscru'table *adj* that cannot be fully understood, mysterious (*wearing an inscrutable expression*).

in'sect *n* a tiny creature with a body divided into sections and usu with six legs.

insec'ticide n a liquid or powder for killing insects (*vegetables that have been sprayed with insecticide*).

insectiv'orous adj insect-eating (*insectivorous animals such as hedgehogs*).

insecure' adj anxious and unsure of oneself, lacking confidence (*children feeling insecure when their parents separated*). 2 (*fml*) not safe, likely to be lost (*an insecure job*). 3 (*fml*) not safe or firmly fixed (*the insecure leg of the table*):—n **insecur'-ity**.

insensibility n lack of feeling.

insen'sible adj 1 too small to be noticed (*an insensible change*). 2 without feeling, indifferent (*insensible to their distress*). 3 unconscious (*knocked insensible by the blow*).

insen'sitive adj 1 not noticing the feelings of others. 2 not quick to feel or notice.

insep'arable adj that cannot be put apart (*the two issues are inseparable/childhood friends who were inseparable*).

insert' vb to put in or among (*insert the key in the lock*).

inser'tion n 1 something inserted (*an advertising insertion in the newspaper*). 2 the act of inserting (*the insertion of the key in the lock*).

in'set n an extra piece set in (e.g. a small picture in a larger one):—vb **inset** (**inset, inset'ting**).

in'shore adj and adv near the shore (*inshore oil workers*).

inside' n 1 the inner side or part (*the inside of the house*). 2 pl (*inf*) the internal organs, stomach, bowels:—adj 1 internal (*an inside toilet*). 2 known only to insiders, secret (*inside information*):—adv 1 on or in the inside, within, indoors. 2 (*inf*) in prison:—prep in or within.

insid'ious adj developing gradually without being noticed and causing harm (*cancer is an insidious disease*).

in'sight n ability to see the real meaning or importance of something, thorough knowledge (*his poverty-stricken childhood gave him an insight into the lives of the homeless*).

insignia [in-sig'-ni-a] npl badges of rank or honour (*the insignia of his regiment*).

insignificant adj of little importance (*an insignificant sum of money/rather an insignificant person*):—**insignif'icance**.

insincere' adj not meaning what one says, false, not truly meant (*his sympathy was insincere/insincere compliments*):—n **in-sincer'ity**.

insin'uate vb 1 to make way gradually and cunningly (*insinuating herself into her aunt's favour in order to receive money*). 2 to hint in an unpleasant way (*she insinuated that he was not honest*).

insinua'tion n a sly hint (*insinuations about his honesty*).

insip'id adj 1 having no taste or flavour (*insipid food*). 2 uninteresting, dull (*an insipid young woman*).

insist' vb 1 to state firmly, to demand or urge strongly (*he insisted on paying the bill*). 2 to keep on saying (*she insisted that she was innocent*).

insis'tent adj 1 firm (*he was insistent that we all go home*). 2 wanting immediate attention (*her insistent demands*):—n **insis'-tence**.

in'solent adj rude, boldly insulting (*an insolent stare*):—n **in'solence**.

insol'uble adj 1 impossible to dissolve (*a chemical insoluble in water*). 2 that cannot be solved (*an insoluble problem*).

insol'vent adj not able to pay debts, having no money (*he had to sell the business because he was insolvent*):—n **insol'vency**.

insom'nia n sleeplessness (*suffering from insomnia*).

inspect' vb to look at closely, to examine (*inspect the work/officials from the insurance company inspecting the damage*).

inspec'tion n an examination (*a school inspection*).

inspec'tor n 1 one who inspects. 2 one who examines the work of others to see that it is done properly. 3 a rank of police officer.

inspec'torate n a body or group of inspectors (*the school inspectorate*).

inspira'tion n 1 (*fml*) the drawing in of breath. 2 a person or thing that encourages one to use one's powers (*the poet's work was an inspiration to young writers*). 3 the encouragement so given (*she provided the inspiration for his latest novel*).

inspire' vb 1 (*fml*) to breathe in (*he was asked by the doctor to inspire*). 2 to encourage someone with the desire and ability to take action by filling with eagerness, confidence, etc (*she was inspired* to work hard by her mother's example). **3** to be the force that produces something, to be the origin of (she inspired his love of poetry). **4** to ar ouse in someone (inspiring confidence in others).

instabil'ity n unsteadiness (the instability of his character).

install' vb **1** to place in office, esp with ceremony (install the new bishop). **2** to put in place (have central heating installed):—n **installa'tion**.

instal'ment n **1** payment of part of a sum of money owed (the first instalment on the TV set). **2** part of a serial story published or broadcast at one time.

in'stance n an example (several instances of car theft in the area):—**for instance** for example:—vb to give or quote as an example (instancing violence as one of the features of modern life).

in'stant adj **1** immediate (demand instant attention). **2** pressing or urgent (an instant need). **3** concentrated or pr e-cooked for quick preparation (instant soup):—n **1** a moment (he did not believe her for an instant). **2** the exact moment (he loved her the instant he saw her). **3** (fml) the present month (your letter of the 3rd inst [= instant]).

in'stantly adv at once (she died instantly).

instanta'neous adj happening or done very quickly (an instantaneous reaction).

instead' adv in place of (he attended the meeting instead of his father).

in'step n the upper part of the foot where it joins the leg.

in'stigate vb **1** to start something happening (the police are instigating a search for the killer). **2** to suggest and encourage, to urge a wrong or evil action (it was he who instigated the bank robbery):—n **in'stigator**.

instiga'tion n **1** encouragement or persuasion, esp to do evil (they carried out the murder at his instigation). **2** the act of starting something (the instigation of the police search).

instil' vb (instilled', instil'ling) to put in little by little into the mind of (instil the need for honesty into him from an early age).

in'stinct n a natural tendency to behave or react in a particular way and without having been taught (in winter swallows fly south by instinct/instinct made them run from danger).

instinc'tive adj done at once without thinking, natural (an instinctive urge to run away).

in'stitute vb to set up for the first time (instituting a new computer system):—n **1** a society working to achieve a certain purpose (the Women's Institute). **2** the building in which it meets or works.

institu'tion n **1** an organization, usu a long-established or well-respected one (schools, hospitals and other institutions). **2** the building used by such an organization. **3** an accepted custom or tradition (the institution of marriage).

instruct' vb **1** to teach (instruct the children in French). **2** to order (she instructed her children to arrive home early).

instruc'tion n **1** teaching (receive instruction in French). **2** an or der (his instructions were to leave immediately). **3** pl information on how to use something correctly (a leaflet giving instructions on how to put the furniture together).

instruc'tive adj giving knowledge or information (an instructive TV documentary).

instruc'tor n a teacher, a coach (a sports instructor).

in'strument n **1** a tool, esp one used for delicate work (surgical instruments). **2** a device producing musical sound (stringed instruments). **3** a device for measuring, recording, controlling, etc, esp in an aircraft. **4** (fml) a document.

instrumen'tal adj **1** being the cause of (she was instrumental in getting him sacked). **2** played on musical instruments (instrumental music).

instrumen'talist n one who plays a musical instrument.

insubor'dinate adj disobedient, rebellious (insubordinate soldiers in the regiment):—n **insubordina'tion**.

insuf'ferable adj that cannot be borne, unbearable (an insufferable bore).

insuffi'cient adj not enough (insufficient evidence):—n **insuffi'ciency**.

in'sular adj **1** (fml) having to do with an island. **2** narrow-minded (an insular outlook on life).

insular'ity n narrow-mindedness.

in'sulate vb **1** to keep apart (a wealthy family insulated from the financial problems of ordinary people). **2** to cover with rubber, etc, in or der to prevent loss of electricity or heat:—n **insula'tion**.

in'sulator *n* a material that does not allow electricity or heat to pass through it.

insulin [in'-sû-lin] *n* a substance that if given as a medicine helps to use up the sugar in the body when there is too much of it (*people suffering from diabetes sometimes have to take insulin*).

insult' *vb* to speak rude or hurtful words to or of (*she was insulted when he called her an old lady*):—*n* **in'sult**.

insu'perable *adj* that cannot be got over, that cannot be overcome (*an insuperable problem*).

insupport'able *adj* unbearable (*insupportable burdens*).

insure' *vb* to pay regular sums to a society on condition that one receives an agreed amount of money in case of loss, accident, death, etc (*insuring his life/insure his house against fire and theft*):—*n* **in-su'rance**.

insur'gent *adj* (*fml*) rebellious (*an insurgent group of soldiers*):—*n* a rebel.

insurmount'able *adj* that cannot be got over (*insurmountable difficulties*).

insurrec'tion *n* a rebellion, a rising against the government.

intact' *adj* untouched, unharmed, with no part missing (*the police recovered the box of jewels intact/her self-confidence remained intact*).

intan'gible *adj* **1** that cannot be touched (*air is intangible*). **2** not able to be clearly defined or understood (*an intangible air of hopelessness*).

integer [in'-te-jèr] *n* a whole number.

in'tegral *adj* necessary to make something complete (*an integral part of the case against him*):—*also n*.

in'tegrate *vb* **1** to join in society as a whole, to mix freely with other groups (*newcomers trying to integrate into village life*). **2** to fit parts together to form a whole (*integrating everyone's comments into the report on the conference*):—*n* **integra'tion**.

integ'rity *n* **1** the state of being whole and undivided, completeness (*their integrity as a nation*). **2** honesty (*a man of absolute integrity*).

in'tellect *n* **1** the mind, the power to think and understand. **2** someone with great intellect (*one of the world's greatest intellects*).

intellec'tual *adj* **1** having a high intellect (*her intellectual friends*). **2** having to do with the intellect (*intellectual interests*):—*also n*.

intell'igence *n* **1** cleverness, quickness of mind or understanding (*the intelligence of the pupils*). **2** (*fml*) news (*receive intelligence of his death*).

intell'igent *adj* having a quick mind, clever (*intelligent pupils*).

intelligent'sia *n* (*fml*) the thoughtful and well-educated people in a country (*she thinks that she belongs to the intelligentsia*).

intell'igible *adj* clear, that can be understood (*instructions that are scarcely intelligible*).

intem'perate *adj* **1** lacking self-control, given to taking too much, esp strong drink (*intemperate habits*). **2** more than is desirable (*an intemperate amount of alcohol*). **3** excessive, unrestrained (*intemperate language*). **4** extreme (*an intemperate climate*):—*n* **intem'perance**.

intend' *vb* **1** to have as a purpose (*she intends to leave tomorrow*). **2** to mean (*the bullet was intended for the president*).

intense' *adj* **1** very great (*intense heat*). **2** very serious (*intense young women*).

inten'sify *vb* to make greater or more severe (*intensified their interest in the subject*).

inten'sity *n* **1** strength (*the intensity of the heat*). **2** seriousness, earnestness (*the intensity of the young poet*).

intent' *adj* **1** attending carefully (*intent on his work/with an intent expression*). **2** eager, planning or wanting to do something (*intent on going abroad*):—*n* (*fml*) purpose (*it was his intent to emigrate*).

inten'tion *n* purpose, aim in doing something (*it was his intention to leave early*).

inten'tional *adj* done on purpose (*intentional damage to his car*).

inter' *vb* (**interred'**, **inter'ring**) (*fml*) to bury (*inter him in the churchyard*).

in'ter- *prefix* between, among.

interact' *vb* to act upon each other (*chemicals that interact*):—*n* **interac'tion**.

intercede' *vb* **1** to try to settle a dispute or quarrel between others (*interceding in the wage dispute between management and the union*). **2** to speak in defence of another (*he interceded with the king to save his friend's life*).

intercept' vb to stop or catch on the way from one place to another (*intercept the enemy message*):—n **intercep'tion**.

interces'sion n act of interceding (*his intercession in the dispute*):—n **interces'sor**:—adj **interces'sory**.

interchange' vb 1 to change places with each other. 2 to give and receive in return (*interchange ideas*).—n an exchange.

interchange'able adj that can be exchanged for each other (*the two words are interchangeable*).

in'tercourse n 1 (fml) a mixing together by people or nations, business dealings (*social intercourse*). 2 sexual inter course.

interdict' vb to forbid:—n **in'terdict** an official order not to do something (*prevented from contacting his ex-wife by court interdict*).

in'terest n 1 something in which one takes part eagerly (*his main interests are tennis and football*). 2 advantage (*it was in our interests to agree*). 3 eager attention (*give the matter all his interest*). 4 concern (*of interest to all of us*). 5 the money paid for the use of a loan of money (*the rate of interest on his bank loan*):—vb to gain the attention of.

in'teresting adj arousing interest (*interesting information*).

in'terface n the point at which two subjects affect each other or are connected (*the interface between production and sales*).

interfere' vb 1 to get in the way of, to prevent from working or happening (*outside interests that interfere with his work*). 2 to force oneself into the affairs of others (*interfering in other people's private business*). 3 to touch or move something that one is not supposed to (*interfere with his private papers*).

interfer'ence n 1 act of interfering (*object to his interference in their affairs*). 2 the interruption of radio broadcasts by atmospherics or other broadcasts.

in'terim n the meantime, the time between two events (*the new head arrives next week—in the interim the deputy head is in charge*):—adj acting for a time only (*an interim marriage/take interim measures*).

inte'rior adj 1 inner. 2 inland:—n 1 the inner part (*the interior of the house*). 2 the inland part (*the interior of the country*).

interject' vb 1 to say something short and sudden. 2 to put in a remark when another is speaking.

interjec'tion n 1 a short word expressing surprise, interest, disapproval, etc (*'Oh' is an interjection*). 2 a remark made when another is speaking (*the speaker objected to his rude interjections*).

interlace' vb to twist together (*branches that are interlacing*).

interleave' vb to put blank sheets of paper between the pages of a book.

interlock' vb 1 to clasp or lock together (*with arms interlocked*). 2 to fit or fasten together (*jigsaw pieces that interlock*).

in'terloper n one who enters a place in which he or she has no right to be (*the older residents regard newcomers to the village as interlopers*).

in'terlude n 1 an interval between the acts of a play, etc. 2 the music or other entertainment provided during such an interval. 3 a period of time that comes between two events or activities (*a brief interlude of peace between the two wars*).

intermar'riage n marriage between members of different groups or countries:—vb **intermar'ry**.

interme'diary n one who goes from one party to another to help to arrange something between them (*appoint an intermediary in the dispute between management and workers*).

interme'diate adj coming between two other things, in the middle (*at an intermediate stage of the language course*).

inter'ment n (fml) burial (*the interment of the soldiers killed in battle*).

intermin'gle vb to mix together (*plain-clothes' policemen intermingling with the crowd*).

intermis'sion n an interval (*have a drink at the theatre bar in the intermission*).

intermit'tent adj stopping for a time, then going on again, happening at intervals (*intermittent showers*).

intern' vb to make people stay within a certain area (e.g. foreigners in time of war) or to put them in prison (*during World War II some German citizens living in Britain were interned*):—n **intern'ment**.

inter'nal adj 1 having to do with the inside, esp of the body (*internal organs*). 2 of one's own country (*internal trade*).

interna'tional adj having to do with several or many countries (an international trading treaty):—n a sporting contest between teams from different countries (a football international).

internecine [in-ter- nee'-sîn] adj 1 causing death and destruction to both sides (an internecine war). 2 involving conflict within a gr oup or organization (the internecine quarrels in the office).

In'ternet n the worldwide system of linked computer networks.

in'terplay n the action of one thing on another (the interplay of light and shade in his painting).

inter'polate vb 1 to put in something additional (an editor interpolating sections into the author's original play). 2 to make a remark while another is speaking ('He's a liar,' she interpolated).

interpola'tion n 1 a short interruption. 2 a passage put into a book by one who did not write the book.

interpose' vb 1 (fml) to put or come between (interposing himself between them to try to stop them fighting). 2 to make a remark or comment while another is speaking (he asked if he could interpose a few comments before the speaker continued).

inter'pret vb 1 to explain the meaning of (how do you interpret these lines of poetry?). 2 to understand the meaning of to be (he interpreted her silence as a refusal). 3 to translate fr om one language into another (he spoke in French and his English assistant interpreted his speech for the audience).

interpreta'tion n 1 act of interpreting. 2 the meaning given to a work of art by a critic or performer.

inter'preter n one who translates from one speaker's language into another's.

interreg'num n the time between the death of a ruler and the beginning of a new reign.

inter'rogate vb to put questions to (police interrogated the accused for several hours).

interroga'tion n 1 the act of interrogating (the interrogation of the accused by the police).

interrogation mark n the punctuation mark put after a direct question (?).

interrog'ative adj asking a question, having to do with questions (an interrogative remark):—n a word used in asking questions (e.g. why).

interrupt' vb 1 to break flow of speech or action (interrupt the broadcast to announce the death of the president/interrupt his lunch break to ask him to move his car). 2 to stop a person while he or she is saying or doing something (he interrupted the speaker to ask a question). 3 (fml) to cut off (build a block of flats that interrupted our view of the lake).

interrup'tion n a remark or action that causes a stoppage (the noisy interruptions by the audience during the politician's speech).

intersect' vb to cut across each other (the roads intersect outside the town).

intersec'tion n the point at which lines or roads cross each other (an intersection without traffic lights).

intersperse' vb to scatter over, to put here and there (green fields interspersed with a few small woods).

interstell'ar adj among or between the stars.

interstice [in-tèr'-stis] n a tiny space between two things close together or parts of the same thing.

intertwine' vb to twist together (roses intertwining round the door).

in'terval n 1 the time or distance between (the interval between snow showers). 2 a br eak, a spell of free time (pupils having a snack in their interval). 3 a short br eak in a play, concert, etc (have a drink at the theatre bar during the interval). 4 the differ ence of pitch between two musical sounds.

intervene' vb 1 to interrupt, to interfer e (intervening to try to stop them quarrelling). 2 to be or to happen between (in time) (a few years intervened before they met again). 3 to happen so as to prevent something (he was going to go to college but the war intervened and he became a soldier):—n interven'tion.

in'terview n 1 a meeting at which a person applying for a job is questioned (several candidates had an interview). 2 a meeting with a person to get information or to do business (the journalist asked for an interview with the president):—also vb.

intes'tate adj (fml) without having made a will (he died intestate):—n intes'tacy.

intestinal [in-tes-tî'-nêl] adj having to do with the intestines (intestinal problems).

intes'tines *npl* the inner parts of the body, esp the bowels (*the intestines consist of the large intestines and the small intestines*).

in'timacy *n* **1** closeness, close relationship (*enjoy the intimacy that exists between old school friends*). **2** (*inf*) sexual intercourse.

intimate [in'-tim-êt] *adj* **1** having a close relationship. **2** having a close knowledge of (*an intimate knowledge of the area*):—*n* a close friend:—*vb* [in'-tim-āt] (*fml*) to make known (*intimating his intention to leave*).

intima'tion *n* **1** (*fml*) a hint (*he gave no intimation of his intention to leave*). **2** an announcement (*intimations of births, marriages and deaths in the newspaper*).

intim'idate *vb* to make afraid, e.g. by making threats (*she was intimidated by the sight of the huge man/the boy intimidating younger boys into giving him money*):—*n* **intimida'tion**.

intol'erable *adj* that cannot or should not be put up with (*intolerable pain/intolerable behaviour*).

intol'erant *adj* not willing to put up with actions or opinions that are different from one's own, narrow-minded (*intolerant people who dislike those who hold views that are different from theirs*):—*n* **intol'erance**.

intona'tion *n* the rise and fall of the voice while speaking (*a monotonous voice with very little intonation*).

intone' *vb* (*fml*) to recite in a high-pitched or singing voice (*the priest intoning a blessing*).

intox'icant *n* a strong drink that can make one drunk (*intoxicants such as whisky and brandy*).

intox'icate *vb* **1** to make drunk (*he had drunk enough beer to intoxicate him*). **2** to excite greatly (*he was intoxicated by his success*):—*n* **intoxica'tion**.

intract'able *adj* (*fml*) **1** hard to control or manage (*intractable children*). **2** difficult to deal with (*intractable problems*).

intran'sigent *adj* (*fml*) unwilling to come to an agreement, not willing to compromise (*the peace talks have come to a halt because both sides were intransigent*):—*n* **intran'sigence**.

intran'sitive *adj* (*of verbs*) not taking an object.

intrep'id *adj* fearless, brave (*the intrepid explorer*).

in'tricate *adj* having many small parts, complicated (*an intricate pattern/an intricate story*):—*n* **in'tricacy.**

intrigue [in-treeg'] *n* **1** a secret plot. **2** a secret love affair:—*vb* **1** to plot secretly. **2** to interest greatly.

intrin'sic *adj* being part of the nature or character of, belonging to a thing as part of its nature (*his intrinsic generosity/furniture of no intrinsic worth*).

introduce' *vb* **1** to bring in or put forward, esp something new (*introducing a new system of accounting*). **2** to make one person known to another (*introduce her two friends to each other*).

introduc'tion *n* **1** act of intr oducing (*the introduction of new methods/ask for an introduction to her friend*). **2** a short section at the beginning of a book to make known its purpose (*an introduction explaining how to use the encyclopedia*).

introduc'tory *adj* coming at the beginning, giving an introduction (*an introductory course/a few introductory remarks*).

introspec'tive *adj* thinking much about one's own actions and ideas (*poetry of an introspective nature/so introspective that she is frequently rather depressed*):—*n* **in-trospec'tion.**

in'trovert *n* one who is always thinking about his or her own ideas and aims (*he is an introvert but his sister is a real extrovert*).

intrude' *vb* to come or go where one is not wanted (*he was intruding since they obviously wanted to be alone/she intruded on their private grief*):—*n* **intru'sion.**

intru'der *n* **1** one who intrudes. **2** a person who breaks into a house to steal, a burglar (*he heard an intruder downstairs*).

intru'sive *adj* tending to intrude (*intrusive neighbours/intrusive questions*).

intui'tion *n* **1** immediate knowledge of the truth gained without having to think (*she had an intuition that he was a wrongdoer, and she was right*). **2** the ability to know things in this way (*she knew by intuition that something was wrong with her sister*):—*adj* **intu'itive.**

In'uit *n* an Eskimo of North America or Greenland.

in'undate *vb* **1** to flow over (*fields inundated with flood water*). **2** to flood, to come in very large amounts (*they were inundated with correspondence*).

inunda'tion *n* (*fml*) a flood.

inure' *vb* (*fml*) to make used to (*she was inured to being ignored by her colleagues*).

invade' *vb* **1** to enter as an enemy, to attack (*the king ordered his army to invade the neighbouring country*). **2** to interfere with (*invading his neighbour's privacy*).

inval'id[1] *adj* **1** not valid (*an invalid ticket*). **2** useless, unreliable (*an invalid argument*).

invalid[2] [in'-val-eed *or* in'-val-id] *adj* weak, sickly (*her invalid aunt*):—*n* a sick person (*her mother is an invalid who rarely gets out of bed*):—*vb* to send away because of illness (*he was invalided out of the army*).

inval'idate *vb* to make to have no value or effect (*his claims to be an expert on local history were completely invalidated*).

inval'uable *adj* of very great value, more valuable than can be paid for (*her invaluable help/the information was invaluable*).

inva'riable *adj* unchanging.

inva'sion *n* **1** entry into a country by enemy forces (*their invasion of a neighbouring country*). **2** interference (*the invasion of his privacy*).

invec'tive *n* insulting language, a violent attack in words (*wept at his bitter invective*).

inveigh [in-vā'] *vb* to attack with words, to speak violently (against) (*the speaker was inveighing against the evils of alcohol*).

inveigle [in-vee'-gêl] *vb* to talk a person into doing something, to tempt (*she was inveigling him into lending her money*).

invent' *vb* **1** to think of and plan something new (*invent the motor car*). **2** to make up (*she invented a story about her car breaking down to account for her lateness*):—*n* **inven'tor**.

inven'tion *n* **1** a thing thought of and made for the first time (*the telephone was one of his inventions*). **2** the ability to think out new ideas (*her powers of invention*).

inven'tive *adj* good at thinking of new or unusual ideas (*an inventive writer*).

in'ventory *n* a list of goods or articles (*take an inventory of the contents of the house before she rented it out*).

inverse' *adj* opposite or reverse (*their enthusiasm for their work seemed to be in inverse proportion to their salaries*).

inver'sion *n* **1** act of turning upside down. **2** a change in the usual order of words in a sentence.

invert' *vb* to turn upside down, to turn the other way round (*he inverted his glass to trap the wasp/ invert the clauses in the sentence*).

inver'tebrate *adj* having no backbone (*invertebrate creatures such as worms*):—*n* an animal without a backbone.

invest' *vb* **1** to mark someone's entry to rank or office by clothing him or her with the robes belonging to it (*invest the new bishop*). **2** to surround a fort with an army. **3** to lend money in order to increase it by interest or a share in profits (*he invested his savings in her new restaurant*).

inves'tigate *vb* to examine, to find out everything about (*police investigating the murder*):—*n* **inves'tigator**.

investiga'tion *n* a careful examination, an inquiry (*the police have mounted a murder investigation*).

inves'titure *n* the ceremony at which new rank or office is conferred (*the investiture of the new bishop*).

invest'ment *n* **1** the act of investing. **2** a sum of money invested (*she has an investment of £14,000 in her husband's business*). **3** the thing bought (*she had to sell all her investments, including her house*).

inves'tor *n* one who invests money (*all the investors in her business lost their money*).

invet'erate *adj* **1** firmly fixed in a habit (*an inveterate liar*). **2** firmly established (*an inveterate dislike of flying*).

invid'ious *adj* (*fml*) likely to cause ill-feeling or envy (*make invidious comparisons*).

invig'ilate *vb* to keep watch over students during examinations:—*n* **invig'ilator**.

invig'orate *vb* to make strong or healthy, to refresh (*his walk in the cold air invigorating him*).

invin'cible *adj* that cannot be defeated (*they thought their army was invincible*):—*n* **invincibility**.

invi'olable *adj* (*fml*) that should not or cannot be harmed, sacred (*their inviolable rights to freedom of speech*).

invi'olate *adj* (*fml*) unharmed, that has been kept sacred (*a temple that has remained inviolate for hundreds of years*).

invis'ible *adj* that cannot be seen (*germs are invisible*):—*n* **invisibil'ity**.

invite' *vb* **1** to ask politely, to ask to come, esp as a guest (*inviting them to dinner/invited them to join their club*). **2** to attract (*the talks invited press attention*):—*n* **invi-ta'tion**.

invit'ing *adj* attractive (*an inviting prospect*).

invoca'tion *n* **1** a prayer . **2** the act of calling upon God or a god.

in'voice *n* **1** a list of goods sent to a buyer , with prices. **2** a list of work done and payment due:— *vb* to send an invoice.

invoke' *vb* **1** to bring into use or operation (*invoking a little-known law to justify their actions*). **2** to call on God in prayer . **3** to r equest or beg for (*invoke their assistance*). **4** to mak e an urgent request to (*invoke the law for their protection*).

invol'untary *adj* unintentional, done without conscious effort or intention (*involuntary movements of the muscles/he gave an involuntary cry*).

involve' *vb* **1** to include (*the accident involved a car and a lorry*). **2** to mix up in (*he became involved in drug-smuggling*). **3** to cause as a result (*a post involving a lot of overtime*).

involved' *adj* complicated (*an involved explanation*).

invul'nerable *adj* that cannot be wounded.

in'ward *adj* **1** inner. **2** having to do with the mind (*a feeling of inward satisfaction*).

in'ward(s) *adv* towards the inside (*the walls fell inwards*).

in'wardly *adv* in the mind (*inwardly disapproving*).

iodine [i'-ō-deen] *n* a chemical element used in medicine (*a solution of iodine used as an antiseptic*).

i'on *n* an electrically charged atom.

iota [i-ō'-ta] *n* **1** a Greek letter. **2** a tiny amount (*not care an iota about his family*).

ipecacuanha [i-pe-ka-kû-a'-na] *n* a plant used as a medicine.

IQ [*abbr for* Intelligence Quotient] *n* a person's level of intelligence as measured by a special test.

iras'cible *adj* easily made angry (*he has become irascible as he has grown older*):—*n* **irascibil'ity**.

irate' *adj* very angry, furious (*the irate farmer chased the boys who had let his cows out*).

ire *n* (*fml or lit*) anger.

irides'cent *adj* coloured like the rainbow, brightly coloured (*iridescent patches of oil on the street*):—*n* **irides'cence.**

i'ris *n* **1** the coloured circle of the eye. **2** a flowering plant. **3** the rainbow.

irk *vb* to annoy, to bother (*it irks her that he earns more than she does*).

irk'some *adj* troublesome, tedious (*irksome household tasks*).

i'ron *n* **1** the most common of metals. **2** a tool or instrument made of iron, esp for smoothing clothes. **3** *pl* chains (*prisoners in irons*):—*adj* **1** made of iron. **2** strong, hard (*an iron will*):— *vb* to smooth (clothes) with an iron (*iron shirts*):—**to have too many irons in the fire** to be trying to do too many things at once.

iron'ic, iron'ical *adjs* expressing irony (*an ironic remark/it was ironic that he stole money that he was going to get as a gift*).

i'ronmonger *n* one who sells metal articles.

i'rony *n* **1** a remark made in such a way that the meaning is understood to be the opposite of what is said (*'A fine fellow you are,' she said with irony*). **2** the result of an action that has the opposite effect to that intended (*the irony of his action was that he stole money that she was going to give him*).

irra'diate *vb* **1** (*fml or lit*) to make bright by throwing light on (*a garden irradiated with light from the lanterns*). **2** to treat with radiation (*irradiating the cancer*).

irra'tional *adj* **1** not r easonable, not sensible (*an irrational decision*). **2** not able to r eason, not using reason (*when she has had a drink she becomes quite irrational*).

irreconcil'able *adj* **1** who cannot be made friendly (*irreconcilable enemies*). **2** that cannot agree or exist together (*policies that are irreconcilable with ours*).

irrecov'erable *adj* that cannot be got back or recovered (*irrecoverable debts*).

irredeem'able *adj* **1** that cannot be saved (*irredeemable sinners*). **2** that cannot be gained again (*irredeemable losses in the fire*).

irrefut'able *adj* (*fml*) that cannot be denied or proved wrong (*irrefutable evidence*).

irreg'ular *adj* **1** not in agreement with the rules, not according to accepted standards (*his behav-*

iour was most irregular). **2** not straight or even (*irregular features/irregular road surfaces/an irregular coastline*). **3** not happening, etc, r egularly (*irregular school attendance*):—*n* **irregularity.**

irrelevant *adj* having nothing to do with the subject, not to the point (*please do not raise irrelevant issues at the meeting*):—*ns* **irrelevance, irrelevancy.**

irreligious *adj* having no interest in religion, showing no respect for God:—*n* **ir-religion.**

irremediable *adj* (*fml*) that cannot be put right, incurable (*irremediable situation/irremediable disease*).

irremovable *adj* that cannot be removed (*irremovable stains*).

irreparable *adj* that cannot be put right, beyond repair (*irreparable damage*).

irrepressible *adj* that cannot be kept down or held back (*irrepressible cheerfulness*).

irreproachable *adj* faultless, that cannot be blamed (*her behaviour throughout was irreproachable*).

irresistible *adj* **1** that cannot be resisted (*an irresistible force*). **2** very strong (*find his argument irresistible*). **3** very attractive, charming (*find newborn babies irresistible*).

irresolute *adj* **1** unable to make up one's mind. **2** hesitating:—*n* **irresolution.**

irrespective *adj* not troubling about.

irresponsible *adj* not caring about the consequences of one's actions (*irresponsible of him to leave the children on their own*).

irretrievable *adj* that cannot be won back (*irretrievable losses/irretrievable marriage breakdown*).

irreverent *adj* not showing proper respect, mocking (*she thought it irreverent of him not to take his hat off in church*):—*n* **ir-reverence.**

irrevocable *adj* that cannot be changed (*an irrevocable decision*).

irrigate *vb* to supply water to dry land by canals, etc:—*n* **irrigation.**

irritable *adj* easily angered or annoyed (*he is always irritable first thing in the morning*):—*n* **irritability.**

irritant *n* something that irritates (*the irritant that caused her sore eye/regard all children as irritants*).

irritate *vb* **1** to annoy, to anger (*irritated by their lack of interest*). **2** to cause to itch (*the washing-up liquid irritating her skin*):—*n* **irritation.**

irruption *n* (*fml*) a bursting in, an invasion.

isinglass [i'-zing-gläs] *n* a type of gelatine.

Islam *n* the religion founded by Mohammed:— *adj* **Islamic.**

island *n* a piece of land surrounded by water (*a desert island*).

isle [il] *n* (*lit*) an island.

islet [i'-lêt] *n* a small island.

isobar *n* a line on a map joining places with equal atmospheric pressure.

isolate *vb* **1** to place apart or alone (*isolate the patient with the unknown fever*). **2** to cut off (*villages isolated in snowy weather*). **3** to separate (*isolating and examining the chemical substance*):—*n* **isolation.**

isosceles [i-so'-sê-leez] *adj* (*of a triangle*) having two sides equal.

isotherm *n* a line on a map joining places with equal temperature.

issue [i'-shö] *vb* **1** to go or come out (*people issuing from the building/noises issuing from the room*). **2** to send out (*issue reminders about unpaid bills*). **3** to flow out (*blood issued from the wound*). **4** to give out (*issue new uniforms to all soldiers*). **5** to publish:—*n* **1** a flowing out (*the issue of blood from the wound*). **2** (*fml*) children (*married couples with no issue*). **3** (*fml*) a result (*await the issue of their debate*). **4** a question under discussion (*this issue is an international one*). **5** the number of books, papers, etc, published at one time (*the Christmas issue of the magazine*).

isthmus *n* a narrow neck of land joining two larger land masses.

italicize *vb* to print in italics (*italicizing the names of books and plays in essays*).

italic(s) *n* in printing, letters in sloping type (e.g. *italics*).

itch *n* **1** an irritation of the skin that causes a desire to scratch (*she has an itch where the flea bit her*). **2** a longing (*an itch to travel*):—*vb* **1** to feel an itch. **2** to feel a strong desire (to do something):—*adj* **itchy.**

item *n* **1** a single one out of a list or number of things (*the items on her shopping list/items of* *clothing*). **2** a piece of news (*an interesting item in the newspaper*):—*adv* also, in the same way.

it'erate *vb* (*fml*) to repeat (*iterating her objections*):—*n* **itera'tion**.

itin'erant *adj* not settling in any one place, moving from place to place (*an itinerant salesman*):—*n* one who is always on the move from place to place.

itin'erary *n* a note of the places visited or to be visited on a journey (*receive an itinerary from the travel agent*).

i'vory *n* the hard white substance forming the tusks of elephants, etc (*ornaments made of ivory*):—*adj* of or like ivory, creamy white (*an ivory blouse*).

i'vy *n* an evergreen climbing plant (*trees covered in ivy*).

J

jab *vb* (**jabbed**', **jab'bing**) to prod or poke suddenly (*she jabbed him in the arm as she spoke*):—*n* 1 a sudden prod or poke. 2 (*inf*) an injection (*get a jab against measles*).

jab'ber *vb* to chatter, to speak quickly and indistinctly (*unable to understand what the excited children were jabbering about*).

jack *n* 1 a tool for lifting heavy weights (*a car jack*). 2 the small white ball aimed at in the game of bowls. 3 the knave in cards. 4 a young pike. 5 a flag:—*vb* to raise with a jack (*jack the car up*):—**every man jack** (*inf*) every single one (*every man jack of us will have to help*).

jack'al *n* a dog-like wild animal.

jack'ass *n* 1 a male donkey. 2 (*inf*) a fool.

jack'boot *n* a high boot reaching over the knee.

jack'daw *n* a type of crow.

jack'et *n* 1 a short coat (*a man's woollen jacket*). 2 a loose paper cover for a book (*the book has a striking design on its jacket*).

jack'-of-all-trades *n* one who is able to do any kind of job (*he is not only a joiner—he is a jack-of-all-trades*).

Jacuz'zi (*trademark*) a kind of whirlpool bath with a system of underwater jets which massage and refresh the body.

jade *n* a green precious stone.

jad'ed *adj* tired, bored, uninterested (*after all the Christmas parties he feels a bit jaded and can't be bothered going out*).

jag'ged *adj* having rough edges or having sharp points (*jagged rocks*).

jag'uar *n* an animal like the leopard, found in South America.

jail *n* a prison (*sentenced and sent to jail*).

jail'er *n* a prison guard (*locked up at night by jailers*).

jam[1] *n* fruit boiled with sugar to preserve it (*spread raspberry jam on the bread*).

jam[2] *vb* (**jammed**', **jam'ming**) 1 to squeeze in, to fix so tightly that movement is impossible, to wedge in (*he jammed his foot in the doorway*). 2 to crowd full (*the hall was jammed with protesters*). 3 to prevent the receiving of radio messages by broadcasting sounds on the same wavelength:—*n* a pile-up of traffic (*bad traffic jams in the town during rush-hour*).

jamb *n* the side post of a door, window, fireplace, etc.

jamboree' *n* 1 a meeting of Scouts from different places. 2 a large, lively gathering (*a family having a jamboree at New Year*).

jan'gle *n* a harsh ringing noise (*hear the jangle of the shop doorbell*):—*vb* 1 to make or cause to make a jangle. 2 (*inf*) to irritate (*jangling one's nerves*).

jan'itor *n* 1 a doorkeeper. 2 one who takes care of a building.

Jan'uary *n* the first month of the year.

japan' *n* a hard black varnish:—*vb* (**japanned**', **japan'ning**) to varnish with japan (*a japanned box*).

jape *n* (*old*) a joke, a trick:—*also vb*.

jar *n* a glass or earthenware vessel with a wide mouth (*a jar of jam*).

jar'gon *n* words special to a group or profession (*the jargon of the advertising business*).

jas'mine, jess'amine *ns* a climbing bush with sweet-smelling flowers.

jas'per *n* a precious stone.

jaun'dice *n* an illness marked by yellowness of the eyes and skin.

jaun'diced *adj* 1 suffering from jaundice. 2 full of envy, disappointment, etc, thinking of everything as bad or unlucky (*have a jaundiced view of life*).

jaunt *n* a short pleasure trip (*go on a jaunt to the seaside*):—*vb* to go from place to place.

jaun'ty *adj* 1 cheerful-looking, confident (*wear his hat at a jaunty angle*). 2 pleased with oneself (*in a jaunty mood*).

jav'elin *n* a light throwing spear.

jaw *n* one of the bones in the mouth that hold the teeth (*get a broken jaw in a fight*).

jay *n*. a bird of the crow family with brightly coloured feathers.

jazz *n* syncopated music and dancing of African-American origin.

jea'lous *adj* 1 disliking rivals in love, having feelings of dislike for any possible rivals (*a jealous* *husband/he is jealous of any man she speaks to*). **2** disliking another because he or she is better off than oneself in some way, envious (*jealous of her friend's beauty*). **3** (*fml*) very careful of (*jealous of her reputation*):—*n* **jea'lousy**.

jean *n* a cotton cloth:—*npl* **jeans** close-fitting trousers often made of denim.

jeep (*trademark*) a light truck, military or otherwise, for going over rough ground.

jeer *vb* to laugh or shout at disrespectfully, to mock, (*jeering at the football player who was playing badly*):—*n* insulting words.

jejune' *adj* **1** childish, naive (*jejune political opinions*). **2** (*fml*) uninteresting, dull (*a jejune piece of prose*).

jel'ly *n* **1** a sweet food made by boiling the juice of fruit with sugar and mixing with gelatine to make it set (*serve ice cream and jelly to the children*). **2** a type of preserved fruit (*spread redcurrant jelly on bread*). **3** a material that is in a state between solid and liquid.

jel'lyfish *n* a jelly-like sea creature.

jem'my *n* an iron tool used by burglars.

jen'net *n* a female donkey or ass.

jen'ny *n* a machine for spinning cotton.

jeopardize [je'-pêr-dîz] *vb* to put in danger, to risk (*jeopardizing the rescue operation by his careless action*).

jeopardy [je'-pêr-di] *n* danger.

jerbo'a *n* an African desert rat, with long hind legs.

jerk *vb* **1** to give a sudden pull or push (*jerk the cord that operates the light*). **2** to move suddenly and quickly (*she jerked back as the car came towards her*):—*n* a sudden, quick movement (*after a series of jerks the car came to a halt*).

jer'kin *n* a close-fitting jacket or short coat.

jerk'y *adj* moving by jerks (*a jerky way of walking*).

jer'ry-built *adj* badly built with cheap materials (*jerry-built tower blocks*):—*n* **jer'ry-builder**.

jer'sey *n* **1** a close-fitting knitted upper garment (*they pulled on jerseys*). **2** a fine wool (*a dress of jersey*).

jest *n* a joke, something done or said in fun (*make a jest about their being newly married/she said it in jest*):—*vb* to joke.

jest'er *n* (*old*) one paid to make jokes, as in a king's or nobleman's household.

Jes'uit *n* a priest or brother in the Society of Jesus, a Roman Catholic religious order.

jet¹ *n* a hard black substance, often used for ornament (*a necklace made of jet*).

jet² *n* **1** a stream of liquid or gas forced through a narrow opening. **2** a spout through which a narrow stream of liquid or gas can be forced (*the water jet is blocked*). **3** a jet plane.

jet'-black *adj* deep black (*jet-black hair*).

jet plane *n* an aeroplane that is jet-propelled, i.e. driven forward by the force of jets of gas forced out to the rear.

jet'sam *n* goods thrown overboard to make a ship lighter.

jet'tison *vb* **1** to throw (goods, etc) overboard. **2** to get rid of (*decide to jettison the idea*).

jet'ty *n* **1** a pier. **2** a wall built to protect a harbour from high seas.

jew'el *n* **1** a precious stone (*diamonds, emeralds and other jewels*). **2** something valued highly (*the jewel of his art collection*).

jew'eller *n* one who buys and sells jewels.

jew'ellery, jew'elry *n* jewels, personal ornaments, as rings, necklaces, etc.

jib¹ *n* **1** a triangular sail raised in front of a ship's foremast. **2** the arm of a crane:—*vb* to pull a sail round to the other side.

jib² *vb* (*jibbed', jib'bing*) **1** to jerk suddenly back from, to stop and refuse to go further (*race horses jibbing at jumps*). **2** to object to and refuse to proceed with (*jib at lending him any more money*).

jibe *same as* **gibe**.

jif'fy *n* (*inf*) a moment, an instant (*she said that she would be down in a jiffy*).

jig *n* a lively dance tune:—*vb* (*jigged, jig'ging*) **1** to dance a jig. **2** to move up and down quickly in a jerky way (*children jigging with excitement*).

jig'saw *n* a picture that has been cut into different shapes and the puzzle is to try to fit them together again (*the jigsaw was of a battle scene*).

jilt *vb* to leave someone after promising to love or marry him or her (*jilted her at the altar*).

jin'gle *n* a light ringing noise made by metal against metal, as by small bells or coins (*the jingle of coins in his pocket*):—*vb* to ring lightly, to clink.

jing'oism *n* a fanatical belief that one's country is better than every other country:—*adj* **jingois'tic.**

jit'ters *npl* (*inf*) great nervousness.

jit'tery *adj* (*inf*) nervous (*in a jittery mood/get jittery at the sight of a policeman*).

jive *n* **1** a type of jazz music. **2** the way of dancing to it—*also vb.*

job *n* **1** a piece of work (*make a good job of mending the table*). **2** one's employment (*a job in an office*). **3** (*inf*) a crime (*serving three years in jail for the job he did*).

job'bing *adj* doing single small jobs (*a jobbing gardener*).

jock'ey *n* a rider in horse races:—*vb* to persuade or manipulate a person gradually and skilfully into doing something he or she is unwilling to do (*succeeded in jockeying him into joining them*).

jocose' *adj* (*fml*) humorous, fond of jokes (*in a jocose mood*).

joc'ular *adj* **1** intended to be humorous (*a few jocular remarks*). **2** fond of joking (*a jocular fellow*).

joc'und *adj* (*fml*) merry, cheerful.

jodh'purs *npl* riding breeches reaching to the ankle.

jog *vb* (**jogged'**, **jog'ging**) **1** to nudge, to prod (*he jogged me and I spilled the coffee/jog one's memory*). **2** to walk or run at a slow, steady pace (*jog round the park for exercise*):—*n* **1** a nudge, a slight shake. **2** a slow walk or trot.

jog'trot *n* a slow steady trot (*set off for the village at a jogtrot*).

join *vb* **1** to put or fasten together (*join the two pieces of string*). **2** to take part in with others (*join the search for the missing child*). **3** to become a member of (*join the golf club*).—*n* a place where things join (*unable to see the join in the wallpaper*):—**join battle** to begin fighting (*the enemies joined battle at dawn*).

join'er *n* a worker in wood, who makes furniture, etc.

joint *n* **1** a place at which two things meet or are fastened together (*seal the joints in the pipe*). **2** a place where two things are joined, but left the power of moving (as at, e.g. the elbow, a hinge) (*old people suffering from stiff joints*). **3** a large piece of meat containing a bone (*roast a joint of beef*):—*adj* **1** shared between two or among all (*a joint bank account*). **2** done by several together (*a joint achievement*):—*also vb.*

joint'ed *adj* having joints.

joint'ly *adv* together (*write the book jointly*).

joist *n* one of the beams of wood supporting the floor or ceiling.

joke *n* something said or done to cause laughter (*a speech full of jokes that were not funny*):—*also vb.*

jollifica'tion *n* merrymaking and feasting (*much jollification when they won the football competition*).

joll'ity *n* gaiety, cheerfulness.

jol'ly *adj* merry, cheerful (*in a jolly mood/jolly, amusing people*).

Jolly Roger *n* the black pirate flag with the skull and crossbones.

jol'lyboat *n* a small boat carried on a ship.

jolt *vb* **1** to give a sudden jerk to (*he jolted my arm as he passed*). **2** to move along jerkily (*a bus jolting along country lanes*):—*n* **1** a sudden jerk (*the car gave a jolt and stopped suddenly*). **2** a shock (*get a jolt when he failed the exam*).

jonquil [jon'-kwil] *n* a small daffodil.

jor'um *n* a large drinking bowl.

joss *n* a Chinese idol.

joss'-house *n* a Chinese temple.

joss'-stick *n* a stick of incense burned in Chinese temples.

jostle [jos'-êl] *vb* to knock or push against (*people jostling to get into the cinema*).

jot *n* a small amount (*have not a jot of sympathy*):—*vb* (**jot'ted**, **jot'ting**) to write down in short form (*jot down his address*).

jot'ter *n* a notebook or exercise book.

jot'ting *n* a short note.

journal [jur'-nêl] *n* **1** (*usu in titles*) a daily newspaper. **2** a weekly or monthly magazine (*The British Medical Journal*). **3** a record of the events of every day (*keep a journal of her travels*).

journalese' *n* the style of writing found in popular newspapers.

jour'nalism *n* the work of preparing or writing for newspapers and magazines (*a career in journalism*).

jour'nalist n one whose job is journalism.

journalis'tic adj having to do with journalism (a journalistic career).

jour'ney n a distance travelled, esp over land (long journeys by train and bus):—vb (fml or old) to travel (journeyed for three days).

jour'neyman n a trained workman.

joust n (old) a contest between two armed knights on horseback at a tournament:—also vb.

jo'vial adj merry, joyful, cheerful (a jovial old man/ in a jovial mood):—n jovial'ity.

jowl n the jaw, the lower part of the cheek (a face with heavy jowls):—cheek by jowl very close together (a meeting to promote peace where terrorists stood cheek by jowl with churchmen).

joy n 1 delight, gladness (bring joy to their lives). 2 a cause of great happiness (their child was a great joy to them).

joy'ful, joy'ous adjs full of joy (a joyful occasion).

joy ride n (inf) a drive for pleasure in a car (often one that does not belong to the driver) (teenagers stealing cars for joy rides):—vb joy'-ride.

joy'stick n 1 the pilot's lever to control an aeroplane. 2 a control lever on a computer.

ju'bilant adj rejoicing greatly, triumphant, very glad (jubilant after winning the match).

jubila'tion n triumphant joy.

ju'bilee n 1 a special anniversary of an event (the firm celebrated its golden jubilee). 2 a celebration of this:—golden jubilee a fiftieth anniversary:—silver jubilee a twenty-fifth anniversary:—diamond jubilee a sixtieth anniversary.

Judaism [jü'-dā-izm] n the religion of the Jews.

judge n 1 one who presides in a court of law giving advice on matters of law and deciding on the punishment for guilty persons (the judge sentenced him to two years in prison). 2 one asked to settle a disagreement (appointed judge in their dispute). 3 one able to distinguish what is good from what is bad (a good judge of wine):—vb 1 to act as judge in a court of law. 2 to decide, to give an opinion on (judging a school by its exam results). 3 to decide which is the best in a competition (judge a singing competition). 4 (fml) to criticize or blame someone (quick to judge others).

judg'ment n 1 act or power of judging (his judgment is not to be trusted). 2 the decision given at the end of a law case. 3 good sense (a business decision showing poor judgment). 4 an opinion (in my judgment he is a good player).

judicature [jü-di-kê-tûr] n all the judges or law courts of a country.

judi'cial adj having to do with a judge or court of law (our judicial system).

judiciary [jü-dish'-i-êri] adj having to do with a court of law:—n judges as a body.

judi'cious adj wise, showing good sense (a judicious decision/an action that was far from being judicious).

ju'do n a Japanese system of unarmed combat adapted as a competitive sport from jujitsu.

jug n a deep vessel for holding liquids, with a handle (a jug of milk):—vb (jugged', jug'ging) (old) to cook in a jar or jug.

jug'gernaut n 1 a large destructive force (the juggernaut of bureaucracy). 2 a very large lorry (juggernauts roaring through country villages from the ports).

jug'gle vb 1 to keep on throwing things up, catching them and throwing them up again with great quickness of hand (an entertainer juggling plates). 2 to change the arrangement of something in order to get a satisfactory result or to deceive (the accountant juggled the company's end-of-year figures):—n jug'gler.

jug'ular adj having to do with the neck or throat.

jug'ular vein n the large vein at the side of the neck.

juice n the liquid of a fruit or plant (orange juice):—adj juic'y.

ju-jit'su n a form of self-defence first used in Japan.

ju'jube n (old) a jelly-like sweet.

jukebox n a machine in a café, pub, etc. that automatically plays a selected record or compact disc when a coin is inserted.

Ju'ly n the seventh month of the year.

jum'ble vb to mix in an untidy heap (a cupboard with shoes and clothes all jumbled up):—n a muddle (a jumble of books and papers).

jumble sale n a sale of second-hand objects (e.g. clothes, crockery, etc), often to raise money for charity (a jumble sale in aid of the Red Cross in the church hall).

jum'bo n something very large of its kind:—adj very large (a jumbo jet).

jump vb **1** to push off the ground with the feet so that the whole body moves through the air (*the dog jumped over the wall*). **2** to make a sudden quick movement or start, as when surprised (*he jumped when the door banged*):—*n* **1** a leap (*a parachute jump*). **2** a sudden, quick movement (*give a jump in his sleep*). **3** an obstacle to be jumped over (*the jumps in a horse race*):—*n* **jump'er**:—**jump at** to accept willingly (*jump at the chance of working abroad*):—**jump to conclusions** to take things as true without waiting for them to be proved so.

jump'er *n* a close-fitting garment put over the head (*wear a warm jumper over his shirt*).

jump'y *adj* (*inf*) nervous, anxious (*feel jumpy when she was alone in the house*):—*n* **jump'iness**.

junc'tion *n* **1** (*fml*) a joining point. **2** a station where several railway lines meet.

junc'ture *n* moment, point, stage (*at this juncture he decided to leave*).

June *n* the sixth month of the year.

jungle [jun(g)'-gêl] *n* land esp in the tropics, covered with trees and matted undergrowth.

ju'nior *adj* **1** younger (*the junior children*). **2** lower in rank (*junior members of staff*):—also *n.*

ju'niper *n* an evergreen shrub.

junk[1] *n* **1** odds and ends, old or unwanted things, rubbish (*the shop is supposed to sell antiques but it's full of junk*). **2** (*inf*) any narcotic drug.

junk[2] *n* a Chinese sailing vessel.

junk'et *n* **1** the thickened part of sour milk sweetened with sugar. **2** a feast:—*vb* to feast.

junk food *n* food which is low in nutritional value, often eaten as snacks (*eating junk food instead of well-balanced meals*).

jurid'ical *adj* having to do with the law.

jurisdic'tion *n* **1** the carrying out of the law. **2** the area over which a judge or court has power.

jurispru'dence *n* the science of law.

ju'rist *n* one possessing a deep knowledge of law.

ju'ror *n* a member of a jury (*the jurors in a murder trial*).

ju'ry *n* a number of persons who have sworn to give a fair and honest opinion of the facts related in a law case (*the jury reached a verdict of not guilty*):—*n* **ju'ryman.**

ju'ry box *n* the part of a court set aside for the jury during a trial.

just *adj* **1** right and fair (*a just decision/it's only just that she pays*). **2** honest, fair, moral (*a just man*). **3** reasonable, based on one's rights (*a just claim*). **4** deserved (*his just reward*):—*adv* **1** exactly (*just what he needs*). **2** on the point of (*just coming in the door*). **3** quite (*a house that is just as nice as theirs*). **4** merely, only (*he's just a child*). **5** barely (*just enough milk for two*). **6** very lately or recently (*she has just left*).

jus'tice *n* **1** fairness or rightness in the treatment of other people (*laws based on justice/there was no justice in her treatment of him*). **2** a judge.

justice of the peace *n* a person appointed to help administer the law in a certain district.

jus'tifi'able *adj* that may be shown right, excusable (*try to make us believe that his behaviour was justifiable*).

justifica'tion *n* a reason for doing something, a defence (*no justification for his bad behaviour*).

jus'tify *vb* to show that something is right, just, reasonable or excusable (*unable to justify spending all that money/try to justify his behaviour*).

jut *vb* (**jut'ted**, **jut'ting**) to stick out (*balconies jutting out over the sea*).

jute *n* a fibre from the bark of certain plants, from which rope, canvas, etc, are made.

ju'venile *adj* **1** having to do with young people (*juvenile courts*). **2** typical of young people, childish (*middle-aged people behaving in a juvenile way*):—*n* a young person.

juxtapose' *vb* to place side by side or close together, esp to show a contrast (*juxtaposing two phrases for effect*).

juxtaposi'tion *n* a placing near, or side by side.

K

kail *see* **kale**.

kale, kail *n* a type of cabbage.

kaleidoscope [ka-lī´-do-skōp] *n* **1** a toy consisting of a tube in which quickly changing colours and shapes are seen through an eyehole. **2** a constantly and quickly changing pattern (*the kaleidoscope of history*).

kaleidoscop'ic *adj* **1** with many changing colours. **2** quickly changing.

kangaroo' *n* an Australian mammal with a pouch for its young and long strong hind legs by means of which it jumps along.

kap'ok *n* a light cotton-like fibre used for stuffing cushions, etc.

karaoke [kä-rä´-ōki] *n* a type of entertainment in which a machine plays a tape of popular music while people take it in turn to sing the words of the songs.

kara'te *n* a Japanese form of unarmed combat using the feet, hands and elbows.

kayak [kī´-ak] *n* an Eskimo canoe, made from seal-skin.

kebab' *n* small pieces of meat or vegetables grilled on a metal or wooden skewer.

ked'geree *n* a dish made of rice, fish and eggs (*serve kedgeree for dinner*).

keel *n* the long beam or girder along the bottom of a ship from which the whole frame is built up:—*vb* **keel over 1** to turn over to one side, to capsize (*the boat keeled over in the storm*). **2** (*inf*) to fall down, to collapse (*people keeling over in the heat*).

keel'haul *vb* (*old*) to punish by dragging through the water under the keel of a ship and up on the other side by ropes.

keen *adj* **1** sharp (*a keen mind/keen eyesight*). **2** eager, very interested (*keen pupils/keen to go/ keen on cooking*):—*n* keen'ness.

keep *vb* (*pt, pp* kept) **1** to have something without being required to give it back (*told to keep the change*). **2** not to give or throw away, to preserve (*keep old family photographs/keep a secret*). **3** to remain in a certain state (*keep calm*). **4** to have charge of, to look after (*keep his watch for him/keep hens*). **5** to pay for and look after

(*keep his family*). **6** to hold back. **7** to carry out (*keep an engagement*). **8** to go on doing (*keep walking*). **9** (*inf*) to remain in good condition (*food that won't keep*):—*n* **1** (*fml*) care (*leave the children in his keep*). **2** a strong tower in the centre of a castle. **3** (*inf*) maintenance, food and lodging (*pay for his keep*):—**keep at** to go on trying to do:—**keep body and soul together** to help to keep alive (*she does two jobs to try to keep body and soul together*):—**keep one's hand in** to practise enough to remain good at (*she no longer plays in an orchestra but she plays the piano enough t o keep her hand in*).

keep'er *n* one who keeps or looks after (*the lock-keeper/the gate-keeper*).

keep'ing *n* care, charge (*money given into the bank's keeping*).

keep'sake *n* a gift valued because of the giver (*she gave him a lock of her hair as a keepsake*).

keg *n* a small barrel (*a keg of beer*).

kelp *n* **1** a type of seaweed. **2** ashes of seaweed, used in making glass, iodine, etc.

ken *n*:—**beyond one's ken** outside the extent of one's understanding (*how he made his money was beyond our ken*).

ken'nel *n* **1** a house for dogs (*a kennel in the garden for the dog*). **2** a pack of hounds.

kerb *n* the stone edging to a pavement (*taxis parked at the kerb outside the hotel*).

ker'chief *n* a cloth for covering the head (*wearing a red kerchief to protect her head from the sun*).

ker'nel *n* **1** the eatable part in the centre of a nut or fruit stone. **2** the most important part (*the kernel of the problem*).

ker'osene *n* an oil made from petroleum, paraffin.

kes'trel *n* a small falcon.

ketch *n* a small two-masted boat.

ketch'up *n* a sauce (*tomato ketchup*).

kettle *n* a metal vessel, with a spout and handle, used for boiling water (*boil water for the tea in an electric kettle*):—**pretty kettle of fish** a great difficulty.

ket'tledrum *n* a drum made of skin or parchment stretched across the mouth of a rounded metal frame.

key [kee] *n* **1** an instrument for opening locks, winding clocks, etc (*turn the key in the lock*). **2** one of the levers struck by the fingers on a piano, typewriter, etc. **3** the relationship of the notes in which a tune is written. **4** something that when known enables one to work out a code, problem, etc (*the key to the puzzle*). **5** a translation. **6** a general mood, tone or style (*in a low key*).

key'board *n* the set of levers struck by the fingers on a piano, typewriter, etc (*the keyboard of the computer*):—*vb* to use a keyboard.

keyed up [keed-] *adj* (*inf*) excited, ready for something to happen (*children all keyed up waiting for the party*).

key'hole *n* the hole through which a key is put in a lock (*looking through the keyhole to see what they were doing*).

key'note *n* **1** the starting note of the musical scale in which a tune is written. **2** a leading fact or idea (*the keynote of the conference*).

key'stone *n* **1** the central stone of an arch, keeping the whole together. **2** something on which everything else depends (*the keystone of the organization*).

khaki [kä'-kee] *adj* dust-coloured:—*n* yellowish-brown cloth originally used in making army uniforms.

khalif *see* **caliph.**

kick *vb* **1** to strike with the foot (*kick the ball*). **2** (*of a gun*) to jerk back when fired:—*n* **1** a blow given with the foot (*his leg injured by a kick from a horse*). **2** the recoil of a gun. **3** (*inf*) a thrill, a feeling of pleasure (*get a kick from fast cars*). **4** strength, effectiveness (*a drink with a kick in it*).

kid *n* **1** a young goat. **2** goatskin leather. **3** (*inf*) a child (*work hard to give his kids everything*):—*vb* (**kid'ded, kid'ding**) (*inf*) to deceive in fun (*she was offended but then she realized that he was only kidding*).

kid'nap *vb* (**kid'napped, kid'napping**) to carry off a person by force (*kidnap the child of the millionaire to get money*):—*n* **kid'napper.**

kid'ney *n* **1** one of two glands that cleanse the blood and pass the waste liquid out of the body. **2** the kidneys of certain animals used as food (*steak and kidney pudding*).

kill *vb* **1** to put to death. **2** to put an end to (*kill all their hopes*):—*n* the animal(s) killed in a hunt:—**kill time** to make time seem to pass more quickly by occupying or amusing oneself in some way (*kill time by looking round the shops*).

kill'joy *n* one who spoils the pleasure of others (*he was a real killjoy who was always complaining about the children's noise*).

kiln *n* a furnace or oven for heating or hardening anything, esp bricks and pottery.

kil'o- *prefix* one thousand.

kil'ogram(me) *n* a measure of weight = 1000 grams (about 2^1/5 lb).

kil'ometre *n* a measure of length = 1000 metres (about ^{5}/8 mile).

kil'owatt *n* a measure of electric power = 1000 watts.

kilt *n* a short pleated skirt worn by Scotsmen as part of Highland dress.

kin *n* (*fml*) one's relatives, by blood or marriage (*all his kin are dead*).

kind [kind] *n* **1** sort, type, variety (*fruit of various kinds/people of that kind*). **2** nature, character (*differ in size but not in kind*):—*adj* thoughtful and friendly, generous (*kind neighbours/kind acts*):—*n* **kind'ness:**—**pay in kind** to pay by goods, etc, not money (*they gave us apples and we paid them in kind by giving them eggs*).

kin'dergarten *n* a school for young children.

kin'dle *vb* **1** to set on fire, to light (*kindling the fire in the hearth*). **2** to stir up (*kindle love*).

kind'ling *n* small pieces of wood used for lighting a fire (*chop kindling for the fire*).

kind'ly *adj* kind, friendly (*a kindly old woman/a kindly smile*):—*also adv*:—*n* **kind'li-ness.**

kin'dred *n* **1** (*fml*) one's relatives, esp by blood (*all his kindred were killed in the battle*). **2** relationship (*claim kindred with him*):—*adj* **1** related (*kindred languages*). **2** congenial (*kindred spirits*).

kinet'ics *n* the study of the connection between force and motion:—*adj* **kinet'ic.**

king *n* **1** the male ruler of a state. **2** a playing card with a king's picture. **3** a piece in chess (*kings and castles and bishops*).

king'dom *n* a state ruled by a king.

king'fisher *n* a small brightly coloured bird that dives for fish.

king'ly adj like a king (with kingly dignity).

king'ship n the state or office of a king.

kink n 1 a backward twist in a rope, chain, etc (a kink in the garden hose). 2 an unusual or strange way of thinking about things (a curious kink in his character).

kins'man n a male relative:—f **kins'woman**.

ki'osk n 1 a small hut or stall for the sale of newspapers, sweets, etc (buy sandwiches at the station kiosk). 2 a public telephone booth.

kip'per vb to preserve by splitting open, salting and drying:—n a fish so preserved, esp a herring, and used as food (have grilled kippers for breakfast).

kirk n (Scot) a church.

kiss vb to touch with the lips as a sign of love or respect (kiss their parents goodnight/kiss each other when they met/he kissed her hand):—also n.

kit n all the tools, etc, needed to do a job (his athletics kit).

kit'bag n a bag for necessary tools, clothes, etc, as carried by soldiers, sailors, etc.

kitch'en n the room in which cooking is done (a kitchen fitted with labour-saving machines).

kitchenette' n a small room where cooking and washing up are done (a flat with a sitting room, bedroom and kitchenette).

kite n 1 a type of hawk. 2 a toy made of paper or cloth stretched on a tight framework, flown in the air at the end of a string (the child was flying a kite in the shape of a dragon).

kit'ten n a young cat.

ki'wi n 1 a wingless tailless bird of New Zealand. 2 the fruit of an Asian vine.

kleptoma'nia n an uncontrollable desire to steal things (she was accused of shoplifting but she was suffering from kelptomania):—n **kleptoma'niac**.

knack [nak] n knowledge of the right way to do a thing, skill gained by practice (there is a knack to tossing pancakes/he has the knack of making people feel welcome).

knap'sack n (old) a bag strapped to the back, worn by soldiers or travellers.

knave [näv] n 1 a rascal, a dishonest rogue (the knaves who stole his horse). 2 the third picture in a pack of cards, the jack.

knead [need] vb to press into a dough or paste (knead the dough to make bread).

knee n the joint between the upper and lower parts of the leg (pray on his knees).

kneel vb (pt, pp **knelt** or **kneeled'**) to go down or rest on the knees.

knell n (fml or lit) the sound of a bell, esp at a funeral:—vb 1 (of a bell) to ring a knell (church bells knelling). 2 to summon by, or as by, a knell.

knick'erbock'ers npl (old) loose breeches ending at the knee.

knick'ers npl a woman's undergarment with elastic round the waist, pants.

knick'-knack n a small or dainty ornament (a row of knick-knacks on her mantelpiece).

knife [nīf] n (pl **knives**) a tool with a sharp edge for cutting (stab him with a knife/carve the meat with a knife/eat his food with a knife and fork):—vb to stab with a knife (he planned to knife her to death).

knight [nīt] n 1 in olden days, one of honourable military rank (knights fighting in a tournament). 2 a rank awarded for service to society, entitling the holder to be called Sir (the Queen made him a knight). 3 a piece in chess:—vb to make (someone) a knight (a famous footballer knighted by the Queen).

knight err'ant n (old) a knight who travelled in search of adventure.

knight'hood n the rank of a knight (receive a knighthood for services to charity).

knight'ly adj having to do with a knight (knightly behaviour).

knit vb (**knit'ted, knit'ting**) 1 to make woollen thread into garments by means of needles (knit a cardigan). 2 to join closely (broken bones that failed to knit).

knit'ting n the thing knitted (leave her knitting on the bus).

knit'ting need'le n a long needle used for knitting.

knives see knife.

knob n 1 a rounded part sticking out from a surface (the knobs on the trunk of a tree). 2 the round handle of something (wooden door knobs). 3 a round control switch (the knobs on the television set). 4 a small lump of something (a knob of butter).

knobb'ly adj covered with lumps, bumpy (knobbly knees).

knock *vb* **1** to strike (*he knocked his head on the low ceiling*). **2** to rap on a door (*knock at the door*). **3** (*inf*) to criticize (*stop knocking him—he's doing his best*):—*n* **1** a blow (*a knock on the head*). **2** a rap on the door.

knock'er *n* a hammer attached to a door for knocking (*brass door-knockers*).

knock'-kneed' *adj* having knees that touch in walking.

knoll [nōl] *n* (*fml or lit*) a little rounded hill (*a grassy knoll*).

knot *n* **1** the twisting of two parts or pieces of string, etc, together so that they will not part until untied (*put a knot in the string to tie the parcel*). **2** a hard piece of the wood of a tree, from which a branch grew out. **3** a small group of people (*a knot of people gossiping at the street corner*). **4** a measure of speed at sea (about 1.15 miles per hour):—*vb* to tie in a knot.

knotty *adj* difficult (*a knotty problem*).

know [nō] *vb* (*pt* **knew**, *pp* **known**) **1** to be aware that (*she knew that he was present*). **2** to have information or knowledge about (*she knows the office system thoroughly/know all the facts*). **3** to have learned and remember (*know a poem by Keats*). **4** to be aware of the identity of, to be acquainted with (*I know Mary Jones*). **5** to recognize or identify (*I would never have known her after all these years*).

knowing *adj* showing secret understanding (*a knowing smile*).

knowledge *n* **1** that which is known, information (*he had considerable knowledge about America*). **2** the whole of what can be learned or found out (*branches of knowledge, such as astronomy*).

knuckle *n* a finger joint (*graze his knuckles*):—*vb* **knuckle down** to start working hard:— **knuckle under** to be forced to accept the authority of someone, to give in to (*he was disobedient but the new teacher made him knuckle under*).

knuckle-dust'er *n* a blunt metal instrument fixed on to the hand as a weapon.

koa'la *n* a small bear-like animal found in Australia.

kook'aburra *n* an Australian bird (the laughing jackass).

Koran' *n* the holy book of Islam.

kosh'er *adj* **1** of food that has been prepared according to the rules of Jewish law. **2** (*inf*) genuine, honest, legal (*I don't think his qualifications are kosher*).

kowtow' *vb* to submit in a base or over-humble manner, to show too much respect to the wishes and views of (*she expects the whole family to kowtow to her*).

ku'dos *n* glory, fame, credit (*gain a lot of kudos in the village from being interviewed on television*).

kung fu' [kung fü] *n* a Chinese form of unarmed combat using the hands and feet, similar to karate.

L

la'bel *n* a piece of paper or card fixed to something to give information about it (*read the ingredients on the label/a label with washing instructions*):—*vb* (**la'belled**, **la'belling**) to fix a label to (*make sure all the parcels are labelled*).

la'bial *adj* having to do with the lips:—*n* a speech sound made with the help of the lips.

labor'atory *n* a workshop used for scientific experiments (*the firm's research laboratory*).

labor'ious *adj* needing hard work, tiring (*laborious tasks such as weeding*).

la'bour *n* **1** hard work (*manual labour/the labour involved in tidying up the garden*). **2** childbirth. **3** all workers as a body (*have difficulty in getting local labour*):—*also adj*:—*vb* **1** to work hard (*labouring away at their homework*). **2** to be employed to do hard and unskilled work (*labouring at the building site*). **3** to do something slowly or with difficulty (*labouring up the hill*).

la'boured *adj* showing much effort or hard work (*a laboured styled of writing*).

la'bourer *n* a person who does unskilled work (*labourers on the building site*).

Labour Party *n* a British political party.

labur'num *n* a tree with hanging yellow flowers.

lab'yrinth *n* a place full of winding passages, a maze (*a labyrinth in the grounds of the Greek temple/the basement was a labyrinth of corridors*).

labyrin'thine *adj* having to do with a labyrinth.

lac *n* a resin giving dark red dye.

lace *n* **1** a cord used for tying opposite edges together (*a shoe lace*). **2** an ornamental network of thread (*handkerchiefs edged with lace*):—*vb* to fasten with a lace (*lacing up her shoes*).

lacerate [la'-sê-rāt] *vb* **1** to tear , to wound (*her leg lacerated by a barbed wire fence*). **2** to hurt badly (*he lacerated her with his cruel words*):—*n* **lacera'tion**.

lachrymose [la'-kri-mōz] *adj* (*fml*) tearful (*lachrymose after her lover left*).

lack *vb* to want, to need, to be without (*she lacks confidence/the organization lacks funds*):—*n* want, need (*a lack of money*).

lackadai'sical *adj* lacking energy or interest (*a lackadaisical attitude to her schoolwork/too lackadaisical to join any of the clubs*).

lack'ey *n* **1** (*old*) a servant. **2** one who behaves like a servant (*she is always surrounded by lackeys*).

lacklus'tre *adj* dull, lacking brightness (*a lacklustre piano recital*).

lacon'ic *adj* using few words to express a meaning (*a laconic way of speaking*).

lacquer [la'-kêr] *n* **1** a varnish. **2** a substance used to keep hair in place (*spray her hair with lacquer*):—*vb* to paint with lacquer.

lacrosse' *n* a team ball game played with long-handled rackets.

lac'tic *adj* having to do with milk.

lacu'na *n* (*pl* **lacu'nae**) (*fml*) a gap, a blank (*a lacuna in the manuscript/a lacuna in her knowledge of the subject*).

lad *n* a boy, a youth (*employ a lad to deliver papers/just a lad*).

lad'der *n* **1** a frame of two poles or planks, joined by short crossbars, used as steps for going up or down (*climb the ladder to get to the roof*). **2** a tear that runs up or down a stocking or tights (*bang her leg and get a ladder in her tights*).

lad'en *adj* loaded (*trees laden with apples/women laden with shopping/laden with worries*).

la'dle *n* a large long-handled spoon for lifting liquids (*a soup ladle*):—*vb* to lift with a ladle (*ladling soup into the plates*).

la'dy *n* **1** a woman of rank or with good manners (*behave like a lady*). **2** the title of the wife of a knight or of a man of higher rank.

la'dybird *n* a small beetle, usu red with black spots.

la'dyship *n* the title used in speaking to or of a lady of high rank.

lag *vb* (**lagged'**, **lag'ging**) **1** to go too slowly , not to keep pace with, to fall behind (*lagging behind the rest of the walkers*). **2** not to k eep up with (*wage increases lagging behind those in other industries*):—*n* (*inf*) an old convict.

lager [lä'-gêr] *n* a light beer (*a pint of lager*).

lag'gard *n* (*fml*) one who falls behind, a person who acts or moves slowly (*laggards who always finish last*).

lagoon' n a shallow salt-water lake cut off from the sea by sandbanks or rocks.

la'ic adj lay, not of the clergy.

laid pt of **lay**.

lair n a wild beast's den (the fox's lair).

laird n a Scottish landowner.

la'ity n the people who are not members of the clergy (the laity in the congregation).

lake[1] n a large stretch of water surrounded by land (Lake Windermere).

lake[2] n a deep red colour (artists using lake).

lamb n a young sheep (newborn lambs frolicking).

lam'bent adj (fml) 1 moving lightly over the surface (lambent flames). 2 flickering, softly shining (lambent lights).

lamb'kin n a small lamb.

lame adj 1 unable to walk well because of an injured or badly formed leg (horses gone lame). 2 not good, inadequate (a lame excuse):—vb to make lame:—n lame'ness.

lament' vb 1 to show grief or sorr ow for, to mourn for (lament the death of the king). 2 to expr ess regret for (lament the passing of old traditions):—n 1 the expressing of great grief. 2 a mournful song or tune:—n lamenta'tion.

lam'entable adj much to be regretted, extremely unsatisfactory (show a lamentable lack of knowledge/the council's lamentable record).

lam'inate vb to put a thin layer (e.g. of plastic) over something (laminating table tops):—also n.

Lamm'as n the first day of August, formerly a harvest festival.

lamp n a vessel for giving light (electric lamps).

lampoon' n something written specially to make another seem foolish or wicked (journalists lampooning the members of the cabinet).

lam'prey n an eel-like fish.

lance n a long spear used by horse soldiers:—vb 1 to wound or hit with a lance. 2 to cut open with a lancet (lancing a boil).

lance-cor'poral n the lowest appointed rank in the British Army, just below that of a corporal.

lan'cet n a pointed two-edged knife used by a surgeon when operating.

land n 1 the solid part of the earth's surface (prefer land to sea). 2 country (visit lands

overseas). 3 ground, soil (the farmer's land is very fertile):—vb to bring, put, or go ashore, to touch down.

landau [lan'-dou] n (old) a four-wheeled carriage.

land'ed adj possessing land (landed gentry).

land'fall n 1 a ship's approach to land at the end of a voyage. 2 the land approached.

landfill site n a place where waste material is buried under layers of earth, often excavated for this purpose.

land'ing n 1 the act of going ashore. 2 a place for going on shore (tie the boat up at the landing). 3 the corridor opening on to the rooms at the top of a flight of stairs (children standing on the landing looking through the bannisters).

land'lady n 1 a woman who k eeps an inn or boarding house (seaside landladies). 2 a woman who rents out rooms, flats or houses (their landlady calls to collect the rent).

land'locked adj almost or wholly enclosed by land (landlocked countries with no ports).

land'lord n 1 a man who rents out rooms, flats or houses (the landlord put up the rent). 2 a man who keeps an inn or boarding house.

land'lubber n (inf) one who prefers dry land to the sea (sailors regarding the rest of us as land-lubbers).

land'mark n 1 an easily recognized object from which travellers can tell where they are. 2 a very important event (a landmark in British history).

land'rail n a bird (the corncrake) with a harsh cry.

land'scape n 1 a view of the country seen from one position. 2 a picture of the countryside (he paints watercolour landscapes).

land'slide n the falling of a mass of earth, etc, down the side of a mountain (the car was buried in the rocks from a landslide).

land'slip n a landslide.

land'ward adj and adv towards land.

lane n 1 a narrow road (country lanes). 2 a narrow passage or alley between buildings, often found in place names (Drury Lane). 3 any of the parallel parts into which roads are divided for a single line of traffic (the fast lane on the motorway). 4 the r oute intended for or regularly used by ships or aircraft (shipping lanes). 5 a mark ed strip of track, water, etc, for a competitor in a race (swimming lanes).

lan'guage n 1 meaningful speech (*humans, unlike animals, use language*). 2 the speech of one people (*the French language*). 3 words (*obscene language*).

lan'guid adj lacking energy, weak, slow-moving (*languid movements*).

lan'guish vb to lose strength, to become weak (*she languishes when her lover is away*). 2 to experience long suffering (*languish in prison*).

lan'guor n faintness, lack of energy, listlessness (*languor caused by extreme heat*).

lank adj 1 tall and thin, lanky. 2 straight and limp (*lank hair*).

lank'y adj ungracefully tall and thin (*lanky male teenagers*).

lan'olin(e) n a soothing ointment made from fat obtained from sheep's wool.

lan'tern n a case, usu of glass, that encloses and protects a light (*the farmer carried a lantern to go out to the barn*).

lan'tern-jawed adj having long thin jaws.

lan'yard n a short cord used for fastening things.

lap¹ n 1 the seat formed by the knees and thighs of a person sitting (*a child sitting on her mother's lap*). 2 one round of a course in a race (*a race of ten laps*).

lap² vb (**lapped**, **lap'ping**) 1 to lick up (*cats lapping milk*). 2 to wash against in little waves (*the sea lapping the rocks*):—n the sound made by small waves.

lap'dog n a small pet dog.

lapel' n the folded back part of the breast of a coat or jacket (*wearing a rose in his lapel*).

lap'idary n one who cuts to shape and polishes precious stones.

lapis lazuli [lap'-is la'-zû-lî] n a blue precious stone.

lapse n 1 a mistake, a small error or fault (*apart from occasional lapses, her work is first class/ brief memory lapses*). 2 the passing (of time) (*with a lapse of several years*):—vb 1 to fall out of use (*local customs that have lapsed*). 2 to come to an end (*their contract has lapsed*). 3 to pass gradually into a less active or less desirable state (*standards have lapsed*).

lap'top n a small, light computer that can be operated by battery and can be used on someone's lap.

lap'wing n a bird (the peewit).

lar'board n the left side of a ship when one faces the bows, the port side.

lar'ceny n stealing, theft (*convicted of larceny*).

larch n a type of deciduous, cone-bearing tree.

lard n the fat of pigs, prepared for use in cooking (*they fry chips in lard, not oil*).

lar'der n a room or cupboard for storing food.

large adj more than usual in size, number or amount, big (*large sums of money/a large lake/ a large house*):—**at large** free, at liberty (*lions wandering at large*).

largess', largesse' n 1 the sharing out of gifts, usu of money, among many, generosity. 2 money or gifts given in this way (*poor people refusing the largess of the rich*).

lar'go adj (*mus*) played in slow time:—also n.

lar'iat n 1 a rope. 2 a rope with a running knot for catching animals, like a lasso.

lark n 1 a songbird. 2 something done for fun:—vb to play tricks.

lar'va n (pl **lar'vae**) the form of an insect on coming out of the egg, a grub.

lar'ynx n the upper part of the windpipe, containing the vocal chords which produce the voice.

lasagne [la-sän'-yê] n an Italian dish made from layers of flat, wide pasta, a meat or vegetable sauce and a cheese sauce.

lascivious [la-siv'-i-ês] adj giving way to immoral desires.

la'ser n a device which produces a narrow beam of concentrated light (*a laser beam*).

lash n 1 the cord of a whip. 2 a blow given with a whip:—vb 1 to whip, to strike hard or often. 2 to fasten by tying tightly.

lass, las'sie n a girl.

lass'itude n faintness, weariness.

lasso [las-ö'] n (pl **lassos'** or **lassoes'**) a rope with a running knot for catching animals:—vb to catch with a lasso.

last¹ adj 1 coming after all others. 2 latest. 3 final:—adv at the last time or place:—**at last** in the end.

last² n a foot-shaped block on which shoes are made or repaired.

last³ vb 1 to go on. 2 to continue.

last'ing adj 1 going on for a long time. 2 remaining in good condition.

latch *n* a small piece of wood or metal for keeping a door shut:—*vb* to fasten with a latch.

lat'chet *n* (*old*) a cord for fastening a shoe, a shoe-lace.

latch'key *n* the key for the main door of a house (*children given latchkeys to let themselves into their homes*).

late *adj* **1** arriving after the time fixed (*late for the meeting*). **2** far on in time (*late afternoon*). **3** now dead (*her late husband*). **4** recent (*her latest novel/the latest news*):—*adv* after the time fixed:—*n* **late'ness**:—**of late** (*fml*) recently (*she seems tired of late*).

late'ly *adv* in recent times, recently (*I have not seen him lately*).

la'tent *adj* present but not yet noticeable, not fully developed (*latent talent*).

lat'eral *adj* on, at or from the side (*lateral movements*).

lath *n* a long thin strip of wood.

lathe *n* a machine for turning around wood, metal, pottery, etc, while it is being shaped (*turn the piece of wood on a lathe*).

lath'er *n* **1** froth of soap and water (*the lather on his face while he is shaving*). **2** froth from sweat (*the lather on a horse after a race*):—*vb* **1** to cover with lather (*lather his face before shaving*). **2** to become frothy (*soap that lathers easily*).

Lat'in *n* the language of ancient Rome:—*adj* **1** having to do with the ancient Romans (*the Latin language*). **2** having to do with the peoples of France, Italy, Portugal and Spain (*Latin peoples*).

lat'itude *n* **1** distance north or south of the equator. **2** freedom from controls (*they give their children a good deal of latitude*).

latrine [la-treen'] *n* a lavatory, esp in a camp or institution.

latt'er *adj* **1** near the end of a period of time (*in the latter part of his life*). **2** second of two just spoken of (*she prefers the former suggestion but I prefer the latter*).

latt'erly *adv* recently, lately, in the last part of a period of time.

latt'ice *n* a network of crossed bars or strips as of wood (*a lattice of pastry on the tart*):—*adj* **latt'iced**.

laud [låd] *vb* (*fml*) to praise (*an article lauding their musical performance*).

laud'able *adj* deserving praise (*a laudable action*).

laudanum [lå'-dê-nêm] *n* a liquid drug made, like opium, from poppy seeds.

laud'atory *adj* (*fml*) full of praise (*laudatory speeches*).

laugh [laf] *vb* to make a sound expressing amusement or pleasure (*laugh at his jokes*):—*n* the sound of laughing.

laugh'able *adj* causing people to laugh, ridiculous (*his laughable attempts to jump the wall*).

laugh'ing-stock *n* a person laughed at and made fun of by everyone (*he was the laughing-stock of the village when the girl slapped his face in public*).

laugh'ter *n* the act or sound of laughing (*listen to the children's laughter*).

launch *vb* **1** to put into motion, to send on its course (*launch a missile*). **2** to cause (a ship) to move into the water (*launch a new liner*). **3** to put into action, to set going (*launch an attack*):—*n* **1** the act of launching. **2** a large motorboat.

laun'der *vb* to wash and iron (*launder his shirts*).

laun'dry *n* a place where clothes, etc, are washed and ironed (*take the sheets to the laundry*).

lau'reate *adj* crowned with laurel as a mark of honour (*poet laureate*).

lau'rel *n* **1** a bay tree whose leaves are used for making wreaths of honour. **2** a special honour (*win academic laurels*).

la'va *n* the melted rock emitted by a volcano.

lav'atory *n* a toilet.

lave *vb* (*lit*) to wash, to bathe.

lav'ender *n* **1** a plant with sweet-smelling flowers (*lavender bushes/branches of dried lavender*). **2** a light purple colour.

lav'ish *adj* **1** giving freely, generous (*a lavish spender*). **2** given or spent in great quantities (*lavish praise*):—*vb* to give or spend lavishly (*lavish money on unsound business schemes/lavish attention on his wife*).

law *n* **1** a rule or set of rules laid down for a people or a group of people by a person or persons with recognized authority (*the laws of the land*). **2** in science, a statement of the way in which objects regularly behave.

law'-abid'ing *adj* obeying the law (*law-abiding people living next door to vandals*).

law court *n* a place where those who are said to have broken laws are brought before a judge.

law'ful *adj* allowed by law (*his lawful wife*).

law'giver *n* one who makes laws.

law'less *adj* not keeping the laws, wild (*a lawless mob destroying property*).

lawn[1] *n* a stretch of carefully kept grass in a garden (*mow the lawn*).

lawn[2] *n* a type of fine linen (*a dress of white lawn*).

lawn'mower *n* a machine for cutting grass.

law'suit *n* claiming before a judge that another has broken the law (*start a lawsuit against the person who slandered her*).

lawn ten'nis *n* an outdoor game played with a ball and rackets (*the lawn tennis finals at Wimbledon*).

law'yer *n* one skilled in the law (*the lawyer who arranged the divorce*).

lax *adj* not sufficiently strict or severe (*lax behaviour*/*lax security*/*teachers too lax with the pupils*).

lax'ative *n* a medicine that causes or helps the bowels to empty:—*also adj.*

lax'ity *n* lack of strictness (*the laxity of his morals*).

lay[1] *pt of* lie.

lay[2] *vb* (*pt, pp* laid) 1 to cause to lie (*lay the injured woman on the ground*). 2 to place (*lay the books on the table*). 3 to make ready (*lay the table*). 4 to produce eggs. 5 to bet:—**lay by, lay up** to store for the future (*lay up trouble for himself*):—**lay oneself open to** to put oneself into the position of receiving (*lay oneself open to accusations of theft*).

lay[3] *n* (*old*) a poem or song.

lay[4] *adj* 1 having to do with people who are not members of the clergy. 2 not expert (*lay people who do not understand technical language*).

lay'er *n* an even spread of one substance over the surface of another (*a cake made of layers of chocolate sponge*).

layette' *n* the clothes prepared for a newly born baby (*knit garments for the baby's layette*).

lay'man *n* 1 one not a clergyman. 2 one not an expert or specialist (*the doctor tried to explain the situation in layman's terms*).

laz'ar *n* (*old*) one suffering from leprosy.

laze *vb* to be lazy, to do nothing (*holiday-makers lazing on the beach*):—*n* **laz'iness**.

laz'y *adj* unwilling to work, liking to do nothing (*too lazy to do any work*/*feel lazy in the heat*).

lea *n* (*lit*) a meadow.

lead[1] [led] *n* 1 a soft heavy metal (*roof covering made of lead*). 2 the stick of black lead or graphite in a pencil. 3 a piece of lead attached to a cord for finding the depth of water. 4 *pl* **leads** the sheets of lead used for covering roofs.

lead[2] [leed] *vb* (*pt, pp* led) 1 to go in front to show the way, to guide (*lead the mountaineers up the cliff face*). 2 to act as a chief or commander (*he was leading the attacking troops*). 3 to influence (*she is easily led*). 4 to spend (life) in a certain way (*lead a quiet life*):—*n* 1 a guiding suggestions or example (*follow their lead*/*police looking for a lead*). 2 a chief part (*she has the lead in a local production of 'Saint Joan'*). 3 the position ahead of all others (*she is in the lead in the race*). 4 a cord, etc, for leading a dog (*put the dog's lead on to take him for a walk*).

leaden [led'ên] *adj* 1 of lead. 2 heavy (*a leaden weight*). 3 dull (*leaden skies*).

lead'er *n* 1 one who shows the way (*act as leader up the mountain track*). 2 one who gives orders or takes charge (*the leader of the attacking force*). 3 a person or thing that is ahead of others (*the leader in the competition*) 4 a newspaper article giving an opinion on a news item of interest (*also* **leading article**):—*n* **lead'ership**.

lead'ing *adj* chief, most important (*leading politicians*).

leading question *n* a question asked in such a way as to suggest the answer desired.

leaf *n* (*pl* **leaves**) 1 one of the thin, flat usu green blades growing out of the stem of a plant or the branch of a tree (*leaves changing colour in autumn*). 2 a single sheet of paper in a book with pages printed on both sides (*turn over the leaves of the book*). 3 the movable part of a table-top or double door (*put in the extra leaf in the table*):—**turn over a new leaf** to begin to live or act in a better way (*he has been in prison but he has decided to turn over a new leaf*).

leaf'let *n* 1 a printed sheet of paper, usu folded and free of charge, containing information (*an advertising leaflet*/*a leaflet on dental care*).

leafy adj full of leaves (leafy lanes).

league[1] [leeg] n a measure of distance (about three miles).

league[2] [leeg] n 1 a group of people or nations bound by agreement to help each other (the League of Nations). 2 a group of sports clubs or players that play matches among themselves (the Football League/a darts league):—vb (fml) to join together, to unite (leaguing together to plot against the king).

leak n 1 a hole by which water escapes (e.g. from a pipe) or enters a dry place. 2 a small accidental hole or crack through which something flows in or out. 3 the accidental or intentional making public of secret information (a leak to the press about confidential government matters):—vb 1 to let water in or out (the roof is leaking). 2 to get out through a hole or crack (gas leaking). 3 to make public that which is secret (leak confidential information to the press).

leakage n act of leaking.

leaky adj (inf) having leaks (leaky roof).

lean[1] vb (pt, pp leaned or leant) 1 to slope to one side (the building leans to the right). 2 to bend (she leant down to pat the dog). 3 to rest against (the ladder was leaning against the wall). 4 to have a preference for (he leans towards the right of the political party).

lean[2] adj 1 not having much fat (lean meat). 2 thin, healthily thin (fit lean athletes):—n meat without fat:—n **leanness**.

leaning n preference, liking (what are his political leanings).

lean-to n a shed built up against a wall or another building (a lean-to for keeping his tools in).

leap vb (pt, pp leaped or leapt) to jump (leap out of bed/the deer leapt the fence):—n 1 a jump (clear the wall in one leap). 2 the height or distance jumped.

leapfrog n a game in which one player leaps over the others while they are bent double.

leap year n a year in which there are 366 days, occurring once every 4 years.

learn vb (pt, pp learned or learnt) 1 to gain knowledge or skill, to find out how to do something (learn French/learn how to swim). 2 to come to understand, to realize (she must learn that

she has to consider others). 3 to memorize, to fix in the memory (learn a poem by Keats).

learned adj having much knowledge, gained by study.

learner n one who is learning (a learner driver/learners of English as a foreign language).

learning n knowledge gained by study (a man of learning).

lease n an agreement by which the use of house or land is given to another in return for a fixed annual amount or rent:—vb to give or take on lease (leasing a house).

leasehold n property held on lease:—n **leaseholder**.

leash n a cord or strap for leading animals (asked to keep her dog on a leash in the park):—vb to hold on a leash.

least adj smallest (the least inconvenience):—also n:—adv in the smallest degree (I don't mind in the least).

leather n material made by preparing animal skins in a certain way (coats made of leather):—also adj:—vb (inf) to beat, to thrash (leathered by his father for lying).

leathering n (inf) a thrashing.

leathery adj like leather, hard and tough (leathery meat/leathery skin).

leave n 1 permission (she received leave to go home early). 2 permitted absence (on sick leave). 3 holiday (on annual leave). 4 farewell (he took his leave from them):—vb (pt, pp left) 1 to give to another at one's death (he left all his money to his son). 2 to cause to be or remain in a particular state or condition (leave the door open/ leave the country without a leader). 3 to go without taking (leave her gloves on the counter). 4 to depart (leave home at an early age). 5 to desert (he has left his wife). 6 to entrust to another (leave getting the food to him). 7 to allow to remain unused, untaken, uneaten, etc (she left most of the meal).

leaven [lev'-ên] n 1 a substance mixed with dough to make it rise, yeast. 2 (fml) anything helping to bring about a change (her friendship acted as a leaven on his hostile attitude):—vb to act as leaven.

leaves see leaf.

leavings npl that which is left as useless (put the leavings in the dustbin).

lech'erous *adj* full of sexual desire, often of a bad kind (*lecherous old men*):—*n* **lech'ery**.

lec'tern *n* a reading desk for standing at (*the lectern on the stage of the hall*).

lec'ture *n* **1** a talk on a certain subject (*go to a lecture on local history*). **2** a scolding (*get a lecture from their mother on good manners*):— *vb* **1** to give a lecture. **2** to scold.

lec'turer *n* **1** one giving a talk (*introduce the lecturer on local history*). **2** one who teaches in a college or university.

lec'tureship *n* employment as a lecturer.

led *pt* of **lead**.

ledge *n* **1** a narrow shelf (*a window ledge*). **2** a ridge (*climbers sheltering on a ledge*).

led'ger *n* the chief account book of a business.

lee *n* **1** the side of an object away from the wind. **2** shelter given by an object from the wind.

leech *n* **1** a blood-sucking worm (*leeches used to be used in medicine*). **2** (*old*) a doctor.

leek *n* a vegetable with broad flat leaves (*a soup made with leeks*).

leer *vb* to look at sideways in a sly or unpleasant way (*a nasty old man leering at girls in their bathing suits*):—also *n*.

lees *npl* tiny bits of matter settling at the bottom of a vessel of liquid (*the lees at the foot of the wine decanter*).

lee'ward *adj and adv* on or to the side sheltered from the wind.

lee'way *n* **1** time or ground lost. **2** room for free movement within limits (*allow them some leeway in their choice of subjects*). **3** a sideways movement of a ship caused by a strong wind:— **make up leeway** to make up lost time (*after missing so much schoolwork she has a lot of leeway to make up*).

left¹ *pp* of **leave**.

left² *n* **1** the side opposite to the right (*drive on the left of the road*). **2** in politics, the Socialist party:—*also adj*:—**the extreme left** the Communist party.

left-hand'ed *adj* better able to use the left hand than the right (*left-handed people*).

leg *n* **1** one of the limbs on which an animal stands or moves. **2** a support for a table, chair, etc (*a table with uneven legs*):—**on one's last legs** near the end of one's power, life, etc (*the*

firm is on its last legs):—**pull a person's leg** to play a joke on someone (*he was pulling her leg when he said there was a bear standing behind her*).

leg'acy *n* that which is left to one by will (*receive a legacy from his uncle*).

leg'al *adj* **1** having to do with the law (*legal proceedings*). **2** allowed by law (*legal activities*).

legal'ity *n* lawfulness (*question the legality of his actions*).

leg'alize *vb* to make lawful (*a suggestion that some drugs should be legalized*).

leg'ate *n* **1** one sent to another country to look after the interests of his own nation. **2** a representative to another country appointed by the pope.

legatee' *n* one to whom a legacy is left.

lega'tion *n* **1** a legate and the officials who assist him or her. **2** the house in which they live.

leg'end *n* **1** an ancient story passed on by word of mouth (*legends about giants*). **2** the words written under a picture, etc (*the legend below the illustration is wrong*).

leg'endary *adj* **1** having to do with ancient legends, famous in story, existing only in story (*legendary beasts/legendary kings*). **2** ver y famous (*legendary folksinger/her legendary beauty*).

legerdemain [le-jêr-dê-mân'] *n* (*fml*) quickness of hand, skill at juggling, etc (*the pickpocket's legerdemain*).

legg'ings *npl* a thick covering for the lower leg (*girls wearing leggings and short skirts*).

leg'gy *adj* (*inf*) having very long legs (*leggy young women*).

leg'horn *n* a type of hen.

leg'ible *adj* possible to read (*handwriting that is scarcely legible*):—*n* **legibil'ity**.

le'gion *n* **1** a Roman regiment or division (3000–6000 soldiers). **2** a great number (*people came to hear him in their legions*).

le'gionary *n* a soldier belonging to a legion.

leg'islate *vb* to make laws (*legislating against smoking in public buildings*).

legisla'tion *n* **1** the act of making laws. **2** the laws made (*new legislation brought in against the import of certain goods*).

leg'islative *adj* having the power or right to make laws (*a legislative assembly*).

leg'islator *n* one who makes laws.

leg'islature *n* the part of a government that makes laws.

legit'imacy *n* being legitimate.

legit'imate *adj* **1** allowed by law, lawful (*a legitimate claim/a legitimate business*). **2** born of married parents (*they married just before their daughter was born so that she would be legitimate*).

legu'minous *adj* having to do with plants that bear seeds in pods (e.g. peas, beans, etc).

lei'sure *n* spare time, time free from work (*little time for leisure/leisure activities*).

lei'sured *adj* having plenty of spare time (*the leisured classes*).

lei'surely *adj* slow, unhurried (*work at a leisurely pace*):—*also adv*.

lemm'ing *n* a small rat-like animal of far northern regions.

lem'on *n* **1** a pale yellow sharp-tasting fruit (*buy lemons to flavour the drinks*). **2** the tree bearing this fruit. **3** a pale yellow colour (*paint the walls lemon*).

lemonade', **lemon squash** *ns* a drink made from or tasting of lemon juice.

lemur [lee'-mûr] *n* a monkey-like animal.

lend *vb* (*pt, pp* **lent**) to give something to another on condition that it is returned after use (*lend her a book/lend my car to my brother*):—*n* **lend'er**.

length *n* measurement from end to end of space or time (*measure the length of the room/estimate the length of a journey*):—**at length 1** at last (*at length we understood what he was trying to say*). **2** taking a long time, in detail (*she explained it at length*).

length'en *vb* to make or become longer (*curtains requiring to be lengthened*).

length'ways, **length'wise** *advs* in the direction of the length (*measure the room lengthways*).

length'y *adj* very long (*a lengthy sermon/a lengthy delay*).

le'nient *adj* **1** merciful (*a lenient judge*). **2** not severe (*a lenient sentence*):—*ns* **le'nience**, **le'niency**.

lens *n* a transparent substance, usu glass, with a surface curved in such a way that objects seen through it appear bigger or smaller.

Lent *n* the period between Ash Wednesday and Easter during which Christ's fast in the desert is commemorated.

len'til *n* the eatable seed of a pea-like plant (*a soup made of lentils*).

le'onine *adj* lion-like (*leonine features*).

leopard [lep'-êrd] *n* a large, spotted animal of the cat family.

lep'er *n* a person with leprosy.

lep'rechaun *n* in fairytales, an elf, esp in Ireland.

lep'rosy *n* an infectious disease that eats away the skin and parts of the body:—*adj* **lep'rous**.

le'sion *n* (*fml*) an injury, a wound (*lesions on his back caused by a beating*).

less *adj* smaller, not so much (*earn less money*):—*n* a smaller amount (*she gave him less*):—*adv* not so greatly, not so much (*she likes him less now*).

lessee' *n* one who rents a house or property.

less'en *vb* to make or become less (*try to lessen the pain*).

less'er *adj* less, smaller (*a lesser problem*).

less'on *n* **1** something that is learned or taught (*give French lessons/take piano lessons*). **2** a period of teaching (*feel ill during the science lesson*). **3** a passage read from the Bible (*read the lesson in church*). **4** an example (*her courage is a lesson to us all*).

lest *conj* (*fml or old*) **1** in order that.. not (*keep hidden lest anyone see us*). **2** for fear that (*lest we forget*).

let *vb* (**let, let'ting**) **1** to allow (*let the children go to the cinema*). **2** to allow the use of for rent or payment (*let a room in their house to a student*):—*n* the act of letting for rent (*a short-term let*).

le'thal *adj* causing death (*a lethal dose of poison*).

lethar'gic *adj* sleepy, slow-moving, lacking interest (*feel lethargic after her illness*).

lethar'gy *n* lack of energy and interest (*the lethargy brought on by extreme heat*).

lett'er *n* **1** a sign standing for a sound (*the letter 'h'*). **2** a written message (*write a letter of apology*). **3** (*fml*) *pl* literature, learning (*men of letters*):—**letter of credit** a letter allowing the holder to draw money when away from home:—**to the letter** exactly (*carry out her instructions to the letter*).

lett'ered *adj* (*fml*) well read.

lett'ering *n* letters that have been drawn, painted, etc (*lettering on shop windows*).

lett'erpress *n* a method of printing in which the words, pictures, etc, to be printed form a raised area on the printing machine.

lett'uce *n* a plant whose leaves are used in salads (*a salad of lettuce and tomatoes*).

leukaemia [lük-ee-mi'-a] *n* a serious disease in which too many white blood cells are produced.

Levant' *n* the eastern coasts of the Mediterranean:—*adj* **Levan'tine**.

levee [li-vee' *or* le-vee'] *n* 1 (*old*) a morning party at which guests were introduced to the king or queen. 2 a raised bank at the side of a river .

lev'el *n* 1 a flat, even surface (*he can walk on the level but not uphill*). 2 an instrument for finding out whether a thing is flat. 3 a general standard of quality or quantity (*a high level of achievement/wages falling below last year's level*). 4 a horizontal division or floor in a house, etc (*a garden on two levels*):—*adj* flat. 2 even. 3 on the same line or height:—*vb* (**lev'elled, lev'elling**) 1 to make flat (*level the ground*). 2 to make equal (*level the score*). 3 to destroy, to demolish (*the bulldozer levelled the block of flats*). 4 to aim (*level his gun at the enemy soldier*).

level crossing *n* a place where a railway line crosses the surface of a road (*the car had to stop at the level crossing until the train passed*).

level-head'ed *adj* sensible (*he is very level-headed and dealt with the emergency calmly and efficiently*).

le'ver *n* a bar for raising heavy objects (*use a lever to remove the tyre from the wheel*).

le'verage *n* power gained by the use of a lever (*not enough leverage to raise the huge metal block*).

lev'eret *n* a young hare.

levi'athan *n* 1 a sea monster. 2 anything very large.

lev'ity *n* (*fml*) lack of seriousness (*treating the matter of her exams with too much levity*).

lev'y *vb* 1 to bring together men to form an army. 2 to collect money for a tax (*levied taxes on alcohol*):—*n* 1 the soldiers thus assembled. 2 the money thus collected.

lewd *adj* 1 having immoral desir es (*lewd old men*). 2 indecent, obscene (*singing lewd songs*):—*n* **lewd'ness**.

lexicog'rapher *n* one who prepares a dictionary.

lex'icon *n* a dictionary.

liabil'ity *n* 1 debt (*liabilities that exceed his assets*). 2 the state of being liable (*his liability to colds/exempt from any liability in the matter*). 3 something for which one is r esponsible (*the dog is his liability*).

li'able *adj* 1 lik ely to have to do or suffer from (*liable to lose her temper/liable to catch cold/liable to flood*). 2 legally r esponsible for (*liable for his wife's debts*). 3 lik ely to get, be punished with, etc (*trespassers are liable to a large fine*).

liaison [lee-āz'-ên(g)] *n* 1 a close connection or working association (*important that the two departments maintain a liaison*). 2 (*fml*) an unlawful sexual relationship (*he had a liaison with a married women*).

liais'on officer *n* an officer who lets one group know what another group is doing (*liaison officer for the two departments*).

li'ar *n* one who tells lies.

liba'tion *n* 1 (*old*) the pouring out of a drink in honour of a god. 2 (*fml or hum*) an alcoholic drink (*a small libation*).

li'bel *n* something written that damages a person's reputation (*being sued for libel*):—*also vb* (**li'belled, li'belling**).

li'bellous *adj* hurtful to one's reputation (*a libellous statement in the newspapers*).

lib'eral *adj* 1 generous (*a liberal supply of food*). 2 ready to accept new ideas (*liberal attitudes*). 3 (*of education*) intended solely to develop the powers of the mind:—*n* one who believes in greater political freedom.

Liberal Party *n* (*old*) a British political party.

liberal'ity *n* (*fml*) readiness to give to others (*the liberality of their host*).

lib'erate *vb* to set free (*liberating the city held by the enemy*):—*n* **libera'tion**.

lib'ertine *n* (*fml*) one who openly leads a wicked, immoral life.

lib'erty *n* 1 freedom (*ex-prisoners enjoying new-found liberty*). 2 the right to do as one likes (*you are at liberty to leave if you wish*). 3 too great freedom of speech or action (*it was taking a liberty to borrow my car without permission*).

libra'rian *n* one in charge of a library.

li'brary *n* 1 a collection of books (*a fiction library and a reference library*). 2 a room or building in which books are kept (*build a new library*).

libret'to n (pl **libret'ti**) the book of words of an opera or musical work (he wrote the music and his wife the libretto).

lice see **louse.**

li'cence n **1** a written permission to do or keep something (a licence to drive a car). **2** (fml) too great freedom of action (allow his children too much licence).

li'cense vb to give a licence to (he is licensed to sell alcohol).

licensee' n one to whom a licence is given (the owner of the pub is the licensee).

licen'tiate n one who, having passed the necessary examinations, is allowed to carry on a certain profession.

licen'tious adj (fml) behaving in an immoral or improper way, indecent (he was licentious as a young man but regrets it now):—n **licen'tiousness.**

lichen [lī'-ken] n a moss that grows on rocks, tree trunks, etc.

lich'-gate same as **lych'-gate.**

licit [lis-êt] adj (fml) lawful (licit pleasures).

lick vb **1** to pass the tongue over (the dog licked her hand). **2** to take (food or drink) into the mouth with the tongue (lick the ice cream). **3** (inf) to defeat (we licked the other team). **4** (inf) to thrash (he will get licked for breaking the window):—n **1** act of passing the tongue over. **2** a blow.

lick'ing n (inf) a thrashing (get a good licking for breaking the window).

licorice see **liquorice.**

lid n the movable cover of a pot, box, etc (the lid of the jar is stiff).

lie[1] n a statement that the maker knows to be untrue (tell a lie to try to avoid being punished):—vb (**lied, ly'ing**) to tell a lie (it was obvious that he was lying).

lie[2] vb (**lay, ly'ing, pp lain**) **1** to put the body full length down (she wants to lie on the beach all day). **2** to be or remain in a certain place (the book was lying on the table):—n the way in which something lies.

liege n (old) **1** one owing certain duties to a lord. **2** a lord.

liege lord n (old) a lord to whom certain duties are owed (the king was the knight's liege lord).

lieu [lō] n:— **in lieu of** instead of (extra holiday in lieu of wages for working overtime).

lieutenant [lef-ten'-ênt] n **1** (fml) one who does the work of another, deputy (sent one of her lieutenants to deal with the complaint). **2** a naval or army officer.

life n (pl **lives**) **1** the state of being alive (there is no life left in the injured man). **2** the force existing in animals and plants that gives them the ability to change with the passing of time. **3** liveliness, activity (a house without life after the children left). **4** the time one has been alive (he worked hard all his life). **5** the stor y of one's life (publish a life of the poet).

life'belt n a belt of a material that floats easily and so helps to prevent the wearer sinking when in water.

life'boat n a boat that goes to the help of those in danger at sea.

life'buoy n an object that floats easily and to which shipwrecked people can hold until help arrives.

life cycle n the series of forms into which a living thing changes during its development (the life cycle of the frog).

life'less adj **1** dead (pull the lifeless bodies from the sea). **2** dull (lifeless hair). **3** not lively (a lifeless performance).

life'like adj seeming to have life (a lifelike portrait).

life'long adj lasting through life (a lifelong friendship).

life'-size, life'-sized adj of the same size as the person or thing represented (a life-size statue of the king).

life span n the length of time that someone is likely to live or something is likely to function (The life span of the average soldier was very short then).

life'style n the way in which someone lives (an affluent lifestyle).

life'time n the length of time a person lives (he experienced several wars in his lifetime).

lift vb **1** to raise up higher (lift the flag above his head). **2** to take up (lift the baby from the pram):—n **1** a machine by which people or goods are carried from floor to floor of a building. **2** a free ride in a private vehicle (get a lift to work from his neighbour).

lig'ament n a band of tough substance joining bones together at joints (strain a ligament).

lig'ature n **1** (fml) a bandage. **2** a cord for tying up the end of a blood vessel during an operation. **3** two letters joined together in type (e.g. æ).

light[1] n **1** that which makes it possible for the eye to see things. **2** anything that gives light, as the sun, a lamp, etc (a bedside light). **3** knowledge, understanding (unable to throw any light on the problem). **4** brightness in the eyes or face (a light in his eye):—adj **1** clear, not dark (it's getting light). **1** not deep or dark in colour (light green/light hair):—vb (pt, pp **lit**) to give light to, to set fire to (light the fire).

light[2] adj **1** not heavy (light loads). **2** not difficult (light tasks). **3** not severe (a light punishment). **4** small in amount (a light rainfall). **5** not serious, for entertainment (light reading). **6** graceful (light on her feet). **7** happy, merry (light of heart).

light[3] vb to come upon by chance (light upon the solution).

light'en[1] vb **1** to make bright (lighten the mood). **2** to flash.

light'en[2] vb to make less heavy (try to lighten the load).

light'er[1] n a device for setting something (e.g. a cigarette) alight.

light'er[2] n a large boat, usu flat-bottomed, for carrying goods from ship to shore.

light'-fin'gered adj (inf) thieving (detectives watching for light-fingered people in shops).

light'-foot'ed adj nimble, quick on one's feet (light-footed dancers).

light'-head'ed adj giddy, dizzy (feel light-headed after drinking the wine).

light'-heart'ed adj **1** merry, cheerful (people on holiday in light-hearted mood). **2** not serious (a light-hearted account of the event).

light'house n a tower with a light to guide ships.

light'ning adj the electric flash seen before thunder is heard (a tree struck by lightning).

light'ning conductor, light'ning rod ns a metal rod that protects a building from lightning by conducting the flash to the earth.

lights npl the lungs of an animal, such as a sheep, used as food.

light'ship n an anchored ship with a light to guide other ships.

light year n the distance light travels in a year.

lig'nite n a type of brown coal.

like[1] adj nearly the same, resembling (have like attitudes/of like mind/they are as like as two peas):—prep in the same way as (she walks like her mother):—n a person or thing nearly the same as or equal to another (you will not see his like again).

like[2] vb **1** to be pleased by (she liked the play). **2** to be fond of (she likes children/she does not like her next-door neighbour).

like'able, lik'able adj attractive, pleasant.

like'lihood n probability (have little likelihood of success).

like'ly adj **1** probable (the likely result). **2** suitable (the more likely of the candidates):—adv probably (they'll very likely arrive late).

lik'en vb to compare (she likened her relationship with him to a battle).

like'ness n **1** resemblance (I saw little likeness between mother and daughter). **2** a picture of a person (the artist's likeness of his wife).

likes npl things pleasing to one (we all have our likes and dislikes).

like'wise adv **1** in the same way (he left early and she did likewise). **2** also (Mr Jones was sacked and likewise Mr Smith).

lik'ing n a fondness or preference for (a liking for classical music/a liking for fast food).

li'lac n **1** a type of small tree with light-purple or white flowers (the sweet smell of lilac). **2** a light purple colour:—adj light purple (lilac wool).

Lillipu'tian adj very small.

lilt vb to sing cheerfully:—n **1** a regular pattern of rising and falling sound (Scots people speaking with a lilt). **2** a cheerful song. **3** a tune with a strongly marked rhythm.

lilt'ing adj having a strongly marked lilt (a lilting voice).

li'ly n a flower grown from a bulb, often white in colour.

lily of the valley n a flower with small white bells and a distinctive sweet smell.

limb [lim] n **1** an arm, leg or wing (fracture a limb). **2** a branch of a tree (a cat stuck on a limb of the oak tree).

lim'ber[1] n (old) a small two-wheeled ammunition carriage that travels with a gun.

lim'ber[2] *adj* moving and bending easily, supple (*he is elderly but still very limber*):—*vb* **lim'ber up** to exercise in order to make more supple (*dancers limbering up for a performance*).

lim'bo[1] *n* **1** a place where, it is supposed, the souls of those who die in complete ignorance of God spend eternity. **2** a place where one is forgotten or neglected, a state of uncertainty (*she is in limbo waiting to get the results of three job interviews*).

lime[1] *n* a white substance got by heating certain kinds of rock.

lime[2] *n* **1** a small lemon-like, yellowish-green fruit (*flavour the dessert with the juice of a lime*). **2** the tree bearing this fruit. **3** the linden tree.

lime juice *n* a drink made from the juice of the lime.

lime'kiln *n* a furnace for making lime.

lime'light *n*:—**in the limelight** in a position in which one's doings are followed with interest by many people (*senior members of the government always in the limelight*).

lim'erick *n* a nonsense poem written in a special five-line stanza.

lime'stone *n* rock containing much lime.

lim'it *n* **1** a boundary (*the limits of his estate*). **2** that which one may not go past (*the limit of his patience*). **3** the greatest or smallest amount or number that is fixed as being correct, legal, necessary, desirable, etc (*the government imposed a 4% limit on pay increases*):—*vb* to keep within bounds (*try to limit their expenditure on entertainment to £10 per week/we must limit the audience to 200*).

limita'tion *n* **1** that which limits (*the limitations imposed by time*). **2** inability to do something, weakness (*all of us have our limitations*).

lim'ited *adj* **1** small in amount (*a limited supply of food*). **2** not very great, large, wide-ranging, etc (*of limited experience*).

limn [lim] *vb* (*old*) to draw or paint.

limp[1] *vb* to walk lamely (*he limps after the accident to his leg*):—*also n*.

limp[2] *adj* **1** not stiff, drooping (*limp lettuce leaves*). **2** without energy or strength (*feel limp after her illness/a limp handshake*).

lim'pet *n* a shellfish that clings tightly to rocks.

lim'pid *adj* clear, transparent (*look into the limpid stream*).

linch'pin *n* **1** the pin passed through the end of an axle to keep the wheel on it. **2** a person who is very important to the running of a form or organization (*the senior secretary is the linchpin of the whole firm*).

lin'den *n* a kind of tree with yellow sweet-smelling flowers, the lime tree.

line *n* **1** a small rope or cord (*washing hanging on the line to dry*). **2** a thin mark made with a pen, pencil, etc (*put a line under the important words*). **3** a row of persons or things (*a line of people waiting to get tickets from the box office*). **4** a row of words on a page (*there were fifty lines on one page of the book*). **5** a short letter (*drop him a line to say hello*). **6** a railway track (*the main London line*). **7** ancestors and descendants (*of the royal line*). **8** a fleet of steamers, aeroplanes, etc, providing regular services (*a passenger line*). **9** (*inf*) the equator. **10** a telephone wire. **11** (*inf*) way of behaving or of earning one's living (*what line is he in?*). **12** *pl* the positions of an army ready to attack or defend (*behind the enemy lines*):—*vb* **1** to mark with lines (*age had lined her face*). **2** to arrange in a row or rows (*lining the children up*). **3** to cover on the inside (*line the dress with silk*).

lin'eage *n* one's ancestors (*of royal lineage*).

lin'eal *adj* passed down from father to son.

lin'eament *n* (*fml*) a noticeable feature of the face (*admire her noble lineaments*).

lin'ear *adj* having to do with lines (*a linear diagram*).

lin'en *n* cloth made of flax (*dresses made of white linen*).

lin'er *n* **1** a large ocean-going passenger ship. **2** something that lines.

lines'man *n* one who assists an umpire or referee by signalling when a ball is out of play (*linesmen on the football pitch*).

ling *n* **1** a fish of the cod family. **2** heather.

lin'ger *vb* **1** to delay before going (*let's not linger—it's getting dark*). **2** to stay about, to last or continue for a long time (*the smell lingered/doubts that lingered*).

lingerie [lân'-zhê-ree] *n* women's underclothing (*the shop's lingerie department*).

ling'o *n* (*inf*) a language (*he didn't learn the language of the country and complained about not understanding the lingo*).

ling'ua fran'ca *n* a mixed language in which people of different languages may speak to each other.

ling'ual *adj* (*fml*) **1** having to do with the tongue. **2** having to do with language.

lin'guist *n* one skilled in foreign languages (*a linguist looking for work as a translator*).

linguis'tic *adj* having to do with the study of languages (*note some linguistic changes*):—*n* **linguis'tics**.

lin'iment *n* an ointment or oil rubbed into the body to prevent stiffness (*athletes rubbing liniment into their legs*).

lin'ing *n* the covering of the inside of something, such as a garment or box.

link *n* **1** one ring of a chain (*break one of the links of the silver chain round her neck*). **2** that which connects one thing with another (*a link between poverty and crime*). **3** ^{1}/$_{100}$ part of a chain (= 7.92 inches):—*vb* to connect, to join (*the police are linking the three murders*).

links *npl* **1** flat sandy, grassy ground by the seashore. **2** a seaside golf course.

lino'leum *n* a floor covering made of cloth coated with linseed oil.

li'notype *n* a machine that prepares whole lines of printing type at a time.

lin'seed *n* the seed of flax.

lint *n* linen specially prepared for dressing open wounds (*cover the grazed knee with lint and a bandage*).

lin'tel *n* the wood or stone across the top of a window or door (*the tall man hit his head on the lintel of the door*).

li'on *n* **1** a large flesh-eating animal of the cat family (*the large tawny mane of the lion*). **2** a famous and important person (*the after-dinner speaker will be one of our literary lions*):—*f* **li'oness:—lion's share** the largest share (*her big brother always took the lion's share of the food*).

li'on-hearted *adj* very brave.

li'onize *vb* to treat a person as if he or she were famous (*he is only a minor poet but he is lionized by the people in the village where he lives*).

lip *n* **1** either of the edges of the opening of the mouth (*she bit her lip to try to stop crying*). **2** the edge or brim of anything (*the lip of the cup*).

lip'-read *vb* to understand what a person is saying

from the movements of his or her lips (*she is deaf and she lip-reads well*).

lip'stick *n* a kind of pencil or crayon used to colour the lips (*wear bright red lipstick*).

liq'uefy *vb* to make or become liquid (*butter that liquefied in the heat of the kitchen*):—*n* **liquefac'tion**.

liqueur [li-kûr'] *n* a sweetly flavoured alcoholic drink.

liq'uid *adj* **1** in the form of a liquid (*liquid soap*). **2** clear (*liquid eyes*). **3** (*of sounds*) smooth and clear, as the letter *r* or *l*:—*n* a substance that flows and has no fixed shape, a substance that is not a solid or gas.

liq'uidate *vb* **1** to pay debts. **2** to close down a business when it has too many debts. **3** to put an end to, to get rid of, to destroy (*liquidating the terrorist leader*):—*n* **liq-uida'tion**.

liquor [li'-kêr] *n* **1** strong drink, such as spirits (*drink beer but not liquor*). **2** the liquid produced from cooked food (*the liquor from the baked ham*).

li'quorice, lic'orice *n* **1** a black sweet-tasting root used in making medicines and sweets. **2** a kind of sweet made from this.

lira, *pl* **lire** *or* **liras** *n* the monetary unit of Turkey. Formerly the currency unit of Italy until the introduction of the euro in January 2002

lisp *vb* **1** to say the sound *th* for *s* when speaking. **2** to speak as a small child does (*a little girl lisping a poem*):—*also n*.

lis'some *adj* graceful, able to bend in any position, supple (*lissome dancers*).

list^1 *n* a series of names, numbers, etc, written down in order one after the other (*making a shopping list*):—*vb* to write down in order (*list the people present*).

list^2 *vb* to lean over to one side (*boats listing in the storm*):—*also n*.

listen [lis'-ên] *vb* **1** to try to hear (*listen to music as she worked*). **2** to pay attention to (*listen to his mother's advice*):—*n* **list'ener**.

list'less *adj* lacking energy, uninterested (*feel listless after the long winter*).

lit *pt* of **light**.

lit'any *n* a form of public prayer with responses given by the worshippers.

lit'eracy *n* ability to read and write (*worried about the lack of literacy in the country*).

lit'eral adj 1 with each word given its ordinary meaning, word for word (a literal translation). 2 following the exact meaning without any exaggeration or anything added from the imagination (a literal account of what happened):—adv **lit'erally**.

lit'erary adj having to do with literature or with writing as a career (have literary tastes).

lit'erate adj 1 able to read and write (a disturbing number of people who are scarcely literate). 2 having read a great deal (literate people who enjoy discussing books).

lit'erature n 1 the books, etc, written on a particular subject (all the literature relating to drug abuse). 2 written works of lasting interest and of fine quality and artistic value (study English literature).

lithe [līth] adj able to bend or twist easily and gracefully (the lithe bodies of the young gymnasts).

lith'ograph n a picture printed from a drawing made on a flat stone or metal plate:—n **lithog'rapher**:—n **lithog'raphy**.

lit'igant n one engaged in a lawsuit (litigants with no hope of winning the case).

litiga'tion n the settling of a disagreement by going to law (consider the expense of getting involved in litigation to get his money back).

lit'igious adj (fml) frequently taking disagreements to courts of law, fond of litigation (a litigious person who has already tried to sue several other firms).

lit'mus n a blue dye turned red by acids.

li'tre n in the metric system, a measure of liquid (about 1¾ pints).

lit'ter n 1 (old) a light bed that can be carried about, a stretcher. 2 bedding of straw, etc, for animals. 3 the young of an animal born at one time (a litter of five pups). 4 scraps of paper and rubbish lying about (pick up the litter and put it in a bin):—vb 1 to throw away untidily (litter the streets with the packaging from fast food). 2 (of animals) to give birth to.

lit'tle adj 1 small (little black birds). 2 short (he was only a little fellow). 3 young (little children):—n 1 a small amount (pay a little at a time). 2 a short time (I'll be there in a little):—adv not much (think little of her work).

lit'toral adj (fml) having to do with the shore or coast:—n the land near the sea.

lit'urgy n the fixed forms of public worship of a church:—adj **litur'gical**.

live[1] vb 1 to have life, to exist, to be alive (everything that lives/the right to live). 2 to continue to be alive (he is very ill but he will live). 3 to dwell, to have one's home (she lives in the country). 4 to behave in a certain way (live dangerously). 5 to keep oneself alive, obtain the food or goods necessary for life (earn barely enough to live/live by hunting). 6 to pass or spend one's life (living a life of luxury):—live down to live in a way that makes others overlook one's past faults (he will never live it down if his neighbours discover he has been in prison).

live[2] adj 1 having life, alive (a cat with a live mouse). 2 full of energy, capable of becoming active (live electrical wires). 3 heard or seen as the event takes place, not recorded (a live broadcast). 4 burning (live coals).

live'lihood n the work by which one earns one's living (earn his livelihood by driving taxis).

live'long adj 1 seeming long (he snored the livelong night). 2 (fml) whole (children playing in the sun the livelong day).

live'ly adj active, energetic, cheerful (a lively child/a lively discussion):—n **live'liness**.

liv'en vb to make more cheerful (try to liven up the party).

liv'er n 1 an organ inside the body that helps to cleanse the blood (get a liver transplant). 2 this organ from certain animals used as food (liver and onions).

liv'ery n a special uniform worn by servants in one household (footmen wearing the queen's livery).

live'stock n animals kept on a farm.

live wire n 1 a wire through which an electric current is passing. 2 a person with a lot of energy (she's a real live wire who's fun to have around).

liv'id adj 1 discoloured, black and blue (livid bruises). 2 (old) pale (a livid face). 3 (inf) very angry (she was livid with her son for being late).

liv'ing n 1 a means of providing oneself with what is necessary for life (what does he do for a living?). 2 employment as a member of clergy in the Church of England.

liz'ard n a four-footed reptile with a long tail.

lla'ma n a South American animal of the camel family.

lla'no n one of the vast grassy plains of South America.

lo interj (old or lit) look! (*lo! a light has suddenly appeared*).

load vb 1 to put a burden on the back of an animal (*load the donkey*). 2 to put goods into a vehicle (*load the van*). 3 to put a heavy weight on (*load him with responsibility*). 4 to put ammunition into a gun (*load his revolver*). 5 to put film into a camera:—n 1 that which is carried (*the lorry's load*). 2 a weight (*a load on her mind*). 3 a cargo (*the ship's load*).

load'star same as **lodestar**.

load'stone same as **lodestone**.

loaf¹ n (*pl* **loaves**) bread made into a shape convenient for selling (*a loaf of brown bread*).

loaf² vb to pass time without doing anything, to laze around (*loafing around street corners instead of going to work*):—n **loaf'er**.

loaf su'gar n sugar cut into small cubes.

loam n a sand and clay soil:—adj **loam'y**.

loan n that which is lent (*get a loan from the bank*).

loath, loth adj unwilling (*she was loath to leave home*).

loathe vb to hate (*she loathed the nasty old man/ loathes living there*).

loath'ing n hate, disgust (*look at him with sheer loathing*).

loath'some adj hateful, disgusting (*a loathsome creature*).

loaves see **loaf**.

lob vb (**lobbed'**, **lob'bing**) to hit, kick or throw a ball gently into the air (*lob the tennis ball over the net*):—also n.

lob'by n 1 an entrance hall (*hotel lobbies*). 2 a group of people trying to influence the decisions of the government (*the anti-motorway lobby*):—vb to try to influence decisions of the government.

lobe n the fleshy hanging part of the ear (*ear-rings are worn on the lobes of the ears*).

lobe'lia n a kind of garden flower, often blue, white or red in colour.

lob'ster n a long-tailed jointed shellfish.

lob'ster pot n a baited basket for trapping lobsters.

lo'cal adj having to do with a particular place (*local history/local people*).

local colour n in a picture or story, accuracy over details of place to make it more realistic (*his descriptions of the village inhabitants added local colour to his novel*).

local'ity n a district, area, neighbourhood (*she has lived in the same locality for years*).

lo'calize vb to keep to one place or district (*the disease seems to be localized*).

locate' vb 1 to find the place of (*try to locate the source of the infection*). 2 to fix or set in a certain place (*the houses are located by the village green*).

loca'tion n 1 place (*live in a pleasant location*). 2 the place where a story is filmed (*the filming was carried out on location in Scotland*).

loch n 1 a lake, esp in Scotland. 2 an arm of the sea.

lock n 1 a fastening bolt moved by a key (*turn the key in the lock*). 2 the part of a gun by which it is fired. 3 a section of a canal, enclosed by gates, in which the amount of water can be increased to raise a ship to a higher level, or vice versa. 4 a firm grasp (*the wrestler held his opponent in a lock*). 5 a curl of hair:—vb 1 to fasten with lock and key (*lock the door/lock the safe*). 2 to hold firmly (*lovers locked in a passionate embrace*). 3 to jam, to become fixed or blocked (*the car's wheels have locked*):—**lock, stock and barrel** altogether, completely (*he moved out of the flat, lock, stock and barrel*).

lock'er n a small cupboard with a lock (*his locker in the changing rooms*).

lock'et n a small metal case, often containing a picture, worn on a chain round the neck as an ornament (*a silver locket containing a lock of her husband's hair*).

lock'jaw n a disease in which the muscles of the jaw become so stiff that the mouth cannot be opened, tetanus.

lock'out n the shutting out by an employer of workers from their place of work (*a lockout to force the workers to accept the new wage offer*).

lock'smith n one who makes or repairs locks.

lock'-up n 1 a cell in a prison (*he's in a lock-up in the local police station*). 2 a garage in which a car can be locked away (*his lock-up is some way from his house*).

locomo'tion n (fml) movement from place to place (*the sideways locomotion of a crab*).

locomo'tive n a railway engine.

lo'cum ten'ens *n* (*usu abbreviated to* **lo'-cum**) one who does the work of another, esp a doctor, during his or her absence (*acting as locum while the usual GP is on holiday*).

lo'cust *n* a large grasshopper that feeds on and destroys crops.

lode *n* a vein of metal in a crack in a rock.

lode'star *n* **1** the star by which one sets a course, the Pole star. **2** a guide or example to follow (*he was so successful that he acted as a lodestar to his fellow workers*).

lode'stone *n* a stone containing magnetic iron, formerly used as a compass.

lodge *n* **1** a small house originally for a gatekeeper at the entrance to a park, church, etc (*he lives in the manor house and his mother in the lodge*). **2** the meeting place of a society (e.g. Freemasons) or the members meeting there (*a Masonic lodge*). **3** a house for a hunting party (*live at the shooting lodge for the stag-hunting season*). **4** a house or cabin used occasionally for some seasonal activity (*a ski lodge*):—*vb* **1** to put in a certain place (*lodge documents with his solicitor*). **2** to stay in another's house on payment (*students lodging with locals*). **3** to fix in (*a bullet lodged in her shoulder*):—**lodge a complaint** to make a complaint before an official.

lod'ger *n* one who stays in hired rooms in another's house (*take in lodgers to make money to live*).

lod'ging *n* a place where one can stay on payment (*look for cheap lodging in town*).

loft *n* **1** the space or room under the roof of a building (*keep old toys and furniture in the loft*). **2** a room over a stable. **3** a gallery in a hall or church:—*vb* to strike upwards (*loft the ball*).

lof'ty *adj* **1** (*lit*) very high (*the lofty walls of the city*). **2** of high moral quality (*lofty aims*). **3** proud, haughty (*with a lofty disregard for other people's feelings*):—*n* **loftiness**.

log *n* **1** a piece sawn from the trunk or one of the large branches of a tree (*cut logs for the fire*). **2** an instrument for measuring the speed of ships. **3** an official written record of a journey (*a ship's log*).

lo'ganberry *n* a fruit like a raspberry.

log'arithms *n* numbers arranged in a table by referring to which calculations can be done quickly.

log'book *n* **1** a book in which the rate of progress of a ship is written daily. **2** an official record of a journey (*details of the flight found in the logbook*). **3** the registration document of a car.

log'gerheads *npl*:—**at loggerheads** quarrelling (*she's been at loggerheads with her neighbours for years*).

lo'gic *n* **1** the art or science of reasoning (*study logic*). **2** a particular way of thinking or reasoning (*we were unable to follow her logic*). **3** (*inf*) reasonable thinking, good sense (*there's no logic in her decision*).

lo'gical *adj* **1** having to do with logic. **2** well-reasoned (*a logical argument*). **3** able to reason correctly (*logical people*).

logi'cian *n* one skilled in logic.

log'o *n* a special symbol or design that an organization uses on its products, notepaper, etc. (*The firm's logo resembled a thistle*).

loin *n* **1** a piece of meat cut from the back of an animal (*a loin chop*). **2** *pl* the part of the human back below the ribs:—**gird up one's loins** to prepare for action.

loin'-cloth *n* a piece of cloth worn round the loins (*loin-clothes are worn in hot countries, usually by poor people*).

loi'ter *vb* **1** to stand about idly (*they were loitering near the bank, looking suspicious*). **2** to go slowly, often stopping (*don't loiter—you'll be late for school*).

loll *vb* **1** to sit back or lie lazily (*they lolled in their armchairs while she washed the dishes*). **2** (*of the tongue*) to hang out (*thirsty dogs with their tongues lolling*).

loll'ipop *n* a sweetmeat on a stick (*children sucking red lollipops*).

lone *adj* alone, single, without others (*a lone piper/ a lone figure on the deserted beach*).

lone'ly *adj* sad because alone (*lonely old people/ lonely since her husband died*).

lone'some *adj* (*inf*) lonely (*feel lonesome when the others are away*).

long *adj* **1** not short, in time or space (*a long meeting/a long journey*). **2** having length, covering a certain distance from one end to the other or a certain time (*a garden 30 metres long/a film two hours long*). **3** (*of drinks*) containing little or no alcohol and served in a long glass:—*adv* for a long time:—*vb* to want very much (*she longs to see her friend again*).

long'boat *n* the largest and strongest boat carried on board a ship.

long'bow *n* a bow, drawn by hand, for firing arrows:—**draw the longbow** to tell untrue and improbable stories.

longev'ity *n* very long life (*a family noted for its longevity*).

longhead'ed *adj* wise, farseeing, shrewd.

long'ing *n* an eager desire (*a longing to be free/a longing for freedom*).

long'ish *adj* (*inf*) quite long (*a longish journey*).

lon'gitude *n* **1** length. **2** distance in degrees east or west of an imaginary line from pole to pole, running through Greenwich (London).

longitu'dinal *adj* having to do with length or longitude.

long'shoreman *n* one who lives or works on the coast or shore.

long-sight'ed *adj* able to see distant objects more clearly than near ones (*he is long-sighted and wears glasses for reading*).

long-suffering *adj* patient, ready to put up with troubles without complaint (*their long-suffering mother tried to sort out all their problems*).

long-wind'ed *adj* speaking or writing in an unnecessarily roundabout way (*a long-winded lecturer who bored the whole audience/a piece of long-winded prose*).

loo *n* (*inf*) a toilet.

loo'fa(h) *n* **1** a marrow-like plant. **2** the fibrous framework of the plant stripped of the fleshy part and used in washing as a sponge (*a loofah at the side of the bath*).

look *vb* **1** to turn the eyes towards so as to see (*look at the picture/look at her with dislike*). **2** to have a certain appearance (*she looks ill/it looks as if it will rain*). **3** to face in a certain direction (*a house looking south*):—*n* **1** act of looking (*do have a look to see if they are coming*). **2** a glance (*have a look at the essay*). **3** the appearance, esp of the face (*the look of one who has seen a ghost*):—**look after** to take care of (*look after the children while their mother is away*):—**look down on** to despise (*look down on people less well-off than she is herself*):—**look for 1** to try to find (*look for the lost book*).

2 to hope for (*look for mercy from the king*):—**look on** to watch (*the other boys looked on while the bully hit the younger boy*):—**look out 1** to be careful (*look out in case you slip*). **2** to watch out for (*look out for my sister at the concert*). **3** to sear ch for and find, to choose (*look out some books for the children to read*):—**look over** to examine:—**look a gift-horse in the mouth** to say that one is not pleased with a present or to criticize it.

look'er-on *n* one who watches or spectates (*the lookers-on should have stopped the boys fighting*).

look'ing glass *n* a mirror.

look'out *n* **1** watchman. **2** a post from which one watches. **3** a careful watch (*be on the lookout for thieves*).

loom¹ *n* a machine for weaving cloth.

loom² *vb* **1** to appear gradually and dimly, as in the dark, to seem larger than natural (*shapes looming out of the mist*). **2** to seem thr eateningly close (*with exams looming*).

loon *n* a northern diving bird.

loop *n* **1** a line that curves back and crosses itself (*the road makes a loop*). **2** a rope, cord, etc, that so curves (*loops of ribbon*):—*vb* **1** to make a loop (*loop the ribbon*). **2** to fasten in a loop.

loop'hole *n* a way of escaping or avoiding something (*a loophole in the contract that meant he could withdraw*).

loose *adj* **1** untied, not packed together in a box, etc (*buy loose tomatoes/the string had come loose*). **2** free, at liberty (*the dog had broken loose from the rope*). **3** not definite (*a loose arrangement*). **4** careless. **5** not tight (*wear loose clothes*). **6** indecent, immoral (*loose behaviour*):—*vb* **1** to untie (*loose the string*). **2** to set free (*loose the cows from the barn/loose the prisoners*).

loose box *n* part of a stable where horses are left untied.

loos'en *vb* to make or become loose or less tight (*loosen his belt after a heavy meal*).

loot *n* that which is stolen or carried off by force (*the police caught the burglar but failed to find his loot*).

lop¹ *vb* (**lopped'**, **lop'ping**) to cut off (*lop branches off the tree/lop a bit off the price*).

lop² *vb* (**lopped'**, **lop'ping**) to hang loosely.

lop-sid'ed adj leaning to one side (she was lop-sided since she carried a heavy bag in one hand/a lop-sided account of the events).

loqua'cious adj (fml) talkative (unable to get away from her loquacious neighbour):—n **loqua'city**.

lord n 1 a master. 2 a ruler. 3 a nobleman. 4 a title of honour given to noblemen and certain high officials (e.g. judges). 5 an owner:—n **Lord God**:—vb to rule strictly or harshly.

lord'ly adj 1 proud, grand. 2 commanding.

Lord's day n Sunday.

Lord's prayer n the 'Our Father'.

Lord's supper n Holy Communion.

lord'ship n 1 the state of being a lord. 2 the power of a lord. 3 the title by which one addresses noblemen, judges, etc.

lore n 1 (old) learning. 2 all that is known about a subject, usu that which is handed down by word of mouth (sea lore).

lorgnette [lorn-yet'] n a pair of eyeglasses with a handle, of a type rarely used now.

lorn adj (old) left alone.

lor'ry n a motor vehicle for carrying goods (lorries carrying loads of coal).

lose [lűz] vb (pt, pp **lost**) 1 to cease to have (lose his eye in an accident). 2 to fail to keep in one's possession (lose her gloves). 3 to be defeated in (lose the battle/lose the match). 4 to fail to use, to waste (lose no time in asking for a loan). 5 to miss (lose an opportunity). 6 (of a watch or clock) to work too slowly (my watch loses about five minutes a day). 7 to have less of (lose weight):—**lose one's head** to become too excited to act sensibly.

lo'ser n one who loses (the loser of the tennis match congratulated the winner).

loss n 1 act of losing (the loss of his wife/the loss of her home). 2 that which is lost (she is a loss to the firm). 3 harm, damage (forced to pay for the losses):—**at a loss** not knowing what to do (at a loss to know what to do).

lost pt of **lose**.

lot n 1 one of a set of objects, a separate part (one lot of clothes). 2 a set of objects sold together at an auction (bid for lot number 3). 3 the way of life that one has to follow (it was his lot in life to work hard and earn little). 4 a large number (a lot of people/a lot of books). 5 a piece of land (a building lot/a parking lot).

loth see **loath**.

lo'tion n a liquid for healing wounds, cleansing the skin, etc (apply a lotion to her sunburn).

lott'ery n a game of chance in which prizes are shared out among those whose tickets are picked out in a public draw (she had the winning numbers in the lottery).

lo'tus n a type of water-lily whose flower was once said to make those who ate it forget everything.

loud adj 1 easily heard (a loud voice). 2 noisy (a loud party). 3 unpleasantly bright, showy (loud colours).

loudspeak'er n a radio apparatus by which sound is transmitted and made louder when necessary (use a loudspeaker to get the competitors to leave the field).

lough n a lake, esp in Ireland.

lounge vb 1 to stand about lazily, to move lazily, to spend time in an idle way (some workers lounging around while others were working hard). 3 to sit or lie back in a comfortable position (lounge in an armchair):—n 1 a comfortably furnished sitting room (take her guests into the lounge). 2 a public room in a hotel (the residents' lounge):—n **loung'er**.

lounge suit n a man's suit of clothes for everyday wear (it's not an occasion for evening wear—a lounge suit will do).

lour same as **lower**.

louse n (pl **lice**) a wingless insect that lives on the bodies of animals (tramps offered baths to get rid of lice).

lous'y adj 1 full of or covered with lice. 2 (inf) very bad, poor (lousy food/lousy weather).

lout n a rude and clumsy fellow (the lout who bumped into the old woman).

lov'able adj worthy of love (a lovable puppy).

love n 1 a strong liking for (a love of good food). 2 a feeling of desire for (full of love for his wife). 3 the person or thing loved (his first love). 4 (in some games) no score (the score was forty love):—vb 1 to be fond of, to like (loving Mexican food). 2 to be strongly attracted to, to be in love with (he loved her and was heartbroken when she left):—n **lov'er**.

love'less adj 1 with no love (a loveless marriage). 2 unloved (when her mother died the child felt completely loveless).

love'lorn *adj* (*old*) sad because left by one's lover.

love'ly *adj* **1** beautiful (*a lovely girl*). **2** (*inf*) very pleasing (*a lovely day/a lovely meal*):—*n* **love'liness.**

lov'ing *adj* full of love, fond (*a loving smile/a loving mother*).

low¹ *vb* **1** to bellow, as an ox. **2** to moo like a cow (*cattle lowing in the field*):—*n* **low'ing.**

low² *adj* **1** not far above the ground (*the picture is too low*). **2** not tall, not high (*low buildings*). **3** small in degree, amount, etc (*low temperatures*). **4** not high in rank or position (*low positions in the firm*). **5** cheap (*low prices*). **6** vulgar, coarse (*low humour*). **7** dishonourable (*a low thing to do*). **8** soft, not loud (*a low voice*). **9** sad, unhappy:— **low spirits** a sad mood.

lower' *vb* **1** to make less high (*lower the height of the ceiling*). **2** to let or bring down (*lower the flag*). **3** to make of less value or worth (*the building of the motorway lowered the value of their property*).

lower², **lour** *vb* **1** to frown (*lower angrily at the news that he had lost*). **2** to become dark (*skies lowering*).

low'land *n* low-lying or level country.

low'lander *n* one born or living in lowlands.

low'ly *adj* **1** (*fml or hum*) humble, not high in rank (*workers too lowly for the owner of the firm to speak to/a lowly clerk*). **2** (*old or lit*) gentle in manner.

loy'al *adj* faithful to one's friends, duty, etc (*loyal followers*). **2** true (*loyal to the cause*):—*n* **loy'alty.**

loyalist *n* one who supports the lawful government of the country.

loz'enge *n* **1** a diamond-shaped figure (*a sweater with a lozenge design*). **2** a small sweetmeat, or medicine in the form of a sweet (*cough lozenges*).

lu'bricant *n* oil or grease used to make machinery run smoothly (*engine lubricant*).

lu'bricate *vb* to oil something to make it run smoothly (*lubricating the parts of the machine*):—*ns* **lubrica'tion, lu'bricator.**

lucerne [lö-sern'] *n* a clover-like plant used as food for cattle.

lu'cid *adj* clear, easily understood (*a lucid explanation*):—*n* **lucid'ity.**

lu'cifer *n* (*old*) a match:—**Lucifer 1** the morning star. **2** Satan.

luck *n* **1** the good or bad things that happen by chance, fate, fortune (*only luck is involved, not skill/she had bad luck/a bit of good luck*). **2** something good that happens by chance, good luck (*luck was with her*).

luck'less *adj* (*fml*) unfortunate (*the luckless loser*).

luck'y *adj* fortunate, having good luck (*she is very lucky and is always winning things*).

lu'crative *adj* bringing in much money or profit (*a lucrative occupation*).

lu'cre *n* (*inf*) money, profit (*often* **filthy lucre**) (*all he's interested in is filthy lucre*).

lu'dicrous *adj* funny, silly and laughable (*she looks ludicrous in that hat/it was ludicrous to think he could win*).

luff *vb* to turn a ship so that it will sail more towards the direction from which the wind is blowing.

lug *vb* (**lugged', lug'ging**) to pull, draw or carry with difficulty (*lug the trunk down from the attic/lug her bags to the station*).

lug'gage *n* a traveller's baggage (*check her luggage in at the airport*).

lug'ger *n* a small sailing boat.

lugu'brious *adj* mournful, gloomy (*always has a lugubrious expression*).

luke'warm *adj* **1** quite warm, neither hot nor cold (*lukewarm water*). **2** not eager (*rather lukewarm about the idea*).

lull *vb* **1** to calm (*hull her fears*). **2** to send to sleep (*the rocking of the cradle lulled the child to sleep*):—*n* an interval of calm.

lull'aby *n* a song sung to a baby to make it sleep.

lumba'go *n* muscular pain in the lower part of the back (*have difficulty in bending because of lumbago*).

lum'bar *adj* having to do with the lower part of the back (*pain in the lumbar region*).

lum'ber *n* **1** unused or useless articles (*clear the lumber out of the attic*). **2** wood of trees cut into timber:—*vb* **1** to move heavily and clumsily (*a bear was lumbering towards them*). **2** to give someone an unpleasant or unwanted responsibility or task (*she got lumbered with taking notes at the meeting*).

lum'berjack *n* in North America, one whose job it is to cut down trees.

lu'minary *n* **1** (*lit*) a body that gives light (e.g the sun). **2** (*fml*) a person well-known for his or her knowledge, expertise or talent (*several luminaries from the world of the theatre were there*).

lu'minous *adj* shining, giving light (*luminous paint/a luminous watch face*).

lump *n* **1** a shapeless mass (*a lump of dough*). **2** a hard swelling (*a lump on his head after being hit with an iron bar*):—*vb* **1** to put together as one, to consider together (*he lumps all women together as inefficient*).

lump sum *n* a single large amount of money instead of several smaller payments (*get a lump sum when he retired instead of monthly amounts*).

lump'ish *adj* heavy, dull (*lumpish, unattractive people*).

lump'y *adj* full of lumps (*lumpy custard*).

lu'nacy *n* madness (*it was lunacy to walk alone in that district at night*).

lu'nar *adj* having to do with the moon.

lu'natic *n* a mad person:—*adj* mad, insane, very foolish (*what a lunatic thing to do*).

lunch *n* a midday meal (*have sandwiches for lunch/have a working lunch*):—*vb* to take lunch (*lunch on fresh salmon*).

lung *n* one of the two bodily organs by means of which we breathe (*have a collapsed lung*).

lunge *n* a sudden move or thrust forward (*make a lunge at her with a knife*):—*vb* to make a sudden onward movement (*she lunged at him with a knife*).

lupin [lŏ'-pên] *n* a kind of garden plant with a tall stem covered in many flowers.

lurch *vb* to roll or sway to one side (*drunks lurching down the road*):—*n* a sudden roll (*the bus gave a sudden lurch*):—**leave in the lurch** to leave (someone) in difficulty (*he left her in the lurch on her own with a baby*).

lure *n* something that attracts or leads on (*a lure to customers of free offers*):—*vb* to attract, to lead on, as by promise or gifts (*try to lure him to join the firm by promises of a high salary*).

lu'rid *n* **1** too brightly coloured, too vivid (*lurid sweaters*). **2** horrifying, shocking (*the lurid details of the accident/a lurid sight*).

lurk *vb* **1** to remain out of sight (*photographers lurking behind trees to try to take shots of the filmstar*). **2** to lie hidden, to exist unseen (*danger might be lurking*).

luscious [lu'-shês] *adj* very sweet in taste (*luscious peaches*).

lush *adj* **1** growing very plentifully, thick (*lush vegetation*). **2** (*inf*) affluent, luxurious (*lush surroundings*).

lust *n* a strong or uncontrollable desire, esp for sexual pleasure:—*vb* to desire eagerly (*older men lusting after young girls*):—*adj* **lust'ful.**

lus'tre *n* **1** brightness (*the lustre of the polished surface*). **2** glory (*his brave actions brought lustre to the family*). **3** dress material with a shiny surface.

lus'treless *adj* dull (*lustreless hair*).

lus'trous *adj* bright, shining (*lustrous eyes*).

lus'ty *adj* **1** str ong and healthy, full of energy (*lusty young men*). **2** str ong or loud (*lusty singing*).

lute *n* (*old*) a stringed musical instrument, rather like the guitar.

luxu'riant *adj* growing in great plenty (*luxuriant vegetation/luxuriant hair*).

luxu'riate *vb* to live in or enjoy great comfort (*luxuriate in a hot, scented bath/luxuriating in the comfort of a high-class hotel*).

luxu'rious *adj* **1** fond of luxury. **2** splendid and affluent (*a luxurious hotel/a luxurious lifestyle*).

lux'ury *n* **1** great ease and comfort (*wealthy people living in luxury*). **2** a desirable or pleasing thing that is not a necessity of life (*afford luxuries such as perfume*).

lych'-gate, lich'-gate *n* the roofed gateway of a churchyard.

Ly'cra [lī'-kra] *n* (trademark) a stretchy, shiny artificial fabric used for swimsuits, sportswear, etc.

lyd'dite *n* a powerful explosive.

ly'ing *pres p* of **lie**:—*also adj.*

lymph *n* a colourless liquid in the body (*the lymph glands*).

lynch *vb* to seize someone, judge him or her on the spot and put to death without a proper trial (*the mob lynched the child's murderer before he could be tried*).

lynx *n* an animal of the cat family noted for keen sight.

lyre *n* (*old*) a U-shaped stringed musical instrument similar to a harp, played by the ancient Greeks.

lyre'-bird *n* a bird with a tail shaped like a lyre.

lyric *n* **1** a short poem expressing the writer's feelings. **2** *pl* the words of a song (*the song has rather sad lyrics*).

lyrical *adj* **1** expressing feeling (*lyrical verse*). **2** enthusiastic, effusive (*lyrical about the beauty of her new baby*).

M

macabre [ma-kābr'] *adj* horrible, causing a shudder of horror (*a macabre murder*).

macaro'ni *n* flour paste rolled into long tubes (*a dish of macaroni and cheese*).

macaroon' *n* a small cake containing powdered almonds or coconut.

macaw' *n* a large type of parrot.

mace *n* 1 (*old*) a spiked club used as a weapon of war. 2 a heavy ornamental stick carried befor e certain officials as a sign of their office (*the mayor's mace*).

Machiavellian [ma-ki-a-ve'-li-ên] *adj* clever and crafty, ready to make use of any means to gain a purpose (*use Machiavellian tactics to achieve his aim*).

machina'tion [ma-ki-nā'-shên] *n* underhand plans, plans for doing something evil (*his machinations to get rid of his boss were successful*).

machine' *n* 1 any apparatus for pr oducing power or doing work (*a washing machine*). 2 a system under which the work of different groups is directed to one end (*the political party's machine*). 3 a vehicle (*ride a fire machine*).

machine gun *n* a gun that fires many bullets in a short time before it has to be reloaded.

machin'ery *n* 1 machines (*buy new machinery for the factory*). 2 parts of a machine (*something wrong with the machinery of the tumble dryer*). 3 or ganization (*the machinery of government*).

machin'ist *n* one who makes, looks after or operates machinery (*she was a machinist in a clothes factory*).

mack'erel *n* an eatable sea fish (*smoked mackerel*).

mack'intosh *n* a waterproof overcoat.

mac'rocosm *n* the universe.

mad *adj* 1 insane (*the murderer pretended to be mad*). 2 out of one's mind with anger , pain, etc (*mad with grief*). 3 (*inf*) very angry (*she was mad at the naughty children*). 4 (*inf*) very unwise, crazy (*a mad plan*).

mad'am *n* the title used in addressing a lady politely.

Madame' *n* the French form of **Mrs**.

mad'cap *n* a wild or reckless person:—*adj* reckless, very thoughtless (*a madcap plan to make money quickly*).

madd'en *vb* to make mad (*an animal maddened with pain*).

madd'er *n* a plant from which red dye is got.

madei'ra *n* a sweet wine made in Madeira.

mad'man *n* one who is mad (*the killer must have been a madman*).

mad'ness *n* 1 insanity. 2 folly.

Madon'na *n* 1 the Vir gin Mary. 2 a pictur e or statue of the Virgin Mary.

mad'rigal *n* 1 a love-song or poem. 2 a part-song for several voices.

mael'strom *n* 1 a whirlpool. 2 a state of confusion and struggle (*in the maelstrom of big-city life*).

mae'stro *n* a master, esp in music (*the maestro bowed to the audience*).

mag'azine *n* 1 a stor e for firearms and explosives (*the military magazine*). 2 a weekly or monthly paper containing articles, stories, etc (*women's magazines*).

magen'ta *n* a crimson dye:—*adj* crimson.

mag'got *n* the grub of certain insects, esp the fly or bluebottle (*find maggots on the rotting meat*).

Magi [mā'-jī] *npl* 1 (*old*) priests of ancient Persia. 2 the wise men fr om the East who visited the infant Jesus.

ma'gic *n* 1 the art of contr olling spirits, and so gaining knowledge of the future or commanding certain things to happen, witchcraft (*black magic*). 2 the art of pr oducing illusions by tricks or sleight of hand (*the magic practised by the stage magician*). 3 fascination (*the magic of the theatre*):—**black magic** magic done with the aid of evil spirits.

ma'gic, ma'gical *adjs* 1 having to do with magic (*a magic spell/a magic act*). 2 (*inf*) marvellous, very good (*the match was magic*).

magi'cian *n* 1 one with magic powers (*the magician in the fairy story*). 2 a person who practises the art of producing illusions by tricks or sleight of hand (*a magician with his own television show*).

magiste'rial *adj* 1 having the manner of one used to giving commands. 2 having to do with magistrates.

ma'gistracy *n* the office of magistrate.

ma'gistrate *n* one with authority to try and sentence those who break the law, a judge (*appear before the magistrate*).

magnan'imous *adj* generous, esp to enemies or dependants, unselfish (*he was magnanimous to forgive those who had attacked him*):—*n* **magnanim'ity**.

mag'nate *n* a person of great wealth or importance (*industrial magnates*).

magne'sia *n* a white powder made from magnesium, used as a medicine (*take milk of magnesia for indigestion*).

magne'sium *n* a white metal that burns with a bright white light.

mag'net *n* 1 a piece of ir on that attracts to it other pieces of iron and that when hung up points to the north. 2 a person or thing that attracts (*he told such interesting stories that he was a magnet for all the children*).

magnet'ic *adj* 1 acting lik e a magnet (*magnetic forces*). 2 attractive (*a magnetic personality*).

mag'netism *n* 1 the power of the magnet. 2 the science that deals with the power of the magnet. 3 personal charm or attraction (*by his sheer magnetism he always took charge of situations*).

magne'to *n* in a petrol engine, the device that produces the spark that sets fire to the gas.

magnifica'tion *n* 1 the act or power of magnif ying. 2 an exaggeration (*the magnification of her troubles*).

magnif'icent *adj* splendid, grand (*a magnificent royal parade/magnificent clothes*):—*n* **magnif'icence**.

mag'nify *vb* 1 to mak e appear larger, to exaggerate (*her parents seemed to magnify the crime that she had committed*). 2 to praise (*magnify God*).

mag'nifying glass *n* a glass with a curved surface that makes things appear larger.

mag'nitude *n* 1 gr eatness of size or extent (*a star of great magnitude*). 2 importance (*the magnitude of the crime*).

magno'lia *n* a tree with beautiful foliage and large flowers.

mag'num *n* a two-quart bottle or container (*a magnum of wine*).

mag'pie *n* a black and white bird of the crow family (*magpies are known for their habit of collecting bright things*).

mahara'ja(h) *n* an Indian prince.

mahara'nee *n* an Indian princess.

mahat'ma *n* an Indian title of respect for a very holy person.

mahog'any *n* a reddish brown wood much used for furniture (*old-fashioned wardrobes made of mahogany*).

mahout' *n* an elephant driver.

maid *n* 1 (*old*) a young girl. 2 a female ser vant (*only very wealthy families have maids nowadays*). 3 (*old*) a virgin.

maid'en *n* (*old*) a young unmarried woman.

maiden name *n* the surname of a married woman before marriage (*Mrs Smith's maiden name is Jones*).

maiden over *n* in cricket, an over during which no runs are hit.

maiden voyage *n* the first voyage of a new ship (*the ship sank on its maiden voyage*).

maid'enhair *n* a fern with light feathery leaves (*a vase of rosebuds and maidenhair*).

maid'enly *adj* modest, gentle.

maid'servant *n* (*old*) a female servant.

mail[1] *n* 1 the postal ser vice (*sent the letter by first-class mail*). 2 letters, par cels, etc, sent by post (*some mail has gone astray*):—*vb* to send by post (*mailed the parcel*).

mail[2] *n* (*old*) armour (*knights clad in mail*).

mail order *n* a system of buying goods from a catalogue and having them delivered to your home.

maim *vb* to disable, to cripple (*maimed for life in the accident*).

main *adj* chief, principal (*his main source of income/the main branch of the store*):—*n* 1 the greater part. 2 the ocean. 3 a pipe under the street for water, gas etc. 4 str ength.

main'land *n* land, as distinct from nearby islands (*the children on the island go to school on the mainland*).

main'ly *adv* chiefly (*they sell mainly magazines and sweets*).

main'sail *n* the chief sail of a ship.

main'sheet *n* the rope attached to the lower corner of the mainsail.

main'spring n 1 the chief spring that when wound sets a mechanism in motion (*the mainspring of the clock*). 2 chief reason for acting (*her children were the mainspring of her life*).

main'stay n 1 the rope holding up the mainmast. 2 the chief support (*the office manager is the mainstay of the firm*).

maintain' vb 1 to feed and clothe (*difficulty in maintaining his family*). 2 to keep up (*maintain a good standard of living*). 3 to keep in good repair (*houses that are expensive to maintain*). 4 to defend a point of view (*maintain his innocence*).

main'tenance n upkeep, support (*pay for the maintenance of his children*).

maize n Indian corn.

majes'tic adj dignified, stately.

ma'jesty n 1 grandeur, dignity (*the majesty of the occasion*). 2 the title given to a king or queen.

ma'jor adj 1 greater in number, size or quantity (*the major part of the audience*). 2 the more important (*the major medical discoveries*):—n an army officer just above a captain in rank.

major'ity n 1 the greater number (*she is liked by the majority of the class*). 2 in voting, the amount by which the number of votes cast for one candidate exceeds that cast for another (*the government won by a majority of twenty*). 3 (*fml*) the age at which one may legally own property (*she has not yet achieved her majority*). 4 (*fml*) the rank of major.

make vb (*pt, pp* **made**) 1 to create (*stories of how God made the earth*). 2 to construct by putting parts or substances together (*make a model aeroplane out of a kit*). 3 to cause to be (*the win made him famous*). 4 to force (*they made her go*). 5 to add up to (*two plus two makes four*). 6. to earn (*he makes £20,000 a year*):—n 1 the way something is made. 2 shape:—**make for** to go towards (*they made for the nearest town*):—**make good** to succeed, to do well (*people from poor backgrounds who make good*):—**make off** to run away:—**make out 1** to decipher (*unable to make out the faint writing*). 2 (*inf*) to succeed:—**make up 1** to invent (a story) (*she made up an excuse for not going to the party*). 2 to put paint, powder, etc (on the face) (*she made up her face in the cloakroom*). 3 to bring (a quarrel) to an end, to try to become friendly with (*she wanted to make up but he was still angry*).

make'-believe n pretence (*it was just make-believe that she was a princess*):—also vb.

make'-over n the process of trying to improve the appearance of a person or place.

mak'er n one who makes (*a maker of model aeroplanes/a tool-maker*):—**Mak'er** God.

make'shift adj used or done because nothing better can be found or thought of (*they made a makeshift shelter on the desert island*):—also n.

make'-up n 1 paint, powder, etc, for the face (*a range of make-up in her bag*). 2 one's character (*it was not in his make-up to be mean*).

mal'achite n a green stone.

maladjust'ed adj fitting in badly (*maladjusted children unhappy at school*):—n **maladjust'ment**.

maladministra'tion n bad government, bad management (*the firm went bankrupt because of maladministration*).

mal'adroit adj clumsy, tactless (*maladroit attempts/a maladroit apology*).

mal'ady n (*fml*) illness, disease (*suffering from an unknown malady*).

mal'apropism n the use of a word in the wrong place or with the wrong meaning.

mala'ria n a fever caused by a mosquito bite.

mal'content n (*fml*) one who is discontented with the state of affairs (*a strike that was caused by malcontents in the industry*).

male adj of the sex that can become a father (*the male of the species*):—also n.

maledic'tion n (*fml*) a curse, a wish that harm may befall another (*utter a malediction against her daughter's murderer*).

malev'olent adj wishing harm to others, spiteful (*give his rival a malevolent glance*):—n **malev'olence**.

malformed' adj out of shape, wrongly shaped (*a malformed foot*):—n **malfor-ma'tion**.

mal'function vb to fail to work correctly (*The machine is malfunctioning*).

mal'ice n pleasure in the misfortunes of others, spite, a desire to harm others (*full of malice towards the person who beat him in the match*).

mali'cious adj spiteful, full of malice.

malign [ma-lìn'] *vb* to speak ill of (*he maligned the person who had helped him*):—*adj* evil, harmful (*a malign influence*).

malig'nancy, malig'nity *ns* 1 great hatred. 2 a desire to do harm.

malig'nant *adj* 1 feeling great hatred (*malignant feelings towards his rival*). 2 very harmful (*a malignant influence*). 3 able to cause death (*a malignant cancer*).

malin'ger *vb* to pretend to be ill.

malin'gerer *n* a person who pretends to be ill in order to avoid duty (*a malingerer who is hardly ever at work*).

mall *see* **shopping mall**.

mal'lard *n* a wild duck.

malleable [ma'-li-êbl] *adj* 1 that which can be hammered into shape (*malleable metals*). 2 easily influenced (*people who are malleable*).

mall'et *n* 1 a wooden hammer (*fix the fence posts in place with a mallet*). 2 the stick used in croquet.

mall'ow *n* a plant with soft leaves and blue-red flowers.

malmsey [mäm'-zee] *n* a sweet white wine.

malnutri'tion *n* a state caused by eating too little food or food that does not supply the needs of the body (*children suffering from malnutrition*).

malprac'tice *n* failure to carry out one's professional duty properly or honestly (*a lawyer accused of malpractice*).

malt *n* barley or other grain prepared for making beer or whisky:—*vb* to make into or become malt:—*adj* **malt'y**.

maltreat' *vb* to treat badly, to ill-use (*accused of maltreating his dog*).

mama', mamma' *n* (*old*) mother.

mam'mal *n* an animal that suckles its young.

mam'mon *n* 1 riches or wealth, esp when thought of as a way to gain power. 2 **Mam'mon** in legend, the god of wealth (*worship Mammon*).

mam'moth *n* a type of large elephant, no longer existing:—*adj* huge (*a mammoth shopping centre*).

man *n* (*pl* **men**) 1 the human race (*man has destroyed much of the environment*). 2 a human being (*all men must die*). 3 a male human being (*men, women and children*). 4 (*inf*) a husband. 5 a male servant (*his man packed his*

suitcase):—*vb* (**manned'**, **man'ning**) to provide with people to go to or to be in the place where a duty is to be performed (*man the lifeboats*).

man'acle *n* an iron ring and chain used to fasten the hands of a prisoner (*slaves in manacles*):—*vb* to put manacles on.

man'age *vb* 1 to control, to be in charge of (*managing the firm*). 2 to succeed (in doing something) (*she managed to get there in time*).

man'ageable *adj* easily controlled (*manageable children/manageable hair*).

man'agement *n* 1 control, direction (*under the management of an experienced businessman*). 2 the group of persons who control or run a business (*management in dispute with the unions*).

man'ager *n* one who controls a business or part of it (*the manager of the accounts department*):—*f* **man'ageress**.

manage'rial *adj* having to do with management of a business (*a managerial post*).

man'darin *n* 1 a Chinese official. 2 the chief dialect of the Chinese language. 3 a small orange.

man'date *n* 1 a command (*by mandate of the queen*). 2 power given to one person, group or nation to act on behalf of another (e.g. by voters to the governing party) (*claim they had a mandate to increase taxes*).

man'datory *adj* compulsory (*attendance is mandatory*).

man'dible *n* the lower jawbone.

man'dolin(e) *n* a musical stringed instrument, like the guitar but with a rounded back.

man'drake *n* a poisonous plant.

man'drill *n* a large type of baboon.

mane *n* the long hair on the neck of certain animals (*the lion's mane*).

man'ful *adj* brave (*a manful attempt*).

man'ganese *n* a hard, easily broken grey metal.

mange *n* a skin disease of dogs, etc.

man'gel-wur'zel *n* a type of beetroot used as food for cattle (*also called* **man'gold**).

man'ger *n* a raised box or trough out of which horses or cattle feed (*the Bible tells us that Jesus lay in a manger*).

man'gle' *n* a machine for pressing washed clothes dry and flat:—*vb* to press with a mangle (*freshly mangled clothes*).

man'gle[2] vb to cut or tear so as to be unrecognizable (*bodies badly mangled in the accident*).

man'go n (pl **man'goes**) **1** an Indian fruit with a large stone (*have fresh mango for dessert*). **2** the tree on which it grows.

man'gold see **mangel-wurzel**.

man'grove n a tropical tree growing in wet or muddy ground.

man'handle vb **1** to move by hand (*manhandling the huge wardrobe up the stairs*). **2** to tr eat roughly (*he complained that the police manhandled him*).

man'hole n a hole in the ground or floor through which a person may enter an underground shaft or tunnel (*get down to the sewer through a manhole*).

man'hood n the state of being a man or of having the qualities of a man (*till he reaches manhood*).

ma'nia n **1** madness (*suffering from mania*). **2** a very great interest (in), an obsession (*he has a mania for fast cars*).

ma'niac n a madman (*killed by a maniac*).

ma'niacal adj completely mad (*a maniacal attack*).

man'icure n the care of the hands and fingernails (*have a manicure*):—also vb.

man'icurist n one whose job it is to care for hands and nails (*train as a manicurist*).

man'ifest adj (fml) easily seen or understood, obvious (*her lack of interest was manifest*):—vb to show clearly (*she manifested very little enthusiasm*).

manifesta'tion n an open showing, a display (*a manifestation of his love for her*).

man'ifestly adv clearly, obviously (*she was manifestly ill*).

manifes'to n a public announcement of future plans (*the political party published its manifesto*).

man'ikin n a very small man.

manil'a, manill'a n **1** a material used for making ropes. **2** a type of thick, str ong brown paper (*manila envelopes*).

manip'ulate vb **1** to handle skilfully (*manipulating the bones back into position*). **2** to manage skilfully (often in a dishonest way) (*a barrister accused of trying to manipulate the jury*):—n **manipula'tion**.

man'ly adj having the qualities of a man (*manly behaviour*).

man'na n **1** the food of the Israelites in the wilderness. **2** something sent by God. **3** a windfall (*the pools win was manna to the poor family*).

mannequin [man'-i-kin] n a woman employed to wear and display new dresses (*mannequins at the fashion show*).

man'ner n **1** the way in which anything is done or happens (*the manner of his dying*). **2** the way a person speaks or behaves to others (*he has an open, frank manner*).

man'nered adj affected, artificial (*a mannered way of walking*).

man'nerism n a way of behaving, writing, etc, that has become a habit (*constantly flicking back his hair is one of his mannerisms*).

mann'ish adj like a man (*mannish women*).

manoeuvre [ma-nö'-vêr] n **1** a planned movement of armies or ships. **2** a skilful or cunning plan intended to make another behave as you want him or her to (*a manoeuvre to get rid of his boss and get the job*). **3** pl practice movements of armies or ships (*troops on manoeuvres*):—vb **1** to move armies or ships. **2** to move or act cunningly to gain one's ends (*she manoeuvred him out of his job to get promotion*).

man'or n the land or house belonging to a lord:— adj **mano'rial**.

manse n (Scot) the house of a clergyman.

man'sion n a large dwelling house.

man'slaughter n the unlawful but unintentional killing of a person (*found guilty of manslaughter rather than murder*).

man'telpiece, man'tel ns **1** an ornamental surr ound built on either side of and above a fireplace. **2** the shelf above a fireplace (*ornaments on the mantelpiece*).

mantil'la n a lace veil used as a head covering (*a Spanish lady wearing a mantilla*).

man'tle n **1** (old) a loose sleeveless cloak (*a velvet mantle over her evening dress*). **2** a chemically treated cotton hood that if fed with gas or oil in a lamp will glow when lit:—vb to cloak, to cover.

man'ual adj done by hand (*manual tasks*):—n **1** a small book containing all the important facts on a certain subject (*have lost the manual for the washing machine*). **2** the k eyboard of an organ.

manufac'ture *n* **1** the making of goods or materials (*the manufacture of computers*). **2** an article so made (*importing many foreign manufactures*):—*vb* to make, esp by machinery, in large quantities (*manufacturing cars*):—*n* **manufac'turer.**

manure' *n* dung or some other substance used to make soil more fertile (*farmers spreading manure on their fields*):—*vb* to treat with manure.

man'uscript *n* **1** a paper or book written by hand (*look at many manuscripts in his research on local history*). **2** the written material sent by an author for publishing.

Manx *adj* having to do with the Isle of Man.

Maori [mou'-ree] *n* one of the brown-skinned original inhabitants of New Zealand:—*also adj.*

map *n* a plan of any part of the earth's surface (*a map of France*):—*vb* (**mapped', map'ping**) to make a map of:—**map out** to plan (*map out their campaign*).

ma'ple *n* a tree from whose sap sugar is made (*pancakes with maple syrup*).

mar *vb* (**marred', mar'ring**) to spoil, to damage (*something marred the performance/mar her beauty*).

mar'athon *n* **1** a long race of about 42 kilometres or 26 miles along roads. **2** something that takes a long time and requires a great deal of effort (*Digging the weed-filled garden was a real marathon*).

marau'der *n* (*fml*) a robber (*marauders raiding the border area*).

mar'ble *n* **1** a type of hard stone used for buildings, statues, etc (*a mantelpiece made of marble*). **2** a small ball of stone or glass used in children's games.

mar'casite *n* a pale yellow mineral used to make jewellery (*a marcasite brooch*).

march¹ *vb* to walk with a regular step (*soldiers marching*):—*n* **1** movement of a body of soldiers on foot. **2** the distance walked (*a march of fifteen miles*). **3** music suitable for marching to (*the band played a stirring march*).

march² *n* the boundary of a county.

March *n* the third month of the year (*the cold winds of March*).

mar'chioness *n* the wife of a marquis.

mare *n* the female of the horse.

mare's nest *n* a discovery that turns out to be worthless (*they thought they'd found treasure trove but it was a mare's nest—the gold coins were fake*).

mar'garine *n* a substance made from vegetable or animal fat, often used instead of butter (*spread margarine on bread*).

mar'gin *n* **1** (*fml*) edge, border (*the margin of the lake*). **2** the part of a page that is not usu printed or written on (*comments in the margin*). **3** an amount more than is necessary, something extra (*leave a margin for error in the estimated calculations*).

mar'ginal *adj* **1** on or near the edge, border or limit. **2** very small or unimportant (*a marginal improvement*). **3** (*of a parliamentary seat*) that may be won or lost by a small number of votes and therefore likely to pass from one political party to another:—*n* a marginal parliamentary seat.

mar'guerite *n* a type of large daisy.

mar'igold *n* a bright yellow flower.

marijuana [mär-i-wän'-a] *n* a drug made from the dried leaves and flowers of hemp and smoked, illegally in many countries, to give a relaxed feeling, also called **pot** (*inf*).

marin'a *n* a harbour for the use of yachts and small boats.

marine' *adj* **1** having to do with the sea (*marine animals*). **2** having to do with shipping (*marine insurance*):—*n* **1** shipping. **2** a soldier serving on board ship.

mar'iner *n* (*fml*) a seaman.

marionette' *n* a doll that can be moved by strings, a puppet.

mar'ital *adj* (*fml*) having to do with marriage (*marital problems*).

mar'itime *adj* of or near the sea (*maritime areas*).

mar'joram *n* a sweet-smelling herb used in cooking (*add marjoram to the sauce*).

mark¹ *n* **1** a sign, spot or stamp that can be seen (*a cat with a white mark on its chest*). **2** a thing aimed at (*the arrow was wide of the mark*). **3** a number or letter indicating the standard reached (*her essay got a mark of 60%*). **4** an acceptable level of quality (*work that is not up to the mark*). **5** a stain or dent (*sooty marks on his white shirt*).

6 an indication, a sign (*give flowers as a mark of respect*):—*vb* **1** to mak e a mark on (*a table-cloth marked with fruit stains*). **2** to indicate by a mark the standard reached (*mark the essays*). **3** (*old*) to watch closely, to pay attention to (*mark my words*). **4** to show the position of (*a cross marks the spot where he died*). **5** to be a sign of (*mark the beginning of change*):—**mark time 1** to move the legs up and down as if walking, but without going backwards or forwards. **2** to fill in time (*mark time while he's waiting to go to college*):—**beside the mark** (*fml*) off the subject (*a guess that was beside the mark*).

mark[2] *n* formerly the currency unit of Germany, until the introduction of the euro in January 2002.

marked *adj* noticeable, important (*a marked change*).

mark'edly *adv* noticeably (*he is markedly healthier*).

mark'er *n* **1** one who k eeps the score. **2** a person or thing used to mark a place (*buoys as mark-ers for the yacht race*).

mar'ket *n* **1** a public place for buying and selling, a coming together of people to buy and sell (*buy fruit at a street market*). **2** a demand or need (*a market for lightweight cotton clothes*):—*vb* to sell in a market (*they market their books all over the world*).

mar'ketable *adj* that can be sold (*products that are no longer easily marketable*).

mar'ket cross *n* (*old*) a cross set up at the place where a market was to be held (*a 14th-century market cross in the village*).

mar'ket gar'den *n* a garden in which vegetables are grown for sale:—*n* **mar'ket gar'dener**.

mar'ketplace *n* the open space where a market is held.

mark'ka *n* formerly the currency unit of Finland, until the introduction of the euro in January 2002.

mark'ing ink *n* ink that does not run or wash out, used for marking linen (*use marking ink for writ-ing names on labels on school clothes*).

marks'man *n* one who shoots well (*a police marks-man*).

marl *n* a rich soil of clay and silt.

mar'line spike[2] *n* an iron tool used for picking apart the strands of a rope.

mar'malade *n* a jam made from oranges or lem-ons (*marmalade on toast*).

mar'moset *n* a type of small monkey.

mar'mot *n* a small squirrel-like animal.

maroon[1] *n* a brownish-crimson colour:—*adj* of this colour (*a book with a maroon cover*).

maroon[2] *vb* to abandon (*marooned on a desert island*).

marquee [mar-kee'] *n* a large tent (*a marquee on the large lawn for a wedding*).

marquess *see* **marquis.**

marquetry [mär'-ki-tri] *n* work in which a design is made by setting differently coloured pieces of wood into another piece of wood.

mar'quis, mar'quess *ns* a nobleman.

mar'riage *n* **1** the cer emony of marrying or being married (*there were sixty guests at their mar-riage*). **2** life together as husband and wife (*their marriage is over*).

mar'riageable *adj* old enough or suitable for marriage (*of marriageable age/a marriageable daughter*).

mar'row *n* **1** a soft fatty substance filling the hol-low parts of bones. **2** a lar ge vegetable (*stuffed marrow*).

mar'ry *vb* **1** to join together as husband and wife (*married by the local minister*). **2** to tak e as husband or wife (*he is marrying his sister's friend*).

Mars *n* **1** a planet. **2** the Roman god of war .

marsh *n* low watery ground, a swamp (*have diffi-culty walking over the marsh*):—*adj* **marsh'y.**

mar'shal *n* **1** an officer of high rank in the army or air force. **2** an official who mak es arrangements for public processions, etc:—*vb* (**mar'shalled, mar'shalling**) to arrange in order (*marshal the troops/marshal your facts*).

marshma'llow *n* **1** a flower that gr ows in marshy land. **2** a type of sweetmeat (*toasted marshmal-lows*).

marsh mar'igold *n* a flower that grows in marshy land.

marsu'pial *n* an animal that carries its young in a pouch (*kangaroos are marsupials*).

mart *n* a market (*a used car mart*).

marten *n* a type of weasel valued for its fur.

mar'tial *adj* **1** (*fml*) warlike (*martial nation*). **2** hav-ing to do with war (*martial arts/martial music*).

Mar'tian n in stories, an inhabitant of Mars.

mar'tin n a bird of the swallow family.

martinet' n one who makes strict rules and punishes severely those who disobey them (*regard her head teacher as a martinet*).

Martinmas n St Martin's day, 11th November.

mar'tyr n 1 one who suffers death for his or her beliefs (*Christian martyrs*). 2 one who suffers continuously from a certain illness (*a martyr to asthma*):—vb to put to death for refusing to give up one's faith (*she was martyred for her faith*):— n **martyrdom**.

mar'vel n a wonder:—vb (**mar'velled, mar'velling**) to wonder (at), to feel astonishment (*marvel at the parachutists' jumping*).

mar'vellous adj 1 wonderful, astonishing, extraordinary (*a marvellous new discovery*). 2 (*inf*) very good, excellent (*a marvellous holiday*).

Marx'ist n a socialist or communist who believes in the teaching of Karl Marx.

mar'zipan' n a sweet made from ground almonds, sugar, etc (*put marzipan on the cake before the icing*).

masca'ra n a substance used for darkening eyelashes (*brush mascara on her lashes*).

mas'cot n a person, animal or thing supposed to bring good luck (*a silver horseshoe as a mascot*).

mas'culine adj 1 of the male sex (*masculine characteristics*). 2 manly (*women who like masculine men*). 3 lik e a man (*a woman with a masculine walk*).

mash vb to crush food until it is soft (*mash potatoes/mash bananas*):—n a mixture of crushed grain, etc, given to animals as food (*prepare a mash for the pigs*).

mask n 1 a cover for the face or part of the face (*surgeons wearing masks to prevent the spread of infection*). 2 an animal or human face painted on paper, etc, and worn at parties or processions (*wear a cat's mask to the Halloween party*). 3 any means of concealing what is really going on (*her smile was a mask for her grief*). 4 (*usu called* **masque**) a poetical play:—vb 1 to cover with a mask. 2 to hide (*try to mask her amusement*).

ma'son n 1 one skilled in shaping stone or building (*a mason making large gravestones*). 2 a freemason:—adj **mason'ic**.

ma'sonry n 1 stonework (*the masonry of the statue is crumbling*). 2 the skill or work of a mason. 3 fr eemasonry.

masque, mask ns a poetical play with music popular at court in the 16th-17th centuries.

masquerade' n a ball at which masks are worn:— vb 1 to go in disguise. 2 to pr etend to be another (*a criminal masquerading as a council worker*).

mass n 1 a lump or quantity of matter (*a land mass*). 2 (*fml*) the quantity of matter in a body (*the mass of the rock*). 3 (*often pl*) a crowd (*there were masses at the protest*). 4 the larger part (*the mass of the people are in favour*):—vb 1 to gather into a mass. 2 to form a crowd.

Mass n the celebration of the Lord's Supper in the RC church.

mass'acre n the killing of large numbers of men, women and children:—vb to kill in large numbers (*the invading army massacred the townspeople*).

massage [ma-säj'] n rubbing and pressing the muscles to strengthen them or make them less stiff (*athletes having a massage after the race*):— also vb.

masseur [ma-sèr'] n one who massages:—f **mas'seuse'**.

mass'ive adj huge, big and heavy (*a massive rock/ a massive rise in unemployment*).

mass produc'tion n the manufacturing of large numbers of the same article for the market (*they made the goods at home but they have gone into mass production*).

mast¹ n on a ship, an upright pole on which sails may be set (*attach a flag to the mast*).

mast² n acorns and beechnuts as food for pigs.

mas'ter n 1 one who is in char ge or gives orders (*the dog's master*). 2 a male teacher (*the French master*). 3 an expert (*a master of the art of conversation*):—vb 1 to gain complete knowledge of (*master the art of public speaking*). 2 to overcome (*master her shyness*):—**old master** a great painter of the past.

mas'terful adj commanding, used to giving orders (*a masterful personality*).

mas'ter key n a key that opens several locks (*she locked her key in her room and had to get the* *hotel manager to open the door with a master key*).

mas'terly adj showing great skill (*a masterly performance*).

mas'terpiece n the best piece of work done by an artist (*regarded as Van Gogh's masterpiece*).

mas'tery n **1** contr ol, command (*gain mastery over the enemy*). **2** thor ough knowledge (*his mastery of foreign languages*).

mas'ticate vb (fml) to chew (*masticating food before swallowing*):—n **mastica'tion**.

mas'tiff n a large powerful dog.

mas'todon n a large elephant-like animal of prehistoric times.

mat n **1** a small piece of coarse cloth or plaited fibre used as a floor covering or foot-wiper (*a mat at the front door*). **2** a piece of cloth or other material placed under a plate or dish (*table mats*):—adj matt:—vb (**matt'ed, matt'ing**) to twist together, to entangle (*matted hair*).

mat'ador n the man who kills the bull in a bullfight.

match[1] n a small stick tipped with a substance that catches fire when rubbed on certain prepared surfaces (*light the fire with a match*).

match[2] n **1** a person or thing the same or nearly the same as another (*find a match for the wool*). **2** an equal (*she was his match in any argument*). **3** a sporting contest or game (*a football match*). **4** a marriage (*a love match*):—vb **1** to be equal to (*the restaurant does not match our local one for home cooking*). **2** to be lik e or to go well with something else (*the dress matches her eyes*).

match'box n a box for holding matches.

match'lock n an old type of musket fired with a match.

match'maker n one who tries to arrange a marriage between others (*try to act as matchmakers by asking her female friend and his male friend to dinner*).

mate n **1** a companion, a colleague (*schoolmates*). **2** (inf or hum) a husband or wife (*she is looking for a mate*). **3** a ship's officer below the captain in rank. **4** a workman 's assistant (*a plumber's mate*). **5** an animal with which another is pair ed for producing offspring (*looking for a suitable mate for her pedigree dog*):—vb to come together for breeding (*animals mating*).

mate'rial adj **1** made of matter . **2** worldly , not spiritual (*a material person/material interests*). **3** (fml) important (*it is not material how he feels about it*):—n **1** the substance out of which a thing is made (*use only good-quality materials in his buildings*). **2** cloth (*coats of a warm material*).

mate'rialism n **1** the belief that nothing exists but matter. **2** the state of being blind to spiritual matters and interested only in worldly things such as wealth (*her materialism led her to marry for money not love*).

mate'rialist n **1** one who believes in materialism. **2** one who is concerned mor e with wealth and comfort than with ideas (*a materialist who has no interest in music or poetry*).

mate'rially adv to a large extent, considerably (*circumstances have changed materially*).

mate'rialize vb **1** to become r eal, to happen (*her dreams of happiness never materialized*). **2** to appear (*a figure of a man materialized out of the mist*).

mater'nal adj of or like a mother (*no maternal feelings*).

mater'nity n motherhood.

mathemat'ical adj having to do with mathematics (*a mathematical problem*).

mathemat'ics n the science of space and number:—n **mathemati'cian**.

mat'ins npl morning prayers.

matinee [mat'-i-nā] n an afternoon performance in a theatre (*the children went to the Saturday matinee of the pantomime*).

mat'ricide n (fml) **1** the killing of one's own mother (*found guilty of matricide*). **2** one who kills his or her mother (*the matricide was jailed for life*).

matriculate vb to enroll or be accepted as a student in a university or college:—n **ma-tricula'tion**.

mat'rimony n (fml) the state of marriage (*joined in holy matrimony*):—adj **matri-mo'nial**.

ma'trix n (pl **ma'trices**) a mould in which hot molten metal is shaped.

ma'tron n **1** (old) an older married woman. **2** (now officially called **senior nursing officer**) a woman in charge of the nursing staff of a hospital. **3** a woman in a school in charge of medical care (*matron bandaged the child's grazed knee*).

ma'tronly adj 1 middle-aged and rather plump (a matronly figure). 2 dignified, serious.

matt, matte adj dull, without gloss or shine (matt paint).

matt'er n 1 that out of which all things ar e made (the different kinds of matter of the universe). 2 a subject of conversation or writings. 3 affair (a family matter/a matter of great importance). 4 the infected liquid contained in a wound or sore (matter oozing from a boil):—vb to be of importance (it doesn't matter if you can't be there).

matt'er-of-fact' adj without imagination or exaggeration, containing facts only (matter-of-fact description).

matt'ing n material used as mats (coconut matting).

matt'ock n a type of pickaxe (break the rocks up with a mattock).

matt'ress n a flat bag filled with soft material or light springs, placed under a sleeper for comfort (prefer a firm mattress).

mature' adj 1 ripe (mature fruit). 2 fully gr own (mature turkeys). 3 fully developed in body or mind (employers looking for mature people):—vb 1 to ripen (fruit maturing early). 2 to become mature (young people beginning to mature). 3 to be due in full (an insurance policy that matures next year).

matu'rity n 1 ripeness. 2 full gr owth or development.

maud'lin adj tearful, foolishly sentimental (maudlin when he is drunk/a maudlin song).

maul vb 1 to injur e badly (mauled by a lion). 2 to handle roughly, often sexually (accuse her boss of mauling her):—n a heavy hammer.

mausoleum [må-sõ-lee'-êm] n a magnificent tomb (mausoleums of ancient kings).

mauve n a purple dye or colour:—adj light purple (mauve eyeshadow).

maw n the mouth or stomach, esp of an animal.

maw'kish adj foolishly sentimental (a mawkish love song).

max'im n a wise saying, a rule for behaviour ('Do as you would be done by' is a well-known maxim).

max'imum n the greatest possible number or amount (the maximum that we can afford):—also adj.

may n hawthorn blossom.

May n the fifth month of the year (the flowers of May).

may'be adv perhaps (maybe he'll come and maybe he won't).

May'day n the first day of May.

mayonnaise [må-yo-nez'] n a sauce of eggs, oil, etc, served with salads or cold dishes (salmon mayonnaise).

may'or n the chief magistrate of a city or borough:—f **may'oress**.

may'pole n a pole decorated with flowers round which people traditionally dance on Mayday.

maze n 1 a confusing system of paths or passages through which it is difficult to find one's way (get lost in the maze at the stately home). 2 a confusing network of streets, etc (lost in a maze of side streets):—vb to confuse, to bewilder.

mazur'ka n 1 a lively dance. 2 music suitable for this dance.

mead n a strong drink made from honey and water (serve pints of mead).

mea'dow n rich grassland (cows grazing in the meadows).

mea'dow-sweet n a sweet-smelling wild plant.

mea'gre adj scanty, not enough (a meagre amount of food/a meagre diet).

meal[1] n food taken at one time (their evening meal).

meal[2] n grain ground to powder.

meal'y adj dry and powdery (mealy potatoes).

meal'y-mouthed' adj not saying what one really thinks (she hinted that she didn't believe us but she was too mealy-mouthed to say it outright).

mean[1] adj 1 (old or lit) poor (mean dwelling). 2 (old or lit) of low birth or behaviour (of mean birth). 3 nasty, unkind over small things (mean to her younger sister). 4 unwilling to spend or give away (too mean to give presents):—n **mean'ness**.

mean[2] vb (pt, pp **meant**) 1 to intend (we did not mean to hurt her). 2 to have a certain purpose (this carpet was meant for the sitting room). 3 to express a certain idea (she did not know what the word meant).

mean[3] adj 1 middle (the mean point). 2 half way between numbers, amounts, extremes, etc, average (the mean annual rainfall):—n 1 the average (the mean of the quantities). 2 a middle state (*finding the mean between being too harsh and too kind*). **3** *pl* that by which something is done or carried out (*means of transport*). **4** *pl* money or property (*a man of means*).

mean'der *vb* to follow a winding course, as a river over very flat land (*paths that meander over the hills*).

mean'ing *n* **1** the idea expressed by a word or words (*a word with several meanings*). **2** the sense in which something is intended to be understood (*the meaning of his action/a look full of meaning*):—*adjs* **mean'ingful**, **mean'ingless**.

mean'time *n* the time between two events (*in the meantime*):—*adv* meanwhile.

mean'while *n* the time between two events, meantime:—*adv* **1** in or during the intervening time. **2** at the same time (*he will be late—meanwhile you will have to wait*).

mea'sles *n* an infectious disease with a red rash (*catch measles from a friend*).

mea'sly *adj* worthless, mean (*a measly sum of money*).

mea'sure *n* **1** a unit by which size, weight etc (*a litre is a measure of capacity*). **2** size, weight, etc, so expressed (*a room of small measure*). **3** an instrument used in finding size, weight, etc (*a tape measure*). **4** (*fml*) the regular rhythm of poetry or music. **5** (*old*) a dance. **6** a course of action (*emergency measures*). **7** a law proposed but not passed (*new taxation measure*):—*vb* **1** to find out size quantity, etc, with an instrument (*measuring the window for new curtains*). **2** to judge (*measure his skill as a pianist*). **3** to weigh out (*measure out a kilo of sugar*):—*n* **mea'surement**.

mea'sured *adj* (*fml*) steady, regular (*a measured pace*).

mea'sureless *adj* too large to be measured.

meat *n* **1** the flesh of animals used as food (*vegetarians who eat no meat*). **2** the essence of something (*the meat of his argument*).

meat'y *adj* **1** full of meat (*meaty pies*). **2** full of information (*a meaty lecture*).

mechan'ic *n* one who looks after a machine (*a car mechanic*).

mechan'ical *adj* **1** done or worked by machine (*mechanical toy cars*). **2** having to do with machinery (*mechanical engineering*). **3** done by

habit, done without awareness (*a mechanical task*).

mechan'ics *n* the science of motion and force.

mech'anism *n* the machinery that makes something work (*something wrong with the mechanism of the washing machine*).

med'al *n* a flat piece of metal with a picture or writing stamped on it, made in memory of some person or event or as a reward of merit (*soldiers given medals for bravery*).

medal'lion *n* a large medal.

med'allist *n.* the winner of a medal (*medallists in the singing competition*).

med'dle *vb* to interfere (*object to her meddling in our private affairs*):—*n* **med'dler**.

med'dlesome *adj* given to interfering (*meddlesome neighbours*).

media *see* **medium.**

mediae'val *same as* **medieval.**

me'dial, **me'dian** *adjs* (*fml*) in the middle (*the medial point*).

me'diate *vb* to try to settle a dispute between others (*mediating between workers and employers*):—*n* **me'diator**.

media'tion *n* an attempt to settle a dispute between others.

med'ical *adj* **1** having to do with medicine (*medical, rather than surgical, treatment*). **2** having to do with the work of a doctor, medicine or healing (*medical care/medical insurance*).

med'icate *vb* (*fml*) **1** to give medicine to. **2** to soak in medicine (*medicated shampoo*).

medica'tion *n* (*fml*) medicine, treatment by medicine (*on medication for a heart condition*).

med'icine *n* **1** the science of bringing the sick back to health (*study medicine*). **2** any substance that cures or heals (*cough medicine*). **3** the science of curing or treating by means other than surgery.

medie'val *adj* having to do with the Middle Ages (*medieval knights*).

me'diocre *adj* not very good, ordinary (*a mediocre performance*):—*n* **medioc'rity**.

med'itate *vb* **1** to think deeply about (*meditating on possible solutions to his problems*). **2** to spend short regular periods in deep, esp religious, thought (*he meditates every day*).

medita'tion *n* deep thought.

med'itative adj (fml) thoughtful (in a meditative mood).

me'dium n 1 (pl **me'dia**) the means by which something is done (expressing his feelings through the medium of paint). 2 (esp in pl) a means by which news is made known (the medium of newspapers/the medium of television/a story put out by the media). 3 (pl **me'diums**) one able to receive messages from spirits at a meeting held for that purpose:—adj middle or average in size, quality, etc (a medium jar of coffee).

med'lar n a tree with a small brown fruit.

med'ley n 1 a mixtur e (a medley of colours). 2 a selection of tunes played as one item (the band played a medley from the 1960s).

meek adj gentle, kind, unresisting (too meek to insist on her rights).

meet vb (pt, pp **met**) 1 to come face to face with, often by chance (I met my neighbour in the local shop). 2 to come together by arrangement (we are meeting for lunch once a week). 3 to pay (unable to meet his debts). 4 to satisf y (meet their requirements/meet their demands). 5 to answer (meet force with force):—n a coming together of huntsmen on horseback with hounds for a hunt.

meet'ing n a coming together for a special purpose (a committee meeting/a meeting of parents and teachers).

meg'alith n a very large stone (often prehistoric):—adj **megalith'ic**.

meg'aphone n a large speaking-trumpet for making the voice louder (the policeman used a megaphone to ask the crowd to move back).

melancho'lia n (old) mental illness caused by worry or depression, depression (a poet who suffered from melancholia).

mel'ancholy n sadness, depression (a tendency to melancholy on dark winter days):—also adj.

mêlée [me'-lā] n (fml) a fight in which everyone seems to be fighting everyone else (police called to a mêlée in the bar).

mellif'luous adj (fml) sweet-sounding (the mellifluous sound of the flute).

mel'low adj 1 soft with ripeness. 2 made kindly by age:—vb to make or become mellow:—n **mell'owness**.

melo'deon n a small hand wind instrument with keys and bellows.

melo'dious adj sweet-sounding (melodious pieces of music).

mel'odrama n a thrilling or sensational play, usu with an improbable plot (Victorian melodramas).

melodramat'ic adj more like a play than real life, theatrical, exaggerated (her melodramatic reaction to the news).

mel'ody n 1 a tune (old-fashioned melodies). 2 the principal part in a piece of harmonized music.

mel'on n a large juicy fruit that grows on the ground (have a slice of melon as the first course of the meal).

melt vb 1 to mak e or become liquid by heat, to soften, to dissolve (melt the butter). 2 to disappear (the crowd melted away). 3 to mak e or become gentler (his heart melted at the sight of the children).

mem'ber n 1 (fml or old) a limb of the body. 2 one of a society or group (become a member of the chess club).

mem'bership n 1 the state of being a member (renew his membership of the chess club). 2 all the members of a society (the membership voted against the idea).

mem'brane n a thin layer of skin covering or connecting parts inside the body (the eyeballs are covered by a thin membrane).

memen'to n an object kept or given to remind one of a person or event (give him a painting of the house as a memento of his holiday).

memo see **memorandum**.

memoir [mem'wär] n 1 a written account of past events. 2 pl the story of a person's life (the memoirs of a famous political leader).

mem'orable adj worth remembering (a memorable occasion/a memorable victory).

memoran'dum n (pl **memoran'da**) (often abbreviated to **me'mo**) a written note of something one wants to remember (a memorandum about staff holidays sent to all heads of department).

memo'rial n an object, often a monument, that helps people to remember a person or event (a memorial to the soldiers who died in the war).

mem'orize vb to learn by heart (memorizing the telephone number/memorize the poem).

mem'ory n **1** the power of the mind to recall past events or to learn things by heart (*have a poor memory*). **2** the mind's store of remembered things (*a memory full of useful facts*). **3** something remembered (*childhood memories*). **4** the part of a computer that stores information.

men'ace n **1** a threat, a person or thing likely to cause harm or danger (*regard him as a menace to their security*). **2** a threat, a show of hostility (*demand money with menaces/ a look full of menace*):—vb (*fml*) to threaten (*a country menaced by talk of war*).

men'acing adj **1** threatening to harm (*menacing letters/a menacing look*). **2** threatening-looking (*a menacing sky*).

mena'gerie n a collection of wild animals for public show.

mend vb **1** to repair (*mend the broken chair*). **2** to improve (*told to mend his ways*). **3** (*inf*) to become well or healthy again (*his broken leg has mended nicely*):—n the hole or crack that has been mended (*see the mend in the shirt*).

menda'cious adj (*fml*) untruthful, given to lying (*taken in by mendacious salesmen*):—n **menda'city**.

men'dicant n (*fml*) a beggar:—n **men'di-cancy**.

me'nial n a servant, esp one who does the more unpleasant jobs in a house (*have a menial to clean up after the party*):—adj humble, unskilled (*have to do all the menial tasks in the hotel*).

meningi'tis n a serious disease affecting the membrane round the brain.

men'struation n a monthly discharge of blood from the womb:—vb **men'struate**.

mensura'tion n (*fml*) the science dealing with ways of measuring size, length, etc.

men'tal adj **1** having to do with the mind (*mental illness*). **2** done in the mind without anything being written (*mental arithmetic*).

mental'ity n **1** mental power (*a person of low mentality*). **2** the way of thinking typical of a person, the character of a person's mind (*I cannot understand the mentality of someone who would attack old women*).

men'thol n a substance made from mint and used as a medicine (*cough sweets containing menthol*).

men'tion vb **1** to speak of, to refer to, to say the name of (*mention various people who had helped him*). **2** to say briefly or indirectly (*she mentioned that she was thinking of leaving*):—n a remark about or reference to.

men'tor n (*fml*) a wise adviser (*his university lecturer was the young writer's mentor*).

men'u n **1** a list of foods that can be ordered for a meal in a restaurant (*the menu was written in French*). **2** a list of options on a computer display.

mer'cantile adj having to do with trade or merchants.

mercantile marine n **1** all the cargo ships of a country. **2** their crews.

mer'cenary adj **1** working for money (*foreign mercenary soldiers*). **2** doing things only to obtain money, greedy for money (*he's too mercenary to help anyone free of charge*):—n a soldier hired to fight for a country not his own.

mer'cer n (*old*) one who buys and sells silks, cottons, etc.

mer'chandise n goods bought and sold (*poor-quality merchandise*).

mer'chant n one who buys and sells goods in large quantities (*a wine merchant*).

mer'ciful adj showing mercy, forgiving (*a merciful judge/be merciful to the criminal because of her youth*).

mer'ciless adj pitiless (*a merciless tyrant*).

mercu'rial adj quickly changing mood (*a mercurial personality*).

mer'cury n a liquid silvery-white metal.

mer'cy n kindness and pity, forgiveness, willingness not to punish (*show mercy to his captured enemy/treat the wrongdoers with mercy because of their youth*).

mere[1] adj no more or less than (*a mere child/win the election by a mere ten votes/learn a mere £3 per hour*).

mere[2] n (*fml*) a lake (*a house by the mere*).

mere'ly adv only (*she's merely a child*).

meretri'cious adj (*fml*) showy, superficially attractive, garish (*meretricious cheap jewellery*).

merge vb **1** to join together to make one (*they merged the two branches of the bank*). **2** to become part of a larger whole (*firms that have merged*).

mer'ger n the joining together of two or more businesses (a merger of two banks).

merid'ian n 1 an imaginary line encircling the earth from pole to pole. 2 the position of the sun at midday. 3 the time of greatest success or power (his fame reached its meridian in his old age).

meringue [me-rang'] n a light sweet or cake made from sugar and white of egg (a pie with a topping of meringue).

meri'no n 1 a type of sheep. 2 its wool, or the soft cloth made from it.

merit n 1 the quality of deserving praise or reward, worth or excellence (recognize the merit of the performance). 2 good point (a merit of the system). 3 pl good qualities:—vb to deserve.

merito'rious adj (fml) deserving praise or reward.

mer'maid n an imaginary sea creature, half woman and half fish:—also **mer'man**.

mer'ry adj joyous, happy, full of fun (a merry mood/a merry evening):—n **mer'riment**.

mer'ry-go-round n a large revolving circular platform with seats in the shape of animals, etc, on which people may ride for amusement at a fair.

mesh n 1 the space between the threads of a net. 2 pl the threads of a net.

mes'merism n the power to mesmerize:—n **mes'merist**.

mes'merize vb 1 (old) to hypnotize. 2 to hold the complete attention of and make seemingly unable to move or speak (they seemed mesmerized by her beauty).

mess¹ n 1 a muddle (the files are in a mess). 2 a dirty or untidy state (the house is in a mess):—vb 1 to make dirty or untidy (mess up the house). 2 to do badly or inefficiently (mess up the job).

mess² n 1 a company of people who take their meals together as in the armed services. 2 the place where they eat (the officers' mess). 3 (old) a dish of food, esp soft or semi-liquid food:—vb to eat in mess.

mess'age n 1 information or news sent to another by word of mouth or in writing (send a message of congratulation/receive a telephone message cancelling the meeting). 2 a piece of instruction, an important idea (a story with a message).

mess'enger n one who bears a message (the king's messenger).

Messi'ah n 1 the deliverer promised by God to the Jews. 2 Jesus Christ.

Messrs [mes'-êrz] npl plural of **Mr**, short for **Messieurs**, usu found in addresses on envelopes (Messrs Jones and Smith).

met pt of **meet**.

meta'bolism n the system of chemical changes in the cells of the body that provide energy (the rate of metabolism has slowed down).

met'al n 1 a class of substances, such as gold, copper, iron, tin, etc (metal boxes). 2 broken stones used in road-making.

metal'lic adj of or like metal (metallic paint).

metal'lurgy n the art of working with metals:—n **metal'lurgist**.

metamor'phosis n (metamor'phoses) 1 a change in form or kind (a caterpillar's metamorphosis into a butterfly). 2 a complete change (she's undergone a metamorphosis since she married).

metaphor n a way of comparing two things by identifying them and speaking about one as if it were the other ('The camel is the ship of the desert' is a metaphor):—adjs **metapho'ric**, **metaphor'ical**.

metaphys'ics n the study of the nature of existence and of the mind:—adj **meta-phys'ical**.

meta'thesis n the changing in order of two successive letters (e.g. lisp for lips).

mete vb (old) to measure (mete out punishment).

me'teor n a shining body that can be seen moving across the sky, a shooting star.

meteor'ic adj rapid but often short-lasting (his meteoric rise to fame).

me'teorite n a meteor that falls to earth as a piece of rock.

meteorolog'ical adj having to do with meteorology (meteorological charts/meteorological changes).

meteorol'ogy n the study or science of the earth's weather:—n **meteorol'ogist**.

me'ter n an instrument for measuring things (a gas meter).

methinks' vb (old or hum) it seems to me (methinks he is not telling the truth).

meth'od n 1 a way of doing something (their method of doing business). 2 an orderly way of arranging or doing things (a system lacking method).

method'ical adj orderly in following a plan or system (a methodical person/a methodical approach).

Meth'odist *n* a member of a Christian sect founded by John Wesley.

meth'yl *n* a substance from which wood-alcohol can be made.

meth'ylated spir'it *n* a type of alcohol unfit for drinking but used for burning, cleaning, etc (*use methylated spirit in a burner to keep the food hot*).

metic'ulous *adj* extremely careful about details or small matters (*prepare the accounts with meticulous attention*).

métier [mā'-ti-ā] *n* **1** one's trade or business (*selling things is his métier*). **2** the thing at which one is best (*making people laugh is his métier*).

meton'ymy *n* a figure of speech in which one word is replaced by another connected with it (e.g. *water* by *glass*).

me'tre *n* **1** the systematic arrangement of stressed and unstressed syllables that give poetic rhythm. **2** a measur e of length (39.37 inches) in the metric system (*measure the cloth in metres*).

met'rical *adj* (*of poetry*) having a regular rhythm or metre.

metric system *n* a system of weights and measures in which each unit is divisible into 10 parts.

met'ronome *n* an instrument with a pendulum that can be set to mark time correctly for a musician (*a metronome on the piano*).

metro'polis *n* (*fml or hum*) a large city, esp the capital (*the metropolises of Europe/our local town is not exactly a metropolis*).

metropol'itan *adj* belonging to a metropolis (*the metropolitan police force/the metropolitan area*):—*n* a bishop with authority over the other bishops in a certain area.

met'tle *n* spirit, courage (*admire their mettle in trying again*):—*adj* **mett'lesome**:—**on one's mettle** trying to do one's best.

mew[1] *n* a seagull.

mew[2], **miaow** *ns* the cry of a cat:—*vb* to emit a high-pitched cry, as a cat (*hear a cat mewing*).

mew[3] *vb* (*fml*) to shut up (in) (*persons mewed up for life*):—*npl* **mews** a row or square formerly containing stables, now often converted into houses (*live in a mews flat*).

mez'zo-sopra'no *n* a female voice between soprano and contralto (*a musical role for a mezzo-soprano*).

mez'zotint *n* **1** a method of engraving on copperplate. **2** a pictur e made from such an engraving (*a mezzotint of the cathedral*).

miaow *see* **mew**.

mias'ma *n* (*pl* **mias'mata** *or* **mias'mas**) **1** a thick unhealthy mist, as from marshes. **2** an evil and weakening influence (*the miasma of despair*).

mica [mī'-ka] *n* a shiny mineral, easily broken into flakes or thin sheets.

mice *see* **mouse**.

Michaelmas [mik'-êl-mas] *n* the feast of St Michael, 29th September.

mi'crobe *n* a tiny living creature, esp one causing disease (*scientists examining microbes under microscopes*).

mic'rochip *n* a very small piece of a material, usually silicon, which acts as a semi-conductor and forms the base on which an electronic circuit is printed.

mi'crocosm *n* a little world, a small copy (*a fish tank that is a microcosm of life on the sea bed*).

micro'meter *n* an instrument for measuring small distances.

mi'crophone *n* in a telephone or radio, the instrument by which the sound of the voice is changed into electric waves, used to make sounds louder (*the news reporter spoke into a microphone/the singer used a microphone so that everyone in the hall could hear*).

mi'croscope *n* an instrument containing an arrangement of curved glasses by means of which very tiny objects can be seen larger and studied.

microscop'ic *adj* **1** ver y small, tiny, seen only with the help of a microscope (*microscopic bacteria*). **2** (*inf*) tiny (*a microscopic improvement*).

mic'rowave *n* a microwave oven, an oven which cooks or heats up food very quickly using electromagnetic radiation:— *vb* to cook or heat in a microwave.

mid *adj* having to do with the middle, in the middle of (*in mid-air, in mid-career*).

mid'day *n* noon or the time about noon (*lunch at midday*).

mid'den *n* a heap of dung or rubbish.

mid'dle *adj* equally distant from the ends or limits (*the middle seat in the row*):—*n* the centre, the middle part or point (*stand in the middle of the circle*).

mid'dle-aged' *adj* neither old nor young, between youth and old age (*a middle-aged man and woman*).

Middle Ages *npl* the period between AD 500 and AD 1500 in European history.

mid'dle class' *n* those who are well enough off to live in comfort, but are neither wealthy nor of noble birth:—*adj* **mid'dle-class** having to do with the middle class (*political policies appealing more to middle-class voters than to the working class*).

Middle East *n* Asiatic countries west of India and China.

mid'dleman *n* a trader who buys goods in large quantities from the maker or producer and sells them again at a profit to shopkeepers.

middle watch *n* (on a ship) the watch between midnight and 4 a.m.

mid'dleweight *n* a boxer who fights in the 10^1/$_2$–11^1/$_2$ stone class.

mid'dling *adj* (*inf*) neither very good nor very bad, average (*of middling ability*).

midge *n* a small flying insect that bites (*she is very itchy from bites by midges*).

mid'get *n* a very small or unusually small person (*she was tiny compared with the rest of her family so they called her the midget*).

mid'land *adj* far from the coasts or borders of a country:—*npl* **Mid'lands** the central parts of England (*the industrial Midlands*).

mid'night *n* twelve o'clock at night (*go to bed at midnight*).

mid'riff *n* the part of the body containing the muscles separating the stomach from the lungs (*a sweater that left her midriff bare*).

mid'shipman *n* a naval rank between cadet and sub-lieutenant.

midst *n* the middle (*in the midst of the battle*).

mid'summer *n* the middle of summer.

Midsummer Day *n* 24th June.

mid'way *n* halfway (*their house is midway between the two towns*):—*also adv*.

mid'wife *n* (*pl* **mid'wives**) a person who assists a mother at the birth of a baby (*the midwife delivered the baby*).

midwif'ery *n* the knowledge or study of the work of a midwife.

midwin'ter *n* the middle of winter, the time about 21st December (*the severe cold of midwinter*).

mien [meen] *n* (*fml or lit*) one's expression or appearance (*of a solemn mien*).

might *n* power, strength (*crushed by the might of the enemy army*).

might'y *adj* **1** powerful, str ong (*a mighty blow/a mighty nation*). **2** huge (*a mighty oak tree*).

mignonette [min-yon-et'] *n* a plant with sweet-smelling flowers.

mi'graine *n* a severe headache, often accompanied by a feeling of sickness.

mi'grant *n* one who migrates:—*also adj*.

migrate' *vb* **1** to move one's home fr om one land to another, to go from one place to another (*tribes that migrated to find food*). **2** (*of birds*) to move to another place at the season when its climate is suitable:—*n* **migra'tion**.

migra'tory *adj* used to migrating (*migratory birds, such as swallows*).

Mika'do *n* a former name for the emperor of Japan.

milch [milsh] *adj* giving milk (*a milch cow*).

mild *adj* **1** gentle, mer ciful, not severe (*a mild punishment/a mild sentence*). **2** calm (*a mild sea*). **3** (*of weather*) not cold (*mild days in late spring*):—*n* **mild'ness**.

mil'dew *n* a tiny but destructive growth that appears and spreads on leaves or on damp paper, leather, etc (*mildew on old books*).

mile *n* a measure of length (= 1760 yards or 16 kilometres) (*distances measured in miles*).

mile'age *n* distance in miles (*what mileage has the car done?*).

mile'stone' *n* **1** a stone by the r oadside telling the distance in miles to places in the neighbourhood. **2** a time at which one can consider the progress made (*reach a milestone in his career*).

mil'itant *adj* **1** fighting, warlik e (*a militant nation*). **2** active in a campaign (*militant members of the feminist movement*).

mil'itarism *n* belief in the use of armies or war in politics (*the militarism of the country in invading others*):—*n* **mil'itarist**.

mil'itary *adj* having to do with soldiers or battles (*a military force*):—*n* the army, soldiers (*join the military*).

mil'itate *vb* **1** to act or stand (against) (*militating against injustice*). **2** to act as a r eason against (*his criminal record militated against him/the recession militated against house sales*).

mili'tia *n* a reserve army, consisting of people trained in the use of arms, and called out in an emergency:—*n* **mili'tiaman**.

milk *n* **1** the secreted liquid on which female mammals feed their young (*a baby getting milk from its mother*). **2** such milk produced by cows or goats and drunk by humans or made into butter and cheese (*have bottles of milk delivered*):—*vb* to draw milk from (e.g. a cow).

milk'maid *n* a woman who milks cows.

milk'man *n* a man who sells milk.

milk'sop *n* a soft, unmanly fellow (*the boy was too much of a milksop to climb the tree with the others*).

milk'tooth *n* one of a child's first set of teeth (*baby's first milktooth came through*).

milk'y *adj* **1** like milk (*a milky liquid*). **2** containing much milk (*a milky drink*).

Milky Way *n* a bright band across the night sky, made up of countless stars.

mill *n* **1** a machine for grinding corn, coffee, etc. **2** the building in which corn is ground into flour. **3** a factory (*steel mills/paper mills/cotton mills*):—*vb* **1** to grind (*mill corn*). **2** to stamp a coin and cut grooves around its edge.

mill'board *n* a thick cardboard.

millen'nium *n* (*pl* **millen'nia** *or* **millen'ni-ums**) **1** a period of 1000 years. **2** according to the Bible, the 1000 years for which Christ will reign on earth. **3** a hoped-for period of perfect happiness (*looking forward to a millennium of full employment*).

mil'lepede *n* an insect with many feet.

mill'er *n* one who keeps a corn mill.

mil'let *n* a grass bearing eatable grain (*buy millet for his budgerigar*).

mill'hand *n* a factory worker (*millhands no longer able to find work*).

mil'liard *n* a thousand million (*a milliard stars in the sky*).

mil'ligram(me) *n* the thousandth part of a gram (*measure the drug in milligrams*).

mil'limetre *n* the thousandth part of a metre.

mil'liner *n* one who makes or sells ladies' hats (*the number of milliners has decreased with the decline in hat-wearing*).

mil'linery *n* hats made or sold by a milliner.

mil'lion *n* **1** a thousand thousand. **2** (*inf*) a very great many (*excuses by the million*).

millionaire' *n* one possessing a million or more pounds or dollars (*lottery winners who are now millionaires*).

mil'lipede *same as* **millepede**.

mill'pond *n* a pond whose water is used to drive a mill (*the sea was as calm as a millpond*).

mill'race *n* the stream of water driving a millwheel.

mill'stone *n* **1** a heavy round stone used for grinding corn into flour. **2** a very heavy load or handicap (*she has the millstone of a lazy husband*).

mill'wheel *n* the large wheel, turned by water power, that drives the machinery inside a mill.

mime *n* **1** a play without words carried on by facial expressions, gestures and actions. **2** using actions without language (*we showed her by mime that we wanted to find a restaurant as we did not speak the language*):—*vb* to act without speaking (*he mimed that he wanted a drink*).

mimet'ic *adj* imitative, copying (*the monkey's mimetic behaviour*).

mim'ic *vb* (**mim'icked, mim'icking**) to imitate, esp in order to make fun of (*mimics his way of walking to amuse her classmates*):—*n* one who imitates.

mim'icry *n* imitation (*impressed by the performer's mimicry of the prime minister*).

mimo'sa *n* a tree with sweet-smelling flowers.

min'aret *n* the tower of a Muslim mosque.

min'atory *adj* (*fml*) threatening (*minatory gestures*).

mince *vb* **1** to cut into very small pieces (*mince up the beef*). **2** to walk with unnaturally short steps (*mincing along in very tight skirts*). **3** (*old*) to pronounce words in an affected way:—*n* minced meat:—**not to mince matters** to speak the plain truth (*not to mince matters, he's a liar*).

mince'meat *n* **1** minced meat. **2** currants, etc, chopped up small and mixed with spices (*pies made with mincemeat for Christmas*).

mince-pie' *n* a pie filled with mincemeat.

mind *n* **1** the power by which human beings understand, think, feel, will, etc (*have a sharp mind/an adult with the mind of a child*). **2** a person of great mental ability (*one of the great minds of the century*). **3** memor y (*unable to call his name to mind*):—*vb* **1** to tak e care of (*mind the baby*). **2** to tak e heed, to be careful (*mind you don't fall on the ice*). **3** to object to (*I do not mind if you leave early*):—**mind one's p's and q's** to be careful what one says or does (*mind your p's and q's when you visit his parents*):—**mind one's own business** not to interfere in another's affairs (*he told his neighbour to mind her own business when she asked him if he was still working*).

mind'ed *adj* desirous, inclined (*serious-minded*).

mind'ful *adj* not forgetful, paying attention to (*always mindful of possible dangers*).

mind'less *adj* unthinking, stupid (*a mindless act of violence*).

mine[1] *poss pron* belonging to me (*the pen is mine*).

mine[2] *n* **1** a deep hole made in the earth so that minerals can be taken from beneath its surface (*a coal mine/a gold mine*). **2** a container filled with explosive charge to blow something up (*military tanks blown up by enemy mines*). **3** a person or place from which much may be obtained (*a mine of information*):—*vb* **1** to mak e tunnels into and under the earth (*the area is extensively mined*). **2** to dig for in a mine (*mining coal*). **3** to place explosive mines in position (*the enemy mined the beaches*). **4** to blow up with mines (*ships mined in the war*).

mine'field *n* **1** an ar ea in which there are many mineral mines. **2** an ar ea in which many explosive mines are placed. **3** something full of hidden dangers (*her situation at work is a minefield*).

mine'layer *n* a ship that places mines in a minefield.

mi'ner *n* one who works in a mine (*a coal-miner*).

min'eral *n* an inorganic substance found naturally in the earth and mined (*coal and salt are minerals*):—*adj* having to do with minerals (*the country's mineral wealth*).

mineral water *n* water that comes from a natural spring and contains minerals, sometimes sold still and sometimes carbonated (*a bottle of fizzy mineral water*).

mineral'ogy *n* the study of minerals:—*n* **mineral'ogist**.

mine'-sweeper *n* a ship that clears an area of mines.

min'gle *vb* **1** to mix together (*comments that mingled praise with blame*). **2** to mix with (*police mingling with the crowds*).

min'iature *n* a very small painting (*a miniature of the artist's mother*):—*adj* very small, tiny (*a miniature bottle of whisky/a miniature model railway*).

min'im *n* a musical note (= $1/2$ semibreve).

min'imize *vb* to make seem less important (*minimizing the problems*).

min'imum *n* the smallest amount possible (*we want the minimum of fuss*).

min'ion *n* **1** a slave-lik e follower or employee, a person who always does as his or her employer orders (*the manager and his minions treated the rest of us badly*).

min'ister *n* **1** a person in char ge of a government department (*Minister of Transport*). **2** the principal representative of a government in another country. **3** a member of the cler gy (*the minister's sermon*):—*vb* to give help, to serve.

ministe'rial *adj* having to do with a minister (*ministerial posts in the government*).

min'istry *n* **1** the cler gy (*join the ministry*). **2** a department of government in charge of a minister (*the Ministry of Defence*).

mink *n* a small stoat-like animal valued for its fur (*breed mink in captivity/a mink coat*).

min'now *n* a very small freshwater fish.

mi'nor *adj* **1** smaller , of less importance (*minor issues*). **2** (*mus*) lower than the corresponding major by a half step (*a minor key*):—*n* **1** a person under age (in Britain, less than 18 years of age) (*he committed murder while still a minor*). **2** a minor k ey, interval or scale (*played in A minor*).

minority *n* **1** the state of being under age. **2** the smaller number in a group or assembly, less than half (*a minority of people voted against the suggestion/the objectors were in the minority*).

min'ster *n* a large church, a cathedral (*York Minster*).

min'strel *n* **1** in olden times, a wandering singer and poet. **2** (*old*) a singer.

min'strelsy *n* a collection of songs.

mint[1] *n* **1** a place wher e coins are made, esp by the government. **2** (*inf*) a large amount (*he* earns a mint):—*vb* to make coins (*mint new 10p pieces*).

mint[2] *n* a sweet-smelling herb whose leaves are used as flavouring in cooking (*lamb flavoured with mint*).

minuet' *n* (*old*) **1** a slow , graceful dance. **2** music for this dance.

mi'nus *prep* less:—*adj* **1** less (*ten minus three is seven*). **2** (*inf*) not having (*we are minus two members of staff*):—*n* the sign of subtraction (–).

minute[1] [mi- *or* mî-nût'] *adj* **1** ver y small (*minute quantities of the drug*). **2** exact (*minute attention to detail*).

minute[2] [mi'-nêt] *n* **1** the sixtieth part of an hour . **2** the sixtieth part of a degr ee. **3** a short time (*I'll be with you in a minute*). **4** a written note or comment. **5** *pl* a short account of what was discussed and decided at a meeting:—*vb* to make a written note of.

minu'tia *n* (*pl* **minu'tiae**) a small detail (*get to the main point and ignore the minutiae*).

minx *n* a forward or cheeky girl (*the minx told her grandmother to keep quiet*).

mir'acle *n* **1** an extraor dinary event brought about by the interference of God with the natural course of events. **2** any extraor dinary event for which there is no known explanation (*it is a miracle that the family can survive on that income*).

miracle play *n* a play that shows part of the Bible story or the life of a saint.

mirac'ulous *adj* **1** caused by a miracle, mar vellous (*the miraculous cures of Christ*). **2** amazing, extraordinary (*his miraculous recovery*).

mirage [mi-räzh'] *n* imaginary objects (e.g. water, trees) that appear real to a traveller because of certain atmospheric conditions, such as shimmer caused by heat (*they thought they saw an oasis in the desert but it was a mirage*).

mire *n* (*fml or lit*) wet, muddy ground, mud (*vehicles stuck in the mire*).

mir'ror *n* a looking-glass:—*vb* to reflect as in a mirror.

mirth *n* laughter, merriment (*collapse with mirth at the antics of the clown*):—*adjs* **mirth'ful**, **mirth'less**.

mi'ry *adj* (*fml or old*) muddy.

misadven'ture *n* (*fml or old*) an unlucky happening (*death by misadventure*).

misalli'ance *n* (*fml*) a marriage between people not suited to each other (*they are now divorced, but it was a misalliance from the start*).

mis'anthrope, misan'thropist *ns* (*fml*) one who hates mankind (*a misanthrope who stays away from other people as much as possible*):—*adj* **misanthrop'ic**:—*n* **mis-an'thropy**.

misapply' *vb* (*fml*) to put to a wrong use (*misapplied the rule*).

misapprehend' *vb* (*fml*) to misunderstand (*misapprehend their intentions*):—*n* **mis-apprehen'sion**.

misappro'priate *vb* (*fml*) to put to a wrong use, to use dishonestly for oneself (*misappropriating the firm's money and running off with it*).

misbehave' *vb* to behave badly:—*n* **mis-beha'viour**.

miscal'culate *vb* to work out an answer or likely result wrongly (*miscalculating the cost of the journey*):—*n* **miscalcula'tion**.

miscall' *vb* to call by the wrong name (*a tendency to miscall the pupils*).

miscar'riage *n* **1** (*fml*) failure (*the miscarriage of his financial schemes*). **2** the loss of a baby fr om the womb before it is able to survive:—**miscarriage of justice** a mistaken finding by a court that an innocent person is guilty of a crime.

miscar'ry *vb* **1** to turn out wr ongly, to be unsuccessful (*his plans miscarried*). **2** to have a miscarriage (*the expectant mother miscarried*).

miscella'neous *adj* mixed, of different kinds (*a miscellaneous collection of old books*).

miscell'any *n* (*fml*) a mixture, a collection of things of different kinds (*a miscellany of old books*).

mischance' *n* (*fml*) an unlucky happening (*killed by mischance*).

mis'chief *n* **1** (*fml*) harm done on purpose (*the mischief done to his property by vandals*). **2** children's naughtiness (*children punished for their mischief*).

mis'chievous *adj* **1** harmful, intended to cause trouble (*mischievous gossip*). **2** naughty (*mischievous children*).

misconceive' *vb* (*fml*) to misunderstand, to have a wrong opinion of.

misconcep'tion *n* a mistaken idea, misunderstanding (*she was under the misconception that he was unmarried*).

miscon'duct n bad or wrong behaviour (*workers sacked for misconduct on duty*):—vb **misconduct'** 1 (*fml*) to conduct wrongly (*misconduct the trial*). 2 to behave (oneself) badly.

misconstrue' vb (*fml*) to give a wrong meaning or significance to (*misconstruing his instructions*):—n **misconstruc'tion**.

miscount' vb to count wrongly (*miscount the number of people present*):—*also n*.

mis'creant n (*fml*) a wicked person (*miscreants sent to prison by the judge*).

misdeal' vb (*pt, pp* **misdealt'**) to make a mistake in giving out playing cards:—*also n*.

misdeed' n (*fml*) a wrongful action, a crime (*punished for their misdeeds*).

misdemean'our n (*fml*) an act that breaks the law, a petty crime (*fined for the misdemeanour*). 2 an act of misbehaviour (*the child's misdemeanour*).

misdirect' vb to give wrong instructions to (*accused of misdirecting the jury*):—n **misdirec'tion**.

mi'ser n one who dislikes spending money (*too much of a miser even to eat properly*).

mis'erable adj 1 very unhappy (*a miserable child/feel miserable*). 2 causing unhappiness or discomfort (*a miserable day/a miserable place to live*). 3 low in quality or quantity (*a miserable performance/a miserable amount of money*).

mi'serly adj very mean (*a miserly employer*).

mis'ery n great unhappiness or suffering (*the misery of their existence*).

misfire' vb 1 (*of guns*) to fail to go off. 2 to fail (*plans that misfired*):—*also n*.

misfit' n a person unsuited to his or her circumstances (*as a shy person, he is a misfit in the sales industry*).

misfor'tune n 1 bad luck (*have the misfortune to have his car break down*). 2 a piece of bad luck (*suffer one misfortune after another*).

misgiving n a feeling of fear, doubt or mistrust (*last-minute misgivings about marrying someone whom he did not know well*).

misguid'ed adj showing bad judgment (*a misguided attempt to help*).

mishan'dle vb (*fml*) to manage badly (*mishandling the situation*).

mis'hap n an unlucky event, usu not serious (*he had a mishap parking the car*).

misinform' vb (*fml*) to give wrong information (*we were misinformed about the time of the meeting*).

misinter'pret vb to give a wrong meaning to (*misinterpreted what they were asked to do*):—n **misinterpreta'tion**.

misjudge' vb to judge wrongly, to form a wrong opinion (*you are misjudging him—he is a very pleasant person*).

mislay' vb (*pt, pp* **mislaid'**) to put (something) down and forget where one has put it (*mislay the book that she was reading*).

mislead' vb (*pt, pp* **misled'**) to deceive, to give the wrong idea to (*he tried to mislead the police by giving wrong evidence*).

misman'age vb to manage badly (*mismanaging his finances*):—n **misman'agement**.

misno'mer n a wrong or unsuitable name ('*assistant' was a misnomer—she never did a thing to help me do the job*).

miso'gynist n one who hates women (*he never married—he's a misogynist who even hates his sister*).

misplace' vb to put in a wrong place (*misplace a book*).

mis'print n a mistake in printing (*correct the misprints before the book is published*):—vb **misprint'**.

mispronounce' vb to pronounce wrongly (*mispronouncing his name*):—n **mispro-nuncia'tion**.

misquote' vb to quote wrongly, to make mistakes in trying to repeat another's words:—n **misquota'tion**.

misread [mis-reed'] vb (*pt, pp* **misread'**) to read wrongly (*misread the instructions*).

misrepresent' vb to give an untrue account of another's ideas or opinions (*in court he misrepresented what I had said*):—n **misrepresenta'tion**.

misrule' vb to rule or govern badly:—*also n*.

miss¹ vb 1 to fail to hit, find, meet, catch or notice (*the batsman missed the ball/we were meant to meet but we missed each other/he missed the bus*). 2 to leave out (*he missed a bit when he was painting*). 3 to regret the loss or absence of (*she missed her friend when he went abroad*):—n a failure to hit or catch.

miss² n (*pl* **mis'ses**) (*old*) an unmarried woman, a girl.

mis'sal n an RC prayerbook containing prayers, etc, for Mass.

mis'sel-thrush' n a large thrush that eats mistletoe berries.

misshap'en adj badly formed, deformed, ugly (*misshapen oak trees*).

mis'sile n 1 any object thr own or fired from a gun to do harm. 2 an explosive flying weapon with its own engine, which can be aimed at distant objects (*nuclear missiles*).

mis'sing adj lost (*the missing letter/his son has gone missing*).

mis'sion n 1 persons sent to carr y out a certain task (*a British trade mission sent to America*). 2 the task itself (*the group's mission was to blow up the enemy bridge*). 3 one's chief aim in life (*her mission is to help people*). 4 a gr oup of persons sent to a foreign land to teach their religion. 5 the building(s) in which they live (*the mission also provides medical services*).

mis'sionary n one sent to a foreign land to teach his or her religion:—*also adj.*

mis'sive n (fml or hum) a letter (*he received a missive from his ex-wife's lawyer*).

misspell' vb to spell wrongly (*she misspelled his name*):—n **misspell'ing**.

misspend' vb (pt, pp **misspent'**) to spend wastefully or unprofitably (*she misspent her dead mother's savings*).

misstate' vb to state wrongly (*misstating his qualifications on the form*):—n **misstate'-ment**.

mist n 1 rain in fine, tiny dr ops. 2 a cloud r esting on the ground (*cars having to drive slowly in the mist*).

mistake' vb 1 to understand wr ongly (*she mistook what he said*). 2 to confuse one person or thing with another (*she mistook him for his brother*):—n an error.

mistak'en adj in error, wrong (*a mistaken interpretation of the situation*).

mis'ter n the title put before a man's name (usu written **Mr**).

mistime' vb to time badly, to do something at a wrong time (*they mistimed their arrival*).

mis'tletoe n an evergreen plant with white berries (*hang bunches of mistletoe at Christmas*).

mis'tress n 1 (*usu written* **Mrs** [mis'-êz]) the title put before the name of a married woman. 2 a woman having charge or control (of) (*she is the mistress of the house*). 3 a woman teacher . 4 a woman who is the lover of a man and sometimes maintained by him but not married to him (*his wife does not know he has a mistress*).

mistrust' vb to suspect, to doubt:—*also n.*

misty adj 1 dark ened or clouded by mist (*misty hills*). 2 not clear (*her eyes were misty with tears*).

misunderstand' vb to take a wrong meaning from (*they misunderstood his directions and got lost*).

misunderstand'ing n a disagreement, esp one due to failure to see another's meaning or intention (*they have not spoken to each other for years, and it was all because of a misunderstanding*).

misuse [mis-ûz'] vb to use in the wrong way, to use badly (*the machine broke because they misused it*):—n [mis-ûs'] improper or wrong use (*his misuse of the firm's money*).

mite n 1 a type of ver y small insect. 2 a small child (*a poor little mite dressed in rags*). 3 a ver y small amount.

mit'igate vb 1 to mak e less serious, to excuse to some extent (*the lawyer hoped that the fact that the accused murdered in self-defence would mitigate the offence*). 2 to mak e less severe (*a drug for mitigating the pain*):—n **mitiga'tion**.

mi'tre n 1 the tall pointed headgear worn by bishops. 2 a way of joining two boar ds meeting at right angles.

mitt, mitt'en ns 1 a type of glove that covers the hand but not the fingers and thumb. 2 a glove without separate places for the fingers (*the little girl wore mittens and a matching hat*).

mix vb 1 to put together to form one (*mix the butter and sugar*). 2 to go together or blend successfully (*oil and water do not mix*). 3 to join in (with others) (*she did not mix at the party*).

mixed adj 1 made up of differ ent things or kinds (*mixed feelings*). 2 r elating to people of different sexes (*a mixed school/mixed doubles at tennis*).

mix'ture n the result of mixing things or people toether (*a mixture of eggs, flour and milk/a mixture of nationalities*).

miz'zen n a sail on the rearmost (mizzen) mast of a ship:—n **miz'zen-mast**.

mnemonic [ne-mon'-ik] adj helping the memory:—n something easily remembered that helps one to remember something else (*mnemonics to remind him how to spell certain words*).

moan *vb* **1** to mak e a low sound expressing sorrow or pain (*moaning in agony*). **2** (*inf*) to complain (*she's always moaning about the weather*):—*also n*.

moat *n* a trench, often filled with water, around a castle or fort.

mob *n* a disorderly crowd (*football mobs*):—*vb* (**mobbed'**, **mob'bing**) to crowd around in a disorderly way (*the filmstar was mobbed by photographers*).

mo'bile *adj* **1** that can be moved (*a mobile library*). **2** easily moved (*mobile office units*). **3** able to move easily, active (*old people no longer mobile*):—*n* **1** a decoration which hangs from the ceiling by threads or wire and which has attached to it several small objects which move when the surrounding air moves (*a mobile made of plastic fish*). **2** a mobile phone.

mobile phone *n* a hand-held, portable phone which works by means of radio networks.

mobil'ity *n* ability to move about (*old people annoyed at their lack of mobility*).

mo'bilize *vb* **1** to call upon to ser ve as soldiers (*officers told to mobilize their men*). **2** to or ganize for a particular reason (*mobilizing supporters for the party rally*).—*n* **mobiliza'tion**.

mocc'asin *n* a shoe or slipper made of deerskin or sheepskin.

mock *vb* **1** to mak e fun of (*they mocked his attempts to improve himself*). **2** to imitate in order to make appear foolish (*the boys mocked the way the lame old man walked*):—*adj* false, not real (*mock leather*).

mock'ery *n* **1** the act of mocking. **2** a person or thing mocked (*make a mockery of his attempts*).

mock hero'ic *adj* imitating the grand style of writing when dealing with an unimportant subject.

mock'ingbird *n* a type of thrush found in North America that imitates the song of other birds, etc.

mock turtle soup *n* a soup made from calf's head.

mode *n* **1** (*fml*) the way of doing something (*his mode of expressing himself*). **2** (*old*) a fashion in clothes (*Paris modes*).

mod'el *n* **1** a person or thing to be copied (*use the essay as a model*). **2** a copy, usu smaller, of a person or thing (*models of aircraft*). **3** a small copy of (e.g. a building or ship made from the plan to show what the finished object will look like) (*show would-be buyers a model of the housing estate*). **4** a living person who sits or stands still to let an artist draw him or her (*act as a model for the art class*). **5** one employed to display clothes by wearing them (*the models at the Paris fashion show*). **6** an artificial figur e used in display (*shop-window models*):—*adj* worth copying, perfect (*model behaviour*):—*vb* (**mod'elled**, **mod'elling**) **1** to give shape to (*model the clay into a bowl*). **2** to mak e a model of (*model the head of the famous man in clay*). **3** to wear clothes to show to possible buyers (*model the new season's fashions*).

mo'dem [mō'-dem] *n* a piece of equipment that links a computer to the telephone system so that information can be sent to other computers.

mod'erate *vb* **1** to pr event from going to extremes (*moderate your demands*). **2** to lessen (*the storm is moderating*):—*adj* **1** not going to extremes (*of moderate views*). **2** within sensible limits (*moderate prices*). **3** average (*someone of only moderate ability*).

modera'tion *n* avoidance of extremes, self-control (*drink alcohol within moderation*).

mod'ern *adj* **1** belonging to the pr esent day (*modern language changes*). **2** belonging to r ecent centuries (*modern history*). **3** up-to -date (*parents who have modern ideas on education*):—*n* **moder'nity**.

mod'ernize *vb* to bring up-to-date (*modernizing machinery to keep ahead of the competition*).

mod'est *adj* **1** not having too high an opinion of oneself (*a very modest young woman*). **2** not boastful (*modest about her success*). **3** decent (*always modest in her dress*). **4** not ver y large (*a modest increase in salary*):—*n* **mod'esty**.

mod'icum *n* (*fml*) a small amount (*not a modicum of truth in what he says*).

modifica'tion *n* alteration, a small change (*minor modifications to the house plans*).

mod'ify *vb* **1** to alter in part (*modified the design*). **2** to mak e less severe (*modify his extreme views*).

mo'dish *adj* (*fml*) fashionable (*a modish style of dress*).

mod'ulate vb **1** to raise or lower the tone or pitch of the voice when speaking or singing (*actors learning to modulate their voices*). **2** in music, to change from one key to another:—*n* **modula'tion**.

mod'ule *n* one of several parts that together form a larger structure.

mo'hair *n* **1** the silky hair of an Angora goat. **2** the wool or cloth made from it (*a mohair sweater*).

Moham'medan *adj* Muslim.

moi'dore *n* an old Portuguese gold coin.

moi'ety *n* (*fml or lit*) the half.

moist *adj* slightly wet, damp (*clean it with a moist cloth/his moist brow*).

moisten [moi'-sên] *vb* to make damp (*moistened a cloth to wipe the child's face*).

mois'ture *n* dampness, wetness caused by tiny drops of water in the atmosphere (*soil in need of moisture*).

mo'lar *n* one of the back teeth that grind food.

molas'ses *n* **1** a dark treacly liquid left over when sugar is made from sugar cane. **2** (*esp Amer*) treacle.

mole[1] *n* a dark spot on the human skin (*he had a mole on his shoulder*).

mole[2] *n* a small furry burrowing animal (*piles of earth on his lawn caused by moles*).

mole[3] *n* a stone pier or breakwater.

mol'ecule *n* the smallest particle of a substance that can exist while still retaining the chemical qualities of that substance.

molec'ular *adj* having to do with molecules (*the molecular structure of the substance*).

mole'hill *n* the heap of earth thrown up by a burrowing mole (*molehills on the lawn*).

mole'skin *n* a strong ribbed cotton cloth.

molest' *vb* **1** to disturb or annoy (*molested by members of the press*). **2** to make a bodily, often sexual, attack upon:—*n* **moles-ta'tion**.

moll'ify *vb* to make less angry, to calm down (*mollified their mother by giving her flowers*).

moll'usc *n* a soft-bodied animal with a hard shell, as a snail, oyster, etc (*edible molluscs*).

moll'ycoddle *vb* to take too great care of (*she mollycoddles her children*).

mol'ten *adj* **1** melted (*molten metal*). **2** made by having been melted (*molten casts*).

mo'ment *n* **1** a very short time (*it took only a moment*). **2** (*fml*) importance (*matters of great moment*).

mo'mentary *adj* lasting only a moment (*a momentary pause*).

momen'tous *adj* very important (*a momentous discovery*).

momen'tum *n* the force of a moving body (*the rock gathered momentum as it rolled downhill*).

mon'arch *n* a single supreme ruler, a sovereign, a king or queen (*the ruling monarch*).

mon'archist *n* one who believes in monarchy (*some people would prefer a republic but he is a monarchist*).

mon'archy *n* a state or system of government in which power is, in appearance or reality, in the hands of a single ruler (*Britain is a monarchy*).

mon'astery *n* a house for monks.

monas'tic *adj* having to do with monks or monasteries (*a monastic way of life*).

Mon'day *n* the second day of the week.

mon'etary *adj* having to do with money (*monetary considerations*).

mon'ey *n* metal coins and printed banknotes used in making payments, buying and selling.

mon'eyed *adj* rich (*the moneyed class*).

mon'eylen'der *n* one who lives by lending money on condition that interest is paid to him or her for the time of the loan.

money order *n* an order for money that can be bought in one post office and cashed at another, thus enabling the buyer to send money safely by post.

mon'goose *n* a small weasel-like animal that kills snakes.

mongrel [mun(g)'-grel] *adj* of mixed breed or race (*a mongrel dog*):—*n* a dog of mixed breed.

mon'itor *n* **1** in school, a senior pupil who helps to keep order. **2** a device for checking electrical transmission without interfering with it. **3** an instrument that receives and shows continuous information about the working of something. **4** a screen for use with a computer. **5** a small screen in a television studio showing the picture that is being broadcast at any given time:—*vb* to observe and check something regularly (*monitor the patient's condition*).

mon'itory adj (fml) warning (a monitory letter).

monk n a man who, with the intention of devoting his life to prayer, joins a religious society and spends his life in a monastery.

mon'key n 1 an animal resembling a human being in shape. 2 (inf) a mischievous child (the little monkey tricked me):—vb to play about (with) (somebody had monkeyed about with the computer).

mon'key puzzle n an evergreen tree whose branches are covered with short prickly leaves.

monks'hood n a poisonous plant (aconite).

mono- prefix one.

mon'ochrome n a picture in one colour.

mon'ocle n a single eyeglass (the old colonel always wore a monocle).

monog'amy n marriage to one husband or wife only:—n **monog'amist**:—adj **mono-g'amous**.

mon'ogram n letters, esp initials, written one on top of another to make a single design (have his monogram on his T-shirt).

mon'ograph n an essay or book on one particular subject (a monograph on Napoleon's death).

mon'olith n a single standing stone as a pillar or ornament:—adj **monolith'ic**.

mon'ologue n a scene or play in which only one person speaks (the play closed with a monologue).

monoma'nia n an obsession with one idea or subject (his monomania centred on butterflies):—n and adj **monoma'niac**.

mon'oplane n an aeroplane with only one pair of wings.

monop'olize vb 1 to have or obtain complete possession or control of (they used to monopolize the ice-cream market there). 2 to take up the whole of (monopolizing the teacher's attention).

monop'oly n 1 complete control of the trade in a certain article by a single person or company (they had a monopoly of the car market once). 2 possession of or control over something that is not shared by others (she thinks that she has a monopoly of beauty).

monosyll'able n a word of one syllable (she was scarcely polite and spoke in monosyllables):—adj **monsyllab'ic**.

mon'otheism n the belief that there is only one God:—n **mon'otheist**.

mon'otone n a single unvarying tone of voice when speaking (an audience almost sent to sleep by the speaker's monotone).

monot'onous adj 1 dull from lack of variety (a monotonous job). 2 in a monotone (a monotonous voice).

monot'ony n dullness, lack of variety, sameness (the monotony of his existence).

monsoon' n a south Asian wind, blowing from the southwest in summer and the northeast in winter, usu bringing heavy rain.

mon'ster n 1 a huge frightening creature (a fairytale about sea monsters). 2 anything huge (the turnip was a monster/a monster turnip). 3 an unnaturally cruel or wicked person (a monster to treat his wife so badly).

mon'strance n in the RC church, a vessel in which the Host, a fragment of consecrated bread, is placed for adoration.

monstros'ity n something, usu large, that is very ugly (my aunt left us a monstrosity of a wardrobe).

mon'strous adj 1 huge (monstrous lorries rushing down the motorway). 2 unnaturally cruel or wicked (a monstrous crime).

month n one of the twelve periods of time into which the year is divided.

month'ly adj happening once a month or every month (a monthly magazine):—also adv.

mon'ument n a statue, stone, etc, set up in memory of a person or event (a monument to the soldiers killed in the war).

monumen'tal adj 1 huge (a monumental painting covering the whole wall). 2 outstanding (a monumental achievement).

mood n 1 a state of the mind and feelings, a person's temper at a certain moment (he is in a bad mood). 2 a state of bad temper (she is in a mood). 3 in grammar, a verb form that tells whether the verb is used to express a command, desire, statement of fact, etc.

mood'y adj tending to change mood suddenly or often, often bad-tempered (moody people).

moon n 1 the heavenly body that moves round the earth and reflects the light of the sun. 2 any smaller heavenly body that moves around a larger one:—vb (inf) to walk about in a dreamy way (mooning about waiting for her boyfriend to ring).

moon'beam *n* a ray of light from the moon.

moon'shine *n* 1 foolish or fantastic ideas (*she says she is going to go round the world but it is just moonshine*). 2 str ong drink made secretly and against the law.

moon'stone *n* a precious stone, bluish-white in colour.

moor[1] *n* a large extent of poor land on which only coarse grass, heather, etc, will grow, a heath (*the Yorkshire moors*).

moor[2] *vb* to fasten a ship by ropes, cables, etc (*moor his yacht at the local harbour*).

Moor *n* an Arab inhabitant of Morocco, or any part of northwest Africa:—*adj* **Moor'ish**.

moor'age *n* a place for mooring a ship (*pay for a moorage near his house*).

moor'cock, moor'fowl *ns* the red grouse.

moor'hen *n* the water-hen.

moor'ing *n*, **moor'ings** *npl* 1 the r opes, cables, etc, by which a ship is fastened (*the moorings came loose*). 2 the place wher e a ship is so fastened.

moor'land *n* a moor, moors (*an area of moorland*).

moose *n* the elk, a type of deer found in North America.

moot *vb* (*fml*) to put forward for discussion:—*n* in the Old English period (before AD 1066), a council or assembly.

moot point *n* a matter on which two or more opinions may be upheld, an undecided matter (*it's a moot point whose land it is*).

mop *n* strips of coarse cloth, yarn, etc, fixed together to a handle and used for washing floors, etc:—*vb* (**mopped'**, **mop'ping**) to clean with a mop, to wipe (*mop the floor*).

mope *vb* to be gloomy or sad (*a dog moping for its owner*).

moraine' *n* the fragments of rock, etc, carried down and deposited by a glacier.

mor'al *adj* 1 having to do with what is right or wrong in action (*a moral problem*). 2 living according to the rules of right conduct (*a very moral person*):—*n* 1 the lesson to be learned from a story (*Aesop's fables had morals*). 2 *pl* one's beliefs as to what is right or wrong in action (*he seems to have no morals*). 3 *pl* standards of behaviour (*complain about the morals of the teenagers*).

morale [mo-räl'] *n* belief in one's ability to do what is asked of one, courage (*he tried to boost the team's morale by telling them how well they were playing*).

mor'alist *n* one who studies questions of right and wrong.

moral'ity *n* 1 moral principles. 2 a particular system of moral principles (*Christian morality*). 3 the quality of an action, as estimated by a standard of right and wrong.

morality play *n* (*old*) a play written to show clearly the difference between right and wrong.

mor'alize *vb* to discuss questions of morals (*the minister used his sermon to moralize to his congregation*).

morass' *n* 1 a marsh, sodden gr ound (*a vehicle stuck in the morass*). 2 a situation that is ver y difficult to deal with or get out of (*a morass of detail associated with the business contract*).

mor'bid *adj* 1 unhealthy, diseased (*a morbid condition of the foot*). 2 thinking too much about what is gloomy or disgusting (*morbid curiosity/have a morbid view of the future*):—*n* **morbid'ity**.

mor'dant *adj* biting, sharp, hurtful.

more *adj* greater in amount, number, etc (*ask for more money*):—*also n*:—*adv* 1 to a gr eater extent or degree (*he has travelled more*). 2 again (*once more*).

moreo'ver *adv* in addition, further (*he is intelligent—moreover he is well qualified*).

morgana'tic *adj*:—**morganatic marriage** a marriage in which a person of low rank marries one of high or royal rank, but is not raised to that rank, nor are any children.

morgue [morg] *n* a mortuary.

mor'ibund *adj* dying, about to die (*a moribund custom/a moribund business*).

Mor'mon *n* a member of a North American religious sect that formerly allowed a man to have more than one wife.

morn *n* (*lit*) morning.

morn'ing *n* the early part of the day (*go to work in the morning*).

morning star *n* the planet Venus when seen before sunrise.

morocc'o *n* a fine goatskin leather originally prepared in Morocco.

mor'on n **1** a feeble-minded person. **2** (*inf*) a very stupid person (*you were a moron to drive without a licence*):—*adj* **moron'ic**.

morose' *adj* gloomy and ill-natured (*in a morose mood after he lost the chess match*).

mor'phia, morphine [mor'-feen] *ns* a drug made from opium that causes sleep and lessens pain (*addicted to morphia*).

mor'ris dance n an English country dance for which the dancers wear traditional dress.

morse n a signalling code in which dots and dashes (or short and long sounds or flashes) represent the letters of the alphabet (*morse code*).

mor'sel n a small piece, a bite (*not able to eat another morsel*).

mor'tal *adj* **1** having to die (*all humans are mortal*). **2** causing death (*a mortal blow*):—*n* a human being (*mortals must die*).

mortal'ity n **1** the state of being mortal (*mortality is one of the few certain things in life*). **2** the number who die from a certain cause (*infant mortality is still high there*).

mor'tar n **1** a bowl in which substances are crushed into powder (by a pestle) (*she ground the spices in a mortar and pestle*). **2** a gun with a short barrel. **3** a cement made of lime and sand and used in building.

mor'tar-board n a square-topped cap worn with an academic gown (*wear a mortar-board for her graduation ceremony*).

mortgage [mor'-gêj] n giving to one who has lent money the control of certain property that he or she may sell if the loan is not repaid but must return when the loan is repaid in full (*take out a mortgage on their new house*):—*vb* to give control over property to another to obtain a loan (*mortgaging the house to the building society*).

mor'tify *vb* **1** to make ashamed (*she was mortified when she discovered that she was wearing non-matching shoes*). **2** (*old*) to gain control over one's body by refusing its desires or causing it suffering:—*n* **mortifica'tion**.

mortise [mor'-tis] n a hole cut in a piece of wood, etc, so that part of another piece (the tenon) may fit into it (*a mortise lock*).

mor'tuary n a building in which dead bodies are kept until burial (*the murdered corpse was removed to the mortuary*).

mosaic [mō-zā'-ik] n a picture or design made by placing together differently coloured pieces of glass, stone, etc.

Moselle' n a kind of German white wine.

Mos'lem *same as* **Muslim**.

mosque [mosk] n a Muslim place of worship.

mosqui'to n (*pl* **mosqui'toes**) a stinging insect that sometimes carries the germs of malaria (*her leg swelled up when the mosquito bit her*).

moss n a tiny flowerless plant growing on walls, tree trunks and in damp places (*stones covered in moss*).

moss'y *adj* overgrown with moss (*mossy rocks*).

most *adj* greatest in number, amount, etc (*she got most votes/most people believed him*):—*also* n:—*adv* **1** in or to the greatest degree or extent (*most importantly*). **2** very (*most accomplished*).

mote n (*old*) a tiny particle, a speck of dust.

motel' n a hotel with special facilities for motorists (*the motel had space for the cars next to the rooms*).

moth n **1** a winged insect that flies by night (*moths are like butterflies but not so brightly coloured*). **2** the clothes moth (*moths had made holes in the clothes stored in the attic*).

mother [mu'-thêr] n **1** a female parent. **2** the female head of a convent of nuns:—*vb* to care for, as would a mother (*mothered the orphans*).

mo'therhood n the state of being a mother.

mother-in-law n the mother of the person to whom one is married.

mo'therless *adj* having no mother (*children left motherless by her death*).

mo'therly *adj* like a mother (*a motherly kind of person*).

mother-of-pearl' n the hard pearl-like lining of certain shells (*a jewel box lined with mother-of-pearl*).

mo'ther tongue n one's native language (*English is his mother tongue*).

mo'tion n **1** act of moving (*the motion of the boat made her feel sick*). **2** a movement (*with a motion of his hand*). **3** an idea put to a meeting so that it can be voted on (*he proposed the motion that fees be raised*):—*vb* to make a movement as a sign.

mo'tionless *adj* unmoving.

mo'tivate *vb* to give a reason or urge to act.

mo'tive adj causing movement:—n a reason for doing something.

mot'ley adj 1 (old) of varied colours (a motley coat). 2 made up of different kinds (a motley collection of people):—n (old) a dress of several colours worn by jesters.

mo'tor n an engine that by changing power into motion drives a machine (the car needs a new motor):—adj causing movement or motion (the accident affected his motor muscles/a motor nerve):—vb to travel by motor car (he motors to work every day).

mo'tor bi'cycle n a bicycle driven by a motor:—similarly **mo'tor-boat**, **mo'tor car**.

mo'torist n one who drives a motor car (a motorist driving without a licence).

mot'orway n a wide road with two or more lanes in each direction, built for fast travel and long distances (motorways such as the M6).

mot'tle vb to mark with spots or blotches (have a mottled complexion).

mot'to n (pl mot'toes) 1 a wise saying that can be used as a rule of life ('Early to bed, early to rise' is his motto). 2 the word or words on a coat of arms. 3 a printed saying or joke (mottoes in Christmas crackers).

mould[1] n loose earth, soil made rich by rotted leaves, etc (leaf mould used as a fertilizer).

mould[2] n a fluffy growth consisting of tiny plants on stale food or damp surfaces.

mould[3] n 1 a shaped vessel into which hot molten metal is poured so that when it cools it has the same shape as the vessel. 2 a vessel used to shape jellies, etc.—vb 1 to form in a mould (the metal is moulded into bars). 2 to work into a shape (mould the clay into a ball). 3 to shape or influence (mould a child's character).

mould'er vb to rot away, to crumble (walls of the old house mouldering away/talent left to moulder away).

mould'ing n 1 anything given shape in a mould. 2 an ornamental pattern on a wall or ceiling or on a picture frame (a moulding on the ceiling in the form of leaves).

mould'y adj 1 covered with mould. 2 (inf) of little value, unpleasant, dull (the child complained about getting a mouldy old five pounds for Christmas).

moult vb to lose the hair or feathers, to fall off (dogs moulting).

mound n 1 a low hill. 2 a heap of earth or stones.

mount n 1 (usu in names) a hill, a mountain (Mount Everest). 2 an animal, esp a horse, for riding (he chose a mount). 3 a card or paper surrounding a picture or photograph:—vb 1 to go up, to climb (mount the ladder). 2 to get on to (mount the bus). 3 to place in position (mount the photograph). 4 to get on horseback (mount the chestnut horse).

moun'tain n 1 a high hill (the highest mountain in Britain). 2 a large heap (a mountain of rubbish).

mountain ash n a type of tree, the rowan.

mountaineer' n one who climbs mountains (mountaineers climbing Everest).

moun'tainous adj 1 having many mountains (a mountainous region). 2 huge (a mountainous man).

moun'tebank n 1 (old) one who, pretending to have special skill as a doctor, sells useless medicines in public. 2 one who falsely claims special knowledge or skill (the lawyer turned out to be a mountebank).

mount'ed adj on horseback (mounted police).

mourn vb to show sorrow, to feel grief, esp after a loss or death (mourn her dead sister/she mourns his death):—n **mourn'er**.

mourn'ful adj sad, sorrowful (a mournful expression).

mourn'ing n 1 sorrow, grief (her mourning for her dead sister) 2 black clothes worn as a sign of grief for another's death (the widow was wearing mourning).

mouse n (pl mice) a small rodent animal found in houses or in the fields (have mice in the kitchen).

moustache [mus-täsh'] n the hair growing on the upper lip (he had a black moustache).

mouth n 1 the opening in the face for eating and uttering sounds (she opened her mouth to scream). 2 the opening into anything hollow (the mouth of the jam jar). 3 the part of a river where it flows into the sea:—vb to twist the mouth into different shapes (mouth the answer silently to him).

mouth'ful n the amount placed in the mouth at one time (eat the cake in two mouthfuls).

mouth'piece n 1 the part of a musical instrument or pipe placed in the mouth. 2 one who speaks for others.

mov'able, move'able adjs able to be moved (movable property):—npl **movables** property that can be moved, esp furniture.

move [möv] vb 1 to cause to change place or position (move the chairs to the next room). 2 to go from one place to another (she moved from the chair to the sofa). 3 to change houses (they are moving to London). 4 to set in motion. 5 to stir up the feelings (her performance moved them deeply). 6 to rouse to action (she moved them to protest). 7 at a meeting, to put forward an idea to be voted on (he moved that they sell the building):—n 1 a change of position or place. 2 a change of house (their second move in one year). 3 an action (wonder what his next move will be). 4 in chess, etc, the act of moving a piece.

move'ment n 1 act of moving (police are watching his movements). 2 change of position (the sudden movement made the dog bark). 3 a number of people working for the same purpose (the women's movement). 4 a complete part of a long musical work (the slow movement).

mov'er n (inf) one who moves or causes movement (the real mover behind the firm).

mov'ing adj stirring up the feelings (a moving film/ the moving sight of the little girl in tears).

mov'ing pic'ture n a cinema picture, a film.

mow vb (pp **mown**) 1 to cut (grass) (mowing the lawn). 2 to knock down, to kill in large numbers (a group of children mown down by a huge lorry).

mow'er n a person or machine that mows (a lawn mower).

much adj great in amount or quantity (not much money):—n a great amount (he does not earn much):—adv greatly.

muck n (inf) wet filth, dirt:—vb (inf) 1 to dirty. 2 to make a mess of (muck up the clean kitchen). 3 to spoil (muck up our plans). 4 to bungle (muck up the interview).

muck'y adj (inf) filthy (children with mucky hands).

mu'cous adj producing mucus, slimy.

mu'cous mem'brane n the inner skin lining the nose, mouth, etc.

mu'cus n the shiny liquid coming from the mucous membrane of the nose (the mucus that comes from your nose when you have a cold).

mud n soft wet earth (cars stuck in the mud).

mud'dle vb 1 to confuse (she felt a bit muddled about the directions). 2 to mix up (she muddled the dates). 3 to act without plan (muddling through the meeting):—n confusion, disorder.

mud'dle-head'ed adj unable to think clearly.

mud'dy adj covered with mud (muddy clothes):—vb 1 to make dirty or muddy (dirt muddying water). 2 to make unclear.

mud'guard n a metal shield over a wheel to catch the mud thrown up by it (the bicycle's mudguards).

muesli [mö'zli] n a kind of breakfast cereal consisting of grains, nuts and dried fruit.

muff[1] n a cover of warm material (often fur) for both hands (gloves are usually worn now instead of muffs).

muff[2] vb (inf) 1 to fail to hold (muff a catch at cricket). 2 to do badly (given an opportunity to succeed but muffed it).

muffin n a teacake eaten hot with butter.

muf'fle vb 1 to wrap up to keep warm (children muffled up in scarves and hats). 2 to deaden sound (a gag muffling his cries). 3 to make a sound less loud (muffle the sound of the car's exhaust).

muffler n a warm scarf.

muf'ti n ordinary clothes worn by a uniformed man when off duty (a policeman in mufti).

mug n 1 a drinking vessel with a handle and more or less straight sides (a mug of cocoa). 2 (inf) one easily made a fool of or cheated (he was a mug to believe that they were genuine policemen).

mug'gy adj unpleasantly warm and damp (muggy weather).

mul'berry n 1 a tree bearing dark red eatable berries. 2 a dark reddish-purple colour.

mulch n a moist mixture of organic material and straw that is spread around the roots of plants to protect and fertilize them.

mulct [mulkt] n (fml or old) money paid in punishment, a fine:—vb (fml or old) to punish by fining or confiscating.

mule n 1 the offspring of an ass and a horse, supposedly famous for its stubborness (use a mule to carry their load/stubborn as a mule). 2 a machine for spinning cotton.

mul'ish *adj* stubborn (*too mulish to admit that she is in the wrong*):—*n* **mul'ishness.**

mull *vb* to heat, sweeten and spice (wine, ale, etc) (*have mulled wine at Christmas*).

mul'let *n* an eatable sea fish.

mulligataw'ny *n* a soup flavoured with curry.

mul'lion *n* an upright bar between the divisions of a window.

mul'ti- *prefix* many.

mul'ti-col'oured *adj* of many colours (*multi-coloured summer shirts*).

multifa'rious *adj* (*fml*) of many kinds (*multifarious activities*).

mul'tiform *adj* (*fml*) having many forms.

multilat'eral *adj* **1** having many sides. **2** (*fml*) concerning more than two groups (*a multilateral agreement*).

mul'timedia *adj* **1** using several different methods and media (*a multimedia approach to advertising*). **2** in computing, using sound and video images as well as data.

mul'tiple *adj* **1** having or affecting many parts (*accident victims receive multiple injuries*). **2** involving many things of the same kind (*a multiple crash on the motorway*):—*n* a number that contains another an exact number of times (*12 is a multiple of 4*).

multiplicand' *n* a number to be multiplied by another.

multiplica'tion *n* act of multiplying.

multiplic'ity *n* (*fml*) a great number (of) (*a tool with a multiplicity of uses*).

mul'tiplier *n* the number by which another is multiplied.

mul'tiply *vb* **1** to incr ease (*their misfortunes seem to multiply/multiplied their chances of success*). **2** to find the number obtained by adding a number to itself a certain number of times (*if you multiply 4 by 3 you get 12*).

mul'titude *n* **1** a gr eat number (*a multitude of objections*). **2** (*old*) a crowd (*the leader spoke to the multitudes*).

multitu'dinous *adj* (*fml or hum*) very many (*his multitudinous relatives*).

mum *adj* silent (*keep mum*):—*n* mother (*short for mummy*).

mum'ble *vb* to speak in a low, indistinct voice (*mumbling the answer so that the teacher could not hear her*).

mum'mer *n* (*old*) one who acts in a play without words.

mum'my[1] *n* (*inf*) mother.

mum'my[2] *n* a human body kept from decay by being treated with certain drugs and wrapped tightly in cloth (*Egyptian mummies*):—*vb* **mum'mify.**

mumps *n* an infectious disease that causes swelling of the neck and face (*off school with mumps*).

munch *vb* to chew noisily, to crush with teeth (*munch biscuits/munch on an apple*).

mun'dane *adj* **1** (*fml*) having to do with this world (*mundane, not spiritual, pleasure*). **2** or dinary, with nothing exciting or unusual (*a mundane job*).

muni'cipal *adj* having to do with a city or town (*municipal buildings*).

municipal'ity *n* **1** a city or town with certain powers of self-government. **2** the body that governs a city or town.

muni'ficent *adj* (*fml*) generous (*a munificent gift of diamonds*):—*n* **muni'ficence.**

muni'tions *npl* the guns, shells, etc, used in making war (*a munitions factory*).

mu'ral *n* a painting that is painted directly on to the walls of a building (*a mural in the hospital corridor showing people being healed*).

mur'der *n* act of unlawfully and intentionally killing another (*commit murder*):—*also vb*:—*ns* **mur'derer, mur'deress.**

mur'derous *adj* **1** used to committing mur der (*murderous thugs*). **2** cruel, savage (*a murderous attack*).

murk *n* (*lit*) darkness, gloom (*unable to recognize the figure in the murk*).

murk'y *adj* dark, gloomy (*a murky night*). **2** vague or obscure (*he has a murky past*).

mur'mur *n* **1** a low, indistinct sound, as of running water (*the murmur of the stream*). **2** a soft low continuous sound (*a murmur of voices in the next room*). **3** a grumble (*murmurs against the his handling of the situation*):—*vb* **1** to make a low indistinct sound. **2** to talk in a low voice (*he murmured something in his sleep*). **3** to grumble (*murmur about their lack of money*).

muscle [mu'-sêl] *n* the elastic fibres in the body that enable it to make movements (*strain a muscle by lifting a heavy weight*).

mus'cular adj **1** having to do with muscles (muscular strain). **2** having well-developed muscles, strong (a muscular young man).

muse[1] n **1** in legend, one of the nine goddesses of the arts and learning. **2** (fml) inspiration to write (e.g. poetry) (the muse deserted him).

muse[2] vb to think deeply about, to ponder (musing on the events of the day).

muse'um n a building in which objects of scientific, artistic or literary interest are kept (the ancient tools in the museum).

mush'room n an eatable plant with a soft whitish pulpy top (steak in mushroom sauce):—vb to grow in size very rapidly (new supermarkets mushrooming).

mu'sic n **1** the art of arranging sounds to give melody or harmony (studying music). **2** the sounds so arranged when played, sung or written down (orchestral music).

mu'sical adj **1** having to do with music. **2** pleasant-sounding (a musical voice).

musi'cian n one skilled in music (the musicians in the orchestra).

musk n **1** a sweet-smelling substance obtained from the musk deer and used in making perfume. **2** a type of plant.

mus'ket n (old) a hand-gun formerly carried by soldiers.

musketeer' n (old) a soldier armed with a musket.

mus'ketry n the art of using muskets, rifles and other small arms.

musk'rat n a large water-rat found in North America.

musk'-rose n a sweet-smelling rose.

musk'y adj smelling of musk (a perfume with a musky smell).

Mus'lim, Mos'lem n a person of the religion known as Islam:—also adj.

mus'lin n a fine thin cotton cloth.

mus'quash n the fur of the muskrat.

mus'sel n an eatable shellfish enclosed in a double shell (have mussels as a first course).

mus'tang n an American wild horse.

mus'tard n **1** a plant with hot-tasting seeds. **2** a type of seasoning made from these for flavouring food, esp meat (spread mustard on the beef sandwiches).

mus'ter vb **1** to bring together (muster the troops/muster his supporters). **2** to call up, to

gather (muster all his courage):—n an assembling, as of troops, etc:—**pass muster** to be good enough.

mus'ty adj stale (a musty smell in the old house/the musty smell of old books).

mu'table adj (fml) changeable (mutable attitudes).

muta'tion n change, alteration (new kinds of plants can sometimes be caused by mutation).

mute adj **1** silent (a mute appeal for mercy). **2** unable to speak (mute since birth). **3** not pronounced (a mute l):—n **1** a dumb person. **2** an attachment that lessens or modifies the sound of a musical instrument.

mu'ted adj **1** having the sound altered by a mute. **2** subdued (muted enthusiasm). **3** soft in hue, shade, etc (muted colours).

mu'tilate vb to damage seriously by removing a part, esp a limb (the murderer mutilated the corpse):—n **mutilation**.

mutineer' n one taking part in a mutiny.

mu'tinous adj **1** taking part in a mutiny (the mutinous sailors). **2** obstinate and sulky, as if going to disobey (mutinous children objecting to the cancellation of the party).

mu'tiny n refusal to obey those in charge, esp a rising of people in the armed services against their officers (a mutiny of sailors protesting about poor food):—also vb.

mut'ter vb to speak in a low voice, without sounding the vowels clearly, esp when grumbling or insulting (mutter a complaint):—also n.

mut'ton n the flesh of sheep as meat (roast mutton).

mu'tual adj **1** common to or shared by two or more persons or parties (a mutual back garden for the set of flats). **2** given and received in the same degree by those concerned (mutual help/their dislike was mutual).

muz'zle n **1** the mouth and nose of an animal (a black dog with a grey muzzle). **2** a cage or set of straps fastened on an animal's mouth to prevent it biting (the dog was apt to attack people and so it was made to wear a muzzle). **3** the open end of a gun:—vb **1** to put a muzzle on an animal's mouth. **2** to prevent from speaking freely.

muz'zy adj confused, dizzy (feel muzzy after having slightly too much to drink).

myo'pia n short-sightedness.

myop'ic adj short-sighted (*too myopic to recognize people across the street*).

myriad n a very large number (*a myriad of reasons*):—also adj.

myr'midon n (*old*) a servant or follower who carries out all orders without question.

myrrh [mèr] n **1** a tree from which is obtained a sweet-smelling gum. **2** the gum so obtained.

myr'tle n an evergreen shrub with sweet-smelling white flowers.

myste'rious adj difficult to understand or explain (*the mysterious stranger/his mysterious behaviour*).

mys'tery n **1** a religious truth that cannot be fully understood by the human mind. **2** anything difficult to understand or explain (*his background was a mystery*). **3** a secret way of doing something, known only to a few (*the mysteries of whisky-making*).

mys'tic adj having to do with religious mysteries or secrets (*mystic rites*):—n one who believes that through prayer or sympathy he or she has understood in part the mysteries of life and of the existence of God.

mys'tical adj mystic (*mystical beliefs*).

mys'ticism n the beliefs or practices of a mystic.

mys'tify vb to puzzle, to bewilder (*mystified by his odd behaviour*):—n **mystifica'tion**.

myth n **1** a story about the gods or goddesses of ancient peoples, esp one containing their beliefs about the facts of nature. **2** something that is popularly thought to be true but is not (*the myth that elephants have good memories*).

myth'ical adj existing in myths or legends, imaginary (*mythical creatures such as dragons*).

mythol'ogist n one who studies myths.

mythol'ogy n **1** a collection of myths (*in Scandinavian mythology*). **2** the study of myths:—adj **mytholog'ical**.

N

nab *vb* (*inf*) (**nabbed'**, **nab'bing**) **1** to catch or seize suddenly (*nab the best seats in the theatre*). **2** to arrest (*police nabbed the criminal*).

nacelle' *n* **1** the casing in which the engine of an aeroplane is contained. **2** the cockpit of an aeroplane or airship.

nacre [na'-kêr] *n* mother-of-pearl (*a jewel box with an inlay of nacre*).

nadir [nā'-dêr] *n* the lowest point or condition (*the political party reached its nadir/standards of cleanliness reached a nadir*).

nag[1] *n* a horse, esp a small, weak or old one (*he hires out horses but they are just nags*).

nag[2] *vb* (**nagged'**, **nag'ging**) to keep on annoying or finding fault with (*his wife is always nagging him/nag her son into getting a haircut*).

naiad [nī'-ad] *n* in legend, a goddess of a river, lake, etc.

nail *n* **1** the horny growth on the tips of the fingers or toes. **2** the claw of a bird or animal. **3** a thin piece of metal with a pointed end and a flattened head, used for joining together pieces of wood (*hammer a nail into the wall to hang the picture from*):—*vb* to fasten with a nail (*nail a sign to the post*).

naïve [na-eev'] *adj* **1** simple and natural, innocent (*naïve young girls*). **2** ignorantly simple, too trustful (*naïve enough to believe he really was a prince*):—*n* **naiveté** [na-eev'-tā].

na'ked *adj* **1** wearing no clothes (*sleep naked/naked children*). **2** uncovered (*a naked flame*). **3** plain, unconcealed (*the naked truth*):—*n* **na'kedness**.

nam'by-pam'by *adj* (*inf*) babyish, unmanly (*boys accused of being namby-pamby by other children because they cry if they get hurt*).

name *n* **1** the word by which a person or thing is known. **2** reputation (*make a name for himself in the art world*):—*vb* **1** to give a name to (*naming the baby Alice*). **2** to speak about by name (*name all the kings of France*).

name'less *adj* **1** unknown (*a nameless poet of the 12th century*). **2** having no name (*nameless graves*). **3** wanting one's name to be concealed (*the giver of the money wishes to remain

nameless*). **4** too bad to be mentioned by name (*nameless acts of cruelty*).

name'ly *adv* that is to say (*only one pupil was absent, namely Peter*).

name'plate *n* a metal plate on which the name of a person, firm, etc, is engraved (*polish the nameplate on the door*).

name'sake *n* a person with the same name as another (*her niece is her namesake*).

nan'ny *n* **1** a woman employed to take care of children, a children's nurse (*their mother works and they have a full-time nanny*). **2** a female goat (*also* **nan'ny-goat**).

nap[1] *n* a short sleep, a doze (*have a nap after lunch*):—*vb* (**napped'**, **nap'ping**) to take a short sleep:—**caught napping** taken by surprise (*the police were caught napping and the bank robbers escaped*).

nap[2] *n* the woolly surface on cloth.

nap[3] *n* a game of cards.

nape *n* the back part of the neck (*hair cut close at the nape of her neck*).

naph'tha *n* an easily lit oil obtained from coal or wood.

naph'thalene *n* an evil-smelling substance obtained from coal, and used for killing moths, etc.

nap'kin *n* **1** a small cloth used at table to keep the clothes clean (*a tablecloth with matching napkins*). **2** a towel put round a baby's bottom to keep it clean (*usu abbr* **nappy**).

narciss'us *n* (*pl* **narciss'i**) a flower of the daffodil family, but with white petals.

narcot'ic *adj* causing sleep.—*n* a drug that causes sleep and eases pain (*addicted to narcotics such as opium*).

narrate' *vb* to tell (a story) (*narrating his adventures in Africa*).

narra'tion *n* a story.

nar'rative *adj* **1** telling a story (*a narrative poem*). **2** having to do with storytelling (*her narrative technique*):—*n* a story.

narra'tor *n* the teller of a story (*the narrator of the nativity play at Christmas*).

nar'row *adj* **1** not broad, measuring little from side to side (*a very narrow bridge/narrow ribbon*).

2 (also **nar'row-mind'ed**) unwilling to accept new ideas or ways of doing things (*narrow views on education*). **3** not extensive, not wide-ranging (*narrow interests*). **4** only just avoiding the opposite result (*a narrow escape*):—*n* (*usu pl*) a narrow part of a river or sea:—*vb* to make or become narrow (*the road suddenly narrows/ narrow the street*).

nar'rowly *adv* barely, only just (*narrowly escape death*).

narwhal [nar'-wêl] *n* a type of whale with one large tusk.

na'sal *adj* **1** having to do with the nose (*nasal infections*). **2** sounded through the nose (*a nasal accent*):—*n* a vowel or consonant so sounded.

nasal organ *n* the nose.

na'scent *adj* (*fml*) just coming into being, beginning to be important (*a nascent political party*).

nastur'tium *n* a quickly spreading garden plant with red and yellow flowers.

nas'ty *adj* **1** unpleasant. **2** dirty. **3** disagreeable. **4** unkind:— *n* **nas'tiness**.

na'tal *adj* (*fml*) having to do with birth.

na'tion *n* all the people belonging to one country and living under the same government (*nations getting together to prevent war*).

na'tional *adj* **1** having to do with a nation (*the maple leaf is the national emblem of Canada*). **2** of concern to all the people in a country (*national rather than local issues*).

na'tionalism *n* the policy or beliefs of a nationalist.

na'tionalist *n* **1** one who demands self-government for his or her country (*Scottish nationalists*). **2** one who has great pride in and love of his or her country and considers it superior to others (*nationalists who get very excited at international football matches*).

national'ity *n* membership of a particular nation (*what nationality is she—French?*).

na'tionalize *vb* to take land, mines, etc, away from private possessors and make them the property of the whole nation (*the electricity industry used to be nationalized*).

na'tive *adj* **1** of the place where one was born (*his native language*). **2** belonging to a country (*a native Scotsman*). **3** born in a person (*native intelligence*):—*n* **1** a person belonging to a place by birth (*a native of Scotland*).

2 (*now often considered offensive*) an original inhabitant of a place.

nativ'ity *n* birth:—**the Nativity** the birth of Jesus Christ.

nat'ty *adj* neat, smart and tidy in appearance (*wear a natty suit*).

nat'ural *adj* **1** in agreement with the laws that seem to govern the universe and existence. **2** born in a person (*natural musical talents*). **3** not caused by Man (*natural resources such as coal*). **4** without pretence, simple and direct (*put them at ease with her natural manner*). **5** normal (*natural in a boy of that age*). **6** real, genuine (*a natural blonde*). **7** (*mus*) neither sharp nor flat:—*n* **1** (*old*) an idiot. **2** (*inf*) a person who is naturally good at something (*as a singer he's a natural*). **3** (*mus*) a natural note and the mark by which it is shown.

natural history *n* the study of the earth and all that grows on it.

nat'uralist *n* one who studies plant and animal life (*naturalists collecting specimens of wild flowers*).

nat'uralize *vb* to accept someone as a member of a nation to which he or she does not belong by birth (*he was not born in Britain but he is a naturalized British citizen*):—*n* **naturaliza'tion**.

nat'urally *adv* **1** in a natural way (*she's naturally beautiful and does not need make-up/behave naturally rather than affectedly*). **2** of course (*naturally he will be paid for the work he has done*).

natural philosophy *n* physics.

na'ture *n* **1** all existing and happening in the universe that is not the work of Man, such as the plants and animals around us. **2** the sum of those qualities that make any creature or thing different from others (*the nature of the new drug*). **3** the character of a person (*a sweet nature*). **4** kind, sort (*the nature of his injuries*).

naught *n* (*old or lit*) nothing (*his plans came to naught*).

naugh'ty *adj* mischievous, badly behaved (*naughty children/children punished for being naughty*):— *n* **naught'iness**.

nausea [nâ'-zee-a] *n* **1** a feeling of sickness (*feel nausea as the boat rocked*). **2** great disgust (*vegetarians filled with nausea at the thought of eating meat*).

nau'seate vb **1** to sick en (*nauseated by the smell of the rotting meat*). **2** to disgust, to loathe (*nauseated by the terrible murder*).

nau'seous adj disgusting.

nau'tical adj having to do with the sea, sailors or ships (*a nautical way of life*).

nautical mile n about 1.8 kilometres (6080 feet).

nau'tilus n a sea creature living in a shell that twists round and round in a spiral.

na'val adj having to do with a navy or warships (*a naval career/a naval officer*).

nave[1] n the main part of a church occupied by the congregation (*the nave in the church is between two aisles*).

nave[2] n the central part of a wheel through which the axle passes.

na'vel n a little hollow in the centre of the belly (*some people wear a jewel in the navel for decoration*).

nav'igable adj that ships can sail through (*navigable waters*).

nav'igate vb **1** to sail (a ship) (*navigating the ship between the dangerous rocks*). **2** to work out the correct course for a ship, aircraft, etc, and direct it on that course (*looking for someone to navigate in the yacht race*).

naviga'tion n **1** the science of working out the course or position of a ship, aircraft, etc. **2** act of sailing a ship.

nav'igator n one who navigates (*employed as a ship's navigator*).

nav'vy n an unskilled labourer (*navvies working on building sites*).

na'vy n the warships of a nation, their crews and equipment.

navy blue adj very dark blue (*a navy blue uniform*).

nay adv and n (*old or lit*) no:—**to say nay** to refuse, to say no to.

Naz'arene adj of Nazareth.

Nazi [nä'-tsee] n a follower of Hitler, the former German dictator.

neap, neap'-tide n the tides in which the distance between low water and high water is smallest, about the times of the new and the full moons.

Neapol'itan adj **1** of Naples. **2** (*without cap*) of various flavours and colours (*neapolitan ice cream*):—n **1** a person fr om Naples. **2** (*without cap*) ice creams of various flavours served together.

near adj **1** close, not distant in time or place (*the station is near/Christmas is near*). **2** only just missed or avoided (*a near miss/a near accident*) **3** (*inf*) mean with money:—prep close to:—adv almost:—vb to approach.

near'ly adv almost (*he nearly died/it's nearly time to go*).

Near East n the countries of southeastern Europe.

near'-sight'ed adj short-sighted (*near-sighted and unable to see numbers on buses as they approach*).

neat adj **1** tidily arranged (*a neat room/neat appearance*). **2** skilfully done or made (*a neat job*). **3** not mixed with anything weak er (*takes his whisky neat*):—n **neat'-ness**.

neb'ula n (*pl* **neb'ulae**) a faintly shiny patch in the night sky, sometimes caused by a number of very distant stars.

neb'ulous adj not clear, vague (*plans that are rather nebulous/only a nebulous idea of the work involved*).

ne'cessary adj needed, unavoidable, that cannot be done without (*have the necessary qualifications/it will be necessary for all of us to go*):—adv **necessar'ily**.

neces'sitate vb to make necessary (*lack of money necessitated a reduction in staff*).

neces'sity n **1** that which one needs (*have money only for the necessities of life*). **2** the condition of being necessary or unavoidable (*is there any necessity to employ more staff*). **3** cir cumstances forcing one to act or behave in a certain way (*necessity made him take a low-paid job*).

neck n **1** the part of the body joining the head to the shoulders (*break his neck in the accident*). **2** the narr ow part near the mouth of a bottle. **3** a narr ow strip of land joining two larger masses of land:—**neck and neck** exactly level (*horses neck and neck approaching the finish*).

neck'erchief n a large handkerchief worn round the neck.

neck'lace n a string of beads or jewels worn round the neck (*diamond necklaces*).

neck'let n a necklace, a covering (e.g of fur) for the neck.

neck'tie n (*usu* **tie**) a band of cloth worn round the neck and under the shirt collar (*wear a black necktie at the funeral*).

nec'romancer *n* one who foretells the future by questioning the spirits of the dead, a wizard:—*n* **nec'romancy.**

necrop'olis *n* (*fml*) a large cemetery.

nec'tar *n* **1** in Greek legend, the drink of the gods. **2** a sweet liquid found in flowers (*bees collecting nectar*). **3** a delicious drink (*a cup of tea seemed nectar to the tired woman*).

nec'tarine *n* a type of peach with a smooth skin.

need *n* **1** a want (*in need of food*). **2** that which one requires (*people with few needs*). **3** poverty (*families living in need*):—*vb* **1** to be in want of, to require (*they need food and warm clothing/need help*). **2** to be obliged (*they will need to work harder*).

need'ful *adj* necessary (*take the needful steps to avoid infection*).

need'le *n* **1** a small sharply pointed piece of steel used for drawing thread through cloth in sewing. **2** a short pointed stick used for knitting wool. **3** a small metal pointer on a dial, compass, etc. **4** the long pointed leaf of a pine tree, fir, etc (*needles falling off the Christmas tree*).

need'less *adj* unnecessary (*inflict needless suffering on animals*).

need'lework *n* sewing (*take needlework at school*).

need'y *adj* poor, living in want (*give parcels of food to needy families*).

ne'er [neer] *adv* (*lit*) never.

ne'er-do-well *adj and n* good for nothing (*a neer-do-well who is in and out of prison*).

nefa'rious *adj* (*fml*) very wicked (*nefarious deeds*).

negate' *vb* (*fml*) **1** to deny (*negate his accuser's statement*). **2** to cause to have no effect (*negating all their attempts to improve the situation*).

nega'tion *n* **1** a denial. **2** a saying no.

neg'ative *adj* **1** saying no (*a negative reply*). **2** criticizing, but putting forward no alternative plan or idea (*a negative report*):—*n* **1** a word like no, not, etc, expressing refusal or denial (*answer in the negative*). **2** the image on a photographic film or plate in which light seems dark and shade light.

neglect' *vb* **1** to fail to take care of (*neglect their children*). **2** to leave undone (*neglected to post the letter*). **3** to pay no or little attention to, to give too little care to (*neglect his work*):—*n* want of care or attention.

neglect'ful *adj* heedless, careless (*neglectful parents*).

négligé(e) [nā'-glee-zhā] *n* a woman's light, thin garment for wearing over a nightdress.

neg'ligence *n* carelessness, lack of proper care (*a driver accused of negligence*).

neg'ligent *adj* careless (*negligent drivers*).

neg'ligible *adj* too little to bother about, unimportant (*the damage to the car was negligible*).

nego'tiable *adj* **1** able to be settled or changed through negotiation (*a negotiable salary*). **2** that can be exchanged for money (*a negotiable cheque*). **3** able to be passed (*icy roads scarcely negotiable*).

nego'tiate *vb* **1** to try to reach agreement, to bargain (*management and workers negotiating over pay*). **2** to arrange, usu after a long discussion (*negotiate a peace treaty*). **3** to obtain or give money for (*negotiate a cheque*). **4** to pass (over, etc) successfully (*negotiate the sharp bend*):—*n* **negotia'tion:**—*n* **nego'tiator.**

Ne'gro *n* (*pl* **Ne'groes**) (*sometimes considered offensive*) a person belonging to a dark-skinned race, esp from the area of Africa south of the Sahara.

ne'gus *n* (*old*) spiced wine and hot water.

neigh *n* the cry of a horse:—*also vb.*

neigh'bour *n* **1** one living near (*all the neighbours collected money to help her*). **2** a person living next door (*speak to her neighbour over the garden wall*).

neigh'bourhood *n* **1** the surrounding area or district (*in the neighbourhood of the lake*). **2** a group of people and their homes forming a small area within a larger one (*live in a quiet neighbourhood of the city*).

neigh'bouring *adj* close at hand, near (*the neighbouring village*).

neigh'bourly *adj* friendly, helpful (*people in the village are very neighbourly*).

nei'ther *adj, pron, conj and adv* not either.

nem'esis *n* the punishment justly suffered by the wrongdoer (*the bully met his nemesis when the older boys beat him*):—**Nemesis** in mythology, the Greek goddess of just punishment.

neolith'ic *adj* having to do with the later Stone Age.

neol'ogism n 1 a new wor d or phrase (*the comput ing industry has brought us several neologisms*). 2 an old wor d used with a new meaning.

ne'on n a gas that glows brightly when electricity passes through it (*neon lighting*).

ne'ophyte n 1 one r ecently converted to a religious belief. 2 a beginner.

nepen'the n in Greek mythology, a drug that killed sorrow.

ne'phew n the son of one's brother or sister.

nep'otism n unjust use of one's power by giving good posts to relations (*he was accused of nepo tism when his daughter got a job in the depart ment that he managed*).

Nep'tune n in Roman mythology, the god of the sea.

nereid [ne'-ree-id] n in mythology, a goddess of the sea.

nerve n 1 one of the thr ead-like fibres along which messages pass to and from the brain (*damage a nerve in his back*). 2 courage (*he was going to walk along a tightrope but he lost his nerve*). 3 (*inf*) self-confidence, cheek (*she had the nerve to come to the party uninvited*). 4 pl ex citement, nervousness (*she suffered from nerves before the exam*):—*vb* to give strength.

nerve'less adj without strength or power.

ner'vous adj easily excited or upset, timid (*too nervous to stay in the house overnight by her self/nervous about her exam results*):—n **ner'vousness**.

ness n (*usu in place names*) a cape, a headland.

nest n 1 a place built by a bir d in which it lays its eggs and brings up its young. 2 the home built by certain small animals and insects (*a wasp's nest/the nest of some fieldmice*). 3 a comfortable shelter. 4 a set of things that fit one inside an other (*a nest of tables*):—*vb* to build a nest and live in it (*birds nesting*).

nest egg n a sum of money laid aside for future use (*try to get a nest egg together for her retire ment*).

nes'tle vb 1 to lie close to (*the children nestled together for warmth*). 2 to settle comfortably (*nestling down in the sofa to read a book*).

nest'ling n a bird too young to leave the nest.

net[1] n 1 criss-cr ossing strings knotted together at the crossing places. 2 an extent of this used

for catching fish, animals, etc, and for many other purposes (*a butterfly net/put the ball in the net*). 3 a fabric made lik e this (*net cur tains*):—*vb* (**net'ted, net'ting**) 1 to catch in a net (*net several fish*). 2 to cover with a net (*net the fruit trees to keep off the birds*). 3 to hit or kick into a net (*net the ball*).

net[2], **nett** adjs left after one has subtracted the amount due for taxes, expenses, etc (*earn £500 net per month*):—*vb* (**net'ted, net'ting**) to bring in as profit (*net a record annual profit*).

net'ball n a game in which goals are scored by throwing a ball through a small net high on a post.

ne'ther adj (*fml or hum*) lower (*the nether re gions*).

nett see **net**[2].

net'ting n material made in the form of a net (*wire netting to keep the chickens in*).

net'tle n a weed covered with stinging hairs (*stung by a nettle*):—*vb* to anger, to annoy (*his remarks nettled her*).

net'tle rash n an irritation of the skin, causing small red sores like nettle stings.

net'work n 1 anything in which lines, r oads, rail ways, etc, cross and recross each other. 2 a wide spread organization (*a radio network*).

neural'gia n pain in a nerve, esp in the face (*in agony with neuralgia*).

neuri'tis n pain from an inflamed nerve.

neurolog'ical adj having to do with the nerves (*a neurological disorder*).

neurol'ogy n the study of the nerves:—n **neurol'ogist**.

neuro'sis n a type of mental illness in which a per son suffers from great anxiety and fear.

neurot'ic adj 1 in a ner vous state, unreasonably anxious or sensitive (*a neurotic man/a neurotic dog*). 2 suffering fr om a neurosis.

neu'ter adj neither masculine nor feminine.

neu'tral adj 1 not taking sides, neither for nor against, impartial (*a country that was neutral in the war/require someone neutral to referee in the match*). 2 not str ong or definite (*neutral col ours*):—n a neutral person or party.

neutral'ity n the state of being neutral.

neu'tralize vb to cause to have no effect, to make useless, to balance by an opposite action or effect (*neutralize the acid*).

nev'er adv at no time.

nevertheless' adv for all that, despite everything (he is young—nevertheless he is highly qualified).

new adj **1** never known befor e (the discovery of a new star/new ideas). **2** just bought or made, fresh (new clothes/new cars). **3** changed fr om an earlier state, different (a new job):—n **new'ness**.

new'comer n one who has recently arrived (newcomers to the village resented by the older residents).

newfan'gled adj (inf) (expressing contempt) very new (dislike his newfangled methods).

new'ly adv recently (newly laid eggs).

news n **1** information about what is going on (we have no news of the missing child). **2** an account of recent events (listen to the news on the radio).

news'agent n a shopkeeper who sells newspapers (get a magazine from the newsagent).

news'letter n a printed sheet of news sent to members of a group, organization, etc (a newsletter sent to all members of staff).

news'paper n a number of printed sheets (usu issued daily) containing the latest news, articles, advertisements, etc.

news'reel n a film showing recent events.

news'vendor n one who sells newspapers (newsvendors standing at street corners).

newt n a small lizard-like creature that can live both on land and in water.

next adj nearest (live in the next street/the next day):—also adv, prep, n.

next of kin n someone's closest relative (contact the dead man's next of kin).

nex'us n (fml) link, connection.

nib n the point of a pen (the nib of a fountain pen).

nib'ble vb to take small bites at (mice nibbling the cheese):—also n.

nib'lick n a golf club with a heavy metal head and deep face.

nice adj **1** pleasing (a nice day/a nice meal). **2** (old) particular when choosing, hard to please. **3** (fml) fine, delicate (a nice distinction/a nice sense of timing).

nice'ty n **1** exactness, pr ecise detail (consider the niceties of the two firms joining together). **2** a very small difference (the nicety of the distinction).

niche [nitsh] n **1** a hollow place in a wall for a statue, etc (a statue of the Virgin Mary in a niche in the church). **2** the work for which one is best suited (find her niche in teaching).

nick n **1** the small hollow left when a piece is cut or chipped out of something, a notch (a nick in the doorpost/a nick in his skin from shaving). **2** (inf) a police station:—vb **1** to cut notches in. **2** (inf) to catch or arrest a criminal (the police nicked him in the act of breaking into the house):—**in the nick of time** just in time (we arrived in the nick of time to catch the train).

nick'el n **1** a har d whitish metal used for plating utensils and in alloys (steel plated with nickel). **2** (Amer) a five-cent piece.

nick'-nack same as **knick-knack**.

nick'name n a name used instead of one's real name in friendship or mockery (the nickname of the red-haired boy is Ginger):—vb to give a nickname to (Scotsmen are often nicknamed Jock).

nic'otine n a toxic oily liquid from tobacco (fingers stained with nicotine).

niece n the daughter of one's brother or sister.

nig'gard n one who dislikes giving anything away, a miser (a niggard who never gives to charity):—adj mean, stingy (also **nig'-gardly**).

nig'gle vb to pay too much attention to unimportant matters (niggling over the details of his account for the joinery work).

nigh [ní] prep (old or lit) near (Christmas is drawing nigh):—also adv.

night n the time between sunset and sunrise, darkness (animals that come out at night).

night'cap n **1** a cap worn in bed. **2** a drink tak en last thing at night (take a glass of hot milk as a nightcap).

night'dress n a garment worn in bed, esp by women and children.

night'fall n evening, the approach of darkness (insist that the children are home by nightfall).

night'gown n same as **nightdress**.

night'ingale n a type of small bird that sings beautifully.

night'ly adj happening every night (listen to the nightly news programme):—adv every night.

night'mare n a frightening dream (a nightmare about being attacked by sharks).

night'shade n deadly nightshade.

night'-watch'man n one who looks after buildings, etc, by night (*the night-watchman disturbed the burglars*).

nihilist [ni'-hi-lêst] n 1 one without any faith. 2 one who is against government of any kind.

nil n nothing (*the score at the end of the football match was three-nil*).

nim'ble adj active, quick-moving (*elderly people who are still nimble/nimble young gymnast.*):—n **nim'bleness**.

nim'ble-wit'ted adj quick-witted (*nimble-witted enough to think of a way of escaping*).

nim'bus n (pl **nim'bi** or **nim'buses**) 1 a rain cloud. 2 the halo r ound the head of an angel in paintings.

nin'compoop n a fool (*he was a complete nincompoop to believe her*).

nine'pins n a game in which a ball is thrown at nine pins to knock down as many as possible.

nin'ny n a fool, a weak and silly person (*Don't be such a ninny!*).

nip vb (**nipped', nip'ping**) 1 to pinch (*nip the child's arm*). 2 to bite (*the dog nipped him on the ankle*). 3 to stop the gr owth (*fruit trees nipped by frost*):—n 1 a pinch (*he gave the other child a nip*). 2 biting cold (*a nip in the air*). 3 a small drink (*a nip of whisky*):—**nip in the bud** to destroy at an early stage (*nip the conspiracy in the bud*).

nip'per n 1 (*inf*) a small child (*he was clever as a nipper*). 2 the claw of a crab. 3 pl a small gripping tool.

nip'ple n 1 the point of the br east (*babies sucking at their mothers' nipples*). 2 anything so shaped. 3 a rubber stopper with a small hole in it through which liquid may pass, a teat.

nirva'na n 1 the Buddhist heaven. 2 complete peace and happiness after death.

nit n the egg of a louse or other small insect (*find nits in her child's hair*).

ni'trate n a salt of nitric acid.

ni'tre n saltpetre, a colourless salt found in the top soil in hot climates.

ni'tric, ni'trous adjs having to do with nitre (*nitric acid*).

ni'trogen n a colourless gas that makes up about four-fifths of the air:—adj **nitro'ge-nous**.

ni'tro-gly'cerine n a powerful explosive.

nitty gritty n the basic or most important details of something (*We must get down to the nitty gritty of the traffic problem*).

nit'wit n a foolish, worthless person (*he was a nitwit to buy a second-hand car without testing it*).

nobil'ity n 1 goodness of character . 2 the nobles of a country (*a member of the nobility*).

no'ble adj 1 fine in character , honourable (*of noble character*). 2 of high rank (*people of noble birth*). 3 stately (*of noble carriage*):—n a person of high rank.

nobleman n a noble.

no'body n 1 no one (*she was warned to tell nobody the secret*). 2 (*inf*) a person of no importance (*she's just a nobody in the firm but she tries to order everyone around*).

noctur'nal adj 1 (*fml*) happening at night (*a nocturnal encounter*). 2 active by night (*nocturnal animals, such as badgers*).

noc'turne n 1 a dr eamy piece of music. 2 a painting of a night scene.

nod vb (**nod'ded, nod'ding**) 1 to bow the head slightly (*she nodded in agreement/nod to her neighbour as he passed*). 2 to let the head dr op forward in tiredness (*old ladies sitting nodding by the fire*):—n a slight bow of the head.

no'dal adj of or like a node.

nod'dle n (*inf*) the head (*Use your noddle!*).

node n 1 the place wher e a leaf joins the stem. 2 the point at which a cur ve crosses itself. 3 a swelling or a roundish lump, as on a tree trunk or a person's body (*lymph nodes*).

nod'ule n a small rounded lump:—adj **nod'ular**.

Noël n Christmas.

nog'gin n a small amount of liquid (*a noggin of rum*).

noise n 1 a sound (*the noise made by a horse on cobbles*). 2 loud or unpleasant sounds, din (*complain about the noise from the party*):—vb (*fml or old*) to make public (*noising the news of his dismissal abroad*):—adjs **noise'less, nois'y**.

nois'ome adj (*fml*) unpleasant, disgusting (*a noisome smell*).

no'mad n 1 a wander er. 2 a member of a tribe that is always on the move.

nomad'ic adj wandering (*nomadic tribes*).

no'-man's-land n **1** land that belongs to no one (*a piece of no-man's-land between the two farms*). **2** land lying between two opposing armies (*the soldier was shot crossing no-man's-land*).

no'menclature n a carefully worked out set of names for things somehow related to one another (*the nomenclature of chemical compounds*).

nom'inal adj existing in name but not in reality (*her father is the nominal head of the firm but she runs it*).

nominal sum n a very small amount of money (*charge his son a nominal sum of money for the car*).

nom'inate vb **1** to put for ward another's name for a certain office (*nominating him for captain*). **2** to appoint (*nominated her brother as her representative*):—n **nomi-na'tion.**

nom'inative n in grammar, the case of the subject of a verb.

nom'inee n a person nominated (*several nominees for the office of president of the society*).

no'nage n (*fml*) being under age (*she was in her nonage and required her parents' permission to marry*).

nonagena'rian n one who is ninety years old or between ninety and a hundred.

nonce n:—**for the nonce** (*lit or hum*) for the present (*let us forget about it for the nonce*).

non'chalant adj calm, unexcited, showing little interest, cool (*nonchalant about the idea of going into battle*):—n **non'chalance.**

non-com'batant n a soldier who does tasks not involving fighting.

non-commis'sioned offic'er n in the army, an officer below the rank of lieutenant.

non-commit'tal adj not definite, saying neither yes nor no (*give a non-committal reply*).

non-conduc'tor n a substance that does not conduct heat, electricity, etc.

nonconform'ist n **1** one who r efuses to follow the accepted ways of doing things (*nonconformists in the political party*). **2** a P rotestant who is not a member of the Church of England:—n **nonconform'ity.**

non'descript adj not easily described, not very interesting (*wear nondescript clothes*).

nonen'tity n a person of no importance, a person of little ability or character (*she considered the party to be full of nonentities and left early*).

non-flam'mable adj not likely to catch fire or burn easily (*non-flammable nightwear for children*).

nonpareil [non-pê-rel'] n (*fml*) a person or thing without equal (*she considered her father a nonpareil*).

nonplus' vb (**nonplussed'**, **nonplus'sing**) to puzzle completely, to leave speechless (*we were nonplussed by her strange behaviour*).

non'sense n foolish or meaningless words, ideas, etc (*talk nonsense/it was nonsense to accuse him of lying*).

nonsen'sical adj meaningless, absurd (*a nonsensical thing to do*).

non-se'quitur n a conclusion that does not logically follow from what has been argued (*it is impossible to have an argument with her—she keeps making non-sequiturs*).

non-smoking adj of a place where people are not allowed to smoke (*a non-smoking area in a restaurant*).

non'-stop adj and adv without any stop or pause (*non-stop pop music*).

non'such, none'such n (*old*) a person or thing without equal.

nood'le n a long thin strip of pasta used especially in Chinese or Italian cooking, often eaten with sauce or soup (*chicken soup with noodles*).

nook n **1** a corner (*a nook by the kitchen fire*). **2** an out- of-the-way place (*shady nooks*).

noon n twelve o'clock, midday (*lunch at noon*).

noon'tide n (*old*) the time about noon.

noose n a cord or rope with a loop at one end fastened by a running knot (*throw a noose round the ball to catch it/hang him with a noose*):—vb to catch in a noose.

norm n the usual rule, an example or standard with which others may be compared (*his height is below the norm for his age/wage increases above the national norm*).

nor'mal adj usual, according to what is expected, average (*normal body temperature/normal behaviour/his normal routine*):—n **normal'ity.**

north n **1** one of the chief points of the com pass, opposite the midday sun as seen from Britain or any other place in the Northern Hemisphere. **2** the northern part of a countr y. **3** the northern regions of the world.

north, north'ern, north'erly adjs 1 having to do with the north. 2 of or from the north (a northern accent/a north wind).

north'-bound adj travelling north (the north-bound train).

northeast' n the point of the compass halfway between north and east:—also adj.

north'erner n one living in or coming from the north (northerners moving south to find work).

northern lights npl bright rays of coloured light sometimes seen in the region of the North Pole.

north'most, north'enmost adjs farthest to the north (the northmost part of Britain).

North Pole n the northern end of the earth, in the middle of the Arctic Regions.

north'ward(s) adv towards the north (trains travelling northwards).

northwest' n the point of the compass halfway between north and west:—also adj.

nose n 1 a jutting- out part of the face containing the organ of smell (a boxer with a broken nose). 2 a sense of smell (dogs with good noses). 3 any jutting- out part in front of anything (the nose of an aeroplane):—vb 1 to smell. 2 to find by smell (the dog nosed out the drugs). 3 to look or search around in (nosing about in her neighbour's shed). 4 to discover by searching (reporters nosing out the details of the scandal). 5 to move slowly (the car nosed out into the traffic).

nose'bag n a bag hung to a horse's head for it to feed from.

nose'dive n 1 a nose-first dive earthwards by an aeroplane. 2 a sudden and great fall or drop (house prices took a nosedive):—vb to take a nosedive.

nose'gay n (old) a bunch of flowers.

nose'y adj (inf) curious about the affairs of others (nosey neighbours).

nostal'gia n a longing or feeling of fondness for things past (music that fills him with nostalgia for his native land):—adj **nos-tal'gic**.

nos'tril n one of the two openings of the nose.

nos'trum n 1 a medicine made up or sold by someone who claims that it works wonderful cures. 2 a favourite remedy (the government's nostrum for unemployment).

no'table adj worthy of notice, deserving to be remembered (notable events of the year/notable achievements):—n **notabil'ity**.

no'tary n one with the power to see that agreements and written documents are made out properly and legally signed by the parties concerned.

nota'tion n a set of signs that stand for letters, numbers, notes in music, etc.

notch n a small V-shaped cut (cut a notch on the stick to mark the child's height):—vb to make a notch in.

note n 1 a short letter (write them a note to thank them). 2 a short written account of what is said or done (taking notes at the committee meeting). 3 a written explanation (a note at the foot of the page). 4 a single musical sound or the sign standing for it. 5 a piece of paper money (ten-pound notes). 6 fame, good reputation (politicians of note):—vb 1 to put down in writing (the policeman noted the details of the accident). 2 to take notice of (they noted a change in their behaviour).

note'book n a book into which notes may be written.

not'ed adj famous, well-known (noted actors).

note'paper n paper for writing letters on (notepaper with matching envelopes).

note'worthy adj deserving to be noticed or remembered (nothing noteworthy occurred).

noth'ing n 1 no thing, not anything (absolutely nothing in the cupboard). 2 a thing of no importance (her friendship's nothing to him).

no'tice n 1 a written or printed announcement (a notice on the wall forbidding smoking). 2 warning (change the rules without notice). 3 attention (he took no notice of the warning). 4 advance information (receive notice about a meeting):—vb 1 to pay attention to. 2 to see.

no'ticeable adj 1 worthy of attention (noticeable improvement). 2 easily seen (she was very noticeable in her red dress).

no'tice board n a board on which notices may be displayed (details of school matches on the notice board).

notifi'able adj that must be reported (notifiable infectious diseases).

no'tify vb to inform, to make known (notified the police about the accident):—n **no-tifica'tion**.

no'tion n 1 idea, opinion, view (old-fashioned notions about what is women's work). 2 a sudden desire (*he took a notion to go to the seaside for the day*).

notori'ety *n* bad reputation.

noto'rious *adj* well-known for something bad (*a notorious criminal/a notorious accident spot*).

noto'riously *adv* as is well known for something bad (*a notoriously inefficient firm*).

notwithstanding (*fml*) *prep* in spite of:—*adv* all the same (*he is active, notwithstanding his age*).

nougat [nŏŏ-ga] *n* a white toffee-like sweet containing nuts.

nought *n* **1** nothing. **2** the figure 0.

noun *n* in grammar, a word that names a person or thing.

nour'ish *vb* **1** to feed, to give what is needed to grow or stay healthy (*foods that will nourish the children/well-nourished babies*). **2** to keep in the mind (*nourish resentment against his rival*).

nour'ishment *n* food, esp food of value to health (*little nourishment in fast foods*).

nous [nŏŏs] *n* (*fml*) common sense (*have the nous to ask the workman for identification*).

nov'el *adj* new and often of an unusual kind (*a novel suggestion/a novel way of dealing with the problem*):—*n* a long story of which all or some of the events are imaginary.

nov'elty *n* **1** newness, the quality of being novel (*the novelty of the idea*). **2** a new or unusual thing (*it was a novelty for him to take a holiday*). **3** an unusual, small, cheap object (*Christmas novelties*).

Novem'ber *n* the eleventh month of the year (*Bonfire Night is 5th November*).

nov'ice *n* **1** a beginner (*just a novice at skiing*). **2** one who has newly joined a religious order but has not yet taken vows (*the novices in the convent*).

novi'tiate, novi'ciate *n* **1** the time spent as a novice (*the novitiate of the nun*). **2** a novice.

now *n* **1** at the present time (*she is living in London now*). **2** at once (*Go now!*).

now'adays *adv* in modern times (*nowadays the rate of unemployment is high*).

no'where *adv* in no place (*he was nowhere to be seen*).

no'xious *adj* (*fml*) harmful, hurtful (*noxious fumes*).

noz'zle *n* a spout or pipe fitted on to the end of a hose, etc, to direct the liquid (*the nozzle of the garden hose*).

nuance [nū'-o(ng)s] *n* a slight difference in meaning, colour, etc (*fail to appreciate the nuances in the arguments*).

nub *n* the most important point (*the nub of the problem*).

nu'clear *adj* having to do with the atomic nucleus (*nuclear power stations*).

nuclear energy *n* the energy in an atomic nucleus.

nuclear physics *n* the science of the forces within the nucleus of the atom.

nuclear reactor *n* a machine for producing atomic energy.

nu'cleus *n* (*pl* **nu'clei**) **1** the central part of an atom, seed, etc. **2** the central part of anything around which the rest grows up (*the nucleus of the library*).

nude *adj* naked, wearing no clothes (*a nude model for the artist*):—*n* a naked person (*a painting of a nude*).

nudge *vb* to push with the elbow (*nudging the child to warn him to keep quiet*):—*also n*.

nu'dist *n* one who believes that it is healthy to wear no clothes (*a nudist colony*).

nu'dity *n* nakedness (*object to the nudity of the characters in the play*).

nug'get *n* a lump, as of gold, silver, etc.

nuis'ance *n* a person, action or thing that annoys.

null *adj*:—**null and void** having no legal force (*a contract declared null and void by the court*).

null'ify *vb* (*fml*) to make of no effect (*the rise in prices nullified their rise in wages*).

numb *adj* unable to feel (*fingers numb with cold/numb with grief*):—*vb* to take away the power of feeling sensations (*hands numbed with cold/numbed by the break-up of her marriage*).

num'ber *n* **1** a word or sign that tells how many (*a phone number*). **2** a collection of several (persons, things, etc) (*a small number of spectators*). **3** a single copy of a magazine, etc, printed at a particular time, an issue (*the current number of the magazine*). **4** a piece of popular music or a popular song usu forming part of a longer performance (*one of the numbers on her latest album*):—*vb* **1** (*fml*) to reach as a total (*the spectators numbered a thousand*). **2** to give a

number to (*number the pages*). **3** to include (*he is numbered among our greatest scientists*):—
back number 1 (*inf*) a person who is no longer important (*once a famous tennis player but now a back number*). **2** a pr evious issue of a magazine.

num'eracy *n* the ability to perform basic mathematical tasks.

nu'meral *n* a word or figure standing for a number (*Roman numerals*).

nu'merate *vb* (*fml*) to count:—*adj* able to do arithmetic and mathematics (*people who are scarcely numerate*):—*n* **numera'tion.**

nu'merator *n* in vulgar fractions, the number above the line which tells how many parts there are.

numer'ical *adj* having to do with numbers (*numerical information/in numerical order*).

nu'merous *adj* many (*numerous reasons for leaving*).

numismat'ics *n* the study of coins and medals:—*n* **numis'matist.**

num'skull *n* a stupid person, a fool (*the teacher accused him of being a numskull*).

nun *n* a woman who joins a convent and vows to devote her life to the service of God.

nuncio [nûn-se-ō] *n* an ambassador appointed to represent the pope.

nun'nery *n* a convent, a house for nuns.

nup'tial *adj* (*fml*) having to do with marriage (*a nuptial ceremony*):—*npl* **nup'tials** a marriage.

nurse *n* one trained to look after the young, sick or aged (*a hospital nurse*):—*vb* **1** to look after as a nurse (*nurse the patient*). **2** to give milk from the breast, to suckle (*mothers nursing babies*). **3** to look after with gr eat care (*nurse his tomato plants*). **4** to k eep in existence (*nurse hopes of success*).

nurs'ery *n* **1** a r oom in a house for children to sleep or play in. **2** a place wher e young children are

looked after (*she takes the child to a nursery before she goes to work*). **3** a place where plants are grown for sale (*buy tomato plants from the local nursery*).

nursery school *n* a school for young children of pre-school age.

nurs'eryman *n* a man who has or looks after a nursery for plants.

nursing home *n* a small private hospital for invalids, convalescent people or old people unable to take care of themselves.

nur'ture *n* care and training (*nurture of children by their parents*):—*vb* **1** to car e for (*parents nurturing children*). **2** to help to gr ow or develop (*nurture ideas of independence*).

nut *n* **1** a fruit with a har d outer shell and an eatable kernel inside it (*crack the nut*). **2** the eatable kernel (*put nuts in the cake*). **3** a scr ew that is turned on to one end of a bolt to fasten it:—**in a nutshell** in a few words.

nut'crackers *npl* an instrument for cracking nuts.

nut'meg *n* the hard seed of an Eastern tree, used as a spice in cooking (*add grated nutmeg to the sauce*).

nu'triment *n* food needed for life and growth (*soil low in nutriments for the plants*).

nutrition *n* **1** food, nourishment (*poor standards of nutrition*). **2** the pr ocess of getting or giving food (*in charge of the children's nutrition*).

nutri'tious, nu'tritive *adjs* good for the health of the body (*nutritious food/a nutritious diet*).

nut'ty *adj* **1** tasting of nuts (*a nutty flavour*). **2** (*inf*) mad, crazy (*one of his nutty ideas*).

nuz'zle *vb* **1** to push or rub with the nose (*a horse nuzzling its owner*). **2** to pr ess close up to (*she nuzzled her head against his shoulder*).

ny'lon *n* **1** a man-made fibr e for thread or cloth (*shirts made of nylon*). **2** a stocking made fr om this (*a pair of nylons*).

nymph *n* in legend, a goddess of forests, rivers, trees, etc.

O

oaf *n* a stupid or clumsy person (*the oaf painted the wrong door*).

oak *n* a hardwood tree that bears acorns.

oak'-apple *n* a diseased growth on the leaves of oak trees.

oak'um *n* the strands of an old rope picked apart and used for stopping up the spaces between planks of ships.

oar *n* a pole with a flat broad end, used for rowing a boat (*he lost one of the oars*).

oars'man *n* a rower (*the oarsmen in the boat race*).

oasis [ō-ā'-sis] *n* (*pl* **oa'ses** [ō-ā'-sez]) **1** a place in the desert where there is water and trees and plants grow. **2** any place of shelter or relief (*her house was an oasis in his busy life*).

oast *n* a large oven for drying hops or malt.

oat *n*, **oats** *npl* a grain much used for food:—**sow one's wild oats** to live a life of unrestrained enjoyment when young (*he is a quiet mature man now that he has sown his wild oats*):—*adj* (*old*) **oat'en**

oat'cake *n* a thin cake made of oatmeal (*serve oatcakes with cheese*).

oath *n* **1** a solemn promise, esp one made in God's name (*take the oath in court*). **2** a swear word (*object to his oaths in front of children*).

oat'meal *n* oats ground to powder (*take some oatmeal to make porridge*).

ob'durate *adj* stubborn, hard-hearted (*there is no point in trying to persuade her not to go—she is obdurate*):—*n* **ob'duracy**.

obe'dient *adj* willing to do what one is told (*obedient children/followers obedient to their leader*):—*n* **obe'dience**.

obeisance [ō-bā'-sêns] *n* (*fml*) a bow of respect (*make obeisance to the emperor*).

ob'elisk *n* a tall four-sided stone monument, narrowing to a point at its top.

obese' *adj* (*fml*) very fat:—*n* **obes'ity**.

obey' *vb* **1** to do what one is told (*when her mother tells her to do something, she obeys*). **2** to carry out (*obey instructions*).

obit'uary *n* **1** a list of deaths. **2** a newspaper account of the life of a person recently dead (*an obituary of the famous poet*).

ob'ject *n* **1** anything that can be perceived by the senses. **2** aim, purpose (*his object is to make money quickly*). **3** in grammar, a word governed by a verb or preposition:—*vb* **object'** **1** to express dislike. **2** to speak against.

objec'tion *n* a reason against (*raise objections against the proposed new road*).

objec'tionable *adj* deserving to be disliked, unpleasant (*a really objectionable young man*).

objec'tive *adj* not depending on, or influenced by, personal opinions (*judges have to be objective*):—*n* aim, purpose (*his objective is a job that he will enjoy*).

objec'tor *n* one who objects (*objectors to the new road scheme*):—**conscientious objector** one who refuses to fight in a war because he or she believes all killing is wrong.

obliga'tion *n* **1** a duty, a promise that must be kept (*he is under an obligation to support his children*). **2** gratitude due to another for kindness or help.

oblig'atory *adj* that has to be done (e.g. as a duty), compulsory (*attendance at the meeting is obligatory*).

oblige *vb* **1** (*fml*) to force or make it necessary to do (*she was obliged to stop working because of ill health*). **2** to do a kindness to or service for (*could you oblige us by lending us your lawn mower*).

oblig'ing *adj* ready to help, kind (*obliging neighbours*).

oblique [o-bleek'] *adj* **1** slanting (*an oblique line*). **2** indirect, roundabout (*an oblique reference to his dishonesty*).

oblit'erate *vb* **1** to destroy utterly (*a town obliterated by enemy bombs*). **2** to blot out (*snow obliterating the footprints in the mud*):—*n* **oblitera'tion**.

obliv'ion *n* **1** the state of being unaware, forgetfulness (*in total oblivion of what had happened*). **2** the state of being forgotten (*he used to be famous but after his death his name sank into oblivion*).

obliv'ious *adj* unaware of, not paying attention to (*completely oblivious to what was happening around him*).

ob'long n 1 a four-sided figure with all angles right angles and one pair of sides longer than the other pair. 2 a figure or object so shaped.

ob'loquy n (fml) insulting language, abuse.

obno'xious adj very unpleasant, hateful (obnoxious people/obnoxious smells).

o'boe n a wooden wind instrument, hautboy:—n **o'boist.**

obscene' adj 1 disgusting, indecent, esp sexual (obscene passages in the film had to be removed):—n **obscen'ity.**

obscure' adj 1 (fml) dark (an obscure corner of the room). 2 not clear in meaning (an obscure reference to an earlier work). 3 not well-known, not famous (an obscure poet):—vb 1 to dark en. 2 to hide from view. 3 to make more difficult.

obscu'rity n the state of being obscure (a once-famous poet now in obscurity).

ob'sequies npl (fml) funeral ceremonies.

obse'quious adj contemptibly eager to please or do service for another (obsequious members of staff trying to please the boss to gain promotion).

obser'vance n 1 the act of obser ving (the observance of religious holidays). 2 the act of obeying (the observance of the law).

obser'vant adj quick to notice things (not observant enough to take the registration number of the car).

observa'tion n 1 the act, power or habit of obser v-ing (the policeman's observation of the criminal's activities). 2 a r emark (he made the observation that things were going badly for the government).

obser'vatory n a place from which scientists study the stars, the planets and the heavens.

observe' vb 1 (fml) to see, to notice (observe a change in the weather). 2 to watch car efully (police told to observe the movements of the accused). 3 to carr y out (observing local customs). 4 to say , to make a remark (he observed that the weather was mild for the time of year).

obser'ver n 1 one who obser ves. 2 one whose job it is to take careful notice of what is going on.

obsess' vb to take up all one's thoughts and interest (obsessed by her rival's activities).

obses'sion n an idea or interest that takes up all one's attention so that one never thinks of other things.

obsid'ian n a glassy rock that may be made into stones for jewellery.

obsoles'cent adj going out of use (obsolescent business methods).

ob'solete adj no longer in use, out of date (obsolete words).

ob'stacle n that which is in the way and prevents progress (lack of money was the obstacle to the firm's plans for expansion).

obstacle race n a race in which the runners have to find their way under, over or through certain objects placed on the course to hinder them.

obstet'ric adj having to do with midwifery or childbirth.

obstet'rics n the study of the means of helping at childbirth (a doctor specializing in obstetrics).

ob'stinate adj 1 determined to hold to one's own opinions, etc, stubborn. 2 not easy to cur e or remove:—n **ob'stinacy.**

obstrep'erous adj noisy and disorderly (people who become obstreperous when they are drunk).

obstruct' vb 1 to stop up. 2 to pr event from moving or acting freely.

obstruc'tion n 1 a cause of delay . 2 an obstacle.

obstruc'tive adj causing delay (obstructive tactics).

obtain' vb 1 to get (interested in obtaining a share of the business). 2 (fml) to be in use (the conditions that currently obtain).

obtain'able adj that can be got (goods no longer obtainable).

obtrude' vb 1 (fml) to push forward though unwanted (obtruding his opinions on the meeting). 2 to enter uninvited (not wishing to obtrude on a family party):—n **obtru'sion.**

obtru'sive adj appearing where unwanted, unpleasantly noticeable (obtrusive cooking smells/ their obtrusive behaviour).

obtuse [ob-tûs'] adj 1 stupid, slow to understand (they accused him of being deliberately obtuse in not understanding the instructions). 2 (of an angle) greater than a right angle.

ob'verse n the 'heads' side of a coin.

ob'viate vb (fml) to get rid of, to remove (succeed in obviating most of the problems).

ob'vious adj easily seen or understood (an obvious solution to the problem).

occa'sion n 1 a particular time (decide not to complain on this occasion). 2 a special event (the *wedding was the occasion of the year for the family*). **3** (*fml*) a reason (*no occasion to be angry*). **4** (*fml*) opportunity (*if the occasion arises*):—*vb* to cause.

occa'sional *adj* **1** happening now and then (*pay the occasional visit*). **2** having to do with a particular event or occasion (*occasional poems*).

occasional table *n* a small easily moved table.

oc'cident *n* (*fml*) the west.

occiden'tal *adj* (*fml*) western.

occult' *adj* secret, mysterious, having to do with magic (*occult powers/occult ceremonies*).

oc'cupancy *n* **1** act of going to live in a house (*their occupancy of the new house*). **2** the time during which one lives there (*an occupancy of five years*).

oc'cupant, oc'cupier *ns* the person living in a house (*owner-occupiers*).

occupa'tion *n* **1** act of occupying (*their occupation of the house/the enemy army's occupation of the city*). **2** the time during which a place is occupied (*during the occupation, many people tried to leave the country*). **3** one's job (*looking for a new occupation*). **4** that which one is doing at a certain time (*various leisure occupations*).

oc'cupy *vb* **1** to tak e possession of (*a town occupied by the enemy*). **2** to live in (*he occupies the whole house*). **3** to fill (*occupying an important post*). **4** to k eep busy (*she keeps herself occupied by doing voluntary work*). **5** to tak e up (space, time, etc) (*his collection of model trains occupies a whole room*).

occur' *vb* (**occurred'**, **occur'ring**) **1** to happen (*accidents occurring*). **2** to come to the mind (*it suddenly occurred to me who he was*). **3** to be found here and there.

occur'rence *n* a happening, an event (*a daily occurrence*).

ocean [ō'-shên] *n* **1** the vast body of salt water surrounding the land on the earth (*on land or in the ocean*). **2** a lar ge sea (*the Pacific Ocean*):—*adj* **ocean'ic**.

o'chre *n* a yellowish clay used for colouring.

oc'tagon *n* a figure or shape with eight angles and sides.

octag'onal *adj* eight-sided.

oc'tave *n* **1** (*mus*) a scale of eight notes beginning and ending with a note of the same tone but a different pitch. **2** a stanza of eight lines.

octa'vo *n* a sheet of paper folded to give eight equal pages when cut.

octet' *n* a piece of music for eight singers or instruments.

Octo'ber *n* the tenth month of the year (*Halloween is 31st October*).

octogena'rian *n* one who is eighty years old or between eighty and ninety.

oc'topus *n* a sea creature with eight arms.

octosyllab'ic *adj* having eight syllables (*an octosyllabic word*).

oc'ular *adj* having to do with the eyes or sight (*ocular problems*).

oc'ulist *n* one skilled in diseases of the eye.

odd *adj* **1** (*of a number*) not even, that cannot be divided by two without leaving a remainder of one (*9 is an odd number*). **2** strange, unusual (*an odd character/an odd thing to say*). **3** unmatched (*six pairs of gloves and one odd one*).

odd'ity *n* something strange or unusual, a queer person (*he's a bit of an oddity*).

odd'ment *n* a piece left over (*oddments of material*).

odds *npl* the chances in favour of a certain happening or result (*the odds are that he will win*):—**at odds with** on bad terms with (*two branches of the firm at odds with each other*):—**make no odds** make no difference (*it makes no odds how many people come—we have plenty of room*):—**odds and ends** extra pieces or things of various kinds (*go shopping for some odds and ends*).

ode *n* a poem in which the writer expresses his ideas or feelings on a certain subject at some length (*Keats's 'Ode to Autumn'*).

o'dious *adj* hateful, disgusting (*an odious smell/ an odious man*).

o'dium *n* (*fml*) hatred, widespread dislike or blame (*bring odium on his family*).

odorif'erous *adj* (*fml*) having an odour (*odoriferous fumes*).

o'dour *n* any smell, pleasant or unpleasant (*the odour of a fish in the boat*):—**in bad odour** unpopular.

o'dourless *adj* having no smell (*odourless face creams*).

o'dorous *adj* having a smell, esp a characteristic one (*the odorous smell of lilies*).

od'yssey n (lit) a long adventurous journey.

o'er (lit) over.

oesophagus [ee-sof´-ê-gês] n (pl **oesophagi** [ee-sof´-ê-gî]) the pipe from the mouth to the stomach (get a piece of food stuck in the oesophagus).

off adv 1 away (they drove off). 2 distant (a few miles off):—adj 1 not happening (the match is off). 2 (inf) not fit to eat, bad, rotten (this meat is off):—prep away from, not on (keep off the grass/take your foot off the table):—n in cricket, the side of the field nearer to the bat than to the batsman when he prepares to strike the ball.

offal n the inner organs of an animal sold as food or regarded as waste matter (offal such as heart and liver).

offence' n 1 a wrongful act (it's an offence to drive in the dark without lights). 2 hurt done to the feelings, a feeling that one has been insulted (a remark that gave offence to his family).

offend' vb 1 to displease, to hurt someone's feelings (she was offended at not being asked to their party). 2 (fml) to do wrong (offend against society). 3 to be unpleasant or disagreeable (his bad language offended her).

offen'der n 1 one who does wrong (a first offender who was not sent to prison). 2 one who causes offence.

offen'sive adj 1 unpleasant (an offensive smell/ an offensive person). 2 insulting (an offensive remark). 3 having to do with attack (offensive weapons):—n an attack (the army took the offensive).

offer vb 1 to give one the chance of taking (offer him a job). 2 to say that one is willing (to do something) (to offer to help). 3 to give as a sacrifice (offer a lamb to God):—n 1 act of offering. 2 the thing or amount offered (an offer of £60,000 for their flat).

offering n 1 (fml or hum) a gift (a humble offering). 2 (old) that which is sacrificed to God. 3 a sum of money given at a religious service, used for the work of the church.

offertory n 1 the collection of money taken at a church service, an offering. 2 a prayer read or sung during the collection.

off'hand' adj careless, thoughtless (his offhand treatment of others).

of'fice n 1 a special duty . 2 a job, esp one in the service of the public (the office of mayor/the political party in office). 3 a room or building in which business is carried on (the head office of the company). 4 (fml) an act of kindness (thanks to his good offices).

officer n one holding a post with certain powers or duties, esp in the armed forces (an army officer).

offi'cial adj 1 having to do with an office or the duties attached to it (his official tasks). 2 given out or announced by those with the right to do so (receive official permission):—n one who holds a post with certain powers or duties.

offi'cialdom n all those holding public office, an unbending attitude of holding to regulations and routine (thanks to officialdom, her visa took weeks to come through).

offi'ciate vb to carry out the duties of an office (officiating at the marriage service).

offi'cious adj too eager to give orders or offer advice (an officious little man who told them they would have to change trains).

offing n the part of the sea some distance from the shore but not out of sight of it:—**in the offing** not far off (a storm in the offing).

off'set vb (**offset, offsetting**) to make up for (her enthusiasm offsets her lack of training).

offshoot n 1 a branch or shoot growing out from the main stem of a plant. 2 something growing out of something else (the firm is an offshoot of a large business).

offside' adv and adj in football or hockey, in a position disallowed by the rules when the ball was last kicked or struck.

offspring n a child (the couple have badly behaved offspring).

oft adv (lit) often.

often adv frequently (we often see them).

o'gee n in architecture, an S-shaped stone decoration.

ogive' n a pointed arch.

o'gle vb to look sideways at, to look or stare at because of admiration or sexual attraction.

o'gre n in fairy tales, a man-eating giant:—f **o'gress**.

ohm [ōm] n the unit of measurement of electrical resistance.

ohm'meter n an instrument for measuring electrical resistance.

oil n **1** a gr easy liquid obtained from vegetable, animal or mineral sources, and used as a fuel, lubricant, etc (*put more oil in the car engine*/*fry the food in sunflower oil*). **2** pl **oils** oil paints or painting (*a portrait in oils*):—vb to put or drop oil on, as on the parts of a machine to make them work smoothly (*oil the hinges of the gate*).

oil'cake n seeds from which the oil has been taken, pressed together and used as food for cattle.

oil'cloth n canvas coated with hardened oil and used as a table-covering.

oil' painting n a picture done in oils (*an oil painting of their house*).

oil'skin n a cloth made waterproof with oil.

oil'y adj **1** cover ed with oil (*oily hands*). **2** gr easy (*oily food*).

oint'ment n an oily paste rubbed on the skin to heal cuts or sores.

old adj **1** not new (*old clothes*). **2** aged (*old people*). **3** belonging to the past (*old customs*). **4** not fresh (*old bread*).

old'en adj (*lit*) of old or ancient times.

old-fash'ioned adj out of date (*old-fashioned clothes*).

olea'ginous adj (*fml*) oily (*oleaginous substances*).

olean'der n an evergreen poisonous flowering shrub.

olfac'tory adj (*fml*) having to do with smelling (*the nose is the olfactory organ*).

ol'igarchy n **1** government by a few people. **2** a state so governed.

olive n **1** an ever green tree bearing a small, sharp-tasting fruit, from which oil can be obtained. **2** its fruit, used as food (*olives stuffed with peppers*):—adj yellowish-green:—n **ol'ive** oil.

olive branch n a sign of peace (*we hadn't spoken to our neighbours for years but we decided to hold out an olive branch to them*).

ol've-skinned' adj having a yellowish-brown skin (*olive-skinned people*).

Olym'pic adj having to do with Olympia in Greece, and the games held there every four years in ancient times.

Olympic Games npl an international athletic contest held every four years, each time in a different country.

omega n the last letter in the Greek alphabet.

om'elette n eggs beaten and fried in a pan.

o'men n a sign of a future event, good or bad (*clouds are an omen of bad weather*).

om'inous adj signifying future trouble or disaster (*ominous black clouds*).

omit' vb (**omit'ted, omit'ting**) **1** to fail to do (*omit to post the letters*). **2** to leave out (*omit a few passages from the report*):—n **omis'sion**.

om'nibus n **1** (*fml*) a bus. **2** a book containing several works by the same author or on the same subject (*an omnibus edition of the crime writer 's works*).

omni'potent adj able to do all things, all-powerful, almighty:—n **omni'potence**.

omnipres'ent adj present in all places at the same time (*Christians believe that God is omnipresent*):—n **omnipres'ence**.

omniscient [om-nish'ênt] adj knowing all things:—n **omnis'cience**.

omni'vorous adj **1** (*fml or hum*) eating all kinds of food (*omnivorous animals*). **2** taking in ever y-thing indiscriminately (*an omnivorous reader*).

once adv **1** on one occasion only (*I met him only once*). **2** formerly (*they were friends once*):—**once and for all** once and never again (*they told her once and for all to go*):—**at once** immediately (*I shall come at once*).

oncol'ogy n the study and treatment of cancer:—**oncol'ogist** n.

on'coming adj approaching (*oncoming traffic*).

one adj single:—pron a person.

on'erous adj difficult to do, burdensome (*onerous tasks*).

one'-sid'ed adj favouring one party or point of view only (*giving a one-sided version of events*).

one'-way' adj of a street, allowing movement of traffic in one direction only.

on'going adj continuing, continuing to develop (*an ongoing process*).

onion [un'-yên] n a strong-smelling eatable bulb, much used in cooking.

on'line' adj controlled by or connected to a central computer or connected to the Internet.

on'looker n a spectator, one who looks at what is happening but takes no part in it (*police asked the onlookers to move from the scene of the accident*).

onomatopoeia [on-ô-ma-tô-pee'-a] n forming words by imitating sounds (e.g. hiss, bang):—adj **onomatopoe'ic**.

on'rush n a rapid advance (*the onrush of the pro-testing demonstrators*).

on'set n the first attack of or the beginning of (*the onset of the illness*).

on'shore adj towards the shore:—adv **onshore'**.

on'slaught n a fierce attack (*try to withstand the enemy onslaught/a politician making an on-slaught on the government*).

o'nus n the duty of doing or proving something, a burden (*the onus is on them to prove his guilt*).

on'ward adj forward:—advs **on'ward, on'-wards**.

on'yx n a precious stone containing layers of different colours.

o'ology n the study of birds' eggs:—n **o'ologist**.

ooze n soft mud, slime:—vb **1** to flow very slowly (*blood oozing from the wound*). **2** to have flowing from (*a wound oozing pus*).

opacity see **opaque**.

o'pal n a white precious stone that changes colour when turned in the light.

opales'cent adj like an opal, changing colour as does an opal.

opaque [o-pāk'] adj that cannot be seen through, letting no light through (*opaque glass*):—n **opa'city**.

o'pen adj **1** not shut, uncovered (*an open gate*). **2** ready for business (*the shops are open*). **3** not hidden (*an open show of affection*). **4** free from obstructions (*the road is open now*). **5** public (*an open meeting*). **6** sincere (*an open manner*). **7** clear:—vb **1** to make or become open (*open the door*). **2** to unlock (*open the safe*). **3** to begin (*open the meeting*):—**keep open house** to welcome all visitors:—**open up** to build roads, etc, in a country to make progress possible.

o'pen-handed adj (*fml*) generous (*an open-handed host*).

o'pening n **1** beginning (*the opening of the fête*). **2** a gap, a way in or out (*an opening in the fence*). **3** an opportunity (*job openings*).

o'penly adv publicly, not secretly (*discuss the matter openly*).

o'pen-mind'ed adj ready to consider new ideas, unprejudiced.

op'era n a musical drama in which all or some of the words are sung (*operas by Wagner*).

op'era glasses npl glasses used in the theatre to magnify the stage and players.

op'erate vb **1** (*of a machine*) to work or to cause to work (*machines operated by hand*). **2** (*of a surgeon*) to cut the body in order to cure or treat a diseased part (*operating to remove her appendix*).

operat'ic adj **1** having to do with opera (*operatic tenors*). **2** exaggerated (*an operatic manner*).

opera'tion n **1** action (*a rescue operation/a plan now in operation*). **2** the way a thing works (*the operation of the machine*). **3** the cutting of the body by a doctor or surgeon to cure or treat a diseased part (*an operation to remove tonsils*).

op'erative adj **1** in action. **2** having effect:—n a worker in a factory.

op'erator n one who looks after a machine (*the lift operator*).

operett'a n a short, not too serious musical play (*an operetta by Gilbert and Sullivan*).

ophthal'mia n a disease of the eye(s).

ophthal'mic adj having to do with the eye(s).

o'piate n a drug that eases pain or helps to sleep (*prescribed an opiate by the doctor*).

opine' vb (*fml*) to think, to suppose.

opin'ion n **1** that which one thinks or believes about something (*listen to the opinions of others*). **2** judgment (*too ill to work in the doctor's opinion*).

opin'ionated, opin'ionative adjs sure that one's opinions are correct (*an opinionated young woman who refuses to listen to the advice of others*).

o'pium n a sleep-producing drug made from poppy seeds.

oposs'um n a small American animal that carries its young in a pouch.

oppo'nent n an enemy, a person whom one tries to overcome in a game, argument, etc (*his opponent in the tennis match*).

op'portune adj happening at the right time (*arrive at the opportune moment*).

oppose' vb **1** to act or speak against (*opposing the bill in Parliament*). **2** to resist (*oppose change*).

oppos'er n one who speaks against.

op'posite adj **1** facing (*the house opposite*). **2** in the same position on the other side. **3** different in every way (*have opposite tastes in music/go in opposite directions*):—n something in every way different (*good is the opposite of bad*):—adv and prep across from.

opposi'tion n 1 the act of going or speaking against, resistance (*their opposition to the new road*). 2 (*often cap*) in parliament, the party that criticizes or resists the governing party (*leader of the Opposition*).

oppress' vb 1 to govern harshly or unjustly , to treat cruelly (*a tyrant who oppressed the people*). 2 to make gloomy or anxious (*oppressed by news of the war*):—n **op-pres'sion**.

oppres'sive adj 1 harsh and unjust (*an oppressive form of government*). 2 (*of the weather*) hot and tiring.

oppro'brious adj (*fml*) insulting (*opprobrious language*).

oppro'brium n (*fml*) public shame or disgrace (*behaviour that brought opprobrium on their family*).

op'tic, op'tical adjs having to do with sight or the eye(s).

opti'cian n one who makes or sells glasses for the eyes (*an appointment at the optician's for an eye test*).

op'tics n the science of light or sight.

op'timism n the belief that all that happens is for the best, cheerful hope that all will go well (*they were full of optimism although we thought they had little chance of success*).

op'timist n a cheerfully hopeful person.

optimis'tic adj having to do with or characterized by optimism (*optimistic people/an optimistic view of life*).

op'tion n choice (*no option but to go*).

op'tional adj that may or may not be done by choice (*some school subjects are optional*).

op'ulence n (*fml*) riches, wealth (*the opulence of the king*).

op'ulent adj (*fml*) rich, wealthy.

op'us n (*pl* **op'uses** *or* **op'era**) 1 (*fml*) a work of art (*the latest opus of the author*). 2 a musical work numbered in order of composition (*Beethoven's opus 106*).

or'acle n 1 in legend, the answer given to a question by or on behalf of a god. 2 the place wher e such answers were given. 3 a person answering on behalf of a god. 4 (*often hum*) a wise or knowledgeable person (*she is the oracle on company law in the office*).

orac'ular n (*fml*) 1 ver y wise. 2 having mor e than one meaning, difficult to understand.

o'ral adj spoken, not written (*an oral exam*).

or'ange n 1 a juicy fruit with a r eddish-yellow skin (*peel the rind from an orange*). 2 the tr ee bearing it. 3 its colour , reddish-yellow:—adj of orange colour.

orangeade' n a drink made with orange juice.

Or'angeman n a member of an Irish Protestant society.

orang'-outang' [-ûtan'] n a large man-like ape with long arms.

ora'tion n (*fml*) a formal public speech (*a funeral oration*).

or'ator n a skilled public speaker (*an eloquent orator*).

orato'rio n a long musical work for choir and orchestra on a religious subject.

or'atory n 1 the art of making speeches (*skilled in oratory*). 2 a small chapel, often for private worship.

orb n 1 (*lit*) a sphere, a round object. 2 (*lit*) a heavenly body. 3 the eyeball. 4 a globe that is part of the British Crown Jewels.

or'bit n 1 the cur ved path of a planet, comet, rocket, etc, around a larger heavenly body (*a satellite in orbit round the earth*). 2 (*fml*) an area of influence (*matters that do not come within the orbit of our department*).

or'chard n a field in which fruit trees are grown (*an apple orchard*).

orchestra [or'-kis-tra] n 1 a gr oup of musicians skilled in different instruments who play together (*she plays the flute in the orchestra*). 2 the place where they sit in a hall or theatre.

orches'tral adj suitable for performance by an orchestra (*orchestral music*).

or'chestrate vb 1 to arrange for an or chestra (*orchestrating the music*). 2 to or ganize or arrange (*orchestrate the campaign*):—n **orchestra'tion**.

orchid [or'-kid] n a showy flower with unusually shaped petals.

or'chis n a type of orchid.

ordain' vb 1 (*fml*) to order (*prisoners freed as the king ordained*). 2 to admit to office as a priest or minister of religion.

or'deal n 1 a difficult, painful experience (*being taken hostage was a terrible ordeal*).

or'der n 1 a methodical arrangement (*put the books in order*). 2 a command (*obey the* *officer's order*). **3** rank, class (*the various orders of plants*). **4** obedience to law (*law and order*). **5** tidiness (*lack of order in the room*). **6** an instruction to mak e or supply something (an order for books). **7** a body or br otherhood of people of the same rank profession, etc, a religious brotherhood obeying a certain rule (*an order of monks*):—*vb* **1** to arrange (*order the book alphabetically*). **2** to command (*order them to leave*). **3** to give an instruction to make or supply (*orders books from them*).

or'derly *adj* **1** tidy, well-arranged (*an orderly room*). **2** well-behaved (*an orderly group of children*):—*n* **1** a soldier who carries the or ders and messages of an officer. **2** a hospital attendant.

or'dinal *adj* showing the place in an order (*first, second, third, etc, are ordinal numbers*).

or'dinance *n* (*fml*) a law, a command (*obey the king's ordinance*).

or'dinary *adj* usual, common, not exceptional (*an ordinary working day*).

ordina'tion *n* the act or ceremony of admitting to office as a priest or minister of religion.

Ordnance Survey *n* the official map-making body of the British government.

or'dure *n* (*fml*) dung.

ore *n* rock from which metal is obtained (*iron ore*).

or'gan *n* **1** part of an animal or plant that ser ves some special purpose (*the respiratory organs*). **2** a lar ge musical instrument supplied with wind through pipes and played by a keyboard (*play the church organ*). **3** a means of conveying views or information to the public (e.g. a newspaper) (*the organ of the political party*).

or'gandie *n* a fine stiffish cotton material like gauze (*bridesmaids' dresses of organdie*).

organ'ic *adj* **1** having to do with an or gan (*an organic disorder*). **2** pr oduced by living organs (*organic compounds*). **3** gr own without the use of artificial fertilizers (*organic vegetables*).

organic chemistry *n* the chemistry of carbon compounds of living things.

or'ganism *n* **1** any living thing (*all the organisms in a pond*). **2** anything in which the parts all work together to serve one purpose.

or'ganist *n* one who plays the organ.

organiza'tion *n* **1** or derly arrangement (*try to establish some organization in the office system*).

2 a gr oup of people working systematically to carry out a common purpose (*a business organization*).

or'ganize *vb* **1** to put together in an or derly way, to make to work systematically (*organizing the office filing system*). **2** to arrange (*organize a party*).

or'gy *n* a wild or drunken feast (*have an orgy while his parents are away*).

or'iel *n* a window built out from a wall.

O'rient *n* the East.

orien'tal *adj* Eastern, Asiatic:—*n* a native of an Eastern or Asiatic country.

Orien'talist *n* one who studies Eastern languages.

or'ientate *vb* **1** to find out north, south, east and west from the point where one is standing (*the climbers were lost in the mist and tried to orientate themselves*). **2** to arrange or dir ect towards (*a course orientated to adult learners*):—*n* **orienta'tion**.

orientee'ring *n* the sport of following a route on foot as quickly as possible, using a map and compass.

or'ifice *n* (*fml*) an opening (*bodily orifices*).

or'igami *n* the Japanese art of paper-folding.

or'igin *n* **1** the place or point at which a thing begins, beginning (*the origin of the river/the origin of the word*). **2** cause (*the origin of his problem*).

orig'inal *adj* **1** new, not thought of before (*an original idea*). **2** first in or der (*the original inhabitants of the country*). **3** r eady to think or act in a new way (*an original thinker*). **4** not copied (*an original painting*):—*n* **1** an original work of art, etc. **2** a cr eative or eccentric person.

original'ity *n* the ability to think or act in a new way.

orig'inate *vb* **1** to bring into being (*originating a new club*). **2** to come into being (*a sport that originated in China*).

or'iole *n* a bird with golden-yellow feathers.

or'ison *n* (*fml*) a prayer.

or'molu *n* bronze that looks like gold, used in decorating furniture (*an ormolu clock*).

or'nament *n* that which decorates or makes more attractive:—*vb* **ornament'** to decorate:—*n* **ornamenta'tion**.

ornamen'tal *adj* decorative (*fireplaces that are purely ornamental*).

ornate' adj with a great deal of ornament, richly decorated (ornate furniture).

ornithol'ogist n one who studies birds (ornithologists going on a bird-watching trip):—n **ornithol'ogy.**

orograph'ic(al) adj (fml) having to do with mountains (an orographical study).

or'phan n a child whose parents are dead (made an orphan by the plane crash):—vb to cause to become an orphan:—also adj.

or'phanage n a home for orphans.

or'rery n a clockwork model of the solar system.

or'thodox adj 1 having the same beliefs or opinions as most other people (orthodox people). 2 agreeing with accepted belief (orthodox views):—n **or'thodoxy.**

orthog'raphy n 1 the art of correct spelling, spelling. 2 the study of spelling.

orthopae'dic adj having to do with injury or diseases of the bones or joints (an orthopaedic surgeon).

os'cillate vb 1 to swing from side to side (an oscillating pendulum). 2 to vary (his opinions tend to oscillate). 3 to give out electro-magnetic waves, so causing bad reception by radio:—n **oscilla'tion.**

os'culate vb (fml) to kiss.

o'sier n willow twigs used in making baskets.

os'prey n a hawk that feeds on fish.

os'seous adj (fml) of or like bone.

os'sify vb to become bone:—n **ossifica'tion.**

osten'sible adj as far as can be seen, apparent (his ostensible reason for leaving).

ostenta'tion n the making of much show to attract attention, a showing off, rich display (their neighbours accused them of ostentation in having a flashy car).

ostenta'tious adj showy, fond of display (an ostentatious wedding despite their lack of money).

osteol'ogy n (fml) the study of bones.

os'teopath n one who practises osteopathy (go to an osteopath with his sore back).

osteop'athy n cure of disease by massage or otherwise handling the bones.

os'tler n (old) a man who looked after horses at an inn.

os'tracize vb to drive out of society, to refuse to have anything to do with (workers ostracizing people who worked during the strike):—n **os'tracism.**

os'trich n a large swift-running bird valued for its feathers.

oth'er adj 1 one of two things (the other hand). 2 addition (we have other problems). 3 those not mentioned, present, etc (other people).

oth'erwise adv 1 in a different way (they think otherwise). 2 if this were not so (you must pay—otherwise they will sue you).

otiose [ō'-ti-ōs or ō'-shi-ōs] adj (fml) idle, lazy.

ot'ter n a fish-eating animal of the weasel family.

Ot'toman adj (old) Turkish:—n 1 (old) a Turk. 2 (without cap) a sofa without back or arms.

ought vb should (she ought to see a doctor).

ounce¹ n 1 a unit of weight ($1/16$ lb or 28.349 grams). 2 a small amount (not an ounce of common sense).

ounce² n a kind of small leopard, the snow leopard.

ousel see **ouzel.**

oust vb to put out, to drive out (oust him from his post).

out adv 1 not inside (the children are out in the garden). 2 away (he was told to get out):—prep out of, out through, outside:—adj 1 external. 2 asleep or unconscious (out to the world).

out-and-out' adj thorough (an out-and-out villain).

out'back n a remote area of Australia with very few inhabitants.

outbid' vb (outbid', outbid'ding) to offer a higher price than another (she outbid him for the antique furniture).

out'board adj attached to the outside of a boat (an outboard motor).

out'break n a sudden beginning, a breaking out (the outbreak of war).

out'burst n a bursting out, an explosion (an outburst of applause/an outburst of anger).

out'cast adj driven away from one's home and friends:—n a person so driven away (an outcast from society).

outclass' vb to do very much better than (they were outclassed by the opposition in the competition).

out'come n the result (the outcome of the discussion).

out'crop n a layer of rock that shows above the surface of the earth.

out'cry n widespread complaint (there was an outcry at the closure of the bridge).

out'dat'ed *adj* old-fashioned, out-of-date (*outdated ideas about childcare*).

outdis'tance *vb* to get ahead of (*outdistancing the rest of the runners*).

outdo' *vb* to do better than (*try to outdo him in giving her expensive presents*).

out'door *adj* done in the open air (*an outdoor display*).

outdoors' *adv* in the open air (*have lunch outdoors*).

out'er *adj* **1** farther out (*outer space*). **2** outside (*the outer layer of clothes*).

out'ermost *adj* farthest out (*the outermost ring of a target*).

out'fall *n* the mouth of a river.

out'field *n* the parts of a field distant from the centre.

out'fit *n* **1** all the articles necessary for a certain job (*a bicycle repair outfit*). **2** a set of articles of clothing (*buy a new outfit for the wedding*).

out'fitter *n* one who sells clothes (*a gents' outfitter*).

outflank' *vb* to go to a position from which one can attack from the side as well as in front (*outflank the enemy army*).

out'goings *npl* the money spent (*their outgoings came to more than their income*).

outgrow' *vb* **1** to grow taller than (*he has outgrown his elder brother*). **2** to grow too big or too old for (*children outgrowing their clothes*).

out'house *n* a small house or building near the main one (*the farm outhouses*).

out'ing *n* a short trip made for pleasure (*take the children on an outing to the seaside*).

outland'ish *adj* strange (*outlandish clothes*).

out'law *n* (*old*) one whose person and property are no longer protected by the law (*Robin Hood was an outlaw*):—*vb* **1** to declare an outlaw. **2** to declare not legal (*outlaw drinking and driving*):—*n* **out'lawry**.

out'lay *n* money spent (*the outlay on new office equipment*).

out'let *n* **1** an opening outwards (*an outlet from the main water tank*). **2** an activity that allows one to make use of one's powers or of a particular ability (*an outlet for his musical talent*).

out'line *n* **1** a line showing the shape of a thing (*children asked to draw the outline of a face*).

2 an account of the most important points, etc (*an outline of the proposals for improvement*):—*vb* **1** to draw in outline. **2** to describe without giving details (*outlining the plans for expansion*).

outlive' *vb* to live longer than (*he outlived his son*).

out'look *n* **1** view (*a house with a beautiful outlook*). **2** what seems likely to happen in future (*the financial outlook for the firm is not good*). **3** point of view (*a gloomy outlook on life*).

outlying *adj* distant, far from the centre (*the outlying areas*).

outmanoe'uvre *vb* to defeat by more skilful movements or planning, to do better than (*outmanoeuvring his opponent to win the match*).

out-mod'ed *adj* out of fashion (*outmoded ideas*).

outnum'ber *vb* to be greater in number than (*the children outnumbered the adults*).

out-of-date' *adj* old-fashioned (*out-of-date clothes*).

out-of-the-way' *adj* **1** not easily reached (*out-of-the-way places*). **2** unusual (*it was not out-of-the-way for him suddenly to disappear*).

out'patient *n* one who visits a hospital for treatment but does not stay there (*attend as an outpatient to have his broken arm attended to*).

out'post *n* **1** a defended place close to enemy territory and in front of the main positions. **2** a settlement far from towns and main roads (*the last outpost of civilization*).

out'pouring *n* the saying all at once of just what one feels (*the outpouring of his grief*).

out'put *n* the total amount produced by a machine, factory, worker, etc (*increase output by 10%*).

out'rage *n* **1** a violent and wicked deed (*outrages committed by enemy soldiers*). **2** a deed that shocks or causes widespread anger (*regard the decision to cut workers' wages as an outrage*):—*vb* **1** to injure. **2** to insult.

outrage'ous *adj* **1** shocking, wicked (*an outrageous crime/it was outrageous to charge so much*). **2** extravagantly unusual (*her outrageous hats*).

out'rider *n* a person who rides on horseback or on a motorcycle beside or in front of a vehicle (*police outriders with a very large lorry*).

out'rigger *n* a light racing boat with special jutting-out rests for the oars or rowlocks).

outright' *adv* **1** completely and at once (*they paid for the funiture outright/kill him outright*).

2 openly, frankly (*tell me outright what you feel*):—*adj* complete (*an outright refusal*).

outrun' *vb* to run faster than (*outrun the other horses in the race*).

out'set *n* beginning (*realize the plan was a failure from the outset*).

outshine' *vb* to do much better than (*his performance outshone all the rest*).

out'side *n* **1** the outer part or parts (*the outside of the orange*). **2** the part farthest from the centre (*standing on the outside of the group*):—*adj* **1** being on the outside, external (*outside help*). **2** outdoor (*an outside lavatory*). **3** slight (*an outside chance*):—*adv* on or to the outside:—*prep* on or to the exterior of, beyond.

outsid'er *n* **1** one who is not accepted as a member of a certain group (*still regarded as an outsider by the family although she is married to one of the sons*). **2** one who is believed to have little chance of winning (*a horse regarded as an outsider won the race*).

outsize' *adj* of a very large size (*outsize clothes*).

out'skirts *npl* the parts of a town or city farthest from the centre (*live on the outskirts of the city*).

outspo'ken *adj* saying just what one thinks, frank (*outspoken people stating their objections*).

outstand'ing *adj* **1** exceptionally good (*an outstanding pupil/an outstanding performance*). **2** (*fml*) still in existence (*outstanding debts*).

outstay' *vb* to stay longer than (*outstay their welcome*).

outstrip' *vb* **1** to pass in running (*outstrip all the other runners*). **2** to do better than (*outstrip their competitors in sales ability*).

outvote' *vb* to defeat by obtaining more votes.

out'ward *adj* **1** on the outside or surface (*her outward cheerfulness*). **2** away from a place (*the outward journey*):—*advs* **out'-ward, out'wards, out'wardly**.

outward-bound *adj* sailing to a foreign port.

outwit' *vb* to outdo or overcome by greater cleverness, to deceive (*succeed in outwitting the police*).

out'work *n* **1** a fort in advance of the main defences. **2** a jutting-out part of a fort. **3** work for a firm that is done outside the firm's premises (*workers doing outwork at home*).

ouzel, ousel [ö́-zêl] *n* **1** a blackbir d. **2** a thrush.

ou'zo *n* an alcoholic drink popular in Greece.

ova *see* **ovum.**

o'val *adj* egg-shaped (*an oval face*):—*n* an oval shape or figure.

o'vary *n* **1** a bodily or gan in which eggs are formed (*a woman's ovaries*). **2** the seed case of a plant.

ova'tion *n* enthusiastic applause (*a standing ovation*).

oven [uv'-ên] *n* a small cupboard heated by a fire or stove and used for cooking (*an electric oven*).

o'ver *prep* **1** above (*a picture over the mantelpiece*). **2** across (*jump over the wall*). **3** more than (*over three miles*):—*adv* **1** above (*planes flying over*). **2** across (*water boiling over*). **3** from one side to the other or another (*roll over*). **4** more than the quantity assigned (*food left over*). **5** completed (*it's all over*). **6** from beginning to end (*think it over*):—*n* the number of successive balls delivered by a bowler in cricket.

o'verall(s) *n* (*pl*) garment(s) worn over one's usual clothes to keep them clean (*workers wearing overalls*).

overawe' *vb* to frighten into obeying or being silent, to fill with silent respect (*children overawed by the great man*).

overbal'ance *vb* **1** to lean too much in one dir ection and fall (*the tightrope walker overbalanced*). **2** to cause to fall in this way.

overbear'ing *adj* proud and commanding (*overbearing people who try to bully others*).

overboard' *adv* over the side of a ship (*fall overboard*).

overbur'den *vb* **1** to put too gr eat a load on (*overburden the donkey*). **2** to give too har d a task to (*overburden the pupils with too much homework*).

overcast' *adj* clouded over (*an overcast sky*).

overcharge' *vb* to ask for too great a price (*he was overcharging customers*):—*n* **o'vercharge** too high a price.

o'vercoat *n* a warm outer garment (*wear an overcoat over his suit*).

overcome' *vb* **1** to defeat (*overcome the enemy*). **2** to get the better of (*overcome difficulties*).

overdo' *vb* **1** to do too much (*the invalid was told not to overdo it*). **2** to cook for too long (*overdo the steak*).

o'verdose *n* too large a dose (*take an overdose of the drug, intending to commit suicide*):—*also vb.*

o'verdraft *n* the amount of money drawn from a bank in excess of what is available in an account (*try to pay off their overdraft*).

overdraw' *vb* **1** to tak e more from a bank than one has in one's account (*overdraw his account*). **2** (*fml*) to add picturesque but not always true details (*overdraw his adventures*).

overdress' *vb* to dress too well for the occasion (*she felt overdressed since everyone else was wearing jeans and sweaters*).

overdue' *adj* after the time fixed or due.

overes'timate *vb* to set too high a value on (*overestimating their ability*).

overexpose' *vb* to admit too much light when taking a photograph.

overflow' *vb* to flood, to flow over the edge or limits of (*the river overflowed its banks*):—*n* **1** what flows over the sides (*a pipe for the overflow*). **2** the amount by which something is too much (*another hall for the overflow of the audience*).

overgrown' *adj* grown beyond the normal size.

overhang' *vb* (*pt, pp* **overhung'**) **1** to jut out over (*cliffs overhanging the sea*). **2** to thr eaten (*the worry of redundancy overhanging them*).

overhaul' *vb* **1** to examine thor oughly and carry out necessary repairs (*overhauling the car engine*). **2** to catch up (*overhaul the other runners*):—*n* **o'verhaul.**

overhead' *adj and adv* in the sky, above (*overhead cables*).

o'verheads *npl* the costs of running a business (*the overheads are too expensive*).

overhear' *vb* to hear what one is not intended to hear (*overhear his parents' conversation*).

overland' *adv* across land (not sea) (*journey overland*):—*adj* **o'verland** passing by land.

overlap' *vb* to cover partly and go beyond it (*tiles overlapping*).

overleaf' *adv* on the reverse side of a page (*turn overleaf*).

overload' *vb* to put too heavy a load on.

overlook' *vb* **1** to look down on fr om above (*balconies overlooking the sea*). **2** to for give, to let off without punishment (*overlook the children's naughtiness*). **3** not to notice, to miss (*defects that are easily overlooked*).

o'verlord *n* a lord, esp one to whom other lords have promised obedience or service.

overmuch' *adj and adv* too much (*she doesn't like him overmuch*).

overnight' *adv* during the night (*have to stay overnight after the party*):—*adj* done in or lasting the night (*an overnight journey*).

overpow'er *vb* to defeat by greater strength (*succeed in overpowering the burglar*).

overpow'ering *adj* too great to bear (*an overpowering urge to scream*).

overrate' *vb* to think a person or thing better than he, she or it really is (*he thinks the artist is overrated*).

overreach' *vb* to fail by trying too much (*overreach themselves by borrowing too much money*).

override' *vb* to decide to pay no attention to (*override their objections*).

overrule' *vb* to use one's power to change the decision or judgement of another (*the appeal court judge overruled the previous judgment*).

overrun' *vb* **1** to spr ead over in large numbers (*a building overrun with rats*). **2** to continue beyond the expected time (*the programme overran*).

oversea(s)' *adj and adv* across the sea (*go overseas to work*).

oversee' *vb* to direct the work of others (*oversee production*):—*n* **o'verseer.**

oversha'dow *vb* **1** to mak e less happy (*a wedding overshadowed by the threat of war*). **2** to mak e seem less important (*her achievements were overshadowed by those of her sister*).

o'vershoe *n* a waterproof shoe for wearing over an ordinary shoe.

overshoot' *vb* to go beyond before stopping (*planes overshooting the runway*).

o'versight *n* a mistake, a failure to do something (*fail to invite her because of an oversight*).

oversleep' *vb* to sleep later than intended (*oversleep and be late for work*).

o'verspill *n* people forced to move to a new area because of redevelopment.

overstate' *vb* to say more than is true, to state too strongly (*overstate the case for his defence*).

overstep' *vb* to go beyond the limits of (*overstep her authority*).

oversubscribed' *adj* with more wanted than is on sale (*the tickets for the concert are oversubscribed*).

overt' adj done or said openly, not hidden (their overt dislike of him).

overtake' vb to catch up with (the car overtook the lorry).

overtax' vb 1 to tax too heavily (he thinks he has been overtaxed by the Inland Revenue). 2 to require too much of (overtax his strength).

overthrow' vb to defeat, to remove from power (overthrow the government):—also n.

o'vertime n time worked beyond the regular hours (be paid extra for overtime):—also adj and adv.

o'verture n 1 a proposal, an offer (overtures of peace). 2 the music played by the orchestra before an opera, etc.

overturn' vb 1 to turn upside down (overturn the bucket). 2 to make fall, to defeat, to ruin (overturn the government).

overween'ing adj unbearably great (his overweening pride).

overweight' adj weighing more than the proper amount:—n excess weight.

overwhelm vb 1 to defeat utterly (overwhelm the enemy). 2 to overcome all one's powers, to make to feel helpless (overwhelmed by the volume of work).

overwork' vb to work too hard (pupils overworking for their exams):—n too much work.

overwrought' adj overexcited, too nervous (too overwrought to think properly).

o'viform, o'void adjs egg-shaped.

ovip'arous adj (fml) egg-laying (oviparous creatures).

ovoid see oviform.

o'vum n (pl o'va) an egg.

owe vb 1 to be in debt to (owe his brother £100). 2 to be obliged to (someone), to feel grateful to (owe his parents a lot):—**owing to** because of (cancelled owing to bad weather).

owl n a night bird of prey.

owl'et n a young owl.

owl'ish adj having a round solemn face and usu glasses (an owlish child).

own adj belonging to oneself:—vb 1 to possess (they own a car). 2 (fml) to admit (she owned that she was guilty):—n own'er:—n own'ership.

ox n 1 a bull or cow. 2 pl ox'en cattle.

ox'eye n a wild chrysanthemum.

oxida'tion n compounding with oxygen.

ox'ide n a compound of oxygen with another element.

ox'idize vb to make unite with oxygen.

ox'lip n a type of primrose.

ox'ygen n a gas without colour, taste or smell that is present in air and water, and is necessary for all life.

ox'ygenate, ox'ygenize vbs to mix with oxygen.

oxymo'ron n a figure of speech in which an adjective seems to contradict the noun it accompanies (e.g. busy idler).

oyez [ō-yes'] interj (old) listen! (the call of a public crier for silence).

oy'ster n an eatable shellfish with a double shell in which pearls are sometimes found (oysters and champagne).

oy'ster-bed n a place where oysters breed.

oy'ster-cat'cher n a bird of the seashore.

o'zone n 1 a kind of colourless gas with a chlorine-like smell. 2 (inf) clean bracing air as found at the seaside.

ozone layer n a layer of ozone in the stratosphere that absorbs ultraviolet rays from the sun.

P

pace n **1** a step with the foot. **2** the distance so covered. **3** speed:— vb **1** to walk slowly. **2** to measure by steps. **3** to run with someone to help him or her judge or improve his or her speed.

pacific adj (fml) peace-loving (a pacific nation).

pacifica'tion n act of bringing peace.

pa'cifism n the belief that war is never right.

pa'cifist n one who works for the end of all war (pacifists who refused to join the armed services).

pa'cify vb **1** to r estore peace, to end a war in. **2** to calm, to soothe (pacified the crying baby).

pack n **1** a bundle of things fastened or strapped together (the pack on the hiker's back). **2** a set of playing cards. **3** a number of animals acting or hunting together (a pack of hounds). **4** a gang (a pack of thieves). **5** a mass of floating pieces of ice:— vb **1** to mak e into a bundle, to put things into a case, etc (pack for their holiday/pack their clothes). **2** to fill. **3** to fill to overflowing (pack the hall). **4** to fill with one's own supporters (pack the jury).

pack'age n a parcel, a bundle (packages delivered by post).

pack'aging n the materials in which objects are wrapped before they are put on sale.

pack an'imal n an animal used for carrying loads (a pack horse).

pack'er n one employed to pack goods (factory packers).

pack'et n **1** a small par cel (a packet containing a watch). **2** a mail boat.

pack'et steam'er n a mail boat.

pack'-ice n a mass of floating pieces of ice.

pack'ing n the paper, cardboard, etc, used to protect goods being delivered (unwrap the china and throw away the packing).

pack'man n (old) one who sells small goods from door to door (buy clothes pegs from the packman).

pact n an agreement (sign a peace pact).

pad[1] n **1** a small cushion (kneel on a pad to scrub the floor). **2** soft material used to pr otect or to alter shape (shoulder pads). **3** sheets of paper fixed together (note pads). **4** the soft flesh on the foot of certain animals (a dog's pad):— vb (**pad'ded, pad'ding**) **1** to fill out with soft material (pad the shoulders of the coat). **2** to mak e longer with unnecessary words (having little to say, she padded out the essay as much as possible).

pad[2] n **1** (also **footpad**) a r obber. **2** a slow-moving horse:— vb to walk steadily and usu softly (children padded down the hall in their slippers).

pad'ding n **1** soft material used for stuffing or fitting out. **2** wor ds, sentences, etc, put in merely to make longer.

pad'dle n a short oar with a broad blade, sometimes at each end:— vb **1** to r ow with a paddle (paddle the boat downstream). **2** to walk in water with bare feet (children paddling at the seaside).

pad'dle steamer n a steamer driven by two large wheels turning in the water to make it move.

pad'dle wheel n the wheel of a paddle steamer.

pad'dock n **1** a small enclosed field (the paddock for the pony near the house). **2** an enclosur e in which horses are assembled before a race.

pad'dy field n a field in which rice is grown.

pad'lock n a metal device that closes over two rings and thus fastens something (the padlock on the gate):— vb to close with a padlock (padlock the trunk).

padre [pä'-drä] n a priest or minister, esp one serving in the forces.

paen [pee'-ên] n (fml or lit) a song of triumph or praise (paens to celebrate the return of the victorious army).

pa'gan n one who does not know about God, a heathen (missionaries sent to convert pagans):— n **pa'ganism**.

page[1] n **1** a boy ser vant, usu uniformed, in a hotel, club, etc (tell the page to take a message). **2** a boy attendant on a bride at a wedding. **3** (old) a boy attendant of a knight or nobleman.

page[2] n one side of a sheet of paper in a book, etc (turn over the pages of the magazine).

pageant [pa'-jênt] n **1** a performance or pr ocession in which scenes from history are presented (a pageant to celebrate the centenary of the village). **2** a fine display or show (a colourful pageant).

pa'geantry n splendid display.

pago'da n a temple of Buddha in Eastern countries.

pail n an open vessel with a handle for carrying liquids (carry a pail of water).

pain n **1** suffering of body or mind (the pain in his back/the pain of her grief). **2** pl trouble, care (be at pains to explain why he refused):—vb (fml) to cause suffering to (it pained him to leave his family):—adjs **pain'ful**, **pain'less**:—**on pain of death** with death as a punishment.

pains'taking adj **1** ver y careful (a painstaking report). **2** taking gr eat trouble (a painstaking student).

paint n a colouring substance spread over the surface of an object with a brush (buy cans of blue paint to decorate the bathroom/the artist's clothes were covered in paint):—vb **1** to put on paint (paint the bathroom/paint a picture). **2** to paint a picture (he paints as a hobby).

paint'er¹ n **1** one who paints (a house painter). **2** an artist (study to be a painter at art college).

paint'er² n a rope for fastening a small boat.

paint'ing n a painted picture (a painting of their house).

pair n **1** two things of the same kind, a set of two (a pair of gloves/two socks that are not a pair). **3** a couple, two people, animals, etc, often one of either sex, who are thought of as being together (a pair of rabbits/our neighbours are an inquisitive pair):—vb **1** to arrange in twos. **2** to join one to another.

pal n (inf) a friend, comrade (his best pal).

pal'ace n a large and splendid house, esp the house of a king or queen (Buckingham Palace).

palaeolith'ic adj having to do with the early Stone Age (palaeolithic remains).

palanquin' n (old) a light covered carriage carried by poles on men's shoulders.

pal'atable adj **1** pleasing to the taste (a palatable meal). **2** pleasant, acceptable (not finding her suggestion palatable).

pal'atal adj pronounced with the tongue touching or near the palate (a palatal sound).

pal'ate n **1** the r oof of the mouth. **2** the sense of taste, the ability to tell good food or wine from bad (get him to choose the wine as he has a good palate). **3** a taste or liking (novels that are not to his palate).

pala'tial adj large and splendid, like a palace (a palatial residence).

pala'ver n **1** idle talk. **2** (inf) fuss (palaver about nothing). **3** (old) a conference (a palaver between leaders):—vb to talk idly.

pale¹ n **1** a pointed stak e of wood driven into the ground as part of a fence. **2** (old) a boundary:—**beyond the pale** beyond the limit of proper behaviour (his drunken behaviour was beyond the pale).

pale² adj **1** lacking colour , whiteish (ill people looking pale). **2** not dark in colour (pale colours):—vb to make or become pale (she paled with fear).

palette [pal'-et] n a thin board on which an artist mixes paints.

palfrey [pāl'-fri] n (old) a horse for riding.

pal'impsest n a parchment from which the writing has been rubbed out to make room for other writing.

pal'indrome n a word whose letters when read from end to beginning spell the same word (e.g. noon).

pa'ling n a fence of stakes (the paling round the school playground).

palisade' n (old) a defensive fence of stakes.

pall¹ n **1** the cloth spr ead over the coffin at a funeral. **2** a cloak (a pall of mist over the fields).

pall² vb to become uninteresting through too much use (he found that watching television all day soon palled).

pall'-bearer n one holding up a corner of the coffin at a funeral.

pall'et n **1** (old) a bed of straw. **2** a wooden platform on which goods can be carried by a fork-lift truck.

palliasse [pa'-li-as] n a straw mattress.

pal'liate vb (fml) **1** to mak e seem serious, to lessen (try to palliate the crime by pointing out his youth). **2** to r elieve pain for a time (palliating the pain).

pal'lid adj pale, white-faced (pallid after her illness).

pal'lor n paleness (the invalid's pallor).

pal'ly adj (inf) friendly (been pally since their schooldays).

palm¹ n the inner part of the hand between the wrist and fingers:—vb **palm off** to get to accept something worthless (palm off the painting as genuine although it was a copy).

palm² [päm] *n* **1** a tall tropical tree with a crown of long broad leaves at the top of the trunk (*coconut palms*). **2** (*old*) a palm leaf as a sign of victory.

palm'er *n* (*old*) one who carried a palm as a sign of having visited the Holy Land.

palm'ist *n* a person who claims to tell one's future from the lines on one's hand (*have her future told by a palmist*):—*n* **palm'istry**.

Palm Sunday *n* the Sunday before Easter.

palm'y *adj* (*old*) successful (*the palmy days of his youth*).

pal'pable *adj* **1** that can be touched (*a palpable lump*). **2** (*fml*) plain, obvious (*the palpable truth*).

pal'pitate *vb* **1** to tremble (*palpitating with excitement*). **2** (*of the heart*) to beat quickly and irregularly:—*n* **palpita'tion**.

pal'sy *n* a disease causing trembling of the limbs:—*adj* **pal'sied**.

pal'ter *vb* **1** to try to trick. **2** not to deal seriously with.

paltry [pâl'-tri] *adj* **1** mean (*a paltry trick*). **2** contemptibly small, worthless (*a paltry sum of money*).

pam'pas *npl* the vast grassy treeless plains of South America.

pam'per *vb* to spoil by trying to please too much (*pamper the child*).

pam'phlet *n* a small paper-covered book (*a pamphlet giving the aims of the campaign*).

pamphleteer' *n* one who writes pamphlets.

pan *n* **1** a metal pot used for cooking (*a frying pan/pans sitting on the stove*). **2** the upper part of the skull. **3** the tray of a balance or set of scales:—*vb* **pan out** to turn out, to result.

Pan *n* in legend, the Greek god of nature and shepherds.

pan- *prefix* all.

panacea [pa-na-see'-a] *n* a cure for all diseases or evils (*look for a panacea for the world's ills*).

panache [pa-näsh'] *n* **1** (*old*) a plume, esp on a helmet. **2** style, a dramatic show of skill, etc (*introduce the guest with great panache*).

pan'cake *n* a thin cake of batter cooked in a pan or on a girdle (*toss the pancakes*).

pan'chromat'ic *adj* able to photograph colours.

pan'creas *n* a gland in the body that produces a fluid that helps digestion (*a disease of the pancreas*).

pan'da *n* a large black and white animal found in China.

pandemo'nium *n* a scene of noisy disorder, uproar (*there was pandemonium when the crowds were refused entrance to the hall to hear the pop stars*).

pan'der *vb* to give in to the desires of a person or group (*pander to the children by letting them stay up late*).

pane *n* a single piece of glass in a window.

panegyr'ic *n* a speech or piece of writing in praise of someone's good qualities (*a funeral panegyric*):—*n* **panegyr'ist**.

pan'el *n* **1** a thin board d fitted into the framework of a door or on a wall or ceiling (*an old house with indoor walls made of wooden panels*). **2** a group of people who discuss or answer questions put to them by others (*a panel of experts answering questions asked by television viewers*).

pang *n* **1** a sudden sharp pain (*pangs of hunger*). **2** a sudden sharp feeling (*pangs of regret*).

pan'ic *n* **1** a sudden uncontrollable fear (*she suffers from panic attacks*). **2** sudden fear spreading through a crowd and causing wild disorder (*there was panic in the cinema when the fire broke out*):—*also adj*.

pan'ic-strick'en *adj* filled with panic (*the panic-stricken crowd*).

pan'nier *n* one of a pair of baskets slung over the back of a horse, mule, etc (*carry his goods in panniers on a donkey*).

pan'oply *n* **1** (*old*) complete armour. **2** all the splendid clothes, equipment, etc, associated with a particular event (*the panoply of a coronation ceremony*).

panora'ma *n* **1** a wide view (*a breathtaking panorama from the top of the mountain*). **2** a scene painted on a strip of material and gradually unrolled before an audience. **3** a general representation in words or pictures (*a book giving a panorama of life in Tudor England*).

pan'sy *n* a large type of violet.

pant *vb* **1** to take short quick breaths (*runners panting at the end of the race*). **2** to long for (*pant for the chance to sing*):—*n* a gasp.

pantaloon' *n* **1** (*old*) a character in pantomime, made fun of by the clowns. **2** *pl* (*old*) wide trousers.

pantech'nicon *n* a large van for moving furniture (*the removal firm's pantechnicon*).

pan'theism *n* the belief that God exists in everything in the universe.

pan'theist *n* one who believes in pantheism.

pan'theon *n* 1 a temple built in honour of all the gods. 2 a building in which ther e are the tombs of or monuments to the famous men of a country.

pan'ther *n* a leopard, esp the black variety.

pan'tomime *n* 1 an amusing Christmas entertainment with music and songs based on a story popular with children (*go to see 'Jack and the Beanstalk' at the pantomime*). 2 mime.

pan'try *n* 1 a small r oom for keeping food (*keep the food cool in the pantry*). 2 a r oom in which food, dishes, cutlery, etc, are stored.

pants *npl* 1 (*esp Amer*) trousers. 2 underpants.

pap *n* 1 (*old*) the nipple of the breast. 2 soft food for children (*pap prepared for babies*).

pa'pacy *n* 1 the office of pope. 2 the method of government of the RC church.

pa'pal *adj* having to do with the pope (*a papal ruling*).

paparaz'zi *npl* (*sing* –zzo) photographers who follow famous people (often intrusively) in order to take their photographs to sell to newspapers and magazines.

pap'aw *n* the fruit of a South American palm tree.

pa'per *n* 1 a material made fr om wood pulp, rags, etc, and used for writing, printing, wrapping and many other purposes (*waste paper*). 2 a newspaper (*a daily paper*). 3 an essay (*write a paper on the poetry of John Keats*). 4 a set of examination questions on a subject or part of a subject (*the maths paper*):—*vb* to cover with paper (*paper the walls*).

pa'perback *n* a soft book with a paper cover (*wait for the novel to come out in paperback*).

pa'per chase *n* a cross-country run in which certain runners throw down a trail of paper for the others to follow.

pa'per-hanger *n* one who puts up wallpaper (*employ a paper-hanger*).

paper money *n* bank notes.

pa'perweight *n* a heavy object placed on top of loose papers to keep them in place.

papier mâché [pap'-yā mä'-shā] *n* a substance consisting of paper pulp and used for making boxes, ornaments, etc (*children making models out of papier mâché*).

papoose' *n* a North American Indian baby.

pap'rika *n* red pepper (*sprinkle paprika on the savouries*).

papy'rus *n* (*pl* papy'ri) 1 a r eed from which paper was made in ancient times. 2 the paper thus made (*manuscripts written on rolls of papyrus*).

par *n* 1 the state of being equal (*cities on a par in terms of tourist popularity*). 2 the normal value, amount or degree of something (*work not up to par*). 3 in golf, the number of str okes that should be taken on a round by a good player (*a score of two over par*).

par'able *n* a simple story made up to make clearer the difference between right and wrong.

para'bola *n* 1 a cur ved line so drawn that it is throughout its length the same distance from both a fixed point and a line. 2 a section obtained by cutting a cone by a plane parallel to its side.

par'achute *n* an apparatus that, by opening like an umbrella, enables people to jump from an aeroplane and drop to earth safely (*killed when his parachute failed to open*).

parade' *n* 1 a public pr ocession (*a parade of decorated lorries*). 2 display, show (*a parade of his knowledge*). 3 soldiers, etc, standing in lines under the command of their officers:—*vb* 1 to show off (*parade his knowledge*). 2 to tak e up places in an orderly body (e.g. of soldiers). 3 to march in procession (*children parading in fancy dress*). 4 to walk up and down (*she paraded up and down impatiently waiting for him*).

par'adise *n* 1 heaven. 2 the gar den of Eden. 3 (*inf*) a place or state of great happiness (*regard a day without work as paradise*).

par'adox *n* a truth stated in words that seem to contradict each other ('*More haste, less speed*' *is a paradox*):—*adj* **paradox'ical**.

par'affin *n* a waxy substance obtained from shale or coal and used for making candles or made into oil for lamps, etc.

par'agon *n* a perfect example of some good quality (*a paragon of good manners*).

par'agraph *n* a distinct division of a piece of writing marked by having its first word slightly in from the left-hand margin.

par'akeet n a small parrot.

par'allel adj **1** (of lines) at the same distance from each other at all points. **2** similar (a parallel case/parallel circumstances):—n **1** a lik e or similar example, a comparison (see a parallel in the two cases). **2** one of the lines drawn on maps through all places at the same distance from the equator.

parallel'ogram n a four-sided figure whose opposite sides are parallel.

par'alyse vb **1** to mak e helpless or powerless (a country paralysed by a transport strike). **2** to strike with paralysis (he has been paralysed since the accident to his spine).

paral'ysis n a condition causing loss of feeling and the power to move in part of the body (suffering from paralysis below the waist).

paraly'tic adj **1** suffering fr om paralysis. **2** (inf) extremely drunk:—also n.

paramed'ic n a person who is trained to give someone a certain amount of medical treatment until the patient can be treated by a doctor.

par'amount adj highest, greatest (of paramount importance).

par'amour n (fml or lit) a lover (she divorced him because of his paramour).

par'apet n a safety wall at the side of a bridge, at the edge of a roof, etc.

parapherna'lia npl a large collection of objects, often personal belongings, or all the tools necessary for a job or hobby (the paraphernalia necessary to take a baby on a journey).

par'aphrase n **1** the expr essing of the sense of a passage in other words (the teacher gave a paraphrase of the difficult poem). **2** a version of a hymn based on a passage of Scripture:—also vb.

par'asite n **1** one who lives at another 's expense (a parasite who moves from one friend's house to another). **2** a plant or animal that lives on or in another (fleas are parasites):—adj parasit'ic.

par'asol n a sunshade in the form of an umbrella (carry a parasol in the midday sun).

par'atroop(er) n a soldier trained to drop from an aeroplane by parachute.

par'boil vb to boil slightly (parboil the potatoes before roasting).

par'cel n **1** a small bundle or package (send the present in a parcel). **2** a small piece of land, esp part of a large piece (the large estate has been divided into parcels of land):—vb (**par'celled**, **par'celling**) **1** to divide into shar es (parcel out the food to the homeless). **2** to wrap up in paper , etc (parcel up the presents).

parch vb to dry up (grass parched by the sun).

parched adj **1** dried out (parched land). **2** (inf) very thirsty (parched after the long walk).

parch'ment n **1** a skin pr epared for writing on. **2** what is written on it.

par'don vb to forgive, to let off without punishment (the king pardoned the wrongdoers):—n forgiveness.

par'donable adj that can be forgiven (crimes that are not pardonable).

pare vb to cut off the skin or edge of (paring the rind from the cheese).

pa'rent n a father or mother.

pa'rentage n parents and ancestors, birth (of noble parentage).

paren'tal adj of a parent (parental responsibilities).

paren'thesis n **1** a gr oup of words put into the middle of a sentence interrupting its sense often enclosed in brackets. **2** brack ets:—adj **parenthet'ical**.

pariah [pa-rī'-a] n **1** a person whom other people will have nothing to do with (treated as a pariah in the district because of his cruel treatment of his children). **2** a dog that has r eturned to wildness.

par'ish n **1** a district with its own chur ch and priest or minister. **2** a division of a county for administrative purposes:—adj having to do with a parish (a parish church/a parish council).

par'ing n a piece of skin cut off (feed vegetable parings to the pigs).

parish'ioner n a member of a parish or parish church.

par'ity n equality, the state of being equal (women seeking salary parity with men).

park n **1** a lar ge enclosed space of open ground round a country house (a mansion with an extensive park). **2** an enclosed piece of gr ound for the use of the public (children playing in the park). **3** a place wher e motor cars, etc, may be left:—vb to leave (a motor car, etc) standing (park his car illegally on a double yellow line).

park-and-ride *adj* of a system, designed to reduce traffic congestion, in which motorists leave their cars on the edge of a town and take a bus or train to the town centre.

par'lance *n* (*fml*) a way of speaking (*in legal parlance*).

par'ley *vb* (*old*) to discuss terms or conditions:— *n* (*old*) a meeting held to discuss terms or conditions (*a parley to discuss peace terms*).

par'liament *n* **1** an assembly that discusses and makes laws. **2** (*usu with cap*) in the UK, the House of Commons and the House of Lords.

parliamenta'rian *n* an experienced member of parliament.

parliamen'tary *adj* having to do with parliament (*parliamentary business/parliamentary constituencies*).

par'lour *n* **1** (*old*) a sitting room. **2** a shop providing some kind of personal service (*a beauty parlour/a massage parlour*).

par'lous *adj* (*fml or hum*) dangerous, uncertain (*the parlous state of international relations*).

paro'chial *adj* **1** having to do with a parish (*parochial issues*). **2** narrow-minded (*parochial people who are interested only in local affairs*).

par'ody *n* **1** a humorous imitation of a serious work of literature. **2** a weak and unsuccessful copy or absurd imitation (*his statement was a parody of the truth*):—*vb* **1** to make a parody of. **2** to imitate in order to make fun of (*he parodied the judge's closing speech*).

parole' *n* the release of a prisoner before the end of his or her sentence on condition that he or she does not break the law (*prisoners released on parole*).

par'oxysm *n* **1** a sudden attack of pain (*a poison that produced violent paroxysms*). **2** a violent outburst (*a paroxysm of rage*).

parquet [par'-kā] *n* flooring made of wooden bricks arranged to form a pattern.

par'ricide *n* (*fml*) **1** the murder of a parent or near relative (*found guilty of parricide*). **2** one who commits such a murder.

par'rot *n* a brightly coloured tropical bird able to imitate human speech (*keep a parrot in a cage as a pet*).

par'ry *vb* to turn aside (*parried the blow/parrying their questions*).

parse *vb* to tell what part of speech a word is and its relation to other words in the sentence:—*n* **pars'ing**.

par'simony *n* (*fml*) meanness about money, stinginess (*the miser's parsimony*):—*adj* **parsimo'nious**.

pars'ley *n* a garden herb used in cooking (*use parsley to flavour the soup*).

pars'nip *n* a vegetable with a yellow eatable root.

par'son *n* a member of clergy (*married by the local parson*).

par'sonage *n* the house provided for a member of clergy serving a church.

part *n* **1** one of the pieces into which a thing can be divided. **2** some but not all. **3** the character played by an actor on the stage. **4** *pl* ability, talents:—*adj and adv* in part:—*vb* **1** to divide. **2** to separate:— *adv* **part'ly:**—**in good part** without being angry (*take the news of the defeat in good part*):—**part and parcel** a necessary part.

partake' *vb* (*fml*) **1** to take a share in, to take part in (*partaking in the decision*). **2** to eat (*partake of a large meal*).

parterre' *n* (*fml*) **1** a piece of ground with flower beds. **2** part of the stalls of a theatre.

partial *adj* **1** in part only (*a partial improvement*). **2** favouring one side or person (*a partial decision/a partial umpire*). **2** fond (of) (*partial to sweet things*).

partial'ity *n* **1** (*fml*) the favouring of one more than others, unfairness (*an umpire accused of partiality*). **2** liking (for) (*a partiality for chocolate*).

partic'ipant, partic'ipator *ns* one who takes a part in (*participants in the quiz*).

partic'ipate *vb* to take part in, to have a share in (*participating in the discussions*):—*n* **participa'tion**.

par'ticiple *n* a part of the verb which does the work of an adjective.

par'ticle *n* a very small part (*particles of dust/not a particle of truth*).

par'ti-coloured *adj* (*fml*) in various colours (*particoloured clothes*).

partic'ular *adj* **1** different from others, special. **2** careful, exact. **3** difficult to please:— *n* a single fact, a detail.

partic'ularize *vb* **1** to name one by one. **2** to describe in detail.

part'ing n 1 separation (*the parting of the ways*). 2 act of going away or leaving (*a sad parting at the station*). 3 the division made when the hair is brushed in two directions (*a centre parting*):— adj done when going away, final (*her parting words*).

par'tisan n 1 an eager supporter . 2 (*old*) a type of spear with a long handle:—adj giving strong, enthusiastic support or loyalty (*a partisan speech*).

parti'tion n 1 a dividing wall or scr een (*a partition dividing the bedroom into two*). 2 division (*the partition of India*). 3 a part divided off fr om the rest (*a partition for changing*):—vb 1 to divide up (*partition the country into states*). 2 to set up a dividing wall, etc.

part'ner n 1 one who works or plays with another in a certain undertaking, game, etc (*business partners/tennis partners*). 2 a husband or wife, someone with whom one lives or is in a long-term relationship (*he and his partner were invited to the party*):—vb to go with or give to as a partner (*she partnered him to the dance*).

part'nership n 1 the state of being partners (*go into partnership*). 2 a gr oup of people working together for the same purpose (*a business partnership*). 3 people playing on the same side in a game (*a successful tennis partnership*).

part'ridge n a type of bird hunted in sport.

part'-song n a song in which several people sing different tunes in harmony.

part'-time adj for some of the time only (*part-time work*).

par'ty n 1 a gr oup of people who have the same or similar beliefs and opinions (*political parties*). 2 a number of people meeting for enjoyment (*a birthday party*). 3 one taking part (*one of the parties involved in the scheme*).

par'venu n a person, previously unimportant, who has suddenly become rich or powerful (*the villagers disliked the wealthy parvenus who bought the manor house*).

paschal [päs'-kêl] adj (*fml*) having to do with Easter or the Jewish feast of the Passover.

pash'a n (*old*) a title formerly given to persons of importance in the Turkish Empire.

pass vb 1 to go past (*pass the church on the way to the station*). 2 to go on one's way (*watch the*

soldiers pass on their way to war*). 3 to move (something) from one place or person to another (*play a game of pass the parcel*). 4 to die (*the invalid passed away*). 5 (*of time*) to go by (*as the hours passed*). 6 to spend (time) (*pass the summer reading*). 7 to overtak e (*a car passing the lorry*). 8 to succeed at examination. 9 to recognize as good enough, to approve (*pass his application for a licence*). 10 to utter (*pass a remark*). 11 to set up as by vote (*parliament passing a new law*). 12 (*fml*) to be too great for (*pass their understanding*):—n 1 a narr ow valley between mountains. 2 a written permission to visit certain places. 3 success in an examination (*get a pass in maths*):—a pretty pass a bad state of affairs (*things have come to a pretty pass when people are begging in the streets*).

pass'able adj 1 fairly good (*a passable pianist*). 2 that can be cr ossed or travelled on (*roads scarcely passable in the winter*).

pass'age n 1 a way thr ough (*force a passage through the crowds*). 2 act of passing (*the passage of time*). 3 a journey, esp by sea (*pay for his passage to America by cooking for the crew*). 4 a lane. 5 a corridor (*a large house with long dark passages*). 6 part of a book, poem, etc (*learn a passage from the poem by heart*):—passage of arms (*fml*) a fight, a quarrel:—bird of passage a bird or person who stays in a place for a time and then leaves again for somewhere else (*our new teacher's a real bird of passage—she has taught all over the world*).

pass'book n a book showing the amounts paid into and drawn from a bank account.

pass'enger n one travelling in a ship, car, train, etc (*a car with room for passengers*).

passe-partout [päs-pär-tö'] n (*fml*) a sticky tape used in framing pictures, photographs, etc.

pass'er-by n one who is walking past (*a beggar ignored by the passers-by*).

pass'ing adj 1 moving or going by (*a passing stranger*). 2 lasting for a short time only (*a passing thought*).

passion [pa-shên] n 1 a str ong feeling, such as love (*their passion for each other*). 2 anger (*a fit of passion*). 3 gr eat enthusiasm (*his passion for football*). 4 (*fml*) great suffering:—the Passion the last sufferings of Christ.

pas'sionate *adj* **1** having or showing strong feelings (*a passionate love of freedom*). **2** very enthusiastic (*a passionate interest in sport*).

pas'sion-flower *n* a flower so-called because of an imagined resemblance to Christ's crown of thorns.

pas'sion-fruit *n* an eatable purple fruit of the passion-flower.

passion play *n* a play representing scenes in the Passion of Christ.

Passion Week *n* the week before Easter.

passive *adj* **1** acted on (*passive verbs*). **2** showing no emotion, interest, etc (*remain passive when she was told the bad news*). **3** unresisting (*accept the situation with passive resignation*):—*n* **passivity**.

passive smoking *n* the breathing in of other people's cigarette smoke (*passive smoking can damage health*).

Pass'over *n* a feast of the Jews in memory of their escape from Egypt.

pass'port *n* a document giving a person permission to travel in foreign countries (*showing their passports at the border*).

pass'word *n* a secret word, knowledge of which shows that a person is friendly.

past *adj* **1** gone by (*in past times*). **2** belonging to an earlier time (*past kings*):—*n* **1** time gone by (*in the past he was very poor*). **2** one's earlier life (*his past is unknown to his present employers*):—*prep* **1** beyond (*the building past the church*). **2** after (*past 3 o'clock*):—*adv* by (*watch the soldiers march past*).

pas'ta *n* an Italian food made from flour, eggs and water and formed into different shapes, such as spaghetti, often dried before use (*pasta and tomato sauce*).

paste *n* **1** flour mixed with water , etc, to make dough for cooking. **2** a sticky mixture of this used as an adhesive (*wallpaper paste*). **3** food crushed so that it can be spread like butter (*fish paste*). **4** the material of which imitation gems are made (*a necklace of paste*):—*vb* to stick with paste (*pasting the pictures to a piece of card*).

paste'board *n* cardboard.

pas'tel *n* **1** a coloured chalk or crayon. **2** a drawing done with pastel:—*adj* soft, quiet, not bright (*pastel colours*).

pas'tern *n* the lowest part of a horse's leg, between the tuft of hair and the hoof.

pas'teurize *vb* to heat in order to kill all harmful germs (*pasteurized milk*).

pas'tille *n* **1** a small sweet. **2** a sweet containing medicine (*cough pastilles*).

pas'time *n* a hobby, a game, an interest for one's spare time (*his pastimes are chess and golf*).

past' master *n* an expert, one with great skill (*a past master at the art of conversation*).

pas'tor *n* the minister of a church.

pas'toral *adj* **1** (*fml*) having to do with the country or country life (*pastoral scenes*). **2** having to do with a member of the clergy or his or her duties (*pastoral duties*):—*n* a poem describing country life.

pas'try *n* **1** paste of flour , water etc, made crisp by baking (*puff pastry*). **2** a pie or tart (*a shop selling pastries*).

pas'ture *n* grassland where farm animals graze:—*vb* **1** to put cattle to graze. **2** to eat grass on.

pas'turage *n* grassland for cattle.

pasty[1] [pās'-ti] *adj* white and unhealthy, pale (*a pasty complexion*).

pasty[2] [pas'-ti] *n* a meat pie.

pat *n* **1** a tap, a light touch (*a pat on the back*). **2** a small lump (*a pat of butter*):—*vb* (**pat'ted**, **pat'ting**) to tap, to hit lightly (*pat the dog*):—*adj* ready, coming too easily (*an explanation that was too pat to be convincing*).

patch *n* **1** a piece of material sewed or put on to cover a hole (*a patch on the knee of her jeans*). **2** a small piece of ground (*a vegetable patch in the garden*):—*vb* to mend by covering over (*patch the elbows of his jacket*).

patch'work *n* many small pieces of material sewn together (*a quilt made of patchwork*).

patch'y *adj* **1** full of patches (*patchy paintwork*). **2** (*inf*) sometimes good, sometimes bad (*his schoolwork is patchy*).

pate *n* (*old or hum*) the top of the head (*a bald pate*).

patel'la *n* (*pl* **patel'lae**) (*fml*) the kneecap.

pat'en *n* a plate for consecrated bread.

pat'ent *n* a written document giving someone the sole right to make or sell a new invention:—*adj* **1** protected by patent (*a patent cough cure*). **2** (*fml*) obvious, clear (*his patent dishonesty*):—*vb* to obtain a patent for (*patenting his new machine*).

patent leather n leather with a very high gloss (*dancing shoes of patent leather*).

pa'tentee n the holder of a patent.

pa'terfamil'ias n (*fml*) the father of a family (*the paterfamilias of a huge family*).

pater'nal adj 1 fatherly, like a father (*paternal love*). 2 r elated by blood to one's father (*his paternal grandmother*).

pater'nity n the state of being a father (*question his paternity of the child*).

pa'ternos'ter n the Lord's Prayer.

path n 1 a narr ow way made by the treading of feet, a track (*mountain paths*). 2 the course followed by a person or thing (*a new career path*).

pathet'ic adj sad, causing pity (*a pathetic sight/a pathetic person*).

path'finder n one who goes ahead to find a suitable route.

path'less adj (*fml*) without a path, unexplored (*pathless tracts of the jungle*).

patholog'ical adj 1 having to do with the study of disease (*pathological research*). 2 (*inf*) unreasonable, unnatural (*a pathological hatred of his brother*).

pathol'ogy n the study of diseases:—n **pa-thol'ogist**.

pa'thos n the quality that excites pity or sadness (*the pathos of the sight of the orphan child*).

path'way n a path (*the mountain pathways/the pathway to fortune*).

pa'tience n 1 the ability to suffer or wait long without complaining, calmness despite delay or difficulty (*bear her long illness with patience/her lack of patience in queues*). 2 a car d game for one person.

pa'tient adj suffering delay, pain, irritation, etc quietly and without complaining (*a patient acceptance of her long illness/be patient and wait your turn in the queue*):—n a person receiving treatment from a doctor (*the general practitioner's patients*).

pat'io n a paved area outside a house where people can sit, plants can be grown in containers, etc.

patois [pat'-wä] n the form of a language spoken in one particular place, a dialect (*cannot understand the local patois*).

pa'triarch n (*fml*) 1 the head of a tribe or family . 2 a senior bishop. 3 a head of the Gr eek church.

4 a ver y old man (*the patriarchs of the village sitting in the square*):—adj **patriar'chal**.

patri'cian n a nobleman in ancient Rome:—adj of noble birth.

pat'ricide n 1 the mur der of one's father (*found guilty of patricide*). 2 one who mur ders his or her father.

pat'rimony n (*fml*) the property received from one's father or ancestors (*have to dispose of his patrimony to pay his taxes*).

pa'triot n one who loves his or her country (*a patriot who died for his country*):—n **pa'triotism**.

patriot'ic adj loving one's country (*sing the national anthem with patriotic enthusiasm*).

patrol' n 1 a gr oup of men, ships, etc, sent out as a moving guard (*enemy aircraft spotted by the patrol*). 2 the act of patr olling (*soldiers on patrol*). 3 a small gr oup of Scouts or Guides:—vb (**patrolled'**, **pa-trol'ling**) to move about on guard or to keep watch (*security guards patrolling the factory grounds*).

pa'tron n 1 one who encourages, helps or pr otects (*a patron of the arts*). 2 a r egular customer (*a patron of the local hairdresser*). 3 one who has the right to appoint someone to a certain office, esp in the church.

pat'ronage n 1 the help or pr otection given by a patron (*his patronage of the arts*). 2 the right of appointing to certain offices (*a church post in the patronage of the local landowner*). 3 a manner that shows that one thinks oneself superior (*her patronage of the younger members of staff*).

pat'ronize vb 1 (*fml*) to encourage or help, as a patron (*patronizing young artists*). 2 to behave to another as if superior to him or her (*the manager's secretary who patronizes the younger secretaries*).

patron saint n a saint believed to give special protection (*Andrew is the patron saint of Scotland*).

patronym'ic n a name handed down from one's father and ancestors, a surname.

patt'en n (*old*) a wooden shoe, a clog.

pat'ter[1] vb 1 to mak e a light tapping sound (*rain pattering on the roof*). 2 to run with quick light steps (*mice pattering around the attic*):—n the sound of pattering (*the patter of rain on the roof*).

pat'ter[2] n fast talk, esp persuasive talk (*the patter of a salesman*).

pat'tern n 1 a model that can be copied (*a dress pattern*). 2 an example (*the pattern of good behaviour*). 3 a design as on cloth, a carpet, etc (*a flower pattern on the curtains*). 4 the way in which something happens or develops (*the pattern of the illness*).

pat'ty n a little pie (*meat patties*).

pau'city n (*fml*) fewness, smallness in amount (*the paucity of suitable candidates for the job*).

paunch n the belly, esp a large protruding one (*develop a paunch from drinking too much beer*).

pau'per n a person too poor to support himself (*he was wealthy once but he died a pauper*).

pau'perize vb (*fml*) to make poor, to ruin (*pauperized by the failure of the stock market*).

pause vb to stop for a time (*pause for a moment before answering*):—n a short stop (*a pause for breath/a pause for a cup of tea*).

pave vb to make a road or pathway by laying down flat stones (*paving the road leading to the new houses*):—**pave the way for** to prepare for (*the opening of the new shopping complex paved the way for further property developments*).

pave'ment n a paved surface, esp a raised footway at the side of the road for pedestrians (*stand on the pavement waiting to cross the road*).

pavil'ion n 1 a building on a playing field for the use of players and spectators (*the cricket pavilion*). 2 a building put up quickly for a special purpose (*the exhibition pavilions*).

paw n the foot of an animal that has claws (*a dog's paws*):—vb 1 to scrape with the foot of (*horses pawing the ground*). 2 to handle clumsily and often sexually (*he was pawing the woman he was dancing with*).

pawl n a short bar that engages in a toothed wheel to prevent it from running back.

pawn[1] n 1 in chess, the piece of least value. 2 a person made use of by another to do his or her will (*the child was used as a pawn in the quarrel between his divorced parents*).

pawn[2] n a thing handed over in return for a loan of money and returned when the loan is repaid:—vb to hand over in return for money lent (*pawning his watch*).

pawn'broker n one who lends money to those who pawn goods with him or her until the loan is repaid (*take his watch to the pawnbroker to get money for Christmas*).

pay vb (*pt, pp* **paid**) 1 to give money for goods, service, etc (*pay for their groceries/paying the gardener for his work*). 2 to suffer for faults, crimes, etc (*murderers who must be made to pay for their crimes*). 3 to give (*pay attention/pay heed*). 4 to produce a profit (*find a product that pays*). 5 to let run out (*pay out the rope to let the boat into the water*):—n wages, salary:—**pay through the nose** (*inf*) to pay too much for something (*he paid through the nose for that old car*).

pay'able adj that must be paid (*debts payable now*).

payee' n one to whom money is to be paid.

pay'master n an officer whose duty it is to pay out wages.

pay'ment n 1 the act of paying (*the payment of their debts*). 2 the amount paid (*payment received in full*).

pay'roll n a list of persons to be paid (*people on the factory payroll*).

PC abbr 1 police constable. 2 personal computer, a computer designed to be used by one person. 3 politically correct.

pea n 1 a climbing plant with pods containing round eatable seeds. 2 one of the seeds (*soup made from peas*).

peace n 1 quiet, calm (*peace reigned after the children went to bed*). 2 freedom from war or disorder (*people in a country at war longing for peace*). 3 the agreement to end a war (*peace talks*).

peace'able adj fond of peace, not liking to fight or quarrel (*a peaceable nation*).

peace'ful adj 1 quiet, calm, untroubled (*a peaceful village in the country*). 2 without war (*peaceful countries*).

peace'maker n one who tries to stop wars, disputes, etc (*a peacemaker trying to bring the quarrelling sides of the family together*).

peace' offering n something offered to bring about peace (*bring his wife flowers as a peace offering after their quarrel*).

peach n a juicy fruit with a rough stone and soft velvety skin (*ripe golden peaches*).

pea'cock n a bird the male of which has a large brightly coloured spreading tail:—f **pea'hen**.

peak[1] n 1 the highest point (the peak of his political career). 2 the pointed top of a mountain (snow-covered peaks). 3 the jutting- out brim at the front of a cap (a blue cap with a red peak):—adj connected with the time of greatest use or demand (peak TV viewing times):—vb to reach the highest point (his career peaked in his early 40s).

peak[2] vb to look ill.

peaked adj having a jutting-out brim in front (a peaked cap).

peak'y adj (inf) ill-looking (children looking peaky).

peal n 1 a sudden noise (a peal of thunder). 2 the loud ringing of bells (the peal of the church bells). 3 a set of bells for ringing together:— vb to sound or ring loudly.

pea'nut n a type of nut, the groundnut or monkey-nut (peanut butter).

pear n a juicy fruit narrower at one end than at the other (pears grow in the orchard).

pearl n 1 a shining white jewel found in shellfish, esp oysters (a necklace of pearls). 2 (inf) something highly valued (the pearl of his collection of antiques). 3 mother- of-pearl (pearl handles).

pea'sant n a person who works on the land, esp in a poor, primitive or underdeveloped area (local peasants ploughing with oxen).

pea'santry n peasants, country people.

peat n turf containing decayed vegetable matter dried and used as fuel (peat fires in the Scottish Highlands).

peb'ble n a small stone made round by the action of water (a beach of pebbles).

peb'bly adj full of or covered with pebbles (a pebbly beach).

peccadil'lo n (pl **peccadil'loes** or **pecca-dil'los**) (fml) an unimportant fault (he regarded lying to his wife as a peccadillo).

peck[1] n a measure for grain, etc (= 2 gallons).

peck[2] vb 1 to strik e with the beak (have his fingers pecked by his pet bird). 2 to pick up with the beak (birds pecking at seed). 3 to eat slowly in small mouthfuls, to nibble (a child who only pecks at her food).

peck'ish adj (inf) hungry (feel peckish about midday).

pec'toral adj (fml) having to do with the breast (pectoral muscles).

pecula'tion n (fml) the taking of public money for one's own use (peculation by council employees).

pecu'liar adj 1 strange, odd (meat that tastes peculiar). 2 belonging to one person, place or thing in particular and to no other (his peculiar style of walking/the peculiar charm of the seaside village).

peculiar'ity n 1 a quality, custom, etc, that belongs to a particular person, thing, etc. 2 an odd way of behaving.

pecu'niary adj (fml) having to do with money (pecuniary difficulties).

pedagogue [pe'-da-gog] n (fml) a teacher (a pedagogue by career).

ped'al n a lever worked by foot to control the working of a machine (the bicycle pedal/the piano pedal):—vb (**ped'alled, ped'alling**) to work a pedal by foot (pedal the bicycle uphill).

ped'ant n 1 one who shows off his or her learning. 2 one who attaches too much importance to small details and unimportant rules (a pedant who kept finding problems with the wording of the contract):—adj **pedan'tic.**

ped'antry n 1 showing off one's learning. 2 overinsistence on rules, etc.

ped'dle vb to sell from door to door (tinkers peddling paper flowers).

ped'estal n the block of stone at the base of a column or under a statue (a bust of Shakespeare on a pedestal):—**put on a pedestal** to treat with very great, often too much, respect (he put his wife on a pedestal but she did not deserve his respect).

pedes'trian adj 1 going on foot (pedestrian passengers on the ferry). 2 dull, uninter esting (a pedestrian style of writing):—n one who goes on foot, a walker (pedestrians looking for a place to cross the street/a pedestrian crossing).

pedes'trianized adj of streets in which traffic is not allowed so that pedestrians can walk safely (a pedestrianized precinct).

ped'igree n 1 a written table showing one's ancestors (get a copy of the dog's pedigree). 2 one's ancestors (a young woman of aristocratic pedigree):—adj of good birth (a pedigree spaniel).

ped'iment *n* the triangular topmost part at the front of a building.

ped'lar *n* one who travels about selling small objects (*pedlars selling things from door to door*).

pedom'eter *n* an instrument that measures distance walked (*walkers carrying pedometers*).

peel *vb* **1** to strip off. **2** to cut the skin off a fruit or vegetable. **3** to come off, as does skin or the bark of a tree (*oranges that peel easily*):—*n* skin, rind, bark.

peeling *n* a piece peeled off.

peel tow'er *n* (*old*) a square fortress.

peep[1] *vb* to chirp, to squeak:—*also n.*

peep[2] *vb* **1** to look at thr ough a narrow opening. **2** to look at for a moment only. **3** to begin to appear:—*n* **1** a quick or secr et look. **2** a look through a narrow opening. **3** a first appearance.

peep'hole *n* a small hole for looking through (*a peephole in the front door*).

peep'show *n* a small show or display looked at through a small hole.

peer[1] *vb* **1** to strain one's eyes to see. **2** to look closely.

peer[2] *n* **1** an equal, one's equal in age, ability , rank (*a child ahead of his peers at school*). **2** a nobleman (*peers in the House of Lords*):—*f* **peer'ess.**

peer'age *n* **1** all the noblemen of a countr y. **2** the rank or title of a nobleman.

peer'less *adj* (*fml*) unequalled (*her peerless beauty*).

peeve *vb* (*inf*) to irritate (*having to wait peeved her*).

peev'ish *adj* irritable, full of complaints (*a peevish old man who is difficult to please*).

pee'wit *n* the lapwing.

peg *n* a nail, pin or fastener (*a clothes peg/tent pegs*):—*vb* (**pegged', peg'ging**) to fasten with a peg (*peg the clothes on the line*):—**peg away** (*inf*) to keep on trying as hard as possible (*peg away at their studying*):—**take down a peg** (*inf*) to humiliate (*she was so conceited that they felt they had to take her down a peg or two*).

pelf *n* money, riches.

pel'ican *n* a water bird with a large beak containing a pouch for storing fish.

pell'et *n* **1** a small ball of anything (*give the birds pellets of bread*). **2** a pill. **3** one of a number of small lead balls packed in a cartridge and fired from a gun.

pell-mell' *adv* in great disorder (*the children ran pell-mell into the playground*).

pellu'cid *adj* very clear, transparent.

pel'met *n* a small curtain or screen above a window to hide the curtain rod.

pelt[1] *n* the raw skin of an animal (*sell mink pelts for profit*).

pelt[2] *vb* **1** to attack by thr owing things at (*the audience pelting the comedian with rotten fruit*). **2** (*of rain*) to fall heavily (*it was pelting down*).

pel'vis *n* the bony frame and the lower end of the trunk, into which the hipbone fits.

pem'mican *n* (*old*) dried crushed meat.

pen[1] *n* an instrument for writing in ink (*a fountain pen*):—*vb* to write.

pen[2] *n* a female swan.

pen[3] *n* a small enclosure, esp for animals (*a sheep pen*):—*vb* (**penned', pen'ning**) to shut up in a small space (*pen the stray dogs up*).

pe'nal *adj* having to do with punishment (*the penal system*).

pe'nalize *vb* to punish (*penalizing the football player/penalize his attempt at cheating*).

penal servitude *n* hard labour done in prison as a punishment for crime.

pen'alty *n* **1** due punishment (*the death penalty*). **2** a disadvantage of some kind that most be suffered for breaking the rules (*a football penalty*).

pen'ance *n* punishment willingly accepted as a sign of sorrow for sin (*do penance for his sins*).

pence *see* **penny.**

penchant [po(ng)'-sho(ng)] *n* (*fml*) a liking for, a preference for (*a penchant for spicy food*).

pen'cil *n* **1** a writing or drawing instrument. **2** a fine paint brush:—*vb* (**pen'cilled, pen'cilling**) to write or draw with pencil (*pencil in a few corrections*).

pen'dant *n* **1** an ornament hanging fr om a necklace or bracelet (*a diamond pendant*). **2** an earring. **3** anything hanging (e.g. a lamp fr om a roof).

pen'dent *adj* hanging, dangling.

pen'ding *adj* not yet decided (*the matter is still pending*):—*prep* waiting for (*pending a decision*).

pen'dulous adj (fml) hanging (branches pendulous with fruit).

pen'dulum n a swinging weight, as in a large clock.

pen'etrable adj that can be penetrated (roads scarcely penetrable in winter).

pen'etrate vb 1 to pass thr ough (light penetrating the thin curtains). 2 to mak e a hole in or through (a bullet penetrated his shoulder). 3 to r each the mind of (it didn't seem to penetrate that her husband was dead).

pen'etrating adj 1 sharp (a penetrating stare). 2 far-seeing (it was penetrating of him to see that she was being dishonest). 3 loud and clear (a penetrating voice).

penetra'tion n 1 act of passing thr ough or making a hole in. 2 clear understanding, intelligence.

pen friend n a person one gets to know only through exchanging letters.

pen'guin n a web-footed bird with very short wings that it uses for swimming, not flying (penguins are found in the Antarctic regions).

penicill'in n a kind of germ-killing drug obtained from mould (take penicillin to cure her sore throat).

penin'sula n a piece of land almost surrounded by water.

pen'itent adj sorrowful for having done wrong (children penitent for having broken the window):—n one who is penitent:—n **pen'itence**.

peniten'tial adj (fml) having to do with penitence (a penitential attitude).

peniten'tiary n a prison.

pen'knife n a folding pocket knife.

pen'manship n (fml) the art of writing (admire his penmanship).

pen name n a pretended name under which an author writes (the author's pen name).

pennant, pen'non ns a long narrow triangular flag.

pen'niless adj having no money (penniless people begging).

pen'ny n (pl **pen'nies, pence**) a British bronze coin worth one twelfth of a shilling until 1971 after which 100 new pence = £1.

pen'sion n money paid regularly to someone for the rest of his or her lifetime after he or she has stopped working or after some misfortune (receive an old-age pension):—vb to give a pension to (pension the older workers off).

pen'sioner n one who receives a pension.

pen'sive adj (fml) thoughtful (in pensive mood `1).

pent adj shut in, confined (pent-up feelings).

pen'tagon n a five-sided figure.

pentam'eter n a line of poetry containing five feet.

Pen'tateuch n the first five books of the Old Testament.

Pen'tecost n a Christian and Jewish festival.

pent'house n 1 a flat, usu luxurious, at the top of a building (a fine view from the penthouse). 2 a shed with down-sloping roof built against a wall.

pent'roof n a roof sloping to one side only.

penul'timate adj (fml) the last but one (salaries paid on the penultimate Thursday of the month).

penu'rious adj (fml) very poor (penurious people begging).

pen'ury n (fml) poverty, want (families living in penury).

pe'on n in South America, a labourer.

pe'ony n a garden plant with large white or red flowers.

people [pee'-pêl] n 1 all those belonging to one nation or country (the people of Britain). 2 the ordinary persons of a country and not their rulers, etc (the people rebelling against their rulers). 3 persons (people who care about others):—vb 1 to fill with people (a building peopled with office workers). 2 to inhabit (tribes who people the plains).

pep'per n 1 a plant whose seeds ar e ground into a hot-tasting powder and used for flavouring food. 2 the powder so used (season the dish with salt and pepper).

pep'percorn n the seed of the pepper plant.

pep'permint n 1 a plant with sharp-tasting oil. 2 a sharp-tasting sweet (suck a peppermint).

pep'pery adj 1 lik e pepper, hot (a peppery sauce). 2 easily anger ed (a peppery old man).

pep'tic adj having to do with the process of digestion (a peptic ulcer).

per prep 1 for each (apples 50p per pound). 2 during each (work 40 hours per week). 3 (inf) according to (as per instructions).

peradven'ture adv (lit) perhaps, by chance.

peram'bulate vb (fml) to walk up and down (holiday-makers perambulating in the sun).

peram'bulator n (abbr **pram**) a child's carriage pushed by hand.

perceive' *vb* to know through one of the senses, to see, to understand (*perceive a reason for their distress*).

per cent in each hundred (%).

percen'tage *n* the number of cases in every hundred (*a percentage of the injured animals die*).

percep'tible *adj* able to be perceived (*no perceptible difference*).

percep'tion *n* 1 the ability to perceive. 2 intelligence.

percep'tive *adj* 1 quick to notice or understand (*perceptive people who reported him to the police*). 2 showing the ability to notice or understand (*perceptive comments*).

perch[1] *n* a freshwater fish.

perch[2] *n* 1 the bar on which a bird stands when resting. 2 a high place. 3 a measure of length (5½ yards):—*vb* 1 to rest on a bar or high place (*parrots perching on bars in their cages*). 2 to put in a high position.

perchance' *adv* (*old*) perhaps.

percip'ient *adj* (*fml*) 1 quick to notice and understand (*percipient observers*). 2 showing the ability to notice or understand (*percipient comments*).

per'colate *vb* 1 to pass slowly through (*water percolating through the soil/information percolating the department*). 2 to put through a strainer.

per'colator *n* 1 a strainer. 2 a coffee pot in which boiling water is passed through coffee grains until the coffee is strong enough to drink.

percus'sion *n* 1 the striking of one thing against another. 2 the sound thus made. 3 the drums and cymbals section of an orchestra.

perdi'tion *n* 1 entire ruin (*an army led to perdition by an incompetent general*). 2 condemnation to hell (*sinners facing perdition*).

per'egrine *n* a type of falcon.

peremp'tory *adj* short and commanding (*a peremptory manner*).

peren'nial *adj* 1 lasting for ever, continual (*their perennial complaints*). 2 (*of a plant*) growing again year after year:—*n* a perennial plant.

per'fect *adj* 1 without fault, excellent (*a perfect piece of work*). 2 exact (*a perfect copy*). 3 complete, utter (*a perfect fool*):—*vb* **perfect'** 1 to finish, to make perfect:—*n* **perfec'tion**.

perfer'vid *adj* (*fml*) very keen, enthusiastic (*perfervid supporters of the cause*).

perfid'ious *adj* treacherous, faithless:—*n* **perfid'iousness**.

per'fidy *n* (*fml*) treachery, unfaithfulness (*followers accused of perfidy*).

per'forate *vb* to make a hole or row of holes through (*perforating paper/a perforated ulcer*).

perfora'tion *n* a row of small holes, often to make tearing easy, as in sheets of stamps, etc.

perforce' *adv* (*old*) of necessity, necessarily.

perform' *vb* 1 to do, to carry out (*perform her duties satisfactorily*). 2 to show in a theatre (*perform a production of 'Hamlet'*). 3 to act in a play (*they performed in a musical production*).

perform'ance *n* 1 act of doing or carrying out (*the performance of their duties*). 2 that which is done (*admire their musical performance*). 3 the acting of a play or part (*see a performance of 'Othello'*).

perform'er *n* an actor, musician, etc.

perform'ing *adj* trained to act, do tricks, etc (*performing animals*).

per'fume *n* 1 a sweet smell (*the perfume of roses*). 2 a sweet-smelling liquid, scent (*buy a bottle of perfume*):—*vb* **perfume'** 1 to put perfume on. 2 to give a pleasant smell to (*roses perfuming the garden*).

perfu'mer *n* one who makes perfume.

perfu'mery *n* 1 a place where perfumes are made or sold. 2 the art of making perfumes (*a training in perfumery*).

perfunc'tory *adj* done carelessly or without interest, badly done (*a perfunctory cleaning of the room*).

perhaps' *adv* it may be, possibly.

per'il *n* risk, danger (*the perils of travel in those parts*).

per'ilous *adj* dangerous (*a perilous journey*).

perim'eter *n* 1 the total length of the line(s) enclosing a certain space or figure. 2 the boundaries of a camp or piece of land (*the perimeter of the city*).

pe'riod *n* 1 a certain length of time (*a period of three months*). 2 an age in history (*the Tudor period*). 3 the dot or full stop marking the end of a sentence. 4 a time of menstruation.

period'ic *adj* happening at regular intervals (*periodic breakdowns in the system*).

period'ical n a newspaper or magazine that appears at regular intervals (e.g. of a week, month, etc) (a scientific periodical):—adj periodic.

peripatet'ic adj going from place to place (a peripatetic music teacher).

periph'ery n a boundary line (on the periphery of the city/on the periphery of the subject that she is studying).

periph'rasis n (fml) a roundabout way of saying something:—adj periphras'tic.

per'iscope n an instrument in which mirrors are so arranged that one can see things on the surface of the land or sea when in a trench or submarine.

perish vb 1 to die (soldiers who perished in the battle). 2 to pass away completely (a way of life that perished). 3 to r ot away (rubber that perished).

per'ishable adj that will rot away under ordinary conditions (perishable food).

peritonit'is n inflammation of the thin skin lining the inside of the abdomen.

per'iwig n a wig.

periwink'le n 1 a small eatable shellfish. 2 a cr eeping evergreen flowering plant.

per'jury n the saying on oath that a statement is true when one knows it to be false (a witness who committed perjury).

perk[1] vb (inf) to cheer up (she perked up when she heard the news).

perk[2] n see perquisite.

perk'y adj lively, cheerful (in a perky mood):—n perk'iness.

per'manent adj lasting (a permanent dye/a permanent job):—n per'manence.

permanent wave n (abbr perm) an artificial wave in the hair.

permanent way n railway track(s).

per'meable adj allowing liquid, gases, etc, to pass through.

per'meate vb 1 to pass thr ough, to spread through every part of (damp permeating the whole house/a club permeated with politics).

permis'sible adj (fml) that can be allowed (it is not permissible to leave school early).

permis'sion n leave, consent (get permission to leave early).

permis'sive adj (fml) allowing freedom (a permissive regime).

permit' vb (permit'ted, permit'ting) to allow (the children are not permitted to leave the school premises):—n per'mit a paper giving the holder the right to do certain things (a permit to sell things in the market).

permuta'tion n 1 all the ways in which a series of things, numbers, etc, can be arranged. 2 one of these ways.

perni'cious adj very harmful, destructive (a pernicious influence on society).

perora'tion n 1 (fml) the closing part of a speech. 2 a grand long speech, often meaningless.

perox'ide n 1 a mixtur e of oxygen with another element to contain the greatest possible amount of oxygen. 2 a substance used for bleaching, e.g. the hair.

perpendic'ular adj 1 at right angles. 2 upright:—n a line at right angles to another.

per'petrate vb to commit, to do (perpetrating a crime):—n perpetra'tion:—n per'petrator.

perpet'ual adj 1 lasting for ever (perpetual life). 2 continuing endlessly, uninterrupted (perpetual noise).

perpet'uate vb to make lasting (a system that perpetuates the old faults):—n per-petua'tion.

perpetu'ity n (fml) everlasting time:—in perpetu'ity for ever.

perplex' vb to puzzle, to bewilder (perplexed by the flashing traffic signals).

perplex'ity n puzzlement, bewilderment.

per'quisite n (usu shortened to perk) money, goods, etc, gained from a job in addition to wages or salary.

per'ry n a drink made from the fermented juice of pears.

per'secute vb to ill-treat, esp because of one's beliefs, to treat cruelly (persecuted for their religious faith):—n persecu'tion:—n per'secutor.

persever'ance n the quality of going on trying until one succeeds.

persevere' vb to keep on trying (if you don't succeed at first, persevere/persevering with singing lessons).

persiflage [per-si-fläzh'] n amusing talk on subjects of no importance.

persist' vb 1 to k eep on doing (persist in telling lies). 2 to last (an infection that persisted). 3 not to give in despite difficulty.

persis'tence n the quality of persisting, obstinacy.

persis'tent adj 1 k eeping on trying, not giving in easily. 2 long, continuing (*a persistent infection*).

per'son n 1 a human being, a man, woman or child. 2 (*fml*) one's body (*drugs about one's person*).

per'sonable adj good-looking (*a very personable young man*).

per'sonage n (*fml*) a person of importance (*the personages on the town council*).

per'sonal adj 1 one's own private (*personal belongings*). 2 (*of remarks*) unkind.

personal identification number see **PIN**.

personal'ity n 1 the union of qualities that mak es one's character different from those of other people (*a cheerful personality*). 2 a str ong, distinct character (*a woman of personality*). 3 a well-known person (*television personalities*). 4 pl unkind remarks about others.

per'sonally adv as far as one is concerned oneself (*personally I think she is honest*).

per'sonate vb (*fml*) to act the part of, to pretend to be (someone else).

person'ify vb 1 to speak or write of a thing, quality, etc, as if it were a human being (*innocence personified as a baby*). 2 to be a perfect example of (*he personifies optimism*):—n **personifica'tion**.

personnel' n the persons employed in a firm (*highly qualified personnel*).

personnel officer n a person whose job it is to interview workers and look after their welfare.

perspec'tive n 1 the art of drawing objects on a flat surface so that they appear farther or nearer as they do to the eye. 2 (*fml*) a view:—**see in perspective** to see the real value or importance of things when compared with others (*so upset that she was unable to see things in perspective*).

Per'spex n a trademark for a tough transparent glass-like plastic.

perspica'cious adj (*fml*) quick to notice or understand (*perspicacious enough to spot the errors*).

perspica'city n quickness or clearness of understanding.

perspire' vb to sweat (*runners perspiring in the heat*):—n **perspira'tion**.

persuade' vb to convince a person or get him or her to do as one wants by argument (*persuading them to take part*).

persua'sion n 1 act of persuading. 2 (*fml*) a belief or set of beliefs (*of the Christian persuasion*). 3 a gr oup holding certain beliefs.

persua'sive adj good at gaining the agreement of others, able to influence others (*a persuasive young man/a persuasive argument*).

pert adj forward, cheeky (*a pert young woman*):—n **pert'ness**.

pertain' vb to belong, to have to do with (*remarks not pertaining to the situation*).

per'tinent adj to the point, having to do with the subject:—ns **pert'inence, per'tinency**.

perturb' vb to make worried or anxious, to disturb (*perturbed by rumours of war*).

perturba'tion n anxiety, worry.

peru'sal n reading, study.

peruse' vb (*fml*) to read through, to examine carefully (*perusing the contract*).

pervade' vb to spread through (*an area pervaded by disease*).

perva'sive adj spreading through all parts.

perverse' adj 1 holding firmly to a wr ong opinion. 2 continuing to do things that one knows to be wrong, unacceptable or forbidden (*it was perverse of her to disobey her father*).

perver'sion n putting to a wrong or evil use (*a sexual perversion*).

perver'sity n the quality of being perverse.

pervert' vb 1 to put to a wr ong use (*perverting the course of justice*). 2 to teach wr ong ways to:— n **per'vert** one who has formed unnatural habits (*a pervert who attacks children*).

per'vious adj (*fml*) that can be passed through.

pese'ta n formerly the monetary unit of Spain, until the introduction of the euro in January 2002.

pes'simism n the belief that things generally turn out for the worst:—n **pes'simist**.

pessimis'tic adj having to do with pessimism, gloomy (*a pessimistic outlook on life*).

pest n 1 something harmful. 2 a nuisance (*the child is just a pest*). 3 a destructive animal, insect, etc (*farmers spraying crops to kill pests*).

pes'ter vb to keep on annoying.

pest'icide n a chemical substance used to kill pests, especially insects which are harmful to crops and other plants (*spray the roses with pesticide*).

pestif'erous *adj* (*fml*) spreading disease or infection, harmful.

pest'ilence *n* any deadly disease that spreads quickly, plague.

pest'ilent *adj* causing pestilence or disease.

pestilen'tial *adj* (*fml*) 1 causing pestilence or disease. 2 annoying (*pestilential children*).

pestle [pes'-êl] *n* an instrument for pounding substances to powder (*a mortar and pestle*).

pet¹ *n* 1 a favourite child (*a teacher's pet*). 2 a tame animal kept in the house as a companion (*keep a dog as a pet*):—*vb* best-loved, favourite:—*vb* (**pet'ted, pet'-ting**) 1 to tr eat lovingly. 2 to fondle.

pet² *n* a fit of sulks:— to sulk.

pet'al *n* the leaf-shaped part of a flower.

pet aversion *n* what one dislikes most (*her pet aversion is fast food*).

pe'ter *vb*:—**peter out** to stop or disappear gradually (*a mild protest that petered out*).

petite [pe-teet'] *adj* tiny, dainty (*a petite blonde*).

peti'tion *n* a r equest. 2 a written r equest signed by a number of people (*sign a petition against the new road being built*). 3 a prayer:— *vb* 1 to make a request to one able to grant it. 2 to put forward a written request:—*n* **peti'tioner**.

pet'rel *n* a sea bird.

petrifac'tion *n* 1 turning into stone. 2 terr or, amazement.

pet'rify *vb* 1 to turn into stone. 2 to terrif y, astound (*children petrified by the eerie music*).

pet'rol *n* a light oil obtained by refining petroleum (*the car ran out of petrol*).

petro'leum *n* a heavy oil obtained from under the surface of the earth.

petrol'ogy *n* the study of the formation, composition and erosion of rocks.

pet'ticoat *n* a woman's undergarment.

pet'tish *adj* sulky (*in a pettish mood*).

pet'ty *adj* 1 small, unimportant, trivial (*petty crime*). 2 mean-spirited (*petty, spiteful people*).

petty cash *n* money held in readiness to meet small expenses (*take the money for stationery from petty cash*).

petty officer *n* in the navy, a non-commissioned officer.

petty sessions *npl* a court for dealing with minor criminal cases.

pet'ulant *adj* easily angered or annoyed, peevish (*get tired of her petulant behaviour*):—*n* **pet'ulance**.

petu'nia *n* 1 a flowering gar den plant of various colours but often purple. 2 the purplish colour of this flower.

pew *n* a seat in a church.

pew'ter *n* a mixture of tin and lead (*goblets made of pewter*).

phae'ton *n* (*old*) an open four-wheeled carriage drawn by a pair of horses.

phal'anx *n* 1 (*fml or old*) a body of foot soldiers standing close to each other in battle. 2 a body of persons or animals standing close to each other (*a phalanx of policemen keeping back the crowds*).

phan'tom *n* a ghost.

phar'isee *n* (*inf*) a hypocrite.

pharmaceutical [får-mê-sû'-tik-êl] *adj* having to do with the making up of drugs or medicines.

phar'macy *n* 1 the making up of drugs or medicines (*study pharmacy*). 2 a shop in which medicines are made up and sold (*buy cough medicine at the pharmacy*):—*n* **phar'macist**.

pharyngi'tis *n* inflammation of the pharynx.

phar'ynx *n* the back part of the mouth.

phase *n* 1 a distinct stage in gr owth or development (*the first phase of the building project*). 2 apparent shape (e.g. of the moon).

pheas'ant *n* a moorland bird hunted for sport (*have roast pheasant for dinner*).

phenom'enon *n* (*pl* **phenom'ena**) 1 any natural happening that can be perceived by the senses. 2 anything unusual or extraor dinary (*snow in that part of the world is a phenomenon*).

phenom'enal *adj* unusual, extraordinary (*a phenomenal talent*).

phi'al *n* a small glass bottle (*a phial of poison*).

philan'der *vb* to flirt (*he is always philandering with married women*):—*n* **philan'-derer**.

philan'thropy *n* love of humankind, shown by giving money, etc, to help those in need or to benefit the public:—*adj* **philan-throp'ic**:—*n* **philan'thropist**.

philat'ely *n* stamp collecting:—*n* **philat'-elist**.

philharmon'ic *adj* musical.

phil'istine n an uncultured person (*a philistine with no interest in books or the arts*).

philol'ogy n the study of languages, their history and development:—n **philol'ogist**.

philos'opher n 1 one who tries to find by reasoning the causes and laws of all things. 2 one who treats life calmly.

philosoph'ic(al) adjs 1 having to do with philosophy. 2 calm, not easily annoyed (*of a philosophical turn of mind*).

philos'ophy n 1 the study of the causes and laws of all things (*study philosophy at university*). 2 a particular way of thinking (*his philosophy of life is to enjoy himself*).

phil'tre n (*fml*) a magic drink supposed to make the drinker fall in love.

phlebi'tis n inflammation of a vein of the body.

phlegm [flem] n 1 the thick slimy liquid coughed up from the throat. 2 coolness of temper, lack of excitement (*admire her phlegm in an emergency*).

phlegmatic [fleg-mat'-ik] adj cool, not easily excited.

phlox n a garden plant with brightly coloured flowers.

pho'bia n. an unreasoning fear or dread (*have a phobia about heights*).

phoenix [fee'-niks] n in ancient fables, a bird said to burn itself and rise again from its own ashes.

phone *the common short form of* **telephone**.

phonet'ic adj having to do with the sounds of speech or pronunciation (*the phonetic alphabet*):—npl **phonet'ics** the study of the sounds of speech.

pho'ney adj (*inf*) not genuine, not sincere, unreal (*a phoney workman/a phoney interest in the arts*).

pho'nic adj having to do with sound.

pho'nograph n (*old*) an instrument for recording sounds and playing them back.

phos'phate n a type of salt mixed into soil to make it more fertile.

phosphores'cence n a faint shining visible only in the dark.

phosphores'cent adj giving out a faint light in the dark (*phosphorescent paint*).

phos'phorous n a yellowish substance, easily set alight, giving out a faint light.

pho'to *short for* **photograph**.

photogen'ic adj suitable for photographing (*photogenic enough to be a professional model*).

pho'tograph n (*abbr* **photo**) a picture taken with a camera by means of the action of light on specially prepared glass or celluloid:—vb to take a photograph:—n **photo-g'rapher**:—adj **photograph'ic**.

photog'raphy n the art of taking photographs.

photo'meter n an instrument for measuring intensity of light.

pho'tostat n a photographed copy (*take a photostat of the document*).

phrase n 1 a small group of connected words expressing a single idea. 2 (*mus*) a group of connected notes:—vb to express in words (*phrase his statement in simple language*).

phraseology [frā-zee-ol'-o-dji] n a manner or style of expressing in words (*expressed in simple phraseology*).

phrenol'ogy n 1 the belief that a person's intelligence and abilities may be judged from the shape of his skull. 2 study of the shape of the skull based on this belief:—n **phrenol'ogist**.

phthisis [thī'-sis] n (*fml*) consumption of the lungs, tuberculosis.

phys'ic n 1 (*old*) the science of healing. 2 (*old*) a medicine.

phys'ical adj 1 having to do with the body (*a physical abnormality*). 2 having to do with the natural world (*the physical sciences*).

physi'cian n a doctor, esp as opposed to a surgeon.

phys'icist n a student of physics.

phys'ics n the study of matter, its properties, and the forces affecting it (e.g. heat, electricity, etc).

physiog'nomy n (*fml* or *hum*) the expression of the face (*deduce his emotions from his physiognomy*).

physiol'ogy n the study of living bodies, their organs and the way they work:—adj **physiolog'ical**:—n **physiol'ogist**.

physique [fi-zeek'] n 1 the structure of a person's body. 2 strength of body (*athletes trying to improve their physique*).

pianiss'imo adv (*mus*) very soft.

pi'anist n one who plays on a piano.

pia'no¹, **pianoforte** [pi-a-nō-for'-ti] ns a musical instrument played by pressing down keys that cause little hammers to strike tuned strings.

pia'no² *adv* (*mus*) softly.

piano'la *n* a piano worked by a machine.

pias'tre *n* a coin in Egypt and elsewhere.

piazza [pee-at'-sa] *n* **1** an open squar e surrounded by buildings (*cafés around the piazza*). **2** a path under a r oof supported by pillars.

pi'broch *n* a type of bagpipe music.

pic'ador *n* a mounted Spanish bullfighter.

picaresque' *adj* telling the story of rogues or adventurers (*a picaresque novel*).

pic'colo *n* a small high-pitched flute.

pick¹ *vb* **1** to choose (*pick a cake from the plateful*). **2** to pull or gather (*pick flowers/pick raspberries*). **3** to eat by small mouthfuls (*pick at one's food*). **4** to open (a lock) with a tool. **5** to steal from (a pocket):—*n* choice, the best:— **pick holes in** to point out the faults in (*pick holes in the argument*):—**pick up 1** to tak e up (*pick up his tools*). **2** to learn as if by chance (*pick up a foreign language*). **3** to come upon by chance (*pick up some interesting jewellery*).

pick², **pick'axe** *ns* a tool with a long pointed head, used for breaking up hard ground. etc (*workers breaking up the road surfaces with picks*).

pick'et *n* **1** a pointed wooden post. **2** a small gr oup of soldiers acting as a guard. **3** a number of people on strike who try to prevent others from going to work (*pickets stopping lorries on the way into the factory*):—*vb* **1** to send out soldiers, strikers, etc, on picket. **2** to tie to a post.

pick'le *n* **1** salt water or vinegar in which food is preserved (*serve pickles with cold roast beef*). **2** (*inf*) a difficult or unpleasant situation (*in a fine old pickle*). **3** *pl* vegetables preserved in vinegar:—*vb* to preserve by putting in salt water, vinegar, etc.

pick'pocket *n* one who steals from pockets.

pic'nic *n* an outing taken for pleasure, during which meals are eaten out of doors:—*also vb*.

Pict *n* one of the ancient Celtic inhabitants of North Britain.

picto'rial *adj* told or illustrated by pictures (*a pictorial description*).

pic'ture *n* a painting, drawing or other likeness, a portrait:—*vb* **1** to imagine clearly (*try to picture their distress*). **2** (*fml*) to represent in a painting (*the artist has pictured him as an old man*).

pic'ture house *n* (*old*) a cinema where films are shown.

picturesque' *adj* that would make a good picture, striking in appearance, beautiful (*a picturesque village*).

pid'gin *n* a language using words and grammar from other languages.

pidgin English *n* pidgin based on English.

pie *n* meat or fruit in or under a crust of pastry (*a steak pie*).

pie'bald *adj* having patches of different colours, esp black and white, spotted (*a piebald pony*):— *also n.*

piece *n* **1** a bit (*a piece of chewing gum*). **2** a distinct part (*put it together piece by piece*). **3** a literar y or musical composition. **4** a gun. **5** a coin (*a 50p piece*):—*vb* **1** to put (together). **2** to patch.

piece'meal *adv* **1** in or by pieces. **2** little by little.

piece'work *n* work paid by the amount done, not by time.

pied [pīd] *adj* (*fml*) of different colours, spotted.

pier [peer] *n* **1** a stone pillar supporting an ar ch, etc. **2** a stone or wooden platform or wall built out into the sea, often used as a landing place by boats.

pierce *vb* **1** to mak e a hole through. **2** to go through (*a dagger pierced her heart*).

pierc'ing *adj* **1** high-sounding (*a piercing scream*). **2** bright and intelligent-looking, staring (*a piercing stare*).

pierrot [pee'-êr-ō] *n* (*old*) a clown with a whitened face and loose-fitting white clothes.

pi'ety *n* devotion to God, love of prayer and religious ceremonies (*nuns are noted for their piety*).

pif'fle *n* (*inf*) nonsense, foolish talk (*Don't talk piffle!*).

pig *n* **1** a common farm animal (*we get pork and bacon from pigs*). **2** a r ough block or bar of smelted metal:—*vb* (pigged', pig'-ging) (*inf*) to live in dirty or untidy surroundings (*pig it in a student flat*):—**buy a pig in a poke** to buy something without examining it first (*buying goods at an auction can be like buying a pig in a poke*).

pi'geon *n* a dove.

pi'geon-hole *n* one of several compartments in a desk for storing papers, letters, etc.

pig'gery *n* a place for pigs.

pig-head'ed *adj* foolishly stubborn (*too pig-headed to listen to advice*).

pig iron *n* iron in rough bars.

pig'ment *n* any substance used for colouring (*a red pigment*).

pig'my *same as* **pygmy**.

pig'skin *n* leather made from the skin of a pig (*a handbag made of pigskin*).

pig'-sticking *n* hunting wild boar with spears.

pig'sty *n* **1** an enclosur e for pigs. **2** a filthy, untidy place (*the house was a pigsty*).

pig'tail *n* a plait of hair hanging down the back of the head (*a girl with pigtails*).

pike[1] *n* a large freshwater fish.

pike[2] *n* (*old*) a long spear.

pike'staff *n* the staff of a pike:—**plain as a pikestaff** very clear.

pilas'ter *n* a rectangular column or pillar.

pil'chard *n* a small eatable sea fish.

pile[1] *n* **1** a heap (*a pile of rubbish*). **2** (*inf*) a large and grand building (*a stately pile*):—*vb* to heap up (*rubbish piling up*):—**atomic pile** the apparatus needed for studying or making use of atomic energy.

pile[2] *n* one of a number of wooden posts driven into the ground as the foundation for a building.

pile[3] *n* the soft woolly hair on cloth, carpets, etc.

pil'fer *vb* to steal small amounts or articles of small value (*pilfer money from the till*):—*n* **pil'ferer**.

pil'grim *n* one who travels to a holy place for pious reasons.

pil'grimage *n* a journey made by a pilgrim (*a pilgrimage to Bethlehem*).

pill *n* a tiny ball of medicine (*sleeping pills*).

pill'age *n* (*fml*) the seizing and carrying off of enemy property after a battle, plunder, spoil:—*vb* to seize and carry off by force (*enemy armies pillaging the border territory*).

pil'lar *n* **1** an upright of stone, wood, etc, for supporting an arch, roof, etc. **2** any person or thing that gives support (*a pillar of the local tennis club*).

pill'ar box *n* a hollow pillar in which letters may be posted.

pill'ion *n* a seat at the back of the saddle of a motorcycle for a passenger (*he was thrown from the pillion in the accident*).

pill'ory *n* (*old*) a board with holes into which the head and hands of wrongdoers were fastened as punishment:—*vb* (*fml*) to mock, to hold up to ridicule (*pilloried the poverty-stricken children for their old-fashioned clothes*).

pill'ow *n* a soft cushion for the head.

pill'owcase *n* the cover put over a pillow.

pi'lot *n* **1** one who guides a ship in and out of harbour. **2** one who steers an aer oplane:—*vb* **1** to guide, to show the way (*piloting the ship into harbour*). **2** to steer an aer oplane (*he pilots military aircraft*).

pimen'to *n* Jamaica pepper.

pim'pernel *n* a low-growing plant with small flowers, often red.

pim'ple *n* a small swelling on the skin.

pim'ply *adj* (*inf*) covered with pimples (*a pimply youth*).

pin *n* **1** a short pointed bar of wir e with a flattened head, used for fastening cloth, paper etc (*put up the hem of the dress with pins*). **2** a wooden, metal, or plastic peg (*have a pin put in his injured arm*). **3** a bolt:— *vb* (*pinned*, *pin'ning*) **1** to fasten or mark (*a silver pin*). **2** to hold firmly (to):—**pins and needles** a tingling feeling in a limb as the blood starts to flow freely through it again.

PIN *abbr* personal identification number, a number, consisting of several digits, used to identify a person (*enter your PIN to get money from the cash machine*).

pin'afore *n* **1** a loose overall worn to pr otect the clothes. **2** a kind of dr ess with no covering for the arms, usu worn over a blouse or sweater.

pince-nez [pèns'-nā] *n* a pair of spectacles that clip on to the nose by means of a spring.

pin'cers *npl* **1** a tool for gripping things firmly , used esp for pulling out nails. **2** claws (e.g. as of a crab).

pinch *vb* **1** to tak e or nip between the finger and thumb (*pinch his arm*). **2** to squeeze the flesh until it hurts (*pinch him to get him to wake up*). **3** (*inf*) to steal (*pinch money from her mother's purse*):—*n* **1** the amount that can be tak en between the finger and thumb. **2** a small amount (*a pinch of salt*). **3** need, distress (*feeling the pinch having no job*).

pinch'beck *n* an alloy of copper and zinc that resembles gold:—*adj* sham.

pine[1] *n* a cone-bearing evergreen tree.

pine[2] *vb* **1** to waste away with sorrow, pain, etc. **2** to long for.

pine'apple *n* a cone-shaped tropical fruit.

pine cone *n* the scaly fruit of the pine (*burn pine cones on the fire*).

ping *n* a sharp sound, as of a bullet in flight.

ping'-pong *n* table tennis.

pin'ion *n* **1** a bird's wing. **2** a small toothed wheel:—*vb* **1** to fasten the arms to the sides (*the burglars pinioned his arms and tied him up*). **2** to clip wings.

pink[1] *n* **1** a garden flower. **2** a light red colour. **3** the best of condition (*in the pink*):—*also adj.*

pink[2] *vb* to cut a zig-zag edge on cloth (*pink the edges of the seams*).

pin money *n* money allowed to a woman to buy clothes and personal effects (*she has a part-time job but it pays only pin money*).

pin'nace *n* (*fml*) a boat with oars and sails. **2** a small boat carried on a warship.

pin'nacle *n* **1** a pointed tower or spire on a building. **2** a pointed mountain. **3** the highest point (*the pinnacle of her success*).

pint *n* the eighth part of a gallon, 0.57 litre.

pioneer' *n* **1** one who goes before the main body to prepare the way, one who is the first to try out new ideas etc (*a pioneer of medical research in cancer*). **2** an explorer:—*vb* **1** to begin (*pioneer the research*). **2** to explore.

pi'ous *adj* loving and worshipping God, religious (*the congregation's pious members*).

pip *n* **1** seed of fruit (*orange pips*). **2** the spot on a card, dice, domino, etc. **3** one of the badges worn on an army officer's shoulder to show his rank:—**give the pip** to make unhappy or depressed.

pipe *n* **1** a musical wind instrument (*the pipes of Pan*). **2** a long tube (*water pipes*). **3** a tube with a bowl at one end for smoking tobacco (*smoke a pipe*). **4** a shrill voice. **5** a bird's note. **6** (*fml*) a measure of wine:—*vb* **1** to play upon a pipe. **2** to make (water, gas, etc) pass through pipes (*piping oil to the refinery*). **3** to

speak in a shrill voice. **4** to whistle:— **piping hot** very hot.

pipe'clay *n* a fine white clay used for making clay pipes and whitening shoes, belts, etc.

pipe'line *n* a long line of pipes to carry water, oil, etc:—**in the pipeline** in preparation (*plans in the pipeline*).

pip'er *n* one who plays a pipe or bagpipes:—**pay the piper** to pay the bill.

pipette' *n* a slender glass tube (*pipettes in the chemistry lab*).

pip'pin *n* a variety of apple.

piquant [pee'-kênt] *adj* **1** sharp-tasting, appetizing (*a piquant sauce*). **2** witty, arousing interest:—*n* **pi'quancy**.

pique [peek] *n* irritation, anger caused by wounded pride:—*vb* to wound the pride of, to offend (*piqued at her lack of interest*).

piquet [pi-ket'] *n* a game of cards.

pi'racy *n* the crime of a pirate.

pi'rate *n* **1** one who attacks and robs ships at sea. **2** a person who does something without legal right (*pirates who publish books without permission*):—*also vb.*

pirouette' *vb* to turn round on the points of the toes, as a ballet-dancer:—*also n.*

piscato'rial *adj* (*fml*) having to do with fish and fishing.

pista'chio *n* a nut with a green kernel.

pis'til *n* the seed-bearing part of a flower.

pis'tol *n* a small firearm fired with one hand.

pis'ton *n* a plug that fits closely into a hollow cylinder inside which it moves up and down (*the pistons in the engine*).

pis'ton rod *n* a rod that moves the piston (e.g. in a pump) or is moved by it (e.g. in an engine).

pit *n* **1** a deep hole in the earth. **2** the passageway leading down to a mine. **3** a mine (for coal, etc). **4** the back seats on the ground floor of a theatre:—*vb* (**pit'ted, pit'ting**) **1** to lay in a pit. **2** to set against in order to outdo (*pit his wits against theirs*).

pit'apat *adv* with quick light steps, with a light tapping sound.

pitch[1] *vb* **1** to set up (*pitch a tent*). **2** to throw (*pitch a ball*). **3** to fall heavily (*he suddenly pitched forward*). **4** to set the keynote of (a tune). **5** (*of a ship*) to dip head-first down after rising on a wave:—*n* **1** a thr ow. **2** the highness or lowness of a note in music. **3** the gr ound marked out for a game (*a cricket pitch*):—**pitched battle** a set battle between two prepared armies.

pitch² *n* a thick dark substance obtained from tar (*as black as pitch*).

pitch'er¹ *n* a container for liquids (*a pitcher of water*).

pitch'er² *n* one who throws the ball to the batter in baseball.

pitch'fork *n* a long-handled tool with prongs for moving hay:—*vb* **1** to move with a pitchfork. **2** to put suddenly into a new situation.

pit'eous *adj* (*fml*) feeling or deserving pity (*a piteous cry*).

pit'fall *n* a trap (*the pitfalls of business*).

pith *n* **1** the soft centr e of the stem of a plant. **2** material just under the skin of an orange etc. **3** the most important part (*the pith of his speech*).

pith'y *adj* short and to the point, forceful.

pit'iable *adj* deserving pity (*a pitiable sight*).

pit'-prop *n* timber used to support walls, roof, etc, in a coal mine.

pit'ta (bread) *n* a kind of oval-shaped flat bread which can be opened to insert a filling.

pit'tance *n* a small allowance or wage (*earn a pittance*).

pit'ted *adj* marked with little hollows, as the skin after smallpox.

pit'y *n* sympathy for the pain or sorrow of others (*feel pity for the homeless*):—*vb* to feel sorry for:—*adjs* **pit'iful, pit'iless**.

piv'ot *n* **1** the pin on which anything (e.g. a wheel) turns. **2** the central point of anything (*the pivot of the organization*).

piv'otal *adj* holding a central or important position (*a pivotal role in the firm*).

pix'ie, pix'y *n* a fairy.

pizza [peet'-zè] *n* a baked dough crust covered with cheese, tomatoes, etc.

plac'ard *n* a notice put up in a public place to announce or advertise something (*carry a placard protesting against the new law*).

placate' *vb* to make calm or peaceful (*placating their angry mother*).

place *n* **1** an open space in a town. **2** a particular part of space. **3** a village, town, etc. **3** the post

or position held by someone. **4** rank in society. **5** a passage in a book:— *vb* **1** to put or set. **2** to decide from where a thing comes or where it ought to be. **3** to r ecognize. **4** to find a job for .

plac'id *adj* calm, not easily angered or upset, gentle (*a placid baby*):—*n* **placid'ity**.

pla'giarism *n* the act of stealing from another author's works:—*n* **pla'giarist**.

pla'giarize *vb* to use the words or ideas of another and pretend they are one's own (*plagiarizing his friend's essay*).

plague [plåg] *n* **1** a ver y infectious and dangerous disease (*the Black Death was a dangerous plague in the Middle Ages*). **2** (*inf*) a nuisance:—*vb* (*inf*) to keep on annoying, to pester (*plaguing us with questions*).

plaice *n* an eatable flat fish (*plaice and chips*).

plaid [plad *or* plåd] *n* a large woollen shawl-like wrap, often of tartan, worn as part of Scottish Highland dress.

plain *adj* **1** clear , easily understood (*plain English*). **2** simple, bar e, undecorated (*plain living*). **3** obvious (*it was plain that she was guilty*):—*n* a stretch of level country.

plain'-clothes *adj* wearing ordinary clothes, not uniform (*a plain-clothes policeman*).

plain' deal'ing *n* honesty, sincerity.

plain' sail'ing *n* something easy (*getting into the building was plain sailing*).

plain'-spo'ken *adj* saying what one thinks, frank.

plaint *n* (*fml*) **1** a complaint. **2** a written r equest for justice to a court of law.

plain'tiff *n* the person who brings a suit before a court of law.

plain'tive *adj* sad, expressing sorrow (*a plaintive sound*).

plait [plat, plåt *or* pleet], **pleat** *ns* **1** a pigtail of intertwined hair. **2** a fold (e.g. in material):—*vb* to twist together into a plait.

plan *n* **1** a drawing of the outlines made by an object on the ground, a map (*a plan of the building*). **2** a scheme of what is to happen on a future occasion (*make plans for defeating the enemy*):—*vb* (*planned', plan'ning*) **1** to draw a plan of. **2** to arrange befor ehand what should happen (*plan their future actions*):—*n* **plan'ner**.

plane¹ *n* **1** a smooth or level surface. **2** a joiner 's tool for giving wood a smooth surface. **3** *a* *common short form of* **aeroplane**:—*adj* level, smooth:—*vb* to make smooth (*planing the rough wood*).

plane² , **plane tree** *n* a tall broad-leaved tree.

plan'et *n* one of the heavenly bodies moving in orbit round the sun.

planeta'rium *n* a model of the planetary system.

plan'etary *adj* having to do with the planets (*planetary influences*).

plan'gent *adj* with loud, deep sound.

plank *n* a long flat piece of timber (*a floor made of planks*).

plank'ton *n* small living organisms found in the sea.

plant *n* **1** anything growing from the earth and feeding on it through its roots (*garden plants*). **2** the machinery and equipment used in a factory (*industrial plant*):—*vb* **1** to put in the ground to grow (*plant potatoes*). **2** to set firmly (*plant his feet on the ground*).

plan'tain¹ *n* a type of herb with broad leaves.

plan'tain² , **plan'tain tree** *n* a tropical tree with fruit like a banana.

planta'tion *n* **1** a wood planted by man. **2** a colony. **3** an estate on which a large amount of sugar, tea, cotton, etc, is cultivated.

plan'ter *n* the owner or manager of a plantation (*a rubber planter*).

plaque [pläk] *n* **1** an ornamental plate of metal, etc (*a plaque on the wall in memory of the dead soldier*). **2** a deposit of saliva and bacteria that forms on the teeth.

plas'ma *n* the liquid part of blood.

plas'ter *n* **1** a mixture of lime, water and sand spread over the walls of buildings to make them smooth. **2** an adhesive bandage used for dressing wounds, etc (*put a plaster on his broken leg*):—*vb* **1** to cover with plaster . **2** to spread over the surface of:—**plaster of Paris** a quickly hardening plaster, used to support broken limbs.

plas'terer *n* one who plasters walls.

plas'tic *adj* easily shaped or moulded:—*n* one of a group of man-made substances that can be moulded into any shape (*chairs made of plastic*).

Plas'ticine *n* the trademark of a clay used to make models (*children play with Plasticine*).

plastic'ity *n* the quality of being easily shaped or moulded.

plastic surgery *n* the reshaping of the human body by surgery (*have plastic surgery to reshape her nose*).

plate *n* **1** a flat piece of metal, glass, etc (*the name of the company engraved on a plate on the wall*). **2** a shallow dish for food (*serve the meat on the plates*). **3** gold and silver household articles (*burglars stole the family plate*). **4** a pictur e printed from an engraved piece of metal, etc:—*vb* to cover with a thin coat of metal.

plat'eau *n* (*pl* **pla'teaux** *or* **pla'teaus**) an extent of high level land, a tableland.

plate'-glass *n* large thick sheets of glass as used for shop windows.

plate'-layer *n* a worker who fixes down railway lines.

plat'form *n* **1** a raised part of the floor (for speakers, etc). **2** a bank built above ground level for those entering trains, etc. **3** statement of the aims of a group (*the animal rights platform*).

plat'ing *n* the art of covering articles with a thin coat of metal (*silver plating*).

plat'inum *n* a valuable heavy greyish-white metal.

plat'itude *n* statement of an obvious truth as if it were important (*people using platitudes to the bereaved family*).

Platon'ic *adj* having to do with Plato, the Greek philosopher.

platonic love *adj* purely spiritual love between two human beings (*a platonic, rather than a sexual, relationship*).

platoon' *n* a small division of a company of infantry.

platt'er *n* a large flat plate or dish (*a platter of cold meat*).

plat'ypus *n* an Australian mammal with jaws like a duck's bill.

plau'dit *n*, **plau'dits** *npl* applause (*performers receiving plaudits from the audience*).

plau'sible *adj* that sounds convincing, seemingly true or truthful (*a plausible excuse*):—*n* **plausibil'ity**.

play *vb* **1** to amuse oneself (*children playing*). **2** to take part in a game (*play darts*). **3** to gamble. **4** to act a part in a drama (*play Hamlet*).

5 to perform on a musical instrument (*to play the piano*). **6** to trifle:— *n* **1** fr ee movement (*the play of the rope*). **2** trifling amusement or sport (*children engaged in play*). **3** gambling. **4** a drama (*go to see a play in the local theatre*).

play'bill *n* a poster advertising a theatrical performance.

play'er *n* **1** one who tak es part in a sport or drama. **2** a musical performer (*piano-player*).

play'fellow *n* (*fml*) a childhood companion.

play'ful *adj* fond of sport or amusement.

play'ground *n* a piece of ground set aside for children to play in.

play'house *n* (*esp in titles*) a theatre.

play'mate *n* a childhood companion (*his playmates at nursery school*).

play'thing *n* a toy.

play'wright *n* one who writes plays.

plea *n* **1** an excuse. **2** an earnest r equest. **3** the prisoner's answer to the charge in a law court (*a plea of not guilty*).

plead *vb* (*pt, pp* **plead'ed** *or* **pled**) **1** to r equest earnestly (*plead for his friend's release*). **2** to put forward in excuse (*plead that he was somewhere else*). **3** to pr esent one's case or one's client's case in a law court.

pleas'ant *adj* agreeable, enjoyable (*a pleasant companion/a pleasant day*).

pleas'antry *n* humorous talk, a joke.

please *vb* **1** to mak e happy or content (*do anything to please her*). **2** to seem good to (*music is pleasing to her*). **3** to be so kind as to (*close the window, please*).

plea'surable *adj* giving pleasure (*a pleasurable occasion*).

plea'sure *n* **1** delight, joy (*get pleasure in her son's happiness*). **2** will (*at their pleasure*).

pleat *see* **plait**.

plebeian [ple-bee-ên] *adj* **1** having to do with the common people. **2** (*derog*) vulgar, common (*a plebeian attitude*):—*n* one of low birth.

pleb'iscite *n* (*fml*) a vote on an important question in which electors are asked whether they approve or disapprove of government policy.

plec'trum *n* a small instrument for plucking the strings of stringed instruments.

pledge *n* **1** an object handed over to another to keep until a debt has been paid back to him or

her. **2** a solemn pr omise (*a pledge that he would look after her*). **3** a toast:— *vb* **1** (*fml*) to give to keep until a debt has been repaid (*pledging his watch at the pawnbroker's*). **2** to pr omise solemnly (*pledge that he would be present*). **3** to drink to the health of.

Pleiads [pli-adz], **Pleiades** *npl* a cluster of stars.

ple'nary *adj* (*fml*) full, complete (*a plenary session*).

plenipoten'tiary *n* an ambassador with full powers to act as he or she thinks fit:—*adj* having full powers.

plen'ish *vb* (*fml*) to provide with what is necessary (*plenish their stores*).

plen'teous *adj* (*fml*) plentiful.

plen'tiful *adj* enough, more than enough (*a plentiful supply*).

plen'ty *n* all that is necessary, more than is necessary (*there is plenty of food*).

ple'onasm *n* (*fml*) use of more words than is necessary.

pleth'ora *n* more than enough of anything (*a plethora of second-hand clothes*).

pleurisy [plö-rê-si] *n* an inflammation of the membrane around the lungs.

pli'able *adj* **1** easily bent. **2** easily influenced (*pliable people doing what she says*):—*n* **pliabil'ity**.

pli'ant *adj* **1** easily bent. **2** easily influenced:— *n* **pli'ancy**.

pli'ers *npl* a small tool for gripping things firmly and for cutting wire (*use pliers to pull out the nail*).

plight[1] *vb* (*fml or old*) to promise (*plight their troth*).

plight[2] *n* a condition, situation (*in a difficult financial plight*).

Plim'soll *n*:—**Plimsoll line** a line on the side of a ship that disappears below water level when the ship is carrying more than the maximum load permitted.

plim'solls *npl* light rubber-soled shoes, gym shoes.

plinth *n* the square slab at the foot of a pillar or under a statue.

plod *vb* (**plod'ded**, **plod'ding**) to walk or work slowly and steadily (*plodding home at the end of the day*).

plod'der *n* one who, though not clever, makes progress by hard work.

plot *n* **1** a small piece of gr ound (*a plot in the cemetery*). **2** the planned arrangement of the events of a story, play, etc. **3** a secr et plan against one or more persons (*conspirators in a plot against the king*):—*vb* (**plot'ted, plot'ting**) **1** to plan. **2** to form a plan against (*plot against the king*). **3** to mark out or set down on paper (*plot a graph*):—*n* **plot'ter**.

plough [plou] *n* an instrument for turning up soil before seeds are sown:—*vb* to turn up with a plough:—**the Plough** a group of seven stars.

plough'man *n* one who ploughs, a farm labourer.

plough'share *n* the cutter or blade of a plough.

plov'er *n* a common wading bird.

pluck *vb* **1** to pick or gather (*pluck roses*). **2** to snatch (*pluck the log from the fire*). **3** to pull the feathers (*pluck the pheasant for dinner*):—*n* courage (*have the pluck to face danger*).

pluck'y *adj* brave (*plucky fighters*).

plug *n* an object that fits into a hole and stops it, a stopper:—*vb* (**plugged', plug'ging**) **1** to stop with a plug. **2** (*inf*) to publicize (*plugging his new book on radio*).

plum *n* **1** a common stone-fruit. **2** a gr eat prize.

plu'mage *n* the feathers of a bird.

plumb [plum] *n* a piece of lead on a string, lowered from the top of a wall to see that it is at right angles to the ground:—*adj* straight up and down:—*adv* **1** exactly (*plumb between the eyes*). **2** straight up and down:—*vb* **1** to measure depth. **2** to study thor oughly (*plumb the human mind*).

plumbago [plum-bā-gō] *n* the black lead used in pencils.

plumber [plum'-êr] *n* a workman skilled in mending or fitting pipes, taps, etc.

plumbing [plum'-ing] *n* **1** the work of a plumber . **2** all the pipes, taps, etc, in a house (*faulty plumbing*).

plumb'line *n* the string by which the plumb is lowered.

plume *n* **1** a feather . **2** an ornament of feathers in a hat, etc:—*vb* (*fml*) **1** to decorate with feathers. **2** to pride (onesel f) (*pluming himself on his building expertise*).

plum'met *n* a line with a piece of lead at its end, used for finding the depth of the sea:—*vb* to drop down, to plunge.

plump[1] *adj* fat and rounded:—*vb* to grow fat, to fatten (*plump the turkeys for Christmas*):—*n* **plump'ness**.

plump[2] *vb* **1** to sit or fall suddenly (*plump down on the sofa*). **2** to choose (*plump for the older candidate*):—*adv* suddenly.

plum pud'ding *n* a pudding containing currants, raisins, etc, flavoured with spices.

plun'der *vb* to steal by force, to rob:—*n* that which is taken away by force (*plunder taken by the enemy from the city*).

plunge *vb* **1** to thrust into water (*plunging the vegetables into boiling water*). **2** to jump or dive into water (*plunge into the lake*). **3** to rush (into) (*plunge into marriage*):—*n* **1** a dive. **2** act of rushing.

plu'perfect *n* a tense indicating that an action took place before a past action (e.g. I had written).

plu'ral *adj* more than one in number:—*n* the form(s) of a word indicating more than one.

plu'ralist *n* (*fml*) one who holds more than one office.

plural'ity *n* (*fml*) **1** a number consisting of mor e than one. **2** the majority.

plus *prep* with the addition of (*brains plus beauty*):—*adj* **1** mor e than (*children who are twelve plus*). **2** to be added, extra (*a plus factor*):—*n* the sign (+) of addition.

plush *n* (*inf*) a velvety kind of cloth.

pluto'cracy *n* **1** a state ruled by the rich. **2** the rich class of people.

plu'tocrat *n* (*fml*) a rich powerful person:—*adj* **plutocrat'ic**.

ply[1] *vb* **1** to work at (*plying his trade*). **2** to go regularly between two places (*a ferry plied between the island and the mainland*). **3** to use skilfully.

ply[2] *n* a layer (*four-ply wood*).

ply'wood *n* strong board made up of several thin layers of wood stuck together.

pneumatic [nû-ma'-tik] *adj* filled with air, moved by air.

pneumonia [nû-mō'-ni-ä] *n* an inflammation of the lungs.

poach[1] *vb* to cook (fish, eggs, etc) lightly in liquid.

poach[2] *vb* to hunt unlawfully on another's land (*poach pheasants*):—*n* **poach'er**.

pock n a small blister on the skin caused by smallpox.

pock'et n **1** a small bag attached to a garment, billiard table, suitcase, etc (*a handkerchief in his top pocket*). **2** a hollow in earth or rock filled with metal ore:—vb **1** to put into a pocket (*pocketing his winnings*). **2** to steal. **3** to conceal (*pocketed his pride*).

pock'etbook n a small case for holding paper money, letters, etc, in one's pocket.

pocket money n money carried about for immediate personal use (*children's pocket money*).

pock'marked adj marked with small hollows on the skin as a result of smallpox.

pod n the covering of the seed of plants, such as peas, beans, etc.

podg'y adj (*inf*) short and fat.

po'em n a piece of writing set down in memorable language and in lines with a recognizable rhythm.

po'esy n (*fml*) **1** the art of writing poetry. **2** poetry.

po'et n one who writes poetry:—f **po'etess**.

poet'ic, poet'ical adjs **1** having to do with poetry. **2** suitable for poetry (*poetic language*).

poet laureate n a title of honour granted by the British monarch to a leading poet and held until death.

po'etry n ideas, feelings, etc, expressed in memorable words and rhythmical language.

pog'rom n a violent attack upon a certain social group or sect, esp the Jews.

poignant [poi'-nênt] adj painful and deeply felt (*poignant memories*).

point n **1** the sharp end of anything (*the point of the knife*). **2** a headland. **3** a dot. **4** the exact place or time. **5** the purpose for which something is said or written (*fail to see the point of his speech*). **6** a single stage in an argument or list. **7** the unit of scoring in certain games (*a team three points ahead*). **8** pl movable rails that enable a train to pass from one railway line to another:—vb **1** to show the direction of with a finger, stick, etc (*point out the house to them*). **2** to sharpen. **3** to aim (*point the gun at them*). **4** (*of dogs*) to show the direction of game with the nose:—**at point-blank range** from a very short distance away:—**make a point of** to attach

special importance to:—**on the point of** about to (*on the point of leaving*).

point duty n the policeman's job of directing traffic at a road junction.

point'ed adj **1** sharp (*with a pointed edge*). **2** meant to be understood in a certain way (*a pointed remark*).

point'er n **1** a rod for pointing with (*indicate the place on the map with a pointer*). **2** a dog trained to point out game.

point'less adj having no meaning, having no sensible purpose (*a pointless exercise*).

points'man n a man in charge of railway points.

poise n **1** balance. **2** calmness and good sense (*enough poise to cope with the situation*):—vb **1** to balance. **2** to hover (*poised ready to intervene*).

poi'son n **1** any substance that taken into a living creature (animal or vegetable), harms or kills it. **2** any idea, etc, that when spread through society causes standards of judgment to become lower:—vb **1** to give poison to. **2** to kill by poison.

poi'sonous adj **1** being or containing poison (*poisonous berries*). **2** having a very harmful influence (*poisonous influences on society*).

poke vb to push with something pointed (e.g. a finger, stick, etc), to prod:—n a prod given with something pointed (*a poke in the ribs*):—**poke fun at** to make fun of:—**poke one's nose into** to interfere in what does not concern one.

po'ker n **1** a metal rod for stirring the coal, etc, in a fire. **2** a card game, usu played for money.

po'ky adj (*inf*) small and confined (*a family living in a poky flat*).

po'lar adj of or near one of the poles of the earth (*the polar regions*).

polar bear n the white bear of Arctic regions.

po'larize vb **1** to make to work in the same direction. **2** to divide into groups based on two completely opposite opinions, attitudes, etc.

pol'der n low-lying land reclaimed from the sea (esp in Holland).

pole[1] n **1** a long rod. **2** a long rounded post. **3** a measure of length (= $5\frac{1}{2}$ yards).

pole[2] n **1** one of the ends of the axis of the earth. **2** one of the points in the sky opposite the poles of the earth (celestial poles). **3** the end of either of the two arms of a magnet.

pole'-axe *n* (*old*) a battle-axe with a long handle.

pole'cat *n* a weasel-like animal that throws out a foul-smelling liquid when attacked.

polem'ic *n* (*fml*) a heated argument (*a polemic against the police*).

polem'ical *adj* attacking the views of another.

Pole Star *n* a particular star at or near the celestial North Pole, used for finding directions.

police' *n* a body of persons whose job is to keep public order and see that the law is kept:—*vb* to see that law and order are kept (*policing the area*):—*ns* police'man, police officer, police'woman.

pol'icy *n* 1 the methods or plans of a government or party. 2 a course of action (*a marketing policy*). 3 a written agreement with an insurance company (*a household policy*).

poliomyeli'tis *n* (*abbr* po'lio) a disease likely to cause paralysis of part of the body.

pol'ish *vb* 1 to make smooth and shining by rubbing (*polish the table*). 2 to improve, to refine (*manners requiring polishing*):—*n* 1 a smooth shiny surface. 2 any substance rubbed on to make smooth and shiny. 3 good manners, refinement (*sent to finishing school to acquire polish*).

polite' *adj* well-mannered, refined (*polite children*):—*n* polite'ness.

pol'itic *adj* wise (*not politic to be rude to her parents*):—**body politic** all the citizens of a state.

polit'ical *adj* having to do with politics (*political motives*).

politically correct *adj* of language that is designed to avoid giving offence to particular groups of people, usually people who are often discriminated against, often abbreviated to **PC**:—**political correctness** *n*.

politi'cian *n* a statesman whose work is concerned with the public affairs or government of a country.

pol'itics *n* the art or study of government, political matters (*go in for politics*).

pol'ka *n* a quick lively dance.

poll *n* 1 an election (*a poll to elect a president*). 2 the number of votes (*a small poll*):—*vb* 1 to vote. 2 to cut off the ends (of hairs, branches, horns, etc).

poll'ard *n* 1 a tree cut off at the top to make new branches grow better. 2 an animal without horns.

poll'en *n* the yellow dust on a flower which, united to seeds, makes them grow.

poll'inate *vb* to make pollen unite with the seed:—*n* pollina'tion.

polling booth *n* the place where people vote in an election.

poll tax *n* a tax in which a certain sum is due for every person in the country.

pollut'ant *n* something which pollutes.

pollute' *vb* to make filthy or unfit for use (*water polluted by industrial waste*):—*n* pollu'tion.

po'lo *n* a game like hockey played on horseback.

polonaise' *n* 1 a stately Polish dance. 2 music for such a dance.

pol'tergeist *n* a mischievous spirit or ghost (*believe that a poltergeist was throwing things around the room*).

poltroon' *n* (*old*) a complete coward.

pol'y- *prefix* many.

polyan'dry *n* the state of having more than one husband at the same time.

polyan'thus *n* a flowering plant of the primrose family.

polyg'amy *n* the state of having more than one wife (or husband) at the same time:—*n* polyg'amist:—*adj* polyg'amous.

pol'yglot *adj* 1 able to speak several languages. 2 printed in several languages.

pol'ygon *n* a figure with many sides.

poly'gyny *n* the state of having more than one wife at the same time.

pol'ysyllable *n* a word with many syllables:—*adj* polysyllab'ic.

polytech'nic *adj* dealing with many arts and skills:—*n* (*old*) a college in which many crafts, sciences and skills are taught.

polythe'ism *n* the belief that there are many gods:—*n* polythe'ist.

pol'ythene *n* a man-made plastic material resistant to chemicals and moisture (*bags made of polythene*).

pomade [po-mäd'] *n* (*fml*) scented ointment for the hair.

pom'egranate *n* a large thick-skinned fruit containing many red eatable seeds.

pom'mel *n* 1 the knob on the handle of a sword. 2 the high front part of a saddle:—*vb*

(**pom'melled, pom'melling**) to beat hard, esp with the fists (*the child pommelled his father's chest*).

pomp *n* splendid show or display, grandeur (*a procession full of pomp*).

pom'pom *n* a woolly ball or tassle (*a child's winter hat with pompoms*).

pompos'ity *n* act of being pompous.

pom'pous *adj* trying to appear dignified or important (*a pompous old fool*).

pond *n* a large pool of standing water.

pon'der *vb* (*fml*) to think deeply, to consider carefully (*ponder the problems of the situation*).

pon'derous *adj* **1** (*fml*) very heavy (*a ponderous load*). **2** slow, dull (*with ponderous steps*).

poniard [pon'-yard] *n* a small dagger.

pon'tiff *n* **1** a bishop. **2** the pope:— **Supreme Pontiff** the pope.

pontifical *adj* **1** having to do with a bishop or the pope. **2** pompous.

pontificate *n* the office or reign of a pontiff:—*vb* **1** to act as a pontiff. **2** (*fml*) to state one's opinions pompously, as if stating undoubted facts (*pontificating on the state of the country*).

pontoon[1] *n* a card game, usu played for money.

pontoon[2] *n* a flat-bottomed boat used as a support for a bridge:—*n* **pontoon' bridge**.

po'ny *n* a small horse.

poo'dle *n* a small pet dog with curly hair, often clipped to leave part of its body bare.

pooh *interj* an exclamation of contempt.

pooh-pooh' *vb* (*inf*) to sneer at, to speak of (an idea) as foolish (*pooh-poohed their efforts to help*).

pool[1] *n* **1** a puddle. **2** a deep place in a str eam or river. **3** an ar ea of still water (*a swimming pool*).

pool[2] *n* **1** all the money bet on a certain game or event. **2** a collection of goods, money, etc, given by many people for reselling, sharing out, etc:—*vb* to put together the goods, etc, of individuals for use by the whole group (*pooling their resources*).

poop *n* the back part of a ship, the stern.

poor *adj* **1** having little money. **2** unfortunate (*sorry for the poor soul*). **3** bad (*poor weather*).

poor'ly *adj* unwell (*too poorly to go to work*).

pop *n* a sharp, low sound (*the pop of a cork being pulled from a bottle*):—*vb* (**popped', pop'ping**) **1** to

make a sharp low sound. **2** to move quickly or suddenly (*the child popped out from behind the door*).

pope *n* the head of the Roman Catholic church.

pop'injay *n* **1** (*fml*) a person who is too proud of his appearance. **2** a parr ot.

pop'lar *n* a tall slender tree.

pop'lin *n* a type of cloth made of silk and wool.

pop music *n* popular tunes of the day.

pop'py *n* a plant with brightly coloured flowers (*red poppies*).

pop'ulace *n* (*fml*) the common people (*ideas disliked by the populace*).

pop'ular *adj* **1** having to do with the people (*popular issues*). **2** well lik ed by most people (*a popular young woman*).

popular'ity *n* the state of being liked by most people.

pop'ularize *vb* to make popular (*popularizing the fashion for short skirts*).

pop'ulate *vb* to provide with inhabitants (*an island mainly populated by old people*).

popula'tion *n* all the people living in a place.

pop'ulous *adj* having many inhabitants (*the more populous areas of the world*).

por'celain *n* fine pottery.

porch *n* a roofed approach to a door.

por'cine *adj* (*fml*) pig-like, swinish.

por'cupine *n* an animal like the rat, covered with prickly quills.

pore[1] *n* a tiny opening, esp in the skin (*blocked pores*).

pore[2] *vb*:—**pore over** to study closely (*poring over the map*).

pork *n* the meat obtained from a pig (*roast pork*).

pork'er *n* (*inf or hum*) a young pig.

pornog'raphy *n* indecent writings, paintings, etc:— *adj* **pornograph'ic.**

por'ous *adj* having small holes through which liquid may pass (*porous substances*).

por'phyry *n* a hard stone, purple and white in colour.

porpoise [por'-pês] *n* a sea animal about 1.5 metres (5 feet) long.

por'ridge *n* a food made from oatmeal boiled in water or milk to make a thick broth (*have porridge for breakfast*).

por'ringer *n* (*old*) a small bowl for porridge, soup, etc.

port[1] n **1** a harbour. **2** a place with a harbour (*a small port in the south of the country*).

port[2] n an opening in the side of a ship.

port[3] n the left side of a ship (looking forward), larboard.

port[4] n (old) the way one stands or walks.

port[5] n a dark sweet red wine (*serve port after dinner*).

port'able adj able to be carried about (*a portable typewriter*).

port'age n **1** act of carrying. **2** the price of having something carried.

por'tal n (fml) a doorway, a gateway.

portcul'lis n a framework of criss-cross iron bars that could be lowered suddenly to close the gate of a castle against attackers.

portend' vb (fml) to be a sign of future happenings (*dark clouds portending a storm*).

por'tent n a sign of future evil.

porten'tous adj (fml) indicating future evil (*portentous events*).

por'ter[1] n a doorkeeper.

por'ter[2] n **1** one who carries loads, baggage, etc, for others (*a station porter*). **2** a dark br own beer.

portfo'lio n **1** a case for carrying loose papers, drawings etc. **2** the office of minister of state (*the trade and industry portfolio*).

port'hole n a small window in the side of a ship.

por'tico n (pl **por'ticoes** or **por'ticos**) **1** a r oof supported by a row of pillars, jutting out at the front of a building. **2** a r oofed approach to a door. **3** a path cover ed by a roof supported by pillars.

por'tion n **1** a shar e (*take a portion of the blame*). **2** a helping (*a large portion of cake*). **3** the money and property given to a woman at the time of her marriage. **4** (*fml or old*) one's fate (*poverty has been her portion*). **5** a part (*the front portion of the train*):—*vb* **1** to divide up. **2** to give a shar e to.

port'ly adj stout (*a portly old gentleman*).

portmanteau [port-man'-tō] n (old) a large suitcase, a trunk.

por'trait n **1** a pictur e of a person (*paint her portrait in oils*). **2** a good description (*a pen portrait of her grandmother*).

por'traiture n **1** the drawing of portraits. **2** describing in words.

portray' vb **1** to draw or paint (*a painting portraying children playing*). **2** to describe (*in her account of the accident the driver of the car is portrayed as a very stupid man*).

portray'al n the act of portraying.

pose vb **1** to put (*posing a question*). **2** to put on or take up a certain attitude (*pose for an artist*). **3** to pr etend to be what one is not (*burglars posing as workmen*):—*n* **1** position, attitude. **2** a pretence of being what one is not. **3** a false manner or attitude.

pos'er n (inf) a difficult problem (*unable to answer such a poser*).

poseur [po-zèr'] n one who pretends to be what he or she is not, a person who behaves unnaturally or affectedly (*a poseur behaving like that to try to impress people*).

pos'it vb (fml) to lay down what is acceptable as true before beginning to argue.

posi'tion n **1** place (*the house's position by the lake*). **2** rank, grade (*finish in second position in the race*). **3** job (*a junior position in the firm*). **4** state of affairs (*their financial position*). **5** a place occupied by troops during battle:—*vb* to place.

pos'itive adj **1** sur e (*positive that she saw him*). **2** certain, definite (*positive proof*). **3** confident (*a positive manner*). **4** gr eater than 0 (*a positive number*). **5** r eally existing. **6** active, leading to practical action (*positive action*).

pos'itively adv completely, really (*positively the last time*).

pos'itivism n the belief that the only trustworthy knowledge is actual human experience.

posse [po'-si] n a small body of people, esp police.

possess' vb **1** to have as one's own (*possess great wealth*). **2** (*fml*) to control the mind of (*possessed by a great rage*):—*adj* **possessed'**.

posses'sion n **1** the act of possessing. **2** ownership. **3** contr ol by evil spirits.

posses'sive adj **1** showing possession (*a possessive pronoun*). **2** liking to possess or own, unwilling to share (*a possessive lover*).

possess'or n one who possesses (*the possessor of a new car*).

poss'et n a drink of hot milk and wine or beer.

possibil'ity n something possible (*no possibility of improvement*).

poss'ible adj **1** that may be true (it is possible that she is dead). **2** that may exist (possible proof). **3** that can be done (possible courses of action).

poss'ibly adv perhaps, maybe.

post[1] n a strong pole or length of wood stuck upright in the ground (posts to make a fence):— vb to put up on a post, noticeboard, etc (post notices about the show).

post[2] n **1** the system by which letters, parcels, etc, are carried from one place to another. **2** one's place of duty (soldiers at their posts). **3** one's job (seek a new post). **4** a military camp. **5** a settlement:—vb **1** to put in a letterbox. **2** to send to a certain place of duty (post soldiers overseas). **3** (old) to hurry. **4** (old) to travel on horseback changing horses at regular intervals. **5** to supply with the latest news (keep them posted).

post- prefix after.

post'age n the charge for sending something by post (postage has gone up).

post'al adj having to do with the carrying of letters, having to do with the post office (postal charges).

post'-boy n (old) a boy riding one of the horses drawing a carriage.

post'card n a card on which a message may be written and posted without an envelope (holiday postcards).

post'-chaise n (old) a hired carriage drawn by post-horses.

post'code n the numbers and letters which are added to an address to enable letters and parcels to be processed faster and more efficiently. Called a **zip code** in the USA.

post'date[1] vb to put on a date later than the actual one (postdating a cheque).

post'er n a large printed notice for public display (a poster advertising the concert).

poste'rior adj (fml) **1** later . **2** placed behind:— n (inf) the buttocks (smack the child's posterior).

poster'ity n one's descendants, later generations (paintings preserved for posterity).

post'ern n (old) a back or private entrance.

post'-haste adv with all possible speed (return post-haste with the reply).

post'humous adj **1** born after the father's death (a posthumous son). **2** published after the author's death (a posthumous novel).

postil'ion n (old) a man who rides one of the leading horses of a carriage.

post'man, post'woman ns one who delivers letters and parcels.

post'master, post'mistress ns one in charge of a post office.

post'-mor'tem adj after death:—n an examination of a body after death to find out the cause of death (a post-mortem after sudden death).

post office n **1** an office where stamps may be bought, letters posted, etc. **2** a government department in charge of postal services.

postpone' vb to put off till a later time (postponing the meeting till next week):—n postpone'ment.

post-pran'dial adj (fml or hum) after dinner (a post-prandial nap).

post'script n something extra written at the end of a letter after the signature.

pos'tulate vb (fml) **1** to accept as true without proof. **2** to require that something should be accepted as true before beginning an argument:—n anything accepted as true without proof.

pos'ture n **1** a way of holding oneself (a slouched posture). **2** an attitude:— vb **1** to hold oneself in a certain way. **2** (fml) to behave in a way not natural to oneself (posturing in front of an audience).

po'sy n a small bunch of flowers (bridesmaids carrying posies).

pot[1] n **1** a vessel for cooking in (a pot of soup). **2** a vessel for holding plants, liquids, etc (a plant pot):—vb (pot'ted, pot'-ting) **1** to put in a pot (pot plants). **2** to shoot at and kill (pot rabbits).

pot[2] see **marijuana**.

pot'ash n a substance obtained from the ashes of certain plants.

potass'ium n the metallic base of potash.

pota'to n (pl pota'toes) a plant the swellings (tubers) on whose roots are eaten as vegetables (mash potatoes).

pot'boiler n (inf) a painting or piece of writing done merely to obtain money (a novelist keeping his family alive with potboilers).

poteen' n whisky made secretly against the law.

po'tency n power.

po'tent adj strong, powerful (a potent influence).

po'tentate n (fml) one who possesses great power, a ruler.

poten'tial *adj* existing but not made use of, possible (*potential trouble*):—*n* the unrealized ability to do something.

potentiality *n* unused or undeveloped power(s) (*the potentiality of the pupils*).

po'ther *n* (*old*) bustle, confusion.

pot'hole *n* **1** a hole in the surface of a r oad (*potholes made driving difficult*). **2** a deep hole in limestone.

pot'holing *n* the exploring of limestone potholes.

po'tion *n* (*lit*) a dose, a liquid medicine (*a love potion*).

pot luck' *n* **1** whatever food is r eady (*come for a meal and take pot luck*). **2** what chance may send (*go to the cinema and take pot luck*).

potpourri [pō-pōo'-ree] *n* **1** (*old*) a dish of several foods cooked together. **2** a mixtur e of dried pieces of sweet-smelling flowers and leaves. **3** (*fml*) a selection of writings or pieces of music, a miscellany.

pot'sherd *n* a piece of a broken earthen pot.

pott'age *n* (*old*) a thick soup or porridge.

pott'er¹ *n* one who makes earthenware vessels.

pott'er² *vb* to work slowly and without much attention (*spend Saturdays pottering about*).

pott'ery *n* **1** cups, plates, etc, made of earthenware (*a shop selling pottery*). **2** a potter 's workshop.

pouch *n* a small bag (*a tobacco pouch*).

pouffe [pōf] *n* a large firm cushion used as a seat (*sit on a pouffe at her mother's side*).

poul'terer *n* one who buys and sells poultry.

poultice [pōl'-tis] *n* a dressing containing some soft material often heated, and placed on or over a sore part of the body (*put a poultice on the boil*):—*vb* to put a poultice on.

poul'try *n* farmyard fowls (*a shop selling poultry*).

pounce *n* the claw of a bird:—*vb* **1** to jump on suddenly (*the cat pouncing on the mouse*). **2** to attack suddenly (*the mugger pounced on the old man*).

pound¹ *vb* **1** to beat har d (*with heart pounding*). **2** to crush into powder or small pieces (*pound the nuts into a paste*). **3** to walk or run heavily (*policeman pounding the beat*).

pound² *n* **1** an enclosur e for lost cattle. **2** a place for holding someone's property until claimed (*a car pound*).

pound³ *n* **1** a measur e of weight (= 16 ounces or 0.454 kilogram). **2** a British unit of money (= 20 shillings until 1971, then = 100 new pence) (*a pound coin*).

pound'age *n* a charge per pound.

pour [pōr] *vb* **1** to cause to flow (*pour milk from the jug*). **2** to flow str ongly (*blood poured from the wound*). **3** to rain heavily (*it was pouring*). **4** to move in gr eat quantity or in large numbers (*children pouring out of school*).

poussette' *vb* in country dances, to swing round in couples with joined hands.

pout *vb* to thrust out the lips in displeasure, to look sulky (*the child pouted when she did not get what she wanted*):—*n* a sulky look.

pout'er *n* a type of pigeon with a puffed-out breast.

pov'erty *n* lack of money or goods, want, the state of being poor (*live in poverty*).

pov'erty-strick'en *adj* very poor.

pow'der *n* **1** any substance in the form of tiny dr y particles (*talcum powder*). **2** gunpowder:— *vb* **1** to mak e into a powder. **2** to put powder on (*powder her face*).

pow'dery *adj* **1** dust-lik e (*powdery snow*). **2** covered with powder.

pow'er *n* **1** the ability to act or do (*the power of speech*). **2** str ength, force (*hit the rock with great power*). **3** influence (*use her power on the committee*). **4** contr ol (*people in his power*). **5** a strong nation (*the great powers of the world*). **6** mechanical ener gy (*the car's power*):—*adjs* **pow'er-ful, pow'erless**.

pow'erhouse *n* **1** a power station. **2** (*inf*) a strong or energetic person, team, etc.

pow'er station *ns* a place where electrical power is generated.

pow'wow' *n* **1** (*inf*) a friendly discussion. **2** (*old*) a conference among North American Indians.

prac'ticable *adj* that can be done, possible (*a plan that is simply not practicable*).

prac'tical *adj* **1** skilful in work, able to deal with things efficiently (*a practical person dealing with household emergencies*). **2** that can be carried out, useful (*practical suggestions*). **3** concerned with action rather than with ideas:—*adv* **prac'tically**.

practical'ity *n* usefulness.

prac'tice *n* **1** (*fml*) habit, frequent use (*it was his practice to walk to work*). **2** the doing of an action often to improve one's skill (*piano practice*). **3** a doctor or lawyer 's business.

prac'tise *vb* **1** to do fr equently (*practising self-control*). **2** to do often in or der to improve one's skill (*practise playing the piano*). **3** to carr y on a profession (*practise medicine*).

practi'tioner *n* one who practises a profession (*a medical practitioner*).

pragmat'ic *adj* concerned with actual results (*a pragmatic solution to the problem*).

prag'matism *n* the judging of actions or events by their results.

prai'rie *n* in North America, an extent of level tree-less grassland.

praise *vb* **1** to speak well of, to speak in honour of (*praising the boy for rescuing his friend/praising his brave action*). **2** to worship, as by singing hymns, etc (*praise God*):—*n* **1** an expr ession of credit or honour. **2** glor y, worship expressed through song.

praise'worthy *adj* deserving to be spoken well of (*a praiseworthy act*).

pram *short for* **perambulator**.

prance *vb* **1** to jump about (*children prancing about with delight/horses prancing*). **2** to walk in a showy manner (*prance about showing off her new shoes*).

prank *n* a trick played in fun (*children playing pranks on their parents*):—*vb* (*old*) to dress up, to decorate.

prate *vb* (*fml*) to talk foolishly, to chatter.

prat'tle *vb* to talk much and foolishly, to chatter, as a young child (*prattling about her holiday*):—*n* foolish or childish talk.

prawn *n* a shellfish like but larger than a shrimp.

pray *vb* **1** to beg for , to ask earnestly (*pray for forgiveness*). **2** to speak to God in worship, thanksgiving, etc.

pray'er *n* **1** an earnest r equest. **2** wor ds addressed to God in worship, thanksgiving, etc.

pray'erbook *n* a book containing prayers, order of services, etc.

pre- *prefix* before.

preach *vb* **1** to speak in public on a r eligious or sacred subject (*ministers preaching to their congregations on Sunday*). **2** to give advice on how to behave correctly (*parents preaching the importance of studying hard*):—*n* **preach'er**.

pream'ble *n* (*fml*) the introductory part of an act of parliament, speech, piece of writing, etc (*bored by the long preamble to the novel*).

prearrange' *vb* to arrange beforehand.

preb'end *n* a share of the income of a cathedral paid to a member of clergy for his or her part in the services.

preb'endary *n* a member of clergy who is paid a prebend, a canon.

preca'rious *adj* uncertain, dangerous (*a precarious existence*).

precau'tion *n* something done to prevent future trouble:—*adj* **precau'tionary**.

precede [pree-seed'] *vb* to come or go before in time, place or importance (*the kings preceding him*).

pre'cedence *n* **1** being earlier in time. **2** gr eater importance (*give precedence to the subject at the meeting*). **3** or der according to rank (*princes take precedence over dukes*).

precedent [pre'-sid-ênt] *n* an earlier case that helps one to decide what to do in like circumstances (*the judge basing his sentence on precedents*).

preced'ing *adj* previous (*during the preceding month*).

precen'tor *n* one who leads the choir or congregational singing in church.

pre'cept *n* a rule of behaviour (*moral precepts*).

precep'tor *n* (*fml*) a teacher.

pre'cinct *n* **1** the land r ound and belonging to a church, government office, etc. **2** *pl* the grounds. **3** a part laid out for a particular use (*a shopping precinct*).

precios'ity *n* (*fml*) too great care in the use of words.

pre'cious *adj* **1** of gr eat worth or value. **2** too deliberate, too concerned with perfection or unimportant detail (*a precious prose style/precious manners*).

prec'ipice *n* a very steep cliff.

precip'itant *adj* (*fml*) **1** falling headlong. **2** rushing, too hasty (*an action that proved precipitant*):—*ns* **precip'itance, precip'i-tancy**.

precip'itate *vb* **1** (*fml*) to throw down headfirst (*the horse precipitated him into the ditch*). **2** to make happen at once (*his speech precipitated war*). **3** to hasten (*his mother's illness* *precipitated his departure*). **4** to cause the solid matter in a liquid to sink to the foot:—*adj* thoughtless, overhasty (*a precipitate action*):—*n* the solid matter that settles at the bottom of a liquid.

precipita'tion *n* **1** too gr eat haste. **2** rainfall.

precip'itous *adj* (*fml*) steep (*precipitous cliff*).

précis, precis [prā'-see] *n* a summary (*give the committee a précis of his report*).

precise *adj* **1** exact, clearly expr essed (*precise instructions*). **2** car eful (*a precise speaker*). **3** exact, particular, very (*at that precise moment*):—*n* preci'sion.

preclude' *vb* (*fml*) to prevent from happening, to make impossible (*he is not precluded from applying again*).

preco'cious *adj* (*of a child*) too clever for one's age, forward:—*n* preco'city.

preconceive' *vb* to form an opinion beforehand (*preconceived attitudes about work*).

precur'sor *n* a person or thing that comes before and leads to another (*inventions that were the precursors of the aeroplane*).

pred'atory *adj* living by killing or robbing others (*predatory animals such as foxes*).

pre'decessor *n* one who held a certain post before another (*younger than his pre-decessors*).

predestina'tion *n* the belief that God has settled beforehand everything that is to happen, including the fate of people in after-life.

predes'tine *vb* to settle or decide beforehand (*the plan seemed predestined to fail*).

predeter'mine *vb* (*fml*) to decide beforehand (*predetermine the problem areas*).

predic'ament *n* a difficulty, an unpleasant situation (*an embarrassing predicament*).

pred'icate *vb* to make a statement about:—*n* the statement so made.

pred'icative *adj* making a statement about someone or something.

predict' *vb* to say what will happen in the future, to foretell (*predict a change in the weather*):—*n* predic'tion.

predilec'tion *n* (*fml*) a preference (*a predilection for expensive perfume*).

predispose' *vb* to influence, to make more likely to be affected by.

predisposi'tion *n* a tendency to be influenced or affected by (*children with a predisposition to asthma*).

predom'inance *n* **1** contr ol (*predominance over other political parties*). **2** superiority in numbers, etc (*the predominance of objectors*).

predom'inant *adj* **1** outstanding (*the predominant colour*). **2** lar gest (*a predominant number of protesters*).

predom'inate *vb* **1** to have contr ol over (*the left wing of the party is said to predominate*). **2** to be most or greatest (*the 'no' votes predominating over the 'yes' votes*).

pre-em'inent *adj* outstanding, better (or worse) than all others:—*n* pre-em'inence.

preen *vb* **1** (*of birds*) to trim the feathers with the beak. **2** to tidy one's hair , clothes, etc (*preening herself in front of the mirror*).

prefab'ricate *vb* to make ready the parts (*esp of a building*) for putting together on site.

pref'ace *n* an explanatory passage at the beginning of a speech or book:—*vb* to begin wlth some explanation or other remarks.

pref'atory *adj* made at the beginning (*prefatory remarks*).

pre'fect *n* **1** one placed over others. **2** a senior pupil who helps to keep order in a school.

prefer' *vb* (**preferred', prefer'ring**) **1** to lik e better, to choose before others (*prefer lamb to beef*/ *prefer his brother to him*). **2** (*fml*) to put forward (*prefer charges against him*). **3** (*fml*) to give a better post to (*accused of preferring his nephew*).

pref'erable *adj* more likeable, chosen before others (*leaving seemed preferable to staying*).

pref'erence *n* a liking for one more than another (*a preference for smaller cars*).

preferen'tial *adj* giving, receiving or showing preference (*accused of giving members of his family preferential treatment in the firm*).

prefer'ment *n* promotion to a higher post.

pre'fix *vb* to put at the beginning:—*n* pre'fix a meaningful syllable or word put at the beginning of a word to alter its meaning.

preg'nant *adj* **1** being with young. **2** full of (*pregnant with meaning*). **3** full of meaning (*a pregnant look*):—*n* preg'nancy.

prehen'sile adj (fml) able to grasp or hold (the prehensile tail of the monkey).

prehistor'ic adj before the time of written records.

prejudge' vb to decide or form an opinion before hearing all the facts (prejudging the issue).

prej'udice n 1 an unr easonable feeling for or against (prejudice on the grounds of race). 2 an opinion formed without full knowledge of the facts (a prejudice against the accused). 3 (fml) harm, injury (to the prejudice of his health):— vb 1 to influence unr easonably for or against (accused of prejudicing the jury). 2 (fml) to harm, to spoil (being late will prejudice her chances of getting the job).

prejudi'cial adj (fml) harmful (actions prejudicial to her career).

prel'acy n 1 the office of bishop. 2 government of the church by bishops.

prel'ate n a bishop or archbishop.

prelim'inary adj coming before what is really important, introductory (preliminary talks):— also n.

prel'ude n 1 a piece of music played befor e and introducing the main musical work. 2 something done or happening before an event, helping to prepare one for it (a prelude to peace negotiations).

pre'mature adj 1 happening or done too soon (their rejoicing was premature). 2 befor e the natural or proper time (premature birth).

premed'itate vb (fml) to plan beforehand (premeditating murder).

premedita'tion n (fml) thought before doing something.

pre'mier adj first, chief:—n the prime minister.

premi'ere n the first public performance of a play, film, etc:—also vb.

prem'ise n 1 (fml) a statement accepted as true for the purpose of an argument based on it (take it as a premise that an accused person is innocent until proved guilty). 2 pl a building, its outhouses and grounds (the builder's premises went on fire).

pre'mium n 1 the amount paid for an insurance policy (the premium for his house insurance). 2 a reward, esp an inducement to buy. 3 something given free or at a reduced price with a purchase:—**at a premium** of greater value than usual, difficult to obtain (tickets for the concert are at a premium).

premoni'tion n a feeling that something particular is about to happen (have a premonition that her son would die in battle).

premon'itory adj (fml) giving warning in advance.

preoccupa'tion n a concern that prevents one thinking of other things (his preoccupation with money).

preocc'upied adj thinking of other things (preoccupied with personal problems).

prepara'tion n 1 the act of pr eparing (the preparation of food). 2 something done to mak e ready (party preparations). 3 that which is made r eady (a medicinal preparation).

prepar'atory adj helping to prepare, making ready for something that is to follow (preparatory steps).

prepare' vb 1 to mak e ready (preparing the meal). 2 to get oneself r eady (prepare for war).

pre'paid adj paid in advance.

prepon'derate vb (fml) to be greater in weight, numbers or influence (those in favour preponderated against those against):—adj **prepon'derant**.

prepon'derance n (fml) the state or quality of preponderating (the preponderance of people in favour over those against).

preposi'tion n a word showing the relation between a noun or pronoun and another word.

prepossess'ing adj pleasing, attractive (hardly a prepossessing young man).

prepos'terous adj completely absurd, foolish (a preposterous suggestion).

prereq'uisite n (fml) an essential, a condition that must be fulfilled in advance (a neat appearance is a prerequisite for the post).

prerog'ative n a special power or right attached to a certain office (the king's prerogative).

presage' vb (fml) to be a sign of a future happening, to foretell (dark clouds presaging a storm):— n **pres'age** a sign of what is to happen.

pres'byter n a minister.

Presbyte'rian adj governed by clergy and lay officials (elders) all of equal rank:—n a member of the Presbyterian Church.

pres'bytery n 1 a chur ch district court consisting of ministers and elders. 2 a priest's house.

prescience [pre'-shi-êns] *n* (*fml*) knowledge of what is to happen in the future:—*adj* **pre'scient**.

prescribe' *vb* **1** (*fml*) to lay down what is to be done (*prescribing how others should behave*). **2** to or der a certain medicine (*prescribe antibiotics for his sore throat*).

prescrip'tion *n* a written order by a doctor for a certain medicine (*get antibiotics on prescription*).

prescrip'tive *adj* indicating how something must be done.

pres'ence *n* **1** the state of being in the place r e-quired. **2** one's appearance and bearing:— **presence of mind** ability to behave calmly in face of difficulty or danger (*her presence of mind pre-vented an accident*).

pres'ent[1] *adj* **1** in the place r equired or mentioned (*they were present at the meeting*). **2** now exist-ing or happening (*the present situation*):—*n* the time in which we live (*think about the present—forget the past*).

pres'ent[2] *n* a gift:—*vb* **present' 1** to give, to offer (*present the queen with flowers*). **2** to intr oduce (one person to another) (*present his wife to his employer*). **3** to show (*present a frightening appearance*). **4** to put for ward (*present the case for the defence*). **5** to point (a rifle).

present'able *adj* fit to be seen or shown (*made himself presentable for the interview*).

presenta'tion *n* **1** the act of handing over a present, esp in public (*the presentation of a gold watch on his retirement*). **2** something given by a group of people to mark a special occa-sion (*a presentation by his colleagues on his retirement*). **3** the way in which things ar e shown or arguments put forward (*a presenta-tion to advertise their new product*).

present'iment *n* a feeling that something unpleas-ant is about to happen (*have a presentiment that she was going to die*).

pres'ently *adv* soon (*he will be here presently*).

preserva'tion *n* **1** the act of pr eserving. **2** safe-guarding.

preserv'ative *adj* keeping from going bad (*put a preservative substance on the wood*):—*also n*.

preserve' *vb* **1** (*fml*) to keep from harm (*pre-serving the children from danger*). **2** to k eep from rotting or decaying (*try to preserve the wood/preserve soft fruit*). **3** to k eep safe or in good condition (*preserve old customs*):—*n* **1** fruit, etc, tr eated so as to prevent it from going bad, jam. **2** a place where animals, birds, etc, are protected.

preside' *vb* to control a meeting, to act as chair-man (*presiding at the board meeting*).

pres'idency *n* the office of president.

pres'ident *n* the elected head of a republic, com-pany, society, etc, a chairman.

presiden'tial *adj* having to do with a president (*American presidential elections*).

press[1] *vb* **1** to push on or against with for ce (*press the doorbell*). **2** to squeeze (*press grapes*). **3** to smooth and flatten (*press trousers*). **4** to tr y to persuade (*press her into joining them*):—*n* **1** a crowd. **2** a printing machine. **3** a machine for crushing or squeezing. **4** the newspapers. **5** a cupboard:—*adj*.

press[2] *vb* (*old*) to force to serve in the armed forces.

press'-gang *n* (*old*) a body of seamen sent out to seize men and force them to serve in the navy.

press'ing *adj* requiring immediate action, urgent (*pressing matters*).

press'ure *n* **1** the act of pr essing force. **2** for ceful influence (*agree to go under pressure from his parents*). **3** str ess (*workers under pressure*).

prestige' *n* good name, high reputation (*his writ-ing brought him prestige*).

presum'ably *adv* apparently.

presume' *vb* **1** to tak e for granted, to accept as true without proof (*we presumed that they would be present/the painting is presumed to be by Renoir*). **2** (*fml*) to act in a bold or forward way (*he presumed to borrow her car without permis-sion*).

presump'tion *n* **1** something supposed to be true. **2** (*fml*) forwardness, boldness of manner.

presump'tive *adj* (*fml*) probable.

presump'tuous *adj* (*fml*) overconfident, bold in manner (*it was presumptuous of him to attend without an invitation*).

presuppose' *vb* to take for granted.

pretence' *n* **1** the act of pr etending. **2** a decep-tion. **3** a false claim.

pretend' *vb* **1** to mak e believe by words or actions that one is other than one really is (*he pretended to be a doctor*). **2** to behave as if one wer e in other circumstances (*she pretends deafness*). **3** to claim (*he does not pretend to understand*).

pretend'er *n* (*fml*) one making a certain claim (*a pretender to the throne*).

preten'sion *n* **1** a claim, true or false (*he has no pretensions to musical skill*). **2** pretentiousness.

preten'tious *adj* claiming much for oneself, too proud (*he is just an ordinary person but he is so pretentious*).

pret'erite *n* the past tense of a verb.

preternat'ural *adj* (*fml*) extraordinary, more than natural (*preternatural sights such as ghosts*).

pre'text *n* a pretended reason, an excuse (*he left under the pretext of feeling ill*).

pret'ty *adj* pleasing to the eye, attractive (*a pretty girl/a pretty dress*):—*adv* quite (*pretty good*):—*n* **pret'tiness.**

prevail' *vb* **1** to over come, to prove better or stronger than (*common sense prevailed*). **2** to be in general use (*customs still prevailing*). **3** to persuade (*prevail on him to stay*).

prevail'ing *adj* **1** common, most widely accepted, etc (*the prevailing fashion*). **2** that usually blows over an area (*the prevailing wind*).

prev'alent *adj* common, widespread (*tuberculosis was prevalent then/prevalent rumours*):—*n* **prev'alence.**

prevar'icate *vb* to avoid giving a direct answer so as not to tell the truth (*politicians said to be prevaricating*):—*n* **prevarica'-tion.**

prevent' *vb* to stop from happening (*prevent an accident/prevent progress*):—*n* **pre-ven'tion.**

preven'tive *adj* helping to prevent (*preventive medical care*):—*also n.*

pre'vious *adj* earlier, happening before (*his previous record*).

prey [prā] *n* **1** an animal or bir d hunted and killed by another animal or bird (*the lion's prey*). **2** one who suffers (from) (*a prey to headaches*):—*vb* **1** to hunt and kill for food (*foxes preying on chicken*). **2** to k eep on attacking and robbing (*frauds preying on old ladies*). **3** to tr ouble greatly (*worries preying on his mind*).

price *n* **1** the money ask ed or paid for something on sale (*the price of a loaf of bread*). **2** what must be done to obtain something (*the price of freedom*).

price'less *adj* of great value (*priceless jewels*).

prick *vb* **1** to stab lightly with the point of a needle, dagger, etc. **2** to mak e a tiny hole in. **3** to make to stand up straight:—*n* **1** a sharp point. **2** a tiny hole. **3** a sting. **4** a thorn.

prick'le *n* a small sharp point growing out from a plant or an animal (*the prickles on a rose tree*).

prick'ly *adj* covered with small sharp points.

prickly heat *n* a skin disease causing severe itching.

pride *n* **1** a feeling of pleasur e at one's own abilities, deeds, etc (*take a pride in her work*). **2** too great an opinion of oneself, one's deeds, etc (*people disliked her because of her pride*). **3** the most valuable person or thing (*the pride of the town*):—**pride oneself on** to take pleasure in.

priest *n* a clergyman, a minister of religion:—*f* **priest'ess.**

priest'hood *n* **1** the office of priest. **2** priests in general.

prig *n* one who acts as if he or she were superior in wisdom or goodness (*accused of being a prig because he would not play truant*):—*adj* **prig'gish:**—*n* **prig'gish-ness.**

prim *adj* **1** stiff in manner, formal and correct (*prim old ladies*). **2** neat, r estrained (*prim clothes*).

pri'macy *n* **1** the office of ar chbishop. **2** the state of being first in time, order, rank, etc.

pri'ma don'na *n* the chief female singer in an opera.

prima facie [prī'-ma fā'-see-ā] *adv* (*fml*) at first sight.

pri'mal *adj* (*fml*) original, having to do with early times (*mankind's primal innocence*).

pri'mary *adj* **1** first (*the primary stages of the disease*). **2** chief (*the primary reason for his absence*):—*adv* **primar'ily.**

primary colours *npl* the colours red, yellow and blue, from which other colours may be made.

primary school *n* a school for children from between five and eleven years of age.

pri'mate *n* **1** an ar chbishop. **2** one of the highest kinds of animals, including men and monkeys.

prime *adj* **1** most important (*her prime reason*). **2** excellent in quality (*prime steak*). **3** that cannot be divided by any smaller number (*prime numbers*):—*n* the best time (*people in their prime*):—*vb* **1** to pr ovide with information (*priming the witness about the kind of questions that she would be asked*). **2** to pr epare (a gun) for firing. **3** to pr epare for painting (*prime the wood*).

prime minister *n* the chief minister in a government.

prime number *n* a number that can be divided only by itself and the number one.

pri'mer *n* **1** the mechanism that sets off the explosive in a shell, etc. **2** (*old*) a child's first reading book. **3** (*old*) a simple book on any subject. **4** an under coat of paint (*put a primer on the new wood*).

prime'val *adj* having to do with the first ages of the world (*primeval Man*).

pri'ming *n* the powder in a gun.

prim'itive *adj* **1** of the earliest times (*primitive tribes*). **2** simple or r ough (*a primitive boat/ camp in primitive conditions*).

primogen'iture *n* the right of the eldest son to title and estate.

primor'dial *adj* (*fml*) existing from the beginning (*primordial forests*).

prim'rose *n* **1** a pale yellow early spring flower . **2** a pale yellow colour:—*adj* pale yellow (*primrose walls*).

prim'ula *n* a flowering plant of the primrose family.

prince *n* **1** a ruler . **2** the son of a king or emper or.

prince'ly *adj* **1** of or lik e a prince. **2** (*fml*) magnificent, splendid (*a princely gift/a princely salary*).

prin'cess *n* **1** the wife of a prince. **2** the daughter of a king or emperor.

prin'cipal *adj* chief, most important (*the principal cause of the dispute*):—*n* **1** the head of a school, college, etc. **2** a amount of money lent at interest.

principal'ity *n* a country ruled by a prince.

prin'cipally *adv* chiefly (*he is principally engaged in research*).

prin'ciple *n* **1** a general truth fr om which other truths follow (*the principle of gravity*). **2** a rule by which one lives (*moral principles*).

print *vb* **1** to mak e a mark by pressure. **2** to r eproduce letters, words, etc, on paper by use of type (*get invitations printed*). **3** to publish in printed form (*his new novel is being printed*). **4** to

write without joining the letters (*print your name*). **5** to stamp. **6** to stamp a design on cloth. **7** to pr oduce a picture from a photographic negative. **8** to write in lar ge clear lettering:—*n* **1** a mark made by pressure (*footprints*). **2** letters, words, etc, reproduced on paper by use of type (*italic print*). **3** a copy of a pictur e taken from a photographic negative or engraving. **4** cloth with a design stamped on it (*a flower print*).

print'er *n* one who prints books, newspapers, etc.

print'ing machine, print'ing press *ns* a machine for printing with type.

pri'or *n* earlier, previous (*a prior engagement*):—*n* **1** the head of a house of monks. **2** a monk next in rank to an abbot.

pri'oress *n* the head of a house of nuns.

prior'ity *n* **1** the state or right of coming befor e others in position or time (*homeless people will get priority for council houses*). **2** something or someone that must be considered or dealt with first (*our first priority is to save the children*).

pri'ory *n* a house of monks or nuns ruled by a prior(ess).

prise, prize *vb* to force open (*prising open the lid of the paint tin*).

prism *n* **1** a solid body with ends the same in shape and size and parallel to each other, and sides that are parallelograms. **2** a triangular glass solid used for breaking up light into colours.

prismat'ic *adj* **1** of or lik e a prism. **2** (*of colours*) very bright.

pris'on *n* a building in which convicted criminals are kept for a time.

pris'oner *n* **1** one k ept in prison. **2** a person captured by the enemy in war (*prisoner-of-war*).

pris'tine *adj* **1** former , of earlier times (*restore the old palace to its pristine splendour*). **2** pur e, undamaged clean (*a book in pristine condition*).

priv'acy *n* **1** undisturbed quiet (*little privacy at a table in a small noisy restaurant*). **2** secr ecy (*the privacy of the government documents*).

pri'vate *adj* **1** belonging to oneself only , not open to other people (*private possessions*). **2** not public (*private houses*). **3** secr et (*private government documents*):—*n* a common soldier who has not been promoted.

privateer' *n* a privately owned ship permitted to carry arms and attack enemy vessels.

priva'tion n lack of food and comforts, hardships (*suffer privation in the war*).

privatise vb to transfer something from public to private ownership (*privatize the steel industry*):—n **privatiza'tion**.

priv'et n an evergreen shrub much used for hedges.

priv'ilege n **1** a right or advantage allowed to a certain person or group only (*old people are given certain privileges*). **2** advantage possessed because of social position, wealth, etc (*people of privilege*):—vb to allow a privilege to.

priv'y adj (*fml*) allowed to share knowledge hidden from others (*not privy to their secrets*):—n an earth or water closet.

Privy Council n a committee that gives private advice to the British sovereign on matters of government.

privy purse n public money set aside for the private use of the British sovereign.

prize¹ n **1** something given as a reward for merit or good work (*awarded a prize for French at school*). **2** that which is won by competition (*win a prize in a travel competition*). **3** anything seized from an enemy:—vb to value highly (*prizing the vase/prize their freedom*).

prize² see **prise**.

prize'-fight n a boxing match for a prize.

pro- prefix **1** befor e. **2** in favour of:— **pros and cons** reasons for and against.

probabil'ity n likelihood.

prob'able adj **1** lik ely to happen, likely to be true (*the probable result/it is probable that he is guilty*). **2** easy to believe (*a probable story*).

prob'ably adv very likely.

pro'bate n proving before a court that a will has been properly and lawfully made.

proba'tion n **1** the testing of a person 's conduct, work or character. **2** a time of trial or testing, esp for a young person found guilty of a crime, but not sentenced on condition that his or her conduct improves (*the young car thieves are on probation*).

probation officer n one whose duty it is to watch over young persons on probation.

proba'tionary adj being tested, on approval (*have the job for a probationary period*).

proba'tioner n **1** one whose fitness for certain work is being tested. **2** one who is on trial for a certain time.

probe n a blunt metal instrument used by doctors when examining a wound closely:—vb **1** to examine with a probe. **2** to examine car efully, to inquire into thoroughly (*police probing the murder case*).

pro'bity [pro'-bi-ti] n (*fml*) honesty, uprightness.

prob'lem n a question or difficulty to which the answer is hard to find (*their problem is lack of staff/financial problems*).

problemat'ic(al) adj doubtful.

probos'cis n (*fml*) **1** the trunk of an ele phant. **2** the tube thr ough which certain animals or insects suck food to their mouths.

proce'dure n way of conducting business (*usual legal procedure*).

proceed' vb **1** to move for ward (*passengers should proceed to gate 5/work is proceeding*). **2** to go on doing, to continue (*give permission to proceed with the scheme*). **4** (*fml*) to go to law (against):—npl **pro'-ceeds** money made on a particular occasion (*the proceeds from the show are going to charity*).

proceed'ing n **1** something happening. **2** a course of action.

pro'cess n **1** the way in which a thing is done or made (*use a new process to waterproof cloth*). **2** a number of actions each of which brings one nearer to the desired end (*the production process/the process of growing up*). **3** (*fml*) a law-court case.

proces'sion n a body of people moving forward in an orderly column (*the carnival procession*).

proces'sional adj having to do with a procession:— n a hymn sung during a religious procession.

proclaim' vb to announce publicly, to tell openly (*proclaim the birth of a prince*).

proclama'tion n a public announcement.

proclivity n a tendency (to behave in a certain way), a natural leaning (*a proclivity towards lying*).

procrastinate vb to put off till later (*procrastinating when there is work to be done*).

procrastina'tion n delay, a habit of putting things off till later.

pro'create vb (*fml*) to produce children:—n **procrea'tion**.

procure' *vb* (*fml*) to obtain (*try to procure a copy of the book*).

prod *vb* (**prod'ded, prod'ding**) 1 to push with something pointed (*prod the cows with a stick to get them to move*). 2 to nudge (*he prodded him to wake him*). 3 to urge into action (*you will have to prod him to get him to work*):—*also n*.

prod'igal *adj* (*fml*) wasteful, spending too freely (*a prodigal young woman*):—*n* a waster, a spendthrift.

prodigal'ity *n* (*fml*) extravagance, great generosity.

prodi'gious *adj* (*fml*) 1 wonderful, extraordinary (*a prodigious sight*). 2 huge (*a prodigious sum of money*).

prod'igy *n* 1 (*fml*) a wonder (*one of nature's prodigies*). 2 a person of extraordinary abilities (*a child prodigy won the music prize*).

produce' *vb* 1 to bring forward, to bring into view (*produce a handkerchief from his pocket*). 2 to bear, to yield (*trees producing rubber*). 3 to cause or bring about (*a remark that produced laughter*). 4 to make or manufacture (*a factory producing furniture*). 5 to give birth to (*the cow produced twin calves*). 6 to cause, to make (*a line*) longer:—*n* **prod'uce** things grown, crops.

produc'er *n* 1 a person or country that grows or makes certain things. 2 one who gets a play or programme ready for performance (*a television producer*).

prod'uct *n* 1 that which grows or is made (*a factory producing wooden products*). 2 result (*the product of much research*). 3 the number given by multiplying other numbers together.

produc'tion *n* 1 the act of making or growing (*the production of furniture*). 2 the amount produced (*increase production*). 3 a performance or series of performances of a programme, play, opera, etc.

produc'tive *adj* 1 fertile (*productive soil*). 2 having results (*a productive meeting*).

productiv'ity *n* the rate of producing something (*increase productivity in the factory*).

profane' *adj* not showing respect for what is holy (*profane language*):—*vb* to treat irreverently.

profan'ity *n* 1 bad language. 2 lack of respect for what is holy.

profess' *vb* 1 to say openly (*profess his love for her*). 2 to claim skill or ability (*he professed to be an expert*). 3 to declare one's beliefs (*profess his religious faith*). 4 to pretend (*he professed that he had been absent because of illness*).

professed' *adj* openly admitted or declared.

profes'sion *n* 1 a public declaration (*a profession of faith*). 2 an employment requiring special learning (*professions such as teaching*). 3 the people involved in such employment (*the teaching profession*).

profes'sional *adj* 1 having to do with a profession (*professional skills*). 2 paid for one's skill (*a professional pianist*). 3 done for a living (*professional singing*). 4 of a very high standard (*a professional performance*):—*n* one who makes his or her living by arts, sports, etc (*opposite of* **amateur**).

profess'or *n* the principal teacher in a university or college (*the professor of French*).

professo'rial *adj* having to do with a professor (*a professorial post*).

profess'orship *n* the office of professor.

proff'er *vb* to offer (*proffer thanks*):—*also n*.

profi'cient *adj* highly skilled, expert (*a proficient pianist*):—*n* **profi'ciency**.

pro'file *n* 1 an outline, a short description (*a profile of the winner of the literary prize*). 2 a head or an outline of it in side view (*a photograph of her profile*).

profit *n* 1 an advantage (*little profit to be had from delaying*). 2 a gain, esp of money (*the profit from the sale*):—*vb* 1 to gain an advantage (*profit from the deal*). 2 to be of use to (*the experience profited her*).

profitable *adj* 1 bringing profit or gain (*a profitable deal*). 2 useful (*a profitable experience*).

profiteer *n* one who makes money by selling scarce goods at very high prices:—*vb* to make money thus.

prof'ligate *adj* 1 living an evil life (*his profligate son*). 2 extravagant, wasteful (*a profligate lifestyle*):—*also n*:—*n* **prof'ligacy**.

profound' *adj* 1 deep (*a profound sleep*). 2 showing much knowledge or intelligence (*a profound thinker*). 3 intense (*a profound love*).

profun'dity *n* 1 depth. 2 the state of being profound.

profuse' *adj* very plentiful (*profuse thanks*).

profu'sion *n* great plenty (*a profusion of flowers*).

progen'itor *n* (*fml*) a forefather, an ancestor.

prog'eny *n* children.

progno'sis *n* a forecast, esp of the progress of a disease (*the prognosis is not good*).

prognos'ticate *vb* (*fml*) to foretell.

prognostica'tion *n* the act of foretelling the future, a prophecy.

pro'gram *n* a sequence of instructions fed into a computer:—*vb* (**pro'grammed, pro'gramming**) **1** to feed a pr ogram into a computer. **2** to write a program.

pro'gramme *n* **1** a plan or scheme (*a programme of social reforms*). **2** a list of the items in a concert, etc (*the conference programme*). **3** a scheduled radio or television broadcast:—*also* *vb.*

pro'gress *n* **1** movement for ward, advance (*the progress of civilization*). **2** impr ovement (*technological progress*):—*vb* **pro-gress' 1** to advance (*the line of cars progressed slowly*). **2** to impr ove (*her condition is progressing*).

progres'sion *n* **1** onwar d movement. **2** a steady and regular advance.

progres'sive *adj* **1** moving for ward, advancing (*the progressive decline in trade*). **2** believing in tr ying new ideas and methods (*progressive educational methods*).

prohib'it *vb* **1** to thr ow (*prohibit smoking in trains*). **2** to pr event (*the high cost of organic food prohibits wide sale*).

prohibi'tion *n* **1** an or der not to do something. **2** the forbidding by law of the making or selling of all strong drink in a country.

prohib'itive *adj* so high (in price) that people are unable to buy (*prohibitive house prices*).

project' *vb* **1** to thr ow (*project a missile into space*). **2** to plan (*project a visit to France*). **3** to stick out (*a sign projecting from the wall*). **4** to operate a projector:—*n* **pro'ject** a plan.

projec'tile *n* **1** something thr own. **2** something fired from a gun, a shell.

projec'tion *n* a part that sticks out.

projec'tor *n* **1** one who forms plans. **2** an apparatus for showing pictures on a screen.

proletariat [prō-le-tā'-ri-at] *n* the lowest class in society, the working people (*the proletariat*

threatening to rebel against the aristocracy*):—* *adj* **proleta'rian.**

prolific *adj* producing much (*a prolific writer*).

pro'lix *adj* using too many words, long-winded (*a prolix prose style*):—*n* **prolix'ity.**

pro'logue *n* **1** (*fml*) an introduction (*the prologue to the poem*). **2** some lines spok en to the audience before a play begins. **3** an event that leads to another (*serve as a prologue to the signing of the treaty*).

prolong' *vb* to make longer (*no point in prolonging the discussion*):—*n* **prolonga'tion.**

prolonged' *adj* very long (*a prolonged stay*).

promenade [pro-me-näd'] *n* **1** (*fml*) a short walk for pleasure (*take a promenade in the evening sunshine*). **2** a wide r oad or pavement, esp along a seafront:—*vb* (*fml*) **1** to tak e a short walk. **2** to walk up and down.

prom'inence *n* **1** the state or act of being pr ominent (*the prominence of his chin/the prominence of the news item*). **2** something that sticks out or is prominent (*prominences on the landscape*).

prom'inent *adj* **1** easily seen. **2** well-known (*prominent local people*). **3** sticking out (*a prominent nose*).

promis'cuous *adj* **1** (*fml*) mixed. **2** having many sexual relationships:—*n* **promiscu'-ity.**

promise *vb* **1** to say that one will or do not do something, to give one's word (*she promised that she would be there/promising to go*). **2** to give hope of a good result (*his work promises well*):—*n* **1** act of giving one's wor d. **2** a sign of futur e success (*a promise of victory*).

prom'ising *adj* likely to do well in the future (*a promising young football player*).

prom'issory *adj* (*fml*) containing a promise.

prom'ontory *n* a headland.

promote' *vb* **1** to raise to a higher position or rank. **2** to help on (*promoting the cause of freedom*). **3** to help to start (*promote a business*):—*n* **promo'ter:**—*n* **promo'tion.**

prompt *adj* **1** r eady, quick to take action (*prompt to criticize other people*). **2** done without delay, quick (*a prompt reply*):—*vb* **1** to tr y to get another to take action (*his behaviour prompted us to call the police*). **2** to help someone (esp an actor) who cannot remember what he or she ought to say.

prompt'er n one whose job it is to whisper words to an actor who cannot remember them.

prompt'itude (fml), **prompt'ness** ns 1 r eadiness. 2 quickness.

prom'ulgate vb (fml) to make known, to publish (promulgating information about the new law):—n **promulga'tion.**

prone adj 1 lying face downwar ds (his prone body/ lying prone). 2 inclined (to) (people who are prone to lose their temper).

prong n the spike of a fork etc:—adj **pronged.**

pro'noun n a word used instead of a noun ('he' is a pronoun).

pronounce' vb 1 to mak e the sound of (pronounce the h). 2 to declar e publicly (pronouncing him dead). 3 to speak.

pronounced' adj very noticeable (a pronounced foreign accent).

pronounce'ment n 1 a statement to an assembly . 2 a firm statement.

pronuncia'tion n the way of making the sounds of a language.

proof n 1 an ar gument, fact, etc, that shows clearly that something is true or untrue (police seeking proof that he was the murderer). 2 (fml) a test or trial (courage put to the proof). 3 (in printing) a first printing for correction before reprinting. 4 the statement of strength of some spirits, e.g. whisky:—adj not affected by, able to resist.

proof'-reader n one whose job it is to read first printings and mark errors.

prop n 1 a support (a roof supported by wooden props/she acted as a prop to the whole family). 2 a piece of stage equipment:— vb (**propped'**, **prop'ping**) to support, to hold up.

propagan'da n a plan for spreading certain ideas, beliefs etc, to large numbers of people (political propaganda).

propagan'dist n one who spreads ideas, etc, by propaganda.

prop'agate vb (fml) 1 to spr ead widely (propagating their political ideas). 2 to incr ease in numbers by sowing seeds or producing young (propagate plants/propagate their species):—n **propaga'tion.**

propel' vb (**propelled'**, **propel'ling**) to drive or push forward (a boat propelled by a diesel engine).

propell'er n a revolving screw with sloping blades attached for moving forward ships, aeroplanes, etc.

propen'sity n a natural leaning or tendency to behave in a certain way (a propensity to drop things).

prop'er adj 1 corr ect, suitable, decent, polite (proper behaviour/the proper method). 2 (inf) thorough, complete (a proper mess).

prop'erly adv 1 corr ectly, suitably (properly dressed). 2 strictly (speaking) (she's not properly speaking qualified).

prop'erty n 1 anything owned, that which belongs to one (the car is his property). 2 one's land (trespassing on his property). 3 a quality or characteristic (properties of the chemical substance). 4 (abbr **prop**) an object needed on the stage during a play.

proph'ecy n 1 the for etelling of future events. 2 something for etold.

proph'esy vb to tell what will happen in the future, to foretell (the old man prophesied that there would be a cold winter).

proph'et n 1 one who for etells the future. 2 one who tells men a message or command from God (Old Testament prophets):—f **proph'etess:**— adj **prophet'ic(al).**

prophylac'tic adj (fml) preventing disease:—n a medicine for preventing disease.

propin'quity n (fml) nearness (the propinquity of their relationship).

propi'tiate n (fml) to gain the favour of, to make less angry (sacrifices to propitiate the gods):—n **propitiation:**—adj **propi-tia'tory.**

propi'tious adj (fml) 1 favourable, friendly (propitious circumstances). 2 signif ying good luck (a propitious sign).

propor'tion n 1 the size of a part when compar ed with the whole (the proportion of his salary that goes in tax). 2 the size of one object, number , etc, when compared with that of another (the proportion of men to women in the firm). 3 a share. 4 pl size (a house of huge proportions).

propor'tional, **propor'tionate** adjs in corr ect or proper proportion.

propo'sal n 1 a suggestion or plan put forward (proposals for expansion). 2 an offer to marr y.

propose' vb 1 to put forward for consideration. 2 to intend. 3 to offer to marr y.

proposi'tion n 1 a plan or suggestion put forward. 2 an offer. 3 a statement, a statement that is to be proved true. 4 (in geometry) a problem to be solved.

propound' vb to put forward for consideration.

propri'etary adj 1 owned by a person or group of persons (proprietary brands of biscuits). 2 possessive (a proprietary manner towards her boyfriend).

propri'etor n an owner:—f propri'etress, propri'etrix.

propri'ety n (fml) correctness of behaviour, fitness (behave with propriety).

propul'sion n a driving or pushing forward (jet propulsion).

prorogue' vb (fml) to put an end to meetings (e.g. of parliament) for a certain time:—n proroga'tion.

prosa'ic adj dull, commonplace, unpoetic (a prosaic piece of writing).

prosce'nium n the front of a stage near the footlights.

proscribe' vb (fml) 1 to declare an outlaw. 2 to forbid the use of (proscribing the sale of alcohol):—n proscrip'tion.

prose n 1 the language of ordinary speech and writing. 2 all writing not in verse.

pros'ecute vb 1 (fml) to carry on (police prosecuting a line of inquiry). 2 to accuse in a court of law (prosecute him for trespassing):—n prosecu'tion.

pros'ecutor n the person who makes the accusation in a court of law.

pros'elyte n (fml) one who has been persuaded to change his or her beliefs, esp in religion.

pros'elytize vb (fml) to try to make one change one's beliefs (members of the religious sect trying to proselytize the townspeople).

pros'ody n (fml) rules for the writing of poetry.

pros'pect n 1 (fml) a view (the prospect from the mountain top). 2 one's idea of what may happen in the future (not much prospect of arriving on time/the prospect of being homeless). 3 chance of future success (a young man with prospects):—vb prospect' to explore, to search for places where mines may be sunk for oil, metals, etc.

prospec'tive adj expected, probable (their prospective son-in-law).

prospec'tor n one who searches for gold or other minerals.

prospec'tus n a written description of some undertaking or of the training offered by a school (a college prospectus).

pros'per vb to do well, to succeed (his business is prospering).

prosper'ity n success, good fortune.

pros'perous adj successful, well off (a prosperous businessman).

pros'tate n (also pros'tate gland) a gland in males in front of the bladder.

pros'titute vb to put to a low or evil use (a musician accused of prostituting his talent by playing in nightclubs):—n a person making a living by immoral means:—n prostitu'tion.

pros'trate adj 1 lying flat with the face to the ground (the prostrate body of the injured man). 2 exhausted (prostrate after climbing the mountain):—vb 1 to throw flat on the ground. 2 to bow in reverence (prostrating themselves before the emperor). 3 to tire out:—n prostra'tion.

protag'onist n 1 one playing a leading part in a drama or in an exciting situation in real life. 2 a leader (one of the protagonists of socialism). 3 someone taking part in a contest.

pro'tean adj (fml) changing frequently.

protect' vb to keep safe from danger, loss, etc, to defend (protect their property/protect rare birds).

protec'tion n 1 defence, watchful care. 2 the taxing of goods brought in from other countries so that goods made at home will be cheaper than them.

protec'tionist n one who believes in taxing goods from abroad to protect home goods.

protec'tive adj giving defence, care or safety (a mother protective of her children).

protec'tor n a person or thing that protects.

protec'torate n a country that is defended and governed by another until it can look after itself.

protégé [pro'-tā-jā] n (fml) one under the care of another (a protégé of the famous ballerina).

protein [prō'-teen] n a substance contained in certain foods (e.g. meat, eggs) which helps the body to grow and become stronger.

protest' vb 1 to object (protest about the building of the new road/protest against the referee's decision). 2 to disapprove. 3 to declare (protest their innocence):—n pro'test a statement of disagreement or disapproval (listen to their protests against his decision).

Prot'estant n a member of one of the Christian groups separated from the Roman Catholic church at the Reformation:—*also adj.*

Prot'estantism n. the Protestant religion.

protesta'tion n **1** an objection (*their protestation against the injustice of the decision*). **2** a declaration (*their protestations of innocence*).

pro'to- *prefix* first.

pro'tocol n **1** a tr eaty. **2** corr ect procedure or behaviour (*diplomatic protocol*).

pro'ton n part of the nucleus of an atom that contains positive electricity.

pro'toplasm n the living substance from which plants and animals grow.

pro'totype n the first model from which others are copied, a pattern (*the prototype of the plan*).

protozo'a npl tiny living creatures, the lowest form of animal life.

protract' vb to make long, to make last longer (*protract the talks unnecessarily*).

protrac'tor n an instrument for measuring angles.

protrude vb (*fml*) to stick out, to stand out from (*his ears protrude too much/a gun protruding from his pocket*):—n **protru'-sion:**—adj **protru'sive.**

protu'berance n (*fml*) a swelling, a part that bulges out (*protruberances on tree trunks*).

protu'berant adj (*fml*) bulging out (*a protruberant stomach*).

proud adj **1** having too high an opinion of oneself, one's deeds or possessions. **2** rightly satisfied with oneself and what one has done.

prove vb **1** to show the truth of (*proving his guilt/they proved that he was guilty*). **2** to turn out to be (*she proved a natural teacher*). **3** to test (*require to prove oneself*).

prov'ender n food, esp for animals.

prov'erb n a popular truth or belief expressed in a short memorable sentence.

prover'bial adj **1** well known to all (*his proverbial bad temper*). **2** expr essed in a proverb.

provide' vb **1** to supply what is needed (*providing food for all*). **2** to mak e ready beforehand, to prepare for (*provide for their future*).

provi'ded (that) conj on condition (that) (*he can stay provided that he keeps quiet*).

prov'idence n **1** car e for the future, foresight. **2** God's car e of his creatures.

prov'ident adj (*fml*) **1** taking car e of the future. **2** not spending too much (*provident housekeepers*).

providen'tial adj **1** ver y fortunate (*it was providential that they gave us a lift*). **2** due to God's car e.

province n **1** a division of a countr y (*a province of Canada*). **2** the limits of one's powers, knowledge, etc (*the administration lies within her province*). **3** pl all the parts of a country outside the capital (*live in the provinces*).

provin'cial adj **1** lik e or in a province (*provincial government*). **2** having limited or local inter ests, unsophisticated (*city people regarding other people as provincial*).

provi'sion n **1** something pr ovided for the future (*the provision of education*). **2** pl food (*buy provisions for the weekend*):—vb to supply with stores of food.

provi'sional adj for a time only, that may be changed (*a provisional arrangement/a provisional government*).

provi'so n (*pl* **provi'sos** or **provi'soes**) a condition (*get the job with the proviso that he provides a reference*).

provoca'tion n a cause of anger or annoyance.

provoc'ative adj intended to anger or annoy, arousing the emotions or passions (*provocative remarks*).

provoke' vb **1** to mak e angry (*provoked by his insulting remark*). **2** to give rise to (*events that provoked a war*).

prov'ost n **1** the chief magistrate of a Scottish town. **2** the head of certain colleges. **3** in the Church of England, a member of clergy in charge of a cathedral.

prow n the front part of a ship or boat.

prow'ess n skill or ability (*admire his prowess as a pianist*).

prowl vb to keep moving about as if searching for something, to move quietly about looking for the chance to do mischief (*hear someone prowling in the garden*).

prowl'er n one who moves stealthily, esp a thief (*hear a prowler in the garden*).

prox see **proximo.**

prox'imate adj (*fml*) nearest.

proxim'ity n nearness, neighbourhood (*the proximity of the house to the station*).

proximo *adv* (*abbr* **prox**) of the next month.

prox'y *n* **1** the right to act or vote for another . **2** one with the right to act or vote for another (*act as a proxy for her mother at the shareholders' meeting*).

prude *n* a person who makes a show of being very modest and correct in behaviour (*too much of a prude to change in a communal changing room*):—*n* **prud'ery**.

pru'dence *n* foresight, caution (*have the prudence to save for their old age*).

pru'dent *adj* thinking carefully before acting, wise, cautious (*it would be prudent to check the times of the train*).

pruden'tial *adj* (*fml*) careful about the future, prudent.

prudery *see* prude.

prud'ish *adj* over-correct in behaviour.

prune[1] *n* a dried plum (*have prunes for breakfast*).

prune[2] *vb* **1** to cut off the dead or over grown parts of a tree (*pruning the rose bushes*). **2** to shorten by cutting out what is unnecessary (*prune the report*).

pru'rient *adj* (*fml*) interested by what is indecent, having too much interest in sex (*a prurient mind*):—*n* **pru'rience**.

pry *vb* to inquire closely, esp into the secrets of others, to examine closely (*pried into her private affairs/neighbours prying into the details of their relationship*).

psalm [säm] *n* a sacred song or hymn.

psalmist [säm'-ist] *n* a writer of sacred songs.

psalmody [sal'-mo-di] *n* **1** psalm-singing. **2** all the psalms.

psalter [sål'-tèr] *n* a book of psalms.

psal'tery *n* a stringed instrument of olden times.

pseudo [sü'-dō] *adj* false, not real (*a pseudo interest in the subject*).

pseudonym [sü'-dō-nim] *n* a name used instead of one's real name (e.g. a pen-name) (*write under a pseudonym*).

pshaw *interj* a sound expressing impatience or disbelief.

psychiatry [sï-kï'-êt-ri] *n* the treatment of diseases of the mind:—*n* **psychi'atrist**.

psychic [sï'-kik], **psy'chical** *adjs* **1** having to do with the mind (*psychic disorders*). **2** (*of influences and forces*) that act on the mind and senses but

have no physical cause (*psychic research*). **3** (*of a person*) sensitive to these influences. **4** able to communicate with spirits.

psy'cho-anal'ysis [sï'-kō-] *n* treatment of mental disease by trying to find out by questioning problems, fears, etc, that exist in the patient's mind without his or her being aware of them:—*n* **psy'cho-an'alyst**.

psychology [sï-ko'-lo-dji] *n* **1** the study of the human mind. **2** the mental pr ocess of a person (*fail to understand his psychology*):—*adj* **psycholog'ical**:—*n* **psychol'ogist**.

ptarmigan [tar'-mi-gên] *n* a type of grouse that turns white in winter.

pterodac'tyl *n* a prehistoric winged reptile known of from fossils.

ptomaine [tō-mān'] *n* a poisonous substance that forms on decaying food.

pub *n* a public house.

pu'berty *n* the age by which a young person has fully developed all the characteristics of his or her sex (*reach puberty*).

pub'lic *adj* **1** open to all (*a public exhibition/public holidays*). **2** having to do with people in general (*a public campaign*). **3** well-known (*a public figure*):—*n* the people in general.

pub'lican *n* **1** one who k eeps a public house. **2** in the Bible, a tax collector.

publica'tion *n* **1** the act of publishing (*the publication of his novel*). **2** a published book, magazine or paper (*weekly publications*).

public house *n* (*abbr* **pub**) a house or inn where alcoholic drink is sold and drunk.

public'ity *n* **1** making something widely known, advertising (*the publicity for her new novel*). **2** the state of being well-known (*filmstars who like publicity*):—*vb* **pub'licize**.

pub'lish *vb* **1** (*fml*) to make widely known (*publish the news of the president's death*). **2** to print for selling to the public (*publish novels*).

pub'lisher *n* one who publishes books, etc.

puce *adj* brownish-purple.

puck *n* a small hard rubber disc used instead of a ball in ice hockey.

puck'er *vb* to gather into small folds or wrinkles (*a material that puckers easily/her face puckered and she began to cry*):—*n* a fold or wrinkle.

pud'ding n 1 a soft sweet cook ed food served at the end of a meal (*Christmas pudding/a fruit pudding*). 2 a type of sausage (*black pudding*).

pud'dle n a small pool of dirty water:—vb to make watertight with clay.

pudg'y adj (*inf*) short and fat (*a pudgy child*).

pu'erile adj childish, silly (*puerile behaviour*):—n pueri'lity.

puff n 1 a short sharp br eath or gust of wind (*a puff of wind blew the letter away*). 2 a small cloud of smoke, steam, etc, blown by a puff (*puffs of smoke from his pipe*). 3 a soft pad for powdering the skin. 4 a kind of light pastr y (*puff pastry*)—vb 1 to br eathe quickly or heavily, as when short of breath (*puffing after climbing the hill*). 2 to blow in small blasts (*puff cigarette smoke in their faces*). 3 to blow up, to swell (*her eyes were puffed up*). 4 to praise too highly (*puff up his role in the rescue*).

puffed-up adj over-proud.

puff'in n a diving bird with a brightly coloured beak.

puffy adj blown out, swollen (*a puffy face*).

pug, pug'-dog ns a type of small dog with an upturned nose.

pu'gilism n (*fml*) boxing.

pu'gilist n a boxer:—adj pugilis'tic.

pugna'cious adj (*fml*) quarrelsome, fond of fighting (*he becomes pugnacious when he has taken too much alcohol*):—n pugna'-city.

pug'-nose n a short upturned nose:—adj pug'-nosed'.

puke vb (*inf*) to bring up the contents of the stomach, to vomit.

pule vb (*fml*) to whine, to cry peevishly (*infants puling*).

pull vb 1 to draw towar ds one, to draw in the same direction as oneself (*pull the door open*). 2 to bring along behind one while moving (*a horse pulling a cart*). 3 to r emove (flowers etc) from the ground (*pull roses*). 4 to gather (*pull raspberries*). 5 to r ow with oars (*pull towards the shore*):—n 1 act of pulling (*give the door a pull/ with a pull of the rope*). 2 (*inf*) advantage, special influence (*have some pull with the council*).

pul'let n a young hen.

pul'ley n a grooved wheel with a cord running over it used for raising weights.

pul'monary adj (*fml*) having to do with the lungs.

pulp n 1 the soft juicy part of a fruit (*peach pulp*). 2 soft substance obtained by crushing rags, wood, etc, and made into paper:—vb to make into pulp, to become pulpy (*pulp the fruit/pulp the rags*).

pul'pit n a raised platform enclosed by a half wall for preaching in church.

pulsate' vb to beat or throb (*the music pulsated through the building*):—n pulsa'-tion.

pulse[1] n 1 the thr ob of the heart or of the blood passing through the arteries (*his pulse is too fast*). 2 a place on the body wher e the throb of the blood can be felt (*find the patient's pulse*):—vb to beat or throb (*blood pulsing through his veins*).

pulse[2] n the eatable seeds of peas, beans, lentils, etc (*make a dish with pulses instead of meat*).

pul'verize vb 1 to mak e into dust or powder (*pulverizing the rock*). 2 (*inf*) to defeat thoroughly (*pulverize his opponent*).

pu'ma n a large American wild cat, the cougar.

pu'mice n a light stone with a rough surface, used for cleansing or polishing.

pum'mel vb (pum'melled, pum'melling) to keep on striking with the fist(s) (*a child pummelling his father's chest with his fists*).

pump[1] n 1 a machine for raising water fr om a well. 2 a machine for raising any liquid to a higher level (*central-heating pump*). 3 a machine for taking air out of or putting air into things (*a bicycle pump*):—vb 1 to work a pump. 2 to raise with a pump. 3 (*inf*) to get information from someone by mixing important with unimportant questions (*pump the children about the details of their parents' income*).

pump[2] n a light shoe for dancing.

pump'kin n a large fleshy fruit with a thick yellow skin (*make a pumpkin into a lantern at Halloween*).

pun n the witty or amusing use of a word like another in sound but different in meaning:—vb (punned', pun'ning) to make a pun.

punch[1] vb 1 to strik e with the fist (*he punched the other boy on the nose*). 2 to mak e a hole with a special tool or machine (*punch holes in the* *papers for filing*):—*n* **1** a blow with the fist. **2** a tool or machine for making holes.

punch² *n* a drink made from wine or spirit mixed with sugar, hot water, fruit, etc (*serve punch at their Christmas party*).

Punch³ *n* a hook-nosed, hunchbacked character in the puppet show *Punch and Judy*.

punctil'ious *adj* very careful over small points of behaviour or ceremonial (*punctilious about diplomatic procedure*).

punc'tual *adj* **1** up to time, not late (*be sure to be punctual*). **2** good at arriving at the corr ect time (*she is always punctual/punctual workers*):—*n* **punctual'ity**.

punc'tuate *vb* **1** to divide up written work with full stops, commas, etc. **2** to interrupt r epeatedly:—*n* **punctua'tion**.

punc'ture *n* a hole made by a sharp point (*a puncture in her bicycle tyre*):—*vb* to make a hole in, to pierce.

pun'dit *n* (*fml*) an expert (*pundits discussing the political situation on television*).

pun'gent *adj* **1** sharp to taste or smell (*the pungent smell of frying onions*). **2** sharp (*pungent criticism*):—*n* **pun'gency**.

pun'ish *vb* **1** to cause someone to suffer for do ing wrong (*punish criminals*). **2** to deal r oughly with (*a punishing exercise schedule*).

pun'ishment *n* pain, loss, etc, inflicted on a wrongdoer (*capital punishment*).

pu'nitive *adj* (*fml*) done by way of punishment, inflicting punishment (*punitive measures such as imprisonment*).

punk'a(h) *n* a large fan used in hot countries.

pun'ster *n* one who makes puns.

punt¹ *n* a flat-bottomed boat moved by means of a pole:—*vb* to move a punt with a pole (*students punting up the river*).

punt² *vb* to kick a ball dropped from the hands before it touches the ground:—*also n*.

punt³ *n* the former currency of the Republic of Ireland, until the introduction of the euro in 2002.

punt'er *n* **1** one who gambles on horse-racing. **2** (*inf*) any ordinary person .

pu'ny *adj* small and weak (*his puny arms*).

pup *n* a puppy, a young dog.

pu'pa *n* (*pl* **pu'pae** *or* **pu'pas**) **1** a stage in the gr owth of an insect just before it develops wings. **2** an insect in this stage.

pu'pil *n* **1** one being taught, a learner (*pupils at the primary school*). **2** the r ound opening in the centre of the eye through which light passes.

pup'pet *n* **1** a doll whose movements ar e controlled by strings, etc. **2** one who obeys without question all the orders given him or her by another (*the king was a mere puppet—the nobles ruled the country*).

pup'pet show *n* a performance by puppets (dolls).

pup'py *n* **1** a young dog. **2** (*inf*) a conceited or impudent young man (*an impertinent young puppy*).

pur'blind *adj* (*fml*) nearly blind.

pur'chase *vb* to buy:—*n* **1** the thing bought (*carry home her purchases*). **2** a position that allows one to apply all one's strength (*the purchase required to lift the iron chest*).

pur'chaser *n* a buyer.

pur'dah *n* **1** in India, a curtain dividing off the part of the house reserved for women. **2** the custom of keeping women from mixing freely in society.

pure *adj* **1** clear (*pure sounds*). **2** unmixed (*a sweater of pure wool*). **3** clean, fr ee from dirt or harmful matter (*pure drinking water*). **4** fr ee from guilt or evil (*pure young girls/pure thoughts*). **5** complete, absolute (*a pure accident*).

purée [pū'-rā] *n* food crushed to pulp and passed through a sieve (*tomato purée/fruit purée*).

pure'ly *adv* **1** wholly (*he passed the exam purely because of hard work*). **2** only , merely (*he did it purely for a joke*). **3** in a pur e manner.

purgation *see* **purge**.

pur'gative *adj* able to clear the body of waste matter:—*n* a purgative medicine.

pur'gatory *n* in Roman Catholic belief, a place where souls suffer for a time in order to be cleansed from all sin before entering heaven.

purge *vb* **1** to mak e pure and clean (*purge your mind of wicked thoughts*). **2** to get rid of unwanted persons (*purging the party of troublemakers*). **3** to clear the body of waste matter, to empty the bowels:—*n* **purga'tion**.

purifica'tion *n* **1** act of purif ying. **2** a cer emonial cleansing.

pu'rify vb **1** to cleanse (*purified the air/purifying the water*). **2** to mak e pure.

pu'ritan n one who is very strict in matters of morals or religion:—*adj* puritan'ic(al):—n **pu'ritanism**.

pu'rity n the state of being pure.

purl[1] n the rippling sound made by a stream:—*vb* to ripple.

purl[2] n a type of knitting stitch:—*also vb.*

purloin' vb (*fml*) to steal (*purloin the firm's property*).

pur'ple n **1** a colour of r ed and blue mixed (*dressed in purple*). **2** (*fml*) the purple robe of a king or cardinal. **3** (*fml*) the rank of king or cardinal:—*adj* of purple colour (*a purple dress*).

pur'port n (*fml*) meaning (*the purport of his remark*):—vb (*fml*) to mean, to intend.

pur'pose n **1** the r eason for an action, an intention or plan (*a journey for business purposes/ his purpose in going*). **2** use or function (*the purpose of the tool*). **3** determination (*a man of purpose*):—vb to intend.

pur'poseful adj **1** having a clear intention in mind (*a purposeful young woman*). **2** determined (*with a purposeful air*).

pur'posely adv intentionally, on purpose.

purr n the low sound made by a cat when pleased:—*also vb.*

purse n **1** a small bag for money . **2** a sum of money offered as a prize:—vb to pull in (*pursing her lips in disapproval*).

purs'er n the officer in charge of money and arrangements for passengers on a ship.

pursue' vb **1** to follow in or der to catch (*police pursuing the escaped prisoner*). **2** to carr y on (an activity) (*pursue studies in French*).

pursu'er n **1** one who chases (*the pursuers of the escaped criminal*). **2** one who mak es an accusation against another before a court of law.

pursuit' n the act of pursuing (*the police in pursuit of a criminal/his pursuit of an interesting career*).

pur'sy adj (*fml*) fat and short-winded.

purvey' vb (*fml*) to provide food or meals:—n **purvey'or.**

pus n yellow matter from an infected sore or wound (*pus exuding from the boil*).

push vb **1** to pr ess against with force (*push the door shut*). **2** to move by for ce, to shove (*push the cart uphill*). **3** to tr y to make someone do

something (*push him into applying*). **4** (*inf*) to sell illegally (*push drugs*). **5** (*inf*) to promote, to advertise (*push his new product*):—n **1** a shove. **2** str ong effort. **3** (*inf*) energy (*people with some push*). **4** an attack by a lar ge army.

push'ing adj **1** ener getic. **2** eager to get on.

pusillan'imous adj (*fml*) timid, cowardly:—n **pusillanim'ity.**

puss, puss'y ns (*inf*) a cat.

pus'tule n (*fml*) a small pimple containing poisonous matter (*the pustules on his face caused by the disease*).

put [püt] vb (**put, put'ting**) **1** to set down in or move into a certain place (*put the cups on the table/put the car in the garage*). **2** to ask (*put a question*). **3** to expr ess in words (*put his refusal politely*):—**put by** to keep for future use:—**put up** to give accommodation to (*put his friend up for the night*):—**put up with** to bear without complaining (*put up with noisy neighbours*):—*see also* **putt.**

pu'tative adj supposed, commonly believed to be (*the putative father of the child*).

pu'trefy vb (*fml*) to become rotten, to decay (*meat putrefied by the heat*):—n **putre-fac'tion.**

pu'trid adj (*fml*) rotten, decayed (*putrid meat*). **2** (*inf*) very bad, poor (*a putrid performance*).

putt, put [put] vb (**putt'ed, putt'ing**) **1** to thr ow from the shoulder with a bent arm. **2** in golf, to hit the ball into the hole on the green:—n **1** act of throwing a weight in sport. **2** in golf a hit intended to send the ball into the hole.

putt'ee n. a long strip of cloth bound around the leg below the knee as a gaiter.

putt'er n a golf club for putting.

putt'ing green n in golf, the smooth green near a hole.

putt'y n a paste made from chalk and linseed oil, used for fitting glass in windows, etc:—vb to cement with putty.

puz'zle vb **1** to pr esent with a difficult problem or situation, to baffle, to perplex (*they were puzzled by the last question in the exam/puzzled by her behaviour*). **2** to think long and car efully about (*puzzling over the instructions*):—n **1** a difficult question or problem (*how they got their was a puzzle*). **2** a toy intended to test one's skill or cleverness (*a crossword puzzle*/*a jigsaw puzzle*):—*n* **puz'zlement**.

PVC *abbr* polyvinyl chloride, a tough kind of plastic (*a waterproof coat made of PVC*).

pyg'my, pig'my *n* **1** a member of a race of very small people in Africa. **2** (*inf*) a very small person or animal:—*also adj*.

pyja'mas *npl* a sleeping suit.

py'lon *n* **1** a hollow skeleton pillar for carrying overhead cables. **2** a tower or pillar built at an aerodrome as a guiding mark.

pyorrhea [pî-or-ce'-a] *n* a disease of the gums.

pyr'amid *n* **1** a solid body with triangular sides meeting in a point at the top. **2** a monument of this shape.

pyre *n* a pile of wood, etc, on which a dead body is placed for burning.

pyrotech'nic *adj* having to do with fireworks.

pyrotech'nics *n* the art of making or using fireworks.

Pyr'rhic *adj*:—**Pyrrhic victory** a victory in which the victors suffer very heavy losses.

Pythagore'an *adj* having to do with Pythagoras or his philosophy, which taught that after death the soul went into another body.

py'thon *n* a large non-poisonous snake that crushes its prey in its coils.

Q

quack[1] *n* the harsh cry of a duck:—*vb* to make the cry of a duck (*ducks quacking by the pond*).

quack[2] *n* **1** one who pretends to knowledge or skill that he or she does not possess, esp in medicine (*illnesses made worse by quacks*). **2** (*inf*) a doctor (*the quack told him to give up smoking*):—*n* **quack'ery**.

quad- *prefix* four:—*n* short for **quadrangle** (of a school or college).

quadran'gle *n* **1** a figure with four sides and four angles. **2** a square or rectangular courtyard enclosed by a building, esp a school or college (*students walking in the quandrangle*).

quad'rant *n* **1** the fourth part of a circle or its circumference. **2** an instrument for measuring angles.

quadrat'ic *adj* in algebra, having to do with the square of an unknown quantity, but with no higher power.

quadrien'nial *adj* **1** happening every four years (*a quadriennial festival*). **2** lasting for four years.

quadrilat'eral *n* a four-sided figure.

quadrille' *n* a dance for four couples, each forming the side of a square.

quad'ruped *n* (*fml*) an animal with four feet (*quadrupeds such as dogs and lions*).

quad'ruple *adj* four times as great:—*vb* to make or become four times greater (*the rent has quadrupled in five years*).

quad'ruplet *n* (*often abbreviated to* **quad**) one of four children born at one birth (*give birth to quadruplets*).

quaff *vb* (*fml*) to drink much at one swallow (*quaffing a goblet of wine*).

quag'mire *n* soft, very wet ground, bog, marsh (*cars stuck in the quagmire*).

quaich *n* (*Scot*) a drinking cup.

quail[1] *vb* to bend or draw back in fear (*children quailing at the sound of angry voices*).

quail[2] *n* a small bird of the partridge family.

quaint *adj* unusual and old-fashioned, pleasingly strange (*quaint customs/quaint thatched cottages*).

quake *vb* to shake, to tremble (*quaking with fear*).

Qua'ker *n* a member of the religious group, the Society of Friends.

qualifica'tion *n* **1** an ability, skill, etc, that fits a person for a certain post or occupation (*study for a teaching qualification*). **2** a remark that in some way alters a statement already made (*unable to recommend him for the post without qualifications*).

qual'ify *vb* **1** to achieve the standards required before one can enter a profession, fill a certain post, etc (*qualified as a doctor*). **2** to make fit (*his low salary qualifies him for a grant*). **3** to change but not alter completely (*qualifying one's statement*). **4** (*of an adjective*) to describe.

qual'itative *adj* (*fml*) having to do with quality (*a qualitative assessment*).

qual'ity *n* **1** a characteristic of a person or thing (*qualities of leadership/the exciting quality of his writing*). **2** the degree to which something is good or excellent, a standard of excellence (*high-quality cloth/low-quality paper*). **3** excellence (*goods of quality*). **4** (*old*) people of high rank.

qualm [kwäm] *n* **1** (*fml or old*) a feeling of sickness. **2** doubt, a fear that one is about to do what is wrong (*have qualms about giving up work in order to write for a living*).

quan'dary *n* a state of uncertainty, doubt as to what one ought to do (*in a quandary about whether to go or stay*).

quan'titative *adj* (*fml*) having to do with quantity (*a quantitative analysis*).

quan'tity *n* **1** size, amount (*state the quantity of paper required*). **2** a large portion (*buy food in quantity*). **3** the length of a vowel sound.

quan'tum *n* an amount.

quantum theory *n* Planck's theory of the nature of energy.

quar'antine *n* a period of time during which a person, animal or ship that may carry infection is kept apart (*dogs coming into Britain have to go into quarantine in case they have rabies*).

quar'rel *n* an angry dispute or disagreement:—*vb* (**quar'relled**, **quar'relling**) **1** to exchange angry words with, to fall out (with) (*quarrel with his business partner over money*). **2** (*fml*) to

386

disagree (*find no reason to quarrel with her account of the event*).

quar'relsome *adj* fond of quarrelling (*quarrelsome children*).

quar'ry[1] *n* that which one is trying to catch, an intended prey (*the mouse was the cat's quarry*).

quar'ry[2] *n* a place from which stone, slate, etc, may be cut:—*vb* to dig or cut from a quarry (*quarried slate*).

quart *n* a measure of liquid (1136 litres, 2 pints or ¼ gallon).

quar'ter *n* 1 the fourth part of anything (*leave a quarter of his fortune to each of his four sons*). 2 a measure of weight, a quarter of a hundredweight (28 lb/177 kg). 3 dir ection. 4 a district in a town (*the business quarter*). 5 a limb and the part where it joins the body. 6 mer cy to an enemy defeated in battle (*show no quarter to the defeated enemy*). 7 (*in heraldry*) one of the four divisions of a shield. 8 *pl* lodgings:—*vb* 1 to divide into four equal parts (*quarter the orange*). 2 (*fml*) to provide with lodgings (*soldiers quartered in the town*).

quar'terday *n* one of the four days in the year on which rent or interest is payable.

quar'terdeck *n* that part of the upper deck of a ship between the main mast and the stern.

quarterings *npl* the various coats of arms of the four divisions of a shield.

quar'terly *adj* happening every three months (*a quarterly magazine*):—*also n*:—*adv* once every three months.

quar'termaster *n* 1 in the navy, a petty officer in charge of steering, signals, etc. 2 in the army, an officer in charge of lodgings, food, stores, etc.

quartet(te)' *n* 1 a piece of music written for four performers (*a Mozart quartet*). 2 a gr oup of four singers or players (*she plays in a quartet*). 3 a set or group of four.

quar'to *n* a size of page obtained by folding a sheet of paper into four.

quartz *n* a type of mineral found in rocks, usu in the form of crystals.

quasar [kwăz-ăr] *n* a distant star-like heavenly body that emits light and radio waves.

quash *vb* 1 to set aside (an or der or judgment), to cancel (*quash the conviction*). 2 to put down, to put an end to (*quash the mutiny*).

quasi- [kwă-zî or kwă-zee] *prefix* almost, to some extent but not really (*quasi-religious faith*).

quassia [kwosh'-ya] *n* a South American tree with a bitter-tasting bark used in medicines.

quatercenten'ary *n* a four-hundredth anniversary.

quat'rain *n* a stanza of four lines, usu rhyming alternately.

qua'ver *vb* 1 to shak e, to tremble (*her voice quavered*). 2 to speak in a tr embling, uncertain voice (*quaver a reply*):—*n* 1 a tr embling of the voice. 2 a note in music (= ½ crotchet).

quay [kee] *n* a landing place for the loading and unloading of ships (*ships moored at the quay*).

que'asy *adj* 1 feeling sick, easily made sick (*feel queasy on the sea voyage*). 2 (*fml*) having fears or doubts, unwilling (*feel rather queasy about accepting his invitation*).

queen *n* 1 the wife of a king (*the king and his queen*). 2 a female ruler of a countr y (*she became queen on her father's death*). 3 the female of the bee, ant, etc. 4 a pictur e playing card. 5 a piece in chess:—**queen it** to behave in an arrogant way (*she tries to queen it over the other women in the department*).

queen bee *n* the only female bee in a hive.

queen'ly *adj* like a queen (*a queenly manner*).

queen mother *n* a former queen who is mother of the reigning king or queen.

queer *adj* 1 strange, unusual (*a queer feeling/a queer fellow*). 2 unwell (*feel rather queer after lunch*). 3 (*inf*) homosexual:—*n* (*inf*) a homosexual male:—*vb* to spoil (*queer his chances of winning*):—**queer the pitch** to spoil the chances:—**in Queer Street** in difficulty.

quell *vb* 1 to put down completely, to crush (*quell the rebellion*). 2 to put an end to (*quell the children's fears*).

quench *vb* 1 to put out (*quench the fire*). 2 to satisfy (*quench one's thirst*). 3 (*fml*) to keep down (*quench a revolt*).

quer'ulous *adj* complaining (*in querulous tones*).

query [kwee'-ri] *n* 1 a question (*answer their queries about her qualifications*). 2 a question mark (?):—*vb* 1 (*fml*) to ask a question. 2 to doubt (*queried the truth of his statement*).

quest (*fml or lit*) *n* a search (*a quest for happiness*):—*vb* to go in search of.

ques'tion *n* 1 a r equest for news, information, knowledge etc (*reply to questions about the* *president's health*). **2** wor ds spoken or arranged in such a way that an answer is called for (*questions rather than statements*). **3** a pr oblem (*exam questions*). **4** the matter under consideration (*questions of international importance*):—*vb* **1** to ask questions. **2** to doubt.— *n* **ques'tioner.**

ques'tionable *adj* **1** doubtful (*it is questionable whether he will arrive on time*). **2** open to suspicion (*of questionable character*).

questionnaire' *n* a set of written questions chosen for a particular purpose (*answer a questionnaire about house-buying*).

queue [kû] *n* an orderly line of persons waiting their turn (*a bus queue/form a queue outside the cinema*):—*vb* to form a queue, to stand in a queue (*queuing for tickets*).

quib'ble *n* an objection or argument, esp an unimportant, trivial objection or argument (*quibbles over the contract holding up the sale*):—*vb* to argue about small unimportant details (*quibbling about the price of some of the items on the restaurant's bill*).

quiche *n* a savoury tart filled with onions and a cheese and egg custard.

quick *adj* **1** fast-moving (*a quick pace*). **2** clever (*a quick pupil/a quick brain*). **3** done in a short time (*a quick drink*). **4** (*old*) living:—*n* the very tender flesh under the nails or just below the skin:—*adv* quickly.

quick'en *vb* **1** to give life to (*quicken his interest*). **2** to become alive or lively. **3** to mak e or become faster (*quicken the pace/his pace quickened*).

quick'lime *n* limestone burned to a powder, but not mixed with water.

quick'ly *adv* at once, rapidly (*read the document quickly*).

quick'sand *n* loose wet sand into which anything of weight (e.g. ships, men) may sink.

quick'set *adj* made up of living, growing plants.

quick'silver *n* mercury.

quick'step *n* a quick ballroom dance, a quick fox-trot.

quid[1] *n* a piece of tobacco for chewing.

quid[2] *n* (*inf*) a pound (*tickets five quid each*).

quies'cent *adj* (*fml*) at rest, still, peaceful (*a volcano currently quiescent*):—*n* **quies'cence.**

qui'et *adj* **1** at r est. **2** noiseless, not noisy . **3** calm, peaceful, gentle. **4** (*of colours*) not bright:—*n* **1** r est, peace. **2** silence:—*vb* **1** to calm. **2** to make silent.

qui'eten *vb* **1** to mak e or become quiet (*quieten the children/children told to quieten down*). **2** to remove or lessen (*quieten their fears*)

qui'etness, qui'etude *ns* rest, peace, silence.

quietus [kwee-â'-tês] *n* (*fml*) **1** a r elease from life or office (*given his quietus at retirement age*). **2** final settlement of an account. **3** something that kills or destroys (*give the false rumour its quietus*).

quiff *n* a tuft of hair, esp one brushed up above the forehead.

quill *n* **1** a lar ge feather from a goose or other bird, used as a pen. **2** the hollow stem of a feather. **3** one of the prickles on the back of a porcupine or hedgehog.

quilt *n* a bedcover padded with feathers, wool, etc (*huddle under the quilt to get warm*):—*vb* to make (a cover, etc) filled with padding separated into small compartments by cross-stitching (*a quilted waistcoat*).

quince *n* **1** a sour pear-shaped fruit much used in jams. **2** a kind of fruit-bearing tr ee.

quinine [kwin-een'] *n* a bitter-tasting drug made from the bark of the cinchona tree, used in treating fevers and malaria.

quinquen'nial *adj* **1** happening ever y five years. **2** lasting five years.

quinquen'nium *n* the space of five years.

quinquereme [kwin'-kwi-reem] *n* (*old*) a ship rowed by five sets of oarsmen.

quin'sy *n* inflammation of the throat or tonsils caused by infection.

quintes'sence *n* the most perfect form of anything, the perfect type or example of (*the quintessence of beauty*):—*adj* **quin-tessen'tial.**

quintet(te) *n* **1** a piece of music written for five performers. **2** a gr oup of five singers or players (*play in a quintet with her four sisters*). **3** a set or group of five.

quin'tuple *adj* five times as great:—*vb* to make or become five times greater (*quintupling the firm's profit in three years*).

quintup'let *n* (*often abbreviated to* **quin**) one of five children born at one birth (*give birth to quintuplets*).

quip *n* a joking or witty remark (*good at making quips*):—*vb* (**quipped'**, **quip'ping**) to make such remarks.

quire *n* twenty-four sheets of paper.

quirk *n* **1** a way of behaving or doing something peculiar to oneself (*one of his quirks is to keep stroking his beard*). **2** a strange or unexpected happening (*by a sudden quirk of fate*).

quit *vb* (**quit'ted** *or* **quit**, **quit'ting**) **1** to leave (*given notice to quit/tired of his job and decided to quit*). **2** to give up (*try to quit smoking*).

quite *adv* **1** completely, wholly (*quite recovered*). **2** fairly, rather (*quite clever*).

quits *adj* on even terms, owing nothing to each other (*call it quits*).

quit'tance *n* (*fml*) a setting free from debt, guilt, etc.

quiver[1] *n* a case for carrying arrows.

quiver[2] *vb* to tremble (*a voice quivering with rage/children quivering with fear*):—*n* a shudder, a slight trembling (*a quiver of fear*).

quixot'ic *adj* trying to achieve impossible or unrealstic aims, esp when these are to help others and bring danger to oneself (*quixotic gestures*).

quiz *vb* (**quizzed'**, **quiz'zing**) **1** (*old*) to make fun of. **2** to examine by questioning (*quiz them about their parents*):—*n* a number of questions set to test one's knowledge (*a television quiz*).

quiz'zical *adj* as if asking a question, esp mockingly or humorously (*a quizzical look*).

quoit [koit] *n* **1** a flat ring for thr owing on to or at a post in the game of quoits. **2** *pl* a game played with these rings.

quon'dam *adj* (*old*) former.

quor'um *n* the least number that must be present at a meeting before any business can be done (*unable to proceed with the annual general meeting without a quorum*).

quo'ta *n* the share of the whole to which each member of a group has a right (*the quota of fish allowed to be caught by the local fishermen*).

quota'tion *n* **1** the wor ds or passage quoted (*a quotation from Shakespeare*). **2** a price stated (*a quotation for painting the house*).

quotation marks *npl* punctuation marks (" " *or* ' ') placed at the beginning and end of a written quotation.

quote *vb* **1** to r epeat or write down the exact words of another person, making it known that they are not one's own (*quoting her mother/quoted Shakespeare*). **2** to say the price of (*quote £500 for decorating the room*):—*n* (*inf*) **1** a quotation. **2** a quotation mark.

quoth *vb* (*old*) said.

quotid'ian *adj* (*fml*) daily.

quo'tient *n* the answer to a division sum.

R

rabbi [rab'-î] *n* one learned in the law and doctrine of the Jews, a Jewish priest.

rab'bit *n* 1 a small long-eared burrowing animal. 2 (*inf*) one who plays a game very badly (*a rabbit at tennis*).

rabbit punch *n* a blow on the back of the neck.

rabbit warren *n* the underground home of many rabbits.

rab'ble *n* a noisy or disorderly crowd (*there was a rabble in the square demanding the president's resignation*).

rab'id *adj* 1 fanatical (*a rabid nationalist*). 2 (*of dogs*) suffering from rabies.

ra'bies *n* a disease that causes madness, and often death, in dogs and other animals.

raccoon' *see* **racoon'**.

race[1] *n* 1 a contest to see who can reach a given mark in the shortest time (*a horse race*). 2 a strong quick-moving current of water:—*vb* 1 to take part in a race. 2 to run or move very quickly (*race to catch the bus*).

race[2] *n* 1 any of the main groups into which human beings can be divided according to their physical characteristics (*the white races*). 2 the fact of belonging to one of these groups (*discrimination on the grounds of race*). 3 a group of people who share the same culture, language, etc (*the Nordic races*). 4 ancestors, family (*a man of noble race*).

race'course, race'track *ns* the ground on which races are run.

race'horse *n* a horse bred for racing.

ra'cial *adj* having to do with a race or nation (*racial characteristics/racial hatred*).

rac'ism *n* prejudice or discrimination against people on the grounds of race, sometimes accompanied by violent behaviour:—*adj* **rac'ist** (*a racist remark*).

rack *n* 1 a frame for holding articles (*a clothes rack*). 2 (*old*) instrument for torturing persons by stretching their joints:—*vb* 1 (*old*) to torture on the rack. 2 to cause great pain or trouble to (*racked by guilt*):—**rack one's brains** to think as hard as possible.

rack'et[1] *n* 1 a bat (usu a frame strung with criss-crossing cords) for playing tennis, badminton, etc. 2 *pl* a ball game like tennis but played against a wall.

rack'et[2] *n* 1 an uproar, a din (*kept awake by a racket from the party next door*). 2 a dishonest method of making a lot of money (*in the drug racket*).

racketeer' *n* one who makes money by dishonest or violent methods.

raconteur [ra-kon-tèr'] *n* (*fml*) one good at telling stories.

racoon', raccoon' *n* an American animal of the bear family.

ra'cy *adj* lively, full of vigour, often slightly indecent (*telling racy stories*).

ra'dar *n* the sending out of radio signals to determine the position of ships, aeroplanes, etc.

ra'dial *adj* 1 of or in rays. 2 arranged like spokes.

ra'diance *n* brightness, brilliance (*the radiance of the sun/the radiance of her smile*).

ra'diant *adj* 1 sending out rays of light or heat (*radiant sun/radiant heat*). 2 glowing. 3 shining. 4 showing great joy or happiness.

ra'diate *vb* 1 to send out rays of light or heat (*heaters radiated warmth*). 2 to shine with (*a face radiating happiness*) 3 to send out or spread from a central point (*roads radiating from the town centre*):—*n* **radia'tion**.

ra'diator *n* 1 an apparatus (an electric or gas fire, hot water pipes, etc) for warming a room by radiating heat. 2 an apparatus for cooling the engine of a motor car.

rad'ical *adj* 1 having to do with the root or basic nature (*radical faults in the system*). 2 seeking great political, social or economic change (*a radical party*). 3 very thorough (*radical changes*):—*n* one who desires to make far-reaching changes in society or in methods of government.

radii *see* **radius**.

ra'dio *n* 1 the sending or receiving of sounds through the air by electric waves. 2 an apparatus for receiving sound broadcast through the air by electric waves. 3 the radio broadcasting industry.

ra'dioactive *adj* giving off rays of force or energy which can be dangerous but which can be used in medicine, etc:—*n* **ra'dioac-tiv'ity**.

ra'diogram *n* **1** a wir eless telegram. **2** (*old*) a radio receiver and gramophone in one cabinet.

ra'diograph *n* a photograph obtained by X-rays, electromagnetic rays able to pierce solid mat ter, an X-ray photograph.

radiog'rapher *n* one trained to take X-ray photo graphs.

radiog'raphy *n* the obtaining of photographs by X-rays.

radiol'ogy *n* the study of radioactivity as a means of treating disease:—*n* **radiol'ogist**.

ra'diotel'egram *n* a telegram sent by radio.

ra'diotel'egraph *n* a message sent by radio.

ra'diotele'graphy *n* the sending of messages by radio.

ra'diotele'phony *n* the carrying on of a conversa tion between people in places far apart by means of radio:—*n* **ra'diotele'phone**.

ra'diother'apy *n* the treatment of disease by rays (e.g. X-rays):—*n* **ra'diother'apist**.

rad'ish *n* a plant with an eatable hot-tasting red root.

ra'dium *n* a rare metallic substance that gives off rays of heat and light made use of in the treatment of disease.

ra'dius *n* (*pl* **radii** [rā'-dee-ī]) **1** a straight line from the centre of a circle to any point on the circumference. **2** a bone in the for earm.

raffia *n* a straw-like string made from the leaves of a type of palm tree (*a basket made of raffia*).

raff'ish *adj* wild and not very respectable (*a raff ish young man*).

raff'le *n* a sale in which people buy tickets for an article that is given to the person whose name or number is drawn by lottery:—*vb* to sell by raffle.

raft *n* logs fastened together to make a floating platform or a flat boat without sides.

raft'er *n* one of the sloping beams supporting a roof (*oak rafters*).

rag *n* **1** a torn or tatter ed piece of cloth, a left-over piece of material (*use a rag to dust the furniture*). **2** *pl* old tattered clothes (*children clad in rags*).

rag'amuffin *n* a dirty, ragged child (*ragamuffins begging in the street*).

rage *n* **1** violent anger , fury. **2** inspiration. **3** something ver y popular or fashionable at a certain time:—*vb* **1** to be furious with anger . **2** to behave or talk violently .

rag'ged *adj* **1** torn or tatter ed. **2** wearing old tattered clothes. **3** r ough-edged. **4** partly good, partly bad.

rag'time *n* a highly syncopated form of music of American negro origin, an early form of jazz.

rag'wort *n* a common weed with a yellow flower.

raid *n* a sudden quick attack made by a group intending to return to their starting point (*a raid behind enemy lines*):—*also vb*:—*n* **raid'er**.

rail[1] *n* **1** a level or sloping bar of wood or metal linking up a line of posts, banisters, etc (*hold on to a ship's rail*). **2** a strip of metal moulded to a certain shape and laid down as part of a railway line or tramline (*the rail to London is blocked by snow*):—*vb* **1** to enclose with railings. **2** to send by railway.

rail[2] *vb* to speak angrily or bitterly (to or about) (*rail against injustices*).

rail'ing *n* a fence made of posts some distance apart linked together by crossbars or a rail.

raill'ery *n* (*fml*) mockery, friendly joking, teasing (*the raillery common in large families*).

rail'road *n* a railway.

rail'way *n* a track laid with parallel metal strips so moulded that a train can run on them.

rai'ment *n* (*old*) clothing.

rain *n* moisture falling from the clouds in drops:—*vb* **1** to fall in dr ops (*it was raining heavily*). **2** to fall or thr ow down in large num bers (*arrows raining down*):—*ns* **rain'drop**, **rain'water**.

rain'bow *n* a semicircular coloured band that of ten appears in the sky when the sun shines through raindrops.

rain'fall *n* the amount of rain that falls in a certain place during a certain length of time (*exceed the average rainfall*).

rain'forest *n* a dense tropical forest where there is a high rainfall.

rain gauge *n* an instrument for measuring rainfall.

rain'y *adj* wet, raining (*a rainy day/rainy weather*).

raise *vb* **1** to lift upwar ds, to move to a higher position (*raise the flag high*) . **2** to br eed (*raise pigs*). **3** to mak e higher (*raise the wall a few metres*). **4** to cause to gr ow, to cultivate (*raise wheat*). **5** to incr ease in amount, size, etc (*raise prices*). **6** to begin to talk about (*raise a new point*). **7** to collect (*raise money for charity*). **8** to make louder (*raise her voice in anger*). **9** to give up (*raise a siege*).

rai'sin *n* a dried grape (*cakes with raisins*).

raj *n* rule.

ra'ja(h) *n* an Indian prince.

rake¹ *n* a metal or wooden toothed crossbar fixed to a pole and used for scraping the ground, pulling together cut grass or hay, smoothing the soil, etc:—*vb* **1** to scrape, pull together , smooth, etc, with a rake (*rake up dead leaves*). **2** to fir e at a long target so that the shot travels its whole length. **3** to sear ch very carefully (*rake through his papers for evidence of guilt*).

rake² *n* (*old*) a person leading a wild and immoral life (*rather a rake in his youth*).

rake³ *vb* (*of a mast*) to slope backwards:—*n* a backward slope.

ra'kish¹ *adj* having sloping masts, swift-looking.

ra'kish² *adj* **1** living wildly and immorally, dissolute (*a rakish young man*). **2** jaunty (*with her hat at a rakish angle*).

rally¹ *vb* **1** to bring or come together again in one body (*rally the troops/troops rallying round the general*). **2** to r egain some of one's strength, health, etc, after weakness or illness (*an invalid who suddenly rallied after the operation*). **3** to call upon for a greater effort (*rally their resolve*):—*n* **1** a coming together in lar ge numbers. **2** r ecovery of strength, health, good spirits, etc.

rally² *vb* to make fun of good-naturedly.

ram *n* **1** a male sheep. **2** any heavy instrument used for breaking down walls, doors, etc (*a battering ram*):—*vb* (**rammed', ram'ming**) **1** to run into with great force. **2** to push down, into or on to with great force (*ram the post into the ground*). **3** (*of a ship*) to strike another ship head-on in order to make a hole in its side. **4** to strike violently. **5** to push a shell into the br eech of a gun.

Ram'adan *n* the ninth month of the Muslim year during which Muslims fast between the hours of sunrise and sunset.

ram'ble *vb* **1** to walk as and wher e one likes for pleasure (*rambling through the woods*). **2** to grow in all directions (*rambling roses*). **3** to change from one subject to another in a foolish, purposeless way (*ramble on about his youth/*

rambling after the knock on his head):—*n* a walk taken for pleasure.

ram'bler *n* **1** a wander er. **2** a climbing plant, esp a type of rose.

ramifica'tion *n* **1** a branch or subdivision, a network of parts or branches (*the ramifications of business*). **2** a consequence, esp one of many and an indirect one (*unable to foresee the ramifications of his actions*).

ramp *n* **1** a slope (*a ramp to allow cars to drive on to the ship*). **2** the upwar d bend in a stair rail:—*vb* to rage.

rampage' *vb* to rush about, to rage (*children rampaging about/elephants rampaging through the jungle*):—*n* great anger or excitement.

ram'pant *adj* **1** in heraldr y, standing on the hind legs (*a lion rampant*). **2** uncontr olled (*rampant violence*). **3** gr owing uncontrollably (*rampant weeds*).

ram'part *n* a defensive wall or mound of earth.

ram'rod *n* a stick for thrusting the shell (formerly the charge) into a gun.

ram'shackle *adj* broken-down, nearly falling down (*ramshackle property*).

ranch *n* a large cattle farm.

ranch'er *n* one who owns or works on a ranch.

ran'cid *adj* bad, unpleasant to taste or smell (*rancid butter*).

ran'cour *n* deep unforgiving hatred, spite (*feel rancour towards his ex-wife*):—*adj* **ran'corous.**

ran'dom *adj* without plan or purpose (*ask a random sample of people*):—**at random** without plan or purpose (*choose people at random*).

range *vb* **1** to set in a line, to place in or der (*range the books on the shelf*). **2** (*fml*) to wander (*country children ranging over the hills*). **3** to extend (*an area ranging from the city boundaries to the next town*). **4** to var y between certain limits (*ages ranging from ten to seventy*):—*n* **1** a line or r ow, e.g. of mountains. **2** extent (*voice range*). **3** a variety (*a range of exotic plants*). **4** the distance between a gun and the fall of the shot, the distance over which an object can be sent or thrown, sound carried, heard, etc (*out of hearing range*). **5** a piece of ground for firing practice. **6** an enclosed kitchen fireplace for cooking and baking (*a stew simmering on the range*).

range'finder n an instrument for measuring distances, e.g. between gun and target.

ran'ger n a keeper in a large or royal park or forest.

ran'gy adj tall and long-legged (*rangy teenage youths*).

rank¹ n **1** a r ow or line (*ranks of policemen keeping back the crowds*). **2** a r ow of soldiers standing side by side. **3** a social class (*the upper ranks of society*). **4** a position of authority, a level of importance (*promoted to the rank of colonel*):— vb **1** to arrange in a r ow or line. **2** to put or be in a certain class or in an order of merit:—**rank and file** the common people.

rank² adj **1** over grown (*a garden rank with weeds*). **2** gr owing thickly and untidily (*rank weeds*). **3** ver y bad (*the rank smell of rotting meat/rank stupidity*). **4** complete (*a rank foul*).

rank'er n a private soldier.

rank'le vb to go on causing anger or dislike (*his defeat still rankles with him*).

ran'sack vb **1** to sear ch thoroughly (*burglars ransacking houses looking for money*). **2** to plunder (*enemy soldiers ransacking the town*).

ran'som n a sum of money paid to free someone from captivity (*asked for a ransom in exchange for their kidnapped children*):—vb to pay to obtain freedom, to redeem.

rant vb to talk in a loud, uncontrolled manner, often using words for fine sound rather than meaning (*ranting on about how badly he was treated*):—also n:—**rant'er**.

rap n **1** a quick light blow , a knock (*a rap on the door*). **2** (*inf*) talk, conversation. **3** a style of popular music in which (usu rhyming) words are spoken in a rhythmic chant over an instrumental backing:—vb (**rapped'**, **rap'ping**) to give a rap (*rap the door*):—**not worth a rap** worthless (*a promise not worth a rap*):— n **rap'per**.

rapa'cious adj (*fml*) greedy for gain, grasping (*rapacious nephews hoping for a share in their uncle's money*):—n **rapa'city**.

rape¹ vb **1** to tak e or carry off by force. **2** to assault sexually (*found guilty of raping the young woman*):—n act of raping.

rape² n a plant like the turnip.

rape oil n an oil made from rape seeds.

rap'id adj very quick-moving (*rapid changes at a rapid pace*):—n (*usu pl*) a quick-flowing stretch of river running downhill:—n **rapid'ity**.

ra'pier n a long thin sword.

rap'ine n (*fml*) plunder, robbery (*the rapine of the royal jewels by the enemy soldiers*).

rapt adj giving one's whole mind (*with rapt attention*).

rap'ture n (*fml*) delight, great joy (*in raptures at the news of their success*).

rap'turous adj full of delight, very happy.

rare adj **1** uncommon, unusual. **2** not thick. **3** ver y lightly cooked. **4** ver y good. **5** valuable:— n **rare'ness**.

rare'fied adj thin, with less oxygen than usual (*the rarefied air of high altitudes*).

rare'ly adv seldom, not often (*we rarely see them*).

rar'ity n **1** rar eness (*stamps valuable because of their rarity*). **2** a thing seldom met with (*such birds are rarities in this area*).

ras'cal n **1** a r ogue, a scoundrel (*a rascal who deserved to be sent to prison*). **2** a naughty boy (*a rascal who tries to avoid going to school*):— adj **ras'cally**.

rase see **raze**.

rash¹ adj **1** acting without for ethought (*she tends to be rash*). **2** hasty (*a rash decision*). **3** foolishly daring (*a rash action*):—n **rash'ness**.

rash² n a redness of the skin caused by illness (*a measles rash*).

rash'er n a thin slice of bacon.

rasp n **1** a file with a ver y rough face. **2** a harsh, grating sound:—vb **1** to rub with a rasp. **2** to make a harsh, grating sound (*a rasping voice/ metal rasping on metal*). **3** to say in a harsh, angry voice.

rasp'berry n **1** a common shrub. **2** its eatable red berry (*raspberry jam*).

rat n a gnawing animal like, but larger than, the mouse:—vb (**rat'ted**, **rat'ting**) to hunt or kill rats (*terriers ratting*).

ratch'et n a toothed wheel with which a catch automatically engages as it is turned, preventing it from being turned in the reverse direction.

rate¹ n **1** the amount of one thing measur ed by its relation to another (*the death rate is the number of people who die yearly to every thousand of the population/a failure rate of ten* *per cent*). **2** speed (*the rate of increase*). **3** price (*charged at the rate of £50 per day*). **4** (*old*) *pl* a tax paid by owners or tenants of houses to the local government of the area or town in which they live:—*vb* **1** (*fml*) to consider (*he is rated by his neighbours as a kind man*). **2** to value (*we rate his abilities highly*). **3** to assign to a position on a scale (*rated number fifteen in the world's tennis players*):—*adj* **rat'able.**

rate² *vb* (*old*) to scold.

ra'ther *adv* **1** pr eferably, more willingly (*she would rather die than marry him*). **2** fairly , quite (*she is rather talented*). **3** mor e exactly, more truly (*she is thoughtless rather than cruel*).

rat'ify *vb* to approve, to confirm:—*n* **rati-fica'tion.**

rat'ing *n* **1** value or rank accor ding to some kind of classification (*his rating as an international ten-nis player*). **2** in the navy , a sailor who is not an officer.

ra'tio *n* one number or amount considered in relation or proportion to another (*the ratio of pupils to teachers*).

ratiocina'tion *n* (*fml*) the process of reasoning.

ra'tion *n* **1** a fixed amount of something allowed every so often (*the child's weekly sweets ration*). **2** *pl* (*old*) food:—*vb* to limit to fixed amounts (*rationed petrol to thirty litres per person*).

ra'tional *adj* **1** having the power to think things out (*man is a rational animal*). **2** r easonable, sensible (*a rational decision*).

ra'tionalist *n* one who tries to find natural causes for all things, including miracles:—*n* **ra'tionalism.**

ra'tionalize *vb* **1** to tr y to find reasons for all actions. **2** to explain as due to natural causes.

rat race *n* the competitive, aggressive struggle to survive and be successful in the modern world (*She is tired of the rat race and has taken early retirement*).

rattan' *n* a cane made from the stem of a Malayan climbing palm (*garden furniture made of rattan*).

rat'tle *vb* **1** to mak e a number of short quick noises one after the other (*windows rattling in the storm*). **2** to shak e something to cause such noises (*collectors rattling their cans*). **3** to speak or say quickly (*rattle off the instructions so that no-one understood*):—*n* **1** an instrument or toy for rattling (*a baby's rattle*). **2** a rattling sound (*the rattle of milk bottles*).

rat'tlesnake *n* an American snake able to make a rattling sound with horny rings on its tail.

rau'cous *adj* hoarse, harsh-sounding (*shout his in-structions in a raucous voice*).

rav'age *vb* to lay waste, to plunder, to destroy far and wide (*crops ravaged by storms*):—*n* dam-age, destruction.

rave *vb* **1** to talk wildly or madly (*he was very ill and was raving in his sleep*). **2** (*inf*) to praise very highly (*critics raving about his new play*).

rav'el *vb* (**ra'velled, ra'velling**) to twist together, to entangle (*the knitting wool became ravelled*):— **ravel out** to untwist, to disentangle.

rav'en *n* a bird of prey of the crow family:—*adj* black (*her raven hair*).

rav'enous *adj* very hungry (*ravenous after their long walk*).

ravine¹ *n* a narrow valley with steep sides.

ravioli¹ *n* an Italian dish consisting of small squares of pasta with a meat or vegetable filling.

rav'ish *vb* **1** to tak e or carry off by force. **2** to de-light (*ravished by her beauty*).

rav'ishing *adj* delightful, wonderful (*her ravish-ing beauty*).

raw *adj* **1** uncook ed (*raw meat*). **2** in its natural state (*raw cotton/a raw recruit*). **3** sor e. **4** (*of part of the body*) uncovered by skin, abraded (*raw wounds*). **5** cold and damp (*a raw day*).

raw'-boned *adj* having little flesh on the bones (*a gaunt, raw-boned woman*).

ray¹ *n* **1** a line of light, heat, etc, getting br oader as it goes further from its origin (*the sun's rays*). **2** a little, a ver y small amount (*a ray of hope*).

ray² *n* a species of flatfish.

ray'on *n* artificial silk.

raze, rase *vb* to destroy completely, to wipe out (*cities razed to the ground by enemy armies*).

ra'zor *n* an implement for shaving hair (*shave his chin with an electric razor*).

ra'zorblade *n* a very sharp blade for use in certain kinds of razor.

ra'zor edge *n* **1** a ver y fine sharp edge. **2** a ver y delicate situation (*peace talks on a razor edge*).

reach *vb* **1** to str etch out (*reach out a hand*). **2** to stretch out a hand or arm for some purpose (*reach for a book*). **3** to obtain by str etching out for (*unable to reach the book on the highest shelf*). **4** to arrive at, to get as far as (*reach the summit* of the mountain). **5** to pass with the hand (*reach him the salt*):—*n* **1** the distance one can extend the hand from the body (*the telephone was within reach*). **2** a distance that can be easily travelled (*an airport within easy reach*). **3** a straight stretch of river (*the upper reaches of the stream*).

react¹ *vb* **1** to act, behave or change in a certain way as a result of something said or done (*react badly to criticism*). **2** to do or think the oppo- site (*react against their strict upbringing*).

reaction *n* **1** action or behaviour given rise to by something said or done (*his reaction to the defeat*). **2** opposition to pr ogress (*reaction against computerization*). **3** in chemistr y, the change in a substance when certain tests are made on it.

reac'tionary *adj* wanting to return to things as they were before, opposed to progress (*reactionary older writers*):—*also n.*

read [reed] *vb* (*pt,pp* **read** [red]) **1** to look at and understand (*read the instructions*). **2** to speak aloud what is written or printed (*read out the message in the letter*). **3** to study (*reading Eng- lish at university*). **4** to be written or wor ded (*his letter reads as follows*).

read'able *adj* easy to read, interesting (*readable books*).

read'er *n* **1** one who enjoys r eading (*children who are not readers*). **2** one whose job it is to r eport on manuscripts sent in to publishers and to read and correct proofs. **3** a grade of university lec- turer. **4** a r eading book for schools (*a basic reader*).

read'ily *adv* willingly, cheerfully (*she readily agreed*).

read'ing *n* **1** the study of books (*reading is her main hobby*). **2** wor ds read out from a book or written paper (*readings from the Bible*). **3** an explanation of what is written (*there is more than one possible reading of the passage*).

readjust' *vb* **1** to put right or in the pr oper place again (*readjust the driving mirror*). **2** to mak e changes needed for altered circumstances (*try to readjust to life at home after life abroad*):—*n* **readjust'ment**.

ready *adj* **1** pr epared and fit for use (*the food is ready*). **2** quick (*people of ready will*). **3** will- ing (*always ready to help people*):—*n* **read'iness**.

ready-made *adj* (*of clothes*) not made specially for the person who buys them (*he buys ready-made rather than tailor-made suits*).

ready money *n* immediate payment (*a discount on the car for ready money*).

ready reckoner *n* a table giving the answers to cer- tain sums.

rea'gent *n* in chemistry, a substance that produces a characteristic reaction to another substance or mixture of substances.

real *adj* **1** actually existing (*real life*). **2** true, genuine, not false or fake (*real gold/his real reason*). **3** utter , complete (*a real idiot*). **4** (*fml*) (*of property*) consisting of lands and houses.

re'alism *n* **1** the belief that only objects per ceptible by the senses actually exist. **2** tr ying to make works of art as true to life as possible (*the school of realism*). **3** the habit of taking a sensible, prac- tical view of life (*forced to think of the future with realism*).

re'alist *n* one who believes in realism.

realis'tic *adj* **1** life-like (*a realistic painting*). **2** tak- ing a sensible, practical view of life (*a realistic idea of what job he is qualified for*).

real'ity *n* **1** that which actually exists (*prefer dreams to reality*). **2** truth. **3** things as they ac- tually are (*the realities of life*).

re'alize *vb* **1** to mak e real (*realize ambitions*). **2** to understand fully (*they realize that he is tell- ing the truth*). **3** to sell for money (*realize their assets*):—*n* **realiza'tion**.

re'ally *adv* **1** actually, in fact (*describes things as they really are*). **2** ver y (*a really pleasant day*).

realm [relm] *n* **1** (*fml*) a kingdom. **2** one particu- lar aspect or sphere of life (*the realm of sport*).

re'alty *n* (*fml*) property consisting of lands and houses.

ream *n* 20 quires of paper.

reap *vb* **1** to cut down (cr ops), to gather in. **2** to receive as a reward (*reap the benefits of hard work*).

reap'er *n* **1** one who r eaps. **2** a machine for reaping.

reappear' *vb* to appear again.

rear¹ *n* **1** the part behind (*the rear of the queue*). **2** the back part of an army or fleet.

rear² *vb* **1** to raise (*the horse reared its head*). **2** to bring up (*rear children*). **3** to br eed (*rearing* *pigs*). **4** to stand on the hind legs (*the horse reared up*).

rear-ad'miral *n* a naval officer just below a vice-admiral in rank.

rear'guard *n* troops protecting the rear of an army.

rear'most *adj* (*fml*) last of all (*the rearmost part of the army*).

rea'son *n* **1** the power to think things out (*lose his reason*). **2** good sense (*he would listen to reason*). **3** cause for acting or believing (*the reason for her sadness/the reason for his actions/the reason why she left*):—*vb* **1** to think out step by step (*we reasoned that they would attack at dawn*). **2** to try to convince by arguing (*reason them into being less hasty*).

rea'sonable *adj* **1** sensible (*a reasonable suggestion*). **2** willing to listen to another's arguments (*a reasonable person*). **3** not excessive (*a reasonable amount to drink*).

rea'soning *n* **1** use of the power of reason. **2** arguments used to convince (*find his reasoning unconvincing*).

reassure' *vb* to take away the doubts or fears of (*reassuring the child that his mother would soon return*):—*n* **reassur'ance**.

re'bate *n* part of a payment given back to the payer (*rent rebate for low-paid workers*).

reb'el *n* one who revolts against authority:—*vb* **rebel' (rebelled', rebell'ing) 1** to take up arms (against) (*rebel against the army leaders*). **2** to refuse to obey those in authority (*children rebelling against strict teachers*).

rebell'ion *n* open resistance to or fighting against authority.

rebell'ious *adj* **1** ready to rebel, disobedient (*at a rebellious age*). **2** fighting against authority (*the rebellious troops*).

rebound' *vb* to bounce back off, to spring back (*the ball rebounded off the wall*).

rebuff' *n* a sharp and unexpected refusal (*offers of help which met a rebuff*).—*vb* to refuse sharply (*rebuffed his attempts at friendship*).

rebuke' *vb* to scold, to find fault with (*rebuke the child for being naughty*):—*n* a scolding.

rebut' *vb* (**rebut'ted, rebut'ting**) to refuse to accept as true (*rebut their accusation*):—*n* **rebutt'al**.

recal'citrant *adj* stubborn, unwilling to obey (*recalcitrant children*):—*also n*.

recall' *vb* **1** to remember (*unable to recall his name*). **2** to call back (*recall certain cars because of a mechanical defect*):—*n* an order to return (*the recall of the ambassador*).

recant' *vb* to say that one no longer holds a certain belief (*he was a Christian who recanted*):—*n* **recantation**.

recapit'ulate *vb* (*often shortened to* **re'cap**) to go over again the chief points, to summarize (*recapitulating the instructions*):—*n* **recapitula'tion**.

recede' *vb* **1** to move back (*his hair is receding at the front*). **2** to slope back (*her chin recedes*).

receipt' *n* **1** a written statement that a sum of money or an article has been received (*ask for a receipt when you pay the bill*). **2** the act of receiving (*her receipt of the goods*):—*vb* to mark as paid or received.

receive' *vb* **1** to come into possession of, to get (*receive a letter/receive good news*). **2** to welcome (*receive guests*). **3** to accept what one knows to be stolen (*receive the jewellery from the burglary*).

receiv'er *n* **1** one who accepts stolen goods from a thief. **2** the earpiece of a telephone. **3** a radio set.

re'cent *adj* not long past (*recent events/recent developments*):—*adv* **re'cently**.

recep'tacle *n* a place or vessel for holding things (*a large receptacle such as a bucket*).

recep'tion *n* **1** the act of receiving or being received, the welcoming of guests (*a room in the building for the reception of visitors/his reception of the news*). **2** a formal party (*invited to a reception for the ambassador*). **3** welcome (*receive a warm reception*). **4** the quality of radio or television signals.

recep'tionist *n* one employed by a hotel, doctor, business, etc, to receive guests, clients, callers, etc.

recep'tive *adj* quick to learn (*a receptive mind*):—*n* **receptivity**.

recess' *n* **1** an interval, a break from work (*the schoolchildren's recess/parliament in recess*). **2** part of a room set back into the wall (*an old-fashioned room with a recess for a bed*).

reces'sion *n* a period of reduced trade and business activity (*people losing their jobs in the recession*).

reces'sional *n* a hymn sung as the clergy retire after a service.

recipe [re'-si-pi] *n* instructions on how to make or prepare a certain dish (*a recipe for chocolate cake*).

recip'ient *n* one who receives (*the recipient of good news*).

recip'rocal *adj* done by each of two parties to the other, affecting both equally (*a reciprocal trade agreement*).

recip'rocate *vb* to give or do something in return (*reciprocate the favour*):—*n* **reci-pro'city**.

reci'tal *n* **1** a detailed account (*a recital of the events at the party*). **2** a public musical performance, esp by one performer (*a piano recital*).

recita'tion *n* that which is recited (e.g. a poem).

recitative [re-si-ta-teev'] *n* speech sung in a plain chant.

recite' *vb* to repeat aloud from memory (*children asked to recite a poem*).

reck *vb* (*old*) to heed, to care.

reck'less *adj* rash, heedless of danger (*a reckless young man/reckless driving*).

reck'on *vb* **1** (*fml*) to count (*reckon the cost*). **2** to consider (*reckoned to be the best worker in the company*). **3** to guess, to estimate (*we reckon they owe us £100*).

reck'oning *n* **1** a calculation, estimate (*by our reckoning we should be there by midnight*). **2** (*old*) a settlement of accounts, a bill.

reclaim' *vb* **1** (*fml*) to win back from evil ways (*reclaim criminals*). **2** to demand the r eturn of (*to reclaim their luggage*). **3** to bring under cultivation waste land, land covered by the sea, etc:—*n* **reclama'tion**.

recline' *n* to sit or lie back at one's ease, to rest (*recline on a sofa*).

recluse [rê-klôs'] *n* one who prefers to live away from human society (*he has become a recluse since his wife's death*).

recogni'tion *n* **1** act of r ecognizing (*he was so ill that he showed no recognition when his family arrived*). **2** acknowledgment (*a medal given in recognition of his courage*).

recogni'zable *adj* that may be recognized (*she was hardly recognizable after going to the beauty salon*).

recognize' *vb* **1** to know again (*recognize an old friend*). **2** to gr eet or salute (*she refused to recognize her ex-husband*). **3** to admit (*recognize his mistakes*). **4** to accept (*qualification not recognized overseas*). **5** to r eward (*recognize the man's courage by giving him a medal*).

recoil' *vb* **1** to go suddenly backwar ds in horror, fear, etc (*recoil in horror at the sight of the corpse*). **2** (*of a gun*) to move sharply backwards on firing:—*n* **1** a shrinking backwar ds. **2** the backward kick of a gun on firing.

recollect' *vb* to remember (*recollect a previous incident*).

recollec'tion *n* **1** memor y. **2** something r emembered.

recommend' *vb* **1** to speak in praise of, to suggest that something or someone is good, suitable, etc (*recommend her for promotion/recommend the medicine as a cure for sore throats*). **2** to advise (*his teacher recommended him to apply for university*).

recommenda'tion *n* **1** act of praising or speaking in favour of (*his recommendation of him as a reliable employee*). **2** a letter praising a person 's good points.

rec'ompense *vb* (*fml*) to pay back or reward for loss, effort, etc (*receive recompense for the damage done*):—*n* repayment, reward.

rec'oncile *vb* **1** to mak e or become friendly again (*they did not become reconciled till several years after the quarrel*). **2** to mak e (*oneself*) accept something new or strange (*try to reconcile oneself to the changes*).

reconcile'ment, reconcilia'tion *ns* a renewal of friendship.

recondite [re-kon'-dît *or* rek'on-dît] *adj* little known, difficult to understand (*recondite information*).

recondi'tion *vb* to improve the appearance and state of (*recondition the old sofa*).

reconn'aissance *n* an examination of the nature of a piece of country, esp for military purposes (e.g. before siting a camp, making an attack, etc).

reconnoi'tre *vb* **1** to examine the enemy 's position and seek information about his strength, etc. **2** to examine unknown territor y before crossing or settling on it.

reconsid'er *vb* to think about again with a view to changing one's mind (*reconsider his resignation*):—*n* **reconsidera'tion.**

reconstruct' *vb* **1** to r ebuild (*reconstruct damaged buildings*). **2** tr y to build up a description or picture of, to work out exactly what happened when all the facts are not known (*police reconstructing the crime*):—*n* **reconstruc'tion.**

record' *vb* **1** to put down in writing (*record the score in a notebook*). **2** to pr eserve sounds or images by mechanical means, on a flat disc, tape, etc (*record the radio concert/record the television programme*). **3** to sing songs, play music, etc, which is recorded on a disc or tape (*record her latest hit*):—*n* **rec'ord 1** a r ecorded account. **2** a book containing written records, a register (*parish records*). **3** the best performance yet known in any type of contest. **4** a vinyl disc for playing on a record-player. **5** what is known about a person 's past (*a good work record*). **6** a criminal r ecord (*his record was well known to the police*).

recorder *n* **1** one who k eeps registers or records. **2** a judge in certain cities. **3** a simple form of flute (*play the recorder*).

rec'ord-player *n* a machine for playing records.

recount' *vb* **1** to tell in detail (*recount their adventures*). **2** to count again:—*n* **re'count** another counting, e.g. of votes after an election.

recoup' *vb* to get back all or part of a loss (*recoup the cost of the car repairs*).

recourse' *n*:—**have recourse to** to go to for help or protection (*have recourse to the courts*).

recov'er *vb* **1** to cover again (*recover the settee*). **2** to get back, to r egain (*recover their strength*). **3** to mak e or become better after illness or weakness (*the accident victim is unlikely to recover*).

recov'erable *adj* that can be regained (*the money paid for the repairs is recoverable from the insurance*).

recov'ery *n* **1** a r eturn to health after illness (*a speedy recovery from flu*). **2** the r egaining of anything after losing some or all of it.

rec'reant *adj* (*old*) cowardly, untrustworthy:—*n* a coward, one who deserts his or her friends, religion, etc.

recy'cle *vb* to put something through some kind of process so that it can be used again (*newspa-*

pers can be placed in that container to be recycled).

recrea'tion *n* **1** r est and amusement after work (*find some form of recreation*). **2** a sport, a pastime (*recreations such as gardening*).

recrim'inate *vb* to accuse in return, to accuse one's accuser

recrimina'tion *n* the act of recriminating, a counter-accusation (*his accusation of his classmates led to recrimination*).

recrudes'cence *n* (*fml*) a fresh outbreak.

recruit' *n* **1** a soldier who has just joined the army . **2** a new member (*the latest recruits to the advertising campaign*):—*vb* to enlist new soldiers, members (*try to recruit new members*):—*n* **recruit'ment.**

rec'tangle *n* a four-sided figure with all its angles right angles and one pair of sides longer than the other:—*adj* **rectang'ular.**

rec'tify *vb* **1** to put right, to corr ect (*rectify the mistake*). **2** (*chemistry*) to purify:—*n* **rectifica'tion.**

rectilin'eal, rectilin'ear *adjs* consisting of straight lines.

rec'titude *n* (*fml*) honesty, uprightness (*people of rectitude*).

rec'tor *n* **1** in the Chur ch of England, a parish clergyman. **2** (*esp in Scotland*) a senior university official elected by the student body. **3** (*in Scotland*) the head teacher of certain senior schools.

rec'tory *n* the house of a rector.

recum'bent *adj* (*fml*) lying down (*a statue of a recumbent lion*).

recu'perate *vb* to regain health or strength after illness (*take a holiday to recuperate*):—*n* **recupera'tion.**

recu'perative *adj* assisting recovery.

recu'perator *n* a mechanical device to restore to its original position something that has sprung back sharply (e.g. a gun on firing).

recur' *vb* (**recurred', recur'ring**) to happen again and again (*a mistake that kept recurring*):—*n* **recur'rence.**

recur'rent *adj* happening or appearing again and again (*a recurrent dream*).

rec'usant *n* (*old*) one who refused to obey former laws commanding everyone to attend Church of England services:—*also adj.*

red adj 1 of a colour lik e blood (a red coat/hands red with cold). 2 of a colour that varies between a golden brown and a reddish brown (red hair). 3 (inf) communist:—n 1 the colour r ed. 2 a communist:—**see red** to become suddenly very angry (she saw red when the child disobeyed).

red'breast n the robin.

Red Cross n an international organization that looks after sick and wounded in time of war and protects the rights of prisoners of war.

red'den vb 1 to mak e or become red (redden her lips). 2 to blush (reddening in embarrassment).

redeem' vb 1 to buy back (redeeming the goods that he had pawned). 2 to buy fr eedom for (redeem the hostages by paying the ransom). 3 to carry out (a promise) (the government being asked to redeem its election promises). 4 to mak e up for (the lead actor's performance redeemed a bad production). 5 to save fr om the punishment due to sin.

Redeem'er n Jesus Christ.

redeem'ing adj cancelling out bad by good (his one redeeming feature).

redemp'tion n act of redeeming.

Red Ensign n the flag flown by ships of the British merchant fleet.

red'-hand'ed adj in the very act of doing wrong (caught red-handed stealing the money).

red herring n something mentioned that takes attention away from the subject being discussed (he said something to the police that made them follow a red herring).

Red Indian n (now considered offensive) a North American Indian.

red lead n red oxide of lead used in making red paint.

red'-letter adj 1 mark ed in the calendar by red letters. 2 notable, memorable (the child's first day at school was a red-letter day).

red'olent adj (fml) 1 smelling or sweet-smelling (a room redolent of expensive perfume). 2 suggesting very strongly (an old house redolent of mystery).

redoubt'able adj to be feared, deserving respect (a redoubtable opponent).

redound' vb (fml) to add to, to end by increasing (his actions redounded to the credit of his family).

red'poll n a bird of the finch family.

redress' vb to set right, to make up for (redress injustices):—n 1 the setting right of a wr ong. 2 something given to mak e up for wrong done or loss caused.

red'shank n a red-legged bird of the snipe family.

red'skin n (offensive) a North American Indian.

red tape n overmuch attention to rules and regulations so that business is delayed.

reduce' vb 1 to mak e less, smaller or less heavy (reducing prices/reduce the load). 2 to change into another, and usu worse state, form, etc (reduce the city to a ruined heap). 3 to bring or for ce to do something less pleasant, etc, than usual (be reduced to begging on the streets):—n reduc'tion.

redun'dant adj 1 more than necessary (redundant words). 2 (of workers) no longer required and so dismissed (redundant workers/workers declared redundant):—n redun'dancy.

redu'plicate vb to double, to repeat (simply reduplicate someone else's work):—n re-dupica'tion.

red'wing n a small thrush.

re-e'cho vb to give back echoes, to repeat.

reed n 1 a tall grass-lik e water plant with a hollow stem. 2 that part of certain wind instruments that vibrates and so causes the sound when the instrument is blown.

reed'y adj 1 cover ed with reeds. 2 high-pitched and thin (a reedy voice).

reef[1] n 1 a ridge of r ock or sand just above or just below the surface of the water (a ship stuck on a reef). 2 a crack in a r ock containing gold.

reef[2] n one of the parts of a sail that can be rolled or folded up:—vb to roll or fold up the reefs of a sail.

reef'er n 1 a short thick jack et worn by sailors. 2 a cigar ette containing marijuana.

reek n a strong unpleasant smell (the reek of tobacco smoke):—vb 1 to give off a smell, esp an unpleasant one (breath reeking of alcohol). 2 to show or suggest str ongly something bad or unpleasant (a situation reeking of bribery).

reel n 1 a frame or r oller around which string, thread, photographic film, etc, may be wound. 2 a lively Scottish dance:— vb 1 to wind on to a reel. 2 to stagger (drunks reeling down the street):—**reel off** to tell without stopping or hesitating (able to reel off the names of every person at the meeting).

reeve *n* a steward, one who looks after property for the owner.

refec'tory *n* a dining hall (*the refectory of the monastery*).

refer' *vb* (**referred'**, **refer'ring**) 1 to pass (a matter) on to another for decision (*refer the complaint to his manager*). 2 to look up a certain item in a book (*refer to a dictionary*). 3 to make mention of (*refer to the help of his parents in his speech*). 4 to advise to consult elsewhere e (*the doctor referred her to a specialist*).

referee' *n* 1 one chosen to give a clear decision in case of doubt (*take the dispute to a referee*). 2 in games, a person who sees that the rules are kept (*the football referee*). 3 one ready to supply information about the character, behaviour, etc, of another (*his former schoolteacher acted as a referee for his job application*).

reference *n* 1 mention (*there was a reference in his speech to his parents' help*). 2 directions as to where to find certain items, passages, etc, in a book (*a map reference*). 3 a letter giving information about the character, behaviour, etc, of one applying for a job (*they refused to give her a reference as her work was so bad*):—**terms of reference** a statement of the range of matters that are to be dealt with in an inquiry (*the terms of reference of the inquiry into the efficiency of the prison system*).

reference book *n* a book (e.g. a dictionary like this one) that supplies information.

referen'dum *n* a vote in which the people of a country are asked to state their opinion on some important matter (*a referendum on whether the country should join the European Union*).

refine' *vb* 1 to purify (*refined oil*). 2 to make more polite and civilized (*a school supposed to produce refined young ladies*).

refine'ment *n* 1 the state of being purified. 2 politeness, good taste, etc (*young ladies of refinement*).

refin'ery *n* a place for purifying sugar, oil, etc.

refit' *vb* (**refit'ted**, **refit'ting**) to repair, to prepare for fresh use (*refit the ship*).

reflect' *vb* 1 to throw back, esp rays of light or heat. 2 (*of a mirror*) to show the image of. 3 to think about carefully (*reflect on the best course of action*). 4 to be a cause (of praise or blame) for (*his behaviour reflects badly on his parents*).

reflection *n* 1 the act of reflecting (light, an image, etc). 2 the image seen in a mirror, etc (*her reflection in the shop window*). 3 a thought, deep or careful thought (*on reflection I think we shall go*). 4 blame (*his bad conduct is a reflection on his parents*).

reflec'tive *adj* thoughtful (*in a reflective mood*).

reflec'tor *n* a polished surface for reflecting light or heat.

re'flex *adj* automatic (*jerking one's leg when the kneecap is tapped is a reflex action*).

reflex action *n* an unintentional movement of the body caused by something outside it.

reflexion *see* **reflection**.

reflex'ive *adj* (*in grammar*) referring back to the subject (*a reflexive verb*).

reform' *vb* 1 to make or become better (*reform the system*). 2 to give up bad habits (*a criminal who promised to reform*):—*n* a change for the better.

reforma'tion *n* a thorough change for the better:—**The Reformation** the religious revolution of the 16th century that ended in the separation between the Protestant and RC churches.

reform'atory *n* (*old*) a school for the improvement of young wrongdoers.

reform'er *n* 1 one who calls for or brings about changes in politics, society, religion, etc (*a reformer of the prison system*) 2 one of the leaders of the Reformation.

refract' *vb* to change the direction of (a ray of light, sound, etc):—*n* **refrac'tion**.

refrac'tory *adj* (*fml*) difficult to control, unwilling to obey (*refractory children*).

refrain' *vb* to hold (oneself) back from doing something (*refrain from saying what they thought*).

refrain *n* a line or phrase that is repeated several times in a song or poem, a tune.

refresh' *vb* to give new strength, energy, power, etc (*feel refreshed after a night's sleep*).

refresh'ment *n* (*often pl*) a light meal, a snack, a drink (*provide refreshments for the party guests*).

refrig'erate *vb* to make cold, to freeze (*refrigerate the meat to keep it fresh*):—*n* **re-frigera'tion**.

refrig'erator *n* an apparatus for preserving food, etc, by keeping it cold.

ref'uge *n* a place of shelter from danger or distress (*a refuge for battered wives*).

ref'ugee *n* one fleeing from danger, one who leaves his or her country to seek shelter in another (*refugees from the famine area*).

reful'gent *adj* (*fml*) shining brightly.

refund' *vb* to repay:—*n* **1** the act of refunding. **2** the amount refunded (*get a refund for the faulty goods*).

refus'al *n* act of refusing (*their refusal of the invitation/his refusal to go*).

refuse' *vb* **1** not to accept (*refuse the invitation*). **2** to say that one will not do or give something (*refuse to plead guilty*):—*n* **refuse** rubbish, that which is left as worthless.

refute' *vb* to prove (an argument) wrong (*refuting the suggestion that he was wrong*):—*n* **refuta'tion**.

regain' *vb* **1** to get possession of again (*regain the throne*). **2** to reach again (*regain the shore*).

re'gal *adj* of or like a king, royal, magnificent (*a regal procession*).

regale' *vb* **1** to supply with plenty of food and drink. **2** to entertain (*regaling them with stories of his adventures*).

rega'lia *npl* objects worn or carried as signs of royalty (e.g. crown, etc) or high office.

regal'ity *n* (*fml*) kingship.

regard' *vb* **1** (*fml*) to look at (*he regarded her questioningly*). **2** to consider (*regarded as a nuisance by his teachers*):—*n* **1** (*fml*) attention (*have regard to the icy roads*). **2** respect (*he is held in high regard*). **3** *pl* good wishes (*send your mother my regards*).

regard'ing *prep* concerning (*suggestions regarding the new plans*).

regard'less *adj* paying no attention, not caring about (*regardless of cost*).

regat'ta *n* a race meeting for boats and yachts.

re'gency *n* **1** rule by a regent. **2** the office of regent. **3** the period during which a regent rules.

regen'erate *vb* to improve after a period of worsening, to give fresh faith or energy to (*try to regenerate the club by bringing in young members*):—*adj* reformed:—*n* **re-genera'tion**.

re'gent *n* one who governs during the youth, absence or illness of a monarch.

reg'icide *n* **1** the murder of a king (*imprisoned for trying to commit regicide*). **2** the murderer of a monarch.

regime [rā-zheem'] *n* a method or system of government (*a military regime*).

reg'imen *n* (*fml*) **1** orderly government. **2** a set of rules to be followed (e.g. on what to eat, etc) (*the athlete's strict regimen*).

reg'iment *n* a body of soldiers commanded by a colonel, an army unit consisting of several battalions:—*vb* **regiment'** to organize, control very strictly (*children regimented by their parents*).

regimen'tal *adj* having to do with a regiment (*a regimental mascot*).

regimen'tals *npl* military dress.

regimenta'tion *n* strict organization and control.

re'gion *n* **1** a part of a country, often a large area of land (*the coastal region*). **2** neighbourhood (*a pain in the region of his kidney/a price in the region of £5000*):—*adj* **re'gional**.

reg'ister *n* **1** an official list (*a register of qualified doctors*). **2** a book in which records (e.g. of births, deaths, school attendance, etc) are kept. **3** the distance from the highest to the lowest note of a singing voice or musical instrument:—*vb* **1** to write down in a register (*register a complaint*). **2** to give details to an official for writing in a register (*register the baby's birth*). **3** to pay extra postage to ensure that a letter or parcel reaches its destination safely (*register the parcel containing the medicine*). **4** to show (what one is feeling) (*her face registered dismay*).

reg'istrar *n* an official who keeps a register.

registra'tion *n* act of registering.

reg'istry *n* an office where official records of births, deaths, marriages, etc, are kept.

re'gius *adj* (*fml*) appointed by the monarch (*a regius professor*).

regress' *vb* to move backwards (*the patient's condition is regressing*):—*adj* **regres'sive**.

regres'sion *n* backward movement, a falling away.

regret' *vb* (**regret'ted**, **regret'ting**) **1** to be sorry for what one has said or done (*he regrets his foolish action*). **2** to remember with sorrow (*regret his criminal days*):—*n* sorrow, grief (*feel regret for* *his foolish actions|feel regret at her absence*):— *adj* **regret'ful**.

regret'table *adj* unfortunate, unwelcome (*it is regrettable that such behaviour is allowed*).

reg'ular *adj* **1** normal, usual (*his regular route*). **2** done always in the same way or at the same time (*regular habits*). **3** occurring acting, etc with equal amounts of space, time, etc between (*a regular pulse|guards placed at regular intervals*). **4** belonging to the r egular army. **5** the same on both or all sides (*a girl with regular features*):—*n* **1** a soldier of the r egular army. **2** a habitual customer (*one of the local pub's regulars*):—*n* **regular'ity**.

regular army *n* that part of the army in which people who wish to make soldiering their career are kept in training.

regular clergy *n* monks.

reg'ulate *vb* **1** to contr ol (*regulate expenditure*). **2** to alter (a machine) until it is working pr operly (*regulate a watch*).

regula'tion *n* a rule, an order, an instruction (*obey the club's regulations*):—*adj* as laid down in the rules (*regulation sports clothes*).

reg'ulator *n* **1** a lever by which one can contr ol a machine. **2** one who contr ols.

regur'gitate *vb* (*fml*) **1** to thr ow up again from the stomach (*the sick dog regurgitated its food*). **2** to r epeat without change (*simply regurgitating what his teacher told him*).

rehabil'itate *vb* to bring back to a normal life or normal standards of behaviour by treatment or instruction (*rehabilitate criminals|rehabilitate soldiers wounded in battle*):—*n* **rehabilita'tion**.

rehear'sal *n* a practice before a performance (*the last rehearsal before the opening night*).

rehearse' *vb* **1** (*fml*) to repeat aloud, to give a list of (*rehearse the various rules*). **2** to practise, esp in preparation for public performance (*rehearse for the performance*).

reign [rān] *n* **1** rule. **2** the time during which a king or queen has ruled:—*vb* **1** to rule as a sovereign. **2** to exist (*silence reigned*).

reimburse' *vb* to repay what someone has lost or spent (*have his travel expenses reimbursed by the company*):—*n* **reim-burse'ment**.

rein [rān] *n* **1** the strap by which a driver or rider directs a horse. **2** contr ol (*keep a tight rein on expenses*):—*vb* to check or control with the rein (*rein in the horse*).

rein'deer *n* a deer found in northern parts of Europe and America.

reinforce' *vb* **1** to mak e stronger (*reinforce the elbows of the jacket with leather patches*). **2** to supply with more soldiers, helpers, etc (*reinforce the aid workers with new recruits*).

reinforced concrete *n* concrete strengthened by thin iron bars running through it.

reinforce'ment *n* **1** the act of r einforcing. **2** *pl* more or fresh troops, etc (*the aid workers require reinforcements*).

reinstate' *vb* to put back in a former position (*he was sacked from his post but has been reinstated*):—*n* **reinstate'ment**.

reit'erate *vb* to repeat again and again (*reiterate the instructions*):—*n* **reitera'tion**.

reject' *vb* **1** to r efuse to accept (*reject the criticism*). **2** to thr ow back or away (*reject goods that were not up to standard*):—*n* **rejec'tion**.

rejoice' *vb* to be glad or joyful, to make glad, to express one's joy (*the team rejoicing at their victory*).

rejoic'ing *n* **1** a feeling or expr ession of joy. **2** *pl* celebrations.

rejoin' *vb* **1** to join again (*soldiers told to rejoin their regiments*). **2** to answer , esp rudely or angrily (*'I will not,' he rejoined*).

rejoin'der *n* an answer, a reply, esp a rude or angry one.

reju'venate *vb* to make feel young again:—*n* **rejuvena'tion**.

relapse' *vb* to fall back into evil or illness after improving (*she was getting better after the operation but she has suffered a relapse*):—*also n*.

relate' *vb* **1** (*fml*) to tell (*relate the story of his escape*). **2** to show or see the connection between (*the rise in crime may be related to poverty*).

rela'tion *n* **1** a stor y, an account. **2** one belonging to the same family by birth or marriage (*invite all their relations to the wedding*). **3** a connection (*a possible relation between crime and unemployment*):—*n* **rela'tionship**.

rel'ative *adj* **1** consider ed in comparison with others (*the relative methods of the two systems*). **2** having to do with (*facts relating to the present situation*). **3** (*fml*) (*in grammar*) referring to an earlier word in the sentence:—*n* one belonging to the same family, by birth or marriage (*relatives on the mother's side*).

rel'atively *adv* **1** quite (*she is still relatively young*). **2** when compar ed with others (*compared with flying, rail travel is relatively cheap*).

relativ'ity *n* Einstein's teaching that, although measurements of position and motion cannot be absolutely correct because of the continuous motion within the universe, it is still possible to lay down correctly laws of physics.

relax' *vb* **1** to loosen (*relax his grip on the rope*). **2** to become or mak e less strict or severe (*relax the rules towards the end of the term*). **3** to take a complete rest, to become less tense or worried (*relax after the working day by listening to music*).

relaxa'tion *n* **1** loosening (*relaxation of his grip*). **2** r est, amusement after work (*go to the cinema for relaxation*). **3** making less sever e (*relaxation of the rules*).

relax'ing *adj* **1** r estful. **2** causing a feeling of tiredness.

re'lay *n* **1** a supply of fr esh men or horses to take over from tired ones (*a relay of firemen*). **2** a relay race. **3** the sending out of a radio or television signal or programme that has been received from somewhere else:—*vb* to rebroadcast a radio message or programme received from elsewhere.

relay race *n* a team race in which each member of a team runs part of the whole distance.

release' *vb* **1** to set fr ee (*release the prisoner*). **2** to let go (*release his hold of the rope*). **3** to unfasten (*release the safety catch on the gun*). **4** to mak e public (*release the details of the president's death*):—*also n*.

rel'egate *vb* to put down to a lower place (*relegate the team to a lower division*):—*n* **relega'tion**.

relent' *vb* to become less severe, to give way (*their mother relented and let the children go to the party*).

relent'less *adj* without pity, unmerciful, continuous (*relentless criticism*).

rel'evant *adj* having to do with the matter under consideration (*discuss matters relevant to the situation*):—*ns* **rel'evance, rel'evancy.**

reliabil'ity *n* trustworthiness.

reli'able *adj* able to be trusted (*reliable witness*).

reli'ance *n* trust, confidence (*put their reliance in his judgment*).

reli'ant *adj* relying on, depending on (*reliant on the financial help of her parents*).

rel'ic *n* **1** something valued because of its close connection with a saint or great person of the past. **2** a souvenir . **3** something old-fashioned that still exists (*a village custom that is a relic of Celtic culture*). **4** *pl* (*fml*) a dead body.

rel'ict *n* (*fml*) a man's widow.

relief' *n* **1** complete or partial fr eeing from pain or worry (*treatment that gave her some relief*). **2** money, etc, given to the poor or those who have lost everything in a disaster (*charitable organizations sent relief to the refugees*). **3** one who takes another's place on duty (*the bus driver waited for his relief*). **4** for cing an enemy to end the siege of a town (*the relief of Mafeking*). **5** a piece of sculptur e in which the design stands out just beyond a flat surface. **6** a clear outline.

relief map *n* a map in which height above sea level is shown by colouring or shading.

relieve' *vb* **1** to set fr ee from or lessen (*pain or worry*) (*a medicine to relieve her back pain*). **2** to give help to. **3** to tak e another's place on duty (*relieve the soldier on duty*). **4** to for ce an enemy to end the siege of a town (*the army marched to relieve the city*).

reli'gion *n* **1** belief in and worship of a god or gods. **2** belief, faith. **3** love of God.

religio'sity *n* love of the services of religion rather than of God.

reli'gious *adj* **1** loving God. **2** holy:— *n* a monk or nun.

relin'quish *vb* to give up (*relinquish his post as manager*).

rel'ish *vb* **1** to enjoy the taste of (*relish a glass of good wine*). **2** to lik e or enjoy (*relish a competitive game of tennis*):—*n* **1** a taste, flavour .

2 enjoyment. **3** a sharp-tasting sauce (*serve a relish with the cold meat*).

reluc'tant *adj* unwilling (*reluctant to speak in public*):—*n* **reluc'tance**.

rely' *vb* **1** to trust in (*relying on his judgment*). **2** to depend on (*relied on her parents for financial help*).

remain' *vb* **1** to stay on in a place (*asked to remain in the house*). **2** to be left over (*a little money remained after the bills had been paid*). **3** to continue to be (*they remained friends*).

remain'der *n* that which is left over or behind (*for the remainder of the evening*).

remains' *npl* **1** that which is left (*the remains of the meal*). **2** (*fml*) a dead body (*bury his remains this afternoon*).

remand' *vb* to send back to prison while further inquiries are being made (*the accused has been remanded*):—*n* **1** act of remanding. **2** the state of being remanded.

remand home *n* (*old*) a place where young persons were kept when awaiting trial or when undergoing punishment.

remark' *vb* **1** to say (*she remarked that it was a pleasant day*). **2** to comment (on) (*he remarked on her beautiful ring*):—*n* **1** something said (*he made a remark about her appearance*). **2** (*fml*) notice, attention (*clothes that could not escape remark*).

remark'able *adj* worthy of notice, extraordinary (*of remarkable intelligence/a remarkable performance*).

reme'dial *adj* intended or helping to cure.

rem'edy *n* **1** a cure (*a remedy for headaches*). **2** a medicine (*herbal remedies*). **3** any way of putting right what is wrong (*seek a remedy for truancy*):—*vb* **1** to cure. **2** to put right (*remedy the injustice*).

remem'ber *vb* **1** to keep in mind (*remember her youth with pleasure*). **2** to recall to the mind (*try to remember his name*). **3** to give greetings from another (*remember me to your father*).

remem'brance *n* **1** memory. **2** a souvenir.

remind' *vb* to cause to remember (*you will have to remind him to come to the meeting*).

remind'er *n* something that helps one to remember (*sent him a reminder about the unpaid bill*).

reminisce' *vb* to tell stories of one's past (*old people reminiscing about their youth*).

reminis'cence *n* **1** a memory of one's past (*a childhood reminiscence*). **2** the remembering of the past. **3** *pl* stories about one's past.

reminis'cent *adj* **1** remembering the past (*in a reminiscent mood*). **2** reminding of the past (*a style reminiscent of Renoir*).

remiss' *adj* (*fml*) careless, not doing one's duty properly (*it was remiss of them to forget their father's birthday*).

remis'sion *n* **1** the reduction of a prison sentence (*given six months' remission for good behaviour*). **2** a period when an illness is less severe (*the cancer patient is in remission at the moment*).

remit' *vb* (**remit'ted, remit'ting**) **1** (*fml*) to lessen or do away with (*remit the sentence*). **2** to send (money) (*please remit your cheque as soon as possible*). **3** to pass back or on for further consideration (*remit the complaint to the manager*).

remitt'ance *n* a sum of money sent.

rem'nant *n* a small piece or part left over, esp of cloth (*make an apron with the remnant*).

remon'strance *n* a strong protest.

rem'onstrate *vb* to protest strongly, to express objections to (*villagers remonstrating about the decision to build new houses*).

remorse' *n* great sorrow for having done wrong (*he showed remorse for his crimes*):—*adj* **remorse'ful**.

remorse'less *adj* feeling no remorse, pitiless (*a remorseless tyrant*).

remote' *adj* **1** distant, far away, out of the way (*a remote village*). **2** not closely related (*a remote cousin/a remote connection*). **3** not friendly, withdrawn (*a remote manner*). **4** slight (*a remote chance of success*).

remote control *n* **1** a system which allows a device or machine to be controlled from a distance, using electrical, electronic or radio signals (*a model boat operated by remote control*). **2** a handheld device that enables the user to operate a television set etc, from a distance.

remov'al *n* **1** act of removing (*the removal of the stain from the cloth*). **2** a change of dwelling place (*the removal will be completed by the weekend*).

remove' vb **1** to tak e from its place (remove a book from the shelf). **2** to tak e off (remove his socks). **3** to dismiss (remove him from the post of manager). **4** (fml) to change one's dwelling place:—adj remov'able.

remu'nerate vb to pay for one's services.

remunera'tion n pay, salary (the level of remuneration was dependent on experience).

remu'nerative adj profitable, bringing in a lot of money (a remunerative post).

renaiss'ance, renas'cence ns a revival, esp of interest in arts and learning, as in the 15th century.

re'nal adj having to do with the kidneys (a renal disease).

renascence see renaissance.

rend vb (old) (pt, pp rent) to tear apart, to split.

ren'der vb **1** to give (for services rendered). **2** to perform in a certain way (a piano solo beautifully rendered). **3** to translate (render the Latin passage into English). **4** to cause to be (her reply rendered him speechless).

ren'dering n **1** a translation. **2** a particular performance.

rendezvous [ro(ng)'-dā-vö] n **1** (fml) an agreed meeting place (the summer house was the lovers' usual rendezvous). **2** a meeting (a midnight rendezvous).

ren'egade n one who deserts his or her party, side, or religion:—also adj.

renew' vb **1** to mak e new again (renew his club membership). **2** to begin again (renew their assault on the town):—n renew'al.

ren'net n a liquid used in curdling milk.

renounce' vb **1** to give up (renounce his claim to the throne). **2** to state that one will have nothing more to do with (renounce his religion):—n renuncia'tion.

ren'ovate vb to make like new, to repair and clean (renovate the old building/renovate the sofa):—n renova'tion.

renown' n fame, glory (he won renown as a writer).

renowned' adj famous (a renowned scientist).

rent[1] n a payment made for the use of land, a house, etc:—vb **1** to get the use of by paying rent (students rent a house from him). **2** to let or hire out for rent (rent his flat to students).

rent[2] n (fml) a tear, a split (a rent in the curtain material).

ren'tal n rent, the sum paid in rent (TV rental).

renunciation see renounce.

reor'ganize vb to organize in a different way (reorganizing the filing system).

rep[1], **repp** n a type of cloth with a corded surface.

rep[2] short for **repertory**.

repair' vb **1** to mend (repair the broken fence). **2** to put right, mak e up for (repair the wrong done to them). **3** to go:—n **1** r eturning to good condition, mending. **2** a mended place (the obvious repair to the dress). **3** condition for using (in poor repair).

rep'arable adj (fml) able to be repaired (wrongs that are scarcely reparable).

repara'tion n (fml) something given to make up for loss or damage suffered (make reparation for her wrecked car).

repartee' n a quick clever reply (admire her witty repartee).

repast' n (old) a meal.

repat'riate vb to send (a person) back to his or her own country (repatriate illegal immigrants):—n repatria'tion.

repay' vb **1** to pay back (repay the money borrowed). **2** to tr eat in a like way (repay her kindness with abuse).

repay'ment n **1** act of r epaying. **2** the sum r epaid.

repeal' vb to withdraw, to set aside, to abolish (to repeal the law):—also n.

repeat' vb **1** to do or say again (repeat the order/repeat the task). **2** to speak aloud something learned by heart (repeat a poem).

repeat'edly adv again and again (he hit the target repeatedly).

repeat'er n **1** a watch that strik es the last hour every time a certain spring is pressed. **2** a fir earm that fires several shots before it has to be reloaded. **3** a decimal fraction that goes on repeating a figure (e.g. 0.333) because it cannot be expressed exactly as a decimal.

repel' vb (repelled', repell'ing) **1** to drive back (repel the enemy army). **2** to cause dislik e (he is so dirty he repels me).

repell'ent adj causing dislike or disgust (a repellent sight):—n that which is able to repel or drive away something (an insect repellent).

repent' vb to feel sorry for having said or done something (repent his wickedness):—n repen'tance:—adj repen'tant.

repercus'sion *n* the after-effects of words or actions, not the immediate effects (*the local dispute had national repercussions*).

repertoire [rep'-er-twär] *n* **1** a performer 's stock of musical pieces, poems, etc (*the comedian's repertoire of jokes*). **2** a company 's stock of plays ready for acting.

rep'ertory theatre *n* a theatre with a permanent company performing a repertoire of plays (*abbr* **rep**).

repeti'tion *n* **1** act of r epeating (*his repetition of the instructions*). **2** saying fr om memory (*the child's repetition of the poem*).

replace' *vb* **1** to put back in place (*replacing the book on the shelf*). **2** to tak e the place of (*she replaced him as head teacher*).

replace'ment *n* **1** act of r eplacing. **2** a person or thing taking the place of another.

replen'ish *vb* to fill up again (*replenish the guests' glasses*):—*n* **replen'ishment**.

replete' *adj* (*fml*) full (*replete after the meal*):—*n* **reple'tion**.

rep'lica *n* **1** an exact copy of a work of art (*a replica of the original piece*). **2** a r eproduction, esp of a smaller size (*a replica of the Statue of Liberty*).

reply' *vb* to answer (*replied to their questions/replying to their initiative*):—*n* an answer.

report' *vb* **1** to give as news or information, to tell (*report a new medical development*). **2** to write an account of, esp for a newspaper (*she reported on foreign affairs for a national newspaper*). **3** to make a complaint about for having done wrong (*report the boys who played truant to the teacher*). **4** to tell someone in authority (*report the theft to the police*):—*n* **1** a spok en or written account of work performed (e.g. by a committee, a pupil). **2** an ac count of something that has been said or done, esp when written for a newspaper. **3** a rumour (*there were reports that he had married*). **4** a loud noise (*a report from a gun*).

report'er *n* one who reports for a newspaper or television/radio broadcast.

repose' *vb* **1** (*fml*) to lay at rest, to lie at rest. **2** to place (*repose her trust in someone not worthy of it*):—*n* **1** r est, sleep (*seek repose*). **2** calmness (*her face in repose*).

repos'itory *n* **1** (*fml*) a store-house (*a furniture repository*). **2** (*old*) a shop.

repp *see* **rep**.

reprehen'sible *adj* (*fml*) blameworthy (*reprehensible conduct*).

represent' *vb* **1** to stand for , or make to stand for, as a sign or likeness (*the white dove representing peace*). **2** to be a pictur e or statue of. **3** to have the right to speak or act for (*the lawyer representing her*). **4** to describe or declar e, perhaps falsely (*he represented himself as someone whom they could trust*). **5** (*fml*) to be, to constitute (*it represented a considerable improvement on previous attendance figures*). **6** to be the r epresentative of (a company).

representa'tion *n* **1** the act of r epresenting or being represented. **2** an image or lik eness (*a representation of the king in oils*). **3** (*fml*) a protest or objection (*make representations about the rise in fees*).

represen'tative *adj* typical, standing for others of the same class (*a representative sample*):—*n* **1** one who acts for another (*the lawyer acted as her representative*). **2** one who sells goods for a business firm (*a representative for a publisher*). **3** an elected member of parliament.

representative government *n* government by an elected assembly.

repress' *vb* to keep under control, to keep down, to restrain (*repress a desire to laugh*).

repres'sion *n* strict control, restraint.

repres'sive *adj* (*fml*) intended to keep down or restrain (*a repressive form of government*).

reprieve' *vb* to let off punishment, to pardon (*he faced the death sentence but was reprieved*):—*also n.*

rep'rimand *n* a severe scolding:—*vb* to scold severely (*reprimand the children for their manners*).

reprint' *vb* to print again:—*n* **re'print** a new printing or edition.

repris'al *n* something done by way of punishment or revenge (*their raid was a reprisal for our earlier attacks*).

reproach' *vb* to accuse and blame, to scold, usu with a suggestion of sadness or disappointment (*she reproached him for letting everyone down*):—*n*

1 scolding, blame (*a look of reproach/words of reproach*). **2** something that brings shame (*his bad conduct brought reproach on his family*).

reproach'ful *adj* accusing, shameful.

rep'robate *adj* (*fml*) very evil, given up to bad ways:—*n* a reprobate person (*a family of reprobates*).

reproduce' *vb* **1** to cause to be heard, seen or done again (*unable to reproduce the results/try to reproduce the atmosphere of the last party/reproduce sound*). **2** to increase by having offspring (*rabbits reproduce rapidly*):—*n* **reproduc'tion**:—*adj* **reproduc'tive**.

reproof' *n* (*fml*) a scolding, blame.

reprove' *vb* (*fml*) to scold, to blame (*reprove the children for their naughtiness*).

rep'tile *n* a class of cold-blooded animals that crawl or creep (e.g. snake, lizard).

repub'lic *n* a state entirely governed by elected persons, there being no sovereign.

repub'lican *adj* having to do with a republic:—*n* one who prefers republican government.

repu'diate *vb* **1** to refuse to recognize as one's own (*repudiate his son in public*). **2** to refuse to accept, to deny (*repudiate the suggestion that he was to blame*):—*n* **repudia'tion**.

repug'nance *n* disgust.

repug'nant *adj* (*fml*) very unpleasant, disgusting (*a repugnant smell*).

repulse' *vb* (*fml*) **1** to drive back, to defeat (*repulse the enemy attacks*). **2** to refuse sharply (*to repulse his offer*):—*n* **1** a defeat. **2** a refusal.

repul'sion *n* dislike, disgust.

repul'sive *adj* hateful, disgusting (*a repulsive sight/a repulsive, dirty old man*).

rep'utable *adj* having a good name, respectable (*a reputable estate agent*).

reputa'tion *n* **1** one's good name, one's character as seen by other people (*damage her reputation to be seen with such a crook*). **2** fame (*establish a reputation as an artist*).

repute' *n* reputation:—*vb* to consider to be.

reput'ed *adj* supposed (to be) (*she is reputed to be very wealthy*).

reput'edly *adv* as is commonly supposed.

request' *vb* to ask for (*request them to order a book/request a piece of music to be played*):—*n* the

act of asking for something (*go there at his request*). **2** a favour asked for (*grant his request*).

requiem [rek'-wi-em] *n* a mass for the dead.

require' *vb* **1** to need (*we have all we require to make the meal*). **2** to demand by right, to order (*the children are required to attend school*).

require'ment *n* **1** a need, something needed (*a shop able to supply all our requirements*). **2** a necessary condition (*a requirement for entry to university*).

req'uisite *adj* needed, necessary (*the requisite amount of money*):—*n* that which is needed or necessary.

requisi'tion *n* a demand or written order for supplies (*a school requisition for paper and pens*):—*vb* to demand or order supplies.

requite' *vb* **1** to repay. **2** to return good for good or evil for evil (*requite our kindness*):—*n* **requi'tal**.

reredos [reer'-dos] *n* the decorated wall or screen behind an altar.

rescind' *vb* to withdraw, to cancel (*rescind the order*).

res'cue *vb* to save from danger or evil (*rescue the dog from drowning*):—*n* act of rescuing:—*n* **res'cuer**.

research' *n* careful study to discover new facts (*engaged in medical research*).

resem'ble *vb* to be like (*she resembled her mother*):—*n* **resem'blance**.

resent' *vb* to be angered by, to take as an insult (*resent their interference in her life*).

resent'ful *adj* showing anger, full of annoyance (*resentful of their interference/a resentful look*).

resent'ment *n* anger, indignation (*feel resentment at their treatment*).

reserva'tion *n* **1** something kept back. **2** a condition. **3** land set aside for some special purpose (e.g. big game). **4** a booked place or seat.

reserve' *vb* **1** (*fml*) to keep back for future use (*reserve some food for later*). **2** to order or book for future use (*reserve seats at the cinema*):—*n* **1** something kept back for future use (*a reserve of money for emergencies*). **2** shyness, unwillingness to show one's feelings (*her reserve made her appear unfriendly*). **3** *pl* troops kept out of battle for use where and when needed.

reserved' adj shy, not showing what one is thinking or feeling (a very reserved young woman).

res'ervoir n 1 a place wher e the water supply of a city is stored. 2 a stor e (a reservoir of oil/a reservoir of information).

reside' vb to dwell, to live (in).

res'idence n dwelling, house.

res'idency n the house of a governor.

residen'tial adj 1 suitable for living in. 2 (of a district) having many dwelling houses.

resid'ual adj (fml) left after the rest has been taken (his residual income after the bills were paid).

res'idue n the remainder, what is left over (he left most of his estate to his sons and the residue was divided among his nephews).

resid'uum n (fml) remainder.

resign' vb 1 to give up (resign his post as manager). 2 to give up an office or post (he threatened to resign). 3 to accept with complaint (he resigned himself to defeat):—n **resigna'tion**.

resigned' adj accepting trouble with complaint, patient (a resigned attitude to trouble/she was resigned to a life of poverty).

resil'ient adj 1 able to spring back to a former position after being bent (rubber is a resilient material). 2 having good powers of r ecovery (she has had much misfortune but has been ve ry resilient):—n resil'-ience.

res'in n a sticky substance that oozes from certain plants, e.g. firs, pines, etc:—adj **res'inous**.

resist' vb 1 to stand against, to fight against, to oppose (resist the enemy advances). 2 to face or allow oneself not to accept (she cannot resist chocolate cake).

resis'tance n the act or power of resisting, opposition (to put up no resistance to the invading army).

resis'tant adj offering resistance.

res'olute adj determined, bold, having the mind made up (resolute in their efforts to succeed).

resolu'tion n 1 determination (proceed with resolution). 2 a firm intention (a New Year resolution to give up smoking). 3 a pr oposal for a meeting to vote on (those in favour of the resolution raised ther hands). 4 the decision of a meeting on a certain matter (pass a resolution to change the rules). 5 (fml) the act of solving (the resolution of the problem).

resolve' vb 1 to determine (resolve to try again). 2 to br eak up into parts or elements (resolve a chemical substance). 3 to solve (resolve the problem):—n 1 a fixed purpose (his resolve was to make a lot of money). 2 determination (proceed with resolve).

res'onant adj 1 echoing. 2 deep-sounding (a resonant voice):—n **res'onance**.

resort' vb to make use of, to turn to (resort to crime to pay his debts):—n 1 a place to which one goes frequently. 2 a place wher e many people go for holidays:—**in the last resort** as a last possibility (in the last resort he can borrow from his father).

resound' vb to echo, to give back the sound of (the cave resounded to the children's shouts).

resound'ing adj 1 echoing. 2 ve ry great (a resounding success).

resource' n 1 ability to think out clever plans (survival on the island would require some resource). 2 a means of obtaining help, something turned to in time of need (the local library was a useful learning resource). 3 (often pl) a source of economic wealth, esp of a country (oil is one of this nation's most valuable resources).

resource'ful adj full of clever plans (his resouceful use of materials saved money).

respect' vb 1 to think highly of (respect him as a writer). 2 to pay attention to (respect their wishes):—n 1 honour (treat older people with respect). 2 car e or attention (treat their wishes with respect). 3 pl good wishes (send his respects to the old man).

respectabil'ity n 1 state of deser ving respect. 2 decency.

respec'table adj 1 deser ving respect, decent (not thought respectable by the neighbours) 2 socially acceptable (respectable clothes). 3 lar ge enough, good enough, etc (a respectable score).

respect'ful adj showing respect or honour to (children told to his be respectful to their elders/a respectful silence at the funeral).

respect'ing prep (fml) having to do with (respecting his position in the firm).

respec'tive adj each to his/her own, proper to each (they all went to their respective homes).

respec'tively adv belonging to each in the order already mentioned (James and John got marks of 70% and 80% respectively).

respira'tion n (fml) breathing.

res'pirator n a mask with a filter worn over the nose and mouth to purify the air breathed in.

res'piratory adj (fml) having to do with breathing (a respiratory infection).

respire' vb (fml) to breathe.

res'pite n a pause, an interval (the storm went on without respite).

resplen'dent adj very bright or splendid (the king was resplendent in his robes).

respond' vb 1 to answer (failed to respond to the question). 2 to do as a reaction to something that has been done (he smiled but she did not respond).

respon'dent n (fml) the defendant in a lawsuit, esp in divorce.

response' n 1 an answer, a reply (in response to the question). 2 a reaction (a magnificent response to the charity's appeal).

respon'sible adj 1 able to be trusted (responsible members of staff). 2 having to say or explain what one has done (he is responsible for his actions). 3 being the cause of something (responsible for the confusion):—n **responsibil'ity**.

respon'sive adj quick to react (responsive to the suggestions).

rest[1] n 1 a pause in work. 2 inactivity. 3 sleep (a good night's rest). 4 a support or prop (he aimed the rifle using the wall as a rest):—vb 1 to cease from action. 2 to stop work for a time (rest for a few minutes). 3 to be still or quiet (young children are resting). 4 to sleep or repose. 5 to be supported (by) (his feet resting on the table).

rest[2] n that which is left, the remainder.

restaurant [res'-tê-ro(ng)] n a place where one may buy and eat meals.

restaurateur n one who keeps a restaurant.

rest'ful adj peaceful, quiet (have a restful holiday).

restitu'tion n the giving back of something taken away or lost (asked to make full restitution for the money lost).

restive adj unable to keep still, impatient (children getting restive at their desks).

rest'less adj 1 always on the move (too restless to stay in one job for long). 2 not restful, giving no rest (spent a restless night).

restor'ative adj (fml) making strong or healthy again (a restorative tonic).

restore' vb 1 to bring back (restore law and order). 2 to put back (they restored him to his former post). 3 to make strong again (restored by his holiday). 4 to bring back to an earlier state or condition (restore old furniture):—n **restora'tion**.

restrain' vb to hold back, to check (restrain the dog from biting people).

restraint' n 1 self-control. 2 lack of freedom.

restrict' vb to set limits to, to keep down (the number or amount of) (restrict the amount of money spent/restrict their freedom).

restric'tion n a rule or condition that lessens freedom.

restric'tive adj (fml) lessening freedom, keeping under control (restrictive clothing).

result' n 1 that which happens as the effect of something else, the outcome (the result of the election/as a result of the accident). 2 the final score in a sports contest:—vb 1 to follow as the effect of a cause (blindness resulting from the accident). 2 to end (in) (the research resulted in a new drug on the market).

result'ant adj following as a result (the resultant confusion).

resume' vb 1 (fml) to begin again (he will resume his studies). 2 to take back (resume his seat after speaking).

resumé [rã-zõ'-mã] n a summary (the resumé of what happened at the meeting).

resump'tion n act of resuming.

resur'gent adj (fml) rising again (resurgent terrorist activity).

resurrect' vb 1 to raise or bring back again (resurrect an old law). 2 to raise to life again (Christians believe Christ was resurrected).

resurrec'tion n a rising again from the dead.

resus'citate vb to bring back to life or consciousness (try to resuscitate the man who had a heart attack):—n **resuscita'tion**.

retail' vb 1 to sell direct to the public in small amounts (he retails tobacco goods). 2 to sell (these sweaters retail at £15 each). 3 (fml) to tell in full, to repeat a story to many (retail the story of his travels):—n the sale of goods in small quantities (the retail trade).

retail'er *n* a shopkeeper.

retain' *vb* **1** to hold back (*a wall built to retain the water*). **2** to continue to use, have, r emember, etc (*retain control of the firm/a town that has retained its churches*). **3** to engage someone's services by paying a fee in advance (*retain a lawyer*).

retain'er *n* **1** (*old*) a follower (*the king's retainers*). **2** an advance fee for someone's ser vices (*the lawyer is paid a retainer*).

retal'iate *vb* to return like for like, to get one's own back (*she retaliated by punching him*):—*n* **retalia'tion**.

retard' *vb* to make slow or late, to make go more slowly, to delay (*the bad weather retarded the growth of the crops*):—*n* **retar-da'tion.**

retch *vb* to try to vomit:—*also n*.

reten'tion *n* (*fml*) act of retaining.

reten'tive *adj* able to keep or retain (*a retentive memory*).

reti'cent *adj* unwilling to speak to others, silent (*a reticent person/reticent about the cause of the quarrel*):—*n* **ret'icence.**

ret'icule *n* (*fml*) a network bag.

ret'ina *n* the inner layer of the eye to which are connected the ends of the nerves that enable us to see.

ret'inue *n* all the followers or attendants of a person of high rank (*the president's retinue*).

retir'al *n* act of retiring (*his retiral from business*).

retire' *vb* **1** (*fml*) to go back or away (*the jury retired to consider their verdict*). **2** to leave one's work for ever because of old age, illness, etc (*he retired at the age of sixty*). **3** to go to bed (*retire shortly after midnight*).

retired *adj* **1** having given up one's business or profession (*a retired businessman*). **2** out- of- the-way, quiet (*a retired country village*).

retire'ment *n* **1** act of r etiring (*his early retirement was due to poor health*). **2** the time after one has finished one's working life (*he spent his retirement enjoying his hobbies*). **3** (*fml*) quiet, privacy (*in the retirement of the countryside*).

retiring *adj* shy, not fond of company (*he was a retiring young man who did not enjoy parties*).

retort' *vb* to reply quickly or sharply:—*n* **1** a quick or sharp reply. **2** a thin glass bottle with a long bent-back neck, used for heating chemicals.

retrace' *vb* to go back over again (*retrace her steps to look for the lost ring*).

retract' *vb* to say that a previous opinion was wrong, to take back what one has said (*retract his accusation*):—*n* **retrac'tion.**

retreat' *vb* **1** to go back (*they had to retreat from the fire*). **2** (*of an army*) to move back away from the enemy:—*n* **1** act of r etreating (*the retreat of the enemy*). **2** a quiet, out- of-the-way place, a place of peace and safety (*a popular country retreat*). **3** a period of r est, meditation, prayer, etc (*spend a week in retreat*).

retrench *vb* to arrange to spend less (*have to retrench on expenses during the recession*):—*n* **retrench'ment.**

retribu'tion *n* just punishment for wrong done (*take retribution on the terrorists*).

retrieve' *vb* **1** to find again (*retrieve the glove she left behind*). **2** to find and bring back (*dogs retrieving birds killed by hunters*) **3** to undo harm or loss undergone (*apologies to try to retrieve the situation*).

retriev'er *n* a dog trained to fetch birds shot by hunters.

retro- *prefix* backward.

ret'rograde *adj* leading to a worse state of affairs (*a retrograde step*).

retrogress' *vb* to become worse (*a state of affairs rapidly retrogressing*):—*n* **retro-gres'sion.**

retrogres'sive *adj* **1** backward d. **2** becoming worse.

ret'rospection *n* a looking back to the past.

retrospec'tive *adj* looking back to the past (*a retrospective mood*).

retroussé [re-trö'-sã] *adj* (*fml*) turned up (*a retroussé nose*).

return' *vb* **1** to come or go back (*they returned to the house*). **2** to give or send back (*return his present unopened*). **3** to elect to parliament (*return him as their MP*):—*n* **1** a coming or going back (*their return from holiday*). **2** what is given or sent back (*the return of the library books*). **3** pr ofit (*a good return from their investment*). **4** a written statement of certain facts, expenses, figures, etc (*their annual tax return*).

return'ing officer *n* the official who sees that an election to parliament is conducted fairly and announces the result.

reu'nion *n* a meeting again of old friends or comrades (*a school reunion*).

reunite' *vb* to join together again (*reunited with her sister whom she had not seen for twenty years*).

rev *vb*:—**rev up** to increase the speed of a motor.

Rev, Rev. *short for* Reverend.

reveal' *vb* 1 to show what was hidden (*open the box to reveal a diamond*). 2 to make known (*reveal what should have been confidential information*).

reveille [rê-va'-lã] *n* a morning call on the bugle, etc, to waken soldiers.

rev'el *n* merry-making, a noisy feast (*student revels*):—*vb* (**rev'elled, rev'elling**) 1 (*old*) to make merry. 2 to take great delight (in) (*she revels in the misfortune of others*):—*n* **rev'eller**.

revela'tion *n* 1 act of making known (*the revelation of her secrets*). 2 a surprising discovery or piece of information (*the revelation caused great dismay*).

rev'elry, *n* noisy feasting or merry-making.

revenge' *n* making someone suffer for a wrong done to another, repaying evil with evil (*he wanted revenge for his brother's death*):—*also vb*:—*adj* **revenge'ful.**

rev'enue *n* money made by a person, business or state (*increase in annual revenue*):—**Inland Revenue** the annual income of a state, obtained through taxes, etc.

rever'berate *vb* to echo (*caves reverberated with the child's laughter*):—*n* **reverbera'-tion.**

revere' *vb* (*fml*) to feel great respect for (*young writers revering the great author*).

rev'erence *n* respect and admiration (*treat the great artist with reverence*).

Rev'erend *n* (*abbr* **Rev., Rev.**) a title given to a member of clergy.

rev'erent *adj* showing or feeling great respect (*a reverent attitude towards writers*).

reveren'tial *adj* full of reverence (*his reverential attitude towards other artists*).

rev'erie *n* 1 a daydream (*pleasant reveries*). 2 a state of dreamy thought (*lost in a reverie about the future*).

reverse' *vb* 1 to turn back to front or upside down (*reverse the tablecloth*). 2 to go or move backwards (*he reversed the car into the garage*). 3 to change to the opposite (*reverse her opinion*):—*n* 1 a defeat (*armies retreating after a major reverse*). 2 a failure (*firms facing a reverse during the recession*). 3 the opposite (*she thinks the reverse of what he does*). 4 the back of a coin, medal, etc:—*adj* 1 opposite. 2 back.

rever'sible *adj* 1 able to be reversed (*a reversible opinion*). 2 that can be turned outside in (*a reversible coat*).

rever'sion *n* 1 going back to a former owner or condition (*reversion of the land to its natural state*). 2 the right to take over property or an office no longer held by another.

revert' *vb* 1 to go back to a former condition, custom or subject (*revert to the old bad habits*). 2 to return or be returned to the previous owner or member of his/her family (*when she dies the land reverts to her brother's family*).

review' *vb* 1 to look over again, to consider with a view to changing (*review the situation*). 2 to inspect (*the queen reviewing the troops*). 3 to write one's opinion of (books, plays, etc):—*n* 1 a looking back on the past (*a review of the year's news*). 2 reconsideration or revision (*a review of company policy*). 3 an article in a newspaper, magazine, etc, giving an opinion on a book, play, etc (*a review of the latest film*). 4 a magazine that reviews books, plays, etc (*a literary review*).

review'er *n* one who writes reviews, a critic (*the play was praised by the reviewer*).

revile' *vb* to speak insultingly about or to (*revile the government*).

revise' *vb* to go over again and correct or improve (*revise the manuscript*):—*n* **re-vis'er.**

revi'sion *n* act of revising.

revi'val *n* 1 act of reviving. 2 the arousing of fresh enthusiasm for.

revi'valist *n* one who tries to arouse fresh enthusiasm for religion.

revive' *vb* 1 to bring back to life, health or consciousness (*able to revive the man who nearly drowned*). 2 to bring back to use or an active state (*revive an old custom*). 3 to give new vigour or energy to (*revive their interest in sport*).

4 to pr oduce an old play in the theatre (*revive an early musical*).

reviv'ify *vb* (*fml*) to give new life or energy to.

rev'ocable *adj* (*fml*) that may be done away with or withdrawn (*decisions that are revocable*).

revoke' *vb* **1** to do away with, to withdraw (*revoke an existing rule*). **2** in car d-playing, to fail to follow suit—*n* **revoca'tion.**

revolt' *vb* **1** to r ebel (*the townspeople revolting against the government*). **2** to shock or disgust (*the sight of blood revolts him*):—*n* a rebellion, a rising against the government.

revolt'ing *adj* disgusting, shocking (*a revolting sight*).

revolu'tion *n* **1** one complete turn of a wheel, etc. **2** a complete change (*the technological revolution*). **3** a movement or r ebellion as a result of which a new method of government is introduced (*the French Revolution*).

revolu'tionary *adj* desiring to bring about a complete change (*revolutionary developments in technology*):—*n* one who works for a complete change of government.

revolu'tionize *vb* to bring about a complete change in (*revolutionize the whole industry*).

revolve' *vb* **1** to turn r ound and round. **2** to move round a centre or axis.

revol'ver, *n* a pistol able to fire several shots without reloading.

revue' *n* a light theatrical entertainment with music, songs, dances, etc.

revul'sion *n* a sudden complete change of feeling, disgust (*feel revulsion at the sight of blood*).

reward' *n* **1** something given in r eturn for work done, good behaviour, bravery, etc (*a reward for saving the drowning man*). **2** a sum of money offered for finding or helping to find a criminal, lost or stolen property, etc (*a reward is offered for the return of his car*):—*vb* to give as a reward.

rey'nard *n* (*old*) the fox.

rhapsodic (*fml*) *see* rhapsody.

rhap'sodize *vb* (*fml*) to talk in an excited, disconnected manner (*rhapsodizing over their holiday abroad*).

rhap'sody *n* **1** a piece of writing or music or a speech full of excited feeling and therefore not following the usual rules of composition **2** (*usu*

pl) an expression of excited approval (*go into rhapsodies over the new baby*):—*adj* **rhapsod'ic.**

rhet'oric *n* **1** the art of speaking and writing well. **2** wor ds that sound well but say little of importance (*they thought the politician's speech was just rhetoric*):—*n* **rhetori'cian.**

rhetor'ical *adj* high-sounding.

rhetorical question *n* a question asked for effect where no answer is expected.

rheum [rōm] *n* a watery fluid prepared by the glands and discharged, esp from the nose.

rheumatism [rōˈ-mē-tizm], **rheuma'tics** *ns* a disease causing painful swelling in the joints (*have difficulty in moving around because of his rheumatism*):—*adj* **rheuma'tic.**

rhino'ceros *n* a large thick-skinned animal with a horn (or two horns) on its nose.

rhododen'dron *n* an evergreen shrub with large brightly coloured flowers (*pink rhododendrons growing along the driveway*).

rhom'bus *n* (*pl* **rhom'buses** *or* **rhom'bi**) a parallelogram with equal sides but angles not right angles.

rhu'barb *n* a garden plant with juicy stalks eatable when cooked and roots sometimes used in medicines (*rhubarb jam*).

rhyme [rīm] *n* **1** sameness of sound at the ends of words or lines of poetry. **2** a wor d that rhymes with another. **3** a poem with r hymes:—*vb* **1** to find words ending in the same sound(s). **2** to end in the same sound(s) as. **3** to write poetry:—**without rhyme or reason** foolish, unreasonable.

rhym'er *n* a poet.

rhythm *n* **1** the r egular beat of words (esp in poetry), music or dancing (*tap her feet to the rhythm of the music*). **2** a r egular repeated pattern of movements, graceful motion (*the rhythm of the dancers*).

rhyth'mic, rhyth'mical *adjs* having a regular beat, regular.

rib *n* **1** one of the cur ved bones of the breast (*crack a rib in the accident*/*a rib of beef*). **2** a curved piece of wood attached to the keel of a ship and going up to the deck. **3** a low narr ow ridge or raised part of a material.

rib'ald *adj* coarse, indecent, vulgar (*ribald jokes*/*ribald laughter*).

rib'aldry *n* coarse talk.

rib'and *n* a ribbon, generally given as a mark of achievement.

rib'bon *n* a narrow decorative band of silk or other material (*tie a ribbon in her hair*).

rice *n* a white eatable grain much grown in hot countries, esp in river valleys (*served with fried rice*).

rice paper *n* **1** a kind of fine paper . **2** a special form of this that can be eaten and is used in cookery.

rich *adj* **1** having much money , wealthy (*a rich man*). **2** fertile (*a rich soil*). **3** valuable (*a rich silk*). **4** plentiful (*a rich source of gold*). **5** containing much fat or sugar (*rich sauces*). **6** deep, strong (*a rich voice/rich colours*)

rich'es *npl* wealth.

rich'ly *adv* **1** in a rich manner (*richly dressed*). **2** with riches (*richly rewarded*).

rick *n* a heap or stack of hay, etc.

rick'ets *npl* a children's disease in which the bones become soft or misshapen.

rick'ety *adj* shaky, unsteady (*a rickety table*).

rick'shaw *n* a light two-wheeled carriage pulled by a man.

ricochet [rik'-o-shā] *n* the skimming of a bullet off a flat surface:—*vb* (*pt* ricocheted [rik'-o-shād]) to hit something and bounce away at an angle (*the bullet ricocheted off the wall*).

rid *vb* (**rid** *or* **rid'ded**, **rid'ding**) to make free from, to clear (*try to rid themselves of their boring guests*).

rid'dle[1] *n* a puzzling question.

rid'dle[2] *n* a large sieve (*use a riddle to seperate stones from the soil*):—*vb* **1** to sift. **2** to fill with holes.

ride *vb* (*pt* **rode**, *pp* **rid'den**) **1** to be carried on the back of an animal or on a vehicle (*ride a donkey*). **2** to be able to ride on and contr ol a horse, bicycle, etc (*she is learning to ride*). **3** to float at anchor (*ships riding on the waves*):—*n* a trip on an animal's back or in a vehicle.

rid'er *n* **1** one who rides (*a horse-rider*). **2** something added to what has already been said or written (*the teacher added the rider that he expected everyone to be on time*).

ridge *n* **1** a long narr ow hill. **2** the raised part between two lower parts (*the ridge of the roof*). **3** a mountain range.

rid'icule *n* mockery:—*vb* to mock, to make fun of (*she was ridiculed by her classmates*).

ridic'ulous *adj* deserving to be laughed at, absurd (*the large hat made her look ridiculous*).

ri'ding habit *n* the clothes worn for riding.

rife *adj* found everywhere or in large numbers or quantities, extremely common (*disease and poverty were rife*).

riff-raff *n* low, badly behaved people (*she was told not to associate with riff-raff*).

ri'fle[1] *n* a handgun with a grooved barrel that makes the bullet spin in flight:—*vb* to make grooves in a gun barrel.

ri'fle[2] *vb* to search through and steal anything valuable (*the burglar rifled through her papers*).

rift *vb* to split:—*n* **1** a split or crack in the gr ound. **2** a disagr eement between two friends (*a rift between neighbours*).

rig *vb* (**rigged**[1], **rig'ging**) **1** to pr ovide clothes (*rig the child out for the party*). **2** to pr ovide tools or equipment. **3** to pr ovide (a ship) with ropes, sails, etc. **4** to set up (*rig up a shelter*). **5** to arrange wrongly to produce a desired result, often an unfair or unlawful one (*rig the election*):—*n* the particular way in which a ship's masts, sails, etc, are arranged.

rig'ging *n* a ship's spars, ropes, etc.

right [rīt] *adj* **1** corr ect (*the right answer*). **2** true (*is it right to say he left early?*). **3** just, morally correct (*it is not right to let him go unpunished*). **4** straight (*go right ahead*). **5** on the side of the right hand (*stand at her right side*). **6** in good condition (*call a plumber to put the washing machine right*). **7** suitable, appr opriate (*the right man for the job*):—*vb* **1** to put back in position, to set in order. **2** to mend, to corr ect:—*n* **1** that which is correct, good or true (*they are in the right*). **2** something to which one has a just claim (*freedom of speech is a right*). **3** the right-hand side (*stand on her right*). **4** in politics, the party or group holding the more traditional, conservative beliefs (*a politician of the right*):—*adv* **1** straight. **2** exactly. **3** to the right-hand side.

right angle *n* an angle of 90 degrees.

righteous [rī'-tyês] *adj* **1** having just cause (*righteous indignation*). **2** good-living, virtuous (*a righteous life/a righteous man*):—*n* **right'eousness**.

right'ful *adj* lawful, just (*the rightful owner*).

right'ly *adv* **1** justly (*rightly or wrongly he was blamed*). **2** correctly (*we rightly assumed he would refuse*).

right of way *n* the right of the public to make use of a certain road, path or track.

ri'gid *adj* **1** that cannot be bent (*a rigid frame*). **2** stern, strict, not willing to change (*rigid in his views*). **3** not to be changed (*rigid rules*):— *n* **rigid'ity**.

rig'marole *n* long and confused or meaningless talk (*give clear instructions, not a rigmarole*).

rig'our *n* (*fml*) strictness, severity, harshness (*the rigours of life in the orphanage*):—*adj* **rig'orous**.

rig-out *n* one's clothes (*a brightly coloured rig-out*).

rill *n* (*lit*) a small stream.

rim *n* **1** the outer hoop of a wheel. **2** the outer edge, brim (*the rim of the glass*).

rime[1] *n* white or hoar frost.

rime[2] *old spelling of* **rhyme**.

ri'my *adj* covered with hoar frost (*rimy fields*).

rind *n* **1** the skin of some fruits (*lemon rind*). **2** the skin of bacon, cheese, etc. **3** the bark of trees.

ring[1] *n* **1** anything in the form of a circle (*the children gathered in a ring*). **2** a hoop of gold or other metal for the finger (*a wedding ring*). **3** a space enclosed by ropes for a boxing match:— *vb* (*pt, pp* **ringed'**) to surround, to encircle.

ring[2] *vb* (*pt* **rang**, *pp* **rung**) **1** to make a clear sound as a bell. **2** to cause a bell to sound (*ring the doorbell*). **3** to echo (*his voice ringing in her ears*):—*n* the sound of a bell.

ring'leader *n* the leader of a gang (*police failed to catch the ringleader*).

ring'let *n* a curl of hair (*a little girl with ringlets falling to her shoulders*).

ring'worm *n* a skin disease causing circular hairless patches.

rink *n* **1** a level stretch of ice for skating or curling. **2** a floor for roller-skating. **3** a level piece of ground for playing bowls.

rinse *vb* **1** to wash by pouring water over (*rinse the cup under the tap*). **2** to dip in water and wash lightly. **3** to put in clean water to remove soap (*wash the clothes by hand and rinse them*).

ri'ot *n* **1** a noisy or violent disorder caused by a crowd (*there was a riot when the police arrested the protester*). **2** (*inf*) something or someone very funny (*the comedian is a riot*). **3** a bright and splendid show (*a riot of colour*):—**read the riot act** give clear warning that unruly behaviour must stop:—**run riot** to go wild, to go out of control (*with the teacher gone the children would run riot*).

ri'otous *adj* noisy, disorderly (*a riotous party*).

rip *vb* (**ripped'**, **rip'ping**) to tear or cut open, to strip off (*she ripped her skirt on the fence*):—*n* a tear, a rent.

rip'cord *n* a cord that when pulled opens a parachute.

ripe *adj* **1** ready to be gathered or picked, ready for eating (*ripe apples*). **2** suitable or ready for (*a company ripe for take-over*):—*n* **ripe'ness**.

ri'pen *vb* **1** to become ripe (*the apples would slowly ripen*). **2** to cause to become ripe (*ripen fruit in a greenhouse*).

rip'ple *n* **1** a little wave (*a ripple on the water*). **2** the sound of shallow water running over stones. **3** a sound resembling this (*a ripple of laughter*):—*vb* **1** to flow in ripples. **2** to cause tiny waves to appear on. **3** to flow with a murmuring sound.

rise *vb* (*pt* **rose**, *pp* **ri'sen**) **1** to get up from bed (*rise early*). **2** to stand up (*she rose to go*). **3** to go upwards (*smoke rising from the chimney*). **4** to increase (*prices rising*). **5** to rebel (*the people rose up against the king*). **6** to move to a higher position (*he has risen to become manager*). **7** (*of a river*) to have its source or beginning:—*n* **1** an increase (*a rise in pay*). **2** an upward slope. **3** a small hill:— **give rise to** to cause or bring about (*their relationship would give rise to scandal*):—**rise to the occasion** to do all that is necessary at a difficult time (*he was nervous about speaking in public but he rose to the occasion*):—**take a rise out of** (*inf*) to play a joke or trick on.

ris'ible *adj* laughable, ridiculous (*a risible suggestion*).

ri'sing *n* **1** the act of rising. **2** a rebellion (*a rising against the tyrant*).

risk *n* **1** danger. **2** possible harm or loss:— *vb* **1** to put in danger, to lay open to the possibility of loss (*risk his health/risk his life*). **2** to tak e the chance of something bad or unpleasant happening (*risk defeat/risk losing his business*).

risk'y *adj* dangerous (*a risky journey*).

ris'sole *n* meat, poultry or fish minced, made into small rolls and fried (*turkey rissoles*).

risot'to *n* an Italian rice dish cooked with meat, vegetables, etc. (*mushroom risotto*).

rite *n* an order or arrangement of proceedings fixed by rule or custom (*marriage rites*).

rit'ual *adj* having to do with or done as a rite (*a ritual sacrifice*):—*n* **1** a set of rites. **2** ceremonies performed to worship God.

ri'val *n* **1** one who is tr ying to do better than another (*rivals for the same girl*). **2** a competitor for the same prize (*rivals in the tennis competition*):—*vb* (**ri'valled, ri'valling**) to be as good or nearly as good as (*her beauty rivals her sister's*):—*n* **ri'valry**.

rive *vb* (*old*) to split.

riv'er *n* a large running stream of water.

riv'et *n* a bolt driven through metal plates, etc, to fasten them together and then hammered flat at both ends:—*vb* **1** to fasten with rivets (*rivet the metal doors together*). **2** to fix (the eyes or mind) firmly upon (*they were riveted by the magician's tricks*).

riv'eter *n* one who rivets.

riv'ulet *n* a small stream.

roach *n* a small freshwater fish.

road *n* **1** a pr epared public way for travelling on (*the road was icy*). **2** a str eet (*he lives in the next road*). **3** a way (*the road to London*). **4** *pl* a place near the shore where ships may anchor.

road'hog *n* (*inf*) a dangerously reckless motorist.

road'house *n* a public house or restaurant on or near a highway.

road'stead *n* roads.

roam *vb* to wander about (*wild animals roam the plain*).

roan *adj* of mixed colour, including much red:—*n* a horse of roan colour.

roar *vb* to give a roar (*roar in pain/roar with laughter*):—*n* **1** a loud shout or cr y (*he gave a roar of pain*). **2** the full loud cr y of a large animal (*the lion's roar*).

roast *vb* to cook before a fire or in an oven (*roast the meat slowly*):—*n* roasted meat (*have a roast for Sunday lunch*).

rob *vb* (**robbed', rob'bing**) **1** to steal fr om (*rob the rich/rob a bank*). **2** (*fml*) to cause someone not to get what he or she ought to get (*war robbed her of her sons*):—*n* **rob'ber**.

rob'bery *n* the act of robbing.

robe *n* **1** a long, loose-fitting garment. **2** *pl* clothes worn as a sign of rank or position:—*vb* to put on robes, to put robes on someone else.

rob'in, rob'in red'breast *n* a small red-breasted bird.

ro'bot *n* **1** a machine made to carr y out certain tasks usu done by people. **2** a person who does his or her work mechanically without thinking or asking questions.

robust' *adj* **1** healthy and str ong (*robust children*). **2** vigor ous, rough (*a robust sense of humour*).

roc *n* in Eastern fables, a huge bird able to carry off an elephant.

rock¹ *vb* **1** to move fr om side to side, or backward and forward in turn (*rock the cradle/rock the baby*). **2** to sway fr om side to side (*boats rocking on the waves*).

rock² *n* **1** the har d, solid part of the earth's crust. **2** a lar ge mass or piece of stone (*a rock fell from the cliff*). **3** a type of sweet made in sticks (*buy rock at the seaside*).

rock'er *n* a curved piece of wood fastened to the foot of a chair, cradle, etc, to enable it to rock (*fix rockers to the chair*).

rock'ery *n* part of a garden consisting of a heap of earth and large stones or small rocks with plants growing between them (*flowers growing in the rockery*).

rock'et *n* **1** a fir ework that flies up into the air as it is burning out, often used as a signal (*rockets went off on November 5th*). **2** a cylinder that is propelled through the air by a backward jet of gas. **3** a spacecraft launched in this way (*send a rocket into orbit*).

rock'ing horse *n* a toy horse on rockers.

rock salt *n* common salt found in solid lumps in the earth.

rock'y *adj* **1** full of r ocks (*a rocky shore*). **2** har d as rock. **3** shak y (*a rocky table*).

roco'co adj (esp of buildings or furniture) very highly or exaggeratedly decorated.

rod n 1 a straight slender stick or bar (a fishing rod). 2 a measur e of length (=5¹/₂ yards).

ro'dent n any animal that gnaws, e.g. a mouse or rat.

rodeo [rō-dā-ō] n 1 a gathering together of cattle for marking. 2 a display of riding skill by cowboys.

roe¹ n 1 a female deer (stags and roes). 2 a small type of deer.

roe² n all the eggs in a female fish (cod roe).

roe'buck n a male roe deer.

rogue [rōg] n 1 a dishonest person (the rogue stole money from the old lady). 2 a naughty mischievous child.

rogue elephant n a savage elephant driven out of its herd.

rogu'ish adj 1 dishonest. 2 mischievous, teasing (a roguish smile).

role n 1 the part played by an actor (he played the role of Hamlet). 2 one's actions or duties (his role in the company).

role model n a person whom some other people admire and try to copy (The footballer was a role model for many teenage boys).

roll vb 1 to move by going r ound and round, like a wheel or ball (roll the stone down the hill). 2 to rock or sway from side to side (ships rolling at anchor). 3 to flatten with a r oller (roll the pastry). 4 to mak e a loud long noise (the drums rolled):—n 1 paper , cloth, etc, rolled into the form of a cylinder. 2 a list of names (the school roll). 3 a ver y small loaf of bread (a roll with butter). 4 a turning or r ocking movement (roll his eyes). 5 a long-drawn- out noise (a roll of thunder).

roll call n the calling over of a list of names (the school roll call).

roll'er n 1 anything made in the form of a cylinder so that it can turn round and round easily (for flattening something) (garden rollers). 2 a long swelling wave.

Rollerblade™ (trademark) n a type of roller skate which has the wheels set in one straight line.

roll'er skate n a skate mounted on small wheels:—vb **roll'er-skate**.

roll'icking adj noisy and merry (a rollicking party).

roll'ing pin n a roller for kneading dough.

rol'y-pol'y n a pudding of paste spread with jam and rolled up for cooking.

Ro'man adj having to do with Rome.

Roman Catholic n a member of that part of the Christian church that is governed by the pope, the Bishop of Rome.

romance' n 1 a stor y of wonderful or fanciful events (a romance about a prince and a princess). 2 a love stor y (a writer of romances). 3 a love affair (she had several romances before she married):—adj (of a language) derived from Latin:—vb 1 to mak e up a story. 2 to tell lies.

Romanesque' n the style of architecture of the late Roman Empire:—also adj.

Roman numerals npl numbers represented by letters (e.g. IV, V, VI for 4, 5, 6, etc).

roman'tic adj 1 imaginative, fanciful (she has romantic notions of becoming a film star). 2 showing feelings of love (a romantic gesture). 3 dealing with love (a romantic novel).

roman type n ordinary upright type (not italics).

Rom'any n 1 a gipsy . 2 the gipsy language:— also adj.

romp vb 1 to play r oughly or noisily (children romping around the garden). 2 to do swiftly and easily (romp through the examinations):—n rough or noisy play.

rom'per n **rom'pers** npl a one-piece garment for a small child.

rood n 1 (old) a cross with an image of Christ fixed to it. 2 a measur e of area (=¹/₄ acre).

roof n 1 the outside upper covering of a house, building, vehicle, etc (mend the roof of the castle). 2 the upper part of the mouth:— vb to cover with a roof (roofed the new house).

rook n 1 a black bir d of the crow family. 2 a piece in chess:—vb (inf) to cheat, to swindle (the shopkeeper rooked many of her customers by over-charging).

rook'ery n a place where many rooks have their nests.

room n 1 an apartment in a house (three rooms upstairs). 2 space (room for three in the back). 3 space for fr ee movement (no room to dance). 4 scope (room for improvement). 5 pl lodgings.

room'y adj having plenty of space (a roomy car).

roost n the pole on which birds rest at night:—vb to rest or sleep on a roost.

roost'er n a cock.

root n 1 the part of a plant that is fixed in the earth and draws nourishment from the soil. 2 the beginning or origin, a first cause from which other things develop (the root of the problem). 3 a word from which other words are formed (from the Latin root). 4 a factor of a number that when multiplied by itself gives the original number:—vb 1 to take root (the plants are not rooting very well). 2 to fix firmly (he felt rooted to the spot). 3 to search about for (rooting around for misplaced keys).

root'ed adj fixed, deep, strongly felt (a rooted objection to people smoking).

rope n a strong thick cord, made by twisting together strands of hemp, wire, etc:—vb 1 to fasten with a rope (rope the donkeys together). 2 to mark off with a rope (rope off an area of the hall for the choir).

ro'sary n in the RC Church, a series of prayers, or a string of beads each of which represents a prayer in the series.

rose n 1 a beautiful, sweet-smelling flower growing on a thorny shrub (a bunch of roses). 2 a shrub bearing roses (plant roses). 3 a light red or pink colour (a dress of pale rose). 4 a nozzle full of holes at the end of the spout of a watering can.

ro'seate adj (fml) rose-coloured.

rose'mary n an evergreen sweet-smelling shrub used as a herb in cooking (lamb flavoured with rosemary).

rosette n 1 a badge, like a rose in shape, made of ribbon (the politicians all wore their rosettes). 2 a rose-shaped ornament carved in stone, etc.

rose'wood n a hard dark-coloured wood smelling of roses when fresh cut (a table made of rosewood).

Rosh Hashana (or **Hashanah**) n the Jewish New Year festival, held in September.

ros'in n resin in solid form.

ros'ter n a list showing the order in which people are to go on duty (the duty roster).

ros'trum n a platform for a public speaker.

ros'y adj 1 red. 2 giving cause for hope.

rot vb (rott'ed, rott'ing) 1 to go bad from age or lack of use, to decay (fruit rotting on the trees). 2 to cause to decay (damp had rotted the woodwork):—n 1 decay (rot in the wood panelling). 2 a disease of sheep. 3 (inf) nonsense (talk rot).

ro'ta n a list showing the order in which people are to go on duty and a list of duties set down in order (a rota for housework).

Rota'rian n a member of the Rotary Club.

ro'tary adj turning round on an axle.

Rotary Club n a world-wide friendly society

rotate' vb 1 to turn as if round a centre or axis (wheels rotating). 2 to move like a wheel (trainees are rotating from department to department)

rota'tion n 1 movement around a centre or axis. 2 a regular order repeated again and again (rotation of crops).

rote n:—**by rote** (fml) learned by heart but not understood (learn spelling rules by rote).

rott'en adj 1 decaying, having gone bad (rotten fruit). 2 (inf) mean (a rotten thing to do).

rott'er n (inf) a worthless person (he was a rotter to his wife and children).

rotund' adj round, fattish (a rotund little man):— n **rotund'ity**.

rotun'da n a round building or room.

rou'ble n a Russian silver coin.

roué [rö'-ā] n (fml) one leading a wild or wicked life (he is a roué who drinks and gambles).

rouge [röj] n red colouring for the cheeks (she wears too much rouge).

rough [ruf] adj 1 not smooth, uneven (a rough road surface). 2 wild, stormy (rough weather). 3 not polite (rough manners). 4 not gentle (a rough voice). 5 coarse, violent (rough hooligan). 6 badly finished (a rough building job). 7 not exact (a rough estimate):—n a violent badly-behaved person.

rough'cast adj covered with a coarse plaster of lime and gravel.

rough'en vb to make or become rough (hands roughened by scrubbing floors).

rough-hew' vb to shape roughly.

rough'-rider n one who breaks in horses.

rough'-shod adj (of horses) having shoes with sticking-out nail heads to prevent slipping on bad roads.

roulette' *n* a gambling game played on a revolving board with a ball that falls into one of a number of holes when the board ceases spinning (*play roulette at the casino*).

round *adj* like a ball or circle in shape:—*n* **1** a round object. **2** a duty visit to all the places under one's care (*the doctor's rounds*). **3** a part song in which singers join at different times and begin again when they have finished. **4** a shell or bullet for firing. **5** a division of a boxing match (*a knockout in the second round*). **6** a complete part of a knock- out competition (e.g. in football). **7** a game of golf. **8** a spell or outburst (*a round of applause*):—*adv* **1** in the opposite direction (*he turned round*). **2** in a circle (*stand all round*). **3** fr om one person to another (*pass the wine round*). **4** fr om place to place (*drive round*):—*prep* **1** on ever y side of (*sit round the table*). **2** with a cir cular movement about (*sail round the world*):—*vb* **1** to give a round shape to (*he rounded the corners with sandpaper*). **2** to go ar ound (*ships rounding the bay*).

round'about *n* **1** a merr y-go-round (*children played on the roundabout in the park*). **2** a meeting place of roads with a circular island which vehicles must go until they turn off (*give way at the roundabout*):—*adj* **1** indir ect. **2** using too many words.

roun'delay *n* a short lively song with a chorus.

roun'ders *npl* a team game played with ball and bat.

Round'head *n* a member of the Puritan or Parliamentary party in the 17th century civil war in England (*Oliver Cromwell's Roundheads*).

round'ly *adv* plainly (*tell her roundly what he thought*).

round robin *n* a written request, protest, etc, with the signatures written to form a circle so as not to show who signed it first.

roup *n* (*Scot*) an auction.

rouse *vb* **1** to awak en (*rouse from sleep*). **2** to stir up to action (*his words roused the crowd to rebellion*).

rous'ing *adj* stirring, exciting.

rout *vb* to defeat and put to disordered flight (*rout the enemy army*):—*n* **1** a disor derly and hasty

retreat after a defeat. **2** complete defeat (*a rout of the enemy*).

route [röt] *n* a way from one place to another (*take the scenic coastal route*).

route march *n* a march done by soldiers as a training exercise.

routine' *n* a regular way or order of doing things (*tired of her working routine*).

rove *vb* **1** to wander about. **2** to wander .

ro'ver *n* **1** a wander er (*too much of a rover to settle down*). **2** (*old*) a pirate. **3** formerly , a senior Boy Scout.

row[1] [rō] *n* a line of people or things (*a row of trees*).

row[2] [rō] *vb* to move a boat by means of oars:—*n* **1** a spell of r owing. **2** a trip in a boat moved by oars (*a row up the river*).

row[3] [rou] *n* **1** noise, disturbance (*the row from the party next door*). **2** a quarr el (*a family row*). **3** a public ar gument (*a row over prison escapes*):—*vb* (*inf*) to quarrel (*husband and wife rowing*).

row'an *n* a tree with bright red berries.

row'dy *adj* noisy and quarrelsome (*a rowdy football crowd*):—*n* a rowdy person, a hooligan (*rowdies fighting in the street*):—*n* **row'dyism**.

row'el *n* the little spiked wheel at the end of a spur.

row'lock *n* a U-shaped rest for an oar on the side of a rowing boat.

roy'al *adj* **1** having to do with a king or queen (*the royal family*). **2** splendid, kingly (*a royal feast*).

roy'alist *n* a supporter of a king or queen.

roy'alty *n* **1** a r oyal person or persons (*royalty was present at the dinner*). **2** a shar e of the profits paid to authors, inventors, etc, for the use of their work (*receive royalties for her work*).

rub *vb* (**rubbed'**, **rub'bing**) to move one thing to and fro against another (*he rubbed his eyes*):—*n* act of rubbing (*a rub with a damp cloth*).

rub'ber[1] *n* **1** a tough elastic substance made fr om the juice of certain tropical trees (*tyres made of rubber*). **2** a piece of rubber used to r emove marks by rubbing (*a rubber to remove her mistake*).

rub'ber[2] *n* an odd number of games in a competition, esp in cards, the person or side winning the greater number being the winner (*a rubber of bridge*).

rub'bish *n* 1 that which is thrown away as useless, useless material (*put the rubbish in the bin*). 2 nonsense (*talk rubbish*).

rub'ble *n* broken pieces of bricks or stones (*search the rubble for earthquake survivors*).

ru'bicund *adj* (*fml*) red-faced.

ru'bric *n* a heading or instruction put into the middle of a text or in the margin, usu in red or otherwise different lettering.

ru'by *n* a red precious stone (*a ring with a valuable ruby*):—*adj* red.

ruck[1] *n* a wrinkle, a crease (*smooth the rucks in the sheet on the bed*):—*vb* to wrinkle or crease.

ruck[2] *n* 1 the mass of or dinary people (*dreams of getting out of the ruck and becoming famous*). 2 the 'also -rans' in a race. 3 in rugby, a loose scrum.

ruck'sack *n* a bag carried on the back and held in position by straps over the shoulders.

rud'der *n* a flat hinged plate at the stern of a ship or the tail of an aircraft for steering.

rud'dy *adj* 1 reddish. 2 a healthy r ed.

rude *adj* 1 impolite (*the child was rude to the teacher*). 2 sudden and unpleasant (*a rude shock*) 3 (*old*) roughly made (*a rude hut*). 4 (*old*) uncivilized, untaught, vulgar.

rudimen'tary *adj* simple, elementary, undeveloped (*a few rudimentary rules*).

ru'diments *npl* simple but necessary things to be learned about a subject before it can be studied thoroughly (*learn the rudiments of cookery*).

rue[1] *vb* (*fml*) to be sorry for (having done something) (*she rued ever having married*).

rue[2] *n* an evergreen plant with bitter-tasting leaves.

rue'ful *adj* sorrowful, regretful (*a rueful smile*).

ruff *n* a stiff frilled collar worn in olden times (*ruffs were worn in Tudor times*).

ruff'ian *n* a rough brutal fellow, a violent lawbreaker (*mugged by a gang of ruffians*):—*adj* **ruffianly**.

ruffle *vb* 1 to disturb the smoothness of, to disarrange (*the wind ruffling her hair*). 2 to anger or annoy (*he was ruffled by her comments*):—*n* a frill (*a party dress with ruffles*).

rug *n* 1 a mat for the floor (*a rug on the floor*). 2 a thick woollen coverlet or blank et (*put a rug over the lady's legs*).

rug'by *n* a form of football in which the ball, oval in shape, may be carried in the hands.

rug'ged *adj* 1 rough, uneven (*rugged coastline*). 2 str ongly built (*rugged young men*).

ru'in *n* 1 destruction (*ancient buildings fallen into ruin*). 2 downfall, overthr ow, state of having lost everything of value (*the company faced ruin during the recession*). 3 r emains of old buildings (*often pl*) (*visit the castle ruins*):—*vb* 1 to destroy (*all chances of success were ruined/the floods ruined her carpets*). 2 to cause to lose everything of value (*he was ruined when he lost the lawsuit*).

ruina'tion *n* 1 destruction. 2 overthr ow.

ru'inous *adj* likely to cause ruin (*ruinous gambling debts*).

rule *n* 1 government (*under foreign rule*). 2 a regulation or order (*school rules*). 3 an official or accepted standard (*as a rule he is home by midnight*). 4 the usual way that something happens (*spelling rules*):—*vb* 1 to govern, to manage (*a king ruling the country*). 2 to give an official decision (*the judge ruled that he go to prison*). 3 to draw a straight line with the help of a ruler.

rul'er *n* 1 one who governs or r eigns (*rebel against their ruler*). 2 a flat r od for measuring length (*draw a straight line with a ruler/measure with a ruler*).

rul'ing *adj* greatest, controlling (*the ruling party*):—*n* a decision (*the ruling of the judge*).

rum *n* spirit made from sugar cane.

rum'ba *n* a dance of Cuban origin.

rum'ble *vb* to make a low rolling noise (*thunder rumbling*):—*also n*.

ru'minant *adj* chewing the cud (*ruminant animals such as cows*):—*n* an animal that chews the cud.

ru'minate *vb* 1 to chew the cud (*cows ruminating*). 2 (*fml*) to think deeply (*ruminating about his chances of success*).

rum'mage *vb* to search thoroughly but untidily (*rummage through her bag for a comb*):—*also n*.

rum'my *n* a card game.

ru'mour n 1 a widely known story that may not be true (*he is not in prison—that was just a rumour*). 2 common talk, gossip (*a story based on rumour*).

rump n 1 the end of an animal's backbone. 2 the buttocks (*smack the horse's rump*).

rum'ple vb to crease, to spoil the smoothness of (*clothes rumpled after the long journey*).

rum'pus n a noisy disturbance or quarrel, an uproar (*there was a rumpus when the concert was cancelled*).

run vb (ran, run'ning, pp run) 1 to move quickly (*run to catch the bus*). 2 to move from one place to another (*a train running from London to Glasgow*). 3 to take part in a race (*he runs in local race meetings*). 4 to flow (*blood running from the wound*). 5 to organize or manage (*she runs the local branch of the company*). 6 to smuggle (*run drugs across the border*). 7 to last or continue (*a play running for a year*):—n 1 act of running (*go for a run*). 2 a trip or journey (*a run in the car*). 3 the length of time for which something runs (*a run of six months*). 4 a widespread demand for (*a sudden run on swimsuits*). 5 an enclosed place for animals or fowls (*a chicken run*). 6 the unit of scoring in cricket (*he made a hundred runs*):—**run down** 1 to say bad things about (*she is supposed to be a friend but she is always running her down*). 2 to stop working because of lack of power (e.g. because a spring is unwound) (*a clock running down*):—**run over** 1 to read or repeat quickly (*run over the words of the poem*). 2 to knock over in a vehicle (*she ran over the dog*).

run'away n 1 a deserter, one running away (*police looking for a runaway*). 2 an animal or vehicle out of control.

rune n a letter of an old Germanic alphabet, used in carving inscriptions:—adj **ru'nic**.

rung n a step of a ladder (*climb the ladder rung by rung*).

run'nel n (*fml*) a small stream.

run'ner n 1 one who runs (*the runners in the race*). 2 a messenger (*a runner for the advertising agency*). 3 a long spreading stem of a plant. 4 a long narrow cloth for a table or carpet for a stair. 5 any device on which something slips or slides along (*the runners on the sledge*).

run'ner-up n the person or team second to the winner.

running adj 1 going on all the time (*a running commentary*). 2 in succession (*two years running*):—n 1 the act of moving quickly. 2 that which runs or flows:—**in the running** with a chance of success.

run'ning board n a footboard running along the side of a car or railway engine.

run'way n a flat road along which an aircraft runs before taking off or after landing.

rupee [rö'-pee] n a silver coin, the unit of value in India and Pakistan.

rup'ture n 1 a clean break. 2 a quarrel or disagreement. 3 the thrusting of part of the intestine through the muscles of the abdomen:—vb 1 to break. 2 to thrust. 3 to quarrel.

ru'ral adj having to do with the country or its way of life (*the rural way of life*).

ruse n a trick (*a ruse to get into the party*).

rush[1] vb 1 to move quickly and with force (*he rushed to help her*). 2 to capture by a sudden quick attack (*rush the enemy fortress*). 3 to do hastily (*rush the job*). 4 to make another hurry (*rush him to make a decision*):—n 1 a fast and forceful move (*a rush towards the exit*). 2 a sudden advance (*a rush by the enemy army*). 3 hurry (*always in a rush*). 4 a sudden demand (*a rush on toys at Christmas*).

rush[2] n a tall grass-like plant growing in damp or marshy ground.

rusk n a light crisp cake or biscuit (*the baby nibbled on the rusk*).

rus'set adj of a reddish-brown colour (*russet hair*):—n a type of apple.

rust n the red coating formed on iron and steel left in a damp place:—vb to decay by gathering rust (*water pipes rusting through*).

rus'tic adj (*fml*) having to do with the country or country people (*a rustic way of life*):—n (*lit*) a countryman, a peasant.

rus'ticate vb 1 (*fml*) to live in the country. 2 to send away from university for a time, as a punishment.

rus'tle[1] vb to make a low whispering sound (*autumn leaves rustling in the wind*):—also n.

rus'tle[2] vb to steal (cattle):—n **rus'tler**.

rust'y adj 1 covered with rust. 2 out of practice

(*her piano playing is a bit rusty*).

rut *n* a deep track made by a wheel (*ruts in the road made by lorries*):—**in a rut** so tied by habits and customs that one is no longer interested in new or better methods (*in a rut and looking for another job*).

ruth'less *adj* cruel, merciless, showing no pity (*a ruthless judge who imposes harsh sentences*).

rye *n* a grain used for making bread.

rye grass *n* a type of grass used as fodder for animals.

S

Sab'bath *n* **1** the holy day of the Jewish week, Saturday. **2** Sunday.

sab'le *n* **1** a type of weasel with dark-coloured fur. **2** its fur:—*adj* black, dark.

sab're *n* a heavy sword with a slightly curved blade.

sac *n* a small bag of liquid inside an animal or plant.

saccharin(e) [sa'-ka-rin(reen)] *n* a very sweet substance used instead of sugar.

sachet [sa'-shā] *n* a small, sealed envelope or bag used to contain shampoo, perfume, etc.

sack¹ *n* **1** a bag made of coarse cloth for holding flour, wool, etc. **2** (*inf*) dismissal from a job (*get the sack*):—*vb* (*inf*) to dismiss someone from his or her job.

sack² *vb* to rob and lay waste (a town) after capturing it:—*also n.*

sack'cloth, sack'ing *ns* cloth from which sacks are made:—**sackcloth and ashes** signs of great sorrow.

sac'rament *n* a religious ceremony that Christians believe brings special blessings to those taking part (e.g. Baptism).

sac'red *adj* holy, set apart for the service of God (*sacred music*).

sac'rifice *n* **1** an offering to a god. **2** the act of giving up of one's own will something desirable. **3** something given up in this way (*parents making sacrifices for their children*):—*vb* **1** to make an offering to God. **2** to give up something held dear:—*adj* **sacrific'ial.**

sac'rilege *n* disrespectful or insulting treatment of something holy:—*adj* **sacri-leg'ious.**

sac'rosanct *adj* **1** very holy. **2** to be treated only with great reverence or respect (*private papers regarded as sacrosanct*).

sad *adj* sorrowful.

sad'den *vb* to make sad.

sad'dle *n* **1** a seat for a rider on a horse or bicycle. **2** meat taken from an animal's back (*saddle of lamb*):—*vb* **1** to put a saddle on. **2** to give (to another) something troublesome (*saddle others with one's responsibilities*):—**in the saddle** in control.

sadist [sā'-dêst] *n* one who takes pleasure in inflicting cruelty:—*n* **sa'dism:**—*adj* **sa-dis'tic.**

safari [sa-fä'-ri] *n* a hunting expedition.

safe *adj* **1** out of harm or danger (*children safe in bed*). **2** not likely to cause harm, danger or risk (*a safe job*):—*n* a strong box or room for valuables:—*adv* **safe'ly.**

safe'guard *n* a protection:—*also vb.*

safe'ty *n* freedom from danger, harm or loss.

safety match *n* a match that lights only on a special surface.

saf'fron *n* a type of crocus, orange-yellow in colour, used to colour or flavour food:—*adj* deep yellow.

sag *vb* (**sagged', sag'ging**) **1** to sink in the middle. **2** to droop.

saga [sä'-gä] *n* **1** an Icelandic tale of legendary heroes. **2** a very long story with many episodes.

sagacious [sa-gā'-shês] *adj* wise, clever:—*n* **saga'city.**

sage¹ *adj* wise:—*n* a wise person.

sage² *n* **1** a sweet-smelling plant, used as a herb in cooking. **2** a greyish-green colour.

sago [sā'-go] *n* a type of flour, used in puddings.

said *pt of* **say.**

sail *n* **1** a canvas spread to catch the wind. **2** a ship. **3** a trip in a boat. **4** the arm of a windmill:—*vb* **1** to travel on water. **2** to move along without effort.

sail'or *n* a seaman.

saint *n* **1** a very good person. **2** a title given to a holy man or woman:—*adj* **saint'ly:**—*adj* **saintlike.**

sake¹ *n:*—**for the sake of** in order to get (*for the sake of peace and quiet*):—**for my sake** in order to please me.

sala'cious *adj* indecent.

sal'ad *n* a dish of lettuce and other raw vegetables, sometimes including meat, fish, cheese or fruit, usu served with a dressing.

salaman'der *n* a lizard-like animal, once believed able to live in fire.

sal'ary *n* the fixed sum of money paid to someone for work over an agreed length of time, usu a month or a year.

sale *n* **1** the act of selling. **2** the exchange of anything for money. **3** a selling of goods more cheaply than usual (*January sales*).

sales'man, sales'woman, sales'person *ns* a person engaged in selling products.

sales'manship *n* skill in selling things.

salient [sā'-li-ênt] *adj* **1** sticking outwards. **2** prominent, most important (*the salient points of his proposal*):—*n* in war, a narrow strip of land jutting into enemy territory.

saline [sā'-līn] *adj* containing salt:—*n* a salt lake or spring.

sali'va *n* the liquid that keeps the mouth moist, spittle:—*adj* **sali'vary**.

sal'low[1] *n* a type of willow tree.

sal'low[2] *adj* having a slightly yellow skin.

sal'ly *n* **1** a sudden attack made by the defenders of a fort, etc, against its attackers. **2** a clever and amusing remark:—*vb* to rush out suddenly.

salmon [sam'-ên] *n* a large fish with pinkish flesh and silver scales, greatly valued for food and sport.

salon [sal'-o(ng)] *n* **1** a reception room. **2** a building or room used for a particular business, such as hairdressing, the selling of fashionable clothes, etc.

saloon' *n* **1** a large public room in a passenger ship. **2** a closed motor car. **3** (*Amer*) a public house.

sal'sa *n* **1** a type of Latin American dance music. **2** a spicy tomato sauce eaten with Mexican food.

salt *n* **1** a white mineral substance, obtained from sea water or by mining, used to give flavour to or to preserve food. **2** a compound produced by the action of acid on the hydrogen atoms of metals. **3** an experienced sailor:—*vb* to flavour or preserve with salt:—*adj* containing or tasting of salt:—*adj* **salt'y**.

salt'cellar *n* a small vessel for holding salt for use at table.

sal'tire *n* a St Andrew's cross (X).

saltpe'tre *n* a white mineral substance used in making gunpowder, as a fertilizer, etc.

salu'brious *adj* health-giving (*a salubrious climate*).

sal'utary *adj* **1** having good effects (*a salutary, if painful, experience*). **2** health-giving.

saluta'tion *n* a greeting.

salute' *vb* **1** to greet. **2** to make a gesture of respect by raising the right hand to the forehead or cap, firing artillery, etc:—*n* **1** the gesture of respect made by saluting. **2** the firing of guns as a welcome or mark of respect.

sal'vage *n* **1** the saving of a ship or its cargo from loss. **2** the saving of property from fire. **3** property saved in this way:—*vb* to save from destruction, shipwreck, fire, etc.

salva'tion *n* **1** the saving from sin and the punishment due to it. **2** the means of this.

salve *n* a healing ointment.

sal'ver *n* a tray.

sam'ba *n* **1** a dance of South American origin. **2** music for this dance.

same *adj* in no way different (*the same person/the same mistake*):—*n* the same person or thing (*I'll have the same*):—*adv* in a like manner.

same'ness *n* lack of change or variety.

samovar' *n* a tea urn or large teapot used in Russia.

sam'pan *n* a small flat-bottomed boat used in China.

sam'ple *n* a part or piece given to show what the whole is like (*a sample of the artist's work*):—*vb* to try something to see what it is like (*sample the cake*).

sanato'rium *n* (*pl* **sanato'riums, sanato'ria**) a hospital for people whose cure requires long rest and special care, esp originally those suffering from disease of the lungs.

sanc'tify *vb* to make holy or sacred:—*n* **sanctifica'tion**.

sanctimo'nious *adj* pretending to be holy or religious.

sanc'tion *n* **1** permission (*with the sanction of the authorities*). **2** a punishment or penalty imposed to make people obey a law (*trade sanctions imposed on countries invading other countries*):—*vb* to permit.

sanc'tity *n* holiness.

sanc'tuary *n* **1** a place where one is safe from pursuit or attack. **2** a place providing protection, such as a reserve for wildlife. **3** the part of the church where the altar is placed.

sanc'tum *n* one's private room.

sand *n* **1** a dust made of tiny particles of rock, shell, etc. **2** *pl* stretches of sand on the seashore.

san'dal *n* a type of shoe to protect the sole, leaving the upper part of the foot largely or wholly uncovered except by cross-straps, etc.

san'dalwood *n* various kinds of scented wood.

sand' martin *n* a small swallow that nests in sandy banks.

sand'paper *n* paper made rough by a coat of sand, used for smoothing and polishing.

sand'piper *n* a wading bird of the snipe family.

sand'shoe *n* a light canvas shoe with a rubber sole, a plimsoll.

sand'stone *n* a stone made up of sand pressed together.

sand'wich *n* two slices of bread with meat, paste, cheese, salad, etc, between:—*vb* to fit between two other things.

sand'y *adj* **1** covered with sand. **2** yellowish-red in colour.

sane *adj* **1** sound in mind. **2** sensible.

sang-froid [so(ng)-frwa'] *n* calmness, self-control.

san'guinary *adj* **1** bloody. **2** blood-thirsty.

san'guine *adj* **1** full of hope, cheerful. **2** red (*a sanguine complexion*).

san'itary *adj* having to do with health or cleanliness.

sanita'tion *n* **1** the process or methods of keeping places clean and hygienic. **2** a drainage or sewage system.

san'ity *n* **1** soundness of mind. **2** good sense.

San'skrit *n* an ancient language of India:—*also adj*.

sap *n* the juice that flows in plants, trees, etc, and nourishes the various parts:—*vb* (**sapped', sap'ping**) to weaken gradually (*sap one's strength*).

sa'pient *adj* wise:—*n* **sa'pience**.

sap'ling *n* a young tree.

sapphire [sa'-fîr] *n* **1** a precious stone of a rich blue colour. **2** its colour:—*also adj*.

sar'casm *n* a mocking remark intended to hurt another's feelings.

sarcas'tic *adj* **1** given to sarcasm. **2** mocking, scornful.

sarcoph'agus *n* (*pl* **sarcoph'agi**) a stone coffin.

sardine' *n* a small fish of the herring family.

sardon'ic *adj* humorous in a grim or bitter way, mocking.

sa'ri *n* the dress of Indian women, consisting of a length of cloth wrapped round and round the body.

sarong' *n* a Malay garment consisting of a length of cloth worn like a skirt by both men and women.

sartor'ial *adj* having to do with a tailor or with clothes (*sartorial elegance*).

sash¹ *n* an ornamental scarf worn round the waist or across the body over one shoulder.

sash² *n* a window frame.

Sa'tan *n* the Devil.

satan'ic *adj* having to do with the Devil.

satch'el *n* a little bag worn on the shoulder or back for carrying books, etc.

sate *vb* to satisfy a desire fully.

sat'ellite *n* **1** a body that moves through the heavens in orbit round a larger body, including artificial bodies launched into orbit by man to collect information or act as part of a communications system. **2** one who depends completely on another. **3** a country that is totally in the power of another.

satellite dish *n* dish-shaped device on the outside of a building for receiving television signals broadcast via satellite.

satellite television *n* the broadcasting of television programmes via satellite rather than by television masts on land.

sa'tiate *vb* **1** to satisfy fully. **2** to give more than enough.

satiety [sã-tî'-ê-ti], **satia'tion** *ns* **1** the state of having more than enough. **2** over-fullness.

sat'in *n* a silk cloth that is shiny on one side.

sat'inwood *n* the smooth wood of a tropical tree.

sat'ire *n* a composition in prose or verse in which persons, customs, actions, etc, are mocked and made to appear ridiculous.

satir'ical *adj* holding up to scorn.

sat'irist *n* one who writes satires.

sat'irize *vb* to ridicule in satire.

satisfac'tion *n* **1** contentment. **2** the feeling of having enough.

satisfac'tory *adj* **1** good enough (*a satisfactory answer*). **2** quite good (*satisfactory work*).

sat'isfy *vb* **1** to give all that is requested or expected (*satisfy her demand*). **2** to be enough (*satisfy their appetites*). **3** to convince (*satisfy them that he was innocent*).

sat'urate *vb* to soak something so thoroughly that it cannot take in any more liquid:—*n* **satura'tion**.

Sat'urday *n* the seventh day of the week.

sat'urnine *adj* gloomy.

sat'yr *adj* a mythical creature, half-man, half-goat.

sauce n 1 a liquid, either savoury or sweet, poured on foods to improve or bring out the flavour. 2 (inf) cheek, impudence.

sauce'pan n a cooking pot with a lid and handle.

sau'cer n a small plate placed under a cup.

sau'cy adj rude, cheeky.

saun'ter vb to walk slowly, to stroll:—also n.

saus'age n a roll of minced meat in a thin skin.

sav'age adj 1 wild, untamed or uncivilized (savage animals or tribes). 2 fierce, cruel (savage blows):—n 1 a member of a savage tribe. 2 a very cruel person.

sav'agery n 1 cruelty. 2 the state of being wild or uncivilized.

savan'na(h) n a grassy treeless plain.

save vb 1 to rescue from danger or harm. 2 to keep for future use (save string from parcels). 3 to keep money instead of spending it (save for one's old age):—prep except.

sa'ving grace n a good quality that helps one to overlook faults.

sa'vings npl money put aside for future use.

sa'viour n one who saves from danger or harm.

sa'vour n taste, flavour:—vb 1 to taste. 2 to have a taste of, to suggest the idea of (savour of disloyalty).

sa'voury adj 1 tasty, arousing appetite (savoury smells). 2 salty or sharp, rather than sweet (savoury pastries):—n an appetizing dish served at the beginning or end of dinner.

savoy' n a type of cabbage.

saw[1] n a tool with a toothed edge for cutting wood, etc:—vb to cut with a saw.

saw[2] n a wise traditional saying.

saw[3] pt of **see**.

saw'dust n small fragments of wood made by sawing.

saw'mill n a mill with a mechanical saw for cutting up wood.

sax'ifrage n a plant that grows among rocks.

sax'ophone n a brass wind instrument with keys.

say vb (pt said) 1 to utter in words, to speak. 2 to state (say what you mean):—n the right to give an opinion.

say'ing n a proverb, a remark commonly made.

scab n a crust that forms over a healing sore.

scab'bard n the sheath of a sword.

sca'bies n an itchy skin disease.

scaffold n the platform on which criminals are executed.

scaffolding n a framework of poles, etc, to support platforms from which people can work above ground level (e.g. when building a house).

scald vb to burn with hot liquid:—n a burn caused by hot liquid.

scale[1] n one of the thin flakes or flat plates on the skin of fish, reptiles, etc:—vb to remove the scales from (scale fish).

scale[2] n 1 the pan of a weighing machine. 2 (often pl) a balance or weighing machine.

scale[3] n 1 a series of successive musical notes between one note and its octave. 2 the size of a map compared with the extent of the area it represents (a scale of ten kilometres to the centimetre). 3 a measure (the scale on a thermometer). 4 a system of units for measuring (the decimal scale). 5 a system of grading (the social scale). 6 size, extent (entertain on a large scale):—vb to climb (scale the wall).

sca'lene adj (of a triangle) having unequal sides and angles.

scall'op n 1 an eatable shellfish with an uneven and toothed edge. 2 a series of even curves:—vb to cut in scallops.

scall'oped adj having an edge like a scallop.

scall'ywag n a rascal.

scalp n the skin and hairs on top of the head:—vb to cut off the scalp.

scal'pel n a light knife used by a surgeon.

scal'y adj covered with scales, like a fish.

scamp n a rascal.

scam'per vb to run quickly or hurriedly, as if afraid:—n a quick or hurried run.

scan vb (scanned', scan'ning) 1 to examine closely or carefully (scan the area for survivors). 2 to obtain an image of an internal part (of the body) by using e.g. X-rays, ultrasonic waves. 3 to mark the weak and strong syllables in a line of poetry:—n a medical examination in which part of the body is scanned (a brain scan).

scan'dal n 1 widespread talk about someone's wrongdoings, real or supposed (listen to scandal). 2 a disgrace (their failure to act is a scandal). 3 disgraceful behaviour that gives rise to widespread talk (a series of corruption scandals).

scan'dalize vb to shock.

scan'dalmonger n one who spreads stories harmful to the character of others.

scan'dalous adj disgraceful.

scan'ner n a piece of electronic medical equipment used to scan part of the body.

scan'sion n analysis of the rhythm of poetry.

scant adj barely enough, very little (*pay scant attention*).

scant'y adj barely enough, very little (*a scanty meal*).

scape'goat n one who takes the blame for wrong done by others.

scap'ula n (*pl* **scap'ulae**) the flat bone of the shoulder or shoulderblade.

scar[1] n the mark left by a healed wound:—*vb* (**scarred'**, **scar'ring**) to leave or cause a scar.

scar[2] n a cliff.

sca'rab n a beetle considered sacred in ancient Egypt.

scarce adj **1** few and har d to find (*such birds are scarce now*). **2** not enough (*food is scarce*).

scarce'ly adv hardly, surely not.

scarc'ity n shortage, lack of what is necessary.

scare vb to frighten:—*n* a fright, panic.

scare'crow n **1** anything (e.g. a dummy man) set up to frighten away birds. **2** someone dr essed in rags.

scarf n (*pl* **scarfs** or **scarves**) a strip of material worn around the neck and over the shoulders.

scar'ify vb to make many scratches or small cuts in.

scar'let n a bright red colour:—*also adj*.

scarlet fe'ver n a very infectious disease causing a red rash on the skin.

scarp n a steep slope.

scath'ing adj hurtful, bitter.

scat'ter vb **1** to thr ow about on all sides (*scatter confetti*). **2** to go away or drive in different directions (*crowds scattering*).

scat'erbrain n a foolish person:—*adj* **scat't'erbrained**.

scav'enger n an animal or person that searches for or lives on discarded or decaying material:—*vb* **sca'venge**.

scenario [shä-në'-ri-o] n a written outline of the main incidents in a play or film.

scene [seen] n **1** the place where something happens (*the scene of the crime*). **2** what one can

see before one from a certain viewpoint. **3** a distinct part of a play. **4** a painted background set up on the stage to represent the place of the action. **5** a quarrel or open show of strong feeling:—**behind the scenes** in private.

scen'ery n **1** the painted backgrounds set up during a play to represent the places of the action. **2** the general appearance of a countryside.

sce'nic adj **1** having to do with scenery. **2** picturesque.

scent n **1** a smell, esp a pleasant one. **2** the smell of an animal left on its tracks. **3** the sense of smell:—*vb* **1** to smell out. **2** to find by smelling. **3** to make smell pleasant.

sceptic [skep'-tik] n one who doubts:—*n* **scep'ticism**.

scep'tical adj having doubts.

sceptre [sep'-têr] n the staff held by a ruler as a sign of authority.

schedule [she'-dûl] n a list of details, a time-table (*production schedules*):—*vb* to plan.

scheme [skeem] n **1** a plan of what is to be done (*a work scheme*). **2** a plot (*a scheme to kill the president*):—*vb* **1** to plan. **2** to plot:—*n* **sche'mer**.

scherzo [skert'-sö] n a playful, lively passage in a musical composition.

schilling n formerly the monetary unit of Austria, until the introduction of the euro in January 2002.

schism [sizm] n a breaking-up into two or more parties.

schismat'ic adj breaking away from the main body:—*also n*.

schist n a rock of slaty structure.

scholar [skol'-êr] n **1** a learned person. **2** a school pupil.

schol'arly adj learned.

schol'arship n **1** learning. **2** wide knowledge. **3** a grant of money given to pupils or students to help pay for their education.

scholas'tic adj having to do with schools or scholars.

school[1] [skül] n **1** an institution in which instruction is given. **2** a group of writers, thinkers, painters, etc, having the same or similar methods, principles, aims, etc:—*vb* to train (*to school horses*):—*ns* **school'-master**, **school'mistress**.

school[2] [skül] n a large number of fish of the same kind swimming together, a shoal.

schoon'er n 1 a large sailing ship with two masts. 2 a kind of large glass (a schooner of sherry).

schottische [sho-teesh'] n a lively dance like a polka.

sciatic [see-at'-ik] adj having to do with the hip.

sciat'ica n pain in the hip or thigh.

sci'ence n 1 all that is known about a subject, arranged in a systematic manner (the science of geography). 2 the study of the laws and principles of nature (biology, physics and other branches of science). 3 trained skill (games requiring science rather than speed).

science fiction n a form of fiction which deals with imaginary future scientific developments or imaginary life in other planets, often abbreviated to **sci-fi**.

scientific adj 1 having to do with science. 2 done in a systematic manner.

sci'entist n one learned in one of the sciences.

sci-fi see science fiction.

scim'itar n a short curved sword, the blade being broadest near the point.

scin'tillate vb 1 to sparkle, to twinkle (diamonds scintillating in the candlelight). 2 to be witty, brilliant, etc (guests scintillating at the party).

scion [si'-on] n a descendant, a young member of a family.

sciss'ors n a cutting-instrument consisting of two blades moving on a central pin.

sclerosis [skle-rō'-sis] n a disease causing hardening of the arteries.

scoff vb to mock (at):—n mocking words, a jeer.

scold vb to find fault with, to rebuke:—n an ill-tempered woman:—n **scold'ing**.

scone [skon] n a small plain cake.

scoop vb 1 to gather and lift up, as with the hands (scoop up sand in one's hands). 2 to hollow out with a knife, etc (to scoop a hollow in the melon half):—n 1 a deep shovel for lifting grain, earth from a hole, etc. 2 a piece of important news known only to one newspaper.

scoot'er n 1 a child's toy vehicle with a footboard and two wheels, moved by pushing off the ground with one foot. 2 a kind of motor cycle.

scope n 1 freedom of movement, thought, etc, within certain limits (require scope to operate). 2 the range of matters being dealt with (the scope of the book). 3 opportunity (scope for improvement).

scorch vb 1 to burn the outside of (scorch the meat). 2 to singe or blacken by burning (scorched the shirt with the iron).

scorch'ing adj 1 very hot. 2 very fast.

score n 1 a set of twenty. 2 a mark or line cut on the surface of. 3 a note of what is to be paid. 4 in games, the runs, goals, points, etc, made by those taking part. 5 a piece of music written down to show the parts played by different instruments:—vb 1 to make marks or scratches on the surface of. 2 to gain an advantage. 3 to keep the score of a game. 4 to arrange music in a score:—**score off** to strike out:—**score' off** to get the better off:—n **scor'er.**

scorn vb 1 to feel contempt for. 2 to refuse to have anything to do with (scorn her friendly advances):—n contempt, complete lack of respect for.

scorn'ful adj mocking, full of contempt.

scor'pion n a small creature with eight legs and a lobster-like tail containing a poisonous sting.

scotch vb to put an end to, to stamp out.

scot'-free adj unharmed, unpunished.

Scots, Scot'tish adjs having to do with Scotland or its people.

scoun'drel n a thoroughly wicked person, a rascal:—adj **scoun'drelly.**

scour[1] vb to clean or brighten by rubbing.

scour[2] vb to go back and forward over, searching carefully (scour the fields for clues).

scourge [skurj] n 1 a whip. 2 a cause of great trouble or suffering:—vb 1 to whip. 2 to make suffer greatly.

scout n 1 one sent in front to see what lies ahead and bring back news. 2 a person employed to find new talent:—vb 1 to go out as a scout. 2 to search or explore (to scout around for an open shop).

Scout n a member of the Scout Association, a youth organization that stresses self-reliance and skill in a wide range of activities.

scowl vb to lower the brows and wrinkle the forehead in anger or disapproval:—also n.

scrag'gy adj thin and bony.

scram'ble vb 1 to climb using both hands and feet. 2 to move awkwardly or with difficulty. 3 to struggle to obtain (*scramble for a seat in the bus*):—*n* a pushing and struggling for something.

scram'bled eggs *npl* eggs beaten up and cooked in butter.

scrap *n* 1 a small piece (*scraps of cloth*). 2 a picture, often cut to shape, for pasting in a book. 3 *pl* what is left over (*dogs feeding on scraps*):—*vb* (**scrapped', scrap'ping**) to throw away as no longer useful (*scrap the plans*).

scrap'book *n* a book for keeping scraps, cuttings from newspapers, etc.

scrape *vb* 1 to clean by rubbing with an edged instrument. 2 to make a harsh, unpleasant sound by rubbing along. 3 to save or gather with difficulty (*scrape together the fare*):—*n* 1 a scratch. 2 something caused by scraping or its sound. 3 (*inf*) a small fight. 4 (*inf*) a difficult situation.

scrap heap *n* a place for waste material, a rubbish heap.

scrap'py *adj* made up of bits and pieces.

scratch *vb* 1 to mark or wound the surface with something pointed. 2 to rub with the nails to stop itching. 3 to tear with the nails or claws. 4 to rub out (*scratch his name from the list*). 5 to withdraw from a competition or contest:—*n* a slight mark or wound, esp one made by scratching:—*adj* 1 without a plus or minus handicap (*scratch golfer*). 2 put together hastily (*scratch meal*):—**up to scratch** as good as usual.

scrawl *vb* to write untidily or carelessly:—*n* untidy or careless handwriting.

scream *vb* to shout in a loud, high-pitched voice, to shriek:—*also n.*

scree *n* loose stones, etc, on a slope or at the foot of a cliff.

screech *vb* to utter a loud high-pitched cry:—*also n.*

screed *n* a long and uninteresting written statement.

screen *n* 1 a movable piece of furniture like a section of a fence that can be used to break a draught, to conceal part of a room, etc. 2 a wooden division in a building (e.g. that between the parts of a church used by the clergy and the laity). 3 a surface on which cinema film is shown. 4 the front glass surface of a television, word processor, etc, on which pictures or items of information are shown. 5 a sieve for separating smaller pieces of coal, etc, from larger:—*vb* 1 to protect (*trees screening the garden from the public gaze*). 2 to hide (*screen his son from the police*). 3 to put through a test (*screen all candidates for posts in the Foreign Office*). 4 to carry out medical tests on a large number of people to check whether they have a particular disease or not (*screen women over 50 for breast cancer*). 5 to show on film or television.

screw *n* 1 a type of nail with a spiral thread so that it can be twisted into wood, etc, instead of hammered. 2 the propeller of a ship. 3 a twist or turn:—*vb* 1 to fasten by means of a screw. 2 to twist. 3 (*inf*) to squeeze, to get everything possible from (*screw a rise out of the boss*):—**screw up one's courage** to be as brave as possible.

screw'driver *n* a tool that can fit into the slot in the head of a screw and turn it.

scrib'ble *vb* to write carelessly or hurriedly:—*n* something written quickly or carelessly.

scrim'mage *n* 1 a confused fight or struggle. 2 a rugby scrum.

scrimp *vb* to give or use too little (*scrimp on food*).

scrip *n* a paper showing that one holds shares in a company.

script *n* 1 handwriting. 2 a printing type like handwriting. 3 a written outline of the incidents in a film. 4 the text of a broadcast talk or play.

scrip'tural *adj* having to do with the Bible.

scrip'ture(s) *n* a holy book, such as the Bible.

scrofula *n* a disease causing swelling of the glands in the neck.

scroll *n* 1 a roll of parchment or paper. 2 in sculpture, a stone ornament like a scroll.

scrub¹ *vb* (**scrubbed', scrub'bing**) 1 to clean by rubbing hard, esp with a stiff brush. 2 (*inf*) to cancel, to remove.

scrub² *n* small stunted bushes or trees, brushwood.

scruff *n* the back of the neck.

scruffy *adj* shabby, untidy.

scrum *n* in rugby, a mass of players packed close together, trying to put the ball in play by making it come out on their own side.

scru'ple n 1 a small weight. 2 doubt or hesitation about doing something because one feels it is wrong:—vb to doubt or hesitate.

scru'pulous adj 1 very careful. 2 hesitating to do what may be wrong (too scrupulous to cheat).

scru'tinize vb to examine closely or carefully:—n **scrutineer'**.

scru'tiny n a close or careful examination.

scud vb (scud'ded, scud'ding) 1 to run quickly. 2 (of a ship) to sail quickly before a following wind:—n loose misty clouds driven along by the wind.

scuf'fle n a confused or disorderly struggle.

scull n one of a pair of short oars:—vb 1 to row with sculls. 2 to move a boat by rowing with one oar at the stern.

scull'ery n a room in which pots, dishes, etc, are washed.

sculp'tor n one skilled in sculpture.

sculp'ture n 1 the art of carving in wood, stone, etc. 2 a work of sculpture.

scum n 1 dirt and froth that gathers on the surface of liquid. 2 wicked or worthless people (the scum who mugged the old man).

scup'per n a hole in a ship's side to let water run off the deck:—vb 1 to sink (a ship) deliberately. 2 to wreck or ruin (scupper our chances).

scurf n small dry flakes of skin.

scurril'ity n dirty and insulting talk.

scur'rilous adj 1 using bad or indecent language. 2 very insulting.

scur'ry vb to run hurriedly:—also n.

scur'vy, n a disease caused by lack of fresh fruit or vegetables:—adj mean, nasty.

scut'tle[1] n a box or pail for keeping coal at the fireside.

scut'tle[2] n a hole with a lid in the deck or side of a ship:—vb to sink (a ship) by making a hole in it.

scut'tle[3] vb to run away hurriedly.

scythe [sîth] n a tool consisting of a long, curving, very sharp blade set at an angle to a long handle, used for cutting grass, etc:—vb to cut with a scythe.

sea n 1 the salt water that covers much of the earth's surface. 2 a large extent of this. 3 the ocean or part of it. 4 the swell of the sea. 5 a large amount or extent of anything (a sea of papers on the desk):—at sea 1 on the sea. 2 puzzled.

sea'board n the coast.

sea breeze n a wind blowing from sea to land.

sea dog n 1 an old sailor. 2 the seal.

sea'farer n 1 one who travels by sea. 2 a sailor.

sea'faring adj going to sea.

sea'going adj able to sail across the sea to other lands.

sea horse n the walrus.

sea kale n a type of vegetable like the cabbage.

seal[1] n 1 wax with a design, etc, stamped on it, used to fasten shut envelopes, boxes, etc. 2 a stamp with a design, initials, etc, engraved on it. 3 a substance or thing that closes, fixes or prevents leakage (a bottle seal):—vb 1 to fasten with a seal. 2 to close firmly. 3 to make airtight (seal jars of preserved fruit). 4 to confirm (seal the agreement).

seal[2] n a sea animal valued for its oil and fur.

sea legs npl the ability to walk on the deck of a tossing ship.

sea level n the level of the sea's surface at halftide.

seal'ing wax n a substance used for sealing letters.

sea lion n a large seal.

seam n 1 the line made by the stitches joining two pieces of cloth. 2 a vein of metal, coal, etc.

sea'man n a sailor.

sea mew n a seagull.

seam'stress n a woman who makes her living by sewing.

seam'y adj 1 marked with seams. 2 unpleasant (the seamy side of life).

seance [sā'-o(ng)s] n a meeting, esp one of spiritualists, people who believe they can call up the spirits of the dead.

sea'plane n an aeroplane with floats enabling it to take off from or to land on water.

sea'port n a town with a harbour.

sear vb 1 to burn with sudden powerful heat. 2 to wither (grass seared by the sun):—adj dry, withered.

search vb to look for, to explore, to examine in order to find:—n act of looking for, an inquiry, an examination:—n **search'er**.

search'ing adj thorough, testing thoroughly.

search'light n a powerful electric lamp able to throw a beam of light on distant objects.

sea'scape *n* a picture of a scene at sea.

sea'sick *adj* sick because of the rocking of a ship at sea.

sea'side *n* the land near or beside the sea.

sea'son[1] *n* **1** one of the divisions of the year into four (e.g. winter). **2** a time of the year noted for a particular activity (*the football season*).

sea'son[2] *vb* **1** to make (wood) hard and fit for use by drying gradually. **2** to add something to food to give it a good taste.

sea'sonable *adj* **1** happening at the right time (*seasonable advice*). **2** suitable to the season of the year (*seasonable weather*).

sea'sonal *adj* having to do with one or all of the seasons (*seasonal variations in the weather*).

sea'soning *n* anything added to food to bring out or improve its taste.

season ticket a ticket that can be used many times over a stated period.

seat *n* **1** anything on which one sits. **2** a piece of furniture for sitting on. **3** a place as member of the House of Commons or of a council. **4** a large house (*his country seat*). **5** the place where something is carried on (*the seat of government*):—*vb* **1** to place on a seat. **2** to have or provide seats for (*a hall seating 500*).

sea urchin *n* a sea creature living in a round prickly shell.

sea wall *n* a wall to keep out the sea.

sea'weed, sea wrack *ns* sea plants.

sea'worthy *adj* fit to go to sea.

secateurs [se'-kê-tèrz] *npl* a pair of shears for pruning.

secede' *vb* to break away from (*seceding from the union of states*).

seces'sion *n* act of seceding.

seclud'ed *adj* **1** out of the way (*a secluded part of the garden*). **2** private, quiet (*a secluded life*).

seclu'sion *n* quietness and privacy.

sec'ond *adj* coming immediately after the first:— *n* **1** one who comes after the first. **2** one who supports and assists another in a fight or duel. **3** the sixtieth part of a minute. **4** *npl* goods that because of some flaw are sold more cheaply:— *vb* **1** to support (*second a proposal*). **2** to assist (*second him in the duel*):—*vb* **second'** to transfer from normal duties to other duties (*second him to the advertising department for a month*).

sec'ondary *adj* **1** of less importance (*secondary considerations*). **2** (*of education*) more advanced, usu for children over 12.

sec'onder *n* one who supports formally a proposal made by another at a meeting.

sec'ond-hand *adj* not new, having been used by another.

sec'ond-rate *adj* not of high quality.

sec'ond sight *n* the ability to see things happening elsewhere or to foresee the future.

second wind the ability to breathe smoothly again after having been out of breath.

se'crecy *n* **1** the habit of keeping information to oneself. **2** concealment (*the secrecy surrounding the meeting*).

se'cret *adj* **1** hidden from others. **2** known or told to few (*a secret drawer/a secret meeting*). **3** private (*secret thoughts*):—*n* **1** a piece of information kept from others. **2** privacy (*a meeting in secret*). **3** a hidden reason or cause (*the secret of their success*).

secreta'rial *adj* having to do with the work of a secretary.

sec'retary *n* **1** one whose job it is to deal with letters and help to carry on the day-to-day business of his or her employer. **2** a high government official or minister (*the Foreign Secretary*).

sec'retaryship *n* the post of secretary.

secrete' *vb* **1** to hide away (*secreting the documents in a locked box*). **2** to produce a substance or fluid within the body by means of glands or other organs.

secre'tion *n* **1** the act of secreting. **2** the substance or fluid secreted (e.g. saliva).

se'cretive *adj* **1** keeping information to oneself. **2** fond of concealing things.

secre'tory *adj* having to do with secretion.

secret service *n* people whose job it is to find out secret information about other countries, and to see that the secrets of their own are kept.

sect *n* a body of persons holding the same beliefs, esp in religion.

secta'rian *adj* **1** having to do with a sect or sects. **2** concerned with or relating to the interests of one's own group, etc.

sec'tion *n* **1** a distinct part. **2** a part cut off (*a section of apple*). **3** the shape of the flat face exposed when something solid is cut clean through.

sec'tional adj **1** made up of sections. **2** in parts.

sec'tor n **1** part of a circle between two radii. **2** one of the parts into which an area is divided (*the Italian sector of the city*). **3** part of a field of activity (*the private sector of industry*).

sec'ular adj **1** having to do with this world (not with heaven), not sacred. **2** having to do with lay, not church, affairs.

secure' adj **1** free from care or danger (*a secure family background*). **2** safe (*a secure place for the jewels*):—vb **1** to make safe. **2** to fasten securely. **3** to seize and hold firmly.

secur'ity n **1** safety. **2** precautions taken to protect someone or something from attack, crime, danger, etc. (*increased security measures at airports*). **3** something given as proof of one's intention to repay a loan. **4** pl documents stating that one has lent a sum of money to a business, etc, and is entitled to receive interest on it.

sedan' n **1** in the 17th-18th centuries, a covered chair for one person, carried on poles by two porters. **2** a car with no division between driver and passengers.

sedate' adj **1** calm and dignified (*a sedate pace*). **2** not easily excited, serious (*sedate middle-aged people*).

sed'ative adj having a calming effect:—n a sedative drug.

sed'entary adj inactive, requiring much sitting.

sedge n a coarse grass growing in wet or marshy places.

sed'iment n the particles of matter that sink to the bottom of liquid.

sedi'tion n words or actions intended to stir up rebellion against the government:—adj **sedi'tious**.

seduce' vb **1** to persuade someone to do what is wrong or immoral. **2** to persuade to have sexual intercourse:—n **sedu'cer**.

seduc'tion n act of seducing.

seduc'tive adj **1** tempting, attracting to do wrong. **2** sexually attractive.

sed'ulous adj working hard, trying one's best.

see¹ vb (pt saw, pp seen) **1** to perceive with the eye. **2** to notice. **3** to understand. **4** to visit or interview:—**see about** to attend to:—**see off 1** to

go so far with one who is leaving. **2** (*inf*) to get rid of:—**see through 1** to keep on with to the end. **2** to understand thoroughly (someone's character, etc):—**seeing that** since, because.

see² n a diocese, the district over which a bishop has control:—**Holy See** the Papacy.

seed n **1** the grain or germ from which, when placed in the ground, a new plant grows. **2** children, descendants:—vb to produce seed:—**go to seed, run to seed 1** (*of a plant*) to shoot up too quickly. **2** to grow careless and lazy. **3** to deteriorate.

seed'ling n a young plant grown from a seed.

seed'y adj **1** shabby (*a seedy part of the town*). **2** unwell.

seek vb (pt, pp sought) **1** to look for. **2** to try to get, to ask.

seem vb to appear to be, look as if.

seem'ing adj having the appearance of, apparent.

seem'ly adj proper, fitting, decent (*seemly behaviour*).

seer n one who foresees the future, a prophet.

see'saw n **1** a plank that is balanced in the middle and on which children sit at either end so that when one end goes up the other end goes down. **2** the act of moving up and down or back and forth:—adj moving up and down like a seesaw:—vb **1** to play on a seesaw. **2** to move up and down or back and forth (*prices continually seesawing*).

seethe vb **1** to boil. **2** to be full of anger, excitement, etc.

seg'ment n **1** a piece cut off. **2** part of a circle cut off by a straight line:—vb to cut into segments.

seg'regate vb to set apart or separate from others (*segregate the girls and boys*):—n **segrega'tion**.

seine [sān] n a large fishing net.

seismic [sīz'-mik] adj having to do with earthquakes.

seis'mograph n an instrument showing the force of an earthquake and the direction in which it has occurred.

seismol'ogy n the science of earthquakes.

seize vb **1** to take by force (*seize a hostage*). **2** to take firm hold of (*seize a branch or an opportunity*).

seizure [see'-zhêr] n **1** act of taking by force. **2** a sudden attack of illness.

sel'dom *adv* rarely.

select' *vb* to choose, to pick out:—*adj* specially chosen:—*n* **select'or**.

selec'tion *n* **1** act of choosing. **2** what is chosen.

selec'tive *adj* choosing carefully, rejecting what is not wanted.

sel'enite *n* clear, colourless crystals of the mineral gypsum.

self *n* (*pl* **selves**) one's own person or interest.

self-cen'tred *adj* selfish, thinking chiefly of oneself and one's interests.

self-con'fident *adj* sure of oneself and one's powers.

self-con'scious *adj* thinking about oneself too much, shy because one thinks others are watching one.

self-contained' *adj* **1** keeping to oneself, not showing one's feelings (*reserved, self-contained people*). **2** (*of a house*) complete in itself and separate from other houses.

self-control' *n* the ability to control one's temper, etc.

self-deni'al *n* refusal to satisfy all one's own desires:—*adj* **self-deny'ing**.

self-esteem' *n* a high opinion of oneself, conceit.

self-ev'ident *adj* obvious, needing no proof.

self-gov'ernment *n* the governing of a country by its own inhabitants or their representatives.

self-impor'tant *adj* full of one's own importance, pompous:—*n* **self-impor'tance**.

self-imposed' *adj* undertaken of one's own free will (*self-imposed exile*).

self-in'terest *n* thought of one's own advantage only, selfishness.

self'ish *adj* thinking only of oneself and one's own advantage:—*adv* **self'ishness**.

self-made' *adj* successful or wealthy as a result of one's own efforts.

self-possessed' *adj* cool, calm:—*n* **self-pos-ses'sion**.

self-reli'ant *adj* depending on one's own efforts rather than the help of others.

self-respect' *n* proper care of one's own character and reputation.

self-right'eous *adj* too aware of what one supposes to be one's own goodness.

self-sac'rificing *adj* ready to give up one's own desires for the good of others.

selfsame' *adj* the very same.

self-sat'isfied *adj* pleased with oneself or one's actions, etc, conceited.

self-seek'ing *adj* doing things for one's own good only.

self-ser'vice *adj* (*of a shop, restaurant, etc*) helping oneself:—*also n*.

self-styled' *adj* so called by oneself (*a self-styled author*).

self-suffic'ient *adj* needing no help from others (*a country self-sufficient in food*).

self-willed' *adj* determined to have one's own way.

sell *vb* (*pt, pp* **sold**) to give in exchange for money.

sell'er *n* one who sells.

sel'vage, selvedge *n* the edge of a piece of cloth, so woven that it does not easily become undone.

selves *see* **self**.

sem'aphore *n* a method of signalling by moving the arms from one position to another.

sem'blance *n* outward appearance (*the semblance of order*).

semes'ter *n* a term of six months.

sem'i- *prefix* half.

sem'ibreve *n* a musical note (= 4 crotchets).

sem'icircle *n* a half circle:—*adj* **semicir'cu-lar**.

sem'icolon *n* a mark of punctuation (;).

sem'i-detached' *adj* (*of a house*) joined to the next house on one side but not on the other.

sem'inal *adj* **1** having to do with seed or semen. **2** influential and original.

sem'inar *n* a small group of students working together under the guidance of a teacher.

sem'inary *n* **1** a school or college, esp one training boys or men to be RC priests. **2** (*old*) a private school.

sem'iquaver *n* a musical note (= ½ quaver).

Semit'ic *adj* **1** having to do with the Jews or Arabs. **2** Jewish.

sem'itone *n* half a tone in music.

semoli'na *n* the hard grain left after wheat has been ground into flour, used to make puddings.

sen'ate *n* **1** the law-making council of ancient Rome. **2** the upper house of the law-making assembly in certain countries, such as the United States. **3** the governing body of certain universities.

sen'ator *n* a member of a senate.

send *vb* (*pt, pp* **sent**) **1** to have taken from one place to another (*send a parcel*). **2** to order to go (*send them away*):—*n* **sen'der:**—**send to Coventry** to refuse to speak to.

send'-off *n* farewell.

se'nile *adj* weak in the mind from old age:—*n* **seni'lity.**

se'nior *adj* **1** older. **2** higher in rank or importance:—*n* **1** one older (*she is her brother's senior/the seniors in the school*). **2** one having longer service or higher rank (*her seniors in the firm*):—*n* **senior'ity.**

sen'na *n* dried leaves of the cassia plant used as a laxative medicine.

sensa'tion *n* **1** the ability to perceive through the senses, feeling (*lose sensation in one's legs*). **2** an impression that cannot be described (*a sensation of being watched*). **3** great excitement (*murder trials causing a sensation*). **4** an event that causes great excitement (*the news article was a sensation*).

sensa'tional *adj* causing great excitement.

sensa'tionalism *n* a liking for exciting news and events.

sense *n* **1** one of the five powers (sight, hearing, taste, smell, touch) by which we gain knowledge of things outside ourselves. **2** wisdom in everyday things (*have the sense to keep warm*). **3** understanding (*no sense of direction*). **4** meaning (*words with several senses*).

sense'less *adj* **1** foolish, pointless (*a senseless act*). **2** unconscious (*senseless after a blow on the head*).

sensibil'ity *n* **1** the ability to feel emotions keenly. **2** delicacy of feeling.

sen'sible *adj* **1** having or showing good judgment, wise (*a sensible decision*). **2** aware (*sensible of the feelings of others*). **3** practical (*sensible shoes*).

sen'sitive *adj* **1** quick to feel things (*too sensitive for the rough and tumble of school life*). **2** easily hurt or damaged (*sensitive skin*). **3** able to feel emotions keenly (*a sensitive reading of the poem*):—*n* **sensi'tivity.**

sen'sory *adj* having to do with the senses.

sen'sual *adj* **1** having to do with the pleasures of the body (*the sensual pleasure of soaking in a scented bath*). **2** fond of the pleasures of the body (*a very sensual man*):—*n* **sensual'ity.**

sen'suous *adj* **1** having to do with the senses.

2 pleasing to the senses (*the sensuous pleasure of music*).

sen'tence *n* **1** a group of words, grammatically correct and making complete sense. **2** a judgment given in a court of law (*pass sentence*). **3** the punishment given to a wrongdoer by a judge (*a sentence of five years*):—*vb* to state the punishment due to a wrongdoer.

senten'tious *adj* pompous and self-righteous (*sententious remarks about his neighbour's behaviour*).

sen'tient *adj* having the power of feeling.

sen'timent *n* **1** what one feels or thinks about something (*I share your sentiments*). **2** an expression of feeling (*a song full of patriotic sentiment*). **3** tender or kindly feeling (*sentiments printed on birthday cards*).

sentimen'tal *adj* **1** showing, causing, etc, excessive tender feeling or emotion (*a sentimental love song*). **2** concerning the emotions rather than reason (*a watch with sentimental value*):—*n* **sentimental'ity.**

sen'tinel *n* a soldier on guard.

sen'try *n* a soldier on guard.

sen'try box *n* a shelter for a sentry.

sep'al *n* one of the leaves growing underneath the petals of a flower.

sep'arate *vb* **1** to put apart. **2** to go away from. **3** to stop living together (*their parents have separated*). **4** to go different ways (*they separated at the crossroads*). **5** to divide into parts:—*adj* unconnected, distinct, apart:—*adj* **sep'arable.**

separa'tion *n* **1** act of separating. **2** an agreement by a married couple to live apart from each other.

se'pia *n* a brown dye or colour made from fluid obtained from the cuttlefish.

sep'sis *n* the poisoning of a wound by germs.

Septem'ber *n* the ninth month of the year.

sep'tic *adj* infected and poisoned by germs.

septuagena'rian *n* one who is seventy years old or between seventy and eighty.

sepul'chral *adj* **1** having to do with a tomb. **2** (*of a voice*) deep and gloomy.

sep'ulchre *n* a tomb, a grave.

se'quel *n* **1** that which follows, a result or consequence (*a sequel to the official inquiry was that standards improved*). **2** a novel, film, etc, that continues the story of an earlier one.

se'quence n a number of things, events, etc, following each other in a natural or correct order.

seques'ter vb to set apart (*sequestering herself in her room to read*).

seques'tered adj quiet and out-of-the-way.

sequestrate [sek'-wes-trat] vb to take control of someone's goods (*sequestrate the man's money until he has paid all his debts*):—n **sequestra'tion**.

sequin [see'-kwin] n a tiny disc of bright metal sewn on to a dress for ornament.

ser'aph n (pl **ser'aphs** or **ser'aphim**) an angel of the highest rank.

seraph'ic adj angelic, pure.

serenade' n a musical work, music played at night by a lover under the window of his lady:—vb to sing or play a serenade.

serene' adj calm, undisturbed.

seren'ity n calmness, peace.

serge n a strong woollen cloth.

sergeant [sar'-jênt] n 1 in the army, a non-commissioned officer a rank above corporal. 2 in the police, a rank above constable.

ser'geant-ma'jor n an army rank above that of sergeant.

se'rial n a story published or broadcast in parts or instalments:—adj 1 happening in a series (*serial murders*). 2 in successive parts (*a serial story*).

se'ries n (pl **se'ries**) a number of things arranged in a definite order.

se'rious adj 1 thoughtful (*in a serious mood*). 2 important (*more serious issues*). 3 likely to cause danger (*a serious wound*).

ser'mon n 1 a talk given by a priest or minister in church on a religious subject. 2 a talk containing advice or warning.

ser'pent n a snake.

ser'pentine adj twisting, winding.

serrat'ed adj having notches like the edge of a saw.

ser'ried adj crowded, packed close together (*serried rows of children in the hall*).

se'rum n 1 the watery part of the blood. 2 liquid taken from the blood of an animal and injected into a person's blood to protect against a disease.

ser'vant n 1 one who works for and obeys another (*politicians regarded as servants of the people*).

2 one employed to do tasks about the house (*houses looked after by a team of servants in Victorian times*).

serve vb 1 to work for and obey . 2 to hand food to at table. 3 to supply with (food, etc). 4 to be helpful. 5 to be of use instead of. 6 (*in tennis*) to hit the ball into play:—**serve you right** that is just what you deserve.

ser'vice n 1 the work of a servant or employee (*five years' service with the company*). 2 time spent in the forces, police, etc. 3 use, help (*people who can be of service to us*). 4 a religious ceremony. 5 a set of dishes for use at table (*a dinner service*). 6 in tennis, the hit intended to put the ball into play. 7 pl the armed forces.

ser'viceable adj useful.

service station n a place which sells petrol, oils, some other car requirements and often drinks and snacks, and usually provides toilet facilities.

serviette' n a table napkin.

ser'vile adj behaving like a slave, too ready to obey:—n **servil'ity**.

ser'vitor n a manservant.

ser'vitude n slavery.

sesame [ses'-ê-mi] n an eastern plant whose seeds are used in cooking and from which an oil, used in cooking and salads, is obtained:—**open sesame** a sure means of gaining admission (*his wealth was an open sesame to all clubs*).

ses'sion n 1 a meeting or sitting of a court or assembly. 2 a school year.

sestet' n the last six lines of a sonnet.

set vb (**set**, **set'ting**) 1 to put. 2 to fix in position (*set a broken bone*). 3 to put to music. 4 to become hard or solid (*leave jellies to set*). 5 (*of the sun, etc*) to sink below the horizon (*the sun setting*):—n 1 a number of things of the same kind. 2 a group of people with similar interests. 3 a group of games in a tennis match:—adj fixed, regular:—**set off**, **set out** to begin a journey:—**set upon** to attack.

set'back n something that hinders one's plans.

set square n a triangular ruler for drawing certain angles.

settee' n a sofa.

set'ter n a dog trained to point out game by standing still and turning its nose towards the animal.

set'ting n 1 surroundings (a house in a woodland setting). 2 background (a story with its setting in Victorian London). 3 music written to go with certain words.

set'tle n a bench with arms and a high back:—vb 1 to set up home in a certain place (decide to settle in the country). 2 to come to rest on (a butterfly settling on a flower). 3 to put an end to by giving a decision or judgment (settle the argument). 4 to make or become quiet or calm (the baby was slow to settle). 5 to pay (a bill, etc). 6 to sink to the bottom of (coffee dregs settling at the bottom of the cup).

set'tlement n 1 a decision or judgment that ends a dispute. 2 money or property given to someone under certain conditions. 3 payment of a bill. 4 a colony.

set'tler n one who makes his or her home in a new colony.

set'-to n a fight.

sev'er vb 1 to cut or tear apart or off (sever his arm from his shoulder). 2 to break (the rope severed in two/sever relations with other countries):—n sev'erance.

sev'eral adj 1 more than two, but not very many. 2 separate, various (go their several ways).

sev'erally adv separately.

severe' adj 1 strict, harsh (a severe punishment). 2 plain and undecorated (a severe dress). 3 very cold (a severe winter):—n sever'ity.

sew [sō] vb (pt sewed', pp sewn) to join by means of needle and thread.

sewage [sō'-êj] n waste matter of a house or town.

sewer [sō'-êr] n an underground drain to carry away water, waste matter, etc.

sew'erage n a system of underground drains or sewers.

sex n 1 the state of being male or female. 2 the qualities by which an animal or plant is seen to be male or female. 3 sexual intercourse.

sexagena'rian n one who is sixty years old or between sixty and seventy.

sex'ism n discrimination on the grounds of sex, especially against women:—adj sex'ist.

sex'tant n an instrument for measuring angles, used for navigating ships and surveying land.

sextet' n a musical composition for six voices.

sex'ton n a person who looks after a church building, ringing the bells and tending graves around it.

sex'ual adj having to do with sex.

shab'by adj 1 untidy through much wear, threadbare, dressed in threadbare or untidy clothes. 2 mean, ungenerous (a shabby trick):—n shab'biness.

shack n a hut.

shack'le vb 1 to fasten with a chain (prisoners with hands shackled together). 2 to restrict freedom of action or speech (shackled by old-fashioned rules):—npl shack'les chains for fastening the limbs.

shad n a fish of the herring family.

shade n 1 to protect from light or sun (shade one's eyes). 2 to darken. 3 to colour (shade wooded parts on the map):—n 1 any device that protects from light or sun. 2 a place in a shadow cast by the sun, half-darkness (tables in the shade). 3 a slight difference (many shades of opinion). 4 a little (a shade warmer). 5 a ghost.

shad'ing n the effects used to suggest darkness in a picture.

sha'dow n 1 a dark patch on the ground caused by the breaking of rays of light by a body (in the shadow of the large building). 2 shade. 3 one who follows another around. 4 a ghost:—vb to follow someone closely without his or her knowing it.

sha'dowy adj 1 in shadow, shaded, dark (shadowy parts of the garden). 2 dark and indistinct (shadowy figures in the mist).

shad'y adj 1 protected from light or sun. 2 dishonest.

shaft n 1 the long handle of any tool or weapon. 2 an arrow. 3 a connecting rod in a machine, one of the poles of a carriage to which a horse is tied. 4 the main part of a pillar. 5 a deep tunnel leading down to a mine. 6 a ray of light.

shag n a sea bird (the cormorant).

shag'gy adj 1 having rough hair (shaggy dogs). 2 rough (a shaggy coat).

shake vb (pt shook, pp shak'en) 1 to move quickly up and down or to and fro (shake the bottle). 2 to tremble (her hands shook). 3 to make weaker or less firm (shake the foundations/shake one's faith):—*n* **1** trembling. **2** a sudden jerk. **3** a shock.

shak'y *adj* **1** not steady (*a chair with a shaky leg*). **2** weak after illness.

shale *n* a soft slaty rock from which oil may be obtained.

shallot' *n* a small onion.

shal'low *adj* **1** not deep (*shallow water*). **2** not thinking deeply (*a shallow writer*):—*n* a place where water is not deep.

sham *n* **1** a person pretending to be what he or she is not (*the doctor turned out to be a sham*). **2** a thing made to look like something else (*trials in that country are a sham*). **3** a pretence (*their marriage was a sham*):—*adj* not real, pretended:—*vb* (**shammed', sham'ming**) to pretend.

sham'ble *vb* to walk clumsily.

sham'bles *npl* a scene of great disorder and confusion (*the burgled house was a shambles*).

shame *n* a feeling of sorrow for wrongdoing or for inability to do something, disgrace:—*vb* to make ashamed, to disgrace.

shame'-faced *adj* showing shame or embarrassment.

shame'ful *adj* disgraceful, shocking.

shame'less *adj* not easily made ashamed, bold.

sham'my *n* chamois leather, a soft leather for polishing.

shampoo' *vb* to wash and rub:—*n* **1** act of shampooing. **2** a preparation used for shampooing (*sachets of shampoo*).

sham'rock *n* a small plant with three leaves on each stem, the national emblem of Ireland.

shan'dy *n* a mixture of beer and ginger beer or lemonade.

shank *n* **1** the leg from the knee to the ankle. **2** the long handle or shaft of certain tools.

shan'ty[1] *n* a poorly built hut.

shan'ty[2], **chan'ty** *n* a song with a chorus, once sung by sailors when working.

shape *n* **1** the form or outline of anything (*clouds of different shapes*). **2** (*inf*) condition, state (*players in good shape*). **3** a dish for giving form to a pudding:—*vb* **1** to form (*shape the sand into a mound*). **2** to give a certain shape to (*shape his career*):—**in good shape** in good condition:—**shape well at** to get on or do well at.

shape'less *adj* ugly or irregular in shape.

shape'ly *adj* well-formed (*shapely legs*).

shard, sherd *n* a piece of broken pottery.

share *n* **1** part of a thing belonging to a particular person. **2** one of the equal parts of the money of a company or business, lent by persons who may then receive a part of the profits. **3** the cutting part of a plough:—*vb* **1** to divide among others. **2** to r eceive a part of.

share'holder *n* one who owns shares in a company or business.

shark *n* **1** a lar ge flesh-eating fish. **2** (*inf*) one ready to use unfair means to get as much money as possible (*a loan shark*).

sharp *adj* **1** having a thin edge for cutting with, having a fine point (*a sharp knife*). **2** quick and intelligent (*a sharp child*). **3** hurtful, unkind (*a sharp tongue*). **4** stinging, keen (*a sharp pain*). **5** in singing, higher than the corr ect note. **6** rather sour (*a sharp taste*):—*n* a musical sign to show that a note is to be raised half a tone (#):—*adv* (*of time*) exactly.

sharp'en *vb* to make sharp (*sharpen knives*).

sharp'er *n* one who cheats, esp at cards.

sharp practice *n* dishonesty.

sharp'-shooter *n* one who shoots well with a rifle.

sharp-sight'ed *adj* having keen eyesight.

sharp-wit'ted *adj* quick and clever.

shat'ter *vb* **1** to br eak into pieces, to smash (*the cups shattered when they were dropped*). **2** to put an end to (*shatter their hopes*).

shave *vb* **1** to cut off hair with a razor (*he shaves every morning*). **2** to cut strips off the surface (*shaving a thin strip from the edge of the door*). **3** to pass ver y close to without touching (*the car shaved the wall*):—*n* **1** act of shaving, esp the face. **2** a close hair cut. **3** a narr ow escape.

shav'ing *n* a thin strip cut off the surface (*wood shavings*).

shawl *n* a cloth folded and worn loosely over the shoulders by women.

sheaf *n* (*pl* **sheaves**) a number of things in a bundle (*a sheaf of paper/sheaves of wheat*).

shear *vb* (*pp* **shorn**) **1** to cut with shears (*shear his curls off*). **2** to clip the wool fr om (*shearing sheep*). **3** to cut or cause to br eak (*the tree fell and sheared through the telephone line*):—*npl* **shears** a pair of large scissors (e.g. for cutting off the wool of a sheep).

shear'er n one who shears (*sheep shearer*).

shear'ling n a sheep whose wool has been cut off only once.

sheath n a close-fitting case or container (*pull the sword from the sheath*).

sheathe vb to put into a sheath (*sheathing the sword*).

sheaves see sheaf.

shed[1] vb (**shed, shed'ding**) **1** to let fall down or off (*trees shedding leaves*). **2** to spread about (*lamps shed a soft light*).

shed[2] n a hut, an outhouse (*a garden shed*).

sheen n brightness (*the sheen on the polished table*).

sheep n **1** a common animal valued for its wool and its meat. **2** a person who follows the lead of others without protesting.

sheep'cote, sheep'fold ns a pen or enclosure for sheep.

sheep'dog n a dog trained to look after sheep.

sheep'ish adj awkward or embarrassed because of having done something wrong (*looked sheepish when they discovered that he was lying*).

sheep'-run, sheep'walk ns grazing ground for sheep.

sheep'shank n a knot tied in the middle of a rope to make it shorter.

sheer[1] adj **1** very steep (*sheer cliffs*). **2** (of material) very fine or transparent (*sheer silk*). **3** thorough, complete (*a sheer accident*).

sheer[2] vb to swerve, to move suddenly in another direction (*the car sheered to the right to avoid the lorry*).

sheet n **1** a broad thin piece of anything. **2** a bedcovering of linen, etc. **3** a broad stretch of water, flame, ice, etc. **4** a rope tied to the lower corner of a sail.

sheet-anchor n **1** a large anchor used only when in danger. **2** a person or thing on which one can rely in time of danger.

sheet'ing n material used for making bed sheets.

sheet light'ning n broad flashes of lightning.

sheik(h) [shāk or sheek] n an Arab chief.

shek'el n **1** an ancient Jewish weight or coin. **2** pl (inf) money (*have run out of shekels*). **3** the unit of currency in Israel.

shelf n (pl **shelves**) **1** a board fixed to a wall or fastened in a cupboard, used for placing things on. **2** a ledge, a long flat rock or sandbank.

shell n **1** a hard outer covering (*a nutshell/the shell of the tortoise*). **2** a thick metal case filled with explosive and fired from a gun:—vb **1** to take the shell off. **2** to fire shells at (*the city shelled by the enemy*).

shell'ac n a type of resin used for making varnish.

shell'fish n a fish with a shell covering (*shellfish such as mussels*).

shel'ter n **1** a place that gives protection from the weather or safety from danger. **2** protection:—vb to protect, to go for protection.

shelve vb **1** to place on a shelf. **2** to put aside for a time. **3** to slope.

shelves see shelf.

shelv'ing n **1** material for shelves. **2** a set of shelves.

shep'herd n a person who looks after sheep:—f **shepherdess:**—vb to guide a flock or group.

sher'bet n a fizzy drink made from fruit juices.

sher'iff n the chief law officer or judge of a county or shire.

sher'ry n a Spanish wine (*have a glass of dry sherry before dinner*).

shew vb old form of show.

shib'boleth n **1** a word or custom, knowledge of which reveals the group, party, sect, etc, to which one belongs. **2** an out-of-date belief.

shield n **1** a piece of metal or strong leather held in front of the body to defend it against sword strokes, etc (*the knight's shield*). **2** a protector or protection (*an eye shield*):—vb to defend, to protect (*put his arm up to shield his eyes from the sun*).

shift vb **1** to change (*shift position*). **2** to move (*shift the blame*). **3** to remove, get rid of (*stains that are difficult to shift*):—n **1** a change (*a shift of emphasis*). **2** a group of workers who carry on a job for a certain time and then hand over to another group. **3** the period during which such a group works. **4** a simple dress or nightgown (*a cotton shift*).

shift'less adj unable to think out ways of doing things, inefficient (*too shiftless to find a job*):—n shift'lessness.

shift'y adj untrustworthy, deceitful (*have a shifty appearance*).

shillelagh [shê-lā'-li] n in Ireland, a short thick club.

shill'ing n a British silver coin ($\frac{1}{20}$ of £1) gradually replaced after 1968 by the 5 pence piece.

shill'y-shall'y vb to be unable to come to a decision, to keep on changing one's mind (*shilly-shallied about whether to go*).

shim'mer vb to shine with a flickering light (*pavements shimmering in the rain*):—also n.

shin n the front part of the leg below the knee:— vb (**shinned'**, **shin'ning**) to climb, gripping with the legs.

shin'dy n (*inf*) a confused noise, trouble (*a shindy at the local pub*).

shine vb (pt, pp **shone**) 1 to give off light (*street lights shining*). 2 to direct a light or lamp (*shine the torch in their eyes*). 3 to polish (*shine his shoes*). 4 (*inf*) to be very good at (*the pupil shines at French*):—n brightness, polish.

shin'gle n loose gravel or pebbles (*the shingle on the seashore*):—vb to cut (a woman's) hair short at the back.

shin'gles npl a skin disease causing a painful rash.

Shin'to n the native religion of Japan.

shin'ty n a Scottish team game played, like hockey, with a ball and sticks.

shin'y adj bright, glossy, as if polished (*a shiny material*).

ship n a large seagoing boat:—vb (**shipped'**, **ship'ping**) 1 to put or take, as on board ship (*ship the goods to their new home*). 2 to go on board a ship.

ship'brok'er n one who buys, sells and insures ships.

ship'building n the act of making ships.

ship chand'ler n one who buys and sells stores and equipment for ships.

ship'mate n a fellow-sailor.

ship'ment n 1 the sending of goods by ship. 2 the goods put on board a ship (*a shipment of fruit*).

ship'ping n 1 all the ships of a port, country, etc. 2 ships in general.

ship'per n one who imports or exports goods by sea.

ship'shape adj in good order, neat and tidy (*have the house shipshape for his mother's return*).

ship'wreck n the loss or destruction of a ship at sea:—also vb.

ship'wright n a carpenter who helps to build ships.

ship'yard n a place where ships are built or repaired.

shire n a county.

shirk vb to avoid (*shirk duty*):—n shirk'er.

shirt n a kind of loose upper garment with a collar (*button up his shirt*).

shirt'ing n material for making shirts.

shiv'er vb 1 to tremble (*shivering with cold*). 2 to break into small pieces:—n 1 a shaking or trembling. 2 a small piece (*a shiver of glass*).

shiv'ery adj trembling, as with cold or fear.

shoal[1] n a shallow place in the sea, a sandbank:— vb to become shallow.

shoal[2] n 1 a large number of fish swimming together. 2 (*inf*) a crowd (*shoals of visitors*).

shock[1] n a mass of long untidy hair (*a shock of black hair*).

shock[2] n 1 the sudden violent striking of one thing against another (e.g. in a collision). 2 weakness of body or confusion of mind caused by a violent blow or collision (*suffer from shock after an accident*). 3 sorrow or a state of upset caused by sudden bad news, etc (*the shock at hearing that she had won the prize*). 4 an involuntary movement of the body, caused by passing electricity through it:—vb 1 to cause sudden pain or sorrow. 2 to horrify, to disgust (*shocked by the treatment of his wife*).

shock'ing adj very bad, disgusting, indecent.

shock troops soldiers specially trained to make a sudden violent attack on an enemy.

shod adj wearing shoes (*shod in leather*).

shod'dy adj cheap, of poor quality (*shoddy clothes*):—n cheap cloth made up from the clippings of other material.

shoe n 1 a covering for the foot (*high-heeled shoes*). 2 a U-shaped metal plate nailed to the hoof of a horse:—vb to fit a horse with shoes.

shoe'black n one who cleans the shoes of passers-by in the street.

shoe'horn n a curved piece of horn, metal, etc, to help the foot to slip easily into a shoe.

shoe'maker n one who makes, repairs or sells shoes.

shoot vb (pt, pp **shot**) 1 to fire a bullet from a gun (*start shooting*). 2 to let fly (*shoot an arrow from a bow*). 3 to move suddenly or quickly (*the child shot across the road*). 4 to hit or kill with a bullet from a gun (*shoot rabbits*). **5** (*in games*) to kick or hit at goal. **6** to begin to grow (*plants shooting up*). **7** to make a moving film (*a film shot in Wales*):—*n* **1** a young branch or bud. **2** a sloping way down which water may flow or objects slide. **3** an outing for shooting and hunting.

shoot'ing *n* land rented to shoot over.

shooting box *n* a small country house for use by members of a shooting party.

shooting star *n* what looks like a moving star, but is really a glowing fragment of a heavenly body flying through space.

shop *n* **1** a place where goods are sold (*a flower shop/the corner shop*). **2** a place where work is done with tools or machines:—*vb* (**shopped**, **shop'ping**) to visit shops to buy things (*shop for groceries*):—**talk shop** to talk about one's work (*she bores everyone by constantly talking shop*).

shop'keeper *n* one who owns a shop where goods are sold.

shop'lifter *n* one who steals from the shops he or she is visiting (*threaten to prosecute all shoplifters*).

shopping mall *n* a covered area which has a number of different shops and is closed to traffic.

shop'walker *n* in a large shop, one who sees that the customers are being properly served and goods not stolen.

shore[1] *n* the land beside the sea, a river, lake, etc.

shore[2] *n* a wooden prop or support:—*vb* to prop up or support (*shoring up the damaged wall*).

shorn *pp of* **shear**.

short *adj* **1** not long or tall (*a short distance/short people*). **2** not enough (*short measures*). **3** without enough of (*short of money*). **4** not lasting long (*a short holiday*). **5** quick and almost impolite (*she was very short on the phone*). **6** (*of pastry, etc*) crumbling easily:—*adv* **short'ly** briefly, soon:—*npl* **shorts** trousers reaching not lower than the knees:—**in short** in a few words.

short'age *n* a lack of, insufficiency (*a staff shortage/shortage of supplies*).

short'bread *n* a biscuit-like cake made of flour, fat and sugar.

short cir'cuit *n* the touching of two electric wires so that current passes from one to the other instead of straight on.

short cut *n* a quicker way (*motorists trying to find a short cut to avoid the heavy traffic*).

shorten *vb* to make less in length or time (*shorten the dress/shorten the working day*).

shor'tening *n* fat for making pastry, etc, crumble easily when cooked.

short'hand *n* a type of signwriting in which one can write as fast as a speaker speaks.

short-hand'ed *adj* not having the number of helpers or workers required (*short-handed at the factory*).

short'horn *n* a breed of cattle with short horns.

short'-lived *adj* living or lasting for a short time only (*her pleasure was short-lived*).

shorts *see* **short**.

short-sight'ed *adj* **1** unable to see clearly things that are distant. **2** lacking for eight (*it was short-sighted of them not to save for their old age*).

short-tem'pered *adj* easily angered (*keep the child away from the short-tempered man*).

shot[1] *pt of* **shoot**:—*n* **1** the firing of a gun, etc (*kill the animal with one shot*). **2** small lead bullets. **3** a solid metal ball fired from a gun. **4** a person able to shoot (*a good shot*). **5** (*inf*) a single attempt at doing something (*have another shot at learning to drive*). **6** a series of pictures of a scene taken at one time by ciné camera. **7** (*inf*) an injection (*an anti-tetanus shot*).

shot[2] *adj* having threads of a different colour interwoven.

shoul'der *n* **1** the joint connecting an arm, wing, or foreleg to the body. **2** anything jutting out like a shoulder (*the hard shoulder of the motorway*):—*vb* **1** to push with the shoulder . **2** to put on to the shoulder (*shoulder the tree*). **3** to bear (*shoulder responsibilities*).

shoulder blade *n* the broad flat bone of the shoulder.

shoulder strap *n* a strap or tape that crosses the shoulder.

shout *vb* to utter a loud cry (*shout for help*):—*n* a loud cry, a call.

shove [shuv] *vb* (*inf*) to push (*shoving him out of the way*):—*also n*.

shov'el *n* a spade with a broad blade for lifting earth, gravel, etc:—*vb* (**shov'elled**, **shov'-elling**) to move with a shovel (*shovel coal*).

shov'elful *n* as much as a shovel will hold.

shov'el-hat n a broad-brimmed hat worn by some clergymen.

show vb **1** to let be seen, to display (*she showed them the new dress*). **2** to point out (*show them the way*). **3** to be in sight (*a light showing*). **4** to pr ove (*it showed the inefficiency of the system*):—n **1** a display . **2** a performance or entertainment (*get tickets for the show*). **3** pr etence. **4** a gathering at which flowers, animals, etc, are displayed to the public (*the agricultural show*).

show'er n **1** a short fall of rain. **2** a gr eat number of things falling or arriving at one time (*a shower of arrows*). **3** a piece of bathroom equipment that produces a spray of water so that people standing underneath it can wash themselves.:—vb **1** to give to or let fall on in large numbers. **2** to take a shower.

show'erproof adj waterproof against light rain only.

show'ery adj rainy, marked by many showers (*showery weather*).

show'man n **1** one who manages a travelling show (e.g. a circus). **2** one who lik es to draw attention to himself.

show'room n a room or shop in which things are on display to the public (*a furniture showroom*).

show'y adj bright and attractive, but not necessarily good (*showy ornaments*).

shrap'nel n **1** a shell pack ed with bullets or pieces of metal that are scattered when it explodes. **2** a fragment of the case of a bomb or shell.

shred vb (**shred'ded, shred'ding**) to tear or cut into small pieces (*shred paper/shred lettuce*):—n a scrap, a rag, a piece cut or torn off.

shrew n **1** a small mouse-lik e animal. **2** a bad-tempered or sharp-tongued woman (*a shrew of a wife*).

shrewd adj clever in practical matters, cunning, good at judging (*too shrewd to be deceived by them*).

shrew'ish adj bad-tempered, sharp-tongued, given to scolding.

shriek vb to scream (*shrieking in agony*):—also n.

shrift n the confession of sins to a priest:—**short shrift** little mercy.

shrill adj high and piercing in sound (*shrill children's voices*).

shrimp n **1** a small eatable shellfish. **2** (*inf*) a very small person (*her shrimp of a son*):—vb to fish for shrimps.

shrine n **1** a box or tomb containing something connected with a holy person. **2** a place r evered because of a connection with a holy person or event.

shrink vb **1** to mak e or become smaller (*clothes that shrink in the wash*). **2** to go back in fear , horror, etc (*shrink at the sight of the burglar*).

shrink'age n the amount by which something becomes smaller.

shrive vb (pt **shrove** or **shrived**, pp **shri'ven**) (*fml or old*) to hear the confession and forgive the sins of (*priests shriving sinners*).

shriv'el vb (**shriv'elled, shriv'elling**) **1** to dr y up and become smaller (*plants shrivelling in the heat*). **2** to become wrinkled (*skin shrivelled with age*).

shroud n **1** a garment or covering for a dead body . **2** pl the set of ropes supporting a mast of a ship:—vb **1** to put in a shr oud. **2** to cover , to hide (*clouds shrouding the sun*).

Shrove'tide n the days just before the beginning of Lent.

Shrove Tuesday the day before the first day of Lent.

shrub n a short tree-like bush with a short trunk.

shrub'bery n a place where many shrubs are growing close together (*children hiding in the shrubbery*).

shrug vb (**shrugged', shrug'ging**) to raise one's shoulders in surprise, doubt, etc (*she shrugged in disbelief*).

shrunk'en adj grown smaller, shrivelled.

shud'der vb to tremble from fear, etc, to shiver with cold (*shudder at the sight of the dead body*):—also n.

shuf'fle vb **1** to mak e a noise by moving the feet on the ground (*old men shuffling around in their slippers*). **2** to mix car ds before giving them out:—also n.

shun vb (**shunned', shun'ning**) to avoid, to keep away from (*she shuns crowds*).

shunt vb (*of a railway engine or train*) to move on to a different track or side line.

shut vb (**shut, shut'ting**) to close (*shut the door/ shut the suitcase*).

shut'ter n a covering that can be placed or closed over a window or other opening to keep out light (*close the wooden shutters*).

shut'tle n the part of a weaving or sewing machine that carries the thread to and fro.

shut'tlecock n a cork rounded at one end and stuck with feathers, used for a ball in badminton.

shy¹ adj timid, easily frightened, retiring in society (*she was too shy to speak to her parents' friends*):—vb to jerk or jump to the side in fear, etc (*horses shying*):—n **shy'ness**.

shy² vb to throw:—n a throw.

sib'ilant adj hissing:—n a letter uttered with a hissing sound, as s or z.

sib'yl n in ancient times, a prophetess.

sick adj 1 ill (*too sick to go to work*). 2 bringing up food from the stomach by vomiting, about to vomit (*always get sick on board ship*). 3 tired of through having too much (*sick of gardening*).

sick'en vb 1 to make or become sick (*she sickened and died*). 2 to disgust (*the sight of the dead rabbit sickened her*).

sick'le n a knife with a curved blade for cutting corn, etc.

sick'ly adj 1 often ill (*a sickly child*). 2 pale (*a sickly complexion*). 3 over-sentimental (*sickly love songs*).

sick'ness n 1 illness. 2 vomiting.

side n 1 one of the surfaces of a body, the part of the body between the shoulders and thighs (*a pain in her side*). 2 edge, border (*the side of the lake*). 3 slope (*the side of the mountain*). 4 one of two opposing parties or teams (*the home side*):—adj on, at or towards the side:—vb to support one party against another.

side'board n a piece of furniture for storing dishes, cutlery, etc.

side'light n 1 a light at one side (*the car's sidelights*). 2 extra information that makes a new point of view possible (*give an interesting sidelight on his character*).

side'line n an activity carried on in addition to one's real job (*he serves in a bar as a sideline*).

side'long adj to the side, slanting (*a sidelong glance*):—also adv.

sidereal [sî-dee'-ri-êl] adj (*fml*) having to do with the stars.

side'-saddle n a saddle for women, on which they can sit on a horse with both legs on the one side.

side'show n a less important show at a fair, circus, exhibition, etc.

side'track vb to turn someone away from what he or she was about to do (*he was going to study but he got sidetracked*).

side'walk n (*Amer*) a footpath at the side of a road.

side'ways adv on or towards one side (*move sideways*).

sid'ing n a short railway track off the main line, used for shunting, etc.

si'dle vb to walk side first, to approach slowly (*sidling up to the tourists to ask for money*).

siege n surrounding a fort, town, etc, with an army to take it or make its garrison surrender.

sien'na n a reddish-brown colouring matter.

sier'ra n a range of mountains with pointed peaks.

sies'ta n a rest taken during the hottest part of the day.

sieve [sêv] n a container with a network bottom or a bottom full of holes, used for separating small particles of anything from larger pieces:—vb to pass through a sieve (*sieving flour*).

sift vb 1 to pass through a sieve. 2 to examine closely (*sifting the evidence*):—n **sift'er**:—**sift out** to separate good from bad.

sigh [sî] vb a long, deep, easily heard breath expressing pain, sadness, unreturned love, etc:—vb 1 to draw such a breath (*sighing with boredom*). 2 (*lit*) to long (for) (*sigh for her lost love*).

sight n 1 the power of seeing (*lose her sight*). 2 that which is seen (*the sight of her in that hat*). 3 something worth seeing (*the sights of the town*). 4 the area within which things can be seen by someone (*the children were out of sight*). 5 (*often pl*) a device attached to a gun to make it easier to aim straight:—vb to see, to notice:—**out of sight** too far away to be seen.

sight'less adj blind.

sight'seeing n going around the places of interest in a town, district, etc:—n **sight'seer**.

sign n 1 a mark, movement, gesture, etc, conveying an accepted meaning (*a sign to indicate her agreement*). 2 a mark or characteristic by which a person or thing can be recognized. 3 a notice to give directions or advertise (*shop* *signs*):—*vb* **1** to write one's name on. **2** to convey meaning by a movement of the head, hands, etc.

sig'nal *n* **1** a sign to give information, or ders, etc, at a distance (*give them a signal to keep quiet*). **2** a mechanism used to give such signs to drivers of railway engines. **3** a message conveyed by such signs:—*adj* notable, important:—*vb* (**sig'nalled, sig'-nalling**) to make signals to (*signal to them to stop*):—*n* **sig'naller.**

signal box *n* a cabin from which railway signals are operated.

sig'nalize *vb* to make remarkable or noteworthy (*her painting is signalized by bold use of colour*).

sig'nally *adv* remarkably.

sig'nalman *n* one who operates railway signals.

sig'natory *n* one who has signed an agreement (*signatories of the contract*).

sig'nature *n* one's name written by oneself.

signature tune *n* a tune used to introduce a particular programme on radio or television.

sign'board *n* a notice giving directions or information (e.g. as to the type of shop, etc).

sig'net *n* a small metal plate on which a sign has been cut for stamping a design on letter seals.

signet ring *n* a ring with a signet set in.

signif'icance *n* meaning, importance (*fail to understand the significance of her words*).

significant *adj* full of meaning, important (*no significant change in the patient's condition/significant events*).

significa'tion *n* (*fml*) exact meaning.

sig'nify *vb* **1** to show by a sign (*she signified her agreement by a nod*). **2** to mean (*what her remark signified*). **3** to be important.

sign language *n* a method of communication using the hands, used especially in communication with deaf people.

signor [seen'-yor] *n* the Italian form of Mr.

signora [seen-yo'-ra] *n* the Italian form of Mrs.

signorina [seen-yo-ree'-na] *n* the Italian form of Miss.

sign'post *n* a post indicating the direction and sometimes also the distance to a place (*see a signpost to the village*).

Sikh *n* a member of an Indian religion called **Sikhism,** originally connected with Hinduism, but now based on a belief that there is only one God.

si'lence *n* absence of sound, quietness:—*vb* to cause to be quiet (*silencing the children with a look*).

si'lencer *n* a device for reducing the noise of an engine, gun, etc (*the car's silencer*).

si'lent *adj* **1** making no sound (*machines that are virtually silent*). **2** not talking, speaking little (*they were silent on the journey*). **3** with no noise or sound (*a silent house*):—**the silent service** the navy.

silhouette [si'-lŏ-et] *n* the dark outline and flat shape of an object as seen with a light behind it.

sil'ica *n* a colourless mineral found as quartz or in flint, etc.

silk *n* **1** the fine thr ead produced by the silkworm. **2** a soft material woven fr om this.

silk'en *adj* (*lit*) made of silk.

silk'worm *n* a caterpillar that spins silk thread to enclose its chrysalis.

silk'y *adj* **1** made of silk. **2** soft, smooth (*silky hair*).

sill *n* the ledge of stone or wood at the foot of a window.

sil'ly *adj* foolish, unwise (*a silly thing to do*).

si'lo *n* a tower or pit in which green fodder (grass, etc) is stored until needed as food for animals.

silt *n* the earth, sand, etc, deposited by a moving river:—*vb* to block or become blocked with silt.

sil'van *see* **sylvan.**

sil'ver *n* **1** a pr ecious metal of shining white colour (*jewellery made of silver*). **2** coins, dishes, etc, made of silver (*the burglar stole the family silver*). **3** (*old*) money:—*adj* made of silver:—*vb* to coat with silver.

sil'verside *n* the underside of a roast of beef.

sil'versmith *n* a worker in silver.

sil'ver-tongued *adj* able to speak well and persuasively.

sil'verware *n* dishes and utensils made of silver.

silver wedding *n* the twenty-fifth anniversary of marriage.

sil'very *adj* **1** lik e silver (*silvery hair*). **2** clear in tone (*her silvery voice*).

sim'ian *adj* like a monkey or ape.

sim'ilar *adj* like, resembling (*have similar attitudes*).

similar'ity n likeness, resemblance (*the similarity of their attitude*).

simile [sim'-i-li] n a striking comparison of one thing with another.

simil'itude n (*fml*) likeness, resemblance.

sim'mer vb to keep on boiling slowly without boiling over (*a sauce simmering in the pan on the stove*).

simoom', simoon' n a hot dry wind blowing off the Sahara desert.

sim'per vb to smile in a silly or insincere way (*girls simpering at the boys*):—also n.

sim'ple adj **1** unmixed, without anything added, pure (*the simple truth*). **2** not complicated (*a simple explanation*). **3** plain (*a simple dress*). **4** trusting, innocent and inexperienced (*simple country girls*). **5** fool ish, easily tricked (*simple enough to believe him*):—n (*old*) a herb used as medicine.

simpli'city n **1** easiness. **2** sincerity. **3** plainness. **4** innocence.

simplifica'tion n the act of making easier to do or understand.

sim'plify vb to make easier to do or understand (*simplified the process*).

sim'ply adv **1** in a clear way (*explained simply*). **2** absolutely (*simply wonderful*). **3** plain (*live simply*). **4** just, mer ely (*do it simply for the money*).

sim'ulate vb (*fml*) to pretend (*simulating interest*):—n **simula'tion**.

simulta'neous adj taking place at the same time (*a simultaneous translation of the play*).

sin n **1** a thought, wor d or action that breaks the law of God. **2** a wick ed act:—vb (**sinned', sin'ning**) **1** to do wr ong. **2** to commit sin:— n **sin'ner**.

since prep from (a certain time till now):—adv ago:—conj **1** fr om the time that. **2** because.

sincere' adj real, genuine, meaning what one says, frank (*sincere friends/a sincere promise/sincere words of thanks*).

sincer'ity n honesty of mind, freedom from pretence.

sin'ecure n a job for which one is paid but which has few or no duties attached to it.

sin'ew n a tough cord-like substance that joins muscle to bone.

sin'ewy adj strong, tough (*sinewy workmen*).

sin'ful adj full of sin, wicked (*sinful thoughts*).

sing vb (*pt* **sang**, *pp* **sung**) to make music with the voice, with or without words (*singing love songs/ be taught to sing*):—n **sing'er**.

singe vb to burn slightly, to burn the surface or ends of:—also n.

sin'gle adj **1** one only, alone (*a single sheet of paper/the single cause*). **2** unmarried (*single people*):—vb to pick out one (for special attention, etc).

sin'gle-mind'ed adj concentrating on one main purpose (*single-minded attempts to get a job*).

sin'glet n a man's vest.

sin'gly adv one by one, one at a time (*leave the meeting singly*).

sing'song adj rising and falling in tone at regular intervals (*a singsong accent*):—n a gathering at which those present sing together for amusement.

sin'gular adj **1** (*fml*) remarkable, unusual, odd, strange (*a singular happening*). **2** (*in grammar*) referring to one only (*a singular noun*).

singular'ity n **1** peculiarity, strangeness. **2** an unusual characteristic.

sin'gularly adv (*fml*) strangely, remarkably (*she was singularly beautiful*).

sin'ister adj **1** evil-looking (*a sinister stranger*). **2** thr eatening harm or evil (*a sinister warning*).

sink vb (*pt* **sank**, *pp* **sunk**) **1** to go slowly down (*the sun was sinking*). **2** to go below the surface of water (*the boat sank*). **3** to become worse or weaker (*the invalid is sinking fast*). **4** (*of an idea*) to be understood gradually (*his death has not sunk in yet*). **5** to dig (*sink a well*). **6** to cause to go underwater:—n a basin with a drainpipe leading from it, used when washing.

sink'er n a weight attached to a fishing line.

sinuos'ity n (*fml*) a wavy line, a bend.

sin'uous adj (*fml*) winding, curving in and out (*sinuous mountain paths*).

si'nus n a small hollow in a bone, esp that connecting the nose with the skull (*have an infection of the sinuses*).

sinusi'tis n illness caused by an infection of the nasal sinus.

sip vb (**sipped', sip'ping**) to drink in small mouthfuls (*sip a cold drink*):—also n.

si'phon n 1 a bent tube for drawing liquids out of one vessel into another. 2 a bottle of aerated water in which the liquid is forced out up a tube by the pressure of the gas.

sir n 1 a wor d of respect used to men. 2 the title given to a knight or baronet.

sire n 1 father . 2 male par ent of a horse or other animal (*the pony's sire*). 3 a title of r espect used on addressing a king:—*vb* (*of animals*) to procreate.

si'ren n 1 a mythical cr eature, half-woman, half-bird, who by the beauty of her song lured sail-ors to destruction. 2 an attractive but danger-ous woman. 3 a loud hooter sounded as a time signal or as a warning of danger (*a siren warn-ing of a bombing raid*).

sir'loin n the upper part of a loin of beef.

siroc'co n a hot wind blowing across Italy from the south.

sir'rah n old form of **sir** (used in anger or con-tempt).

sis'ter n 1 a female born of the same par ents as another person. 2 nun. 3 the nurse in char ge of a ward in a hospital.

sis'terhood n a society of women, usu carrying out religious or charitable works.

sis'ter-in-law n 1 the sister of a husband or wife. 2 the wife of one's br other.

sis'terly adj like a sister.

sit vb (**sat, sit'ting**) 1 to tak e a rest on a seat. 2 to rest upon eggs to hatch them. 3 (*of parliament, courts, etc*) to meet to do business. 4 to r est upon (*books sitting on the table*):—**sit up 1** to sit straight. 2 to stay out of bed when it is time to sleep (*parents sitting up until their children come in*).

site n the ground on which a building or number of buildings stands or is to stand (*the site of the new block of flats*):—*vb* to choose a place for.

sit'ter n one who visits an artist to have his or her portrait done.

sit'ting n 1 a single uninterrupted meeting. 2 one's seat in chur ch. 3 a single visit to an artist doing one's portrait.

sitting room n the room in which a family sit when not working.

sit'uated adj placed.

situa'tion n 1 a place or position (*a house in a picturesque situation*). 2 (*fml*) a job (*seek a*

new situation). 3 cir cumstances (*their financial situation*).

six'pence n a British silver coin (=6 pennies) in use until 1971.

six'penny adj worth or costing sixpence.

size[1] n bigness, bulk:—*vb* to arrange in order according to size (*sizing the eggs*):—**size up** to form an opinion about (*size up the opposition*).

size[2] n a thin glue used as a varnish on paper, cloth, etc.

siz'zle vb to make a hissing or spluttering sound, as when frying (*sausages sizzling on the grill*).

skate[1] n a steel blade fastened to a boot to allow a gliding movement on ice:—*vb* to move on skates or roller skates.

skate[2] n a large eatable flatfish.

skate'board n a short narrow board on small wheels on which people stand and move rapidly or perform jumps and stunts:—n **skate'boarding**.

skat'ing rink n an area of ice prepared for skating.

skein [skeen] n a coil or bundle of thread tied in a loose knot.

skel'eton n 1 the bony framework of a body . 2 an outline of a plot or plan (*give a skeleton of the scheme to the committee*):—**skeleton in the cup-board** something in one's past life that one keeps secret for fear of disgrace (*newspaper reporters anxious to find a skeleton in the filmstar's cupboard*).

skeleton key a key that will open a number of dif-ferent locks of similar pattern (*the skeleton key held by the hotel manager*).

skeleton staff the least number of people needed to keep a factory, etc, working.

sketch n 1 a r ough drawing or painting, some-times to be finished later. 2 an outline or short account (*a sketch of their future plans*). 3 a short amusing play:—*vb* 1 to mak e a quick or rough drawing. 2 to give a short account or outline of, to draw (*sketching out their plans*).

sketch'y adj incomplete, leaving out details (*a sketchy description of their plans*).

skew adj slanting, not straight.

skew'er n a wooden or metal pin for fastening meat in shape while cooking (*meat cooked on skewers*).

ski n a long shaped strip of wood, metal, etc, fixed to the feet to allow gliding movement over snow:—ns **ski'er, ski'ing**.

skid n 1 a wooden or metal block put under a wheel to stop it turning. 2 a sort of runner fixed to the under part of an aeroplane. 3 a sideways movement of a wheel on the ground:—vb (**skid'ded, skid'ding**) 1 to move sideways on wheels that fail to turn (cars skidding on the ice). 2 to stop turning by placing a block under (a wheel).

skiff n a small light boat.

skilful adj expert, clever (at doing something) (she was a skilful pianist).

skill n ability gained by practice, natural cleverness at doing something (her skill as a pianist/improve her typing skills).

skilled adj expert.

skill'et n a small pot with a long handle.

skim vb (**skimmed', skim'ming**) 1 to remove anything floating on the surface of a liquid (skim the grease off the stew). 2 to pass quickly over the surface of. 3 to read quickly and without attention (skim the headlines).

skim milk, skimmed milk n milk from which the cream has been skimmed.

skimp vb to give less than is needed, to give or use sparingly (skimp on the curtain material).

skimp'y adj insufficient (a skimpy dress/skimpy helpings of food).

skin n 1 the natural outer covering of animal or vegetable (apple skins). 2 a thin layer or covering (the skin on rice pudding). 3 a container made of skin:—vb (**skinned', skin'ning**) to take the skin off.

skin'flint n (inf) a miser, a mean person.

skin'ny adj (inf) very thin (children who are too skinny).

skip[1] vb (**skipped', skip'ping**) 1 to jump about lightly. 2 to keep on jumping over a rope swung over the head and then under the feet alternately. 3 to leave out parts of a book when reading it (skip the descriptive parts in the novel):—n a light jump.

skip[2] n the captain of a curling or bowling team.

skip'per n the captain of a ship or team.

skir'mish n 1 a fight in which the main armies are not engaged. 2 a fight broken off before serious harm is done to either side:—vb to fight in small parties.

skirt n 1 the part of a garment below the waist (the skirt of the ball dress). 2 a woman's gar-

ment stretching from the waist down. 3 the border or outer edge:—vb to pass along the edge or border.

skirt'ing n 1 material for skirts. 2 skirting board.

skirting board n a board round the bottom of a room wall (paint the skirting board with gloss paint).

skit n a piece of writing in which persons, events, etc, are imitated in a way that makes fun of them.

skit'tish adj playful (in a skittish mood).

skit'tle vb to knock down.

skit'tles npl a game in which one bowls a ball at nine pins or skittles to knock them down.

skulk vb to try to keep out of sight for fear or with evil intentions (burglars skulking in the garden watching the empty house).

skull n the bony case that contains the brain.

skunk n 1 a weasel-like animal that gives out an evil-smelling fluid when attacked. 2 (inf) a mean or contemptible person (he was a skunk to betray his friend).

sky n the space around the earth as visible to our eyes.

sky'-blue adj light blue, azure.

sky'lark n a small bird that sings as it flies upwards:—vb to play about noisily, to play tricks.

sky'light n a window in the roof of a building (the skylight in the attic).

sky'line n the horizon.

sky'scraper n a very tall building.

sky'wards adv upwards from the earth.

slab n a large flat piece of anything (a slab of cheese).

slack[1] adj 1 loose, not tight (a slack waistband). 2 careless, lazy (workers becoming slack under poor management). 3 not busy (their slack time of year):—n the loose part of a rope, etc:—vb 1 to work lazily or carelessly. 2 to lose speed.

slack[2] n coal dust and tiny pieces of coal.

slack'en vb 1 to loosen. 2 to lose force or speed (trains slackening speed). 3 to become less (demand slackening).

slack'er n (inf) one who does not work hard.

slack'ness n 1 looseness (the slackness of the waistband). 2 carelessness.

slacks npl loose-fitting trousers.

slag n 1 the waste matter from melted metal. 2 waste cinders from a furnace.

slag'heap *n* a heap of waste cinders.

slake *vb* **1** to satisf y (thirst). **2** to mix lime with water (when making cement).

slam¹ *vb* (**slammed'**, **slam'ming**) to shut or put down noisily (*slam the door angrily*):—*n* a bang.

slam² *n* in a card game, the winning of all or all but one of the tricks.

slan'der *n* an untrue story put about to injure a person's character (*take them to court on a charge of slander*):—*vb* to spread such a story.

slan'derous *adj* harmful to the reputation.

slang *n* words and phrases in common use but not accepted as good English:—*vb* to scold, to abuse.

slang'y *adj* (*inf*) using slang.

slant *n* slope (*draw a line at a slant*):—*vb* **1** to slope or cause to slope. **2** to expr ess or describe something in such a way as to emphasize a cer tain point or show favour towards a particular point of view.

slap *n* a blow with the open hand:—*vb* (**slapped'**, **slap'ping**) to strike with the flat of the hand or anything flat.

slap'dash *adj* careless, done in a hurry (*slapdash in their attitude to their work*):—*adv* carelessly.

slap'stick *adj* causing laughter by absurd ac tions:—*also n*.

slash *vb* **1** to mak e a sweeping cut at with a knife, etc, to make long cuts in. **2** to r educe sharply (*slash prices*):—*n* a long cut.

slat *n* a thin strip of wood, etc.

slate¹ *n* **1** a type of r ock that splits easily into thin layers. **2** a shaped piece of slate for covering a roof or for writing on:—*vb* to cover with slate (*slating the roof*).

slate² *vb* **1** to scold angrily . **2** to criticize sever ely (*a play slated by the critics*).

slat'er *n* one who slates buildings.

slat'tern *n* a dirty and untidy woman.

slat'ternly *adj* dirty, untidy.

slat'y *adj* of or like slate (*a slaty blue*).

slaughter [slä'-têr] *n* **1** killing in gr eat numbers. **2** the act of killing:— *vb* **1** to kill in gr eat num bers (*slaughter every soldier*). **2** to kill for food (*slaughter cattle*).

slaughter'house *n* a place where animals are killed for food.

slave *n* **1** one who is the pr operty of another per son and has to work for him or her. **2** one who has to do the dirty or unpleasant work:—*vb* to work very hard (*slaving away to try to pass the exam*).

slave'-driver *n* **1** one whose job it is to see that slaves work hard. **2** one who mak es those un der him or her work very hard.

slaver [sla'vêr] *vb* to let saliva drop from the mouth, to dribble:—*n* saliva running from the mouth.

slavery [slāv'eree] *n* **1** the state of being a slave. **2** har d, unpleasant and badly paid work (*it was sheer slavery working in the hotel kitchen*). **3** absence of all freedom.

slave trade *n* the buying and selling of people as slaves.

slav'ish *adj* **1** lik e a slave. **2** accepting without question (*a slavish attitude to fashion*).

slay *vb* (*pt* **slew**, *pp* **slain**) to kill.

sledge *n* a vehicle on runners for use in snow.

sledge'hammer *n* the heavy hammer used by a blacksmith.

sleek *adj* **1** smooth and shiny (*sleek hair*). **2** well fed and cared for (*sleek cats*).

sleep *vb* to rest the body, with the eyes shut, unaware of one's surroundings:—*n* a complete rest for the body, as at night.

sleep'er *n* **1** one who is asleep. **2** a long r ectan gular block that supports railway lines. **3** a coach on a train with bunks for sleeping passengers.

sleeping partner *n* one who owns part of a busi ness but does not work in it.

sleeping pill *n* a drug that makes one sleep.

sleep'less *adj* **1** unable to sleep (*lie sleepless all night*). **2** without sleep (*a sleepless night*).

sleep'walker *n* one who walks about in his or her sleep.

sleep'y *adj* wanting to sleep, drowsy (*feel sleepy after a large meal*).

sleep'y-head *n* (*inf*) a sleepy or lazy person.

sleet *n* falling snow mixed with rain or hail:—*adj* **sleet'y**.

sleeve *n* the part of a garment that covers the arm:—**laugh up one's sleeve** to be amused with out showing it (*she pretended to admire his efforts but was really laughing up her sleeve at him*).

sleigh [slā] *n* a vehicle on runners for use in snow, a sledge.

sleight of hand *n* quickness with the hands, jugglery (*admire the conjuror's sleight of hand*).

slen'der *adj* **1** thin, scanty, only just enough (*of slender means*). **2** slim (*a slender figure*).

sleuth [slöth] *n* a detective (*the sleuth in the crime story*).

slice *vb* **1** to cut into thin pieces (*slicing bread*). **2** to strik e a ball a glancing blow that makes it spin:—*n* **1** a thin br oad piece cut off (*a slice of bread*). **2** a flat utensil for ser ving food (*a fish slice*).

slick *adj* **1** quick and clever (*turn the pancake with a slick movement*). **2** smart but deceitful (*a slick salesman*).

slide *vb* (*pt,pp* **slid**) to move smoothly over a surface, as of ice, to slip:—*n* **1** a slope or track for sliding on (*the children's slide in the park*). **2** a small glass plate with an object to be examined through a microscope or a picture to be shown on a screen (*scientists examining bacteria on a slide*).

slide rule *n* a ruler with a central section that can be adjusted to perform calculations.

sliding scale *n* a rate (of wages, etc) that can be varied to suit existing conditions.

slight *adj* **1** small, lightly built (*too slight to push the heavy car*). **2** small, not gr eat, not serious (*matters of slight importance/a slight problem*):—*n* an insult:—*vb* to treat as unimportant, to treat insultingly.

slim *adj* thin, lightly built, small (*slim young women*):—*vb* (**slimmed', slim'ming**) to reduce weight by exercises, not eating certain foods, etc (*go on a diet to try to slim*).

slime *n* sticky mud.

slim'y *adj* **1** cover ed with slime, slippery. **2** untrustworthy (*a slimy character*).

sling *vb* (*pt, pp* **slung**) **1** to thr ow with the outstretched arm (*sling a stone in the river*). **2** to cause to hang from (*a gun slung from his shoulder*):—*n* **1** a strap or band used for hurling stones. **2** a bandage hanging fr om the neck to support an injured arm. **3** a band passed ar ound something to help to lift or support it (*a baby sling*).

slink *vb* (*pt, pp* **slunk**) to go away quietly as if ashamed (*the dog slunk away after being punished*).

slip *vb* (**slipped', slip'ping**) **1** to move smoothly along. **2** to go quietly or unseen. **3** to lose one's footing. **4** to escape (the memor y):—*n* **1** the act of slipping. **2** a car eless mistake. **3** a narrow piece of paper. **4** a twig. **5** a loose cover (e.g. a pillowcase). **6** a woman 's undergarment or petticoat. **7** a pr epared downward slope along which newly built, repaired, or laid-up ships can slide into the sea:—**give the slip to** to go away from without being noticed.

slip'knot *n* a knot that can be moved.

slip'per *n* a loose shoe for wear in the house.

slip'pery *adj* **1** har d to stand on without sliding or falling (*slippery ground*). **2** har d to hold without one's grip sliding (*slippery fish*). **3** (*inf*) untrustworthy (*a slippery character*).

slip'shod *adj* careless, untidy.

slip'way *n* a downward slope in a shipyard.

slit *vb* (**slit'ted, slit'ting**) to make a long cut in (*slit the envelope open*):—*n* a long narrow cut or opening.

slith'er *vb* to slide clumsily or without control (*people slithering on icy pavements*).

sli'ver *n* a thin piece cut off, a splinter (*a sliver of cheese*).

slob'ber *vb* to let saliva run or fall from the mouth.

sloe *n* **1** the blackthorn. **2** its black plum-lik e fruit.

slog *vb* (**slogged', slog'ging**) (*inf*) **1** to hit har d. **2** to work hard (*slogging away at his homework*):—*n* **slog'ger**.

slo'gan *n* **1** a war cr y. **2** a party cr y or catchword. **3** an easily memorized saying used to advertise a product or campaign.

sloop *n* a small sailing boat with one mast.

slop *vb* (**slopped', slop'ping**) to spill through carelessness, to overflow a little at a time:—*n* **1** a puddle of spilled liquid. **2** (*usu pl*) dirty or waste water. **3** (*usu pl*) liquid food.

slope *n* **1** a rise or fall fr om the level. **2** a slant:—*vb* **1** to rise or fall fr om the level (*fields sloping down to the sea*). **2** to slant.

slop'py *adj* (*inf*) **1** wet, muddy . **2** car eless and untidy (*sloppy work*). **2** foolishly sentimental (*sloppy love stories*).

slot n a narrow oblong opening or hole, esp one made to receive coins (*the slot in a gas meter*).

sloth n 1 laziness. 2 a slow-moving South American animal that lives in trees.

sloth'ful adj very lazy.

slot machine n a machine worked by placing coins in a slot.

slouch vb to stand, walk or sit with bent back and head and shoulders sloping inwards (*slouching in his chair*):—n a lazy and ugly way of standing and walking.

slouch hat n a hat with a soft drooping brim.

slough[1] [slou] n a bog, a wet and muddy place.

slough[2] [sluf] n the cast-off skin of a snake:—vb 1 to cast off (*snakes sloughing their skin*). 2 to throw off (*slough off a feeling of depression*).

slov'en n an untidy and dirty person.

slov'enly adj dirty and untidy, very careless (*slovenly habits/a slovenly housekeeper*).

slow adj 1 not quick or fast. 2 taking a long time to do things. 3 not clever (*slow pupils*). 4 behind the correct time (*the clock is slow*):—vb to go or cause to go less quickly.

slow'coach n one who does things slowly.

sludge n soft, thick mud.

slug[1] n a shell-less snail, harmful to plants.

slug[2] vb (**slugged'**, **slug'ging**) 1 to shoot. 2 to hit hard:—n a small solid metal bullet.

slug'gish adj slow-moving (*feel sluggish in the morning/trade is sluggish*).

sluice [slös] n 1 a sliding gate to contr ol the flow of water. 2 the water way so controlled:—vb to wash out with running water (*sluicing out the animal's feeding bowl*).

slum n part of a town in which people live in overcrowded, dirty and unhealthy houses.

slum'ber vb to sleep:—n sleep.

slump n a sudden fall in prices, wages, etc (*a slump in house prices*):—vb 1 to go suddenly down in price, etc. 2 to fall suddenly or heavily (*she slumped into a chair*).

slur vb (**slurred'**, **slur'ring**) 1 to pass over quickly or without attention. 2 to mak e (sounds) indistinct by running them together (*a drunk slurring his words*):—n 1 a bad point in one's character or reputation. 2 (*mus*) a curved mark over two notes to be played smoothly one after the other.

slush n 1 half-melted snow , soft mud. 2 (*inf*) foolishly sentimental writing or talk (*the slush on some greetings cards*):—adj **slush'y**.

slut n a dirty and untidy woman:—adj **slut'tish**.

sly adj cunning, deceitful, doing things in a secret and deceitful way:—**on the sly** secretly.

smack[1] vb 1 to hit with the flat of the hand (*mothers smacking children*). 2 to part the lips so as to make a sharp noise:—n a 1 slap. 2 a loud kiss.

smack[2] n a taste, a flavour or suggestion of:—vb 1 to taste (of). 2 to r emind of, to suggest (*the situation smacks of bribery*).

smack[3] n a small fishing boat with sails.

small adj 1 little (*small people*). 2 not much (*small reason to rejoice*):—n the narrow part of the back.

small arms n firearms that can be carried by one person (e.g. rifles, etc).

small beer n something unimportant.

small hours npl the hours just after midnight.

small'pox n a dangerous infectious disease that leaves little pocks on the skin.

small talk n conversation about unimportant matters (*trying to make small talk with his neighbour*).

smart adj 1 quick, clever (*smart pupils/smart thinking*). 2 well-dr essed (*smart wedding guests*):—vb to feel or cause a quick keen pain (*a burn that was smarting*).

smart'en vb to make smart or smarter (*told to smarten up his appearance*).

smash vb to break into pieces (*smash crockery*):—n 1 act of br eaking into pieces. 2 the noise caused by breakage. 3 an accident involving one or more vehicles (*a motorway smash*). 4 a disaster, downfall:—**smash and grab** a theft carried out by smashing a shop window and taking articles behind it.

smat'tering n a very slight knowledge (*have a smattering of German*).

smear vb 1 to spr ead (something sticky or dirty) over the surface (*smear jam over his face*). 2 to smudge, to make or become blurred (*smear the lettering*):—n 1 a dirty mark, a blot. 2 a stor y intended to harm a person's good name (*a smear campaign*).

smell n 1 the sense that enables animals to perceive by breathing in through the nose (*dogs finding the criminal by smell*). 2 scent, odour:— vb (pt, pp **smelled** or **smelt**) 1 to perceive by smell. 2 to give off an odour:— **smell a rat** to be suspicious.

smell'ing salts n a strong-smelling medicine that helps to revive a person feeling faint or ill.

smell'y adj (inf) having an unpleasant odour (*smelly socks*).

smelt[1] vb to melt metal out of rock:—n **smelt'er**.

smelt[2] n a small eatable fish of the salmon family.

smile vb 1 to show joy, amusement, etc, by a movement of the lips. 2 to be favourable (*the future smiling on them*):—n a look of pleasure or amusement.

smirch vb to make dirty, to stain (*smirch his reputation*).

smirk vb to smile in a silly or unnatural manner (*stand smirking while being photographed*):—n a smug or scornful smile (*a self-satisfied smirk*).

smite vb (**smote**, **smi'ting**, pp **smit'ten**) (*old or fml*) 1 to strike hard. 2 to cause to suffer from (*smitten with flu*).

smith n one who works in metals.

smith'y n the workshop of a blacksmith.

smock n 1 a loose overall worn to protect one's clothes. 2 a woman's loose dress.

smog n a smoky fog.

smoke n the sooty vapour rising from a burning substance (*smoke rising from the chimney*):— vb 1 to give off smoke (*fires smoking*). 2 to draw in the tobacco smoke from a cigarette, pipe, etc. 3 to preserve in smoke (*smoke fish*). 4 to drive out by smoke:—adj **smoke'less**.

smok'er n 1 one who smokes tobacco. 2 a compartment in a train in which smoking is allowed.

smoke screen n 1 thick clouds of smoke sent out to conceal movements. 2 something intended to conceal one's actual activities (*his shop was a smoke screen for his drug-smuggling*).

smoke'stack n the chimney of a steamer or factory.

smok'y adj 1 full of smoke (*smoky rooms*). 2 giving off smoke (*smoky fires*).

smolt n a salmon a year or two old.

smooth adj 1 having an even surface, not rough. 2 free from difficulties (*the smooth running of*

the organization). 3 having good yet not pleasing manners:—vb to make smooth or level (*smooth the rough wooden surface*).

smooth'-tongued adj able to speak in a very polite or flattering manner.

smoth'er vb to kill by keeping air from (*smother the old woman with a pillow*).

smoul'der vb to burn without flame.

smudge n a dirty mark, a stain:—vb 1 to make a dirty mark on. 2 to make or become blurred or smeared (*smudging the painting*):—adj **smudg'y**.

smug adj self-satisfied, too pleased with oneself.

smug'gle vb 1 to bring goods into the country secretly, without paying customs duties on them. 2 to bring in or pass secretly (*smuggling food into the dormitory*).

smug'gler n one who smuggles goods.

smut n 1 a flake of soot. 2 a dirty mark or stain. 3 dirty or indecent talk (*object to the smut of the comedian*):—adj **smut'ty**.

snack n a light quick meal (*a mid-morning snack*) 2 something, such as a biscuit or chocolate bar eaten between meals:—vb to eat between meals.

snaf'fle n a metal bit put in a horse's mouth to control it when riding.

snag n 1 an unexpected difficulty or hindrance (*their plans hit a snag*). 2 a log just below water surface, dangerous to boats.

snail n a slow-moving soft-bodied creature with a shell on its back.

snake n 1 a long crawling creature with no legs and a scaly skin, a serpent. 2 an untrustworthy or deceitful person (*the snake betrayed his friend*).

snak'y adj snake-like (*snaky movements*).

snap vb (**snapped'**, **snap'ping**) 1 to bite or seize suddenly. 2 to break with a sharp sound (*twigs snapping as they walked*). 3 to speak in a quick, angry manner (*mothers snapping at their children*). 4 to take a photograph of with a hand camera:—n 1 a sudden bite. 2 a short sharp sound. 3 a lock that springs shut when released. 4 a spell of weather (*a cold snap*). 5 a card game. 6 a snapshot.

snap'pish adj irritable, short-tempered.

snap'py adj 1 snappish (*a snappy remark*). 2 (*inf*) quick (*ask for a snappy response*).

snap'shot n **1** a quick shot. **2** a photograph taken with a hand camera.

snare n **1** a trap for catching birds or animals, esp one made with a running noose. **2** a temptation (*her beauty was a snare*):—vb to catch by a snare (*snaring rabbits*).

snarl vb **1** to growl angrily and show the teeth (*dogs snarling*). **2** to speak rudely or angrily (*an old man snarling at the children*):—also n.

snatch vb to seize quickly or suddenly:—n **1** a sudden seizing. **2** a small part.

sneak vb **1** to go quietly, as a thief (*sneak up the stairs at midnight*). **2** to tell of another 's wrongdoing to one in authority (*children sneaking on their friends*). **3** to behave meanly:— n **1** a telltale. **2** a mean person.

sneak'ing adj underhand, secret.

sneak'y adj mean.

sneer vb to show contempt by a look or remark (*sneer at his attempts to row the boat*):—n a mocking smile or remark.

sneeze vb to expel air noisily through the nose (*people with colds sneezing*):—n the act or sound of sneezing.

snick vb to cut a small piece out of (*snick his face while shaving*):—n a small cut, a notch.

snick'er same as **snigger**.

sniff vb **1** to breathe noisily inwards. **2** to smell (*sniff the smell of the sea*):—n **1** the act or sound of sniffing. **2** a slight smell:— **sniff at** to show scorn for.

snig'ger vb to laugh under the breath or secretly, to giggle nervously or unpleasantly:—also n.

snip vb (**snipped'**, **snip'ping**) to cut as with scissors, to cut off with one sharp movement (*snip off a lock of her hair*):—n **1** the act or sound of scissors closing to cut. **2** a small piece cut off (*a snip of the material*).

snipe[1] n a game bird with a long bill, found in marshy places.

snipe[2] vb to shoot at from a hiding place:—n **snip'er**.

snip'pet n **1** a small piece cut off. **2** a short item of news (*snippets of gossip*).

sniv'el vb (**sniv'elled**, **sniv'elling**) **1** to run at the nose. **2** to go on crying or complaining, to whimper (*snivel about being cold*) .

snob n one who looks down on others because they are less wealthy or of lower rank in society (*his former friends accuse him of being a snob*):— n **snob'bery**.

snob'bish adj behaving like a snob.

snood n a band for the hair, a hairnet, a hood.

snook'er n a billiards game in which players have to knock, with a white cue ball, 15 red and then in order 6 coloured balls into pockets on a table.

snoop vb to go about secretly or stealthily in order to find out something (*snooping among her friend's papers*):—n **snoop'er**.

snoot'y adj (*inf*) haughty, proud and distant in manner (*snooty neighbours who won't speak to other people*).

snooze n (*inf*) a short light sleep:—vb to take a short nap (*snoozing on the plane*).

snore vb to breathe noisily while asleep, as if grunting:—n the noise so made.

snor'kel n a tube that extends above the water through which one can breathe while swimming just below the surface.

snort vb to blow air out noisily through the nose (*snort with disbelief*):—also n.

snot n the mucus of the nose.

snout n **1** the long nose and mouth of an animal (*the pig's snout*). **2** the nozzle of a pipe.

snow [snō] n vapour frozen in the air and falling in flakes:—vb to fall as snow, to cover as with snow.

snow'ball n snow pressed into a hard ball.

snow blind'ness n dullness of sight caused by the glare from snow:—adj **snow'blind**.

snow'board n a long wide board with bindings for the feet on which people slide down slow slopes:—n **snow'boarding**.

snow'drift n snow heaped up by the wind to form a bank.

snow'drop n a small white flower that grows in early spring.

snow'flake n a single piece of snow.

snow line n the level above which snow never melts.

snow'plough n an implement for clearing snow from roads or railways.

snow'shoe n a light broad frame worn on the feet for walking on snow.

snow'y adj **1** of or lik e snow. **2** pur e white (*snowy sheets on the washing line*).

snub vb (**snubbed', snub'bing**) to show dislike or disapproval of a person by taking no notice of or speaking rudely to him or her (*she was snubbed when she tried to be friendly to them*):—n rude lack of notice, an unfriendly act or speech:—adj (*of a nose*) short and turned up.

snuff' vb **1** to br eathe in through the nose. **2** to sniff powdered tobacco, etc, up the nose:—n **1** tobacco powder ed for sniffing up the nose. **2** a sniff.

snuff' vb to cut off the burnt part of the wick of a candle.

snuff'box n a box for carrying snuff in the pocket.

snuf'fle vb **1** to mak e sniffing noises. **2** to speak through the nose (*children with colds snuffling*).

snug adj warm and comfortable, cosy (*children snug in their beds/a snug room*).

snug'gle vb to lie close for warmth, to settle comfortably (*children snuggling under the bed-clothes*).

so adv **1** in this or that manner (*do it so*). **2** to that extent (*so wet that we stayed in*). **3** thus (*she was tired and so left the party*). **4** ver y (*so happy*):—conj therefore (*be quiet so I can think*).

soak vb **1** to wet thor oughly. **2** to steep (*soak the stained clothing*). **3** to suck up (*blotting paper soaking up ink*).

soak'ing n a thorough wetting.

soap n **1** a substance made of oil or fat and certain chemicals, used in washing **2** a soap opera:—vb to rub with soap.

soap opera n a radio or television drama serial which deals with the day-to-day lives and problems of the same group of characters [originates from the soap-powder-selling sponsors of such shows in the 1950s in the USA].

soap'suds npl the froth on soapy water.

soap'y adj having to do with soap (*soapy water*).

soar vb **1** to fly upwar ds. **2** to tower up (*mountains soaring above the town*).

sob vb (**sobbed', sob'bing**) to draw in the breath noisily when weeping or short of breath:—also n.

so'ber adj **1** not drunk (*not quite sober*). **2** serious, quiet (*a sober person*). **3** dark in colour (*wear sober clothes to the funeral*).

sobri'ety n the state of being sober.

so'-called adj given a name or title to which one has no right (*a so-called lady*).

soc'cer n association football.

so'ciable adj fond of company.

so'cial adj **1** having to do with society (*social problems*). **2** living in an or ganized group (*social creatures*).

so'cialism n the belief that all means of producing national wealth (e.g. mines, etc) are the property of the community and should be used for the benefit of all.

so'cialist n one who believes in socialism.

soci'ety n **1** a gr oup of people living together in a single organized community. **2** a gr oup of people who meet regularly for a special purpose, mixing with other people (*a debating society*). **3** the wealthy or high-ranking members of a community (*mix in society*).

socio'logy n the study of the nature, growth and problems of human society:—n soci-o'logist.

sock n a short stocking.

sock'et n a hole or hollow for something to fit into or turn in (*an electric socket/an eye socket*).

sod n a piece of earth held together by the roots of the grass growing in it.

so'da n an alkali (carbonate of soda) made into a powder and used in washing, baking, etc.

soda water n water containing bicarbonate of soda and made fizzy by gas.

sod'den adj wet through, soaking (*their sodden clothes*).

so'dium n a soft light silvery metal that burns in water.

so'fa n a couch with cushioned seat, back and arms.

soft adj **1** not har d (*soft cheese*). **2** easily r eshaped by pressing (*a soft substance*). **3** not loud (*soft music*). **4** (*of colour*) not bright. **5** gentle (*a soft breeze*). **6** not strict (*teachers who are too soft*). **7** not alcoholic (*soft drinks*). **8** foolishly kind (*Don't be soft!*):—adv quietly, gently.

soft drink a non-alcoholic drink, like lemonade.

soften [så'-fên] vb **1** to mak e or become soft. **2** to become less harsh or angry (*her attitude softened*).

soft goods cloth and articles made of cloth.

soft-spok'en adj having a low or gentle voice.

soft'ware *n* the programs used in computers.

sog'gy *adj* soft and wet (*soggy toast/soggy ground*).

soil *n* the ground, earth, esp that in which plants are grown:—*vb* to dirty, to spoil (*children told not to soil their clothes in the sand*).

sojourn [sŏ'-jêrn] *vb* (*fml*) to stay (in a place) for a time:—*n* (*fml*) a temporary stay (*a sojourn of three weeks by the sea*).

sol'ace *vb* to cheer, to comfort:—*n* that which gives cheer or comfort (*the widow found her child a solace*).

so'lar *adj* having to do with the sun (*solar power*).

solar plex'us *n* the network of nerves behind the stomach.

solar system the sun and the planets that move round it.

sold *pt of* **sell.**

sol'der *n* a metal alloy that when melted can be used for cementing together pieces of metal:—*vb* to join with solder.

sol'dier *n* a person serving in an army.

sol'dierly *adj* like or of a soldier (*a soldierly stance*).

sole[1] *n* the underside of the foot, stocking or shoe (*boots with leather soles*):—*vb* to put a sole on (a shoe).

sole[2] *n* a small flatfish.

sole[3] *adj* only, single (*his sole objection*):—*adv* **sole'ly.**

sol'ecism *n* a mistake in grammar, speech or behaviour.

sol'emn *adj* **1** serious in manner or appearance (*a solemn child*). **2** slow , stately (*a solemn procession*).

solem'nity *n* seriousness.

sol'-fa *n* the use of the sounds *doh, ray, me, fah, soh, lah, te* in singing the scale:—*also adj.*

soli'cit *vb* to ask earnestly or repeatedly (*soliciting a loan*):—*n* **solicita'tion.**

soli'citor *n* a lawyer who advises people on matters concerned with the law and prepares cases for presentation in court by a barrister or advocate.

soli'citous *adj* anxious, full of concern (for) (*solicitous about her mother's health*).

soli'citude *n* anxiety, care, concern.

sol'id *adj* **1** not hollow , consisting of hard matter throughout (*solid pieces of metal*). **2** not liquid or gaseous (*solid substances*). **3** firm (*solid*

flesh). **4** r eliable (*a solid citizen*):—*n* a body consisting of hard matter throughout.

solidar'ity *n* sameness of interests (*workers joined by solidarity*).

solid'ify *vb* to make or become solid (*water solidified in the pipes*).

solid'ity *n* the state of being solid.

solil'oquy *n* (*fml*) a speaking to oneself (*the actor's soliloquy*).

solitaire' *n* a game for one player, esp one with marbles on a board with holes.

sol'itary *adj* **1** alone, without companions (*solitary travellers/a solitary tree*). **2** living or being alone by habit or preference (*solitary people*). **3** single (*a solitary reason*):—*n* one who lives alone and away from others.

sol'itude *n* loneliness, being alone, a lonely place.

so'lo *n* **1** a piece of music for a single performer . **2** a performance by one person (*a piano solo*). **3** a single person 's unaccompanied flight in an aeroplane.

so'loist *n* a solo singer or performer.

sol'stice *n* the time when the sun is farthest north (21st June) or south (21st December), giving in the Northern Hemisphere the longest and shortest days respectively.

sol'uble *adj* **1** able to be melted or dissolved in liquid. **2** (*fml*) to which an answer or solution can be found (*soluble problems*):—*n* **solubil'ity.**

solu'tion *n* **1** a liquid containing another substance dissolved in it (*a salty solution*). **2** the answer to or explanation of a problem, etc (*the solution to a crossword puzzle*).

solve *vb* to find the right answer to or explanation of (*solving the problem/solved the puzzle*).

sol'vency *n* ability to pay one's debts.

sol'vent *adj* **1** able to pay one's debts (*firms that are scarcely solvent*). **2** able to dissolve:— *n* a liquid able to dissolve another substance (*get some solvent to remove the grease from his shirt*).

som'bre *adj* dark, gloomy, cheerless (*sombre colours/in a sombre mood*).

sombre'ro *n* a broad-brimmed felt hat.

some *adj* a certain number or amount (of):—*pron* **1** certain people (*some would not agree*). **2** a little (*have some*):—*ns and prons* **some'one, some'thing.**

some'body n and pron **1** some person. **2** a person of importance.

some'how adv in some way or other (we'll get there somehow).

somersault [sum'-êr-sålt] n a leap or roll in which the heels turn completely over the head.

some'time adj (fml) former (his sometime lover).

some'times adv now and then.

some'what adv in some degree, a little (somewhat annoyed).

some'where adv in some place (they have to live somewhere).

somnam'bulism n the act of walking about while asleep:—n **somnam'bulist**.

som'nolent adj (fml) sleepy:—n **som'no-lence**.

son [sun] n a male child.

sonar' n an apparatus that detects objects underwater by reflecting sound waves.

sona'ta n a musical composition in several movements, usu for a solo instrument.

song n **1** wor ds set to music for the voice. **2** the sounds uttered by a bird. **3** a short poem, poetry.

song'ster n **1** a singer . **2** a singing bir d:—f **song'stress**.

son'-in-law n the man married to one's daughter.

son'net n a poem of fourteen lines, usu following fixed rhyming patterns.

son'orous adj having a deep, clear sound or tone (the sonorous voice of the minister).

soon adv **1** in a short time (they'll be here soon). **2** early (it's too soon to know). **3** willingly (I would just as soon go).

soot n black particles that rise with the smoke from burning matter.

soothe vb to calm, to comfort (soothing the baby/ soothe the pain).

sooth'sayer n one who foretells the future.

sooty adj **1** lik e soot. **2** black (a sooty cat).

sop n **1** a piece of br ead dipped in liquid before being eaten. **2** a money gift or bribe given to make less angry or unfriendly (give the workers a sop to stop them striking):—vb (**sopped'**, **sop'ping**) to soak.

soph'ist n one who reasons falsely but persuasively:—adj **sophis'tic(al)**.

sophis'ticated adj **1** (fml) not natural. **2** having a great deal of experience and wordly wisdom, knowledge of how to dress elegantly, etc:—n **sophistica'tion**.

soph'istry n false reasoning.

soporific adj (fml) causing sleep:—n a drug that causes sleep.

sop'py adj **1** wet thr ough. **2** foolishly sentimental (soppy love songs).

sopra'no n **1** the highest female or boy 's singing voice. **2** a singer with such a voice.

sor'cerer n one who works magic, an enchanter.

sor'cery n magic, witchcraft.

sor'did adj mean, dirty, disgusting (a sordid neighbourhood/a sordid crime).

sore adj painful, hurtful (sore legs):—n a painful cut or growth on the body (old people with bed sores).

sore'ly adv **1** ver y much. **2** painfully .

sor'rel n **1** a plant with sour-tasting leaves. **2** a reddish brown colour. **3** a horse of that colour.

sor'row n sadness caused by loss or suffering, grief (her sorrow at the death of her friend):—vb to mourn, to grieve:—adj **sor'rowful**.

sor'ry adj **1** feeling pity or r egret, sad because of wrongdoing (sorry for what he had done). **2** wr etched (a sorry sight).

sort n a kind, class or set:—vb to arrange in classes or sets (sorting the library books):—**out of sorts** not well.

sort'er n one who sorts, esp letters in a post office.

sor'tie n **1** a sudden quick attack made by the defenders of a fort upon their attackers. **2** a short expedition or trip.

so-so' adj fairly good, not bad (his work is only so-so).

sot n a drunkard.

sot'tish adj **1** foolish. **2** given to drink.

sou n an old French coin (=halfpenny).

soufflé [söf'-lä] n a light dish made from beaten whites of eggs (a cheese soufflé).

sough [suf, sou, soch (Scot)] n (of the wind) to make a moaning or sighing sound.

sought pt of seek.

soul n **1** the spiritual part of a person. **2** (inf) a person (poor souls).

soul'ful adj full of feeling (soulful music).

soul'less adj lacking nobility of mind, meanspirited.

sound[1] *adj* **1** healthy (*sound in mind and body*). **2** str ong (*sound reasons for going*). **3** without serious error or weakness (*his work is quite sound*):—*adv* completely.

sound[2] *n* **1** a noise. **2** that which is hear d:—*vb* **1** to mak e a noise (*alarms sounding*). **2** to touch or strike so as to cause a noise (*sound the dinner gong*).

sound[3] *n* a long narrow piece of water between two land masses, a strait:—*vb* **1** to find depth by lowering a lead weight on a cord. **2** to tr y to discover someone's opinion by questioning (*sound out his views on the new project*).

sound barrier *n* speed in motion equal to or greater than the speed of sound.

sound'ing board *n* **1** a boar d over a platform, etc, to direct the sound towards the audience. **2** a means used for testing thoughts, opinions, etc (*use her as a sounding board for his artistic ideas*).

sound'ings *npl* measurements of the depth of the sea made by sounding.

sound'less *adj* noiseless (*machines that are practically soundless*).

sound'track *n* the part of a film on which sounds are recorded.

soup [sōp] *n* a liquid food made by boiling meat, vegetables, etc (*leek soup*).

sour *adj* **1** sharp or bitter in taste (*the sour taste of lemons*). **2** ill-temper ed and hard to please (*a sour old man complaining about the child's noise*):—*vb* to make sour.

source *n* **1** that fr om which anything begins. **2** the spring from which a river flows. **3** origin or cause.

souse *vb* **1** to pickle in salted water (*soused herring*). **2** to plunge into water .

soutane [sö-tän] *n* a long black gown worn by RC priests, a cassock.

south *n* **1** one of the four car dinal points of the compass opposite north. **2** the position of the sun at noon (in Britain):—*adj* being in the south, facing south:—*also adv*:—*adj and adv* **south'ward**.

south'east *n* the point midway between south and east:—*also adj*:—*adjs* **south-east'erly**, **southeast'ern**.

sou'therly *adj* lying towards or coming from the south (*southerly winds*).

sou'thern *adj* in or of the south (*the southern part of the country*).

south'west *n* the point midway between south and west:—*also adj*:—*adjs* **south-west'erly**, **southwest'ern**.

sou'venir *n* an object kept to remind one of a person or event (*a souvenir of their holiday*).

sou'wester *n* **1** a str ong southwest wind. **2** a waterproof hat with a large flap at the back to cover the neck.

sov'ereign *adj* above all others, chief:—*n* **1** ruler , a king or queen. **2** an old British gold coin (= £1).

sov'ereignty *n* supreme power.

sow[1] [sou] *n* a female pig (*sows with their piglets*).

sow[2] [sō] *vb* (*pp* **sown**) **1** to scatter (*sow seeds*). **2** to plant with seeds (*sow a new lawn*).

sow'er *n* one who sows.

soy'a bean *n* a type of bean grown in the East, used for making flour or oil, as fodder for cattle and in food that is free of dairy products, such as **soya milk**.

spa *n* a place at which natural mineral waters may be drunk for the health.

space *n* **1** the whole extent of the universe not occupied by solid bodies. **2** the distance between one body or object and another. **3** the place occupied by a person or thing. **4** a length of time (*in the space of a year*):—*vb* to arrange with intervals between (*spacing the new trees out across the field*).

space'craft *n* a vehicle used for space travel.

spa'cious *adj* roomy (*spacious cars*).

spade *n* **1** a tool with a br oad blade, used for digging. **2** *pl* a suit of playing cards:—**call a spade a spade** to say exactly what one thinks.

spade'work, *n* the hard work needed to start an enterprise (*do all the spadework when they opened the office*).

spaghetti [spä-ge'-ti] *n* long thin tubes of paste made from flour (*spaghetti with tomato sauce*).

spake *old form of* **spoke**.

span *n* **1** the distance between the tip of the thumb and the little finger fully extended (about 23 cms in an adult). **2** the spr ead of an arch. **3** the distance fr om end to end of a bridge. **4** a space of time (*a span of five years*). **5** a number of horses or oxen yoked together to draw a cart, etc:—*vb* (**spanned'**, **span'ning**) **1** to extend fr om one point in space or time to another (*his criminal record spans ten years*). **2** to measur e with outstretched fingers.

span'gle *n* a small glittering metal ornament.

spaniel [span'-yêl] *n* a sporting or pet dog with long silky hair and drooping ears.

spank *vb* **1** to slap with the hand (*the child was spanked by her mother*). **2** to move along quickly .

span'ner *n* a tool fitted on to the head of a nut and used for tightening or loosening it.

spar[1] *n* **1** a long piece of wood. **2** a pole attached to the mast, used for holding sails in position.

spar[2] *vb* (**sparred'**, **spar'ring**) to box, to fight with the fists, to argue.

spare *adj* **1** scar ce. **2** thin. **3** mor e than is needed, kept in reserve:—*vb* **1** to let off punishment or suffering, to show mercy to. **2** to do without. **3** to use up slowly and car efully.

spark *n* **1** a tiny piece of burning matter . **2** a tiny flash made by electricity passing from one wire to another. **3** a bright or clever young person:— *vb* to give off sparks.

spark'ing plug a device for causing an electric spark to ignite the gas that drives an engine.

spark'le *vb* **1** to seem to give off sparks, to glitter (*lights sparkling*). **2** to be lively and intelligent (*she was sparkling at the party*):—*n* glitter, liveliness, brilliance.

sparring part'ner *n* one who takes part in practice fights with a boxer.

spar'row *n* a common small bird.

spar'rowhawk *n* a small type of hawk.

sparse *adj* **1** thinly scatter ed (*sparse vegetation*). **2** scanty , scarcely enough (*our information is rather sparse*):—*n* **spar'sity**.

Spar'tan *n* an inhabitant of the ancient Greek state of Sparta:—*adj* hardy, suffering much without complaint (*a Spartan existence with no luxuries*).

spasm *n* **1** a sudden involuntar y movement of the body, caused by a tightening of muscles, as in cramp, a fit (*an epileptic spasm*). **2** a feeling or activity that does not last long (*a spasm of coughing*).

spasmod'ic *adj* done occasionally for short periods (*spasmodic bouts of coughing*).

spas'tic *n* one suffering from a nervous disorder that causes continual jerky movements of the muscles:—*also adj.*

spate *n* **1** a flood, the overflow of a river . **2** a lar ge number or amount (*a spate of letters*).

spa'tial *adj* (*fml*) having to do with space (*spatial problems*).

spats *npl* a cloth covering for the upper part of the feet and ankles.

spat'ter *vb* to throw or scatter (liquid, mud, etc) in drops, to splash (*cars spattering pedestrians with mud*).

spat'ula *n* a broad thin blade used in spreading or scraping plaster, paint, ointment, etc (*a spatula for turning eggs in the pan*).

spa'vin *n* a disease of horses affecting the leg joints.

spawn *n* the eggs of fish, frogs, etc:—*vb* **1** to pr oduce spawn. **2** to pr oduce, usu in large numbers (*a lot of new committees have been spawned*).

speak *vb* (*pt* **spoke**, *pp* **spok'en**) **1** to utter words, to talk (*children learning to speak*). **2** to mak e a speech (*speak after dinner*). **3** to pr onounce.

speak'er *n* **1** one who speaks. **2** a member of the House of Commons elected to be its chairperson.

spear *n* a weapon with a long straight handle and a pointed metal head:—*vb* to pierce with a spear.

spe'cial *adj* **1** having to do with one particular thing, person or occasion (*a special tool for the job*). **2** not common or usual, distinctive (*a special occasion*):—*n* **special'ty.**

spe'cialist *n* one who makes a particular study of one subject or of one branch of a subject (*a cookery specialist*).

special'ity *n* **1** a special field of work or study (*cosmetic surgery is his speciality*). **2** something made or sold only by a certain trader (*the speciality of the house*).

spe'cialize *vb* to make a particular study of (one subject) (*a doctor specializing in skin disorders*).

spe'cie *n* metal money, coins.

spe'cies *n* kind, sort, a group of things (e.g. plants, animals) with certain characteristics in common.

specif'ic *adj* **1** definite (*something specific he wants to ask*). **2** exact (*specific instructions*).

3 particular (*a specific tool for the job*):—*n* a remedy for a particular disease.

specifica'tion *n* an exact statement of the details of a piece of work to be done (measurements, materials to be used, etc) (*the specifications for the new factory*).

spec'ify *vb* to state exactly or in detail (*specified his reasons for leaving*).

spec'imen *n* a sample, a part taken as an example of the whole (*take a blood specimen*).

spe'cious *adj* (*fml*) seeming true or right but really false.

speck *n* a tiny particle, spot or stain (*a speck of soot*).

speck'le *n* a small spot on a differently coloured background.

speck'led *adj* marked with speckles (*the speckled breast of the bird*).

spec'tacle *n* **1** something worth looking at, a wonderful or magnificent sight (*crowds gathering to see the spectacle of the military parade*). **2** *pl* glasses worn in front of the eyes to assist the eyesight.

spectac'ular *adj* **1** magnificent or splendid to look at (*a spectacular parade*). **2** impr essive, dramatic (*a spectacular change in his appearance*).

specta'tor *n* one who looks on.

spec'tral *adj* ghostly (*spectral figures*).

spec'tre *n* a ghost.

spec'troscope *n* an instrument used to break up rays of light into the colours of the rainbow.

spec'trum *n* a band of colours, as in a rainbow, produced by passing light through a prism.

spec'ulate *vb* **1** to think about, to guess without having the necessary facts (*speculating on his reasons for leaving*). **2** to buy shar es in the hope of selling them later at a profit.

specula'tion *n* **1** act of speculating. **2** a guess or theory (*some speculation that they were getting married*).

spec'ulative *adj* **1** risk y (*a speculative venture*). **2** hesitant, uncertain. **3** given to tr ying to think out the reasons for things (*some speculative thinking*).

spec'ulator *n* one who buys things (esp of uncertain value) in the hope of making a large profit on them.

speech *n* **1** the ability to speak (*children acquiring speech*). **2** a talk given in public (*an after-dinner speech*).

speech'less *adj* unable to speak for love, surprise, fear, etc (*speechless with rage*).

speed *n* **1** quickness of movement (*the speed of the car*). **2** haste (*move with speed*):—*vb* (*pt* **sped**) **1** to go fast. **2** to drive a motor car ver y fast, often illegally fast (*fined for speeding*). **3** to succeed or make succeed.

speedom'eter *n* an indicator to show how fast a car, motor cycle, etc, is travelling.

speed'well *n* a plant with small blue flowers.

speed'y *adj* fast, quick-moving (*seek a speedy end to the strike*).

spell[1] *vb* (*pt, pp* **spelt** *or* **spelled'**) to say or write the letters of a word in order.

spell[2] *n* certain words uttered in order to make something happen by magic, a charm, a strange or magical power.

spell[3] *n* **1** a length of time (*spells of bad weather*). **2** a turn at doing work (*a spell at digging the garden*).

spell'bound *adj* fascinated, made still by wonder or magic.

spel'ter *n* zinc, usu impure.

spen'cer *n* a short woollen coat or jacket.

spend *vb* (*pt, pp* **spent**) **1** to pay out (money). **2** to use or use up. **3** to pass (time).

spend'thrift *n* one who spends money wastefully and carelessly.

spent *adj* **1** tir ed out (*spent after the day's work*). **2** used up (*spent energy*).

sperm *n* spawn or eggs.

sperm whale *n* a type of whale from which is obtained **spermaceti**, an oily substance used in ointments.

spew *vb* **1** (*inf*) to vomit. **2** to come out in a flood (*lava spewed out of the volcano*).

sphere *n* **1** a ball. **2** a sun, star or planet. **3** the extent of one's work, knowledge, influence, etc (*in the sphere of television*).

spher'ical *adj* round like a sphere.

Sphinx *n* a mythical monster, half-woman, half-lion, said to put riddles to travellers and to destroy those who could not answer.

spice *n* **1** a sharp-tasting substance used to flavour food (*add spices to the sauce*). **2** something

spin't[ ]

spine[ ]

ani[ ]

spine'less [ ]

determi[ ]

himself).

spin'et, spin'n[ ]

harpsichord.

exciting or interesting (*add a bit of spice to life*):—*vb* to flavour with spice, etc.

spick'-and-span' *adj* neat and tidy, smart.

spic'y *adj* **1** sharp-tasting (*spicy food*). **2** lively and witty (*spicy stories*).

spi'der *n* an eight-legged creature that spins a web to catch the insects on which it lives.

spi'dery *adj* long and thin.

spig'ot *n* a peg to stop the hole in a cask.

spike *n* **1** a short piece of pointed metal, a lar ge nail (*spikes along the top of the wall to keep people out*). **2** an ear of corn. **3** many small flowers forming a single head along a stalk:—*vb* **1** to fasten with spik es. **2** to pier ce with a spike. **3** to put a gun out of action by driving a spike into it:—**spike someone's guns** to spoil someone's plans (*she tried to get her colleague sacked but we succeeded in spiking her guns*).

spike'nard *n* a sweet-smelling Eastern plant from which oil is obtained.

spill[1] *vb* (*pt, pp* **spilled'** *or* **spilt**) to let run out or overflow (*spill the tea as she pours it*):—*n* **1** a fall. **2** something spilled.

spill[2] *n* a thin strip of wood or twisted paper for lighting cigarettes, candles, etc.

spin *vb* (**spun, spin'ning**) **1** to draw out (wool, cotton, etc) and twist into threads. **2** to turn quickly round and round one point (*she spun round to face him*). **3** (*inf*) to make up (*spin a yarn about being attacked*):—*n* **1** a short or rapid trip. **2** a dive made by an aeroplane turning round and round at the same time.

spin'ach *n* a vegetable whose leaves are eaten as food.

spin'al *adj* having to do with the spine (*spinal injuries*).

spin'dle *n* in a spinning machine, the bar on to which the newly made thread is wound.

spin'dly *adj* very long and thin (*spindly legs*).

⋯ift *n* the spray blown from the tops of waves.

⋯ *n* **1** the backbone. **2** a pointed spik e on an ⋯nal or fish. **3** a thorn.

⋯adj 1 having no spine. **2** weak, lacking ⋯mination (*too spineless to stand up for*

⋯et *n* an early type of piano, like the

spin'naker *n* a triangular sail sometimes used on racing yachts.

spin'ney *n* a small wood.

spin'ning jen'ny *n* an early type of spinning machine.

spin'ning wheel *n* a home spinning machine operated by a wheel driven by a pedal.

spin'ster *n* a woman who has never been married.

spin'y *adj* full of prickles or thorns (*spiny bushes*).

spir'al *adj* winding round and round like the thread of a screw (*a spiral staircase*):—*also n*.

spire *n* a tall tower, tapering to a pointed top.

spir'it *n* **1** the soul. **2** a ghost. **3** courage, liveliness (*sing with spirit*). **4** mood (*the spirit of the times*). **5** the intention underlying (*the spirit, not the letter, of the law*). **6** *pl* strong alcoholic liquor:—*vb* to remove in a mysterious way.

spir'ited *adj* **1** lively (*a spirited musical performance*). **2** showing courage (*a spirited defence of her tennis title*).

spirit lamp *n* a lamp that burns methylated spirits.

spir'itless *adj* without courage or liveliness.

spirit level *n* a sealed tube filled with alcohol and containing an air bubble that is stationar y in the middle of the tube when it is level with the ground.

spir'itual *adj* **1** having to do with the soul or spirit (*the children's spiritual welfare*). **2** r eligious, holy:—*n* a religious song of the American Blacks.

spir'itualism *n* the belief that the soul or spirit only has real existence, the belief that it is possible to communicate with the souls of the dead:—*n* **spir'itualist**.

spirituality *n* concern with religion and matters concerning the soul.

spir'ituous *adj* containing alcohol.

spit[1] *n* **1** a long thick pin on which meat is r oasted over a fire (*a pig turning on a spit*). **2** a long piece of lowland running out into the sea:—*vb* (**spit'ted, spit'ting**) to put on a spit, to pierce.

spit[2] *vb* (**spat, spit'ting**) **1** to blow fr om the mouth (*spit out chewing gum*). **2** to put saliva, etc, out of the mouth (*he spat on the pavement*):—*n* a quantity of saliva put out of the mouth.

spite *n* ill-feeling against another, a desire to hurt or harm another:—*vb* to do something to hurt or harm another:—**in spite of** without paying attention to (*she got the job in spite of her lack of qualifications*).

spite'ful *adj* desiring or intended to hurt or harm another (*a spiteful person/a spiteful action*).

spit'fire *n* a quick-tempered person.

spit'tle *n* saliva, the liquid of the mouth.

spittoon' *n* a vessel for spitting into.

splash *vb* to throw or scatter drops of mud or liquid on to (*splash bath oil into the water/rain splashing in the puddles*):—*n* **1** act of splashing. **2** the sound made by a heavy body striking water. **3** a spot of mud or li-quid (*splashes on her white dress*).

splay *vb* to slope or turn outwards:—*adj* (*of feet*) turned outwards and flat.

spleen *n* **1** an or gan near the stomach that helps purify the blood. **2** ill-temper , gloom (*vent his spleen on his colleagues*).

splen'did *adj* **1** bright, shining, brilliant (*a splendid palace*). **2** excellent (*a spendid performance*).

splen'dour *n* brightness, magnificence.

splenet'ic *adj* ill-natured, gloomy, easily angered.

splice *vb* **1** to join the ends of two r opes together by interweaving their strands. **2** to fit one piece of wood into another so as to join them:—*n* a joint so made.

splint *n* a piece of wood to keep a broken bone in position (*the ambulance driver put a splint on the injured man's leg*).

splin'ter *n* a sharp-edged or pointed piece of glass, wood, metal, etc, broken off a larger piece:—*vb* to break into small pieces (*the shop window splintered*).

split *vb* (**split, split'ting**) **1** to cut or br eak from end to end. **2** to separate into parts or smaller groups (*split the class into teams*):—*n* **1** a long break or crack (*a split in the wood*). **2** a division (*a split on the committee*). **3** *pl* the trick of going down upright on the ground with the legs spread out at each side at right angles to the body.

splut'ter *vb* **1** to utter confused, indistinct sounds (*spluttering in rage*). **2** to mak e a spitting noise (*the candle spluttered*):—*also n.*

spoil *vb* (*pt, pp* **spoiled'** or **spoilt**) **1** to mak e or become useless or unpleasant (*food spoiling in the heat/spoil his chances of getting the*

job). **2** to r ob, to plunder. **3** to harm someone's character by always allowing him or her his or her own way (*spoil the children*):—*n* things stolen or taken by force.

spoil'sport *n* one who spoils the pleasure of others.

spoke[1] *pt of* **speak**:—*pp* **spok'en.**

spoke[2] *n* one of the bars running from the hub to the rim of a wheel:—**put a spoke in someone's wheel** to do something to prevent a person from carrying out a plan.

spoke'shave *n* a planing tool for giving wood a curving shape.

spokes'man, spokes'woman, spokes'person *n* one who speaks for others (*the workers elected a spokesperson to talk to management*).

spolia'tion *n* plundering, robbing.

spon'dee *n* in poetry, a metrical foot of two long syllables.

sponge [spunj] *n* **1** a type of sea animal. **2** a kind of light absorbent washcloth made from the soft frame of a sponge (*a child's sponge in the shape of a bear*). **3** one who lives on the money or favours of another:—*vb* **1** to wipe with a sponge. **2** to live on the money or favours of another (*sponging on his friends*):—**throw in the sponge** to withdraw from a contest and allow victory to another.

spongy [spun'-ji] *adj* soft and absorbent, soft.

spon'sor *n* **1** one who intr oduces someone or something and takes responsibility for it (*the sponsor of a new parliamentary bill*). **2** a business that pays for an event, show, etc, in return for advertising. **3** a person who agr ees to pay someone money for charity if he or she completes a specified activity. **4** a godfather or godmother:—*vb* **1** to put for ward and support (*sponsor the new bill*). **2** act as a sponsor (*a soft-drinks firm sponsoring the football match/ sponsor the child in a charity swim*).

sponta'neous *adj* **1** done willingly . **2** not caus▓ by an outside agency. **3** done without pr evi▓ thought:—*n* **spontane'ity.**

spook *n* (*inf*) a ghost.

spool *n* a reel on which thread, film, ▓ wound.

spoon *n* **1** a domestic utensil consis▓ low bowl and a handle, used feeding. **2** a wooden golf club:— *vb* to lift with a spoon.

spoon'ful *n* the amount that a spoon contains.

spoor *n* the track or trail of an animal.

sporad'ic *adj* occasional, happening only here and there or now and then (*sporadic outbreaks of the disease*).

spore *n* the seed of a flowerless plant.

spor'ran *n* a pouch or purse worn suspended in front of a kilt.

sport *n* **1** outdoor or athletic indoor games in which certain rules are obeyed (*children interested in sport*). **2** one of these games (*sports such as football and swimming*). **3** (*fml*) something done for fun or amusement (*tease the dog for sport*). **4** (*fml*) one fond of fun or amusement:— *vb* to play, to have fun.

sport'ing *adj* **1** fond of sports. **2** used in sport (*sporting equipment*). **3** fair-minded and generous, esp in sports (*it was sporting of him to admit the ball was out*).

sporting chance *n* a fair chance of success (*they have a sporting chance of reaching the summit of the mountain*).

spor'tive *adj* playful.

sports'man, sports'woman, sports'person *n* **1** one who takes part in a sport. **2** one who likes to see every person or group given an equal chance of success:— *adj* **sports'manlike**.

sports'manship *n* the spirit of fair play.

spot *n* **1** a small mark, stain or blot (*a black spot on her new dress*). **2** a tiny piece. **3** a pimple (*spots on his chin*). **4** the exact place where something happened (*the murder spot*):— *vb* (**spot'ted, spot'ting**) **1** to stain. **2** to see or catch sight of.

spot'less *adj* unmarked, very clean (*a spotless floor*).

spot'light *n* a strong beam of light shone on a particular person or place on a stage.

spot'ty *adj* covered with spots.

spouse *n* a husband or wife.

spout *n* **1** a long tube sticking out from a pot, jug, pipe, etc, through which liquid can flow (*the spout of the teapot*). **2** a jet or gush of liquid:— *vb* **1** to gush or make to gush in a jet. **2** (*inf*) to talk at length (*spouting on about his holiday*).

sprain *n* the painful twisting of a joint in the body, causing damage to muscles or ligaments:— *vb* to twist a joint in such a way (*sprain her ankle*).

sprat *n* a small sea fish.

sprawl *vb* **1** to sit or lie with the limbs spread out awkwardly. **2** to be spread out untidily (*towns sprawled along the seashore*).

spray[1] *n* **1** a twig or stem with several leaves or flowers growing out from it (*a spray of cherry blossom*). **2** an arrangement of flowers (*a bridal spray*).

spray[2] *n* **1** a cloud of small drops of liquid moving through the air. **2** liquid to be sprayed under pressure. **3** a can or container holding this:— *vb* to sprinkle with fine drops of liquid (*sprayed the roses with insecticide*).

spread *vb* (*pt, pp* **spread**) **1** to lay out over an area (*spread butter on bread*). **2** to grow bigger, so covering more space (*towns spreading rapidly*). **3** to make or become more widely known or believed (*spread the information*). **4** to affect more people (*the disease is spreading*):— *n* **1** an area covered, extent. **2** a good meal, a feast.

spread-eag'led *adj* **1** with arms and legs spread out. **2** scattered.

spree *n* **1** a noisy feast. **2** a bout of drinking.

sprig *n* **1** a small shoot or twig (*a sprig of cherry blossom*). **2** a small nail without a head.

spright'ly *adj* lively (*people sprightly for their age*):— *n* **spright'liness**.

spring *vb* (*pt* **sprang**, *pp* **sprung**) **1** to jump. **2** to flow up from under the ground. **3** to be caused by (*his lack of confidence sprang from his unhappy childhood*). **4** to bud. **5** to cause (a mine) to explode:— *n* **1** a jump. **2** a piece or coil of metal that after being compressed returns to its earlier shape or position. **3** water flowing up from under the ground (*hot springs*). **4** the season following winter when plants begin to grow again:— **spring a leak** to have a hole through which water can come in:— **spring a surprise** to give a surprise.

spring'board *n* a springy board for jumping or diving from (*the springboard at the swimming pool*).

spring'bok *n* a type of deer found in South Africa.

springe *n* **1** a trap. **2** a noose set as a trap.

spring'tide, spring'time *n* the season of spring.

spring tide the high tide at new and full moon.

spring'y adj **1** having elasticity . **2** light on one's feet.

sprink'le vb to scatter in small drops or tiny pieces (*sprinkling water on the dry clothes before ironing them*).

sprink'ling n a very small number or quantity (*a sprinkling of snow*).

sprint vb to run as fast as possible for a short distance:—n **1** a short foot race. **2** a short fast run (*a sprint for the bus*).

sprite n an elf or fairy.

sprock'et n a cog on a wheel to carry a chain.

sprout vb to begin to grow, to bud (*bulbs sprouting*):—n a young plant, a shoot of a plant.

spruce[1] adj neat, smart and tidy (*look spruce for his job interview*).

spruce[2] n a type of fir tree, valued for its white timber.

spry adj quick and active, lively (*spry old ladies*).

spume n froth, foam.

spunk n (*inf*) courage.

spur n **1** a pointed instrument or spik ed wheel attached to a rider's heel and dug into the horse's side to make it move more quickly. **2** anything that ur ges on to greater effort (*the promise of a good job acted as a spur to his studying*). **3** the sharp point on the back of the leg of cocks and certain other birds. **4** a ridge or line of hills running out at an angle from a larger hill or hills:—vb (**spurred'**, **spur'ring**) **1** to prick with a spur. **2** to ur ge to greater effort:—**on the spur of the moment** without previous thought.

spu'rious adj false (*a spurious interest in her opinions*).

spurn vb **1** to push away, as with the foot. **2** to refuse with contempt (*spurn their offers of help*).

spurt vb to burst out in a jet:—n **1** a gush of liquid. **2** a special effort. **3** a sudden short burst of extra speed (*put on a spurt at the end of a race*).

sput'ter vb **1** to spit when speaking. **2** to thr ow out small drops of liquid. **3** to mak e spitting and hissing noises (*sausages sputtering in the pan*).

spu'tum n that which is spat from the mouth and throat.

spy n **1** one who tries to obtain secr et information about one country on behalf of an enemy country. **2** one who tries to find out another 's

secrets (*an industrial spy*):—vb **1** to catch sight of (*she spied her friend in the distance*). **2** to act as a spy.

spy'glass n a small telescope.

squab'ble vb to quarrel over unimportant matters (*children squabbling over their toys*):—also n.

squad n a small party of soldiers or workers.

squad'ron n **1** a gr oup of warships under the one commander. **2** a gr oup of twelve aeroplanes commanded by a squadron leader. **3** a unit of cavalry.

squal'id adj dirty and unpleasant, wretched (*squalid living conditions*).

squall vb to scream loudly (*kept awake by a cat squalling*):—n **1** a loud scr eam. **2** a sudden violent gust of wind.

squal'ly adj gusty, stormy and windy (*squally weather*).

squal'or n excessive dirt, filth.

squa'mous adj (*fml*) covered with scales.

squan'der vb to spend wastefully, to use up needlessly (*squander her savings*).

square adj **1** having four equal sides and four right angles. **2** forming a right angle. **3** just, fair (*a square deal*). **4** even, equal (*the two teams are now square*):—n **1** a squar e figure. **2** an open space in a town with buildings on its four sides (*a war monument in the town square*). **3** the number obtained when a number is multiplied by itself. **4** an L- or T-shaped instrument for drawing right angles:—vb **1** to mak e square. **2** to pay money due. **3** to bribe. **4** to multiply (a number) by itself. **5** to agr ee with.

square meal n a large or satisfying meal.

square root n the number that must be multiplied by itself to obtain a given number (*2 is the square root of 4*).

squash vb **1** to crush, to pr ess or squeeze into pulp (*squash fruit*). **2** to speak sharply or rudely to someone to silence him or her (*the speaker squashed the people who were shouting criticisms*):—n **1** a cr owd, a crush. **2** a drink from fruit juice. **3** squash-rack ets.

squash-rackets n a game played against a wall with rackets and a of the ball.

squat vb (**squat'ted**, **squat'ting**) **1** to sit down on the heels. **2** to mak e one's home on a piece of land or in a building to which one has no legal right:—*adj* short and broad.

squat'ter *n* one who settles on land or in a building without legal right to do so.

squaw *n* the wife of a North American Indian.

squawk *vb* to utter a harsh cry (*parrots squawking*):—*also n.*

squeak *vb* to utter a short, high-pitched sound (*mice squeaking*):—*also n:*—**narrow squeak** an escape that almost fails.

squeal *vb* to cry with a sharp shrill voice:—*also n.*

squeam'ish *adj* 1 easily made sick, feeling sick (*squeamish at the sight of blood*). 2 easily shocked or upset.

squeeze *vb* 1 to press from more than one side (*squeezing oranges*). 2 to hug. 3 to push through a narrow space (*squeeze into the crowded hall*):—*n* 1 the act of squeezing. 2 a hug. 3 a tight fit.

squelch *vb* to make a sucking noise, as when walking over sodden ground (*squelch up the muddy road in wellingtons*):—*also n.*

squib *n* a small firework.

squid *n* a cuttlefish.

squint *vb* 1 to have eyes that look in different directions. 2 to look sideways without turning the head:—*n* 1 eyes looking in different directions. 2 (*inf*) a quick look (*take a squint at the papers on the boss's desk*).

squire *n* 1 a land-owning country gentleman. 2 (*old*) one who attended on a knight:—*vb* to accompany (a woman) in public (*squiring her to the dance*).

squirm *vb* to wriggle about, to move by wriggling (*fish squirming in the nets/squirm with embarrassment*).

squir'rel *n* a small bushy-tailed animal living in trees.

squirt *vb* to force or be forced out in a thin fast stream (*squirt water on the dry clothes*):—*n* 1 a jet. 2 an instrument for throwing out a jet of liquid.

stab *vb* (**stabbed'**, **stab'bing**) to wound with a pointed weapon:—*n* 1 a wound made with a pointed weapon. 2 a thrust with a dagger or pointed knife (*kill him with one stab*). 3 a sharp feeling (*a stab of pain/a stab of fear*).

stabil'ity *n* steadiness, security.

stab'ilize *vb* to make firm or steady.

sta'ble[1] *n* a building or shelter for horses, cattle, etc:—*vb* to keep in a stable.

sta'ble[2] *adj* 1 firm, secure, not easily moved, upset or changed (*stable shelves/stable marriages/stable institutions*). 2 likely to behave reasonably (*he's not very stable*).

sta'ble-boy, sta'ble-man *ns* one who works in a stable.

stab'ling *n* buildings available as stables.

stacca'to *adj* in music, having each note sounded clearly and distinctly:—*also n.*

stack *n* 1 a large orderly pile of hay, wood, etc. 2 a group of chimneys built in together. 3 a very tall chimney:—*vb* to pile together.

stack'yard *n* a yard for stacks of hay, etc.

sta'dium *n* (*pl* **sta'dia** *or* **stadiums**) a large ground for sports and athletics.

staff *n* 1 a stick or rod used as a support. 2 a stick as a sign of office. 3 the set of five parallel lines on and between which musical notes are written. 4 a group of officers chosen to assist a general. 5 any body of employees (*the office staff*):—*vb* to provide with workers or employees (*an office staffed mainly by women*).

staff-officer *n* a member of a general's staff.

stag *n* a male red deer.

stage *n* 1 a raised platform for actors, performers, speakers, etc. 2 the theatre (*she went on the stage*). 3 a halting place. 4 the distance that maybe travelled after paying a certain fare. 5 a certain point in development or progress (*stages in the production process*):—*vb* to produce (a play) on a stage (*staging 'Hamlet'*).

stage'coach *n* formerly, a coach providing a regular service for passengers.

stage fright *n* the nervousness felt on appearing on the stage in public.

stage'-struck *adj* very eager to appear on the stage.

stage whis'per *n* a loud, easily heard whisper.

stag'ger *vb* 1 to walk unsteadily, to lurch to the side, to reel. 2 to amaze. 3 to arrange holidays, etc, so that they do not begin and end at the same times as those of others (*stagger the staff's lunch hours so that there are always people in the office*).

stag'nant *adj* 1 not flowing and often foul (*stagnant water*). 2 not developing or growing, inactive (*a production process that remained stagnant*).

stagnate' *vb* 1 to cease to flow. 2 to cease to develop or make progress. 3 to become dull:— *n* **stagna'tion**.

stag party *n* a party for men only (*he had a stag party the night before his wedding*).

staid *adj* serious, steady, unwilling to move with the times.

stain *vb* 1 to mak e dirty (*stain their hands*). 2 to change the colour of (*stain the table dark brown*). 3 to mak e marks of a different colour on. 4 to spoil, to disgrace (*stain her reputation*):—*n* 1 a dirty mark or discoloration that cannot be removed. 2 a paint or dye. 3 disgrace.

stain'less *adj* 1 not easily stained or rusted. 2 without fault or disgrace (*a stainless reputation*).

stair *n* a series of connected steps leading from one place to another on a different level.

stair'case *n* a flight or successive flights of stairs.

stake[1] *n* 1 a stout piece of wood pointed at one end for driving into the ground. 2 formerly , the post to which was tied a person condemned to death by burning:—*vb* to mark with stakes.

stake[2] *n* the amount of money bet:—*vb* to bet (money), to risk:—**at stake** able to be lost.

stalactite *n* a mass of limy matter hanging like an icicle from the roof of a cave (caused by dripping water that gradually deposits the lime).

stalagmite *n* a mass of limy matter rising like a spike from the floor of a cave.

stale *adj* 1 not fr esh (*stale bread*). 2 not new (*stale news*). 3 uninter esting (*a stale piece of writing*).

stale'mate *n* 1 in chess, a position fr om which neither player can win. 2 a situation or ar gument in which neither side can gain an advantage over the other (*management and workers reached stalemate on the subject of wages*).

stalk[1] [ståk] *n* 1 the stem of a plant. 2 a tall chimney.

stalk[2] [ståk] *vb* 1 to walk holding oneself stiffly upright (*stalk out of the room in anger*). 2 to approach an animal quietly and without being seen when hunting it (*stalking stags*) 3 to follow someone around, often someone famous,

regularly and annoy or frighten him/her with unwanted attention (*accused of stalking the filmstar*):—*n* **stalking, stalk'er**.

stall *n* 1 a division of a stable or byr e in which one animal is kept. 2 a counter on which goods are laid out for sale. 3 a small, sometimes temporary, shop set up in an open place. 4 a ground-floor seat in a theatre. 5 a seat in the choir of a church:—*vb* 1 (*of an aeroplane*) to lose speed and get out of control. 2 (*of a motor car engine*) to stop working (*the car stalled at the traffic lights*). 3 to avoid giving a dir ect answer (*the politician stalled when he was asked about unemployment*).

stal'lion *n* a male horse, esp one kept for breeding.

stal'wart *adj* tall and strong, sturdy:—*n* a person on whom one can rely (*one of the firm's stalwarts*).

sta'men *n* one of the little pollen-bearing stalks in the middle of a flower.

stam'ina *n* staying power, ability to endure (*he does not have the stamina to have a full-time job*).

stam'mer *vb* to have difficulty in uttering the sounds at the beginning of words, sometimes attempting them several times before succeeding:—*n* such difficulty in speaking.

stamp *vb* 1 to strik e the foot forcefully or noisily downwards. 2 to print a mark on (*have his passport stamped*). 3 to put a postage stamp on:— *n* 1 a for ceful or noisy downward movement of the foot. 2 a mark or paper affixed to a letter or package to show that postage has been paid. 3 a mark consisting of letters, numbers, a pattern, etc, printed on paper, cloth, coins, etc. 4 a machine for making such a mark. 5 (*fml*) a kind or sort (*men of a different stamp*).

stamp al'bum *n* a book for a collection of postage stamps.

stampede' *n* a sudden panic-stricken rush of many people or animals:—*vb* to take sudden flight (*the buffaloes stampeded/people stampeding to get free tickets*).

stanch *see* **staunch**[2].

stan'chion *n* a supporting prop or post.

stand *vb* (*pt* **stood**) 1 to be upright on the feet, legs or end (*boys standing at the corner*). 2 to rise up (*she stood and left*). 3 to set upright (*stand the tables up*). **4** to stop moving. **5** to stay motionless. **6** to be in a certain place (*a house standing on the river bank*). **7** to bear , to put up with (*unable to stand the loud noise*). **8** to become a candidate for election. **9** (*inf*) to pay for (*stand his friend a drink*):—*n* **1** a halt. **2** a small table, rack, etc, on which things may be placed or hung. **3** a structur e with seats arranged in tiers for spectators (*the stands in football grounds*). **4** a base or support on which an object may be placed upright (*a stand for the statue*). **5** r esistance to an attack (*take a stand against the enemy/take a stand against racism*):—**stand by** to support, to be ready to help (*stood by their friend*):—**stand down** to withdraw:—**stand fast** to remain firm:—**stand out 1** to be pr ominent (*the new building stands out in the old square*). **2** to refuse to give in (*stand out against the enemy*):—**stand up** to get to one's feet:—**stand up for** to defend:—**stand up to** to resist.

stan'dard *n* **1** a fixed measur e. **2** an average level of accomplishment with which others' work is compared (*work below standard*). **3** a lar ge flag or banner (*raise the regiment's standard*). **4** an upright post, etc. **5** a class or stage in primar y school:—*adj* **1** fixed. **2** fixed by rule. **3** usual. **4** standing upright.

stan'dard-bear'er *n* one who carries a standard or banner.

stan'dardize *vb* to see that all things are made or done in the same way (*standardizing the marking system in schools*).

stand'ing *n* rank, position, reputation (*her standing in the community*):—*adj* **1** up right (*standing stones*). **2** not flowing (*standing water*). **3** permanent, fixed (*a standing joke*).

stand-off'ish *adj* unfriendly, unwilling to mix with others.

stand'point *n* a point of view (*from the average person's standpoint*).

stand'still *n* a stoppage (*work at the factory is at a standstill*).

stan'za *n* in poetry, a number of lines arranged in a certain pattern that is repeated throughout the poem.

sta'ple *n* **1** a U-shaped nail or pin. **2** a principal product or article of trade. **3** a main item (*the staples of her diet*):—*adj* chief, principal.

star *n* **1** a heavenly body seen as a twinkling point of light in the night sky. **2** any object lik e a twinkling star in shape. **3** an asterisk (*). **4** a leading actor or actress:—*vb* (**starred'**, **star'ring**) to have the leading part in a play, etc (*star in the new film*).

star'board *n* the right-hand side of a ship as one faces the bows:—*also adj*.

starch *n* **1** a vegetable substance found in potatoes, cereals, etc. **2** a white powder mixed with water and used to make cloth stiff.

starch'y *adj* **1** containing star ch. **2** stiff with starch (*starchy collars*). **3** stiff or unfriendly in manner (*her grandmother is rather starchy*).

star'dom *n* fame as an entertainer, sportsman, etc.

stare *vb* to look at fixedly, to look at with wideopen eyes (*staring at him in amazement*):—*also n*.

star'fish *n* a star-shaped sea creature.

star'gazer *n* **1** (*inf*) one who studies the stars. **2** a dreamer.

stark *adj* **1** bar e or simple, often in a severe way (*the stark landscape/the stark truth*). **2** utter , complete (*stark idiocy*):—*adv* completely.

stark-na'ked *adj* completely bare.

star'less *adj* with no stars visible (*a starless night*).

star'ling *n* a bird, with black-brown feathers, of the crow family.

star'ry *adj* full of stars, like stars (*a starry sky*).

start *vb* **1** to begin (*start working/start to work*). **2** to set in motion (*start a new business*). **3** to jump or make a sudden movement (*start in alarm at the eerie sound*):—*n* **1** a beginning (*at the start of the working day*). **2** a sudden sharp movement (*give a start at the noise*). **3** the distance certain runners are allowed to start a race in front of the others.

start'er *n* **1** a device for starting a motor engine. **2** one who gives the signal to begin. **3** one who takes part in a race.

start'ing line, start'ing post *ns* the place from which competitors in a race begin.

star'tle *vb* to frighten, to give a sudden surprise to (*animals startled by the sudden noise*).

starve *vb* **1** to die of hunger , to suffer greatly from hunger. **2** to k eep without food. **3** to suffer for want of something necessary (*children starved of affection*):—*n* **starva'tion**.

star'veling *n* one weak and thin from lack of nourishment.

state *n* **1** condition, cir cumstances (*the state of the house/the state of the housing market*). **2** the people of a country organized under a form of government. **3** the governmental institutions of a country. **4** (*fml*) pomp or ceremonious display:—*adj* **1** having to do with the government. **2** public:— *vb* **1** to say as a fact. **2** to put clearly into words, spoken or written.

state'ly *adj* dignified, grand in manner or behaviour.

state'ment *n* **1** a clear spok en or written account of facts (*an official statement about the king's illness*). **2** an account of money due or held (*a bank statement*).

state-of-the-art *adj* using the most modern, advanced methods (*using state-of-the-art computing equipment*)

state'room *n* a large private cabin aboard ship.

states'man, states'woman *n* **1** one skilled in the art of government. **2** one who has held high political office.

stat'ic *adj* motionless, at rest (*static electricity*).

sta'tion *n* **1** (*old*) position, rank (*his station in life*). **2** a r egular stopping place for trains, buses, etc. **3** a headquarters fr om which a public service is operated (*fire station, police station*):—*vb* to put in or send to a certain place.

sta'tionary *adj* fixed, not moving (*stationary traffic*).

sta'tioner *n* one who sells stationery.

sta'tionery *n* paper, pens, and all other writing materials (*a shop selling stationery*).

station master *n* the official in charge of a railway station.

statisti'cian *n* one who makes up or studies statistics.

statis'tics *n* **1** the science of turning facts into figures and then classifying them. **2** the study of figures in order to deduce facts. **3** figur es giving information about something (*unemployment statistics*).

stat'uary *n* **1** the art of statue-making. **2** a collection of statues.

stat'ue *n* the carved or moulded figure of a person or animal in stone, etc (*a statue of the famous writer in the town square*).

statuesque' *adj* **1** lik e a statue. **2** motionless, not showing changes in expression.

statuette' *n* a small statue.

stat'ure *n* **1** height of the body . **2** impor tance, reputation (*a writer gaining in stature*).

sta'tus *n* rank, social position.

status quo *n* an unchanged state of affairs (*wish to return to the status quo after the changes*).

status symbol *n* a possession that seems to confirm or confer higher social position.

stat'ute *n* **1** a law. **2** a law passed by parliament.

stat'utory *adj* required by law or statute (*the statutory conditions of employment*).

staunch[1] *adj* loyal, firm, reliable (*staunch followers of the king*):—*vb* see **staunch**[2].

staunch[2]**, stanch** *vb* to stop blood flowing from a cut, etc (*apply a tourniquet to staunch the blood*).

stave *n* **1** one of the strips of wood forming the sides of a barrel. **2** the set of five parallel lines on and between which musical notes are written. **3** a verse of a song, a stanza:— *vb* to break inwards:—**stave off** to keep away, to put off.

stay *vb* **1** to r emain (*stay calm*). **2** to live in a place for a time (*stayed in New York for a few years*). **3** (*fml*) to delay, to stop (*stay the execution*):—*n* **1** time spent in a place. **2** a delay . **3** one of the r opes supporting the mast in its upright position. **4** *pl* a woman's undergarment stiffened to support the muscles of the abdomen, corsets.

stead [sted] *n*:—**in one's stead** in one's place:—**stand one in good stead** to be of great help to one.

stead'fast *adj* loyal, firm, unmoving.

stead'y *adj* **1** firm (*hold the ladder steady*). **2** not easily changing (*steady temperatures*). **3** r egular (*steady work*). **4** r eliable, sensible (*steady workers*):—*n* **stead'iness**.

steak [stāk] *n* a slice of meat or fish for cooking (*cod steak*).

steal [steel] *vb* (*pt* **stole**, *pp* **sto'len**) **1** to tak e what belongs to another. **2** to move slowly and quietly (*steal upstairs late at night*).

stealth *n* **1** secr ecy. **2** acting quietly or slyly so as not to be seen or heard.

stealth'y *adj* quiet, sly, secretive (*stealthy footsteps*).

steam *n* the vapour of hot liquid, esp water:—*vb* **1** to give off steam. **2** to cook in steam (*steam* *vegetables*). **3** to move driven by steam power (*a ship steamed into harbour*).

steam'boat, steam'er, steam'ship *ns* a ship driven by steam power.

steam engine *n* an engine driven by steam power.

steam'roller *n* a steam-driven vehicle with wide heavy wheels, used for flattening road surfaces.

steed *n* (*old*) a horse.

steel *n* **1** an alloy consisting of iron hardened by carbon. **2** a steel bar on which knives may be sharpened:—*adj* made of steel:—*vb* to harden, to strengthen (*steeling herself to sack the boy*).

steel'y *adj* hard, unsympathetic (*a steely gaze*).

steep[1] *adj* having a rapid slope up or down (*steep cliffs*):—*n* a cliff or precipice.

steep[2] *vb* to soak, to leave in water for a time (*steep stained clothes*).

steep'le *n* a tall church tower, sometimes tapering to a point.

steep'lechase *n* a cross-country race over obstacles for horses or runners.

steep'lejack *n* one who climbs steeples, tall chimneys, etc, to repair them.

steer[1] *n* a young ox.

steer[2] *vb* to keep a moving object pointed in the desired direction, to guide or control (*steer the car/steer the conversation to the question of holidays*).

steer'age *n* the part of a ship for passengers who pay the lowest fares.

stell'ar *adj* having to do with the stars.

stem[1] *n* **1** the trunk of a tree, the stalk of a flower, leaf, etc. **2** the front part of a ship. **3** the main unchanging part of a word, prefixes and suffixes left out.

stem[2] *vb* (**stemmed', stem'ming**) to check, to delay, to stop (something) flowing (*stem the flow of blood*).

stench *n* a foul smell (*the stench from the sewer*).

sten'cil *n* **1** a thin plate or card with a design cut through it so that patterned markings can be painted or printed on a surface beneath. **2** a waxed paper from which copies of typewritten material can be printed:—*vb* (**sten'cilled, sten'cilling**) to make a design or copy by using a stencil.

stenog'raphy *n* (*old*) shorthand, a type of writing using signs for letters and words so that one can write as fast as a speaker speaks:—*n* **stenog'rapher**.

stento'rian *adj* (*of the voice*) very loud (*stentorian snoring*).

step *n* **1** a pace taken by one foot. **2** the distance covered by such a pace. **3** a footprint. **4** the sound of a footfall (*hear steps on the stair*). **5** a complete series of steps in a dance. **6** one of a series of rungs or small graded platforms that allow one to climb or walk from one level to another (*the steps of a ladder*). **7** *pl* a flight of stairs. **8** *pl* a stepladder:—*vb* (**stepped', step'ping**) to walk:—**out of step 1** out of time with others in performing a regular movement. **2** behaving or thinking differently from others (*older workers are out of step with the ideas of the young people*):—**step out** to move boldly or quickly forward:—**step up** to increase (*step up the interest payments on the loan*):—**take steps** to take action.

step'child *n* the child of a husband or wife by a previous marriage:—*also* **step'daughter, step'father, step'mother, step'son.**

step'ladder *n* a portable self-supporting ladder.

steppe *n* in Russia or Asia, a vast treeless uncultivated plain.

step'ping stone *n* **1** one of a series of stones that rise above the surface of a stream, enabling one to cross it. **2** a means of making progress (*stepping stones in his career*).

ste'reoscope *n* an instrument through which two pictures can be seen as one in such a way as to give the combined picture the appearance of depth:—*adj* **stereoscop'ic.**

stereoscopic sound *n* sound relayed from two transmitters so that it seems to come from an area and not one point.

ste'reotype *n* **1** a metal plate on which type is reproduced so that it may be reprinted over and over again. **2** an idea, image, etc, that has become fixed and unchanging.

ste'reotyped *adj* fixed and unchanging (*actors worried about becoming stereotyped by playing the same kind of role too often*).

ste'rile *adj* **1** bearing no fruit or children, barren. **2** germ-free (*sterile operating theatres*):—*n* **steril'ity.**

ster'ilize *vb* **1** to make sterile. **2** to get rid of germs (by boiling, etc).

ster'ling *n* British coinage:—*adj* genuine, of worth.

stern[1] *adj* severe, strict, harsh.

stern[2] *n* the back part of a ship.

ster'torous *adj* (*of breathing*) noisy and requiring effort.

steth'oscope *n* an instrument by means of which one can listen to the sound of another's breathing or heartbeats.

stevedore [stee'-vê-dâr] *n* one who loads or unloads ships.

stew *vb* to boil slowly in little liquid in a closed vessel:—*n* 1 stewed meat and vegetables. 2 (*inf*) a state of anxiety (*in a stew about the exams*).

stew'ard *n* 1 one paid to manage another's land or property. 2 a manservant on a ship or aeroplane. 3 an official at a concert, race meeting, show, etc:—*f* **stew'ardess**.

stick[1] *vb* (*pt, pp* **stuck**) 1 to pierce or stab (*stick a knife in him*). 2 to fasten or be fastened to, as with glue (*stick pictures on a piece of card*). 3 to be unable to move (*cars stuck in the mud*).

stick[2] *n* 1 a rod, a long thin piece of wood, esp one carried when walking. 2 a bar of toffee, etc.

stick'ing plaster *n* a type of bandage, sticky on one side, used for closing or covering wounds, etc.

stick-in-the-mud *n* one who has become set in his or her ways and refuses to change them.

stick'leback *n* a tiny freshwater fish with a spiny back.

stick'ler *n* one who is fussy about details or unimportant matters (*a stickler for the school rules*).

stick'y *adj* 1 smeared with glue, etc, for fixing to other things (*sticky paper*). 2 tending to fasten on by sticking. 3 (*inf*) difficult (*a sticky situation*).

stiff *adj* 1 hard to bend. 2 firm. 3 unable to move easily (*feel stiff after the unaccustomed exercise*). 4 cold and severe in manner. 5 difficult (*a stiff exam*).

stiff'en *vb* to make or become stiff.

stiff'-necked *adj* stubborn, unwilling to give in or obey.

sti'fle *vb* 1 to smother (*stifling the old woman with a pillow*). 2 to prevent from expressing (*stifle the child's natural talent*). 3 to keep down by force (*stifle a laugh*).

stig'ma *n* (*pl* **stig'mas**) 1 a mark of shame or disgrace (*the stigma of having been in prison*).

2 the part of a flower that receives the pollen. 3 (*pl* **stig'mata**) marks like those of the wounds on Christ's body.

stig'matize *vb* to blame as being shameful or disgraceful (*stigmatized as cowardly*).

stile *n* a set of steps over a fence or wall.

stilet'to *n* a short dagger.

still[1] *adj* 1 at rest, motionless (*still water*). 2 calm, silent:—*n* a single photograph out of a series taken by a moving camera:—*vb* to make still:—*adj* 1 even so (*he is old—still he wants to go on working*). 2 up to this moment (*they are still quarrelling*).

still[2] *n* an apparatus for distilling spirits (*a whisky still*).

still'born *adj* born dead (*stillborn babies*).

still life *n* (*pl* **still lifes**) inanimate objects (e.g. fruit, ornaments, etc) as subjects for painting.

still'y *adj* (*lit*) silent, peaceful.

stilt *n* one of a pair of poles with footrests so that one can walk some height above the ground.

stilt'ed *adj* 1 unnatural or pompous in manner. 2 awkwardly expressed (*stilted English*).

stim'ulant *n* something that increases energy for a time (*coffee is a stimulant*):—*also adj*.

stim'ulate *vb* 1 to rouse or make more alert, active, etc (*stimulating her into learning to paint*). 2 to stir up, cause (*the teacher stimulated a discussion on the arts*):—*adj* **stim'ulating**.

stim'ulus *n* (*pl* **stim'uli**) something that arouses one's feelings or excites one to action (*the competition acted as a stimulus to get him to practise running*).

sting *n* 1 a sharp-pointed defensive organ of certain animals or insects by means of which they can inject poison into an attacker. 2 in plants, a hair containing poison. 3 the pain caused by a sting (*a wasp sting*). 4 any sharp pain:— *vb* (*pt, pp* **stung**). 1 to pierce or wound with a sting. 2 to pierce painfully with a sharp point. 3 to drive or provoke (a person) to act (*stung into making an angry reply*).

stingy [stin'-ji] *adj* mean, unwilling to spend or give money.

stink *vb* (*pt* **stank** *or* **stunk**, *pp* **stunk**) to give off an unpleasant smell:—*n* an unpleasant smell (*the stink of rotten meat*).

stint vb to give or allow only a small amount of (stinted on materials):—n limit, a set amount of work.

sti'pend n a salary, esp of a member of the clergy.

stipen'diary adj paid:—n a paid magistrate.

stip'ple vb to paint or draw in very small dots instead of lines.

stip'ulate vb to lay down conditions in advance (stipulating the terms of her employment in writing).

stipula'tion n conditions demanded as part of an agreement.

stir vb (**stirred'**, **stir'ring**) 1 to move or set in motion (stir the sauce). 2 to arouse (stir up hatred):—n excitement, noisy movement, a sensation (their divorce caused quite a stir).

stir'ring adj rousing, exciting (a stirring song).

stir'rup n a metal foot support hung from the saddle for a horse-rider.

stirrup cup n a parting drink taken on horseback.

stitch n 1 a single movement of the needle in knitting, sewing, etc. 2 the thread, wool, etc, used in such a movement. 3 a sharp pain in the side as a result of running, etc:— vb to join by stitches (a wound requiring stitching).

stoat n a type of weasel, valued for its fur.

stock n 1 the main stem of a plant, the trunk of a tree. 2 the wooden handle of a gun. 3 a band of cloth worn round the neck, sometimes also covering the shirt front. 4 the families from which one is descended. 5 goods kept for selling (have a varied stock of sweets). 6 shares in a business. 7 the animals of a farm. 8 liquid in which marrow bones, vegetables, etc, have been boiled. 9 a sweet-smelling garden flower. 10 pl (old) a frame with holes for the hands and feet into which lawbreakers could be fastened for punishment. 11 pl the wooden frame on which a ship rests while being built:—adj always in use or ready for use:— vb to provide with necessary goods, to keep a store of (stock greeting cards):—**take stock 1** to list and check goods. 2 to consider all the aspects of a situation (take stock of his future prospects).

stockade' n a fence of strong posts built for defence.

stock'broker n one who buys and sells shares in business companies on behalf of others.

stock exchange, stock market ns a place where shares are bought and sold.

stock'ing n a close-fitting covering for the foot and leg.

stock'-in-trade' n 1 all the goods stored by a shopkeeper. 2 something habitually used (charm is part of his stock-in-trade).

stock'man n a man employed to look after cattle.

stock' pot n the pot in which soup stock is made.

stock'-still adj motionless, completely still (she stood stock-still in terror).

stock'taking n the checking of all the goods held in a shop or store (undertake a stocktaking of their winter stock).

stock'whip n a whip with a short handle and a long lash.

stock'y adj short and broad (a stocky young man).

stock'yard n an enclosed yard for cattle at a market or slaughterhouse.

stodg'y adj 1 dull (a stodgy piece of prose). 2 (of food) heavy or hard to digest.

sto'ic n one who accepts good and bad, pleasure and pain without excitement or complaint:— adj **sto'ical:**—n **sto'icism**.

stoke vb to put fuel on a fire.

stok'er n one who stokes a furnace.

stole[1] n 1 a band of cloth worn round the neck by a priest when officiating. 2 a long scarf worn round the shoulders by women (wearing a fur stole over her evening dress).

stole[2] pt of **steal**.

sto'len pp of **steal:**—also adj.

stol'id adj dull, not easily moved, impassive (rather a stolid child):—n **stolid'ity**.

stomach [stum'-ak] n 1 the bag-like bodily organ that receives and digests food. 2 courage (not have the stomach for battle):—vb to bear with, to put up with (could not stomach his treatment of animals).

stone n 1 a hard mass of rock. 2 a piece of rock, a pebble. 3 the hard centre of some fruits (cherry stones). 4 a piece of hard matter that forms in the body in certain diseases (kidney stones). 5 a precious stone or gem. 6 a measure of weight (14 lbs, 6.35 kilograms):—adj made of stone:— vb 1 to throw stones at. 2 to remove the stones from (fruit) (*stoning the cherries*):—**leave no stone unturned** to do everything possible (*the police left no stone unturned in the search for the murderer*).

Stone Age *n* an early period in history during which humans made tools, weapons, etc, of stone.

stone'-blind *adj* quite blind.

stone'-deaf *adj* quite deaf.

stone'ware *n* a coarse pottery with a glazed finish.

ston'y *adj* **1** like stone. **2** covered with stones (*a stony beach*). **3** hard, unsympathetic (*listen in stony silence*).

ston'y-hearted *adj* pitiless (*stony-hearted judges*).

stood *pt of* **stand.**

stooge *n* **1** one made a fool of in a farce, etc (*a comedian's stooge*). **2** one who does the unpleasant work for another, one who takes the blame due to others.

stook *n* a set of sheaves of corn, etc, standing on end.

stool *n* a low backless seat.

stoop *vb* **1** to bend forward and downward. **2** to agree to do something unworthy, to give in (*refuse to stoop to lying*):—*n* a downward bending of the head and shoulders.

stop *vb* (**stopped'**, **stop'ping**) **1** to cease or prevent from moving or doing something. **2** to come or bring to a standstill. **3** to block or close up (*stop the hole in the pipe*):—*n* **1** a pause. **2** a place where a bus, etc, halts to pick up passengers. **3** time spent standing still or doing nothing (*a stop for lunch*). **4** a punctuation mark at the end of a sentence (.). **5** one of the knobs controlling the flow of air in the pipes of an organ, so regulating the sounds produced.

stop'cock *n* a tap to regulate the flow of water, gas, etc.

stop'gap *n* a person or thing that acts as a temporary substitute until a better can be found.

stop'page *n* **1** a halt. **2** a ceasing of work. **3** something blocking a tube or pipe.

stop'per *n* something closing a small hole (e.g. in the neck of a bottle).

stop press *n* late news added in a special column after the rest of a newspaper has been printed.

stop'watch *n* an accurate watch, used for timing events, that can be started or stopped at will (*use a stopwatch to time the race*).

stor'age *n* **1** the putting of goods in warehouses, etc, until they are required (*the storage of their furniture while they were abroad*). **2** the charge for storing goods.

store *n* **1** a large quantity. **2** a supply of goods that can be drawn on when necessary. **3** a room or building where such goods are kept. **4** a shop selling many different kinds of articles (*a department store*):—*vb* **1** to keep for future use (*storing her summer clothes in the attic*). **2** to put in warehouses, etc:—**set store by** to regard as valuable.

store'house, **store'room** *ns* places for storing goods.

stor'ey *n* (*pl* **stor'eys**) any floor of a building from the ground floor upwards.

stor'ied *adj* (*old*) told of or famous in stories.

stork *n* a white wading bird of the heron family, with long legs and bill.

storm *n* **1** a spell of very bad weather (e.g. rain, wind, snow, etc). **2** a display of violent emotion, public anger:—*vb* **1** to make a sudden violent attack on a defended place (*the enemy storming the castle*). **2** to rage (*storming about the damage to his car*):—**storm in a teacup** much fuss over an unimportant matter:—**take by storm** to capture by sudden violent attack.

storm'y *adj* **1** liable to or troubled by storms. **2** violent, marked by angry feelings (*a stormy reaction to his defeat*).

stor'y *n* **1** an account of events, real or imagined. **2** (*inf*) a lie (*feel that his account of the event was just a story*).

stoup *n* **1** a drinking vessel. **2** a basin for holy water.

stout *adj* **1** strong or thick (*a stout stick*). **2** fat (*so stout that he was breathless walking along the road*). **3** brave and resolute (*a stout attempt*):—*n* a strong dark beer.

stout-heart'ed *adj* courageous, not giving in easily.

stove *n* a closed-in fireplace or metal apparatus for warming a room, cooking, etc.

stow *vb* to put away, to pack tightly (*stow the luggage in the boot of the car*).

stow'away *n* one who hides on a ship, etc, so as to travel without paying the fare.

strad'dle *vb* **1** to spread the legs wide apart. **2** to sit or stand with a leg on either side of.

strag'gle *vb* **1** to move in widely scatter ed formation. **2** to fall behind the main body .

strag'gler *n* one who wanders from the main body.

straight [strāt] *adj* **1** not cur ving or crooked. **2** honest:—*adv* directly, at once.

straight'en *vb* to make straight (*straighten the bedclothes*).

straightfor'ward *adj* **1** simple, not compli cated. **2** honest (*a straightforward person*).

straight'way *adv* at once.

strain[1] *vb* **1** to str etch tightly (*a dress straining at the seams*). **2** to mak e the utmost effort. **3** to harm by trying to do too much with (*strain themselves by pushing the cart*). **4** to put in a sieve to draw liquid off (*strain the sauce*):—*n* **1** violent effort. **2** harm caused to muscles, etc, by straining them. **3** manner or style of speaking or writing. **4** a tune.

strain[2] *n* **1** br eed, stock (*a strain of plant*). **2** an element of character (*a family with an artistic strain*). **3** a tune.

strained *adj* **1** str etched too far. **2** not natural (*a strained comparison*).

strain'er *n* a small sieve or filter (*a metal strainer*).

strait *adj* narrow, strict:—*n* **1** a narr ow strip of water between two land masses. **2** *pl* distress, difficulties.

strait'ened *adj* distressed, made difficult by lack of money (*in straitened circumstances*).

strait'-jacket *n* a strong tightly fitting garment that can be laced on to violent persons to make them helpless or to people with a back injury for support.

strait'-laced *adj* having strict rules of behaviour for oneself and others.

strand[1] *n* (*fml*) the shore:—*vb* **1** to run agr ound. **2** to be left helpless without money , friends, etc (*find herself stranded with nowhere to stay*).

strand[2] *n* one of the threads of a rope or string.

strange *adj* **1** unusual, odd (*strange beasts*). **2** unfamiliar (*strange to the job*). **3** (*lit*) foreign (*strange lands*). **4** (peculiar , uncomfortable, unwell (*feel strange*).

stran'ger *n* **1** one pr eviously unknown. **2** a new arrival to a place, town, etc. **3** one who is unfamiliar with or ignorant of something (*a stranger to the truth*).

strang'le *vb* to kill by pressing the throat tightly, to choke (*strangling his victim with her scarf*).

stran'gulate *vb* to strangle:—*n* **stran'gula-tion.**

strap *n* **1** a narr ow band of leather or other material (*a strap round the suitcase*). **2** a leather belt:—*vb* (**strapped'**, **strap'ping**) **1** to fasten with a strap (*strap the load to the donkey*). **2** to beat with a strap.

strap'ping *adj* tall and strong (*strapping athletes*).

strata *see* **stratum.**

strat'agem *n* a trick intended to deceive (*a stratagem to get into the house unnoticed*).

strate'gic(al) *adjs* having to do with strategy.

strat'egist *n* one skilled in strategy.

strat'egy *n* **1** the art of dealing with a situation in such a way as to gain from it the greatest advantage possible (*the strategy required to get the council to agree to the building of the new road*). **2** in war , the planning of a campaign.

strath *n* (*Scot*) a broad valley.

strat'ify *vb* to form into or set out in layers:—*n* **stratifica'tion.**

strat'osphere *n* a layer of the earth's atmosphere (5–10 miles up) in which temperature does not become lower as one goes higher.

stra'tum *n* (*pl* **strata**) **1** a layer of r ock, earth, etc, forming part of the earth's surface. **2** a level (*a stratum of society*).

stra'tus *n* (*pl* **stra'ti**) a long low horizontal layer of cloud.

straw *n* **1** the dried stalks of corn, etc (*lay straw for the cattle to lie on*). **2** one such stalk or something resembling it (*suck lemonade through straws*). **3** something of no worth (*not worth a straw*).

straw'berry *n* **1** a wild or gar den plant. **2** the juicy red fruit it bears.

stray *vb* to wander, to lose the way (*find the animal that had strayed*):—*adj* **1** lost, off the right path (*stray animals*). **2** occasional (*stray flowers in the wood*):—*n* a lost or wandering person, animal or thing.

streak *n* **1** a long narr ow mark or stain, a stripe, a narrow band (*streaks of red in the sky*). **2** part of one's character (*a streak of nastiness*):—*vb* to mark with streaks.

streak'y *adj* consisting of or marked with streaks (*streaky bacon*).

stream n 1 a curr ent of any liquid or gas. 2 a small river. 3 a succession of people moving in one direction (*a stream of people leaving the office*):—vb 1 to move in a str eam. 2 to flow freely.

stream'er n 1 a long narr ow flag. 2 a narr ow strip of ribbon or coloured paper for flying in the wind (*streamers flying from the bus window*).

stream'let n a small stream.

stream'line vb 1 to build so as to offer minimum resistance to air or water. 2 to mak e more efficient.

street n a road lined with buildings in a village or town.

strength n 1 bodily power (*not have the strength to lift the load*). 2 might, for ce. 3 the number of persons of a class, army, etc, present or on the roll (*when the staff is at full strength*).

strength'en vb to make or become stronger (*strengthen the wall/strengthen our case*).

stren'uous adj requiring much energy or vigour (*a strenuous task*).

stress vb 1 to point out the importance of. 2 to emphasize with the voice (*stress the second syllable*):—n 1 importance (*put some stress on the cost of the project*). 2 strain, pr essure (*not coping with the stress of the job*). 3 the special emphasis given in speaking to particular syllables, words, etc.

stretch vb 1 to mak e or become longer or broader by pulling. 2 to draw out to the fullest extent. 3 to put or r each out (*stretch out for the salt*). 4 to exaggerate:— n a full length of time or space.

stretch'er n a light frame for carrying a sick or wounded person.

strew vb (pp **strewn**) to scatter about, to spread at intervals over (*strewed flowers in the bride's path*).

strick'en adj affected by (*stricken with a fatal illness*).

strict adj 1 sever e. 2 demanding obedience to rules (*a strict teacher*).

stric'ture n 1 blame, unfavourable criticism of a person. 2 limit (*impose strictures on their freedom*).

stride vb (pt **strode**) to walk with long steps:—n a long step.

stri'dent adj loud and harsh in sound (*strident voices*).

strife n open disagreement, quarrelling, fighting.

strike vb (pt, pp **struck**) 1 to hit (*he struck his opponent*). 2 (*of a clock*) to sound the hours or quarters. 3 to stop work to tr y to make employers grant better pay or conditions. 4 to come suddenly to mind (*it struck me that they were late*). 5 to mak e and stamp (a coin or medal). 6 to tak e down (a flag or tent). 7 to light (a match) by rubbing. 8 to come upon by chance (*strike a bad patch*):—n a stopping of work.

strik'er n a worker on strike.

strik'ing adj attracting attention because fine or unusual (*a striking dress*).

string n 1 a cor d or strong thread. 2 the cor d or wire of a musical instrument. 3 a number of persons or things, one following the other (*a string of applicants for the job*):—vb 1 to put on a string. 2 to put a string into (a musical instrument).

strin'gent adj 1 sever e, strict, laying down precise rules to be obeyed (*stringent measures*). 2 mark ed by severe lack of money or firm control (*stringent economic conditions*):—n **strin'gency**.

string'y adj 1 lik e string (*stringy beans*). 2 thin and muscular (*stringy arms*).

strip vb (**stripped'**, **strip'ping**) 1 to pull off the outer covering. 2 to undr ess (*they stripped in order to swim*). 3 to tak e everything from (*strip the room of everything valuable*):—n 1 a long narrow piece. 2 special clothes for games, athletics, etc.

stripe[1] n 1 a band or str eak of different colour from those on either side of it (*a pattern of blue and white stripes*). 2 a str oke from a whip, rod, etc.

striped adj having stripes.

strip'ling n a boy, a youth.

strive vb (pt **strove** or **strived**, pp **striv'en**) to try as hard as possible, to struggle (*strive to reach the top*).

stroke[1] n 1 a blow . 2 a sudden turn of luck, good or bad. 3 a sudden attack of illness, esp one affecting the brain. 4 a line made by a pen, pencil, etc. 5 one sound fr om a bell (*at the stroke of ten*). 6 in a boat, the oarsman with whom the others keep time when rowing.

stroke² vb to rub gently with the hand in one direction (*stroking the cat's fur*).

stroll vb to walk in a leisurely way (*stroll along the promenade*):—n a short leisurely walk.

strong adj **1** powerful (*a strong influence*). **2** healthy (*children getting strong after their illness*). **3** possessing bodily power or vigour.

strong'hold n **1** a fort. **2** a place difficult to capture by attack.

strong'-minded adj determined, not easily influenced by others.

strong'room n a room with reinforced walls and door for storing valuables.

stron'tium n a silvery-white metal.

strop n a strip of leather for sharpening razors:—vb (**stropped'**, **strop'ping**) to sharpen on a strop.

struc'tural adj having to do with structure (*the storm caused structural damage*).

struc'ture n **1** a building. **2** anything consisting of parts put together according to a plan. **3** the way in which a thing is put together (*the structure of the organization*).

strug'gle vb **1** to try hard. **2** to fight:— n **1** a hard effort (*put up a struggle*). **2** a fight.

strum vb (**strummed'**, **strum'ming**) **1** to play a tune carelessly. **2** to play on a stringed instrument by plucking the strings (*strum on a guitar*).

strut¹ vb (**strut'ted**, **strut'ting**) to walk stiffly, as if trying to look important (*the MP was strutting round the charity fair*):—also n.

strut² n a supporting bar, a prop or support.

strychnine [strik'-neen] n a highly poisonous drug.

stub n **1** a short piece left when the rest is cut off or used up (*cigarette stubs*). **2** the retained section of a cheque, etc:—vb (**stubbed'**, **stub'bing**) to strike (the toes) against by accident.

stub'ble n **1** the stumps of the corn stalks left in the ground after reaping. **2** the short bristly hairs that grow on a man's face after he has shaved.

stub'born adj unwilling to change one's point of view, not ready to give in, obstinate.

stub'by adj short and broad, short and thick (*stubby fingers*).

stuc'co n a fine plaster used to cover and ornament the walls of a building.

stuck'-up adj too proud of oneself (*too stuck-up to speak to her neighbours*).

stud¹ n **1** a nail with a large head or knob. **2** a fastener with a head at each end for linking two buttonholes (*collar stubs*):—vb (**stud'ded**, **stud'ding**) **1** to decorate with many small ornaments. **2** to cover with (*a dress studded with sequins*).

stud² n a number of horses kept for breeding.

stu'dent n one who studies (*university students*).

stud'ied adj done with care, deliberate (*with studied politeness*).

stu'dio n **1** the room in which a painter, sculptor, photographer, etc, works. **2** a building in which films are made. **3** a workshop in which records are made or from which programmes are broadcast.

stu'dious adj fond of studying (*studious pupils*).

stud'y vb **1** to read about or examine in order to obtain knowledge (*studied local history*). **2** to examine closely, to think deeply about (*studying the evidence*):—n **1** the obtaining of information, esp by reading. **2** a subject studied. **3** an office, a room set aside for reading and learning (*the headmaster's study*). **4** a work of art done to improve one's skill.

stuff n **1** the material of which something is made. **2** cloth (*clothes of hard-wearing stuff*):—vb **1** to fill full or tightly. **2** to fill something hollow with another material.

stuffing n **1** material used to stuff something hollow (*stuffing for cushions*). **2** a paste of breadcrumbs, minced meat, etc, put inside fowls, etc, when cooking (*turkey stuffing*).

stuff'y adj hot and airless (*a stuffy room*).

stul'tify vb to make seem useless.

stum'ble vb **1** to trip and nearly fall (*stumbling over an uneven piece or road*). **2** to make an error, to do wrong. **3** to come upon by chance (*stumble upon the solution*):—n a trip, a false step when walking, nearly causing one to fall.

stum'bling block n a hindrance, something that prevents progress.

stump n **1** the part of a tree left above ground when the rest is cut down. **2** the part of a limb left after the rest has been amputated. **3** one of the wickets stuck in the ground at cricket:—vb **1** to walk heavily (*she stumped out of the room* angrily). **2** to ask someone a question that he or she is unable to answer. **3** in crick et, to put a batsman out by knocking down his wicket when he is out of his ground.

stump'y *adj* short and thick, short and broad (*stumpy fingers*).

stun *vb* (**stunned'**, **stun'ning**) **1** to knock senseless. **2** to amaze (*stunned by the changes in the city centre*).

stunt[1] *vb* to prevent the full growth of (*plants stunted because of frost*).

stunt[2] *n* **1** a trick to display special skill or daring. **2** anything done to attract attention or gain publicity (*a publicity stunt for their new product*).

stunt'ed *adj* undersized.

stupefac'tion *n* (*fml*) amazement.

stu'pefy *vb* **1** to mak e stupid, to make the senses less acute (*stupefied by the drug*). **2** to amaze.

stupen'dous *adj* extraordinary, so large or powerful that it amazes.

stu'pid *adj* foolish, not intelligent, slow to understand:—*n* **stupid'ity**.

stu'por *n* temporary inability to think clearly, confusion of mind (*in a drunken stupor*).

stur'dy *adj* strong, well-built (*sturdy country children*).

stur'geon *n* a large fish from whose roe caviar is made.

stut'ter *vb* to speak with difficulty, to repeat the first sound of a word several times before saying the whole word:—*n* a stammer.

sty[1] *n* an enclosure in which pigs are kept.

sty[2]**, stye** *n* a poisoned swelling on the edge of the eyelid.

Styg'ian *adj* **1** dark, gloomy . **2** having to do with hell.

style *n* **1** manner of doing anything (*her style of teaching*). **2** a way of writing, painting, etc, by which works of art can be recognized as the work of a particular artist, school or period (*discuss the style of the writer in one's essay*). **3** a fashion (*the style of the 1920s*). **4** elegance (*dress with style*). **5** (*old*) a pointed instrument for engraving or writing on wax.

styl'ish *adj* well-dressed, smart, fashionable.

styp'tic *n* a substance that stops bleeding:—*adj* acting to stop bleeding by contracting the blood vessels (*a styptic pencil to stop bleeding after shaving*).

suave [swäv *or* swāv] *adj* agreeable in manner, esp in an insincere way:—*n* **suav'ity**.

sub- *prefix* under, below.

sub'altern *n* in the army, a commissioned officer below the rank of captain.

sub'class *n* one of the subdivisions of a class.

subcon'scious *adj* not fully aware of what one is doing (*a subconscious hatred of his father*):—*n* mental processes that go on without one's being fully aware of.

subdivide' *vb* to divide into smaller parts or groups.

subdivi'sion *n* a part of a larger part.

subdue' *vb* to conquer, to force to be tame or obedient.

subdued' *adj* not bright, not loud (*subdued lighting*).

subed'it *vb* to prepare for immediate publication.

subed'itor *n* an assistant editor.

sub'ject *adj* **1** ruled by another . **2** liable to (*subject to colds*):—*n* **1** one who owes loyalty to a ruler or government. **2** that about which something is said or written (*he was the subject of the newspaper article*). **3** something studied (*French and other school subjects*). **4** in a clause or sentence, the word with which the verb agrees grammatically:—*vb* **subject'** **1** to bring under the power of (*a country subjected to tyranny*). **2** to expose to (*subject them to ridicule*).

subjec'tion *n* control, the state of being under another's rule or power.

subjec'tive *adj* having to do with one's own ideas and feelings rather than with objects outside one (*a subjective judgment*).

subject matter *n* the ideas under consideration.

sub'jugate *vb* to conquer, to bring under another's power or rule:—*n* **subjuga'tion**.

subjunc'tive *n* the forms of the verb that express doubt, condition or improbability.

sub'let *vb* to let to another what one is already paying a rent for oneself:—*also n*.

sublieuten'ant *n* in the navy, an officer below the rank of lieutenant.

sub'limate *vb* **1** to change a solid into vapour by heating it, and then solidify the vapour by cooling it. **2** to mak e pure, to direct the lower instincts towards more noble ends (*sublimating* *his animal instincts into hard work*):—*n* what is produced by sublimating:—*n* subli**ma'tion**.

sublime' *adj* noble, awe-inspiring, grand and lofty.

sublim'ity *n* grandeur of feeling or expression.

submarine' *adj* under the surface of the sea:—*n* a ship that can travel under the surface of the sea.

submerge' *vb* to put or sink under water:—*n* **submer'gence**.

submer'sion *n* the act of putting or sinking under water.

submis'sion *n* **1** surrender, obedience. **2** a proposal or opinion (*their submission was rejected*).

submis'sive *adj* willing to accept orders, ready to give in.

submit' *vb* (**submit'ted, submit'ting**) **1** to give in (*submit to the enemy*). **2** to put forward for consideration (*submit a claim for expenses*).

subor'dinate *adj* **1** less important (*subordinate issues*). **2** of lower rank:— *n* one who is lower in rank, one who is working under the orders of another:—*vb* **1** to place in a lower rank, to put under the command of. **2** to regard as less important:—*n* **subordi-na'tion**.

suborn' *vb* (*fml*) to bribe to do what is wrong or unlawful.

subpoena [sub-pee'-na] *n* an order to appear as a witness in a law court.

subscribe' *vb* **1** to sign one's name under. **2** to agree with (*unable to subscribe to his views*). **3** to give or promise to give money to a fund or collection (*subscribing to a children's charity*):—*n* **subscrib'er**.

subscrip'tion *n* **1** a signature. **2** a sum of money given to a fund or collection.

sub'sequent *adj* following, later (*on subsequent occasions*).

subserve' *vb* (*fml*) to help towards carrying out a certain purpose.

subser'vient *adj* ready to do all one is told in order to gain favour (*subservient members of staff*).

subside' *vb* **1** to sink gradually down (*buildings subsiding*). **2** to become less, to disappear gradually (*the wind subsided*).

sub'sidence *n* a gradual sinking down, esp of land.

subsid'iary *adj* of less importance (*subsidiary issues*).

sub'sidize *vb* to pay a subsidy to (*subsidizing the children's theatre*).

sub'sidy *n* money paid by the government to certain groups, trades, etc, to enable them to provide the public with necessary services without losing money (*subsidies for renovating old property*).

subsist' *vb* to live or exist, to have the means of living (*subsisting on very little money*).

subsis'tence *n* existence, that which is necessary to support life.

subsistence allowance *n* a payment made to enable someone to buy the necessities of life.

sub'soil *n* the layer of earth just below the surface.

sub'stance *n* **1** the material of which a thing is made (*a waterproof substance*). **2** that which really exists (not what is imagined). **3** the chief ideas in a speech or written work. **4** (*fml*) wealth (*a man of substance*).

substan'tial *adj* **1** really existing. **2** solid. **3** fairly large or important (*a substantial improvement*).

substan'tiate *vb* to prove the truth of (*substantiating his claim to the truth*).

sub'stitute *vb* to put in place of (*substituting a soya substance instead of meat*):—*n* a person or thing put in the place of another:—*n* **substitu'tion**.

substra'tum *n* a lower layer, a foundation or basis.

subten'ant *n* one who pays rent to a person who is paying rent for the same thing to another.

sub'terfuge *n* a trick or pretence to get one out of a difficulty (*use subterfuge to get into the filmstar's house*).

subterra'nean *adj* underground (*subterranean caves*).

subti'tle *n* **1** a second, less important, title of a book. **2** explanatory comments, etc, printed on silent or foreign-language films.

subtle [sut'-l] *adj* **1** cunning, clever (*he succeeded in persuading her by subtle means*). **2** difficult to understand completely (*a subtle difference*). **3** faint or delicate (*subtle colours*).

subtlety [sut'-l-ti] *n* **1** skill, cleverness. **2** refinement.

subtract' *vb* to take (one number) from another:—*n* **subtrac'tion**.

sub'urb *n* an outlying part of a city:—*adj* **subur'ban**.

subver'sive *adj* intended or likely to overthrow or destroy, directed against the government, management, organization, etc (*a subversive section of the club*).

subvert' vb (fml) to overthrow, to try to destroy (try to subvert the monarchy):—n **subver'sion**.

sub'way n 1 an under ground passage (use the subway to get across the busy road). 2 an underground railway.

succeed' vb 1 to do what one has attempted or desired to do (succeeded in climbing the mountain). 2 to come after , to follow in order and take the place of (the monarch who succeeded King Henry VIII/he succeeded his father as chairman).

success' n 1 the doing of what one has attempted or desired to do. 2 a favourable r esult or outcome. 3 a person or thing that does as well as was hoped or expected.

success'ful adj doing well, doing what was attempted or desired (a successful attempt/they were successful in their attempt).

succes'sion n 1 a number of persons or things following one another in order (a succession of candidates for the post). 2 the or der in which people may inherit a title when it becomes vacant.

success'ive adj coming in order, following one after another (on successive occasions).

success'or n one who comes after or takes the place of another (the president's successor).

succinct' adj short and to the point, concise (a succinct account of the meeting).

suc'cour vb (fml) to help when in difficulty:—n aid, help (give succour to the injured).

suc'culent adj juicy (succulent peaches).

succumb' vb 1 to give way to, to be over come. 2 to die.

such adj of a like kind or degree, similar.

suck vb 1 to draw into or in with the mouth (suck juice from an orange). 2 to draw the liquid fr om the mouth or something in it with the tongue (suck sweets):—also n.

suck'er n 1 a shoot other than the main stem growing up from the root of a plant. 2 (inf) a foolish or gullible person.

suck'le vb to allow to suck milk from the breast (sows suckling their piglets).

suck'ling n a baby or animal still feeding from its mother's breast.

suc'tion n the act of sucking, the drawing up of a fluid into a tube, etc, by expelling the air so that the fluid fills the vacuum.

sud'den adj happening without warning, unexpected, hurried (a sudden change in the weather).

suds npl the froth on soapy water.

sue vb 1 to bring a case against in a court of law (sue him for slander). 2 (fml) to beg for (suing for mercy).

suede [swãd] n a soft kind of leather made from undressed kidskin:—also adj.

su'et n the hard fat around the kidneys and loins of cattle, sheep, etc.

suffer vb 1 to under go pain or great anxiety (families suffering during the strike). 2 to experience or undergo (suffer defeat). 3 to put up with (unable to suffer the noise).

sufferance n permission that is given unwillingly, or that may be withdrawn if one behaves badly.

suffice' vb (fml) to be enough (a little will suffice).

suffi'ciency n a big enough supply.

suffi'cient adj enough (not sufficient money to buy food).

suffix n a syllable added to the end of a word (e.g. -ness,-ly).

suffocate vb 1 to chok e for lack of air (people suffocating in the heat). 2 to kill by pr eventing from breathing (suffocated the old man with a pillow):—n **suffocation**.

suffragan n an assistant bishop.

suffrage n (fml) the right to vote in parliamentary elections.

suffragette' n a woman who claimed and obtained the right for women to vote.

suffuse' vb (fml) to spread over (a blush suffusing her cheek):—n **suffu'sion**.

su'gar n a sweet substance manufactured from sugar cane, beet, etc:—vb 1 to sweeten with sugar (sugared the strawberries) 2 to try to make more acceptable (try to sugar the insult).

sugar beet n a plant with a root from which sugar is obtained.

su'garcane n a tall stiff reed from which sugar is obtained.

su'gary adj sweet (sugary desserts).

suggest' vb 1 to put for ward (suggest some improvements). 2 to hint (she thought that he was suggesting that she was a liar). 3 to cause an idea to come into the mind (*a perfume suggesting roses*).

sugges'tion *n* 1 a pr oposal. 2 a hint.

sugges'tive *adj* 1 putting ideas into the mind (*suggestive of Victorian times*). 2 rather indecent (*suggestive remarks*).

suici'dal *adj* 1 liable to commit suicide. 2 putting one' s life in danger.

su'icide *n* 1 the deliberate killing of oneself. 2 one who kills himself or herself deliberately (*the police found the suicide*).

suit *vb* 1 to please or satisf y (*it suits him to go*). 2 to go well with. 3 to look nice on (*a dress that suits her*):—*n* 1 a set of clothes of the same material (*a business suit*). 2 (*fml*) a request (*her suit to the king for mercy*). 3 attentions paid to a lady with the intention of marrying her. 4 one of the four sets (hearts, clubs, etc) in a pack of playing cards. 5 the taking of a case to a court of law:—**follow suit 1** to play a card from the same suit. **2** to do the same as or follow the example of another (*he left and she followed suit*).

suit'able *adj* what is wanted for the purpose, fitting the occasion (*suitable clothes for the job*).

suit'case *n* a portable travelling bag for clothes.

suite [sweet] *n* 1 a set of r ooms or furniture (*the bridal suite in the hotel*). 2 all the attendants who wait upon a certain person. 3 a series of connected pieces of music.

suit'or *n* 1 one making a r equest or asking for a favour. 2 a man paying attention to a lady with the intention of marrying her.

sulk *vb* to behave in an ill-humoured, unfriendly way, to refuse to speak to others because of ill-temper (*she sulked when she didn't get her own way*).

sulks *npl* a silent ill-humoured mood.

sulk'y *adj* ill-natured, not mixing with others because of ill-humour (*sulky because he didn't get his own way*).

sul'len *adj* ill-natured, silently bad-tempered.

sul'ly *vb* to dirty, to stain, to spoil (*sullied her good name*).

sul'phate *n* a salt of sulphuric acid.

sul'phur *n* a yellow non-metallic element.

sulphu'ric *adj* having to do with or containing sulphur.

sul'phurous *adj* having to do with or like sulphur.

sul'tan *n* the ruler of a Muslim country.

sulta'na *n* 1 the wife of a sultan. 2 a type of raisin.

sul'try *adj* very hot and close (*sultry weather*).

sum *n* 1 the answer obtained by adding several numbers together. 2 the total or entir e amount, esp of money (*the sum gathered for the charity*). 3 a pr oblem in arithmetic:—*vb* (**summed'**, **sum'ming**) to add up:—**sum up** to summarize.

sum'marize *vb* to give a brief account of the main points (*summarizing the discussion of the committee*).

sum'mary *n* a brief account of the main points (*summaries of their speeches*):—*adj* 1 short. 2 done quickly or by a short method (*their summary dismissal of him*).

sum'marily *adv* quickly, without long consideration.

sum'mer *n* the warmest season of the year.

sum'merhouse *n* a kind of hut in the garden for sitting in.

sum'mit *n* 1 the highest point, the top. 2 a meeting of heads of government, or other high-ranking officials, of several countries to discuss matters of great importance (*a summit on environment pollution*).

sum'mon *vb* 1 to call upon to appear befor e an official (*summoned by the court*). 2 to call upon to do something (*summon all his strength*).

sum'mons *n* an order to appear for trial by a court of law:—*vb* to present with such an order.

sump *n* a hole or hollow in which liquid collects (e.g. an oil sump in an engine).

sump'tuous *adj* splendid, very expensive, luxurious (*a sumptuous palace*).

sun *n* 1 the heavenly body that gives light and heat to the earth and other planets in the same system. 2 the warmth or light given by the sun.

sun'beam *n* a ray of light from the sun.

sun'burn *n* a darkening of the skin's colour caused by exposure to the sun:—*also vb*.

sun'dae *n* ice cream served with fruit, nuts, syrup, etc.

Sun'day *n* the first day of the week.

sun'der *vb* (*fml*) to part, to separate (*sunder relations between them*).

sun'dial *n* an instrument that tells the time by casting the shadow of an indicator on a face marked with the hours.

sun'dry *adj* (*fml*) several, of different kinds (*sundry other matters*):—*npl* **sun'dries** odds and ends of different kinds.

sun'flower *n* a tall plant with a large yellow flower.

sun'ny *adj* **1** brightly lit by the sun. **2** cheerful, happy (*a sunny nature*).

sun'rise *n* the first appearance of the sun in the morning.

sun'set *n* the disappearance of the sun below the horizon in the evening.

sun'shine *n* **1** the light or warmth of the sun. **2** cheerfulness (*the sunshine of her nature*).

sun'spot *n* a dark patch sometimes to be seen on the surface of the sun.

sun'stroke *n* a severe illness caused by the effect of the sun's heat on the body.

sup *vb* (**supped'**, **sup'ping**) **1** (*old*) to take supper. **2** to eat or drink in small mouthfuls:— *n* a small mouthful.

super- *prefix* above, over.

superabun'dance *n* great plenty (*a superabundance of fish*).

superabun'dant *adj* more than enough.

superan'nuate *vb* to cause to retire from a job with a pension because of old age:—*n* **superannua'tion**.

superb' *adj* magnificent, excellent (*a superb performance*).

su'percargo *n* the officer in charge of a ship's cargo.

supercil'ious *adj* **1** over-pr oud, having a scornful manner (*a supercilious young woman*). **2** disdainful, scornful (*a supercilious look*).

superfi'cial *adj* **1** on the surface (*superficial wounds*). **2** not deeply felt or thought about (*a superficial knowledge*). **3** shallow , incapable of deep thought or feeling (*a superficial person*):—*n* **superficial'ity**.

super'fluous *adj* more than enough, unnecessary (*his advice was superfluous*):—*n* **superflu'ity**.

superhu'man *adj* more than human, extraordinary, divine (*make a superhuman effort*).

superimpose' *vb* to lay on top of something else (*superimposing one photograph on another*).

superintend' *vb* to watch others to see that they do their job properly, to direct, to be in charge of (*superintend the making of goods in the factory*).

superinten'dent *n* **1** one who superintends. **2** a high-ranking police officer.

supe'rior *adj* **1** higher in rank (*his superior officer*). **2** better (*a superior player*):—*n* **1** one higher in rank. **2** one better than others (*he is his brother's superior on the football pitch*). **3** the head of a monastery or convent:—*n* **superior'ity**.

super'lative *adj* **1** excellent, above all others in quality (*a superlative musical performance*). **2** expressing the highest degree (*best is the superlative degree of good*).

su'perman *n* a man of extraordinary powers, the imagined perfect human being of the future.

su'permarket *n* a large shop selling (usu by self-service) food and household goods.

supernat'ural *adj* **1** not to be explained by natural causes (*supernatural forces*). **2** caused by direct divine intervention in human affairs:—*n* immortal beings existing outside the known universe and having the power to intervene in human affairs.

supernu'merary *adj* (*fml*) more than the number needed (*supernumerary volunteers*):—*n* an extra person.

superscrip'tion *n* what is written above or on something.

supersede' *vb* to take the place of, to put another in the place of (*some hobbies have been superseded by television viewing*).

superson'ic *adj* faster than sound (*supersonic aircraft*).

supersti'tion *n* **1** a tendency to believe that certain human beings or objects have more than natural powers. **2** belief in magic, luck, etc (*the superstition that black cats are lucky*).

supersti'tious *adj* believing in magic, etc (*too superstitious to walk under a ladder*).

superstruc'ture *n* **1** anything r esting on a foundation. **2** a building.

su'pertax *n* an extra tax payable on large incomes.

supervene' *vb* to happen while something else is going on, to happen in addition (*the MP's death supervened during the election campaign*).

su'pervise *vb* **1** to watch others to see that they do their work properly (*supervising the pupils doing homework*). **2** to be in char ge of (*supervised the dress department*):—*n* **supervi'sion**:— *n* **supervi'sor**.

su'pine *adj* (*fml*) **1** lying on the back (*the injured man was lying supine*). **2** lazy, doing nothing (*too supine to take action*).

sup'per *n* a light evening meal.

supplant' *vb* to gain the place or position of another, esp by deceit.

sup'ple *adj* **1** (*fml*) easily bent. **2** bending or moving easily and gracefully (*supple gymnasts*).

sup'plement *n* **1** something added to make up what is lacking (*vitamin supplements*). **2** an addition:—*vb* **supplement'** to make additions to.

supplemen'tary *adj* given in addition, given to make up what is lacking (*supplementary income*).

sup'pliant *adj* (*fml*) begging for as a favour:—*n* (*fml*) one begging for a favour (*suppliants asking the emperor for mercy*).

sup'plicate *vb* (*fml*) to beg humbly for, to pray.

supplica'tion *n* (*fml*) earnest request, prayer.

supply' *vb* to provide what is needed (*supplied food for the party*):—*n* **1** a store of what is needed. **2** *pl* stores.

support' *vb* **1** to help to hold up (*struts supporting the bridge*). **2** to give help or encouragement to (*support the cause*). **3** to provide the necessities of life for (*support a family*). **4** to put up with (*unable to support the noise of the machinery*):—*n* **1** a prop. **2** assistance, encouragement. **3** a person or thing that supports.

support'er *n* one who helps or encourages (*supporters of the king's cause*).

suppose' *vb* **1** to believe to be true without sure evidence (*we suppose that he is honest*). **2** to imagine. **3** to think probable (*I suppose she has gone home*).

supposi'tion *n* **1** a guess. **2** something taken as true or imagined.

suppress' *vb* **1** to put down, to crush (*suppress the rebellion*). **2** to prevent from being known (*suppress information*):—*n* **suppres'sion**.

sup'purate *vb* to gather or form poisonous matter (*wounds suppurating*):—*n* **suppu-ra'tion**.

suprem'acy *n* the highest power or authority.

supreme' *adj* **1** highest in power or authority. **2** greatest (*supreme happiness*).

sur'charge *n* an extra charge (*a surcharge for taxis ordered after midnight*).

sur'cingle *n* a strap for holding the saddle in position on a horse's back.

sure *adj* **1** certain (*I'm sure he'll come*). **2** convinced of (*sure of her own ability*). **3** unfailing (*a sure remedy*).

sure-footed *adj* good at keeping one's feet, even on difficult ground.

sure'ly *adv* without doubt.

sure'ty *n* **1** (*fml*) certainty. **2** one ready to vouch for the truth of another's promise to pay (*stand surety for her sister's bank loan*). **3** something given into the possession of another by a debtor until such time as the money due is paid.

surf *n* the foamy water caused by waves breaking on a sloping shore.

surfboard *see* **surfing**.

sur'face *n* **1** the outside or top part of anything. **2** outside appearance (*she seems happy on the surface*):—*vb* to rise to the surface (*divers surfacing*).

sur'faceman *n* a workman whose job it is to keep railway tracks in good order.

sur'feit *n* too much of anything (*a surfeit of rich food*):—*vb* to overfeed.

surf'ing *n* **1** the sport of riding on the crest of large waves while standing on a long, narrow board with a rounded or pointed front end, called a **surfboard**. **2** the act of moving from site to site on the Internet looking for something interesting:—*v* **surf**.

surge *n* the rising of a wave, the up-and-down movement of the surface of the sea:—*vb* to rise, to well up, as a wave.

sur'geon *n* a doctor skilled in surgery.

sur'gery *n* **1** the art or science of curing disease by cutting the body. **2** a doctor's consulting room (*the general practitioner's surgery*).

sur'gical *adj* having to do with surgery (*surgical treatment*).

sur'ly *adj* gloomy and ill-humoured:—*n* **sur'liness**.

surmise' *vb* to guess, to suppose (*I surmised that she was telling the truth*):—*n* a guess.

surmount' *vb* to overcome (*surmount the difficulty*).

sur'name *n* a person's family name.

surpass' *vb* to do better than (*his performance surpassed that of the others*).

surpas'sing *adj* excellent.

sur'plice *n* a loose white garment worn during a service by members of the clergy, of the choir, etc.

sur'plus *n* the amount by which anything is more than is required (*a surplus of apples that autumn*).

surprise' *n* **1** the feeling caused by what is sudden or unexpected. **2** a sudden or unexpected event, gift, piece of news, etc (*it was a surprise when she arrived*):—*vb* **1** to come upon when not expected. **2** to tak e unawares, to startle, to astonish (*surprising the enemy*).

surren'der *vb* **1** to stop fighting and accept the enemy's terms, to give up. **2** to hand over (*have to surrender his passport at the border*):—also *n*.

surrepti'tious *adj* underhand, done secretly or slyly (*have a surreptitious look at the answers at the back of the book*).

surround' *vb* to go, put or be on all sides of (*trees surrounding the house/an army surrounding the city*).

surround'ings *npl* the objects or country round a person or place (*live in beautiful surroundings*).

sur'tax *n* an extra tax.

surveillance [sêr-vāl'-êns] *n* a careful watch (*he was under police surveillance*).

survey' *vb* **1** to look over . **2** to look at car efully. **3** to measur e an area of land and make a plan of it:—*n* **sur'vey 1** a general view. **2** the measuring of a piece of land. **3** a plan made of a piece of land.

survey'or *n* one who surveys land.

survi'val *n* **1** act of sur viving. **2** a person or thing that has lived on from a past age:—**survival of the fittest** the belief that only those kinds of plants, animals, etc, live on that have been able to adapt themselves to their surroundings.

survive' *vb* **1** to live on after (*she survived her husband*). **2** to continue to live or exist (*several were killed but she survived*).

survi'vor *n* one who has lived on, esp after a disaster (*survivors of the plane crash*).

suscep'tible *adj* easily influenced or affected by (*susceptible to colds/susceptible children*):—*n* **susceptibil'ity**.

suspect' *vb* **1** to think something is the case but have no proof (*I suspect that he is leaving*). **2** to mistrust, to doubt the truth or genuineness of. **3** to believe to be guilty (*suspect him of murder*):—*n* **sus'pect** one who is suspected:—*adj* **sus'pect** doubtful, not worthy of trust.

suspend' *vb* **1** to hang fr om (*hooks suspended from the roof*). **2** to cause to stop for a time (*sales of the product have been suspended*).

suspen'der *n* an elastic support for socks or stockings.

suspense' *n* uncertainty or anxiety about what may happen in the future (*the suspense of waiting for exam results*).

suspen'sion *n* the state of being suspended.

suspension bridge *n* a bridge suspended by chains or steel ropes from towers or arches.

suspi'cion *n* a feeling of doubt or mistrust.

suspi'cious *adj* doubtful, mistrustful (*suspicious about his neighbour's activities*).

sustain' *vb* **1** to k eep up, to support (*sustain the weight of the statue*). **2** to give str ength to (*sustained by a good meal*). **3** to k eep in existence over a long period (*sustain his interest*). **4** to undergo (*sustain damage*).

sus'tenance *n* food, nourishment.

sut'tee *n* a former Hindu custom by which a widow burned herself on her husband's funeral fire.

su'zerainty *n* (*fml*) the power to rule over.

swab *n* **1** a mop for cleaning decks, etc. **2** a pad of cotton wool (sometimes wrapped round a stick) used for cleansing wounds, applying medicines, etc:—*vb* (**swabbed'**, **swab'bing**) to clean with a swab.

swad'dle *vb* to wrap up tightly with clothes.

swad'dling clothes *npl* baby clothes.

swag *n* (*inf*) stolen goods (*the burglar's swag*).

swag'ger *vb* to walk proudly, to behave boastfully (*swagger down the road after winning the fight*):—also *n*.

swain *n* (*old*) **1** a lover . **2** a young countr yman.

swal'low' *vb* **1** to draw down the thr oat and into the stomach (*swallow pills*). **2** to enclose in the middle of something bigger (*villages swallowed up by the growing city*). **3** to believe without question (*did not swallow the story*):—*n* the act of swallowing.

swal'low² *n* a bird with long wings and a forked tail which flies to a warmer country in winter.

swal'lowtail *n* a man's dress jacket with a long tail at the back.

swamp *n* wet, marshy ground:—*vb* **1** to flood. **2** to over whelm by greater numbers or strength (*swamped by letters of application*).

swamp'y adj soft and wet, marshy.

swan n a long-necked bird of the duck family.

swan song n one's final work or achievement before death, retirement, etc (his appearance in 'Hamlet' was his swan song).

swap, swop vb (**swapped'**, **swap'ping**) to exchange (one thing for another) (the children are swapping model cars).

sward n the grassy surface of land, a lawn.

swarm n 1 a large number of insects (e.g. bees) moving as a group. 2 a large closely packed crowd (swarms of people going to the sales):— vb 1 to come together in large numbers. 2 (of bees, etc) to leave the hive in a body. 3 to climb, gripping with the arms and legs.

swar'thy adj dark-skinned.

swash'buckler n a noisy quarrelsome fellow, a bully.

swat vb (**swat'ted**, **swat'ting**) to hit sharply, to crush (swat the flies).

swath n a strip of cut grass or corn.

swathe [swāth] vb to wrap up in bandages or clothing:—n swathe or swath.

sway vb 1 to move with a rocking motion from side to side or backwards and forwards (trees swaying in the wind). 2 to rule, to have influence over (he's easily swayed):—n 1 a rocking movement. 2 contr ol, rule.

swear vb (pt swore, pp sworn) 1 to promise solemnly to tell the truth, calling on God as witness to one's good faith. 2 to declar e something is true. 3 to use bad wor ds or language insulting to God, to use words that are considered offensive and socially unacceptable.

sweat n the moisture that oozes from the body when it is overheated, perspiration:—vb 1 to perspire. 2 to work ver y hard (sweat to pass the exams). 3 to employ for low wages.

sweat'er n a heavy woollen jersey.

sweat'y adj (inf) damp with perspiration (sweaty feet).

swede n a large yellow turnip.

sweep vb (pt, pp swept) 1 to clean with a brush or broom (sweep the floor). 2 to move over swiftly and smoothly (the waves swept towards the shore/panic swept through the crowd). 3 to remove with an extensive or curving movement (sweep the papers into the drawer):—n 1 an extensive or curving movement. 2 a quick look over. 3 one who cleans chimneys:—**sweep the board** to win everything offered or at stake.

sweep'ing adj 1 wide, extensive (sweeping changes). 2 not taking sufficient account of exceptions (a sweeping generalization).

sweep'stake n a gambling game in which the buyers of winning tickets win prizes.

sweet adj 1 tasting lik e honey or sugar (sweet fruit). 2 having a pleasing smell (the sweet smell of roses). 3 pleasing to the senses (sweet music). 4 gentle and lik eable (she's a sweet old lady). 5 pr etty (a sweet dress):—n 1 a sweetmeat. 2 a pudding:— adv **sweet'ly**:—**have a sweet tooth** to like eating sweet-tasting things.

sweet'bread n part of the stomach of a calf used as food.

sweet'-briar, sweet'-brier n a wild rose tree.

sweetcorn n 1 a type of maize consisting of juicy yellow kernels growing on thick stems 2 the kernels eaten as a vegetable.

sweet'en vb to make or become sweet (sweeten the pudding with honey).

sweet'heart n one dearly loved, a lover.

sweet'meat n a piece of toffee, chocolate, boiled sugar, etc.

sweet pea n a garden plant with sweet-smelling flowers.

sweet william n a garden plant with flowers growing in clusters.

swell vb (pp swoll'en) 1 to gr ow larger (the lump is swelling). 2 to mak e or become louder (the music swelled). 3 to bulge out (with stomach swelling). 4 (of the sea) to rise and fall in large waves that do not break:—n 1 movement of the sea in large waves that do not break. 2 (inf) a very well-dressed person.

swell'ing n a lump raised for a time on the body by a bruise, infected cut, etc (a swelling on her neck).

swel'ter vb to be very hot, to be uncomfortable because of great heat (tourists sweltering in high temperatures):—adj **swel'tering**.

swerve vb to turn or move suddenly to one side (the driver swerved to avoid the dog):— also n.

swift adj quick-moving, speedy:—n a bird like the swallow.

swig *vb* (**swigged'**, **swig'ging**) (*inf*) to drink in large mouthfuls:—*n* (*inf*) a large mouthful (*a swig of beer*).

swill *vb* **1** to wash out (*swill the cellar floor out*). **2** (*inf*) to drink greedily (*swilled beer*):—*n* liquid food for pigs.

swim *vb* (**swam**, **swim'ming**, *pp* **swum**) **1** to move through the water by moving the arms and legs. **2** to float in or on the top of (*a stew swimming with fat*). **3** to be dizzy (*with head swimming*):—*n* act of swimming, a bathe spent swimming:—*n* **swim'-mer**:—**in the swim** knowing what is going on, knowing important or influential people.

swimming baths *npl* a building containing a **swimming pool** a pond made for swimming in.

swim'mingly *adv* smoothly, with great success (*everything went swimmingly*).

swin'dle *vb* to cheat:—*n* a deception intended to cheat people, a fraud (*the cheap holiday offer was a swindle*).

swind'ler *n* a cheat, one who tricks people out of money.

swine *n* (*pl* **swine**) **1** a pig. **2** (*inf*) a very nasty person.

swine'herd *n* one who looks after pigs.

swin'ish *adj* beastly.

swing *vb* (*pt*, *pp* **swung**) **1** to move to and fro, esp when suspended from above (*children swinging from a branch*). **2** to whirl round (*dancers swinging*). **3** to turn round when at anchor. **4** to walk quickly with a swaying movement (*swing along the promenade*):—*n* **1** a seat suspended by ropes, etc, on which a child can swing to and fro (*the swings in the park*). **2** a swinging movement. **3** a long-range blow given with a curved arm:—**swing the lead** to pretend to be ill (*his boss thinks he is swinging the lead*):—**go with a swing** to take place well without difficulties arising (*the conference went with a swing*):—**in full swing** in progress (*the party was in full swing*).

swinge *vb* to beat hard.

swing music *n* a type of jazz.

swipe *vb* **1** to hit har d with a swinging movement (*swipe the mosquito*). **2** (*inf*) to steal:—*n* a hard, sweeping blow.

swirl *vb* to flow or move with a circular motion (*water swirling*/*her skirt swirled*):—*n* a circular motion of water.

swish *n* the sound made by a light or thin object moving through the air (*the swish of her skirt*):—*vb* **1** to move thr ough the air with a swish. **2** to beat with a cane or birch.

switch *n* **1** an easily bent stick. **2** a small le ver for turning on and off electric current (*the light switch*):—*vb* **1** to hit with a switch. **2** to turn electric current (on or off). **3** to change suddenly (*switch courses*).

switch'back *n* a road or railway over an up-and-down course:—*also adj*.

switch'board *n* a board at which connection can be made between one telephone line and another.

swiv'el *n* a ring that turns freely round a pin, so that what the one is connected to can remain stationary while the other turns:—*vb* (**swiv'elled**, **swiv'elling**) to turn round, as on a swivel.

swoon *vb* to faint:—*n* a fainting turn.

swoop *vb* **1** to fly down upon with a sudden swift movement (*hawks swooping*). **2** to come upon swiftly and suddenly (*the police swooped on the smugglers in a dawn raid*):—*n* **1** a sudden downward rush. **2** a sudden attack.

swop (**swopped'**, **swop'ping**) *see* **swap**.

sword [sord] *n* a weapon with a long blade and sharp point for cutting or thrusting.

sword'fish *n* a large fish whose upper jaw sticks out and comes to a point like a sword.

swords'man *n* one skilled in the use of a sword.

swords'manship *n* the art of fighting with a sword.

syb'arite *n* one who likes to live in luxury and ease:—*adj* **syba'ritic**.

syc'amore *n* a large tree, of the same family as the maple and fig tree.

syc'ophant *n* one who flatters another to gain his or her favour:—*adj* **sycophan'tic**.

syllab'ic *adj* having to do with syllables.

syl'lable *n* a part of a word or a word containing one vowel sound.

syl'labus *n* a plan for a course of studies, giving subjects to be studied, times of classes, etc.

syl'logism *n* a method of testing the genuineness of an argument by seeing if it can be set out in a series of three statements in accordance with certain rules.

sylph *n* **1** a spirit of the air , a fairy. **2** a slim, graceful girl.

sylph'-like *adj* slim and graceful.

syl'van, sil'van *adj* having to do with woods or forests.

sym'bol *n* 1 an emblem or sign made to stand for or represent something else (*Ag is the symbol for silver*). 2 a sign that all r ecognize as bearing a certain meaning (*the symbol of peace is an olive branch*).

symbol'ic *adj* standing for or representing something else:—*adv* **symbol'ically**.

sym'bolism *n* the use of symbols.

sym'bolize *vb* to stand as a sign for (*an olive branch symbolizing peace*).

symmet'rical *adj* 1 having a balanced or regular design (*symmetrical patterns*). 2 graceful because the parts are in pleasing proportion to each other and to the whole.

sym'metry *n* 1 sameness between the two halves of a design. 2 a pleasing similarity or contrast between parts, beauty resulting from graceful proportions.

sympathet'ic *adj* showing or feeling understanding or pity.

sym'pathize *vb* 1 to feel with and for another . 2 to be in agreement with.

sym'pathy *n* 1 understanding of the sorr ow or distress of another, pity. 2 agr eement with the opinion of another (*in sympathy with his views on hanging*).

sym'phony *n* 1 a piece of music written for a full orchestra. 2 (*lit*) a pleasant unison of sounds, colours, etc:—*adj* **symphon'ic**.

sympo'sium *n* (*pl* **sympo'sia** *or* **sympo'si-ums**) 1 a conference at which specialists deliver short addresses on a topic. 1 a collection of written papers on a set subject.

symp'tom *n* 1 a sign or mark by which something can be recognized. 2 one of the signs by which a doctor is able to recognize the disease affecting a patient:—*adj* **symptomat'ic**.

syn'agogue *n* a Jewish church.

syn'chronize *vb* 1 to happen or cause to happen at the same time (*synchronize our plans*). 2 to set to exactly the same time (*synchronizing watches*).

syn'copate *vb* to change the rhythm of music by beginning or ending notes slightly sooner or later than is strictly correct:—*n* **syncopa'tion**.

syn'dicate *n* 1 a gr oup of persons or companies who are working together for business reasons or financial gain:—*vb* 1 to join together in a syndicate. 2 to sell for publication in mor e than one journal, newspaper, etc (*syndicating his column across the United States*).

synecdoche [si-nek'-do-kee] *n* a figure of speech in which a part is made to stand for the whole, or a whole for the part (e.g. a *sail* for a *ship*).

syn'od *n* a meeting or assembly of members of clergy.

syn'onym *n* a word having the same or nearly the same meaning as another word.

synon'ymous *adj* having the same meaning.

synop'sis *n* a summary, a short account of the main happenings or ideas in a book.

synop'tic *adj* giving a general view of the whole.

Synoptic Gospels *npl* the gospels of Matthew, Mark, and Luke in the Bible.

syn'tax *n* the putting of words in a sentence in order and in the correct relation to each other:—*adjs* **syntac'tic(al)**.

syn'thesis *n* the putting together of parts to make a whole.

synthet'ic *adj* made or put together by artificial means, not natural (*synthetic materials*).

sy'phon *n* same as **siphon**.

syringe' *n* a tube filled with a piston by means of which fluid can be drawn up or squirted out:—*vb* to squirt or spray with a syringe.

syr'up *n* 1 any thick sweet-tasting liquid (*syrup of figs*). 2 the thick liquid obtained when r efining cane sugar.

sys'tem *n* 1 a method by which a number of parts of different kinds are made to work together as a unified whole (*the nervous system*/*a transport system*/*the solar system*). 2 a r egular method of doing things (*he has no system in working*). 3 a plan (*a system for winning the lottery*).

systemat'ic *adj* methodical, arranged in an orderly or reasonable manner, following a pre-arranged plan.

sys'tematize *vb* to reduce to a system.

T

tab *n* a small piece of paper, cloth, etc sticking out from something larger, a small flap (*the tab on the packet of soap powder*).

tab'ard *n* (*old*) a herald's coat.

tab'by *n* a female cat.

tab'ernacle *n* a place of worship.

ta'ble *n* **1** an article of furniture with legs and a flat top, used for placing or resting things on (*the kitchen table*). **2** a list of figures, names, facts, etc, arranged in columns (*a table showing the times of the buses*):—*vb* to put forward for discussion (*tabling a motion*):—**turn the tables on** to begin doing to another what he or she has been doing to you.

tab'leau *n* (*pl* **tab'leaux** [tab'-lōz]) a scene in which people stand motionless as if figures in a picture (*the pageant consisted of a series of historical tableaux*).

table d'hôte [täbl dōt] *n* a meal with a limited choice of dishes served at a fixed price in a restaurant or hotel.

ta'bleland *n* a wide extent of flat land at the top of a hill.

ta'blespoon *n* a large spoon used for serving at table or as a measure in cooking.

tab'let *n* **1** a piece of cardboard or flat piece of metal or stone with some writing or signs on it (*a tablet on the wall in memory of a local hero*). **2** a small flat slab (*a tablet of soap*). **3** a pill (*sleeping tablets*).

table talk *n* friendly conversation.

tab'loid *n* a small-format newspaper usu with emphasis on photographs and news in condensed form.

taboo', **tabu'** *adj* set apart so as not to be touched or used, forbidden for religious reasons or because it is against social custom (*alcohol is taboo in Muslim countries*):—*n* an order not to touch or use something:—*vb* to forbid to touch or use.

ta'bor *n* a small drum.

tab'ular *adj* set out in columns or tables (*information in tabular form*).

tab'ulate *vb* to arrange in columns or tables in a systematic way (*tabulate the results of the experiment*):—*n* **tabula'tion**.

ta'cit *adj* thought or intended, but not spoken (*tacit agreement*).

ta'citurn *adj* speaking little, silent by nature (*he was so taciturn that it was difficult to get to know him*):—*n* **tacitur'nity**.

tack *n* **1** a small sharp nail with a broad head. **2** a long loose stitch. **3** the zigzag course of a sailing ship when sailing against the wind:—*vb* **1** to nail with tacks (*tack the notice to the wall*). **2** to sew with long loose stitches. **3** (*of a sailing ship*) to change course to catch the wind. **4** to add on (*they had tacked an extra question on to the exam paper*):—**on the wrong tack** on the wrong trail (*the police were on the wrong tack in the murder investigation*).

tack'le *n* **1** all the equipment needed for some sport or game (*fishing tackle*). **2** all the things necessary for a task. **3** a series of ropes, pulleys, etc, for raising weights, sails, etc:—*vb* **1** to struggle with, to seize and pull down (*tackle the bank robber*). **2** (*in football*) to prevent from advancing with the ball. **3** to try to do (*tackle the job*). **3** to speak to or put questions to (*he tackled him about the unemployment issue*).

tack'y *adj* **1** sticky (*the paint is still tacky*). **2** (*inf*) cheap, in bad taste (*tacky furniture*).

tact *n* the ability to speak or behave without hurting the feelings of others, consideration (*husband and wife are not speaking to each other and so act with tact*):—*adjs* **tact'ful**, **tact'less**.

tac'tical *adj* having to do with tactics (*tactical military manoeuvres*).

tacti'cian *n* **1** one skilled in tactics. **2** one quick to see a possible advantage.

tac'tics *npl* **1** the art of moving armies or other warlike forces during battle. **2** any actions intended to gain an immediate advantage (*tactics required to win the match*).

tac'tile *adj* having to do with the sense of touch (*the tactile qualities*).

tad'pole *n* the young of a frog, toad, etc, just after it has come out of the egg.

taf'feta *n* a shiny silk material.

taf'frail *n* the rail round the stern of a ship.

tag *n* **1** the metal point at the end of a shoe-lace. **2** an address label. **3** a common quotation or saying:—*vb* (**tagged', tag'ging**) to fasten on.

tail *n* 1 a long hanging part of an animal's body, situated at the end of the spine. 2 the back part of anything (*the tail of the queue*).

tail'back *n* a long line of very slow-moving or stationary traffic caused by something blocking the road ahead.

tail'board *n* a board for closing the back of a cart or lorry.

tail'coat *n* a man's jacket, short in front, long and divided down the middle at the back.

tail end *n* the last or back part (*the tail end of his speech*).

tail'light *n* the light at the back of a vehicle.

tail'or *n* one who makes clothes, esp for men:—*vb* to make clothes.

tail'or-made *adj* 1 made by a tailor to a person's measurements (*a tailor-made suit*). 2 just what is needed (*a tailor-made job*).

tail'piece *n* 1 a design sometimes placed at the end of a chapter. 2 a later happening.

tails *npl* the reverse side of a coin.

tail'spin *n* a dive made by an aeroplane while twisting round and round (*the plane went into a tailspin*).

taint *vb* to spoil or make bad (*tainted meat/taint his reputation*):—*n* 1 a stain, an evil element that spoils the rest. 2 a mark of shame or disgrace.

take *vb* (*pt* **took**, *pp* **tak'en**) 1 to seize or grasp. 2 to receive or accept. 3 to capture (*the army took the city*). 4 to carry. 5 to travel by (bus, etc). 6 to eat (*take fruit*). 7 to be infected by (*take flu*). 8 to require (numbers, time, material, etc):—**take after** to be like:—**take down** to write (notes, etc):—**take for** to think to be (*they took him for a fool*):—**take heart** to become braver:—**take in** 1 to deceive (*they pretended to be workmen and took in the old lady*). 2 to understand (*scarcely able to take in the news*). 3 to make (a garment) smaller:—**take off** 1 to remove. 2 to leave the ground when beginning to fly. 3 to imitate mockingly (*to take off their boss*):—**take on** to agree to play or fight against:—**take over** to get control of (*take over the running of the shop*):—**take place** to happen:—**take to** to begin to like (*he did not take to her*):—**take up** to begin

to do or study:—**take up with** to begin to go about with.

take'-away *n* 1 ready-cooked food bought from a restaurant to be eaten elsewhere. 2 a restaurant selling this kind of food.

tak'ing *adj* (*fml*) pleasing, attractive (*a taking little girl*).

tak'ings *n* money received for goods, admission, etc (*the day's takings were stolen*).

talc *n* 1 a glass-like mineral. 2 a fine powder for the skin made from this.

talc'um *n* a fine powder made from talc (*powder the baby with talcum*).

tale *n* 1 a story. 2 (*old*) a number.

tale'-bearer, tale'-teller *ns* one who reports another's wrongdoings in order to get him or her into trouble.

tal'ent *n* 1 special ability or skill (*a talent for dealing with people*). 2 an ancient coin or measure of weight.

tal'ented *adj* very clever.

tal'isman *n* (*pl* **talismans**) an object, word or words supposed to possess magic powers.

talk [tåk] *vb* to speak:—*n* 1 a conversation. 2 a lecture (*a talk on local history*). 3 gossip (*there is a lot of talk about their affair*):—**talk over** to discuss:—**talk (someone) round** to convince:—**talk to** to scold.

talk'ative *adj* fond of talking.

tall *adj* 1 high (*he was over six feet tall*). 2 above the usual height.

tall'boy *n* a high chest of drawers.

tal'low *n* the melted fat of animals.

tal'ly *n* 1 an account. 2 formerly, an account kept by cutting notches on wood. 3 a score or count (*keep a tally of money spent*):—*vb* to agree with, to fit (*his account of events does not tally with hers*).

tally-ho' *interj* and *n* a huntsman's cry to urge on hounds.

Tal'mud *n* the Jewish system of law.

tal'on *n* the claw of a bird of prey (*the eagle's talons*).

tam'arind *n* 1 a tropical tree. 2 its fruit.

tam'arisk *n* an evergreen shrub with feathery leaves.

tam'bour *n* 1 a drum. 2 a drumlike frame on which embroidery is worked.

tambourine' *n* a small one-sided drum with rattling metal discs around its sides, played by hand.

tame *adj* **1** not wild. **2** trained to be obedient. **3** not exciting, dull (*life in the little village was considered tame*):—*vb* to make tame.

tam'my, tam-o'-shan'ter *ns* a round flat-topped Scottish cap.

tam'per *vb* to meddle with, to interfere with dishonestly or unlawfully (*tamper with the evidence*).

tan *n* **1** bark of trees crushed for use in preparing leather. **2** a light-brown colour. **3** suntan (*hope to get a tan on holiday*):—*vb* (**tanned' tan'ning**) **1** to treat animal skins so as to turn them into leather. **2** to make or become brown from sunburn:—*adj* light brown in colour (*tan shoes*).

tan'dem *adj* one behind the other:—*n* **1** a pair of horses harnessed one behind the other. **2** a bicycle for two persons, one sitting behind the other.

tang *n* **1** a sharp taste (*the tang of the sea air*). **2** a characteristic flavour.

tan'gent *n* a straight line touching a circle but not cutting it:—**go off at a tangent** to begin talking about something quite different (*his speech was difficult to follow as he would often go off at a tangent*).

tan'gible *adj* **1** able to be touched. **2** real, actual (*no tangible evidence*).

tan'gle *vb* **1** to interweave in a confused way, difficult to undo. **2** to muddle:—*n* **1** a mass of confusedly interwoven thread, string, etc. **2** a muddle, a complication.

tan'go *n* a South American dance.

tank *n* **1** a large container for storing water, oil, etc. **2** a fighting vehicle protected by thick metal plates and moving on caterpillar tracks (*the advance of enemy tanks*).

tank'ard *n* a large metal drinking mug (*a tankard of beer*).

tank'er *n* a cargo ship with tanks for carrying oil.

tanned *adj* **1** made brown by the sun (*they were tanned after their holiday*). **2** made into leather.

tan'nery *n* a place where leather is made.

tan'nic *adj* having to do with tannin (*tannic acid*).

tan'nin *n* a substance found in the bark of the oak and certain other trees, used in tanning leather.

tan'sy *n* a herb with yellow flowers and bitter-tasting leaves.

tan'talize *vb* to torment by raising false hopes (*hungry people tantalized by the cooking smells*).

tan'tamount *adj* as good as (*his remark was tantamount to a dismissal*).

tan'trum *n* a fit of bad temper or ill-humour (*the child had a tantrum*).

tap¹ *n* **1** a short pipe containing a stopper that can be opened by a handle to allow liquid to flow out. **2** a stopper:—*vb* (**tapped', tap'ping**) **1** to fit with a tap. **2** to draw liquid out of. **3** to obtain information from.

tap² *vb* (**tapped', tap'ping**) **1** to strike lightly (*tap him on the shoulder*). **2** to knock gently (*tap the door*):—also *n.*

tape *n* **1** a long narrow strip of cloth, paper or sticky material (*he used tape to seal the parcel*). **2** a sensitized strip for recording and transmitting sound or pictures (*audio-tape*):—also *vb.*

tape mea'sure *n* a strong tape of cloth, metal, etc, used for measuring (*measure her waist with a tape-measure*).

ta'per *n* a long wick coated with wax, like a thin candle:—*vb* to become narrow or thinner at one end.

tape record'er *n* a machine for recording and transmitting sounds on tape.

tap'estry *n* a large piece of cloth in which different coloured threads are worked together to make a picture, sometimes hung on walls as a decoration.

tape'worm *n* a long tape-like worm sometimes found in the intestines.

tapio'ca *n* **1** an eatable grain obtained from a West Indian plant. **2** a pudding made from it.

ta'pir *n* a pig-like animal of South America.

tap'room *n* (*old*) a room in a public house in which drinks are served.

tap'root *n* the main root of a plant.

tap'ster *n* (*old*) a barman, one whose job it is to serve drinks in a public house.

tar *n* **1** a thick black sticky substance obtained from wood or coal (*get tar on his shoes from the road*). **2** (*old*) a sailor:—*vb* (**tarred', tar'ring**) to coat with tar.

tarantel'la n a lively Italian dance.

taran'tula n a large poisonous spider.

tar'dy adj (old) slow, late (tardy in making a decision):—n **tar'diness**.

tare n **1** a plant of the bean family, used as fodder. **2** a weed. **3** the weight of a package, vehicle, etc, when empty.

targe n (old) a small round shield.

tar'get n **1** something set up for aiming or shooting at (the archers set up a target). **2** a goal or result that one hopes to achieve (the charity's target was £ 20,000):—vb to make someone the object or focus of something (target single parents with their advertising campaign).

tar'iff n **1** the tax to be paid on an imported commodity. **2** a list of the taxes to be paid on imported goods. **3** a list of charges.

Tar'mac, Tarmaca'dam (trademark) ns a road surface material made of tar and fragmented stone.

tarn n a small mountain lake.

tar'nish vb **1** to make less bright, to discolour (it tarnished with age). **2** to spoil (tarnish their reputation).

tarpaul'in n strong cloth or canvas covered with tar to make it waterproof (cover the load in the trailer with a tarpaulin).

tar'ry[1] adj coated with tar.

tar'ry[2] vb (old or lit) to stay, to delay, to wait behind.

tart[1] n a pastry containing jam or fruit.

tart[2] adj **1** sharp-tasting (a tart sauce). **2** sour , biting, sarcastic (tart remarks).

tar'tan n a cloth with stripes and squares of different colours, esp. when worn as part of Scottish highland dress.

tar'tar n **1** a crust of lime left by wine in a barrel. **2** a hard substance that forms on the teeth. **3** a hot-tempered person, a person who is hard to manage (everyone is frightened of her, she is a real tartar).

tartar'ic adj having to do with tartar.

task n a piece of work to be done (given the task of washing the dishes):—vb to lay upon as a burden.

task force n a group of people brought together to deal with a particular problem (a police task force appointed to reduce youth crime).

task'master n (old) one who sets work to be done and sees that it is done properly.

tas'sel n an ornamental knot with loose threads hanging down from it (a beret with a tassel on it).

taste n **1** the sense by which one judges whether food is pleasant or unpleasant (have a cold and lose her sense of taste). **2** the ability to distinguish what is fine, beautiful or correct from what is not so (have good taste in décor). **3** the flavour of food when eaten (soup lacking in taste). **4** a small portion of food for testing:—vb **1** to eat to see whether pleasant or unpleasant. **2** to have a flavour (of) (taste of soup).

taste'ful adj showing good taste or judgment (tasteful wallpaper).

taste'less adj **1** having no flavour (tasteless food). **2** showing bad taste or judgment (a tasteless remark).

tas'ty adj having a pleasing flavour (tasty food).

tat vb (**tat'ted, tat'ting**) to weave lace by hand.

tat'ter n **1** a loose torn rag. **2** pl ragged clothes.

tat'tered adj ragged (tattered clothes).

tat'ting n lace woven by hand.

tat'tle n idle talk, gossip (tattle in the village about his affair):—vb to chatter, to gossip.

tattoo'[1] n **1** beating of a drum, blowing of a bugle, etc, to recall soldiers to camp at night. **2** a night display of military drill, exercises, etc, to music.

tattoo'[2] vb to make a coloured design on the skin by pricking holes in it and filling them with coloured matter (get her arm tattooed with a red butterfly):—also n.

taught pt of **teach**.

taunt vb to make fun of in order to hurt, to mock, to sneer at (taunt the boy because he is poor):—n a mocking or hurtful remark.

taut adj stretched tight (pull the rope taut).

tautol'ogy n saying the same thing again in different words:—adj **tautolog'ical**.

tav'ern n an inn, a public house.

taw'dry adj showy but cheap or of bad quality (a shop selling tawdry souvenirs).

taw'ny adj yellowish-brown.

tax n **1** money paid to the government to help pay for public services. **2** an unpleasant or difficult task (it was his tax to expell the child):—vb **1** to raise a tax. **2** to charge a tax on. **3** to accuse (tax him with cruelty). **4** to be a hard test for (tax his strength).

taxa'tion *n* **1** all the taxes paid. **2** the charging of taxes.

tax'i *n* a motor car for hire, esp one fitted with a machine (**tax'imeter**) showing the amount to be paid as a fare:—*also* **tax'i-cab**:—*vb* (*of an aeroplane*) to run along the ground (*planes taxied down the runway*).

tax'idermist *n* one skilled in taxidermy.

tax'idermy *n* the art of stuffing the skins of dead animals to make them look like living animals.

tea *n* **1** a shrub found in India and China. **2** its leaves dried. **3** a drink made by pouring boiling water on dried tea leaves (*a cup of tea*). **4** a light afternoon or evening meal (*invite them to tea*):—**high tea** tea with one main dish of meat, fish, eggs, etc (*have high tea at about six o'clock*).

tea caddy *n* a box for keeping tea dry in the house.

teach *vb* (*pt, pp* **taught**) **1** to give information about (*teach English*). **2** to show how to do something (*teach him how to drive*). **3** to give lessons to (*teach primary pupils*).

teach'able *adj* able to be taught, able to learn (*the pupils are scarcely teachable*).

teach'er *n* **1** one who teaches (*a piano teacher*). **2** a schoolmaster or schoolmistress.

tea chest *n* a box in which tea is packed for transport.

teak *n* an Indian tree producing very hard timber (*a table made of teak*).

teal *n* a small freshwater wild duck.

team *n* **1** a number of persons working together for the same purpose (*a team of workers*). **2** a set of players on one side in a game (*a football team*). **3** a number of horses, oxen, etc, harnessed together.

team'work, united effort for the common good.

tear[1] [teer] *n* a drop of water appearing in or falling from the eyes (*the tragedy brought tears to his eyes*).

tear[2] [tēr] *vb* (*pt* **tore**, *pp* **torn**) **1** to pull apart or into pieces (*tear paper*). **2** to pull with violence (*tear her hair*). **3** (*inf*) to rush (*tear upstairs*):— *n* a hole or division made by tearing.

tear'ful *adj* weeping (*in a tearful mood*).

tease *vb* **1** to annoy by making fun of. **2** to pull apart wool, etc, into separate strands. **3** to comb wool to give it a hairy surface:—*n* one who annoys another by teasing.

teas'el, teaz'el *n* a plant with prickly thistle-like heads, used for combing the surface of woollen clothes.

teas'er *n* a difficult problem.

tea'spoon *n* a small spoon for use with tea.

teat *n* **1** the part of the breast from which milk may be sucked or drawn. **2** a rubber attachment through which a baby sucks milk from a bottle.

teazel *see* teasel.

tech'nical *adj* having to do with a particular art, science or craft (*the manual was full of technical language*).

technical'ity *n* **1** a technical word or phrase. **2** a small detail or rule (*disqualified on a technicality*)

techni'cian *n* one skilled in a particular art or craft.

technique [tek-neek'] *n* the method of doing something that requires skill (*his technique as a portrait painter*).

techno'logy *n* the study of methods of manufacturing:—*n* **techno'logist**.

ted'dy, ted'dy bear *n* a child's toy bear.

te'dious *adj* long and boring, tiresome (*it was a tedious job*).

te'dium *n* boredom, long-drawn-out dullness (*the tedium of factory work*).

Te Deum [tā dā'-um] *n* a hymn of thanksgiving to God.

tee *n* **1** the starting place for each 'hole' in golf. **2** a peg or small mound on which the ball may be placed for the first shot at each 'hole' in golf. **3** the target in quoits, curling, etc.

teem *vb* to be full of (*rivers teeming with fish*).

teen'ager *n* one aged between 13 and 19.

teens *npl* the ages from 13 to 19.

teeth *see* tooth.

teethe *vb* to grow one's first teeth (*babies teething*).

teeto'tal *adj* taking no strong drink:—*n* **tee-to'taller**.

teg'ment *n* (*fml*) a covering.

tele- *prefix* far, at or to a distance.

telecommunications *n* the technology or industry involved in transmitting information electronically over long distances by means of wires, radio signals, satellite, etc.

tel'egram *n* a message sent by telegraph.

tel'egraph *n* an apparatus for sending messages to a distance, esp by means of electricity:—*vb* to send by telegraph:—*n* **teleg'raphy**.

telegraph'ic adj 1 having to do with telegraph. 2 with unnecessary information, words, etc, omitted (a telegraphic way of giving the information).

telep'athy n the power to pass thoughts to or receive them from another, even if far away, without the use of words or signs (he knew by telepathy that his sister was ill).

tel'ephone n (abbr **phone**) an apparatus by means of which one may speak with a person at a distance by means of electric currents carried along wires:—vb to speak with or communicate by telephone (he telephoned his doctor).

telephon'ic adj having to do with telephone.

teleph'onist n one who operates a telephone.

telephotog'raphy n the taking of photographs of distant objects by using special equipment.

tel'eprinter n a typewriter that takes down messages sent from elsewhere by means of electricity.

tel'escope n an instrument consisting of lenses set in a tube or tubes that, when looked through, makes distant objects appear larger:—vb 1 to slide together, one section fitting into another, as with a telescope. 2 to become shorter by one part sliding over the other.

telescop'ic adj 1 having to do with a telescope. 2 able to be seen only by means of a telescope (a telescopic image). 3 some thing that telescopes (a telescopic umbrella).

tel'evise vb to transmit by television.

tel'evision n the transmitting of pictures by sound waves so as to reproduce them on a screen.

tell vb (pt, pp **told**) 1 to give an account of (tell about the accident). 2 to let another know of by speaking. 3 to count. 4 to have an effect (his illness is telling on him).

tell'er n 1 a bank clerk who receives and pays out cash. 2 one appointed to count votes. 3 one who tells.

tell'ing adj very effective (a telling remark).

tell'-tale adj 1 giving information (tell-tale signs). 2 revealing what was meant to be secret:—n one who tells what another has done to get him or her into trouble.

temer'ity n boldness, rashness (have the temerity to question the judge).

tem'per vb 1 to mix in proper proportions. 2 to make less severe. 3 to harden (metal):—n

1 mood, state of mind (in a good temper). 2 anger (in a real temper). 3 the correct hardness of metal.

tem'perament n 1 one's character. 2 the usual state of one's mind or feelings.

temperamen'tal adj easily excited, changing mood quickly.

tem'perance n 1 not taking too much strong drink. 2 taking no strong drink.

tem'perate adj 1 taking neither too much nor too little. 2 neither too hot nor too cold (a temperate climate).

tem'perature n degree of heat or cold:—**take one's temperature** to find the degree of heat of one's body (take the baby's temperature).

tem'pest n a violent storm.

tempes'tuous adj 1 very stormy. 2 violent (a tempestuous relationship).

tem'ple¹ n 1 a place of worship. 2 a church.

tem'ple² n the side of the head above the end of the cheekbone and between the ear and the forehead.

tem'po n (pl **tempos** or **tempi**) the speed at which a piece of music is played.

tem'poral adj 1 (fml) having to do with time. 2 worldly. 3 having to do with life on earth.

tem'porary adj lasting for a time only, not permanent (a temporary job).

tem'porize vb to try to gain time by delays, etc, to put off action or decision (she tried to temporize but he wanted a decision).

tempt vb 1 to try to get someone to do what he feels he ought not to do (he tried to tempt her with another drink). 2 to arouse desire in:—ns **tempt'er**, **tempt'ress**.

tempta'tion n attraction to what is wrong or forbidden.

tempt'ing adj 1 attractive. 2 arousing desire.

ten'able adj able to be believed or defended against criticism (tenable theories).

tena'cious adj 1 holding on firmly (a tenacious hold on the branch). 2 not giving in easily, stubborn (a tenacious fighter):—n **tena'city**.

ten'ancy n 1 the renting of property. 2 property for which a rent is paid. 3 the time during which one rents property.

ten'ant n one who occupies rented property.

ten'antry n all the tenants on an estate, etc.

tench *n* a freshwater fish.

tend[1] *vb* **1** to incline to (*tend to get angry easily*). **2** to have a leaning towards.

tend[2] *vb* to care for, to look after (*tend sheep*).

ten'dency *n* a leaning towards, an inclination, liability to do certain things more than others (*a tendency to drink too much*).

tenden'tious *adj* done with a hidden purpose, biased (*a tendentious statement*).

ten'der[1] *vb* (*fml*) to offer or present (*to tender his resignation*):—*n* an offer, esp one to do work at a certain price.

ten'der[2] *adj* **1** soft, gentle and loving. **2** easily hurt:—*n* **ten'derness**.

ten'der[3] *n* **1** a small boat carrying stores, etc, to a larger one. **2** a wagon or truck attached to a locomotive to carry coal, water, etc, for it.

ten'derfoot *n* (*pl* **ten'derfoots** *or* **ten'derfeet**) **1** an inexperienced person. **2** (*old*) a newly joined member of the Scout movement.

ten'der-heart'ed *adj* full of pity, easily moved.

ten'don *n* a strong cord-like band joining a muscle to a bone.

ten'dril *n* a slender curling shoot by which some plants cling to supports when climbing.

ten'ement *n* **1** a building containing a number of separate houses. **2** a single house in such a building.

ten'et *n* a belief, a principle (*the tenets of Christianity*).

ten'nis *n* a game played across a net by striking a ball to and fro with rackets.

ten'on *n* the end of a piece of wood, etc, shaped to fit into a hole (mortise) cut in another piece.

ten'or *n* **1** the higher of two kinds of men's singing voices. **2** the general meaning (*the tenor of his speech*). **3** one's ordinary way of life (*the tenor of one's way*).

tense[1] *n* a set of forms of the verb that indicate time.

tense[2] *adj* **1** stretched tight (*keep the rope tense*). **2** strained (*his job makes him feel tense*). **3** excited from expectation (*tense with excitement*).

ten'sion *n* **1** act of stretching. **2** tightness, strain. **3** excitement due to expectation.

tent *n* a portable shelter of canvas, supported by a pole or poles and stretched and held in position by cords.

ten'tacle *n* a slender boneless limb of various creatures, used for feeling, gripping or moving (*the tentacles of an octopus*).

ten'tative *adj* done as an experiment or trial (*a tentative approach*).

ten'terhook *n*:—**on tenterhooks** anxious or excited because of doubt or suspense (*on tenterhooks waiting for the exam results*).

ten'uous *adj* thin, slender (*a tenuous connection between the events*).

ten'ure *n* the holding or conditions of holding land, office, etc.

tepee' *n* an American Indian tent of skins.

tep'id *adj* lukewarm (*a tepid bath*).

tercente'nary *n* the three-hundredth anniversary.

ter'ebinth *n* the turpentine tree.

term *n* **1** a limited period of time (*during the term of the contract*). **2** a division of the school year. **3** a time when law courts are dealing with cases. **4** a word or phrase used in a particular study (*a technical term he did not understand*). **5** *pl* conditions, charge, price (*the terms of the loan agreement*):—*vb* to name, to call (*he is not what you would term a friendly person*):—**come to terms** to make an agreement:—**on good terms** friendly.

ter'magant *n* a bad-tempered scolding woman.

ter'minal *adj* having to do with the end or last part (*a terminal illness*):—*n* **1** one of the screws to which an electric wire is attached to make a connection. **2** the station at the end of a line or route.

ter'minate *vb* to bring or come to an end (*terminate the agreement*).

termina'tion *n* end, ending.

termino'logy *n* the words, phrases, etc, special to a particular branch of study (*the terminology of computing*).

ter'minus *n* (*pl* **termini** *or* **terminuses**) the station at the end of a line or route.

ter'mite *n* a white ant.

tern *n* a sea bird like a gull, but smaller.

ter'race *n* **1** a raised bank of earth with a flat area on top. **2** a row of houses.

ter'raced *adj* having terraces (*terraced houses*).

ter'racot'ta *n* **1** a reddish-brown pottery. **2** its colour:—*also adj.*

terrain' *n* a stretch of country (*rocky terrain*).

ter'rapin *n* a type of tortoise.

terres'trial *adj* having to do with the earth.

ter'rible adj **1** frightening, causing dread (a terrible scream). **2** very bad (a terrible experience).

ter'rier n a small dog good at hunting.

terri'fic adj **1** frightening, causing dread. **2** exceptionally good (a terrific concert).

ter'rify vb to make very frightened (she was terrified of the dog).

territo'rial adj having to do with a certain district or piece of land:—n formerly, a member of the Territorial Army, a body of men who trained as soldiers in their spare time.

ter'ror n great fear, dread.

ter'rorism n the use of, or the threat of, extreme violence for political purposes (The bombing was an act of terrorism).

ter'rorist n a person who uses, or threatens to use, extreme violence for political purposes.

ter'rorize vb **1** to make very frightened. **2** to make do what is desired by causing fear.

ter'ror-strick'en adj full of fear or dread.

terse adj short and to the point (a terse statement of resignation):—n terse'ness.

Ter'ylene n the trademark of an artificial fibre used to make cloth.

tes'selated adj having a pattern made up of different-coloured tiles, blocks, etc.

test n an examination or trial intended to reveal quality, ability, progress, etc:—vb **1** to try the quality of (test the new car). **2** to examine (test his French).

tes'tament n **1** in law, a person's will. **2** one of the two main divisions of the Bible (Old Testament, New Testament).

testamen'tary adj having to do with a will.

tes'tate adj leaving a will.

testa'tor n one who leaves a will at death:—f **testa'trix**.

tes'tify vb **1** to give evidence. **2** to say publicly what one believes to be true (he testified to her honesty).

testimo'nial n **1** a letter stating a person's good qualities and abilities. **2** a gift presented as a sign of respect.

tes'timony n evidence, a public statement of belief (give his testimony in court).

test match n one of a series of sporting contests, esp in cricket, between teams representing two countries.

test pi'lot n one who tests an aircraft by making it perform difficult manoeuvres.

test tube n a glass tube open at one end, used for scientific experiments.

tes'ty adj irritable, easily angered (a testy old man).

tet'anus n a disease causing cramp in the muscles and making the jaw so stiff that it cannot move.

tête-à-tête n a private talk between two people.

teth'er vb to tie an animal by a rope to a stake or peg:—n a stake, etc:—**at the end of one's tether** at the end of one's strength or endurance (she left the job because she was at the end of her tether).

tet'ra- prefix four.

tet'ragon n a four-sided figure.

tetrahe'dron n a solid figure with four sides shaped like a pyramid.

tetram'eter n a line of poetry containing four metrical feet.

tet'rarch n the governor of the fourth part of a Roman province.

text n **1** the words actually written by the author (not including notes, drawings, etc). **2** a short passage from the Bible. **3** subject, topic (the text of his speech).

text'book n a book about a subject written for those studying it (a maths textbook).

tex'tile n a cloth made by weaving:—adj having to do with or made by weaving.

tex'ture n **1** the way in which a fabric or cloth, etc, is woven. **2** the quality of woven cloth.

thane n in Anglo-Saxon times, a nobleman below the rank of earl.

thank vb to express pleasure to another for something done, etc, to express gratitude.

thank'ful adj grateful, full of gratitude (thankful that the children were safe).

thank'less adj ungrateful, for which one will receive no thanks (a thankless task).

thanks npl an expression of gratitude.

thanks'giving n act of giving thanks, esp to God at harvest time (a service in the church for thanksgiving).

thatch n straw used as a cover for the roof of a house:—vb to put thatch on (thatch the cottage roof):—n thatch'er.

thaw vb **1** to melt (the snow began to melt in the sun). **2** to become more friendly:—n a state or time of thawing.

the'atre *n* **1** a building or hall in which plays are acted. **2** a lecture hall. **3** in a hospital, a room in which surgeons perform operations. **4** a scene of action (*the theatre of war*).

theat'rical *adj* **1** having to do with plays or the theatre. **2** behaving as if acting in a play (*her theatrical reaction to the news*).

theat'ricals *npl* dramatic performances.

thee *pron* you (*sing*).

theft *n* act of stealing (*the theft of her car*).

their, theirs *poss adj and pron* belonging to them.

the'ism *n* belief in the existence of God:—*n* **the'ist**.

theme *n* **1** subject, topic (*the theme of his talk*). **2** a set of notes played several times in a piece of music.

then *adv* **1** at that time. **2** after that. **3** therefore.

thence *adv* **1** from that time or place. **2** for that reason.

thencefor'ward *adv* from that time onward.

theoc'racy *n* government of a state by those who claim to speak with the voice of God.

theod'olite *n* an instrument used to measure angles in surveying land.

theolo'gian *n* an expert in or a student of theology.

theolo'gical *adj* having to do with theology.

theo'logy *n* the study of the existence of God and man's beliefs about God.

theorem [thee'-rêm] *n* an idea that can be proved true by reasoning (*geometrical theorem*).

theoret'ical *adj* based on ideas, not on practice (*a theoretical solution to the problem*).

the'orist *n* one who holds or forms a theory.

the'orize *vb* **1** to suggest explanations. **2** to put forward theories (*he was theorizing on the problem*).

the'ory *n* **1** an explanation that seems satisfactory but has not been proved true. **2** a set of ideas or rules on how something should be done.

therapeu'tic *adj* having to do with therapy.

therapeu'tics *n* the study of therapy.

ther'apy *n* the treatment and cure of disease (*cancer therapy*).

there *adv* in that place.

thereaf'ter *adv* after that.

thereby' *adv* by that means.

there'fore *adv* for this or that reason.

therein' *adv* in that or this.

thereupon' *adv* immediately after that.

therewith' *adv* with that or this.

therm *n* a unit of measurement of heat, used in measuring the amount of gas used.

therm'al *adj* having to do with heat, hot (*thermal currents*).

thermodynam'ics *n* the study of heat as a source of power.

thermo'meter *n* an instrument for measuring degree of heat (*an oven thermometer*).

Ther'mos *n* a trademark of a flask for keeping hot liquid hot or cold liquid cold.

therm'ostat *n* an instrument that mechanically controls temperature and keeps it steady (*a central heating thermostat*).

thesau'rus *n* a reference book containing synonyms and antonyms.

the'sis *n* **1** an opinion to be defended in writing or discussion. **2** an essay on a subject submitted for a higher university degree.

thews *npl* muscles, strength.

thick *adj* **1** broad (*thick slices of meat*). **2** fat. **3** not easily seen through (*thick fog*). **4** slow to understand (*the people were rather thick*):—*n* the most crowded part (*the thick of the crowd*):—*n* **thick'ness**.

thick'en *vb* to make or become thicker (*the sauce would not thicken*).

thick'et *n* a group of trees, shrubs, etc, growing close together.

thick'set *adj* broad and strong of body.

thick'-skinned' *adj* slow to feel or resent insults.

thief *n* (*pl* **thieves**) one who steals (*the thief took her purse*).

thieve *vb* to steal.

thiev'ish *adj* given to stealing.

thigh *n* the part of the leg above the knee.

thim'ble *n* a metal or plastic cap to protect the finger in sewing.

thin *adj* **1** not thick. **2** not fat, lean, skinny, slim. **3** not crowded (*the audience was a little thin*). **4** not convincing (*a thin excuse*):—*vb* to make or become thin:—*n* **thin'ness**.

thing *n* **1** any single existing object. **2** whatever may be thought of or spoken about. **3** a happening. **4** *pl* one's belongings.

think *vb* (**thought, thinking**) **1** to form ideas in the mind, to consider (*no time to think*). **2** to believe, to hold as an opinion (*he thinks it is wrong*).

think'ing adj able to think or reason.

think'er n 1 one who thinks. 2 one who tries to work out an explanation of life, etc, for himself or herself.

thin'-skinned' adj quick to feel or resent insult, easily upset.

third adj coming after second:—n one of three equal parts.

thirst n 1 the need or desire to drink. 2 a strong desire for anything (a thirst for learning):—vb to feel thirst, to desire strongly.

thirst'y adj 1 wanting or needing a drink. 2 dry. 3 causing thirst (thirsty work).

this'tle n a prickly plant with a purple head, the national emblem of Scotland.

this'tledown n the light feathery carrier of thistle seeds.

thi'ther adv to that place.

thole, thole'-pin ns one of two pins stuck in the side of a boat to keep the oars steady while rowing.

thong n 1 a strap of hide or leather. 2 the lash of a whip.

tho'rax n the human chest (have an operation on his thorax).

thorn n 1 a prickle on the stem of a plant. 2 a bush or plant with prickles:—**thorn in the flesh** a cause of trouble or difficulty (he thinks his sister is a thorn in his flesh).

thorn'y adj 1 prickly. 2 difficult, troublesome (a thorny situation).

thorough [thur'-ê] 1 complete (a thorough job). 2 doing work with gr eat care (a thorough person):—n thor'oughness.

thor'oughbred adj (of an animal) having parents that have been specially bred and trained:—also n.

thor'oughfare n a road open to the public and to traffic.

thor'ough-go'ing adj complete.

thorp n a village.

though [thô] prep despite the fact that.

thought pt of **think**:—n 1 the power or act of thinking. 2 what one thinks, an idea (a sad thought).

thought'ful adj 1 given to thinking (a thoughtful mood). 2 considerate, thinking of others (the gift was typical of such a thoughtful person).

thought'less adj 1 not thinking before acting. 2 inconsiderate, not thinking of others (a thoughtless remark that hurt her mother).

thou'sand adj and n ten hundred.

thral'dom n slavery.

thrall n (old) a slave, slavery.

thrash vb to beat hard, to flog.

thrash'ing n a good beating, a flogging.

thread n 1 a fine strand of any substance (e.g. cotton, wool, etc) drawn out and twisted to make a cord. 2 the spiral ridge running round and round a screw, etc. 3 the main connected points running through an argument (lose the thread of the speech):—vb 1 to pass thread or fine cord through. 2 to make one's way through.

thread'bare adj (of clothes) having the fluffy surface worn off, shabby, frequently used and so no longer fresh or new.

threat n 1 a promise to hurt or punish another in future. 2 a warning of harm to come (the threat of unemployment).

threat'en vb 1 to make threats to. 2 to be a sign of coming harm, evil, etc (it was threatening to snow).

three'-ply adj consisting of three layers or strands (three-ply wool).

thresh vb to separate corn from chaff by beating it or putting it through a machine.

thresh'ing machine n a machine that beats the corn out of the chaff.

thresh'old n 1 the plank or stone one crosses when passing through a door. 2 the beginning (on the threshold of a new career).

threw pt of **throw**.

thrice adv three times.

thrift n care in spending or using up, the habit of saving and not wasting.

thrift'less adj wasteful.

thrift'y adj careful in spending, saving (a thrifty attitude to money).

thrill n a sudden feeling of excitement or emotion:—vb to excite, to cause a thrill in.

thrill'er n a story written to excite or horrify.

thrill'ing adj very exciting (a thrilling experience).

thrive vb 1 to do well (the baby continues to thrive). 2 to be or become strong or successful (a business that was thriving).

throat n 1 the front of the neck. 2 the opening downward at the back of the mouth and the pipe leading down from it.

throb vb 1 to beat, as the heart. 2 (of pain) to increase and decrease at short regular intervals:—also n.

throe n:—**in the throes of** in the middle of doing something difficult (in the throes of moving house).

throne n the chair occupied by a monarch or bishop.

throng n a crowd:—vb to go in crowds, to crowd together (people thronged to the hall).

throt'tle n 1 the throat or windpipe. 2 a lever working a valve that controls the supply of steam, petrol, etc, to an engine:—vb 1 to choke or strangle. 2 to cut down the supply of steam, etc, by using a throttle.

through [thrû] prep 1 from end to end. 2 from beginning to end. 3 by means of (get to the top through hard work). 4 because of:—adv from end to end:—adj going all the way without requiring changes.

throughout' adv in every way or part (a house painted throughout):—prep right through (throughout the day).

throw vb (pt threw, pp thrown) 1 to fling or cast (throw a stone in the river). 2 to make to fall on the ground (e.g. in wrestling):—n 1 act of throwing. 2 the distance to which something can move or be flung through the air.

thrum vb (thrummed', thrum'ming) 1 to play (a musical instrument) carelessly. 2 to play by pulling the strings of.

thrush[1] n a song-bird.

thrush[2] n a disease of the mouth and throat.

thrust vb 1 to push with force (thrust the door open). 2 to stab at or into. 3 to push forward (thrust himself to the front of the queue):—n 1 a sudden or violent push. 2 a stab.

thud n a low dull sound, as of a muffled blow (the thud of the heavy parcel hitting the floor):—also vb (thud'ded, thud'ding).

thug n 1 a ruffian. 2 (old) in India, a member of a sect of ritual stranglers.

thumb n the shortest and thickest of the fingers:—vb to dirty with marks of the thumb or fingers:—**rule of thumb** a rough rule based on

practice:—**under someone's thumb** under the control or influence of someone (he is said to under his girlfriend's thumb).

thump n a dull heavy blow:—vb to beat heavily.

thun'der n 1 the sound that follows lightning. 2 any loud rumbling noise (the thunder of passing lorries):—vb 1 to make thunder. 2 to make a loud noise.

thun'derbolt n a flash of lightning.

thun'derclap n a peal of thunder.

thun'derous adj like thunder, very loud (thunderous applause).

thun'derstruck adj amazed, astonished (thunderstruck at the news).

thun'dery adj (of weather) hot and close, as before a thunderstorm.

Thurs'day n the fifth day of the week.

thus adv in this way.

thwack vb to beat hard:—n a heavy blow.

thwart vb to prevent from succeeding (thwart him in his attempts to gain promotion):—n a rower's seat from side to side of a boat.

thyme [tîm] n a herb with sweet-smelling leaves, used in cooking.

tia'ra n a jewelled band, like a small crown, worn on the head by ladies.

tib'ia n the shin-bone (a fracture of the tibia).

tick[1] n a small blood-sucking insect.

tick[2] n 1 the sound made by a watch or clock (he heard the tick of the clock). 2 a mark made when checking or correcting:—also vb.

tick'et n 1 a marked card giving its possessor the right to do something (e.g. travel by train, enter a theatre, etc) (his weekly rail ticket). 2 a label.

tick'le vb 1 to cause discomfort or make laugh by touching or prodding lightly a sensitive part of the body. 2 (inf) to please, to amuse.

tick'lish adj 1 easily tickled. 2 difficult, requiring careful management (a ticklish problem).

tid'al adj having to do with tides.

tide n 1 the regular rise and fall, or ebb and flow, of the sea. 2 time, season.

ti'dings npl (old or fml) news (bring tidings of his death).

ti'dy adj neatly arranged, orderly:—vb to arrange neatly (tidy the room).

tie vb 1 to fasten with cord, rope, etc (tie the dog up). 2 to make a knot in. 3 (in a game or *contest*) to be equal with:—*n* **1** a band of cloth, usu coloured, worn round the neck. **2** a connection, bond (*family ties*). **3** a match in a knock-out competition (*the third-round tie*). **4** a draw (i.e. an equal score).

tier *n* one of a series of rows of seats arranged on the slope, so that each row is slightly higher than the one below it.

tiff *n* a slight quarrel (*a lover's tiff*).

ti'ger *n* a large fierce striped animal of the cat family:—*f* **ti'gress**.

ti'gerish *adj* fierce as a tiger.

ti'ger lily *n* a lily with spotted orange flowers.

tight *adj* **1** close-fitting (*a tight dress*). **2** closely packed (*a tight fit*). **3** (*inf*) difficult, esp because of shortage of money. **5** (*inf*) drunk (*get tight at the office party*).

tight'en *vb* to make or become tight (*tighten the rope*).

tight'rope *n* a tightly stretched rope on which an acrobat walks and performs tricks.

tights *n* a light, close-fitting garment covering the lower trunk and legs.

tike *see* **tyke**.

tile *n* a thin slab of baked clay or other suitable material for covering roofs, floors, etc:—*vb* to cover with tiles (*tile the wall*).

till[1] *n* in a shop, a drawer for money.

till[2] *prep* up to the time of:—*conj* up to the time when.

till[3] *vb* to plough and prepare for seed (*farmer tilling the land*).

till'age *n* **1** the tilling of land. **2** land tilled. **3** agriculture.

till'er *n* the handle of a rudder, a blade at the back of a boat by means of which it is steered.

tilt *vb* to make to slope to one side, to lean (*a floor that tilts*). **2** (*old*) to charge on horseback with a lance (*knights tilting*):—*n* **1** a slant, a sloping position. **2** act of charging on horseback with a lance.

tim'ber *n* **1** wood for building, carpentry, etc. **2** trees from which such wood can be obtained. **3** a wooden beam used in the framework of a house or ship.

timbre [tim'-bêr] *n* (*fml*) the recognizable quality of a sound, musical note, voice, etc.

tim'brel *n* a small drum played by hand.

time *n* **1** the measure of the passage of past, present and future. **2** the moment of the hour, day, year, etc. **3** a season. **4** an occasion (*a happy time*). **5** the rhythm of a piece of music:—*vb* **1** to see how long something lasts (*time the race*). **2** to see that something happens at the right moment (*time his arrival well*):—**for the time being** meanwhile.

time-hon'oured *adj* respected because of age.

time'keeper *n* one who notes the times at which something begins and ends.

time'ly *adj* (*inf*) happening at the right time (*his timely arrival*).

time'ous *adj* (*inf*) happening at a suitable time.

time'piece *n* a watch or clock.

time'server *n* one who does things only if they will bring immediate advantage.

time'table *n* **1** a list of classes, giving times when they begin and end. **2** a list giving the times of arrival and departure of trains, buses, etc.

tim'id *adj* easily made afraid, shy (*too timid to complain*):—*n* **timid'ity**.

tim'orous *same as* **timid**.

tin *n* **1** a soft, light white metal. **2** a can or box made from thin iron coated with tin (*a tin of baked beans*):—*vb* (**tinned'**, **tin'ning**) **1** to coat with tin. **2** to put or pack in tins (*tin the raspberries*).

tinc'ture *n* **1** a shade of colour. **2** a slight taste or flavour of something. **3** a drug dissolved in alcohol:—*vb* **1** to colour slightly. **2** to have a slight effect on.

tin'der *n* an easily lit substance that catches light from a spark (used before the invention of matches).

tin'foil *n* tin beaten into a very thin sheet and used for wrapping.

tinge *vb* **1** to colour slightly. **2** to have a slight effect on:—*n* **1** a shade, a slight colour (*a reddish tinge*). **2** a small amount.

tingle [ting'-gêl] *vb* to feel a prickly or thrilling sensation (*her fingers tingled with cold*).

tink'er *n* **1** one who goes from door to door, mending pots, kettles, etc. **2** a vagabond:—*vb* **1** to mend roughly. **2** to work at unskilfully (*tinker with the car*).

tinkle [ting'-kêl] *vb* to make soft, bell-like sounds (*the doorbell tinkled*):—*also n*.

tin'ny *adj* sharp and harsh in sound.

tinned *adj* in a tin (*tinned peas*).

tin'-opener *n* an instrument for cutting open tin cans.

tin'sel *n* **1** thin strips, threads, discs, etc, of shiny metal. **2** anything showy but of little value.

tin'selly *adj* showy.

tin'smith *n* one who works in tin.

tint *n* **1** a shade of colour (*a bluish tint*). **2** a faint colour:—*vb* to colour slightly.

tintinnabula'tion *n* the ringing of bells.

ti'ny *adj* very small (*tiny insects*).

tip *n* **1** a narrow end or point. **2** a light blow. **3** money given as a present or for special help (*a tip for the waiters*). **4** a helpful hint (*tips on removing stains*). **5** a place where rubbish, etc, is heaped:—*vb* (**tipped', tip'-ping**) **1** to put a tip on. **2** to make to tilt. **3** to give a money tip to (*tip the waiter*). **4** to give a useful hint to. **5** to throw out (of) (*tip the peas out of the tin*).

tip'pet *n* a short cloak to cover the shoulders.

tip'ple *vb* to make a habit of taking strong drink, to drink often.

tip'pler *n* one who is fond of strong drink.

tip'ster *n* one who tries to foretell which horse will win a race.

tip'sy *adj* drunk, confused by strong drink (*tipsy after the office party*).

tip'toe *n* the point of the toe:—*vb* **1** to walk on the points of the toes. **2** to walk very quietly (*tiptoe out of the room*).

tip'top' *adj* splendid, excellent (*in tiptop condition*).

ti'rade *n* a long angry speech, a violently critical speech (*a tirade on the subject of punctuality*).

tire[1] *vb* to make or become weary (*the long journey was tiring her*).

tire[2] *vb* (*old*) to dress.

tired *adj* weary.

tire'less *adj* not easily wearied, having much energy.

tire'some *adj* boring, annoying (*a tiresome day*).

ti'ro, ty'ro *n* a beginner.

tis'sue *n* **1** any fine woven material. **2** substance (fat, muscle, etc) of which the parts of animals and plants are made. **3** a complete connected set.

tis'sue paper *n* thin soft paper for wrapping (*wrap the china in tissue paper*).

tit[1] *n* a small bird (*blue tit*).

tit[2] *n*:—**tit for tat** getting one's own back.

tit[3] *same as* **teat**.

titan'ic *adj* huge, gigantic.

tit'bit *n* a tasty piece of food (*titbits for the dog*).

tithe *n* **1** a tenth part of one's crops, livestock, etc, paid to the church as a tax. **2** a tenth part.

titian [tish-yên] *adj* of a reddish-brown colour (*titian hair*).

tit'illate *vb* **1** to tickle. **2** to give pleasure to (*titillate the audience*):—*n* **titilla'tion**.

tit'ivate *vb* to make neat or smart (*titivating herself for the party*).

ti'tle *n* **1** the name of a book, piece of writing or music, picture, etc. **2** a name or word used in addressing someone, to indicate rank, office, etc. **3** a claim to ownership, a right.

ti'tled *adj* being a member of the nobility.

ti'tle deed *n* a document stating that one owns certain property.

title page *n* a page at the beginning of a book, stating its name and that of the author and publisher.

ti'tle role *n* the part of a character in a play whose name is the same as that of the play, e.g. Macbeth in *Macbeth*.

tit'mouse *n* a small bird, commonly called a tit.

tit'ter *vb* to giggle (*they tittered behind his back*):—*also n*.

tit'tle *n* a very small piece.

tit'tle-tat'tle *n* gossip, foolish talk.

tit'ular *adj* having the rank or title but no powers (*the titular head of the country*).

toad *n* a frog-like animal that lives both on land and in water.

toad'-in-the-hole *n* meat cooked in flour mixed with eggs and milk.

toad'stool *n* a poisonous fungus, like a mushroom in shape.

toad'y *n* (*inf*) one who flatters another in order to gain his or her favour:—*vb* to flatter or try to please in order to gain favour (*toadied to the boss*).

toast *vb* **1** to dry and brown by heat. **2** to warm at the fire (*toast themselves by the fire*). **3** to drink the health of (*toast his friends*):—*n* **1** sliced bread browned by heat. **2** a person whose health is drunk. **3** a sentiment or thing to which one drinks.

toast'er *n* an electrical implement for toasting bread.

tobac'co *n* the dried leaves of the tobacco plant, used for smoking or taken as snuff.

tobac'conist *n* one who sells tobacco, cigarettes, etc.

tobog'gan *n* a narrow sledge for sliding down snow-covered slopes:—*vb* (**tobog'ganned**, **tobag'ganning**) to go on a toboggan.

toc'sin *n* an alarm bell.

today' *adv* on this day.

tod'dle *vb* to walk with short unsteady steps, as a small child.

tod'dler *n* a small child just beginning to walk.

tod'dy *n* a mixture of whisky or brandy, sugar and hot water.

toe *n* one of the five finger-like members at the end of the foot:—**toe the line** to behave as one is told.

toffee *n* a sweetmeat made of sugar and butter.

to'ga *n* in ancient times, the cloak of a Roman citizen.

togeth'er *adv* with another or others, in company.

toil *vb* to work hard:—*n* hard work:—*n* **toil'er**.

toil'et *n* 1 a lavatory. 2 (*old*) the act of making oneself clean and tidy. 3 (*old*) one's dress.

toilet soap *n* soap for washing the body.

toil'some *adj* (*old*) needing hard work.

to'ken *n* 1 a mark or sign (*a token of his friendship*). 2 an object often to help to remember. 3 something used instead of money (*bus token*).

told *pt of* tell.

tol'erable *adj* 1 able to be put up with. 2 fairly good (*work of a tolerable standard*).

tol'erance, tolera'tion *ns* 1 patience. 2 readiness to allow what is displeasing, strange or different to continue to exist.

tol'erant *adj* ready to tolerate, broad-minded (*tolerant of their beliefs*).

tol'erate *vb* 1 to put up with (*he could not tolerate the noise*). 2 to allow (*she will not tolerate shoddy work*).

toll¹ *n* a tax charged for the use of a bridge, road, etc.

toll² *vb* to ring slowly, as a bell at a funeral (*church bells tolling*):—*n* a single stroke of a large bell.

tom'ahawk *n* a battle-axe used by North American Indians.

toma'to *n* (*pl* **toma'toes**) 1 a plant with a soft eatable fruit. 2 the fruit of the tomato.

tomb [töm] *n* 1 a grave. 2 a cellar in which dead bodies are placed.

tom'boy *n* an energetic girl who is fond of boyish games and sports.

tomb'stone *n* a stone placed over a grave giving the name, etc, of the person buried underneath.

tome *n* a large heavy book (*a tome on philosophy*).

tomfool'ery *n* nonsense, silly behaviour.

tomor'row *adv* the day after today.

tom'-tit *n* a small bird, the titmouse.

ton *n* a measure of weight (=20 hundredweight).

tone *n* 1 a sound. 2 the quality or pitch of a voice or sound. 3 the prevailing spirit or atmosphere (*the tone of the meeting*). 4 a shade of colour (*in tones of blue*):—*vb* to fit in with:—**tone down** to soften, to make less harsh.

tongs *npl* an instrument with two arms between which things can be gripped for moving (*lift the coal with tongs*).

tongue [tung] *n* 1 an organ in the mouth with the help of which one speaks or tastes. 2 anything shaped like a tongue (e.g. a leather flap in a shoe). 3 a language (*a foreign tongue*). 4 the clapper of a bell:—**give tongue 1** to make a noise. 2 to speak:—**hold one's tongue** to remain silent.

tongue'-tied *adj* unable to speak because of excitement or nervousness.

tongue'-twist'er *n* a group of words that it is difficult to pronounce quickly.

ton'ic *adj* 1 strengthening, giving vigour or health. 2 having to do with musical tones:—*n* a strengthening medicine (*the sick boy was given a tonic*).

tonight' *adv* on this night.

ton'nage *n* the weight of goods a ship can carry.

tonne *n* a metric ton.

ton'sil *n* one of the two glands at the back of the mouth.

tons'ili'tis *n* a disease causing the tonsils to become swollen and sore.

ton'sure *n* 1 the shaving of the hair off the head or part of the head of a monk. 2 the part of the head so shaven.

took *pt of* take.

tool *n* **1** an instrument for working with. **2** a person who does exactly what another wants him or her to do (*a tool of the company's management*).

toot *n* the sound of a horn.—*also vb* (*drivers tooting their horns in impatience*).

tooth *n* (*pl* **teeth**) **1** one of the bony projections rooted in the jaw, used for biting or chewing. **2** any tooth-shaped projection, as on a saw, comb, etc:—**have a sweet tooth** to like eating sweet things:—**long in the tooth** (*inf*) old (*he is a bit long in the tooth to be at a disco*):—**tooth and nail** with great violence or fury (*fight tooth and nail*).

tooth'ache *n* a pain in a tooth (*go to the dentist with a toothache*).

tooth'comb *n* a small comb with the teeth very close together.

toothed *adj* **1** having teeth. **2** having a jagged edge (*a jagged instrument*).

tooth'pick *n* a small stick used for removing anything stuck in or between the teeth.

tooth'some *adj* (*old*) pleasant to taste.

tooth'y *adj* having or showing large or sticking-out teeth (*a toothy grin*).

top *n* **1** the highest part or place (*the top of the tree*). **2** the summit (*the top of the mountain*). **3** a toy for spinning:—*adj* **1** highest. **2** most important:—*vb* (**topped'**, **top'ping**) **1** to be at the top of. **2** to hit the top of. **3** to do better than.

to'paz *n* a precious stone.

top boot *n* a high boot with a white or light-coloured band around its top.

top'coat *n* an overcoat.

top dressing *n* **1** a covering of manure laid on the surface of land. **2** any type of covering on top of something else.

topee *see* **topi**.

top'gall'ant *n* the part of the mast above the topmast.

top hat *n* a tall cylindrical hat covered with silk (*the wedding guests wore top hats*).

top'-heavy *adj* so heavy at the top that it may fall over (*the load was top-heavy*).

topi, topee [tō'-pee] *n* a light hat to protect the head from the sun (*men wearing topis in the tropics*).

top'ic *n* a subject of discussion.

top'ical *adj* having to do with events of the present day (*topical stories*).

top'mast *n* the part of the mast above the lower mast.

top'most *adj* highest.

topog'raphy *n* a detailed description of a small area or district:—*adj* **topograph'ical**.

top'ple *vb* **1** to fall over, to overbalance (*much of the load toppled off*). **2** to cause to fall.

top'sy-tur'vy *adj* confused, upside-down.

toque [tōk] *n* a woman's close-fitting hat without a brim.

tor *n* a rocky hill.

torch *n* **1** a light to be carried in the hand, a flashlight (*use a torch to see in the dark*). **2** (*old*) a piece of blazing wood carried or stuck up to give light.

tore *pt of* **tear**.

toreador' *n* a Spanish bullfighter.

tor'ment *n* **1** great suffering or agony. **2** great anxiety (*the torment of waiting for the results of the test*):—*vb* **torment'** **1** to cause distress or suffering to, to torture. **2** to tease (*pupils tormenting the new boy*):—*n* **tormen'tor**.

torn *pp of* **tear**.

torna'do *n* (*pl* **torna'does**) a violent swirling wind or hurricane.

torpe'do *n* (*pl* **torpe'does**) **1** a long fish-shaped shell that can be fired along the surface of the water to hit another ship and explode on touching it. **2** a fish able to paralyse its prey by giving it an electric shock:—*vb* **1** to hit or damage with a torpedo. **2** to spoil or ruin (*his actions torpedoed our plans*).

tor'pid *adj* lacking energy, numb, inactive, dull (*feeling torpid in the extreme heat*).

tor'por *n* lack of energy or interest, inactivity.

tor'rent *n* **1** a rushing stream. **2** a heavy downpour (*rain came down in a torrent*).

torren'tial *adj* flowing with great violence, falling heavily and steadily (*torrential rain*).

tor'rid *adj* **1** extremely hot. **2** dried up by heat.

tor'so *n* the body without the head or limbs (*police have found a torso*).

tortilla *n* a thin pancake usually made with maize flour and wrapped round a filling, used in Mexican cooking.

tor'toise *n* a four-footed reptile almost entirely covered by a hard shell.

tor'toiseshell n the shell of a type of sea turtle used to make combs, rims of spectacles, etc, coloured brown and yellow.

tor'tuous adj crooked, twisting (tortuous mountain roads).

tor'ture vb 1 to cause great suffering or anxiety to. 2 to cause pain to as a punishment or in order to obtain information from (he was tortured by the enemy):—n extreme pain or anxiety.

Tor'y n a member of the British Conservative political party.

toss vb 1 to throw upwards, to jerk upwards, as the head (toss a coin in the air). 2 (of a ship) to roll about in rough seas. 3 to drink (off) quickly (toss off his beer):—n 1 a throw. 2 a fall:—**toss up** to throw up a coin to decide something by chance.

tot n 1 a small child. 2 a small quantity (a tot of rum):—vb (tot'ted, tot'ting) to add up (tot up the cost of the meal).

total adj 1 whole (the total cost). 2 complete (the car was a total wreck):—n 1 the whole amount. 2 the result when everything has been added up:—vb (totalled, total'ling) 1 to add up (total the items on the bill). 2 to add up to.

totalisa'tor n (abbr **tote**) a machine used on a racecourse to work out the sums due to those betting on winning horses.

totalita'rian adj allowing only one political party.

total'ity n the complete amount.

tote see totalisator.

to'tem n an animal or plant taken by a tribe as an emblem and regarded as mysteriously connected with the tribe.

to'tem pole n a pole on which the totem or symbols of it are carried.

tot'ter vb to stand or walk unsteadily, to stagger (tottering down the street in high-heeled shoes).

toucan [tö'-kan] n a South American bird with a huge bill.

touch vb 1 to come to rest against with any part of the body, esp the hand. 2 to be in contact. 3 to cause to feel emotion (touched by the poem). 4 to make a difference to, to concern (the changes in management did not touch her):—n 1 act of coming against or being in contact with. 2 the ability to do really well something requiring skill. 3 the sense of feeling. 4 (in football)

the ground at the side of the marked field of play:—**touch on** to mention briefly:—**touch up**, to improve by making small changes.

touch'ing adj moving the feelings, causing pity:—prep having to do with (information touching his employment).

touch'line n (in football) the side lines of the marked field of play.

touch'stone n something by comparison with which one judge's other things, ideas, etc (a touchstone for the other pupils' work).

touch'y adj easily angered or hurt (in a touchy mood).

tough [tuf] adj 1 hard to cut, tear or chew (tough meat). 2 hardy strong (people living there have to be tough). 3 rough-mannered (a tough neighbourhood). 4 difficult to deal with (a tough problem):—n a street ruffian.

tough'en vb 1 to make tough. 2 to make better able to resist (toughen the plastic).

tour [tör] n a journey, made for pleasure, to various places, usu ending up at the starting point:—vb to go for a tour, to travel here and there (tour the Highlands).

tour'ism n the providing of hotels, routes, etc, for tourists.

tour'ist n one who travels for pleasure, a sightseer.

tour'nament n 1 a series of games between different competitors to see which is the best player or team (a tennis tournament). 2 in olden times, a display of fighting on horseback in which the warriors carried blunted arms.

tour'ney n a tournament of mock fighting.

tourniquet [tör'-ni-ket or -kā] n a bandage twisted tightly round a limb to prevent the flow of blood from a cut artery.

tou'sle vb 1 to disarrange, esp the hair (the wind had tousled her hair). 2 to make untidy.

tout vb to go about looking for customers or buyers (tout for business):—n one who touts (a ticket tout).

tow¹ [tö]vb to pull along with a rope, chain, etc:—n 1 anything towed. 2 the act of being towed.

tow² [tö] n fibres of flax or hemp.

toward, towards preps in the direction of.

tow'el n a cloth for drying the body:—vb (tow'elled, tow'elling) to rub with a towel (towel the child after the bath).

tow'elling *n* material for making towels, etc (*a dressing gown made of towelling*).

tow'er *n* 1 a building much higher than it is broad. 2 a high part of another building, projecting above it. 3 a fortress:—*vb* to rise high into the air (*the mountains tower above the village*)

tow'ering *adj* 1 very high or tall (*towering mountain*). 2 very great (*a towering rage*).

tow'line, tow'rope *ns* the rope used in towing.

town *n* a group of houses, shops, etc, larger than a village but smaller than a city.

town coun'cil *n* a number of people elected to look after the affairs of the town.

town hall, town house *ns* the offices in which the business of the town council is carried on.

town'ship *n* the territory or district of a town.

towns'man *n* one who lives in a town.

tow'path *n* a path beside a canal for a horse towing a barge.

tox'ic *adj* poisonous (*the toxic substance in some plants*).

toxicol'ogy *n* the study of poisons.

tox'in *n* a poison (*the toxins in some plants*).

toy *n* a plaything:—*vb* to play with (*the dog was toying with the kitten*).

trace *n* 1 a mark left behind (*a trace of blood on the knife*). 2 a footstep. 3 a trace, a sign of something that has happened or existed (*there were traces of a struggle*). 4 one of the two straps by which a horse is joined to a carriage:—*vb* 1 to copy a drawing on to transparent paper laid on top of it. 2 to follow the tracks of (*the police traced him to his hide-out*).

tra'cery *n* 1 stone carved to form an open design, as in the windows of old churches. 2 a design of criss-crossing lines.

trachea [tra-kee'-a] *n* the wind pipe in the throat (*an infection of the trachea*).

tra'cing *n* a drawing made by copying another drawing on to transparent paper laid on top of it.

track *n* 1 a footprint. 2 the mark or rut left by a wheel. 3 a path made by coming and going (*a track up the mountain*). 4 a railway line. 5 a course for races:—*vb* 1 to follow the marks left by (*track the wolf to its lair*). 2 to pursue or search for someone or something until found (*track down the source of the gas leak*).

track'less *adj* without paths.

tract *n* 1 a wide area of land. 2 a short booklet, esp one about religion.

trac'table *adj* easily managed (*he was used to tractable children*).

trac'tion *n* the drawing of vehicles.

traction engine *n* a steam engine for dragging loads on roads.

trac'tor *n* a heavy motor vehicle used for drawing other vehicles or farm implements.

trade *n* 1 the buying and selling of goods. 2 the exchanging of goods in large quantities:—*vb* 1 to buy and sell. 2 to exchange in large quantities.

trade'mark *n* an officially registered mark or name put on goods to show who manufactured them and not to be used by any other party.

trad'er *n* one who buys and sells goods, a merchant.

trades'man *n* 1 a shopkeeper. 2 a skilled workman (*the joiner and other tradesmen*).

trade union *n* the banding together in an association of people engaged in a certain trade to protect their interests.

trade wind *n* a wind that is always blowing towards the equator (from northeast or southeast).

tradi'tion *n* 1 the handing down of knowledge, customs, etc, from age to age by word of mouth (*according to traditions*). 2 any story, custom, etc, so handed down (*village traditions*).

tradi'tional *adj* according to or handed down by tradition (*traditional Christmas customs*).

traduce' *vb* (*fml*) to speak evil of, to slander.

traf'fic *n* 1 the coming and going of persons, vehicles, etc, between places. 2 trade. 3 the carrying of goods or persons in vehicles, etc. 4 all the vehicles on the roads (*motorway traffic*):—*vb* (**traf'ficked, traf'ficking**) to trade.

tra'gedy *n* 1 a sad event, a disaster (*his death was a tragedy*). 2 a play showing the suffering caused by man's inability to overcome evil (*Shakespeare's tragedies*).

trage'dian *n* a writer or actor of tragedy.

tragedienne [tra-jee'-dee-en] *n* an actress of tragedy.

tra'gic *adj* 1 having to do with tragedy (*a tragic actor*). 2 very sad (*a tragic story*).

tra'gi-com'edy *n* a play in which the happy and sad are mixed together.

trail n 1 the track or scent left by a moving creature (*the stag's trail*). 2 a path or track made by coming and going (*the mountain trail*):—vb 1 to drag along the ground (*the child trailing its teddy-bear*). 2 to draw along behind. 3 to walk wearily (*children trail home from school*). 4 to follow the tracks of (*trail the fox to its lair*):— **blaze a trail** to make a path that can be followed by others.

trail'er n 1 a climbing plant. 2 a vehicle without an engine towed by another. 3 a short part of a film shown in advance by way of advertisement.

train vb 1 to prepare or make to prepare by constant practice or teaching (*train the football team*). 2 to aim (*train his gun on them*). 3 to make to grow in a particular direction (*train the vine along the wall*):—n 1 railway carriages or trucks drawn by an engine. 2 part of a dress that trails behind the wearer (*the bride's train*). 3 (*old*) persons in attendance (*the king's train*). 4 a series (*train of thought*). 5 a thin line of gunpowder lit to set off an explosion, etc.

train'-bear'er n one who holds up the train of a dress or robe (*the bride's train-bearer*).

train'er n 1 a person who teaches animals or people to do something, often a sport, well (*a trainer of racehorses*). 2 a kind of sports shoe often used for general casual wear.

train'ing n education, practice (*football training*).

train'ing col'lege n a place where people are prepared for some job (e.g. teaching).

trait [trã *or* trãt] n a special characteristic by which one may know a person (*his humour was his most endearing trait*).

trai'tor n one who helps an enemy against his or her own country or friends:—adj **trai'-torous.**

tra'jectory n the path of a moving body (e.g. a bullet, a comet, etc).

tram, tramcar ns a vehicle running on rails laid in the streets.

tram'mel n 1 a net for catching birds or fishes. 2 anything that prevents free action:—vb (**tram'melled, tram'melling**) to prevent from moving freely (*trammelled by her long dress*).

tramp vb 1 to walk heavily. 2 to travel on foot (*it was a day's tramp for the army*):—n 1 a journey on foot. 2 one who has no home and walks about the countryside begging (*the tramp begged for spare change*). 3 the sound of heavy steps or many steps together (*the tramp of soldiers*). 4 cargo vessel with no regular run.

tram'ple vb to walk heavily on top of (*the animals trampled the crops*).

tram'way n rails laid for tramcars.

trance n a state in which one is unconscious of one's surroundings (*the hypnotist put her into a trance*).

tran'quil adj 1 calm, peaceful. 2 still:—n. **tranquil'lity.**

tran'quillize vb to calm (someone) down (*tranquillize the patient before surgery*).

tran'quillizer n anything (e.g. a pill) that calms a person down.

transact' vb to carry on or put through (*transact business with his company*).

transac'tion n 1 a piece of business (*property transaction*). 2 pl a written record of the doings of a society.

transatlan'tic adj across or crossing the Atlantic (*transatlantic flight*).

transcend' vb 1 to rise above (*his desire for power transcends everything else*). 2 to be superior to (*his new symphony transcends his other musical works*).

transcen'dent adj marvellous (*her transcendent beauty*).

transcenden'tal adj beyond human understanding, supernatural.

transcribe' vb to copy in writing.

tran'script n a written copy (*a transcript of the broadcast*).

transcrip'tion n 1 act of copying. 2 a copy.

tran'sept n one of the two parts representing the arms in a cross-shaped church.

transfer' vb (**transferred', transfer'ring**) to send or remove from one place or owner to another:— n **trans'fer** 1 act of transferring (*seek a transfer from one company to another*). 2 a design that can be pressed from one surface on to another.

transfer'able adj that can be transferred (*his property is transferable to his wife*).

trans'ference n act of transferring.

transfig'ure vb 1 to change in form, shape or appearance. 2 to make more beautiful or splendid (*a face transfigured with happiness*):—n **transfigura'tion.**

transfix' *vb* **1** to pier ce through (*transfixed by a spear*). **2** to cause to be unable to move (*transfixed with terror*).

transform' *vb* **1** to change the form of. **2** to change completely (*computers transformed the office system*):—*n* **transforma'tion**.

transform'er *n* a machine for changing the voltage of an electric current.

transfuse' *vb* to transfer from one thing to another (e.g. by pouring).

transfu'sion *n* **1** the act of transfusing. **2** the passing of the blood of one person into another.

transgress' *vb* **1** (*fml*) to break a rule or law. **2** to do wrong.

transgres'sion *n* **1** fault. **2** wrong-doing.

transgres'sor *n* **1** a wrongdoer. **2** a sinner.

trans'ient *adj* **1** not lasting for long, passing quickly (*transient pleasures*). **2** not staying for long (*a transient population*):—*n* **trans'ience**.

transis'tor *n* a simple radio receiving set in which the current is produced by sensitive wires in contact with a crystal.

trans'it *n* **1** going or being moved from one place to another (*passengers in transit at the airport*). **2** the passing of a planet between the sun and the earth.

transi'tion *n* changing from one state or condition to another (*in transition between school and university*).

trans'itive *adj*:—**transitive verb** a verb taking a direct object.

trans'itory *adj* passing quickly, not lasting for long (*transitory pleasures*).

translate' *vb* **1** to give the meaning of what is said or written in one language in another language. **2** (*fml*) to remove from one place to another:—*n* **transla'tor**.

transla'tion *n* **1** a turning from one language into another. **2** (*fml*) removal.

translu'cent *adj* allowing light to pass through (*translucent glass*).

transmigra'tion *n* passing of the soul into another body after death.

transmis'sion *n* **1** the act of sending messages, etc. **2** a radio or television broadcast.

transmit' *vb* (**transmit'ted, transmit'ting**) **1** to send (a message, news, etc). **2** to send by radio or television. **3** to send or pass fr om one person

to another (*a disease transmitted by mosquitoes*).

transmit'ter *n* a radio apparatus able to send messages or make broadcasts.

transmute' *vb* (*fml*) to change from one form into another.

tran'som *n* a strengthening crossbeam over a door or window.

transpa'rent *adj* **1** that can be clearly seen through. **2** obvious (*her misery was transparent to all*):—*ns* **transpa'rence, trans-pa'rency.**

transpire' *vb* **1** to become known (*it later transpired that he was not there*). **2** to happen (*wait and see what transpires*). **3** to exhale.

transplant' *vb* **1** to uproot and plant in another place. **2** to replace an organ of the body by one belonging to someone else (*transplant a kidney*):—*n* **trans'plant.**

transport' *vb* **1** to carry from one place to another (*transport children to school*). **2** (*old*) to convey to another country as a punishment. **3** (*fml*) to fill with emotions, anger, etc:—*n* **trans'port 1** any means of carrying persons or goods from one place to another. **2** a ship for carrying troops. **3** (*fml*) great delight, ecstasy (*in transports after their victory*).

transporta'tion *n* the conveying of convicts to another country as a punishment.

transpose' *vb* **1** to interchange the places of. **2** to change the order of (*transpose the words in the sentence*):—*n* **transposi'tion.**

transubstan'tiate *vb* to change the substance of.

transubstantia'tion *n* the belief that (in the Mass) bread and wine offered by the priest are changed into the substance of the body and blood of Christ.

transverse' *adj* lying across.

trap *n* **1** an instrument or device for catching wild animals and holding them alive or dead. **2** any device that, by its appearance, deceives one into advancing or progressing into unseen difficulties (*he walked into the trap*). **3** an S-shaped bend in drainpipes to prevent foul air rising. **4** a light two-wheeled horse carriage. **5** *pl* luggage:—*vb* (**trapped', trap'ping**) **1** to catch in a trap or snare. **2** to deceive (*they trapped her into admitting her guilt*).

trap'door *n* a door in a floor, ceiling or roof.

trapeze' n a bar suspended from two swinging ropes, some distance above the ground, and used in gymnastic or acrobatic exercises.

trape'zium n a four-sided figure of which two sides are parallel and unequal in length.

trap'per n one who traps animals, esp for their furs.

trapp'ings npl 1 finery, decoration. 2 ornamental harness for a horse.

Trap'pist n a monk who has taken a vow of silence.

trash n 1 (esp Amer) rubbish. 2 (inf) something worthless (his essay was trash):—adj **trash'y**.

trav'ail n 1 hard work or effort. 2 the pains of childbirth:—vb to labour, to toil.

trav'el vb (**trav'elled, trav'elling**) 1 to make a journey (travel by train to the city). 2 to move on one's way (the speed at which light travels).

trav'eller n 1 one who journeys. 2 one who goes from place to place trying to obtain orders for a business firm (also **commercial traveller**).

traverse vb 1 to go across (traversing the desert). 2 to journey through (traverse the country):—n a crosspiece.

trav'esty vb to imitate in such a way as to make appear ridiculous:—n a silly imitation, a burlesque.

trawl n a large wide-mouthed net for deep-sea fishing:—vb to fish by drawing a trawl through the water.

trawl'er n a fishing boat using a trawl.

tray n a flat piece of wood, metal, etc, with a rim, used for carrying dishes, etc.

treach'erous adj 1 faithless, disloyal, deceitful (treacherous followers). 2 dangerous, but seeming safe (a treacherous beach full of mines).

treach'ery n 1 unfaithfulness to those who have placed trust in one, disloyalty.

trea'cle n a dark-coloured syrup obtained when refining sugar.

tread vb (pt **trod**, pp **trod'den** or **trod**) 1 to step or walk (tread softly). 2 to walk heavily on (tread grapes to crush them). 3 (old) to dance:—n 1 a step (hear her tread on the stairs). 2 one's way of walking. 3 the sound of walking. 4 the flat part of the step of a stair. 5 the part of a tyre that touches the ground.

tread'le n a pedal used for operating a machine.

tread'mill n a millwheel turned by persons treading on steps sticking out from it.

trea'son n disloyalty to one's country or ruler.

trea'sonable adj having to do with treason (treasonable actions).

trea'sure n 1 something greatly valued (family treasures such as photographs). 2 a store of great wealth:—vb to value greatly.

trea'surer n one in charge of the money of a society, business firm, etc.

trea'sure trove n treasure found hidden and ownerless (the children dug up some treasure trove on the beach).

trea'sury n 1 the government department in charge of a nation's finances. 2 a store where public money is kept. 3 (old) a book containing a collection of facts, poems, etc.

treat vb 1 to deal with. 2 to act towards. 3 to talk or write about. 4 to try to cure by certain remedies. 5 to pay for another's entertainment. 6 to discuss conditions for an agreement:—n 1 an entertainment. 2 something that gives great pleasure.

treat'ise n a piece of writing giving information on a certain subject (a treatise on diseases transmitted by mosquitoes).

treat'ment n the way of treating anything.

treat'y n an agreement between two nations (a treaty that ended the war).

treb'le adj threefold, three times:—vb to multiply by three:—n the highest part in singing, soprano.

tree n a plant with a trunk and branches of wood:—**family tree** a table showing the growth of a family from a pair of common ancestors.

tre'foil n a plant with three leaves growing on one stem.

trek vb (**trekked', trek'king**) 1 (old) to journey by ox wagon. 2 (old) to hike and camp, dragging equipment in a cart. 3 to journey on foot, often wearily (trek around the shops buying presents):—also n.

trell'is n a light framework of criss-crossing bars of wood or metal for supporting climbing plants.

trem'ble vb 1 to shake with fear, cold, fever, etc. 2 to feel great fear.

tremen'dous adj 1 huge. 2 very great, impressive (a tremendous achievement).

trem'or n a slight shaking or shivering (earth tremors).

trem'ulous adj (fml) trembling, shaking, fearful, timid.

trench n a long narrow hole or ditch dug in the ground, esp one to shelter soldiers from enemy gunfire:—vb 1 to dig a long narrow hole or ditch. 2 to turn over and mix soil by digging trenches.

tren'chant adj 1 (of remarks) sharp and forceful (trenchant criticism).

tren'cher n 1 a wooden plate. 2 a cap with a square top, worn in certain colleges.

trend n 1 tendency. 2 a general inclination towards (a trend towards smaller families).

tren'dy adj (inf) very fashionable (a trendy wine bar).

trepan' vb (trepanned', trepan'ning) to remove part of the skull:—n a surgeon's saw for this purpose.

trepida'tion n fear.

tres'pass vb 1 to go unlawfully on another's land (walkers trespassing on the farmer's land). 2 (old) to sin:—also n:—n tres'passer.

tress n a lock of hair.

tres'tle n a movable wooden stand for supporting a table top, platform, etc.

trews npl tartan trousers.

tri- prefix three.

tri'al n 1 a test (give the young woman a trial as a secretary). 2 hardship or distress undergone (the trials of being homeless). 3 the examining of a prisoner in a court of law.

trian'gle n 1 a figure with three sides and three angles. 2 a musical instrument consisting of a triangle-shaped steel rod, played by striking it with a small rod.

trian'gular adj having three sides and three angles.

tri'athlon n an athletic contest consisting of three events, usually swimming, cycling and long-distance running.

tribe n a group of people or families living together under the rule of a chief:—adj trib'al:—n tribes'man.

tribula'tion n great suffering or trouble (the trials and tribulations of the refugees).

tribu'nal n 1 a court of justice. 2 a body appointed to look into and report on a matter of public interest.

trib'une n a Roman magistrate chosen by the people.

trib'utary adj 1 paying tribute. 2 flowing into a larger stream or river:—also n.

trib'ute n 1 deserved praise (pay tribute to her bravery). 2 money paid by a defeated nation to its conquerors.

trice n:—in a trice in a moment.

tricenten'ary n a three hundredth anniversary.

trick n 1 something said or done in order to deceive (gain entry to the house by a trick). 2 something done quickly and skilfully in order to amuse (a conjurer's trick). 3 a special way of doing something (the trick of getting the car to start). 4 cards played and won in a round:—vb to deceive, to cheat.

trick'ery n cheating, deceitful conduct (use trickery to get the old woman's money).

trick'le vb to flow very slowly (blood trickling from the wound):—n a thin stream of liquid.

trick'ster n a cheat.

trick'y adj 1 cunning (a tricky customer). 2 requiring skill (a tricky piece of engineering). 3 difficult (a tricky situation).

tri'colour n a three-coloured flag, esp that of France.

tri'cycle n a three-wheeled cycle.

tri'dent n a spear with three prongs.

tried pt of **try**:—adj reliable, proved good.

trien'nial adj 1 happening every three years. 2 lasting three years.

tri'fle n 1 a thing of little value or importance (worry about trifles). 2 a small amount (she was a trifle annoyed). 3 a pudding consisting of sponge cake, fruit and cream:—vb 1 to treat without seriousness. 2 to idle.

tri'fling adj 1 of no value or importance. 2 very small (a trifling animal).

trig adj (old) neat, smart.

trig'ger n a small lever that when pulled fires a gun:—vb 1 to cause something to happen (trigger an allergic reaction), 2 to cause something to start functioning (trigger the alarm).

trigonom'etry n the science dealing with the measurement of triangles, and the relation between their sides and angles.

trilat'eral adj having three sides.

tril'by n a soft felt hat.

trill vb in music, to play or sing in rapid succession two sounds that are close together:—also n.

tril'lion n a million million.

tril'ogy n a series of three connected plays, novels, etc.

trim vb (**trimmed**, **trim'ming**) **1** to make neat, esp by cutting (*have her hair trimmed*). **2** to decorate (*trim the jacket with fake fur*). **3** to rearrange cargo so that a ship is properly balanced. **4** to make ready for sailing:—adj neat, tidy:—**in good trim 1** in good condition. **2** well prepared.

trimes'ter n **1** an academic term. **2** three months.

trim'eter n a line of poetry consisting of three metrical feet.

trim'ming n something added as an ornament (*gold trimming on the evening dress*).

trin'ity n a union of three in one:—**the Trinity** the Christian belief that in one God there are three persons—the Father, Son and Holy Spirit.

trin'ket n an ornament of little value, a piece of cheap jewellery.

tri'o n **1** a set of three (*the trio of rascals who broke the windows*). **2** a piece of music for three performers.

trip vb (**tripped**, **trip'ping**) **1** (*fml*) to move with quick light steps (*trip upstairs*). **2** to stumble or fall over (*she tripped getting off the bus*). **3** to cause to stumble or fall (*they deliberately tripped her up*):—n **1** a stumble. **2** a short journey or outing.

tripar'tite adj **1** divided into three parts. **2** concerning three parties.

tripe n **1** part of the stomach of a sheep, cow, etc, prepared as food. **2** (*inf*) nonsense, rubbish (*the film was just tripe*).

trip'le adj made up of three parts, threefold:—vb to make or become three times as large or many (*triple his income in a year*).

trip'let n **1** a set of three. **2** one of three children born at one birth.

trip'licate adj threefold:—**in triplicate** with three copies.

tri'pod n a three-legged stand or support (e.g. for a camera).

tri'pos n a Cambridge University honours examination.

trip'per n (*inf*) one on a holiday or outing for pleasure (*the trippers set out for the seaside*).

trisect' vb to cut into three equal parts.

trite adj often used, commonplace (*her words of comfort were rather trite*).

tri'umph n **1** joy at success or victory. **2** a great success or victory (*the crowd cheered her triumph*). **3** in ancient Rome, a procession in honour of a victorious general:—vb to gain a great success or victory (*triumphed over the opposition*).

trium'phal adj having to do with a victory (*a triumphal procession*).

trium'phant adj **1** successful, victorious (*the triumphant team*). **2** joyous at success or victory (*triumphant at the team's win*).

trium'virate n a group of three men sharing the power of government.

triv'et n a three-legged stand for a pot, kettle, etc:—**right as a trivet** perfectly all right.

triv'ial adj of small importance, trifling (*waste time on trivial matters*):—n **triv-ial'ity**.

trochee [trō'-kee] n a metric foot of one long and one short syllable:—adj **trocha'ic**.

trog'lodyte n a cave-dweller.

Tro'jan n **1** an inhabitant of ancient Troy. **2** a hard-working person:—also adj.

troll n a dwarfish elf or goblin.

trol'ley n (*pl* **trol'leys**) **1** a small truck. **2** a type of handcart with two wheels (*luggage trolleys at the airport*). **3** a serving table on wheels (*bring the food in on a trolley*). **4** a pole that conveys electric current from an overhead wire to a bus or tramcar.

trol'lop n a dirty and untidy woman.

trombone' n a deep-toned type of trumpet with a sliding tube moved in and out when it is being played.

troop n **1** a collection or group of people or animals (*a troop of monkeys in the circus*). **2** an organized group of soldiers, Scouts, etc. **3** *pl* soldiers:—vb to move or gather in large numbers:—**trooping the colour** a ceremony at which soldiers honour their own special flag.

troop'er n a horse-soldier.

troop'ship n a ship for carrying soldiers.

tro'phy n something given or kept as a reward for or reminder of success or victory (*a trophy for winning the tournament*).

trop'ic *n* one of two imaginary lines round the earth marking the farthest distance north and south of the equator at which the sun rises and sets during the year:—*npl.* **trop'ics** the hot regions north and south of the equator.

trop'ical *adj* 1 having to do with the tropics (*tropical fruit*). 2 very hot.

trot *vb* (**trot'ted, trot'ting**) 1 to run with short steps (*a child trotting behind his mother*). 2 (*of a horse*) to go at a pace between a walk and a gallop:—*n* a medium pace.

troth *n* (*old*) truth, faith:—**plight one's troth** (*old*) to promise to marry.

trot'ter *n* the foot of a pig or sheep.

trou'badour *n* a wandering poet and minstrel in the south of France in the Middle Ages.

trouble [trubl] *vb* 1 to cause anxiety, difficulty or distress to (*she was troubled by her daughter's absence*). 2 to disturb (*please don't trouble to get up*):—*n* 1 worry, anxiety, distress (*her daughter causes her a lot of trouble*). 2 difficulty (*having trouble closing the door*).

trou'blesome *adj* causing trouble (*a troublesome task*).

troub'lous *adj* (*old*) disturbed.

trough [trof] *n* 1 a long narrow vessel to hold water or food for animals. 2 a hollow (e.g. between two waves).

trounce *vb* to beat severely (*they trounced the opposing team*).

troupe [tröp] *n* a company of actors or other performers.

trou'sers *n* a garment originally for men, reaching from waist to ankles and covering each leg separately (*a pair of trousers*).

trousseau [trö'-sō] *n* (*pl* **trousseaux** *or* **trousseaus**) a bride's outfit.

trout *n* an eatable freshwater fish.

trow [trö *or* trou] *vb* (*old*) to think, to suppose.

trow'el *n* 1 a tool with a flat blade used for spreading mortar, plaster, etc. 2 a tool with a curved blade used in gardening.

troy, troy' weight *n* a system of measures used in weighing precious metals or gems.

tru'ant *n* a child who stays off school without leave (*the teacher saw the truants at the supermarket*):—**play truant** to stay off school without leave.

truce *n* an agreement to stop fighting for a time (*both armies agreed on a truce at Christmas*).

truck[1] *n* 1 a large motor vehicle for carrying goods, a lorry. 2 a railway goods wagon.

truck[2] *n* 1 dealings (*have no truck with the people next door*). 2 trade:—*vb* to trade, to exchange for other goods.

truck'le *n* a small wheel or castor:—*vb* (*old*) to try to please by obeying slavishly.

truckle bed *n* a low bed that moves on castors.

truc'ulent *adj* quarrelsome, trying to find a cause for quarrelling or fighting (*children in a truculent mood*):—*n* **truc'ulence**.

trudge *vb* to walk, esp with heavy steps, to walk in a tired manner (*trudge home after a hard day's work*):—*also n*.

true *adj* 1 in agreement with fact, not false (*the true facts*). 2 genuine (*the true heir*). 3 honest. 4 faithful, loyal (*true friends*). 5 exact, close (*a true copy*):—*adv* **tru'ly**.

truffle *n* an eatable fungus that grows underground (*truffles are an expensive delicacy*).

tru'ism *n* a remark that is obviously true and therefore unnecessary ('*look before you leap*' *is a truism*).

trump *n* one of a suit of cards that, in a particular hand, beats a card of any other suit:—*vb* to play a trump on a card of another suit:—**trump up** to make up, to invent.

trump card *n* a means of ensuring success.

trum'pery *n* (*old*) worthless finery (*she wears a lot of trumpery to go out*):—*adj* showy but worthless.

trum'pet *n* a metal wind instrument:—*vb* 1 to make known far and wide. 2 to make a noise, as an elephant (*trumpet as he blew his nose*).

trum'peter *n* one who plays the trumpet.

truncate *vb* to cut off, to cut short (*a truncated meeting*).

trun'cheon *n* 1 a policeman's baton. 2 a short staff carried as a sign of authority.

trun'dle *vb* to roll, push or bowl along (*the bus trundled along the country road*).

trunk *n* 1 the main stem of a tree. 2 the body without the head or limbs (*the rash was confined to his trunk*). 3 the long tube-like nose of an elephant. 4 a box or chest for clothes, etc (*store the clothes in the trunk*).

trunk call n (old) a telephone call from one town or district to another.

trunk line n 1 a main railway line between two main stations. 2 (old) a telephone line between one large exchange and another.

trunk road n a main road.

truss n 1 a bundle of hay or straw. 2 a supporting bandage (a truss for a hernia):—vb 1 to tie (the burglars trussed up the guard). 2 to tie up (a fowl) for cooking.

trust n 1 a firm belief that another person or a thing is what it claims or is claimed to be, confidence (put your trust in him). 2 a union of several firms to advance their business interests. 3 the holding and controlling of money or property for the advantage of someone (money held in trust until she is twenty-one). 4 care or responsibility (a child placed in her trust):—vb 1 to rely upon, to have faith in. 2 to hope:—**take on trust** to accept without examination or inquiry.

trustee' n one appointed to hold and look after property on behalf of another:—n **trustee'ship**.

trust'ful, trust'ing adjs ready to trust.

trust'worthy adj deserving trust or confidence, reliable.

trust'y adj (fml) that can be trusted, reliable (his trusty followers).

truth n that which is true (always tell the truth).

try vb (tried', try'ing) 1 to attempt (try to climb the tree). 2 to test (try the new flavour). 3 to examine and judge in a court of law.

try'ing adj difficult, worrying, annoying (a trying time for all).

tryst [trĭst] n 1 an appointment to meet. 2 an arranged meeting place.

tsar, tzar, czar n the title of the emperor of Russia:—f **tsarina**.

tse'tse n an African fly whose bite is fatal to horses, cattle, etc, and which carries the disease of sleeping sickness.

tub n 1 a large open container used for bathing, washing clothes, growing things etc (an old wooden washing tub). 2 a bath tub.

tu'ba n a low-pitched brass wind instrument.

tub'by adj (inf) round and fat (a tubby child).

tube n 1 a pipe. 2 a hollow cylinder. 3 an underground electric railway.

tu'ber n a swelling on the root of a plant (e.g. a potato).

tu'bercle n 1 a small tuber. 2 a small mass of diseased matter on the lungs or other organs.

tuberculo'sis n a wasting disease caused by the growth of tubercles on the lungs or other organs, consumption:—adj **tuber'cular**.

tub'ing n 1 a length of tube. 2 a series of tubes.

tub'-thumper n (inf) a speaker who tries to excite his or her audience by skill in using words.

tub'ular adj 1 like a tube. 2 consisting of tubes (tubular construction/tubular bells).

tuck vb 1 to push, to stuff (tuck his shirt into his trousers). 2 to put in a secure or private place (tuck his book under his arm):—n 1 a fold in a garment. 2 (inf) food, esp cakes and sweetmeats:—**tuck in 1** to cover up comfortably (tuck the baby in). 2 (inf) to eat hungrily (tuck into tea and cakes).

tuck'er n (old) a frill round the top of a woman's dress.

tuck'shop n a shop selling food, esp cakes and sweets, often near a school.

Tues'day n the third day of the week.

tuft n 1 a bunch or clump of grass, hair, etc, growing together. 2 a bunch of threads, etc, held together.

tuft'y adj growing in tufts (tufty hair).

tug vb (tugged', tug'ging) 1 to pull with effort (tug the gate open). 2 to pull sharply (tug his sister's hair):—n 1 a strong sharp pull. 2 a small boat used to pull larger ones.

tug-of-war' n a contest in which two teams pull opposite ways on a rope until one is pulled across a mark.

tui'tion n teaching (private tuition in French).

tu'lip n a plant growing from a bulb and having a single brightly coloured flower.

tulle [tūl] n a thin soft silk material.

tum'ble vb 1 to fall (the child tumbled down the hill). 2 to do acrobatic and jumping tricks:—n a fall.

tumbledown' adj in a ruined state, falling apart (a tumbledown cottage).

tum'bler n 1 a drinking glass (a tumbler of cold water). 2 an acrobat (tumblers in the circus). 3 a type of pigeon.

tum'brel, tum'bril n a dungcart.

tu'mid adj (fml) swollen.

tu'mour n a mass of diseased cells in the body causing swelling (a brain tumour/a cancer tumour).

tu'mult n 1 noisy confusion, uproar (his statement went unheard in the tumult). 2 disorderly behaviour by a crowd.

tumul'tuous adj noisy and disorderly (a tumultuous welcome).

tun n a large cask.

tu'na n a large eatable fish of the mackerel family.

tun'dra n a wide plain of frozen marshy land in northern Siberia or North America.

tune n 1 the melody or air of a piece of music. 2 a short pleasing piece of music. 3 the correct relation of one musical note to others:—vb 1 to see that the strings of an instrument are adjusted to play the correct notes. 2 to adjust a radio, etc, until it is receiving as clearly as possible.

tune'ful adj having a pleasing air or melody (a tuneful air).

tung'sten n a rare metallic element, used for filaments in electric light bulbs.

tu'nic n 1 a loose upper garment covering the body, sometimes to below the waist (a school gym tunic). 2 a soldier's uniform jacket.

tu'ning fork n a two-pronged fork that, when struck, gives a musical note to which instruments can be adjusted.

tun'nel n an underground passage, esp one that enables a road or railway to pass under or through an obstacle (the train went through a tunnel).

tur'ban n a headdress, common in the East, made by winding a band of cloth round and round the head.

tur'bid adj 1 muddy (the turbid waters of the lake). 2 thick (turbid smoke).

tur'bine n a type of wheel that, when moved by steam or water power, drives an engine.

tur'bot n a large eatable flatfish.

tur'bulent adj disorderly, hard to control or rule, rebellious (a turbulent crowd of protestors):—n **tur'bulence**.

tureen' n a large deep dish for soup.

turf n 1 earth covered thickly with short grass (the turf of the golf course). 2 a single piece of turf cut out:—vb to cover with turf:—**the Turf** horseracing.

turf accountant n a bookmaker.

tur'gid adj swollen.

tur'key n a large farmyard fowl (roast a turkey at Christmas).

Tur'kish bath n a bath in which one bathes in hot steam.

tur'moil n noisy confusion, disorder (the office was in turmoil after she left).

turn vb 1 to move or cause to move round (she turned to face him). 2 to shape wood by cutting it as it revolves. 3 to change (turn into a beautiful young woman). 4 (of milk) to become sour:—n 1 a change of direction. 2 (of a wheel) a revolution. 3 a bend (the accident happened at the turn in the road). 4 an act (she did him a good turn). 5 a short walk (take a turn along the promenade). 6 a sudden feeling of sickness:—**turn down** to refuse (turn down the invitation):—**turn in** (inf) to go to bed:—**turn out** 1 to have (good or bad) results (it turned out for the best). 2 to attend a meeting, etc (very few turned out because of the weather):—**turn over a new leaf** to change oneself for the better:—**turn turtle** to turn completely over, to capsize:—**turn up** to appear unexpectedly (she did not turn up at the meeting):—**turn upon** to attack suddenly (the dog turned upon its master):—**in turn** one after the other, in the proper order (they drove the car in turns).

turn'coat n one who gives up party or belief for his or her own advantage.

turn'ing n 1 a bend in the road. 2 a corner leading off to another road.

tur'nip n a plant with a large eatable root (serve mashed turnip with the dinner).

turn'key n a person in charge of the keys of a prison.

turn'out n the number of people in an assembly (a large turnout at the concert).

turn'over n in business, the amount of money paid in and out in a certain period (the shop's turnover is down this year).

turn'pike n a gate or bar across a road at which travellers must pay a tax for the use of the road.

turn'stile n a revolving gate through which only one person can pass at a time (pay at the turnstile).

turn'table n 1 a r evolving platform for turning round railway engines, etc. 2 a r ound spinning surface on a record-player on which the record is placed.

tur'pentine n 1 a resin obtained from certain trees. 2 an oil made from this.

tur'pitude n (fml) wickedness.

tur'quoise n a greenish-blue precious stone or its colour (a turquoise dress):—also adj.

tur'ret n 1 a small tower forming part of a building (a castle with many turrets). 2 a revolving tower to protect guns and gunners on a warship or in a fort.

tur'tle n a large sea tortoise.

tur'tle dove ns a dove with a soft, cooing note.

tusk n a long pointed tooth sticking out from the mouth, as in an elephant, walrus, etc.

tus'sle n a short struggle, a disorderly fight (the children had a tussle over the toys):—vb to struggle.

tus'sock n a clump of grass.

tus'sore n an Indian silk.

tut interj an exclamation expressing disappointment or disapproval.

tu'telage n (fml) care, protection (under the tutelage).

tu'telary adj protecting.

tu'tor n a private teacher (have a tutor to help with the subjects with which she is having difficulty):—vb to teach, to act as tutor.

tuto'rial adj having to do with a tutor or teaching:—n 1 a group of students who study with a tutor. 2 study time spent with a tutor.

twad'dle n nonsense, foolish talk (he was talking twaddle).

twain adj two:—n a pair.

twang n 1 the sound made by plucking a tightly stretched string or wire. 2 a tone that sounds as if one were speaking through one's nose:—vb to pluck a tightly stretched string or wire.

tweak vb to twist sharply, to pinch (he tweaked his ear in fun):—also n.

tweed n a rough woollen cloth, suitable for outer garments.

twee'zers npl small pincers for pulling out hairs, lifting tiny things, etc (pluck her eyebrows with tweezers).

twice adv two times (he has been beaten only twice).

twid'dle vb to play with (sit twiddling one's fingers with nothing to do).

twig n a small shoot or branch of a tree or shrub.

twi'light n the faint light just after sunset or before dawn.

twill n a strong cloth with ribbed lines or ridges running from end to end (trousers made of twill).

twin n 1 one of two children born at one birth. 2 a person or thing looking exactly the same as another (the twin of her china vase):—adj 1 born at one birth (twin babies). 2 double. 3 consisting of two like parts or things (twin engines):—vb (twinned', twin'ning) to pair together.

twine n strong string (garden twine):—vb 1 to twist or wind around. 2 to twist together (garden plants twining around each other).

twinge n a sudden sharp pain (a twinge in his back when he bent down).

twink'le vb 1 to sparkle. 2 to shine with a light that very quickly increases and decreases (stars twinkling in the sky):—n 1 a gleam of light. 2 a quick look of amusement in the eyes:—**in a twink'ling** in a moment.

twirl vb to spin or turn round rapidly (she twirled the baton):—also n.

twist vb 1 to turn quickly out of shape or position. 2 to wind strands round each other (to make a cord). 3 to put a wrong meaning on (she deliberately twisted his words):—n 1 something made by twisting. 2 a sudden turning out of shape or position.

twit vb (twit'ted, twit'ting) 1 to make fun of. 2 (old) to blame.

twitch n 1 a jerk. 2 a sudden quick movement:—vb 1 to pull sharply (twitch her dress into position). 2 to make a quick movement unintentionally (her eye twitches).

twit'ter vb to chirp, as a bird:—n 1 a chirp. 2 a state of nervous excitement (in a twitter about the party).

two [tö] adj and n one more than one.

two-faced' adj deceitful, not sincere (a supposed loyal supporter who turned out to be two-faced).

tycoon' n a very successful and influential business man, a business magnate.

tyke, tike n a dog, a low fellow.

tym'panum *n* (*pl* **tym'pana** *or* **tym'panums**) the eardrum, a tightly stretched skin inside the ear, by means of which we hear.

type *n* **1** a person or thing possessing most of the qualities of a certain group, class, nationality, etc. **2** a class or kind (*a kind of vegetable*). **3** a letter or symbol cut in metal, etc, and used for printing. **4** the kind and size of a set of letters used in printing:—*vb* to use a typewriter (*he is learning to type*).

type'script *n* typewritten material (*send the typescript to her publisher*).

type'writer *n* a machine operated by keys that, when struck, cause letters or symbols to be printed through an inked ribbon on to paper.

ty'phoid *n* an infectious disease causing acute pain in the intestines (*get typhoid from infected food*).

typhoon' *n* a violent storm of wind and rain, esp in the China seas.

ty'phus *n* a dangerous infectious fever.

typ'ical *adj* **1** serving as an example of a class or group (*a typical village store*). **2** characteristic (*it was typical of him not to apologize*).

typ'ify *vb* to serve as an example of.

typ'ist *n* one who uses a typewriter.

typog'raphy *n* the art of printing:—*n* **ty-pog'rapher.**

tyran'nical, tyr'annous *adjs* cruel, ruling unjustly (*a tyrannical emperor*).

tyr'annize *vb* to use power cruelly or unjustly (*the dictator was known to tyrannize the people*).

tyran'nosaurus *n* a very large meat-eating dinosaur that walked on its hind legs and had two small front legs.

tyr'anny *n* cruel or unjust use of power.

ty'rant *n* **1** one who uses power cruelly. **2** an unjust ruler.

tyre, tire *n* a ring of iron or rubber around the outside rim of a wheel.

tyro *see* **tiro.**

tzar *see* **tsar:**—*f* **tzarina.**

U

ubi'quitous *adj* being or seeming to be in more than one place at the same time, seemingly occurring everywhere (*broccoli seems to be ubiquitous in restaurants these days*):—*n* **ubi'quity**.

ud'der *n* the organ containing the milk-producing gland of a cow, sheep, etc.

UFO *abbr* **unidentified flying object**, a strange, unidentified object seen in the sky, believed by some people to be an alien spacecraft.

ug'ly *adj* **1** unpleasant to see or hear. **2** unpleasant, dangerous (*an unpleasant incident in the bar*):—*n* **ug'liness**.

ukulele [u-kê-lā'-li] *n* a stringed musical instrument played by plucking the strings.

ul'cer *n* an infected sore containing poisonous matter (*mouth ulcers*).

ul'cerated, ul'cerous *adjs* having an ulcer or ulcers.

ul'ster *n* a long loose overcoat.

ulte'rior *adj* further, secret, hidden.

ulterior motive *n* a reason for action that one does not make known to others.

ul'timate *adj* last, final (*his ultimate destination*).

ul'timately *adv* in the end.

ultima'tum *n* (*pl* **ultima'tums** *or* **ultima'ta**) a last offer of conditions, to be followed, if refused, by action without more discussion (*she gave an ultimatum that if he did not stop bothering her she would call the police*).

ul'tra- *prefix* **1** very, extremely (*ultra cautious*). **2** beyond (*ultra microscopic*).

ultramarine' *n* a bright sky-blue colour:—*also adj.*

ultravi'olet *adj* beyond the violet end of the spectrum.

um'ber *n* a reddish-brown colour.

umbil'icus *n* (*pl* **umbil'ici**) the navel:—*adj* **umbil'ical.**

um'bra *n* (*pl* **um'brae** *or* **um'bras**) the dark central part of a shadow (e.g. of the earth on the moon).

um'brage *n*—**take umbrage** to be offended or made angry by.

umbrel'la *n* a folding frame covered with waterproof material, that can be opened out and held over the head at the end of a stick as protection against rain.

um'pire *n* one who acts as judge in a dispute or contest, a referee (*a tennis umpire*).

un- *prefix* not.

unabashed' *adj* not ashamed, not put off (*she was unabashed by the criticism*).

unabridged' *adj* not shortened, complete (*unabridged edition of the book*).

unaccept'able *adj* unwelcome.

unaccom'modating *adj* not ready to oblige.

unaccount'able *adj* that cannot be explained (*for some unaccountable reason*).

unaccus'tomed *adj* not usual (*the unaccustomed warmth of a March day*).

unacknow'ledged *adj* not recognized, ignored (*his unacknowledged skill*).

unadorned' *adj* plain, simple.

unaffect'ed *adj* **1** simple, sincere (*his unaffected manner*). **2** unmoved (*unaffected by the child's tears*).

unalloyed' *adj* unmixed, pure (*unalloyed joy*).

unanim'ity *n* complete agreement.

unan'imous *adj* **1** being all of the same opinion (*they were unanimous in their decision*). **2** agreed to by all present (*a unanimous decision*).

unan'swerable *adj* that cannot be easily argued against or proved wrong (*an unanswerable charge*).

unapproach'able *adj* unfriendly in manner.

unassum'ing *adj* modest, not boastful.

unauth'orized *adj* done without permission.

unaware' *adj* not knowing, ignorant (of).

unawares' *adv* unexpectedly (*catch the thief unawares*).

unbal'anced *adj* **1** not steady. **2** mentally unstable (*he was unbalanced when he committed the crime*).

unbecom'ing *adj* not suitable, not proper (*her behaviour was unbecoming*).

unbelief' *n* lack of faith, doubt.

unbeliev'er *n* one who does not believe in the accepted religion.

unbend' *vb* **1** to make straight. **2** to behave in a more friendly way (*unfriendly at first but she unbent later*).

unbi'as(s)ed *adj* fair to all parties, just (*the judge made an unbiased decision*).

unbo'som vb (old) to tell one's secret thoughts, etc.

unbound'ed adj great, without limits (unbounded enthusiasm).

unbri'dled adj uncontrolled (umbridled rage).

unbur'den vb 1 (fml) to take a load off. 2 to tell about something that has caused worry or anxiety (unburden himself of his worries).

uncalled'-for adj unnecessary and rude (uncalled-for comments).

uncan'ny adj strange, mysterious.

uncer'tain adj 1 not sure (uncertain about how to proceed). 2 doubtful (uncertain plans):—n **uncer'tainty**.

unchar'itable adj unkind, ungenerous (uncharitable thoughts).

un'cle n 1 the brother of one's father or mother. 2 the husband of one's aunt.

unclean' adj not pure (unclean thoughts).

uncoil' vb to unwind (the rope was uncoiled).

uncom'fortable adj 1 uneasy (feel uncomfortable about going alone). 2 giving no comfort (an uncomfortable chair).

uncommu'nicative adj not speaking much to others.

uncomplimen'tary adj critical, insulting.

uncom'promising adj firm, not ready to give in (both sides had uncompromising attitudes).

unconcerned' adj 1 unmoved. 2 uninterested.

uncondi'tional adj without conditions (unconditional surrender).

uncon'scionable adj (fml) unreasonable, excessive (an unconscionable length of time).

uncon'scious adj 1 not knowing, unaware (unconscious of what was going on). 2 stunned, as by a blow, etc, and so unaware of what is going on (knocked unconscious by the blow).

unconstitu'tional adj against the principles of the constitution, unlawful.

unconven'tional adj not bound by custom, natural, free and easy (unconventional dress and manners).

uncouth' adj rough in manner, awkward, clumsy (uncouth manners).

unc'tious adj (fml) so polite as to be displeasing (an unctious willingness to obey).

uncul'tivated adj 1 not prepared for crops (uncultivated land). 2 uncivilized, crude (an uncultivated people).

undaun'ted adj bold, fearless (undaunted they went through the jungle).

undecid'ed adj not having made up one's mind, doubtful (undecided about how to vote).

undemon'strative adj not showing one's feelings, calm by nature (the judge was an undemonstrative man).

undeni'able adj that cannot be argued against, certain (his undeniable guilt).

un'der prep 1 below. 2 beneath. 3 subject to. 4 less good than:—adv in a lower condition, degree or place.

un'dercarriage n the wheels or other parts on the underside of an aircraft needed for landing.

undercharge' vb to ask less than the correct price (it is unusual for shopkeepers to undercharge).

un'derclothes, un'derclothing n clothes worn under others or next to the skin.

un'dercurrent n 1 a current flowing beneath the surface. 2 an influence or popular feeling that cannot easily be noticed (undercurrent of discontent in the office).

undercut' vb to offer to sell at a lower price (than):—n **un'dercut** 1 the underside of a loin of beef. 2 in a fight, a blow from below.

underdone' adj not sufficiently cooked, lightly cooked (the beef was underdone).

underes'timate vb to have too low an opinion of (underestimate his ability).

undergo' vb to bear, to suffer (undergo much pain).

undergrad'uate n a university student who has not yet taken a degree.

underground' adj and adv 1 beneath the ground. 2 secret (an underground political organization):—n **un'derground** 1 a place below the surface of the earth. 2 a railway running through underground tunnels.

un'dergrowth n shrubs and low bushes growing among trees.

underhand' adj sly, secret, dishonest (an underhand action).

underline' vb 1 to draw a line under. 2 to emphasize (underline the need).

un'derling n one who is under the orders of another (the underlings of the leisure industry).

undermine' vb 1 to make holes underground. 2 to destroy gradually, to seek to harm by underhand methods (undermine his confidence).

un'derpass *n* part of a road or footpath that goes underneath a road or railway.

underrate' *vb* to have too low an opinion of (*underrate their ability*).

undersell' *vb* to sell at a lower price (than) (*he tried to undersell his competitors*).

undersized' *adj* less than the normal size, very small.

understand' *vb* 1 to see the meaning of (*understand the poem*). 2 to know thoroughly (*understand the filing system*). 3 to work out the truth from what has been said. (*understand his motives*).

understand'ing *n* 1 intelligence, powers of judgment. 2 an agreement, esp an unwritten one (*an understanding that the money would be paid every month*).

understate' *vb* to talk of something as smaller or less important than it really is (*understate his role in the events*).

un'derstudy *n* one who learns the same part as another actor in order to be able to take his place if necessary (*the understudy took the place of the sick actor*).

undertake' *vb* to take upon oneself to do, to attempt.

un'dertaker *n* one who manages funerals.

un'dertaking *n* 1 a task (*an undertaking requiring great skill*). 2 a promise (*he gave an undertaking that he would be present*).

un'dertone *n* a low voice (*give his opinion in an undertone*).

un'dertow *n* the backward flow of a wave breaking on the shore, an undercurrent.

un'derwear *n* underclothes.

un'derwood *n* low bushes or shrubs growing at the foot of larger trees.

un'derworld *n* 1 the mythical place to which the spirits of people went after death. 2 those members of society who live by violence and crime.

underwrite' *vb* to accept money in return for a guarantee of insurance:—*n* **un'der-writer**.

undisguised' *adj* open, not hidden (*her undisguised jealousy*).

undisturbed' *adj* calm, tranquil (*an undisturbed night*).

undo' *vb* to reverse what has been done, to untie or unfasten, to ruin (*undo the damage*).

undo'ing *n* ruin (*lying was her undoing*).

undone' *pp* of **undo**:—*adj* 1 not done. 2 ruined.

undoubt'ed *adj* certain, undeniable (*her undoubted honesty*).

undress' *vb* 1 to take one's clothes off (*she undressed in private*). 2 to take off the clothes of (*undress the doll*).

undue' *adj* greater than is necessary (*an undue panic*).

un'dulate *vb* 1 to rise and fall like waves. 2 to have a wavy appearance.

undu'ly *adv* more than is necessary, excessively (*not unduly worried*).

unearth' *vb* 1 to discover by searching (*unearth the truth*). 2 to dig up (*police unearthed the corpse*).

unearth'ly *adj* weird, supernatural, ghostly (*there was an unearthly scream*).

uneas'y *adj* uncomfortable, worried, anxious (*an uneasy feeling that all was not well*).

unemployed' *adj* having no paid job, out of work.

unequi'vocal *adj* clear, that cannot be misunderstood (*an unequivocal reply*).

unerr'ing *adj* true, going straight to the target (*with unerring accuracy*).

une'ven *adj* 1 not flat, not smooth (*uneven ground*). 2 sometimes not so good as at other times (*his work is uneven*).

unfail'ing *adj* sure, reliable (*an unfailing remedy*).

unfamil'iar *adj* strange (*unfamiliar territory*).

unfas'ten *vb* to undo, to unfix, to set loose (*unfasten the belt*).

unfath'omable *adj* 1 very deep. 2 mysterious.

unforeseen' *adj* unexpected (*unforeseen circumstances*).

unfor'tunate *adj* unlucky (*it was unfortunate that she was late*).

unfound'ed *adj* not based on fact (*unfounded allegations*).

unfurl' *vb* to spread out (*unfurl the flag*).

ungain'ly *adj* clumsy, awkward (*her ungainly way of walking*).

ungrate'ful *adj* not showing due thanks (*an ungrateful remark*).

unguent [ung'-gwênt] *n* (*fml*) an ointment.

unhap'piness *n* misfortune, misery.

unhap'py *adj* 1 miserable, sad (*unhappy that she had failed*). 2 unlucky (*an unhappy set of circumstances*).

unhealth'y adj **1** not having good health. **2** bad for health (*unhealthy diet*). **3** having a bad influence.

u'nicorn n in fables, an animal like a horse with a single straight horn on its head.

u'niform adj **1** unchanging. **2** of the one kind, shape, size, etc:—n distinctive clothing worn by all members of the same organization, institution, etc (*school uniform*).

u'nify vb to unite, to form into one (*unify the political factions*):—n unifica'tion.

unilat'eral adj affecting one side or party only (*a unilateral attitude to nuclear weapons*).

u'nion n **1** a putting together to make one. **2** act of joining together. **3** a trade union (*the print unions*).

Union Jack n the national flag of the United Kingdom of Great Britain and Northern Ireland.

unique [û-neek'] adj being the only one of its kind, unequalled (*she has a unique beauty*).

un'isex adj designed for use by both man and women (*a unisex hair salon*).

u'nison n agreement:—**sing in unison** all to sing the same tune together.

u'nit n **1** the number 1. **2** a single person, thing, or group. **3** a fixed amount, etc, taken as a standard in measuring.

unite' vb **1** to make or become one (*unite the two organizations*). **2** to join together, to act or work together (*the people united to defeat the tyrant*).

u'nity n **1** oneness. **2** agreement.

univer'sal adj **1** total, whole. **2** affecting all, done by everyone (*a universal effort*).

universa'ity n the state of being universal.

u'niverse n **1** the whole of creation. **2** the world.

univer'sity n an educational institution in which advanced study in all branches of knowledge is carried on, and by which degrees are awarded to those showing merit in their subjects.

unkempt' adj (of hair) uncombed.

unleav'ened adj not mixed with yeast (*unleavened bread*).

unless' conj if not.

unlim'ited adj **1** as much as is wanted, that cannot be used up (*unlimited supply of money*).

unload' vb to remove the load or burden from (*unload the lorry*).

unman' vb to take away the courage of (*unmanned by their severe criticism*).

unman'ly adj cowardly, timid, weak (*unmanly behaviour*).

unmit'igated adj complete, with no good qualities, thorough (*an unmitigated disaster*).

unmoved' adj firm, calm, not affected (by) (*unmoved by the child's plea*).

unnerve' vb to take away the strength or courage of (*unnerved by the confidence of the opposition*).

unobtru'sive adj not attracting attention, modest.

unoc'cupied adj empty (*unoccupied houses*).

unor'thodox adj holding unusual views, differing from the accepted view.

unostenta'tious adj not showy, not trying to draw attention to oneself/itself (*an unostentatious dresser*).

unpal'atable adj **1** unpleasant to taste (*unpalatable food*). **2** unpleasant (*an unpalatable set of events*).

unpop'ular adj widely disliked.

unpreced'ent'ed adj without a previous example of the same kind (*an unprecedented set of circumstances*).

unpre'judiced adj fair, showing favour to no one.

unpremed'itated adj done without forethought (*an unpremeditated crime*).

unprepossess'ing adj unattractive at first sight (*an unprepossessing sight*).

unpreten'tious adj modest, not attracting attention.

unprin'cipled adj immoral, wicked, recognizing no standards of right and wrong.

unproduc'tive adj **1** yielding no crops, etc. **2** giving no profit (*an unproductive scheme*).

unprofes'sional adj against the rules or customs of a profession (*unprofessional conduct*).

unqual'ified adj **1** not having the necessary training or skill. **2** complete (*an unqualified success*).

unques'tionable adj undoubted, certain (*unquestionable proof*).

unrav'el vb **1** to disentangle. **2** to solve (*unravelled the problem*).

unrelieved' adj **1** without relief (from pain, etc). **2** lacking variety (*unrelieved monotony*).

unremitt'ing adj without pause, ceaseless (*his unremitting effort*).

unrequit'ed adj not rewarded, not returned (*unrequited love*).

unresolved' adj not settled, undecided (*the matter remains unresolved*).

unrest' n discontent, rebellion.

unru'ly adj disorderly, badly behaved (*the unruly behaviour of the schoolchildren*).

unsa'voury adj unpleasant (*an unsavoury incident*).

unscathed' adj unhurt (*he emerged from the wreck unscathed*).

unscru'pulous adj having no standards of good and evil, wicked (*an unscrupulous criminal*).

unseem'ly adj not fitting, improper (*unseemly behaviour*).

unset'tle vb to upset, to disturb (*the incident unsettled them*).

unsheathe' vb to draw from a sheath or scabbard (*unsheathe his sword*).

unsight'ly adj ugly, unpleasant to look at (*an unsightly scar*).

unskilled' adj having no special skill or training.

unsoli'cited adj not asked for (*unsolicited advice*).

unsophis'ticated adj simple, natural, innocent.

unsound' adj 1 not healthy. 2 faulty (*equipment that is unsound*).

unspeak'able adj better or worse than can easily be expressed in words (*his unspeakable rudeness*).

unstud'ied adj natural (*with unstudied grace*).

unsuspect'ing adj free from fear of danger or evil, trusting (*too unsuspecting to think he was lying*).

until' prep up to the time of:—conj up to the time when.

untime'ly adj happening at the wrong or an inconvenient time (*an untimely visit*).

untold' adj 1 not related, not told (*untold stories*). 2 vast (*untold wealth*).

untouch'able n a member of the lowest Hindu caste, whom a higher-caste Hindu may not touch.

untoward' adj awkward, unsuitable, undesirable (*a journey in which nothing untoward happened*).

untrue' adj 1 not true. 2 not loyal, faithless (*untrue followers*).

untruth' n (*fml*) a lie, a falsehood (*tell an untruth*).

untruth'ful adj given to lying.

unu'sual adj rare, peculiar (*unusual patterns*).

unut'terable adj that cannot be described in words (*his unutterable rudeness*).

unveil' vb to uncover, to reveal, to disclose to view (*unveil the portrait*).

unversed' adj (*fml*) having no skill or knowledge (*unversed in computers*).

unwar'rantable adj unjustifiable, not able to be defended with good reasons (*his unwarrantable interference*).

unwa'ry adj not cautious enough, rash.

unwhole'some adj not good for health.

unwiel'dy adj 1 huge. 2 hard to move. 3 clumsy.

unwill'ing adj not willing, reluctant (*unwilling to get involved*).

unwit'ting adj not knowing (*the unwitting cause of her injury*).

unwont'ed adj (*fml*) rare, unusual (*his unwonted enthusiasm*).

unworld'ly adj 1 not interested in things in this life. 2 lacking experience of public life.

unwor'thy adj 1 not deserving (*a remark unworthy of comment*). 2 dishonourable (*unworthy thoughts*).

up adv 1 in or to a higher place, amount, etc. 2 above:—prep from below to.

upbraid' vb to scold, to blame (*upbraid the children for being late*).

up'bringing n one's early training at home and school.

upheav'al n 1 the pushing up of part of the earth's surface by forces below it. 2 a great change (*the upheaval of moving houses*).

uphill' adv in an upward direction:—adj 1 sloping upwards. 2 very difficult (*an uphill task*).

uphold' vb 1 to support (*upholding the right of free speech*). 2 to defend as correct (*the appeal judge upheld the original sentence*).

uphol'ster vb to provide (chairs, sofas, etc) with springs, stuffing, covering, etc:—n uphol'stery:—n uphol'sterer.

up'keep n 1 the money needed to keep anything in good condition. 2 the act of keeping in good health or condition (*the upkeep of the large house*).

uplift' vb 1 to raise. 2 to make to think of higher things:—n up'lift.

up'per *adj* higher in place or rank:—*n* the upper part of a shoe.

up'permost *adj* highest in place or rank (*the thought was uppermost in his mind*).

up'pish *adj* (*inf*) rather proud of oneself.

up'right *adj* **1** standing straight up. **2** honest (*an upright member of the community*):—*n* a vertical post.

up'roar *adj* confused noise (*there was an uproar when the concert was cancelled*).

uproar'ious *adj* noisy (*an uproarious party*).

uproot' *vb* to tear up by the roots (*the trees were uprooted in the gales*).

upset' *vb* **1** to overturn, to knock over (*tables upset during the fight in the bar*). **2** to spoil completely (*plans upset because of a change in the weather*). **3** to cause to be sad, worried etc (*his remarks upset her*):—*adj* **1** worried. **2** ill:—*n* **up'set 1** disturbance. **2** trouble. **3** a sudden misfortune.

upset price *n* the starting price at an auction sale.

up'shot *n* result, outcome (*the upshot of the negotiations was a pay rise for the workers*).

up'side-down *adv* with the top down and the bottom upwards.

up'stairs' *adv* on an upper floor of a house with stairs.

up'start *n* one who has risen quickly to a position of wealth or importance (*older members regard him as an upstart*).

up'tight *adj* tense and worried (*uptight about the exam results due tomorrow*).

ura'nium *n* a heavy white radioactive metal.

Ura'nus *n* the name of a planet.

ur'ban *adj* having to do with a city or city life (*urban areas of the country*).

urbane' *adj* polite, refined, smooth (*his urbane manner charmed everyone*):—*n* **ur-ban'ity**.

ur'chin *n* **1** (*old*) a ragged street boy. **2** a sea creature with a prickly shell.

urge *vb* **1** to press to do (*urge her to take the job*). **2** to suggest strongly (*urge caution*).

ur'gent *adj* requiring to be done quickly or at once, needing immediate attention (*it is an urgent matter*):—*n* **ur'gency**.

u'rinal, uri'nal *n* a place for passing urine.

u'rine *n* fluid passed from the kidneys and bladder.

urn *n* **1** a vase for the ashes of the dead. **2** a large container with a tap for making and serving tea, etc.

u'sage *n* treatment (*furniture subjected to rough usage*).

use *vb* **1** to do something with for a purpose (*use a knife to cut the butter*). **2** to employ (*use a great many long words*). **3** consume (*use all the butter*):—*n* **1** the act of using, the state of being used (*for use in emergencies*). **2** advantage, benefit, value (*a book that is of no use to us*). **3** the power of using (*lose the use of her legs*). **4** permission to use, the right to use (*give them the use of the car*):—**use up** to consume or exhaust, leaving nothing.

use'ful *adj* **1** of help (*useful advice*). **2** able to be used (*tools no longer useful*).

use'less *adj* **1** of no help. **2** not any use.

user-friendly *adj* designed to be used easily by a wide range of people who are not experts (*a user-friendly computer program*).

ush'er *n* one who meets people at the door (of a church, hall, etc) and shows them to their seats (*usher the guests to their seats*):—*vb* to show in:—*f* **usherette'**.

u'sual *adj* common, normal (*the usual price*).

u'surer *n* one whose business consists of lending money at high interest.

usurp' *vb* to seize power or property to which one has no right (*attempt to usurp the king's authority*):—*n* **usurpa'tion**:—*n* **usurp'er**.

u'sury *n* (*fml*) the lending of money at high interest.

uten'sil *n* a vessel or object in common household use (*kitchen utensils*).

utilita'rian *n* one who considers that a thing or action is good only if useful:—*also adj*.

utilita'rianism *n* the belief that only what is useful is good.

util'ity *n* **1** usefulness. **2** benefit. **3** a public service (*gas and other utilities*).

u'tilize *vb* (*fml*) to make use of (*utilize her powers of observation*).

ut'most *adj* **1** the farthest (*the utmost parts of the earth*). **2** the greatest (*utmost tact*).

uto'pia *n* an imaginary state in which everything is perfect.

uto'pian *adj* perfect but impossible to achieve.

ut'ter[1] *adj* complete, total (*he is an utter fool*).

ut'ter[2] *vb* to speak, to pronounce (*utter his first words*).

ut'terance *n* **1** something said. **2** a way of speaking.

ut'termost *adj* **1** farthest (*the uttermost parts of the earth*). **3** greatest (*the uttermost care*).

u'vula *n* a small piece of flesh hanging inside the back of the mouth.

uxo'rious *adj* foolishly fond of one's wife, always giving in to one's wife.

V

va'cancy *n* 1 an empty space. 2 a job to be filled (*advertise vacancies in the paper*).

va'cant *adj* 1 empty, not occupied (*vacant flats*). 2 unthinking (*in a vacant mood*).

vacate' *vb* 1 (*fml*) to leave empty (*vacate the flat*). 2 to give up (*vacate his position in the firm*).

vaca'tion *n* a period of holiday.

vac'cinate *vb* to inject with vaccine or with fluids giving protection against diseases:—*n* **vaccina'tion**.

vac'cine *n* 1 fluid tak en from a cow infected with cowpox and injected into a person's bloodstream to cause a mild attack of smallpox and so protect against worse attacks later. 2 a substance made from the germs that cause a particular disease and given to someone to prevent the disease.

vac'illate *vb* (*inf*) to keep on changing one's mind, to hesitate to come to a decision (*vacillate about moving house*):—*n* **vacilla'tion**.

vacu'ity *n* (*fml*) emptiness.

vac'uous *adj* 1 (*fml*) empty, meaningless (*a vacuous life*). 2 without expr ession (*look vacuous*).

vac'uum *n* a space from which all the air has been taken.

vacuum clean'er *n* a machine that cleans carpets, etc, by sucking dust into a bag.

vacuum flask *n* a container with two walls with a vacuum between them so that hot food keeps hot or cold food remains cold.

vag'abond *n* one who wanders aimlessly from place to place:—*adj* wandering.

vaga'ry *n* a piece of odd or unexpected behaviour (*the vagaries of human life/the vagaries of the weather*).

va'grant *adj* wandering:—*n* a wanderer or tramp:—*n* **va'grancy**.

vague *adj* not clear, not definite (*a vague idea of where he might be*):—*n* **vague'ness**.

vain *adj* 1 having no meaning or value (*vain words*). 2 too proud of oneself (*so vain that he is always looking in the mirror*). 3 useless (*a vain attempt to swim the river*):—**in vain** without result or effect.

vainglo'rious *adj* (*old*) boastfully proud.

vainglo'ry *n* (*old*) boastful pride.

val'ance *n* a short curtain hanging from a couch, bedstead, etc.

vale *n* (*fml*) a valley.

valedic'tion *n* (*fml*) a farewell:—*adj* **val-edic'tory**.

val'ency *n* the power of chemical elements to combine.

val'entine *n* 1 one chosen as a lover or beloved on St Valentine's day, 14 February. 2 a card expressing love sent on this day.

val'et *n* a man's personal servant.

valetudina'rian *n* (*old*) one who is always worrying about the state of his or her health.

val'iant *adj* brave (*a valiant attempt to save the drowning man*).

val'id *adj* 1 correct according to law (*a regulation no longer valid*). 2 good, sound (*asked to validate her husband's alibi*):—*n* **valid'ity**.

val'idate *vb* (*fml*) to make valid.

valise [va-leez'] *n* a travelling bag for holding belongings.

val'ley *n* the low ground between neighbouring hills or mountains, often watered by a river.

val'our *n* bravery, courage (*pay tribute to the valour of the soldiers*):—*adj* **val'orous**.

val'uable *adj* 1 of great worth or importance (*valuable advice*). 2 costly (*valuable jewels*).

val'uables *npl* precious things (*have her valuables insured*).

val'uate *vb* to estimate the worth of:—*n* **val'uator**.

valua'tion *n* the estimated worth, price or importance of a thing (*ask for a valuation of the property*).

val'ue *n* 1 worth, importance (*information that was of value to the police*). 2 price, cost (*the marked value of the vase*). 3 *pl* the standards by which one judges the worth of things (*moral values*).

val'uer *n* one who estimates the value of things.

valve *n* 1 a device that, when opened, allows gas, air, fluid, etc, to pass through in one direction only. 2 in radio sets, a device by which one can control the power of waves transmitted or received.

vamp *n* the upper part of a boot or shoe:—*vb* to play music made up as one plays.

vam'pire n 1 in old stories, a ghost supposed to suck the blood of the living. 2 a bloodsucking bat.

van[1] short fot **vanguard**.

van[2] n a covered car or wagon for goods (*the van that delivers bread*).

van'dal n one who purposefully and pointlessly destroys or damages public buildings or other property:—n **van'dalism**.

vane n 1 a weathercock. 2 the blade of a windmill, propeller, etc.

van'guard n (*abbr* **van**) 1 the front part of an army or fleet. 2 those leading the way.

vanill'a n a flavouring prepared from a tropical plant (*a dessert flavoured with vanilla essence*).

van'ish vb 1 to disappear (*the chill seems to have vanished*). 2 to pass out of sight (*the car vanished round the corner*).

van'ity n 1 lack of meaning or value (*the vanity of human ambition*). 2 too great pride in oneself, conceit (*she was disliked for her vanity*).

van'quish vb to defeat completely (*vanquish the enemy*).

van'tage n 1 (*old*) advantage. 2 a point in lawn tennis (after deuce).

vantage point n a good position (*the hill was a good vantage point from which to see the procession*).

vap'id adj lacking in spirit, dull (*so vapid as to bore everyone*).

va'porize vb to turn into vapour.

va'pour n 1 the gas given off by a body when sufficiently heated. 2 mist.

va'riable adj 1 quick to change (*variable in her opinions*). 2 changing often or easily (*variable temperature*).

va'riance n:—**at variance with** in disagreement with.

va'riant n a different or alternative form:—adj different (*variant spellings of the word*).

varia'tion n change, difference (*variations in temperature*).

va'ricose adj:—**varicose veins** swollen veins.

va'riegate vb to mark with different colours (*the leaves were variegated*).

vari'ety n 1 the state of being different. 2 a collection of different or slightly different things. 3 a class or species. 4 a theatre show with performers of different kinds.

var'let n (*old*) 1 a servant. 2 a rascal.

var'nish n a clear, sticky liquid used to give a shiny surface to wood, metal, paper, etc:—vb to coat with varnish (*varnish her nails in red*).

va'ry vb to make or become different, to change (*his rate of work never varies*).

vase [väz] n a vessel used for holding flowers or as an ornament.

Vas'eline n the trademark of a soothing jelly made from petroleum.

vas'sal n in the feudal system, one who held land from a lord on condition that he performed certain services for the lord.

vast adj 1 of great extent (*vast plans*). 2 huge (*a vast improvement*).

vat n a large tub or tank.

Vat'ican n the Pope's palace in Rome.

vaudeville [vōd'-ê-vil] n an entertainment including songs and dances, usu comic, a light variety entertainment.

vault[1] n. 1 an arched roof. 2 a room, usu underground, with an arched roof (e.g. a cellar, a tomb, etc).

vault[2] vb to jump over while resting the hand on something for support (*vault over the fences*):—n a leap (over something).

vaunt vb (*old*) to boast:—*also n*.

veal n the flesh of a calf.

veer vb to change direction (*the wind has veered to the north*).

veg'an [vee'gan] n a person who eats no food made from animal products.

veg'etable n a plant grown for food (*soup made with fresh vegetables*).

vegeta'rian n one who eats only vegetable food, taking no meat.

veg'etate vb 1 to live a plant's life. 2 to lead a dull, inactive life (*she is vegetating staying in her house all day*).

vegeta'tion n 1 plants in general. 2 the plants of a particular region (*jungle vegetation*).

ve'hement adj 1 full of strong feeling, passionate (*a vehement protest*). 2 having a forceful way of speaking:—n **ve'hemence**.

ve'hicle n 1 any type of carriage, cart, etc, used on land for carrying people or things. 2 (*fml*) a means of doing something (*the newspaper is a vehicle of communication*):—adj **vehic'ular**.

veil *n* **1** a cloth worn over the face to hide or protect it (*a bridal veil*). **2** something that hides or conceals (*a veil of mist*):—*vb* **1** to conceal (*try to conceal her dislike of him*). **2** to cover (*mist veiling the hill*):—**take the veil** to become a nun.

vein *n* **1** one of the blood vessels through which blood flows back to the heart. **2** a sap tube or small rib of a leaf. **3** a layer of mineral in a rock. **4** a mood (*in a lighthearted vein*).

Vel'cro (*trademark*) *n* a type of fastening for clothes, etc. consisting of two strips of fabric which stick to each other when pressed together.

veld, veldt [velt] *n* in South Africa, a wide expanse of grassy country with few trees.

vel'lum *n* a fine parchment made from the skin of calves, lambs or kids.

velo'cipede *n* an early form of bicycle.

velo'city *n* speed.

velours [vê-lör] *n* a material like velvet.

vel'vet *n* a thick silk fabric or substitute, with a soft pile on one side.

velveteen' *n* an imitation velvet made from cotton or cotton and silk mixed.

vel'vety *adj* soft and smooth, like velvet (*the velvety skin of a peach*).

ve'nal *adj* ready to take bribes, corrupt.

vend *vb* (*old*) to sell.

vendet'ta *n* a feud between two families in which each is bound to revenge the death of any of its members killed by the other.

vending machine *n* a machine from which certain items can be bought by putting coins in it (*chocolate from a vending machine*).

ven'dor *n* one who sells (*a street vendor selling newspapers*).

veneer' *n* **1** a thin layer (of fine wood, plastic, etc) glued on the surface of another inferior one. **2** something that appears fine but is not deep or lasting (*a veneer of sincerity*):—*vb* to cover with veneer.

ven'erable *adj* worthy of respect because of age or goodness, old and honourable.

ven'erate *vb* to feel great respect for, to show one's respect for (*venerate the old soldiers*):—*n* **venera'tion.**

Vene'tian *adj* from or of Venice.

Venetian blind *n* a window blind made from horizontal strips of thin wood, plastic, etc.

ven'geance *n* harm done in return for harm or injury received, revenge (*seek vengeance for his brother's death*).

venge'ful *adj* desiring revenge.

ve'nial *adj* that can be forgiven, slight (*venial sins*).

ven'ison *n* the flesh of deer.

ven'om *n* **1** (*fml*) poison (*the venom of the cobra*). **2** spite (*a look full of venom*).

ven'omous *adj* **1** poisonous (*venomous reptile*). **2** spiteful (*venomous remarks*).

vent *n* **1** a hole or opening through which air, smoke, etc, can pass. **2** an outlet. **3** expression (*give vent to his rage*):—*vb* to give free expression to (*vent his rage on the children*).

ven'tilate *vb* **1** to allow fresh air to pass into or through (*ventilate the room by opening the windows*). **2** to discuss freely (*ventilate topics of interest to all*):—*n* **ventila'tion.**

ven'tilator *n* any device to let in fresh air.

ventril'oquist *n* one able to speak without moving the lips, in such a way that the voice seems to come from another person:—*n* **ventril'oquism.**

ven'ture *n* an undertaking that may lead one into loss or danger (*a business venture*):—*vb* **1** to dare (*venture to go into the jungle alone*). **2** to risk (*venture his savings on the scheme*).

ven'turesome *adj* (*fml*) ready to take risks, daring.

ven'ue *n* the place appointed for a trial or public event (*the venue of the match*).

Ve'nus *n* **1** the Roman goddess of love. **2** one of the planets in the solar system.

vera'cious *adj* (*fml*) true, truthful.

vera'city *n* (*fml*) truthfulness (*doubt the veracity of his statement*).

veran'da, veran'dah *n* a covered platform or open balcony along the wall of a house.

verb *n* a word that tells of the action or state of the subject of a sentence.

verb'al *adj* **1** of or in words. **2** by word of mouth. **3** word for word:—*adv* **verb'ally.**

verba'tim *adv* word for word (*he wrote down the statement verbatim*).

verbe'na *n* a flowering plant with lemon-scented leaves.

ver'biage *n* (*fml*) **1** the use of more words than are necessary. **2** too many words (*get rid of much of the verbiage in the report*).

verbose' *adj* (*fml*) using too many words, using more words than are necessary (*a verbose style*):—*n* **verbos'ity**.

ver'dant *adj* (*fml*) **1** green with leaves, grass, etc (*the verdant lawns*). **2** fresh and green.

ver'dict *n* **1** the decision of a jury. **2** a considered opinion or judgment (*their verdict on the food at the new restaurant*).

verdigris [ver'-di-grês] *n* the green rust on metals of various kinds.

ver'dure *n* (*fml*) fresh green grass, leaves, etc, green vegetation.

verge *n* **1** the edging of a road etc (*the grass verges of the motorway*). **2** edge, brink (*on the verge of losing his temper*):—*also vb*.

ver'ger *n* a church attendant or usher.

ver'ify *vb* **1** confirm (*verify the statement*). **2** to prove to be true:—*n* **verifica'tion**.

ver'ily *adv* in truth.

versimil'itude *n* (*fml*) the appearance of truth, truth to life.

ver'itable *adj* (*fml* or *hum*) true, real, actual (*a veritable feast*).

ver'ity *n* (*fml*) truth.

vermicel'li *n* long thin threads of paste made from wheaten flour.

vermil'ion *n* a bright red colour.

ver'min *n*. **1** small animals that do harm (e.g. to crops), as rats, mice, etc. **2** insects connected with discomfort to human beings or dirt.

ver'minous *adj* covered by or full of vermin.

vernac'ular *n* the language spoken from infancy by the people of a certain country or district.

ver'nal *adj* (*fml*) having to do with the spring.

veron'ica *n* a flowering plant.

ver'satile *adj* able to do many different kinds of things (*a versatile tool*):—*n* **ver-satil'ity**.

verse *n* **1** poetry. **2** writing set down in the form of poetry. **3** a stanza. **4** a short division of a chapter of the Bible.

versed *adj* skilled, having knowledge (*a student versed in Latin*).

versifica'tion *n* the act or art of making verse or verses.

ver'sify *vb* (*fml*) **1** to write poetry or verse. **2** to turn into verse:—*n* **ver'sifier**.

ver'sion *n* **1** an account or description peculiar to a particular person (*his version of the events before the accident*). **2** a translation.

ver'sus *prep* against.

ver'tebra *n* (*pl* **ver'tebrae**) one of the bones of the spine.

ver'tebrate *adj* having a backbone.

ver'tex *n* (*pl* **vertices**) the highest point, the top (*the vertex of the pyramid*).

ver'tical *adj* upright, at right angles to the bottom or ground level, running straight from top to bottom.

ver'tigo *n* dizziness, giddiness (*suffer from vertigo at the top of the ladder*).

verve *n* enthusiasm, liveliness (*set about the task with verve*).

ver'y *adj* true, real (*the very person we were looking for*):—*adv* extremely.

ves'pers *npl* evening service in church.

ves'sel *n* **1** a container for holding things. **2** a ship or boat.

vest *n* **1** an undergarment worn next the skin. **2** (*esp Amer*) a waistcoat.

ves'tal *adj* pure, devoted to chastity.

vested interests *npl* rights that have been long held and will not readily be given up.

ves'tibule *n* a porch or small compartment between the outer and inner front doors of a house, a small entrance hall.

ves'tige *n* **1** a mark or trace (*vestiges of old customs*). **2** a very small amount (*not a vestige of the truth*).

vest'ment *n* a garment or robe, esp that worn by a priest or official.

ves'try *n* a room in a church where the robes of priests, etc, are kept.

ves'ture *n* (*fml*) dress, clothing (*the bishop's vesture*).

vet¹ short for **veterinary surgeon**.

vet² *vb* (**vet'ted**, **vet'ting**) to approve, to pass as sound (*have to have his application vetted by the committee*).

vetch *n* **1** a plant of the bean family used as fodder. **2** a common hedgerow plant.

vet'eran *n* an old person having long experience, esp as a soldier (*a veteran of the last war*):—*also adj*.

vet'erinary adj having to do with the diseases of domestic animals.

vet'erinary sur'geon n (abbr **vet**) an animal doctor.

ve'to n (pl **ve'toes**) the right to refuse or forbid:—vb to forbid, to refuse to allow discussion of (vetoing the suggestion).

vex vb to make angry, to annoy (their mother was vexed by the children's behaviour):—n **vexa'tion**.

vexa'tious adj annoying, troublesome.

via [vee'-a] prep by way of.

vi'able adj **1** able to exist or survive (viable foetus). **2** workable (viable proposition).

vi'aduct n a long arched bridge carrying a road or railway over a valley, etc.

vi'al n a small bottle (a vial of perfume).

vi'ands npl (fml or old) food.

vi'brant adj **1** quivering (singing in a vibrant voice). **2** full of ener gy (a vibrant personality). **3** bright, shining (vibrant colours).

vibrate' vb **1** to move quickly backwards and forwards. **2** to shake, to quiver:—n **vi-bra'tion**.

vic'ar n the priest or minister in charge of a parish.

vic'arage n the house of a vicar.

vica'rious adj **1** suffered or undergone in place of another. **2** enjoyed or experienced thr ough the medium of other people (vicarious pleasures).

vice[1] n a fault, a bad habit (smoking was his only vice).

vice[2] n an instrument for holding something (a piece of wood, metal, etc) steady while one is working on it.

vice[3] [vī'-si] prep in place of.

vice- [vīs] prefix in the place of, next in order to (vice-admiral, vice-chairman, etc).

vice versa [vī'-si ver'-sa] adv the other way round (dogs dislike cats and vice versa).

vicere'gal adj having to do with a viceroy.

vice'roy n one who rules on behalf of a king or queen.

vicin'ity n neighbourhood (look for a restaurant in the vicinity of the hotel).

vi'cious adj wicked, evil, ill-tempered (a vicious temper/a vicious dog).

vicious circle n a series in which each bad event or action or argument leads on to a worse one.

viciss'itude n a sudden change in fortune (the vicissitudes of the stock market).

vic'tim n **1** one who suffers either from his or her own faults or from outside circumstances (the police have not named the victims killed in the explosion). **2** a person or animal killed and offered in sacrifice.

vic'timize vb to make to suffer, to treat unfairly (people victimized for their beliefs):—n **victimiza'tion**.

vic'tor n one who wins or conquers.

victo'rious adj successful in a war, battle, contest or match (the victorious team).

vic'tory n the winning of a war, battle, contest or match (victory in the tennis tournament).

victual [vitl] vb (old) **1** to supply with food. **2** to take in supplies of food:—n **victualler** [vit'-lêr].

victuals [vitls] npl food.

vi'deo n the transmission or recording of television programmes or films using a television set and a **video recorder** and **videotape**:—also vb.

vie vb to try hard to do better than, to compete with (the two boys spent the evening vying for her attention).

view n **1** all that can be seen at one look or from one point, a scene (the view from the hill). **2** opinion (in his view she is not suitable for the job). **3** intention (buy the house with the intention of building an extension):—vb **1** to look at (view the property). **2** to examine, to consider (view all possible solutions to the problem).

view'point n **1** a place from which one can see the surroundings well. **2** the way in which one considers or thinks of something (try to see the problem from the viewpoint of the teacher).

vi'gil n an act of staying awake all night or remaining watchful (keep a vigil at his injured son's bedside).

vi'gilance n watchfulness, care.

vi'gilant adj watchful, careful (the police asked the public to remain vigilant).

vignette [veen-yet] n (fml) **1** a small printed ornament in a book. **2** a portrait of the head and bust against a light or shaded background, with no border. **3** a character sketch (a vignette of Queen Victoria).

vig'orous adj full of strength or energy, active (vigorous young athletes/a vigorous attack on her writing).

vig'our n strength and energy, power of mind.

Viking [vī'-king] *n* a Norse pirate or sea rover of the 8th-10th centuries.

vile *adj* 1 wicked, evil (*a vile crime/a vile old man*). 2 disgusting, horrible (*a vile meal at the new restaurant*).

vil'ify *vb* to speak ill of (*he was vilified by the press for his part in the affair*):—*n* vilifica'tion.

vil'la *n* 1 a country house. 2 in a town, a house with a garden and a space between it and the houses on either side.

vill'age *n* a group of houses, shops, etc, smaller than a town.

vill'ager *n* one who lives in a village.

vill'ain *n* a bad or wicked person, a scoundrel (*police are looking for the dangerous villain*).

vill'ainous *adj* wicked.

vill'ainy *n* wickedness.

vill'ein *n* in the Middle Ages, one occupying some land, and obliged in return for it to perform certain services for his lord.

vim *n* energy, strength, force (*a gymnastic performance that was full of vim*).

vin'dicate *vb* 1 to show that charges made are untrue, to free from blame (*the testimony of the witness completely vindicated him*). 2 to prove that something is true or right, to justify (*her success vindicates his faith in her*):—*n* vindica'tion.

vindic'tive *adj* eager to obtain revenge, spiteful (*have a vindictive streak*).

vine *n* a climbing plant that bears grapes.

vin'egar *n* a sour liquid, made from wine or malt and used in cooking or for seasoning.

vin'egary *adj* sour.

vin'ery *n* a heated glasshouse for growing grapes.

vineyard [vin'-yärd] *n* a field or area in which vines are cultivated.

vin'tage *n* 1 the number of grapes or amount of wine obtained from one vineyard in a year. 2 all the wine made from the grapes grown in a certain year.

vint'ner *n* (*old*) a wine-seller.

vinyl *n* a kind of strong plastic that can bend easily, used to make wall and floor coverings, etc, and, especially formerly, records.

vi'ol *n* an old form of violin.

vio'la[1] *n* a large type of violin.

vio'la[2] *n* a family of plants, including the violet, pansy, etc.

vi'olate *vb* 1 (*old*) to treat with violence, to rape. 2 to break (*violate the peace treaty*):—*n* viola'tion.

vi'olence *n* 1 great force (*the violence of the wind*). 2 harm, injury (*he was so angry that he resorted to violence*).

vi'olent *adj* 1 strong (*a violent quarrel*). 2 using force (*the man grew more violent*).

vi'olet *n* 1 a small bluish-purple flower. 2 a bluish-purple colour:—*adj* bluish-purple (*violet eyes*).

violin' *n* a four-stringed musical instrument played with a bow:—*n* vi'olinist.

violoncello [vī-ê-lên-chel'-ō] *n* (*abbr* cello) a large violin giving deep notes:—*n* vio-loncell'ist.

vi'per *n* 1 a poisonous snake. 2 (*lit*) a treacherous or spiteful person.

vira'go *n* (*pl* vira'goes *or* vira'gos) a bad-tempered scolding woman.

vir'gin *n* a chaste unmarried girl or woman:—*adj* 1 pure. 2 still in its original condition (*virgin territory*):—*n* virgin'ity.

vir'ginal[1] *adj* pure.

vir'ginal[2] *n* an old type of piano.

vir'ile *adj* manly, strong (*virile athletes*):—*n* viril'ity.

vir'tual *adj* being so in fact but not in name or title (*her husband is so weak that she is virtual head of the company*).

virtual reality *n* the simulation by a computer of three-dimensional images which creates the impression of surrounding the person looking at them and which allows him/her to interact with the images, using special electronic equipment.

vir'tue *n* 1 goodness of life or character. 2 a good quality, power, strength (*generosity is her greatest virtue*).

virtuo'so *n* (*pl* virtuo'si *or* virtuo'sos) an exceptionally highly skilled musician or other artist:—*n* virtuos'ity.

vir'tuous *adj* morally good, of good character, leading a good life.

vir'ulent *adj* 1 powerful, dangerous (*virulent passions*). 2 full of hatred, spiteful (*virulent criticisms*):—*n* vir'ulence.

vi'rus *n* any of various types of germ that are smaller than bacteria and cause infectious diseases in the body.

visa [vee'-za] *n* a permit stamped on a passport, giving the owner the right to enter or leave a particular country.

vis'age *n* (*fml*) the face.

vis-à-vis [veez-a-vee'] *prep* (*fml*) with regard to (*the committee's position vis-à-vis the proposed changes*).

viscid [vis'-id] *adj* sticky (*a viscid substance*).

viscount [vī'-kount] *n* a nobleman of the rank below an earl.

vis'cous *adj* sticky (*viscous substances*):—*n* **viscos'ity**.

visibil'ity *n* **1** clearness to sight. **2** the state of weather, atmosphere, etc, as they affect one's ability to see clearly (*visibility was poor on the motorway*).

vis'ible *adj* able to be seen.

vi'sion *n* **1** the ability to see, sight (*have poor vision in one eye*). **2** something imagined as in a dream (*God came to him in a vision*). **3** something seen that has no bodily existence (*see a ghostly vision*). **4** the power to foresee consequences (*he had a vision of the result*).

vi'sionary *adj* **1** existing only in the imagination (*visionary scheme*). **2** full of fancies or hopes of perfection (*a visionary writer*):—*n* one who believes in ideals that cannot be achieved in his or her lifetime.

vis'it *vb* **1** to go to see or stay with (*visiting his parents*). **2** to call upon (*the minister visited his congregation*):—*n* **1** a call upon. **2** a short stay.

vis'itor *n* one who visits.

visita'tion *n* **1** an official visit. **2** suffering believed to be sent by God as punishment.

vi'sor, vi'zor *n* **1** (*old*) a movable part of a helmet, protecting the face when closed. **2** the peak of a cap.

vis'ta *n* a narrow view, as seen between rows of houses, trees, etc.

vi'tal *adj* **1** very important (*a meeting vital to the peace treaty*). **2** unable to be done without, necessary to life (*vital organs*).

vital'ity *n* energy, vigour, liveliness.

vi'tals *npl* the organs of the body necessary to life.

vit'amin *n* one of several substances found in food, necessary to the health of the body.

vi'tiate *vb* (*fml*) to make faulty, to spoil completely (*the strength of his argument was vitiated by its impracticality*).

vit'reous *adj* of or like glass.

vit'riol *n* sulphuric acid.

vitriol'ic *adj* using violent language, full of hatred (*a vitriolic attack on the government policy*).

vitu'perate *vb* to abuse, to speak ill of (*he vituperated against the politician*):—*n* **vi·tupera'tion**:—*adj* **vitu'perative**.

viva voce [vee'-va vō'-see] *adj* (*fml*) by word of mouth (*a viva voce exam*).

viva'cious *adj* lively, bright and talkative (*a vivacious personality*).

viva'city *n* liveliness (*the girl's vivacity*).

viv'id *adj* **1** bright, striking. **2** appearing true to life (*a vivid dream/a vivid description*).

viv'ify *vb* (*fml*) to make lively or lifelike.

vivisec'tion *n* the cutting up of a living animal to assist scientific experiment.

vix'en *n* **1** a female fox. **2** a bad-tempered woman.

vix'enish *adj* bad-tempered.

viz *adv* (short for Latin *videlicet*) that is, namely.

vizier [vi-zeer'] *n* a high political official in Moslem countries.

vizor *see* **visor**.

vocab'ulary *n* **1** all the words used by a certain person or a certain work (*a child with a large vocabulary*). **2** a list of words with their meaning (*a vocabulary at the back of the book*).

vo'cal *adj* **1** having to do with the voice, spoken or sung (*the vocal organs*). **2** intended to be heard (*vocal opposition to the plan*).

vo'calist *n* a singer.

voca'tion *n* **1** one's employment, profession or trade. **2** the particular work one feels one is especially fitted for (*being a minister of the church is a vocation*).

voca'tional *adj* concerned with one's profession or trade.

vocif'erate *vb* (*fml*) to shout.

vocif'erous *adj* **1** noisy. **2** expressing opinions loudly or openly (*a vociferous protest from the crowd*).

vod'ka *n* a strong drink, made from rye, originating in Russia.

vogue [vōg] *n* a popular or passing fashion (*the length of skirt currently in vogue*).

voice *n* **1** the sound produced through the mouth when speaking or singing (*the choir boy has a lovely voice*). **2** a vote, an opinion (*the voice of the people*). **3** the right to speak or express an opinion (*the workers had no voice*). **4** (*gram*) a grouping of forms of the verb according to whether they are active or passive:—*vb* **1** to say. **2** to express (*voice their disapproval*).

voice'mail *n* an electronic system for storing telephone messages so that they can be listened to later.

void *adj* **1** (*fml*) empty (*a statement void of meaning*). **2** having no effect, having no force (*regulations that are now void*):—*n* empty space.

vol'atile *adj* **1** easily changing into gas. **2** able to evaporate readily. **3** changing moods or ideas often (*a volatile personality*).

volca'no *n* (*pl* **volca'noes**) a mountain with an opening at its summit through which molten rock, metals, etc, are occasionally forced up in a red-hot stream from beneath the surface of the earth:—*adj* **volcan'ic**.

vole *n* the water-rat.

voli'tion *n* will-power (*leave of his own volition*).

voll'ey *n* **1** the firing of several guns or throwing of many things at the same time. **2** the speaking of a number of words in quick succession (*a volley of questions addressed to the speaker*). **3** in tennis, the hitting of a ball before it touches the ground:—*vb* **1** to send a volley. **2** to hit (a ball) before it touches the ground.

volt *n* the unit used in measuring electrical power or force.

volt'age *n* electrical power measured in volts.

vol'uble *adj* speaking much (*she is voluble on the subject of her son's education*):—*n* **volubil'ity**.

vol'ume *n* **1** a book. **2** one of a series in a set of books (*volume three of the encyclopedia*). **3** the amount of space taken up by anything (*the volume of water in the tank*). **4** a large mass or amount (*the volume of trade*). **5** level of sound (*turn up the volume on the radio*).

volu'minous *adj* **1** taking up much space (*a voluminous skirt*). **2** very big, holding a lot (*a voluminous suitcase*).

vol'untary *adj* done of one's own free will, not forced (*face voluntary early retirement*):—*n* an organ solo before or after a church service.

volunteer' *n* one who offers to do something without being asked or ordered (*volunteers required to visit the elderly*):—*vb* **1** to offer one's services. **2** to give (information) unasked (*she*

volunteered that she had no experience of doing the job).

volup'tuary *n* (*fml*) one who gives himself up to bodily pleasures.

volup'tuous *adj* **1** tempting to bodily pleasures (*the voluptuous movements of the dancers*). **2** giving pleasure to the senses (*the voluptuous feel of velvet*). **3** having a full, rounded figure (*voluptuous women*).

vom'it *vb* **1** to throw up from the stomach through the mouth, to be sick. **2** to put out in large clouds, e.g. of smoke (*factory chimneys vomiting black smoke*).

voo'doo *n* a primitive and degraded form of worship, witchcraft.

vora'cious *adj* very greedy:—*n* **vora'city**.

vor'tex *n* **1** a whirlpool. **2** a whirlwind.

vo'tary *n* (*fml*) **1** one bound to an intention by vows. **2** an enthusiastic supporter (*a votary of classical music*):—*f* **vo'taress**.

vote *n* **1** an expression of opinion for or against a proposal (*sixty votes for the proposal and ten against*). **2** the support given by an individual to a person contesting an election:—*vb* **1** to give a vote. **2** to decide by vote:—*n* **vo'ter**.

vo'tive *adj* (*fml*) given to fulfil a vow or solemn promise.

vouch *vb* to speak (on behalf of) with confidence, to confirm, to guarantee (*able to vouch for his friend's statement*).

vouch'er *n* **1** a paper handed over in exchange for goods instead of cash (*the company provided staff with luncheon vouchers*). **2** a receipt.

vouchsafe' *vb* (*fml*) to be good enough to give or grant (*reluctant to vouchsafe a reply*).

vow *n* a solemn promise, a promise made to God:—*vb* to promise solemnly.

vow'el *n* **1** a simple sound (*a, e, i, o, u*) made by the voice without obstruction to the air passage. **2** the letter representing it.

voy'age *n* a long journey, esp by sea (*a voyage to Australia*).

vul'canite *n* rubber hardened by treating with sulphur.

vul'canize *vb* to treat rubber with sulphur.

vul'gar *adj* **1** coarse in manners or behaviour, rude (*a vulgar comment*/*it is vulgar to eat with your* *mouth open*). **2** (*old*) having to do with ordinary people, low.

vulgar fraction *n* a fraction other than a decimal fraction (e.g. ⁵/₈).

vulgarity *n* rudeness, coarseness.

vulgarize *vb* to make less polite or refined, to spoil by trying to make widely popular (*she considers the town has been vulgarized by the new shopping centre*).

Vulgate *n* an ancient Latin version of the Bible.

vulnerable *adj* **1** able to be wounded or hurt (*he liked to pick on vulnerable people*). **2** weakly defended against attack (*the vulnerable position of the army*).

vulpine *adj* (*fml*) **1** of or like a fox. **2** crafty, cunning.

vulture *n* a large bird that feeds on the flesh of dead animals.

W

wad *n* **1** a lump of soft fibrous material for padding garments, stopping holes, etc. **2** a bundle (*a wad of bank notes*).

wad'ding *n* soft material used for padding, etc.

wad'dle *vb* to walk, rolling from side to side, as a duck (*she was so fat she waddled*):—also *n*.

wade *vb* **1** to walk through water. **2** to walk slowly and with difficulty. **3** to read through with difficulty.

wa'der *n* **1** any long-legged bird that wades in water in search of food. **2** *pl* high waterproof boots worn by fishermen, etc.

wa'fer *n* **1** a very thin cake or biscuit. **2** a thin disc of paper, etc, stuck on the back of a letter to seal it.

waffle [wǎf'-êl] *n* a batter cake baked in a mould.

waft *vb* to bear along gently through the air.

wag *vb* (**wagged'**, **wag'ging**) to shake up and down or to and fro (*he wagged his finger while giving the children a warning*):—*n* **1** a wagging movement. **2** one fond of telling jokes or making amusing comments.

wage *n* money paid regularly for work done (*often pl*):—*vb* to carry on (*wage war*).

wa'ger *n* a bet:—*vb* to bet.

wag'gle *vb* to wag.

wag'on, wag'gon *n* **1** a four-wheeled cart. **2** a railway truck.

wag'tail *n* a small bird with a long tail that it wags constantly.

waif *n* a homeless child or animal.

wail *vb* to cry aloud in grief, distress (*the children wailed when their parents went away*):—*n* a loud cry of grief, a moaning cry.

wain *n* (*old*) a wagon.

wains'cot, wains'coting *ns* **1** a wooden board running around the foot of the walls of a room. **2** wooden panelling on walls.

waist *n* the narrowest part of the human trunk, just below the ribs.

waist'coat *n* a sleeveless garment worn by men below the jacket.

wait *vb* to stay in a place in the hope or expectation of something happening (*wait for the lights to change*). **2** to serve at table:—*n* time spent waiting (*a wait of five hours*).

wait'er *n* a person employed to serve food at table:—*f* **wait'ress**.

waits *npl* (*old*) a group of singers who go from house to house at Christmastime singing carols.

waive *vb* to give up, not to insist on (*waive his usual fee*).

wake¹ *vb* (*pt* **woke**, *pp* **wo'ken**) **1** to arouse from sleep (*wake the baby with the loud music*). **2** to return to full consciousness after sleep (*she woke early*):—*n* a watch kept over a dead body until the time of burial, sometimes with feasting.

wake² *n* the track left on water by a moving ship:—**in the wake of** behind, following.

wake'ful *adj* not sleeping (*a wakeful child*).

wa'ken *vb* to wake.

walk *vb* **1** to advance step by step. **2** to go on foot:—*n* **1** an outing on foot. **2** one's manner of walking. **3** a road or path:—**walk of life** one's rank or work in life (*people in a humble walk of life*).

walk'ing stick *n* a stick carried when walking.

walk'over *n* **1** an easy victory (*they were so bad that our team had a walkover*). **2** a victory granted because there has been no opposition (*she had a walkover in the match because her opponent did not turn up*).

wall *n* **1** a barrier of stone, brick, etc. **2** one of the sides of a building, room, etc:—*vb* to provide with a wall (*the garden was walled in*).

wall'aby *n* a type of small kangaroo.

wall'et *n* a pocket-case for money, papers, etc.

wall'flower *n* **1** a sweet-smelling garden flower. **2** a person who is not dancing because he or she has no partner.

wal'lop *vb* to thrash soundly, to strike heavily:—also *n*.

wal'low *vb* **1** to roll about in mud, dirt, etc. **2** to enjoy what is dirty or unpleasant (*wallow in his rival's misfortune*).

wall'paper *n* coloured or decorative paper covering the walls of rooms.

wal'nut *n* **1** a tree whose wood is much used for making furniture. **2** its eatable nut.

wal'rus *n* a large tusked sea mammal that can live on both land and sea.

waltz *n* **1** a dance for two people. **2** music for such a dance:—*vb* to dance a waltz (*dancers waltzing round the room*).

wan *adj* pale, sickly-looking (*wan after her long illness*).

wand *n* **1** a long thin stick. **2** the rod of a magician or conjurer (*wave his magic wand*).

wan'der *vb* **1** to go purposelessly from place to place. **2** to lose one's way (*wander off the path*). **3** to talk in a disconnected manner (*the lecturer began to wander*). **4** to go off the point:—*n* **wan'derer**.

wane *vb* **1** to grow less or smaller. **2** to lose strength or power:—**on the wane** growing less.

wan'gle *vb* to arrange cleverly or by trickery (*try to wangle a ticket for the game*):—*also n:—n* **wan'gler**.

want *n* **1** need. **2** longing. **3** shortage. **4** poverty:—*vb* **1** to lack. **2** to need. **3** to desire.

want'ing *adj* **1** not as good as required (*he found his work wanting*). **2** lacking (*a car wanting a tyre*). **3** foolish-minded.

wan'ton *adj* **1** immoral. **2** malicious:—*n* an immoral person.

war *n* **1** a state of fighting and enmity between nations or within a nation. **2** an active campaign against something (*the war against racism*):—*vb* (**warred'**, **war'ring**) to make war.

war'ble *vb* to sing, as a bird.

war'bler *n* a songbird.

war cry *n* **1** a rallying cry used in battle. **2** a word or phrase used to express the aim of an active group or movement.

ward *vb* (*with* **off**) **1** to defend oneself against (*ward off the blow with his arm*). **2** to defeat (an attack) for the time being:—*n* **1** in a hospital, a large room containing several beds. **2** a division of a town for the purposes of local government. **3** a person under the legal care of another until he or she is old enough to manage his or her own affairs (*he is the ward of his uncle*).

war'den *n* **1** one who guards or helps to protect. **2** the head of a college or hostel.

war'der *n* a guard in a prison:—*f* **war'dress**.

war'drobe *n* **1** a cupboard for hanging clothes. **2** all a person's clothes (*get a new spring wardrobe*).

ward'room *n* the officers' room on a warship.

ware *n* **1** articles manufactured out of some material (e.g. *hardware*). **2** *pl* goods for sale (*a flowergirl selling her wares*).

ware'house *n* a building for storing goods.

war'fare *n* the carrying on of fighting in war.

war'like *adj* **1** fond of fighting. **2** ready to do battle.

warlock *n* one having magical powers (*witches and warlocks*).

warm *adj* **1** quite hot (*warm water*). **2** affectionate (*a warm greeting*). **3** sincere (*with warm regards*):—*vb* to make or become warm.

warm-heart'ed *adj* kindly, generous.

warmth *n* **1** gentle heat. **2** excitement. **3** sincerity.

warn *vb* **1** to advise against possible danger or error (*warn against walking home alone*). **2** to tell to be careful (*warn the children not to cross the road*).

warn'ing *n* **1** advice to be careful. **2** advice that danger or trouble lies ahead.

warp *vb* **1** to twist or bend out of shape (*warp the metal rod*). **2** to become twisted or bent. **3** to spoil the nature or character of (*the unhappy childhood warped her*). **4** to haul a ship along by pulling on a rope attached to a point on shore:—*n* **1** the lengthwise threads in a loom (a weaving-machine). **2** a strong rope.

war'path *n:*—**on the warpath** ready to fight, quarrel or scold.

war'rant *n* a written document giving the right to do certain things (*a warrant for his arrest*):—*vb* **1** to give the right or permission to. **2** to be good reason for, to justify (*that does not warrant his rudeness*) **3** (*fml*) to be sure (that) (*I warrant that he has run away*).

warrant of'ficer *n* in the services, an officer appointed by warrant but not holding a commission.

war'ren *n* many rabbit burrows in one piece of land.

war'rior *n* **1** one good at fighting. **2** a soldier.

wart *n* a hard dry growth on the skin.

wart'hog *n* a type of wild pig found in Africa.

war'y adj careful, cautious, not rushing into danger (wary of trusting strangers).

wash vb 1 to clean with water (wash her hair). 2 to flow against or over (waves washing against the rocks). 3 to carry away (on a rush of liquid) (wash the mud away). 4 to colour lightly:—n 1 the act of cleaning with water. 2 a washing, the flow or dash of water. 3 a healing liquid. 4 a thin coat of colour:—**wash one's hands of** to refuse to have anything more to do with.

wash'er n a ring of metal, rubber, etc, to keep a bolt, etc, firmly in position (top washer).

wash'erwoman n a woman who washes clothes, etc.

wash'ing n 1 dirty clothes or linen to be washed. 2 clothes newly washed.

wash'stand n a table for a basin of water.

wasp n a stinging winged insect, with black and yellow stripes on its body.

wasp'ish adj sharp-tempered, spiteful (a waspish remark).

was'sail n (old) a drinking party.

wast'age n that which is lost by waste (the wallpaper wastage when decorating).

waste vb 1 to fail to put to a useful purpose (waste talent). 2 to spend or use foolishly (waste money). 3 to destroy, to damage. 4 to make or become weaker (muscles wasting without exercise):—adj 1 left over (waste product). 2 uncultivated, undeveloped (waste land):—n 1 what is left over as useless (industrial waste). 2 useless spending.

waste'ful adj spending foolishly or uselessly.

waste pa'per n paper thrown away as useless.

waste pipe n a pipe to carry away dirty water.

wast'er, wast'rel ns (inf) a lazy useless person.

watch vb 1 to look at or observe with care (watch how he changes the tyre). 2 to look at (watch television). 3 to guard (watch the princess). 4 to look after (watch the children). 5 (old) to stay awake:—n 1 a guard. 2 a careful look-out. 3 a four-hour spell of duty for half the crew on board a ship. 4 a clock carried in the pocket or on the wrist.

watch'ful adj keeping a look-out, observant, alert (under watchful eyes).

watch'maker n one who makes or repairs watches.

watch'man n a man employed to look after a building or site when it is unoccupied (a night watchman).

watch'word n 1 a word known only to members of a group so that by using it they may be recognized as members (only let them in if they know the watchword). 2 a motto.

wa'ter n 1 the clear liquid that falls as rain and flows in streams and rivers. 2 a large area of water, as a lake, sea, etc. 3 the degree of brightness of a diamond (diamonds of the first water):—vb 1 to supply with water. 2 to pour or sprinkle water on (water the garden). 3 to mix water with illegally (water the whisky).

wa'tercol'our n 1 colouring matter to be mixed with water, not oil. 2 a painting in watercolours (a watercolour of the old mill).

wa'tercourse n a channel in which water gathers and flows as a stream.

wa'tercress n an eatable water plant.

wa'terfall n a stream falling over steep rocks or stones to a lower level.

wa'terfowl n birds that live in or near water.

wa'terglass n a thick clear liquid in which eggs are placed to stop them going bad.

wa'tering place n 1 a holiday place at which mineral waters are found. 2 (old) a seaside holiday place.

wa'ter-lily n a plant with floating flowers and leaves, found in ponds, etc.

wa'terlogged adj soaked or filled with water (waterlogged field).

wa'terman n a boatman.

wa'termark n the faint trademark on a piece of paper.

wa'termelon n a large juicy type of melon.

water po'lo n a ball game for swimmers.

water pow'er n mechanical power got from running water.

wa'terproof adj able to keep out water, that water cannot pass through (waterproof tents/waterproof coat):—n 1 waterproof cloth. 2 a raincoat.

wa'tershed n 1 a ridge or hill separating two river valleys. 2 a point at which events take a different turn (a watershed in the war).

wa'ter-ski n a board on which a person can stand and be towed over water by a speedboat:—also vb:—n **wa'terski'er**.

wa'terspout n a column of water sucked by a whirlwind.

wa'tertight adj so tight that water can pass neither in nor out (a watertight container).

wa'terworks n an apparatus for supplying water through pipes to a town, etc.

wa'tery adj 1 full of water (watery eyes). 2 tasteless, weak, thin (watery soup).

watt n a unit of measurement of electric power.

wattle [wǎt'-l] n 1 a twig. 2 a fence made of twigs woven together. 3 an Australian tree that is the country's emblem.

wave n 1 a moving ridge of water rising above the surface of the sea and then sinking down again. 2 any movement resembling this (light waves/sound waves). 3 one of several ridges in the hair. 4 a moving of the hand as a signal (a friendly wave):—vb 1 to move or make to move up and down or to and fro. 2 to shake in the air as a sign. 3 to put waves in hair. 4 to signal with one's hand.

wave'length n the distance (on the sea or in the air) between the crest of one wave and that of the next.

wa'ver vb 1 to be uncertain, to hesitate (wavering about whether to be good or not). 2 to move unsteadily. 3 to flicker (candle flame wavering).

wa'vy adj 1 rising and falling in waves (wavy hair). 2 covered with waves.

wax[1] vb (old) 1 to grow larger (the moon waxing). 2 to become (wax eloquent).

wax[2] n 1 a sticky yellow substance made by bees. 2 any material resembling this. 3 a substance used to seal letters, parcels, etc.

wax'en adj like wax (a waxen skin).

wax'work n 1 the image of a famous person made in wax for showing to the public. 2 the place where these are exhibited.

way n 1 a track, path or road (the way of passage). 2 a method of doing something (a new way of teaching). 3 distance travelled (it is a long way to the next village). 4 the route to a place (the way to the station). 5 a custom or habit (have an unpleasant way):—**have a way with one** to be attractive in character (he has a way with women):—**under way** in movement (the expansion of the firm is under way):—**ways and means** methods.

way'farer n a traveller, esp on foot.

waylay' vb to hide and wait for in order to surprise or attack (they waylaid the enemy).

way'side n (old) the side of the road.

way'ward adj fond of one's own way, not heeding the advice or orders of others (wayward children).

weak adj 1 not strong, feeble. 2 giving in too easily to others. 3 not good at (weak at foreign languages).

weak'en vb to make or become weak (she was determined not to go but finally weakened).

weak'ling n one who is weak in body or character.

weak'ly adj not strong, not having good health (weakly children).

weak'ness n 1 lack of strength or determination. 2 a bad point in one's character (telling white lies is her major weakness). 3 a foolish liking for (a weakness for ice cream).

weal[1] n (old) 1 welfare. 2 being well off. 3 happiness:—**the public weal** the good of the whole country.

weal[2] n a raised mark on the skin caused by a blow from a whip, thin stick, etc.

weald n (old) open or wooded country.

wealth n 1 riches (the miser's great riches). 2 plenty (a wealth of talent).

wealth'y adj very rich (wealthy enough not to have to work).

wean vb 1 to change from feeding (an infant) only on milk to more solid food. 2 to get someone to change his or her habits or desires (wean him from his criminal ways).

wea'pon n any instrument that can be used in fighting or attack (weapons such as guns and knives).

wear [wǎr] vb (pt wore, pp worn) 1 to have on the body as clothing. 2 to put or stick on one's clothes for show (wear a badge). 3 to damage or waste by rubbing or use (the waves wear away at the rocks). 4 to tire out (worn by his continual complaining):—n 1 clothing. 2 damage caused by rubbing or use:—n wear'er:—**wear away** to become gradually less, to rub or be rubbed away:—**wear on** to pass slowly (time is wearing):—**wear off** to become gradually less (the effects of the painkillers wore off):—**wear out** 1 to exhaust. 2 to make useless by using too often.

wea'risome adj tiring, boring (a wearisome journey).

weary [wee'-ri] *adj* **1** tired by continued effort, exhausted (*weary from the long journey*). **2** fed up, bored (*weary of listening to complaints*).

wea'sel *n* a small bloodthirsty reddish-brown animal that eats frogs, mice, birds, etc.

wea'ther *n* the general conditions of the atmosphere (e.g. sunshine, rain, wind, etc) at any particular time:—*vb* **1** to come safely through (*succeed in weathering the selection process*). **2** to be damaged or discoloured by the effects of weather (*stone weathered with age*):—**make heavy weather of** to find difficulty in doing (*he made heavy weather of the work*):—**under the weather** feeling unwell.

wea'ther-beaten *adj* marred or coloured by the effects of the weather.

wea'ther-bound *adj* held up or delayed by bad weather (*motorists weather-bound on the motorway*).

wea'thercock *n* a pointer, often in the shape of a cock, that turns round to show the direction from which the wind is blowing.

wea'therglass *n* a barometer for indicating the weather.

wea'thervane *same as* **weathercock**.

weave *vb* (*pt* **wove**, *pp* **wov'en**) **1** to form cloth by intertwining threads. **2** to put together sticks, twigs, etc, by interlacing them. **3** to make up (*weave a story about his childhood*):—*n* **weav'er**.

web *n* **1** cloth made by weaving. **2** the net of fine threads made by a spider. **3** the skin between the toes of water-birds.

web'bing *n* a narrow band of strong material used for belts, etc.

web-foot'ed *adj* having skin between the toes.

web'site *n* an Internet location that consists of a number of related documents about a particular subject (*a website about allergies*).

wed *vb* (**wed'ded**, **wed'ding**) to marry (*he promised to wed her*).

wed'ding *n* a marriage.

wedge *n* a piece of wood, metal, etc, thick at one end and narrowing to a sharp edge at the other:—*vb* to split open, fix or fasten with a wedge (*wedge the door open*).

wed'lock *n* the married state.

Wednesday [Wed'-âns-dā] *n* the fourth or middle day of the week.

wee *adj* (*Scot*) very small.

weed *n* **1** a useless plant growing in a garden or field. **2** (*inf*) a thin person with little strength or energy (*a strong woman married to a weed*):—*vb* **1** to clear of weeds (*weed the garden*). **2** to pull up weeds (*pay him to weed*).

weeds *npl* the black clothes worn by a widow in mourning.

weed'y *adj* thin and weak-looking (*a weedy youth*).

week *n* a period of seven days.

week'day *n* any day of the week except Sunday and often Saturday.

weekend' *n* the period from the time one's work ceases on Friday or Saturday until one begins it again on Monday.

week'ly *adj* happening once a week (*a weekly meeting*):—*n* a newspaper or magazine published once a week.

ween *vb* (*old*) to think.

weep *vb* (*pt*, *pp* **wept**) **1** to shed tears, to cry. **2** to mourn (*weep for a lost cause*).

weep'ing *adj* **1** crying. **2** (*of a tree*) having drooping branches (*a weeping willow*).

weev'il *n* a type of beetle that destroys stored grain.

weft *n* the cross-threads of a piece of cloth.

weigh [wā] *vb* **1** to measure the heaviness of (*measure the weight of the load*). **2** to consider carefully. **3** to raise (anchor). **4** to be of a certain heaviness. **5** to have importance (*her opinion does not carry much weight*):—**weigh down** to trouble:—**weigh up** to consider carefully:—**weigh with** to seem important to.

weigh'bridge *n* a machine for weighing a vehicle and its load.

weight [wāt] *n* **1** heaviness. **2** a piece of metal, etc, of known heaviness, used in finding how heavy another object is. **3** importance, influence. **4** a heavy load.

weight'y *adj* **1** heavy (*weighty load*). **2** important, deserving careful consideration (*weighty matters*).

weir [weer] *n* a barrier built across a stream to make the water approaching it deeper.

weird [weerd] *adj* **1** strange, eerie, unearthly (*a weird scream*). **2** odd, very strange (*she looks weird in that outfit*):—*n* fate.

wel'come *adj* **1** pleasing. **2** allowed to use or take at any time:—*n* a kindly greeting or reception:—

vb **1** to greet kindly (*welcome the guests*). **2** to receive or hear with pleasure (*welcome the news*):—**make welcome** to make (a guest) feel at home.

weld *vb* **1** to join two pieces of metal by heating them and hammering them together. **2** to unite closely (*families welded in friendship*):—*n* **weld'er**.

wel'fare *n* **1** happiness, success. **2** health, good living conditions (*the department concerned with the welfare of the community*).

wel'kin *n* the sky.

well[1] *n* **1** a spring of water. **2** a hole in the ground from which water can be drawn. **3** a pit made in the ground to reach oil. **4** a fountain:—*vb* **1** to come up as from a spring. **2** to gush out (*tears welling from her eyes*).

well[2] *adv* **1** in a good way or style (*he does his job well*). **2** thoroughly (*examine the house well before buying*). **3** rightly (*you may well apologize*). **4** with appr oval (*speak well of him*):—*adj* **1** in good health. **2** all right:—**as well as** in addition to.

well-appoint'ed *adj* provided with all that is necessary (*a well-appointed kitchen*).

well-being *n* success, happiness (*only interested in his wife's well-being*).

well-informed' *adj* having much knowledge.

well'ingtons *npl* loose-fitting rubber boots reaching up to the knees.

well-known' *adj* famous (*well-known actors*).

well'-nigh *adv* (*old* or *fml*) almost (*it was well-nigh impossible to take him seriously*).

well-off' *adj* rich.

well-read' *adj* having read much.

well-spok'en *adj* always pronouncing clearly with a pleasing, educated accent.

well'-spring *n* **1** a fountain. **2** a sour ce (*a well-spring of knowledge*).

well-to-do' *adj* rich.

well-turned' *adj* well-expressed (*a well-turned phrase*).

well'-wisher *n* a friendly supporter (*well-wishers giving donations to charity*).

well-worn' *adj* much worn, much used (*well-worn phrases*).

welt *n* the strip of leather round the shoe upper and joined to the sole:—*vb* to provide with a welt.

wel'ter *vb* to roll about:—*n* a confused mass, disorder (*a welter of useless information*).

wel'terweight *n* a boxer between middleweight and heavyweight.

wen *n* a harmless swelling below the skin.

wench *n* (*old*) a young woman.

wend *vb* (*old*) to go, to make (one's way).

west *n* one of the four principal points of the compass, the direction in which the sun sets.

west'erly *adj* from or towards the west (*a westerly wind*).

west'ern *adj* in or from the west.

west'ward(s) *adv* towards the west.

wet *adj* **1** covered or soaked with water or other liquid (*get wet standing in the rain at the bus-stop*). **2** not dry, moist. **3** rainy (*a wet day*):—*n* rainy weather:—*vb* (**wet'ted, wet'ting**) to make wet.

whack *vb* (*inf*) to strike sharply, to beat severely (*he was whacked by his father*):—*n* **1** a blow. **2** a share.

whack'ing *adj* very large.

whale *n* a large sea mammal:—*vb* to hunt whales.

whale'bone *n* an elastic horny substance got from the jaw of a whale.

whal'er *n* a ship engaged in whale hunting.

wharf *n* (*pl* **wharfs** *or* **wharves**) a platform or quay at which ships are loaded and unloaded.

wharf'age *n* the money paid for the use of a wharf.

wharf'inger *n* one who owns or looks after a wharf.

what'not *n* **1** an object not easily described or defined (*buy a few whatnots for her holiday*). **2** a piece of furniture to hold odds and ends.

wheat *n* the grain from which bread flour is obtained.

wheat'en *adj* made from wheat (*wheaten bread*).

whee'dle *vb* to try to please a person in order to get him or her to do something, to coax (*he tried to wheedle more pocket money out of his father*).

wheel *n* **1** a round frame, often strengthened by spokes, turning on an axis. **2** a change of direction by a line of marching men moving like the spoke of a wheel:—*vb* **1** to move on wheels. **2** to turn like a wheel. **3** to change direction by a wheeling movement when marching in line.

wheel'barrow *n* a handcart, usu with one wheel, two legs, and handles.

wheel'wright *n* a maker of wheels and carts.

wheeze *vb* to breathe with a hoarse or hissing sound (*she is asthmatic and wheezes badly*):—*also n*:—*adj* **wheez'y.**

whelk *n* a small shellfish in a spiral shell.

whelp *n* a puppy, a lion cub—*vb* (*of certain animals*) to give birth to young.

when *adv and conj* at what or which time.

whence *adv and conj* from what place.

whenev'er, whensoev'er *advs and conjs* at no matter what time.

where *adv and conj* at, to or in what place.

where'abouts *n* the place one is in (*the police want to know the accused's whereabouts*).

whereas' *conj* since, although.

whereby' *adv and conj* by which.

where'fore *adv and conj* for which or what reason.

wherein', whereon' *advs and conjs* in or on which or what.

whereupon' *adv* after which.

wherev'er *adv and conj* at, to or in whatever place.

wherewith' *adv* with which or what.

where'withal *n* the money needed for a certain purpose.

wher'ry *n* a light shallow boat.

whet *vb* 1 to sharpen. 2 to make (a desire) more strongly felt (*whet their appetites*).

wheth'er *conj* if:—*pron* which of two.

whet'stone *n* a stone on which knives, tools, etc, may be sharpened.

whey *n* the watery part of the milk, separated from the curd.

whiff *n* 1 a puff of air or smoke. 2 a quick or slight smell (*think she smelt a whiff of gas*):—*vb* 1 to puff. 2 to smell.

while *n* a space of time:—*conj* during the time that:—*vb* to pass (time) in pleasure or leisure (*while away the afternoon reading*).

whi'lom *adj* (*old*) former.

whilst *conj* while.

whim *n* a sudden strange desire or idea, a passing fancy.

whim'per *vb* to cry brokenly, to whine (*the child was whimpering in his cot*):—*also n.*

whim'sical *adj* full of whims, odd, unusual, fantastic.

whim'sy *n* whim (*she went to the seaside for the day on a sudden whimsy*).

whin¹ *n* a prickly bush with bright yellow flowers, gorse, furze.

whin², whin'stone *ns* a hard rock.

whine *n* a long cry of complaint, a wail:—*vb* 1 to utter a sad or complaining cry (*dogs whining*). 2 to speak in a complaining voice (*whine about her misfortune*).

whin'ny *n* the high-pitched cry of a horse:—*also vb*

whip *n* 1 a cord attached to a stick for beating or driving animals. 2 (*old*) a coachman. 3 a party official whose duty it is to see that members attend and vote in parliamentary debates:—*vb* (**whipped', whip'ping**) 1 to strike with a whip (*whip the wrongdoers*). 2 to beat eggs, cream, etc, into a froth (*whip the mixture*). 3 to take or move (something) quickly (*she whipped her apron off*).

whip'cord *n* a strong hard cloth for making clothes.

whip hand *n* an advantage, the mastery (*since she discovered his secret she has had the whip hand*).

whip'persnapper *n* an unimportant person who is always trying to seem important.

whip'pet *n* a dog like a greyhound used for racing.

whir(r) *vb* (**whirred', whir'ring**) to move through the air or spin with a buzzing or clicking sound (*the propellers whirred*):—*also n.*

whirl *vb* to move quickly round and round, to spin quickly (*the dancers whirl around the dancefloor*):—*n* a quick round-and-round movement, confusion.

whirl'igig *n* a type of spinning toy.

whirl'pool *n* a current of water turning round and round with a circular motion.

whirl'wind *n* a violent wind blowing round and round in a circle.

whisk *vb* 1 to knock or brush with a quick light movement. 2 to beat lightly into a froth (*whisk the eggs*). 3 to take with a quick movement (*whisk her apron off*):—*n* 1 a quick or jerky movement. 2 an implement for beating eggs, etc (*an electric whisk*). 3 a bunch of hair, etc, for brushing away flies, dust, etc.

whis'ker *n* 1 the hair growing on the cheeks, the stiff hairs growing on the cheeks of men. 2 the stiff hairs growing above the mouth of certain animals (*the cat's whiskers*).

whis'kered *adj* having whiskers.

whis'key *n* an Irish and North American form of whisky.

whis'ky *n* a strong alcoholic drink made in Scotland from barley, rye, etc.

whis'per *vb* **1** to speak very softly, using the breath instead of the voice. **2** to rustle (*silk skirts whispering as she walked*):—*n* **1** a very soft voice. **2** what is whispered (*he heard her whispers*). **3** a rumour (*there is a whisper that he embezzled money*).

whist *n* a game of cards for four persons.

whistle [whis'-él] *vb* **1** to make a high, shrill sound with the lips or a special instrument. **2** to play a tune by whistling:—*n* **1** a shrill sound made with the lips or a special instrument. **2** an instrument that makes a whistling sound when blown (*the policeman blew his whistle*).

whit *n* a tiny piece (*not a whit of truth in his statement*).

white *adj* **1** of the colour of clean snow or milk. **2** pale (*her illness has made her look rather white*). **3** having a pale skin (as opposed to yellow, brown or black):—*also n.*

white'bait *n* a very small eatable sea fish.

white lie *n* a lie told for what is believed to be a good purpose.

whit'en *vb* to make or become white (*buy something to whiten the sheets*).

white'wash *n* a mixture of lime or chalk and water used for painting walls, etc, white:—*vb* **1** to paint with whitewash (*whitewash the walls of the shed*). **2** to try to make what is wrong appear blameless, to try to make a guilty person seem innocent (*they tried to whitewash the crime*).

whith'er *adv and conj* to which or what place.

whi'ting *n* a small eatable sea fish.

whit'low *n* an infected swelling on the finger.

Whitsun'day *n* the seventh Sunday after Easter.

Whit'suntide, Whit'sun *ns* the time immediately after Whitsunday.

whit'tle *vb* **1** to pare off short strips with a knife. **2** to make smaller or thinner (*whittle the budget*). **3** to cut down or reduce a little at a time (*the bills are whittling away at our budget*).

whiz(z) *vb* (**whizzed', whiz'zing**) to make a hissing or swishing sound when moving through the air (*children whizzing down our road on roller-skates*):—*also n.*

whizz'kid *n* (*inf*) a young person who is exceptionally successful at something, often in business (*The financial world is full of whizzkids*).

who *pron* which person (*the man who died*).

whole [hōl] *adj* **1** complete, entire (*tired of the whole affair*). **2** unharmed (*escape whole from the accident*). **3** (*old*) in good health:—*n* the total, all.

whole'food *n* food which has not been refined or processed very much and which does not contain artificial substances.

wholeheart'ed *adj* enthusiastic, keen (*give the cause his wholehearted support*).

wholemeal *adj* of flour or bread, made from the complete grain of wheat, including the husk.

whole'sale *n* the selling of goods in large quantities to those who will re-sell them to others:—*adj* on a large scale (*wholesale slaughter*).

whole'some *adj* **1** having a good effect on health (*wholesome food*). **2** healthy, morally healthy (*a wholesome young girl*).

whol'ly *adv* completely (*not wholly committed*).

whoop *n* a loud shout:—*vb* to make a whoop (*whooping with joy*).

whoop'ing cough *n* a disease, chiefly of children, with long fits of coughing, during which the breath is taken in again with a gasping sound.

whorl *n* **1** a ring of leaves round a stem. **2** one turn of a spiral shell.

whor'tleberry *n* the bilberry.

whosoev'er *pron* no matter who, any person concerned.

why *adv and conj* for what reason.

wick *n* the thread in a candle, in an oil-lamp or oil heater, the band of cloth that draws up the oil and is burned to give light.

wick'ed *adj* bad, sinful, evil (*wicked people*):—*n* **wick'edness**.

wick'er *n* a willow twig:—*adj* made of willow twigs woven together.

wick'erwork *n* basket-work.

wick'et *n* **1** a small gate, a small door in or near a larger one. **2** in cricket, the sticks that the batsman stands at and defends. **3** a piece of turf specially prepared for the game of cricket (*a wicket too wet to play*).

wick'et-keep'er n in cricket, one who fields behind the stumps.

wide adj broad, extending far in all directions:—adv **1** missing the target by passing beside it (shoot wide). **2** fully (wide awake).

wid'en vb to make or become wide (widen the garden).

wide'spread adj occurring or found far and wide (a widespread belief).

wid'ow n a woman whose husband is dead.

wid'ower n a man whose wife is dead.

width n breadth (measure the room's width).

wield vb **1** to use with the hands (wield a knife in self-defence). **2** to use or put into practice (wield power).

wife n (pl wives) a married woman.

wife'ly adj like a wife (wifely affection).

wig n an artificial covering of hair for the head (he wore a wig to cover his baldness).

wig'ging n a severe scolding.

wig'gle vb to wag, to shake from side to side (wiggle her hips as she walked).

wig'wam n the hut or tent of a North American Indian.

wild adj **1** not tamed or civilized. **2** not cultivated (wild stretch of countryside). **3** savage. **4** uncontrolled (wild passions). **5** very excited (crowds growing wild at the arrival of the pop star):—n a desert area, an area unaltered by man.

wild'cat n **1** a fierce wild animal of the cat family. **2** a fierce person:—adj foolish, reckless, risky (a wildcat strike).

wil'debeest n a gnu.

wil'derness n a desert, an uncultivated or uninhabited area (the place is a wilderness since it was bombed).

wild'fire n broad sheets of lightning.

wild-goose chase n an undertaking that cannot possibly succeed.

wild'life n animals, birds and insects, and sometimes plants, which live in their natural environment (damaging the forest wildlife).

wile n a trick (use her wiles to get her own way):—vb to persuade, to coax.

wil'ful adj always wanting one's own way, done deliberately.

will n **1** one's power to make decisions or choices, self-control (believe in freedom of the will). **2** desire (done against her will). **3** a written document made by a person to say what is to be done with his or her property after death:—vb **1** to desire (we are willing her to win). **2** to leave property to others by a signed will.

will'ing adj ready, eager (willing helpers).

will-o'-the-wisp' n **1** a moving flickering light seen over marshy ground. **2** one hard to catch.

will'ow n **1** a tree with slender, easily bent branches. **2** a cricket bat.

will'owy adj **1** easily bent. **2** slender, graceful (a willowy figure).

wil'ly-nil'ly adv whether willing or unwilling (he has decided to leave willy-nilly).

wilt vb **1** to droop (plants wilting). **2** to lose freshness or vigour (people wilting in the heat).

wil'y adj cunning (a wily plan to get into the building).

wim'ple n (old) a headdress, fitting closely around the face, worn by nuns.

win vb (won, winning) **1** to be successful in a match or contest, to be victorious (he is bound to win against the younger player). **2** to obtain in a competition (win a prize). **3** (old) to reach (win the shore):—n **1** a success. **2** a victory:—n **win'ner**.

wince vb **1** to make a quick movement back because of pain or fear. **2** to twist the face from pain (she winced as the dentist touched her sore tooth).

winceyette' n a plain cotton and fine wool cloth (pyjamas of winceyette).

winch n **1** a handle for turning a wheel. **2** a device for moving a heavy object by winding a rope attached to it round a drum or wheel, so drawing the object up or along.

wind[1] [wind] n **1** air moving. **2** a current of air, a breeze or gale. **3** breath:—vb (pt, pp win'ded) to put out of breath by a blow in the stomach (the boxer was winded and fell).

wind[2] [wind] vb (pt, pp wound) **1** to twist. **2** to coil. **3** to gather up by turning. **4** to follow a twisting course (the path winding up the mountain):—**wind up 1** to bring to an end. **2** to turn a handle to tighten a spring in a machine. **3** to bring to an end (wind up the firm).

wind[3] [wind] vb (pt, pp wind'ed or wound) to blow (a horn).

wind'bag n (inf) one who talks too much (bored listening to the old windbag).

wind'fall n 1 fruit blown down (gather windfalls in the orchard). 2 a piece of unexpected luck, an unexpected gift of money.

winding sheet n a cloth in which a dead body is placed for burial.

wind'jammer n a sailing ship.

wind'lass n a winch.

wind'mill n a mill with sails driven by wind.

win'dow n an opening in the wall of a house, etc, to let in light (usu filled with a sheet of glass) (bay windows).

wind'pipe n the air passage from the mouth to the lungs.

wind'screen n the glass panel at the front of a motor car that acts as a shield (a windscreen shattered by a pebble).

wind'surfing n a sport involving moving along the surface of the sea or a stretch of water while standing on a board with a sail attached to it:—n **wind'surfer**.

wind'ward n the direction from which the wind is blowing:—also adj.

wind'y adj open to the winds, breezy, gusty (a windy day/a windy stretch of countryside).

wine n a strong drink made from the fermented juice of grapes.

wine'press n a machine for squeezing the juice out of grapes.

wing n 1 the limb with the help of which birds, insects, etc, fly. 2 a side part or extension of a building, stage, etc (one wing of the building was burnt down). 3 the supporting parts of an aeroplane. 4 the side part of an army when drawn up for battle:—vb 1 to fly (swallows winging their way south). 2 to wound in the wing or arm:—**on the wing** in flight.

wing' command'er n a high-ranking officer in the Royal Air Force.

wink vb 1 to shut and open one eyelid with a quick movement. 2 to flicker, to twinkle (lights winking). 3 (fml) (usu with at) to pretend not to see (wink at her son's misdeeds):—n 1 the act of winking. 2 a hint given by winking:—**forty winks** a nap, a short sleep.

winner see win.

win'ning adj 1 successful (a winning formation). 2 charming (winning manners).

win'now vb to separate the grain from the chaff by a draught of air.

win'some adj (fml) attractive, pleasant.

win'ter n the cold season of the year:—vb to spend the winter (wintering in Italy).

win'try adj like winter, cold, stormy (wintry weather).

wipe vb to clean or dry by gentle rubbing (wipe the kitchen worktops):—n a rub intended to clean or dry:—**wipe out** to destroy, to cause to cease to exist (an entire city wiped out by the war).

wi'per n a device for wiping rain from a car windscreen (a windscreen wiper).

wire n 1 a thread or cord of metal. 2 a telegram:—vb 1 to provide with wire. 2 to send a telegram.

wire'less n 1 the sending or receiving of messages between two places by means of sound waves without the use of wires. 2 an apparatus for this purpose, radio:—vb to send a message by wireless.

wire-net'ting n a network of thin wire used in fencing, etc (put wire-netting on the fruit trees to keep the birds off).

wire'-puller n one who gets important people to help or support him or her.

wi'ry adj thin but muscular (the boxer did not look strong but he had a wiry build).

wis'dom n 1 the ability to make good use of one's knowledge and experience. 2 good sense.

wise¹ adj 1 having or showing wisdom (a wise man). 2 sensible (a wise decision).

wise² n (fml) way, manner.

wise'acre n (old) one who pretends to know more than he or she really does.

wish vb to have a desire, to want (to do), to long:—n 1 a desire. 2 the thing wanted.

wish'ful adj wanting (something), desirous.

wishful thinking n something believed in spite of the facts because one wants it to be true (she said she was going to the Caribbean but it was only wishful thinking).

wish'y-wash'y adj weak and pale, feeble (too wishy-washy to defend herself).

wisp n a small bundle of straw, hay, etc (wisps of hair).

wist'ful adj thoughtful, longing (she looked wistful as the other children left on holiday).

wit n 1 intelligence, understanding. 2 the ability to say things shortly, neatly and cleverly, often in a way that makes them amusing. 3 one having this ability:—**at one's wits' end** so worried that one does not know what to do next:—**to wit** namely, that is to say.

witch n 1 a woman believed to have magical powers granted by the devil. 2 an ugly old woman.

witch'craft n magic performed with the aid of the devil.

witch'-doctor n among certain African tribes, a man believed to be able to control evil spirits and cure illness by magic.

withal' adv (old) also, moreover.

withdraw' vb 1 to draw or pull back, to retreat. 2 to take back (something said) as not meant (withdraw his apology). 3 to take money, etc, from one's bank or stock (withdrew money from his current account):—n **withdraw'al**.

with'er vb to make or become dry and faded, to shrivel, to rot away (flowers withering without water).

with'ering adj 1 drying, fading. 2 hurtful, sarcastic (a withering reply).

with'ers npl the ridge between the shoulder blades of a horse.

withhold' vb to refuse to grant or give, to keep back (withhold information).

within' prep inside:—adv 1 indoors. 2 inwardly.

without' prep 1 not having. 2 (old) outside:—adv (old) outside.

withstand' vb to resist, to oppose.

wit'less adj (fml) foolish, stupid.

wit'ness n 1 a person who sees an event taking place. 2 one who tells in a court of law what took place on an occasion at which he or she was present. 3 (fml) evidence pointing to the truth:—vb 1 to see happening (witness the accident). 2 to sign a document to confirm that another has signed it in one's presence (witness the signature on the agreement):—**bear witness** to give evidence.

wit'ticism n a clever or humorous saying, shortly and neatly expressed.

wit'tingly adv with knowledge or understanding of what one is doing (he did not wittingly hurt her).

wit'ty adj able to say clever things briefly and often amusingly (a witty after-dinner speech).

wives see **wife**.

wiz'ard n 1 a man who claims magical powers. 2 a conjurer.

wiz'ardry n 1 magic. 2 great skill.

wiz'ened adj dried up and wrinkled (a wizened old lady).

woad n a blue dye obtained from a plant.

wob'ble vb to sway from side to side, move unsteadily (cyclists wobbling along the street):—also n.

wob'bly adj unsteady (a wobbly table).

woe n (fml) grief, sorrow, misery (tell a tale of woe).

woe'begone adj (fml) full of sorrow or grief (she felt woebegone when they left).

woe'ful adj sad.

woke pt of **wake**.

wold n a stretch of open uncultivated hill country.

wolf n (pl wolves) a fierce wild animal of the dog family.

wolf'ish adj 1 fierce. 2 very greedy or hungry (a wolfish appetite).

wolverene', wolverine' n a small greedy animal.

wolves see **wolf**.

wo'man n (pl women) a grown-up female human being.

wo'manhood n the state or qualities of a woman (the age at which girls reach womanhood).

wo'manish adj 1 having the qualities of a woman. 2 unmanly.

wo'mankind, wo'manfolk ns women in general.

wo'manly adj having the good qualities of a woman, gentle.

women's movement n a movement whose aim is to improve the position of women in society and obtain equality with men.

womb n the female organ in which the young are kept and fed until birth.

wom'bat n a pouched Australian animal, like a small bear.

women see **woman**.

won pt of **win**.

won'der n 1 great surprise or astonishment (*look at the sight with wonder*). 2 anything giving rise to such feelings, a marvel or miracle (*the wonders of the world*):—vb 1 to feel surprise or astonishment. 2 to think about the reasons for something (*wonder why he behaved like that*).

won'derful adj very surprising, extraordinary (*a wonderful gift/a wonderful surprise*).

won'derment n surprise, astonishment.

wont [wŏnt] n custom, habit:—adj accustomed.

wont'ed adj (*fml*) usual (*his wonted route*).

woo vb to make love to, to seek to marry:—n **woo'er**.

wood n 1 a large collection of growing trees (*the pine wood below the hill*). 2 the hard substance of which the trunks and branches of trees are made, timber.

wood'bine n the honeysuckle.

wood'cock n a game bird of the snipe family.

wood'craft n knowledge of forests and forest life.

wood'cut n a print made from a picture carved on wood.

wood'cutter n one whose job it is to cut wood.

wood'ed adj covered with trees or woods (*wooded areas*).

wood'en adj 1 made of wood. 2 dull, lacking feeling (*wooden acting*).

wood'land n country covered with trees or woods.

wood'man n a man who works in woods or forests, one who cuts down trees.

wood'pecker n a bird that taps holes in trees with its long pointed beak and takes out insects from them with its tongue.

wood'work n 1 the art of making objects out of wood (*woodwork is taught at the school*). 2 objects so made.

wood'worm n a grub that eats its way into wood and destroys it.

wood'y adj 1 made of wood. 2 covered with woods (*a woody area*).

woof n the cross-threads of a piece of cloth, the weft.

wool n 1 the soft, wavy hair covering the body of certain animals (e.g. sheep, goats, etc). 2 thread or cloth made from wool (*knit a sweater with wool*).

wool'-gath'ering n daydreaming, absent-mindedness (*wool-gathering instead of working*).

wool'len adj made of wool (*woollen sweaters*):—also n.

wool'ly adj 1 covered with wool. 2 like wool.

wool'sack n 1 the bag filled with wool on which the Lord Chancellor sits in the House of Lords. 2 the office of Lord Chancellor.

word [wèrd] n 1 a sound or group of sounds expressing an idea. 2 a message, information (*send him word about his wife's health*). 3 a promise (*he gave his word that he would be there*):—vb to express in words:—**the Word** Jesus Christ or His teaching:—**have words with** to quarrel with:—**word for word** in exactly the same words as those used before.

word-per'fect adj able to say without an error the words of something learnt (*actors who were not word-perfect*).

word'-picture n a clear description.

word'y adj using more words than are necessary (*a wordy letter*).

wore pt of **wear**.

work n 1 effort (*put a lot of work into the project*). 2 a task, tasks (*bring work home from the office*). 3 that which one does for a living (*she is at work seven hours a day*). 4 a book, picture, piece of music, etc. 5 pl a factory. 6 pl the parts of a machine that make it go:—vb 1 to labour, to toil (*they really worked at getting the house ready*). 2 to be in a job. 3 to make to do work (*to work the servants hard*). 4 to have the desired effect or result (*the painkillers did not work*). 5 to cause, to bring about. 6 to give shape to (*work the clay into a pot*):—**work up** to excite.

work'able adj that can be done or used (*a workable plan*).

work'aday adj everyday, ordinary (*wear her workaday clothes*).

work'bag, work'basket, work'box ns containers for materials and tools or implements.

work'er n 1 a person who works (*the factory workers*). 2 an insect (e.g. a bee) that does all the work.

work'force n the number of people who work in a particular firm, place, industry, etc.

work'house n (*old*) a place in which the homeless and aged poor can live.

work'ing class n those who work with their hands:—also adj.

work'ing model *n* a small model of a machine that works just as the original does.

work'man *n* one who works, esp with the hands (*get a workman to repair the roof*).

work'manship *n* **1** the skill of a worker. **2** the quality of a piece of work.

work'-out *n* a session of physical exercise or training (*Regular work-outs at the gym keep her fit*):—*vb* **work out**.

work'shop *n* a building or room in which work is carried on (*mending the radio in the workshop*).

world *n* **1** the earth on which we live. **2** any planet or star. **3** the universe and all created things. **4** all human beings. **5** any sphere of activity, study, etc (*the world of science*). **6** a great amount (*a world of difference*).

world'ling *n* (*old*) one interested only in doing well in this life.

world'ly *adj* **1** having to do with this world or life (*worldly pleasures*). **2** interested only in the things of this life (*worldly people*).

worldwide' *adj* spread throughout or found everywhere in the world (*a worldwide organization*).

worldwide web *n* (*abbr* **WWW**) the Internet network that stretches across the world. Each Internet page is indexed (by a function called hypertext) and can be linked to a related document and searched for using search engines.

worm *n* **1** a small backbone-less creeping animal. **2** the thread of a screw. **3** (*inf*) a despicable person (*he is an absolute worm*):—*vb* **1** to wriggle or crawl along. **2** to do something slowly and secretly (*worm his way into her favour*). **3** to persuade to tell by persistent questioning (*worm the truth out of her*).

worm'-eaten *adj* full of holes made by woodworms.

worm'wood *n* a bitter-tasting plant.

worn *pp* of **wear**:—*adj* showing signs of wear (*worn furniture*).

wor'ry *vb* **1** to feel anxiety (*she worries when the children are late*). **2** to trouble, to vex (*the child's behaviour worries her*). **3** to tear with the teeth (*the dog worrying a bone*):—*n* **1** anxiety, trouble. **2** a cause of anxiety.

worse *adj* more bad, less good, more ill or sick:—*adv* more badly.

wors'en *vb* to make or become worse (*interference would only worsen the situation*).

wor'ship *n* **1** prayers and praise offered to God. **2** a religious service. **3** great love or reverence for. **4** a title of respect for magistrates:—*vb* (**wor'shipped, wor'shipping**) **1** to pray to. **2** to honour greatly. **3** to join in a religious service (*the congregation worships every Sunday*):—*n* **wor'shipper**.

wor'shipful *adj* (*fml*) honourable.

worst *adj* most bad or ill:—*adv* most badly:—*n* the greatest evil or ill possible:—*vb* to defeat (*he was worsted by his opponent*).

wor'sted *n* a woollen thread used in knitting.

worth *adj* **1** equal in value to (*a vase worth £200*). **2** deserving of (*a film worth seeing*). **3** having such-and-such an amount of money or property (*he's worth millions*):—*n* **1** value (*the painting's worth is incalculable*). **2** price (*£10 worth of petrol*). **3** merit, excellence (*he proved his worth by going*).

worth'less *adj* of no use or value.

worthwhile' *adj* profitable, repaying the money, work, etc, expended (*a worthwhile job*).

worth'y *adj* deserving, deserving respect (*worthy of respect/a worthy cause*):—*n* (*inf*) a notable person (*one of the local worthies*).

would'-be *adj* wishing to be, intending (*a would-be doctor*).

wound[1] [wŏnd] *n* a hurt, cut or bruise, an injury:—*vb* **1** to injure, to cause a wound to (*wounded in battle*). **2** to hurt the feelings of (*wounded by his nasty remarks*).

wound[2] [wound] *pt* of **wind**:—**wound-up** over-excited (*she was wound-up before the job interview*).

wove *pt* of **weave**:—*pp* **woven**.

wrack *n* **1** seaweed cast up on the shore. **2** a wreck.

wraith *n* (*fml*) a ghost.

wran'gle *vb* to quarrel, to argue angrily (*wrangle over their father's will*):—*n* a quarrel, a dispute:—*n* **wrang'ler**.

wrap *vb* (**wrapped', wrap'ping**) to fold paper, cloth etc around so as to cover (*wrap presents*):—*n* **1** a shawl, a loose cloak. **2** a sandwich consisting of a tortilla with a filling inside.

wrap'per *n* **1** a loose outer garment for wear indoors. **2** a cover for books, etc.

wrath *n* great anger, rage (*show her wrath by walking out*).

wrath'ful *adj* very angry.

wreak *vb* to carry out, to put into effect (*wreak revenge*).

wreath *n* 1 flowers, leaves, etc, woven together to form a ring or crown (*put a wreath on her grave*). 2 a curling or spiral cloud (*wreaths of smoke*).

wreathe *vb* 1 to put a wreath on or round. 2 to weave together to make a wreath.

wreck *n* 1 destruction, esp of a ship at sea. 2 a ruin (*a wreck of a car*). 3 the remains of a ship destroyed by the sea. 4 a person weakened by ill health or evil living:—*vb* to ruin, to destroy (*wreck their plans*).

wreck'age *n* the broken parts of a wrecked ship.

wreck'er *n* one who deliberately causes a wreck or destruction.

wren *n* a very small songbird.

wrench *n* 1 a violent twist (*open the bottle with a wrench*). 2 the sorrow caused by parting from or giving away (*leaving her children was a wrench*). 3 a tool for gripping and turning nuts, bolts, etc:—*vb* 1 to give a sudden twist or pull to. 2 to sprain.

wrest *vb* 1 to twist, to pull violently from (*wrest the property from his hands*). 2 to alter (from the true meaning).

wres'tle *vb* 1 to struggle with another by gripping and trying to throw down. 2 to try hard to solve (*wrestle with the problem*).

wrest'ler *n* one who wrestles for sport.

wrest'ling *n* the sport of wrestling.

wretch *n* 1 a very unfortunate or miserable person (*the poor wretch has lost everything*). 2 a wicked or worthless person (*that wretch stole my money*).

wretch'ed *adj* 1 miserable. 2 worthless.

wrig'gle *vb* 1 to twist from side to side (*children wriggling with impatience*). 2 to move with a wriggling movement:—*also n.*

-wright *suffix* worker at, maker of (*shipwright/ playwright*).

wring *vb* (*pt, pp* **wrung**) 1 to squeeze hard, to twist tightly. 2 to get by pressure or persuasion (*wring a confession from him*).

wring'er *n* a machine for squeezing the water out of clothes.

wrink'le *n* a fold or furrow in the skin, or in cloth, etc (*have wrinkles in her skirt after sitting for so long*):—*vb* to make wrinkles in.

wrist *n* the joint between the hand and the arm.

wrist'let *n* a band worn round the wrist, a bracelet.

wrist'watch *ns* a watch attached to a band worn round the wrist.

writ *n* a written order from a law court to do or not to do certain acts (*issue a writ for his arrest*):—**Holy Writ** the Bible.

write *vb* (*pt* **wrote**, *pp* **writ'ten**) 1 to make marks standing for sounds, letters or words on paper, etc, with a pen or pencil (*learn to read and write*). 2 to make up stories, poems, etc, for publication (*writing fairy stories*). 3 to write a letter to (*I wrote to him yesterday*).

writ'er *n* 1 an author. 2 one who writes.

writ'ing paper *n* paper for writing letters on.

writ'ings *npl* the written works of an author.

writhe *vb* to twist and turn the body about, (*writhe in agony*).

wrong *adj* 1 not correct, false (*the wrong set of figures*). 2 incorrect in one's opinion, etc (*she was proved wrong*). 3 not good, not morally right, evil (*wrong deeds*):—*vb* 1 to treat unjustly (*wrong his wife*). 2 to do harm to:—*n* 1 an injustice. 2 harm.

wrong'doer *n* a criminal, a sinner:—*n* **wrong'doing.**

wrong'ful *adj* 1 unjust (*wrongful arrest*). 2 criminal, wrong (*wrongful actions*).

wrong-headed *adj* obstinate.

wrote *pt* of **write.**

wrought *old pt of* **work:**—*adj* beaten or rolled into shape (*wrought iron*).

wrought i'ron *n* hammered iron.

wry *adj* 1 twisted, turned to one side (*a wry neck*). 2 slightly mocking (*a wry smile*).

X

xenophobia [ze-nŏ-fō'-bee-ā] *n* hatred of foreigners and their ways.

xero- [zee'-rō] *prefix* dry.

xerophytic [zee-rō-fi'-tik] *adj* (*fml*) suited to dry conditions (*xerophytic plants*).

xe'rox *vb* to make photograph copies by machine (*xeroxing the documents for each of the committee*).

Xmas [ex'-mês] short for **Christmas**.

X'-rays *npl* electric rays that are able to pass through solid substances and so can be used in photographing broken bones, or other objects hidden behind a solid surface.

xylophone [zī'-lō-fōn] *n* a musical instrument of hanging wooden bars that give notes when struck with a wooden hammer.

Y

yacht [yot] *n* a ship, esp a sailing ship, used for pleasure or racing.

yachts'man, yachts'woman *n* one who sails a yacht.

yak *n* a type of ox with long silky hair, found in Tibet.

yam *n* a tropical plant with an eatable root, a sweet potato.

yank *vb* to move suddenly or with a jerk (*yank the door open*).

Yank'ee *n* a citizen of the USA.

yap *vb* (**yapped'**, **yap'ping**) to yelp, to bark shrilly (*little dogs yapping*).

yard *n* **1** a measure of length (=3 feet or 0.9144 metres). **2** a pole fixed across a mast for supporting a sail. **3** an enclosed piece of ground near or behind a building. **4** a piece of ground enclosed for a particular purpose (*a building yard*).

yard'arm *n* either end of a ship's yard.

yard'stick *n* a standard by which one measures or judges other things (*use her mother's behaviour as a yardstick for her own*).

yarn *n* **1** any type of spun thread. **2** (*inf*) a made-up or improbable story (*the old man was spinning a yarn about his days as a sailor*):—*vb* (*inf*) to tell a story.

yash'mak *n* a veil worn by Muslim women in public.

yawl *n* **1** a ship's small boat. **2** a small sailing ship.

yawn *vb* **1** to open the mouth wide because of tiredness or boredom. **2** to be wide open (*the cave yawned below them*):— *n* act of yawning.

ye *pron* old form of you (*pl*).

yea [yā] *adv* yes.

year *n* the time taken by the earth to travel once around the sun, 365 days, esp from 1 January to 31 December, twelve months.

year'ling *n* a one-year-old animal.

yearly *adj* **1** happening once a year. **2** happening every year:— *also adv.*

yearn *vb* to desire greatly, to long (for) (*yearn for a better way of life*).

yearn'ing *n* a strong desire, a longing.

yeast *n* a frothy substance used for making bread rise and in making beer, etc.

yell *vb* to scream, to shout loudly and suddenly (*yell for help*):—*also n.*

yellow *n* a bright golden colour, as of daffodils:— *adj* **1** of golden colour. **2** (*inf*) cowardly (*too yellow to stand up for himself*).

yellow-fe'ver *n* a dangerous tropical disease spread by mosquitoes.

yellowhammer *n* a small yellow songbird.

yelp *vb* to utter a sharp cry, as a dog in pain (*she yelped as the boulder fell on her foot*):—*also n.*

yen¹ *n* (*pl* **yen**) a Japanese coin.

yen² *n* (*inf*) desire (*have a yen for sunshine*).

yeoman [yō-man] *n* a farmer, one who owns a small farm of his own.

yeo'manry *n* (*old*) a force of volunteer soldiers, formerly esp cavalry.

yeoman service *n* (*old*) strong support or assistance.

yes'terday *n* the day before today:—*also adv.*

yes'teryear *n* (*fml*) **1** last year. **2** the past (*all their yesteryears*).

yet *adv* **1** still. **2** in addition. **3** up to the present. **4** however. **5** all the same.

yew [yû] *n* a large evergreen tree often grown in churchyards.

Yid'dish *n* a language, partly German and Hebrew, spoken by modern Jews.

yield *vb* **1** to produce (fruit, crops, profit, etc) (*the milk yielded by the cattle*). **2** to give in, to surrender (*the soldiers yield to the enemy*). **3** to give way (*the door finally yielded to pressure*):— *n* **1** the amount produced or made in profit. **2** a crop.

yield'ing *adj* giving in easily, easily influenced or managed.

yo'del *vb* (**yo'delled**, **yo'delling**) to sing with frequent changes from one's ordinary voice to a higher-pitched one.

yo'ga *n* a Hindu belief that by prayer and complete control over the body and its desires, one may become one with God.

yoghourt [yō-gêrt] *n* a food made from fermented milk (*have yoghourt and fruit for breakfast*).

yo'gi *n* one who practises yoga.

yoke *n* **1** a frame of wood that fits over the necks of two oxen, making them work together when pulling a plough, cart, etc. **2** the part of a garment that fits over the shoulders and round the neck (*a black dress with a white yolk*). **3** something that forces people to do something (*the yoke of slavery*):—*vb* **1** to put together under a yoke. **2** to link together.

yo'kel *n* (*derog*) a country fellow.

yolk *n* the yellow part of an egg.

yon, yon'der *adjs* (*old*) that (one) over there:— *adv* **yon'der** over there.

yore *n* (*old*) olden times:—**of yore** (*old*) in olden times.

young *adj* not old, not grown up, childish,

youthful:—*n* **1** all the children or offspring (of) (*the lioness and her young*). **2** young people in general (*entertainments for the young*).

young'ster *n* a young person.

youth *n* **1** the early part of one's life (*she lived abroad in her youth*). **2** a young man (*youths who have just left school*). **3** young people (*clothes designed for youth*).

youth'ful *adj* young, young-looking (*youthful old people*).

yowl *vb* to cry or howl like a dog:—*also n*.

yule *n* Christmas.

yule'-tide *n* the Christmas season.

Z

za'ny *n* a clown, a jester:—*adj* crazy (*a zany comedy*).

zeal *n* keenness, eagerness, enthusiasm (*show a great deal of zeal for keeping fit*).

zealot [zel'-ot] *n* one so keen on a cause or idea that he can talk of nothing else.

zea'lous *adj* very keen, eager (*zealous supporters of the cause*).

zeb'ra *n* a striped horse-like animal found in Africa.

zebra cros'sing *n* a street crossing place for pedestrians, marked by black and white stripes.

zen'ith *n* **1** the point of the heavens directly overhead. **2** the highest point (*the zenith of his career*).

zeph'yr *n* (*lit*) a gentle breeze.

zep'pelin *n* (*old*) a large cigar-shaped airship.

ze'ro *n* **1** the figure 0. **2** the 0-mark on a measuring scale.

zero hour *n* the time fixed for the beginning of something, such as a military attack.

zest *n* keen enjoyment, enthusiasm (*the old lady's zest for life*):—*adj* **zest'ful**.

zig'zag *adj* turning sharply to the left, following a straight line, then turning sharply to the right, and so on:—*n* a zigzag line or course:—*vb* (**zig'zagged**, **zig'zagging**) to follow a zigzag course (*the path zigzags up the hill*).

zinc *n* a bluish-white metal

Zi'on *n* **1** a hill in Jerusalem. **2** Heaven.

Zi'onism *n* the movement to found and develop Israel.

zip *vb* (**zipped'**, **zip'ping**) **1** (*inf*) to whizz (*zipping to the corner shop*). **2** to fasten with a zip (*zip up her dress*).

zip-fas'tener, zip'per *ns* a sliding fastener that causes two strips of metal teeth to engage in or disengage from each other as it moves.

zith'er *n* a flat stringed musical instrument played with the fingers.

zo'diac *n* the band of the heavens within which the sun, moon and planets seem to move, and containing the twelve groups of stars known as the signs of the zodiac.

zone *n* **1** a belt or stripe. **2** any region with distinctive characteristics of its own. **3** one of the five great belts running around the earth (e.g. *Arctic zone*).

zoo *n* a park in which animals are kept in cages, enclosures, ponds, etc, for show.

zoolo'gical *adj* having to do with the study of animals.

zoological gardens *n* a zoo.

zool'ogist *n* one who studies animals.

zool'ogy *n* the study of animals.

zoom *vb* **1** to climb rapidly at a steep angle. **2** (*inf*) to increase rapidly (*prices have zoomed*). **3** (*inf*) to move very quickly (*cars zooming along the road*).

zounds *interj* short for **God's wounds**, formerly an exclamation of anger or surprise.

zucchini [zu-keen'-ī] *see* **courgette**.

Zu'lu *n* **1** a member of an African tribe. **2** its language.

zythum [zi'-thêm] *n* (*old*) a type of beer made by the Ancient Egyptians.